International Handbook of Practical Theology

International Handbook of Practical Theology

Edited by
Birgit Weyel, Wilhelm Gräb,
Emmanuel Lartey and Cas Wepener

DE GRUYTER

ISBN 978-3-11-151874-9
e-ISBN (PDF) 978-3-11-061815-0
e-ISBN (EPUB) 978-3-11-061839-6
DOI https://
doi.org/10.1515/9783110618150

This work is licensed under the Creative Commons Attribution-NonCommercial-NoDerivatives 4.0 International License. For details go to https://creativecommons.org/licenses/by-nc-nd/4.0/.

Library of Congress Control Number: 2022935345

Bibliographic information published by the Deutsche Nationalbibliothek
The Deutsche Nationalbibliothek lists this publication in the Deutsche Nationalbibliografie; detailed bibliographic data are available on the Internet at http://dnb.dnb.de.

© 2024 with the authors, editing © 2024 Birgit Weyel, Wilhelm Gräb, Emmanuel Lartey and Cas Wepener, published by Walter de Gruyter GmbH, Berlin/Boston. This book is published with open access at www.degruyter.com.
This volume is text- and page-identical with the hardback published in 2022.

Cover image: Studio Light and Shade / iStock / Getty Images Plus

www.degruyter.com

Preface

Beyond its rather encyclopaedic preliminary considerations, a preface offers the opportunity for personal remarks. First and foremost are our thanks. We would like to thank our publisher De Gruyter, namely Albrecht Döhnert, who believed in this project from the outset and supported us over the years with advice going beyond the publishing side of things.

The cultural plurality of our discipline presents formidable challenges for bibliographical compilations. We would like to thank the students and research assistants who have worked hard to standardize the contributions and references without making them uniform. Of these we mention only a few names from the Tübingen community Dr. Katharina Krause, Lea Stolz and Marcel Brenner whilst recognizing the many others in different countries without whom this volume would not have been compiled.

We would like to heartily thank all the authors who embarked on this venture offering their texts. We are especially grateful that all authors adopted English as the common language. Not writing in one's native language is fraught with uncertainties, unpredictable connotations, and ambiguities not always under an author's control. While we offered English language editing, which many authors were happy to make use of, we accepted a wide range of English usage, bearing in mind that we, as editors, are not all native English speakers ourselves.

Through the generous support of the Evangelical Church in Germany (EKD), and the Calwer Verlag-Stiftung we are fortunate to be able to make the contributions of this book available to readers for free on the publisher's website. We are convinced that access to knowledge resources should not depend on the funds of individuals or educational institutions.

Finally, a personal word about our motivation as editors. We would like the conceptual work of the Handbook to contribute to the debate on the decolonization of practical theology. With the global approach this Handbook pursues, our hope is to be able to show how much the culturally situated religious practices and discourses which are subject of the book's chapters are shaped by international, intercultural, and interreligious processes of exchange.

May the readers also enjoy being part of such an exchange.

Birgit Weyel (Tübingen)
Wilhelm Gräb (Berlin)
Emmanuel Lartey (Atlanta)
Cas Wepener (Stellenbosch)

Contents

Birgit Weyel, Wilhelm Gräb, Emmanuel Y. Lartey, and Cas Wepener
Introduction —— 1

Part I: **Concepts of Religion in a Practical-Theological Perspective**

Marcel Barnard
Aesthetics and Religion —— 13

Angela Treiber
Anthropology and Religion —— 29

Heather Walton
Life Writing and Religion —— 47

Jaesung Ha
Communication and Religion —— 61

Birgit Weyel
Community and Religion —— 75

Nadine Bowers Du Toit
Development and Religion —— 89

Mutaz al Khatib
Ethics and Religion —— 103

Annemie Dillen
Family and Religion —— 117

Indukuri John Mohan Razu
Human Rights and Religion —— 129

Ignatius Swart
Institution and Religion —— 143

Mouez Khalfaoui
Law and Religion —— 155

Wilhelm Gräb
Life Interpretation and Religion —— 169

Júlio César Adam
Lived Religion and Religion —— 183

Johanna Sumiala
Media and Religion —— 195

Asonzeh Ukah
Politics and Religion —— 205

Birgit Weyel
Practical Theology and Religion —— 219

Matthew Ryan Robinson
Sociability and Religion —— 233

Part II: Religious Practices in the Perspective of Agency

Hans-Ulrich Probst
Artefact / Personal Belongings / Things —— 249

Albin Masarik
Commemoration / Remembrance / Reconciliation —— 261

Thomas Schlag
Confirmation Ceremonies / Maturity / Processes of Faith and Life —— 275

Brendan Ozawa-de Silva and Chikako Ozawa-de Silva
Contemplative Practice / Sacred Spaces / Cultural Resilience —— 289

Katharina Krause
Conversion / Change / Transformation of Lifestyle —— 301

Trygve Wyller
Diaconia / Empowering / Social Development —— 313

Thias Kgatla
Exorcism / Envy / Witchcraft —— 327

Michel Clasquin-Johnson
Fasting / Asceticism / Feasting —— 341

Manuel Stetter
Funerals / Death / Grief —— 353

Cas Wepener
Holy Supper / Meal / Sharing Food —— 367

J. Kwabena Asamoah-Gyadu
Initiation Ceremonies / Incorporating / Identity Formation —— 379

Faustino Cruz
Leadership / Embodied Knowledge / Resistance —— 393

R. Simangaliso Kumalo
Pulpit / Power / People / Publics —— 405

Mahmoud Abdallah
Pilgrimage / Journey / Practice of Hajj —— 417

Theo Pleizier
Praying / Pastoral Care / Spirituality —— 431

Sunggu Yang
Preaching / Hermeneutics and Rhetoric / Religious Speech —— 445

Herbert Moyo
Priestly Office / Spirit Mediums / Pastoral Care —— 457

Harold D. Horell and Mai-Anh Le Tran
Religious Formation / Educating / Religious Knowledge —— 467

Marcel Barnard, Johan Cilliers and Cas Wepener
Rituals / Liturgies / Performances —— 481

HyeRan Kim-Cragg
Holy Scripture / Hermeneutical Practice / Oral Literature —— 495

Dalia Marx
Sacred Times / Rites of Passage / The Talmudic Ritual for Awakening —— 509

Henry Mbaya and Cas Wepener
Sacrifice / Violence / Isitshisa —— 521

David Plüss and Dorothea Haspelmath-Finatti
Singing / Embodiment / Resonance —— 533

Daniel S. Schipani
Spiritual Care / Counselling / Religious Coping —— 547

Volker Küster
Storytelling / Minjung Theology / Identity Formation —— 561

Rima Nasrallah
Symbolizing / Meaning / Ambiguity —— 575

Auli Vähäkangas and Kirstine Helboe Johansen
Wedding Ceremonies / Blessings / Partnership —— 587

Part III: Theoretical Approaches towards a Global Practical Theology

Jun'ichi Isomae
Anthropology of Religion —— 601

Ulrike E. Auga
Gender Studies —— 615

R. Ruard Ganzevoort
Cultural Hermeneutics of Religion —— 633

Hans-Günter Heimbrock
Phenomenology —— 647

Emmanuel Y. Lartey
Postcolonial Studies in Practical Theology —— 661

Geir Sigmund Afdal
Practice Theory —— 677

Tõnu Lehtsaar
Psychology of Religion —— 691

Bonnie J. Miller-McLemore
Religion and the Social Sciences —— 703

Ana Thea Filipović
Religious Education —— 717

Anita Louisa Cloete
Religious Literacy —— 731

Paul Post
Ritual Studies —— 743

Federico Settler
Sociology of Religion —— 761

Terry A. Veling
Theology of Religion —— 775

Jaco Beyers
Theories of Religious Communication —— 787

Contributors —— 801
Images, Figures and Tables —— 809
Index of Names —— 811
Index of Subjects —— 817

Birgit Weyel, Wilhelm Gräb, Emmanuel Y. Lartey, and
Cas Wepener

Introduction

1 Preliminary Considerations

Calling a collection of chapters an International Handbook of Practical Theology requires careful consideration. Practical Theology indicates a consistent academic discourse although the term refers to a variety of concepts, contexts, and approaches. The designation as handbook suggests comprehensiveness and a well-considered selection of key topics. However, if one really takes diversity seriously, it quickly becomes clear that with each topic considered in the book, the number of blind spots and blanks becomes even more obvious. Editing a book always means limiting the number and variety of all kinds of topics, approaches, and authors. As editors, we cannot escape this imperative, since this kind of decision making also involves excluding topics, approaches, scholars, and contexts from being part of such a project. Every handbook is merely a snapshot and is rounded up by other books.

In a way, this description can be claimed for almost all academic discourses. However, Practical Theology does not always assume the guise of academic discourse with corresponding institutional frameworks: rather, in some contexts, it is seen to be wisdom, practical knowledge. We, the four editors who met each other and maintained conversations in the International Academy of Practical Theology, cannot cover the complexity and messiness of all approaches in Practical Theology, but we appreciate the openness for conversations (Cahalan and Mikosi 2014, 7) and are aware of our self-limitation to academic discourses in this Handbook. Our concept of Practical Theology therefore always means Practical Theologies in the plural. We owe this insight to conversations with colleagues in the International Academy of Practical Theology (IAPT). Examples are those with whom we had the opportunity to discuss the concept of this book in two paper sessions in Sao Leopoldo, Brazil in 2019.

Last but not least, the term 'international' needs some explanation. At one point, we were thinking of eliminating it altogether. The concept of nations is, like Benedict Anderson (1963) shows, an invented tradition in terms of the nationalism and imperialism of North America and Europe in the nineteenth century. Over the last decade the self-reflection of Practical Theology has focused on plurality and diversity, but that is still very much only beginning. In this light we made three editorial decisions:

First, Practical Theology does not only refer to the Christian Tradition. Even though we as editors and most of our authors are Christian theologians and Christianity itself is split into many different ecclesial traditions, we have also collected chapters from scholars who belong to or refer to non-Christian religious traditions and communities. These chapters do not only enrich Practical Theology and make it more diverse, but they also help our epistemology. The respective communities of practice and theological concepts (values, norms, traditions, communities) cannot be tacitly assumed, references must be made explicit and accessible to description and reflection.

Secondly, there are many overlaps and common approaches between Practical Theology and Religious Studies including empirical research on religion. There is a whole range of disciplines that form important interlocutors for Practical Theology. A question that is asked again and again is: What is theological about theology? The discussion of disciplinary belongings seems to be an open field to us and containing many ambiguities in which strict boundaries are not helpful. Following these considerations, we invited contributions from colleagues who do not necessarily self-define as theologians and who are not linked to any institutional theological background.

Finally, from our point of view, the issue of limitation, which we considered from many different viewpoints, can lead to making explicit one's own perspective and scope of representation. This includes not obscuring or objectifying one's own self-image, but rather disclosing it. Limiting becomes a problem if it is made as if it were ever possible to cover all possibilities or to ignore concrete contexts. As noted above, the term 'internationality' is associated with hegemonic claims which have their roots in Europe and North America. With this in mind, we encouraged authors to make their affiliation, subject relation, and context-boundness transparent, even though in some academic traditions doing so is considered a non-academic writing style. However, the question of what Practical Theology means and for what purpose it is practiced finds different answers depending on local, institutional, cultural, and religious environments. Therefore, from our point of view, it is a proof of epistemological honesty to make one's own knowledge recognizable as situational knowledge. In the following therefore we would like to further discuss our context and the issue of Practical Theology.

2 Practical Theology – The Subject Matter

It is not surprising that Practical Theology, as an academic discipline, is involved in ongoing discourse about its self-understanding, its tasks, its methods, and subjects. The discourse on the epistemology of Practical Theology reflects the fact that the interests and questions pursued by this discipline are closely related to contextually specific challenges posed by religious communities, and practices. As to the subject matter of Practical Theology an important question is one of relevance: Does what academic practical theologians do have any relevance for people in their religious and social communities? The concept of collaborative empirical research is one example of handling the question of relevance regarding research (de Roest 2020). Does academic Practical Theology contribute to the training of professions, while the focus on professions may be broader than the pastoral paradigm? In which ways is research in Practical Theology also of interest to other religion-related disciplines, such as empirical religious research, sociology, or psychology?

A Practical Theology that faces the complexity, plurality and diversity of situations and contexts of religious practices in a global horizon has to make visible the discourses which identify and shape these religious practices in a specific sense. In this volume the term *religion* is taken to refer to a field of cultures, ritual practices, and symbolic orders whose boundaries are not well defined and whose contents are shifting. To describe a practice, an experience, an event, an institution, or a community as being 'religious' depends on the respective religio-cultural context and the related framework of interpretation.

3 Encyclopaedia

We assume that the assignment of religious practices to certain religio-cultural traditions, communities, and organisations already presupposes their discursive construction. As such, we did not choose classifications and categorisations which are related to fixed traditions, regions, or religions. From our point of view this leads again to generalization and essentialization. We are not interested in an *overview* of knowledge, which disregards the situatedness of knowledge and the positionality of representation. In our conversations about the concept, we agreed that we did not wish to allocate the chapters of this Handbook to denominational or religious traditions and organisations, nor did we want to divide the volume according to the chapters' affiliation to countries or continents. Such allocations resemble tidying up a messy subject. We recognise that denominational and religious, regional, and national affiliations have a marked influence on the conceptions and formations of religious communities and religious practices. We assume that these interrelations are fundamental. The chapters of this Handbook portray the discussions which shape institutions, religious communities, and religious practice as such. They show the embeddedness of religion.

In the light of these considerations, we chose a lean encyclopaedic system and divided the Handbook into three sections. In the first section, titled 'concepts of religion', we present seventeen examples of fields in which religion is conceptualized. Family or biography are not religious in any way, but the contours of the religious become visible in these contexts with reference to certain discourses. In the second section, the chapters explore strategies of religious practices with respect to their actors in a variety of twenty-eight case studies. These include e.g., rites of passages, sacred space, and praying. These case studies not only refer to human beings when talking about actors: They also include material objects. The third section presents a selection of fourteen key discourses Practical Theology refers to, such as Gender Studies, Hermeneutics, and Philosophy. Of course, the series of topics and and contributions could easily be extended. However, the fact that the middle section is the most extensive is no coincidence. The heart of Practical Theology lies in the religious practices themselves.

To bring out the situatedness and contextuality of discourses conceptualizing religious practices, imaginations, and strategies of individuals and religious communities, we tried hard to invite authors from all over the world. The Handbook aims to contribute to the international network of Practical Theology. We are very grateful to the authors for embarking on this adventure with us. Especially those who did not know us as editors at all. In this sense, it builds on the activities of the International Academy of Practical Theology (IAPT). We experienced the biennial meetings as an inspiring hub of conversations and encounters. We also owe much to the International Journal of Practical Theology (IJPT), which has been published by De Gruyter since 1997. In almost every issue of the IJPT there is an "International Report" which describes practical-theological discourses in relation to a particular region of the world and the ecclesial and religious situation there. Much can be learned from these International Reports about how different perceptions of the ecclesial and religious situation also give rise to different practical-theological problems and theoretical procedures. Nevertheless, for this Handbook we made the decision not to report on the practical-theological discourses in their international affiliations, but to let the authors each take their situationally conditioned perspective on their topic, moving in the conceptualization of a particular ecclesial, religious, and cultural context.

Due to the different regional, ecclesiastical, religious, and cultural affiliations of the authors, it was our hope that the global approach of this Handbook would emerge. It was particularly important to us to include perspectives from authors living and working in the Global South and to represent as broad a spectrum as possible in their religious belongings and cultural orientations. To have achieved this more fully, our circle of editors, all Christian theologians, should have probably been composed differently. In this respect, this Handbook represents a first step to a global approach to Practical Theology in international discourse. Perhaps it already makes visible how cultural and religious boundaries are becoming more and more fluid and permeable within this discourse. We have therefore refrained from a detailed labelling of the ecclesiastical and religious affiliations and situational contexts of the authors. A few traces can be read beyond the articles in the (short) author biographies. Instead, chapter authors were asked to make explicit their personal experiences and views in their articles.

We have relied on the fact that denominational, religious, and cultural affiliations become apparent from the author's discourse, but that this kind of crossover discourse is also open to readers with other denominational, religious, and cultural affiliations. In the best case, we gain new insights into what we initially perceived as different: on denominational, religious, and cultural levels.

4 Concepts of Religion in the Perspective of Practical Theology (Part 1)

The International Handbook of Practical Theology enters the arena of the disciplines of Practical Theology assuming that Practical Theology is an empirically grounded and hermeneutically elaborated theory of religious practice. The primary interest as practical theologians is the focus on 'doing religion'. What people call 'religion' or 'spirituality' is not only vague and fluid but is related to culture and the ways in which individuals make use of the term. The question of religion is also open and controversial in academic discourse. When things go well, it becomes clear that the question is indeed answered differently by the discourse partners. When things go poorly, religion is talked about as if it were a fixed object. Is religion an experience, an event, an institution, a community, a practice, a collection of sacred literature, or a historical movement? Is Buddhism a religion? What is meant by African Heritage Religion? Are there many Christianities, African religions or just one "Christianity" or African Traditional Religion? Can practitioners of one shaping of Islam recognize and legitimize practices of Islam in all other parts of the world? It is the stated task of the first part of the Handbook to 'clarify its notion of religion'.

These chapters include considerations of 'anthropology and religion', 'community and religion', 'family and religion', 'institution and religion', 'law and religion', 'media and religion', 'politics and religion' and so on – all aimed at clarifying the conceptualizing of religion in a variety of fields.

The chapters, moreover, are written by authors from different parts of the globe. The contributors engage their topics from within their own context and culture, which is made abundantly clear, recognizing that no one speaks for all but instead our situatedness gives us grounding from which to explore any subject. Aware of the historical danger of universalizing from one's particularity – the peril of colonialist discourse – from these vantage points they each explore possible meanings of religion in a wider, transcultural, globalizing, and decolonializing world.

What we have then in this first part is a collection of essays which illuminate the problem of 'religion' in our world in its current fragmented and fluid state, and then offers ways in which practical theologians may frame and explore their interest in religious practices and in doing religion.

5 Religious Practices in the Perspective of Agency (Part 2)

Whatever definition of religion is used, religion is also something people do. People living their religion implies practitioners involved in embodied practices. This conception of the Handbook becomes abundantly clear in Part 2 where twenty-eight sets of keywords closely connected to practices are discussed. They are ordered alphabetically, beginning with Artifacts and Confirmation, including Praying and Rituals, and ending with Symbolizing and Weddings. A reader will encounter a description of animal sacrifices in South Africa within a spiritual worldview, music performed in traditional mainline churches in a more secularized Europe, and pilgrimages undertaken by Muslims from all over the world.

Part 2 widens the scope of practical-theological reflection, transcending traditional teaching, preaching, and pastoral care. It includes practices of traditional communities, such as the Lutheran or Roman Catholic Churches as well as for example practices of African Independent Churches. In the past, practices of the latter would only have been the discussed in contexts of Religious Studies, Anthropology, and Missiology, reflecting a clear bias on the side of Practical Theology in respect to which churches' practices were deemed important for scholarly reflection. In addition, Part 2 also includes a range of practices with no relation to any specific church or religion. This is because the choice of what to include was not about what constitutes religious, Christian, or theological practice, and what does not. Instead, the choice about what to include in Part 2, was an indication of what counts in the Handbook as knowledge and, in addition, whose knowledge should be included amid the fluidity of church and religion today.

In Part 2, as in Parts 1 and 3, the authors represent scholars from many parts of the world, and a variety of disciplines and backgrounds. Apart from the religious practices readers encounter in the chapters in Part 2, they will also, importantly, encounter the authors of each chapter who very deliberately situated themselves in their socio-cultural contexts and disciplinary fields whilst exploring these practices. This situatedness of the practices and the positionality of those reflecting on the practices, makes for a transcultural approach as it uncovers the struggles of each author and the resources at their disposal. The practices open up windows to the lifeworld of the authors, their challenges, and privileges in a very particular time in history in specific contexts. It also allows for the individual author's idiosyncratic understandings or definitions of religion to surface in their chapters, which is critical for a transcultural Practical Theology. In this regard, methodologically, it is important that the chapters deliberately take an emic perspective and provide idiographic rather than nomothetic accounts of the practices.

This methodological approach implies that the practices reflected upon are executed by humans with agency. In Ted. A. Smith's discussion of theories of practice in The Wiley-Blackwell Companion to Practical Theology (Smith 2014), he refers to Pierre Bourdieu's work on the topic and his distinction between "subjective" (focus on freedom of human action) and "objective" (social structures determining actions) which is critical for the notion of human agency in relation to practices. The chapters in Part 2 provide a variety of perspectives on human agency as human beings doing religion by means of their involvement in practices. And the actors in these practices include a wide variety of people in religious communities, academia, and society, often reflecting on practices as they relate to problems, struggling to enhance the life of individuals and communities.

The largest portion of the Handbook is devoted to Part 2 and thus to practices. This is due to the conviction that Practical Theology is reflection on the relation of practice and theory. With this emphasis on practices, the Handbook wants to move beyond a practice-theory dichotomy and a privileged position of theory in academic reflection. Instead, it positions practice at the core of practical-theological endeavours, thus not as a secondary task, but as primary and integral. In Conundrums in Practical Theology Bonnie Miller-McLemore (2016) shows how deeply entrenched the theory-practice binary is, also in our academic institutions.

With practices at the core of Practical Theology, and religion as doing, important sources of knowledge can be included into the picture, such as embodied knowledge. Regarding practices it includes, importantly, human bodies. In his classic article "On ritual knowledge" Theodore Jennings Jr. (Jennings 1996) discusses a (religious) practice, namely ritual, as well as the importance of a bodily based epistemology and the human body as a site of knowledge production. This knowledge is knowledge gained through practice such as rituals. The knowledge gained through ritual action is "knowledge gained in action of action"; aimed at finding out how to act. In recent years, the material turn has contributed to a focus on materiality, spatial arrangements, and the collaboration of things in practices. Theology in many parts of the world has a strong focus on the subject. The focus on religious practices and on agency distributed among different actors, including non-human actors is worth pursuing further.

6 Discourses in Practical Theology (Part 3)

In the third part of the Handbook, theoretical approaches and scientific-methodological procedures are presented. They are already referenced in the critical and constructive analysis, reflection, and presentation of religious discourses and practices in Part 1 and 2 of the Handbook. In Part 3 they are explicitly named and developed in context: Sociology of Religion, Hermeneutics of Culture, Gender Studies, Postcolonial Studies, Phenomenology of Religion, Psychology of Religion. This list is unfinished, because it is our view that all approaches which help in the understanding of and reflection upon religious practices, are relevant to Practical Theology. The reader may notice that Practical Theology is not part of the theoretical approaches as such. Practical Theology as one chapter in addition to the list of academic discourses presented in a handbook of Practical Theology looks like a meta-discourse. Therefore, we put Practical Theology as a matter of subject in Part 1.

Practical Theology, as an academic reflection on the practices of religion is part of this practice. So, ultimately, we understand Practical Theology as both, the subject, and the object of its self-reflection. This reflection cannot stay in an inner space of one cultural and religious tradition only. The principle aim of this Handbook, therefore, is to bring religious and denominational traditions and cultures into a conversation.

A central question which has concerned us in the conception of this Handbook, is what Practical Theology can contribute to the perception of lived religion in different cultural contexts and religious traditions. Is not the distinction between religion and culture rather blurred and therefore inappropriate? How can Practical Theology refer to other religions and relationships without othering? In our academic context, very often Religious Studies relate to the claim of a supposedly 'objective perspective' on religious phenomena. As editors, we are convinced that it is helpful to disclose one's own self-relation to the object of research. This is also part of a process of learning in ethnographic research.

The answers we give in this Handbook attempt to culturally situate every description of practice and discourse of religion. The position of the author, his or her cultural context, and his or her religious affiliation and individual religious conviction must be made explicit in the processing of the topic. However, this can be at the expense of the general scope of the representation again and lead to the fact that Practical Theology merely makes positional statements. Therefore, we presuppose, those who belong to other traditions or religious communities or who move in different cultural and social contexts must also be able to understand the practical-theological analysis and reflection of religious practices and communities. We hope that the global perspective transcends boundaries between cultures and religions by making visible connecting themes beyond distinction. Therefore we talk about a global approach instead of intercultural or interreligious theology. Talking of inter-culturalism and inter-religiosity starts from the assumption of religions and cultures as more or less fixed social bodies, and space of intersection in-between. Instead, we assume that there are no fixed boundaries between religions and cultures. Rather, in the globalized world we are involved in dynamic processes of cultural and religious transformation creating a complex entanglement between different religious traditions, cultures, discourses, communities, and practices. This entanglement is what we seek to highlight in this anthology.

Bibliography

Anderson, Benedict. 1983. *Imagined Communities. Reflections on the Origin and Spread of Nationalism*. London: Verso.

Cahalan, Kathleen A., and Gordon S. Mikoski, eds. 2014. *Opening the Field of Practical Theology: An Introduction*. Lanham: Rowman & Littlefield.

Jennings, T.W. Jr. 1996. "On Ritual Knowledge." In *Readings in Ritual Studies*, edited by Ronald L. Grimes, Upper Saddle River: Prentice Hall, 324–334.

Mercer, Joyce Ann, and Bonnie J. Miller-McLemore, eds. 2016. *Conundrums in Practical Theology*. Leiden / Boston: Brill.

Miller-McLemore, Bonnie J. 2014. *The Wiley-Blackwell Companion to Practical Theology*. Chichester: Wiley-Blackwell.

Roest, Henk de. 2020. *Collaborative Practical Theology: Engaging Practitioners in Research on Christian Practices*. Leiden / Boston: Brill.

Smith, Ted, A. 2014. "Theories of Practice." In *The Wiley-Blackwell Companion to Practical Theology*, edited by Bonnie J. Miller-McLemore, Chichester: Wiley-Blackwell, 244–254.

Part I: **Concepts of Religion in a Practical-Theological Perspective**

Marcel Barnard
Aesthetics and Religion

1 Introduction

1.1 Aesthetics

The notion of aesthetics derives from the Greek word αἴσθησθαι – 'to perceive' or 'relating to the senses' – and at first sight this seems to have little to do with its other meaning – 'philosophy of art'.

In its first meaning – 'relating to the senses' – aesthetics belongs inextricably to the field of religion. Lived religion is literally sensed religion. Religion is never separate from the senses and the body; it is always embodied. Whether it concerns Buddhist, Hindu, Greek or Roman temples, Romanesque churches or Gothic Cathedrals; whether sound bowls, mantras, organs, praise bands, talking drums or choirs; whether bread, wine, sacrificial meat or *umqombothi* (traditional beer in Xhosa rituals); whether a laying on of hands, rustling ritual garments, anointing oil, holy water or baptismal water; whether incense or scented spices, – religion is a sensory phenomenon. The senses, seeing and hearing, touching, tasting, and smelling, are hermeneutical instruments we use to interpret the world around us and also the world which we ordinarily perceive to be beyond this one, the domain of religion.

Aesthetics in the sense of 'philosophy of art' is also associated with religion. In the Western world, the Enlightenment assigned religion its legitimate place "within the bounds of bare reason", as Immanuel Kant said at the end of the eighteenth century (Kant 2009). From a theological perspective, we can say that with the breakthrough of pure reason, the demolition of the metaphysical domain and of onto-theology began to gain momentum. At the same time, the spiritual, religious, or sacred is re-localized in the arts, whereas, to quote anthropologist Carol Duncan, "the appearance of art galleries and museums gave the aesthetic cult its own ritual precinct" (Duncan 1995, 14). It is here that the aesthetic becomes connected with beauty. The aesthetic experience is "a moment of moral and rational disengagement that leads to or produces some kind of revelation or transformation" (Duncan 1995, 14).

The re-localizing of the spiritual, the religious or the sacred in the arts developed into the dominant conception of the museum in the twentieth century. It became a contemplative space for the meditation of art, that results in, as Ives Gilman of the Boston Museum of Fine Arts formulated in 1918, "a profoundly transforming experience, [...], an intense and joyous emotion, an overwhelming and 'absolutely serious' pleasure that contains a profound spiritual revelation" (Duncan 1995, 16). The museum visitor in turn becomes a "devotee who achieves a kind of secular grace through communion with artistic geniuses of the past" (Duncan 1995, 17). It is striking that

Gilman and Duncan talk about the museum in emphatically religious terms: spiritual revelation, devotee, grace, and communion.

In our late-modern time the concept of religion was broken open, as we will see below. Religion no longer refers as self-evident to accurately delimited beliefs and practices that create 'model believers'. The same applies to the concept of the museum. It is no longer assumed that museums produce model visitors, but that social identities are negotiated between exhibited objects, visitors, museum staff and affiliates etc., in short: they are negotiated through museum culture (Bouquet and Porto 2005, 5). The museum includes objects as well as social networks in which objects are at the centre of a "signifying process" (Bouquet and Porto 2005, 21). Here, religion comes to the fore.

It is claimed that the much-discussed disenchantment of the world is answered by a deliberately sought magic or re-enchantment of secular rituals that "[...] seem in some sense to fill a void created by the 'crossed-out God' of rational, post-Enlightenment mankind" (Bouquet and Porto 2005, 3. 20–22). Museums are partners in this re-enchantment; it has been demonstrated how "museum collections are constituted and technologically manipulated [...] through the interplay of science and magic" to achieve this aim (Bouquet and Porto 2005, 4).

We can, of course, wonder whether this is still about religion. So, the question remains: what is religion exactly?

1.2 Religion

Religion is inextricably linked to the physical world that we inhabit bodily and perceive with our senses, as mentioned above. But it is precisely the relocation of religion into the aesthetic domain that results in religion not always immediately being recognizable as such; or that makes one consider certain phenomena as being religious, while another might view it very differently. The relocation of religion, and the movement of religion away from traditional domains such as the church and temple (among other spaces) towards the field of the arts (but also for example into daily life), makes religion a rather invisible phenomenon: Religion hides in the world and cannot be distinguished from it. So much so, that in contemporary Religious Studies it is even questioned whether religion does indeed 'exist'.

From this follows a matter of principle in the contemporary practice of Practical Theology. Religion is hiding in the world, we said. But 'the world' is always a specific world, a specific time and specific place, in short, a specific culture. I am a white, Protestant, Western European, strongly influenced by secularism, and that determines my view of the world. The way I 'know' the world is determined by my locality and temporality. Put differently, my epistemology is determined by my ontology. There is no such thing as 'objective' positivistic knowledge (Dreyer 2016, 102–103). More than that, my knowledge is driven by values, in my case, more specifically, by the desire to embed Protestant-Christian religiosity, into a broader, multi-layered, pluralistic post-secular religious discourse. I do so because I believe that the globalization and pluralization of our world requires such an approach: in the end peace is served by an understanding of the other, the stranger, who undoubtedly has a different view of the same world as I do. The case study that I present in a moment is an example in which, in my opinion, that desire takes on a good form.

Religious Studies, and certainly academic theology, are, at least in the Western world, involuntarily dominated by an ecclesiastical, even Protestant, comprehension of concepts and convictions (Nongbri 2013, 18, comp. 85–105). What we understood by religion in the Western world was for a long time akin to the Protestant faith, driven by accurately delineated and isolated beliefs and convictions. Nowadays, Practical Theology sees it increasingly as its task to give a podium voices and phenomena that have not been conceived of before as religious, and that move beyond the demarcation lines of the past. In that context, religion is being sought more and more in a non-isolated domain, for example in everyday life, in the domestic realm, in the public domain and in sports, in justice and peace, for women and children, in health, and in collective memory and museums, as well as in the arts. Thus, theologians and scholars of religion investigate a part of the social and cultural reality that cannot easily be isolated, but that in everyday language points to something that we call 'religion' and that intuitively also means something. In other words, religion is a discourse rather than an isolated phenomenon. Religion is not so much 'something out there', but the notion of religion is of use to approach an existential phenomenon that cannot easily be understood in other conceptualizations (Nongbri 2013).

Religion often cannot be identified as a demarcated domain or as an independent category, and yet within half a second, Google gives more than a billion results for 'religion'. The notion of religion is 'of use', although its 'existence' is scientifically more difficult to establish. Whether a phenomenon is a religious phenomenon depends to a large extent on how it is named or, abstractly formulated, on the discourse in which it is incorporated. Religion hides and at the same time reveals itself in ritual and artistic expressions, thoughts, and actions. These expressions, thoughts and actions can be determined as religious either through popular discourse, or in isolation, through analysis and investigation with academic theological methods and concepts. It is quite possible to consider a museum as a completely secular institution, but at the same time, to see it as loaded with religious meanings.

The world of arts and museums is a symbolic one. It consists of symbols that have multi-layered meanings and that are valid within a certain culture. In other words, symbols only have diction within a specific cultural code. It thus requires an active attitude of the viewer or visitor in order to generate and understand these meanings. 'Objective symbolic forms' and 'subjective meaningful orientations' go together in culture and in everyday life. Religion is a symbolic world as well, its symbols refer to the ultimate, or the absolute, or the infinite. Lived religion is "the culture of symbolizing ultimate horizons of meaning" (Gräb 2006, 33). In other words, in religious discourses culture is interpreted "in terms of the infinite or of an absolute sense" (Gräb 2006, 68). Or, again, in other words, a religious discourse makes use of "symbolic statements [...] which cannot be proved using encyclopaedic knowledge, knowledge which informs our normal understanding of the world" (Stringer 2011, 16). Symbols and artistic expressions accomplish "more than its context would suggest" (Long 2010, 70–71) and so point to a 'beyond', to which a religious discourse adheres. That also applies to the Christian religion, which is a 'subjective meaningful orientation', a discourse that can incorporate many phenomena. God is God in the midst of the gods; Jesus is Lord in the midst of the rulers; the feast of liturgy is celebrated in the midst of other festivals; the inspiration of the Pentecostal spirit blows through artistic inspiration.

Finally, at the end of the previous section we asked whether magic such as late-modern museums evoke it is also religious. In fact, this magic is about 'conjuring magic', a manipulation of the public, which in turn knows it is being manipulated (Luhrmann 1998, 299). It is illusion, which can nevertheless evoke or keep awake the hope of a supernatural cause. So, yes indeed, 'magic' may also be religious.

1.3 Aesthetics, Arts, Religion and Practical Theology

The connection between the arts and religion is almost inherent to Practical Theology. Only decades after the relocation of the religious, spiritual, or sacred to the domain of the arts, the father of Practical Theology, Friedrich Schleiermacher, states that the two are inextricably linked (Barnard 2001).

In his conceptual framework, *self-consciousness* (*Selbstbewußtsein*) is the relationship between the pure self and Infinity or God. *Infinity*, or God, touches or – again in the terminology of Schleiermacher – 'heightens' (*erhöht*) the self-consciousness that, as a consequence, expresses or represents itself (in an indirect way)[1] in artistic forms. Thus, Infinity manifests itself in an act of representation. 'Self-consciousness' is therefore a dynamic concept that exists in the activity of manifesting itself, or, in German, in a *darstellende Tätigkeit* (Schleiermacher [1821/1822] 1980, §9; [1830/1831] 2003, §§4–5; comp. 1850, 71–72; [1832/1833] 2021, 120). According to Schleiermacher, manifestations or *Darstellungen* of the religious mood are possible in a subjective way by means of artistic and ritual forms, and in an objective way by means of discursive beliefs. In this article we focus on what he calls the subjective way. Self-consciousness can also be touched or 'heightened' by a *finite* cause – for example visiting a museum, looking at art or participating in worship. This 'heightening' also leads to a manifestation.

Worship – sermon, song, and music – and the arts are manifestations of the heightened mood and, as a consequence, are closely related to each other. It will

---

[1] A representation of heightened consciousness is tempered by intermediate moments of mood and prototype. Mood or *Stimmung* places the momentary impulse in a bed of constant affection. Furthermore, there are prototypes or ideal models of representation in the human mind under which direct representations of self-consciousness are subsumed (Barnard 2001, 191–192).

be clear that these expressions are eminently *symbolic* in nature: they hold together two domains, the infinite and the known physical world.

Rooted in the individual, these manifestations ask for an understanding community or 'an identity of life' so they can be *shared* (Schleiermacher 2021, 12). As we said above, a symbolic order can only be activated and understood within a specific culture with a specific cultural code. For that reason, the aim of worship is 'the representative communication of a more stimulated religious consciousness' (*die darstellende Mitteilung des stärker erregten religiösen Bewußtseins*) (Schleiermacher 1850, 65). The perception of a manifestation of a heightened mood activates the perceiver and heightens their consciousness. This is comparable to the consideration of the German-American theologian Paul Tillich, that art has the unique characteristic of deepening religious experiences. "For the arts do both: they open up a dimension of reality that is otherwise hidden, and they open up our own being for receiving this reality" (Tillich 1987, 247).

1.4 Religious and Artistic Expressions Are Gratuitous

According to Schleiermacher, touched or heightened self-awareness reaches its goal in the *Darstellung* or manifestation. For that reason, the arts and also worship are goals in themselves, they are gratuitous. They rest in themselves and serve no purpose at all (Schleiermacher 1850, 37. 75; 2021, 42). Religious mediation – through elements from this sensual world – is stripped of all functionality and instrumentality. This also applies to the arts. The religious sensory experience rests in itself and the same applies to the religious ritual of worship. In that sense they are separate from the everyday world, or, better still, from the everyday world in which functionality and instrumentality are dominant.

This theory returns in its own way in the existential philosophy of Martin Heidegger, which in turn underlies the sacramental theology of the French theologian Louis-Marie Chauvet, probably the most prominent sacrament theologian at the moment. With Heidegger, the open-minded vision of the pair of farmer's shoes that Van Gogh painted grants a passage to being itself; with Chauvet, by analogy, an open-minded taking, and especially breaking or opening of the bread in the Eucharist grants passage to Christ himself.

Without going into Heidegger's philosophy here, we point to a famous passage that the philosopher dedicates to this painting by Vincent van Gogh, now in the Van Gogh Museum in Amsterdam, of a pair of farmer's shoes (Heidegger [1950] 2002, 13–16). In Heidegger's interpretation not what we already know is at stake, that shoes serve to cover the feet and that their shape depends on their function: dancing, working the land or walking. Rather, these functional aspects of the farmer's shoes rest in 'the fullness of an essential being' (Heidegger 2002, 14), in what they are 'in truth' (Heidegger 2002, 15).

> From out of the dark opening of the well-worn insides of the shoes the toil of the worker's tread stares forth. In the crudely solid heaviness of the shoes accumulates the tenacity of the slow trudge through the far-stretching and ever-uniform furrows of the field swept by a raw wind. On the leather lies the dampness and richness of the soil. Under the soles slides the loneliness of the field-path as evening falls. The shoes vibrate with the silent call of the earth, its silent gift of the ripening grain, its unexplained self-refusal in the wintry field. This equipment is pervaded by uncomplaining worry as to the certainty of bread, wordless joy at having once more withstood want, trembling before the impending birth, and shivering at the surrounding menace of death. This equipment belongs *to the earth* and finds protection in the *world* of the peasant woman. From out of this protected belonging the equipment itself rises to its resting-within-itself (Heidegger 2002, 14).

Analogous to how with Schleiermacher, expressions of heightened self-consciousness are indirect representations of the infinite or God (without the infinite ever being able to be fixed or detached from the manifestation), with Heidegger the work of art gives passage to being itself (that cannot be fixed either).

1.5 Also the Sensory Act of Celebrating the Sacraments Is Gratuitous

If the senses play a role somewhere in the Christian religion, then in the sacraments: we feel the baptismal water, take, and eat bread, smell and drink wine. Referring to the philosophy of Heidegger, Chauvet elaborated on the Eucharistic gift of the bread. How could we understand the moment that we touch, break, taste, chew and swallow the Eucharistic bread? The 'reality' of the bread is not primarily its biological and chemical qualities, but its symbolic characteristic, that is, the way in which it is socially or culturally (in culture *and* in the cult) instituted. Thus, bread, at least in the Western world, feeds and fuels the body, but it is also socially instituted as a symbol for what one shares (precisely during a meal). Bread "is the *mediation of fellowship as much as of the maintenance of biological life*" (Chauvet 1995, 397). Moreover, within the Christian community the bread is offered to God as giver of the grain and bread. In other words, "it is presented to *God* as the highest word of recognition by humankind: recognition *of* God as God" (Chauvet 1995, 397). Finally, in the Christian cult and faith, the bread is recognized as "the gift of God's very self, as the *autocommunication of God's very self in Christ*" (Chauvet 1995, 398). This is the very essence of bread (Chauvet 1995, 400) that happens in the act of the breaking, of the opening of the bread: it reveals the coming of Christ that however never can be fixed or preserved; it is advent and retreat at the same moment.

> Presence-as-trace; trace of a passing always-already past; trace thus of something absent. But still trace, that is, the sign of a happening which calls us to be attentive to something new still to come (Chauvet 1995, 58).

Faith is always mediated, as the sacraments show; it does "not exist except as inscribed somewhere" (Chauvet 1995, 402). Thus, faith and especially the sacraments are inescapably embedded in human existence and in specific cultural settings.

From these considerations, it is a relatively small step to a case of a medieval city church in Amsterdam that became a museum of modern art, but in which an ecclesial congregation still meets and celebrates the Eucharist weekly on Sunday.

2 Art Installations in the Old Church in Amsterdam[2]

The medieval Old Church in the heart of Amsterdam's red-light district is owned by a foundation and used on Sunday as a place for worship, but also has official status as a museum. High-profile and controversial exhibitions of modern art are organized by director Jacqueline Grandjean in the church. As the exhibitions are always site-specific, they are excellent examples of the interweaving of religion and art. The discussions that the shows evoke among art lovers, churchgoers, and advocates of cultural heritage at the same time make clear that this interweaving is not self-evident and undisputed. We present three examples.

In 2015 the Japanese artist Taturo Atzu constructed a huge platform on top of the building, *The Garden Which is the Nearest to God*. Through staircases on a scaffolding that led up along the walls and the huge gothic windows of the church, the visitor ended up on a platform where the roof-turret stood out. The artist stated: "I want to activate people to look more actively and freely. [...] That old church is a strange, fascinating place, surrounded by prostitutes and urinals. As I walked through those narrow alleys, I realized that I wanted to create a space that was large and open: the largest roof terrace in the distant environment" (Smallenburg 2015). And a reviewer from a national newspaper:

> The Red Light District was clean, sweet, well-arranged and cool from here, and the condom hats from the British bachelor's clubs seemed to be cute, dangling. But the best thing was the lead work and the pattern of drop-shaped slates on the church roof, so close at once. Long ago laid by many hands, only to please the birds (and the Lord, if you want). It was thoughtful and relativizing, a bit astronaut (Prisser 2015).

The uselessness of the project is striking and generated a lot of discussion. In other words, the cultural code was being challenged and the work contested. The title of the work of art alone, *The Garden Which is Nearest to God*, is a religious reference, no longer specifically Christian, but much more generally religious. The same could be said of the space and openness that it realized above the spatial narrowness of the neighbourhood. Probably, it even deepens the understanding of infinity and per-

---

2 I used the artworks and the here presented interpretations also in other publications: Barnard 2019, Barnard 2020.

Image 1: Taturo Atzu, The Garden Which is Nearest to God (2015), printed with friendly permission of Museum De Oude Kerk, Amsterdam.

haps of absoluteness in the middle of a busy populated city-centre which is to a large extend devoted to the immediate satisfaction of lusts. The work clearly refers to a 'beyond' the daily reality of the red-light District. As far as I know, the work did not actively interact with the Sunday services of the Christian congregation meeting in the church.

In 2017 the French artist Christian Boltanski carried out the exposition NA (Dutch for 'AFTER'). He designed site-specific installations in the church building that referred to the many names remembered in the church, especially on the tomb slabs. He also constructed enormous towers of agricultural plastic on the graves, which were higher as more people had been buried there. The visitor walked between the towers and came into contact with coats hung on a wooden skeleton, which when you approached asked very personal questions, such as 'Are you lonely?' Jackets of local residents spread out on the floor served as reminders for what a human being leaves behind after their death. At the Lord's Table in the choir of the church lay a thick layer of flowers that were slowly wilting.

On one of the last Sundays before Advent, at the end of the liturgical year, where traditional themes such as death and resurrection, destruction and purification, restoration, and return (of Jesus) are central, the ecclesiastical congregation designed a church service in which the churchgoers passed singing between the towers of agricultural plastic. I was one of the presiders in the service. I composed the prayers from excerpts of Jesus' sermons about the last things, prescribed for that Sunday. Thus, the artwork was emphatically brought into the Christian liturgical narrative, and the art-

Image 2: Christian Boltanski, NA (2017), printed with friendly permission of Museum De Oude Kerk, Amsterdam.

work also allowed for this. The NA/AFTER to which the title of the work of art refers is given an interpretation within a biblical liturgical narrative: the coming of the Son of Man. The installations deepened the understanding of the NA/AFTER: death is a massive force and power, and the voluminous presence of the plastic towers emphasized the non-obviousness of an AFTER. Or, framed in the language of the liturgical discourse, the revelation of the Son of Man is a radical break with the familiar and with what lies within human power.

The Kyrie-litany:
Minister: Holy places are being desecrated,
                temples will all be thrown down,
                not one stone will be left upon the other (Matt 24:1).
All (sung):   The end is still to come (Matt 24:6).
                AFTER the horrors
                the sign that heralds the Son of Man
                will appear in heaven (Matt 24:30).
Minister: Refugees
                — they flee into the mountains,
                leave behind their homes and possessions,

	their coats on the land,
	— coats, jackets, everywhere,
	who were wearing them, where are they?
	Fled, disappeared, killed, drowned. (Matt 24:16, 18, 20)
All:	The end is still to come.
	AFTER the horrors
	the sign that heralds the Son of Man
	will appear in heaven.
Minister:	They flee, pregnant women
	with a child at the breast;
	they flee in the cutting wind
	through an ice cold winter. (Matt 24:19)
All:	The end is still to come.
	AFTER the horrors
	the sign that heralds the Son of Man
	will appear in heaven.
Minster:	Wars and rumours of wars,
	nation that goes to war against nation,
	kingdom against kingdom (Matt 24:6a, 7).
All:	The end is still to come.
	AFTER the horrors
	the sign that heralds the Son of Man
	will appear in heaven.
Minister:	Famines in many places (Matt 24:7).
All:	AFTER the horrors
	the sign that heralds the Son of Man
	will appear in heaven.
	The end is still to come.
Minster:	The earth trembles (Matt 24:7).
All:	AFTER the horrors
	the sign that heralds the Son of Man
	will appear in heaven.
	The end is still to come.
Minister:	False messiahs and false prophets
	produce great signs and wonders,
	mislead God's chosen ones. (Matt 24:24)
All:	AFTER the horrors
	the sign that heralds the Son of Man
	will appear in heaven.
	The end is still to come.
Minister:	Death everywhere,
	dead everywhere,
	a labyrinth of tombs,

	a jungle of towering black tombs,
	as high as the number of deaths underneath.
All:	The end is still to come.

When we celebrated the Eucharist, the cups and plates of Holy Supper stood in the midst of the wilting flowers on the table, and its looks and smells gave deep meaning to the Eucharistic prayer, which included this clause:

Minister:	O Lord, come to our aid!
All:	The configuration of this world will pass.
Minister:	O God make us alive
All:	and sanctify your name.
Minister:	Thanks to the God of David
All:	through Jesus his servant,
Minister:	who in the same night that he was betrayed
	…

In 2018 the Italian artist Giorgio Calò transformed all the windows of the church by covering them with red transparent foil. The Reformation, in 1578, turned the church into – as Milan Kundera says in *The Unbearable Lightness of Being* – a 'white hangar', a void of no significance. Calò 'teared up' the decor of that emptiness by reddening it, to an impressive effect, especially when on the longest day in June the church stayed open until the sun had set and the red light became more and more intense, until it slowly dissolved in the dark night.

One could say that completely new meanings were unlocked. Red has, to quote the color teacher Johannes Itten, 'an irresistible radiation power', it is 'a fiery force',

Image 3: Giorgio Calò, Anastasis (2018), printed with friendly permission of Museum de Oude Kerk, Amsterdam.

and can express a 'feverish-like, combative passion'. It is connected 'with war and demons', but also with the colour of 'spiritualized love'. And a more extensive quote:

> There are a lot of red-modulations, because one can vary it to cold – warm, dull – radiating, and light – dark, without destroying its red character. From the demonic and gloomy vermilion red on black, to sweet angelic Madonna-rose, red can express all the stages from the subterranean to the celestial life. Only the etheric, spiritual, transparent-airy remains inaccessible to the red, because in that area the blue prevails (Itten 1961, 134–135, o.t.).

The red, like every colour, is full of ambivalences: It consumes, and it warms, it is the colour of fire and of blood, of death and life, of enthusiasm and ire. In a medieval church building like this it also evokes references to the ecclesial canonical colours, to the liturgical red of the Holy Spirit and of the faith witnesses, the martyrs. But unmistakably in this specific church building it also refers to the district in which the church stands, and which is named by this same colour, the Red Light District. At night the church mimics the brothels around it. No illusions, the artwork seems to say, the boundaries between church and square are wafer thin and the red therefore evokes "all the stages from the subterranean to the celestial life". The red has meaning both from the cultural code in which the church is set, and the spiritual code within the church. And at the same time, it transcends all that through its powerful rule. It is this world, but different, this world in the perspective "of the infinite or of an absolute sense" (Gräb 2006, 68): *Anastasis*, Resurrection.

3 Anthropological and Theological Considerations

Earlier in this chapter we outlined a general theological and philosophical framework in which senses, art and museums were kept together in their coherence. We mainly referred to fundamental theological and philosophical thinkers such as Schleiermacher, Heidegger, and Chauvet. After a description of several art installations in the museum and church building of the Old Church in Amsterdam, we now introduce the exemplary in a contemporary theological-philosophical discourse, in order to show the relevance of the encounter between art and religion.

3.1 Radical Theology

In the first section of this chapter, we refer to the religious dimensions of the museum, in the ways that Carol Duncan, Mary Bouquet and Nuno Porto describe. Carol Duncan develops her narrative starting with the development of the public art museum in the Enlightenment, through nineteenth-century bourgeois culture that conferred an educational and civilizing value to the art museum. This story culminates in the narrative of the twentieth-century modern art museum and its corresponding search for spiritual transcendence of the nothing-beyond-the-empirical-observable earthly world. The religious language that frames the narrative of Mary Bouquet and Nuno Porto is far more fragmented, due to the changes that museums underwent and the complex apparatuses into which they developed. The encyclopaedic oversight is diversified, the public pluralized, the museum entered into dialogue, there is no overarching unified idea anymore (Bal 2011, 530–531, 540).

It is here that postmodern, so-called *Radical Theology* joins the debate. 'The holy' is 'the complete other' that manifests itself to people and phenomena (Otto [1917] 2014), *and especially in art*, which Richard Kearney calls 'the poetics of the possible' (Kearney 1988, 371). The 'poetics of the possible' point to the non-available, the non-representable, in short, the stranger. One could also say: the incalculable (Chauvet 1995, 49). Or, in other words, the 'indeconstructable', the promised for, the called for. It is always to come, never a fixed entity. It is an event that uncovers or constitutes 'truth' (Chauvet 1995, 49; Caputo 2006, 6). Eventually the three installations in the Old Church of Amsterdam escape description and only poetry suffices to trace their meanings. Art evokes art. Or, to frame it in the language of Schleiermacher: being touched by an expression of heightened self-consciousness heightens the self-consciousness of the one who is touched, which evokes a new expression.

Analogous to Bouquet and Porto, but unlike Tillich, Kearney speaks of art as referring to 'a *quasi*-belief in a *quasi*-God. It suspends the question of God' (Kearney 2011, 130). When speaking about God, he speaks of a 'God-perhaps' and joins the notion of 'the radical other' in which religiosity was caught in twentieth-century discourse. He proposes his project as "an invitation to revisit what might be termed a primary scene of religion: the encounter with a radical Stranger who we choose, or don't choose, to call God" (Kearney 2011, 7). It is precisely the arts that are pre-eminently a place where the question of God can be asked without having to be answered. Again, whether the encounter with art is interpreted as religious depends on the viewer and the discourse in which he or she participates. Because a discourse is never individual, the community and culture in which the viewer participates plays a role in that interpretation.

Further, Kearney refers in his work to sacramentality. "Imagining the other as other is what enables the self to become a host and the stranger a guest" (Kearney 2011, 41–42). The notion of the 'sacramental' refers to welcoming 'the stranger into the here and now' (Kearney 2011, 85); it refers to the artistic process of 'consecrating' whatever 'corporeal situation' into 'a second order reference of creative possibility'. Kearney names this proceeding the 'aesthetic of transubstantiation' or 'eucharistic aesthetic' (Kearney 2011, 90–91. 97). It is: "The word made everyday flesh" (Kearney 2011, 87). Whether this sacramentality is religious aesthetics or aesthetic religion, remains undecided (Kearney 2011, 99). Going one step further, opening to God's condescension in the sensory and physical remains dependent on a human response "to the sacred summons of the moment" (Kearney 2011, 87).

Kearney makes a correct reference to Francis of Assisi, and especially to his *Cantico delle Creature*. His "mystical panentheism [...] was a way of restoring God to the world, of rediscovering a living God amidst the ashes of a dead one" (Kearney 2011,

100). The question of ultimate meaning, of God perhaps, can arise on a roof terrace on a medieval church building high above the narrow alleys of the city, between towering tombs of agricultural plastic in the same building, and in a mysterious red light that illuminates the oldest church of Amsterdam. Religious aesthetics may turn into an aesthetic religion.

3.2 Final Practical Theological Considerations

Christian theology can be defined as the border traffic on the roads between the areas of 'church' and 'culture'. In order to be able to carry out their task, the theologian must participate in both areas, wholeheartedly and with a critical sense. We belong to both areas, to two regimes. *Practical* Theology can be defined as the border traffic between ecclesiastical and cultural practices. Practical Theology that deals with the aesthetic and the arts can be described as the border traffic between ecclesiastical and cultural *artistic* practices. In the late modernity in which we live, the boundaries between both areas are not always clear (if they have ever been). In the 'true' work of art a way opens up for being to disclose itself, in the 'true' ritual or sacrament, a path opens up for Christ to reveal himself. But their coming cannot be fixed or empirically established; it is 'Presence-as-trace; trace of a passing always-already past; trace thus of something absent'.

Bibliography

Bal, Mieke. 2011. "Exposing the Public." In *A Companion to Museum Studies*, edited by Carol Duncan, Chichester: Blackwell Publishing, 525–542.

Barnard, Marcel. 2001. "Secular Feast and Christian Feast in Schleiermacher's *Practical Theology and Aesthetics:* A Theoretical Contribution to the Study of Liturgy and the Arts." In *Christian Feast and Festival: The Dynamics of Western Liturgy and Culture*. Liturgia Condenda 12, edited by Paulus G. Post, Gerard Rouwhorst, Louis van Tongeren, Alexander Scheer, Leuven / Sterling: Peeters, 185–203.

Barnard, Marcel. 2019. "Art as Sacrament." *Stellenbosch Theological Journal Supplementum* 5:13–28.

Barnard, Marcel. 2020. "Il vuoto rosso. La tomba deserta" / "The Red Void. The Empty Grave." In *Anastasis*, edited by Giorgio Andreotta Calò, Amsterdam: Roma Publications 2020, 27–32.

Barnard, Marcel. 2020. "Il vuoto rosso. La tomba deserta" / "The Red Void. The Empty Grave." In Anastasis, edited by Giorgio Andreotta Calò, Amsterdam: Roma Publications 2020, 27–32.

Bouquet, Mary, and Nuno Porto, eds. 2005. *Science, Magic and Religion: The Ritual Process of Museum Magic*. New Directions in Anthropology 23. New York / Oxford: Berghahn Books.

Caputo, John. 2006. *The Weakness of God: A Theology of the Event*. Bloomington: Indiana University Press.

Chauvet, Louis-Marie. 1995. *Symbol and Sacrament: A Sacramental Reinterpretation of Christian Existence*. Collegeville: The Liturgical Press.

Dreyer, Jacco. 2016. "(De)coloniality and the Conundrum of Reflexivity." In *Conundrums in Practical Theology,* edited by Joyce Ann Mercer and Bonnie J. Miller-McLemore, Leiden / Boston: Brill, 90–109.

Duncan, Carol. 1995. *Civilizing Rituals: Inside Public Art Museums.* Re Visions: Critical Studies in the History and Theory of Art. London: Routledge.

Gräb, Wilhelm. 2006. *Religion als Deutung des Lebens: Perspektiven einer Praktischen Theologie gelebter Religion,* Gütersloh: Gütersloher Verlagshaus.

Heidegger, Martin. [1950] 2002. *Off the Beaten Track*, trans. Julian Young and Kenneth Haynes. Cambridge: Cambridge University Press.

Itten, Johannes. 1961. *Die Kunst der Farbe: Subjektives Erleben und objektives Erkennen als Wege zur Kunst.* Ravensburg: Otto Maier Verlag.

Kant, Immanuel. [1739] 2009. *Religion within the Bounds of Bare Reason*, trans. Werner S. Pluhar. Indianapolis / Cambridge: Hackett Publishing Company.

Kearney, Richard. 1988. *The Wake of Imagination: Ideas of Creativity in Western Culture*, London / Melbourne: Routledge. Oxford / Malden: Blackwell Publishers.

Kearney, Richard. 2011. *Anatheism: Returning to God after God.* Insurrections: Critical Studies in Religion, Politics, and Culture. New York: Columbia University Press.

Long, D. Stephen. 2010. "Making Sense of Christian Worship: Language, Truth, and Metaphysics." *Liturgy* 25:62–71.

Luhrmann, Tanya. 1998. "Magic." In *The Dictionary of Anthropology,* edited by Thomas Barfield, 298–299.

Nongbri, Brent. 2013. *Before Religion: A History of a Modern Concept*, New Haven / London: Yale University Press.

Otto, Rudolf. [1917] 2014. *Das Heilige: Über das Irrationale in der Idee des Göttlichen und sein Verhältnis zum Rationalen.* München: Verlag C.H. Beck.

Prisser, Jeanne. 2015. "Doorbreken van een cliché kan een cliché worden." *De Volkskrant.* https://www.volkskrant.nl/nieuws-achtergrond/doorbreken-van-een-cliche-kan-een-cliche-worden~b4955b32/ (29.11.2021).

Schleiermacher, Friedrich D. E. [1821/1822] 1980. *Der christliche Glaube nach den Grundsätzen der evangelischen Kirche im Zusammenhange dargestellt.* Vol. 1,7,1, Kritische Gesamtausgabe, edited by Hans-Joachim Birkner. Berlin: De Gruyter.

Schleiermacher, Friedrich D. E. [1830/1831] 2003. *Der christliche Glaube nach den Grundsätzen der evangelischen Kirche im Zusammenhange dargestellt.* Vol. 1,13,1, *Kritische Gesamtausgabe*, edited by Rolf Schäfer, Berlin: De Gruyter.

Schleiermacher, Friedrich D. E. [1832/1833] 2021. *Vorlesungen über die Ästhetik. Nachschrift Schweizer.* Vol. 2,14, *Kritische Gesamtausgabe*, edited by Holden Kelm. Berlin / Boston: De Gruyter.

Schleiermacher, Friedrich D. E. 1850. *Die praktische Theologie nach den Grundsätzen der evangelischen Kirche im Zusammenhange dargestellt,* edited by Jacob Frerichs. Berlin: Reimer.

Smallenburg, Sandra. 2015. "Kunstenaar maakt op Oude Kerk dakterras". *NRC Handelsblad.* https://www.nrc.nl/nieuws/2015/06/26/kunstenaar-maakt-op-oude-kerk-dakterras-1508351-a882286 (29.11.2021).

Stringer, Martin. 2011. *Contemporary Western Ethnography and the Definition of Religion.* London / New York: Continuum.

Tillich, Paul. 1987. "Address on the Occasion of the Opening of the New Galleries and Sculpture Garden at the Museum of Modern Art." In *On Art and Architecture*, edited by John Dillenberger, New York: Crossroad, 246–249.

Angela Treiber
Anthropology and Religion

1 Culture and Religion

Starting from the anthropologically orientated conception that culture, as the world of things, and of people's relationships with them, "does make human subjects what they are" (Scharfe 2002, 22; o.t.), the issue outlines the most important theoretical tendencies, methodological specificities, and positions in scholarly discussions about culture and religion. The focus is on the field of Cultural anthropology/European ethnology and in the German-language field once called *Volkskunde* since the late 1950s.

This historical view underlines subtextual implications of imprinting through internalised denominational, theological knowledge in the sciences of Religion. For an ethnographic approach within cultural anthropology, and for analysis from the perspective of historical, social, and cultural studies, there is a need to explore the terminological structures determining these disciplines to seek to identify how religion becomes visible as the object of communication. In this way, we can understand and accept the polyphony and hybridity of academic discourse and its practices in connection with Religion.

1.1 The Concept of the Human Being

If we ask 'What is a human being?', and we are a cultural anthropologist, an ethnologist, a specialist in cultural studies, we are always simultaneously asking: 'What is culture?' Researchers in these disciplines focus on the cultural contingency of humanity and of human individuals; they regard culture as a product of human action, as the 'work of human hands'. Culture, as the world of things, of cultural objectivisations and of people's relationships with them, calls for our careful and thorough consideration "because not only does it make human subjects what they are, it makes them in the first place" (Scharfe 2002, 22; o.t.).

The roots of this concept of the human being and of culture are traceable to the specific approach taken by what is known as philosophical anthropology, which began to emerge in the 1920s and for which Max Scheler (1874–1928), Arnold Gehlen (1904–1976) and Helmuth Plessner (1892–1985) laid the foundations. It developed a long-term impact on what came to be called cultural anthropology or European ethnology and in German sociology as it regrouped and re-established itself after 1945 (Fischer 2006; Greverus 1978).

A decisive influence came from the field's response to and adoption of the conceptualisation of a human being as possessed of 'world-openness', which is "in principle tantamount to shedding the spell of the environment" (Scheler 1928). Human beings achieve this via their capacity for self-distancing (*Fernstellung*) from conditions in their environment and, in so doing, for making them into 'objects'; this is their 'ability to objectify' (*Gegenstandsfähigkeit*). This is the ability of human beings to distance themselves via words, images, symbols, representations; that is, via a concept or idea removed from immediate experience. In this theory, then, human engagement with the self and the world takes place through interpretations of perceptions and experiences upon which active, lived experience and self-expression are contingent. From this it follows that the act of understanding is an integral part of the act of living.

Regardless of their critique of the generation of anthropological universals, the questions raised by what has been called philosophical anthropology have been constitutive of approaches in social theory. The reason therefore laid not least in the manner in which they have – while respecting the factuality of variability and change – linked questions around the natural biological foundations on which human beings' lives and activities are based and those relating to the cultural and historical dimensions of human experience.

1.2 Religion as a Part or a Specific Form of Culture

The doubtless most influential response from the realm of cultural studies to the question of what culture is has been the proposal by Clifford Geertz in the form of an "interpretive theory of culture", drawing on the semiotic, symbolic facet of culture as a tendency in human expression and communication. It presents an image of man as "suspended in webs of significance", that is, culture, which "he himself has spun" (Geertz [1966] 1973, 5). Geertz sees the sum of these webs as an 'acted document' created via mimesis and participation in the life of a society. Progressing from this concept, he defines religion as a cultural "system of symbols which acts to establish powerful, pervasive, and long-lasting moods and motivations in men by formulating conceptions of a general order of existence and clothing these conceptions with such an aura of factuality that the moods and motivations seem uniquely realistic." (Geertz 1973, 90) Geertz further suggests:

> For an anthropologist, the importance of religion lies in its capacity to serve, for an individual or for a group, as a source of general, yet distinctive, conceptions of the world, the self, and the relations between them, on the one hand – its model of aspect – and of rooted, no less distinctive 'mental' dispositions – its model for aspect – on the other (Geertz 1973, 123).

Geertz' approach, distinguishing religion's 'model of aspect' and its 'model for aspect', points simultaneously to entanglements of meaning (cultures / religions), produced in continuous social practice, and to the character of these enmeshments as a resource driving that social practice. In this view, then, we can conceive of religion as a cultural and social fact. In defining its general function as one of the creation of meaning, however, Geertz does not intend to raise it to the status of an absolute and universal principle. His assertions do not exclude the possibility that there are other 'webs' generating significance, other symbolic systems, nor that people in all societies adopt and share in the specific system of religion (Geertz 1973, 108–109, note 33)[1].

In his ethnological studies on material religious culture, whose emphasis centred on cultural history and phenomenology of religion, Lenz Kriss-Rettenbeck was an early responder to Geertz. Kriss-Rettenbeck's exemplary exploration of devotional objects as material objects and specific entities representing actions demonstrated the possibility of "constructing ideal types both of entities and of devotional styles" from stable fields of meaning limited to specific situations, to the end of identifying instances of the performative. In his view, understanding such phenomena requires the researcher to examine and illuminate her own interpretive, behavioural, and expressive schemata as well as those of the 'others', her subjects (Kriss-Rettenbeck 1983, 219–220; o.t.), accompanied by the foundational necessity of – to speak with Geertz – "look[ing] for systematic relationships among diverse phenomena, not for substantive identities among similar ones. And to do that with any effectiveness, we need to replace the 'stratigraphic' conception of the relations between the various aspects of human existence with a synthetic one." (Geertz 1973, 44) This is critique of comparative anthropology and religious studies, that assumed, in analogy to assumptions drawn from evolutionary biology, the existence of a series of ascending cultural levels in human society (magic → religion → Christianity). That also suggested relationships among cultural phenomena that occurred at great geographical distances from one another but appeared to bear similarities; and in so doing presumed the identifiability of specific stages of age or development in the phenomenon in question.

As early as the late 1950s, long before research in religious studies had taken the step, Kriss-Rettenbeck's work, in particular, had renounced the habit of attributing magical, that is, irrational, and primitive properties to religious rituals that evade our own understanding. Citing as an example the Christian use of amulets and votives, Kriss-Rettenbeck concluded, in a manner which called the leading assumptions of contemporary comparative religious studies into question: "We may without difficulty trace the creation and use of all Western amulets to *participation mystique* (as in Lévy-Bruhl), but only if we restrict ourselves to a superficial interpretation of

---

[1] Asad (1993) emphatically critiqued Geertz' conception, protesting that its terminology was largely influenced by developments in modern Christianity and was therefore of limited use to the analysis of other traditions, as well as showing a particular tendency to leave aside matters of the exercise of social and political power (Asad 1993). Fundamentally, this position corresponded to Asad's call, in opposition to Geertz' 'universal' definition of religion, for the exploration of what symbols mean in relation to the practical contexts of their use, to authority, and to forms of the exercise of power in society (Asad 1993, 53).

the outer appearance, negate all historicity and turn to a naïve psychologism in our interpretation." (Hansmann and Kriss-Rettenbeck [1966] 1999, 8; o.t.)

Kriss-Rettenbeck's exploration and interpretation of medieval Christian sources enabled him to develop productive theoretical starting points for work on religion from a cultural studies perspective. Via the question of how we might conceive of religiosity, specifically popular religiosity, he asserted the centrality of identifying and illuminating the "notion, valid in the main for the whole Church, of the relationship between teaching ('liturgical/sacramental religiosity'), religious experience, cognition ('spiritual religiosity' as a *causa monachorum*) and human capacity ('religious sensitivity')", each in their historical context (Kriss-Rettenbeck 1963, 14; o.t.). It is not by chance that this approach corresponds on a theoretical level with the theorems proposed by Peter L. Berger und Thomas Luckmann (1966) on the 'social construction of reality' (the objective reality with which one is presented, subjective reality, internalisation, and externalisation).

Unlike Kriss-Rettenbeck's work, Luckmann's theoretical concept of 'the invisible religion', with its philosophical and phenomenological basis, and the manner in which he conceives of religion (Luckmann 1967, 1991), did not directly elicit a great response until cultural anthropology became increasingly interested in topics relating to what were called alternative forms of faith and began to focus on empirical approaches. Luckmann's afterword to the German edition of *The Invisible Religion* (1991) was of particular influence in this regard. It defines religion as founded in the fundamental anthropological constant of the human capacity to transcend the immediate environment and experience other, extra-ordinary 'realities' beyond the everyday empirical sphere. The act of transcending alone does not amount to religion; instead, religion provides a framework for the interpretive attachment of meaning to experiences of the transcendental and shapes the ways in which a culture engages with these experiences. Religious consensus arises through the passing down as tradition of conventions, both canonical and non-canonical and varying in the degree of their binding force (Luckmann 1967, 1991, 167–172). Put succinctly, it is via religion that "experiences of transcendence [are] socially constructed" (Knoblauch 1997, 186; o.t.), are "formed and ma[de] the subject of rules, with varying degrees of success" (Luckmann 1985, 34; o.t.). Cultural studies may draw on this in forming a concept of religion as a "part or specific form of human-created culture" (Scharfe 2004, ix; o.t.).

In light of the increasing difficulty of gaining a clear picture of 'lived religion' in complex, pluralistic societies with strong cultures of individualism, this broad concept of religion promises to add precision to our analysis and interpretation of what is religious and what is not. 'Small' and 'intermediate transcendences', which transcend the actual direct experience, as in the journey of memory through time and space or the indirect experiences of the other (Luckmann 1991,164–183), reveal their religious or spiritual character when an actor interprets them, from within her worldview, as pertinent to an extra-ordinary region of meaning and when they find expression via discursive practices and acts of materialisation. In this way, we conceive of theoretical approaches to understanding religion as models that raise our awareness and enable us to analytically access practices a society interprets in a religious context, rather than as universal definitions.

2 Self-Consciousness

2.1 Understanding Other People

What has been called the 'ethnological paradigm', and its approach, based on understanding other people via the methodology of participant-observation-based fieldwork, cast light on actions and products subjectively deemed to hold meaning, as interpretations of the world, and on the conceptions that attach to these products and actions. This attempt to draw near to the view from within, to modes of experience, made the sensitivity and the emotional constitution of religion visible, laying the groundwork for the insight "that the categories of function and functional rationality alone are insufficient for the attainment of a more profound understanding of notions of faith and acts of religion." (Kohl 2001; 171, o.t.) It was the emergence of an anthropology of understanding that enabled us to describe the acts of others in terms that ascribed to them and credited them with a proper logic and rationality within their own cultural and religious systems of meaning; this was understanding in the sense of recognition of grounds for actions that were invested with meaning and therefore rationality.

How do people, facing their objective realities, their environment, the things, actions, practices and linguistic expressions around them, garner meaning from them and create meaning in the act of their interpretation? How do they come to understand the fabric, woven of knowledge and the attribution of meaning, of ideas and notions communicated to them and passed down the generations and of which they are part, in all its symbolic complexity? And how does this fabric come to be; how does it constitute itself through a shared understanding of shared symbolic practices? Interpretive ethnology, led by the desire to understand, has come to focus on these questions. It is a field closely associated with Clifford Geertz, who drew directly on the hermeneutics of biblical exegesis. After the turn of the nineteenth and twentieth centuries, when Hermann Gunkel had sought to identify the "Sitz im Leben" (place in the life of people) of Old Testament texts, this area of scholarship had gained influence and significance for a historically driven *Volkskunde* that was increasingly taking on the character of cultural anthropology, and for a religious ethnology of practical theology (Gunkel [1925] 1963).

Geertz asserted a contextualising, perspective-centred approach via complementary or mutually commenting upon, contradicting, questioning interpretations of social discourses and practices enables the generation of a 'thick description' of reality. The core of this exploration, therefore, is the understanding and interpretation via hermeneutic means of human cultural creativity – of how humans understand their world (Geertz 1973).[2]

In terms of theories of knowledge, this technique of standing back from the subject/object, positioning oneself as distanced, other, as part of the hermeneutic process and to the end of avoiding 'going native' in total identification, creates a point at which the approaches of historically focused cultural anthropology and ethnological fieldwork meet and intersect. Stepping back and distancing oneself from others' religious worlds of ideas and worldviews calls for us to reflect thoroughly upon ourselves, for it entails standing apart from our own – in the broadest sense of the term – religious experiences, those experiences which go to the heart of our humanity and act as powerful codeterminants of our identity. It may be that in so doing, we gain a particularly clear, perhaps painful sense of our own relativity.

2.2 Estrangement – Making the Familiar Strange

The discourse around knowledge in ethnology/cultural anthropology has accorded a key role to the researcher's understanding of her own emotional access to her subject and to uncovering its initially unconscious undergirding with her own values (Clifford and Marcus 1986).[3] Klaus Peter Köpping proposes the centrality to understanding during fieldwork of comprehending the dialectical relationship "in which the researcher, in the encounter with the other, meets the boundaries of [her] self and [in which] that self becomes conscious both of its prejudices and of the values it holds most dear" (Köpping 1990, 14; o.t.).

In this context, Köpping and Heike Kämpf have pointed to the heuristic relevance of Helmuth Plessner's hermeneutics to interpretive praxis in ethnology and cultural anthropology (Köpping 1990, 14; Kämpf 2003). The human position in the world that Plessner terms 'eccentric positionality' is about a capacity for reflexivity; a human being is able to step back from herself and to take an attitude to herself with which she acts in accordance, and, in understanding, to step back in distance from the act of understanding itself. In 1948, drawing on his experience as an emigré, Plessner speaks of painful experiences which led him out of the sphere of the familiar and opened up a view to the discovery of the Other; experiences acting as catalysts to a 'cognisant comprehension' which brings about consciousness of an interpretive approach to the world:

---

[2] The scope of this article prohibits a discussion of the 'writing culture' debate and its critique of the approach to culture as 'text' (Clifford and Marcus 1986), which primarily emphasises the discursive nature of writing in ethnography, or of the postcolonial 'writing against culture' approach (Abu-Lughod 1991).

[3] For an overview of the debate see Berg and Fuchs (1993).

That is why the estranged vision of the artist fulfils an indispensable condition for all genuine understanding. It lifts what is invisible in human relations because it is familiar, into visibility; in this new encounter, understanding is brought into play; so that what is in fact familiar becomes accessible by virtue of being estranged. Without this estrangement there is no understanding; it constitutes a roundabout approach to the familiar, the counterfoil which puts the familiar into perspective as foreground and background and makes it comprehensible (Plessner 1978, 31).

There is now no way back to the former state of unconsciousness, of taking things as read: "Instead, the knowledge of the provisionality and constructed character of the comprehension [we have] achieved is inherent to this act of understanding." (Kämpf 2012, 398, o.t.)

Following this argument, we as cultural anthropologists must abandon any notion of our research aiming towards a final and thereafter immovable understanding and therefore definition of the Other – specifically here the Other of religious practice – in its difference to what we identify as our own. For, were we to continue to seek such finality, we would lose our insight into the interrelationships and interreferentialities among perspectives drawn from our own cultural horizons in the practices with which we approach understanding the Other.

3 Making Religion: Approaches to Interpretation

3.1 Thing-World

The influence of phenomenological approaches and the methodological repertoire of research in the field effected a turn towards subjective components of religious experience which has enabled insights into the interrelationships among fields of significance pertaining to religious teachings and the specific experiential worlds of actors. At this juncture, the question has arisen of the extent to which cultural anthropology and ethnology can seek to explore subjective religiosity. Around the end of the 1990s the emphasis on the subject observable up to that point in the field's evident focus on personal, internal experiences of reality was challenged. Calls emerged for a new concentration on their "externalisations, in which [these experiences] become visible and which arise, are shaped anew, and invented in [subjects'] engagement with the culture passed down [to them]" (Scharfe 1997, 149; o.t.). The 'thing-world', the performative praxis of rituals and gestures, of images and signs, habitual religious practices as the embodied substructure of group-specific acts of making the world – in other words, 'lived religion' in its material visibility and its historical making – are key points of departure for work on religion in cultural anthropology and ethnology. As previously indicated, the roots of this approach lie in a constructivist view of cultural and religious phenomena (objectivations) in their constructed entanglements of interrelationships. These phenomena come into being through practices of adoption and of the imposition of a specific character on such rituals and acts, upon the sediment of attributions of meaning passed down the generations and enacted by, for example, religion constituted in the form of a church and / or via individual access to other corpora of knowledge.

This approach corresponds overall to the more recent notion of material religion, which conceives of images, objects, songs, and specific bodily movements as mediating the transcendental and seeks to understand the interconnections between religious experience and materiality, with the aim of achieving an "integrated approach that includes the mental dimension within a material approach" (Meyer 2012, 11; o.t.). This concept came to be in a context of increasing critique levelled from representatives of the humanities and cultural studies at tendencies towards de-materialisation perceived as being at work in constructivism and semiotic interpretive methods: "[I]nstead of prioritizing semantic approaches that look through concrete manifestations so as to get at the abstract meanings behind, it is key to approach religion as a mundane, practical and material affair – as present in and making a world" (Meyer 2012, 20; o.t.). Attributions of meaning are nevertheless directly related to the materiality of a thing's physical shape and form, in which are 'inscribed' societal prescriptions for courses of action; the entanglements of meaning created by human hands materialise in an open-ended process.

There is a view that the perception of a process of de-materialisation being at work on religion has emerged, *inter alia*, from the response to Thomas Luckmann's work, a response whose concomitant has been a concentration on individual religious cosmoses of meaning which form in the personal sphere, beyond and aside from institutional forms of religious socialisation. This tendency may also be responding to the observable decline in the institutionally linked 'visible' practice of faith (Meyer 2011, XV). This said, Luckmann does not suggest that religion is dissolving, disappearing from modern, pluralistic societies, but rather that it is manifesting in other new socio-cultural forms outside institutional religion lived via churches and other similar bodies, diffusing through areas of society, such as sport, politics, and entertainment, which we do not associate with traditional ideas of what religion is. This process, suggests Luckmann, makes religion 'invisible', that is, no longer recognised for what it is (Luckmann 1991; cf. Scheer 2015, 90).

In the context of research into religion from the perspective of Protestant theology, which explores religion as an institutional phenomenon, of ecclesial studies, of sociology and what was once *Volkskunde*, likewise for research into Protestant religiosity, we can indeed perceive a neglect of 'lived religion', leading to its invisibility. The origin of this development lies in the Protestant conception of the personal sphere and of the inward nature of faith (inner belief) alongside freedom of conscience to be exercised in accordance with one's judgement (free conscience). Studies by Anglo-American cultural anthropologists/ethnologists on Christianity refer in this context to a 'mentalistic' or 'Protestant bias', which denotes self-perception as more modern or progressive than other confessional communities or denominations due to the assumed ability to be religious without material aids. It is in line with the tradition, theologically initiated in the Reformation, of rejecting the use of mediating forms to tackle the problem of presence and materiality. Another influence here is a hangover from a religious aesthetic prized by a middle-class Protestant milieu, which defines a correct way to practise religious emotionality to the ultimate end of attaining the proverbial 'Protestant inwardness of faith'. This has entailed a narrative which, in line with a specific denominational culture-critical theology, degraded the use of things, rituals and the physicality associated therewith as ephemeral, superficial, and devoid of true meaning.

From the late nineteenth century onward, forms of religious externalisation, through the influence of evolutionist notions in religious studies, fell under the essentially age-old suspicion of being tantamount to magic, superstition and fetishism, as therefore essentially archaic, pre-modern, primitive stages of culture. This claim to superiority over the use of things, perceived as 'irrational', failed to take account of the dynamics of religious actions and practices as conferring meaning. Rituals performed within a community or collective, accompanied by the transferral of a cultural knowledge held by those involved and consciously reflected upon to a (greater or lesser) degree ('tacit knowing'; Polanyi 1958), generate sensory dispositions and moods which provide the required conditions for acts of transcending. This takes place via the perceptible, or put differently, experiencable, appresentation (*Mitvergegenwärtigung*) of the symbolic practice's referent. This appresentation points to extra-ordinary experiences and realities, which may, for instance, find themselves endowed with eschatological interpretations, and likewise to mediated experience of a close, intense connection to a community, or to immediate experience of remembering the past or planning the future. It may indeed occur as presentation, in which instance symbolic practice itself becomes reality and is conceived of as such (Soeffner 2004, 42).

There have doubtless historically been boundaries, drawn in the context of ecclesial canonisation, between the faithful and those without faith. These notwithstanding, taken-as-read experiences of rootedness or incorporation into a community, proceeding with little or no awareness of self and unfolding via mimetic practices in communicated action, without knowledge of a meaning to this expression founded in religion or theology and without the powerful transcendental experience of *communitas* (Turner 2003), but accompanied by a community or group experience, belong to the category of the religious.

Approaches that foreground the aesthetics of religion are gaining traction in work on religion from cultural anthropology and ethnology. These approaches place emphasis on a sensory anthropology which seeks to explore the use of the senses, sensory perceptions, the interpretive horizons of what subjects see, hear, taste, and touch, mindful of their mediated character and their historicity. In its mimesis of the interpreted narrative of salvation via the employment of the physical mode and the Church calendar, Christian *praxis pietatis*, particularly in its pre-Reformation traditions, has made use of the constitutive function that attaches to human physicality in engagement with things accessible to experience via the senses and their embodiments as extensions of human embodiedness. And at an early stage, what is known as Jesuit anthropology had recognised that the presentation, the making present, of the transcendental requires the deployment of the senses and the generation of an emotional mode of expression, and that the sensory embodiment of a *religio carnalis* is what creates religious experience (Lundberg 1966; Daxelmüller 2000, 221).

Post-Reformation traditions of teaching in Protestantism, with their emphasis on a direct personal relationship to God and on self-responsibility, are reticent towards or actively reject the use of expressive practices with bodily character and material objects as media of the transcendental. This said, these traditions, too, render religion tangible or palpable in materialised expressions of a field of discourses and things, to which end they employ communicable, mediated repertoires of forms and practices, passed down through the generations. Practices, such as Bible study, which revolve around internalisation and self-examination, are core expressions of 'Protestant inwardness'. The attention to the appropriateness or otherwise of emotional states reveals itself as a process of the 'cultivation of emotions', which, experienced as mediating the experience of the divine, find expression in emotional concepts and practices learned in the context of the traditional body/soul dichotomy. This tradition cultivates a critique of the bodily aspect of religious sensibility and embodies it in the subject's physical disposition and habitus, their gestures, and expressions. The particular emotionality found in the religious practices of the Pentecostal and charismatic movements are no exception to this; they turn the body into the core medium of the transcendental in the form of the 'Holy Spirit', of its presence and immediacy (Scheer 2014, 2015).

3.2 Ambiguities

The onward march of modernisation in the European setting has increasingly weakened the social normativity of religious symbols, images, rituals, and their use and has increased the scope of their ambiguity, their significative plurality. Encounters between people with divergent cultural and religious orientations and in many instances clashing sets of attitudes and expectations are no longer limited to the exceptional contexts of regionally specific urban settings. In our day, acting in concert with the occurrence and accessibility of heterogeneous bodies of religious knowledge from a wide range of interpretive contexts on the multimedia stage, people find themselves increasingly challenged to live with ambiguities and multiple potential interpretations of cultural, religious, and attitudinal factors. What positions do they take up relative to one another in these settings, and what positions are assigned to objects? We are called to pinpoint the cultural techniques and strategies which people employ to fill the space opening up through religious plurality and ambiguity for new standpoints and identifications. Likewise, we seek to explore people's responses to this emergent situation; do we find tolerance, a search for certainties and an associated rejection or indeed violent repudiation of the 'foreign' and new, or an assumption of cultural ambiguity?

In a striking 'alternative history of Islam', specifically of Islamic culture of the post-formative but pre-modern period, Thomas Bauer, a researcher on literature and on Islam, has applied the term 'cultural ambiguity' to the phenomenon, of unperturbed attitudes to vagueness and ambiguity, among scholars as well as elsewhere, and indeed of the conscious generation of ambiguities as a cultural technique. "Where one social group simultaneously draws norms and attributions of significance for specific areas of life from opposed or highly divergent discourses, or when differing interpretations of a phenomenon find acceptance at one and the same time within a particular group, without either or any of these interpretations gaining exclusive primacy" (Bauer 2011, 27; o.t.).

In this, Bauer is referring to a concept, originating in psychology (Frenkel-Brunswik 1949), termed 'tolerance [or intolerance] of ambiguity'. Later work in this area identified a connection between intolerance of ambiguity and feelings of psychological discomfort, such as fear and threat, alongside characteristics of ethnocentrism, dogmatism, authoritarianism, and rigidity. These authors came to the conclusion "that religiosity, as a dogmatic attitude, is typically concomitant with increased intolerance of ambiguity" (Reis 1997, 112; o.t.). People with a synthetic one, by contrast, tend to remain calm even in situations that to them appear unfamiliar, unstructured and difficult to exert control over, thereby managing the situation, and show attitudes characterised by circular thought patterns that rather than falling into an 'either/or' scheme, will tend to prefer both.

The ethnologist Dieter Narr formulated similar 'diagnoses', or, put differently, characterisations of lived religion. He refers to undividedness/decidedness as a conspicuous characteristic of popular piety, explaining "that it neither seeks to achieve a balance of ideas, eliminating contradictions, nor attempts a timid severance between the sacred and the profane spheres" (Narr 1959/60, 70; o.t.). The historical anthropologist Carlo Ginzburg characterised the idiosyncratic 'theology' proposed by the sixteenth-century miller Menocchio, who fell victim to the Inquisition, as an 'imbroglio' in an attempt to illuminate that which was flamboyant, ambivalent, new and striking, un-decided, about his 'simplified religion' (Ginzburg 1979, 84, 163–164). Ginzburg reads this phenomenon of 'religious living' as a "plebeian reduction and correction of official theology", implying that a counter-cultural tendency attaches to it (Scharfe 2004, 226; o.t.). This is also the context in which the sociology of religion, drawing on Bourdieu, characterises 'popular religion' as 'heterodox': "It does not align itself with an orthodox worldview, but diverges from it, indeed may at times oppose it" (Knoblauch 2009, 240; o.t.).

Likewise, the type of religious practice which, defined as popular, spiritually based religiosity, has emerged on the scene in recent decades places people's "conscious, emotionally experienced individual concept[s] of meaning, translated into real-life action", at its centre (Polak 2008, 98; o.t.). This conceptualisation is one way in which people seek to express themselves in antithesis to the reified character of their everyday lives and to religious practices defined and determined by others, dominated by 'experts', similarly in opposition to the radical practical concept of dominion over nature embodied in science and academic study (Heimbrock 1998, 33). Read thus, popular religion and spirituality resist academic (or, more precisely, scientific) and rationalist worldviews as well as those founded in rationalist theology, along with their orthodoxies of perception.

Similarly oriented perceptions have emerged from the sociology of religion in relation to everyday religiosity as it manifests itself in our day. In this context, Armin Nassehi refers to the figure of the 'composer' of religion, which an ethnologist would term 'bricoleur' ('DIYer'); this denotes a type of religious experience "which is accustomed to living in an inconsistent world", living a form of religiosity which "can get along with inconsistencies"; this attitude renders inconsistencies simultaneously a problem and a solution (Nassehi 2007, 119; o.t.).

Studies on migration have shown that people employ diverse individual coping strategies in response to the emergent awareness of their socio-cultural religious socialisation that is concomitant to the self-alienation inherent in the migration process. These strategies may range from re-arrangement, adjustment, and re-orientation to the taking of a completely new direction and/or conversion of their prior religious identification. In some instances, such developments may bear definition as distinct spiritual paths, as 'process-based religious doing' or 'religioning' (Nye 2000, 21; Jaciuk 2019, 48), which pushes the matter of a specific, actual location within a particular tradition into the background or renders it redundant. We might well describe this manner of engaging with religion as a strategy revolving around psychologically balancing out deficits or limitations in societal participation.

We may conceive of cultural ambiguity as part of the human condition; we find it ubiquitous as we go about and manage our daily lives, for the things and the norms we encounter require our interpretation and we may find ourselves in metaphorical battle around contradictory sets of values. The setting of the everyday is a distinctly rich source of situations which call for action beyond the routine. The space a culture creates for the 'undecided', for ambiguity, provides a potential path to a solution. One of the central properties of cultural ambiguity is a lack of exclusive claims to the definition of an unambiguity within a particular group or society; instead, the group or society includes and encompasses divergent interpretive patterns stemming from competing norms and accepts them. This means that there is no description of norm versus deviance at work; instead, an instance of cultural ambiguity in this context may be conceived of as the result of strategies of boundary-drawing and exclusion between historically established religious fields. Such results include the "genealogy of the distinctly modern, secular category of 'religion'" and the "classifying taxonomy of religion" (Casanova 2009, 91; o.t.), likewise the various, historically located variations on the images of self and other produced by professionals (theologians and scholars in the humanities) and also laypeople whose classifications gravitate towards unambiguity, in terms of popular piety, vernacular religion, superstition and magic (Treiber 1996).

This means that, for an ethnographic approach within cultural anthropology, and for analysis from the perspective of historical, social, and cultural studies, there is a need to explore the terminological structures determining these disciplines, to seek to identify how, on a socio-cultural level, religion becomes visible as the object of communication. We would also do well to retrace the boundaries drawn – where they are drawn at all – around defined 'reality' via the oppositions religious / secular, sacred / profane, and rational / irrational in each relevant socio-historical context.

3.3 Forms of Speeching about Religion

Paul Mecheril and Oscar Thomas-Olalde (2011, 38) have turned a spotlight on the binary way of speaking about religion within academia, with one type of speech rooted in a 'model of appropriation/adoption' (*Aneignungsmodell*) and the other proceeding from the 'model of religious identity as destiny'. The first of these conceptions of religion appears to relate more substantively to the 'native population' of the society the migrant enters; it describes individual subjects' religiosities "as dynamic, hybrid and contingent elements of identity, [or,] better still, as preferences" (Mecheril and Thomas-Olalde 2011, 36).[4] By contrast, Mecheril and Thomas-Olalde continue, numerous studies around migration resort 'in a reductive manner' to the concept of 'religion' in order to present, explain and position the Other as they see fit. A focus on concepts of diversity and ethnicity, on the specific groups of migrants in question, and a funnelling of the relevant issues down to religious organisations and institutions will lead to the attribution of a central role to religion alongside and in this segment of society and the subliminal application of an ethno-cultural label. In this way, the praxis of hegemonic discourse effectively produces a group via "essentialisation, attribution and representation" and in so doing posits a religious identity (Mecheril and Thomas-Olalde 2011, 45; o.t.), with the effect that research on religion often finds itself perpetuating 'religion' as a popular topos without realising it.

The layers of interpretation of 'religion' and 'culture' outlined here and emerging through competing discourses call for us to make clear distinctions in our academic use of the terms. We need to distinguish the concept of religion as a "part or specific form of human-created culture", alongside the notion of religiosity/spirituality as particular modes of subjectively lived religion accessed by communicable, 'traditional' forms of practice, from the deterministic equivocation of religion with/as culture, which turns religion into culture's sole determinant or, conversely, in the perceived relativity of a coherent field of interpretation, makes religion appear as culture (Nassehi 2007).

---

[4] We are unable here to explore more closely the theoretical concepts of hybridity (Bhabha 1994), creolisation (Hannerz 1987) and transculturation (Ortiz 1940).

In day-to-day reality, the categories, of course, are blurred; these academic constructs nevertheless require analytical distinction from concepts and strategies around categorising culture and religion that draw on everyday manifestations of these phenomena and which serve to aid individuals' self-positionings in their specific lifeworld within their societal surroundings, satisfy their spiritual needs and, in so doing, generate an individual sense of self-identification or self-stabilisation. For instance, people may participate in religious traditions consciously estranged from the spiritual/transcendental significance they carry; this participation serves instead as a strategy for the individual to lay down roots in the tradition's specifically located function as a repository of cultural memory. Alternatively, the separation of religion from culture, that is, from religious traditions, may become part of a distinct spiritual stance, what we might term a practical, everyday cultural technique of differentiation between culture and religion.

3.4 Final Review: 'to Find a Language in Difference'

When academics use the category of 'religion', they, like non-academics, very often do not mean the same thing as their peers. Culture and religion are dynamic fields of reference and significance within a world of things, which structure people's perceptions and experience. Merely speaking the same language carries no guarantees; we must be aware of the position from which the act of speaking is taking place. Every encounter, then, calls for translation from one cultural/linguistic field of reference into another. The sociologist Encarnación Gutiérrez Rodríguez describes the encounter of conversation as a transcultural space, an interstice between the divergent socialisations that shape language. Connotations of linguistic expressions that are specific to particular cultural or group-based settings or contingent upon specific situations or that emerge from the individual's sets of associations give birth to semantic lacunae which hinder decoding (Enzenhofer and Resch 2011). Gutiérrez Rodríguez observes in this context: "The translation project that emerges from this encounter does not pursue the goal of articulating a universal commonality but rather attempts to find a language in difference." (Guiterrez-Rodriguez 2008, 3) Similarly, when we encounter one another across academic disciplines, we need to act in the spirit of interpretive understanding in cultural anthropology, recognising and reflecting upon the cultural codes that arise through our academic and general socialisation and determine our perspective on the world and the ways of speaking we have adopted and assimilated – including our own. In so doing, we bring to light our implicit, heterogeneous prior conceptions of religion and religious practice. If we are to comprehend one another and perhaps reach consensus, we need to accept and tolerate the polyphony and hybridity of academic discourse and its practices.

Bibliography

Abu-Lughod, Lila. 1991. "Writing Against Culture." In *Recapturing Anthropology: Working in the Present*, edited by Richard G. Fox, Santa Fe: School for Advanced Research Press, 137–162.

Asad, Talal. 1993. "Anthropological Conceptions of Religion: Reflections on Geertz." In *Genealogies of Religion: Disciplines and Reasons of Power in Christianity and Islam*, edited by Talal Asad, Baltimore: Johns Hopkins University Press, 27–54.

Bauer, Thomas. 2011. *Die Kultur der Ambiguität: Eine andere Geschichte des Islam*. Berlin: Verlag der Weltreligionen im Insel Verlag.

Berg, Eberhard, and Martin Fuchs, eds. 1993. *Kultur, soziale Praxis, Text: Die Krise der ethnographischen Repräsentation*. Frankfurt am Main: Suhrkamp.

Berger, Peter L., and Thomas Luckmann. 1966. *The Social Construction of Reality: A Treatise in the Sociology of Knowledge*. New York: Doubleday.

Bhabha, Homi. 1994. *The Location of Culture*. London: Routledge.

Casanova, José. 2009. *Europas Angst vor der Religion*. Berlin: University Press.

Clifford, James, and George E. Marcus, eds. 1986. *Writing Culture: The Poetics and Politics of Ethnography*. Berkeley / Los Angeles: University of California Press.

Daxelmüller, Christoph. 2000. "Volksfrömmigkeit als Gegenstand der Lehre in der Empirischen Kulturwissenschaft." In *Hochschullehre und Religion: Perspektiven verschiedener Fachdisziplinen*, edited by Dieter Fauth und Ulrich Bubenheimer, Würzburg: Religion-und-Kultur-Verlag, 213–240.

Enzenhofer, Edith, and Katharina Resch. "Übersetzungsprozesse und deren Qualitätssicherung in der qualitativen Sozialforschung." *Forum Qualitative Sozialforschung / Forum: Qualitative Social Research* 12. https://www.qualitative-research.net/index.php/fqs/article/view/1652/3177 (29.11.2021).

Fischer, Joachim. "Philosophische Anthropologie: Ein wirkungsvoller Denkansatz in der deutschen Soziologie nach 1945." *Zeitschrift für Soziologie* 35:322–347.

Frenkel-Brunswik, Else. 1949. "Intolerance of Ambiguity as an Emotional and Perceptual Personality Variable." *Journal of Personality* 18:108–143.

Geertz, Clifford. [1966] 1973. "The Impact of the Concept of Culture on the Concept of Man." In *The Interpretation of Culture: Selected Essays*, edited by Clifford Geertz, New York: Basic Books, 33–54.

Geertz, Clifford. 1973. "Religion as a Cultural System." In *The Interpretation of Culture: Selected Essays*, edited by Clifford Geertz, New York: Basic Books, 87–125.

Gehlen, Arnold. 1986. *Anthropologische und sozialpsychologische Untersuchungen*. Reinbek: Rowohlt.

Ginzburg, Carlo. 1979. *Der Käse und die Würmer: Die Welt eines Müllers*. Frankfurt am Main: Wagenbach.

Greverus, Ina-Maria. 1978. *Kultur und Alltagswelt: Eine Einführung in Fragen der Kulturanthropologie*. München: Beck.

Gunkel, Hermann. [1925] 1963. *Die israelitische Literatur*. Darmstadt: Wissenschaftliche Buchgesellschaft.

Gutiérrez Rodríguez, Encarnación. 2008. "'Lost in Translation' – Transcultural Translation and Decolonialization of Knowledge." *transversal texts* 6. http://eipcp.net/transversal/0608/gutierrez-rodriguez/de (29.11.2021).

Hannerz, Ulf. 1987. "The World in Creolisation." *Africa* 57:547–559.

Hansmann, Liselotte, and Lenz Kriss-Rettenbeck, eds. [1966] 1999. *Amulett und Talismann: Erscheinungsform und Geschichte*. München: Callwey.

Heimbrock, Hans-Günter. 1998. "Welches Interesse hat Theologie an der Wirklichkeit? Von der Handlungstheorie zur Wahrnehmungswissenschaft." In *Gelebte Religion wahrnehmen: Lebenswelt – Alltagskultur – Religionspraxis*, edited by Wolf-Eckhart Failing and Hans-Günter Heimbrock, Stuttgart / Berlin: Kohlhammer, 11–36.

Jaciuk, Marina. 2019. *"Es war ein langsamer Prozess des Bewusstseins": Erfahrungshorizonte, Identität und Religion lateinamerikanischer MigrantInnen in Deutschland*. Würzburg: Königshausen & Neumann.

Kämpf, Heike. 2003. *Die Exzentrizität des Verstehens: Zur Debatte um die Verstehbarkeit des Fremden zwischen Hermeneutik und Ethnologie*. Berlin: Parerga.

Kämpf, Heike. 2012. "Verstehen." In *Handbuch Kulturphilosophie*, edited by Ralf Konersmann, Stuttgart: J. B. Metzler, 398–402.

Knoblauch, Hubert. 1997. "Die Sichtbarkeit der unsichtbaren Religion: Subjektivierung, Märkte und die religiöse Kommunikation." *Zeitschrift für Religionswissenschaft* 5:179–202.

Knoblauch, Hubert. 2009. *Populäre Religion: Auf dem Weg in eine neue spirituelle Gesellschaft*. Frankfurt am Main: Campus.

Kohl, Karl-Heinz. 2001 "Adolf Ellegard Jensen." In *Hauptwerke der Ethnologie*, edited by Christian Feest and Karl-Heinz Kohl, Stuttgart: Kröner, 166–172.

Köpping, Klaus-Peter. 1990. "Authentizität in der Dialektik Selbst/Anderer." *kea* 1:6–20.

Kriss-Rettenbeck, Lenz. 1963. *Bilder und Zeichen religiösen Volksglaubens*. München: Verlag Georg D.W. Callwey.

Kriss-Rettenbeck, Lenz. 1983. "Zur Bedeutungsgeschichte der Devotionalien." In *Umgang mit Sachen: Zur Kulturgeschichte des Dinggebrauchs: 23. Deutscher Volkskunde-Kongress in Regensburg vom 6.–10.10.1981*, edited by Konrad Köstlin and Hermann Bausinger, Regensburg: Universität Regensburg, Lehrstuhl für Volkskunde, 213–233.

Luckmann, Thomas. 1967. *The Invisible Religion*. New York: Macmillan.

Luckmann, Thomas. 1985. "Über die Funktion der Religion." In *Die religiöse Dimension der Gesellschaft: Religion und ihre Theorie*, edited by Peter Koslowski, Tübingen: Mohr Siebeck, 26–41.

Luckmann, Thomas. 1991. *Die unsichtbare Religion*, trans. Hubert Knoblauch. Frankfurt am Main: Suhrkamp.

Lundberg, Mabel. 1966. *Jesuitische Anthropologie und Erziehungslehre in der Frühzeit des Ordens (ca. 1540 bis ca. 1650)*. Uppsala: Universität.

Mecheril, Paul, and Oscar Thomas-Olalde. 2011. "Die Religion der Anderen." In *Jugend, Migration und Religion: Interdisziplinäre Perspektiven. Religion – Wirtschaft – Politik 4*, edited by Birgit Allenbach, Urmila Goel, Merle Hummerich, and Cordula Weissköppel, Baden-Baden: Nomos Verlag, 35–66.

Meyer, Birgit 2012. *Mediation and the Genesis of Presence: Towards a Material Approach to Religion*. Utrecht: Universiteit Utrecht. http://dspace.library.uu.nl/handle/1874/257546 (29.11.2021).

Narr, Dieter. 1959/1960. "Volksfrömmigkeit." In *Württembergisches Jahrbuch für Volkskunde*, edited by Friedrich Heinz Schmidt-Ebhausen, Stuttgart: Kohlhammer, 68–71.

Nassehi, Armin. 2007. "Erstaunliche religiöse Kompetenz: Qualitative Ergebnisse des Religionsmonitors." In *Religionsmonitor 2008*, edited by Bertelsmannstiftung, Gütersloh: Hans Kock Buch- und Offsetdruck GmbH, 113–134.

Nye, Malory. 2000. "Religion, Post-Religionism and Religioning: Religious Studies and Contemporary Cultural Debates." *Method and Theory in the Study of Religion* 12: 447–476.

Ortiz, Fernando. 1940. "El Fenómeno Social de la Transculturación y su Importancia en Cuba." *Revista Bimestre Cubana* 46:273–278.

Plessner, Helmuth. 1978. "With Different Eyes." In *Phenomenology and Sociology*, edited by Thomas Luckmann, Harmondsworth: Penguin Books, 25–41.

Plessner, Helmuth. 1982. *Mit anderen Augen: Aspekte einer philosophischen Anthropologie.* Stuttgart: Reclam.
Polak, Regina. 2008. "Spiritualität – Neuere Transformationen im Religiösen Feld." In *Individualisierung, Spiritualität, Religion: Transformationsprozesse auf dem religiösen Feld in interdisziplinärer Perspektive,* edited by Wilhelm Gräb, Münster: LIT, 89–116.
Polanyi, Michael. 1958. *Personal Knowledge: Towards a Post-Critical Philosophy.* London: University of Chicago Press.
Reis, Jack. 1997. *Ambiguitätstoleranz: Beiträge zur Entwicklung eines Persönlichkeitskonstruktes.* Heidelberg: Asanger.
Scharfe, Martin. 1997. "Soll und kann die Erforschung subjektiver Frömmigkeit das Ziel volkskundlich-kulturwissenschaftlicher Tätigkeit sein?" In *Individuum und Frömmigkeit: Volkskundliche Studien im 19. und 20. Jahrhundert,* edited by Ruth-E. Mohrmann, Münster: Waxmann, 145–151.
Scharfe, Martin. 2002. *Menschenwerk: Erkundungen über Kultur.* Köln: Böhlau Verlag.
Scharfe, Martin. 2004. *Über die Religion: Glaube und Zweifel in der Volkskultur.* Köln / Weimar: Böhlau Verlag.
Scheer, Monique. 2014. "Von Herzen glauben: Performanzen der Aufrichtigkeit in protestantischen Gemeinden." In *Religiosität und Spiritualität: Fragen, Kompetenzen, Ergebnisse,* edited by Anja Schöne and Helmut Groschwitz, Münster: Waxmann, 111–130.
Scheer, Monique. 2015. "Das Unsichtbare wieder sichtbar machen: Für einen rematerialisierten Zugang zu Religion in der Empirischen Kulturwissenschaft." In *Materialisierung von Kultur: Diskurse Dinge Praktiken,* edited by Karl Braun, Claus-Marco Dieterich, and Angela Treiber, Würzburg: Königshausen & Neumann, 88–103.
Scheler, Max. 1928. "Die Stellung des Menschen im Kosmos." In *Späte Schriften.* Vol. 9, *Gesammelte Werke,* edited by Manfred Frings, Bonn: Bouvier, 7–72.
Soeffner, Hans Georg. 2004. "Symbole in der Theorie: Protosoziologische Überlegungen zur Soziologie des Symbols und des Rituals." In *Die Wirklichkeit der Symbole: Grundlagen der Kommunikation in historischen und gegenwärtigen Gesellschaften,* edited by Rudolf Schlögl, Konstanz: UVK, 41–73.
Treiber, Angela. 1996. "Interpretamente historischer Forschung über Superstitionen und magische Mentalitäten." *Jahrbuch für Volkskunde NF* 19:81–125.
Turner, Victor. 2003. "Liminalität und Communitas." In *Ritualtheorien: Ein einführendes Handbuch,* edited by André Belliger and David J. Krieger, Wiesbaden: Springer VS, 251–262.

Heather Walton
Life Writing and Religion

1 Prologue: Letters in My Luggage

As a student I enthusiastically embraced the challenges of liberation theology, became involved in activist politics, and joined international solidarity movements. The resistance to apartheid particularly captured my imagination as it was justice-seeking and also generating new theological thinking. I ached to understand more, engage more, and share in this political/ideological struggle. I was 21 years old when I packed my rucksack, travelled by coach to London and boarded an evening flight from Heathrow to Johannesburg. I had been awarded a WCC Scholarship to study at the famous black theological seminary *FedSem* – then located in the sprawling township of Edendale.[1] That, as a white person, I gained a visa to study at the seminary now seems incredible. At the time I was too excited (and too naïve) to appreciate the strangeness of my situation. I also had some distracting practical concerns. What to take with me from home to sustain me on this life transforming journey?

My sleeping bag and the lovely dress my mother bought me for graduation were obvious essentials. I rolled up a spare pair of Jeans with some tee-shirts and a long cheesecloth skirt. I remember carefully choosing a little broach in the shape of a rose. But what books to take? In the end only two; my Bible and Dietrich Bonhoeffer's *Letters and Papers from Prison* (1973).

During the year I spent in South Africa I lived in the pages of this book. I loved Bonhoeffer's fine theological mind – formed by a classical education and rooted in the great I traditions of the Church – a background very different from my own. But while enchanted by him I was also irritated by his deeply bourgeois sentiments, his at-homeness in a world of man-friendships, cigars and courteous, but quaintly patriarchal, attitudes to women. I suspect if meeting in person conversation would have been awkward. But on paper his life became open to mine and, in my new context, revelatory.

I was young. I was in South Africa in the middle of a war. I was living in a township on a campus surrounded by a high wire fence and sharing a small room (actually the converted 'ladies' end of a toilet block) with Lindiwe – the only other woman student. I was beginning to get to know people who were 'involved' and at risk. I was also living alongside Bonhoeffer in the last days of the Reich and the last days of his life. There is not space here to list all that this particular collision of worlds generated for me, but some things are particularly important.

---

[1] The seminary had been exiled from its previous campus for political reasons and was in temporary accommodation.

 OpenAccess. © 2022 Heather Walton, published by De Gruyter. This work is licensed under the Creative Commons Attribution-NonCommercial-NoDerivatives 4.0 International License.
https://doi.org/10.1515/9783110618150-004

Image 4: Dietrich Bonhoeffer, Letters and Papers from Prison; SCM-Edition 1973 in possession of the author, © Heather Walton.

I was learning that in a struggle you must live with deception, silences, the acknowledgement that informers are your friends, and your friends might be informers. You become oddly close to your enemies and simultaneously distanced from people whose lives are not dominated by the ongoing conflict. What I grasped about Bonhoeffer's letters in this context was that they are written by a committed activist whose famous celebration of 'worldly' Christianity is constituted out of experiences of deep ambiguity and irregular intimacies. The man on paper knows he is a 'guilty' actor not an innocent victim. He must always dissemble and remain silent about matters of fundamental significance. The voice that reaches us strains to speak and cannot do so clearly:

> Am I then really all that which other men tell of? Or am I only what I know of myself [...] struggling for breath, as though hands were compressing my throat. (Bonhoeffer 1973, 349)

What South Africa was also teaching me, and which I found reflected in the letters, was the peculiar intensity of relationships forged under pressure. I have never been to better parties than those in which people segregated by the state drank together and banned persons broke their banning orders to come dancing. When Bonhoeffer writes that despite everything he would not 'wish to live in any other time' I understand it. His deep love for friends is palpable but so also are the realities of separation. Separation of distance but also of circumstances. Bonhoeffer has taken sides, but he is still not suffering in the same way as those without any power who do not await trial but are casually condemned. Pondering Bonhoeffer's writing I became acutely aware that although I settled down each night into my camp bed (the sleeping bag had proved a wise choice) only a few feet away from where my friend Lindiwe lay down to sleep, in reality, we still inhabited different worlds. Furthermore, Bonhoeffer and many of the other activists I met in South Africa had made irrevocable choices with their lives. I was passing through.

The time I spent in South Africa formed me as a person and shaped my theological work. The way I think and the ideals I cherish are entangled with strong sense impressions and body-memories out of which they were generated. As I write this paper I am standing again at the open door of my room as evening falls in the township. I can hear fellow students singing hymns as they chant their way out of chapel. I can smell cigarette smoke and cooking fires and the particular clear amber soap and coconut oil skin cream that Lindiwe used. I can taste the pink-sweetness of guava juice. In *Letters and Papers* Bonhoeffer's theology does not come cleansed of its context. It is a theology that communicates the feel of rough woollen blankets, the smell of men in confined spaces, the taste of a 'glorious liver sausage' (1973, 100) sent by his mother, the sound of sirens and the sweep of light across the sky, a sense of Spring in the air outside and the noise of a fellow prisoner weeping. And most of all it comes from a small and restricted space. Bonhoeffer compared his prison cell to the cell of a monk. A place confined and apparently set apart. Yet also one in which the life of the world is compressed into spiritual and theological energy; as a magnifying glass turns light into fire.

2 Reading Religious Lives

In a context in which analyses of secularisation, postsecularisation, enchantment, re-ritualisation, religious fundamentalism and religious decline endlessly contend together, it is easy to understand why the study and representation of particular lives appears an increasingly attractive way to reflect upon questions of religious identity. It has also proved a creative means to engage theologically with the complex nature of contemporary faith. Within practical theology there has been a significant and productive turn towards employing life narratives as 'data' for social analysis and for theological reflection (e.g., Ganzevoort, De Haardt, and Scherer-Rath 2013; Moschella 2016; Couture 2016; Wolfteich 2017).

Although, until recently, our academic use of personal life experience has been relatively uncommon it has enabled some very important developments to take place within the discipline (e.g., McLemore 1994). Today, however, more and more practical theologians are placing elements of their own life narratives within their texts (e.g., Beaudoin 2010; Couture 2017; Graham 2017; Walton 2018; Wigg-Stevenson 2017). This is in part due to a (rather belated) acknowledgement of the necessity for reflexivity in research practice (Dreyer 2016; Goto 2018; Bennett et al. 2018). Although our use of life writing is still often cautious and circumscribed, there is also growing recognition of how fruitful an epistemic resource personal experience might become. Practical theologians are hard-wired to make deep connections between faith and practice and life writing is a fertile space in which to explore this process.

Published works in practical theology that employ life writing are thus increasing exponentially. However, to date there has been very little focussed exploration into the nature of life writing itself. Nor has there been substantial critical engagement with the work of scholars from other disciplines who are bringing their own methodological insights to this discursive form. In the sections that follow I will refer to some of these methodological developments – while illustratively referring back to the personal narrative with which I began this chapter. I shall then focus in Part Three upon my own work and what I hope this contributes to developing project of practical theology

2.1 Literary Studies

Life writing is one of the oldest and most engaging literary forms but comprehending life writing 'as literature' is a challenging process. For example, many practical theologians take for granted that their task is to empirically represent lived religious experience and then hermeneutically elaborate upon it. However, when we consider life writing through a literary lens it begins to appear that experience itself is constructed within the narrative process. As Paul Ricœur has famously argued it is through the constructive work of 'enplotment' that experience is shaped into a form that enables us to access and comprehend it. To become intelligible at all it must be placed within a narrative frame:

> It seems that our life, enveloped in one single glance, appears to us as the field of a constructive activity, deriving from the narrative intelligence through which we attempt to recover [...] the narrative identity which constitutes us [...]. It is exactly the kind of identity which the narrative composition alone, by means of its dynamism, can create. (Ricœur 1991, 437)

So, although my South African story is a sincere attempt to communicate experience it has been constructed to achieve a particular end and the experiences themselves receive their form through the story I have told. It is true. But it is also 'fictive' and this quality marks all life writing as it is as dependent as any other literary form upon the plotting devices out of which narrative is formed.

But literary critics challenge us further by pointing out that enplotment is not a creative act that takes place ex nihilo. We fashion our own stories according to the narratives we inherit and the patterns they have laid down. For many literary scholars the starting point for exploring this process is St Augustine's *Confessions* which is frequently taken as initiating the autobiographical genre within Western culture (Anderson 2004). Augustine's work borrows the structure of a quest myth from the legends of battles and heroes, exiles and homecomings that were the cultural currency of his time.

This form became the pattern through which countless spiritual writers who followed him were to express their own stories of travail, transition, and transfiguration.[2]

Romanticism, emerging within late eighteenth century as an aesthetic response to the rationalist ethos of the enlightenment, radically inverted Augustine's narrative of the soul's journey towards the divine. Instead, it imaged the human quest as a self-creating journey towards personal authenticity. It is this romantic quest narrative that many influential cultural theorists identify as shaping notions of the self and spiritual identity in contemporary Western culture – whether or not people identify as religious (e.g., Taylor 1989; Heelas and Woodhead 2005). When I ask my students to describe their own spiritual journey's they speak of: 'being true to myself', 'discovering who I was meant to be', 'needing to find *my own* way through' etc. As they do so they are standing within a narrative tradition that stretches from Augustine to the present day, but which has taken many twists and turns through history. However, although we employ a common script it does not imply that our spiritual narratives are nothing but shallow repetitions of received ideas.

First it has to be said that the script endures because it remains meaningful to many people. Whether employed to describe a struggle with cancer, gender transitioning, becoming a poet or religious conversion – a story that tells of a difficult journey to positive selfhood can be a powerful way to frame identity. Second, as the generative work of Judith Butler has enabled us to understand, in the day-to-day performance of socially inscribed scripts individuals find themselves unable to fully achieve the roles ascribed to them. We improvise and make changes and these small performative gestures mean that the scripts are not as stable as might be imagined and are, themselves, implicated in creative processes of social change. Third, as literary critics have delighted to point out, in the inherited tradition the quest for a coherent narrative self is never achieved – it deconstructs before our eyes. The 'I' Augustine establishes is continually on the edge of toppling into chaos; anxiety wrestles with faith throughout his text (Anderson 2004, 27). Even within the romantic tradition, in which huge energy is devoted to the social performance of the expressive self, there is consistent uncertainty that this has been adequately achieved. Life writing is writing that both constructs identity and displays the contradictions and incongruities out of which it is formed.

The literary insight that our personal narratives are both scripted and unstable might be thought of as undermining their theological use. However, in my opinion, it opens up much more depth and complexity to the form. If I simply read Bonhoeffer's letter as the saintly musings of a man boldly facing martyrdom, they might be inspiring. However, they became revelatory for me precisely because of the intense struggles they embody and the silences they contain – hands 'compressing my throat'. There are things he cannot speak and things he does not know how to say, and they mark the text just as surely as the faith and hope he seeks to commu-

---

[2] See Walton (2015) for a detailed exploration of this mimetic process.

nicate. This partial and often contradictory narration of Christian experience makes sense to me. I am always conscious of mispronouncing the sacred script and that the border between belief and betrayal is never a wall but a very fine line.

I write these words aware that theologians are still rather inclined to seek the inspiration of virtuous and exemplary lives as data for theological reflection. However, some very interesting theological reflections emerge when we admit the ambiguities that haunt religious life narratives. For example, in her recent work on women's life writing practical theologian Clare Wolfteich (2017) takes the risk of writing about Dorothy Day's separation from/neglect of her daughter as she struggled to fulfil her religious vocation. A tragic tension in the life of this iconic woman is revealed. This is a very hard account to write and to read. However, Wolfteich has gifted me with a narrative of Day that I find I can now place next to my own life in powerful communication with my own struggles and dilemmas. Similarly, in my life writing I always seek to make evident the points of tension and contradiction in my faith life in order that the frayed edges of my own story can become threads my readers might connect with.

2.2 Epistemology

Reflection upon the ambiguities, gaps, and silences inherent within narrative construction was fundamental to the massive epistemological shift generated by second wave feminism. Women began to question why so many aspects of their experience were culturally invisible and, indeed, whether they were unnarratable in a patriarchal frame. Convinced that male experience had shaped ways knowing the world the movement was symbolically rooted in constellations of small consciousness raising groups in which women began to share personal narratives and to explore their political significance. Those involved cherished the conviction that narrative agency could produce both personal healing and new knowledge.

Pressing this insight further feminist cultural theorists developed standpoint epistemologies. Opposing traditional conventions of critical neutrality Sandra Harding (1991) argued that 'strong objectivity' is achieved when those bear the impact of social marginalisation are recognised to have a privileged understanding – and are enabled to explore their insights in conversation with others. Donna Haraway's generative work on situated knowledge similarly emphasised that vantage point informs viewpoint. Her vision was that networks of persons differently located, yet in dialogue with each other, might together produce ever more 'truthful' understandings of embodied experience:

> So feminists don't need a doctrine of objectivity that promises transcendence [...] but we do need an earth-wide network of connections, including the ability to partially translate knowledges among very different power differentiated communities. [...] Feminist objectivity means quite simply situated knowledge (Haraway 1988, 579–80).

Views of epistemology as both located and dialogical have now gained currency across a range of different fields and, to return to life writing, encourage us to read our own lives in relation to those of other people in different contexts whose insights challenge and enrich our own. This work does not entail abstraction or generalisation but delving deeper into the particularity of persons and lives in order create relational wisdom. Encountering Bonhoeffer's soul-searching reflections in South Africa was transformative for me – deepening my perception and giving me keys to interpret my own experiences. However, I return to Haraway's assertion that we should seek the translation of knowledges 'among very different power differentiated communities' to question how we might understand the limits of such dialogue. Although separated by time, gender, and class I shared with Bonhoeffer a saturation in Western culture and a privileged social location. In some ways it was easier for me to engage with his reality than that of the good friend with whom I shared a cramped an intimate space for several months. A genuine desire for meaningful communication does not mean it is easily achieved.

As we are increasingly aware political silencing is achieved through processes which render personal narratives inadmissible: stories of the forced removal of indigenous children, child abuse and the sexual victimisation of women were often told in the past but remained *as if* untold by their narrators. Coloniality as a cultural mechanism similarly renders many contemporary experiences unaccountable. Decolonial thinkers are now calling for the "unveiling of epistemic silences" and the creation of a "geo and body politics of knowledge hidden from western epistemology" (Mignolo 2009, 4). This will entail engaging with a reservoir "of ways of life and modes of thinking that have been disqualified by Christian theology" (Mignolo 2013, 133) and post-enlightenment thinking. Yet to access such a reservoir of understanding entails more than the silenced gaining the power to speak. Coloniality does not simply divide us from others but also create fissures within the self as people struggle to find modes of communication between the diverse worlds they inhabit. Kwok Pui Lan names the difficulties encountered:

> What is the process of self-fashioning that is going on in the story-telling process? 'Speaking for oneself' is never an easy and unambiguous process, especially when one constantly navigates between two cultures and languages. For example, are there silences and ellipses in the narratives? [...] Can one deal with the moral ambiguities and inconsistencies when one worldview collides with another in the process of negotiating multiple identities? (Kwok 2011, 35)

Practical theologian Courtney Goto has reflected deeply upon the fact that the fractured stories of people experiencing oppression do not easily find a space within a discipline dominated by white western voices and modes of expression (Goto 2018). She questions whether practical theologians possess the capability to engage with voices that resist incorporation into conventional frames of academic credibility and coherence. Convinced that 'empirical' research can become another form of cultural imperialism through which personal stories are colonised within an alienating interpretative framework she argues that people must, nevertheless, be enabled to share their lived experience. Referring to her own pedagogical practice she advocates that instead of withdrawing in disillusion students resisting coloniality should be encouraged to enter this communicative process *more deeply but differently*. First of all, there should be appreciation of epistemic advantage, "*a critical, perspectival edge created by experiencing oppression personally or empathically, enabling a knower to stand in multiple places, discern what others might neglect, and challenge ignorance or violence*" (Goto 2018, 202 italics original). With the recognition of this advantage students may gain confidence to write with forms of hyper-reflexivity and embodied rhetoric that reveal how they have been integrally formed by their contexts and display their affective as well as their intellectual means of grasping the world. It is Goto's hopeful vision that writing which is courageously open is paradoxically less vulnerable to objectivization for it "invites readers to engage in a parallel process" of self-examination and to consider the ways in which their own experiences have "been shaped by patterns of prejudice, privilege and violence". In other words, it invites relationship; "author and reader are in conversation in the space created by writing and reading" (Goto 2018, 216).

2.3 Social Research

Goto's hope for a relational narrative connection also stands behind the turn to forms of life writing which are becoming hugely influential within contemporary qualitative research. Norman Denzin and Yvonna Lincoln, leading scholars in this field, argue that an encounter with the narratives of those resisting 'epistemic silencing' should prompt qualitative researchers in all fields to "construct stories that [...] will be dialogical counternarratives [...] stories that create spaces for multicultural conversations, stories embedded in the critical democratic imagination" (Denzin and Lincoln 2008, 6). Specifically, the development of autoethnography as a lively and productive methodology facilitates this form of encounter as it "provides a framework to critically reflect upon the ways in which our personal lives intersect, collide and commune with others in the body politic" (Spry 2011, 54).

Autoethnography, which is a relatively recent arrival within the field of qualitative research, encourages deep critical attention to personal life narratives as a means to gain understanding of issues that have a collective cultural significance. Not only does it esteem 'insider' knowledge, but it also pays attention to the form in which this understanding is communicated. Pioneers in the field Carolyn Ellis and Art Bochner have repeatedly emphasised that autoethnographic writing must be evocative; framed to engage intellectual and also affective, embodied responses.[3] Norman Denzin goes further and argues autoethnography not only communicates

---

[3] See Walton (2014) for an overview of 'evocative autoethnography' which builds upon the foundations established by Ellis and Bochner.

but 'performs' transformation as it embodies "a way of writing, hearing and listening [...] a return to narrative as a political act. [...] It uses the words and stories people tell to imagine new worlds" (Denzin 2003, 105).

The subject matter of autoethnography varies hugely. I have used this methodology to reflect upon motherhood and secularisation (Walton 2014, 21–30), political activism and the work of preaching (Walton 2014, 10–20). However, as a form of life writing it shares the concerns of this genre with two distinct but overlapping foci: the epiphanic and the everyday. In reference to the first Ellis and Bochner encourage researchers to write about epiphanic insights that emerge from their particular cultural identity or social location. Norman Denzin also advises autoethnographers to focus on moments of revelatory significance that construct identity; "always write out of those spaces and experiences that carry the sting of memory, those epiphanies, and turning point moments that leave a mark on you"[4]

This is good advice because what a writer communicates with passion about moments of clarity and awe (including fearful moments of pain and grief) presses into the imaginations of their readers and generates intense responses. Interestingly these responses are not tied to the subject matter that evoked them. When I read about Bonhoeffer's prison experiences, I understood that they were very different indeed from my own encounters with the confining power and 'banal' evil of the apartheid regime. However, they spoke so powerfully to my context that it seemed natural to me to use his prayers and memorise his poetry as a means to express my own developing spiritual / political understanding. When I write about my own particular and personal 'epiphanic' experiences I am asking my readers to engage with different experiences from their own contexts which provoke similar intense, hyper-reflexive energy. I am asking them to seek out the epiphanies present in their everyday lives.

Attention to the significance of everyday life is fundamental to autoethnographic writing – and part of a turn to the everyday within social research more generally. Recognition has grown that the ofttimes neglected sphere of daily living is where most people exercise agency and construct selfhood. It is the plane on which our most meaningful life experiences unfold and also where the impacts of economic and political forces are most keenly felt – and, in some cases, resisted (Walton 2014, 170–85). The multi-layered nature of everyday living is what inspires radical autoethnographic researchers who continually seek to delve deeper into the particularity of experience as a means of voicing their political challenges. It is also why a turn to everyday life is also proving theologically generative.

For example, in the work of mujerista theologian Ada María Isasi-Díaz we are presented with a powerful articulation of the importance of *lo cotidiano* as the place in which Hispanic women engage in caring and cooking, shopping and sex but also social struggles and meaning-making work that "has descriptive, hermeneutical and epistemological importance" (Isasi-Díaz 1996, 67). It is from the every-

---

[4] https://www.dur.ac.uk/writingacrossboundaries/writingonwriting/normandenzin (08.10.2019).

day that vibrant theological understandings emerge out of lived religion. These incarnate epistemologies appear as very different from the 'normative' perspectives of ecclesial and academic traditions and encourage a reconceptualization of theology itself making it "possible for us to see our theological knowledge as well as all our knowledge as fragmentary, partisan, conjectural and provisional" (Isasi-Díaz1996, 72).

Isasi-Díaz is articulating here points about the nature of theological thinking through life narratives that I have been at pains to stress throughout this chapter. However, I would wish to add that theology generated in this form is not only fragmented plural and provisional it may also be rich, colourful, and vital. In Bonhoeffer's letters his unsystematic reflections are not separable from the cultural textile and personal texture of the man who wrote them. As such what they offer is not abstracted understanding what the cultural theorist Bruno Latour describes as truth 'warmly clothed, incarnated and strong' (Latour 1989, 115). As practical theologian Natalie Wigg Stevenson (2017) has argued we need to develop more nuanced ways of approaching where truth lies in our theological reflections. Older understandings of normativity are difficult to operationalise in relation to autoethnographic writing. However, as their evident epistemological significance cannot be denied we will need to discover new means of appraising value. Significant work on this topic is underway in qualitative research but is only just beginning within practical theology.

3 Writing My Life

Up to this point I have been at pains to stress the rich potential of life writing as we seek to understand contemporary religious practice and also as we seek to become more creative in our theological reflections. I have argued that we are not engaging with coherent and reliable (so-called empirical) accounts that can be easily processed into conventional theological statements. Quite the contrary. Life narratives are unwieldy and difficult to tame for our own ends. They reveal things we might prefer to ignore such as:
- The constructed, fictive, and mimetic nature of narrated experience.
- The gasp, silences and fissures narration contains.
- The difficulty of representing trauma and pain – or indeed any deeply disruptive experience within a conventionally 'storied' framework.

However, the revelatory power of life narratives also sheds light on things that we are learning to celebrate. These include:
- The dialogical and relational nature of meaning making.
- The importance of everyday life and the epiphanies it contains.
- The located and embodied nature of our understanding.
- The potential of an intense focus upon the particular to illuminate wider cultural, political, and theological issues.

- The vivid and compelling nature of theological reflection that is 'incarnate and strong'.

I now turn back to my own practice to explore how I seek express these qualities of life writing in my own work. I would like to highlight three practices that have become particularly important to me as my engagement with theological life writing has developed and deepened.

The first relates to making explicit links between life experience and theoretical thinking. I am a life writer, but this does not mean that I wish to repudiate theoretical thinking and embrace a moist and moody immanence. I am someone who is, by temperament, perhaps a little too analytical – I love a good theory. It is rather that I now seek to tie my theoretical reflections back into the life situations out of which epistemic challenges arise. In recent years I have made it my custom to include short life writing extracts in my most 'abstract' scholarly articles. The incident retold gestures towards the existential elements the theoretical argument addresses. So, for example, an article on postsecularism begins with an account of going to church one Sunday morning (Walton, 2018) and a discussion of new materialist thinking begins with an account of clearing up after putting my daughter to bed:

> Blossom, the favourite doll, was sprawled face down on the carpet. Her stiff limbs outstretched, and her long golden nylon hair tangled. I bent to pick her up and it was as if a current ran through me. A small but perceptible force that made me shiver slightly. This doll could not be impersonally handled but commanded respect. She was animated and something of my child's life was bounded up in her. I combed her hair with my fingers, smoothed her dress and sat her in my daughter's little chair where she could be found and loved again next morning (Walton 2014, 31).

Secondly, I now seek to make evident the relational nature of understanding by addressing very directly (as I have done in this chapter) the ways in which my own ideas are formed out of intense encounters with others – which may be personal, political and/or textual. I treat authors I admire as friends and write about my friends in ways that acknowledge their shaping influence upon me. In my book *Not Eden* (Walton 2015) I employ an extended, 'relational' metaphor to describe my experience of becoming politically engaged in South Africa.

> I read newspapers and cut out bits to file. I wrote down tables of statistics noting infant mortality, malaria, and TB. I studied philosophy and wrote my diary. I liked this serious person I was playing. She had taken her vows and was dedicated like a nun. But then I went to visit. I stayed in [the Young Christian Workers] house. There was no place for me there. I had to sleep in the bed of whichever person was away that night or in the space that was left when two people shared one bed [...]. I was sleeping in the hollows other bodies had left in the mattress, in rooms where clothes other people had worn were scattered on the floor and where the cigarettes they had smoked were still in the ashtray (Walton 2015, 120).

This image illuminates a process leading from observation to involvement – literally a living-in-the-life-space that others have created. I think this metaphor holds good for my academic theological practice also.

A third important aspect of life writing that is increasingly becoming part of my academic discipline is the active disclosure of the many spheres in which I dwell and the overlaps as well as the tensions between them. This is facilitated by the generative capacity of life writing and, in particular, the practice of journaling. I have published edited extracts from my journals that demonstrate ways in which being a partner, a mother, a friend, an academic, a lover-of-lovely things, a writer, a gardener and someone who enjoys wrestling hard with a dense theory (particularly if it is French/ and or Marxist) all tumble together in my theological thinking. Some of my 'journaled-articles' are about specific challenging issues in my life such as an extended period of infertility, a personal bereavement and suffering from anxiety. The fragmented heterogeneity of journal writing naturally lends itself to exposing the 'unresolvement' that these experiences entail and to experimental theological work as steps in the development (or not) of understanding can be noted and transcribed.

Working in these ways, writing in these ways, still feels a little transgressive within practical theology. It is therefore deeply enjoyable! However, I have to concede that I am only gradually learning ways of proceeding that are taken for granted in other spheres. Artists have always opened themselves up to the inspiration of the 'found object'; something happened upon in the midst of life that becomes epiphanic to them. Poets and creative writers have similarly found that great power lies in the improper mixing of things that should remain apart. What is metaphor other than relational thinking with revelatory effect?

What artistic work in all spheres teaches is that particular experience, compressed through intense focus upon it, can become incandescent. Light into fire. This was what I found in Bonhoeffer's *Letters and Papers* and which so caught my imagination. The personal writing of a man in a particular and prescribed environment combusted old ways of thinking and sent sparks flying far beyond their prison. I covet this incendiary art for contemporary practical theology and am excited by the challenge of working to develop a theopoetics of practice within our discipline (Walton 2019).

Bibliography

Anderson, Linda. 2004. *Autobiography*. London / New York: Routledge.
Beaudoin, Tom. 2010. *Witness to Dispossession: The Vocation of the Post-Modern Theologian*. Maryknoll: Orbis.
Bennett, Zoe, Elaine Graham, Stephen Pattison, and Heather Walton. 2018. *Invitation to Research in Practical Theology*. London / New York: Routledge.
Bonhoeffer, Dietrich. 1973. *Letters and Papers from Prison*. London: SCM Press.
Couture, Pamela. 2016. *We Are Not All Victims: Local Peacebuilding in the Democratic Republic of Congo*. Münster: LIT Verlag.

Denzin, Norman. 2003. *Performance Ethnography: Critical Pedagogy and the Politics of Culture.* London: Sage.

Denzin, Norman. "Mystories." https://www.dur.ac.uk/writingacrossboundaries/writingonwriting/normandenzin (08.10.2019).

Denzin, Norman, and Yvonna Lincoln. 2008. "Introduction: Critical Methodologies and Indigenous Inquiry." In *Handbook of Critical and Indigenous Methodologies*, edited by Norman K. Denzin, Yvonna S. Lincolm, and Linda Tuhiwai Smith, London: Sage, 1–20.

Dreyer, Jaco. 2016. "Knowledge, Subjectivity, (De)Coloniality and the Conundrum of Reflexivity." In *Conundrums in Practical Theology*, edited by Joyce Ann Mercer and Bonnie Miller-McLemore, Leiden: Brill, 90–109.

Ganzevoort, R. Ruard, Maaike De Haardt, and Michael Scherer-Rath. 2013. *Religious Stories We Live By: Narrative Approaches in Theology and Religious Studies.* Leiden: Brill.

Graham, Elaine. 2017. "On Becoming a Practical Theologian: Past, Present and Future Tenses." *HTS Teologiese Studies / Theological Studies* 73:1–9.

Goto, Courtney. 2018. *Taking on Practical Theology: The Idolization of Context in the Hope of Community.* Leiden: Brill.

Haraway, Donna. 1988. "Situated Knowledge: The Science Question in Feminism and the Privilege of Partial Perspective." *Feminist Studies* 14:575–599.

Harding, Sandra. 1991. *Whose Science? Whose Knowledge? Thinking from Womens' Lives.* Ithaca: Cornell University Press.

Heelas, Paul, and Linda Woodhead. 2005. *The Spiritual Revolution: Why Religion Is Giving Way to Spirituality.* Oxford: Blackwell Publishing.

Isasi-Dìaz, Ada María. 1996. *Mujerista Theology: A Theology for the 21st Century.* Maryknoll: Orbis.

Latour, Bruno. 1989. "Clothing the Naked Truth." In *Dismantling Truth: Reality in the Post-Modern World*, edited by Hilary Lawson and Lisa Appignanesi, New York: St Martin's Press, 101–126.

Kwok, Pui Lan. 2011. "The Politics and Poetics of Ada María Isasi-Díaz." *Feminist Theology* 20:33–38.

Mignolo, Walter D. 2009. "Epistemic Disobedience, Independent Thought and De-Colonial Freedom." *Theory, Culture & Society* 26:1–23.

Mignolo, Walter D. 2013. "Geopolitics of Sensing and Knowing: On (De)coloniality, Border Thinking, and Epistemic Disobedience." *Confero* 1:129–150.

Miller McLemore, Bonnie. 1994. *Also a Mother: Work and Family as Theological Dilemma.* Nashville: Abingdon.

Moschella, Mary Clark. 2016. *Caring for Joy: Narrative, Theology and Practice.* Leiden: Brill.

Ricœur, Paul. 1991. *A Ricoeur Reader: Reflection and Imagination*, edited by Mario Valde, Hemel Hempstead: Harvester Wheatsheaf.

Spry, Tami. 2011. *Body, Paper, Stage: Writing and Preforming Autoethnography.* Walnut Creek: Left Coast Press.

Taylor, Charles. 1989. *Sources of the Self: The Making of the Modern Identity.* Cambridge: Cambridge University Press.

Walton, Heather. 2014. *Writing Methods in Theological Reflection.* London: SCM Press.

Walton, Heather. 2015. *Not Eden: Spiritual Life Writing for this World.* London: SCM Press.

Walton, Heather. 2018. "We Have Never Been Theologians: Postsecularism and Practical Theology." *Practical Theology* 11:218–230.

Walton, Heather. 2019. "A Theopoetics of Practice: Reforming in Practical Theology." *International Journal of Practical Theology* 23:1–21.

Wigg-Stevenson, Natalie. 2017. "You Don't Look Like a Baptist Minister: An Autoethnographic Retrieval of 'Women's Experience' as an Analytic Category for Feminist Theology." *Feminist Theology* 25:182–197.

Wolfteich, Claire. 2017. *Mothering, Public Leadership, and Women's Life Writing.* Leiden: Brill.

Jaesung Ha
Communication and Religion

1 Practical Theology as Communication

From the beginning, practical theology itself has been an effort to communicate with the world outside the church and contemporary society. Don Browning introduces practical wisdom as useful for practical reasoning with the concept of *phronesis* that Aristotle and the Gospel of Luke commonly used. It distinguishes itself from *theoria* or *techne* and religious communities often demonstrate it in a powerful way by constituting practical rationality and conveying it to the world. Christianity has practical reason with a narrative envelope "about God's creation, governance, and redemption of the world," in which "the life and death of Jesus Christ further God's plan for the world" (Browning 1995, 10).

Browning has well demonstrated how practical communication might happen since he developed a practical reasoning in the postmodern society or in the post-Christian culture. In the postmodern "deconstructionism" of pluralistic society, people "are all suspicious of all truth claims." (Meracadante 2014, 183) He argues that religious communities must "exhibit reason or, more specifically, practical reason" to make sense to the outside world (Browning 1995, 1).[1] In the post-Christian era of high reflection and communication, people do not feel that they are living in the present, but rather as deferred between past memory and future hope. The culture is rapidly changing into nihilism, and the church has lost its power to reform the world, let alone itself. Communication of religious faith has come to an end from within. The Church's voices have lost its authenticity and rather received backlash from the public about its corrupt inside. Society, culture, and politics univocally stand against the church throughout the world, especially in Korea's current society.

There is, however, one instigator for religious involvement in this atheistic era, that is, an individual's suffering. "Suffering is pervasive, intrinsic to the human condition," (Hunter 1991, 1230) and no one is able to escape from the vulnerability to suffer. Tim Keller, a preacher and Christian thinker, once said, "there is nothing more certain than the fact that you are going to suffer and/or people around you are going to be suffering" (Keller 2008). Suffering to those who tolerate pain is real; therefore, people are "not interested in the theoretical issue of suffering [...] [but] are torn apart by what is happening to real people, to those we know and love." (Hauerwas 1990, 2)

---

[1] Especially, about a form of speech, Browning introduces Habermas' three competences, that is, "to speak the truth, establish normative claims, and express oneself authentically" (Browning 1995, 200). Even among the uneducated people, according to Habermas, these communicative competences are essential not to break down the communicative action.

A Korean church introduced in this paper insists to grow because it has been dealing with human suffering in a unique way. It does not communicate practical wisdom with the society in a sophisticated way; instead, it has radical means to communicate with suffering individuals and connect them to God, that is, interpreting life in the light of the Scripture. This church follows "a classic expression of the *theory-to-practice model*" by "conform[ing] itself totally to the Word of God revealed in Scripture" (Browning 1995, 7). At first glance, it seems naïve and subjective process of appropriating biblical instructions for one's benefit.

However, the church exceptionally uses human suffering as a means to communicate with the world with biblical interpretations. Struggling with questions of *why* for a deep meaning functions as a path to faith in God. Regardless of the negative impressions of churches during the post-revival era in Korea, the church's model of practical theology that interprets personal suffering is being used as a guide to faith. Its confessional theology in the form of universality per se is a remarkable way of communicating with the gospel to society by offering a spiritual meaning. Although Browning and Edward Farley commonly slam the confessional theology "as a hamper in practical theological thinking" (Ha 2011, 206) Korean churches that include this principle have been thriving with confessionalism among the past persecution and ongoing pluralism.

2 Suffering and Interpreting in Narrative Community

At the gate of Seoul in Korea, from the busiest No. 1 highway from the south, no one can miss the church to the left on the hillside with its large billboard sign saying, "Marriage is not for happiness, but for holiness," which reminds us of a popular Christian author, Gary Thomas, and his bestselling book *Sacred Marriage* (Thomas 2015). The church is well-known for many peculiarities. first of all, the senior pastor is a woman who established the church in 2002, a time period when Korea did not have many female pastors. The church started its gatherings in a high school gymnasium in Seoul, but now it has two places to gather on Sundays. It is the *Wooridle Church*, which means *our church*. The church has been known for its magnetic power, especially for those who have suffered multiple afflictions in life including illness, abuse, or affairs. Its members are not usually local residents: they mostly come from distant cities within two, three, even five hours by car.

The church presently has more than a thousand 'powerful' small groups for looking after souls, which they call "pastures". They are a vital part of the church in which meetings are composed of Scripture readings and applications. There are pastures for couples, for women, and for workplaces; the size of each group is typically from seven to fourteen people. Once or twice a week, they gather at home, work, or church, doing Bible study and communal dialogues, which takes at least three hours.

Regardless of some resentments of the long meeting hours, the majority of the members still have a strong desire to attend the pasture meetings.

After reading the Bible, they share their life stories in light of the word for which they term this activity the *interpretation of life*. This allows for them to share their sufferings and ultimately seek spiritual meanings. Browning summarizes that "hermeneutics is basically a conversation" (Browning 1983, 49) as a process of interpretation, e.g., between theology and psychology. Biblical hermeneutics of life, however, is the church's unique process of finding the underlying message suffering brings through the intersubjective group process. The church finds it effective regarding communicative and collective healing to practice Bible meditation, confession of sins, and resolution for holiness in life. By helping those who suffer interpret their lives based on scripture, the church facilitates spiritual growth of individuals and rebuilding of families.

The church has also begun seminars for ministers since 2014, which is called, "THINK Bathtub Ministry Seminar". Public baths are common in Korea, in which everyone is expected to be naked, although sex-specific.[2] This metaphor makes it clear that the church prioritizes confession of sins, revealing wounds and weaknesses, while enabling rehabilitation from relational brokenness.

Victor Frankl, a survivor of a concentration camp during World War II, created the logotherapy based on his first-person experience of fatal sufferings and life-threatening fears among fellow inmates. He accepts the reality of "the unavoidability of suffering," (Frankl 1963, 181) but believed that a person's suffering has a meaning in itself. In the face of his own sufferings, including high chances of death, he bravely and rationally observed people's responses to their own detrimental destinies. He kept asking questions about the meanings of suffering while most other prisoners became hopeless in sustaining their interpretations.

> The question which beset me was, "Has all this suffering, this dying around us, a meaning? For, if not, then ultimately there is no meaning to survival; for a life whose meaning depends upon such a happenstance-whether one escapes or not-ultimately would not be worth living at all. (Frankl 1963, 183)

Frankl's concern in the camp was not survival itself. Instead, he believed that his suffering certainly had a meaning up to the moment of death. At the site of struggle for survival, he spawned the idea of logotherapy to help "the patient regain his (or her) capacity to suffer," (Frankl 1963, 180) not simply to enjoy life.

His ideas of suffering and meaning have made an important shift in therapy: rather than getting rid of pain itself, the therapist can help illuminate a meaning or purpose hidden under the surface of hopeless situations of the patient. The pur-

---

[2] It is not 'gender-specific' in Korea yet, legally or commonly. It has been a big dispute between progressivists and conservatives about the issue, but Korea still keeps its original constitutional position on 'sex' instead of 'gender'.

suit of happiness by regarding unhappiness as a symptom of maladjustment is a result of the 'mental-hygiene philosophy'. Instead of endeavoring to find pleasure or avoid pain, he sees a human as one who can embrace sufferings as long as hardships are meaningful.

Pastoral ministry is expected to accomplish a hermeneutical task by concerning "itself with ways of seeing and responding to situations of contemporary life that comfort with the vision of life that emerges from Scripture and tradition." (Hunter 1991, 592) The church has paved its way for the search for meaning through its peculiar practice for sufferers. The church does not only try to comfort those who mourn to make them happy again, but it also actively welcomes suffering in an individual's life and gets involved with it to make it meaningful. Instead of helping people overcome afflictions instantly, the church first teaches how to change themselves rather than changing their surrounding situations or related others.

By getting involved with people's sufferings communally and spiritually, the church encourages them to *interpret* their lives in light of the scripture. It provides a way of seeing life's predicaments, whose purposes and meanings can be found only in faith. The church functions as a pastoral guide for those in chaos by presenting a way of individual but biblical hermeneutics to find spiritual meanings.

The church values the interpretation of individual life based on the interpretation of the Bible. It is interesting to see how the church members do not just depend on sermons of the pastor. Instead, they actively participate in the process of interpreting the Bible in their own words. The church likes to use the term *interpretation of life* instead of the scriptural interpretation.

Rosemary Ruether once found that Korean women's life experiences and their views of scripture are closely integrated: "it is they and their lives that are the text, and the various scriptures and traditions provide material by which women can interpret their lives" (Ruether 1998, 271). The integration of their life stories in the form of particularity with Bible stories is respected and shared, which ends up becoming an active interpretation of life. The Bible is not simply one of the many reading materials but the one true resource that makes them obedient even during the suffering.

Once people register as a church member, they will be taught how to interpret their lives based on a personal and communal application. They are encouraged to seek individualized meanings for their suffering. Life situations such as broken relationships may not be easily altered, but the confessing of sins within small groups is necessary because they believe a person's suffering is not bigger than the graceful purpose of God. The authority of the Bible is universal and is accepted as absolute: theodicy always prevails over individual sufferings. It is natural in this situation that no other voice can be bigger than that of the Scripture. The church welcomes whomever suffers: it practices hospitality especially for those with broken relationships. Therefore, it is not strange for the church to be called "the shelter for sufferers."

3 Hermeneutics of Scriptures and Sufferings: Encounter of Universality and Particularity

Instead of taking a western medical paradigm to get rid of pain, the church targets the extraction of messages from God. One of the common words that people like to mention is "my sinfulness" in the midst of suffering. In appearance, the church wrongly imposes a sense of guilt on the sufferers or victims. However, the habit actually began with the pastor's personal experience before the church existed. As a matter of fact, the whole church is repeating the healing process of the pastor's individual afflictions in the past.

The pastor had a distinctive biography: she was not a welcome baby at birth. Her parents gave her a boy's name before she was born[3], expecting a boy to inherit the family's name in the Confucian patriarchy. Her growth was full of disappointment because she felt ashamed as a girl and was resented by the family.

Regardless of the negative attitude in the family, she grew up well and went to a prestigious college. She married a medical doctor and lived with parents-in-law for five years. As defectives from North Korea during the Korean War, they were beyond harsh and oppressive to her. She experienced serious verbal abuse and unforgiving demands from the family. She tried to kill herself in depression which finally made her run away from home.

As a runaway, she experienced a spiritual conversion. In an interview with the author, she said she had met Jesus Christ in person and returned home. She reconciled with the family by confessing her sins and asking for forgiveness. At the same time, she began studying scriptures with the Daily Bible, a Christian magazine for a quiet time. She has not skipped even a single day for more than forty years thereafter. Under the supervision of her pastor, she also began to lead a Quiet Time group in a local church.

Her husband died in her late thirties due to a sudden rupture of the liver. As a single mother, she founded Quiet Time Mission for biblical meditation and went to a seminary, sensing the limitations in her ministry as a lay person. She was ordained as a minister in order to facilitate God's ministry without interruption.

Following the pastor's model, church members share their life stories in depth; she often introduces some of the cases to the whole congregation under their consent. The church is always added up with novelties of the first-person experience and keeps up to date in terms of taking care of a person, which only reinforces its priority of the Bible. For the pastor and the congregation, "God is always right!" Whenever they share their particular stories, they commonly accept them as part of the universal and providential will of God. Theodicy prevails at all times among the congregation.

---

[3] Rev. Yang Jae Kim has a boy's name that is not common among Korean women.

There are rules of thumb for the community to practice: no future divorce, no marriage to a person without faith, no abortion, no silence in revealing sufferings, and no financial interaction between church members. The pastor insists these are essential for a person's real change.

When Browning defines hermeneutics as a conversation, he refers to bringing something foreign to a familiar understanding, based on Hans Gadamer, David Tracy, and Richard Rorty. He emphasizes it as a process in which a necessary conversation happens "for understanding the depths of one's own faith [...] And understanding the perspectives and meanings of the other people" (Browning 1983, 49). Distinguished from Browning, the church does not use mutually critical hermeneutics between two equal partners in a rational conversation. Rather, it resonates the method of Tillich, which states that people have questions from life and the Bible proposes the answer. Foreign to Tillich, the church members themselves actively participate in the hermeneutical process and willingly accept the will of God in the midst of sufferings through obedience.

Hermeneutics of life in the church is not simply a cognitive theological process. Although it looks like a simple one-way application of faith or theology, it is the fruit of painstaking engagements between suffering and faith, life and the scripture, meditation and confession, human desire and God's will, and furthermore, particularity and universality. Its uniquely embodied hermeneutics of life has helped people experiencing suffering keep discussing between those poles conversely and communally.

A new meaning discovered through interpretation reduces the depth of suffering. Howard Brody says that the "relief of suffering comes most often by changing the meaning of the experience for the sufferer and restoring the disrupted connectedness of the sufferer with herself and with those around her" (Brody 2002, 30). By finding meanings, a person is capable of suffering deeper and thus can endure longer, regardless of life's unfavorable fortunes. The community with empathic acceptance facilitates healing by interpreting the meaning of individual suffering in particularity; it helps relieve the pain by seriously considering "the multiple aspects of personhood and personal meaning" (Brody 2002, 30).

4 Narrative, Interpretation, and Community

One important difference between this church and the charismatic movement is that the former does not follow the model of medicine to remove the pain. Rather, it seeks "a narrative unity," as Stanley Hauerwas suggests, as an alternative (or supplementary) model of healing the charismatic or medical tradition (Hauerwas 1990, 120). The narrative is simply a story of our life, but it has a multitude of forms of expression that convey our stories of ordinary life. It is necessary that "our lives [...] have a narrative unity" (Hauerwas 1990, 119). Our life is not laid out as is lived in a way of mere chronicity; instead, it expresses itself by maintaining a pattern of narrative unity that is bound up with stories.

> The situation is graver when patients themselves lack any sense of narrative unity, for medicine becomes impotent to bring about or enhance patient well-being, even by accident, if there is no "intelligible narrative" to ground questions about better or worse: treatments (Long 1986, 80).

Thus, storytelling by a person in suffering is a crucial part of becoming or recovering herself. Especially "intelligible narratives" are an effective (or essential) way of promoting the well-being of the sufferer. Narrative unity may build and grow "out of a kind of belief system that not everyone has" (Hauerwas 1990, 120).

Christian stories in the past contributed to the growth of Christian communities and to the maintenance of its tradition regardless of multitudes of counterforces against the church. However, by storytelling of the narratives, the church was able to avoid Christian *amnesis* and continue to reaffirm its identities. In its tradition, the story has been a way and a tool "to invite those outside to join our family and become renewed by sharing our memories" (Culbertson 2000, 44).

On the other hand, stories of a person in the family can help form an interpretive community because "a commonality of interpretation creates the sense of belonging or family loyalty" (Culbertson 2000, 51). People in the *Wooridle Church* have explored the spiritual meanings by interpreting both the daily texts and the individual narratives, which reinforces their communal identity. For them, interpretation is considered prior or superior to objective facts of sufferings, in which the faith community is worth being maintained in order to pass its beliefs and values to those who are not aware of their meaning. Beyond individual and particular narratives, the church offers a universal canopy of faith that covers their shame and discovers a common hope through biblical interpretation that meaningfully binds them together. By sharing the interpretive strategies among members, the church "becomes a social unit [...] (of) an interpretive community" like a family does (Culbertson 2000, 51).

> How can any one of us know whether or not he is a member of the same interpretive community as any other of us? [...] The only 'proof' of membership is fellowship, the nod of recognition from someone in the same community, someone who says to you what neither of us could ever prove to a third party: 'we know' (Fish 1980, 173).

When the whole church shares common religious belief systems, however, the communication of religious meanings in a narrative unity gains powerful effects on the individual and the community. It makes the community build itself by connecting individuals as a common unit of particular narratives and general interpretations. It also expands itself by repeating its own script, that is, a sequence of repetitive practices of listening and empathizing. In this context, shared stories of enduring sufferings end up with a powerful community of interpretive communication, which reduces their formidable sufferings into tolerable pieces.

Instead of existing for themselves as an end, communities "are created in response to a call" (Kornfeld 2001, 17). The sense of calling strengthens the motivation to serve and care for others as well as themselves. Because all communities, whether religious or not, take care of each other as their root for existence, they are 'spiritual' by nature.[4] The church, however, prioritizes God's call first and its members share their visions of healing based on the common confession of faith as a general theological property. The scripture and the confessional tradition function as bases for the current community progressing towards a meaningful interpretation of life both individually and communally.

5 Practical Theology that Creates, Cultivates, and Cares for Community

Introducing a revisionist model for contemporary theology, Tracy argues that "the two principal sources for theology are Christian texts and common human experience and language" (Tracy 1975, 43). He does not ignore the importance of "appropriate interpretations" of the scriptures and "a theologian's responsibility to the tradition" (Tracy 1975, 44). However, he regards both coherence in articulating reality and adequacy for common human experience as more important values of today's practical theology. As with Browning, he goes beyond Tillich's correlational model for intrinsic conviction and consistency of the task of theology in order to explicate the ultimate meaning of the existential everyday life.

The *Wooridle Church*'s approach to interpretation of life considering scriptures may look simple or naïve in this respect: it does not allow any mutually critical position on the scripture or on the redemptive historical faith in Jesus. The orthodox theology that most Korean churches represent has a major strength in its "ability to develop sophisticated models for providing systematic understanding of the basic beliefs of [the] church community," with its weakness in making "intrinsic use of the other scholarly disciplines" (Tracy 1975, 25). That is why Browning draws a line between confessional theology and practical theology: "Confessionally-oriented religious interpreters may stop the process here" (Browning 1995, 6). In his mind, practical theology must be critical in order to develop its own religious motivation and test its adequacy for communication of meanings with the world outside. Confessional interpreters, however, may not be able to continue the process of critical hermeneutics on the traditional text regardless of having well-organized theological properties to be effectively transferred to others.

Therefore, Browning recommends practical theologians to think in religious and philosophical terms with/using a narrative envelope outside. It is important for Christian churches and theologians to cultivate a new way to communicate with the secular world on the level of common human reason. However, it is still crucial that Christianity keeps its tradition and identity within the society with its faith-

---

[4] Annie Dillard defines community as a 'spiritual fact' before it is built as a social or political reality. She says we have to begin with contemplation instead of activity in order to experience a sense of a common life, our "hidden wholeness." Quoted in Kornfeld 2001, 19.

ful presence and servanthood without compromising its core values as manifest in the scripture.

Hermeneutics of classic texts must "be a community effort involving several people and their respective horizons in a dialogue with the classic texts" (Browning 1995, 50). Widely leaning on Gadamer's works, he defines hermeneutics as "a community process" in which the community and its members actively – but each in a different degree – participate in a dialogue or conversation to attain a consensus that is still fluid and open (Browning 1995, 50). Concerning the church as a community of interpretation, he illustrates Josiah Royce's image of the church as the "beloved community" that is "committed to the process of loving interpretation to achieve the good and true" (Browning 1995, 51). Communal understanding of conversation, nevertheless, must be a mutually critical or correcting process so that it incorporates both the present praxis questions and the past textual hermeneutics. Anton Boisen's metaphor, the living human document, is a good example of a correlational revisionist theology integrating the individual's archaeological stories and the biblical and theological texts.

The *Wooridle Church* tries to communicate with Korean society in its own way, saying "the family is not for happiness but for holiness." Although the secular society may not understand what this means, the church tries to communicate a meaning of family in a different way and embrace those who suffer from it with its strong, conservative, and text-oriented practical (or pastoral) theology. The church keeps a practical intention to integrate its conservative values in practicing care for specificities of individual, interpersonal, and socio-cultural problems.

Although it is not mutual or critical enough as Browning expects for *phronesis*, the Korean church communicates the practical issues about abortion, divorce, feminism, or homosexuality based on the orthodox scriptural readings. Confessing the inspiration and inerrancy of the Bible, the pastor simply but faithfully performs her duty as "a Christian pastor by bringing men into the obedience of the Gospel, to offer them as it were in sacrifice unto God" as John Calvin appointed" (Taylor 1989, 228).

Although different from this radical openness among congregations, most other Korean churches accept the authority of the Bible like this church. Their communication with society is largely limited to personal evangelism and charities, which still falls short in terms of the practical theological expectations. However, their conservative values seem to be hardly compromised, considering the church and political history that perpetuate the status quo of today's practical theology in Korea (Ha 2015).

6 Hermeneutical Particularity and Particular Hermeneutics

Paying attention to particularity in pastoral and practical theology has accomplished a spectacular paradigm shift in theology in which a specific human experience gains eligibility to be part of an academic status. Considering the stronghold of *academia* throughout history, generality or universality with objectivity has always prevailed over particularity with subjectivity due to the nature of human understanding, that is, it is easier to grasp the overview than the smallest details. That is why Martin Heidegger defends particularity against metaphysical generality: a loss of particularity in the modern technological era means a loss of subject (Heidegger 1982).

Traditionally, theoretical theologians have overlooked practical theologians who actively include and participate in messy details of life as non-academic or less worthy for systematic speculations. Miller-McLemore raises a significant question about practical theology's tendency of abstraction and objectivity that may obscure certain voices of truths in order to get some scholarly validity (Miller-McLemore 1999). Due to loyal commitments and efforts of many practical theologians, practice and reality of life have intruded in the academic fortress, being planted yet to grow.

On the contrary, the propensity toward practice and particularity brings about a relative disregard of the traditional texts including scriptures, which Korean churches and theologians are critically concerned about. Some radical proponents of particularity even require to change scriptural texts instead of changing of situation. Although Christian theology has a wide spectrum in Korea, simply erasing or correcting the essential Christian resources upon the need of sufferers may provoke a critical opposition from the majority of Christian believers.

By criticizing Rebecca Chopp's theory of "a hermeneutic of marginality," Anthony C. Thiselton, a renowned British scholar in biblical hermeneutics, regards it as a "restless 'hermeneutics' that leaves behind any foundationalism, and moves through the endless polyvalency of language" (Thiselton 1992, 461). The scriptures, according to Chopp, must be "de-centered" for "an experience of emancipatory transformation" (Chopp 1989, 126). However, Thiselton is concerned that it is hard to "establish adequate criteria for determining how far a tradition can be transformed before it ceases to remain *this* tradition" (Thiselton 1992, 461). He raises an important question about her priority to the present particularity over the traditional text.

> Might it be that many pastoral theologians, by concentrating on the segment of the process that concerns the *present*, have fallen into *the very same trap of objectifying pastoral phenomena in ways which give privilege to the present as over against the biblical text?* (Thiselton 1992, 557)

Thiselton pays critical attention to Browning's note on contingent particularities and *diversity* in the public world, whose terms are found also in Tracy and Farley. Although Thiselton is "extremely cautious about George Lindbeck's tendency to locate the meaning of biblical texts in intralinguistic or 'intratextual' categories," both of them give a doubt together to "this tendency to give privilege to the present" (Thiselton 1992, 557).

He understands the fluidity of hermeneutics between the text and the present experience. He mentions that "the flow of interpretation between the horizons of biblical texts and those of pastoral situations assumes different forms and different functions as the two sets of *particularities* change" (Thiselton 1992, 557). He resents that many books on hermeneutics fall short in expectation because of simply generalizing the situation or being ignorant of diversity and even the text itself. The old text of scripture contains different types of texts such as didactic, narrative, poetic, boundary situation, apocalyptic and so on. He maintains that these different texts "perform *different, though often overlapping, hermeneutical functions, especially in relation to different reading-situations*" (Thiselton 1992, 558).

He warns about the existential understanding of the text and particularity for its danger of making the text of the Bible "*individuating* vehicles" (Thiselton 1992, 563) in pastoral theology. Existential readers like to use the "boundary situation" of Karl Jaspers, but they may lack "the social and communal perspectives of socio-pragmatic or even speech-act models" (Thiselton 1992, 563). It is important for him to reconstruct the lifeworld that is bound to the author with the text's directed goal first. Therefore, not only is pastoral theology using the essential "listening skills" with patience in respect of others, but also do the historical biblical studies expand critical "objective" methods into "re-live" or "reconstruct its life-world and [...] seek to enter it by sharing its form" (Thiselton 1992, 559).

Most of all, Thiselton points out that "the relation between biblical material and the present situation *cannot be regarded as fully symmetrical*" (Thiselton 1992, 606). By quoting Pannenberg's argument that "the *present* can be *understood* only in the light of the *past history of traditions*," he summarizes that "*divine promise shapes both the nature of reality and how the present is to be understood*" (Thiselton 1992, 606). He objects the trend of "over-privileging of the present in pastoral theology" (Thiselton 1992, 606), that is, the inclination of giving too much emphasis on the present situation.

Korean churches including the *Wooridle Church* have demonstrated a strong dedication to the biblical text, which is closer to Thiselton than to other theologians. They take particular hermeneutics of the individual in a situation by giving preference to the text, not without giving attention to the particularities of human suffering. Although Korean pastors, pastoral counselors, or pastoral theologians offer proper significance to the present issues of suicide, poverty, or injustice, they are still expected to stay within the priority of biblical authority by the churches.

7 A Practical 'Biblical' Thinking

Although Browning always prioritizes practical moral reasoning in practical theology, he still pays attention to the postmodern trend of ignoring the biblical axis. Considering the issue of homosexuality in the 1980s, he thought it deserves a "calm, careful, loving, unanxious, and undogmatic reflection" (Browning 1983, 74). However, he finds that supporters of homosexuality are "all [taking] a modern scholarly critical view of the Bible" (Browning 1983, 82). Although he takes a position of a non-dogmatic approach to homosexuality, he is still marveled at the asymmetry in understanding of God.

> [S]ome of the higher-level metaphors (God as love) are used, but others (God as creator and governor) are neglected. Neighbor love as a principle of obligation is affirmed, but on the whole it is disconnected from principles of justice and unsupported by understandings of human nature (human tendencies and needs) as articulated in the arguments either from orders of creation or from natural law (Browning 1983, 86–87).

Browning resents that the movement attracts great attention within the present social context. Within practical moral rules and social roles at the lowest levels, biblical patterns are gone, and new ones have replaced them in their place. He asserts that it should be properly balanced with "parental, familial, and societal expectations with respect to sexual preference" (Browning 1983, 89). He does not mean that it cannot be tolerated; instead, he does not want it to be advocated.

Many Korean churches are currently advocating against the upcoming movement of legislating gay marriage by the progressive government and its major Democratic lawmakers. Churches and lay leaders including lawmakers, lawyers, medical doctors, professors, and college students have been working together to communicate with the secular society in stopping the legislation. It has been successful so far to slow down the rushing political movement. With Christian fundamentalism, they have sound practical reasons to execute social resistance. Founded on the teachings of the scripture, their communications to the secular society are translated into the scientific data of public health.[5]

Korean churches have accomplished a peculiar progress in communicating with society while carefully balancing between the universality of faith and the particularity of care. They prioritize the scriptures as God's word and confess their belief in Jesus Christ as a savior and moral standard. However, they are not simply naïve in communication.

---

[5] HIV patients have been rapidly increasing in Korea for the last two decades due to a failure of public health policies for control on a socio-political level. In 2017, the number of teenage HIV patients expanded up to 600% compared to 2001. Korea has been in danger of AIDS expansion since 2013 when the total number of patients exceeded a ten thousand according to the *Kukmin-ilbo* daily newspaper in October 10, 2018: http://news.kmib.co.kr/article/view.asp?arcid=0012749709&code=61221111&cp=du (29.11.2021).

They have actively participated in particularity of individual sufferings in order to take care of people and to rebuild their surroundings based on the universality of faith.

Bibliography

Brody, Howard. 2002. *Stories of Sickness*. New Haven: Yale University Press.
Browning, Don S. 1983. *Religious Ethics and Pastoral Care*. Philadelphia: Fortress Press.
Browning, Don S. 1995. *A Fundamental Practical Theology: Descriptive and Strategic Proposals*. Minneapolis: Fortress Press.
Chopp, Rebekah S. 2009. "Practical Theology and Liberation." In *Formation and Reflection: The Promise of Practical Theology*, edited by Lewis S. Mudge and James Newtin Poling. Minneapolis: Augsburg Press, 120–138.
Culbertson, Philip. 2000. *Caring for God's People: Counseling and Christian Wholeness*. Minneapolis: Fortress Press.
Fish, Stanley. 1980. *Is There a Text in This Class? The Authority of Interpretive Communities*. Cambridge: Harvard University Press.
Frankl, Viktor E. 1963. *Man's Search for Meaning: An Introduction to Logotherapy*. New York: Pocket Books.
Ha, Jaesung. 2011. "The Revised Correlational Method of Don Browning and Edward Farley: A Comparative Essay on the Interpretation of Situation." *The Gospel and Counseling* 16:203–224.
Ha, Jaesung. 2015. "A Practical Theological Idea of Social Justice: A Study of Inequality Envisaged in Gangnam Style." In *Complex Identities in a Shifting World: Practical Theological Perspectives*, edited by Pamela Couture, Robert Mager, Pamela McCarroll, and Natalie Wigg-Stevenson, Zürich: LIT, 219–229.
Hauerwas, Stanley. 1990. *God, Medicine, and Suffering*. Grand Rapids: Eerdmans Publishing.
Heidegger, Martin. 1982. *The Question Concerning Technology and Other Essays*. New York: Harper and Collins.
Keller, Tim. 2008. *Questions of Suffering*. https://www.youtube.com/watch?v=XCzd0qF3Mlg (29.11.2021).
Kornfeld, Margaret. 2000. *Cultivating Wholeness: A Guide to Care and Counseling in Faith Communities*. New York / London: Continuum.
Long, Thomas A. 1986. "Narrative Unity and Clinical Judgement." *Theoretical Medicine and Bioethics* 7:75–92.
Mercadante, Linda A. 2014. *Belief without Borders: Inside the Minds of the Spiritual but not Religious*. London: Oxford University Press.
Miller-McLemore, Bonnie, and Brita L. Gill-Austern. 1999. *Feminist and Womanist Pastoral Theology*. Nashville: Abingdon Press.
Ruether, Rosemary. 1998. *Women and Redemption: A Theological History*. Minneapolis: Fortress Press.
Hunter, Rodney, ed. 1991. *Dictionary of Pastoral Care and Counseling*. Nashville: Abingdon.
Taylor, Charles. 2000. *Sources of the Self: The Making of the Modern Identity*. Cambridge, MA: Harvard University Press.
Thiselton, Anthony C. 1992. *New Horizons in Hermeneutics: Theory and Practice of Transforming Biblical Reading*. New York City: HarperCollins.
Thomas, Gary L. 2015. *Sacred Marriage: What if God Designed Marriage to Make us Holy More Than to Make us Happy*. Grand Rapids: Zondervan.
Tracy, David. 1996. *Blessed Rage for Order: The New Pluralism in Theology*. Chicago / London: The University of Chicago Press.

Birgit Weyel
Community and Religion

1 Introduction

One of the central questions of practical ecclesiology is what social forms lived religion takes on. Since the 1970s, this question has caused much debate in the German-speaking academic world. The debate has been spurred by social changes that have affected membership in the two mainline German churches: the Catholic and the Protestant church. Particularly, these churches have seen a significant decline in membership, which they are now seeking to address through church policy. Church leaders in the Evangelical Church in Germany (EKD) have a strong interest in research that considers the causes for this as well as ways they can influence future developments. Thus, they are in support of this research field of practical theology both financially and ideationally by expressing interest in the research results of practical and systematic theology and by inviting researchers to lectures and consultations. The Church Membership Surveys, which the EKD has conducted every ten years since 1972, are a prominent example of how church itself engages as a research actor and incorporates scholars in the conceptualization and interpretation of data.

On the level of broader scientific reflections, sociological theoretical concepts that combine empirical methods with theory formation have proven stimulating and garnered much acclaim during this time. Practical theology draws heavily on the sociology of religion in developing its theoretical impulses. In addition to classic concepts by Max Weber, Georg Simmel, Émile Durkheim, Ferdinand Tönnies, and Niklas Luhmann, contemporary scholars have also introduced important recent developments such as the role of media and network theory. Examples for these contemporary scholars are Andreas Hepp, Markus Hero, Christian Stegbauer, and Roger Häußling. They provide theoretical concepts that relate to the sociology of technology as well as the sociology of religion. By considering and collaborating with sociology, practical theology has developed impulses that are not limited to the level of theory but have also found expression in empirical methodological approaches, both quantitative and qualitative. Therefore, concepts of sociality and empirical studies that consider various forms of religious community formation interact closely. In this way sociological approaches are helpful lenses through which scholars can perceive religious sociality.

During the fifth *Kirchenmitgliedschaftsuntersuchung* (Church Membership Survey; short: KMU) conducted in 2012, I was part of the scientific advisory board which investigated the concept of church as a network. In my view, this conceptualization is an obvious choice based on practical ecclesiology, since it acknowledges how transformative processes of digitization have been. Furthermore, practical ecclesiology heuristically benefits from representing relationality in various forms (Hermelink and Weyel 2015; Roleder and Weyel 2019; Weyel 2016, 2018). In addition to working on the 5th KMU, I supervised three Ph.D. students in a doctoral network together with my two practical-theological colleagues Peter Bubmann (Erlangen) and Kristian Fechtner (Mainz). On behalf of the church, we conducted research on the concept of a 'temporary congregation' (Bubmann et al. 2019; Weyel 2019). This involved actors from within the church who helped to consult and to evaluate the results of this collaborative research (de Roest 2020). The experiences and findings of these two projects significantly shape my approach in this field. In the following, I will first establish contextual background by outlining social transformation processes (2.). Then, I will lay out the organizational role the church holds when faced with the recent membership developments (3.) to develop new perspectives on religious community formation through networks. This is also the focus of my reflections (4.) and synopsis (5.), which again hark back to the role of religion as a social practice. In the conclusion, I will touch on the implications this holds for practical theology within the current discourse (6.).

2 The Institutional Nature of the Protestant Church Faced with Processes of Social Transformation

Since the end of the 1960s, German churches have seen a decline in membership occurring in waves. In response to this trend, the Evangelical Church in Germany (EKD) initiated a membership survey, which they conducted for the first time in 1972 and every ten years since then (Hild 1974; Bedford-Strohm and Jung 2015). When considering the twentieth century as a whole, the number of members leaving the Church at the end of the 1960s was significantly lower than, for example, during the Weimar Republic, when, following World War I, the church ceded to exert governmental sovereignty in Germany and church and state separated on an organizational level. Many also left the church during the National Socialist era (Hanselmann, Hild, and Lohse 1984, 36). However, even with these earlier trends, the decline in membership since the end of the 1960s shook the self-perception of the Protestant Church. In 1956, 96% of the total population in the German Federal Republic were members of one of the two Christian churches; only a minority of 4% claimed another religion or no religion at all. The Protestant Church held a slight majority over the Catholic Church with 50.1% Protestants compared to 45.9% Catholics (Eicken and Schmitz-Veltin 2010). These statistics underline that the Christian churches understood themselves as *people's churches* in the sense of *Churches of the people of the Federal Republic of Germany (West)*. In a period of 65 years the membership statistics have since changed dramatically. As of 2020, Protestant and Catholic church members represent a combined 51% of the German population (both West and East); another 2.9% of Germans identify as Christians that belong to other Christian communities like the Baptists, the Methodists, and Orthodox churches (Russian, Greek, etc.).

The Catholic Church holds a slight majority over the Protestant Church: They make up 26.7% of Germans whereas Protestants make up 24.3% (Kirchenamt der Evangelischen Kirche in Deutschland 2021). A major factor for this development can be found in the way the communist regime in East Germany broke with church tradition. After the reunification, the developments in East Germany greatly impacted religious ratios in unified Germany. Other factors include waves of migration from predominantly Catholic (Italy, Spain, etc.) and Islamic countries (e.g., Turkey). In addition, demographic changes, i.e., changes in gender roles, declining birthrates, and more women in the workplace, must also be considered as a significant factor. In recent years (2021/22), church membership has again drastically decreased. While the motives for this cannot be boiled down to a single event, this new trend has surely been significantly spurred on by the sexual abuse crisis in the Catholic Church. By handling this crisis inappropriately, the church has revealed an unwillingness for transparency and self-criticism as well as a tendency to systematically isolate clergy. For the Protestant Church, on the other hand, it seems like the institution has lost its relevance and become more alienated from modern Germany. As of now, there have not been sufficiently detailed analyses on how the Covid-19 pandemic has impacted the relationship to the church. Overall, however, we can observe complex transformation processes that have considerably influenced the relationship Germans have to the church, which cannot be summed up by secularization alone. It should be noted that federal German statistics do not provide information about individual parts of the country. In fact, there are significant religious-cultural differences between federal states, regions, and state churches. In some regions (e.g., Brandenburg), the popular structures of the Protestant Church are thinning out in such a manner that the church can barely uphold the comprehensive system of parochial congregations. Kristian Fechtner has thus diagnostically declared that the people's church is currently undergoing the late stages of its transition (Fechtner 2011, 207), whereby its future social form remains open. However, although the church is losing its institutional character as a people's church, it is still able at present to incorporate different forms of religious sociality. Eberhard Hauschildt and Uta Pohl-Patalong therefore speak of the church as a "hybrid" (Hauschildt and Pohl-Patalong 2013, 218). As a result of the transformation processes outlined above, however, the organizational character of the church is becoming more prominent whereas its institutional character is losing importance.

3 The Church as an Organization

Coming from sociology, the concept of organization, developed by Niklas Luhmann, was made strong in practical ecclesiology. Within a plural and differentiated society communally exercised interactions of a *congregatio sanctorum* not only depend on but also presuppose organization. "Specifically, functional systems and organizations must create opportunities for interactions, that is, they must provide appropriate temporal, spatial, social, and, not least, thematic arrangements." (Hermelink 2011, 112; o.t.) Religious practice remains dependent on the frameworks of church organization. Past and present criticisms of the church as an organization therefore come to nothing if generally directed towards character of the Church as an organization. It would be more precise to criticize the church as an organization only when it dysfunctionally relates to the enabling of religious practice. Tensions in the concept of church are to be kept alive for the benefit of enabling religious practice, because critical and constructive potential can be found in it in the determination of the relationship between organization and religious practice. Against the background of the previously outlined processes of social change and the accompanying decline in church membership, the EKD is increasingly presenting itself nationally to the regional churches and to the public as an organization. The thesis paper *Kirche der Freiheit* (English: *Church of Freedom*) (Kirchenamt der Evangelischen Kirche in Deutschland 2006) has become a symbol of the church's increased development into an organization (*Organisationswerdung*) and how this comes into tension with the self-understanding of the church as an institution by threatening to call into question the latencies of a public church. The paper assesses the actions of church leadership according to organizational-sociological paradigms, such as quality and personnel management, in other words, business management tools (Meyns 2013). In view of the decline in membership and staff resources this is an obvious approach. The paper appeals to pastors, volunteers, and full-time staff to change their mentality in order to set free a willingness to reform and a spirit of optimism within the congregations. There have been many criticisms of this from a practical theology perspective (Karle 2011). I would like to emphasize two aspects.

First, according to the Protestant understanding, the task of the church is functionally determined by the proclamation of the gospel (Confessio Augustana Art. 5 in Dingel 2014, 100–101). A self-preservation of the church as an organization, on the other hand, cannot be justified theologically. The organizational character must be kept in contact with this function, otherwise there is a danger that the functional logics of business will gain the upper hand in the church.

Second, church members could be turned into consumers who are viewed by the means of market research. In the logic of supply and demand, the religious subject and the church are pulled apart. Here the church as *congregatio sanctorum* remains hidden; both the individual and the congregation itself bear responsibility for their church life within the framework of the theological concept of a *priesthood of all baptized Christians*. Church life includes, in addition to church services, a variety of other occasions, public and private, in which religion is practiced.

The self-understanding of church as a business enterprise orientates church organization towards an economic concept of organization designed for businesses, "which see themselves under pressure to compete and perform." (Hermelink 2011, 90; o.t.) Church membership, which is institutionally supported by occasional participation in worship, is measured by the church against the idea of involvement. This notion originates in the theory of volunteerism and leads to commitment to church community life becoming the norm for the church concept. The expectation of the church as an organization towards its members changes by differentiating between commitment and indifference. This distinction reflects a critique of how most church members participate (or do not participate) in church life. The statement of Thies Gundlach, Vice President in the Church Office of the EKD regarding the 5th Church Membership Survey entitled "Engagement and Indifference" is an example of how the church considers the ways church membership is lived out as deficient:

> The "extremes" are being strengthened, members are either actively committed or predominantly passively involved through their biographical situation. This means, however, that the mild, moderate form of evangelical piety and church involvement – the so-called majority religion for which our church is widely designed – is on the wane. Accordingly, what is expected from the church is increasingly diverging: some want clearly recognizable communities shaped by religion, while others want situational pastoral care that is reliable and individually oriented. Are these mutually exclusive expectations towards the church on the part of different groups increasing? Do the actions of church leadership increasingly get caught in a quandary of irreconcilable polarities? (Gundlach 2014, 130–131; o.t.)

From my point of view, Gundlach's dramatization of the situation in the final sentence can only be understood against the background of perspectives led by organizational theory. As a matter of fact, the polarization within the church stated here is produced rhetorically and cannot be reconstructed from the survey data. Church membership has always been diverse, and participation in church life has always been affected by the current biographical situation of its members. The intrinsic plurality of the church is, in fact, a characteristic of the church as a people's church. The organization of the church, however, casts a devaluing view of popular church life and the diversity of its membership forms because membership numbers are declining.

With the decline in church tax revenues and membership, reform processes that target the church as an organization and demand further organizational processes have become necessary: Congregations will have to merge, church buildings will have to be used alternatively, staff numbers will have to be cut, and areas of work will have to be closed down. In any case, there is a need for church leaders to respond to the decline through organization. However, a central question of practical ecclesiology is whether the churches will reflect their organizational actions in such a way that allows different social forms of lived religion to be integrated (Gräb 2006; Gräb 2016).

4 The Church as a Network

The concept of the network brings another way of perceiving and describing sociality into view, which complements previous approaches instead of providing an alternative. In general terms, the 'network' is a transdisciplinary concept, which needs to be investigated by considering more or less complex phenomena as relational entities. In the theories of sociology, the concept is not limited to constellations of people. A key element of actor-network theory is that it also includes things (objects) that take part in social processes through the interaction of people and things. This hybridization of actants is one of the pivotal components in Bruno Latour's Actor-Network-Theory (short: ANT). I understand his famous text *We Have Never Been Modern*, published in French with the subtitle *Essais d'anthropologie symmétrique*, as a critique of a modern style of thinking, which is characterized by a paradox. On the one hand, modernity is associated with practices of "translation" (Latour 1993, 10), in which new mixtures – hybrids – emerge, not only but especially through technological innovations. On the other hand, modernity is associated with practices that aim to distinctly separate the spheres of the human and the non-human. Latour calls them purification practices. Mixtures (or 'translations') and separations (or 'purifications') are closely related to each other.

> The hypothesis of this essay is that the word "modern" designates two sets of entirely different practices which must remain distinct if they are to remain effective, but have recently begun to be confused. The first set of practices, by "translation", creates mixtures between entirely new types of beings, hybrids od nature and culture. The second, by "purification", creates two entirely distinct ontological zones: that of human beings on the one hand, that od nonhumans on the other. Without the first set, the practices of purification would be fruitless or pointless. Without the second, the work of translation would be slowed down, limited, or even ruled out. The first set corresponds to what I have called networks; the second to what I shall call the modern critical stance. (Latour 1993, 10 – 11)

At this point, I quote Bruno Latour at length to show that his network theory is a very comprehensive critique of modernity and has far-reaching consequences for a theory of the social. In light of this the agency of things and the role of technologies in social processes come into view. This becomes more plausible considering not only but especially the digitization of the workplace and daily life. Beyond that, however, the critique is also a dialectical critique of critique itself, because critical thinking is always connected with separation and differentiation. Thus, there cannot be an exit from modern thinking *en passant*.

I also refer explicitly to Bruno Latour at this point to hint at the depth of the theory's background when using the concept of the network in practical ecclesiology. A network theory of religious community formation can go further than just incorporating the relations between humans into practical ecclesiology. It is also a self-critique of a style of thinking whose research-practical and theory-flexive implications are at least hinted at when the material dimension of religious practices is considered. However, in my view this does not exhaust the theoretical potential of Actor-Network-Theory. The use of the network category to describe religious community formation is, in my view, of heuristic interest.

A first aspect is the option of looking at social interactions and relational structures in the cultural transmission of religion with the help of the theory design. Sociality processes, friendship networks, etc. become visible as social structures in which religiosity emerges and is lived. Religious communication, which needs to be defined in more detail, can be traced online and offline in the context of social networks. Online practices form part of the connections found in everyday life, resulting in fluid transitions. In other words, the separation between online and offline practices seems less and less plausible. Research must react to this through a "conceptual shift" (Przybylski 2021, 4) that focuses on the "in-between". "The main attraction of digital sociology is precisely that it enables the development of experimental forms of inquiry that cut across the divides between the sciences and the humanities. It may develop and inform richer approaches to 'data interpretation', more adventurous ways of introducing social theory into the space of digital research" (Marres 2017, 6).

Secondly, the entry point of network research can also be reversed by examining the role of religious practices in the formation of social networks. The interdependencies of religious communication and sociality come to the fore. Thus, the way religion is socially embedded comes into view. Lived religion can be understood through social links both within and outside the church as an institution. According to this understanding, the religious network is not a specific form of sociality, but rather joins sociality concepts such as institution and organization as an empirical and theoretical model of description. Moreover, the network has already been established as a descriptive model for online communities.

The impulses that arise from network theory are therefore on several levels. On the one hand, the impulses are on a methodological level, which investigates the relationship between the individual and sociality under conditions that include translocal mediatized communication. These interdependencies have been described in a differentiated way for the friendship networks of young people (Hugger 2018, 16–17). According to this description youth scenes can be considered as thematically focused networks that are constituted through mediatized communication. They are thereby dependent on permanent communicative self-assurance through processes of assignment and delimitation (Krotz and Schulz 2014, 34). Further impulses also arise from terms and theoretical concepts associated with network analysis. Network theory can build on classics of interpretative sociology. Christian Stegbauer's work, for example, builds on Georg Simmel's theory of social circles. Stegbauer's reception of Simmel offers an explanatory model for the development of culture from the concatenation of situations (Stegbauer 2016, 79–90). Situations enable interactions and their correlating processes of negotiation that are needed for behavioral assimilations or deviations. Here, negotiation is referring to "the process that aligns behavior with the situation and its specific requirements on the one hand, and with the other attendants on the other, thereby making them compatible with each other." (Stegbauer 2016, 82; o.t.) Through the concatenation of situations culture develops. At the same time, relationships are formed "which provide the materials for determining structures in network research" (Stegbauer 2016, 83; o.t.).

In the context of network research, the nodes of the links, the *ties*, can be determined as social actors. The concept of networks thus aims at representing the socialities that are found at the meso level. The concept of a network can also be used to capture and describe small social structures. A classic example can be found in conversion research, which can show how specific changes in a person's relationship constellation can favor or impede conversion (Roleder 2019). The concept of networks also makes it possible to analyze the structure of individual social occasions in detail (Roleder and Weyel 2019). In this case the analysis is on the micro level: the personal network of relationships of an individual person which is characterized by friendship and kinship is represented. It is also possible to survey very large networks. An example of this are global flows of communication on social-media platforms (Merle 2019, 330–351). Network research has its heuristic value for practical ecclesiology at the meso level, i.e., in the 'in-between' space between close contacts (such as family and friends) and large organizations (such as church, political parties, etc.). Community formation through regular face-to-face communication as well as communication via social media, the regular use of cell phones, IP telephony, computer games and mobile broadband can be considered with the network paradigm. It brings a key factor of communicative practices into the picture: online and offline forms of sociality can be considered together and as crossovers. Andreas Hepp and others have coined the concept of "communicative figurations" (Hepp and Hasebrink 2018, 31) for this purpose. It takes up the developments of "deep mediatization". "With deep mediatization, the very elements and building blocks from which a sense of the social is constructed become themselves based on technologically based processes of mediation. In such a sense, deep mediatization is an advanced stage of mediatization." (Hepp, Breiter, and Hasebrink 2018, 6; see also Hepp 2020) Hepp and others focus primarily on the trends of a changing media environment in their cross-media research approach. They list the following as possible consequences for individual social domains: optionality, opportunities for social contingency and participation, spatial expansion, the blurring of boundaries, acceleration and immediacy, concealment of agency, stabilization of sociality, social surveillance and segmentation, and exclusion and division. It should be noted that this overview outlines possible consequences that still need to be empirically investigated and described for social fields such as religion (Hepp and Hasebrink 2018, 31).

In a study of religious online communities, Anna Neumaier has shown that the characteristics of community classically assigned to traditional communities by Max Weber and Ferdinand Tönnies can also be found in online communities. Neumaier mentions the symbolic sense of belonging but also refers to characteristics of communities that are 'action-related' such as shared rituals, internal interaction, and support (Neumaier 2019, 24). Neumaier presents a differentiated picture of community formation in her work as she highlights that online communities do not exhibit characteristics of post traditional community formation *per se*. Both the attributes of community formation that Ferdinand Tönnies ascribes to the traditional village community, as well as the characteristics assigned to post traditional, deterritorialized forms of religious community formation in media sociology can be found in online communities. This description of Neumaier can also be understood to support the notion that community building in networked communities does not have a fundamentally different quality to other networks, such as e.g., Campbell and Sheldon suggest. "Rather than living in a single, static religious community, the study of religious online community shows many people in contemporary society live among multiple religious networks that are emergent, varying in depth, and highly personalized." (Campbell and Sheldon 2022, 76)

5 Summary: Religion as a Social Practice

The manifestations of sociality and the terms and theoretical concepts for sociality are to be distinguished on the one hand, but also to be related to each other on the other hand. Institution, organization, and network are concepts of sociality that relate to different logics of the functioning of the church and can be complemented by further concepts. In my view the relational approach to processes of religious community formation is a key field of research for practical theology because it allows the relevance of mediatized communication for religious practice to be considered. Concepts of sociality always have theoretical implications that make statements about the emergence of socialities, their integrative power, the relationship to the environment, and their modes of functioning.

The church structures religious communication and many other church and non-church activities. This relationality-orientated research approach perceives the respondents in their interconnectedness with others, i.e., with the social roles they hold. Moreover, the structure of institutional places that provide opportunities for (religious) interactions can be made visible. Such places can be understood as situations in which culture emerges and relationships are developed.

In this way, the inner diversity of a Protestant church congregation and its communicative densification and structural gaps, as well as its interconnections with structures outside of church organization can be shown. The results cannot be presented in detail here, but examples can be found in the following in Roleder and Weyel (2019). The network survey clearly showed that the community of the church is embedded in its social environment. It was demonstrated that the wider community of the church consists of a multitude of more or less densely interconnected communities in which religious communication takes place but that it also transcends its own boundaries and is part of trans-local networks of relationships.

This method calls for an important change of perspective in practical ecclesiology. Religion can be located in multiple areas of life; faith is communicated, in, but also beyond the church community. As Volker Drehsen has stated building upon Max Weber, religion has its own social value (Drehsen 2009). Church members are actors that carry their religious interest and their religious knowledge with them in many places. Their main role is not to present the church with motives and expectations it must react to. Church members do not form a counterpart to the church as an organization but rather play their own part in forming the church.

The idea of network formations in the church also has rhetorical value. It suggests that 'the church congregation' (singular) represents a polycentric entity, which, put pointedly, consists of many congregations as social microcosms. With the help of network theory, we can speak of 'the church congregation' as an organizational unit and at the same time see the diversity of different communities. The church congregation does not appear to be distinctly delimitable, even to the outside world: It is 'open at the edges'. Various events, associations, and groups, etc. are linked to each other through joint participation: The community food bank and the sports club, the support association for a children's home and the music club. These informal, everyday situations, have their own occasionality, but naturally remain related to the organization of the church, because they tie to their congregation.

6 Concluding Remarks: The Role of Practical Theology and Practical Ecclesiology

Concepts of sociality, empirical perceptions, practical-theological church theory and church-guiding strategy drafts have all been closely related to each other in this discourse over the last 50 years, sometimes in a tense way. The sociologist Herbert Kalthoff aptly writes in his introduction to the volume *Theoretische Empirie: Zur Relevanz qualitativer Forschung* (English: *Theoretical Empiricism: On the Relevance of Qualitative Research*):

> The theories [...] open up different approaches to the observed empirical world. Thus, they stand in a complementary as well as in a competitive relationship to each other. Complementary relationship means that the approaches complement each other in explaining the social world and are also used to break down its empirical data. At the same time, which theory is referenced in qualitative research is determined by both the data collection method and the empirical data. The interplay of research question, methods, and data collected generates plausibility for particular theoretical approaches. (Kalthoff 2015, 19; o.t.)

This is also true for practical ecclesiology. I wanted to make clear that empirical perceptions both presuppose and present very different images of the church. When methods are proven in the field their implications are reproduced. They offer possibilities of perception, but they also have limits. Therefore, it seems important to me to make the interactions between empirical perceptions and images of the church more explicit in the process, and especially in the presentation, of research by
- making the theoretical backgrounds and their assumptions about the social world more transparent to recipients;
- highlighting the methodologically conditioned one-sidedness of the approach to ecclesiastical reality more strongly;

- fanning out the ambiguities of both quantitative and qualitative research, and
- relating the perception of church and the conceptual-strategic images of church to each other without confusing them.

Bibliography

Bedford-Strohm, Heinrich, and Volker Jung, eds. 2015. *Vernetzte Vielfalt: Kirche angesichts von Individualisierung und Säkularisierung: Die fünfte EKD-Erhebung über Kirchenmitgliedschaft.* Gütersloh: Gütersloher Verlagshaus.

Bubmann, Peter, Kristian Fechtner, Konrad Merzyn, Stefan Ark Nitsche, and Birgit Weyel, eds. 2019. *Gemeinde auf Zeit: Gelebte Kirchlichkeit wahrnehmen.* Praktische Theologie heute 160. Stuttgart: Kohlhammer.

Campbell, Heidi A., and Zachary Sheldon. 2022. "Community." In *Digital Religion: Understanding Religious Practice in Digital Media.* New York: Routledge, 71–86.

Dingel, Irene. 2014. *Die Bekenntnisschriften der Evangelisch-Lutherischen Kirche.* Göttingen: Vandenhoeck & Ruprecht.

Drehsen, Volker. ^{2}2009. "Religion – der verborgene Zusammenhalt der Gesellschaft: Émile Durkheim und Georg Simmel." In *Der Sozialwert der Religion: Aufsätze zur Religionssoziologie*, edited by Christian Albrecht, Hans Martin Dober, and Birgit Weyel, Berlin / New York: De Gruyter, 15–40.

Eicken, Joachim, and Ansgar Schmitz-Veltin. 2010. "Die Entwicklung der Kirchenmitglieder in Deutschland: Statistische Anmerkungen zu Umfang und Ursachen des Mitgliederrückgangs in den beiden christlichen Volkskirchen." *Wirtschaft und Statistik* 6:576–589.

Fechtner, Kristian. 2011. "Späte Zeit der Volkskirche." In *Kirche.* Themen der Theologie 1, edited by Christian Albrecht, Tübingen: UTB, 197–218.

Gräb, Wilhelm. 2006. *Sinnfragen: Transformationen des Religiösen in der modernen Kultur.* Gütersloh: Gütersloher Verlagshaus.

Gräb, Wilhelm. 2016. "Lebenssinndeutung als Aufgabe der Theologie." *Zeitschrift für Theologie und Kirche* 113:366–383.

Gundlach, Thies. 2014. "Handlungsherausforderungen: Erste Überlegungen zu den Ergebnissen der V. KMU." In *Engagement und Indifferenz*, edited by Kirchenamt der Evangelischen Kirche in Deutschland, Hannover: no publisher, 128–132.

Hanselmann, Johannes, Helmut Hild, and Eduard Lohse. 1984. *Was wird aus der Kirche? Ergebnisse der zweiten EKD-Umfrage über Kirchenmitgliedschaft.* Gütersloh: Gütersloher Verlagshaus.

Hauschildt, Eberhard, and Uta Pohl-Patalong. 2013. *Kirche.* Lehrbuch Praktische Theologie 4. Gütersloh: Gütersloher Verlagshaus.

Hepp, Andreas. 2020. *Deep Mediatization.* New York: Routledge.

Hepp, Andreas, Andreas Breiter, and Uwe Hasebrink. 2018. "Rethinking Transforming Communications: An Introduction." In *Communicative Figurations: Transforming Communication in Times of Deep Mediatization*, edited by Andreas Hepp, Andreas Breiter, and Uwe Hasebrink, Cham: Palgrave Macmillan, 3–13.

Hepp, Andreas, and Uwe Hasebrink. 2018. "Researching Transforming Communications in Times of Deep Mediatization: A Figurational Approach." In *Communicative Figurations: Transforming Communication in Times of Deep Mediatization*, edited by Andreas Hepp, Andreas Breiter, and Uwe Hasebrink, Cham: Palgrave Macmillan, 15–48.

Hermelink, Jan. 2011. *Kirchliche Organisation und das Jenseits des Glaubens: Eine praktisch-theologische Theorie der evangelischen Kirche.* Gütersloh: Gütersloher Verlagshaus.

Hermelink, Jan, and Birgit Weyel. 2015. "Vernetzte Vielfalt: Eine Einführung in den theoretischen Ansatz, die methodischen Grundentscheidungen und zentrale Ergebnisse der V. KMU." In *Vernetzte Vielfalt: Kirche angesichts von Individualisierung und Säkularisierung: Die fünfte EKD-Erhebung über Kirchenmitgliedschaft*, edited by Heinrich Bedford-Strohm and Volker Jung, Gütersloh: Gütersloher Verlagshaus, 16–32.

Hild, Helmut. 1974. *Wie stabil ist die Kirche? Bestand und Erneuerung: Ergebnisse einer Umfrage*. Gelnhausen / Berlin: Burckhardthaus-Verlag.

Hugger, Kai-Uwe. ²2018. "Digitale Jugendkulturen: Von der Homogenisierungsperspektive zur Anerkennung des Partikularen." In *Digitale Jugendkulturen*. Digitale Kultur und Kommunikation 2, edited by Kai-Uwe Hugger, Wiesbaden: Springer VS, 11–28.

Kalthoff, Herbert. 2015. "Einleitung: Zur Dialektik von qualitativer Forschung und soziologischer Theoriearbeit." In *Theoretische Empirie: Zur Relevanz qualitativer Forschung*, edited by Herbert Kalthoff, Stefan Hirschauer, and Gesa Lindemann, Frankfurt am Main: Suhrkamp Taschenbuch Wissenschaft, 8–32.

Karle, Isolde. ²2011. *Kirche im Reformstress*. Gütersloh: Gütersloher Verlagshaus.

Kirchenamt der Evangelischen Kirche in Deutschland. 2006. *Kirche der Freiheit: Perspektiven für die evangelische Kirche im 21. Jahrhundert: Ein Impulspapier des Rates der EKD*. Hannover: no publisher.

Kirchenamt der Evangelischen Kirche in Deutschland. 2021. *Gezählt 2021: Zahlen und Fakten zum kirchlichen Leben*. https://www.ekd.de/ekd_de/ds_doc/Gezaehlt_zahlen_und_fakten_2021.pdf (03.01.2022).

Krotz, Friedrich, and Iren Schulz. 2014. "Youth Cultures in the Age of Mediatization." In *Digitale Jugendkulturen*. Digitale Kultur und Kommunikation 2, edited by Kai-Uwe Hugger, Wiesbaden: Springer VS, 31–44.

Latour, Bruno. 1993. *We Have Never Been Modern*, trans. Harvester Wheatsheaf. Cambridge, MA: Harvard University Press.

Marres, Noortje. 2017. *Digital Sociology: The Reinvention of Social Research*. Malden: Polity.

Merle, Kristin. 2019. *Religion in der Öffentlichkeit: Digitalisierung als Herausforderung für kirchliche Kommunikationskulturen*. Berlin / Boston: De Gruyter.

Meyns, Christoph. 2013. *Kirchenreform und betriebswirtschaftliches Denken: Modelle, Erfahrungen, Alternativen*. Gütersloh: Gütersloher Verlagshaus.

Neumaier, Anna. 2019. "Christian Online Communities – Insights from Qualitative and Quantitative Data." In *The Dynamics of Religion, Media, and Community: Special Issue 14*, edited by Andrea Rota and Oliver Krüger, Heidelberg: Heidelberg University Publishing, 20–40.

Przybylski, Liz. 2021. *Hybrid Ethnography: Online, Offline, and In Between*. London: Sage.

Roleder, Felix. 2020. *Die relationale Gestalt von Kirche: Der Beitrag der Netzwerkforschung zur Kirchentheorie*. Praktische Theologie heute 169. Stuttgart: Kohlhammer.

Roleder, Felix, and Birgit Weyel. 2019. *Vernetzte Kirchengemeinde: Analysen zur Netzwerkerhebung der V. Kirchenmitgliedschaftsuntersuchung der EKD*. Leipzig: Evangelische Verlagsanstalt.

Roest, Henk de. 2020. *Collaborative Practical Theology: Engaging Practitioners in Research on Christian Practices*. Leiden: Brill.

Stegbauer, Christian. 2016. *Grundlagen der Netzwerkforschung: Situation, Mikronetzwerke und Kultur*. Wiesbaden: Springer VS.

Weyel, Birgit. 2016. "Kirchenmitgliedschaft als soziale Praxis: Die V. EKD-Kirchenmitgliedschaftsuntersuchung in kirchentheoretischer Perspektive." In *Kirche und Gesellschaft: Kommunikation – Institution – Organisation*, edited by Christof Landmesser and Enno Edzard Popkes, Leipzig: Evangelische Verlagsanstalt, 13–26.

Weyel, Birgit. 2018. "Reflektierte Praxis dynamischer Selbststeuerung: Kirche als Organisation". In *Reflektierte Kirche: Beiträge zur Kirchentheorie*. Arbeiten zur Praktischen Theologie 72, edited by Konrad Merzyn, Ricarda Schnelle, and Christian Stäblein, Leipzig: Evangelische Verlagsanstalt, 15–29.

Weyel, Birgit. 2019. "Gemeinde als Netzwerk: Perspektiven der Netzwerktheorie für eine Kirche bei Gelegenheit." In *Gemeinde auf Zeit: Gelebte Kirchlichkeit wahrnehmen*. Praktische Theologie heute 160, edited by Peter Bubmann, Kristian Fechtner, Konrad Merzyn, Stefan Ark Nitsche, and Birgit Weyel, Stuttgart: Kohlhammer, 73–83.

Nadine Bowers Du Toit
Development and Religion

1 Introduction

Discourse on Religion and Development has witnessed a shift in recent years with a distinct move from religion as a threat to social welfare and development, towards the recognition of the role played by religion or spirituality in promoting development. The 'turn' towards religion as being beneficial to development, has largely arisen from the recognition that for the global South "spirituality is integral to their understanding of the world and their place in it, and so is central to the decisions that they make about their own and their communities' development" (ver Beek 2000, 31). It should be noted, however, that while development discourse has only recently recognized the value of religion, it is religious practitioners that have been at the forefront of mitigating the effects of poverty for centuries.

As a woman of colour, writing from the perspective of the Global South and more specifically from an African context, both constructs of religion and of development are contested notions. By placing this on the table, the intersection of religion and development as a growing field – also within Practical Theology – becomes dialogical and produces a creative tension within this exploration. This chapter explores three key points of engagement within the discussion of religion and development, namely: poverty alleviation, social capital and agency. It is important to note, however, that as a South African working in the field of Theology and Development, these concepts are explored with reference both to recent discourse on these concepts and contextualized with regards to African and, at times, South African praxis with main references to Christian praxis. Although the chapter's contextualization takes place largely within an African context, there are many points of contact with other contexts in the Global South, as well as tensions with, and perspectives from, the Global North.

The chapter begins with various critical perspectives on the notion of poverty alleviation by exploring the tensions between charity and development, the 'double legacy' of missionary colonialism and development for Africa and the importance of holism and the decolonial debate for religious engagement with poverty in an African context. These discussions recognize the intersections of gender, religion and culture as being key to poverty alleviation. The section also deals with the importance of Faith Based Organizations (FBOs) as agents of poverty alleviation and their contribution. The second part of this exploration deals with the way in which religion is argued as being central to social change and poverty alleviation, through the manner in which it generates high levels of social capital. This discussion is also contextualized within a sub-Saharan African context in particular and explores the way in which churches and church groups, act as core assets in mobilizing bonding, bridging and linking capital in service of poorer communities in particular. The final section deals with the notion of agency and the ways in which religion can promote social transformation, by highlighting in particular the importance of recognizing theological notions of power and justice in seeking such transformation. The section highlights the need to problematize development projects themselves by questioning whether they are truly liberative as well as being aware of the ways in which our ecclesiology of development could be challenged.[1]

2 Poverty Alleviation

2.1 Charity versus Development?

While discourse on religion and development is more recent, religious responses to poverty alleviation has a long history. In fact, all religions "have a long tradition of charitable work, including giving food and other items to the poorest and caring for orphans and the sick and dying" (Tomalin 2013, 20). Moreover, disaster relief as well as provision in the areas of education, health and the strengthening of livelihoods has been central to religious work. These actions are rooted in the fact that most religious traditions have "mechanisms of helping the poor as a central feature". For example, in Buddhism it is "selfless giving", in Islam the practice of "Zakat" as pillar of the religion and in the Judeo-Christian religions "love of neighbour" (Tomalin 2013, 20). The engagement of religions with poverty has, however, been critiqued as more firmly located within a 'charity' – rather than 'development' paradigm. The charitable approach often entails the provision of basic needs to relieve the plight of the poor, such as: food, clothing and the provision of welfare services in the form of care homes for the elderly and orphanages. Although not wrong in and of themselves, these 'first generation' development strategies, as popularly identified by development scholar David Korten (1990, 115) and framed within Christianity as an example of 'service' to the poor, may lead to dependency if not combined with the empowerment strategies of development (Korten 1990, 115; Swart 2006, 24.25). Swart (2006, 24) also notes that in this way, charity work may even represent "a form of paternalism of which the net result has been the historical, almost complete estrangement between the Christian churches, on the one hand, and the working classes and poor on the other".

Tomalin (2013, 20), nevertheless, acknowledges that while many religious actions may fall more firmly into the charitable paradigm, religious actors do ask questions as to the roots of poverty and inequality and how these should be overcome, which she argues "bridges the gap" between development work and charity work.

---

[1] It should be noted that this contribution does not seek to deal with all mainstream religions, but largely focuses on Christian faith communities.

The 2012 Busan gathering of the World Council of Churches, for example, saw a watershed in the ecumenical understanding of *diaconia*, a term which had come to dominate ecumenical development discourse and had largely been understood as compassionate service to the poor and marginalized. Ecumenical scholars in the field now point towards the importance of not reducing the notion of diaconia to compassionate service or acts of charity: "ecumenical diakonia today requires a critical analysis of what causes poverty and human suffering and bold action in defense of the excluded and their rights". In this way Christian understandings must be shaped by equal notions of compassion and justice (Phiri and Donsung 2014, 253; Nordstokke 2014, 265).[2]

2.2 The Colonial Era: A Double Legacy

The notion of ambivalence with regards to religions' engagement with poverty alleviation occurs from several perspectives, not least of which is what may be termed the "double legacy" of colonial missionary endeavors. Christian approaches towards poverty alleviation during the colonial era in the Global South, for example, are acknowledged as much for establishing basic welfare infrastructure such as schools and hospitals, as they are for the manner in which colonialism stands at the very root of the systemic impoverishment of the Global South. Manji and O'Coil's (2002) seminal article entitled "The missionary position: NGOs and development in Africa", for example notes that during the colonial era, missionary societies and other voluntary organizations are identified as providing "a cheap form of private welfare" in order to control the black populace as the wealth of their countries flowed to the Global North. They further note that charity of this kind was not only intended to assist the poor, but also to serve the rich in their quest to quell social unrest that would affect colonial interests (Manji and O'Coil 2002, 570). While Xaba (2015, 5) acknowledges this, he notes not only the role played by missionaries in establishing soft infrastructure, but also in standing "in support of Africans against colonial interests". This double legacy remains relevant within today's continuing dynamic between global North donors and their global South recipients as discussed in the section that follows pertaining to Faith Based Organizations.

2.3 Faith Based Organizations as Active Agents in Addressing Poverty Alleviation

In terms of poverty alleviation, the most active agents of development have certainly been Faith Based Organizations. Their contribution to development and the allevia-

---

[2] This discussion is taken further in the section on religious agency.

tion of poverty, are perhaps most popularly identified by James (2011, 111) as the following:
- providing efficient development services;
- reaching the poorest at grassroots;
- having a long-term sustainable presence;
- being legitimate and valued by the poorest;
- providing an alternative to a secular theory of development;
- eliciting motivated and voluntary service;
- encouraging civil society advocacy.

Indeed, "existing studies appear to show that Faith Based Organizations (hereafter referred to as FBOs) are more likely to score highly in terms of moral and ethical standing, understanding of the local context, flexibility and the ability to mobilize energy and resources" (Tomalin 2012, 699). The term FBO, however, is itself contested – even by FBOs themselves – and has come to refer to a wide range of organizations including: congregations, mission organizations, aid and NGO[3] type organizations, denominations, networks and even training institutions. Clarke and Jennings (2008, 6) provide perhaps the broadest definition: "any organization that derives inspiration and guidance for its activities from the teaching or principles of faith or from a particular interpretation or school of thought within the faith". This contestation has resulted on the one hand in some scholars arguing that congregations, for example, should not be included in this definition. On the other hand, arguments exist that "to limit the definition of FBOs to formally registered organizations that resemble NGOs would exclude much religiously inspired development work with which donors might usefully engage" (Clarke and Jennings 2008, 6). Although congregations have at times been critiqued for engaging more in charitable relief and welfare responses, congregations remain important as they are often the first point of contact, since they are often made up of the poor themselves.

Various typologies have also emerged in order to seek to categorize FBOs, according for example with regards to their faith-centeredness or characteristics, however, due to the complex and contested nature of FBOs, this is no easy task (see Sider and Unruh 2004). Tomalin (2012, 694) makes the important point that in the Global South many organizations "operate in contexts where the relationship between the religious and secular are not clearly differentiated". Unlike the Global North, which makes a clear distinction between the material and the spiritual realms and may not always acknowledge the manner in which religious behaviors and values lie at the roots of issues such as poverty and marginalization as being religiously influenced, development in the Global South cannot ignore the importance of religion. In fact, FBOs in the Global South may be expected to engage the civic realm from the perspective of faith (James 2009, 10). James (2011, 11) adds that it is in fact faith that

---
[3] Non-Governmental Organizations.

"provides fuel for action" in many FBOs and that the unique contribution of FBOs is indeed their faith basis, which he argues "offers hope, meaning, purpose and transcendental power" to the work of poverty alleviation. Tensions remain, however, with regards to the intersection of religion and development as evidenced within the work of FBOs. On the one hand, FBOs use of relief and development work to proselytize has been identified as problematic, while on the other hand FBOs themselves find the pressure of donors to downplay their faith ethos equally challenging (Thaut 2009, 329). Tomalin (2012, 696) highlights the ways in which Western donor agencies, while claiming their "engagement with FBOs as evidence of their acceptance of the importance of incorporating cultural and religious values and practices into development policy and practice", in fact prove the exact opposite by requiring that there be little to no evangelical faith expression. The emerging findings of my own current research entitled "Does Faith Matter? The role of Faith Based Organizations as civil society role players in South Africa", however, appears to indicate that South African Christian FBOs are not swayed by donor calls from the North to downplay their Christian ethos, with one respondent of the study claiming that this would be like "disowning my own mother or father". While scholars remain divided as to whether FBOs can claim to possess a comparative advantage to secular organizations in terms of their outcomes, FBOs have and do continue to play a key role in addressing the alleviation of poverty worldwide.

2.4 Holism, Decolonizing and Intersectionality in Addressing Poverty

As already alluded to, development in the Global South has highlighted the importance of values and spirituality within development work, as there is no separation between the physical and spiritual realms within most cultures in the South. Indeed, August (2014, 46) argues that "followers of Jesus Christ who engage in social action should never have to choose between satisfying physical hunger and spiritual hunger or between healing bodies and saving souls". This has served as a critique to the dominant secular economic Modernization development models of the North, which conceived of development as an "inevitable, unilinear process that operates neutrally in every culture" and which reduces the meeting of human need to the physical alone (August 2014, 62). Perhaps most problematic about this model of development, was that it was based on the flawed assumption that in order for development to occur, western values, worldviews and goals were to be pursued (August 2014, 63). African scholars such as Adenay (1987, 96) highlighted this issue over 30 years ago. She argued that while Christian development projects should not be uncritical of cultural practices that dehumanize, it should ask the following questions: 'Does the project fit with local worldviews, concepts and values?', 'Does the project fit with local structures?' and 'does the project fit with local economic resources?' Such questions, she argued, are key in placing local people at the centre of the development agenda and thus ensuing the sustainability of development work (Adenay 1987, 96–106).

Current discourse, however, demands that we move one step further: how could African Initiated Church grassroots praxis for example unearth points of critique 'from below' to decolonize current western development praxis? In what ways does its holistic cosmology challenge western notions of development and promote grassroots agency of the kind that is rooted in Africa? These questions challenge us to ask in what ways indigenous culture can not only be valued but be placed at the center of development praxis in Global South contexts and pose a challenge to Western models.

African development scholars and practitioners also recognize the manner in which religion and culture highlights the intersectional nature of poverty. Several African scholars, for example, highlight the manner in which patriarchal religious beliefs re-inforce cultural practices, resulting in women's increased vulnerability to poverty (Fagbeminiyi and Oluwatoyin 2010; Para-Mallam 2006, 413). In addressing women's social disadvantage, it is, therefore, "also important to examine and to attempt to transform religious attitudes" (Tomalin 2013, 157). In addition, poverty alleviation work must "disentangle patriarchal values from their justification as religious and promote alternative (many would argue 'authentic') interpretations of religious traditions that are supportive of women's human's rights and empowerment" (Tomalin 2013, 167). This would include the notion of gender partnership and mutuality in development work, as promoted by African Christian womanist scholars such as Mercy Amba Oduyoye who argue that the "partnership of women and men are both necessary if the church is to be whole and to be the light of Christ for the world" (Onwunta and August 2012, 3). This partnership, it is argued, could see faith leaders, who are still largely male, stand in solidarity with women on key development issues such as maternal health, HIV/AIDS and Gender Based Violence (GBV).

3 Social Capital

3.1 The Value of Religion within the Social Capital Debate

The centrality of social capital to development is largely shaped by the way in which empirical studies show that increased levels of social capital directly reduce levels of poverty, increase wellbeing, reduce crime rates, increase economic productivity and intensify political participation amongst others. In fact, some scholars have argued that communities with both higher and more diverse stocks of social capital "will be in a stronger position to confront poverty and vulnerability" (Traunmüller and Freitag 2011, 253). Fukayama (2001, 18) notes that beyond the role of the state, there are only two "other potential external sources of social capital": religion and globalization. He goes on to state that while secularization applies largely to western Europe, other parts of the world are seeing new forms of religiosity and religiously inspired social change.⁴

The central role of religion in building social capital, is largely due to the fact that religious organizations are able to generate significant amounts of social capital. Three major arguments are identified as supporting this notion. Firstly, religious organizations, such as churches, play a central role in community life – often performing "social, cultural and educational services". This includes access to basic services such as healthcare and education. They also serve as places where community members develop civic skills as volunteers and they offer spaces for those often-marginalized groups in community (such as the poor, women, migrants, the elderly) to participate civically (Traunmüller and Freitag 2011, 254; Ruben 2011, 232). It could be argued that these actions are based on religious teachings, which promote such activities as aspects of religious capital.

It has also been argued that participation in civic organizations, such as religious organizations, create social bonds and social trust – "making collective action much easier" as well as advancing "values and mores regarding communal life, such as reciprocity, trustworthiness and friendship". Some scholars refer to 'spiritual capital', which they view as providing a theological identity and worshipping tradition, undergirded by a "value system, moral vision and basis for faith". This form of capital is embedded within groups but expressed through individuals and enhances social capital (Olney and Burton 2011, 29).⁵ While both Fukayama (2001, 18) and Traunmüller and Freitag (2011, 254) recognize the fact that religious organizations could also generate 'negative' social capital in the form of exclusivist or sectarian groups that foster intolerance, distrust and even violence – they appear to argue that the benefit for the 'common good' far outweighs the bad.

The benefit of religions in the development of social capital for the common good is supported by recent studies. In the US context, almost half of all associational members, personal philanthropy and volunteering is within a religious context (Traunmüller and Freitag 2011, 255) This is no different in Europe, where "faith-based volunteering and faith-based donations comprise a substantial part of active involvement and philanthropy in Europe" – despite the differences in variation across neighboring countries (Traunmüller and Freitag 2011, 255.256). Such findings were not only acknowledged by governments, such as the UK's ruling Labour Party in the early 2000's but promoted within their policy documents. FBOs were viewed as "contributing to community and empowerment and engagement through their net-

---

4 This, however, is tempered by the fact that social capital also has negative outcomes such as sectarianism which breeds "intolerance, hatred and violence" (Fukayama 2001, 18).
5 It should be noted that this identification has also come under fire from some scholars who argue that it fails to recognize group hierarchy, neglects reflection on the "dynamics between ritual action and social action and fails to distinguish between spiritually motivated social action and politically or culturally motivated social action" (Montemaggi 2011, 68).

works, organizational capacity and resources, local knowledge and voluntary action" (Montemaggi 2011, 70), thus not only assisting to deliver basic services but also to promote community cohesion in partnership with the state.

In sub-Saharan Africa, churches and FBOs deliver up to 40 % of basic health care provision and have extensive reach into poor households due to their long term relationships with the civic cause and strong identification with the demands of the poor. Churches/FBOs are also recognized for their contribution to the protection of human rights and, more recently, with regards to reconciliation and reconstruction after civic conflict (Ruben 2011, 232). In a South African context, religious actors are identified as generating considerable amounts of social trust through their volunteer work, care work and involvement in social services. So much so that one of the provincial governments recognized the religious sector as the key role player in their 'Social Capital Formation strategy' (Eigelaar-Meets, Gomulia, and Geldenhuys 2010, 53). The role played by religious communities in moral formation and the development of values is also viewed as valuable within the South African context.

This is affirmed by scholars in other African contexts who view religious beliefs as "associated with solidarity, altruism, humane values, charity etc., thus promoting co-operation with others and positive attitudes towards others" (Kaasa 2013, 580). Adogame (2013, 114) for example points out the way in which African Christians in the diaspora, harness spiritual and social capital to "lift themselves out of poverty" through church-based savings and loan schemes which pool resources to provide resources such as microfinance to small business owners. In an unequal context such as South Africa, with high levels of race-based inequality rooted in its Apartheid legacy, religious actors are viewed as possibly providing both bridging and linking social capital by fostering the dismantling of racial, cultural and socio-economic barriers (Eigelaar-Meets, Gomulia, and Geldenhuys 2010, 54). The latter, however, has not been realized fully in our context and remains a challenge in order to bridge the race-based inequality. How could partnerships between largely rich white congregations and poorer black congregations be encouraged in a way that fosters the dismantling of those barriers in order to give rise to reciprocity, trust and empowerment? This is not an easy question to answer in our context, but it is one which must be dealt with, as much current generation of social capital focuses on bridging (within communities, homogenous race and economic groups) rather than linking social capital (towards other communities, racial and economic groups).

3.2 Approaches to Poverty Alleviation that Build on the Social Capital Debate

Perhaps the most well-known recent approach to community development that builds on discourse around Social Capital is Assets Based Community Development (ABCD). ABCD is a strengths-based approach, premised on the understanding that local communities can drive the development processes themselves through the utilization and mobilization of their own (often unrecognized) assets (Mathie and Cunningham 2003, 474; De Gruchy 2015, 78). In fact, ABCD is identified as "a practical application of the concept of social capital" as ABCD recognizes for example the "potential of community associations to mobilize bonding social capital and increase bridging social capital" (Mathie and Cunningham 2003, 478). With regards to religion's role in promoting this approach, De Gruchy (2015, 82) notes the following:

> Each particular religious institution offers a unique configuration of specific resources which can be utilized in the process of community building. Yet every religious institution, whether large or small, urban or rural, Protestant, Catholic, Jewish, Muslim or Buddhist, or other always offers certain common sets of resources which can be mobilized.

Churches and church groups, then, act as core assets in mobilizing bonding and bridging and linking capital for the community. Haddad (2010, 129), for example, notes the manner in which networks of religious women in rural South Africa serve as places where women "find courage, strength and resources to persevere in the face of near death" by "harnessing the physical and spiritual resources" within these networks. Perhaps one of the most interesting ways in which the social capital debate intersects with praxis – is the manner in which the African Independent Churches (AICs) may be viewed as generators of social capital in order to address poverty and marginalization. While AICs, could not be said to be applying ABCD as an approach, it is clear that they bond, bridge and link for the good of the communities in which they reside. The development projects of AICs are "small scale, self-generated, resourced by local congregants and internally funded" (Masondo 2014, 10). AICs, therefore, may be termed generators of social and spiritual capital, because their development work is not centered on financial capital, but rather on their extensive social networks and shared spiritual and cultural values, which they use to bridge and link their people to the resources needed for development.

4 Religious Agency

4.1 Agency, Power and Participation in the Context of Religion and Development

Religious agency is part of the way in which both individuals and collectives contribute to social change. It is also tied to dimensions of human action and identity. The notion of agency within development discourse has perhaps most popularly been defined by Amartya Sen's book *Development as Freedom* (1999). Sen argues that freedom is both the end and means of development. In his definition, freedom is "not the opposite of oppression", but is rather opposed to *unfreedom*, a word he defines to include the full range of hindrances to human flourishing or "capability deprivation" (De Gruchy 2015, 73; Sen 1999, 23). While Sen defines freedom *from* in terms of common development indicators such as: from starvation, malnourishment, escapable morbidity and premature mortality, he also defines it as freedom *to*, for example literacy and numeracy, political participation, freedom of speech etc., (Sen 1999, 36). He sees freedom as central in enhancing "the ability of people to help themselves and also to influence the world" (De Gruchy 2015, 73), as a means of development:

> With adequate social opportunities, individuals can effectively shape their own destiny and help each other. They need not be seen primarily as passive recipients of the benefits of cunning development programmes. There is a strong rationale for recognizing the positive role of free and sustainable agency – and even of constructive impatience. (Sen 1999, 21)

Underlying this is the assumption that all citizens – not just the elites – should be active participants in their own social, political and economic life. In advocating for this kind of participation, power must be central to development discourse and practice. A "more egalitarian pattern of distribution" must be promoted by encouraging the participation of the poorest of the poor in their own development, challenging rich Christians to "critically examine their own power base" (Swart 2006, 47–48). This is not unlike the call of Liberation Theology, which should be re-explored in order to provide theological critique to current engagement with the poor and marginalized in many contexts. Where Christian development practice attempts to understand power only in terms of empowerment as skills transfer and 'projectized' development, then people are reduced to objects of development rather than as agents and subjects of their own development. This kind of projectized development could thus be seen as retaining the "relationships of power that were characteristic of the missionary and charity services of the churches" (Elliot 1987, 17–23) which promoted dependency and the abandonment of indigenous knowledge systems in the past. In a South African context, for example, Christian development practitioners seeking to 'do' development that is sustainable and just, must recognize the manner in which our racially-skewed poverty and inequality calls into question our practice. In a recent article on the need to decolonise the development praxis of Christian Development Organisations (CDOs) in a South African context I noted the following:

> CDOs will need to reflect on whether they are truly contextually engaged and valuing local knowledge systems and cultures or whether their own policies and practices continue to "enshrine white superiority and black inferiority" (Vellum 2016, 2; Tshaka and Mafokane 2010, 535). How do they read the bible and do they read the bible with those they serve? What kinds of spirituality inform their practices? Do they take black experiences as their point of departure when designing projects and programmes? (Bowers Du Toit 2018, 31–32)

If CDOs fail to take such issues into account – and this includes Global North CDOs working in the Global South – rather than promoting agency and self-reliance, they will reproduce dependency and disempowerment.

It is also important to note that often development that focuses on projectized notions of development that do not recognize power – and which may be termed 'pragmatic' – encourage close partnership with the state. In many contexts, however, this partnership may be with a corrupt state that seeks to oppress the very people who should benefit from development. In such contexts, the role of the church in development, must include a prophetic element that recognizes the roots of poverty and inequality in such contexts and not only seeks to promote development through its daily development work, but also through its solidarity with the poorest of the poor.

4.2 Social Movements as Examples of Religious Agency

Some of the most prominent examples of the role of religious agency in social change is that of the Civil Rights and Anti-Apartheid movements respectively – movements which sought to stand in solidarity with the poor and oppressed. Prominent development scholar, David Korten, argues that in order for development praxis to be values-driven, social movements often take the lead in "promoting an alternative vision of a more just society" (Korten 1990, 124). He argues this as the 'Fourth Generation of development'. These movements are not driven by "budgets or organizational structures", but rather by an "idea, by a vision of a better world". They are well positioned to drive social change as they possess the ability to "rapidly and flexibly network diverse and dispersed individuals and organizations that are motivated by voluntary commitments" (Korten 1995, 55). South African scholar, Ignatius Swart, argues that as a role player in global civil society, the church has a unique role to play in the intersection between development and civil society discourse (Swart 2006, 144). And, indeed, economic justice and resistance to the global forces of neo-liberalism are macro development agenda's which a civil society role player with global reach, such as the church, can and must address.

Such social movements are most commonly exemplified by global campaigns such as Jubilee 2000/Drop the Debt, which drew on biblical notions of justice to call for an end to the crippling debt imposed by the Bretton Woods institutions on the Global South. Movements such as this one used the power and reach of the global church to activate and mobilize a global advocacy campaign by promoting an alternative vision of a more just society. More recently the #Feesmustfall student movement in South Africa has tackled the issues of inequality, neoliberalism and lack of transformation in the Higher Education sector in SA. Although the social movement itself was not a religious one, in a country that is 80% Christian, some of the student activists who participated identified as Christians and saw their activism as an outworking of their theology. Their activism was viewed as rooted in their vision of a just God as found in scripture, a God who had compassion for the marginalized and oppressed and called them to do likewise. However, they also critiqued mainstream Christianity for subscribing to the kind of theological dualism that focuses life only on the 'world hereafter' and results in passivity and inaction from the church (Lee 2017). Such social movements, as fourth generation actors driven by agency often fueled by religious motivations, then play an important role in re-activating what may be termed as a prophetic vision of a more just society.

5 Conclusion: The Challenge of this Contribution for Contemporary Practical Theological Discourse

Practical Theology stands at intersections – of faith and life, of theory and practice, of church and society – and this contribution embodies much of that ambiguous, yet exciting, tension in seeking to discuss the intersection between religion and development. The latter field is itself an emerging one largely populated by scholars within the fields of Sociology of Religion and Development Studies, and this chapter also acknowledges this placement, while seeking to engage faith praxis from diaconal, grassroots and contextual perspectives. Religion and Development discourse remains a fairly open field with much still to be explored. The global and local complexities within which faith-based development practitioners work are challenging and in need of greater engagement from the perspective of Practical Theology and this chapter sought to highlight some key points of departure in current discourse. It also seeks to give voice to some of the critical discourses and issues in the study and practice of the field. Notions such as decolonization and the manner in which development itself is implicated in the colonial project; the subtle difference between empowerment and power / charity and liberation; the need to center culture and gender in development discourse and the manner in which religion complicates and implicates faith-based development are all highlighted.

Through exploring these critical perspectives in this contribution, Practical Theology is interpreted as a form of Public Theology – and voice is given to often unheard perspectives emerging from the Global South at the intersection of church and society. There remain, however, many unheard voices in the intersection between religion and development as this is both an emerging sub-field within the fields of Development and Theology respectively. These are also key challenges for the larger field of Practical Theology itself, as it highlights the importance of intersectionality within the field. Are, for example, notions of power and gender (in both research and practice) foregrounded in our research as Practical Theologians? Do we, as scholars in Practical Theology, acknowledge our own positionality with sufficient emphasis? Is there an acknowledgement within the academy that the most prominent Practical Theological voices are still from the Global North, and how can these power dynamics be acknowledged and addressed? Perhaps even the manner in which my own contribution is written, still betrays my bias in working at times from Global North definitions towards the South so the challenge to decenter the North – even as a Global South scholar in such an emerging field – remains. Perhaps this is the 'elephant in the room' as we seek to produce Practical Theology that centers our own practical theological realities and not only Northern discourse and practice.

Bibliography

Adenay, Miriam. 1987. "Culture and Planned Change." In *The Church in Response to Human Need*, edited by Vinay Samuel and Chris Sugden, Grand Rapids: Eerdmans, 85–108.

Adogame, Afe. 2013. *Christian Diaspora: New Currents and Emerging Trends in World Christianity*. New York: Bloomsbury.

August, Karel Thomas. 2014. *Equipping the Saints: God's Measure for Development*. Bellville: The Print Man.

Beek, Kurt Alan ver. 2000. "Spirituality: A Development Taboo." *Development in Practice* 10:31–43.

Bowers Du Toit, Nadine. 2018. "Decolonising Development? Re-claiming Biko and a Black Theology of Liberation within the Context of Faith Based Organizations in South Africa." *Missionalia* 46:24–35.

Clarke, Gerard, and Michael Jennings, eds. 2008. *Development, Civil Society and Faith-based Organizations: Bridging the Sacred and the Secular*. Hampshire / New York: Palgrave Macmillan.

Eigelaar-Meets, Ilse, Carolin Gomulia, and Almo Geldenhuys. 2010. "An Emerging Strategy of Social Capital Formation: Opportunity and Challenge for the Religious Sector." In *Religion and Development in Post-Apartheid South Africa*, edited by Ignatius Swart, Hermann Rocher, Sulina Green, and Johannes Erasmus, Stellenbosch: Sun Press, 121–136.

Elliot, Charles. 1987. *Comfortable Compassion: Poverty, Power and the Church*. Hodder & Staughton: London.

Fagbeminiyi, Fasina, and Matthew Oluwatoyin. 2010. "Religion, Gender and Development: Emerging Issues." *Gender and Behaviour* 8:2789–2802.

Fukayama, Francis. 2001. "Social Capital, Civil Society and Development." *Third World Quarterly* 22:7–20.

De Gruchy, Steve. 2015. "Of Agency, Assets and Appreciation: Seeking some Commonalities between Theology and Development." In *Keeping Body and Soul Together: Reflections by Steve de Gruchy on Theology and Development*, edited by Beverly Haddad, Pietermartizberg: Cluster Publications, 66–87.

Haddad, Beverly. 2010. "Gender, Development and Faith: Religious Networks and Women's Struggle." In *Religion and Development in Post-Apartheid South Africa*, edited by Ignatius Swart, Hermann Rocher, Sulina Green, and Johannes Erasmus, Stellenbosch: Sun Press, 121–136.

James, Rick. 2009. "What is Distinctive about FBOs? How European FBOs Define and Operationalize their Faith." Praxis Paper 22. https://www.intrac.org/resources/praxis-paper-22-distinctive-fbos-european-fbos-define-operationalise-faith/ (29.11.2021).

James, Rick. 2011. "Handle with Care: Engaging with Faith-Based Organizations in Development." *Development in Practice* 21:109–117.

Kaasa, Anneli. 2013. "Religion and Social Capital: Evidence from European Countries." *International Review of Sociology* 23:578–596.

Korten, David. 1990. *Getting to the 21st Century: Voluntary Action and the Global Agenda*. Connecticut: Kumarian Press.

Lee, Jennifer. 2017. *Hope Has Two Daughters: The Intersections of Faith and Activism for Christian Fallists in South Africa*. Unpublished Masters thesis. Eastern Mennonite University.

Manji, Firoze, and Carl O'Coil. 2002. "The Missionary Position: NGOs and Development in Africa." *International Affairs* 178:567–583.

Mathie, Alison, and Gord Cunningham. 2003. "From Clients to Citizens: Asset Based Community Development as a Strategy for Community-Driven Development." *Development in Practice* 13:474–486.

Masondo, Sibusiso. 2014. "The African Indigenous Churches' Spiritual Resources for Democracy and Social Cohesion." *Verbum et Ecclesia* 35:1–15.

Montemaggi, Franscesca. 2011. "The Enchanting Dream of 'Spiritual Capital'." *Implicit Religion* 14:67–86.

Nordstokke, Kjell. 2014. "Ecumenical Diakonia." *The Ecumenical Review* 66:265–273.

Olney, Fred, and Lewis Burton. 2011. "Parish Church and Village Community: The Interchange of Social Capital in a Rural Setting." *Rural Theology* 9:27–38.

Onwunta, Esther, and Karel August. 2012. "(Gender) Partnership as Transforming Paradigm for Development in Church and Society." *HTS Teologiese Studies / Theological Studies* 68:1–9.

Para-Mallam, Oluwafunmilayo Josephine. 2006. "Faith, Gender and Development Agendas in Nigeria: Conflicts, Challenges, and Opportunities." *Gender and Development* 14:409–421.

Phiri, Isabel, and Kim Dongsung. 2014. "Called to Be a Diaconical Community through a Pilgrimage of Justice and Peace." *The Ecumenical Review* 66:252–264.

Ruben, Ruerd. 2011. "Can Religion Contribute to Development? The Road from 'Truth' to 'Trust'." *Exchange* 40:225–234.

Sider, Ronald, and Heidi Unruh. 2004. "Typology of Religious Characteristics of Social Services and Educational Organizations and Programs." *Non-Profit and Voluntary Sector Quarterly* 33:109–134.

Sen, Amyrta. 1999. *Development as Freedom*. Oxford: Oxford University Press.

Swart, Ignatius. 2006. *The Churches and the Development Debate: Perspectives on a Fourth Generation Approach*. Stellenbosch: Sun Press.

Thaut, Laura. 2009. "The Role of Faith in Christin Faith-Based Humanitarian Agencies: Constructing the Taxonomy." *Voluntas* 20:319–350.

Tomalin, Emma. 2012. "Thinking about Faith-Based Organisations in Development: Where Have we Got to and what Next?" *Development in Practice* 22:689–703.

Tomalin, Emma. 2013. *Religions and Development*. London: Routledge.

Traunmüller, Richard, and Markus Freitag. 2011. "State Support of Religion: Making or Breaking Faith-Based Social Capital?" *Comparative Politics* 43:253–269.

Vellum, Vuyani. 2016. *The Decolonization of Theology: An Epistemological Challenge and Opportunity*. Decolonizing Theology Conference at the University of Stellenbosch. Unpublished paper.

Xaba, Thokozani. 2015. "From Public-Private Partnerships to Private-Public Stick'em Ups! NGOism, Neoliberalism, and Social Development in Post-Apartheid South Africa." *International Social Work* 58:1–11.

Mutaz al Khatib
Ethics and Religion

1 Introduction

This article[1] focuses on the concept of ethics and its link to religion from the "practical theology" perspective. It highlights the scope of overlap between the concepts of ethics and religion at two levels: a) the theoretical level represented in meta-ethics and other central concepts, and b) the applied level highlighting the deep debates of good or morally and religiously justifiable forms of practice. This is to be addressed through a modern and complex issue called "geneticization". It is the phenomenon of the genetic approach to the human body, including genetic intervention (GI).

2 Islamic Ethics: Concept and Theoretical Framework

Classical Islamic philosophical thought defined ethics as a condition, or a well-established characteristic of the soul, that drives the actions of the body (Miskawayh no date, 41; al-Māwardī 1981, 5; al-Ghazālī 2004, 3:53). Following the Greek philosophical sources, these types of writings were inclined to describe the nature of the soul and its characteristics in addition to defining the virtue and its divisions (Draz 2008, 2; Walzer 1962, 236–252). However, this early perception limits ethics to Greek philosophy only, whereas the modern concept of ethics has witnessed two developments. Firstly, it went beyond the classical concept due to being transitioned to normative sciences (i.e., logic, epistemology, and ontology), which comprehensively study human behaviour making ethical judgements the outcome of accumulated knowledge from studying human behaviour. Secondly, the possibility of ethical evaluation is no longer an axiomatic issue, given the complexity, expansion, and multiplicity of knowledge. This has led to research in meta-ethics, i.e., the study of ethical systems from an external perspective, to understand their differences, similarities, and operational mechanisms (Arkoun 2007, 83–84).

If the traditional notion, which considers ethics as a branch of philosophy (Phronesis, commonly known as practical wisdom), is adopted, it cannot be seen as a dis-

---

[1] This research was made possible by the NPRP grant *Indigenizing Genomics in the Gulf Region (IGGR): The Missing Islamic Bioethical Discourse*, no. NPRP8–1620–6–057 from the Qatar National Research Fund (a member of The Qatar Foundation). The statements made herein are solely the responsibility of the author.

tinct discipline within the classical Islamic classifications of science (al-Nadīm 2009). Moreover, the sources on this issue from such perspective are limited because they will depend on the philosophical writing style and its development throughout Islamic history (Mūsā 1953, 225; al-Jābirī 2014, 9–10). In fact, the number of Arab-Islamic sources in the field of ethics is enormous, if we exclude, in our approach, the Greek philosophical conception (Fakhry 1994; Fakhry 1978, 1:9–10). Ethics addresses the goals of human acts and living a good life. On this basis, it is more comprehensive than the dualistic conception of *ḥalāl* (permissible) vs. *ḥarām* (prohibition), or the dualistic concept of righteousness vs. wrongfulness. Consequently, the concept of ethics is complex because the sciences that address human conduct at all levels are numerous. Hence, this explains, partially, why ethics as a domain has not witnessed independence from the rest of the known fields of Islamic studies. Ethics, as we understand it today, intersects with several fields in Islamic studies, including: *fiqh* (Islamic law), *uṣūl al-fiqh* (Islamic legal theory), *kalām* (theology) and Sufism, as well as *adab* (a genre explaining the ideal behavior or code of ethics for specific professional groups like scholars, students, jurisconsults, jurists, physicians, etc.).

The concept of good deed has two divisions: ontological and epistemological. These divisions seek to answer the questions, "Who are we? How should we behave?" Traditional Islamic theology was preoccupied with two main issues. The first is the human attitude towards the Divine Act and the human act itself, including the issues of free will and obligations in addition to the relationship between reasons and causes, salvation and happiness. The second issue is obligation, including the source of obligation, evaluation of acts, whether reason-based evaluation or tradition-based evaluation, and the nature of good and evil. Muslim theologians, therefore, formulated a debate on the basis of ontological vs. epistemological aspects. Does revelation establish the provisions on ethical evaluation, or is it only for explanation and demonstration? Here, we have two major theories. The first theory, advocated by the Muʿtazila, is ethical objectivism. This means that ethical foundations have an existence independent from the Divine Will, and thus they precede the existence of the divine command and prohibition. Command and prohibition are of the requirements of good and bad; i.e., command comes according to the good and prohibition comes according to the bad, where the function of revelation here is only revealing and explanatory. The second theory, advocated by the Ashʿarites, is the ethical voluntarism or the Divine command theory. Its advocates argue that good and bad are pre-determined by the Divine Will; therefore, there are no normative bases before the revelation; i.e., command makes the deed good and prohibition makes it bad. This is, however, the doctrine of the Ashʿarites ('Abd al-Jabbār no date, 6:1:7–8; 6:2:323; al-Taftāzānī 1998, 4:282–3; Hourani 1985, 57–66).

It must be made clear that the concept of good vs. bad involves three possible interpretations: A) being appropriate to behavior or contradictory to it (*mulā'iman li-l-ṭabʿ aw munāffiran*), B) perfect or imperfect, where these two interpretations are unarguably rational, and C) where act is subject to being righteous or wrongful to God (reward and sanction), which raises controversy (al-Rāzī 1997, 1:123; al-Shahristānī 2009, 363; al-Taftāzānī 1998, 4:282; al-Qarāfī 1973, 88).

The foregoing analysis falls within meta-ethics and the sources of normative provisions. Although the mainstream approach throughout history is the Ashʻarite approach, the development of theological and doctrinal debates led to the crystallization of the higher objectives of sharīʻa (*maqāṣid al-sharīʻa*). This theory was built on the idea that Divine commands and prohibitions are rational and not arbitrary, as "the commands are compatible with the overriding interests (*maṣlaḥah*), while its prohibitions are directed against the overriding harm (*mafsadah*)" (al-Qarāfī no date, 2:126). In other words, the interests on which rewards and sanctions are based, namely, the interests for the Hereafter and the common interests between the worldly life and the Hereafter, are known only through command and prohibition (al-ʻIzz, 1991, 1:5, 10). It was possible to build this theory, which was founded by a number of Ashʻarite scholars, by deducting the various jurisprudential rulings and knowing their reasons or objectives, and linking them to inclusive interpretations which set them in order. The interest here is not determined by reason independently. Rather, it is determined by sharīʻa, which is the only source of obligation and prohibition according to the Ashʻarites. From a different perspective, Muʻtazila believe in obligation stemming from human reason (*al-taklīf al-ʻaqlī*).

These debates took the form of a concrete and comprehensive methodology through Islamic legal theory (*uṣūl al-fiqh*), dealing with the normative rulings, their sources, and the methods of deriving them. It is a discipline that combines revelation and reason. There are differences between the legal theorists (*uṣūliyyūn*) from different schools in terms of inclusiveness and exclusiveness, but the higher objectives of sharīʻa highlights holistically the philosophy of sharīʻa and provides a rational justification for the system of normative rulings presented by the jurists of the schools (*fuqahāʼ al-madhāhib*).

3 Geneticization and Genetic Intervention

How can the previous conceptual and theoretical framework operate in a topic such as genetics? Why genes in particular? The topic of genes is linked to the achievements of modernity on the one hand, while, on the other hand, it is characterized by the complexity of the concepts of ethics and religion according to the new perspective of practical theology. The topic of genes, moreover, belongs to the field of interdisciplinary studies, as the subject of genes today relates to the fields of moral philosophy, biomedical ethics, social sciences, and Islamic law (*fiqh*).

With regards to the issue of genes, three concepts can be highlighted: geneticization, genetic intervention and genetic enhancement. Geneticization is the most comprehensive among them, with different types of GI, e.g., treatment and enhancement.

> The concept of geneticization has been introduced in the scholarly literature to describe the various interlocking and imperceptible mechanisms of interaction between medicine, genetics, society, and culture. It is argued that Western culture currently is deeply involved in a process of geneticization. This process implies a redefinition of individuals in terms of DNA codes, a new language to describe and interpret human life and behavior in a genomic vocabulary of codes, blueprints, traits, dispositions, genetic mapping, and a gentechnological approach to disease, health, and the body. (ten Have 2001, 4: 295)

GI includes all processes that are subject to human genes, including therapy and enhancement. GI is implemented on two types of cells: a) reproductive cells, where intervention is often implemented on an embryo / foetus, either by modifying an (un)desirable characteristic, and b) somatic cells, where intervention is implemented on someone who already exists and his/her characteristics are stabilized, such as the newborn.

The most problematic practice in GI, presumably, is enhancement, which refers to "any change in the biology of a person which increases the chances of leading a good life in the relevant set of circumstances" (Savulescu, Sandberg, and Kahane 2011, 7).

4 Genetic Intervention according to Contemporary Fiqh Discourse

Islamic legal opinions are the applied field that is supposed to reflect theological and ethical perceptions in the form of normative rulings that address the behavior of the believer. The jurist's examination of the methods used, and discussion of the objectives is based on a specific conception of two aspects: genetic techniques and their ability to make a difference, and the objective of the lawgiver or the Divine Will. The jurist reaches the ruling by *ijtihād* (independent legal reasoning), which is meant to reveal the Divine Will. How has the topic of genes been discussed in contemporary *fatwas*? Three of the main institutions, which addressed this issue, are featured here to highlight the topic of this article. The first institution is the International Islamic Fiqh Academy (IIFA) in Jeddah, affiliated with the Organization of Islamic Cooperation, which brings together the members representing their countries and experts appointed by the IIFA and belonging to different disciplines. The second institution is the Islamic Fiqh Academy (IFA), affiliated with the Muslim World League based in Mecca. The third institution is the Islamic Organization for Medical Sciences (IOMS), based in Kuwait.

The IOMS has reacted positively to genetics by considering it "part of humankind's self-identification and the manifestation of God's Will in His creation", and, consequently, the IOMS introduced this into the area of collective duties (*furūḍ al-kifāya*) that countries or institutions must abide by. From a holistic view, genetic engineering can be employed by good and evil means, as their lawful use is limited to the prevention or treatment of diseases, except for germ cells because of their problematic issues related to lineages. It is religiously prohibited to use them for the purposes of experiment. The general rule here is that, according to the IOMS statement, genetic research and its applications should not go beyond the commitment to "the rulings of sharīʿa and respect for human rights recognized by Islam and not detract from fundamental freedoms and human dignity".[2] The IFA in Mecca has a similar but more conservative stance. It believes that no research, treatment or diagnosis of human genes should be conducted except as a matter of necessity (ḍarūra) after an accurate and prior assessment of the risks and potential benefits, preceded by obtaining the religiously accepted consent, while maintaining the full confidentiality of the results and adherence to sharīʿa rulings.[3] The IIFA, however, confirmed the decision of the IOMS and allowed the examination of germ cells, but prohibited the therapy in its current form because it does not take into account sharīʿa rulings. It only allowed for therapeutic intervention in somatic cells but under certain conditions, as long as it does not lead to greater harm, and is definitely used for healing or alleviating pain; when there is absolutely no alternative approach. However, GI is prohibited for enhancement purposes because it interferes with the essence of the creation (aṣl al-khilqa) and changes it, which is a violation of human dignity and does not come out of a religiously considered necessity or need.[4]

The concern of the muftīs in dealing with the uses of genetic technology is the search for the Divine Will in terms of commands and prohibitions as explained above, especially in Muslim societies, where great importance is given to the dichotomy of ḥalāl vs. ḥarām. The problem here, however, is in the absence of a scriptural reference that reveals God's will, which means that the muftī must practice ijtihād. If any fiqhī parallel (naẓīr) or classical paradigm is found, relevant rulings are to be considered, but if the issue is novel and has no precedent, the muftī resorts to the general principles historically set by the Islamic legal schools after studying scriptural texts and the Islamic practice in the formative period and analysing the commands and prohibitions that embody the lawgiver's will (al-Khatib 2018).

Fatwas on genetics, can be classified into two categories. The first includes the fatwas on therapeutic treatment, which was extensively discussed by classical jurists. Contemporary muftīs, however, set restrictions and conditions to permit this modern pattern of treatment, e.g., the likelihood that it will yield good results and that it does not cause greater harm. The second category of fatwas depends on the concept of maṣlaḥ mursala (undefined interest). If the interest is what the lawgiver's will defines as but the scriptural text showing this will is not available, then it is considered undefined interest. In this case, a new ruling is to be derived based on general principles of sharīʿa because human reason does not judge independently as it is in the

---

[2] This symposium was held under the title *Genetics, Genetic Engineering and Human Genome* in Kuwait, 13–15 October 1998 (al-Jundī 2000, 1045–1049).
[3] IFA, 15th Session, Mecca, October 31, 1998.
[4] IIFA, 21st Session, Riyāḍ, November 18–22, 2013.

mainstream doctrine, but this juristic deduction is governed by a specific perception of the gene and this, as a result, will affect how to estimate its benefits and harms at two levels. The first level includes the psychological, social, and cultural influences associated with the individual, society and human species in general (geneticization). The second level comprises the effects of the use of genetics on the juristic rulings, which relate to other parts such as the rulings on therapeutic treatment, diseases, human dignity, rights, guardianship, lineage, and others. However, they all fall under two higher objectives,[5] Namely preserving the offspring (*ḥifẓ al-nasl*) and protecting the human life (*ḥifẓ al-nafs*), where it seems that jurists encounter three major rules: A) all things are in principle permissible (*al-aṣl fī al-ashyā' al-ibāḥa*). This rule applies to the genetic technique, B) preservation of the self and offspring, will also touch upon the network of related *fiqhī* rulings, and C) the main purpose of Sharīʻa is to achieve what is beneficial and avoid what is harmful (*jalb al-manāfiʻ wa dar' al-mafāsid*), which research on genomics promises to offer. The jurist's analysis, therefore, falls between these rules based on his own perception and understanding of the of gene as a thick concept. His analysis is also based on his estimation of possible benefits and harms in the light of the broad scheme of *fiqh*; because, at the end, he seeks the Divine Will that covers all human actions, not just benefit in general, as "achieving what is beneficial does not exempt from the adherence to the sharīʻa rulings; lest the material damage be eliminated at the expense of the moral damage by neglecting the standard of lawful vs. unlawful." (Abū Ghudda 2000, 574)

Three remarks can be raised on the previously mentioned collective *fatwas* issued by institutions. First, the absence of the theological dimension; although genetic enhancement, in particular, relates to the principle of creation and its qualities, which relate to issues of Divine destiny and human freedom. Second, the jurists viewed the genetic techniques purely from a "utilitarian" perspective arguing that technology can be used for both good and harm. However, genetic technology refers to a network of possibilities related to changes and effects which are difficult to be separated from each other, or to control all of them, without bearing the consequences and their results. For example, permitting genetic examination is meaningless without accepting what is based on this examination. The beneficial use of genetic technology would not exist without having incidental consequences that might cause psychosocial and social problems and so on. In other words, the distance between the means and the consequences may be narrowed and complicated and might involve several parties that the owner of the gene himself/herself becomes outside the process of geneticization, which is considerably understudied by those institutions (al-Khatib 2019, 175–178).

The third point is that the collective approach revolves around therapy and benefits; two concepts that are complex in the context of modern medicine. Medicine no

---

[5] There are five major objectives of *sharīʻa* which are considered essentials: the preservation of religion, self, reason, offspring, and property. The system of juristic rulings relies on them.

longer revolves around health and disease. It is, rather, on "enhancing the quality of life" (Veatch, 2012, 146–147), dominating, controlling, and re-shaping it (genetic engineering) according to new conditions dictated by the circumstances of modernity and their standards and philosophy on humans and life. On this basis, therapy is no longer a simple concept as may be suggested by those fatwas, but is subject to cultural and social impacts, especially in the presence of geneticization.

5 Genome and Thick Ethics

Against the above-mentioned background, how can we reform the ethical discourse on genetics? This can be achieved by integrating four disciplines rooted in the Islamic tradition, namely theology, philosophy, *fiqh* and legal theory. This is to build a thick ethics perspective towards geneticization. Such a stance will help us include the moral status of man in the universe as part of the debate, where genome relates to two major questions: Who am I? What do I want? This will help us understand the overlap between the practical and theological aspects of jurisprudence. They are interrelated and form what is called, in the present time, practical theology. Moreover, GI is not evaluated as a mere act or practice with questionable uses, in which we balance between temporary and individual benefits and harm. Rather, it is a complex act which can be evaluated based on its drives, motivations, goals, and effects on the individual, and on the community and the species as a whole.

5.1 Geneticization and Theological Ethics

Previous juristic debates neglected the theological aspect in genetics. In fact, the Christian discourse towards the challenges posed by the gene to traditional Christian theology has been delayed for two and a half decades (Chapman 1998, 297). Christian theological debates in this context focused on human nature and human behaviour. This includes the presentation of views based on the evolutionary perspective, the question of man's composition and whether he/she is the sum of his/her parts or has a transcendental dimension, the dualistic soul—body conception, the definition of human beings as biocultural creatures, the conflict between our individual and social nature, the assessment of the extent to which genes shape human nature and determine human behaviour, playing God, criticizing the alleged genetic essentialism, or gene myth to assert the idea of human creativity, moral responsibility and freedom (Chapman 1998, 296–299; Peters 1997; Peters 1998).

From the Islamic theological perspective, geneticization can be discussed through two main angles, a) the concept of human and human nature, and b) the human act and its relation to the Divine Act.

5.1.1 The Concept of Human and Human Nature:

Three conceptions of the human can be identified in this regard. The first one is the Greek conception which is based on the classical belief of the powers of the soul, where *these powers* are the efficient causes of the body's acts. According to this conception, the human soul has three faculties, namely the concupiscent which motivates the human being to achieve his desires; the irascible which motivates the human being to protect himself; and the rational which is supposed to make balance between the other powers. Each faculty generates one virtue which means that we will have three virtues: moderation, courage, and wisdom. It is from the control of the rational power over the faculties of concupiscent and irascible that we get balance in the soul and generate a fourth virtue called justice.[6] Greek ethics was founded on this perception because it is a school that focuses on self-management after self-knowledge, and knowledge of how acts are generated from it (Ḥājī Khalīfa 1941, 1:13–4). Subsequently, the Sufi perspective emanated to build its belief on this conception in purifying the self. The second conception of human is presented by the genetic technique that transferred the centre of the human, from soul to body, until the following question was raised: are we the sum of our genes? (Kaye 1992, 77–84) The third conception refers to the growing belief that man is more than just the sum of genes. This perception dominated the debates after the appearance of the Human Genome Project. It revealed that certain environmental factors, lifestyle factors and cultural factors related to upbringing and education contribute to the activation of certain genes.

Theology in general, and Islamic theology in particular, cannot neglect the spiritual and metaphysical dimensions of its conception of humans. This should also be taken into consideration in building practical stances and discussing the moral arguments of any GI.

5.1.2 Divine Action and Human Action

Genetic enhancement does not, in any way, mean the ability to create or to 'play God'. It is, rather, an extension of God's activity. On this basis, it is necessary to state that the Divine Will is of two kinds. The first is the Will related to the commands by God (*irādat al-amr*); i.e., God wants the human under obligation (*al-mukallaf*) to do what he/she is commanded to do. This is the religious Will and includes the love of God to those who obey these obligations. The second is the Will of Creation (*irādat al-khalq*), which is the Divine Cosmic Will that includes all the actions. It means that nothing in existence that is contrary to His Cosmic Will (the Will of Creation), but it

---

6 For more details about the cardinal virtues see Schofield (2013, 11–28).

may be at odds with His religious will (Ibn Taymiyya 1995, 8:131; Ibn Taymiyya 1986, 3:156).

While the Qur'ān states that God is the Creator, it does not deny the possibility of man's changing the creation of God which can occur through the Cosmic Will but not the religious will. Qur'ān exegetes differ in clarifying the meaning of "changing the creation of God" (*taghyīr khalq Allāh*). For some, the change can be either beneficial or harmful; where only beneficial change is good (Ibn 'Aṭiyya 2001, 2:115). Nonetheless, "changing the creation of God" can mean change in the body and nature, or moral change; for instance, between faith and disbelief. The change in question is, in principle, materialistic and refers to the change of nature, which goes out of its stable characteristics and natural biological biography. This, nevertheless, does not include the partial change that returns the organ or the body to its nature which is represented in two matters: form (image) and function (characteristics) that he/she was created for. Any change in the organ's image or predetermined function is consequently a change in its nature. Genetic enhancement is morally unjustified for two reasons. The first is that it is a negative intervention, which is based on individual and cultural choices and preferences that affect the human species and its balance (natural engineering), since the decision to change is not built on a rational or religious basis in determining what is beneficial or harmful. It is, rather, based on personal views and cultural or social prejudices, and involves a negative attitude towards a specific natural characteristic determined by God's Will of Creation. Change, in this case, seeks to gain another characteristic that man desires. The second reason is that genetic enhancing threatens the stable concept of being natural and is referenced as a standard that is culturally or individually agreed upon, despite the great diversity that exists among humans. However, therapeutic intervention means returning what is abnormal back to its normal nature, and the concept of prevention in preventive intervention means the prevention of what will lead to the change from what is normal and stable in time, place, and age.

5.2 Geneticization and Jurisprudential Systematic Approach

Instead of the abovementioned thin "utilitarian" conception of genetic technology, the thick concept, which includes the link between theological and jurisprudential aspects, strives for the ethicization of *fiqh* through two channels: A) the transition from legal reasoning to ethical reasoning, and B) the connection between the vast *fiqhī* traditions, along with its historical settings and debates found in dialogues within various ethical discourses. The approach of the *fiqhī* tradition is carried out through a method characterized by three features: A) the connection between its many parts and components, B) tracking the various juristic rulings, and C) linking the branches of jurisprudence with the theoretical fundamentals of it.

GI relates to a system of primary concepts that Islamic jurisprudence has historically analysed through various forms of applied studies on some issues. This includes the beginning of life, inviolability of the body, the system of rights, self-preservation and birth control (al-Khatib 2019, 186–198). GI can be implemented on the fertilized egg, foetus and body. When performed on the fertilized egg and the foetus, it is related to the moral rectification of the beginning of life and whether life in this case is inviolable. Some contemporary *muftīs* believe that the fertilized egg has no inviolability because it is not a foetus.[7] This reasoning revolves around the inviolability of the foetus only, as the foetus exists only in the womb, which is an explicit or textual reasoning because life is not associated with a place or is described outside of what it is. In fact, due to its limited potentials historically, the *fiqhī* tradition did not explore the presence of a fertilized egg outside the womb, while modern knowledge reveals that life starts from the fertilized egg, and the same is true for the issue of the foetus, where many jurists proved to be of a potential life (*ḥayāt i'tibāriyya*) (al-Ramlī 1984, 8:442; Ibn al-Jawzī 1981, 374; Ibn 'Ābidīn 1992, 3:176; al-Shubramallisī 1984, 6:182). As for the intervention in the body, this raises the question of the inviolability of the human (*al-ādamiyya*), which is different from human life (*al-ḥayāt al-ādamiyya*). Human is the value of the human body regardless of whether it is alive or dead. Classical jurists debated on the issue of the embryonic stage, and the initial appearance of a human image in the foetus. Additionally, they prohibited the forms of intervention and mutilating a corpse, because human dignity is attached to the creation of man in all stages (Ibn Mufliḥ 1997, 7:74; al-Nawawī 1991, 9:370; al-Ḥaṭṭāb 1992, 3:353).

GI affects two major objectives of Sharī'a: A) self-preservation (*ḥifẓ al-nafs*) and B) preserving the offspring (*ḥifẓ al-nasl*). Self-preservation includes the aspect of existence to fully preserve it and the aspect of the absence of any imbalance, whether immediate or expected (al-Shāṭibī 1997, 2:18). It also includes the real self and the potential self, which means that GI is governed by this principle, and the concept of preserving the human nature is applied as explained before. Preserving the offspring overlaps with self-preservation as it includes preservation at both the individual level, and at the level of humankind, which both relate to GI in germ cells. In addition, our moral responsibility necessitates that we do not force them or impose on them our preferences and cultural or individual choices. GI may maintain human nature but does not take into account the maintenance of lineage, which is a religious duty upon which many juristic rulings are built.

The process of reproduction is linked to a system of rights that must be observed, including religious and socio-financial rights.[8]

---

[7] IOMS in Kuwait, 3rd Symposium, April 18–21, 1987. See: al-Ashqar (2001, 305–310).
[8] For more details about these rights see al-Khatib (2019, 191–193).

5.3 Biology and Medical Authority

The field of jurisprudence is concerned with studying the rulings of intervention and its means by taking the method of analogy in relation to the counterparts (*naẓā'ir*) or based on the method of interest (*maṣlaḥa*). It is a methodology that seeks the Will of God in relation to the specific case but does not help to evaluate the overall picture of the issue and the complexities of the human act which is subject to multi-disciplinary knowledge. The jurist deals with the use of technology, without questioning the technique itself, as it is considered to be the most prominent manifestation of the principle of evolution or continuous progress. Some theologians have warned that "technology is power, unnatural power" (Simmons 1983, 211). It is, rather, a tool in which market and political considerations interfere. The concept of ongoing evolution imposes many more problematic aspects than the mere question of benefits and harms, as argued by Habermas. Nevertheless, from this perspective, and according to Helmuth Plessner, there is a difference between being a body and having a body with a soul (Plessner 1969, 9–10). This, as a result, will affect the human understanding of the self and being responsible for one's own actions, such as the evolution of biological techniques posing a threat to the clarity of human nature in its structure and relations. Its inherent quality, however, is in being natural and distinct from others and equal in conditions of reproduction without economic, cultural or biological interventions or biases. These GIs are an act of self-control that will enable the present generations to dominate the destiny of future generations. The other side of today's authority will be future slavery of the living people towards the dead (Habermas 2003, 16–74). It is true that the methodology of the jurist contains a systematic mechanism called blocking the means (*sadd al-dharā'i'*) or slippery slope. However, this methodology is not as robust and multilayered as the system of "thick ethics" which comprises philosophical components.

Geneticization raises three major complexities that preoccupy philosophy as well. The first is that it undermines the concept of independence, which threatens man's morality because all human actions are linked to the concept of being a moral entity. Hence, if it undermines its independence, it means that its effectiveness is undermined too which will violate man's ethics where his/her action becomes no longer free. The second complexity is that it will affect the ability to understand own self or identity. The last challenge is on the attitude towards pre-personal life and human dignity (al-Khatib 2019, 179–186), where it is related to the understanding of human nature; an area that belongs to the domain of the philosopher's work as well.

Experimental science seeks to take developments to the extreme and expand the circle of the potential that turns over time into an existing reality and then re-opens the possibility of another promising emergence and so on. Islamic Jurisprudence, according to the existing methodology, deals with these changes and results, and adapts to the constraints. However, the concept of thick ethics in its philosophical dimension can help us pre-empt developments by discussing the principle of evolution, allowing moral thinking to transcend science, restricting its movement, and limiting the attempt to dominate and control human nature rather than simply pursuing science and finding solutions and ways out for its outputs.

6 Conclusion

Employing a practical theology approach helps us understand the interaction between revelation and reality, tradition, and modernity. This interaction is reflected in the studies of scholars in different disciplines who provide answers to the questions posed by the developments in reality. Conceptually, religion is a dynamic concept in which tradition, diverse experiences and knowledge contribute to confront a changing and dynamic reality. It is a concept in which several components interact, including Islamic jurisprudence as an applied field which focuses on the specific and partial act, and Islamic legal theory (*uṣūl al-fiqh*) and theology as being two theoretical areas of normative rulings and their scriptural and rational sources. Within this, the cultural and social elements overlap with the religious perceptions and beliefs that are no longer mere rigid or static components. Based on this complex concept of religion, the concept of thick ethics has broadened the ethical discourse to a multidisciplinary approach that recognizes the partial within the holistic, as it does recognize the holistic through the partial in the form of a two-way movement. It deals with the *fiqh* tradition in a systemic approach without neglecting its historical dimensions and treats humankind in accordance with a complex approach that does not see man as a mere body or a sum of genes, but maintaining both his / her visible and internal dimensions; as a microcosm in which the Divine Will is reflected upon. According to this perspective, a human being is entrusted with the task of protecting his / her body and not as the owner of this body. In addition, his / her moral mission is reflected in the rhythm of his / her will in accordance with the Divine Will that he / she constantly strives to know through a developing and dynamic knowledge so that the Cosmic Will meets the religious will and is manifested in his/her actions.

Bibliography

'Abd al-Jabbār, Abū al-Ḥasan. No date. *Al-Mughnī fī abwāb al-tawḥīd wa-l-'adl*, edited by Maḥmūd Muḥammad Qāsim, Cairo: no publisher.

Abū Ghudda, 'Abd al-Sattār. 2000. "Al-Muwākaba al-shar'iyya li mu'ṭayāt al-handasa al-wirāthiyya." In *Ru'ya Islāmiyya li-ba'ḍ al-mushkilāt al-ṭibbiyya al-mu'āṣira*, edited by Aḥmad Rajā'ī al-Jundī, Kuwait: Silisilat maṭbū'āt al-Munaẓẓama al-Islāmiyya li-l-'Ulūm al-Ṭibbiyya, 571–594.

Al-Ashqar, 'Umar, 'Abd al-Nāṣir Abū al-Baṣal, Muḥammad 'Uthmān Shabīr, Alī 'Ārif 'Ārif, and 'Abbās Al-Bāz. 2001. *Dirāsāt fiqhiyya fī qaḍāya ṭibbiyya mu'āṣira*. Amman: Dār al-Nafā'is.

Al-Ghazālī, Abū Ḥāmid. 2004. *Iḥyā' 'ulūm al-dīn*. Beirut: Dār al-Ma'rifa.

Al-Ḥaṭṭāb, Abū 'Abd Allāh. 1992. *Mawāhib al-Jalīl fī sharḥ mukhtaṣar Khalīl*. Beirut: Dār al-Fikr.

Al-'Izz ibn 'Abd al-Salām. 1991. *Qawā'id al-aḥkām fī maṣāliḥ al-anām*, edited by. Ṭāhā 'Abd al-Ra'ūf Sa'd, Cairo: Maktabat al-Kulliyyāt al-Azhariyya.
Al-Jābirī, Muḥammad 'Ābid. 2014. *Al-'Aql al-akhlāqī al-'arabī*. Beirut: Markaz Dirāsāt al-Wiḥda al-'Arabiyya.
Al-Jundī, Aḥmad Rajā'ī. 2000. *Ru'ya Islāmiyya li-ba'ḍ al-mushkilāt al-ṭibbiyya al-mu'āṣira*. Kuwait: Silisilat Maṭbū'āt al-Munaẓẓama al-Islāmiyya li-l-'Ulūm al-Ṭibbiyya.
Al-Khatib, Mutaz. 2018. "Legal Opinion." In *The Encyclopedia of Islamic Bioethics*, edited by Ayman Shabana, Oxford: Oxford University Press. http://www.oxfordislamicstudies.com/article/opr/t9002/e0279 (29.11.2021).
Al-Khatib, Mutaz. 2019. "The Ethical Limits of Genetic Intervention: Genethics in Philosophical and Fiqhi Discourses." In *Islamic Ethics and the Genome Question*, edited by Mohammad Ghaly, Leiden: Brill, 169–200.
Al-Māwardī, Abū al-Ḥasan. 1981. *Tashīl al-naẓar wa-ta'jīl al-ẓafar fī akhlāq al-malik wa siyāsat al-Mulk*, edited by Muḥyī Hilāl al-Sarḥān, Beirut: Dār al-Nahḍa al-'Arabiyya.
Al-Nadīm, Muḥammad ibn Isḥāq. 2009. *Kitāb al-fihrist*, edited by Ayman Fu'ād Sayyid, London: Mu'assasat al-Furqān li-l-Turāth al-Islāmī.
Al-Nawawī, Muḥyī al-Dīn. 1991. *Rawḍat al-ṭālibīn wa 'umdat al-muftīn*, edited by Zuhayr al-Shāwīsh, Beirut: al-Maktab al-Islāmī.
Al-Qarāfī, Shihāb al-Dīn. 1973. *Sharḥ tanqīḥ al-fuṣūl*, edited by Ṭāhā 'Abd al-Ra'ūf Sa'd, Beirut: Sharikat al-Ṭibā'a al-Fanniyya al-Muttaḥida.
Al-Qarāfī, Shihāb al-Dīn. No date. *Anwār al-burūq fī anwā' al-furūq*. Beirut: Dār 'Ālam al-Kutub.
Al-Ramlī, Shams al-Dīn. 1984. *Nihāyat al-muḥtāj ilā sharḥ al-minhāj*. Beirut: Dār al-Fikr.
Al-Rāzī, Fakhr al-Dīn. 1997. *Al-Maḥṣūl*, edited by Ṭāhā al-'Ilwānī, Beirut: Mu'assasat al-Risāla.
Al-Shahristānī, 'Abd al-Karīm. 2009. *Nihāyat al-iqdām fī 'ilm al-kalām*, edited by Alfred Guem, Cairo: Maktabat al-Thaqāfa al-Dīniyya.
Al-Shāṭibī, Abū Isḥāq. 1997. *Al-Muwāfaqāt*, edited by Mashhūr ibn Ḥasan Āl Salmān, al-Khubr: Dār Ibn 'Affān.
Al-Shubrāmallisī, Nūr al-Dīn. 1984. *Ḥāshiya 'alā nihāyat al-muḥtāj ilā sharḥ al-minhāj li al-Ramlī*. Beirut: Dār al-Fikr.
Al-Taftāzānī, Sa'd al-Dīn. 1998. *Sharḥ al-maqāṣid*, edited by 'Abd al-Raḥmān 'Umayra, Beirut: 'Ālam al-Kutub.
Al-Taftāzānī, Sa'd al-Dīn. n.d. *Sharḥ al-talwīḥ 'alā al-tawḍīḥ*. Cairo: Maṭba'at Ṣubaiḥ.
Arkoun, Mohammed. 2007. *Al-Islām, al-akhlāq wa-l-siyāsa*. Beirut: Dār al-Nahḍa al-Arabiyya.
Chapman, Audrey. 1998. "Ethics and Human Genetics." *Society of Christian Ethics* 18:293–303.
Draz, Mohammed A. 2008. *The Moral World of the Quran*, trans. Danielle Robinson and Rebecca Masterton. London / New York: Tauris.
Fakhry, Majid. 1978. *Al-Fikr al-akhlāqī al-'arabī*. Beirut: al-Ahliyya li-l-Nashr.
Fakhry, Majid. 1994. *Ethical Theories in Islam*. Leiden: Brill.
Habermas, Jurgen. 2003. *The Future of Human Nature*. Cambridge: Polity Press.
Ḥājī Khalīfa. 1941. *Kashf al-ẓunūn 'an asāmī al-kutub wa-l-funūn*. Baghdad: Maktabat al-Muthannā.
Have, Henk A.M.J. ten. 2001. "Genetics and Culture: The Geneticization Thesis." *Medicine, Health Care, and Philosophy* 4:295–304.
Ibn 'Ābidīn, Muḥammad Amīn. 1992. *Radd al-muḥtār 'alā al-durr al-mukhtār*. Beirut: Dār al-Fikr.
Ibn 'Aṭiyya, Abū Muḥammad. 2001. *Al-Muḥarrar al-wajīz fī tafsīr al-kitāb al-'azīz*, edited by 'Abd al-Salām 'Abd al-Shāfī, Beirut: Dār al-Kutub al-'Ilmiyya.
Ibn al-Jawzī, Abū al-Faraj. 1981. *Aḥkām al-nisā'*, edited by. 'Alī al-Muḥammadī, Beirut: Manshūrāt al-Maktaba al-'Aṣriyya.
Ibn Mufliḥ, Muḥammad. 1997. *Al-Mubdi' fī sharḥ al-muqni'*, Beirut: Dār al-Kutub al-'Ilmiyya.

Ibn Taymiyya, Taqī al-Dīn. 1986. *Minhāj al-sunna al-nabawiyya fī naqḍ kalām al-shīʿa al-qadariyya*, edited Muḥammad Rashād Sālim, Riyad: Jāmiʿat al-Imām Muḥammad ibn Suʿūd.

Ibn Taymiyya, Taqī al-Dīn. 1995. *Majmūʿ al-fatāwā*, edited by ʿAbd al-Raḥmān ibn Muḥammad ibn Qāsim, Medina: Majmaʿ al-Malik Fahd.

Kaye, Howard L. 1992. "Are we the Sum of Our Genes?" *Wilson Quarterly* 16:77–84.

Miskawayh, Aḥmad ibn Muḥammad. No date. *Tahdhīb al-akhlāq wa taṭhīr al-aʿrāq*, edited by Ibn al-Khaṭīb, Cairo: Maktabat al-Thaqāfa al-Dīniyya.

Mūsā, Muḥammad Yūsuf. 1953. *Tārīkh al-akhlāq*. Cairo: Dār al-Kitāb al-ʿArabī.

Peters, Ted. 1997. *Playing God? Genetic Determinism and Human Freedom*. New York: Routledge.

Peters, Ted, ed. 1998. *Genetics: Genes, Religion, and Society*. Cleveland: The Pilgrim Press.

Plessner, Helmuth. 1969. "Al-Insān bi-waṣfihi kāʾinan ḥayyan (The Living Human Being).", trans. Magdi Youssef. *Fikr wa Fann* 13:9–10.

Savulescu, Julian, Ruud ter Meulen, and Guy Kahane. 2011. *Enhancing Human Capacities*. Chichester: Wiley-Blackwell.

Schofield, Malcolm. 2013. "Cardinal Virtues: A Contested Socratic Inheritance." In *Plato and the Stoics*, edited by Alex G. Long, Cambridge: Cambridge University Press, 11–28.

Simmons, Paul D. 1983. *Birth and Death: Bioethical Decision Making*. London: Westminster Press.

Veatch, Robert M. 2012. *The Basics of Bioethics*. Upper Saddle River: Pearson Education.

Walzer, Richard. 1962. *Greek into Arabic: Essays on Islamic Philosophy*. Cambridge, MA: Harvard University Press.

Annemie Dillen
Family and Religion

1 Introduction

In 2001 I started writing a PhD on families, theology, ethics, and religious education (Dillen 2009). At that moment, a few major works on families and practical theology, were published. The American protestant practical theologian Don Browning was leading a large project on families and theology, called the *Religion, Culture and Family project*. One of the most famous outcomes of the project was the book 'From Culture Wars to Common Grounds', which he co-published with leading practical theologians Bonnie Miller-McLemore and Pamela Couture (2000), who each also published other books on practical theology in relation to family issues (Miller-McLemore 1994; Couture 1991). In the French speaking world, Catholic moral theologian Xavier Lacroix published several books on family and ethics, most of them focused on the value of heteronormative marriage (e.g., 2001). The Austrian Catholic ethicist Gerhard Marschütz published on family and ethics (2000), and several authors wrote about their empirical research on family religious education (Elshof 2009). Since the beginning of this century, a lot more has been published on all issues related to families. Interesting overviews and up to date articles can be found in the journal *Marriage, Families and Spirituality* (edited by Intams – the International Academy for Marital Spirituality, published by Peeters, Leuven).

In 2008 I became the chairholder of the Catholic inter-diocesan council for family ministry in Flanders, the Dutch speaking part of Belgium. Having this (unpaid) church-related function, in addition to a function as professor in practical theology at a faculty of theology and religious studies in a Catholic University (Leuven, Belgium) in a pluralist country, influences my own theology, as well as my own family experiences and those of people around me.

In this chapter, I will answer the question how a practical theology of families can be conceived, knowing that this is only one possible path, influenced by my own Belgian Catholic context and theological views developed in dialogue with international protestant and catholic scholars from various disciplines and backgrounds, among which also explicit feminist theologians. By developing the core elements of a practical theological reflection on families, I will also explain how 'religion' is conceived in this view.

2 Lived Religion and Families

Don Browning and his co-authors developed their practical theological approach on the family in relation to their own definition on practical theology (Browning, Miller-

McLemore, and Couture 2000). Browning developed earlier a 'fundamental practical theology' and explained how in fact all forms of theology fall under 'practical theology' (Browning 1991, 7 ff). His idea about 'fundamental practical theology' includes four steps: 'descriptive theology', 'historical theology', 'systematic theology' and 'strategic practical theology'. This last step is what is often considered as practical theology. Browning refers to David Tracy's critical correlation as an important methodological characteristic for practical theology (Tracy 1975).

Within the global field of practical theology there are various paradigms. Browning's approach is one of them, which is considered as a form of 'public theology' that tries to influence a broader audience with ethical positions on family issues. The South African practical theologian Jaco Dreyer describes an 'intradisciplinary diversity' within practical theology (Dreyer 2012, 34–35). He cautions about an approach that tries to overcome all the differences and wants to unify all kind of approaches; but he also warns against a pluralist position where the variety in practical theological approaches is "accepted but ignored" (Dreyer 2012, 34–35). In line with this 'intradisciplinary diversity', I do not want to deepen the differences between a more strategic form of practical theology, or a correlational approach on the one hand, and an approach in line with 'lived religion' on the other hand. I will develop my arguments below in dialogue with a 'lived religion' approach of practical theology, but I do recognize the value of other approaches and do not want to position them as totally different from what I suggest. Thus, rather than discussing particular nuances, tensions, differences and communalities between Browning's approach and an approach of practical theology which focuses on 'lived religion', I will discuss how I conceive a practical theology of families in line with a lived religion approach.

Within practical theological discussions, the study of lived religion refers to an empirical approach, which considers practical theology merely in line with the academic paradigm of practical theology, less in line with the clerical paradigm – as they are distinguished by Ed Farley (1988) and discussed by Bonnie Miller-McLemore (2007, 19–38). Studying lived religion focuses on the descriptive aspect of practical theology, whereas a more clerical paradigm discusses the 'how to' or the more pragmatic or strategic approach of practical theology, sometimes even considered as applied theology. This distinction between 'descriptive' and 'strategic' refers to Osmer's fourfold approach of practical theology, where he describes a descriptive – interpretive – normative – and strategic aspect of practical theology (2008). In more classical terms, it refers to the see – judge – act triad as it became popular in Catholic Social Teaching. These approaches received critical comments, as the reality and the diversity of practical theological research cannot be grasped in such a schematic form. Other critical questions are whether these schemes do not easily presuppose a form of 'correlation' between practices or experiences and theory, or whether they might neglect the friction between them or even reinforce a dualistic view where theory/theology and practices/experiences can be clearly distinguished, or a view where theory/theology seems to be fixed.

We need terms and schematic views in order to think, and thus I go on with using existing terminology. Although a lived religion approach of practical theology will often focus on a more descriptive character of the discipline, I take the position that studying lived religion is as such also transformative (and thus also 'strategic') and loaded with theological presumptions and explicit theological choices. Every description of a lived experience or a viewpoint is always colored. A neutral, purely objective description does not exist, as researchers make interpretative choices in what they describe and how they describe it. These choices are influenced by and also influence more formal elaborated theological (or ideological) views.

Starting from the idea that the 'lived religion' has to be studied and is itself a real theological endeavor, the question is: what does this mean concretely in relation to families?

Family life is more and more a topic within theological studies since the beginning of the twenty-first century. However, when it comes to empirical research and the study of family life as it is lived, and not only as it ought to be, most studies focus on aspects of religious initiation or religious communication. Some others integrate the reflection on their own family experience within their practical theology. Daily family life of partners, parents or children has received relatively little scholarly attention of practical theologians, in comparison to professional practices such as teaching religion, hospital chaplaincy or the study of the spirituality of children, adolescents or patients in order to conceive good (professional) practices. However, a theological study of the way in which family members experience family life and religion or spirituality related to their family life, is relevant for these family members, but also for teachers, religious leaders, pastoral ministers, and academic theologians. Studying family life and religion is however more than only a 'mean' to make sure that churches or schools would thrive. It helps religious leaders and theologians to discover the diversity of religious views between and within families. In this way, a practical theology, as the study of lived religion in families, can function within an intercultural and interreligious context, stimulating dialogue and understanding first of all, and not so much the continuation or renewal of existing church-based practices.

3 Towards a Practical Theology of Families

Choosing which aspects of lived religion in families have to be investigated and discussed, reflects a specific position. I focus here on how people experience 'religion' as life giving, but also as a hindrance to their flourishing, as oppressing even. Thereby I use the term 'religion' in reference to institutionalized religion while personal experiences of religion are often named 'spirituality' or 'religiosity'. The term 'lived religion' refers to the personal way to deal with one's own spirituality, but also with forms of institutionalized religion. Lived religion cannot be considered as the opposite of institutionalized religion. Such a position would start from a more dualistic interpretation of what is happening in Western societies like Belgium. It is all too easy to suppose that our society is characterized by secularization (decline of institutionalized religion) on the one hand and a revival of spirituality (individual level) on the other hand. At least in my own context, in Belgium, the institutionalized religion, especially Catholicism, is present in parts and fragments within many persons' lived religion, although it is clear that only very few people will go to the church on Sundays. Within Islam, protestants and other groups, the commitment to forms of 'institutionalized religion' (communities, doctrines, leaders) is often stronger as they are in a minority position in Belgium. Here, I will focus on how 'religion' is experienced, in its various forms. Two remarks have to be made, however. First, studying 'lived religion' does not entail an exclusive focus on individuals, but suggests major trends within society and church as well. Second, I will discuss aspects of lived religion that I consider as important for a 'practical theology of families', with the question how formal theology (as expressed by academic theologians) and lived religion can be most 'life-giving' or empowering for individuals and for the whole society. In this perspective, I will discuss three major aspects.

A first important experience is the tension between the official religious institution and its doctrinal views, normative practices or texts, or authoritative leaders on the one hand, and the lived religion and lived experiences that are influenced by these institutionalized aspects of religion on the other hand. Here topics such as divorce, homosexuality or cohabitation are at stake. Specific family forms or experiences will be discussed in this context.

A second way to study lived religion in families relates to specific experiences within families, which I summarize under the key terms family violence and gender issues. The role of normative theological views and practices and experiences of family members and their operant and espoused theology might be ambiguous (Cameron, et al. 2010, 54), working in a positive or rather negative way. I explicitly choose to name family violence, as this is one of the most widespread problems in the world and endangers many families but is at the same time a taboo and an underdeveloped topic in formal religious texts and theological research.

A third main element in the study of lived religion within a practical theology of families, refers to daily experiences of care by family members. Here I will discuss research on giving birth, breastfeeding, and parenting in families. I could focus on marriage and partner relations as well, but from a practical theological perspective it seems that issues related to parenting and lived religion received more attention recently than the experiences of partner relationships. Much more has been written on partner relationships as such from the perspectives of sacramental theology (marriage), ethics or pastoral care.

3.1 Dealing with Difficult Religious Views

A major question is how family members can deal with the tension between 'ideal' and 'reality'. The Louvain ethicist Roger Burggraeve developed an 'ethics of mercy' in relation to classical topics on sexual and relational ethics (2016).[1] He speaks about an 'ethics of growth', which recognizes the value of little steps towards the larger ideal as proposed by the Roman Catholic Church (sexuality and relationality embedded within a heterosexual marriage). In my own approach I focus on the resilience of families and criticize a monolithic idea of what an 'ideal family' could be. Influenced by narratives from family therapists and personal encounters, I warn in various publications of an all too idealistic view on the family.

The tensions between people's experiences and the normative teachings of the Roman Catholic Church are more and more recognized by church leaders. In 2014 and 2015 two synods were organized on family issues and the difficulties people in some countries have with some traditional views of the church were recognized, especially in relation to issues on divorce and remarriage. Pope Francis wrote on the value of 'discernment' for pastoral leaders and believers, as a way to support persons (AL 2016, 19).

This tension between what is expected from the perspective of the institutionalized religion and the way in which people experience family issues, has been studied within other denominations and religions as well. Recently, the American sociologist Samuel Perry wrote about the reasons people give for their divorce, and the moderating role of their conservative protestant beliefs and practices. He concluded that divorced persons in the USA, with a stronger (conservative protestant) religious practice (church attendance) usually tend to indicate that the other, the ex-partner, was more responsible for the divorce. In the 2018 article "Their fault, not mine", Perry explained these empirical findings partly by referring to the difficulty religious people experience when their life situation does not match with doctrines of the church. In his words: "Given the stigma against divorce in many religious communities, I argue that divorcées in such communities likely feel internal pressure to account for their divorce in ways that deflect blame" (Perry 2018, 1). This is one way to cope with the tension between church teachings and personal experiences, and a way to stay loyal to the teachings. It can be considered as a way to 'adapt the experiences' in order to minimize the gap.

This can be noticed in studies on Islam and homosexuality as well. Some persons who experience themselves as homosexual or lesbian, will choose not to engage in such relations or might even choose for a heterosexual marriage, to stay loyal to what their religious leaders or their families tell them. Within the Catholic Church in

---

[1] This was originally published in Dutch, and later reworked and adapted as: R. Burggraeve. 2016. *An Ethics of Mercy. On the Way to Meaningful Living and Loving.* Leuven / Dudley: Peeters.

Belgium, there is a small minority of divorced people who explicitly choose not to enter in a new sexual relationship to stay honest to the church teachings.

However, there are many other strategies to deal with the gap between official religious expectations and personal experiences. The British sociologist Andrew Yip studied, among others, how British non-heterosexual Christians and Muslims deal with the tension between ideal and reality. He describes how they re-interpret scriptural texts and consider them more in line with their own homosexual experiences (Yip 2005).

Similar results are found in relation to gender issues. Many adolescents in various religious do not support gender-unequal practices in their religion and do not consider this as essential for religion (Page and Yip 2017). Various other results of empirical research and daily experience show how religion is fluid and how various interpretations and practices are conceived by persons, living in complex family situations that do not necessary fit within the normative discourse of the institutionalized religion but who consider themselves as belonging to this religion. What 'belonging' means, is very diverse – from taking up leadership positions to weekly attendance at religious services to only praying occasionally to a vague sense of belonging without strong commitment. These 'reinterpretations' of institutional teachings might go together with a longing for change by a much broader group of religious people, not only those who experience specific family situations that are stigmatized by the institutional religion. In 2014 my colleague Thomas Knieps and I asked a large group of Belgians active as volunteers or professionals within the Catholic Church about their views on issues such as homosexuality, remarriage after divorce, sex before marriage and cohabitation. A majority of respondents in this survey answered that they would like the teachings to change; these were clearly not only those in these specific family situations. Whether these respondents agreed or disagreed with church teachings and practices on family issues or wanted change, was also related to their general religious views and practices. Those who believed in a more 'literal way' were less inclined to disagree or to expect change of church teachings than those who interpreted catholic teachings in a more symbolic way. The way in which religion is interpreted and experienced matters a lot and prevents generalizations when we describe people's experiences.

Practical theologians are confronted with the challenge to search for ways that support people in their flourishing. They have to juggle between a strong focus on ideals that might be stigmatizing or oppressing on the one hand, and an inclination to give up normative speech by proposing a relativistic view where everything is ok. The focus of Pope Francis on the Jesuit principle of 'discernment' can be considered as a way out of the gap between ideals and experiences, but it leaves some questions unanswered. Discernment, as is the case with speaking about grace or mercy in theological and pastoral debates, does not erase the stigmatizing effects of church teachings as such. It supports the personal experience of being cared for, being loved, and welcomed within a church community. However, church teachings might be oppressive or exclusive for some people. Most often, there is a good reason why these teachings have developed and are still defended, but if one cares about individual experiences as well, a form of transformation is needed. We need a theology that focuses on the positive strengths of people in situations that are considered as deviant from norms and that names how ideals can also have negative sites (as marriage is not always so ideal, all forms of violence can happen within marriage and might stay unnoticed, or women and children may be oppressed in some situations). Resilience, flourishing and searching for new narratives are key concepts in such a theology. It is important to avoid positions of 'cheap grace' (someone commits a sin, but forgiveness or grace is always there as a way out). Reading the bible, listening to stories of people from long ago and from today, and reinterpreting them time and again, in search of what they tell us for a better future, is important here. In all forms of religious education and pastoral care, it is important to deal with narratives and to show the fluidity and flexibility of people's dealing with religion, rather than only present aspects of normative theology or institutionalized religion. In terms of church practice, it is important to pay attention to the diversity within experiences of family lives and to notice that people who are living in families that do not fully match the religious norms, also practice their religious faith in various ways and are often partly, and critically, loyal to religious institutions. This could be reflected in catechetical practices and materials, where various types of families are presented and addressed, not only the traditional heterosexual married couple with children.

3.2 Wrestling with Difficult Aspects of Reality: Family Violence

So far, I discussed people's wrestling with difficult aspects of institutionalized religions (gender issues, views on homosexuality, …). I explained how a form of transformation is important, but I also warned against 'relativism': not everything is good. This is especially important when we consider aspects of domestic violence. Although this reality is gaining more and more attention within society, there is only limited attention for domestic violence within official Catholic teachings. Some (practical) theologians have taken up the topic of domestic abuse. One example is James Poling, who has to be acknowledged for putting domestic violence on the theological agenda. He challenged classical theological views and urges the reader to rethink them in light of the violence and the abuse of power that are happening. He paid explicit attention to male offenders in *Understanding Male Violence: Pastoral Care Issues* (2003). Michael O'Sullivan, the Irish Jesuit expert in spirituality studies, published *How Roman Catholic Theology Can Transform Male Violence Against Women: Explaining the Role of Religion in Cultural Assumptions about Gender'* in 2010.

Most practical theological works on domestic violence challenge practices (what is the role of the church/pastoral minister?) or theologies. They explain how theologies on sacrifice, family, gender, male/female complementarity, forgiveness, or atonement can be used as legitimations of domestic violence and suggest critical reflections and transformation of these theologies and the way they are preached or used in catechetical settings (Ganzevoort 2009). An adequate theology can have a public, prophetic function. Especially in contexts where gender equality needs more acceptance in society, churches and theology could have a very important role, under the condition that they critically and continuously rethink their own theology in light of its possible dangerous consequences.

Some recent practical theological books give an explicit voice to survivors of violence. Susan Shooter (2016), for example, was using grounded theory as an empirical method and she started from the experiences of women themselves. Shooter speaks about all forms of abuse, and how it influences the spiritual lives of survivors. Abuse most often has devastating consequences and, as trust becomes difficult, might also lead to questioning the relation someone has with God. Yet survivors interviewed by Shooter also explain how their spirituality helps them, how they find strength in their faith and how they reconsider God's caring presence now, after the abuse. The Canadian Catholic practical theologian Jean-Guy Nadeau (Nadeau, Rochon, Golding, 2012) explains how the religious education received by many victims of sexual abuse raises lots of doubts. Survivors wrestle with many difficult questions about evil and God's goodness and support. Most of the studies where survivors of violence have a voice indicate that it is often difficult to speak about 'religion' and much more preferred to speak about 'spirituality' because the automatic association of the term 'religion' with institutionalized religion is not always helpful when one becomes a victim of abuse. Some survivors do not feel welcome in the church or feel very lonely in their experiences – they expected more from the church or might even be misused by persons with a strong link to the church. Still, they might find support in their personal spirituality.

Noteworthy in this (limited) overview of recent studies is the virtual absence of male victims and female offenders. More attention should also go to them, as the taboo here is even much larger. It would be very interesting to study how 'bystanders' experience domestic violence and religion. Which religious arguments do they use to care for victims, to defend offenders, to justify their own passive attitude or to be involved in domestic violence policy issues? More attention could also go to survivors of family violence, especially (adult) children, male and female, who experienced all forms of violence (sexual, psychological, physical, …) by their parents or siblings, or who used violence against their parents. Most important for a practical theologian, reflecting on care issues, on religious education and on narratives is that the experience of domestic violence is named and made visible in all kinds of writings, theologies, catechetical settings. A good practice I experience in the university parish in Leuven (Belgium) is lighting a candle for all victims of violence before the liturgy really starts. If from time to time the presider reminds the people present in the liturgy that these are victims of violence during war, structural violence as in racism or poverty, but also domestic violence, people might feel that leaders in the church at least acknowledge this reality. If domestic violence is not made a taboo but explicitly mentioned, people might feel more inclined to speak up about their own experiences, doubts, etc. Only then can adequate care be given or searched for.

3.3 Wrestling with Family Experiences: Spirituality, Giving Birth and Parenting

Studying lived religion is important for discussing family life and religion. In 2017, a new series of books was established: *Palgrave Studies in Lived Religion and Societal Challenges*. The first titles dealt with tolerance and intolerance, and violence and trauma after mass shootings. Newer titles will deal with homosexuality and Islam, bisexuality, and trauma; issues related to the two previous sections of this chapter. In this third part of this chapter, I will expand the focus and indicate how thinking about 'lived religion' and 'family life' can focus our attention on other aspects, on experiences of giving birth and parenting, especially on practices of care in family contexts.

Within the Roman Catholic Church, family metaphors get a lot of attention. The church is presented as a woman, the bride of Christ, and as a mother; frequent references are made to Mary, as mother of the Church, mother of Jesus. More infrequently, references are made to Joseph, the father of Jesus. The church itself is sometimes presented as a family (Gomez 2018).

Mostly, these theological metaphors are based on essentialized or idealistic views of the family, motherhood, or fatherhood. Studying experiences of family life from the perspective of lived religion might nuance these all too idealistic views. When results of these 'lived religion' approaches are used more in church contexts, people might be able to identify with what is being said, as they will be able to recognize their own struggles. I will show below how parenting can be experienced as a spiritual practice and how this can and should be considered as a very ambiguous and wrestling experience.

Not only explicit religious practices in families can be considered as aspects of lived religion in families. Evidently, when time is made for common prayer, attending liturgical services or speaking about theological questions among partners or parents and children, the religiosity in the family is clearly noticed. Bonnie Miller-McLemore (2006) and others argued persuasively however that the daily practices of care in family life can be considered as 'spirituality' (2006). They are not only an expression of someone's Christian, or more vague spirituality, but they can be called 'spiritual practices' as such. For Christians, preparing food for a partner, parent or children can be read in line of Mt 25:31–46, and be considered as a practice where Christ is present.

This may sound rather idealistic and strongly focused on ethical responsibilities. Parents or partners have to care. But when is it good enough? Many suffer from the idea, coming from others or from themselves, that they have to be perfect. And this might be suffocating, leading to 'burn out', maybe even in a family context. Many family members however also experience God's grace and love. They experience how they are accepted, loved, and cared for by God, even if they are not perfect themselves. And most of all: they trust that God will also care for the other. It does not only depend on them. Particularly pregnant mothers and expecting fathers, who feel powerless in waiting for the birth of the child, speak about how they may light a candle and ask God or 'Someone' or 'the higher power' to care for the unborn child as they are unable to prevent all potential risks for such a vulnerable child. That is learned from the empirical research of Judith Cockx, who interviewed twelve Belgian heterosexual couples about the pregnancy and the birth of their child in relation to aspects of a broad spirituality (Cockx, Dillen, and Spitz 2017). The concept of 'grace' is seldom used by these parents, living in a secularized culture. They speak however about thankfulness, about the gift of the child and the gift to have the opportunity to become a parent. They also wrestle with this responsibility and the high expectations, and the balance between the search for having some control and the necessity to 'let it go' – to trust and to abandon the quest for control. They have to live with vulnerability, and to experience that this is far from romantic. Experiences of grace in daily family life can be related to what is beautiful, what is considered as a present – from God or from a partner or a child – but it can also be experienced in the midst of trouble, difficulties, mourning.

Biblical stories, which are full of narratives about family situations, notably in the First Testament, show how people have experienced God's grace and presence even in the midst of chaotic or sad circumstances, as the story of Abraham and Sarah who receive a son shows. These biblical stories and other texts (such as psalms) might support people in their daily family life. They deserve critical reflection of course as well; the bible should not be read as a legitimation of sexual violence, corporal punishment, or oppression of women, as is – sadly enough – sometimes happening.

Some experiences in families cannot be considered only as 'practices of spirituality' or even 'lived religion', but they also give rise to theological reflections. This is what Elisabeth Gandolfo (2013) shows in relation to breastfeeding, which is called a 'contemplative practice' but is also a source for theological reflection. Cristina Traina (2011) wrote in a similar way, when she considered the practice of breastfeeding as a challenge for ethical thinking and reflections on self-love and neighbor-love.

4 Conclusion

This chapter gives an overview of what is discussed in the field of practical theology and families, with references to literature in various contexts. I am fully aware of the fact that I did not do justice to the work of many other authors, who are not named here but have contributed a lot. The choices in this chapter were partly made based on my own biographical and academic context, partly on the three main areas I wanted to cover with this chapter. Three main aspects have to be seen by religious leaders and scholars in relation to family and lived religion. This is, first of all, the fact that many people wrestle with institutionalized forms of religion, doctrinal and ethical views of family life and sexuality, but nevertheless find ways to cope with these 'difficult views' and call themselves religious or spiritual. Secondly, violence happens in families and studying lived religion and families asks for more attention for this reality. Thirdly, there are also many beautiful and ambiguous experiences that deserve attention from the perspective of lived religion and practical theology. Shortly, people wrestle with religions and institutions, they wrestle with difficult aspects of life (such as violence) and they wrestle with family life itself, as experiences in families are mostly ambiguous. This can be demonstrated with the example of pregnancy and childbirth.

In conclusion, studying family life from the perspective of practical theology as the study of lived religion asks for a study of the 'wrestling' of people on a daily basis, and for taking this 'wrestling' seriously as a fruitful ground for theologizing.

Bibliography

Browning, Don. 1991. *A Fundamental Practical Theology*. Minneapolis: Fortress Press.
Browning, Don, Bonnie Miller-McLemore, Pamela Couture, K. Brynolf Lyon, and Robert M. Franklin. 2000. *From Culture Wars to Common Ground: Religion and the American Family Debate*. Louisville: Westminster John Knox.
Burggraeve, Roger. 2016. *An Ethics of Mercy: On the Way to Meaningful Living and Loving*. Leuven / Dudley: Peeters.
Cameron, Helen, Deborah Bhatti, Catherine Duce, James Sweeney, and Clare Watkins. 2010. *Talking about God in Practice: Theological Action Research and Practical Theology*. London: SCM Press.
Cockx, Judith, Annemie Dillen, and Bernard Spitz. 2017. *Een kind beleven: over kinderwens, zwangerschap, geboorte en pril ouderschap*. Leuven / Den Haag: Acco.
Couture, Pamela. 1991. *Blessed Are the Poor? Women's Poverty, Family Policy and Practical Theology*. Nashville: Abingdon Press.
Dillen, Annemie. 2009. *Het gezin: à Dieu? Een contextuele benadering van gezinnen in ethisch, pedagogisch en pastoraaltheologisch perspectief*. Brussel: Koninklijke Vlaamse Academie voor Wetenschappen en Kunsten.
Dillen, Annemie, Thomas Knieps-Port le Roi, and Karolina Krysinska. 2015. "A Growing Gap? Catholic Pastoral Workers and Volunteers' Perceptions of Family Life and Church Teaching in Flanders." In *The Contemporary Family: Local and European Perspectives*. Vol. 2, Krakow: The Pontifical University of John Paul II in Krakow Press, 159–177.
Dreyer, Jaco. 2012. "Practical Theology and Intradisciplinary Diversity: A Response to Miller-McLemore's 'Five Misunderstandings about Practical Theology'." *International Journal of Practical Theology*. 16:34–54.
Elshof, Toke. 2009. *Van huis uit katholiek: Een praktisch theologisch, semiotisch onderzoek naar de ontwikkeling van religiositeit in drie generaties van rooms-katholieke families*. Delft: Eburon Academic Publishers.
Farley, Ed. 1988. *The Fragility of Knowledge: Theological Education in the Church and University*. Philadelphia: Fortress Press.

Gandolfo, Elisabeth. 2013. "Mary Kept These Things, Pondering Them in her Heart: Breastfeeding as Contemplative Practice and Source for Theology." *Spiritus: A Journal of Christian Spirituality* 13:163–186.

Ganzevoort, Ruard. 2009. "Domestic Violence Against Children: Pastoral-Theological Reflections." In *When 'Love' Strikes: Social Sciences, Ethics and Theology on Family Violence,* edited by Annemie Dillen, Leuven: Peeters, 2009, 219–232.

Gomez, Cristina. 2018. *The Church as Women and Mother.* New York: Paulist Press.

Holtman, Catherine, and Nancy Nason-Clark. 2018. *Religion, Gender, and Family Violence: When Prayers Are Not Enough.* Leiden: Brill.

Lacroix, Xavier. 2001. *L'amour du semblable, questions sur l'homosexualité.* Paris: Cerf.

Marschütz, Gerhard. 2000. *Familie Humanökologisch: Theologisch-Ethische Perspektiven,* Münster: LIT.

Miller-McLemore, Bonnie. 1994. *Also a Mother: Work and Family as Theological Dilemma.* Nashville: Abingdon Press.

Miller-McLemore, Bonnie. 2007. "The 'Clerical Paradigm': A Fallacy of Misplaced Concreteness?" *International Journal of Practical Theology* 11:19–38.

Nadeau, Jean-Guy, Claude Rochon, and Carol Golding. 2012. *Autrement que victims: Dieu, enfer et résistance chez les victimes d'abus sexuels.* Montreal: Novalis Canada.

Osmer, Richard. 2008. *Practical Theology: An Introduction.* Grand Rapids: Eerdmans.

O'Sullivan, Michael Francis. 2010. *How Roman Catholic Theology Can Transform Male Violence Against Women: Explaining the Role of Religion in Shaping Cultural Assumptions about Gender.* Lewiston / New York: Edwin Mellen Press.

Page, Sarah-Jane, and Andrew K. T. Yip. 2017. "Gender Equality and Religion: A Multi-Faith Exploration of Young Adults' Narratives." *European Journal of Women's Studies* 24:249–265.

Perry, Samuel. 2018. "Their Fault, Not Mine: Religious Commitment, Theological Conservatism, and Americans' Retrospective Reasons for Divorce." *Religions* 9:1–18.

Poling, James. 2003. *Understanding Male Violence: Pastoral Care Issues.* St. Louis, Missouri: Chalice Press.

Shooter, Sharon. 2016. *How Survivors of Abuse Relate to God: The Authentic Spirituality of the Annihilated Soul.* London: Routledge.

Tracy, David. 1975. *Blessed Rage for Order.* Minneapolis: Seabury Press.

Traina, Christina L.H. 2011. *Erotic Attunement: Parenthood and the Ethics of Sensuality between Unequals.* Chicago: University of Chicago Press.

Yip, Andrew K.T. 2005. "Queering Religious Texts: An Exploration of British Non-Heterosexual Christians' and Muslims' Strategy of Constructing Sexuality-Affirming Hermeneutics," *Sociology* 39:47–65.

Roman Catholic Church Documents

AL Amoris Laetitia. Apostolic Exhortation of Pope Francis, 19.03.2016. https://w2.vatican.va/content/dam/francesco/pdf/apost_exhortations/documents/papa-francesco_esortazione-ap_20160319_amoris-laetitia_en.pdf (01.12.2021).

Indukuri John Mohan Razu
Human Rights and Religion

1 Introduction

India is known for its religious plurality and cultural multiplicity and thus has come to characterize unity in diversity and harmonious co-habitation. However, in recent times, Hindu fundamentalism aided by the ruling dispensation, the Bhartya Janata Party (BJP), a far-right conservative nationalist party and its ideological nerve centre Rashtriya Swayamsevak Sangh (RSS) premised on the credo of 'Hindu majoritarianism', is set to realize its vision of making India a 'Hindu nation'. In order to realize its vision, BJP-RSS is engaged in polarizing and fuelling hatred against those who belong to other religions and cultures. Consequently, human rights and human dignity of minorities, the subaltern communities particularly the Dalits, the (Untouchables) have increasingly been violated and trampled upon. Plurality and inclusivity are undermined, posing serious threat and contestation as the country keeps witnessing a spate of incidences leading to intolerance and indignation. Moreover, spewing venom, fuelling religious and communal hatred against those who have different belief systems, political ideologies, value orientations, traditions, and cultures, has become the order of the day.

Against this backdrop, this paper brings to the foreground the ways with which the fundamental tenets of religion vis-à-vis Hinduism are abused and subverted. And in the process, the paper examines and analyses the forms of intolerance perpetrated by the ruling party BJP, its cultural wing RSS and far-right Hindu outfits who are engaged in the program that violates the fundamental and constitutional rights of the citizens of India enshrined in the Constitution and UNDHR Charter. More importantly, this paper invokes, argues and essentializes one of the core theological and ethical principles of human dignity within broader notions of human rights.

2 Positing Plural and Diverse India

India is a constitutional democracy. For a Republic to function, the Constitution plays the most crucial part. India as a constitutional democracy is expected to adhere to the principles enshrined in the Constitution prescribed to all its citizens. Nonetheless, a question that arises at this juncture is: Do all the citizens of the Indian Republic enjoy the fundamental principles enshrined in the Constitution? India's Constitution starts with "We the citizens of the Indian Republic" which is unique and distinct. However, the enshrined principles of the Constitution in spirit and practice are losing their essence and relevance and are under intense contestation. The word 'citizens' that appears in the preamble of the Constitution is under serious threat to those who belong to minorities, Dalits and other vulnerable communities. For the government to run and to govern, basic requisites – principles, mechanisms, and processes – are meticulously elucidated in the Constitution. Therefore, the Constitution is the light house or sacred book that elucidates each and every aspect of governance in a comprehensive manner.

India's democracy is still alive by virtue of having its Constitution securing to all the citizens of the country – the fundamental and constitutional rights. The architect of India's constitution, Bhimrao Ramji Ambedkar warned that however good the constitution may be, it is sure to turn out bad if those who are called to make it work are a bad lot. For Ambedkar, those in power and authority are expected to put the constitution into practice through their governance, and in the process the people are transformed and thus become citizens. Citizenship and democracy go hand in hand and complement each other. But, in recent times the citizenship of those belonging to other communities and identities are being increasing questioned and threatened. The current impasse sends signals that amplify whether the Indian republic is clouded with misplaced religious, political, and cultural aberrations, fear, and insecurity.

3 Shifting Terrains – Rising Populism and Hindu Fundamentalism

The majority of Indians are Hindus, but live side by side with others respecting each other's differences. Since 2014, we have been witnessing a radical shift taking place due to the fact that the ruling dispensation is engaged in divisive politics pitched on binaries: majority versus minority, us versus them. It has spread its tentacles against select communities spewing venom and hatred throughout Indian society. The emergence and rapid rise of the political ideology, Hindutva, is perhaps the most striking feature of contemporary Indian politics. An understanding of the origin of the discourse on Hindutva is imperative in understanding the phenomenon as it is presented today. The discourse on Hindutva has to be located in the complex set of processes in motion with the onset of colonial rule in India.

The ideology of Hindutva was founded and constructed on 'Hindu nationalism'. The idea of a homogenous 'Hindu', 'nation', and 'culture', transcending caste, class and sectarian differences is a product of the ideology of Hindutva. By homogenizing the Hindutva ideology, it hegemonizes the interests of certain castes and classes. The ideology of Hindu nationalism is becoming an ideological tool that absorbs, assimilates, articulates as well as rewrites, reinterprets and reconstructs the nation's history in furthering its agenda of 'one nation', 'one culture', 'one language', and 'one religion'. It has even gone to the extent of opening its fold to Dalits and Tribals to establish a majoritarian democracy to further their own interests in creating Hindu Rashtra vis-à-vis pan-Indian raj. The construction of a nation based on the ideology of Hindutva in its definition, consolidation, and articulation underlines "Hindu-ness".

Over the past few years, a series of lynchings, inflammatory speeches, desecration of mosques and churches and a distribution of highly provocative literature against minorities, Dalits and Tribals, reconversion drives, the bid to saffronise educational materials, an attempt to rewrite Indian history, and a tampering with the Constitution clearly portrays a well-planned political project of the Hindutva forces. It is deeply rooted in BJP-RSS ideology and political praxis. For instance, Savarkar, an ideologue of this tenet articulates, "Hindutva entails the religious, cultural, linguistic, social and political aspects of the life of Hindus" (Baird 1981, 466). It believes in establishing "one nation, one people, one religion, one language, one culture and one executive". (Baird 1981, 466) This 'Hindu-ness' seeks to establish the political, cultural, and religious supremacy of Hinduism and the Hindu nation (Ganguly 1999). At the same time those who are outside the ambit of Hindutva, Christians and Muslims are labelled and identified as 'aliens', 'infiltrators', 'aggressors', and 'enemies'.

Golwalkar, one of the architects and ideologues, reiterates that "[t]o keep up the purity of [the] Nation and its culture, Germany shocked the world by her purging the country of the Semitic races. [...] Germany has also shown how well-nigh impossible it is for races and cultures having differences going to the root, to be assimilated into one united whole, a good lesson for us in Hindustan to learn and profit by" (quoted by D'Souza 1999, 185). For Golwalkar, Hitler's Germany and an anti-Semitic stance became tools for pushing the ideology of Hindutva. He was against pluralism and secularism enshrined in the Indian Constitution. Instead, he spoke for nationalism[1] and the preservation of the pure Aryan culture engrained in Hinduism. The same ideology and political project are being transplanted by the BJP-RSS: combined using religion and politics for the wrong reasons. For example, Golwalkar emphasized that,

> [t]he non-Hindu people in Hindustan must either adopt the Hindu culture and language, must learn to respect and revere Hindu religion, must entertain no idea but the glorification of the

---

1 Conceptions and notions of nationalism by Hindutva forces contravene the majority consensus of nationalism. "True, nationalism as the embodiment of collective aspiration can move people and inspire them to engage in meaningful social reconstruction. [...] But the real essence of nationalism, it has to be realized, is the tangible experience of togetherness, the ability to fight internal inequalities and divisions so that the unity of people can be felt in every sphere of life. In other words, true nationalism means, as Gandhi sought to argue, real Swaraj: creating a society that is egalitarian and free from inequality, exploitation, and violence. Nationalism is not, as Tagore repeatedly warned us, chauvinism: a narcissistic assertion against the 'external' enemy. Nationalism is not wild passion. Instead, it is a sincere, honest, committed practice for constructing a just society. The irony is that the crude logic of election politics has killed this humanistic spirit of nationalism. Nationalism has become particularly after Pokhran 11 and Kargil, a mighty weapon the ruling party need to assert the power of the narcissistic nation" (Pathak 1999, 10).

Hindu nation [...] but also cultivate the positive of love and devotion [...] they must cease to be foreigners or may stay in the country, wholly subordinated to the Hindu nation, claiming nothing, deserving no privileges, far less any preferential treatment, not even citizen's rights. (Quoted by D'Souza 1999, 186)

4 Changing Templates of India – Hindu Nationalism

The Indian Constitution acquires secular character and credentials not only in letter, but also from the collective reality of many provisions that appear in the constitution that guarantee citizens and community in letter and spirit. Indian society is secular meaning that religions tend to co-exist side by side with other ideologies, belief systems, cultures, and traditions. These principles are increasingly in contestation in recent times. For instance, on December 24, 2017, in a public address, Minister of State for Employment and Skills Development, Ananthkumar Hegde said, "Secular people do not have an identity of their parental blood" and we, the BJP, he added "are here to change the constitution" (this appeared in all the dailies the following day). By this statement the fundamental guarantees such as right to freedom, right to religion, right to equality and right to dignity of those who belong to the other are to be negated and under contestation.

What is happening in India is the absorption of religion into the ideology of Hindutva. The synthesis of religion and politics is becoming deeply entrenched into the plural kaleidoscopic milieu. When the State attempts to prioritize and hegemonize Hindus of different shades of Hinduism in a religiously plural society like India, minorities are bound to suffer. Since communal political parties and organizations are prioritizing Hinduism over other religions, the secular fabric of Indian society is now cracking up. This is a most disturbing trend, which gravely affects the fine balance, which India as a country has maintained thus far. A secular democracy is bound to have the presence and practice of many religions and they can co-exist without any conflict if the nation-state maintains its plural character by equally respecting, protecting and accommodating all religions. The Indian State under RSS-BJP is pushing its project of majoritarian politics as its point of governance.

The present scenario has created insecurity amongst the minorities who feel threatened by state-sponsored religious fundamentalism and cultural nationalism. What is happening now is the polarization of communities on the basis of the religious persuasion to which they adhere. The communal parties, in order to secure Hindu votes, are polarizing society and in the process creating a Hindu vote bank. The Hindutva phenomena should not be reduced to political battle between "majority" and "minority" or be assumed that the problem has been exaggerated and therefore is not an immediate threat. What is at stake is India's constitutional democracy – a project in which a wide range of social, cultural groups and identities, have perennially interacted and been juxtaposed. Added to this, the capacity of the Indian nation to retain its character vis-à-vis a plural entity, is in jeopardy.

It is also equally important to observe that the secular character and composite nature of the Indian Constitution, which is democratic in its entirety, is in grave danger. The reason being: the very words that are being used by the proponents of Hindutva such as nation, culture, language, and religion imply uniformity and division. But in reality, it is diversity and plurality that brings richness and beauty to the world and to the human family. It is not unity in uniformity but unity in diversity. As time and space in which Indian people live becomes increasingly constricted and conformed in the current political and cultural space, it is apparent that the domains of inter-relatedness, cultural diversity, plurality, and inter-dependence between one another become obsolete and redundant. BJP-RSS's notions of the homogenization and unification of Hindu culture are being promoted and preserved, and in the process their vision of a Hindu Nation will be realized. BJP-RSS is using religion and culture effectively in order to realize its vision.

5 De-Coding the Terrains – the Complex Web of Lynching

The spate of lynchings across India since 2014 is on the rise. The social conditions presently prevailing, characterized by intolerance and hatred, is horrifying. Those involved in such dastardly acts keep committing them without any fear and restraint, because the current social and political climate favours them. Groups involved in lynching are well-connected, highly organized, and politically influential. Those who defy their political, socio-cultural, and moral views have to face their wrath. Mob lynching stems from its core ideological underpinning that the other ought to be eliminated by all means. Mob killings have become the new normal in India. The mob quickly gathers, executes their lynching, and then disappears. The ruling dispensation keeps spreading the idea that Hinduism is under attack and for this the minorities are responsible for spreading hatred. This has reposed 'majority Hindus' to create the 'other' and treat them as outsiders of the Hindu society.

97 percent of the incidents occurred after BJP came to power in 2014. 84 percent of those killed in the related mob lynching incidents were Muslims. The rest, 16 percent, accused of cow slaughter are Dalits and marginal sections (Parambil 2018, 29). The word "lynching" has occupied centre stage in all areas of Indian society. This leads us to ask: what then is lynching? It is best described as "a pre-mediated extra judicial killing by a group. It is most often used to characterize informal public executions by a mob in order to punish an alleged transgressor, or to intimidate a group. It is an extreme form of informal group social control and often conducted with the display of a public spectacle for – maximum intimidation" (quoted by Prakash 2018, 26). Mob lynching is horrifying and creates frenzy and horror for the vic-

tims surrounded by a mob who systematically take on the victims who belong to the other.

Grotesque brutality once again hit the national headlines when cow vigilantes lynched a 31-year-old Muslim man from Haryana's Mewat district in Raajasthan's Alwar on Friday the 20th of July 2018. Rakbar Khan was attacked allegedly by a group of 8–10 cow vigilantes. He succumbed to his injuries in hospital after a few hours. In his dying statement, Rakbar told police that he and his friend Aslam were walking back with two cows they had bought when they came under attack in Alwar's Ramgarh area by the mob which accused them of being smugglers taking the cattle for slaughter. It is an irony that for a distance of 5 to 6 kilometres to the nearby hospital which usually takes less than 30 minutes, the Rajasthan police had taken more than 3 hours. He could have been saved if they had brought him a little earlier. Two ministers of the BJP Government honoured those accused of lynching; one stood vigil over the body of a lynching accused draped in the national flag, and the other garlanded several people accused of lynching. Both were honoured due to the fact that they went all out in defence of the cows (Arun 2018, 16).

Junior Union Home minister Arjun Ram Meghwal justified lynching as being due to the rising popularity of Prime Minster Narendra Modi. Cow Politics continues to polarize Indian society with clear messages that until there's a total ban on cow slaughter, lynchings will continue. Lynching of Muslims, Dalits and vulnerable identities and communities is certainly a large plan of the ruling dispensation and should not be viewed through the prism of the letter of the law. Instead, these chauvinistic nationalists should be dealt with severely for blatantly defying and violating the basic rights of the citizens. As Satwana Bhattacharya (2017) rightly asks: "Who's this threatening to usurp my identity? Tainting and twisting my faith and beliefs? Destroying the values I hold dear? Who's this who kills mercilessly? […] How did they become the law unto themselves and the order of the day and arbiters of destiny and life and meaning, deciding what shall be eaten, how one has to dress, what health care to opt for."[2]

When mob lynching grows and becomes toxic, India's democratic and secular fabric is undermined. In such context-specificities, the citizens are to invoke moral revulsion and seek justice under the provisions of basic and fundamental human rights. Nonetheless, "We see a macabre festival of violence around us, a relapse into the baser human capacities, whether it is in Kashmir or Kerala or Jharkhand … where the usual constitutional niceties do not apply and everything goes—is now beginning to be applicable everywhere" (Bhatacharya 2017). In the pretext of protecting the cows, attacking Christians, Muslims and Dalits is rapidly spreading and becoming toxic.

---

2 For an in-depth analysis read the Bhatacharya column (2017). Bhatacharya is political editor of the Indian Express.

6 Essentialising Human Rights

In recent times, India's democracy and the rule of constitutional law is increasingly contested by the self-styled cow protectors conveying a clear message that cows have more value and are more precious than minorities such as Muslims, Dalits, Tribals, and Christians. According to the data released by IndiaSpend, 28 people were killed and 123 were injured in the attacks unleashed by the 'cow vigilantes'. What is more disturbing is that out of the 28 deaths, 24 were Muslims, which is a whopping 86 percent of the total fatalities. 97 percent of these attacks were reported after BJP took over the government at the Centre in 2014. On a similar vein, about half of the cow-related violence – 32 out of 63 cases were reported from states governed by BJP, eight run by Congress and the rest by other political parties (The Hindu 2018). India has drastically changed and now symbolizes binaries based on religion, ideology, and culture. Santawana Bhattacharya (2017) aptly characterizes that: "Is the Indian cow just an empty symbol then, an instrumental token for a society that is angry and brutalized? A society that does not know how to find legitimate mechanism to voice its angst—all the angst produced by the modern living and its alienating effect [...] has to resort to violence merely to find a sense of power and meaning?" Basic rights of humans have been violated and throttled.

The gap between the rhetoric and practice in letter and spirit that we find in the Universal Declaration of Human Rights (UDHR)[3] evokes concern and dismay to the citizens as we look around the happenings in the world that we live in. In all the spheres of our existence, particularly political and religious spheres, we cannot undermine or ignore the alacrity and gravity of human rights violations that manifest daily in the form of torture, genocide, social and economic asymmetries, custodial deaths, ethnic cleansing, political prisoners, suppression of democratic rights and expressions and a host of others. Although all the countries of the world are signatories of UDHR, the gap between words and action creates a sense of optimism and a feeling of pessimism. However, optimism and hope continue to ignite the simmering light/spirit. Discourses and actions should continue on human rights in the areas of historical, philosophical, legal, political, theological or ethical domains.

For more than sixty years discourses at different levels on the legitimate claims for universal human rights have been justified and sustained (Chandran 1997, 138).[4]

---

3 Some opine that the Declaration as a resolution of the General Assembly has no legal binding effect, while others view that the Declaration is a living document that has acquired credible authority. In general, there is an expression of hope, cf. Bajwa (1995, 136) and Dutta (1998, 275). For example, cf. Panikar (1959) and Adas (1989). Hence, we see a number of works that describe the colonial and imperial motif woven into the structures of popular culture, fiction and the rhetoric of history, philosophy and geography.

4 The division of Human Rights into the three generations, namely the first world, second world, and the third world was initially proposed in 1979 by the Czech jurist Karel Vasak at the International Institute of Human Rights in Strasbourg. His divisions follow the three great watchwords of the French

At the same time, it should be noted that the thrusts and foci of these discourses kept changing at each historical epoch. As the context changes, the conceptual, definitional, and perspectival understandings should change. In the twenty-first century, new forms of atrocities and rights violations are taking place. Given the ambiguities and ambivalences of rights discourse, rights' discourse needs to be nuanced so that the responses that are offered will be apt and relevant. We live in a world in which the perpetrators of injustice inflict all sorts of violations and yet justify their actions. Particularly, the State uses its machinery to silence those who use the provisions extended by the human rights' charter. However, it is important to invoke human rights at this juncture because,

> Analytically, a right is considered a 'remedial' category, a deterrent against the possibility, or a redressal of the fact, of some wrong being inflicted upon its bearer. As such, rights cannot but be relational since they imply, at the very least, a link between the bearer of rights and the state. Moreover, since rights never take shape in a social vacuum – other, competing rights are always already present in society – they are contextual in a readily visible fashion. Thus, when considered as theoretical categories, rights are not the essence-like, intrinsic attributes that they are often made out to be, but products of their milieu. In a different, less obvious sense, rights can be shown to be context-dependent even when considered as historically-specific phenomena. Contrary to the universalistic claims [...] all rights involve explicit (and more often implicit) exclusions. In other words, every historically-specific instance of a right carries within itself its own apparatus of inclusion/exclusion. These devices defining those endowed with or denied rights are the products of the particular conjunction of historical forces obtaining at the time, and it is in this sense that every right is inevitably contextual. (Deshpande 1998)

Any discussion on the challenges to human rights in the twenty-first century will be meaningful only when we look at the historical-contextual processes in which each society's search for equality and human dignity are taken in realistic ways. The forces of equality, freedom and dignity countered by the ideological propaganda that there is no alternative (TINA) is a clever strategy to push the matter into subjugation and could perhaps be considered to be the greatest challenge of the twenty-first century to the theory and practice of human rights. In a world of populism and nationalism the conceptual understanding of basic and fundamental rights, democracy, and freedom seems to be in danger. In a scenario where rights are violated, we need to have clear understanding of the following:

Revolution: Liberty, Equality, and Fraternity (Ife 2001, 2006; Shimray 1994, 28; Balasuriva 2000, 75). The Universal Declaration of Human Rights included all the three generations of rights (UNESCO 1953; UN 1998). It was enshrined at the global level by the 1948 Universal Declaration of Human Rights, Articles 3–21 of the Universal Declaration and the International Covenant on Civil and Political Rights. It derives primarily from the seventeenth- and eighteenth-century political theories associated with the English, American, and French revolutions. Major political theory consisted of life, liberty, and pursuit of happiness, which favoured limiting the government by placing restrictions on state action.

> When democracy becomes devoted to the maintenance of the existing structures of power, the first causality is, naturally, freedom: for without freedom to imagine, to dare to conceive alternatives– including also alternative ways of answering human need [...]. To set 'freedom to choose' at the heart of our culture, and to deny the possibility of choosing any other way of being in the world is a denial of the 'pluralism' and 'diversity' to which the West asserts its devotion these are evidently mere ornaments decorations on the surface of an increasingly showy, image-conscious, appearance-manipulating culture. (Seabrook 1996)

Politics over lynching has reached alarming heights in India with slogans such as: "Leave India, if you don't like cows", "respect cows, love Hinduism", "respect cows or leave Hinduism" and "lynching will continue till cow Slaughter and beef eating stops". Human life has value and in no way has lesser value than a cow. Attacks are based on an ideology of polarization leading to hatred and antagonism. In such a climate, it is important for Christians to invoke faith which is rooted in the authority of scripture. There is no direct reference to or usage of Human Rights in the Bible. But the Christian Scripture brings out clearly human wrongs and substantiates explicitly why they are wrong.

7 Human Dignity. An Essential Component of Human Rights

The materials we find in the Bible need to be complimented by non-scriptural materials to address the contemporary issues concerning human rights. Humans represent the image of God and so it is implied that co-humans are treated with respect and dignity. Therefore, treating each other as co-humans is the core principle of God's creation. The essence of human rights acquires greater value and fuller meaning precisely due to this. For instance:

> The atonement has been powerful grounding of human dignity and consequently of human rights for several reasons. It is universal, containing a dignity which applies to all people. Human rights are claims any individual can place upon the community solely on the grounds of being human. The dignity of those for whom the Son of God died rests not on individual characteristics, which distinguish one person from another. No characteristic, which commends one person as being greater than another, provides status before God or a claim upon God's mercy. Those crushed by human power are able to know that neither colour nor sex. (Mott 1985, 6)

Human dignity acquires a fuller status in and through incarnation, crucifixion, and resurrection. As human beings we have failed and also fallen short of representing God's image. We are clothed with human dignity and a set of human rights. It is embedded in us as God's gift from whom the rights flow. The God of righteousness is the provider of rights and expects us to respect the rights of humans because we are bestowed with human rights that are inalienable and inviolable. In this sense, everyone before the sight of God is equally endowed with human dignity and human worth.

Differences, exclusions, and segregations based on caste, colour, gender, and ethnicity are considered unbiblical and un-Christian. Further,

> [d]rawing upon dignity through the creation has the advantage of being more widely accepted and understood beyond the Christian circle. Those who do not respond to Jesus as the dying and propitiatory Son of God may accept the conception of a creating God. This basis of human worth thus provides a broader value basis for human rights. The advantage of drawing upon the atonement is that it brings human dignity and human rights into the very heart of Christian faith and experience, dispelling the dichotomy of piety and social commitment. (Mott 1985, 7)

As human deprivations and violations of human rights are on the rise we need to commit towards the restoration of life. It begins with basic education, awareness, and commitment eventually leading to action. How are we to set right human wrongs, so that human dignity and human worth may be retrieved? Human rights undoubtedly are one of the vehicles or instruments that could address the human wrongs effectively and thereby the deprivations of millions of people would be set right. We live in miserable times and our identities are questioned, challenged, and contested. In such a scenario, "Human rights are an expression, channel, and control of the power which limits and ameliorates exploitation. Because exploitation arises out of the depth and pervasiveness of sin, voluntary efforts are insufficient. Exploitive power is never adequately controlled by reason and conscience alone." (Mott 1985, 6) Concretely speaking, Human rights are the Magna Carta for a global future of human dignity. They are the foundation of a new world order. They are also a prerequisite for the transition to sustainable societies, where future generations can live in political and economic security. Partially due to this vigorous development some care must be taken towards conceptual clarity, in order to better promote human rights. Oppression literally means, pushing people down "below a certain existential threshold or not allowing them to come" to satisfy existential needs – which need not be material needs. The victims of oppression suffer deprivation. They live below their existential threshold, and existential needs are not satisfied. One of the most vicious arguments of oppressors of all sorts is to call oppression normal and present it as a law of nature (FIAN 1995, 14–15).

Rights of human beings are existential and real. But, in reality these rights hardly work and therefore rights have to be pursued all the time and by all means. The dominant and the powerful keep inventing new instruments, meanings, and mechanisms to justify their wrongs. As people of faith, we are called to set right the human wrongs that the dominant and the powerful inflict upon the weak and the vulnerable. Those in power and authority wield their power in socio-political and religious structures and systems that obstruct the rights that are due to every citizen irrespective of gender, caste, creed, and class. Therefore, realizing fuller and authentic humanity and restoring human rights that are due to them is of utmost importance. Those with power and authority continue to deny those on the bottom rungs their full and authentic humanity and negate their basic identity as persons. The very notion of human rights is precisely entrenched in humans and thus upholds human rights against human wrongs. Christian Scripture adds value to human dignity. It endorses infinite worth because the concept of humanity is enmeshed in its letter and spirit. So, it is expected that victims are to be treated and respected as humans, persons, and people whose stature is far above and far higher than other creatures. It is in this context that the goal of human rights is to give people their dignity, help them regain lost personhood and reiterate peoplehood, so that they become as subjects of history and fulfil their own destiny. M. M. Thomas, the revered and renowned Indian Christian theologian, has delved into human rights in-depth and thus offers two typologies that consist of the rights of people or "people-hood" which in the Indian context refers to minorities and other weaker sections of Indian society (1977, 33).

Two concepts surface more powerfully in M. M. Thomas' theology i.e., personhood and people-hood encompassing – individuals and community respectively. These two concepts have to be theologically nuanced because they clearly state that each and every individual before the sight of God is endowed with the highest order considered as the crown of God's creation representing the image of God (*imago dei*). In that human dignity (self-esteem or self-respect) is indeed part and parcel of all humans. Hence, human dignity is intrinsic and inalienable and therefore no one has the right to take it away from anyone. Accordingly, even the Universal Declaration of Human Rights and the Indian Constitution categorically insist that the core of these two concepts is humanity. 'Humanity' in this context becomes essential and central. In and around humanity human dignity hangs on, so tightly and deeply entrenched since each and every human being represents the image of God, and therefore, are above all creatures intrinsic and thus sacred.

Human rights and human dignity are value loaded and deeply entrenched and intertwined with each other and therefore inseparable concepts. Rights and dignity are within us and ingrained in us and so no one has given them to us because they are natural, indivisible, and indelible. Amidst a number of facets in the sphere of human rights, human dignity is undoubtedly the most important because it touches upon the very being of each and every human. M. M. Thomas develops personhood theologically and reasons that the dignity of every human being is personified in personhood that adds to other related aspects of rights. Therefore, whether singular personhood or plural "people-hood", each is embedded in self-esteem / self-worth. Accordingly, minorities and the marginalized have been victims of rising majoritarianism and populism.

The very purpose of creating humans in God's image pre-supposes the worth and dignity extended to all humans and certainly not only to a select few. When the very purposes of God are violated, and the basic rights of humans negated then we have to correct the wrongs by employing the instruments of human rights. It further endorses that God's covenantal relationship with humans symbolizes God's gracious mediating effort to redeem the fallen world and created order. M. M. Thomas (1996, 31) issues a clarion call for all people to participate in establishing human dignity and thus restoring equality of all and for all. God so loved the world and the humanity and so sent His Son to the world in flesh and blood so that the fractured and alienated humanity by His birth, death and resurrection could be redeemed, renewed, and thus become a new community of persons (Thomas 1996, 31).

According to M. M. Thomas, Christ brought anew the lost and fractured humanity. He substantiates the New Humanity as "the restoration of the human person in Christ as God's free creative agent in the divine act of new creation to restore the wholeness of the entire universe throughout history" (Rajaiah 2017, 141). Reiterating, "The new humanity revealed in Jesus Christ is the instrument of constant revolution in social history, exerting pressure aimed at creating universal brotherhood/sisterhood" (Rajaiah 2017, 141). Retrieving lost humanity or redeeming de-humanized humanity is possible in and through human rights that are inalienable and inviolable of all humans. Let us strive to reclaim the personhood and peoplehood at the individual (personal) and communitarian (community) levels that are premised in human dignity because their worth is infinite and incontrovertible.

Bibliography

Adas, Michael. 1989. *Machines as the Measure of Men: Science, Technology, and Ideologies of Western Dominance.* Ithaca: Cornwell University Press.
Arun, Thalekkara K. 2018. "Politics to Stop Lynching." *The Economic Times*, 25.07.2018.
Baird, Robert D., ed. 1981. *Religion in Modern India.* New Delhi: Manohar.
Bajwa, Gumohindor P. S. 1995. *Human Rights in India, Implementation and Violation.* New Delhi: Anmol Publications.
Balasuriya, Tissa. 2000. *Globalization and Human Solidarity.* Tiruvalla: Christava Sahitya Samithi.
Bhatacharya, Satwana. 2017. "Mobocracy in the Name of New India." *The Indian Express*, 30.06.2017.
Chandran, Joshua R. 1997. *Christian Ethics.* Delhi: ISPCK.
Deshpande, Satish. 1998. "Current Impasse in Language of Rights: Questions of Context." *Economic and Political Weekly* 33:11–15.
D'Souza, Andreas. 1999. "Hindutva and the Indian Churches' Response." In *Preparing for Witness in Context*, edited by Jean S. Stoner, Louisville: Presbyterian Church, 81–195.
Dutta, Nilanjam. 1998. "From Subject to Citizen: Towards a History of the Indian Civil Rights Movement." In *Changing Concepts of Rights and Justice in South Asia,* edited by Michael R. Anderson and Sunit Guha, Delhi: Oxford University Press, 275–288.
FoodFirst Informations- und Aktions-Netzwerk (FIAN). 1995. *Economic Human Rights: Their Time Has Come.* Heidelberg: FoodFirst Information and Action Network / International Secretariat.
Ganguly, Amulya. 1999. "Hinduism and Hindutva." *Hindustan Times*, 08.02.1999.
Ife, Jim. 2001. *Human Rights and Social Work: Towards Rights-Based Practice.* Cambridge: Cambridge University Press.
Ife, Jim. 2006. "Human Rights Beyond the 'Three Generation'". In *Activating Human Rights*, edited by Elisabeth Porter and Baden Offord, Peter Lang: Bern, 29–45.
Mott, Stephen C. 1985. "The Contribution of the Bible to Human Rights" In *Human Rights and the Global Mission of the Church*, edited by Lorine M. Getz, Cambridge, MA: Boston Theological Institute, 5–12.
Panikar, Kavalam M. 1959. *Asia and Western Dominance.* New York: Macmillan.
Parambil, Jacob P. 2018. "Mob Lynching Fuelled by Whats App." *Indian Currents*, 16–22.07.2018.

Pathak, Avijit. 1999. "From Secularism to Nationalism: Fate of Grand Ideal." *Deccan Herald*, 27.08.1999.
Prakash, Cedric. 2018. "India@lynching.com." *Indian Currents*, 16–22.07.2018.
Rajaiah, Jeyaraj. 2016. *Dalit Humanization: A Quest Based on M.M. Thomas' Theology of Salvation and Humanization*. Utrecht: Doctoral Dissertation. https://www.narcis.nl/publication/Record ID/oai%3Adspace.library.uu.nl%3A1874%2F341387 (29.11.2021).
Sanajaoba, Naorem. 1994. *Human Rights: Norms and Standard*. New Delhi: Osmons Publications.
Seabrook, Jeremy. 1996. "Human Rights in Western Terms." *Deccan Herald*, 13.02.1996.
Shimray, Shimreingam. 2002. *Theology of Human Rights: A Critique on Politics*. Jorhat: Barkataki & Company.
Thomas, Madathilparampil M. 1977. *Towards an Evangelical Social Gospel*. Madras: Christian Literature Society.
Thomas, Madathilparampil M. 1992–1996. *The Church's Mission and Post-Modern Humanism: Collection of Essays and Talk*. Delhi: ISPCK.
The Hindu. 2018. "Human Life is Less Than Cow." *The Hindu*, 26.07.2018.
UNESCO. 1953. *The Universal Declaration of Human Rights: A Guide for Teachers*. Paris: UNESCO.
UN. 1998. *1948–1998: The Universal Declaration of Human Rights*. Geneva: The United Nations Department of Public Information.

Ignatius Swart
Institution and Religion

1 Institution and Religion: Directing a Debate to a Different Contextual Reality

Judged by the debate among some of the most prominent scholars in the field of international practical theology today, the topic of institution and religion may well be regarded as of lesser importance. Here I particularly have in mind the prevailing debate conducted under the rubric: "Practical theology as a hermeneutical science of lived religion" (Weyel 2014; see also Ganzevoort 2009; Ganzevoort and Roeland 2014; Gräb 2014; Schweitzer 2014). Under this topical focus, the argument developed is that practical theology is assigned the essential task of illuminating the concept and practices of "lived religion". Ruard Ganzevoort and Johan Roeland, two exponents of this approach to practical theology explain:

> The concepts of praxis and lived religion focus on what people do rather than on 'official' religion, its sacred sources, its institutes, and its doctrines. As such, practical theology has much in common with what in disciplines like anthropology, sociology, and media studies, is known as 'the practical turn': the *turn away from institutes* and (cultural) texts to the everyday social and cultural practices of ordinary people (Ganzevoort and Roeland 2014, 93; italics added).

It becomes necessary to emphasise that Ganzevoort and Roeland's reference to "the turn away from institutes" should not be understood as a complete turn away from such institutes. This emerges in the way in which the institution of the church is recognised as a prevailing site of lived religion in more than one contribution to the debate. Of particular significance, however, is that this recognition is at the same time relativised by the relatively small role afforded to the church in the production of religion in everyday life (see Miller-McLemore 2012, 105–107). It is postulated that much, if not most, of what is produced as lived religion happens outside the realm of the church. "Lived religion does not refer primarily to forms of belonging to a Christian community or to the church. Lived religion is a sense of the religious dimension of human life" (Gräb 2014, 109; cf. Ganzevoort and Roeland 2014, 96; Schweitzer 2014, 144; Weyel 2014, 154).

The direction in which I am seeking to take the discussion in this chapter should not be understood as an attempt to devaluate or undermine the claims and perspectives on lived religion arising from the international debate on practical theology. The insight that religious meaning, experiences, and practices can be found *outside* the institutional domain of the church, and that as such they remain distinctive features that are by no means being dissipated as a result of processes of secularisation and deinstitutionalisation (Weyel 2014; Ganzevoort and Roeland 2014), is compelling and relevant. Yet I want to argue at the same time that this insight needs to be understood and appreciated in terms of its *situatedness*. While scholars from the Global North are not the sole contributors to the practical theological debate on lived religion (see e. g., Charbonnier et al. 2018), it is nevertheless a debate that is dominated by scholars from this part of the world – i. e., noticeably from continental Europe. Clearly, it is this group of scholars whose ideas on the matter are mostly advanced in prominent outlets such as the *International Journal of Practical Theology*, and whose situatedness is constituted through their self-orientation within their contexts of advanced secularisation and deinstitutionalisation (see e. g., Ganzevoort 2009, 2; Ganzevoort and Roeland 2014, 97; Weyel 2014, 158).

My point of orientation in this practical theological debate – which predominantly reflects an outlook on institution and religion in the Global North – leads me to direct the deliberation towards a conspicuously *different* reality in the rest of this chapter. This is the reality of the Global South, Africa, and South Africa, which determines my own situatedness. As such, I am a South African scholar of practical theology and religious studies who cannot deny my own upbringing in a theological and ecclesial tradition that has to a large extent looked northwards for generating its own ideas and its socio-institutional location. Yet at the same time I have found this orientation to be increasingly challenged by my own growth in decolonial sensibility, my related exposure to the academic and social worlds across the South-North spectrum and, not least, my own plain observation and sense-making of the dynamics of far-reaching religious and social change in my own society and beyond. From this vantage point, I want to advance the thesis that a situatedness such as my own calls for a far more pointed practical theological concern with the *institutional* dimensions of lived religion. Contrary to what may be offered as a wholly legitimate perspective by practical theological scholars from the Global North in the light of their own situatedness, the argument that I want to proffer is that my own contextual reality is one where the institutional dimension ought to be taken very seriously as a major, if not *the* dominant, domain where lived religion is practised and produced. As such, this is a context of ongoing religious change where a religious institution such as the Christian church is flourishing in multiple, diverse, and fluid ways; by implication, it is a context where lived religion ought to be sought and studied more than anything else *inside* or *within* the institutional domain.

I will now continue to in the rest of this chapter draw selectively on perspectives from the broad field of religious studies research that I perceive as significant to support and inform my line of argumentation on institution and religion. These are perspectives that are in one way or another all concerned with the contemporary reality of far-reaching religious change that accordingly take us to a contextual reality far removed from the one presented by practical theological scholars from the Global North. Representative of my own situatedness, this is the world of Global South

Christianities,[1] in which the churches of Africa occupy a central place; but closer to home, incorporated is also my own South African religious context where scholarly undertakings to track (or map) the sacred and carry out other forms of empirical work reveal images of an institutional geography and dynamics reminiscent of developments within a larger southern Christian presence, not least on the wider African continent.

2 Looking South: Fragments of a New Christian Synthesis

If the Christian church, historically the most powerful religious institution in that part of the world known as the Global North, is in decline because of ongoing processes of advanced secularisation and deinstitutionalisation, this is not the case in that part of the world referred to as the Global South. This is the message conveyed by a growing chorus of commentators and scholars in the field of religious studies internationally, which in a very direct way supports the argument I am pursuing in this chapter. In a nutshell, it is a message that (at least in the explicit case of some contributors) does not ignore the presence of another major force shaping the contours of ongoing religious change, namely Islam (Jenkins 2007, 189–221; Kim 2012, xxxiv, 19–20, 78, 364–65; Mwashinga 2016, 35, 48–49). Yet, at the same time, it is a message that wants to open our eyes to an epoch-making transformative moment in the history of religion worldwide whereby the centre of gravity of the Christian world is shifting from the Global North to the Global South, to Africa, Latin America and parts of Asia (see e.g. Anderson 2013; Daughrity 2018; Jenkins 2007; Johnson and Chung 2004; Johnson and Kim 2005; Johnson and Ross 2009; Kim 2012; Lamport 2018; Mwashinga 2016; Tryggestad 2010). To quote from Philip Jenkins's magisterial work (2007, 1–2) theorising about this shift in the centre of gravity:

> Today, the largest Christian communities on the planet are to be found in those regions. If we want to visualize a 'typical' contemporary Christian, we should think of a woman living in a village in Nigeria, or in a Brazilian favela. In parts of Asia too, churches are growing rapidly, in numbers and self-confidence. As Kenyan scholar John Mbiti has observed, 'the centers of the church's universality [are] no longer in Geneva, Rome, Athens, Paris, London, New York, but Kinshasa, Buenos Aires, Addis Ababa and Manila'.

The important point arising from this quotation does not only reflect the fact about Christianity's extraordinary growth in distinctive parts of the world known collective-

---

[1] I accept the premise that there "is no single southern Christianity" and that the plural reference far more appropriately does justice to "the vast and diverse world" of *Christianities* in the Global South (Jenkins 2006, 13; Jenkins 2007, 8; see also Johnson and Ross 2010, 12).

ly as the Global South. It also affirms a larger scholarly recognition that such growth becomes manifested first and foremost in the ongoing proliferation of the *church* as institution (see e.g., Johnson and Kim 2005, 80; Kim 2012, 4). In other words, through this scholarly recognition we encounter a perspective on religious change that is steeped in socio-historical reality and for this reason can be considered as of paramount importance for a contemporary practical theological scholarship that rightly aspires to prioritise the practice of lived religion as its object of study. For such scholarship it implies that a concern with lived religion in those parts of the world where the Christian religion is flourishing ought to take us back to prioritising research and study of practices *within* and *by* the Christian church. Unmistakably, however, this has become a daunting task, perhaps more than ever before given the myriad of manifestations that may count as church within the domain of institution and religion.

The recognition of the immense diversity and plurality of what may count as being church in the Global South today (Jenkins 2006, 13; Jenkins 2007, 8; Johnson and Ross 2010, 12; Kim 2012, 8, 20–21) – in other words church as a carrier of lived religion in its plurality of expressions – brings us to the important question then of whether it may in fact be possible to draw any converging lines from this diverse but proliferating institutional phenomenon. In this respect, I find compelling the idea or thesis of a "new Christian synthesis", which is central to Jenkins's (2007, 7) argument, but also finds resonance in a considerable body of complementary literature. In what can be considered at the most as addressing fragments of this *synthesis*, I am confining myself to a few observations in trying to capture essential elements of the phenomenon of the rising churches of the South.

A significant point of departure is that one can only come to a reliable understanding of the phenomenon of the rising Southern churches by not projecting onto them the "familiar realities and desires" (Jenkins 2007, 15) emanating from the Global North. This highlights the expectation of Western liberal but socially committed Christians that the rising churches from the Global South could become the vehicles of a kind of emancipation and leadership that, in the mould of liberation theology, "would be fervently liberal, activist, and even revolutionary" (Jenkins 2006, 13; Jenkins 2007, 7). Jenkins, however, explains why this expectation could be considered a fallacy:

> In this view, the new Christianity would chiefly be concerned with pulling down the mighty from their seats, through political action or even armed struggle. All too often, though, these hopes have proved illusory. Frequently, the liberationist voices emanating from the Third World proved to derive from clerics trained in Europe and North America, and their ideas won only limited local appeal. Southern Christians would not avoid political activism, but they would become involved strictly on their own terms (2006, 13; 2007, 7).

The fundamental issue is that it has become crucially important to recognise that while many Southern Christians and their churches have embraced the cause of political liberation, they have "made it inseparable from *deliverance* from supernatural evil" (Jenkins 2006, 13; Jenkins 2007, 7). It is this distinctive feature – an emphasis that reverberates in a considerable body of literature – that should be regarded as the "single key area of faith and practice that divides Northern and Southern Christians" (Jenkins 2007, 143): the belief in spiritual forces, the effect of such forces on everyday human life, and the way they shape the existence of the churches (see e.g., Adogame 2004; Anderson 2003; Chitando, Gunda, and Kügler 2014; Ilo 2018; Jenkins 2007, 143– 147; Jenkins 2006, 16; ter Haar 2009). While such beliefs may be rejected by a Northern secular mindset as superstitious and a manifestation of a pre-Enlightenment worldview, they align with a cultural orientation and worldview that perceive the realities of evil, sickness and repression to be directly influenced by *supernatural* forces. This explains, for instance, why the practice of healing – through spiritual means – takes such a central place especially in the newer Southern churches. But it also explains these churches' fervent identification with *biblical worldviews*, which in turn give rise to ritual and worship practices that emulate the practices of the ancient Hebrew and early Christian communities of the Bible. As observed by Jenkins, "(c)ultural affinities with the biblical world" lead many contemporary Christians from Africa and Asia especially to see the Old Testament "as their story, their book" (2006, 14; see also Gunda 2014), an identification that in turn finds concrete expression in the way in which worship and social events frequently evolve around practices of animal sacrifice (see Wepener et al. 2019) as well as in celebrations of key events in the ceremonial year (Jenkins 2006, 14; cf. 151–153). At the same time, however, this does not rule out the New Testament as equally influential, since texts such as the Letter to the Hebrews, the Book of Revelation and the Gospels all in their respective ways appeal to a Christian life world in which veneration of the living dead, ritual practices of blood sacrifice, and the power to perform prophetic revelation, miracles, exorcism and faith-healing constitute core ingredients of a lived religion (Jenkins 2006, 14–17; cf. Jenkins 2007, 148–149, 151–153; see also Gunda 2014).

A major argument advanced by Jenkins therefore is that we may today find ourselves at the beginning of a new epoch whereby the rising churches of the South will in fact take us "back to the future" (Jenkins 2007, 6–9). The dominant churches of the future, he contends, may well be seen as sharing many commonalities with those of the *medieval* or early European period (Jenkins 2007, 8; cf. 2006, 17). In what I consider to be a valuable part of his discussion, he also introduces the distinction between churches and sects in support of his argument (Jenkins 2007, 156–160). By drawing on the related theoretical distinctions of sociologists Max Weber and Ernst Troeltsch, the thrust of the argument is that the newer churches of the South could be seen as holding much in common with the classic features of sects vis-à-vis those of churches. These include the inclination of sects toward overt emotionalism, spontaneity and mystical experience that are not easily accommodated by the intellectualism, suppressed emotionalism and formalism that characterise the teachings and liturgical arrangements of churches. Moreover, they also include the way in which the members of sects are typically voluntary converts, often from a lower educational and social status, whose lives are strongly controlled by the organisation, in comparison with the members of churches whose members are often better educated and as a rule born into the organisation. And, last but not least, a prominent feature crucially also pertains to the nature of leadership, in the way in which sects demand that their leaders demonstrate spiritual and charismatic gifts, compared to churches who are run by formally trained ministers within a distinctively bureaucratic framework (Jenkins 2007, 157–158). Jenkins summarises the significance of this perspective:

> In terms of the sociology of religion [...] [the rising churches of the South] are classic sects, with all that implies for leadership, worship style, and degree of commitment. They are fundamentalist and charismatic by nature, theologically conservative, with a powerful belief in the spiritual dimension, in visions and spiritual healing. With their claims to prophetic status, figures such as Simon Kimbangu and Isaiah Shembe exactly fit the classic profile of sect leaders. In practice, leadership roles in Pentecostal and independent churches are open to anyone who is accepted as having spiritual gifts, regardless of any form of education or theological training (Jenkins 2007, 158).

To conclude this part of the discussion, it certainly is worth alluding to another pertinent observation in Jenkins's argument. His prediction is that Southern churches may over time, as they grow and mature, "loose something of their sectarian character, and become more like the major churches" (Jenkins 2007, 159). He even contends that the "new churches" could become "key agents" of modernisation themselves (Jenkins 2007, 159). And yet, as the argument above suggests, what will remain an influential force for a considerable time to come are the "sectarian features" that are giving rise to the unparalleled institutional proliferation and presence of *Pentecostal* and so-called *independent* churches[2] (Jenkins 2007, 8, 70–76, 78–84). In this respect, here it could meaningfully be noted how Jenkins's analysis corresponds favourably with that of many other academic commentaries that identify the latter churches as the institutional representatives that will to a large extent dominate the face of global Christianity in the future (see e.g., Anderson 2013; Cox 2009; Johnson and Ross 2009; Kim 2012; Pew Forum 2007). These are expressions of 'institution and religion' that are flourishing in their great variety in the Global South today, are increasingly also expanding their reach toward the Global North and will continue with this dual dynamic for the unforeseeable future, albeit with some qualifications.

---

[2] According to Jenkins, "independent churches" are flourishing in the Global South. They do not fit the label of being Protestant, Catholic, Anglican, or Orthodox, but are comprised of "a wide variety of denominations, often (but not always) included under the label of Pentecostal." This may include churches that "are affiliated with Northern Hemisphere denominations", although a large majority "are indigenous with roots entirely in Africa, Asia, and Latin America" (2007, 70). In this respect, Jenkins also devotes considerable space to singling out the importance of the African Independent Churches (AICs) (which may otherwise also be referred to as African Indigenous or African Initiated Churches) (Jenkins 2007, 56–62, 78–80). He emphasises the fact that the AICs "collectively represent one of the most impressive stories in the whole history of Christianity". They have been successful in adapting the Christian faith to local cultures and traditions. As such, "[t]hey are African churches with African leaders for African people" (Jenkins 2007, 61).

According to Jenkins, such flourishing does not mean that the so-called "mission" or *mainstream* churches will simply disappear. He highlights the fact that "leading churches" in the Global South will continue to be Anglican, Methodist and most prominently Roman Catholic (Jenkins 2007, 8, 65–70, 76–78, 226–231), though in a garment much different from their erstwhile mainstream manifestations. As a result of processes of "inculturation" and "Pentecostalisation", they will increasingly take on features of the *newer* Global South churches (Jenkins 2007, 8, 65–69, 76–78, 125–142).

3 From the Global South in General to Africa and South Africa: The Case of Institution and Religion in the Unsecular City

I would like to continue briefly with Jenkins's commentary at this point in my discussion by drawing on another captivating idea from his work: the notion of the *unsecular city* (Jenkins 2007, 107–108). One of the important themes running through his work – a theme that effectively reverses Harvey Cox's famous coinage, the "secular city" (Cox 1965) – is that the dynamic of the rising Southern churches will to a large extent play itself out in the cities of the Global South (cf. Johnson and Kim 2005, 80). Jenkins stresses the fact that most of the population growth in the coming decades will be urban, albeit with some qualification as this will by and large be a development in the Global South, giving rise to an increasing number of vast metropolitan complexes with populations totalling tens of millions. He writes:

> We think of cities such as Cairo, Mumbai (Bombay), Dhaka, Karachi, Jakarta, Lagos, and Mexico City, each with perhaps 30 to 40 million people, and next to nothing in working government services. Tens of millions of new urban dwellers will in effect be living and working totally outside the legal economy or any effective relationship with officialdom. And there will be other future colossi, giant cities with names hitherto unfamiliar to Westerners, centers such as Kampala, Kinshasa, Dar-es-Salaam, and Sana'a (Jenkins 2007, 107–108).

It is against this backdrop that Jenkins gives an account of the striking *urban* presence of the rising churches of the Global South, especially of the Pentecostal and independent type. He comments that the success of these churches can be seen as a by-product of modernisation and urbanisation (Jenkins 2007, 85). While there are among them also denominations that cater for sections of the middle classes, it is among the very poor that these churches are finding special appeal. Accordingly, it is at the *fringes* of the cities of the Global South – in the city margins and shantytowns where millions of illegal squatters, migrants and socio-economically disenfranchised try to eke out a living – where the rising churches are particularly visible and mushrooming. In these environments – in addition to performing their spiritual functions – they emerge as providers of "functional alternative arrangements for health, welfare, and education" (Jenkins 2007, 85), as "radical communities" (Jenkins 2007, 87) where their members may find a sense of family and fellowship, but also the social network support to improve their lives (Jenkins 2007, 85–90; for a similar perspective cf. Rakodi 2014). As postulated by Jenkins, this is the way that the new churches of the Global South play a role strikingly similar to that of the early Christian communities in offered support to their members, in situations similarly devoid of any official aid. He makes the significant point:

> As historian Peter Brown observes of the third and fourth centuries, 'The appeal of Christianity still lay in its radical sense of community: it absorbed people because the individual could drop from a wide impersonal world into a miniature community, whose demands and relations were explicit.' Every word in this sentence could be wholeheartedly applied to modern Africa or Latin America. The provision of social services that were otherwise unobtainable also goes far to explaining the growth of urban Christianity during Roman times, just like today [...] To be a member of an active Christian church today might well bring more tangible benefits than being a citizen of Nigeria or Peru (Jenkins 2007, 90; cf. 2006, 17).

I find in the above notion of the unsecular city and the perspectives that inform it a significant point of connection to also bring the discussion home to my own immediate South African context, a society that in its own right features a high level of religiosity and a considerable but diverse Christian institutional presence when compared to other societies elsewhere in Africa and the Global South (see e.g., Chipkin and Leatt 2011). In making this connection, I find no better way than to start doing this by drawing from one of the outstanding more recent scholarly books on the social place and significance of religion and its institutions in contemporary (post-apartheid) South Africa. This is David Chidester's *Wild Religion: Tracking the Sacred in South Africa* (2012), in which his aim to "track the sacred" has led him to also undertake a "preliminary mapping of the religious meanings" (Chidester 2012, 17) of the city where he has worked as a distinguished professor of religious studies for many years, namely Cape Town.

What Chidester's tracking of the sacred in Cape Town strikingly reveals is an image that does not differ much from Jenkins's notion of the unsecular city. One of the prominent themes running through his analysis is that of 'centre' and 'periphery' to make the point that any 'mapping of the sacred' cannot escape the heritage of Cape Town's colonial and apartheid history. He states as a key observation: "While a European Architectonics seems firmly established at the city center, most Christians have been relegated to the periphery, the urban townships around Cape Town, where the so-called African-initiated churches in particular have redefined the meanings of urban space by sacralising not only ordinary homes but also what may be called the leftover spaces[3] of the city" (Chidester 2012, 18).

---

[3] Such "leftover spaces", Chidester specifies, included open lots, the areas beneath motorways and even beaches, "where a 'line on the ground is often the only edge between sacred space and the city'" (Chidester 2012, 37).

Chidester's undertaking has therefore led him, in a way remarkably similar to Jenkins's, to also appreciate the *city margins* as the space where institutional expressions of religion are flourishing and leaving their mark. He acknowledges that this identification should not ignore the prevailing dominant presence of the European mission churches in Cape Town's city centre – churches from the Reformed, Anglican, and German Lutheran traditions (2012, 36–37). Yet he emphasises in the same breath that by the late twentieth century this was not the space where most Christians (and also Muslims) in greater Cape Town practised their religion. They were practising their religion in the black townships, informal settlements and peripheral neighbourhoods that included the Coloured residential areas of the Cape Flats. These areas had become the spaces where Christian churches of a great variety – noticeably of the African Independent and Pentecostal charismatic types – were not only flourishing, but where European mission churches were themselves "essentially converted to African Christianity" (Chidester 2012, 37, 48–49). As a result, Chidester significantly concludes that "although it might appear to be anchored at the city center [...] Christian space in Cape Town was actually dispersed through multiple centers that had emerged on the city's periphery" (Chidester 2012, 37).

I want to begin closing this part of my discussion by also relating to James Cochrane's similar focus on Cape Town in a contribution some years ago in order to (re)frame "the political economy of the sacred" in post-apartheid Christianity (Cochrane 2009). A close colleague of Chidester's at the time and in his own right a distinguished South African scholar of religious studies, Cochrane arrived at a perspective that shows strong similarities with that of Chidester. For Cochrane, a "proliferation of religious phenomena that claim some kind of Christian identity" had become an outstanding feature of the "religious spaces of the city of Cape Town". Yet, in a way even more explicitly than Chidester, he found it necessary and appropriate to assert that such *multiplying* painted "a picture that may be *generalized* across contemporary South African society" (Cochrane 2009, 103–104; italics added).

I take from Cochrane's claim to generalisation a valuable pointer to in conclusion also allude to a wider body of ever-growing empirically based research work offering insights into the dynamics of religious and social change across a broad South African urban reality. Including contributions that beyond those of Chidester and Cochrane take us to other major South African metropolises such as the cities of Johannesburg and Tshwane (Pretoria), this body of research work may be valued for its interdisciplinary and transdisciplinary span across the disciplines of religious studies, practical theology, and the social sciences and humanities more broadly speaking. Of even greater significance, however, at the centre of the different explorations is also a similar interest in how a multitude of institutional representations from the Christian church are especially from the margins transforming their city environments and in the process providing spaces of refuge, belonging and support for their members, albeit with an important qualification. Whereas in the case of Chidester and Cochrane's mappings, the so-called *migrant*-dominated Pentecostal charismatic churches are recognised as a part of the institutional representation, these churches constitute a *dominant* focus in much of the ongoing research work (see e. g., Landau 2017; Nzayabino 2010; Ribbens and De Beer 2017; Wilhelm-Solomon et al. 2017).

4 A Brief Concluding Word

My aim in this chapter was to show how the conceptual framework of 'institution and religion' acquires new relevance for practical theological scholarship when the focus is directed to the contextual reality that determines my own situatedness: the Global South, Africa and South Africa. While practical theological scholars especially from the Global North may, for understandable reasons, find lesser relevance in this conceptual framework, my discussion has attempted to make clear why such lesser estimation cannot hold in contexts where the rise of prolific new institutional formations points instead to churches across the Pentecostal-charismatic, independent and inculturated mainline spectrum as *privileged* sites of lived religion – perhaps most pointedly for the very poor and disenfranchised.

I want to take into account, however, that my line of argumentation could easily be read as a presentation of an oversimplified South-North juxtaposition. This, I want to make clear, was not the intention. Rather, my aim was to present an argument from my own situatedness, an argument that is of *limited scope* and cannot give account of how contemporary global processes of social and religious change are also impacting on societies of the Global North. As Jenkins acknowledges himself, secularisation and religious deinstitutionalisation cannot capture the full story of the Global North today. In this story account has to be given of how a new Christian institutional presence is affirming itself in the heartlands of Global North societies through ongoing processes of mass migration from the Global South (see Jenkins 2007, 111–124). And, not least, in this story a specific chapter also needs to be written on how, within European Christianity in particular, the decline of "national or folk churches" coincides with "the survival of belief among smaller, often very committed, groups of believers", both Catholic and Protestant (Jenkins 2007, xiii). These are parts of the story that my chapter could in no way do justice to, but that nevertheless call for the serious attention of a practical theological scholarship prioritising the concept of "lived religion" as its subject focus (cf. Weyel, 2014, 153).

Bibliography

Adogame, Afe. 2004. "Engaging the Rhetoric of Spiritual Warfare: The Public Face of Aladura in Diaspora." *Journal of Religion in Africa* 34:493–522.

Anderson, Allan 2003. "African Initiated Churches of the Spirit and Pneumatology." *Word & World* 23:178–186.

Anderson, Allan 2013. "Global Pentecostalism, Charismatic Movements and Independent Churches." Lecture for the Ecumenical Institute, Bossey, Switzerland, 18.11.2013.

Charbonnier, Lars, Johan Cilliers, Matthias Mader, Cas Wepener, and Birgit Weyel, eds. 2018. *Pluralisation and Social Change: Dynamics of Lived Religion in South Africa and in Germany.* Praktische Theologie im Wissenschaftsdiskurs 21. Berlin: De Gruyter.

Chidester, David. 2012. *Wild Religion: Tracking the Sacred in South Africa.* Berkeley: University of California Press.

Chipkin, Ivor, and Annie Leatt. 2011. "Religion and Revival in Post-Apartheid South Africa." *Focus* 62:39–46.

Chitando, Ezra, Masiiwa Gunda, and Joachim Kügler, eds. 2014. *Multiplying in the Spirit: African Initiated Churches in Zimbabwe.* Bible in Africa Studies 15. Bamberg: University of Bamberg Press.

Cochrane, James 2009. "Reframing the Political Economy of the Sacred: Readings of Post-Apartheid Christianity." In *Falling Walls: The Years 1989/90 as a Turning Point in the History of World Christianity.* Studies in the History of Christianity in the Non-Western World 15, edited by Klaus Koschorke and Johannes Meier, Wiesbaden: Harrassowitz Verlag, 95–116.

Cox, Harvey. 1965. *The Secular City: Secularization and Urbanization in Theological Perspective.* New York: Macmillan.

Cox, Harvey. 2009. *Fire from Heaven: The Rise of Pentecostal Spirituality and the Reshaping of Religion in the 21st Century.* Cambridge, MA: Da Capo Press.

Daughrity, Dyron 2018. *Rising: The Amazing Story of Christianity's Resurrection in the Global South.* Minneapolis: Augsburg Fortress.

Ganzevoort, Ruard. 2009. "Forks in the Road When Tracing the Sacred: Practical Theology as Hermeneutics of Lived Religion." Presidential Address to the Ninth Conference of the International Academy of Practical Theology, Chicago.

Ganzevoort, Ruard, and Johan Roeland. 2014. "Lived Religion: The Praxis of Practical Theology." *International Journal of Practical Theology* 18:91–101.

Gräb, Wilhelm. 2014. "Practical Theology as a Theory of Lived Religion Conceptualizing Church Leadership." *International Journal of Practical Theology* 18:102–112.

Gunda, Masiiwa 2014. "African Biblical Christianity: Understanding the 'Spirit-Type' African Initiated Churches in Zimbabwe." In *Multiplying in the Spirit: African Initiated Churches in Zimbabwe.* Bible in Africa Studies 15, edited by Ezra Chitando, Masiiwa Gunda, and Joachim Kügler, Bamberg: University of Bamberg Press, 145–160.

Haar, Gerrie ter. 2009. *How God Became African: African Spirituality and Western Secular Thought.* Philadelphia: University of Pennsylvania Press.

Ilo, Stan 2018. *Wealth, Health, and Hope in African Christian Religion: The Search for Abundant Life.* Lanham: Lexington Books.

Jenkins, Philip. 2006. "Believing in the Global South." *First Things* 168:12–18.

Jenkins, Philip. 2007. *The Next Christendom: The Coming of Global Christianity.* New York: Oxford University Press.

Johnson, Todd, and Sun Young Chung. 2004. "Tracking Global Christianity's Statistical Centre of Gravity, AD 33–AD 2100." *International Review of Mission* 59:166–181.

Johnson, Todd, and Sandra Kim. 2005. "Describing the Worldwide Christian Phenomenon." *International Bulletin of Missionary Research* 29:80–84.

Johnson, Todd, and Kenneth Ross. 2009. *Atlas of Global Christianity 1910–2010.* Edinburgh: Edinburgh University Press.

Johnson, Todd, and Kenneth Ross. 2010. "The Making of the Atlas of Global Christianity." *International Bulletin of Missionary Research* 34:12–16.

Kim, Elijah. 2012. *The Rise of the Global South: The Decline of Western Christendom and the Rise of Majority World Christianity.* Eugene: Wipf & Stock.

Lamport, Mark, ed. 2018. *Encyclopaedia of Christianity in the Global South.* Lanham: Rowman & Littlefield.

Landau, Loren. 2014. "Religion and the Foundation of Urban Difference: Belief, Transcendence and Transgression in South Africa and Johannesburg." *Global Networks* 14:291–305.

Miller-McLemore, Bonnie. 2012. "Toward Greater Understanding of Practical Theology." *International Journal of Practical Theology* 16:104–123.

Mwashinga, Christopher. 2016. "Global South Christianity and Adventism: Trends and Implications." *Andrews University Seminary Student Journal* 2:33–51.

Nzayabino, Vedaste. 2010. "The Role of Refugee-Established Churches in Integrating Forced Migrants: A Case Study of Word of Life Assembly in Yeoville, Johannesburg." *HTS Teologiese Studies/Theological Studies* 66:1–9.

Pew Forum. 2007. *Spirit and Power: A 10-Country Survey of Pentecostals*. The Pew Forum on Religion and Public Life. Washington: Pew Research Centre.

Rakodi, Carole. 2014. "Religion and Social Life in African Cities." In *Africa's Urban Revolution*, edited by Susan Parnell and Edgar Pieterse, London: Zed Books, 82–109.

Ribbens, Michael, and Stephan de Beer. 2017. "Churches Claiming a Right to the City? Lived Urbanisms in the City of Tshwane." HTS *Teologiese Studies/Theological Studies* 73:1–11.

Schweitzer, Friedrich. 2014. "Professional Praxis in Practical Theology: Theoretical and Methodological Considerations." *International Journal of Practical Theology* 18:139–149.

Tryggestad, Erik. 2010. "Rise of the Global South." *The Christian Chronicle*, 24.06.2010. https://christianchronicle.org/rise-of-the-global-south/ (29.11.2021).

Wepener, Cas, Ignatius Swart, Gerrie ter Haar, and Marcel Barnard, eds. 2019. *Bonding in Worship: A Ritual Lens on Social Capital in Africa Independent Churches in South Africa*. Liturgia Condenda 30. Leuven: Peeters.

Weyel, Birgit. 2014. "Practical Theology as a Hermeneutical Science of Lived Religion." *International Journal of Practical Theology* 18:150–159.

Wilhelm-Solomon, Matthew, Lorena Núñes, Peter Busaka, and Bettina Malcomess, eds. 2017. *Routes and Rites to the City: Mobility, Diversity and Religious Space in Johannesburg*. London: Palgrave Macmillan.

Mouez Khalfaoui
Law and Religion

1 Introduction

Several events that took place at the turn of the twenty-first century signalled 'the return of religion' to the political and social spotlight with serious consequences for religious institutions, practitioners, and for secular political systems. Ignoring the debates concerning whether or not this 'return of religion' is a myth, or if modern societies are indeed turning more religious, the paradigm of state-church separation (Barzilai 2007, xi) is currently facing grave challenges with the increased visibility of religion within the public sphere in comparison with previous decades. This trend unsettles established norms regulating the public sphere in modern democratic states, which are almost always founded on secular paradigms. Accordingly, religions that have been strongly represented in Europe and Western states for centuries – albeit shaped by sweeping waves of secularisation and emancipation throughout Europe (i.e., Christian churches) – have developed a modus-vivendi over decades to cope and live peacefully within secularly dominated contexts (Roy 2005, 39–41). The concept of secularism has been uprooted. On the one hand, the idea of secularism has expanded, transforming into an ideology that concerns both secular and religious affairs in many global contexts so that it became a global prescription for regulating ties – or lack thereof – between religion and the state. This transformation has led to harsh debates that are still taking place between religious and secular actors. The Islamic world is one of the main regions where this debate is reaching its apex.

Moreover, there have been extremely high rates of migration of religious and cultural groups from the Islamic world to Western states over the past decades. These flows unearth challenges to secular and religious concepts domestically as well as to existing paradigms that maintain the coexistence of secular and religious doctrines. Current debates concerning Sharia and secular law, the Islamic headscarf, male circumcision, interfaith marriage, and religious education illustrate this challenging issue. Secularism is mainly found in legal concepts related to the regulation of public space and the role and place of religion and religious symbols within that space. Thus, any debate concerning religious law concentrates mainly on the question of how and to what extent secular civil legal concepts can accommodate excessive religious symbols in public space and state institutions. This discussion is currently focussed on Islam, due to the visibility of Islamic religious symbols in public, to the relatively recent introduction of Islam into Western societies and thus to the ambiguity of several aspects of Islamic doctrine both to Muslims and non-Muslims. This has led to many misunderstandings and false assumptions. Tension arises from secular legal concepts that assign the 'righteous' role and place of religion in the public sphere, allocating it exclusively to the private sphere (Casanova 1994, 35). Therefore, the appearance of Islamic religious symbols in Western public space is doubly difficult: These symbols were previously unknown to the West, and religion is not expected to be confronted in public. Debates concerning religious norms and values in the Muslim world present several similarities with debates taking place in Western contexts. Since the mid-nineteenth century there has been continuous dialogue between secular and religious actors regarding the interpretation of religious law and its interaction with secular legal concepts. This dialogue has not yet reached its conclusion, and the interchange between these parties has been deteriorating (Asad 2003, 205).

This chapter[1] deals with the interchange between religious and civil legal norms. I shall take up the elements of Islam, Muslim individuals, and Islamic legal concepts in my case study. It seems that the corresponding debate that is currently dominating Western discourse, as well as discussion in many Muslim states, will continue far into the future. It offers a touchstone for a broader discussion on the interchange of religion and secular concepts. I will argue that the reconciliation of God's law and secular law cannot be approached through a comparative methodology. I shall further submit that the secular paradigm of tolerance of religious law can be seen as an interim solution but cannot be used as a permanent one for modern societies as it does not encompass all aspects of the interchange between religious law and secular law. Therefore, other methodological and legal approaches are needed. In other words, dominating secular concepts that regulate the public sphere need to be expanded in order to encompass other (and even opposing) concepts. Moreover, there is a need to rethink the position of religion and religious law in our understanding of modern secular societies. In terms of Islamic legal concepts and Muslims, I would like to argue that the debate on God's law and civil law both in Western societies as well as in societies with a Muslim majority has been shaped by several misunderstandings and assumptions both among non-Muslims and Muslims, and which are not limited to mainstream thinking. This state of the art requires an epistemological clarification of terminologies associated with Islamic law, religious law and God's law, and the history of Islamic law. Likewise, clarification of the current debate on religious law in the Islamic world is helpful as well. Therefore, reconciling religious and secular law – which is frequently presented as being a conflict between God's law and civil law – cannot be approached exclusively through western paradigms. Other models of secularism exemplified in India or Indonesia, as well as other models of religion and state interchange, refute the habitual assumption that secularism is an exclusively Western achievement. These models also offer proof that secularism can and should be manifested in a variety of forms (An Na'im 2008, 140. 223). The debate regarding religious and civil norms has focused

---

[1] I am very grateful to the Luxembourg School of Religion & Societey for the support I received to prepare this article during my period as visiting professor.

in the last decades on finding solutions for existing conflicts. It can transform into a fruitful debate if other paradigms and contexts are considered and mistrust between actors reduced; the Euro-American model may be opened and enriched by other concepts so that it may be applied globally.

2 God's Law and Civil Law or Religious versus Secular Norms

To understand the link between God's law and civil law, one should bear in mind that a comparison of both concepts does not help. Such an undertaking requires an understanding of both concepts separately, without limiting them or changing their character. The scientific approach of comparative legal studies, which has become a prominent discipline in Western academia, rests on a comparison of different legal concepts from different states and backgrounds, such as American and French law or Jewish and Islamic legal concepts. Such a comparison cannot be considered an ideal choice according to academic standards because these two concepts (religious and secular) cannot be put on equal footing. Secular law has dominated modern democratic societies for decades; it is being continuously developed and has become the prototype for political and social concepts worldwide (Salaymeh 2015, 153). Religious law, in stark comparison, has been marginalized and allocated in many cases to the private sphere, resulting in its stagnation. Thus, religious law cannot be in use without modernisation. In addition to the dominance of secular law in modern democratic societies, the self-perception of secular and religious people regarding their respective legal concepts makes any discussion very difficult: Religious conservative groups still believe the absolute superiority of religious norms and imbue them with sanctity. They make the argument that it is God's law and is thus neither comparable with man-made law nor able to be changed. Secular institutions and actors, on the contrary, demonstrate pride in secular legal concepts and do not see any benefit of bringing religion back to the sphere of public debate. Furthermore, they understand religious law as a rigid conception that is unable to cope with change and development (Zubaida 2005, 338).

The accumulation of concepts and definitions for religious and secular concepts such as 'religious', 'secular', and 'civil' accompanied the development of modern legal studies in the last decades, and has contributed in many cases and regions to a confusing situation (Casanova 2011; van der Ven 2014, 278). Thus, religious law, God's law, secular, civil, positive, common, and private law are now used interchangeably – not only in current discourse – but also within academic spheres. The concepts of God's law and religious law are therefore often employed in a confusing way. To clarify this, let us assume that God's law and religious law are not the same; God and God's law are two distinct entities and should be distinguished. God's law is currently understood as religious law and religious scriptures as the exclusive sources of religious law. Therefore, God's law automatically refers to a sacred legal concept. Accordingly, if religious law is understood as sacred and unchangeable, this closes the door to any interpretation or debate. Therefore, dialogue shifts from debating the contents of religious law and secular law to a superficial discussion about the potential for religious law to be interpreted or changed. This last point instils fear in both religious and secular groups. Religious groups largely believe that the opening of religious legal concepts for discussion would allow secularists to attack these concepts and introduce changes. Secularists, in turn, fear that any attempt to develop or discuss religious law would allow classical legal concepts to return to the centre of public interest. The ongoing debate on Sharia law and civil law illustrates this situation both in Western States and the Islamic World. This debate is always rife with misunderstandings: On one hand Muslim conservative groups strongly believe that Sharia is God's law and therefore sacred, and cannot be modified (Zubaida 2005, 440). On the other hand, their secular counterparts see Sharia as a closed, unchangeable concept, thus arguing to keep it outside of the debate because it is considered to be inviolable (Duderija 2011, 63). Both understandings are in error, however: God's law, as it is manifested in Sharia law, is not necessarily religious and it is largely not considered to be sacred. Sharia, which is wrongly considered as God's law, consists mainly of two parts: The first consists of Quranic norms which comprise a small number of verses – between 200 and 500 verses out of more than 6000 verses. These verses are not comprehensible without a linguistic and religious explanation and consist mainly of general guidance that needs to be accommodated to the modern life of Muslims (Rohe 2014, 10–21). This has led to the proliferation of Islamic legal concepts in different regions. The second part consists of legal literature, which comprises interpretations of general norms by legal experts according to various contexts (Zubaida 2005, 440). This latter part is the most important component of Islamic law and needs to be interpreted in order to accommodate lived reality (Rohe 2014, 97–209). Thus, God's law is not as sacred as people may believe, but this should not be a reason to mistreat it, or to mistreat religious people. One should distinguish between God as a meta-legal concept and God's law or Sharia law as a concept developed by human beings over centuries. Rafael Domingo argues for an appropriate distinction between God and religion to reintroduce God into secular society. He calls on secular legal systems to understand God as a meta-legal concept and hypothesises that this will contribute to the reconciliation of religion with secular systems. It would thus be the first step to the integration of religion into a secular legal system (Domingo 2016, 8).

The discussion on God and God's law applies to other monotheistic religions. There are many parallels and similarities between Islamic, Jewish, and Christian legal understandings in this regard (Salaymeh 2015, 160). The first consequence of this argument is to recognize a similarity between God's law, that is to say religious law, and civil or secular law as legal concepts. These two latter concepts (secular and religious legal conceptions) have been mostly elaborated and developed by human beings, so that the law of Islam, as it is used by Muslims, is created by legal experts.

The law of the church, as is used by Christians, is created by human beings. This clarification contributes to the de-specialisation of religious law without depriving it of its sacred character (Casanova 1994, 211–234). The sacred aspect of religious law is not manifested in the mummification of God's words, but rather in the moral dimension of engaging with these norms and taking them as guidelines. This general dimension of religion is currently reflected in the main goals of the religion (*maqāṣid*) in the debate on Islamic law. These *maqāṣid* tackle Sharia from its general ethical perspective and not from its legal perspective (Kamali 1999, 193). This perspective can open this concept to new interpretations and positive change – unfortunately, this trend is still nascent and is not very popular among Muslims. The legal systems of most of the Islamic states are Western-oriented and not dominated by religious law. Even considering family law in Islamic states as being rooted in religious concepts or as being strongly influenced by the law of Islam, is incorrect. Family law in most of the Islamic states underwent several reforms and codifications so that it looks different to classical concepts and is strongly influenced by Western secular conceptions.

Be that as it may, let us envisage the dispute regarding public space, which constitutes the main subject of debate between religious and civil legal concepts. The apex of this debate is the concept of human rights and its principles. Human rights are based in the International Declaration of Human Rights of 1948 and have been the basis of several regional and bilateral legal conventions. A human rights framework is the leading reference for legal concepts of democratic societies and provides guidelines for other international legal concepts (An Na'im 2008, 83–85). Encased within human rights concepts is the principle of religious freedom – a critical point for navigating the relationship between civil and religious law. This principle is consistently used as an argument whenever the principle of neutrality of the public space is discussed. The principle of neutrality is the basis for the main element of secular law that is employed in this debate. Freedom of religion generally means the right to display both religious faith and religious symbols. The principle of equality demands the equal treatment of all religions and of believers and non-believers. In discussions of pluralistic societies, the principle of neutrality is employed to reconcile this. In modern societies, neutrality is understood as the neutrality of the state, which means that the state does not interfere in any religion. Yet, it also has a responsibility to limit absolute religious freedom to prioritise the neutrality of the public sphere. The principle of religious freedom encompasses the right to both active and passive belief i.e., to believe or not to believe and to demonstrate this in public. Furthermore, religious freedom guarantees the presentation of one's own faith in an active way, such as wearing religious clothing, building religious structures, celebrating holidays, as well as implementing religious education and carrying out circumcision and animal slaughter as part of religious ceremonies. All these rights may be limited or in some way restricted by other principles of human rights such as human dignity and physical integrity (Rohe 2007, 79).

The Islamic headscarf, animal slaughter, religious and secular law, and religious education at public schools are all under intense scrutiny in Western societies. While this debate mainly focuses on contradictory understandings of religious freedom in Western democratic societies, the debate in Muslim states mainly revolves around principles of gender equality as well as the equality between people from different religious backgrounds. The principle of equality involves issues of inheritance and family law, such as marriage and divorce. In contrast to civil law where religious actors are still arguing for the adoption of several Sharia norms and see them as still valid; trade law as well as several aspects of the economy and scientific areas are mostly secular and 'Westernised' to a wide extent not only in states where religious law has been reformed such as Tunisia, but also in those Muslim states where Sharia law is still active and represents the main reference of legal norms, such as Saudi Arabia. Noteworthy in this regard is that both secularists and moderate religious people in Muslim states argue for changing the law to accommodate and promote equality between men and women. Conservatives, on the contrary, argue for conserving classical concepts and see their preservation as a sign of identity. The debate between these two groups has reached its apex in the last years, when new legal concepts – such as in Tunisia and Morocco etc. – suggested the equality between men and women in view of inheritance and responsibility and have been passed to parliament to be signed.

3 Islamic Legal Concept as a Touchstone for the Relation between Religious and Civil Legal Concepts

The ongoing debate concerning public space in Western societies is mainly focused on the interchange between Muslims and the Islamic legal concepts with secular law. I will therefore focus the following discussion on the main issues of the debate on Sharia and public space. In Western Europe, the debate on Sharia and civil law is shaped by the permanent existence of Muslim minorities in Europe over the last decades. Their presence has engendered more visibility of Muslim religious symbols and rituals such as prayer-houses, headscarves, etc. Regardless of whether those symbols are legally recognized by European states, they do exist and are challenging even in those states where the relationship between religious communities and the nation state is harmonious. The pinnacle of the debate is the resilience of the principle of religious freedom when it is applied to new religious groups. To distil the arguments used in this debate at least in one aspect, both concepts of law are inspired by their respective understanding of human rights. This often results in greater confusion, in that every group, including the state, attempts their own distinctive interpretation of human rights as opposed to a common one. On the one hand, religious freedom is meant to guarantee the free exercise of religious rituals. On the other hand, secular legal concepts are designed to regulate this freedom such that every religious group has the same rights and space. In fact, the ideology of the state in this regard is based on the principle of neutrality. Neutrality is achieved by regulating public space and limiting any religious or cultural imagery that would disturb that neutrality. An alternative concept that manages the public sphere and allows the existence of all religious symbols does not yet exist. Therefore, neutrality of public space can be understood as the limitation of religious freedom. This modality is not always effective and constructive, especially for those religious groups that did not experience such limitation before.

As mentioned, the discussion on religious freedom described above has its roots in human rights. Human rights defend freedom of religion without limitation, so that any religious group and individual can practice his or her religion based on this principle. The issues of the Islamic headscarf, male circumcision, religious education, minarets for mosques, as well as religious marriage are all being debated in this framework. The arguments of those who call for a limitation of these rituals are related to the principle of neutrality of the public space, which is a secular virtue. Nevertheless, neutrality has different meanings and cannot be limited to a restrictive interpretation. There exist at least three different models of secularism and its reconciliation with religious freedom regarding the relationship between church and state in Western democratic societies: the British-American model, the French, and the German model (Asad 2003, 6). All these models have adopted different solutions to the question of Muslim religious symbols and their visibility in public space. The appearance of the headscarf in the public sphere has been seen as a threat to the principle of secularity in France and has led to a ban of the hijab in the public sphere and public administration. On the contrary, the wearing of religious symbols is accepted and not questioned in Britain and the USA. In Germany, the issue is still up for debate and all suggested solutions are still under consideration (Rohe 2016, 279).[2] It is quite interesting that both religious groups and the secular state base their arguments on human rights. Muslims who wear a headscarf or circumcise their male children understand these rituals and symbols as a religious obligation and they justify their decisions with religious arguments from the religious scriptures as well as other legal concepts. By performing these rituals, they follow a strict religious obligation. More precisely, for religious people who want to fulfil their religious duties, but suffer from a number of restrictions in this regard, the question becomes clear: Which shall I obey, God's law or man-made law? The answer to this question is well-known: "Then Peter and the other apostles answered and said, we ought to obey God rather than men" (Acts 5:29). This question and the answer are both over-simplified. Many religious obligations have different interpretations within

---

[2] The Yearbook of Muslims in Europe is currently one of the leading references for this subject. It appears almost yearly and contains the state of the art on the situation of Muslim minorities in Europe.

the religious legal tradition so that one can distinguish between different categories of obligation. Yet secular legal systems have promised every citizen a margin of freedom such that everyone can live peacefully and have sufficient religious liberty to practice their religion. Moreover, the lives of religious minorities who have always benefitted from religious freedom as a guarantee and understood it as a non-limited right to freedom are disrupted whenever they are limited in the extent or manner in which they may exercise this right. This question reflects conflicting understandings of religious freedom: While religious minorities consider religious freedom as guaranteed and unlimited, local authorities refer to human rights and local civil law to argue against this religious understanding of freedom. This can lead to clashes on both sides of the debate. The situation has become more problematic within the last years because of the issues of child marriage, polygamy and domestic violence which are both related to religious Islamic law. All acts are justified in religious scriptures of Islam and conservative religious groups see them as a part of the religious dogmas, while Muslim mainstream society does not understand them as such, and many Muslim intellectuals see the need to change them to meet the international norms of life in the modern world. Thus, the debate shifted from dealing with separated cases on a regional and local level to a general question that affects the stability of entire societies. Because the rules of the game are still written by secular legal systems, religious groups are currently given three solutions to cope with secular systems. The final report of the research project ReligioWest (2016) summarises the situation for religious groups in three options; it argues that religious communities

> are confronted with a choice between three options: 1) to withdraw into private sphere for individuals, or to the 'ghetto' for communities (Amish, Lubavitch), 2) to acknowledge the divorce and to claim, for mainstream churches, 'clear exemptions' and 'consciousness objection', 3) to reformulate religious norms in a way that is acceptable by the secular rationality, in a word, to 'reform' religion (a constant call addressed to Islam, but also to the Catholic Church). (Roy 2016, 6)

These options are still on the table for Muslim communities as well. The debate among Muslim communities regarding this issue is still lacking consistent answers. The fundamentalist approach does not recognize the modern state but is practiced by a small minority of Muslims (Rohe 2016, 280). Rather, it seems that most of the Muslims living in western societies is interested in finding a balance between religion and civil law in term of establishing a modus-vivendi that takes into consideration the specific character of the Islamic faith. While Muslim communities and official institutions do not provide answers to the question of how state-religion interchange should be and how Muslims should behave regarding this issue, some Muslim intellectuals try to advance some solutions. Abdullahi An-Na'im proposes ideas to establish a symbiosis with the concept of secularity and secular states. He emphasizes that Muslims should distinguish between secular state and secular society; that a secular state is a guarantee for everyone so that secularism does not present any threat to the Muslim faith (An Na'im 2008, 1).

In addition to the practical issues related to the current questions of secular and religious law, there is a theoretical one: How Muslims see the law of Islam and how they understand it. This question is relevant for both Western states where Muslim minorities live and in the Islamic word. The available data on this subject are somewhat confusing. The available quantitative data about Muslims, which were mostly gathered by European and American research institutions, insist on the fact that Islam is resistant to secularism and that most Muslims are religious or consider themselves as religious (Pew Research Center 2013, 2–5). This research presents this religiosity as a sign of the preference of religious law over secular law among Muslims. Sami Zubaida summarises these assumptions as follows:

> The idea that Islam is particularly resistant to secularization is common in public discourse, both in the West and in the "Islamic world", but with different evaluations. For religious and political Muslims, it is held with pride, as a steadfast attachment to God and his revelations, valid for all times. For Western commentators, it is part of Muslim (and Arab) exceptionalism – impervious to the march of modernity and progress, heralded by the West and followed in so many parts of the world, most recently South and East Asia and China. (Zubaida 2005, 438)

This assumption needs more clarification and specification, particularly because of the strong lack of religious information and knowledge among Muslims and non-Muslims about Islamic law, so that Sharia in many cases, appears to be tantamount to the Quran and the literal interpretation of the scripture. This perspective is gaining more ground through modern media (Powell 2016, 124). When we debate this issue from the perspective of the Muslims, we should always mention the existence of different positions and groups. Adis Duderija has presented two main groups and conceptions which are diametrically opposed to each other on the issue of religious law: The new salafi (traditionalist) one, which argues for conserving the traditional understanding of religious law and claims that this is the best way to preserve Muslim faith, while the progressive liberal interpreter argues for the adoption of Western legal concepts instead of insisting on the validity of the classical one (Duderija 2011, 63). A third group can be added; namely, specialists who try to strike a balance. This group could be identified as reformers i.e., Muslim specialists in Islamic law who argue for a reform of classical Islamic legal concepts to meet international standards while trying to find a balance between religious faith and modern legal concepts. However, this last group is very small, still understudied and has no weight in the debate.

The legal concepts of the majority of the Muslim modern states have been inspired by western legal conceptions (Otto 2010, 14). Further, secularism has been often seen as a sign of modernisation in that region, yet secularisation was not – in contrast to the European case – reached through the ban of religion, but through cooperation between secular and religious authorities. Thus, it may be said that the local debate on religious law and secular law manifests other dimensions than those in the European case (Asad 2003, 205).³ Moreover, the majority of Muslim states are employing Western concepts of secular law, which is mostly the result either of the importation of Western legal concepts such as the Turkish case after 1924 or a sort of reformed Sharia-law as the case in Egypt and many other states. Additionally, the thesis of the contradiction between reality and theory in Islamic law which dominated the reception of Islamic law in Western academia for long time has been disproved by recent scholars such as Hallaq and Johansen (Johansen 1999, 189–191; Hallaq 2009, 1419). Accordingly, Sharia is now defined in its whole theoretical and practical conception. The debate on legal concepts and the linkage between secular and religious norms in Muslim states has focused on a small area of a larger terrain of legal discourse. While branches of law related to purely secular sectors such as trade and natural sciences are exclusively dominated by secular norms, the area of private law and civil law do encompass some issues in relation to religion and religious law. Historically speaking, this debate began after the process of secularisation had already started. Secularisation commenced in the nineteenth century in the Islamic world and accompanied the establishment of the nation state; it has likewise led to the establishment of secular oriented constitutions and legal systems (Asad 2003, 208).

4 Beyond the Myth of Religious versus Secular Law

Within the debate on religious and secular legal norms, we can ascertain the existence of a state of stagnation both in Europe and the Islamic world. This is not only due to the mistrust and misunderstandings between secular states and religious groups, but also to the fact that these subjects are still being debated within classical models and paradigms, where new approaches and methodological statements are expected. This leads to the question: Is secularism the last word in this debate? Does the concept of secularism appear to be as dogmatically unchangeable as religious scriptures? Is religious law not changeable? And in the event of its malleability, in which dimension is this possible?

The evidence that secularism and secular systems have become the leading concepts for managing life in modern societies is so clear that even several Muslim thinkers and theologians consider secularism as the best concept for Muslims because it guarantees the separation between state and religion. Abdullahi An-Na'im calls on Muslims both in the West and the Islamic world to adopt and acknowledge secularity because it guarantees religious freedom (An Na'im 2008, 1–4). He distinguishes between secular states and secular societies, incites Muslims to adopt secularism and sees it as very helpful to Muslims in modern contexts (An Na'im 2008, 1–44). Other leading Western thinkers have suggested some solutions for managing

---

3 Asad focusses on the transformation that occurred in Egypt.

the relation between religion and secular states. Charles Taylor has proposed a campaign of reasonable accommodation, meaning that the secular individual should accept religious signs and practice that do not mean anything for them "while religious communities should not try to impose their norms on secular society [...] both sides must make concessions" (Roy 2016, 8). Taylor's recommendation for the region of Quebec explains how this principle should work (Bouchard and Taylor 2008, 51). In another issue Taylor suggests symbiosis as a moral, political, and social ideology for the future (Taylor 2006, 117–142). The solution proposed by Habermas for fruitful living together in modern societies consists of the fact that

> the secular character of the state is a necessary though not a sufficient condition for guaranteeing equal religious freedom for everybody. It is not enough to rely on the condescending benevolence of a secularized authority that comes to tolerate minorities hitherto discriminated against. The parties themselves must reach agreement on the always contested delimitations between a positive liberty to practice a religion of one's own and the negative liberty to remain spared from the religious practices of the others. (Habermas 2006, 4)

He states further:

> Fair arrangements can only be found if the parties involved learn to take the perspectives of the others. The procedure that fits this purpose best is the deliberative mode of democratic will formation. In the secular state, government has to be placed on a non-religious footing anyway. The liberal constitution must flesh out the loss of legitimation caused by a secularization that deprives the state of deriving its authority from God. From the practice of constitution-making, there emerge those basic rights that free and equal citizens must accord one another if they wish to regulate their co-existence reasonably on their own and by means of positive law. (Habermas 2006, 4–5)

The three solutions presented above to religious groups which were differently adopted by secular legal systems seem to be insufficient and the debate is currently stagnating. This stagnation contributed in Western societies to the strengthening of many extremist parties on both sides and secular states are still looking for solutions. In the Islamic world, the debate consists obviously of a reinterpretation of those ideas and arguments about the relation between Sharia and secular law which were presented decades before. As a way to get out of the vicious cycle of religious vs. secular the authors of the EU- report *Rethinking the place of religion in European secularized societies: the need for more open societies* (2016), argue for adopting a multi-level approach that reconsiders the liberal understanding of religious freedom and reconciles religion with human rights and modern societies. This consists of 1) defending freedom of religion as a specific freedom; 2) maintaining the separation of Church and State, because "The separation protects the State from the Church, but it also prevents secular states from interfering with theology." 3) understanding religion as an autonomous sphere, 4) looking at human rights as truly universal, rather than European (Roy 2016, 9–10). Regarding the concept of God's law, Raphael Domingo argues that the secular legal system should protect the right to religion and not only a right to freedom of religion (Domingo 2016, 113–114). He also insists on the need to have different approaches to the interchange between state and religion, so that we have a better understanding of the situation, instead of having a closed and exclusive secular Western system (Domingo 2016, 2). Domingo argues further for the replacement of the principle of neutrality – as a principle of behaviour within a secular system – by pluralism. Accordingly, God's law would then be a legal system within a multiplicity of systems.

As mentioned before, both secular and religious actors need to confront the fact that God's law does not exist as a sacred unchangeable law. As far as Islam and European Muslims are concerned, the debate is currently dominated by the permanent discussion on the relation of Muslim religious organisations and communities to secular states and secular legal conceptions. This discussion also touches on the relation of these Muslim organisations to Muslim states, the so-called homeland, such as Turkey or Morocco. In this regard one can say that the relation of Muslim European communities to the states where they live is still impacted by scepticism. This character shadows almost all aspects of the debate and cooperation between both parties. As a case in point, the question related to Islamic education at state schools has been declining for decades, due to the lack of trust between both sides (Khalfaoui 2019, 71–81). This is due not only to the mistrust of Western states vis-à-vis certain Muslim religious organisations and groups; it is also due to the lack of structures and channels of communication between both Muslim organisation and stakeholders. As far as Muslim communities are concerned, one can say that scepticism vis-à-vis rulers and politicians is rooted in the Muslim social history and still shadows their relation to politics even today. This is due to the repressive ideology adopted by several Muslim dynasties and states vis-à-vis their populations and religious organisations. The problematic behaviour of several Muslim modern national states with religion since the downfall of the Ottoman Empire 1022 is a case in point (Khalfaoui 2017, 89–101). Within a short time, religion and religious organisation have been marginalized and lost their value both in politics and religious affairs. This was a shock for them, and it still has an impact on their relation to politics. On the other hand, the relation of Muslim communities to Western states is shaped by what we can call a politic of take and give. On the one hand, European states still think of relations to minorities within the framework of how many rights can be given to these minorities. This often leads to the fact that minorities strive to get as many rights as possible. This strategy of both parties is not constructive and contra productive; it strengthens particularism and completion between minorities and harms pluralism and plurality. On the other hand, negotiation with every minority separately has proven inefficient for stakeholders worldwide, because it weakens the central state. Therefore, I would like to argue that it would be far more helpful for Muslims living in Western democratic societies to avoid particularism. Particularism leads to marginalisation and loss of any common sense with other groups. Muslims must stop exclusively defending the Muslim faith and Muslim cause; they should understand the Muslim faith as being an intrinsic part of the entire system of values and norms that exists in society (Khalfaoui 2018, 281). Strengthening one strong right for all groups would contribute to a better debate on religion and secularism; this will offer more rights both for religious and non-religious people. Though problematic in several ways, secularism has proven to be one of the most efficient models and frameworks for regulating the relation between religious and secular groups as well between individuals, regardless of their religious background. Secularism could be improved by political participation and debate to fit to the recommendations of a modern democratic and pluralistic society.

Bibliography

An Na'im, Abdullahi Ahmad. 2008. *Islam and the Secular State: Negotiating the Future of Shariʿa*. Cambridge, MA: Harvard University Press.

Asad, Talal. 2003. *Formations of the Secular: Christianity, Islam, Modernity*. Stanford: Stanford University Press.

Barzilai, Gad. 2007. *Law and Religion*. Aldershot: Ashgate.

Bouchard, Gérard, and Charles Taylor. 2008. *Building the Future: A Time for Reconciliation: Abridges Report*. Québec: Commission de consultation sur les pratiques d'accomodement reliées aux différences culturelles.

Casanova, José. 1994. *Public Religions in the Modern World*. Chicago: The University of Chicago Press.

Casanova, José. 2011. "The Secular, Secularisations, Secularism." In *Rethinking Secularism*, edited by Mark Juergensmeyer, Jonathan VanAntwerpen, and Craig J. Calhoun, Oxford / New York: Oxford University Press, 56–74.

Domingo, Rafael. 2016. *God and the Secular Legal System*. Cambridge / New York: Cambridge University Press.

Duderija, Adis. 2011. *Constructing a Religiously Ideal 'Believer' and 'Woman' in Islam: Neo-Traditional Salafi and Progressive Muslims' Methods of Interpretation*. New York: Palgrave Macmillan.

Habermas, Jürgen. 2006. "Religion in the Public Sphere." *European Journal of Philosophy* 14:1–25.

Hallaq, Wael B. 2009. *An Introduction to Islamic Law*. Cambridge / New York: Cambridge University Press.

Johansen, Baber. 1999. *Contingency in a Sacred Law: Legal and Ethical Norms in the Muslim Fiqh*. Studies in Islamic Law and Society 7. Leiden: Brill.

Kamali, Muhamad Hashim. 1999. "'Maqāṣid al-Sharīʿah': The Objectives of Islamic Law." *Islamic Studies* 38:193–208.

Khalfaoui, Mouez. 2017. "Public Theology and Democracy." In: *Religion and Democracy: Studies in Public Theology*, edited by Torsten Meireis and Rolf Schieder, Baden-Baden: Nomos, 89–101.

Khalfaoui, Mouez. 2018. "Maqasid ash-Shariʿa as Legitimization for the Muslim Minorities Law." In *The Objectives of Islamic Law: The Promises and Challenges of the Maqāṣid al-Shariʿa*, edited by Idris Nassery, Rumee Ahmed, and Muna Tatari, Lanham: Lexington Books, 271–284.

Khalfaoui, Mouez. 2019. "Zwischen Vertrauen und Skepsis. Die Beziehungen von Staat und Religion im Islam." In *Rechtliche Optionen für Kooperationen zwischen deutschem Staat und muslimischen Gemeinschaften*, edited by Karlies Abmeier, Andreas Jacobs, and Thomas Köhler, Münster: Aschendorff Verlag, 71–81.

Otto, Jan Michiel. 2010. *Sharia Incorporated: A Comparative Overview of the Legal Systems of Twelve Muslim Countries in Past and Present*, Leiden: Leiden University Press.

Pew Research Center. 2013. The World's Muslims: Religion, Politics and Society, 41–58. http://www.pewforum.org/2013/04/30/the-worlds-muslims-religion-politics-society-beliefs-about-sharia/ (29.11.2021).

Powell, Russell. 2016. *Shari'a in the Secular State Evolving Meanings of Islamic Jurisprudence in Turkey*. Law, Language and Communication. New York: Routledge.

Rohe, Mathias. 2007. *Muslim Minorities and the Law in Europe: Chances and Challenges*. New Delhi: Global Media Publications.

Rohe, Mathias. 2014. *Islamic Law in Past and Present*. Themes in Islamic Studies 8. Leiden: Brill.

Rohe, Mathias. 2016. "Germany." *Yearbook of Muslims in Europe* 7:272–288.

Roy, Olivier. 2016. "Rethinking the Place of Religion in European Secularized Societies: The Need for More Open Societies." Florence: European University Institute. http://www.eurel.info/IMG/pdf/rw-rethinking_the_place_of_religion.pdf (29.11.2021).

Salaymeh, Lena. 2015. "'Comparing' Jewish and Islamic Legal Traditions: Between Disciplinar and Critical Historical Jurisprudence." *Critical Analysis of Law* 2:153–172.

Taylor, Charles. 2006. *Symbiosism*. Lanham: Hamilton Books.

Ven, Johannes A. van der. 2014. "From Divine Law to Positive Law. A Perspective from the Science of Religion." In *Secular and Sacred? The Scandinavian Case of Religion in Human Rights, Law and Public Space*, edited by Rosemarie van den Breemer, José Casanova, and Trygve Wyller, Göttingen: Vandenhoeck & Ruprecht, 278–311.

Zubaida, Sami. 2005. "Islam and Secularization." *Asian Journal of Social Science* 33:438–448.

Wilhelm Gräb
Life Interpretation and Religion

1 Introduction

Religion places our lives within a larger frame of interpretation. It relates life to a higher, transcendent order. It gives life a deeper meaning and a sense of the unconditional. Religion makes it possible to remain capable of action even when events occur in which no more meaning can be found, and when challenging transitions and crises have to be overcome.

If religion is understood as an interpretation of life, then religion belongs to the sociality of humans (Luckmann 2014; Hoult 1967). However, in the cultural context of Germany and Europe, which are the primary focus of this chapter, this understanding of religion seems to have lost its persuasive power. Many speak of an inexorably advancing secularization (Pollack 2012). They refer here above all to the continuing loss of members of the churches and a forgetting of the Christian message of God (Taylor 2007), which they interpret as lack of interest in lived religion in general.

This chapter presents arguments that prove the cultural presence of lived religion as an interpretation of life, even in supposedly secularized Europe. The change in values in modern Western societies has a strong impact on religious behaviour. Lived religion has become individualized and pluralized. However, just as it is a place for the communication of a religious interpretation of life, the church remains socially relevant. Participation in the church's life rituals (*Kasualien*) is also changing significantly. Nevertheless, the church continues to be a cultural site of symbolic and ritual interpretations of life.

2 Transformation of Values

Many sociologists agree that since the 1970s values have significantly changed, both in Germany and in Western societies in general (Klages 1985; Inglehart 1989, 1997; Reckwitz 2017). There was a massively increased emphasis on the importance of values such as freedom, autonomy, equality and humanity. This shows a clear devaluation of the values associated with tradition and convention, loyalty, deference, and conformity.

The new values of autonomy and self-development are far more open to a wide range of definitions than the earlier values of convention and tradition were. They refer to each individual's own subjectivity and require continuous self-examination and discursive negotiation. Ultimately, others do not have the right to decide which life path, which partnership, which friends are the right ones for me, or to whom I want to commit myself for how long, and where I want to be involved and how intensively. The self-confidence that something is right and appropriate for me becomes an important criterion for the relationship to my life partners or friends, and decisions about the course of education, profession or search for job offers.

Since the 1970s lived religion has also been drawn into the wake of this claim to autonomy. Religion is no longer just what is objectively referred to as 'religion' or 'church'. Religion is now also what the individual understands by the notion, so that the reference that the individual makes to what he or she understands by religion and communicates as religion is also part of the concept of religion. 'Religion' has become synonymous with interpretations of life related to one's own subjectivity (Gräb 2006a, 46–55).

'Religion' – the term used in the singular – means a human capacity that should be understood as a dimension of human life evoking the questions of where we come from and where we are going, and what makes our lives meaningful in a greater context. This religious attitude to life we can perform or ignore, but there is no doubt that it is part of us as self-conscious human beings. In order to distinguish 'religion' in the singular, understood as a human capacity and as a human attitude to the transcendent wholeness of reality, from the institutionalized 'religions' in the plural, the concept of spirituality has been pervasive in the religious field and in the studies of religion as well. The term 'spirituality' is increasingly used to describe religion as a form of life interpretation not only open to the transcendent wholeness of reality, but also realizing expressions of a deep feeling of connectedness with that dimension grounding one's own existence and fulfilling it with a deeper sense of meaning (Gräb 2008; Knoblauch 2007). Nevertheless, although spiritual attitude knows itself to be free in its relation to the ideas and practices of different religions and of the church, we would be misguided not to recognize that in modern societies, the behaviour of the majority of church members in their religious practices also more or less actualizes the concept of spirituality. They practice their relationship to the church not in accordance with traditional churchly norms, but rather in terms of whether they feel moved themselves by its spiritual dimensions.

The spiritual interest in specific occasions during the course of life, marked by the stages of a normal biography, determines their relationship to the church for the majority of church members. Most church members come to the church for baptisms and confirmations, weddings, and funerals, at school enrolment celebrations, at Christmas and other church holidays, as long as they also have a cultural significance for society. What moves these members to take part in these church rituals? If we are to get a deeper theological understanding of this, we have to see it is the integration of fragmented identity and an acknowledgment of the individual searching within a broader context for the interpretation that the Christian story of salvation is offering (Weyel 2008).

3 Transformation of Values and Lived Religion

As we know from church membership studies (Bedford-Strohm and Jung 2015), despite individualization and secularization church membership in Germany is still largely based on convention and tradition. People come to the church especially at the transitional stages in the life and annual cycle. Then they demand symbols and rituals that place the life of the individual within the frame of the Christian story and thereby in a larger wholeness of reality embracing the physical and metaphysical context, promising God's blessing, protection, and guidance.

One can certainly say that what holds most people in church is their interest in life rituals with which the church stages symbols of the Christian interpretation of life in an aesthetically appealing and personally engaging way. Even if people are in the church predominantly because of tradition and convention, their behaviour as church members engages spiritual interest that seeks an integration of personal identity into a broader horizon of meaning represented by religious symbols and rituals. Nobody forces people to stay in church; if they do so, it is because they do not want to lose the Christian-religious framework of a worldview, life interpretation and production of meaning that for them belongs to the cultural setting of their way of life.

Insofar as the church itself can do something to be or remain attractive for its members and those who might become members, it must therefore start with an acknowledgement of the potential of the rituals of life for a spiritually meaningful interpretation of life. Those who attend church do so ultimately based on their life-oriented spiritual interests. However, the dissolution of church membership must not be understood as an act of spiritual lack of interest. Most often, before leaving the church, people take stock. A cost-benefit calculation is made. What is my personal benefit of staying in the church? Is the effort, including the financial effort, justified? Obviously, their spiritual interests remain active, but the church may no longer be the place where people search for satisfaction of their spiritual needs.

The transformation of values in modern culture is also becoming increasingly prevalent in religious relations. Instead of orienting oneself in terms of tradition and convention, people follow their own spiritual aspirations much more. Correspondingly, those who are responsible for church leadership now see their responsibility for reflecting on the spiritual needs of the people. What makes the church important for the people is that it helps them to enlarge their capacities for coping with life's crises and the disruptive experiences of contingencies by opening the transcendent dimension of reality and witnessing God's faithful presence. The service of the church is called upon when previous orientations become fragile or are lost and existential questions of meaning arise.

On the one hand, religion lived in this way is highly individualized, partly under the roof of the large, institutionalized church, and on the other hand, it is free-floating, producing hybrid forms. The formerly binding forces of religious communities have become rather fluid energies. Thus, new religious energy centres are constantly forming from which high levels of spiritual, social and/or cultural attractiveness emanates, but mostly only for a limited time, bound to special places and special, charismatic personalities. These are global trends, but in Europe, too, free churches may reach higher numbers locally and temporarily, but seldom for a longer period of time and hardly ever on a broad scale.

In view of the declining number of church members and the loosened form of membership by the majority of church members in Germany and the broader European context, it is sometimes also argued that the future could belong to fundamentalist and charismatic forms of religion, because they offer a clear and strong sense of commitment and orientation (Riesebrodt [2000] 2001; Graf 2014; Graf and Hartmann 2018). It is true that the churches, which are growing dynamically in the case in sub-Saharan Africa, Latin America, and East Asia, for example, give the impression that they can convince their followers by a strong message of faith and can discipline them by imposing rigid norms of behaviour. However, their success is largely also based on helping individuals to gain an identity that makes them feel better and able to cope with the challenges of life. The binding forces that these churches release do not result primarily from normative demands and commitments, but from the promise that new forms of life empowerment arise from the energy of faith (Berger 2010; Cox 1995).

The success of the Pentecostal and Charismatic churches in the global South is essentially based on their ability to respond to spiritual, social, and economic needs. However, the aim is not to silence people with their message, but to release the self-activation of people through the aesthetic, emotionally moving staging of their symbols and rituals. In the foreground are not doctrine and dogma, nor church-institutional claims to obligations and normative concepts, but a decisive focus on what people need and what they can do to be fulfilled with the Holy Spirit in spiritual, social, and economic terms. These churches offer people the chance to thrive in precarious situations and contexts as people possessed of their own dignity and their enormous capacity for action (Öhlmann, Gräb, and Frost 2020).

What is different in the global South? There the churches stand for a particular way of life. They accompany people not only over the course of their lives; they convey a spiritual interpretation of life, a concept of meaning and a set of values in the light of the Christian faith. In largely unstable social, economic, and political conditions, the churches and religions play an important role to promote the sustainable development of society as a whole (Öhlmann, Frost, and Gräb 2016).

In enormously functionally differentiated Western societies religion fulfils its specific function as vigorously as possible. Religion deals with the questions we humans face when we are confronted with the limits of our human capacities and contingencies that we cannot transform into meaningful actions (Luhmann and Kieserling 2007). Religion arises in the awareness of our finiteness, of sin and guilt, and today above all in the light of the doubt about the meaning of the whole. Religion deals with the question of how life can reach its fullness and be experienced as a potential of human flourishing despite finiteness, sin, and guilt (Gräb 2006b).

The themes of religion are the themes of a religious interpretation of life that reaches down to the depths of reality. They are the themes that we encounter in the Christian story of the triune God: The Creator, Reconciler, and Redeemer. The experience of finiteness corresponds to faith in God the Creator. The fate of sin and guilt is overcome by the orientation towards the reconciling work of Christ. Doubt about the meaning of the whole is countered by trust in the encouraging and renewing power of the Holy Spirit.

The church is expected to work on a sustainable interpretation of life even in crises and at the turning points of life. At the same time, however, these questions also arise for people in their everyday lives. Responses to these questions are negotiated in the networks of the lifeworld, yet any reference to the Christian story is usually not explicitly established. However, it would again be wrong to come to the conclusion that, as a result of the increasing disappearance of the traditional language of the Christian faith in terms narrating the Christian story, the desire for and work on the topics of a spiritual interpretation of life would also have been lost.

4 'Lived Religion' and Church Relationship

Practical Theology in the German-speaking world has long been engaged in a heated debate about whether the decline in the number of church members, the weak participation in Sunday services, the loss of social relevance of the churches is leading to a gradual disappearance of religion (Wegner 2015; Pollack and Wegner 2017). Some Practical Theologians affirm this, now also in the evaluation of the last Church Membership Survey of the "Evangelische Kirche in Deutschland" (EKD) (Bedford-Strohm and Jung 2015), although they no longer speak of religious "indifference" in the title, as the provisional publication does (Evangelische Kirche in Deutschland 2014). Nevertheless, it continues to use this terminology in a central place. Gert Pickel and Tabea Spieß confirm the non-denominational "religious indifference" which they see as equivalent to "lack of religion" (Pickel and Spieß 2015, 263). Maintaining a distance from the church is equated with a lack of interest in religion and ultimately with lack of religion per se. They do not ask how people respond to the experiences of life that demand the encouragement of meaning making by religious interpretation. Religiousness is most often measured in terms of the knowledge of and agreement with elements of the doctrines and creeds of the Church, but not by the way people behave towards themselves and their lives in terms of self-interpretation open to a transcendent dimension of reality (Pollack 1995, 186).

In an empirical research design that looks to religion as separate from the act of communication, people cannot be understood as possible subjects of their own religious self-understanding. However, what people understand as religion or as their relationship to religion must be discerned according to what they perceive as religiously or spiritually relevant life issues (Nassehi 2009).

5 Lived Religion as Free-Floating Network Communication

The last Church Membership Survey of the EKD (Bedford-Strohm and Jung 2015) adopted a different approach to empirical research on religion and the church. A research team led by Birgit Weyel (Weyel 2015, 339–43) wanted to ascertain in what kinds of social relationships church members address religious issues. The research team initiated a network survey to find out with whom, when and where people talk about religious issues (Weyel, Hermelink and Grubauer 2015, 435–37).

The analysis of this network survey revealed that church members occasionally bring up religious topics, but not so often. They do so mainly in the family, in their circle of friends and at work. Religion becomes a topic of conversation where people can rely on a personal relationship of trust, precisely because it is always a matter of personal questions of life interpretation. That religion is a question of life interpretation also explains why this question is not raised so often in closer contacts. For explicit forms of interpretation, one needs an appropriate vocabulary, which is not so easy to establish. The language used in the church is most often too far removed from the expression of ones' own experiences and thoughts. Therefore, researchers must reflect on the fact that the marginal number of occasions for religious communication in everyday life mirrors the fact that people are not trained to articulate religious experiences, feelings, thoughts and attitudes. Nevertheless, the central question of life which seems open for a religious interpretation is the "question about the meaning of life" (Stegbauer, Grubauer, and Weyel 2015, 414).

This network study regarded church members not only as consumers of the activities of the church, but as religious agents following their own agenda of communicating their personal affairs and also their spiritual interests whenever it seems necessary for them. This marks a new approach in empirical religious studies that offers significant starting points for looking at the occurrence of religious communication beyond the practices of a church relationship (Weyel, Gräb, and Heimbrock 2013).

This explains too why church members do indeed seek contact with the church and the congregation, especially with the pastor, in the context of rituals anchored in life cycles. Apart from its occurrence in everyday life, religious communication takes place in the intimate social relationships of partnership, marriage, family, and circles of friends, but at major turning points, the need for a religious interpretation of life calls for an ecclesiastical elucidation. Then the liturgy of the church is called for, which with its symbols of creation and justification, reconciliation, and redemption, involving the individuals in an interpretative framework that at the same time collectively unites Christianity.

Church and congregations are for church members – this can be stated as a conclusion of the network survey. Church and community will then find access to members (and, I think, far beyond that) when they make an effort to be there to meet the needs.

6 Life Interpretation as Identity- and Self-Formation

There is no reason to assume a growing lack of interest in religion – even in the so-called 'secularized' Western societies. One need not even speak of increasing religious indifference, despite the increasing number of those who do not belong to any church or religious community. On the contrary, if one's basic premise is in people's life interests then a social need for religious communication becomes apparent, but this need is one that derives from the existential questions of life.

As far as the church is concerned, this means that the church should recognize people as sovereign subjects not only of their lives but also of the interpretation of their lives. The church must accept that people are also self-determined in matters of religious or spiritual life. This by no means makes the church's proclamations superfluous, but people want to be able to relate the church's message constructively to the questions of life that arise for them personally.

This is impressively demonstrated by a study by the Institute for the Study of Religions in Bayreuth, which was headed by Christoph Bochinger (Bochinger, Engelbrecht, and Gebhardt 2009).This empirical religious study focused on a new, highly individualized generation of 'believers'. Many people more or less tacitly alluded to the binding claims of the churches and the orthodox demands of theology. They wanted to fulfil their religious needs in an individual way and under their own direction. In doing so, they were convinced of their own competence in religious interpretation. However, this new generation of 'believers' was characterized not only by their sovereign handling of church traditions, teachings and truth claims; they also aimed to test the wide range of spiritual teachings and techniques that are now available in global culture and to examine their suitability for meeting their personal needs. In doing so, novel constellations are created in which Christian and non-Christian ideas and practices are combined, even if they appear incompatible from the perspective of theology and the church.

The Bayreuth study hypothesises that within the Christian churches, and even more so on their periphery and far beyond, new religious patterns of interpretation of life are developing which subtly transform established Christianity and especially its ecclesiastical expressions. It is not religious indifference which is the consequence of a weakening of the church binding forces and the much-lamented breaking off traditions. On the contrary, with the decline of the bonding forces of the church, other powers of religious interpretation have emerged, but above all individuals see themselves increasingly induced, as well as entitled, to behave in religiously self-determined ways. In addition, this fact can be taken up for the theoretically founded and here represented thesis that it is short-sighted to see lived religion solely as a product of socialization. Lived Religion is rather to be understood as a humane act of interpretation of life into which people are repeatedly pushed, one way or another, to explain the experiences of their lives. That is because as human beings they have to lead their lives in a self-conscious way. People cannot avoid the question of what the whole of their own existence in this world is all about – even if there are many, many ways of keeping this question in the background of consciousness.

We see that contemporary religious diagnosis that investigates increasing religious indifference suffers from an inability to distinguish between objective and subjective religion. Undoubtedly, the traditional forms of religious practice have become fragile. They have lost their closeness to people and their everyday lives. Theology and the church can take up this interest by rendering visible the symbols of the Christian faith (creation, sin, reconciliation, redemption) as means of life interpretation. However, if these symbols are to acquire an understandable and convincing meaning for people, they must be recognizable as a form of a deeper self-interpretation.

One does not learn much about the religion lived in everyday life if one looks only at whether people agree with the church's creeds or follow other doctrines and practices of faith (e.g., Zen meditation, anthroposophy, astrology, reincarnation, etc.). It is important to draw people into a conversation about what is convincing to them by addressing what gives meaning to their lives, when they can no longer find such meaning for themselves. What is your trust in life ultimately based on? What gives stability in life when all certainties are shattered? These are the decisive religious questions of life because they cannot be answered without taking recourse to a transcendent dimension or to the divine, representing the incomprehensible wholeness of meaning. The discursive fact that people themselves raise the question of meaning, or relate to it in any way, is already a religious process. Conscious of the fragility and vulnerability of finite existence, people express their longing for the infinite fullness of life.

7 Church Life Rituals and Religious Life Interpretation

The binding force of life rituals offered by the church is not strong enough to prevent the loss of members. Nevertheless, the vast majority of church members still seek contact with the church and participate in its worship services when life rituals are performed, or services are celebrated at turning points in the life cycle or in the religious calendar.

The behaviour of church members shows that transitions and crises in life still call for Christian interpretation. Understood more deeply, theologically speaking, this means that, where the finiteness of life, the incomprehensible gift of life, its needs and its happiness become conscious, or where we have to deal with illness and pressure, dying and death, the compelling need for interpretation, accompaniment and ritualistic treatment arises.

The church life rituals (*Kasualien*) are attached to the passages and transitions in the life course (Gräb 2006a; Albrecht 2006; Fechtner 2011). These are essentially baptism, confirmation, marriage, and funerals. Baptism is also the sacrament of formal entry into the Christian Church, but at the same time, it celebrates the gift of life. Confirmation is the personal reception of the baptismal confession, but also the celebration of the transition to adulthood. The ecclesiastical wedding is a service linked to the marriage contracted at the registry office, but also the religious ceremony for the celebration of life and love. Burial is the ritual for coping with death, but also a service in which the life of the deceased is located in the light of the Gospel and to which Christian message of hope is directed.

What happens in these services is a religious or theological interpretation of life that works with the symbols of the Christian faith (creation and sin, justification and reconciliation, resurrection, and redemption). This interpretation is carried out in such a way that those who celebrate the service and find their way into their own self-understanding can appropriate it. In this way, the services relate to critical transitions in life to shape the attitudes and ideas towards life.

8 Modern Culture and the Transformation of Religious Communication

Church communication is strongly affected by the change in values described at the beginning of this chapter. Individualization always results in a pluralization of life-oriented attitudes. Traditions and conventions lose their normative power. Instead, they can and must be purposefully selected. Individual decision-making plays a greater role than social induction. Also, as far as church weddings, baptisms, confirmation, and church funerals are concerned, they are no longer chosen only because it is so usual, but because one consciously acknowledges oneself as a member of the church or wants to become one, and also because one wants to pass on Christian values and attitudes to the next generation. However, these are decisions that are made largely in the awareness of having alternatives. Everyone recognizes that he or she can also refrain from participation in these rituals without having to face socially disadvantageous consequences. In some places the non-church alternatives also appear more attractive: the festive ambience of the civil wedding, the seemingly plausible value orientation of the post-socialist youth celebrations, the personal address of the secular funeral orator who appreciates the life of the deceased, the selection of one's own music, and aesthetic staging.

As social conditions become more complex, there is clearly a need to create fixed markers for the individual life story by ritually celebrating life's turning points. What is always sought is the opportunity to place one's own individual life into a larger context of interpretation that is connected to what is generally valid. It is about the reassurance of personal identity and the experience of social recognition. Thus, children's milestones are celebrated within a lager framework, the round-number birthdays and silver marriage anniversaries. Everywhere the church with its offers of rituals and thus also with the symbolization of the Christian interpretation of life, finds itself in a market where a variety of interpretations of life, conceptions of lifestyles, formations of values and worldviews are offered.

The considerations of the ethnologist Victor Turner regarding the transformative value of rites of passage in modern Western societies are enlightening in any reflection on the changes in church ritual practice and thus the socio-cultural mediation of the Christian-religious interpretation of life under the conditions of modern culture (Turner [1982] 2008).

In contrast to simple, agrarian societies, on the basis of which Arnold van Gennep (1909) developed his theory of *Les rites de passage* (van Gennep, Vizedom, and Caffee 2019), Turner asks how these rites come to operate under the conditions of functionally differentiated and religiously individualized and pluralized societies. He notes that they lose their unconditional obligatory character. It is no longer necessary for members of society to commit and submit to them. They now assume a pluralistic, fragmentary, and experimental character. They also lose their collective commitment. They no longer have the same intellectual and emotional significance for all members of society.

The traditional rites of passage organized by churches and religious movements are facing competition. Rites are formed that fulfil a similar social function as the traditional rites of passage do. Turner calls them 'liminoid' phenomena (Turner 2008, 53–55), because they merely resemble the ritualization of the liminal, the threshold transitions. He identifies these 'liminoid' phenomena in the fields of art and sport, games and entertainment, leisure, and vacation. According to Turner, these areas of art and culture, leisure time and sport fulfil a function in modern Western societies that is comparable to that of rites of passage in traditional, agrarian societies.

Film and literature, theatre and football, hobbies and holidays also interrupt the everyday, formed by work and professional practice, by fixed roles and functions. They can – much like the traditional rites of passage based on the life cycle – create the temporary – but during this period – real transition into a transcendent symbolic order that attributes a new meaning to the whole.

These 'liminoid' rituals of cultural and leisure activities enable threshold experiences. They lead into transitions. They represent passages that temporarily push members of society beyond the status and functions they occupy and perform in society. As a phased interruption of the everyday world, they enable the construction of an imaginative, but at the same time real, experience of an "anti-structure". Those who are otherwise only interested in, for example, their economic, political, family, professional functions can potentially experience a transcendence of the structure framing their life attitudes and life interpretations. 'Liminoid' rituals still have the power to initiate what Turner calls – following the sociologist Mihály Csikszentmihalyi – a "flow-experience" (Turner 2008, 56).

Turner points out that a strong tendency towards the phenomenon of the 'liminoid' can also be observed in church ritual practice (Turner 2008, 55). Church life rituals increasingly come to resemble the liminal rites of passage in traditional societies. In modern culture, the experience of the interruption of everyday reality can be encountered in many ways; people can immerse themselves in worlds of meaning that motivate them to cultivate their own attitudes towards life and their own ideas about the significance of life.

The attractiveness of the church's life rituals draws attention to the fact that what the church offers to people and what they expect from the church are particularly well matched. The church's rituals of life resonate far beyond the circle of committed parishioners and faithful churchgoers. The theologically deeper reason for the resonance of church life rituals lies in the fact that the church generates an elementary existential interest in a certainty of life that is fed by the interpretive potential of the Christian faith.

On all occasions of worship and preaching, those who are responsible for shaping the church service know that they have to raise the questions, what is the case here and now in people's lives? What can be said about that in the light of the Christian faith? What does faith give us to enable us to understand our lives?

Bibliography

Albrecht, Christian. 2006. *Kasualtheorie: Geschichte, Bedeutung und Gestaltung kirchlicher Amtshandlungen.* Praktische Theologie in Geschichte und Gegenwart 2. Tübingen: Mohr Siebeck.
Bedford-Strohm, Heinrich, and Volker Jung, eds. 2015. *Vernetzte Vielfalt: Kirche angesichts von Individualisierung und Säkularisierung; die fünfte EKD-Erhebung über Kirchenmitgliedschaft.* Hannover: Evangelische Kirche in Deutschland / Gütersloh: Gütersloher Verlagshaus.
Berger, Peter L. 2010. "Max Weber Is Alive and Well, and Living in Guatemala: The Protestant Ethic Today." *The Review of Faith & International Affairs* 8:3–9.
Bochinger, Christoph, Martin Engelbrecht, and Winfried Gebhardt. 2009. *Die unsichtbare Religion in der sichtbaren Religion: Formen spiritueller Orientierung in der religiösen Gegenwartskultur.* Religionswissenschaft heute 3. Stuttgart: Kohlhammer.
Cox, Harvey G. 1995. *Fire from Heaven: The Rise of Pentecostal Spirituality and the Reshaping of Religion in the Twenty-First Century.* Reading: Addison-Wesley Publishing Company.
Evangelische Kirche in Deutschland, ed. 2014. *Engagement und Indifferenz – Kirchenmitgliedschaft als soziale Praxis: V. EKD-Erhebung über Kirchenmitgliedschaft.* Hannover: Evangelische Kirche in Deutschland.

Fechtner, Kristian. ²2011. *Kirche von Fall zu Fall: Kasualien wahrnehmen und gestalten.* Gütersloh: Gütersloher Verlagshaus.

Gennep, Arnold van. [1909] 2019. *The Rites of Passage*, trans. Monika B. Vizedom and Gabrielle L. Caffee. Chicago / London: The University of Chicago Press

Gräb, Wilhelm. 2006a. *Religion als Deutung des Lebens: Perspektiven einer Praktischen Theologie gelebter Religion.* Gütersloh: Gütersloher Verlagshaus.

Gräb, Wilhelm. 2006b. *Sinnfragen: Transformationen des Religiösen in der modernen Kultur.* Gütersloh: Gütersloher Verlagshaus.

Gräb, Wilhelm, ed. 2008. *Individualisierung – Spiritualität – Religion: Transformationsprozesse auf dem religiösen Feld in interdisziplinärer Perspektive.* Studien zu Religion und Kultur 1, edited by Wilhelm Gräb, Berlin / Münster: LIT.

Graf, Friedrich Wilhelm. 2014. *Götter global: Wie die Welt zum Supermarkt der Religionen wird.* C.H. Beck Paperback 6126. München: Beck.

Graf, Friedrich Wilhelm, and Jens-Uwe Hartmann, eds. 2018. *Religion und Gesellschaft: Sinnstiftungssysteme im Konflikt.* Berlin / Boston: De Gruyter.

Hoult, Thomas F. 1967. "The Invisible Religion: The Problem of Religion in Modern Society." By Thomas Luckmann. *Social Forces* 46:302–303.

Inglehart, Ronald. 1989. *Kultureller Umbruch: Wertwandel in der westlichen Welt.* Frankfurt am Main / New York: Campus Verlag.

Inglehart, Ronald. 1997. *Modernization and Postmodernization: Cultural, Economic, and Political Change in 43 Societies.* Princeton: Princeton University Press.

Klages, Helmut. ²1985. *Wertorientierungen im Wandel: Rückblick, Gegenwartsanalyse, Prognosen.* Frankfurt am Main / New York: Campus Verlag.

Knoblauch, Hubert. 2007. *Populäre Religion: Auf dem Weg in eine spirituelle Gesellschaft.* Frankfurt am Main / New York: Campus Verlag.

Luckmann, Thomas. [1967] 2014. *Die unsichtbare Religion.* Suhrkamp-Taschenbuch Wissenschaft 947. Frankfurt am Main: Suhrkamp.

Luhmann, Niklas, and André Kieserling, eds. 2007. *Die Religion der Gesellschaft.* Suhrkamp-Taschenbuch Wissenschaft 1581. Frankfurt am Main: Suhrkamp.

Nassehi, Arnim. 2009. "Religiöse Kommunikation: Religionssoziologische Konsequenzen Einer Qualitativen Untersuchung." In *Woran glaubt die Welt? Analysen und Kommentare zum Religionsmonitor 2008*, edited by Bertelsmann Stiftung, Gütersloh: Bertelsmann, 169–204.

Öhlmann, Philipp, Marie-Luise Frost, and Wilhelm Gräb. 2016. "African Initiated Churches' Potential as Development Actors." *HTS Theological Studies / Teologiese Studies* 72:1–12.

Öhlmann, Philipp, Wilhelm Gräb, and Marie-Luise Frost, eds. 2020. *African Initiated Christianity and the Decolonisation of Development: Sustainable Development in Pentecostal and Independent Churches.* London: Routledge.

Pickel, Gert, and Tabea Spieß. 2015. "Religiöse Indifferenz – Konfessionslosigkeit als Religionslosigkeit?" In *Vernetzte Vielfalt: Kirche angesichts von Individualisierung und Säkularisierung: Die fünfte EKD-Erhebung über Kirchenmitgliedschaft*, edited by Heinrich Bedford-Strohm, and Volker Jung, Hannover: Evangelische Kirche in Deutschland / Gütersloh: Gütersloher Verlagshaus, 248–266.

Pollack, Detlef. 1995. "Was ist Religion? Probleme der Definition." *Zeitschrift für Religionswissenschaft* 3:163–190.

Pollack, Detlef. ²2012. *Säkularisierung – ein moderner Mythos?* Studien zum religiösen Wandel in Deutschland 1. Tübingen: Mohr Siebeck.

Pollack, Detlef, and Gerhard Wegner, eds. 2017. *Die soziale Reichweite von Religion und Kirche: Beiträge zu einer Debatte in Theologie und Soziologie.* Religion in der Gesellschaft 40. Würzburg: Ergon Verlag.

Reckwitz, Andreas. 2017. *Die Gesellschaft der Singularitäten: Zum Strukturwandel der Moderne.* Berlin: Suhrkamp Verlag.
Riesebrodt, Martin. ²2001. *Die Rückkehr der Religionen: Fundamentalismus und der "Kampf der Kulturen".* Beck'sche Reihe 1388. München: Beck.
Stegbauer, Christian, Franz Grubauer, and Birgit Weyel. 2015. "Gemeinde in netzwerkanalytischer Perspektive: Drei Beispielauswertungen." In *Vernetzte Vielfalt: Kirche angesichts von Individualisierung und Säkularisierung: Die fünfte EKD-Erhebung über Kirchenmitgliedschaft,* edited by Heinrich Bedford-Strohm and Volker Jung, Hannover: Evangelische Kirche in Deutschland / Gütersloh: Gütersloher Verlagshaus, 400–434.
Taylor, Charles. 2007. *A Secular Age.* Cambridge, MA: Belknap Press of Harvard University Press.
Turner, Victor. [1982] 2008. *From Ritual to Theatre: The Human Seriousness of Play.* Performance Studies Series 1. New York: Performing Arts Journal Publications.
Wegner, Gerhard. 2015. *Religiöse Kommunikation und Kirchenbindung: Ende des liberalen Paradigmas?* Leipzig: Evangelische Verlagsanstalt.
Weyel, Birgit. 2008. "Individualisierung und die Transformation des Religiösen am Beispiel der Kasualien." In *Individualisierung – Spiritualität – Religion: Transformationsprozesse auf dem religiösen Feld in interdisziplinärer Perspektive,* edited by Wilhelm Gräb, Studien zu Religion und Kultur 1. Berlin / Münster: LIT, 23–30.
Weyel, Birgit. 2015. "Vernetzte Vielfalt: Gesamtnetzwerkerhebung einer evangelischen Kirchengemeinde." In *Vernetzte Vielfalt: Kirche angesichts von Individualisierung und Säkularisierung: Die fünfte EKD-Erhebung über Kirchenmitgliedschaft,* edited by Heinrich Bedford-Strohm and Volker Jung, Hannover: Evangelische Kirche in Deutschland / Gütersloh: Gütersloher Verlagshaus, 339–343.
Weyel, Birgit, Wilhelm Gräb, and Hans-Günther Heimbrock. 2013. *Praktische Theologie und empirische Religionsforschung.* Veröffentlichungen der Wissenschaftlichen Gesellschaft für Theologie 39. Leipzig: Evangelische Verlagsanstalt.
Weyel, Birgit, Jan Hermelink, and Franz Grubauer. 2015. "Kirchentheoretische Konsequenzen der Netzwerkerhebung." In *Vernetzte Vielfalt: Kirche angesichts von Individualisierung und Säkularisierung: Die fünfte EKD-Erhebung über Kirchenmitgliedschaft,* edited by Heinrich Bedford-Strohm and Volker Jung, Hannover: Evangelische Kirche in Deutschland / Gütersloh: Gütersloher Verlagshaus, 435–437.

Júlio César Adam
Lived Religion and Religion

1 Introduction

In the second half of the twentieth century a deliberate shift of perspective occurred in practical theology. The discipline started to give special attention to reality, not only of the church and ministry, but also of culture, society, and religion in general as an empirical realm to be considered. The way in which the individual experiences their religiosity and spirituality inside and outside the institutional and traditional sphere of the church or other religious tradition began to acquire greater relevance, whether their experience related to a religious system or not. The concept of lived religion emerged from this empirical turn as a way of observing and reading the context of life and of religion outside the strictly institutional, normative, traditional, and dogmatic realm of the church. Thus, lived religion has become for practical theology at the same time a kind of hermeneutics, a key to read the context, but also a phenomenon of expression of religiosity and religion in a broader sense. This article intends to contribute to the reflection on the hermeneutics and the phenomenon of lived religion in its relation with practical theology with particular attention to the Brazilian and Latin American context, where religion, religiosity and also lived religion exist in an exuberant manner, and where, however, there has been little reflection on the basis of the concept of lived religion.

I learned about the possibility of an interest in the investigation of religious expressions and experiences outside of the ecclesiastical and theological institutional realm when I was doing my doctorate in Germany, at the University of Hamburg, at the end of the 1990s and beginning of the 2000s. Professor Hans-Martin Gutmann (1998, 2009, 2013) had recently come to that university and it was from him that I heard for the first time about the potential relation between theology and pop culture, particularly cinema, but also music and literature. This combination was something uncommon and strange for me, but fascinating at the same time, because it enabled me to combine two things in which I was deeply interested, which are theology and contemporary culture. The first texts in which I came across the concept of lived religion as such were the works of Failing and Heimbrock (1998) and Gräb (1995, 2000, 2002, 2006). At that time, I still wasn't aware of the fact that in the Brazilian and Latin American context, where religion and religiosity are very much present, one could also feel the pulsing of something like a lived religion outside of religious institutions, and that several studies, although they did not explicitly use this concept, analyzed, in different ways, religion and religiosity in a manner that was similar to the investigations of lived religion.

After finishing my studies in Germany, my church sent me to my first field of ministry. Contrary to all my expectations and personal projects, my first field of work was a pastoral ministry at a Lutheran school in southern Brazil. I was standing, on a daily basis, in front of children and youths who experienced life and religion in a de-institutionalized, de-traditionalized, pragmatic and individualized manner, with little involvement or interest in the church or formal religious issues, who were resistant to classical traditions of theology, indifferent to orthodox biblical and theological questions. At the same time, they showed openness to messages about the meaning of life, broader forms of spirituality and mystical experience, and overcoming crises and fears.

In this article, then, I intend, as mentioned above, to define lived religion in its relation with practical theology taking into account the changes – or at least the change of perception – in religion, culture and society in recent decades, in particular taking into consideration the Brazilian and Latin American context. I try to point out possibilities of a practical theology in dialogue with lived religion that may contribute towards rethinking the role of the church in a context in need of meaning and social transformation. The article is organized as follows: First I discuss aspects of the change in research on religion and culture as the backdrop of what later came to be defined as lived religion. Next, I attempt to delineate a concept of lived religion in its relation to practical theology. In the third section I reflect on the possibilities of a lived religion in the Brazilian and Latin American context. Finally, I discuss some consequences of this study for practical theology.[1]

2 Religion, Culture and Context in Change – the Backdrop of Lived Religion

The backdrop of the concept of lived religion emerged from a change in culture and society and, at the same time, from a change in theory and research, especially in sociology of religion, in the twentieth century. This was a cultural turn in which empirical, cultural, and hermeneutical perspectives began to play a preponderant role (Herrmann 2007, 45; McGuire, 2008; Ammerman 2007). These changes have been articulated on the basis of new assumptions in sociological research and assimilated by theology, to a great extent, through a change of the role of the church and the relation of people with religion and the church, especially in the post-industrial European context (Herrmann 2007, 45). In a general way, facing the profound changes in the view of the world and of reality: pluralization, diversity, globalization and, at the same time, the individualization of the conceptions of life, traditional and institutional models of religion were all no longer able to respond effectively to the permanent human longing for meaning in life (Gräb 2000, 23–35).

---

[1] Some of the authors I'm citing in this article, have written their texts in German and other languages. As I quote them, I translated the excerpts into English, so that the text can be understood in its entirety. Those quotes are marked with "o.t." for "own translation".

In 1967, Thomas Luckmann published a small book in the form of an essay called *The Invisible Religion* in which he tried, starting from sociology, to broaden the concept of religion beyond a sociology of religion, by including other forms of religiosity in modern society in that concept. According to this author, secularization did not mean an overcoming of religiosity and religion in society and in people's mindset, but rather a change and broadening of religious experience in the form of a syncretic, secular, and private religion – something that empirical research on religion should take into account. The displacement of religion towards the outside of what sociology used to define as religion took place, basically, because of the freedom that modern individuals have to organize their understanding and experience of religion independently of sociostructural determinations (Luckmann 2014, 1996).

The essay on invisible religion led Luckmann to a functionalist and anthropological definition of religion according to which human beings transcend biological beings to become human. In other words, the religious phenomenon is part of the human process of socialization, in the objectivation of subjective experiences and in each one's individuation. In his Postscript, added nearly 25 years later, Luckmann states:

> I continue to hold the view that the basic function of 'religion' consists in transforming members of a natural species into protagonists inside a historically grown social order. Religion is found everywhere where the behavior of members of the species becomes actions that can be morally evaluated, where a Self is in a world inhabited by other beings for whom and against whom he acts in a way that can be morally evaluated. (Luckmann 2014, 138; o.t.)

The idea of invisible religion would be given many other names in sociology, such as modern religion, diffuse religion, individual, civil, popular, mediatic (Herrmann 2000; Gräb 2002), everyday religion (Ammerman 2007) or even lived religion (McGuire 2008) and would enable sociological research of religion to not only look at what is outside traditional and institutional religious expressions, but also to rethink its own closed and objective conceptions of religion (Asad 1993; Port 2011). The way people live, experience and express religious convictions and views acquires value, be it in the realm of religion itself, in daily life, in the world of labor and business, in consumption, leisure and entertainment, in the search for life quality and health, or in the new views on spirituality (Streib 2008).

McGuire raises the following question:

> Scholars of religion, especially sociologists, must reexamine their assumptions about individuals' religious lives. What might we discover if, instead of looking at affiliation or organization participation, we focused first on individuals, the experiences they consider most important, and the concrete practices that make up their personal religious experience and expression? What if we think of religion, at the individual level, as an ever-changing, multifaceted, often messy – even contradictory – amalgam of beliefs and practices that are not necessarily those religious institutions consider important? (McGuire 2008, 4)

In this article I do not operate with a concept of religion as a set of values, beliefs, rites and symbols around the transcendent or numinous. In my view, that does not equate to the concept of lived religion. Lived religion is instead a way of perceiving religion in its practical, every day, cultural experience, in a dynamic and contextual manner, providing people with a meaning for life (Gräb 2000, 13–22). Therefore, I consider those investigations that open up the individual experiences and practices that are equivalent or come close to what I understand by religion in a broad sense, to be particularly important. Along with the works of Luckmann (2014, 1996), Asad (1993) and Van de Port (2011), I value specific studies on lived religion that do not adopt a concept of religion as a trans-historical, isolated, and timeless essence. Religion is, rather, something that lies in people's views and experiences and therefore changes along with time, culture, and society.

3 Lived Religion and Practical Theology

These changes in sociology of religion have also had an impact on practical theology, mainly as far as the relation between theology, culture and the individual are concerned. It is important to note that in theology there was already at least one articulation of the correlation between theology and culture, which is Paul Tillich's theology of culture. These changes led not only to the question about a correlation between culture and religion, but also to the great question about whether religion exists and lives outside of and beyond institutions such as the church. Can one identify religious phenomena in spaces that do not see themselves as being religious, but can be understood as such from a theological-religious perspective?

The concept of lived religion in practical theology appears as a way of corroborating the insight that there are actually forms of lived religion in everyday life, in culture, individuality and in people's life stories, which sometimes are conscious and related to a particular traditional religion and other times are unconscious and experienced without a religious connotation by a person or human group. Practical theology, now understood as the theory of religious practice (Steck 2000, 100), has an interest in these expressions as a way of rethinking itself and the church's role in the present. Thus, lived religion is understood as a way of seeing and perceiving religion and theology not primarily based not on its theoretical, dogmatic traditions, and on the tradition of the church, but of what culture and people do and call religion and religious, as pointed out by Ganzevoort and Roeland:

> The concepts of praxis and lived religion focus on *what people do* rather than on 'official' religion, its sacred sources, its institutes, and its doctrines. As such, practical theology has much in common with what in disciplines like anthropology, sociology, and media studies, is known as 'the practical turn': the turn away from institutes and (cultural) texts to the everyday social and cultural practices of ordinary people. (Ganzevoort and Roeland 2014, 93; o.t.)

Lived religion is a way of perceiving religious elements, contents and forms in the sphere of life, be it in everyday and personal experiences, or special moments of celebrations or crises, in various relationships, in leisure and entertainment. In sum, it is experienced outside of the domain of the religious institution: the worship service, the sacred sphere itself – although sometimes related to it. "This empirical orientation means that the attitude taken is more descriptive and analytical than normative. Another common ground seems to me that the textual side of religion can be understood in the sense of a cultural system of codes of meaning, with the help of which people interpret their lives." (Herrmann 2007, 46; o.t.) The possibilities of perceiving this expression of lived religiosity can take place in the realm of a religious tradition, such as the church, by evaluating how people interpret and experience religion independently of the institution and its precepts, but also without relation to a particular religion.

This second possibility has to do with expressions in culture, in the media and in daily life, in elements, contents and forms where one perceives relations with religious elements. As pointed out by Gräb (2000, 39; o.t.) "lived religion, also Christian lived religion, is not simply found in the church." These relations may be of a more explicit nature, such as references to religious contents and practices: lyrics of the U2 Band based on biblical references (40, for example), or the movie *Noah* by Darren Aronofsky (2014), based on the biblical narrative of the flood. Or they may contain more implicit expressions of religiosity that can be interpreted as a religious equivalent such as the devotion to the singer Madonna or touristic visits to places of memory such as the house of Anne Frank in Amsterdam.

In Gräb's view, this lived religion can be seen in communication as an expression of the search for meaning for human existence.

> Lived religion is constituted by communication [...]. The term functions as a 'mental category of interpretation'. And its historical reality results from cultural interpretations of what this world and our life is all about, where we come from and where we are going – including the answers found and given in the contexts of the institutionalized churches. It is practiced religion there, but then also wherever socio-culturally mediated ways of interpreting life pass into one's own life-style practice, which determines and orientates it. (Gräb 2000, 39; o.t.)

According to this author, the human search for meaning in life, mainly through relationships and belonging – "Meaning is relationship, is connection, is connectedness." (Gräb 2000, 13; o.t.) – takes place in a context of loss of value-related references, on the one hand, and on the other hand the pressure to guarantee a life in fulness vis-à-vis a diversity of roles on offer. In this sense, the reference of the Christian faith, which for generations has provided meaning for people, has become weaker in its role as a master key vis-à-vis the diversity of offers and possibilities of meaning (Gräb 2000, 14, 42–43; 2006, 17–23). Failing and Heimbrock (2001), although more focused on Christian practice in daily life, corroborate this proposal by reinforcing perception (*Wahrnehmung*) as a basic principle for present practical theology. According to these authors, the reason leading to this proposal has to do with the loss of relevance of theology as a whole in the present, on the one hand, and the relevance of everyday life, on the other, mainly on the basis of Henning Luther's work (1992), as a space of the subject's experience of religiosity in the search for meaning and transcendence within the immanence of life.

It is important to note that lived religion is related not only with implicit forms of religion and religiosity, but also with explicit ones. In both cases religious traditions and matrices are important because it is on their foundations that lived religion can be understood and put into dialogue with practical theology itself. Sometimes one may have the impression that the phenomenon of lived religion is something new. McGuire (2008, 25–26) refutes this idea by showing that in the Late Middle Ages both Catholicism and Protestantism were not unified and homogeneous entities and that there were projects of consolidation of theological and practical patterns about people's religious beliefs and experiences of an authoritarian nature. In other words, it seems that there have always been, even in biblical tradition, forms of religion that were lived at the margins of the official religion.

In the discussion on practical theology as hermeneutics of lived religion, Ganzevoort and Roeland define religion itself in an open and broad manner, i.e., "religion as the transcending patterns of action and meaning, emerging from and contributing to the relation with the sacred" (2014, 96). For these authors, this is a primarily functional definition that aims at a maximum of malleability so that we may be open to new and different forms of religion (Ganzevoort and Roeland 2014). For them, patterns of the transcendent should not be confused with a transcendent being but are processes of a *transcending* of borders in the relationship with something that involves us completely. In Luckmann's view, transcendence is precisely that which surpasses the immediate evidence of the experience of the world of life (Luckmann 2014, 138). The core of Ganzevoort's and Roeland's definition, however, is the relation with the holy, which is not an infinitely open concept. For them, the notion of the holy implies at least a center around which our lives gravitate as well as a presence that evokes reverence and passion. This is often determined by the cultural context in which we live and follows the model of a religious tradition (Ganzevoort 2014, 322).

It must be added that from the very beginning the concept of lived religion has been treated as a complex and controversial concept, or, as Rössler puts it: "lived religion remains indeterminate, vague, unclear and difficult to demarcate." (Rössler 1976, 67; o.t.) The uncertainty and unease brought by lived religion as a hermeneutics of practical theology are due to reasons that can be imagined, such as the opening of theology to the concept of religion, the complexification of the concept of religion itself and, last but not least, the decision to interpret it based on the transitoriness of concrete practices, individual practical, daily and cultural wisdom. Consequently, lived religion implies a change of perspective in theology: from theory to concrete practice, which is something that, as noted by Miller-McLemore, causes resistance and insecurity of various kinds (2016, 37–38). Using the hermeneutics of lived religion and recognizing the phenomenon of lived religion always involves the risk of thinking about religion and theology beyond what has been standardized as a system or a truth.

Besides that, for theology and practical theology lived religion is just a contextual hermeneutics of change of religion and culture, a reading of people's individual expressions and experiences, of the search for meaning expressed through aesthetics and communication. At a second moment, they dialogue with the basis of meaning, with the communication and tradition of theology and the church, as pointed out by Gräb (2000, 45; o.t.): "Practical-theological hermeneutics of religion is meant to orientate the life of the Church and of the Christians building it. It must therefore always connect lived religion in its plural meanings to the traditional stock of meaning of the Christian faith."

4 Lived Religion and Religion in Brazil and Latin America

In contrast with the European context, in which the concept of lived religion emerged and which is marked by a certain secularism and individualization of religion, Brazilian reality is marked not only by religion and the church, but mainly by the manifestation of religion in the traditional and popular forms in all spheres of life. The first action undertaken by the Portuguese when they invaded the territory of what is now Brazil was to hold a mass, which was an emblematic event for religion and its later development. In spite of this Catholic liturgical inscription, it was not only the official form of the Catholic Christian faith that prevailed in the country, but also, from the very beginning, forms of religious syncretism with indigenous religions and later with religions of African origin, which have marked the Brazilian religious context in a permanent, unique and effervescent cultural and religious hybridity. The Protestant (beginning in the nineteenth century) and later Pentecostal (beginning in the twentieth century) contribution became a part of this religious hybridity and syncretism even when opposing them.

At present one can experience in Brazil – and, with due regard for the differences, in several other Latin American countries – the effects of this religious diversity and effervescence on a daily basis. One could almost say that what is experienced here is an excess of religion that goes beyond the religious field itself. Religion is part of culture, of society, of intimacy, of the body, of sexuality, of politics and the economy, of pop culture, of daily life. Besides the surprising emergence of new churches and religious movements in recent decades, syncretism, religious mobility, bricolage, and hybridity are part of trends that can be observed in the religious field. In the case of the growth of evangelicals, which Peter Berger (1999) calls "evangelical explosion" in his text on the desecularization of the world. It is significant that "already at the beginning of the 1990s one new church was founded on each workday only in the Greater Rio area" (Bartz, Bobsin and von Sinner 2012, 232).

On the other hand, there are studies indicating a significant decline of the historical denominations, such as Lutheranism and Catholicism, besides a growing lack of interest in the more traditional forms of religion, particularly Christianity, as I showed in the introduction when talking about my experience in the school pastoral ministry. In line with this trend, there is a considerable growth of the group of those without religion, for instance, according to data of the population census (Ribeiro 2013). Either with or without connection to this trend of a certain secularization and religious decline, the adhesion to practices and experiences of pop culture such as soccer, cinema, television, internet, and music, mainly among young people, has become widespread in Brazil. To what extent people look also for something religious or equivalent to religion in these environments is a question worth considering.

Is it possible to speak of a lived religion in this context? Certainly yes, considering its peculiarities. I think we can speak of a lived religion in the Brazilian context considering both popular religiosities and religious syncretism and hybridity as well as the explicit and implicit expressions of religiosity in everyday life, in the media and in pop culture. Regarding the first case, Adilson Schultz proposes a way of thinking about theological structure in Brazil based on the religious imaginary, which he defines as a *nebula*. He uses the term "nebula" because he believes that there is no base on which the religions or the Brazilian religious matrix is constructed, but rather something, meanings that move between the religions and their matrices (Schultz 2008, 31). According to the author, at least three references feed this nebula.

The main references of the Brazilian religious matrix are the religious meanings that come from Catholicism, from African-Brazilian religions and from Spiritualism – besides the indigenous meanings in the aspects in which they influence Umbanda, Spiritualism and Candomblé (Schultz 2008, 28).

According to him, this nebula, forged in a slow historical process, hovers over the country and is constantly repeated in a continuous process of resignification of values and principles, which is something that makes a lot of sense for the reflection on the various forms and contents of lived religion. The author complements his idea by taking the rhizomatic theory from Gilles Deleuze. As it is different from roots, that are connected to a same point, "the logic of the rhizome operates at the same time by ruptures and interconnections" (Schultz 2008, 33; o.t.).

Thus, lived religion has a lot of space in the perception of these popular phenomena, of syncretism and hybridity. The second space where lived religion can be observed is related to culture, daily life, life in its spontaneity, dynamism and needs. Beginning in the 1960s, with the articulation of a more contextual theology, which is liberation theology, a perception of and interest in the reality and expression of religion beyond the institutional realm arose in Latin America. The seeing-judging-acting method, as an analytical, hermeneutical, and practical process, shifted the doing of theology towards concrete life, towards practice, mainly where there was suffering under oppression, economic misery and discrimination of the poor, women, blacks and indigenous people. Doing theology meant considering and transforming this reality: "The presence of the church in society occurs not only through religious (devotional, cultic, liturgical) practice; the religious practice has to be connected to ethical, social practices and to the promotion of human being as a whole and all human beings." (Boff 1979, 13; o.t.) Theology starts from practice and returns to the practice of life.

In the following decades liberation theologies broadened and at the same time specified their perspective, going beyond economic, social, and political concerns. Gender theologies, for instance, pay great attention to everyday life. In recent years the feminist theologian Ivone Gebara, for example, has contrasted an epistemology of ordinary life with reflective, philosophical, and scientific epistemology, proposing everyday knowledge, mainly of people in a situation of vulnerability and invisibility, as the starting point for an authentic theology of life: "The originary place of theology is not logos about God, but human experience in its complexity and in its irreducibility to a single explanatory reason." (Gebara 2015, 37; o.t.)

Rubem Alves articulated in a very explicit way a form of lived religion in the relation with everyday life, art and culture, a theology that unfolds in simple and concrete life. According to Alves, religion arises from the human need to imagine possibilities that overcome the harshness of life's reality. In his words, "religion is the proclamation of the axiological priority of the heart over the raw facts of reality […] in the name of a vision, of a passion, of a love." (Alves 1988, 19; o.t.) For him, theology permeates daily life and is intertwined in ordinary life, in the subject's spirituality and religiosity in the different spaces of life, as a way of giving life meaning and beauty.

"For those who love, theology is a natural function just like dreaming, listening to music, drinking a good wine, weeping, suffering, protesting, hoping […]. Perhaps theology is nothing but a way of talking about these things by giving them a name and is only distinguished from poetry because theology is always made with a prayer. No, it doesn't result from the 'cogito' in the same way as poems and prayers. It just sprouts and unfolds, as a manifestation of a way of being: 'sigh of the oppressed creature'– would a better definition be possible?" (Alves 1985, 21; o.t.)

Also, in the 1980s, the Dutch anthropologist André Droogers, then living in Brazil, wrote a small text proposing the existence in Brazil of what he called Minimal Brazilian Religiosity (MBR). "It is a religiosity that manifests itself publicly in secular contexts, that is conveyed by the mass media, but also by everyday language. It is part of Brazilian culture." (Droogers 1987, 65; o.t.) This MBR is very similar to what I understand as lived religion in the sense that Droogers considers it as a set of religious and spiritual expressions present in the everyday life of Brazilian culture and free, general forms with which people express their beliefs and belonging, in a way that is independent of religious institutions. The author analyzes this MBR in politics, sports, television, radio, advertisements, sayings on bumpers, in everyday language and popular sayings.

Much more recently, in the last decade, a new concept has entered the scene, which is postcoloniality or decoloniality. Rather than a concept, postcoloniality or decoloniality is a new way of perceiving local (and global) reality on the basis of its differences, subtleties, fragmentariness, alterities, ruptures and social, cultural, sexual, political and religious alternatives, rather than just on the basis of what is already established and standardized.

> [...] speaking of postcoloniality means to challenge and deconstruct the dynamics of identification pursued by the colonial forces by exposing their own weaknesses through the heterogeneities inscribed in that Subject, with the purpose of making visible the intrinsic bifurcations that characterize the global context, which enable its constant malleability, transformation and openness to new forms of sociocultural construction. (Panotto 2016, 34–35; o.t.)

Here we have a great potential to think about lived religion in the Latin American context, since postcoloniality intensifies the gaze at culture, daily life, the body, highlighting particularly the difference, those aspects that do not fit into the homogeneous standards of the systems and absolute truths and are, for this reason, seen as weak, fragile, and vulnerable.

5 Consequences of a Hermeneutics of Lived Religion for Practical Theology

Practical theology is a critical reflection about *praxis*, about theories and perceptions of practice aiming at communicating the Gospel to the world. In this sense, the hermeneutics of religion is an indispensable way of understanding society, culture and human beings and their manners of experiencing and understanding life on the basis of religion. Lived religion is a way of initially observing a person's religious reality to – based on this observation – take the way back into the communication of the Gospel (Ernst Lange), taking into account the theological, biblical, historical heritage and the church tradition. The hermeneutics of lived religion is not closed upon itself but serves as an instrument of reflection on the practical religion of individuals, cultures, and societies.

In this sense, one can see in the hermeneutics of lived religion at least three major consequences for practical theology. (1) Institutional religion, the church, no longer offers the whole meaning for the lives of people and societies today. As Gräb puts it: "Christian faith can no longer claim to give the definite answers to what is happening in the world as a whole and the history of mankind on the tiny earth on the edge of the immeasurable universe." (Gräb 2000, 17; o.t.) The human search for meaning, however, remains. (2) It is necessary to understand other offers of meaning present in individualized, plural, and experiential society. Lived religion in its varied forms expresses and shapes the human search for meaning in life (Adam, 2017). Thus, lived religion makes it possible to rethink ways in which practical theology can help human beings to find the meaning offered by the Christian faith. Finally, (3) observing lived religion in its implicit and explicit forms is a way of expanding practical theology itself as a discipline and of reinventing new forms of evangelism, mission, and experience of the Christian faith in today's world.

Bibliography

Adam, Júlio Cézar. 2017. "Deus e o Diabo na Terra do Sol: Lived Religion, Conflict and Intolerance in Brazilian Films." In *Lived Religion and the Politics of (In)Tolerance*, edited by R. Ruard. Ganzevoort and Srdjan Sremac, Cham: Palgrave, 111–132.
Alves, Rubem. ⁴1988. *O enigma da religião*. Campinas: Papirus.
Alves, Rubem. ²1985. *Variações sobre a vida e a norte: o feitiço erótico-herético da teologia*. São Paulo: Paulinas.
Ammerman, Nancy T. 2007. *Everyday Religion: Observing Modern Religious Lives*. New York: Oxford University Press.
Asad, Talal. 1993. *Genealogies of Religion: Discipline and Reasons of Power in Christianity and Islam*. Baltimore / London: The Johns Hopkins University Press.
Berger, Peter. 2001. "A dessecularização do mundo: uma visão global." *Religião e Sociedade* 21:9–23.
Bartz, Alessandro, Oneide Bobsin, and Rudolf von Sinner. 2012. "Mobilidade religiosa no Brasil: conversão ou trânsito religioso." In *Religião e sociedade: desafios contemporâneos*, edited by Iuri A. Reblin and Rudolf von Sinner, São Leopoldo: Sinodal, 231–268.
Boff, Leonardo. 1979. *Da libertação: o teológico das libertações sócio-históricas*. Petrópolis: Vozes.
Droogers, André. 1987. "A religiosidade mínima brasileira." *Religião e Sociedade* 14:111–128.
Failing, Wolf-Eckart, and Hans-Günter Heimbrock. 1998. *Gelebte Religion wahrnehmen: Lebenswelt, Alltagskultur, Religionspraxis*. Stuttgart: Kohlhammer.
Ganzevoort, R. Ruard, and Johan Roeland. 2014. "Lived Religion: The Praxis of Practical Theology." *International Journal of Practical Theology* 18:91–101.
Ganzevoort, R. Ruard. 2014. "Narrative Approaches." In *The Wiley-Blackwell Companion to Practical Theology*, edited by Bonnie Miller-McLemore, Chichester: Wiley-Blackwell, 214–223.
Gebara, Ivone. 2015. "As epistemologias teológicas e suas consequências." In *Epistemologia, violência e sexualidade: olhares do II Congresso Latino-Americano de Gênero e Religião*, edited by Elaine Neuenfeldt, Karen Bergesch, and Mara Parlow, São Leopoldo: Sinodal / EST 31–50.
Gräb, Wilhelm. ²2000. *Lebensgeschichten, Lebensentwürfe, Sinndeutungen: Eine Praktische Theologie gelebter Religion*. Gütersloh: Kaiser / Gütersloher Verlagshaus.
Gräb, Wilhelm. 2006. *Religion als Deutung des Lebens: Perspektiven einer Praktischen Theologie gelebter Religion*. Gütersloh: Gütersloher Verlag.
Gräb, Wilhelm. 2002. *Sinn fürs Unendliche: Religion in der Mediengesellschaft*. Gütersloh: Kaiser / Gütersloher Verlagshaus.
Gräb, Wilhelm. 1995. "Auf den Spuren der Religion." *Zeitschrift für Evangelische Ethik* 39:43–56.
Gutmann, Hans-Martin. 2013. *"Irgendwas ist immer": Durchs Leben Kommen: Sprüche und Kleinrituale, die Alltagsreligion der Leute*. Berlin: EB-Verlag.
Gutmann, Hans-Martin. 1998. *Der Herr der Heerscharen, die Prinzessin der Herzen und der König der Löwen: Religion Lehren zwischen Kirche, Schule und Populärer Kultur*. Gütersloh: Gütersloher Verlag.
Gutmann, Hans-Martin. 2009. "Theologische Hermeneutik populärer Kultur – Phänomenologisch." In *Sinnspiegel: Theologische Hermeneutik populärer Kultur*, edited by Joachim Kunstmann and Ingo Reuter, Paderborn: Ferdinand Schöningh, 37–46.

Herrmann, Jörg. 2007. *Medienerfahrung und Religion: Eine empirische-qualitative Studie zur Medienreligion.* Göttingen: Vandenhoeck & Ruprecht.
Luckmann, Thomas. 1967. *The Invisible Religion.* New York: MacMillan Publishing Company. (Postscript in the Brasilian edition 2014. *A religião invisível.* São Paulo: Olho d'Água / Loyola.)
Luckmann, Thomas. 1996. "Religion – Gesellschaft – Transzendenz." In *Krise der Immanenz: Religion an den Grenzen der Moderne*, edited by Hans-Joachim Höhn, Frankfurt am Main: Fischer, 112–127.
Luther, Henning. 1992. *Religion und Alltag: Bausteine zu einer Praktischen Theologie des Subjekts.* Stuttgart: Radius Tekla.
McGuire, Meredith B. 2008. *Lived Religion: Faith and Practice in Everyday Life.* Oxford: Oxford University Press.
Miller-McLemore, Bonnie J. 2016. "Teologia Prática: Reforma e transformação na epistemologia teológica." In *Reforma: tradição e transformação*, edited by Iuri A. Reblin and Rudolf von Sinner, São Leopoldo: Sinodal / EST, 35–67.
Panotto, Nicolás. 2016. *Religión, política y poscolonialidad en América Latina: hacia una teología posfundacional de lo público.* Madrid / Buenos Aires: Miño y Dávila.
Ribeiro, Jorge Cláudio. 2013. "Sem-religião no Brasil: dois estranhos sob o guarda-chuva." *Cadernos do IHU* 11:3–12.
Rössler, Dietrich. 1976. *Die Vernunft der Religion.* München: Piper Verlag.
Schultz, Adilson. 2008. "Estrutura teológica do imaginário religioso brasileiro." In *Uma religião chamada Brasil: estudos sobre religião e contexto brasileiro*, edited by Oneide Bobsin, Rogério Sávio Lin, Nivia Ivette Núñez de la Paz, Iuri Andréas Reblin, São Leopoldo: Faculdades EST / Oikos, 27–60.
Steck, Wolfgang. 2000. *Praktische Theologie: Horizonte der Religion – Konturen des Neuzeitlichen Christentums – Strukturen des Lebenswelt.* Stuttgart: Kohlhammer.
Streib, Heinz. 2008. "More Spiritual than Religious: Changes in the Religious Field Require New Approaches." In *Lived Religion: Conceptual, Empirical and Practical-theological Approaches: Essays in Honor of Hans-Günter Heimbrock*, edited by Heinz Streib, Astrid Dinter, and Kerstin Söderblom, Leiden: Brill, 53–70.
Tillich, Paul. 2009. *Teologia da cultura*, trans. Jaci Maraschin. São Paulo: Fonte Editorial.
Port, Matitijs van de. 2011. *Ecstatic Encounters: Bahian Candomblé and the Quest for the Really Real.* Amsterdam: Amsterdam University Press.

Johanna Sumiala
Media and Religion

1 Study of Religion and Media – Many Beginnings

The history of the study of media and religion can be argued to have many beginnings depending on the disciplinary orientation guiding the interpretation. For an anthropologist of communication, rock paintings, smoke signals and ritual dance can well qualify as early examples of religious communication carried out via premodern media. For a theologian, handwritten sacred texts can represent the very starting point of the study of religion and (written) media. A media historian and a church historian might point to the development of the printing press in Gutenberg's time and argue for its relevance in starting a new tradition of research investigating the relationship between religion (namely, Protestantism) and media (namely, the printing press; see, e.g., Eisenstein 1979; Meyer 2013; Stolow 2005). Moreover, the order in which these two concepts – religion and media – appear in research most likely varies by the scholarly orientation, that is, whether the main focus is on media or religion.

The purpose of this chapter is to provide an overview of some key developments in the field and to discuss them in the context of historical and theoretical developments relevant to the growth of this research field. In addition to an historical analysis of the development of the research field, two key theoretical frameworks are discussed: the study of religion in the *public sphere* and the study of *mediatization* of religion in late modern society. My approach to the study of media and religion (in this order) in this chapter is best characterised as interdisciplinary. Although I draw on various scholarly traditions, I mainly focus on and combine media and communication studies and sociology of religion. Theories are never created in a vacuum. I acknowledge that my scholarly thinking as a Nordic academic is influenced by European/Western social thought and related ideas about the role of religion (in particular Lutheran Church) and media (public broadcasting) in society. In this framework, the study of media and religion can be seen to evolve alongside the modernisation of Western society (embedded in secularisation) and the development of modern mass communication technology (newspapers first, followed by radio and finally television) and the related public sphere (Meyer and Moors 2006). In recent years, the digitalisation of communication has radically shaped the field, and concepts such as *digital religion* have gained emerging interest in the field, so we may call digital religion the third key theoretical framework in the study of media and religion (see, e.g., Campbell and Lövheim 2017).

I begin this chapter by providing a short overview of the history of the research field of media and religion. I then move to discuss in more detail how the concepts of the public sphere and mediatization have shaped research on media and religion.

The last section of this chapter focuses on reflecting on the present context of the global and digital media ecology and how it shapes current and future research on media and religion.

2 From Impact to Meaning – Two Key Phases in the History of the Field

The first phase of the study of media and religion is often referred to as the so-called mass communication era, which has its origins in the United States. In the 1960s, various evangelical dominations and churches with Protestant backgrounds in the United States began to purchase airtime from television stations. In the 1980s, some central themes in the field were the electronic church and the phenomenon of televangelism, which increased the visibility of religion in American media and made evangelicalism a potential worldview among others. Peter Horsfield's *Religious Television* (1984) was a classic study in that era and looked at the phenomenon from the perspectives of media history and media culture and different religious communities' theological viewpoints.

Research in this first phase typically was motivated by *mass communication research*, also called the MCR research tradition. Famous in the field of media studies, it had the aim to explore and explain media's effects on their audiences and the surrounding society (Pietilä 2005). Many studies from this period focused on how religious messages could be most effectively delivered to audiences through media, particularly television. In this line of thinking, religion and media appeared to be independent, separate categories, and the role of media was understood to be primarily an instrument for delivering messages.

The beginning of the second phase of the study of media and religion can be dated to the 1990s. This phase was characterised by a desire to gain a wider understanding of both religion and media as social and cultural phenomena and categories. Thus, this intellectual tradition is often referred to as the media, religion, and culture paradigm. It was born from cooperation among certain Nordic (Alf Linderman and Knut Lundby), British (Jolyon Mitchell) and American (Stewart Hoover, David Morgan, and Lynn Schofield Clark) researchers. The key ideas of this school of thought were collected in the book *Rethinking Media, Religion and Culture*, published in 1997 and edited by Hoover and Lundby. Later, the Center for Media, Religion, and Culture, directed by Hoover at the University of Colorado, became one of the most important research centres in this field. This school of thought raised *meaning* as a key concept. Within the school, there was a debate between substantivist (often referring to institutional religion) and functionalist (focusing on religious practices and duties) conceptions of religion. There was also some shift from studying religion to studying religiosity. In this phase, it was crucial for researchers to study the kinds of forms religiosity took in media, who had the right to define religion, what was considered to be religious and how media made sense of religious practices.

Instead of studying traditional institutions, researchers in this strand focused on audiences and recipients and how people made sense of their lives in and through media. Rather than separate categories, media and religion appeared in this research tradition to be social and cultural phenomena intertwined in many ways. In media studies, this tradition drew ideas from the research field of cultural studies (see e.g., Pietilä 2005). Researchers were especially inspired by the ritual view of communication developed by a key figure in interpretive cultural studies, James Carey (1989). This idea emphasised the ritual significance of communication, referring to communication as a phenomenon that built community and kept it together. In the sociology of religion discourse, these ritual aspects of communication typically were interpreted as manifestations of functionalist religion (see, e.g., Hoover and Lundby 1997). Furthermore, media and communications studies scholar Roger Silverstone's (1981) research applying theories of myth to study television and its role in everyday life was well received among scholars adhering to what was later called the media, religion, and culture paradigm. This school of thought inspired researchers to turn their gaze from institutional and organised religion to everyday life and its religious dimensions. This school marked a paradigm shift from the impact- to the meaning-oriented study of media (see e.g., Pietilä 2005).

3 Religion(s) in the Public Sphere

Other important factors to explain the key phases in the development of the research field of media and religion are the main conceptual debates and the different positions scholars in the field have taken in these debates. Perhaps the most important debate within European intellectual history deals with conceptualising the role and place of religion in modern public life. Philosopher and social theorist Jürgen Habermas is considered to be the most famous theoretician on the birth of the modern public sphere, which often is argued to be the most crucial arena of public life. Habermas ([1962] 1989) was especially interested in the public sphere in which issues of important public relevance such as politics were discussed. For Habermas, the press marked the public sphere. He considered a politically and religiously independent press to be a central factor in the birth of the modern public sphere. The press provided a platform for free social debate based on which citizens could participate in and commit to building a democratic society. This original public sphere theory thus downplayed the importance of religion in modern public life. Consequently, many studies discussing the role and place of religion in contemporary, secular Western news media considered religion to be a topic unimportant to modern secular news (Winston 2012).

Moreover, the idea of secularisation influenced not only the place of religion in news media but also the ways in which religion was covered and reported in the news when it was given attention. As scholar of religion and news Diane Winston reminds us, "news is current and consequential information on matters that affect and interest its consumers" (Winston 2012, 5). The defining news criteria – impact, timeliness, prominence, proximity, bizarreness, conflict, and currency – are indirectly related to secularisation. Thus, if and when religion makes the news in secular media, it must meet these criteria, which explicitly influences the conditions under which religion makes the news (when it does!) in secular news media (Winston 2012, 5). Furthermore, according to Winston (2012, 14), secular news outlets often define religion in rather conventional and institutional terms. For example, in the news, Judaism is perceived as a religion, but extreme suffering is not, though they both share aspects of community, ritual and transcendence (Winston 2012). News on religion thus tends to focus on prominent religious institutions (e.g., large churches) and powerful people (e.g., the pope and the Dalai Lama) instead of small, marginal religious groups and their followers. This focus, of course, has the exception of violent religious movements and curiosities concerning religious practices that are considered to be bizarre in news media and make headlines in secular news media, such as polygamy in the Mormon religion and celebrity-driven scandals in Scientology.

With the rise of post-9/11 terrorism, the questions of radicalisation of religion and fundamentalism have invited scholars of media and religion to provide new explanations for the growing visibility of religion in the global and digital public sphere. An early explanation was given by Manuel Castells (1996), interpreting the rise of Muslim (but also Christian and Hindu) fundamentalism in the public sphere as a defensive reaction to insecurities and inequalities caused by globalisation and digitalisation. In more recent scholarly debates, Castells' (1996) explanation has been challenged by more progressive views on Islam and the public sphere. For example, Eickelman and Anderson (2003) have argued for Islam's constructive role in a transnational, even global public sphere in which Islam is seen to develop not against but with new digital media technologies. This view enables development of what can be called a Muslim public sphere in which new Muslim publics have new possibilities to challenge the authority of the state and more conventional religious authorities and to establish and maintain new transnational relations and forms of civil society (Meyer and Moors 2006, 5). In this frame of analysis, new public debates may emerge not only between Islam and the secular public sphere but also within the Muslim public sphere.

In recent years, the development of communication technologies, increasing multiculturalism of societies, growth of migration and globalisation of economics, politics and culture have challenged scholars of media and religion to re-think secularisation theory and the related place of religion in the public sphere (Walters and Kersley 2018). Consequently, Habermas (2006), as well as many of his colleagues and contemporaries, have reinterpreted the secularisation paradigm. For instance, José Casanova (1994) has had a central role in raising discussion on what kinds of conditions are set for practicing public religion. Birgit Meyer and Annelie Moors

(2006) have shaken up the secularisation paradigm and critiqued its inability to recognise religious phenomena in the public sphere. The discussion on the post-secular has also built new bridges for research oriented to sociology of religion in today's public sphere (Frisk and Nynäs 2012).

Within these discussions, an increasing number of scholars in media studies and the study of religion share the idea that on a global scale, the role and significance of religion have not merely decreased in the public sphere as assumed, and religion has not unequivocally shifted from the public sphere to the private sphere of the family as many scholars earlier predicted. The secular way of life has not gained a position as the global norm as once anticipated. The secularisation paradigm still has its supporters, of course, and its explanatory power is continuously debated in the field of the sociology of religion. In an example of this ongoing debate, in the book *Secularization*, Steve Bruce (2011) defends the theory's explanatory power when studying the role of religion in modern Western societies from the perspective of social structures and cultural changes.

4 Towards the Study of Mediatization of Religion

In addition to the vital debate on the role and place of religion in the public sphere, another key debate has emerged at the intersection of the study of media and religion. This debate was triggered by the concept, idea, and theory of mediatization (of religion). From the perspective of media studies, the mediatization agenda grew out of a need to better capture the significance of the all-encompassing presence of media in contemporary social life (see e.g., Couldry and Hepp 2017; Lundby 2014). Today, many scholars of media and religion agree that what we have witnessed over recent centuries is the growing media influence of religion in society (Hjarvard and Lövheim 2012). Mediatization, perceived as a process, is thought to have profoundly transformed the patterns of social interactions and the workings of social institutions in a given society. This development also applies to religion (Lundby 2018, 5). Mediatization theory was first used to analyse religion in the work of media scholar Stig Hjarvard (2016). Since then, it has had a strong influence in the study of media and religion in the Northern European Protestant context and within a certain type of public broadcasting media system (Hjarvard and Lövheim 2012). The application of mediatization theory to religion refers to the processes 'through which religious beliefs, agency, and symbols are becoming influenced by the workings of various media' (Hjarvard 2016, 8; see also Lövheim and Hjarvard 2019, 208). Moreover, as a theory, the mediatization of religion investigates how religion and related changes take place at the structural level (institutions) and the level of social interaction (practices; Lövheim and Hjarvard 2019, 208).

One key debate within research on the mediatization of religion has to do with whether mediatization reinforces the secularisation of society as it is argued to diminish the influence of religious institutions in society. The debate on *banal religion* resonates with the debate on secularisation. With this concept of banal religion, Hjarvard (2016) refers to various forms of popular religiosity that break away from institutions and different dogmatic systems and are typical of religious expressions produced and represented by media. Various film and book genres including supernatural elements, such as the vampire-themed Twilight Saga, are examples of banal religion in Hjarvard's concept. A counterargument to this perception of banal religion highlights the concept's lack of historical perspective (Lied 2012; Lövheim and Lynch 2011). As many scholars of 'folk religion' would argue, forms of religious beliefs and practices established and experienced in various non-institutional contexts have long existed side by side with institutional religions and often contesting orthodox religious dogma of representatives of religious institutions (see e.g., Utriainen and Salmesvuori 2014). In this line of thinking, the different forms of banal religion do not indicate secularisation but, instead, the fragmentation, pluralisation and contestation of religious authority in society.

Yet another debate in the study of media and religion concerns the concept of mediatization or mediation (see e.g., Lundby 2014). Researchers who emphasise the mediated instead of the mediatized nature of religion and belief stress slightly different aspects than those working on the concept of mediatization. Representatives of the mediation school of thought include media scholars Hoover (2013) and Stolow (2005), anthropologist Meyer (2013) and material religion and visual studies scholar Morgan (2008). This school holds that all phenomena and cultural practices that are somehow religious in nature are bound to become mediated, whether in the form of texts, images or any material or immaterial means of communication. Instead of focusing on a particular medium (e.g., mass media), scholars interested in the mediation of religion pay attention to the mediation of meaning, that is, to meanings, places and practices linked to mediation and how they change in different contexts. This approach does not assume that modern media are exceptional but, instead, sees them as part of historical continuities and discontinuities (Hoover 2014; Martin-Barberon 1993). From the perspective of Hjarvard's mediatization theory, the problem in the mediation of religion approach is that its broad definition of religion as a "culturally meaningful belief system" (Schofield Clark and Hoover 1997, 17) weakens its potential to analytically explain "how mediation shapes the particularities of religious beliefs, practices and organisations as forms of meaning making and social interaction" (Lövheim and Hjarvard 2019, 209).

From the perspective of observing religion in today's society, one may conclude that both approaches – research emphasising mediatization or mediation – raise essential questions about the relationship between religion and media in the contemporary media-saturated society. It is impossible to interpret contemporary Western society without comprehending the processes of modernisation and their impacts shaping society, individuals, and different institutions. Thus, mediatization is a necessary concept for interpreting Western societies penetrated by modernisation on every level, but at the same time, the more subtle dynamics of the mediation of religiously inspired meanings in different places and practices should also be taken into consideration.

New research that analyses the mediatization of religion outside Western contexts also has made relevant contributions to bringing the two concepts into fruitful interplay. Patrick Eisenlohr's (2017) research stands out as an example. His work on Islamic televangelism in India clarifies that it is important to analytically differentiate the mediatization of religion – or religion in the public sphere – connecting interactions between human actors through the circulation of religious discourse and images from the mediation of religion as interactions between human and divine actors. The level of mediatization thus depends on the interactions between public religion and religious mediation. Furthermore, Eisenlohr (2017) notes that in such contexts, religious mediation may also function as a form of resistance to changes induced by the use of media technology and related mediatization of religion (see also Lövheim and Hjarvard 2019). In recent years, radical changes in the media environment, namely, the vast influence of the Internet and social media, have challenged scholars of media and religion to begin to ask new questions about the relationship between media and religion in this digital age (Campbell and Lövheim 2017). The last section of this chapter focuses on the growing influence of the digitalisation of media communication in the study of media and religion.

5 Digital Media – Digital Religion

Today's digital media environment can best be described as networked, fragmented and in constant flux. In this type of communication environment, local communication on religion intersects with national and global communication. Issues of power, structure, agency and authority related to religion are constantly re-negotiated as professional news media and journalism have lost the privilege to act as gatekeepers and agenda setters for the global flows of communication on religion (see e.g., Evolvi 2018; Sumiala et al. 2018).

Heidi Campbell's (2017) work on digital religion is an important attempt to better grasp religion in the present media environment. According to Campbell (2017, 16): "digital religion explores the intersection of new media technologies, religion, and digital culture. It encompasses topics such as how religious communities engage with the Internet to ways religiosity is expressed through digital practices and the extent to which technological engagement can be seen as a spiritual enterprise." Digital religion can be argued to exist in three particular ways. First, digital media characteristically generate new patterns of communication within religious groups and thus transform or even destabilise their traditional communication flows (Campbell 2017, 18). Second, digital media provide opportunities for digital religion to gain visibility in the digital public sphere and thus allow different religious communities and individuals to voice their views in ways not possible in the era characterised by mass communication (Campbell 2017, 18). Third, digital media shape religious authority as digital religion has potential to destabilise the authority of traditional religious institutions and related actors (Campbell 2017, 19). Digital media, in this type of reading, can be argued, on one hand, to shape digital religion in ways that promise to give religion more visibility in the present digital media environment and related society. On the other hand, digital media also provide tools to challenge traditional religious authority and order and thus may well threaten religious institutions while making room for new types of religious activities and re-structuring of religious hierarchy.

In recent years, a key debate in digital religion studies has concerned the blending and blurring of what have been called the online and the offline religious spheres and how this intermingling of the online and the offline shapes existing religious practices and triggers new practices of spirituality (Campbell 2017). This debate has pushed scholars to further think about the interplay between the concepts of the digital and the religious. Following Hoover's (2012, ix) insight, instead of simply looking at the "digitalisation of religion" – that is, how digital media push religious groups to adapt to changing conditions in approaching and practicing religion – scholars of digital religion should be more interested in considering "the actual contribution 'the digital' is making to 'the religious'". Lövheim and Campbell (2017, 11–12) reflected on the future of research on media and religion in today's digital context and suggested that what is needed is a shift of perspective from looking at religious communities, organised religion and individual believers and their communicative practices to a more explicit focus on how other communities, organisations and individuals apply religious symbols and ideas in their communication and how these communicative practices shape the public presence of religion in the present digital sphere (see e.g., Evolvi 2018).

In concluding this chapter, I wish to illustrate how this shift in the study of media and religion can be applied in empirical research. A recently growing area of research on digital media and religion focuses on public controversies and contested religion in the present digital age (Lundby 2018; Sumiala 2017). A subarea in this research field looks at religiously inspired terrorist attacks as hybrid media events (Sumiala et al. 2018). This research strand gives special focus to the complex ways in which the phenomenon of religiously inspired terrorism circulates in various digital media platforms and how this flow of violence shapes the social construction of religion in the digital context. This research stream thus looks at not only the actors triggering communication on religion but also communicative structures and how they shape communication on religion. The hybrid concept is applied to emphasise how certain elements such as the multiplication of actors (e.g. journalists, ordinary media users, politicians, terrorists and nongovernmental organisations), diverse affordances (e.g., for different purposes for police and terrorists), constant fights over attention (e.g., professional news media and ordinary social media users), a strong emphasis on affective messages (e.g., memes and hashtags associated with religious meanings) and acceleration of communication (e.g., the intensified flow of messages across different platforms) all shape communication on religion and, consequently, affect the public presence of religion in the digital media environment, thereby contributing to the social construction of Religion as a global threat (Sumiala et al. 2018). One of the main challenges for future research on digital media and religion is to better understand how such public understandings of religion may shape the role and place of not only particular religions but also religion in more general in the digitally saturated and highly mediatized public sphere we occupy today.

Bibliography

Bruce, Steve. 2011. *Secularization: In Defence of an Unfashionable Theory*. Oxford: Oxford University Press.
Campbell, Heidi. 2017. "Surveying Theoretical Approaches within Digital Religion Studies." *New Media & Society* 19:15–24.
Campbell, Heidi, and Mia Lövheim. 2017. "Considering Critical Methods and Theoretical Lenses in Digital Religion Studies." *New Media & Society* 19:5–14.
Carey, James W. 1989. *Communication as Culture: Essays on Media and Society*. London / New York: Routledge.
Casanova, José. 1994. *Public Religions in the Modern World*. Chicago: University of Chicago Press.
Castells, Manuel. 1996. *The Rise of Network Society*. Vol. 1, *The Information Age: Economy, Society, and Culture*. Oxford: Blackwell.
Couldry, Nick, and Andreas Hepp. 2017. *The Mediated Construction of Reality*. Cambridge: Polity Press.
Eickelman, Dale F., and Jon W. Anderson. 2003. *New Media in the Muslim World: The Emerging Public Sphere*. Bloomington: Indiana University Press.
Eisenlohr, Patrick. 2017. "Reconsidering Mediatization of Religion: Islamic Televangelism in India." *Media, Culture & Society* 39:869–84.
Eisenstein, Elizabeth. 1979. *The Printing Press as an Agent of Change*. Cambridge, MA: Cambridge University Press.
Evolvi, Giulia. 2018. *Blogging My Religion: Secular, Muslim, and Catholic Media Spaces in Europe*. Oxon: Routledge.
Frisk, Liselotte, and Peter Nynäs. 2012. "Characteristics of Contemporary Religious Change: Globalization, Neoliberalism, and Interpretative Tendencies." In *Post-Secular Society*, edited by Peter Nynäs, Mika Lassander, and Terhi Utriainen, New Brunswick: Transaction Publishers, 47–70.
Habermas, Jürgen. [1962] 1989. *The Structural Transformation of the Public Sphere: An Inquiry into a Category of Bourgeois Society*, trans. Thomas Burger. Cambridge: Polity Press.
Habermas, Jürgen. 2006. "Religion in the Public Sphere." *European Journal of Philosophy* 14:1–25.
Hjarvard, Stig. 2016. "Mediatization and the Changing Authority of Religion." *Media, Culture & Society* 38:8–17.
Hjarvard, Stig, and Mia Lövheim, eds. 2012. *Mediatization and Religion: Nordic Perspectives*. Göteborg: Nordicom.
Hoover, Stewart. 2012. "Forward: Practice, Autonomy and Authority in the Digitally Religious and Digitally Spiritual." In *Digital Religion, Social Media and Culture: Perspectives, Practices and Rituals*, edited by Pauline H. Cheong, Peter Fischer-Nielsen, and Stefan Gelfgren, New York: Peter Lang, 6–12.
Hoover, Stewart. 2013. "Evolving Religion in the Digital Media." In *Religion across Media: From Early Antiquity to Late Modernity*, edited by Knut Lundby, New York: Peter Lang, 169–184.

Hoover, Stewart. 2014. "Media, Culture and the Imagination of Religion." In *Communication Theories in a Multicultural World*, edited by Clifford Christians and Kaarle Nordengstren, New York: Peter Lang, 197–212.
Hoover, Stewart, and Knut Lundby, eds. 1997. *Rethinking Media, Religion, and Culture*. London: Sage.
Horsfield, Peter G. 1984. *Religious Television: The American Experience*. New York: Longman.
Lied, Liv Ingeborg. 2012. "Religious Change and Popular Culture: With a Nod to a Mediatization of Religion Debate." In *Mediatization and Religion: Nordic Perspectives*, edited by Stig Hjarvard and Mia Lövheim, Göteborg: Nordicom, 183–201.
Lövheim, Mia, and Gordon Lynch. 2011. "The Mediatisation of Religion Debate: An Introduction." *Culture and Religion* 12:111–117.
Lövheim, Mia, and Stig Hjarvard. 2019. "The Mediatized Conditions of Contemporary Religion: Critical Status and Future Directions." *Journal of Religion, Media and Digital Culture* 8:206–225.
Lundby, Knut, ed. 2014. *Mediatization of Communication*. Berlin / Boston: De Gruyter Mouton.
Lundby, Knut, ed. 2018. *Contesting Religion: The Media Dynamics of Cultural Conflicts in Scandinavia*. Berlin / Boston: De Gruyter.
Martín-Barberon, Jesús. 1993. *Communication, Culture and Hegemony*. London: Sage.
Meyer, Birgit. 2013. "Material Mediations and Religious Practices of World Making." In *Religion across Media: From Early Antiquity to Late Modernity*, edited by Knut Lundby, New York: Peter Lang, 1–19.
Meyer, Birgit, and Annelies Moors, eds. 2006. *Religion, Media, and the Public Sphere*. Bloomington: Indiana University Press.
Morgan, David. 2008. "Introduction. Religion, Media, Culture: The Shape of the 'Field'." In *Key Words in Religion, Media, and Culture*, edited by David Morgan, New York: Routledge, 1–19.
Pietilä, Veikko. 2005. *On the Highway of Mass Communication Studies*. Cresskill: Hampton Press.
Schofield Clark, Lynn, and Stewart Hoover. 1997. "At the Intersection of Media, Religion, and Culture: A Bibliographic Essay." In *Rethinking Media, Religion, and Culture*, edited by Stewart Hoover and Knut Lundby, Thousand Oaks: Sage, 37–64.
Silverstone, Roger. 1981. *Message of Television: Myth and Narrative in Contemporary Culture*. London: Heineman Educational Books.
Stolow, Jeremy. 2005. "Religion and / as Media." *Theory, Culture & Society* 22:119–45.
Sumiala, Johanna. 2017. "Introduction: Mediatization in Post-Secular Society – New Perspectives in the Study of Media, Religion and Politics." *Journal of Religion in Europe* 10:361–365.
Sumiala, Johanna, Katja Valaskivi, Minttu Tikka, and Jukka Huhtamäki. 2018. *Hybrid Media Events: The Charlie Hebdo Attacks and the Global Circulation of Terrorist Violence*. Bingley: Emerald Publishing Limited.
Utriainen, Terhi, and Päivi Salmesvuori. 2014. *Finnish Women Making Religion: Between Ancestors and Angels*. New York: Palgrave Macmillan.
Walters, James, and Esther Kersley. 2018. *Religion and the Public Sphere: New Conversations*. Abingdon: Routledge.
Winston, Diane. 2012. "Introduction: Mapping the Royal Road." In *The Oxford Handbook of Religion and the American News Media*, edited by Diane Winston, Oxford: Oxford University Press, 3–32.

Asonzeh Ukah
Politics and Religion

1 Introduction

This chapter analyses the complex and changing relationships between religion and politics in contemporary societies and nation-states.[1] It also examines the dimensions of these complex relationships as well as some specific aspects of the relationships such as civil religion, theocracy, the secular / sacred distinction and the separation between the state and religion. The approach employed here is historical, analytical, and conceptual. Each of these relationships is an attempt at conceptualising the meaning, definition and theory of religion and politics and how they interlink in practice in specific social contexts. The cultural context of this analysis is the post-colonial societies of countries in Africa where Euro-western colonialism imposed a colonial model of the nation-state, with a (formal but impactable) separation of state and religion.

In different countries and societies, the relationship between politics and religion, faith, and polity, is constantly debated and contested. In contemporary times, this is more so due to the increased visibility and resilience of religion in the face of, or rather despite, secularisation assumptions undergirding the formation of the modern nation-state. In an era of globalisation, inherited ideas and notions of politics, religion and their relationship have come under increasing scrutiny as society changes. In the face of increasing global interconnection and interpenetration as well as ethnoreligious or cultural nationalism around the world, some scholars, following the lead of Hannah Arendt ([1951] 1979), argue that the power and role of the nation-state (and hence polity and politics) are increasingly declining. However, as concepts that predominate in interdisciplinary research, 'politics' and 'religion' are both contested categories, differently defined across disciplines and according to scholars' interests. That religion and politics have shifting and indeterminate meanings is what Bryan Turner describes as "the problem of the cultural specificity of our basic concepts" (Turner 2011, 3); these concepts are deployed differently in different contexts, cultures and societies. Definitions are important, as Jeppe Sinding Jensen (2003, 63) makes clear because they embody, and are shortened forms of, theorisation. A definition of politics or religion subscribes to an implicit theory of action and practice about how these concepts perform and are expected to perform in real-world situations and within cultures. In both popular and scholarly usage, the

---

[1] Research for this essay was supported by the National Research Foundation of South Africa (Reference number [UID] 85397). The opinions, findings, and conclusions expressed are those of the author; the NRF accepts no liability whatsoever in this regard. I am grateful to Banchileyew Silewondim Getahun for assistance during the revision and editing of this paper. The usual caveats hold.

meaning of politics as well as religion is part of what Willi Braun describes as "experience-near" and "untaught learning" (Braun 2000, 4) which people absorb from their cultural environments and social representations. Because these two concepts are frequently used in a context-specific manner – although driven by transcultural and transreligious goals – it is challenging to determine where their respective boundaries lie, "or what constitutes religion [or politics] as opposed to some other type of activity or thought" (Ellis and ter Haar 2012, 457). For religion and politics, the root of this challenge, among others, is "the problem of excess and spectrality: there are too many meanings and meanings are too indeterminate" (Braun 2000, 4).

In the case of religion, because of the multiplicity of meanings, and the historical association of the concept with Christianity, colonialism and western imperialism (Chidester 1996, 30–72; Chidester 2014, 59–89; Turner 2011, 3–5), Toyin Falola postulates the use of the different concept of "ritual archive" to designate what in the African world religion represents: "the conglomeration of words as well as texts, ideas, symbols, shrines, images, performances, and indeed objects that document as well as speak to those religious experiences and practices that allow us to understand the African world through various bodies of philosophers, literatures, languages, histories and much more" (Falola 2017, 703). Ritual archive, therefore, means much more than what the western-derived concepts such as 'religion', 'the holy' and 'the sacred' designate. Furthermore, ritual archive seems more faithful to the etymology of religion, *relegere* (as against the more frequently referenced Latin root, *religare*, to bind, see Idowu 1973, 22–75), to pay heed, to have a care for (spiritual and godly matters [Hoyt 1912, 127]). This perspective on religion recognises and unites the historic traditions of religion as "a pervasive dimension in human life" (Smith 1994, 1). Similarly, politics, while dealing with formal and informal contestations and control of managing a civil sphere through so-called rational legal structures, is construed as the arena of power involving much more than formal domination of state governance infrastructure to include "power to", "power over", "power for" as well as "domination" (Lukes 2005, 27; 64). It may also mean the mobilisation of non-legal, other-worldly, resources in influencing decisively these worldly structures and affairs, for example, under theocracy, to be discussed below. According to this conceptualisation – and because politics is about the distribution of power in a society – power is at the core of politics; it is the locomotive that propels and determines political activities, organisations, and objectives.

The relationship between politics (understood broadly as power archives) and religion (understood as ritual archives) is multifaceted and complex. While religion provides a moral, metasocial conceptual framework for the organisation of perception and social structure and ethical stability, politics as the sphere of (the exercise of) power depicts the arena of real interests and social capacity for action, as "productive, transformative, authoritative [domination which can be] compatible with dignity" (Lukes 2005, 109). For the purposes of this chapter, religion is conceived as "the political economy of the sacred" (Chidester 2012, 4; 44) and ritual archive; the sacred is variously referenced as the metasocial, the other-worldly or the meta-empirical world, or the ritual economy that guides, motivates, or inspires a group or a people to interpretations, practices and perspectives related to their surrounding environment and experiences of being in the world. Framed in this broad sense, religion constitutes the tangible and intangible sociocultural and eco-political heritage of a people and society. Similarly, politics, etymologically derives from the Greek πολιτικός, which relates to the affairs of the πόλις, the assembly of free citizens or the ἐκκλησία (Seiwert 2016, 430). In both common, everyday usage and scholarly discourse, it is often understood as the political economy of power, power being variously referenced as domination, and real interest in the sphere of social reality that is separate from economics, family, or religion. The social sphere of politics, therefore, concerns the formal contestation over control of (the formation of) state policies and their implementation, political parties, and governance structure. Though the two spheres of politics and religion are diffused and protean in conceptualisation, they are also differentiated social realities. Even so, they are related and overlap in many respects. In this chapter, the relationships between politics and religion are examined in respect to the concept of civil religion, theocracy, secularisms, and the separation between state, as a formal structure of governance, and religion, as a meta-social sphere that relates citizens to extra-empirical entities and realities.

2 Civil Religion

In contemporary societies and nations, politics relates to religion in different ways, one of which is usually termed civil religion. This concept captures a set of values and norms, practices and attitudes and beliefs which a society recognises that sacralise and impose upon it a transcendental mission. In such a society, the political authorities or structure, in addition to being informed by a legal-rational ethos, also express a charismatic aura. Civil religion expresses aspects of the overarching dimensions of social reality in society. Under the ethos of civil religion, the object of belief is not the invisible realm but the social sphere where the nation becomes the transcendental repertoire of consent, loyalty and emotion that holds citizens together and, according to the famous definition of religion provided by Émile Durkheim, "unite [them] into a single moral community [...] all those who adhere to them" (Durkheim [1915] 2008, 47). In civil religion, the nation-state is set up both as a dimension of social reality and a "conception of destiny" as the "ultimate object of loyalty and devotion" (Smith 1994, 8). In the context of the secularisation debate of the mid-1960s which posited increasing disenchantment of modernity because of the consequences of technological and scientific thinking and application (Wilson 2016), Robert Bellah, borrowing the phrase of 'civil religion' from the title of the last chapter of Jean-Jacques Rousseau's *The Social Contract* (Rousseau [1762] 1994), proposed what amounted to arguably the most powerful articulation of a civil religion thesis within the American context. Rousseau's (Rousseau 1994, 158–168) version aimed at sacralising the state to avoid the divisiveness and half-hearted civil commitment which multiple religious traditions and institutions create in terms of citizens' allegiances. In the seminal essay "Civil Religion in America" Bellah (1967, 1970, 168–189), inspired by Durkheimian sociology (rather than Rousseau's ideas), examines the American nation as an entity that transcends itself as an embodiment of critical ethical principles under which its citizens are subordinate. He compares how the dominant religion of America, which is Protestant Christianity, has shaped and informed social and civic consciousness of Americans, which is evident in the ritual components, metaphors, and religious ideas within political culture. Civil religion is the concept that captures what he terms "a clearly differentiated [...] religious dimension [that is] elaborate and well-institutionalized" (Bellah 1970, 167) which exists alongside traditional religion. In Bellah's repurposing of the concept of 'civil religion' core Christian (read: British Puritanistic) ideas and the belief in a moral God who is the creator of humanity are the driving imperative and objective of political practice and goals. Through this concept, he undergirds the religious dimension of American political culture and social discourse and how the nation could be an object of self-idolisation and self-worship.

Every nation and society articulate specific relationships between dominant religious values and institutions and organisation of civil and political life and culture; civil religion refers to the institutionalised collection of sacred beliefs, rituals, and symbols of a nation. Bellah offers a loose definition of the concept as "a collection of beliefs, symbols, and rituals with respect to sacred things and institutionalized in a collectivity" (Bellah 1967, 175) called a nation. In this conceptualisation, civil religion is distinct and distinguishable from denominational religion even though the former borrows extensively from the latter. The ritual objects of civil religion include founding documents and constitutions which function symbolically as civil scriptures, inaugural speeches of political leaders which are likened to religious sermons. Important national celebrations such as anniversaries and Independence Day take on the value of rituals in terms of solidarity and the re-enactment of divine intervention or transcendental ethics in the life of the nation. In this sense, civil religion is a social fact that exists, a social reality that can be perceived and analysed and reconstructed; more importantly, it affects and structures how individuals relate to one another and to the state. It is a specific objective realm of action and perception, a site of convergence between politics and religion.

While it may be debated whether civil religion is a delineated realm of 'social facts' – defined by Durkheim as "the clearest thing in the world [which] vary with the social system of which they form a part; they cannot be understood when detached from it" (Durkheim 2008, 27, 94) – as Bellah had conceived, the concept expresses a specific manner in which politics and religion relate as social realities or objective social facts, shaping the public sphere and discourses. Consistent with Durkheimian sociology, civil religion as social fact influences – though not in a deterministic way – categories of thought in a society (Durkheim 2008, 145). In different societies, civil and political culture interpenetrates with the religious and spiritual or mythic realm, each reinforcing and strengthening the other, sharing symbols, ideas, motifs, ethics, and concepts such as "the values of liberty, justice, charity, and personal virtue" (Christiano, Swatos, and Kivisto 2016, 65). Religion in subtle ways frames political purposes, interests, and agenda (Martin 2010).

The debates on the analytical character and utility of civil religion and the application of the concept in socio-political contexts other than the United States are still ongoing. If religions usually and definitionally reference a transcendence and are articulated in creeds, what is the creed of civil religion? According to Bellah, "[t]here is no formal creed in civil religion" (Bellah 1970, 183), and because of this, the concept is nebulous, assimilating or accommodating of anything anyone wants to describe as civil religion, "a secularized 'cult of man'" (Thompson 1998, 104). A creedless civil religion suffers from similar conceptual and analytical muddles in the definitions of belief found in the work of David Hume, one of which is that a "belief is nothing but a more vivid, lively, forcible, firm, steady conception of an object, than what the imagination alone is ever able to attain." (Hume [1748] 2007, 48). How is civil religion conceptualised in societies where there is a plurality of institutional or organised religions or where the state enforces a specific religion rather than have religious solidarity emerge from a voluntary polity? While these questions deserve more elaborate analysis than is possible in this chapter, the explanatory utility of the concept could be found in the diverse ways in which contemporary society is reified and transcendentalised, for example, in constitutional patriotism or hyper nationalism where devotional fervours and unconditional, absolute allegiances to the nation-state are demanded of citizens. The concept also sheds some light on the boundaries between religious resurgence within spiritual communities and political nationalism that have emerged in the context of globalisation and its discontents. Furthermore, the concept is applicable outside of western democracies, for example, in the debates surrounding the possibility of Confucianism emerging as a form of "Chinese civil religion" in contemporary China (Zhe 2013, 48).

In contemporary societies under the influence of globalisation, civil religion is a veritable structure and process in which political discourses and ideas are revitalised and reinfused with moral vigour and energy. In an era of populist politics and religious hyper nationalism across the world (for example, the controversies about the faith and pastor of Barack Obama (Mansfield 2008), Conservative Protestant Trumpism, Hindu nationalism, etc.), civil religion as non-religious sacred nationalism offers some insights into the relationship between political discourse, the public sphere and religious ideas and imagination. Similarly, the raging debates surrounding homosexuality and same-sex relationship as well as the criminalisation of such behaviours in Africa, which are evidently driven by religious morality and ethical apocalypticism (Ukah 2016b, 2018a), can be analysed under the rubric of African civil religion. Also, widespread instances of religiously infused and motivated virulent hate speech (Ukah 2019) in Africa may be viewed as a form of political interaction with religion in a rapidly changing media environment. This sort of religion increasingly re-enchants political discourses with sacred and transcendental values. As Grave Davie (Davie 2001) argues, there are growing examples of what could be conceptualised as a 'global civil religion' constituted by strands of institutions and religious practices from different parts of the world.

3 Theocracy

"Originally men had no kings except their gods, and no government except theocracy" (Rousseau 1994, 158). If Rousseau's statement is accepted as historical and factual, theocracy becomes the oldest form of governance system. Further, if this statement is interpreted to mean that at some point in human history deities *personally* presided over human affairs as 'kings' or rulers, then it is indeed difficult to understand with any degree of analytical precision what the concept of theocracy means. However, the concept has a long and complex history, with many layers of meaning: "The theocratic form of government is particularly difficult to understand, partly because the word can be taken to mean so many different things and also because the regimes which can be labelled theocratic in one sense or another appear too different" (Ferrero and Wintrobe 2009, 1). Etymologically, theocracy is the system of government of gods and deities and their representatives of human society. Derived from the Greek θεοκρατία, meaning 'rule by god', the word was coined by the Jewish priest-historian, Joseph Ben Mattias better known as Titus Flavius Josephus (37/38–100 CE) specifically in reference to preferred Jewish systems of governance and the role of Moses as a lawgiver, a divine personality or 'man of God', and an interpreter of the will of Yahweh, the Hebrew God. According to Josephus, for the Jews, "the God of Israel was allowed to be supreme King of Israel, and his directions to be their authentic guides, God gave them such directions as their supreme king and governor; and they were properly under a theocracy" (A. J. 2.6–24, 3.180, 4.13, 150, 156; C. Ap. 2.75, 145, 154; see Josephus 1974, 1137; 2006, 663; on Moses as the initiator of theocracy, see van Seters 2005, 6199). Originally, theocracy defines "divine government of the Jewish nation" (Josephus 1974, 507), which is the only way in which Josephus was able to explain and compare the Jewish political organisation and system to Hellenistic systems such as monarchy, oligarchy, or a republic. Understood as the rule of gods over humans, theocracy is an extreme form of the relationship between politics and religion or the supernatural.

Theocracy does not literally mean that gods and deities assume governmental power over humans but that individuals, particularly a sacerdotal order, assume political control of a society claiming divine mandate or commission. For this class of actors, ascribing authority to a meta-social or metapolitical order guarantees obedience and allegiance for divine guidance and precept. Theocracy, therefore, is an intensely contested system in which a class of religious officials exercise political power and authority or even rule directly. The class of religio-political actors ascend their position in their capacity as interpreters or translators of a divine will. As a rule of gods through a sacerdotal order, theocracy is also a hierocracy or an "ecclesiocracy" (Salmon 2009, 57). In a theocracy, the divine will override and overwrites the will of the δῆμος, the people; and the source of authority is assumed to be invisible and inscrutable: god, gods, deities, the sacred, the supernatural, ancestors/ancestresses, in other words, the meta-social. Theocracy is a government based on and circumscribed by a theological faith, implicitly or explicitly, which may be derived from institutional religion or rational ideologies that Smith characterise as quasi-religions – "ultimate object[s] of loyalty and devotion" (Smith 1994, 8). These rational ideologies include humanism, nationalism, communism, or Marxism. According to Mario Ferrero (Ferrero 2009), although theocracy is transreligious and transcultural, the theocratic ruling class is historically male. Theocracies, therefore, correlate negatively with women's participation in public power; this is especially the case with Islamic theocracies in Sharia states.

It is not infrequent that the mention of theocracy is associated with Muslim majority countries or Islamic regimes such as the Iranian state government or the Taliban during their rule in Afghanistan. Theocratic strains can, however, be noted in almost every society and type of government from the British monarchy and its relationship with the Church of England to the American system of democracy with its conservative evangelical political resurgence. Sometimes what appears as a constitutional democracy is, in fact, a disguised theocracy. Nigeria is a good example: the debate whether it is a secular or a multireligious state is a perennial one. Christians claim and insist that the operative 1999 Constitution is a secular document; Muslims decry even the use of the word 'secular' because to them, it means irreligious. Nigerian Muslims claim their faith does not permit them to live in an irreligious state. Furthermore, the Preamble to the Constitution states thus: "We the people of the Federal Republic of Nigeria Having firmly and solemnly resolved, to live in unity and harmony as one indivisible and indissoluble sovereign nation under God".[2] To live "under God" is precisely what a theocracy means in its original Josephusian sense even though the nature and character of this 'God', used seven times in the document, is never elaborated. Even more confounding for those who believe that the Constitution is a secular document is that while 'Christian' or 'Christianity' does not occur in the document, "Islam/ic" occurs 28 times; "Muslim/s" occurs 10 times and "Sharia" occurs a staggering 73 times. The mere appearance of words may seem insignificant but cumulatively, it is plausible to argue that they point to a major discursive, legislative, and interpretative direction, which is towards upholding, reinforcing and signposting Islamic legal and religious ideas, purposes, interests and agenda. Because these Islamic concepts predominate and are used in strategic contexts, 12 of the 36 (sub-national) states of the country have adopted expanded versions of Sharia penal codes since 1999/2000 (Ostien, Nasir, and Kogelmann 2005; Harnischfeger 2008; Chesworth and Kogelmann 2014), effectively practising a version of theocracy that may be called 'theodemocracy' or theocratic democracy.

---

[2] For the Constitution of the Federal Republic of Nigeria (1999, as amended), cf. https://nigerian-constitution.com/s (30.11.2021).

The response of Nigeria's large Christian population to the increasing 'Shariafication' of the country's sociolegal environment and the crowding out of competing religious communities, symbols, ideas, and discourses has been confounding, too. As expected, Christians decry the imposition of Sharia penal codes in large swaths of northern Nigeria, but they fail to provide a viable alternative other than following the pathway defined by Muslims. Christians, in particular the Pentecostal community, designate the country as a 'Christian nation' whose leaders, especially at the national level, must be born-again Christians and 'servants of God' imbued with divine guidance based on the Judeo-Christian scripture. Nigerian Christians, basing their argument on articles 10 and 38(1) of the Constitution which contains the disestablishment and free exercise of religion clauses,[3] insist that the nation is a secular State; they have still proceeded to supply religious arguments and rhetoric for wanting to Christianise a secular State (Ukah 2014; 2018b). In this articulation, the electorate is reduced to giving accent to divine choice rather than expressing their own will in choosing a leader through the exercise of electoral politics. For both Nigerian Muslims and Christians, therefore, politics is a religious vocation and exercise by other means. Inversely, religion is a political practice by other means. When they speak of 'democracy', they in practice mean and prefer a theocracy where the will and guidance of a god supersedes the will of the electorate. Theocracy shows the degree to which a government approximates to religion in its structures, ideologies, and practices. The Nigerian example, which can be multiplied across countries and continents, illustrates that a theocratic impulse could still be evident even in an ostensible liberal democracy.

4 Secular / Sacred Distinction

The concepts of religion and politics are, in theory, conceived to represent two distinct, even if related social spheres and realities. This analytic distinction is not a given or obvious in many societies. Historically, the distinction is recent. The phenomenologist of religion, Mircea Eliade postulates about "two modes of being in the world, two existential situations assumed by man in the course of his history" (Eliade [1957] 1987, 14), these he calls 'the sacred' and 'the profane'. This distinction is necessary, according to Eliade, because it better brings out "the specific characteristics of life in a world capable of becoming sacred" (Eliade 1987, 15). The sacred is the experience of the nonworld, the meta-world, while the profane is the experience of the world; both types of experiences occur within corresponding types of spaces;

---

[3] Art.§10: "The Government of the Federation or of a State shall not adopt any religion as State Religion". Art. §31(1): "Every person shall be entitled to freedom of thought, conscience and religion, including freedom to change his religion or belief, and freedom (either alone or in community with others, and in public or in private) to manifest and propagate his religion or belief in worship, teaching, practice and observance."

sacred experience occurs within "strong, significant space" while profane experience occurs within "amorphous, neutral space" (Eliade 1987, 20). By extension of Eliade's distinction, the sacred space is the religious space where structured, significant experience occurs while the profane of this world is the space of amorphous experience of politics or political mystique that degenerates human religious imagination.

Before Eliade's writing, the distinction between the sacred and the secular was already at the root of the theory, controversies and debates about 'secularisation', a concept that Max Weber (1864–1920) invented and introduced to the sociology of religion (Weber 1946, 307, 311; 1991 [1922], 47). Etymologically, both secular and secularisation came from the Latin root of *sæculum*, which means an age or an era, and by extension "a spirit of an age" (Christiano, Swatos, and Kivisto 2016, 55). The secular thus means the physical, social world with all its trappings and temptations. In Weber's theorisation, the greatest engine of secularisation is the rationalisation of thought and action which produces demystification or de-magicalisation of thought and action; it is *die Entzauberung der Welt*, or "the disenchantment of the world" (Hanson 2001, 105). Disenchantment is "a transformation of structures of consciousness in terms of their rationalization" (Riesebrodt 2010, 175). Rationalisation process produces secularisation and results in the disenchantment of the world in which religion, its gods and structures lose their influence on people's imagination and the organisation of the social world. Secularisation dereligionizes the world, exiles magic and miracle and produces a declining sphere of religious influence, power, authority, institutions on human action and social organisation (Wilson 2016, 3–7) by freeing institutions from religious control and domination.

While Weber believed that the distinction between the sacred and the secular, and its consequent disenchantment of the world, is necessary to produce progress and development, Durkheim believes that such a distinction is necessary for the formation of society itself, a more radically foundational and fundamental idea. According to the interpretation of the German sociologist, Martin Riesebrodt,

> For Durkheim, human beings and society have two dimensions, a profane and a sacred. Man is profane in his bodily needs and desires, in his egotism and self-centeredness. He is sacred as a moral, social being who is able to transcend these limitations. Society is profane in its everyday economic life, which primarily serves the needs of physical reproduction. (Riesebrodt 2010, 62–63)

A completely profane person or society is impossible; so also, is a completely sacred person or society. It takes the coexistence of both dimensions to coordinate and cooperate for either humans or society to exist, interact, network, produce and reproduce. The sacred realm of society represents religion while the profane sphere represents its political yearnings and ambition. Even for many societies, (for example, in Africa) where there are no words for 'religion' (Ukah 2016a, 48; 49 Shaw 1990, 339), this spiritual dimension exists and articulates the peoples' non-worldly desires but exists in tension with the mundane and profane concerns that make life and living possible. The distinction between the sacred and the profane or secular is analytical;

the existence of one sphere makes the other possible. Similarly, the distinction between politics and religion is amorphous, nebulous, and analytically useful but as dimensions of social reality, hard to concretely demarcate.

5 Separation between State and Religion

A nation-state is a collective formed by a government that assumes a legal and moral right to control and reserves the use of force as a last resort in exercising jurisdiction over a territory and its citizens (Cohen, Kennedy, and Perrier 2013, 85). In many parts of the world, the nation-state is a recent phenomenon, although in Europe and Japan it predates modernity. The State is (presumed to be) the core sphere of politics, the realm of the secular and this-worldly organisation and distribution of power and the exercise of authority over commonly owned resources through legal-rational legitimation. Religion, on the other hand, is the realm of non-worldly power and exercise of authority through charismatic (or in some instances, traditional / cultural), non-legal-rational legitimation. The modern state makes claims, demands allegiance, and exercises its power and sovereignty on territories and populations, while religion does not make a similar claim to territorial sovereignty but demands loyalty and allegiance over populations. The separation between the state and religion in western countries as well as in many non-western nations is recent and varies from one state to another. The arguments and purpose of such separation are subject to debate. Some scholars argue separation constitutionally provides a level playing ground for a plurality of religious groups and traditions, allowing the state to be the guarantor of freedoms and rights of all citizens (Laborde 2016). Perhaps, more important in the separation of state from church – considering the long-drawn-out religious wars in Europe – is to protect the state from religious interference in the running of government and statecraft. Separation is, therefore, a response to the fact and reality of religious plurality and diversity and the inevitable competition to control instruments of state. It is easy to point out inconsistencies and contradictions in both the conceptualisation and application of the doctrine of separation of spheres of operations. In many instances, the wall of separation is a flexible, porous, and permeable one that permits mutual interaction and influence.

In European countries, the state performs services that benefit institutional religious organisations, a practice that is not possible in the United States where the disestablishment of state and church is aggressively policed. However, religious organisations active in the provision of social welfare increasingly benefit from government funds in the United States. Also, in recent years, state officials promulgate and justify policies based on sacred scriptures (Miller and Shimron 2018). Such services which some states provide for religious, mainly Christian, organisations in Europe include the collection of church tax and help with maintenance of church property. In Nigeria which claims to be an electoral and constitutional democracy, the state spends more on religious buildings and pilgrimages than it does on the provision of education and healthcare put together.

Aside from Muslim majority states that are avowed Islamic republics, where there is an intimately intermingled circulation of power between the spheres, in many other modern states, the doctrine of separation of state structures, policies and practices from religious ideologies and organisations is the norm of political and philosophical orthodoxy (Martin 2010). In practice, however, many states – such as South Africa where religious organisations are powerful social actors and power brokers – find it impracticable to keep government policies away from religion, or religion away from the state. The overarching function of the state is partly to exercise oversight even on the legitimate exercise of the freedom of religion and other religious rights. Another factor that poses a strong challenge to divorcing the state from religious practice is the rise of religious hypernationalism across many countries (Europe and Asia; in Africa, Pentecostalism – and in the United States, the rise of Alt-Right (or Alternative Right) in its merging with conservative evangelical Christians) and its interaction with visible political roles. In the case of the Alt Right, an amorphous collection of white supremacist groups, neo-Nazis, racist ideological formations and white conservative Christians, the election of President Donald Trump has helped in no small measure to boost the visibility and embolden its online voice and influence over US State policy formulation and implementation (Futrell and Simi 2018). In this new unfolding environment, and in many other countries, old inhibitions against the mixing of state policies and support with religion is waning and old barriers are breaking down with powerful religious organisations infiltrating and controlling state organs and facilities. The principle of separation of state and religion will remain in place but will be likely observed in breaches, a point to underscore the intricate and inextricable relationship between politics and religion and the circulation of power between different domains in society.

6 Conclusion

Politics and religion are spheres of human practice and performance that exist in mutual tension. As spheres of power and domination, there are many dimensions to their relationship. Some of those analytical spheres have been discussed in this chapter, drawing examples from several societies and countries but especially from Africa where the postcolonial state is frail and fragile, often contending with residual religious institutions and attitudes. Religion as the political economy of the sacred and ritual archive is not *a priori* apolitical; it is intimately connected with power that claims to transcend the sphere of the social. Claiming that it is or should be separated from politics, a core and foundational domain of power, is to obfuscate complex imbrications of the mutual reinforcement of politics and religion. As the above discussions illustrate, the intersection between politics and religion is complex, complicated, and intricate because both spheres of social reality and experience are potential sources and structures of moral purpose, real interests, and social action. As dimensions of social reality, the relationship between politics and religion is a continuum. Politics and religion are structures to explain the world, providing moral meaning between events and peoples or groups and their total environment (social, economic, cultural, physical, ethical, geopolitical). Religion generates communities of belief; politics creates communities of real interest. Both domains have a direct bearing on power structures, circulation of power and ways of gaining access to and controlling or dominating these structures. Like modernity, the relationship and intersection between politics and religion embody some contradictions and tensions that can be seen in civil religion, theocracy, the conceptual attempts to distinguish between the secular and the sacred, and the constitutional separation between the state and religion in liberal and constitutional democracies; between separation/disestablishment and recognition/establishment. Through politics and religion, real "needs and interests are articulated and pursued in the framework of structural possibilities and ideological orientations" (Riesebrodt 2010, 181) inevitably resulting in contradictory outcomes and social realities.

Bibliography

Arendt, Hannah. [1951] 1979. *The Origins of Totalitarianism*. London: A Harvest Book.
Bellah, Robert. 1967. "Civil Religion in America." *Daedalus: Journal of the American Arts and Sciences* 96:1–21.
Bellah, Robert. 1970. *Beyond Belief: Essays on Religion in a Post-Traditionalist World*. Berkeley: University of California Press.
Braun, Willi, 2000. "Religion." In *Guide to the Study of Religion*, edited by Willi Braun and Russell T. McCutcheon, London / New York: Cassell, 3–18.
Chesworth, John, and Franz Kogelmann, eds. 2014. *Shari'a in Africa Today: Reactions and Responses*, Leiden: Brill.
Chidester, David. 1996. *Savage System: Colonialism and Comparative Religion in Southern Africa*. London: University Press of Virginia.
Chidester, David. 2012. *Wild Religion: Tracking the Sacred in South Africa*. Berkeley: University of California Press.
Chidester, David. 2014. *Empire of Religion: Imperialism and Comparative Religion*, Chicago: University of Chicago Press.
Christiano, Kevin J., William H. Swatos, Jr., and Peter Kivisto. ³2016. *Sociology of Religion: Contemporary Developments*. London: Rowman & Littlefield.
Cohen, Robin, Paul Kennedy, and Maud Perrier. ³2013. *Global Sociology*. London: Palgrave Macmillan.
Davie, Grace. 2001. "Global Civil Religion: A European Perspective." *Sociology of Religion* 62:455–473.
Durkheim, Émile. [1915] 2008. *The Elementary Forms of the Religious Life*. New York: Dover Publications.
Eliade, Mircea. [1957] 1987. *The Sacred and the Profane: The Nature of Religion*, trans. Willard R. Trask. London: A Harvest Book.

Ellis, Stephen, and Gerrie ter Haar. 2012. "Religion and Politics in Africa." In *The Wiley-Blackwell Companion to African Religions* edited by Elias Kifon Bongmba, West Sussex: Wiley-Blackwell Publishing, 457–465.
Falola, Toyin. 2017. "Ritual Archives." In *The Palgrave Handbook of African Philosophy*, edited by Adeshina Afolayan and Toyin Falola, New York: Palgrave Macmillan, 703–728.
Ferrero, Mario. 2009. "The Economics of Theocracy." In *The Political Economy of Theocracy*, edited by Mario Ferrero and Ronald Wintrobe, New York: Palgrave Macmillan, 31–55.
Ferrero, Mario, and Roland Wintrobe. 2009. "Introduction." In *The Political Economy of Theocracy*, edited by Mario Ferrero and Ronald Wintrobe, New York: Palgrave Macmillan, 1–5.
Futrell, Robert, and Pete Simi. 2018. "The [Un]Surprising Alt-right." *Context* 16:76.
Hanson, George P. 2001. *The Trickster and the Paranormal*. Philadelphia: Xlibris Publications.
Harnischfeger, Johannes. 2008. *Democratization and Islamic Law: The Sharia Conflicts in Nigeria*. Frankfurt: Campus Verlag.
Hoyt, Sarah F. 1912. "The Etymology of Religion." *Journal of the American Oriental Society* 32:126–129.
Hume, David. [1748] 2007. *An Enquiry Concerning Human Understanding and Other Writing*, edited by Stephen Buckle, Cambridge, MA: Cambridge University Press.
Idowu, Bolaji E. 1973. *African Traditional Religion: A Definition*, London: SCM.
Jensen, Jeppe Sinding. 2003. *The Study of Religion in a New Key: Theoretical and Philosophical Soundings in the Comparative and General Study of Religion*. Aarhus: Aarhus University Press.
Josephus, Flavius. 1974. *The Complete Works of Josephus*, trans. William Whiston. Grand Rapids: Kregel Publications.
Josephus, Flavius. 2006. *The Antiquities of the Jews*, trans. William Whiston. Teddington: Echo Library.
Laborde, Cécile. 2016. "Political Liberalism, Separation and Establishment." In *The Social Equality of Religion or Belief: A New View of Religion's Place in Society*, edited by Alan Carling, London: Palgrave Macmillan, 183–199.
Lukes, Steven. ^{2}2005. *Power: A Radical View*. New York: Palgrave Macmillan.
Mansfield, Stephen. 2008. *The Faith of Barack Obama*. Nashville: Thomas Nelson.
Martin, Craig. 2010. *Masking Hegemony: The Genealogy of Liberalism, Religion and the Private Sphere*. London: Equinox.
McFarlan Miller, Emily, and Yonat Shimron. 2018. "Why is Jeff Sessions Quoting Romans 13 and Why is the Bible Verse so Often Invoked?" In *USA Today*, 16.06.2018 (updated 29.11.2021). https://eu.usatoday.com/story/news/2018/06/16/jeff-sessions-bible-romans-13-trump-immigration-policy/707749002/ (30.11.2021).
Ostien, Philip, Jamila M. Nasir, and Franz Kogelmann, eds. 2005. *Comparative Perspectives on Shari'ah in Nigeria*. Ibadan: Spectrum Books Limited.
Riesebrodt, Martin. 2010. *The Promise of Salvation: A Theory of Religion*, trans. Steven Rendall. Chicago: The University of Chicago Press.
Rousseau, Jean-Jacques. [1762] 1994. *The Social Contract*, trans. Christopher Betts, Oxford: Oxford University Press.
Salmon, Pierre. 2009. "Serving God in a Largely Theocratic Society: Rivalry and Cooperation between Church and King." In *The Political Economy of Theocracy*, edited by Mario Ferrero and Ronald Wintrobe, New York: Palgrave Macmillan, 57–80.
Seiwert, Hubert. 2016. "Politics." In *The Oxford Handbook of The Study of Religion*, edited by Michael Stausberg and Steven Engler, Oxford: Oxford University Press, 430–449.
Seters, John van. ^{2}2005. "Moses." In *Encyclopedia of Religion*. Vol. 9, edited by Lindsay Jones, Farmington Hills: Thomson Gale: 6199–6204.
Shaw, Rosalind. 1990. "The Invention of 'African Traditional Religion'." *Religion* 20:339–353.

Smith, John E. 1994. *Quasi-Religions: Humanism, Marxism and Nationalism*. New York: Macmillan Education.

Thompson, Kenneth. 1998. "Durkheim and Sacred Identity." In *On Durkheim's Elementary Forms of Religious Life*, edited by Nicholas J. Allen, William S. F. Pickering, and William Watts Miller, London: Routledge, 92–104.

Turner, Bryan S. 2011. *Religion and Modern Society: Citizenship, Secularisation and the State*. Cambridge, MA: Cambridge University Press.

Ukah, Asonzeh. 2014. "The Midwife or the Handmaid? Religion in Political Advertising in Nigeria." In *Religion and Society in the 21st Century*, edited by Joachim Küpper, Klaus W. Hempfer, and Erika Fischer-Lichte, Berlin / Boston: De Gruyter: 87–114.

Ukah, Asonzeh. 2016a. "Religion in the Pre-Contact World: Africa." In *The Cambridge History of Religions in Latin America*, edited by Virginia Garrard-Burnett, Paul Freston, and Stephen C. Dove, Cambridge, MA: Cambridge University Press: 47–61.

Ukah, Asonzeh. 2016b. "Sexual Bodies, Sacred Vessels: Pentecostal Discourses on Homosexuality in Nigeria." In *Christianity and Controversies over Homosexuality in Contemporary Africa*, edited by Ezra Chitando and Adriaan van Klinken, Surrey: Ashgate Publishers, 21–37.

Ukah, Asonzeh. 2018a. "Pentecostal Apocalypticism: Hate Speech, Contested Citizenship, and Religious Discourses on Same-Sex Relations in Nigeria." *Journal of Citizenship Studies* 22:633–649.

Ukah, Asonzeh. 2018b. "Vox Dei, Vox Populi: Pentecostal Citizenship and Political Participation in Nigeria since 1999." In *Christian Citizenship and the Moral Regeneration of the African State: Locating the Relationship between Religion, Society and Political Transformation in Africa*, edited by Barbara Bompani and Caroline Valois, London: Ashgate, 35–48.

Ukah, Asonzeh. 2019. "Africa and Free / Hate Speech." *Immanent Frame: Secularism, Religion, and the Public Square*. https://tif.ssrc.org/2019/01/04/africa-and-free-hate-speech/ (30.11.2021).

Weber, Max. 1946. *From Max Weber: Essays in Sociology*, trans. H. H. Gerth and C. Wright Mills. New York: Oxford University Press.

Weber, Max. [1922] 1991. *The Sociology of Religion*, trans. Ephraim Fischoff. London: Methuen & Company Limited.

Wilson, Bryan R. 2016. *Religion in Secular Society: Fifty Years On*, edited by Steve Bruce, Oxford: Oxford University Press.

Zhe, Ji. 2013. "Return to Durkheim: Civil Religion and the Moral Reconstruction of China." In *Durkheim In Dialogue. A Centenary Celebration of the Elementary Forms of Religious Life*, edited by Sondra L. Hauser, New York: Berghahn Books, 47–66.

Birgit Weyel
Practical Theology and Religion

1 Introduction

What is practical theology? What religious practice does it refer to? These definitions are highly relevant to me. As a chaired professor in Practical Theology at an old university in southern Germany, my work depends heavily on the answers to these questions. What subjects for research should I select and where do I find them? From what perspectives and with which methods should I proceed? For whom do I write? For what audience and with what goal? What is the relationship between the topics of my teaching/speaking engagements and the shifting interests of my research? At this point in my academic career, I have answered these questions with considerable diversity (Weyel 2006a, 2013, 2014, 2016). In addressing these matters, I also have to account for the shifting contexts and expectations which are brought to me and in which I conduct myself. Practical theology cannot be separated from religious practice – they must be sought and found together because together they form a common context. My understanding of religious practice informs my practical theology and vice versa. The proceeding discussion will unfold as follows: First, I will go deeper with these encyclopedic questions and bring them into contact with my particular framework. (2) In doing so, the topic at hand will fan out in various directions, unfolding intrinsic tensions in the field (3). Then, I will treat explicitly the topic of practical theology, lived religion (4.1), the concept of religious practice (4.2) and from there I will inquire about the theory-formation of practical theology.

2 The Encyclopedic Question

What from case to case we ought to understand by "practical theology" depends on several factors and their dynamic relationships: institutional setting, different methodological approaches, and corresponding theory-development, the overlapping of various contexts into which practical theology is speaking, the various expectations brought to practical theology, and last but not least the subjects who pursue practical theology *as* practical theology. The same may be said of other academic fields, but the complexity of the issue is often understated when speaking about practical theology. Hence Brett C. Hoover describes practical theology as a "hub of intersecting activities" (Hoover 2019, 7). The following sketch will be one that both serves the current understanding of the field and allows room for new models. This contribution operates against the background assumption that practical theology is an academic form of knowledge that cannot be – nor should be – considered apart from its constructive character and embedded context.

How one classifies or delineates a particular field of study is a central question. The outcome of this sort of reflection on the nature of practical theology helps not only the one practicing to obtain information but it can also strengthen the possibility for dialogue in inter-cultural and global contexts. Kathleen A. Cahalan und Gordon S. Mikoski have chosen a similar approach, in that they liken the field of practical theology to a conversation consisting of many voices (Cahalan and Mikoski 2014, 271), the similarities and differences of which they can only make explicit in the conclusion at the end of their book. However, the foundations and presentation of practical theology are in many ways confined to a particular framework. This expresses itself in select processes and decisions. What issues and what objects are being dealt with – and which are excluded? What literature is consulted? What names are mentioned, and which names are not? How is the material organized and what logic does the ordering of chapters follow? The problem is not that these decisions must be made, but rather that they are not known to authors. It is not as if these have been made transparent and key features have been established as norms. Against the background of this only hinted-at problem, I have made two basic decisions for my presentation. First it seems helpful to me in the first place to state the tensions and ambiguities in practical theology, without having to clarify them in one way, or disambiguate them in another (cf. the approach of Mercer and Miller-McLemore 2016). This therefore takes into account what has often been described in the history of practical theology as the "constitutive uncertainty of its foundations and objectives" (Krause 1972, xx). This uncertainty is not a flaw; it lies established in the very dynamic of the discipline: its openness to practical issues in the Church and in Christianity (Albrecht 2000, 321). Second, on the other hand, this treatment of practical theology does not claim to cover the (singular!) practical theology for the German-speaking world or even continental Europe. While a surface-level representation such as this might offer some orientation, it also brings with it unsatisfactory oversimplification.

Furthermore, one must avoid the risk of eurocentrism, by, for example, singling out Continental Europe as the home of major theological developments. "It is probably not claiming too much to say that Continental Europe was the cradle of practical theology, at least of practical theology as an academic discipline" (Schweitzer 2012, 465). Indeed, there very well may be comparable developments, similarities, parallels, and mutual influences in other countries. Overview-sketch presentations frequently unfold master narratives, which assert claims of origins and simple cause and effect relationships. In these historical arch-narratives, the reciprocity of influences, as well as the complexity of practices often go ignored. To avoid this, the following sketch only attempts to describe the constitutive challenges which arise when considering the task of Protestant practical theology in a specific institutional context – namely a public university in southern Germany. It does intend to project these issues unilaterally.

3 Tensions due to the History of Practical Theology in Germany

I understand practical theology to be an academic discipline which in the German-speaking context is taught within a theology department. The encyclopedic rationale for the field is closely tied to its institutionalization in the historical context of the Berlin University reform in 1810. Friedrich Schleiermacher, who at the time worked as an advisor to Wilhelm von Humboldt, contributed substantially to the model of the reform (Weyel 2006b, 51–55). Although Schleiermacher himself was opposed to the formation of an independent chair for practical theology, his vision for the university (Schleiermacher [1808] 1964) and his theological encyclopedia, the brief outline (Schleiermacher [1810/11] 1998), led to the establishment of practical theology as a discipline and the scientification of its theory and practice (Barth 2017; Gräb 2017; Weyel 2022). The scientific reformulation of theology that occurred in this neo-humanist university context continues to shape the understanding and regulation of practical theology in the German state-church today. In proceeding I will go deeper into this historical background.

3.1 The Scientification of the Relationship between Theory and Practice

The Prussian university reform was characterized by the neo-humanist education ideal, which sought to train people in independent, scientific work, as opposed to a more general formation. Related to this was the view that one can only react to societal changes sustainably through self-education and the ability to make independent judgments. Academic study accordingly intended to make a long-lasting and high-quality contribution to one's qualification for a given job, thereby doing away with strict qualification requirements. This is also the case for theology, which at the institutional level of the university is regarded as a positive science. The object of theology – insofar as it concerns the action-oriented side of Christianity – is "the qualification of competent leadership for the Christian Church" (Gräb 2017, 399).

This readjustment of theology brought about long-lasting effects, which, although they were a reaction to societal changes in the 19th and 20th century (Drehsen 1988; Drehsen 2007), continue to shape today. Some of the ramifications of this shift include the differentiation between the Church and Christianity – a concept which brought about the strict separation of religious practice from theological reflection – as well as the relativization of various claims to validity through a growing historical consciousness (Laube 2007, 64–68). Against the backdrop of the growing need for reflection and orientation, religious practice was raised to the rank of a narrowly defined and institutionalized object of academic study. This vision took as a prerequisite the awareness of a necessary differentiation between theology as a form of reflection and religious practice as the exercise of religion. Schleiermacher placed religious practice at the center of all theology where it formed the connection between the various theological disciplines: "Theology is a positive science the parts of which are only connected to a whole by their common relationship to a specific faith i.e., by their relationship to Christianity" (Schleiermacher 1998, §1; o.t.). In light of today's growing religious pluralization, it is worth noting that this model does not only apply to Christianity but rather can speak to any number of faiths. The understanding of theology as reflection on religious practice by religious communities was not, for Schleiermacher, an explicitly Christian or Protestant model. It requires only a commitment to community building and an interest in scientific self-reflection. Certainly, this theological model impacts how various religious communities in Germany operate – for example various Islamic groups. Nowadays if these groups wish to achieve official state recognition, they must abide by this model. Hence, we hear people speaking today of the "churchification" of Islam (von Sydow 2010).

The relationship between theology and Christianity in Schleiermacher's model contains both a functional as well as a substantial aspect; these are rooted in the material essence-defining of Christianity. The unity of theology consists in the "substantial-functional dual constitution of the *Wissenschaft* of Christianity for the promotion of Christianity" (Laube 2007, 81; o.t.). By this essence-defining of Christianity we are not to understand some speculative principle or dogmatic which is subject to critical, empirical verification. For Schleiermacher Christianity comes into view as a historical phenomenon; its essence is determined by historical analyses of the status quo, not by metaphysical or supernatural characteristics. The essence of Christianity is obtained in the analysis of its historical manifestations. It consists of a "reflected historicity" (Laube 2007, 81; o.t.). The essence of Christianity, therefore, cannot be located outside of history; it is woven into history and can only be derived from it through processes of reconstructive interpretation. Dogmatics is therefore properly considered part of practical theology, in that it leads to critical self-reflection of how Christianity developed and became what it is

This course set out in the early 19th century continues to have an impact in many respects. Practical theology is an academic field whose relationship to its subject is in need of constant re-explanation. In Germany the academic field of practical theology is somewhat of a balancing act: it must emphasize its relationship to practice, while at the same time maintaining proper distance. Practical theology does not understand itself as applied science. On the one hand it must uphold its practical relevance for its practitioners, while at the same time maintaining its academic integrity with other fields at the university.

3.2 Formation for Clergy and Teachers as res mixta (The Working together of Religious Communities with State Involvement)

To this day, the churches in Germany hold that the training for pastoral ministry should mirror that of other careers; theological study at a (state) university should be a prerequisite for the obtaining of a church office. This decision was maintained even after the Church and State in Germany separated from one another in 1919. Still today the participation of religious communities (churches) and the state involvement in the education of religious teachers and clergy are intimately intertwined through legal relations (Christoph 2009). The state's interest in the academic training for religious teachers and ministers (pastoral jobs) has been recently renewed (2014) through the establishment of centers for Islamic theology in Germany. On the one hand, this historical state-church model is expanding to encompass other religious communities (and is therefore strengthened); on the other hand, there are political voices emerging who, in light of growing religious pluralization and diminishing numbers of church membership, plead for a reduction of state involvement in religious education and to allow for self-management among religious communities.

Different theologies are confronted with both the expectations of the church community and those studying for religious occupations (for example those who are doing apprentices in a church). Theologies are therefore faced with the challenge of integrating the practical-religious needs for the general community, while keeping in view the professional interests (especially course curriculum) of the students who are training to become teachers, ministers, and to occupy other professions in the religious fields. These occupations have the central task of determining the proper subject matter for practical theology, as well as the objectives of doctrine and research. For this reason, the current model for the study of Protestant practical theology is oriented toward the tasks of preaching, pastoral ministry, and education. Even recent practical theology textbooks which attempt to closely conform to curricular requirements follow this profession-oriented principle (Karle 2020; Fechtner et al. 2017). In a way, the pastoral paradigm is reproduced in class and the body of knowledge of practical theology is connected back to its assumed relevance for career preparation. In order to ensure the development of practical theology is oriented solely toward profession preparation, textbooks have been expanded to include reflections on the general framework of religious practice (e.g., religion in modern and late modern era, individualization, and secularism (e.g., Fechtner et al. 2017). The constructive character of practical theology is especially evident in these descriptions. On the one hand, the character of practical theology remains abstract. On the other hand, theories in practical theology are contextualized – developed in light of the descriptive categories of modern, late modern, and postmodern. One theoretical model by Wolfgang Steck takes an inductive approach – it integrates numerous independent theoretical elements into his presentation and in a detailed manner seeks to identify the core profile of specific and selective manifestations of actualized, lived out religion.

"In order to maintain the authenticity of practical religion and at the same time shield it from theoretical alienation, empirical manifestations of contemporary Christian practice are not observed from the distant perspective of academic theorist, rather they are represented as they are themselves: partly in their immediate social-cultural expression, partly as presented in its own reflective self-description" (Steck 2000, 16; o.t.). Only in the subsequent interpretation of this system of categories is a practice theory drafted that aims to integrate reflections developed in the practice itself.

3.3 Practical Theology as Theology

By virtue of its institutional context, practical theology is placed alongside her theological sister-disciplines as part of an organized whole (a theology faculty or department). Administrative matters that pertain to the teaching of and commitment to evangelical theology (for example granting degrees, conferring *venia legendi*, establishing study regulations) fall under the jurisdiction of confessional theology and are shielded from outside influence. What falls into the area of facility administration and what should be left to the influences of confessional principles remains to be negotiated by the university administration, state department of science, and the evangelical churches. Since education policy in Germany lies within the sovereignty of each specific federal state (*Bundesland*) and the status of the Faculty of Theology belongs to the *res mixta* of the church and state, church agreements are negotiated and closed at the state level (for Tübingen: Baden-Württemberg). In the Evangelical Church Contract Baden-Württemberg (Evangelischer Kirchenvertrag Baden-Württemberg), which merged the church territories of Baden and Württemberg, it was established that evangelical theology would be taught at the University of Tübingen, and an adequate endowment would be granted on the part of the state:

> The Evangelical-theological departments at the Universities of Heidelberg and Tübingen remain for the cultivation of the teaching and research of evangelical theology – an integral part of European academic culture – and for the academic formation of pastors and teachers in school religious education. An adequate representation of the five core theological subjects ranging from philosophy of Christian religion to ancient languages is guaranteed. These five core subjects include Old Testament, New Testament, Church History, Systematic Theology, and Practical Theology. (Evangelischer Kirchenvertrag 2007, Art. 3; o.t.)

The number of appointed chairs (15) was explicitly noted at the time of the unification; it remains to be seen whether this specification is to be understood as normative or descriptive. There is also the question of whether the state interest in maintaining academic theology will remain in the future and whether the cost for its maintenance will increase as the number of students decrease. Among interdisciplinary classes, courses of study, support agreements, and research societies, there are numerous models that do not question academic theology itself as an organizational unit. Since theology is represented at the *Universitas Litterarum*, it is viewed by other disciplines as a cooperation partner and vice versa. As such, theological study can pair itself with other disciplines and form combined degrees or courses of study and research societies for which there exist third party funding opportunities.

The institutional framework of the state church treats protestant theology as a science to which practical theology belongs as a core subject. This means that practical theology is permanently linked to the sister disciplines with whom it forms course plans and degree programs and with whom it enters conversation. In this interdisciplinary vision we get a better glimpse of theology as a whole as well as what protestant theology actually is, when it is viewed as its own subject and not merely as a husk. The question of what makes practical theology *theology* is not seldom informed by the competition between the theological disciplines, especially when it comes to question of relevance and orientation (Gräb 1988). For practical theology's self-understanding, it is important that it is perceived as a unique discipline with its own theory; it should not be treated as merely a bridge builder between other theological disciplines and church practice. The move toward empirical methods in the past centuries has contributed to the establishment of practical theology's independence from systematic theology and exegesis. Reception arenas also help; this sort of empirical research frequently arouses interests in church settings (pastoral conventions, academies, church administrations). Additionally, by using shared methods and closely connected theoretical approaches, opportunities arise for cooperation with other empirically oriented fields apart from theology. Despite this, however, the "fundamental problem" is still not totally resolved (Albrecht 2011, 23; o.t.). The problem "lies in the tension between the goal of practical theology to have specified rules for its craft which do not raise scientific claims and the expectation to have scientific justifications for these rules on hand, which do not collide or compete with the goals, procedures, or topics of concern for other theological disciplines" (Albrecht 2011, 23; o.t.).

3.4 Practical Theology and Other Forms of Knowledge

While reflections on the relationship between theory and practice find their place in the academy, other forms of knowledge which do not conform to academic standards or follow academic rules of discourse are directed to other institutions. Following the model whereby one begins with university study followed by hands-on training in field (paid internships, apprenticeship) and keeping the commitment to the principle of life-long learning, further education in other forms of knowledge can be added onto one's course of education. From the perspective of the academy, the standards of knowledge in the non-university, church contexts (for example in seminary) fall far short. From the perspective of the churches, academic practical theology is out of touch with real life and its relevance to practice is questioned. From the history of practical theology, many examples of this can be called to mind. Of course, these are not limited to mutual criticism or the juxtaposition of different forms of knowledge. The integration of internships as part of academic study, the appointing of practitioners to university teaching positions, the reading of academic literature in seminary courses, the invitation of professors to courses for professional development of pastors and other church-related professionals and seminars, are all ways examples of attempts to bridge the gap between different forms of knowledge, even if through such encounters the differences between them are made more evident. On the one hand, practical theologians can provide insight when invited to serve on advisory councils and boards in churches, on the hand these visits could be occasions for their own knowledge acquisition.

Approaches that apply the concept of theology to religious subjects with programmatic intention can also be classified as attempts at integration and bridge-building (Luther 1987). For example, academic theologians often take statements gathered empirically from children and youth and link these to theological concepts (children's theology, youth theology) (Schweitzer and Schlag 2012; Zimmermann 2016). Paradoxically, in doing so, the theories developed from within an academic culture and constructed according to its own inner logic, are undermined at the same time they are carried on. In proceeding, the concept of theology will first be made ambiguous, so that by detailing the criticism of children's theology it will in turn be clarified.

The concept of a collaborative practical theology integrates different forms of knowledge that work together constructively, by differentiating their respective roles in the pursuit of knowledge (e. g., de Roest 2019). Academic practical theology can bring practitioners into the research process who can provide different perspectives from their various communities. The knowledge of these practitioners is valuable – increasing both the utility and the benefits that the research can then contribute back to the practice. In my assessment, this integrative approach is particularly strong. It allows me as a scholar to systematically reflect on the discussions in my field and consider how they are present in ethnographic contexts. At the same time, however, when practical theology proceeds collaboratively, it remains open to tensions. Said otherwise: the practice of research requires one to reflect on the constructing and manufacturing character of sociality and intersubjectivity while keeping view toward practitioners. Ethnomethodology has brought attention to problems regarding the governing rules of the field, particularly as they relate to conversations with bureaucratic organizations and entities. Often in my work I find myself in "situations of justification" (Bohnsack 2017, 42; o.t.), whose definitional fixations and interpretations I do not carry over to the realm of research. The envisioned practical utility assumes that the researcher improves and adapts according to the needs of practitioners in the field. I will take up again the question of the object of practical theology and its character as theology in a line of thought which attempts to present the object and theory of practical theology via the concept of religious practice.

4 Religious Practice: The Subject and Formation of Practical Theology

4.1 Religion as Lived Religion

What we identify as religion in a pluralistic society must be marked and identified in connection to a concept of religion as religion (Matthes 1992). The variety and diversity of religious practice correspond to contexts in which we live. In our case, religion is embedded in conditions marked by individualization and pluralization. The concept of "lived religion" takes up as its object the embedding of religion in various life contexts (see the chapter of Ruard Gaanzevoort in this book). Since practical theology identifies "lived religion" as its object, it carries with this claim the assertion that it makes a principal contribution to an overall theory of Christianity. Practical theology assumes, "that there is no phenotype of religious people which exists independent from the construction of a normative, scientific concept of religion" (Pfleiderer 2002, 33; o.t.). Theories of a lived religion are "strategies to make religion visible." (Pfleiderer 2002, 33; o.t.) These strategies are critical toward theories of secularization, which attach themselves to the dwindling of institutionalized religion and the disappearance of religions as a whole. A large part of the empirical-qualitative work in practical theology (which has emerged in the last twenty years) is connected to the work of Thomas Luckmann (1991) – namely the making visible of what he describes as "invisible religion." This approach surveys processes of constructing religion, structures of everyday life (Merle 2011), and biographical interpretations (Gräb 1998). Since religion is lived out in various and individualized ways, it must be first named and identified as religion. It belongs to the very nature of practical theology that both in research and when working with its subjects, it is always developing its understanding of religion anew. Any work on the concept of religion is in principle interminable since our understanding of religion cannot be explained apart from the concrete manifestations of its practitioners. In this context there is also the task of the operationalization of religion, which seeks to treat these in a methodologically controlled manner, according to their various contexts. The research processes, between the work on the concept of religion and empirical survey, lead to a hermeneutical circle of mutual clarification (Weyel 2013).

4.2 Religion as Social Practice: Perspectives on the Social Nature of Religion

Against the focus on the religious subject and the individualized forms of religion beyond institutional contexts (e.g., churches), the question of the social and cultural embeddedness of religion also presents itself. An empirical-phenomenological approach to religion maintains a constant reference to cultural interpretive patterns, narratives, etc. without reconstructing some underlying phenomenon of consciousness of the surveyed subjects. Interpretations of religious experience are tied to the signs, images, and texts transmitted by a given society or culture. In the wake of *material, special, and digital turns,* artifacts, spaces, and technologies also come into view. Following and building on the concept of "lived religion" is the more recently developed emphasis on religion as social practice. The stress on social practice seeks to integrate the social dimension of religion into our understanding of religion as a concept. Religion is something that is always lived in specific forms, from within certain culturally transmitted norms; it is given to an individual, but the individual can adjust its form and modify it in an individual way. The religious person is thus characterized neither as an individual purely shaped by their own subjectivity nor a "marionette in a theater of social practice" (Laube 2015, 47; o.t.). Religious practice is embedded in concrete social relations determined by "doings and sayings" (Laube 2015, 47; o.t.; according to Schatzki 2002). These *social interdependences* provide patterns of religious practice that are fairly stable. In addition to the doings and sayings, the concept of social practice also conceptualizes mindset as part of interactive i.e., mutual practices. Alongside the interactivity of social practice, its reflexivity is also important. What should be identified as religion is not always strictly determined. Rather it is constantly identified anew amidst various social practices – even when it is not explicitly identified, it remains implicit.

4.3 A Theory of Religious Practice as Theology

Practical theology shares methodological approaches and vocabulary with religious studies, sociology of religion, psychology of religion, cultural studies, and others. One might ask then whether there is an essential difference between the discipline of theology and the study of religion, or whether all empirical religious research should rather be shared among participants of all possible disciplines. The fields of theology do not possess research methods that are exclusive to them alone; rather theology shares the canon of methods with the humanities, social, and cultural sciences. The institutional expansion of the theological disciplines is a foundational decision that promotes scientific reflection on religion – it seeks to understand how religions are lived out in communities of faith in Germany. The fact that theology has a scientific nature and at the same time confessional-religious "ties" is thus viewed positively. Theology as an academic discipline does not exist solely to serve the self-understanding of religions in society or to work against the emigration of religious communities out of society. The presence of a religious scholar in the field should therefore not be viewed as a hindrance to research and teaching, rather the opposite: an occasion for productivity. The personal commitment between the scholar and the object of her study is made transparent by the institutional setting of theology. It is possibly this transparency with one's personal commitments that sets theology apart from other academic fields dealing with religion. The freedom and potential for reflection that practical theology holds towards confessing communities is owed to its conversations with other disciplines and its institutional location, which places it both near and far from the lived religion of these communities. One might ask then whether this same transparency of a scholar's personal commitment to her field of study might be a useful methodological move in other fields. In ethnology, proximity and distance to the object of research is both reflected upon and methodologically enacted. The clarification of the social position of the researcher plays an important role, especially in connection with the methodology of the participatory observation. Participation and observation are conceived as an "ongoing changing of registers" (Breidenstein et al. 2013, 67; o.t.) which make it possible to approximate and observe cultural practices and trace the meaning and relevance attributed to these practices. On the other hand, however, it must at the same time be possible to take the perspective of reflective distance. Neither proximity nor distance alone allows for good ethnography; it is rather the "double movement" between participation and observation, proximity, and distance. "Both ethnographers, the 'native' and the 'foreigner' confront this demand, only from different starting points" (Breidenstein et al. 2013, 68; o.t.). The oscillation between proximity and distance and the reflection on changing registers is an epistemic model for those disciplines concerned with lived religion. In any case, as I understand it, it is the model for practical theology. Theoretical approaches under the umbrella of practice-theory which have provoked a wide resonance in practical theology in recent years are, in my view, helpful, precisely because they create space for multi-perspective research approaches and bring practical theology as itself a form of practice into consideration.

Bibliography

Albrecht, Christian. 2000. *Historische Kulturwissenschaft neuzeitlicher Christentumspraxis.* Tübingen: Mohr Siebeck.

Albrecht, Christian. 2011. *Enzyklopädische Probleme der Praktischen Theologie:* Tübingen: Mohr Siebeck.

Barth, Ulrich. 2017. "Theorie der Theologie." In *Schleiermacher Handbuch*, edited by Martin Ohst, Tübingen: Mohr Siebeck, 316–327.

Bohnsack, Ralf. 2017. *Praxeologische Wissenssoziologie.* Opladen / Toronto: Verlag Barbara Budrich.

Breidenstein, Georg, Stefan Hirschauer, Herbert Kalthoff, and Boris Nieswand. 2013. *Ethnografie: Die Praxis der Feldforschung.* Konstanz / München: UVK.

Cahalan, Kathleen A., and Gordon S. Mikoski. 2014. "Conclusion." In *Opening the Field of Practical Theology: An Introduction*, edited by Kathleen A. Cahalan and Gordon S. Mikoski, Lanham: Rowman & Littlefield, 271–273.

Christoph, Joachim E. 2009. *Kirchen- und staatsrechtliche Probleme der evangelisch-theologischen Fakultäten in Deutschland.* Jus ecclesiasticum 91. Tübingen: Mohr Siebeck.

Drehsen, Volker. 1988. *Neuzeitliche Konstitutionsbedingungen der Praktischen Theologie: Aspekte der theologischen Wende zur sozialkulturellen Lebenswelt christlicher Religion*. Gütersloh: Gütersloher Verlagshaus.

Drehsen, Volker. 2007. "Praktische Theologie." In *Handbuch Praktische Theologie*, edited by Wilhelm Gräb and Birgit Weyel, Gütersloh: Gütersloher Verlagshaus, 174–187.

Evangelischer Kirchenvertrag. 2007. *Vertrag des Landes Baden-Württemberg mit der Evangelischen Landeskirche in Baden und mit der Evangelischen Landeskirche in Württemberg (EvKiVBW) vom 17. Oktober 2007*. https://www.kirchenrecht-wuerttemberg.de/document/17130/search/t%25C3%25BCbingen#s1530004 (20.01.2022).

Fechtner, Kristian, Jan Hermelink, Martina Kumlehn, and Ulrike Wagner-Rau. 2017. *Praktische Theologie: Ein Lehrbuch*. Stuttgart: Kohlhammer.

Gräb, Wilhelm. 1988. "Dogmatik als Stück der Praktischen Theologie: Das normative Grundproblem in der praktisch-theologischen Theoriebildung." *Zeitschrift für Theologie und Kirche* 85:474–492.

Gräb, Wilhelm. 1998. *Lebensgeschichten, Lebensentwürfe, Sinndeutungen: eine praktische Theologie gelebter Religion*. Gütersloh: Gütersloher Verlagshaus.

Gräb, Wilhelm. 2017. "Praktische Theologie." In *Schleiermacher Handbuch*, edited by Martin Ohst, Tübingen: Mohr Siebeck, 399–410.

Hoover, Brett C. 2019. "Practical Theology in the United States." *Zeitschrift für Pastoraltheologie* 39:7–18.

Karle, Isolde. 2020. *Praktische Theologie*. Lehrwerk Evangelische Theologie 7. Leipzig: Evangelische Verlagsanstalt.

Krause, Gerhard. 1972. "Vorwort." In *Praktische Theologie: Texte zum Werden und Selbstverständnis der praktischen Disziplin der evangelischen Theologie*, edited by Gerhard Krause, Darmstadt: Wissenschaftliche Buchgesellschaft, xi–xxiv.

Laube, Martin. 2007. "Zur Stellung der Praktischen Theologie innerhalb der Theologie – aus systematisch-theologischer Sicht." In *Praktische Theologie. Eine Theorie- und Problemgeschichte*, edited by Christian Grethlein and Helmut Schwier, Leipzig: Evangelische Verlagsanstalt, 61–136.

Laube, Martin. 2015. "Religion als Praxis: Zur Fortschreibung des christentumssoziologischen Rahmens der EKD-Mitgliedschaftsstudien." In *Vernetzte Vielfalt: Kirche angesichts von Individualisierung und Säkularisierung: Die fünfte EKD-Erhebung über Kirchenmitgliedschaft*, edited by Heinrich Bedford-Strohm, and Volker Jung, Gütersloh: Gütersloher Verlagshaus, 35–49.

Luckmann, Thomas. 1991. *Die unsichtbare Religion*. Frankfurt am Main: Suhrkamp.

Luther, Henning. 1987. "Praktische Theologie für alle: Individualität und Kirche in Friedrich Schleiermachers Verständnis Praktischer Theologie." *Zeitschrift für Theologie und Kirche* 84:371–393.

Matthes, Joachim. 1992. "Auf der Suche nach dem Religiösen: Reflexionen zu Theorie und Empirie religionssoziologischer Forschung." *Sociologica Internationalis* 30:129–142.

Mercer, Joyce A., and Bonnie J. Miller-McLemore. 2016. "Introduction." In *Conundrums in Practical Theology*, edited by Joyce A. Mercer and Bonnie J. Miller-McLemore, Leiden / Boston: Brill, 1–7.

Merle, Kristin. 2011. *Alltagsrelevanz: Zur Frage nach dem Sinn in der Seelsorge*, Göttingen: Vandenhoeck & Ruprecht.

Pfleiderer, Georg. 2002. "Gelebte Religion – Notizen zu einem Theoriephänomen." In *"Gelebte Religion" als Programmbegriff systematischer und praktischer Theologie*. Christentum und Kultur 1, edited by Albrecht Grözinger and Georg Pfleiderer, Zürich: Theologischer Verlag Zürich, 23–41.

Roest, Henk de. 2019. *Collaborative Practical Theology: Engaging Practitioners in Research on Christian Practices*. Leiden: Brill.
Schatzki, Theodore R. 2002. *The Site of the Social: A Philosophical Account of the Constitution of Social Life and Change*. Philadelphia: The Pennsylvania State University Press.
Schleiermacher, Friedrich. [1808] 1964. "Gelegentliche Gedanken über Universitäten in deutschem Sinne: Nebst einem Anhang über eine neu zu errichtende." In *Die Idee der deutschen Universität: Die fünf Grundschriften aus der Zeit ihrer Neubegründung durch klassischen Idealismus und romantischen Realismus*, edited by Ernst Anrich, Darmstadt: Wissenschaftliche Buchgesellschaft, 221–293.
Schleiermacher, Friedrich. [1810/11] 1998. "Kurze Darstellung des Theologischen Studiums zum Behuf einleitender Vorlesungen." First Edition. Vol. 1.6, *Kritische Schleiermacher-Gesamtausgabe*, edited by Dirk Schmid, Berlin: Walter de Gruyter, 243–315.
Schweitzer, Friedrich. 2012. "Continental Europe." In *The Wiley-Blackwell Companion to Practical Theology*, edited by Bonnie J. Miller-McLemore, Malden: Wiley Blackwell, 465–474.
Schweitzer, Friedrich, and Thomas Schlag. 2012. *Jugendtheologie: Grundlagen – Beispiele – kritische Diskussion*. Neukirchen-Vluyn: Neukirchener Verlagsgesellschaft.
Steck, Wolfgang. 2000. *Praktische Theologie: Horizonte der Religion – Konturen des neuzeitlichen Christentums – Strukturen der religiösen Lebenswelt*. Vol. 1, Stuttgart: Kohlhammer.
Sydow, Gernot von. 2010. "Pressemitteilung: Staatskirchenrecht auch für Muslime geeignet?" https://www.uni-muenster.de/imperia/md/content/religion_und_politik/aktuelles/2010/07_2010/pm_staatskirchenrecht_und_islam.pdf (20.01.2022).
Weyel, Birgit. 2006a. "Religion in der modernen Lebenswelt – Erscheinungsformen." In *Religion in der modernen Lebenswelt*, edited by Birgit Weyel and Wilhelm Gräb, Göttingen: Vandenhoeck & Ruprecht, 13–26.
Weyel, Birgit. 2006b. *Praktische Bildung zum Pfarrberuf: Das Predigerseminar Wittenberg und die Entstehung einer zweiten Ausbildungsphase evangelischer Pfarrer in Preußen*. Beiträge zur Historischen Theologie 134. Tübingen: Mohr Siebeck.
Weyel, Birgit. 2013. "Netzwerkanalyse – ein empirisches Paradigma zur Konzeptualisierung von religiöser Sozialität? Überlegungen zur wechselseitigen Erhellung von empirischen Methoden und praktisch-theologischen Konzepten." In *Praktische Theologie und empirische Religionsforschung*, edited by Birgit Weyel, Wilhelm Gräb, and Hans-Günter Heimbrock, Leipzig: Evangelische Verlagsanstalt, 157–169.
Weyel, Birgit. 2014. "Practical Theology as a Hermeneutical Science of Lived Religion." *International Journal of Practical Theology* 18:150–159.
Weyel, Birgit. 2016. "Religion in praktisch-theologischer Perspektive." In *Die Bedeutung der Religionswissenschaft und ihrer Subdisziplinen als Bezugswissenschaften für die Theologie*. Reihe für Osnabrücker Islamstudien 26, edited by Rauf Ceylan and Coşkun Sağlam, Frankfurt am Main: Peter Lang, 377–390.
Weyel, Birgit. 2022. "Schleiermacher's Practical Theology." In *Oxford Handbook of Friedrich Schleiermacher*, edited by Andrew Dole, Shelli Poe, and Kevin Vander Schel. Oxford: Oxford University Press (in print).
Zimmermann, Mirjam. 2016. "Kann Kindertheologie auch unwahr sein? Ein Plädoyer für differenzierte Bewertungskriterien in der Kindertheologie." *Zeitschrift für Pädagogik und Theologie* 68:58–72.

Matthew Ryan Robinson
Sociability and Religion

1 Introduction: On Sociability and Method in Theological Research

Whatever else it may be, religion under the pen of a scholar is always also the scholar's own construction. That construction will be conditioned by each particular scholar's personal background and experience, as well as by the particular ways through which she or he has sought to control for those limiting conditions. The present volume recognizes these challenges and seeks to address them head-on by explicitly inviting us, the contributing authors, to reflect on our own research backgrounds and orientations and how they filter our scholarly analyses in as self-aware a manner as we can.

A perhaps curious acknowledgement must, however, come along with the selection of this hermeneutical approach. Not only does it resist the top-down assertion of concepts and scholarly paradigms from some outside source onto peoples and their traditions that are animated by unique forms of life and deserving of their own correspondingly specific presentation. That very resistance is the methodological conclusion of denying that scholars can ever capture the 'essence' or articulate with complete 'accuracy' the beliefs, values, and practices that animate any community's or tradition's modes of life. This results in the awkward acknowledgement that the denial of universality sets the scholar at an equal distance from particularity, leaving the study of religion floating in a kind of outer-space-like limbo between seeking to neutralize as many of one's own prejudices and universal concepts as possible, on the one hand, while affording untouchable uniqueness and independence to the communities and traditions one studies on the other.

A practical theology of the kind that seeks to develop an empirically founded and hermeneutically reflected theory of lived religion out of the highly particularized individual experiences of the individual scholar participants needs to address itself to this challenge. I want to suggest that a particular orientation to the dynamics of human 'sociability' is helpful for working through *methodological challenges* in theological research for practical theologians who are interested in a transcultural and transreligious approach to lived religion. Specifically, thinking of theological research as a sociable task can help theologians to inhabit the hermeneutical problem that arises in the tension between universality and particularity.

In this article, I define and then outline 'sociability' as *meaningful participation in human community*. To conduct theological research 'sociably' in the development of a hermeneutics of lived religion in diverse contexts requires unusual methods, specifically, embedded methods. This will raise questions related to the appropriate degree of distance and involvement between scholars and communities. But it can also help us to reflect more deeply on the nature of what theology is, what it does and how it functions in and for communities. Paying greater attention to the dynamics of participation in community can help theologians in general and practical theologians in particular to thematize the phenomena that individuals and communities themselves identify as religious in a way that preserves a high degree of independence between scholar and subject, seeking to preserve the authenticity of both subjects' experience and the scholar's descriptive analysis. At the same time, practical theologians are called to the recognition that they continue to interpret those phenomena, contextualize them, and thereby participate in the process of producing them as historically positive traditions. An orientation to the sociable nature of theology leads not to lament or cynicism that this participation is unavoidable but rather to responsible recognition and engagement with it.

In what follows, I introduce Friedrich Schleiermacher's early Romantic *Attempt at a Theory of Sociable Conduct* (Schleiermacher [1799] 2011) in part one as the primary reference work for the reflections on sociability and theological method outlined in parts two and three.

2 Schleiermacher on Religion and Sociability

In the spring of 1799, Schleiermacher was occupied with bringing his first major literary project to completion, namely, *On Religion: Speeches to Its Cultured Despisers*. In this text, Schleiermacher theorizes religion as a "sensibility and taste" for the infinite, for the universe, and the cultivation of "feeling" for "the relation of humanity to it [the universe]" (Schleiermacher [1799] 1996, 23, 22, 19). Less well-known, however, is that he had already anonymously published, in the January and February 1799 issues of the Enlightenment periodical *Berlinisches Archiv der Zeit und ihres Geschmacks*, a text in two parts outlining an "Attempt at a Theory of Sociable Conduct" (Schleiermacher 2011).[1] In this latter text, Schleiermacher describes the experience of late Enlightenment *salon* culture, where in the context of open homes men and women of differing social classes, levels of education and professional engagements could interact on equal footing, engaging one another on issues of science, art, politics, religion, travel and any number of other topics. Through this exchange, one's world expanded – opened to the universe, one might say – and new possibilities were created. The relevance of Schleiermacher's "Attempt" to the writing of the *Speeches* is that Schleiermacher repurposed many of the arguments from his "At-

---

[1] For a philosophical contextualization of Schleiermacher's essay in the German Enlightenment and overview of its broad reception in the twentieth century, as well as an interpretation of Schleiermacher's theological development of the concept of sociability, see Robinson (2018).

tempt" for use throughout the *Speeches*, particularly in the fourth speech which he titled, "On the Sociable Element in Religion" (Robinson 2018).

In the fourth speech of *On Religion*, Schleiermacher calls religion "the most complete result of human sociability" (Schleiermacher 1996, 75). The reason for this is that Schleiermacher saw human experience as caught up in a perpetual dialectic between, on the one hand, encountering one's own limitations and thereby being brought to an awareness of something more which surpasses and encompasses oneself or one's community and, on the other hand, moving beyond the self into what Robert Orsi and Tyler Roberts have described as an excessive "more" (Orsi 2011, 97–104; Roberts 2006, 705–706) through interactive relationships with other persons and groups that can confirm, correct, or otherwise help one overcome one's limitations. The latter movement, of course, quickly becomes a new instance of the former, and the process repeats. In other words, it is through a certain kind of participatory interaction with diverse others that individuals and communities develop themselves into particular individualities. This interaction possesses an inherently "religious" quality in the sense (and to the extent) that it is driven by an orientation, not only toward what exceeds the self, but toward giving a *complete, integrated account* of that excess and, finally, *of all things*. Every coming into community both is an attempt at giving such an account and, by virtue of its finitude, becomes a reaffirmation that one has not done so. While this is especially evident in communities traditionally identified as 'religious', it is true to some extent of all forms of human community in Schleiermacher's view.

Sociable interactions thus constitute the primary site of *religious formation* for Schleiermacher. In order to understand this hermeneutical position, it will be helpful to summarize some of the main arguments of Schleiermacher's theory of sociability. Long before a community becomes self-reflectedly religious in the sense of intentionally seeking to develop a comprehensive orientation toward reality as such, individual persons and small groups perceive a fundamental need for what Schleiermacher theorizes in the "Attempt" as *freie Geselligkeit*, or "free sociability." He writes, "Sociability that is free and not bound or determined by some external purpose is demanded by all human beings as one of their most primary and most noble needs" (Schleiermacher 2011, 165).[2] Schleiermacher explicates this basic need by reference to commonplace experiences of professional and private life. The former brings with it the tendency to see and interpret life from the point of view of a predetermined interest and to implement the necessary methods for accomplishing a specific end. The latter tends to make life just as simple by means of routinization and habituation of behaviors and attitudes. Those who are "thrown back and forth" between these two modes find themselves in a situation not unlike that of the hapless scholar

---

2 All translations of the *Attempt* are my own and follow the text of the critical edition (Schleiermacher [1799] 2011). Two English translations exist, see Schleiermacher ([1799] 1995) by Jeffrey Hoover and Schleiermacher ([1799] 2006) by Peter Foley.

floating between unjustified universals and meaningless particulars: One's view into the "diverse insights of humanity" – one's understanding of what being human could be like, beyond the limits of one's own circumscribed experience – becomes more and more narrow (Schleiermacher 2011, 165). These mutually compounding limitations give one the overwhelming sense that

> there must be some way to make these two complementary to one another such that the sphere of one individual is placed into a position where it can be intersected as diversely as possible by the spheres of other individuals, and each individual's points of limitation can become viewpoints into another strange world for one another, so that all appearances of humanity eventually become familiar to one and even the strangest orientations and relationships become like friends and neighbors (Schleiermacher 2011, 165).

What is that way? 'Free sociability' *(freie Geselligkeit)*. And what is free sociability? Free sociability is simply the thoroughgoing practice of *reciprocity* among persons in community with one another. The form of any freely sociable relationship, "should be a reciprocity that permeates all participants but that is also wholly determined and completed by them" (Schleiermacher 2011, 169). Schleiermacher then proceeds to outline the ideal form of free sociability as a thought experiment; if it were possible to implement this ideal in practice, it would mean: (a) that no external purpose or goal contextualizes the relationship other than the "natural tendency" (Schleiermacher 2011, 168) driving free sociability, namely, the drive to learn as much as possible about being humans; (b) that participants engage in a "free play of thoughts and feelings" as a method and form for revealing the group's sum total of exposure to and insights into humanity (Schleiermacher 2011, 170); (c) that this *form* of exchanging thoughts and feelings itself also constitutes the *material content* for the exchange such that participants are sharing their own experiences with the others, who in turn draw upon their own experiences in reaction; (d) that all participants enjoy full, unimpaired freedom in sharing their own experiences and perspectives as well as commit to being transparent and comprehensive in their sharing in order that no exposures to humanity be held back, limited, or otherwise conditioned and covered; and finally (e) that all participants continuously engage in this reciprocal communicative practice until the 'amount' of humanity which the group collectively contains and can produce is exhausted.

Such *reciprocity*, as early German Romantics (like Schleiermacher) as well as German literary elites (like Schiller [1795] 1971) and Idealists (like Fichte [1794/95], 1982) were recognizing, is not simply an idea of taking turns, but a social and epistemological ethics, that, when fully developed, implies robust civic virtues and duties, including rights to self-determination such as free speech, public assembly, tolerant and open public debate, and transparency in civic institutions. Early classical sociologist Georg Simmel, who may have known Schleiermacher's essay but only as an anonymous piece (possibly via Wilhelm Dilthey), saw the theory of sociability as a paradigm for the interpretation of basic social dynamics (Simmel [1911] 1997, 120–130), while later sociologists and philosophers in the twentieth century found in this theory and the social form of the *salon* both an index of the evolution of a new form of public space (Habermas [1962] 1989, 43) as well as evidence for the functional differentiation of society under conditions of modernity (Luhmann 1980, 158). Even though Schleiermacher also uses the terminology of sociability more narrowly to refer to concrete settings of private life among family and friends, the form and practice of sociability create for him a kind of universal environment for human interactions and development in general. They outline basic conditions for the possibility of human beings learning about and realizing more fully the conditions of good life in pluralistic communities of the most diverse orientations and perspectives on the fullness of human life in the world in relation to the vastness of all things (Robinson 2018, 98–99).

3 Comparative and Ethical Aspects of a Sociable Paradigm for Theological Research

As a lens for theological research, a focus on human sociability does not offer any definition of what religion *is*, in some kind of essentialist sense. Rather sociability directs the attention toward the media through which the *relationships* which people regard as most meaningful and significant are formed, expressed, articulated, and circulated. That is, sociability directs the attention toward *communications* that form and maintain communities' modes of life. And theological research participates unavoidably in these communications. In our interconnected, globalized present, the question is not how to avoid this form of sociability but how to engage in it responsibly and fairly in theological research. Personally, as a scholar with an odd pedigree in two disciplines that have often viewed one another with skepticism, if not downright antipathy – namely, Religious Studies and Christian Systematic Theology – my own view is that ideas and practices labeled 'religious', when viewed through scholarly paradigms, are to be treated as indeed non-necessary, historical accidents, but that scientific analysis of these things nevertheless functions as a normative, ethical task. Of course, many scholars of religion and Christian systematic theologians alike will find such a position deeply dissatisfying, though likely for opposite reasons. I would outline my reasons for taking it, in brief, as follows.

3.1 Communication-Based Theology Means Comparative Theology

As Ernst Troeltsch worried over one hundred years ago, "when Christianity is treated systematically, the historical-critical approach is abandoned" (Troeltsch [1898] 1991, 11). A sociologist, philosopher, and theologian, Troeltsch observed that Christian systematic theology has a long history of attempting "to validate the old authoritarian concept of revelation" by means of focusing on "postulates, claims, theories of knowledge, or other intangible generalities" (Troeltsch [1898] 1991, 11). Troeltsch found especially frustrating that theologians would do this and simply ignore the serious questions posed to Christian theology from new findings in the natural sciences and humanities, not least among them, the emerging discipline of the History of Religions. He thus devoted extensive attention to the challenges raised by critical, historical inquiry for *theological method,* and his outline of the implications for theology of "the modern view of history" presents a moment of reckoning to theology echoing down to this day (Troeltsch [1898] 1971, 45). In his essay on *Historical and Dogmatic Method in Theology,* Troeltsch presented three critical-constructive principles for a theological method that seeks to be as honest as possible about the limitations on the kinds of claims it makes, as informed by modern scientific methods (Troeltsch [1898] 1991, 13–14): (1.) historical judgements are judgements of probability not certainty; (2.) facts and events can only be defined in historical and sociological analysis by means of distinctions, analogies and comparisons; (3.) and any knowledge at all is conditional upon the presupposition of an interconnectedness, and thus non-randomness, of all historical phenomena. For theology, this means it should seek to describe phenomena in an orderly, measurable manner that can be checked, verified, and criticized, moreover, again and again and by anyone – just as in the natural sciences. Theological arguments might be said to be stronger and weaker as accounts of a community's reflected modeling of itself to itself and to that degree deserving of corresponding acknowledgment even from the outside. But no theology can expect scientific recognition of the correspondence of its claims to some ultimate reality.

Human knowledge, including theological knowledge, forms by means of collecting human experiences, indeed, as many experiences as possible, and communicating, comparing, and organizing them. For Troeltsch, this meant that all theology would have to work a bit more empirically than it had in the past. The position for which Troeltsch was arguing, though innovative with respect to its scientific applications, is consistent with the outline prepared by Schleiermacher who defined even dogmatic theology descriptively as the organized presentation of the prevailing views of a particular community at a particular time (Schleiermacher [1830] 2011, § 97). In keeping with this view, Schleiermacher was among the first to develop the science of *Church Statistics* – essentially a first experiment in comparative theology of the Christian churches. He observed that the more churches multiply and spread, "the more linguistic and cultural areas" they encompass. Correspondingly, "the more numerous are the different notions and ways of living that theology must take into account" and "the more diverse are the historical data to which it must refer" when doing so (Schleiermacher 2011, § 4). In short, the more time, the greater the geographical territory, and the more complex the socio-cultural factors, the more empirical theology has to become. In the pluralistic and globalized world of the twenty-first century, I do not see how, pragmatically speaking, it could be possible to work with any other paradigm: The only available options are descriptions and comparisons or fundamentalisms. Faced with this choice, comparison of the most diverse traditions, communication across them, and, in situations where mutual understanding is necessary, a complete *translatability* of concepts and symbols between traditions form a most pressing set of theological responsibilities.

3.2 Comparative Theology Presupposes and Practices Some Ethic of Participation

The normative and ethical do not disappear in this descriptive-comparative paradigm; quite to the contrary, they are heightened.[3] Description and comparison entail *interpretation*, for, as far as we can judge within the horizons of human experience, connections between events do not 'exist' in any metaphysically real order but must rather be drawn by a subject or subjects who, moreover, are doing so on the basis of incomplete information. The scientific analysis and presentation of the religious lives of others presents itself as a deeply ethical task *in the sense that* and *on the recognition that* both what we say and what we do not say, the ways we choose to engage communities and to (remain) disengage(d), all contribute directly to the formation of the scholarly knowledge gained. This then becomes part of the corpus of scientific literature that exercises more and less (functionally, not metaphysically) normative authority, depending on the extent of its reception. Humanities scholars generally and theologians specifically are embedded and participate, not only in the processes of knowledge production and exchange, but in the contexts and communities about whom and for whom that knowledge is developed.

For work in the humanities, including theology, the inextricable historical embeddedness of all knowledge summons scholars to persistent *contextualization*, and an openness to new information and perspectives – above all from those with a nearer historical, geographical, and traditional proximity – holds paramount importance.

4 Responsibilities and Methods for a Sociable Theology

Which leads us back to the matter at hand, namely, sociability. As discussed in relating Schleiermacher's theory of sociability, the limitations of individual human ex-

---

[3] In this essay, I am focusing on issues of research method, and thus can only mention in passing the issue of the ethics of theological knowledge. But this is a point of fundamental importance, indeed, with specific relevance to the topic of sociability. Dietrich Bonhoeffer's doctoral dissertation *Sanctorum Communio* remains one of the most important studies of what he called human 'sociality' (*Sozialität*) and the church. See Bonhoeffer ([1930] 1998); Green (1997).

perience, combined with human needs and desires to live as well as possible, compel us to sociable life with others. Flourishing must not be threatened but can be enhanced by *meaningful participation in community* with diverse others. I want to conclude by reflecting on the implications of a *sociable approach* to contemporary hermeneutical theology for practical and systematic theological research. Practically speaking, the drive toward meaningful participation in community with others creates certain responsibilities, which in turn can function as vectors for guiding new methodological directions in theological research.

4.1 Responsibility 1 – Transcultural Research as Essential, Not Optional

First, a transcultural and transreligious orientation can no longer be seen as optional but must be recognized as essential to practical- and systematic-theological work going forward. Theological research has a responsibility to seek out and incorporate as many perspectives and experiences as possible, à la Schleiermacher's interest in a reciprocal exchange of thoughts and feelings. This implies a general warning against the acceptance of "willful epistemologies" (Fishbane 2008, ix) – whether in theology or any intellectual pursuit – and a general openness to the world. This is, on the one hand, a basic observation about human living and knowing that is modelled in the modern scientific method's principled commitment to accepting nothing on the basis of unquestionable orthodoxies and rather to testing old hypotheses against new experience, exploring the unknown, and re-calibrating old knowledge while developing new. But the vitally important point is a socio-ethical one: As human beings, we think and know only in community with other people, and what we think and know depends on who is present (or not) in the communities we create. Not too long ago, one's own life and the lives of culturally and religiously distant others held much less significance for one another than they presently do – certainly there was nothing approaching the concrete presence of distant others in daily life that many people experience today, at work, in the neighborhood, and even at home, not to mention virtually. Smaller spheres of interaction correspondingly limited the perspectives on what it means to be human and to live well that individuals and local communities could reasonably incorporate into their own self-understanding vis-à-vis their understanding of the totality of reality. Today, however, people all around the world, from every cultural and religious context, live under conditions of a continuous and simultaneous interconnectedness of economic and social media networks. In this situation, the question of human flourishing has taken on a complexity that is orders of magnitude greater than the same question presented just a few generations ago. It is thus a pressing challenge for theological research today to innovate *new methods* for and angles on studying the ways in which religious communities process this transcultural and transreligious complexity and incorporate it into the particularity of their communal life.

4.2 Responsibility 2 – Cultivating Meaningful Co-Participations in Research

Second, the transcultural and transreligious focus in theological research must itself be recognized as being just as much about meaningful participation in community life – and thus about economic participation, access to education and inclusion in communication networks – as about culture or religion *per se*. Seeking out and incorporating the perspectives of others requires striving for their full *participation* – in this case, *participation in theological research* – and this presents difficulties on several levels. To the degree that the perspectives of others are absent or limited, constrained, qualified, or marginalized from our theological investigations, we can be sure that we are cultivating our *complete* orientation toward reality on the basis of the particular, limited imagination of one *incomplete* perspective – which unavoidably results in error and, more gravely, harm (Robinson 2017, 241). Where participation is missing, there arises a responsibility to ensure the opportunity for its cultivation and to support its formation. But what can this mean for scholarship? What might it look like? One simple implication can be to further incorporate intercultural and interreligious paradigms and methods into the core of theological education curricula, rather than viewing them as elective or areas of specialization. But more radically, it will become increasingly important to foster the incorporation into theological work of the thoughts, feelings, and experiences – the visions of life and experiences of well-being or lack thereof – of communities in disadvantaged and excluded social, cultural or geographical locations in a more material way. Are we to engage in theology as activism? Theology as development? Perhaps. But only if we understand development as freedom. As Martha Nussbaum and Amartya Sen have argued in outlining their economic philosophy of human capabilities, *meaningful* participation in community requires that persons and groups have the *capabilities* necessary for creating and conducting a self-determining life (Nussbaum 2011). In *Development as Freedom,* Amartya Sen described the same principle as people's ability "to lead the kind of lives they have reason to value" (Sen 1999, 10). This is similar to what Schleiermacher, in his essay on sociability, called following only those laws which one gives oneself (Schleiermacher 2011, 165). For transcultural and transreligious theological research based in Western contexts this would mean not only including non-Western perspectives in teaching and scholarship but encouraging the articulation of those perspectives through supporting self-determining theological education where the resources, forms and platforms for it are lacking. Thus, a transcultural and transreligious focus in theological research, if it is to support such meaningful participation in community, may require methods for bringing the theological reflection of disadvantaged others to speech.

A primary challenge for theological research in the first quarter of the twenty-first century, it seems to me, has been that the Christian churches and movements around the world who are among the largest, most influential, and fastest growing are also among the least represented in (particularly Western) higher-education contexts. Here I have in mind, especially but not only, Pentecostal Christian movements and Christian churches among the world's poorest, in both "developed" and "developing" contexts. These two groups are in many instances overlapping populations. Encounters between much academic theology and various Pentecostal movements around the world carry significant potential for political, cultural, and theological division (Haustein and Maltese 2014, 15–65), and the meanings and goals of "mutual recognition" in these encounters may seem uncertain in many cases. Nevertheless, a transcultural and transreligious theological paradigm, will need to cultivate these encounters. The self-determining participation of the poor and other socially marginalized persons, on the other hand, presents different, especially administrative-logistical complications for higher-education contexts. Academic and scholarly recognition of study programs and degrees or scientific products (publications and research projects, for instance) requires a fund of opportunities, resources, and capabilities often far exceeding what those living in poorer and developing locations have reliably available to them. Nevertheless, both Pentecostal traditions and the world's poorest Christians have in common that they are communities rich with theological reflection.

5 Concluding Methodological Proposal – Observant Participation and Co-writing Living Theologies

The challenge of incorporating these voices into theological research is in fact twofold, namely, a challenge of bringing to voice those currently without a presence in global theological conversations and a challenge of discerning appropriate responses of theologies in global conversations to one another. First, regarding the poor and those lacking the capabilities needed for meaningful participation, there is the challenge that – to borrow terminology from another practical-theological context – theological reflection in contexts lacking the infrastructure needed for meaningful participation in global conversations often takes form as a "theology through *living human documents*" (Nouwen 1968) rather than through the media of publications and institutions more familiar to Western academic theology.[4] That is, these theologies do exist, but in order to participate meaningfully in global conversations that concern them, they need to be written. The writing of them could be seen as a promising frontier in theological research. In part, this can be encouraged by supporting local theological education that is oriented toward the specific historical, material, and cultural situation of local contexts. But it would also be appropriate to employ

---

[4] The term "living human documents" refers back to the pioneering work in "empirical theology" (Nouwen 1968, 60) of Anton T. Boisen, a founding figure in the Clinical Pastoral Education movement of the latter twentieth century. More recently, Sarah Coakley has taken up the concept in calling for a systematic theology that is more pastoral (Coakley 2017).

empirical and ethnographic methods and share them in the life of poor and disadvantaged Christian communities in a kind of reverse coding of fieldwork as traditionally understood in the humanities and social sciences.

Namely, rather than 'participant observation' where an anthropologist or scholar of religion seeks to observe while influencing the context as little as possible, theologians can engage in 'observant participation'. Here the mode is not only one of observation in the sense of watching but in the sense of recognizing, honoring, and respecting a particular community's experience of the world, vision of ultimate reality, and how the latter organizes its confrontation with the former. In the course of shared life, such a theologian, joining as an outside collaborator, does not seek to bracket-off his or her particularity and isolate the "pure community". Rather, both recognize that no communal or individual *Urbild* exists, but both have formed and continue to form in and through life in a shared world. Theological terms, symbols, practices, and beliefs shared by virtue of a common, broadly Christian identity are to be discussed, as well as the various ways each would understand their relevance to the community's particular political and cultural situation. Nevertheless, the emphasis should remain on capacity-creation for the expression of the self-understanding of that particular community or group as a Christian group in and for its specific situation. Some may worry that this approach would push beyond the bounds of best practices in Religious Studies; this is a reasonable question to debate. But such a practice works in a mode in which self-aware theological research can feel right at home. The resulting theology would not be one that is to be seen as normative or valid for any other than that particular community or group, but it can support meaningful participation in global discourses that have direct and significant impact on their communal life.

In short, more first-order theologies need to be written, and this can be done in part through various modes of supporting, amplifying and partnering with local voices. These theologies can then be set alongside one another, in ways that preserve and reflect all of the socio-political particularity of each respective instance. Such comparative work might make clearer the function of theology in and for the communities in which reflected, intentional religious communications are circulating and, in this way, contribute to scientific understanding of religious self-understandings in the contemporary world. Practically, this would require transcultural, "trans-traditional" (that is, both ecumenical and interreligious) comparative research based, in turn, on extensive embedded observant theological participation of the kind described above. Affirmation is not a requirement of mutuality, but understanding is, and mutual, meaningful participation in one another's community lives and in global discussions – in a word, *sociability* or meaningful participation in community – is critical and indispensable for transcultural, transreligious research on theology and religion in the contemporary world.

Bibliography

Bonhoeffer, Dietrich. [1930] 1998. *Sanctorum Communio: A Theological Study of the Sociology of the Church.* Vol. 1, Dietrich Bonhoeffer Works, edited by Clifford J. Green and trans. Reinhard Krauss and Nancy Lukens. Minneapolis: Fortress Press.

Coakley, Sarah. 2017. "Can Systematic Theology become Pastoral Again, and Pastoral Theology Theological?" *ABC Religion & Ethics*, https://www.realclearreligion.org/2017/07/25/can_systematic_theology_become_pastoral_again_278045.html (29.11.2021).

Fichte, Johann Gottlieb. [1795] 1982. *The Science of Knowledge*, edited and trans. Peter Heath and John Lachs. Cambridge / New York: Cambridge University Press.

Fishbane, Michael. 2008. *Sacred Attunement: A Jewish Theology.* Chicago: University of Chicago Press.

Green, Clifford J. 1997. *Bonhoeffer: A Theology of Sociality.* Grand Rapids / Cambridge: William B. Eerdmans.

Habermas, Jürgen. [1962] 1989. *The Structural Transformation of the Public Sphere: An Inquiry into a Category of Bourgeoisie Society*, trans. Thomas Burger and Frederick Lawrence. Cambridge: Polity Press.

Haustein, Jörg, and Giovanni Maltese, eds. 2014. *Handbuch pfingstliche und charismatische Theologie.* Göttingen: Vandenhoeck & Ruprecht.

Luhmann, Niklas. 1980. *Gesellschaftsstruktur und Semantik: Studien zur Wissenssoziologie der modernen Gesellschaft.* Vol. 1, Frankfurt am Main: Suhrkamp.

Nouwen, Henri. 1968. "Anton T. Boisen and Theology Through Living Human Documents." *Pastoral Psychology* 19:49–63.

Nussbaum, Martha. 2011. *Creating Capabilities: The Human Development Approach.* Cambridge, MA: Harvard Belknap Press.

Orsi, Robert. 2011. "The Problem of the Holy." In *The Cambridge Companion to Religious Studies*, edited by Robert A. Orsi, Cambridge: Cambridge University Press, 84–106.

Roberts, Tyler. 2006. "Between the Lines: Exceeding Historicism in the Study of Religion." *Journal of the American Academy of Religion* 74:697–719.

Robinson, Matthew Ryan. 2017. "Schleiermacher on Evil as Social Evil." *Itinerari*, special issue "Il Male e le sue forme: Riconsiderazioni modern e contemporanee di un problema antico.", edited by Roberto Garaventa and Omar Brino, 225–246.

Robinson, Matthew Ryan. 2018. *Redeeming Relationship, Relationships that Redeem: Free Sociability and the Completion of Humanity in the Thought of Friedrich Schleiermacher.* Tübingen: Mohr Siebeck.

Schiller, Friedrich. [1795] 1971. *On the Aesthetic Education of Man in a Series of Letters*, edited and trans. Reginald Snell. New York: Friedrich Ungar Publishing Co.

Schleiermacher, Friedrich. [1830] 2011. *Brief Outline of Theology as a Field of Study: Revised Translation of the 1811 and 1830 Editions*, edited and trans. Terrence N. Tice. Louisville: Westminster John Knox Press.

Schleiermacher, Friedrich. [1799] 2006. "Essay on a Theory of Sociable Behavior." In *Friedrich Schleiermacher's Essay on a Theory of Sociable Behavior (1799): A Contextual Interpretation*, edited and trans. Peter Foley. Lewiston: Edwin Mellen Press, 153–176.

Schleiermacher, Friedrich. [1799] 1996. *On Religion: Speeches to its Cultured Despisers*, edited and trans. Richard Crouter. Cambridge: Cambridge University Press.

Schleiermacher, Friedrich. [1799] 1995. "Toward a Theory of Sociable Conduct." In *Friedrich Schleiermacher's 'Toward a Theory of Sociable Conduct', and Essays on its Intellectual-Cultural Context*, edited by Ruth Richardson, trans. Jeffrey Hoover. New Athenaeum / Neues Athenaeum 4. Lewiston: Edwin Mellen Press, 22–40.

Schleiermacher, Friedrich. [1799] 2011. "Versuch einer Theorie des geselligen Betragens (1799)." In *Schriften aus der Berliner Zeit 1796–1799*. Vol. 2, *Kritische Gesamtausgabe Abteilung 1*, edited by Günter Meckenstock. Berlin: De Gruyter, 163–184.
Sen, Amartya. 1999. *Development as Freedom*. Oxford: Oxford University Press.
Simmel, Georg. [1911] 1997. *Simmel on Culture: Selected Writings*, edited by David Frisby and Mike Featherstone. London / Thousand Oaks: Sage Publications.
Troeltsch, Ernst. [1898] 1971. *The Absoluteness of Christianity and the History of Religions*, trans. David Reid. Richmond: John Knox Press.
Troeltsch, Ernst. 1991. *Religion in History*, trans. James Luther Adams and Walter F. Bense. Minneapolis: Fortress Press.

Part II: **Religious Practices in the Perspective of Agency**

Hans-Ulrich Probst
Artefact / Personal Belongings / Things

1 Things Matter! The Stone of the Anointing in the Church of the Holy Sepulchre

For one year I was lucky enough to study at the Hebrew University in Jerusalem while living in a quarter close to the Church of the Holy Sepulchre in the Old City. Being a German student of Protestant theology at that time, I was fascinated by the dialogue between Jewry and Church and decided to enrich my academic education by taking a programme in Jewish studies. Beside the intensive and inspiring courses in Rabbinic literature and Jewish history, I enjoyed observing daily religious practices as they took place in this city, indeed, the melting pot of Abrahamic religions.

For this article I would like to refer to a situation I experienced while sitting close to the entrance of the Church of the Holy Sepulchre, which one might call one of the most important places in the Christian tradition. Many pilgrims from all over the world enter this place and I was overwhelmed and impressed by the acts that I witnessed at the Stone of the Anointing, a marble slab which is located close to the entrance, embedded into the floor and is a point of interest for many pilgrims. Opposite the stone you find a mosaic depicting the body of Jesus Christ receiving the last rites after death. Many people, mostly women, kneel in front of the stone, touch it, and put different things on top of it, such as small candles that you can buy in souvenir shops around the church, miniature icons of Christian saints, or private photographs depicting loved ones that are not with them or little jewels like bracelets or chains. An Orthodox guide from Russia gives a piece of advice: "Do not leave your things in the plastic bag. Otherwise, the effect of the stone won't work!" While personal belongings are placed on top of the stone, the owners start praying, most of them leaning their bodies down to the slab and kissing it tenderly. Some of the women wipe the surface of the stone intensely with white towels. Afterwards all items are tentatively put back into bags and people move on to the next place of holiness in the church.

The Stone of the Anointing is linked to the Christian tradition of the Passion narrative according to the Gospel of Saint John (19:39–40) and represents the last place where a human touched Jesus' dead body before his resurrection. The power and effect of this stone seems to be present even today, at least in the eyes of the pilgrims. Thus, the personal belongings which are put on top of this stone change in value and incorporate a part of the stone's meaning. The pilgrims' behaviour is influenced by different objects in this example: They encounter the stone in a submissive attitude by kneeling down and interact by putting personal belongings on top of the stone with the slab.

Things matter – not only – for religious practices; they are essential (inter)actors in the field of religion. The pilgrims I witnessed at the Church of the Holy Sepulchre are only one example of many. Religion is far more than a spiritual or verbal system. Religious practices are full of tangible or visible things that play a significant role in religion and are important for human life. Thus, the question arises: What is a 'religious' or a 'sacred' material object and how does it interact with people exactly? In other words: How does a thing become so meaningful as the Stone of the Anointing and the objects placed on top of it, such that we end up describing it as 'religious' or 'sacred'?

In the following chapter I will present a short introduction of the discussion about artefacts and objects by outlining the relevance of material culture studies for empirical religious studies. Furthermore, I will reflect on some methodological considerations and instructions on how to deal with artefacts and objects in the field of religious studies. To conclude, I will show paradigmatically what kind of theoretical impact and benefit the study of material objects could have for Practical Theology if it integrates the research of artefacts and things into its own research programme.

2 Traditions of Material Analysis

Throughout history material objects have played a prominent role in European philosophy. Rooted in Platonic contemplation, a neo-Platonic tradition postulated a dualistic division between mind and body which was formative for many centuries. In modern times Renes Descartes renewed this dualism in his *Meditationes* through his distinction between the immaterial mind as a *res cogitans* (thinking thing) and the material body as a *res extensa* (existing thing). Even though Descartes described both entities in a way of interaction, in Cartesian rationalism the material body was devalued through a dualism of the body and spirit. Referring to the same neo-Platonic philosophical tradition, Christian scholasticism received the human mind as immortal and spiritual, whereas the body and tangible goods were an expression of transience. Religion was an "interior spiritual experience" and "study of religion, yielding a focus on beliefs." (Meyer and Houtman 2012, 1) Following this antagonistic concept, a Christian moral against greed was developed, referring also to Biblical sources criticising excessive material possessions as an unchristian immoral way of life. Even though tangible things in religious life were always apparent in history, the Christian doctrine adopted an ambivalent and negative stance towards material objects, which could become human idols and induce mankind to destructive dependencies. The tradition of Lutheran reformation and its highlighting focus on the spiritual biblical word can be understood as a strengthening of these tendencies.

Not only in Christian theology does one find a fundamental scepticism regarding material things, but also in the beginning of non-confessional religious studies this scepticism can be seen, where the analysis of fetishism in 'primitive' religious practices received a lot of attention. Charles de Brosses (1760) depicted in his book *Du culte des dieux fétiches* that objects are worshipped as gods, a characterisation which is also outlined in Émile Durkheim's (1912) great work *Les formes élémentaires de la vie religieuse*. The examination of material artefacts and objects was preluded, but their unprejudiced in-depth analysis was integrated into other fields of research. Cultural material artefacts were a topic of interest in the field of archaeology (archaeological findings), ethnology (everyday items) or anthropology and induced various theoretical concepts about material culture (Miller 1998).

As part of a cultural turn the *material turn* argued strongly for the social relevance of things and artefacts and had a strong impact on social sciences and humanities to focus on material cultural representations (Appadurai 1986). At least since the 1980s material objects as constitutive elements for culture were considered in a participating position of interaction with all humankind and as an indicator of their social status. Thus, not only the function of material things should be analysed but also their symbolic meaning and content as emanations of a cultural location. An additional step was taken by the actor-network theory emphasising an active and creative power of things in a pattern of agency. These reflections of the material turn can be understood as a change of paradigm in which no longer exclusively human beings are in the position to act but also material artefacts and things (Latour 1993). The *theory of practice* is related to that change of paradigm and a fruitful approach for a new perspective on material culture. Material objects are of different though equal entities of arrangements and are connected and constitutive for practises as the basic element of social life (Schatzki 2010).

A philosophical tradition that reconstructs the attribution of meaning to artefacts and things is the *Phenomenology* which "[...] is an attempt to study in a systematic manner our different subjective perspectives, our different ways of experiencing reality." (Føllesdal 2010, 32) Edmund Husserl, the founder of Phenomenology, took the connection between the human mind and the appearance of material things as the starting point for a transcendental philosophy and returned to the things themselves and described their reception through human mind. The ambiguous meaning of a thing is a product of the intentionality of the human consciousness that receives objects not as what they are but as what they appear to humans. Humans do not perceive things as they are but in a dependency with an intentional focused consciousness (Held 1996, 454–456). The experience and the perception of material things is embedded in a structure of appresentation, i.e., the addition of hidden aspects which are connected to previous experiences and knowledge about an object. Husserl concludes that things are constantly in a transcendental position in human's mind whereby the task of a phenomenological analysis is to describe the constitution of this position. No material object can be received as isolated but is embedded into patterns of space and time. Therefore, all things are in references to existing senses of an universal horizon in the surrounding world, and act inside this horizon. The Husserlian concept of *lifeworld* (*Lebenswelt*) emphasises the corporal experienced world and things in it, too. The lifeworld is the pre-reflexive and dynamic horizon of all our lived experiences in the world, thus, it is that scene on which all things appear for human's consciousness. Material things are in the view of the phenomenological tradition effective elements in all human lifeworlds and give impetus to people to act and interact. Another merit is the phenomenological accordant perception between the human body and material things as related corporal appearances (Waldenfels 2015).

3 Material Religion, 'Sacralised' Things, and Artefacts

The research on artefacts in the field of religion(s) is strongly stimulated by the phenomenologically sensitised insights of *material culture studies* which led to overcoming the traditional antagonism between mind and body (Thomas 2006). The perspective of material culture studies can be described as a new understanding of the interaction between humankind and things in all aspects of culture and as a new sensibility to examine the meaning of material objects (Hahn 2014). Material culture is visible in all parts of human life and therefore a constitutive player in society. Close to the described programme of Phenomenology, material objects are understood in a relation of meaning for people in contact with them. The meaning of material objects becomes apparent by analysing the human perception and dealing with them and the impact of things on humankind's activities (Hahn 2015, 9). Another instructive awareness emerging from material culture studies is the postulation to differentiate between things (*Dinge*) and artefacts/items (*Sachen*). *Dinge* are defined as natural materials that are unavailable to the human realm, whereas *Sachen* are defined as available objects having been produced by humans. This distinction will also be used throughout this chapter, whilst attempting not to reify the nature/culture dichotomy.

Some researchers see an academic programme of material religion closely linked to an aesthetic approach in the context of material culture. In this field, religion is understood heuristically as a materially bounded practice in that belief, rituals and other religious practices are carried out in a perceivable way. All religious actors appear through religious practices or rituals that deal with transcendence or sacredness through different kinds of materiality, such as artefacts or their own corporeality (Morgan 2010). To study material religion means seeking a connection between humans' corporal and religious practices or experiences and focusing on the sensory and material signifiers within this correlation. These signifiers can be colours, olfactory and visible dimensions, elements of architecture, tangible objects, or corporal movements of religious agents. Thus, everything that is perceivable via bodily senses, in the area of religion is of interest for material religion studies. The international journal *Material Religion: The Journal of Objects, Art and Belief* publishes much in this domain. Of course, the research on "religious" or "sacred" material objects is challenged by a pre-existing shared assumption and understanding of the phenomena of religion and sacredness. Through exploration of different examples of material objects, we will begin to see an underlying fluid concept of religion that is not restricted to explicit religion.

A basic understanding in material culture studies is that things and artefacts can pose a symbolic meaning beyond the functional, in their own horizon that is inscribed into them through cultural and social practices (Csikszentmihalyi and Halton 1981). The multitude of symbolic meanings can be described as a polysemy which is characteristic for all material objects: A tree can be perceived as a peaceful place providing shade, as a material expression of God's creation as well as an emblematic symbol for the ecological movement. All different semantic dimensions and attributed symbolic meanings cause different emotions, responses, and reactions. Thus, the symbolic meaning of a tree is closely linked to different patterns of human interpretations and actions associated with it. Thus, no thing is inherently religious, instead it is always perceived as a thing which is attributed with a specific symbolic religious meaning. Artefacts as well as things are not unambiguous but equivocal. Hence the vagueness of their meaning is the basic condition for a religious attribution. To be more specific: The candles on top of the Stone of the Anointing described above could be lit to illuminate, for example, a room, the wax would last for a few hours and one possible functional sense of the candle would be fulfilled. But in this example another dimension of content and meaning is inscribed on the candle through a social context and an individual belief that the contact with the stone changes the value of the items on top. One can assume that the owner will not light this candle like any other and their activities are guided by the candle, hence the functional sense of this artefact is reduced or even liquidated through a new meaningful attribution. The candles are transfigured into symbols of this meaningful experience in life and can remind of this specific moment. Ultimately therefore, all objects and artefacts are open to be categorised as religious and may be objects of practiced intersubjective *transfiguration* leading to a separation of these objects from less valued things or artefacts. This process can be understood as a practice of sacralisation (Cress 2021, 33-35). Sacred things in explicit religion can be described as extraordinary, worthy of protection, integral parts of cultic practices at a tabooed place (Kohl 2003, 151–158). Furthermore, material objects (both, artefacts, and things) can occupy an integral function in religious life and play distinct roles within it: some of them embody and represent a deity or saints and serve as a go-between to unreachable figures enabling communication and relation between humankind and transcendental divinities. Others can be described as a memory of religious history giving deep insights into specific historical steps of lived and experienced religion (Cress 2014). Through material objects people remember meaningful narrations and can experience them through *immediacy*. Sacred artefacts in this sense, authentically transport a religious narrative which is then perceivable in a haptic way and increases its comprehensibility for a religious group. Thus, artefacts and things represent an important aspect of religious identity and sense of belonging to a social group.

The Stone of the Anointing evokes pilgrims' intersubjective imagination to be close to the Passion and Resurrection after Jesus' death. Even though the Stone of the Anointing was placed into the Church of the Holy Sepulchre not earlier than in 1811, in the eyes of the believer this artefact is the place where they are corporeally very close to the final step during the Passion. This individual assumption – to be a part of an authentic immediacy in the presence of a materialised religious narrative – seems to be a key moment for a religious attribution of material objects. In a similar way a sacred host during Communion or a collection of relics can be received as sacred artefacts (Laube 2011). They materialise and actualise a religious narrative and – in the perception of the believer – make it visual and perceptible. Artefacts and things transport religious knowledge and serve as vehicles of culturally remembered religious narratives. All these artefacts cannot be characterised as sacred by their functional sense or by their materiality but by a culturally developed meaning and sense, which formats the horizon for a thing's religious attribution.

As pointed out above, personal belongings and everyday items (candles, photographs etc.) can obtain a new meaning by being brought into contact with "sacred" objects. This emanation is neither a magical charging nor 'auratising' of metaphysical power but simply a change in the human perception of the object. Thus, a sacred meaning can be inscribed into all kinds of personal things leaving it to the individual to convey a religious attribution. In this process they become part of a religious sphere and, indeed, sacred from an individual point of view through contact with intersubjectively recognized sacred objects. These moments of transfiguration of the personal items' meaning can evoke intimate emotional experiences, embodied in these personal objects. Thus, personal items can be a materialised memory of key moments in life; they represent and embody situations of imagined immediacy.

Having this in mind, one can see phenomena of sacralisation not only in explicitly religious fields but in different cultural situations, for instance in *pop-culture* or in sports. In my current research project, I analyse the social lifeworlds of people who are fanatic about football and focus on the meaning of material objects in this field as well (Probst 2022). The analogy between objects, as described above, and valorised things in this field is evident in my point of view: A jersey worn by a football player during a match and afterwards thrown to a group of fans in the stands – all the fans trying to get a hold on this valuable item – can be seen as a sacred thing as well. In a fan's perception, this jersey is much more than a piece of clothing. Indeed, in their eyes it is connected to a single player, his performance and effort on the pitch. A specific value is inscribed to this jersey, so that on the one hand the object is a materialised memory of a specific story. On the other, the jersey evokes a specific treatment (e.g., it is hung on the wall or used only during visits to the stadium perhaps never being washed).

Thus, it is not only things and artefacts that get constructed as valorised religious objects, narratives or persons can also be perceived as transfigured sacralised objects. Research points to ways in which religious attribution of everyday items is shown in response to the question "to what is your heart committed" (Mädler 2006; o.t.). Here it is shown that everyday items can be transfigured to presenting materialised symbols which represent a moment of individual identity and gain a deeper meaning because they mirror processes of life's consummation. Valorised everyday belongings as representations of their owners' identity enable these to cope with human contingency vis a vis the unconditional in life. Through this kind of attribution an everyday item is changed not in its material substance but in its symbolic meaning and is shifted into a new horizon. Tracks of implicit religiosity and sacralisation through meaningful things and artefacts can be recognised in daily life, which requires an open view into social processes of people's everyday lifeworld.

Hence, things and artefacts in different cultural contexts can gain sacred attribution. It is not only material objects in explicit religions that can be objects of transfiguration, but rather, everyday items can also be understood as religious objects. To focus only on explicitly religious institutions reduces our perception of cultural phenomena in daily life that gain a comparable meaning and attribution. Material objects in an institutional system of religion represent, remember, or embody important experiences in life, but all things and artefacts in daily life are in the position to do so as well. *Sacredness* (and religion) is therefore neither a stable phenomenon nor fixed to a specific site or moment, but liquid and transferable through human practices (Keenan and Arweck 2006). The dispersion of religion in modernity into other cultural contexts, postulated by many researchers, states that the strict distinction between the profane and sacredness is not maintainable (Luckmann 1967). As a more open and wider perspective for religious phenomena it is postulated that practices which transcend human's life are essential moments for religion. Material things and artefacts are important actors for all kinds of transcending because there is no (religious) practice without materialisation.

4 Analysis of Sacred Things

For an appropriate analysis of all kinds of transfigured things and artefacts in the field of religion I suggest operating with a plurality of empirical methods as it has been proposed and implemented in numerous research projects on artefacts and things within the field of cultural and social sciences (Eisewicht 2016; Hahn and Soentgen 2011). The described multidimensional process of interactions between things, artefacts and humankind in different areas of life is a substantial reason for a plurality of methods to focus on an artefact's or thing's meaning and their materiality in their specific context. For this attempt at reconstructing meaning, it is important to reflect on human perception and handling of material objects. Thus, not only is the bare materiality of things and artefacts the leading topic of this research but rather the materialised meaning in a wider horizon for actors interacting with material objects. To study things and artefacts means not only concentrating on the material object itself but rather on reconstructing the attribution of meaning through cultural and social practices. An interesting proper starting point for a detailed artefact-analysis could be the recognition and perception of things or artefacts in people's lifeworld as I indicated above. An examination of artefacts or things is therefore basically linked to an analysing approach into processes and dimensions of meaning within social lifeworlds.

Four different aspects (analysis of material composition, aesthetic dimensions, functional usage, and the question about symbolic meaning of artefacts and things) that are rather circularly integrated into each other and not to be understood as a chronological or distinct research process could be instructive for an in-depth analysis of artefacts. A first step is the physical and chemical material matter of artefacts or objects, so that the shape of artefacts or things is investigated by scientific research. A second aspect of an artefact-analysis would be a description of human aesthetic and sensitive experiences in the presence of the object, e.g., to analyze human consciousness in different modes of perception (auditory, visual, tactile, olfactory, or gustatory). In a third dimension, the researcher observes the different modes of functional use following the question for which purpose an artefact, or a thing is utilised or used in a specific situation. A last perspective thematises the diverse symbolic meanings that can be inscribed onto or attributed to an artefact or thing. These four aspects should be seen in a reciprocal relationship and not as isolated steps.

In the field of sacralised artefacts and objects it is essential to adopt a perspective that helps to reconstruct the interaction between material objects and mankind. To explain how artefacts can gain a religious meaning by representing, symbolizing, or revealing aspects of a deity or a transcending moment in life, the point of view in a specific social lifeworld must be considered. Therefore, different kinds of empirical data that open the perspective for multiple expressions of experiences can be considered. A central method of data gathering is the participating observation that is a key instrument of all kinds of non-standardised ethnographies. Focusing on the meaning of artefacts or things, all data in this research setting such as interview transcripts, observational protocols or other kinds of documents can reflect experiences with material objects and the effect on humankind emanating from them. Thus, the undertaking to reconstruct perspectives of human and non-human actors in the wake of ethnographies can be achieved through personal approaches to the primary context of interaction between things, artefacts, and people. Hence, the detailed description in the beginning attempts to be a stimulating starting point for an in-depth analysis of artefacts and things and their dimensions of interaction. At best, the researcher should acquire specific modes of meaning and interactions between things, artefacts, and people by participating and entering into their social lifeworlds. Taking the thing's and artefact's meaning into account as an expression and result of social practices means to challenge the examination as a reconstruction of individual perspectives in a social context. Therefore, data that reflects dimensions of social experiences is suitable and appropriate for a closer specification of things' and artefacts' meaning. An integrated self-reflection analysis of one's own perspectives and handlings with things and artefacts can also supplement a reconstruction and interpretation of things' and artefacts' (sacralised) meaning in a social lifeworld's setting. This research approach is understood as a part of a sensory ethnography that uses human's corporality and the senses as effective research instruments (Pink 2010).

All methodological considerations are based in a phenomenological sensitised cultural-hermeneutic approach that is not censorious of any religious rituals or practiced cults and avoids prejudging them. An intentional unknowing attitude can rather enable a heuristic exploration of unexpected contents of meaning that are connected and attributed to things and artefacts. Thus, a phenomenological based cultural-hermeneutic research remains open-minded for individual attribution of things' and artefacts' meaning.

5 Contribution for Practical Theology

Practical Theology – as an academic theological discipline – thematises, reflects and interprets religious practices in all parts of life's consummation and has its startingpoint in human experiences along with the theological reflection on these everyday experiences. Even though the practical theological tradition has previously not focussed on things and artefacts in religious acts, aspects of a cultural and material turn should be integrated into the field of Practical Theology. One of Practical Theology's endeavours is to observe material culture and to elucidate explicit and implicit religious dimensions of material objects. It was shown above that artefacts and things play a significant role in all religious processes and, therefore, should be more strongly integrated as substantial objects of research into a phenomenologically grounded examination of lived religion in the field of Practical Theology. Finally, the religious attribution of things and artefacts is an evident argument understanding sacredness as an ongoing practice of sacralization that shifts former postulated distinct borders between profanity and sacredness. In summary, three topics can contribute towards an orientation for a materially informed Practical Theology in different religious denominations (Beckmayer 2021, 44-46).

Firstly, material culture was – historically and still today – an integral part of manifold religious practices and should be recognized as an object of high interest into Practical Theology. Practical Theology should adopt a wider and more forthright position to examine all aspects of religious consummation and should not constrict lived religion as a simple expression of inner faith. Social and cultural sciences offer a thoughtful access to human society and culture and are appropriate dialogic partners for a practical theological approach to material religion. The analysis of material aspects of religious practices and materialization of religious meaning into things and artefacts was proposed as a qualitative research program above. In this way, Practical Theology uses these research tools, developed in the fields of cultural and social sciences in an unbiased way. To reconstruct and analyse things' and artefacts' substantial composition and symbolic meaning – not in a moral position but with a curious and acknowledging attitude – challenges the practical theological researcher to acquire and apply qualitative and empirical methods from social sciences into their own field of interest. Practical Theology is thus positioned in a hinge function between the dynamic variety of religious practices and an academic description and reflection on these human processes. Following this understanding, Practical Theology examines which horizons of meaning and religious attribution are inscribed into material objects and how they influence and interact with human practices.

Secondly, Practical Theology should include not only qualitative and empirical dimensions of social and cultural studies but phenomenologically grounded reflections on human experiences in daily life. Human beings are corporeal creatures and situated in a contingent context of space, time, and social interaction. Religious practices are bound to humans' social lifeworld that is at all times encompassed with religious contents and transcending dimensions that everybody must interpret. Practical Theology learns about offered interpretations of religious institutions and observes considerations of religious and transcending moments. To name experiences 'religious' results from a specific lifeworld-positioned standpoint of interpretation. In the same way, religious symbolic meanings of artefacts and things can be taken as a reasonable example of a socially determined and content-related attribution of human experience. Hence, Practical Theology is an experiencing lifeworld-related academic program that requires cultural hermeneutics of human experiences and their standpoint-based interpretations of symbolic meanings. A phenomenologically sensitive Practical Theology describes and examines contexts in which material objects receive a religious meaning. The continued interest in this analysis focuses on human handlings and interactions that are led by materialised meanings of artefacts and objects.

Finally, Practical Theology integrates the significant insight of material culture studies, namely that the processes and practices of things' and artefacts' sacralisation are fluid, and depend on the interactions between objects and human beings. All kinds of material objects, not only in religious institutions, are open to be received as symbolically religious. As shown above, things and artefacts are variable and transformable in their polysemy and their multiple symbolic meanings. For a thing's or artefact's attribution with the symbolic meaning "sacred" or "religious", specific continuous practices and narrations are required: in religious institutions, ritualised consecrations of things or artefacts may be seen, everyday sacred items could be kept in a safe place or used only during special moments. Practical Theology analyses not only the intersubjective sacralisation through social practices and institutional narratives, such as a postulated material symbolic representation of a deity or the participation of material objects in institutional consummation but also focuses on human everyday and individual sacralising attributions of things and artefacts. The insights of sacralisation-processes with material objects can be integrated into a wider understanding regarding the concept of sacredness and profanity. The often-postulated distinction between different spheres that structure phenomena of religious practices and experiences should be left behind. The dispersion of religion into different cultural and social fields can be perceived on the topic of artefacts' and things' sacralisation like under a burning glass. Transfigured and sacralised material objects are apparent not only in religious institutions but in all social lifeworlds.

Bibliography

Appadurai, Arjun, ed. 1986. *The Social Life of Things: Commodities in Cultural Perspective.* Cambridge, MA: Cambridge University Press.
Beckmayer, Sonja. 2021. "Materielle Kulturforschung und Praktische Theologie" In Die religiöse Positionierung der Dinge: Zur Materialität und Performativität religiöser Praxis, edited by Ursula Roth and Anne Gilly, Stuttgart: Kohlhammer, 37–46.
Brosses, Charles de. 1760. *Du Culte Des Dieux Fétiches, Ou Parallèle de l'ancienne Religion de l'Egypte avec la religion actuelle de Nigritie.* Paris: no publisher.
Cress, Torsten. 2021. "Soziale Praktiken und die Sakralisierung der Dinge" In Die religiöse Positionierung der Dinge: Zur Materialität und Performativität religiöser Praxis, edited by Ursula Roth and Anne Gilly, Stuttgart: Kohlhammer, 27–36.
Cress, Torsten. 2014. "Religiöse Dinge." In *Handbuch materielle Kultur: Bedeutungen, Konzepte, Disziplinen*, edited by Stefanie Samida, Darmstadt: Wissenschaftliche Buchgesellschaft, 241–244.
Csikszentmihalyi, Mihaly, and Eugene Halton. 1981. *The Meaning of Things: Domestic Symbols and the Self.* Cambridge / New York: Cambridge University Press.
Durkheim, Emile. [1912] 1990. *Les formes élémentaires de la vie religieuse: Le système totémique en Australie.* Quadrige 77. Paris: Presses Universitaires de France.
Eisewicht, Paul. 2016. "Die Sicht der Dinge: Konzeptualisierung einer ethnographischen Artefaktanalyse anhand der Frage nach der Materialität von Zugehörigkeit." In *Materiale Analysen: Methodenfragen in Projekten*, edited by Nicole Burzan, Ronald Hitzler, and Heiko Kirschner, Wiesbaden: Springer Fachmedien Wiesbaden, 111–128.
Føllesdal, Dagfinn. 2010. "Lebenswelt in Husserl." In *Science and the Life-World: Essays on Husserl's Crisis of European Sciences*, edited by David J. Hyder and Hans-Jörg Rheinberger, Stanford: Stanford University Press, 32–43.
Hahn, Hans P. ²2014. *Materielle Kultur: Eine Einführung.* Berlin: Reimer.
Hahn, Hans P. 2015. "Der Eigensinn der Dinge – Einleitung." In *Vom Eigensinn der Dinge: Für eine neue Perspektive auf die Welt des Materiellen*, edited by Hans P. Hahn, Berlin: Neofelis Verlag, 9–56.
Hahn, Hans P., and Jens Soentgen. 2011. "Acknowledging Substances." *Philosophy & Technology* 24:19–33.
Held, Klaus. 1996. "Phänomenologie: I. Philosophisch." In *Theologische Realenzyklopädie.* Vol. 25, edited by Gerhard Müller, Berlin / New York: Walter de Gruyter, 454–458.
Keenan, William J. F., and Elisabeth Arweck. 2006. "Introduction: Material Varieties of Religious Expression." In *Materializing Religion: Expression, Performance and Ritual*, edited by Elisabeth Arweck and William J. F. Keenan, Aldershot: Ashgate, 1–20.
Kohl, Karl-Heinz. 2003. *Die Macht der Dinge: Geschichte und Theorie sakraler Objekte.* München: Beck.
Latour, Bruno. 1993. *We Have Never Been Modern.* Cambridge, MA: Harvard University Press.
Laube, Stefan. 2011. *Von der Reliquie zum Ding: Heiliger Ort – Wunderkammer – Museum.* Berlin: Akademie-Verlag.

Luckmann, Thomas. 1967. *The Invisible Religion: The Problem of Religion in Modern Society*. New York / London: Macmillan Co.

Mädler, Inken. 2006. *Transfigurationen: Materielle Kultur in praktisch-theologischer Perspektive*. Praktische Theologie und Kultur 17. Gütersloh: Gütersloher Verlagshaus.

Meyer, Birgit, and Dick Houtman. 2012. "Material Religion: How Things Matter." In *Things: Religion and the Question of Materiality*, edited by Dick Houtman, Birgit Meyer, and Hent de Vries, New York: Fordham University Press, 1–23.

Miller, Daniel, ed. 1998. *Material Cultures: Why Some Things Matter*. London: UCL Press.

Morgan, David, ed. 2010. *Religion and Material Culture: The Matter of Belief*. London / New York: Routledge.

Pink, Sarah. 2010. *Doing Sensory Ethnography*. Los Angeles: SAGE.

Probst, Hans-Ulrich. 2022. *Fußball als Religion? Eine lebensweltanalytische Ethnographie*, Bielefeld: Transcript.

Schatzki, Theodore. 2010. "Materiality and Social Life." *Nature and Culture* 5:123–149.

Thomas, Julian. 2006. "Phenomenology and Material Culture." In *Handbook of Material Culture*, edited by Christopher Tilley, Webb Keane, Susanne Küchler, Michael Rowlands, and Patricia Spyer, London: SAGE, 43–59.

Waldenfels, Bernhard. 2015. "Die Mitwirkung der Dinge in der Erfahrung." In *Vom Eigensinn der Dinge: Für eine neue Perspektive auf die Welt des Materiellen*, edited by Hans P. Hahn, Berlin: Neofelis, 57–79.

Albin Masarik
Commemoration / Remembrance / Reconciliation

1 Introduction

There are events in the lives of individuals, communities, and even entire nations, which have a serious impact. Tragic events. Some of these affect many people. Among these, for example, are military conflicts, terrorist incidents, natural disasters, mining accidents[1], air disasters, ship and ferry wrecks and mass traffic accidents. Events originally experienced as individual losses make up another group, but families affected in this way, remember them together. Commemorative acts remembering traffic accidents or mountaineering victims[2] are one such example. We must not overlook commemorations for loved ones who have died naturally and whose family members honour them in commemorative acts, often carried out in private in a pastoral context.

Political prisoners who died or were executed in prison during the rise of socialism in Czechoslovakia may be considered a special group; commemorations take place as part of memorial gatherings for political prisoners. Similar in character are commemorative acts in significant places of human suffering. As examples of such we can mention Auschwitz concentration camp in Poland; the execution room with a guillotine and equipment for execution by hanging in Prague Pankrác prison, where 1,075 people were executed under German occupation (referred to in the Czech Republic as sekyrárna (the axe-room) from the word sekera (axe)), or the Czech village Lidice, whose inhabitants were massacred after an assassination attempt on Heydrich during the Second World War and the village was razed to the ground. In such places, memorials take place on anniversaries even several decades later, and these are intended as a reminder and a show of respect for the memory of the victims. This article will explore such intentions, as well as the array of additional goals of commemoration, remembrance, and reconciliation.

---

[1] For example, the mining disaster on 8th August 1956 where 262 miners died in the Bois du Cazier mine in the Marcinelle parish, which is part of the town Charleroi in Belgium.
[2] For example, a memorial service takes place annually at the Symbolic Cemetery near Popradské mountain-lake in the High Tatras (Slovakia).

OpenAccess. © 2022 Albin Masarik, published by De Gruyter. This work is licensed under the Creative Commons Attribution-NonCommercial-NoDerivatives 4.0 International License.
https://doi.org/10.1515/9783110618150-020

2 Types of Commemorative Ceremonies

From research interviews with church leaders and military chaplains it appears that from the liturgical point of view, we can divide commemorative acts as follows:

a) Church commemorative ceremonies – in the shape of (1.) a church service (or mass) by one church, (2.) a church service (or mass) according to the liturgical rules of one church with room for an address and prayer of clergy by a different Christian church, or (3.) an ecumenical service with equal room for active participation of representatives from two or more churches. Besides this, there is also the possibility of commemorating the dead within the framework of church life (for example, commemorating the dead on All Souls' Day, Sheppy 2005, 70–79), or individual commemorations on anniversaries of death, which the clergy can carry out in a narrower or wider family circle in homes, at the graveside or in church (Sheppy 2005, 80–83).

b) Secular commemorations with clergy participation in a variety of forms (1.) state memorials, within the framework of which clergy of the Christian church have one point in the programme; (2.) military memorials with active participation from the clergy; (3.) commemorations of professional bodies (for example, mining, firefighters, river transportation workers, etc.) in which we also come across active clergy participation.

3 Periodicity of Commemorations

Regarding commemorations, we come across various approaches to their periodic repetition. In some cases, they take place annually on a set day of the year. Others take place on the jubilee anniversary or without any noticeable regularity. In practice we also come across commemorations which remind us of tragic events from decades or centuries ago which, because of their local significance take place regardless of whether it is a "milestone" anniversary or not.

3.1 Annual Commemorations

Belonging in this group are commemorations on All Souls' Day and important historical national events, connected with loss of life.

Commemoration on All Souls' Day (November 2nd): Since human society is continually bidding farewell to its members, this commemoration also takes place annually with the aim of remembering those who have departed from us, not only in the particular year, but also in the past. This opportunity tends to be reflected in various forms: (a) in the liturgical forms of the church commemorating them; (b) with ecumenical worship; (c) with a secular commemoration (in rare cases also with room for active clergy participation).

Important historical national events, which are connected with a loss of life (for example, in the Dutch context a national day of mourning and remembrance on 4th May, or in the Slovak context commemoration of the heavy fighting on Dukla during the Second World War, where thousands of Soviet and Czechoslovak soldiers died. Each year there are also services of remembrance for important tragic events of less significance for society as a whole. The Slovak Armed Forces stop organizing this type of commemorations after the 10th anniversary of the event.

3.2 Commemorations on Jubilee Anniversaries

Belonging to this category are reminders of events that have significance for the history of humanity in general, for a nation or some national or religious group and which were connected with loss of life. As an example of these events, we can mention the memorial ceremonies and commemorations on the 600th anniversary of John Hus being burnt at the stake or, from the point of view of the so-called radical reformation, the 480th anniversary, commemorated with international participation, of the arrival in Slovakia of Anabaptist preacher Andreas Fischer, who was later executed by being thrown from the walls of Krásna Hôrka castle (in what is now Slovakia). These anniversaries are not remembered with commemorative ceremonies every year. When there are significant jubilees, it is appropriate to give them both commemorative and media attention.

4 Specific Examples of Commemorations

As examples of commemoration we mention: (1.) Commemoration of Second World War victims; (2.) Commemoration of air disaster victims, Hejce, Hungary; (3.) Commemoration of traffic accident victims, Liptovský Mikuláš, Slovakia; (4.) Commemoration of mining disaster victims, Kremnica, Slovakia.

4.1 Commemoration of Second World War Victims

In this group of commemorations, we mention (1.) the commemoration of the massacre of the inhabitants of Lidice village (CR) and (2.) the state commemoration of Second World War victims in Amsterdam, Holland.

4.1.1 Commemoration of the Victims of the Massacred Village – Lidice, Czech Republic

The commemoration is carried out to honour the victims.

After the assassination attempt in Prague on the acting Reich protector Reinhard Heydrich during the Second World War, Adolf Hitler decided to make an example out of the punishment of this act. The Czech village Lidice was selected for this purpose and on 10.6.1942 German soldiers gathered the men over 15 years of age and shot them in this place. The women were transported to Ravensbrück concentration camp, and 82 children were slaughtered in a gas van in Chelm extermination camp. The village was burned and razed to the ground.

Following the commemoration on the 76th anniversary of this event, we can begin the creation of a theory of commemorations:

The commemoration began with mass on the foundations of the ruined church, and then continued with laying wreaths at a mass grave. We highlight a few emphases in the content of the addresses which were spoken there:

In his address, Andrej Babiš, the Czech Prime Minister, offered a point of view on the slaughter of hundreds of people from a political perspective. He observed the appalling dimension of the historical event. He used expressions like "victims of the Nazi self-will", "the appalling nature of the German occupiers' action", "They wanted to demonstrate that they could with impunity determine the fate of completely innocent people [...]. They wanted to demonstrate in their own awful and malicious way that no power could restrain them in their senseless cruelty and give the citizens of the protectorate a warning." (Babiš, 2018)

Immediately after this address, military chaplain, Lt-Col Kloubek, was called upon to pray. He saw his role in our moving on in our view of this tragedy – to a humane way of life in forgiveness, respect, and cooperation. In his prayer, after introductory words of thanks to God, he expressed his requests:

> And I pray that this place would be a place symbolizing unification, connection, cooperation, and mutual understanding. I pray that we may be able to forgive one another and that we not renew hostility again and again. I pray that our path to Lidice means a new path in our lives, that it might be a path towards one another, that it be a path of love, encouragement, understanding and friendship [...]. I pray that every reminder of evil things would ignite in us a new longing for approaching one another amicably, for mutual tolerance and love of one another. May our Heavenly Father in the Lord Jesus Christ help us to do so. Amen. (Kloubek, 2018)

Although the prayer by itself apparently offers only limited possibilities for communication with those present, practical observation shows that the opposite is true. In our study of this commemoration, we arrive at the observation that individual parts of the programme also affect those present in their mutual synergy. What the chairman of the government expressed was necessary, that what happened in Lidice was appalling and evil. But what the chaplain expressed in the prayer was also necessary, that consciousness of evil should lead people in the present day to pursue positive approaches to living together in a community of nations. It is precisely in an expression of the need for forgiveness and in the pursuit of peaceful co-existence that we can see the clergyman's role.

4.1.2 Commemoration of Second World War Victims – Amsterdam / Soesterberg, Holland

Dutch protestant chaplain, Lieutenant Colonel Jan Tom Schneider, serving at Airforce (Dutch military) describes this memorial ceremony and the role of the military chaplain in it as follows:

> The fourth of May is a national day of mourning and remembrance. In the evening the King is present at the national monument in Amsterdam, remembering all victims of the Second World War (a chief of the military chaplaincy prays or speaks a few reflective words there). On the morning of that day the Airforce has its own intimate gathering at the Airforce monument in Soesterberg. Retired military, delegates from all over the country and the Airforce orchestra all surround the monument. The General usually highlights one or two service members for acts of bravery against the Germans in the first days of the war in May 1940. After music, the national anthem, and two minutes of silence, the chaplain has a seven-minute contribution. This can be anything; a general theme around the struggle for freedom, followed by a short prayer. And then four F16 fighter planes fly over in 'missing man' formation. Very moving. (Schneider 2019)

In relation to the religious element in a secular ceremony's framework, chaplain Schneider observes that the secular context in his country "is different from that of the UK or the US, where the church's contribution, prayer and the pastor are still very evident in daily life. In the Netherlands this is no longer the case". In the Dutch context, therefore, "prayer for the troops has become a rarity. Now and again a script for a ceremony might still reserve room for it." In view of the secularized context, he considers it important that the minister prepares his audience before actually delivering the prayer and explains what he is going to do asking "for a listening ear from those who are not used to praying in their daily lives." At the same time, he recommends the use of simple expressions.

4.2 Commemoration of Air Disaster Victims – Hejce, Hungary

On 19.1.2006 soldiers of the Slovak Armed Forces were returning by air from a mission in Kosovo. Approximately 20 km from their planned landing in Slovakia, they crashed near the Hungarian village Hejce. 42 of 43 people died on board the plane. Every year the most senior representatives of the SR army, and also relatives and loved ones of the victims, along with Catholic and Evangelical military chaplains visit the site of the tragedy.

In 2019 there was a commemoration on the 13th anniversary of this tragic event. It began with Catholic mass. During it there was also opportunity for an address and a prayer by an Evangelical minister. After mass the participants moved to the tragedy's memorial site, where the Slovak and Hungarian Ministers for Defence gave speeches. This was followed by the laying of wreaths. Within the framework of the programme at the memorial site, where speeches are delivered, there is only scope for prayer from the military chaplains. In some cases, only one slot is possible for all churches, and sometimes it is possible to provide space for ministers from two churches. But such a degree of church involvement is not the general experience in the framework of international studies.

Regarding commemorations related to air disasters, as time goes by, we can observe the beginnings of a narrative of increasing distrust and doubt of official investigation results and the propagation of conspiracy theories. Not only in the case of this disaster, but also after the fall of a Polish aeroplane with a government delegation on its flight to Smolensk on 10.4.2010, a similar trend can be observed. Therefore, the theme of loss is still current among most of the bereaved and complicates their coming to terms with it. The minister needs to find his bearings in his tasks. His task is to bring a spiritual dimension to the commemoration and not to stand in for investigators of the tragedy. If he wants to contribute to solving controversial questions, he must remember that a commemoration is not the appropriate place for this.

4.3 Commemoration for Traffic Accident Victims – Liptovský Mikuláš, Slovakia

On the basis of a resolution of the United Nations General Assembly from 26th October 2005, the third Sunday in November is World Day of Remembrance for Traffic Victims. On this day police chaplains organize commemorations together with the clergy of the firefighters' corps in the Slovak Republic. Catholic clergy usually perform them in the east of the country, and protestant usually in central Slovakia, in the town of Liptovský Mikuláš. This division does not arise from the commemoration itself but rather from the fact that these two pastoral ministries of the Slovak Armed Forces are organized independently. This type of commemoration has several goals:
- to express an awareness of the fragility of human life;
- to honour all victims of traffic accidents;
- to express sympathy to the bereaved for their pain and loss;
- to express gratitude to the rescue services, who are always prepared and intervene when accidents occur;
- a preventative function: to warn of danger and encourage responsible traffic behaviour based on a respect for life;
- to offer an opportunity for medical and fire rescue workers, and police staff to be able to come humbly before God at commemorations with a religious character

to come to terms, spiritually, with the stress that they experience when encountering accident victims.

After an address and prayers, and the reading out of traffic accident statistics (victims' names also at regional commemorations), candles are lit for each traffic accident victim as a reminder of the light of the world – Jesus Christ.

As far as prayer is concerned, Catholic clergy pray primarily for the dead. Protestant clergy do not pray for the dead. In both streams of Christianity, we find the following thoughts in their prayers:
- the consciousness that our time is in God's hands;
- people do not know when and how they will die;
- the request that Christ be with us in our hour of death;
- a request for comfort for the bereaved;
- an eschatological perspective: faith in the resurrection and eternal life;
- an expression of thanks to God for rescue service workers (medical rescue workers, fire fighters, police workers), who are active at accident scenes and have saved many lives. (A commemoration as a whole does not only express thanks on their behalf but also to them.)

4.4 Commemoration for Victims of an Ancient Mining Accident – Kremnica, Slovakia

In some localities we also come across commemorations for mass tragic events which happened centuries ago. An example of this practice is the Slovak town of Kremnica, where, for several years, commemorations took place on the anniversary of the mining disaster of the year 1443 (for example the 572nd anniversary in 2015). Šturec hill, under which were the richest gold-bearing veins, collapsed during an earthquake. The ceilings in the mine collapsed and sources conclude that more than 500 miners died in the tragedy.[3]

5 Identifying the Goals of a Commemoration

The goals fulfilled by a minister in his service at commemorations emanate (1.) from the forms of participation and time allocation, (2.) from the time that has elapsed from the event, of which the commemoration is a reminder.

---

[3] For more on themes that dominate this kind of commemoration see section 5.2.3 Commemorations for tragedies in the distant past.

5.1 Types of Participation and Allocation of Time

The minister takes part in the commemoration in a variety of ways.

Ecclesiastical forms of commemoration. Sometimes it is an entire church service (according to the liturgical precepts of one church or ecumenical) with its customary length. The minister sometimes has an opportunity to deliver an address in a limited timeslot within the framework of a different Christian church's liturgy. When the framework is a church service, the entire commemoration has an ecclesiastical character and on occasions with national significance, this is sometimes part of a more extensive commemorative programme.

Secular forms with clergy participation. Ministers have an opportunity to participate in secular commemorations. This possibility is shared by ministers from parishes as well as military chaplains. Concerning commemorations organized by the Slovak Ministry of Defence, according to its Communication Department, they are given the opportunity, for example, to participate by way of prayer and this in an approximately four-minute timeslot. Some ministers introduce prayer with three to five sentences. With some, it is more. Clergy, inexperienced in this area need to be reminded that time allotted at state-organized commemorations must be handled carefully, especially if a military aircraft flyover is also to be part of the ceremony. Authorized individuals behind the scenes of the ceremony communicate with pilots and guides who are waiting for the signal to fly military aircraft over the location of the commemoration at a specific time. Due to this synchronization, everyone, including clergy, is expected not to exceed the time allotted him.

5.2 The Influence of the Time-Lapse from the Event on Determining Goals

The less time that elapses between the event and the commemoration, the more similar the emerging goals will be to a funeral ceremony's pastoral goals. As more time elapses, individual grief decreases. But studies show that clergy must not assume that the notion of the loss and grief will fade after ten years. It is more appropriate to determine whether any of the bereaved who had had to deal with the loss of the particular accident's victims will be present or not.

5.2.1 Commemorations during the Grieving (or Painful Period) of the Bereaved

If the commemoration takes place at such a period that the bereaved of the victims are also participating in it, the structure of goals must naturally consider dealing with loss and mourning and must express sympathy for their pain and point to the comfort of faith.

Conversations with bereaved individuals who have participated in commemorations reveal that, even after ten or more years, some of them (above all the victims' parents) state that their loss is still painful. A father who lost his son, said 13 years after the event: "Even after so many years it is impossible to forget. I think about my son even several times a day." (Bodolló 2019) Wherever there is a clearly guilty party in the tragedy, anger, or helplessness, as the case may be, may also persist.

Therefore, regarding commemorations it seems that it is more appropriate to distinguish between periods where bereaved parties, who are still processing their grief in some way, are present, and commemorations which occur after such an interval of time that direct relatives of the victims are no longer present.

Besides this, where serious losses are concerned, some bereaved individuals are confronted with secondary losses connected to the event. For example, the mother of a female soldier who died in the aeroplane crash, lost her husband, who did not live to see the first anniversary of the tragedy (Bodolló 2019).

Studies show that, with the increase of time from the event, what occurs is not necessarily a lessening in the difficulty of the grief but that in fact the opposite trend can be observed. While the tragic event itself might represent a primary source of pain and grief for the bereaved, other events, connected to the tragedy, often become a secondary source of traumatizing grief. Therefore, their situation might actually deteriorate. Here we can have in mind the following:

(a) Coming to terms with the results of an official investigation into events and a distrust of the results. This distrust can be if after the investigation, the results are deemed secret (for example, the investigation into the Hejce air disaster, Hungary in 2006). This encourages the rise of a variety of questions and even several conspiracy theories.

(b) Coming to terms with public opinion, shaped by the media and speculation about blame for the tragic event, e. g., the widow of the pilot from the tragic event, suffers the loss of her husband, but also suffers from information passed on to her that the tragedy was caused by her deceased husband, although, according to some, it may well have simply been a technical failure;

(c) Coming to terms with the way the victims' bodily remains were handled (one victim's mother complained that her son's body was incomplete in the coffin; according to her, DNA identification was not provided for torn off sections of the bodies, but only for the biggest parts);

(d) The bereaved of victims of a bus and train collision (Polomka, Slovakia, 21. 2. 2009) stated ten years later that this event had changed their lives, bringing them a great deal of pain, with which they must live somehow. They complain that the guilty party has neither contacted them nor apologized to them. They consider it an injustice that his prison term was shortened and that he is living his life freely while the victims of the tragedy do not have this possibility.

The minister who makes an address on the site of a tragedy or who is performing an ecumenical church service must have realistic expectations about the possibilities of his address. He must use to good theological purpose the few moments he has available for the address as a gospel support for the bereaved and to help them become reconciled to their loss. At the same time, he must count on facing a secularized audience. A segment of them may possess a critical attitude toward the church.[4]

Although funeral sermon theory envisages comforting the bereaved, responders to empirical research in Slovakia did not confirm that this goal is actually achieved (Masarik 2015, 143–156; 2018, 504–512). We can assume the same thing with commemorations. Therefore, effective approaches must be sought both from the perspective of the address or prayer as well as from the perspective of the programme structure (in secular forms) and the liturgical structure (in ecclesiastical forms). Effective communication of comfort can be observed where the minister has personally come to terms with difficult problems and has learnt to find comfort in faith in God. This experience behind the scenes of his ministry can work to enhance what he offers in addresses or prayers.

In relation to individual types of events the following goals are included:
- With mining disasters: respect for the victims, realization of one's own mortality and an increased sensitivity to technological and natural factors that might lead to tragic events in the future, leading to improved work safety.
- With traffic accidents in various transport modes: respect for the victims and realization of one's own mortality. Motivation to drive responsibly and show consideration in traffic.
- With victims of military conflicts and political persecution: the need for a constant reminder that a negative turn in political developments may take on even monstrous proportions, which horrify us as we remember the commemorated events. Therefore, it is necessary to seek peaceful solutions as a starting point.

With all these types of commemorative events, religious goals also take shape; the consciousness that human life is fragile, whether due to natural phenomena (avalanches, earthquakes, tsunami), or technological tragedies (shipwrecks, air disasters, bridge collapses etc.) Therefore, in our religious contribution to these commemorative events we remember our own ephemerality and ask for God's protection. A part of this is also a motivation towards an ethical lifestyle because the event we are commemorating reveals the fragility of human life and we do not know when and how our days will come to an end.

In conversations before and after commemorative events, where the bereaved have shown interest in a pastoral conversation, the minister has ample opportunities to offer them this help. This is the practice of the military chaplains in the Slovak context, and they meet with interest among the bereaved. The head of the Ecumenical Pastoral Service of the Slovak armed forces, Colonel Bodolló noted: "Bereaved families are thankful for the involvement of the clergy in their grief; repeatedly, there-

---

[4] "The church 'stinks', a chaplain wants to conquer you with his faith […] This is what I sense with a lot of people. And it makes us careful and sometimes too modest." (Schneider 2019)

fore, they want to meet with the clergy at other opportunities also. We ask ourselves what next, how to stand by them in their grief and also how to help them practically." (Bodolló 2019)

5.2.2 Commemorations after a Greater Lapse of Time

When much time has elapsed since the event, when widowed individuals form relationships with new partners, or later when only some of the bereaved are still living, motives like coming to terms with pain and comfort of the bereaved disappear from among the commemorative ceremony's objectives. The particular tragic event's message takes on greater prominence. For example:
- When commemorating distant accidents, like the disaster in the Bois du Cazier mine, in Belgium, 1956 (TASR 2016) – the fragility of human life may be reflected upon;
- On the anniversaries of military events; the need for peaceful solutions to conflicts and reconciliation between opposing nations, motivation to prevent similar tragedies (here military chaplains also see the necessity of working with youth and young teens in order to avoid unnecessary conflicts). The more time that elapses, the more open the minister can be and the more easily the need for reconciliation can be pointed out than would be possible immediately after the conflict in question (although it is precisely then that it tends to be very important). Historical records from post-war years in communist Czechoslovakia show that hinting at friendly attitudes towards people from "Western" (that is capitalist countries), led to political reprisals and long-term imprisonment. Therefore, it was necessary to wisely seek out forms of influence that would attain goals and minimize victims.
- At commemorations where professional bodies remember the loss of their colleagues, to pay their respects, to exalt their honesty, diligence, sacrifice, solidarity, and professionality.
- At commemorations for victims of political persecution – the need to transfer this experience across the generations to grandchildren and greatgrandchildren so that knowledge about the abuse of power (e. g., about communist oppression) is conveyed to the next generation. In this context, the minister points to the need to seek life attitudes which correspond to faith in God, whether someone is on the side of those in power, or of those who may be endangered by this power.

5.2.3 Commemorations of Tragedies from the Distant Past

When it is a question of a long historical interval, at least several centuries from the tragedy (as in the case of the commemoration of the Kremnica mine tragedy of 1443) themes that dominate the commemorative services are the fragility of human life, fatal work accidents and development of professional solidarity, when those belonging to a certain profession remember together with the public their deceased colleagues from the (long-distant) past. In a religious sense, it is an awareness of the fragility of human life and the need to remember that people will stand before God responsible for themselves in the end that stands out as important. Ján Ondrejčin, an evangelical pastor, who was one of the organizers of the commemorative ceremony for the Kremnica tragedy for several years, said in a research interview: "Usually I used as my source materials from the week of prayer for Christian unity. The goals emanated from the recommended texts. One year we preached and the next the Catholic priest. Because the miners worked hard, he used to preach about work [...] It was a question of drawing some spiritual goal from the memorial, which we placed before the nation." (Ondrejčin 2019)

5.3 General Remarks

Regardless of its form and how much time has elapsed since the commemorated event, the minister brings Christian spiritual elements into the commemorative act. At the same time, he must also remember that they stand before a secularized society. His task is not to indoctrinate those present, but to enrich the particular commemoration with a spiritual dimension in such a way that it will be comprehensible and culturally acceptable. Therefore, he must be sensitive not to overdo the religious content. In the case of ecumenical commemorations, it is necessary to pay attention to an ecumenically conciliatory approach and to anticipate that participants from other Christian traditions will critically evaluate the presence or absence of some elements (e. g., orthodox participants asked the evangelical chaplain in Slovakia why he did not pray for the dead). The ministers should formulate their speech so that its departure points and content suggest Christian values and that they are not only present in the use of religious terminology.

The minister must also pay attention to not overloading their speech with superfluous details. According to Schneider, "many technical details, many explanations about the military mission or propaganda about the great effort made by the troops", are not the chaplain's task. They can "leave all technical details to the military speaker [...] (and) concentrate on their task: expressing the words that fail us all when a young person has just died and focus on the relatives, their feelings, insecurity etc." (Schneider 2019)

In an attempt to connect with the surroundings' typical elements, a minister sometimes connects with impulses that he later uses metaphorically in the religious address. For example, one military unit's emblem was a horse. The minister wanted to connect with this at the commemoration and said that the dead soldier left his unit to go to heaven on a white horse. Clergy attending from his church considered this inappropriate. The preacher should consider his line of content in his speech accurately and not succumb to making an aesthetic statement to the detriment of its theological and pastoral suitability.

Regardless of the scope of their involvement (whether it is service or just a prayer), they must remember that their actions are part of a particular commemoration, therefore they must anticipate their actions being evaluated from the point of view of the event being remembered. The impulses which I have observed in my preparation in the Slovak context show that the minister needs wisdom to know which themes he can touch and which he should not introduce in his address.

6 Controversial Questions and Risky Impulses

6.1 Unethical Acts and Crimes on the Victors' Part

Ladislav Lanštiak, who worked as a clergyman during the Second World War, wrote in 1948: "The post-war person has much to repair and reform in his character. This is also true of the soldier in full measure." (Lanštiak 1948, 58) My German teacher reminisced about an experience from the end of the Second World War when a woman walking in a German town was shouting that she had been raped by a group of Russian soldiers. But at the commemorative ceremony at the end of the Second World War soldiers like these were also standing among the victors and were listening to expressions of thanks. A clergyman aware of this tension would look for effective opportunities and ways of solving it. A commemorative event is not one of them. Regarding his participation in it he must consider how he should approach the theme in order to honour the event and the people who suffered and lost their lives for the good of future generations – and meanwhile stay truthful to Christianity.

6.2 The Impact of the Political Context on an Evaluation of Historical Phenomena

Soviet soldiers were long considered the liberators of central Europe, which was much emphasized in the former socialist states. The historical fact that thousands of them died during the Second World War at Dukla (the border region between Poland and Slovakia) is still true. But the change in the political climate and Russia's status in international relations, leads to a more reserved view of their country. This is also reflected in a perplexed attitude towards their victims.

Bibliography

Babiš, Andrej. 2018. *Address of the Czech Prime Minister.* https://www.youtube.com/watch?v=clvVe10sfzU (29.11.2021).
Kloubek, Miloslav. 2018. *The Prayer.* https://www.youtube.com/watch?v=clvVe10sfzU (29.11.2021).
Lanštiak, Ladislav. 1948. "Bratom vojakom, rotmajstrom a dôstojníkom." *Cirkevné listy, venované záujmom Evanjelickej a.v. cirkvi na Slovensku* 4:58–59. In *Duchovní na bojiskách európskych a svetových vojen: V službe milosrdenstva I.* edited by Marian Bodollo et al. Bratislava: Ústredie ekumenickej pastoračnej služby v OS SR a OZ SR.
Masarik, Albin. 2018. "The Problem of Comforting the Grieving in the Funeral Sermon." *Expository Times* 129:504–512.
Masarik, Albin. 2015. "Verstorbenentrauer unter Mitgliedern der Baptistengemeinden in der Slowakei." In *Trauerbegleitung in unterschiedlichen kulturellen, sozialen und religiösen Kontexten*, edited by Patricia Dobríková, Walter Gebhardt, Grzegorz Giemza, Vasile Grajdian, and Adrian Kacian, Dziegielów: Warto, 143–156.
Sheppy, Paul P. 2005. *In Sure and Certain Hope: Liturgies, Prayers and Readings for Funerals and Memorials.* Nashville: Abingdon Press.
TASR. 2016. "Pred 60 rokmi sa v Belgicku stalo najväčšie banské nešťastie." https://www.teraz.sk/zahranicie/pred-60-rokmi-sa-v-belgicku-stalo-najva/211051-clanok.html (29.11.2021).
United Nations General Assembly. 2005. *General Assembly Designates Day of Remembrance for Road Traffic Victims.* https://www.un.org/press/en/2005/ga10409.doc.htm (29.11.2021).

Research interviews and research correspondence

Colonel ThDr. Marian Bodolló, Chaplain General of the Slovak Armed Forces and Armed Corps. Research Interview: Bratislava, 19.2.2019.
Lieutenant Colonel Jan Tom Schneider, Dutch military chaplain, Coordinator of spiritual care of veterans. He answered questions on the theme by email on 26.2.2019
Ján Ondrejčin, Lutheran pastor, Chancellor of the Centre for Ecumenical Pastoral Service of the Slovak armed forces. Research interview: Bratislava, 19.2.2019

Thomas Schlag
Confirmation Ceremonies / Maturity / Processes of Faith and Life

1 Introduction

1.1 Basic Information

Confirmation work is one of the core fields and topics of Protestant pedagogical work. Far beyond this, the self-understanding of Protestant Theology and Protestant Church is reflected in the historical developments, the theological justifications, and the current pedagogical and ritual forms of practice of this programme offered for young people. For Practical Theology as an academic discipline and for church life the challenges of future-oriented practices are dynamically reflected in confirmation work.

Since the practice of confirmation varies greatly from one country to another, the following considerations are essentially geared to the challenges and characteristics in the German-speaking countries and, with a sideways glance, to other European countries as well. In terms of empirical insights, this article refers especially to the so called Second Study on Confirmation work, which was conducted 2012–2014 in Austria, Denmark, Finland, Germany, Hungary, Norway, Poland, Sweden, and Switzerland (Schweitzer, Koch, and Maaß 2015a; Schweitzer et al. 2017; for Germany see esp. Schweitzer et al. 2015b, for Switzerland Schlag, Koch, and Maaß 2016). A new third study is currently under way and results can be expected in 2022.[1] References to the situation in the USA are not made in this article since confirmation work there differs significantly in various respects from what is offered in the European context (Osmer 1996) and results from the U.S. survey, conducted in collaboration with the European Second Study (Osmer and Douglass 2018).

It is important to know that confirmation work in the European countries, participating in the study, takes place in groups that are largely homogeneous in age (ranging from about 13 to 16 years) with a regular cycle and over a period of one to two years. Confirmation has as its theological basis the connection with baptism and from there aims at the maturity of young people's own faith. Within this goal horizon, the confirmation period includes insight into the essential contents of the Protestant faith. Confirmation work is characterised by a variety of different contexts of discovery, which include pedagogical and ritual, pastoral and congregational, as well as pastoral care elements. In all these contexts, the aim is for young people to become

---

1 Cf. http://konfirmandenarbeit.eu/en/network/ (30.11.2021).

familiar with the core contents and the practice of shaping the church through their own experiences. In this sense, confirmation work aims at individual insights into the meaning of church, the ability to position oneself religiously and the practice of liturgical-ritual practice. Confirmation work is a complex experience- and dialogue-oriented educational process that is open to participation and resonance (Ebinger et al. 2018).

In this context, the ritual dimension of 'Confirmation Ceremonies', which is central to this paper, plays an essential role. This classically refers to the confirmation service, which marks the end of the confirmation period. In theological terms, the confirmation service ceremony represents a symbolic interface between the young people's life so far and their future life and faith. Through this final service, the young people are publicly addressed as mature members of the congregation and become recognisable in their relationship to faith and the church.

In addition to this theologically and biographically highly significant ceremony at the end of the confirmation period, which will be discussed in more detail, it should be pointed out that other ritual elements are included in the churches' pedagogical programmes. These range from regular participation of the young people in 'normal' Sunday services, the so-called presentation service at the beginning of the confirmation period, baptismal services for the young people in the confirmation group who have not yet been baptised, the celebration of the Lord's Supper – which nowadays very often already takes place at confirmation camps or group weekends – to smaller liturgical and ritual elements during confirmation classes – such as common prayer or meditation, musical elements or even a blessing ritual at the end of the respective group meetings.

At the same time, and in connection with this expansion of ritual practice, it should already be pointed out that in recent decades the instructional character of confirmation work, has changed in favour of a more experiential, experimental, and developmental character. As a result, the aim is actively to include age-specific conditions and potentials as constitutive factors in the planning and design of this programme. From a ritual point of view, this has led to considerable dynamics in the shaping of confirmation time and its liturgical-ritual practice in recent decades, which will be discussed in more detail below.

1.2 Theological-Cultural Roots

In confirmation work pedagogical and ritual-liturgical aspects are closely linked from the beginning (Grethlein 2001). The theological logic of confirmation ties in with the early Christian tradition of baptismal catechesis, in which individual Christian formation was closely linked to ritual admission into the community of believers from the very beginning. One of the most important achievements of the Reformation was indeed the introduction of confirmation, which spread from Ziegenhain in Hesse, Germany all over the world. In the *Ziegenhain Church Discipline*, which was issued in 1539 by Landgrave Philipp with the cooperation of the reformer Martin Bucer, it was stipulated that children should be systematically taught catechism before they were confirmed and thus admitted to the Lord's Supper. The introduction to Christian doctrine, the individual confession, the – *nota bene* changed – ritual of anointing those willing to be admitted, as well as the admission to the Lord's Supper, are elements that still form essential components of the Protestant understanding of confirmation today. In contrast to the Catholic tradition and its practice of confirmation (*Firmung*), however, confirmation is not a sacramental act. Rather, in the confirmation service, the divine promise already given in baptism is symbolically confirmed and celebrated. In this sense, instruction in the Christian faith and the confirmation service have been closely linked since the time Reformation.

Until recently, the catechetical significance of the confirmation period was expressed in the fact that in the final service, the catechism – i.e., the core of the Christian faith – had to be learned by heart and recited in front of the congregation as a kind of exam. This was not infrequently associated with stressful situations and often downright traumatic experiences on the part of the young people and their families.

The strong theological charge of this ritual-liturgical event can still be seen today in many church orders of the Protestant Churches, and especially in the liturgical agendas for the confirmation service. In addition, in many church contexts it is still only through confirmation that admission as a godparent and the right to participate in church elections, as well as the right to be elected to honorary church offices, are opened up. The right to participate in the Lord's Supper, which for centuries was only connected with confirmation, is now hardly common due to a greatly changed church practice of celebrating the Lord's Supper with children. The confirmation service can thus be characterised as a ritual-liturgical celebration with several sacrament-like aspects (creed, confession/affirmation, blessing, release into future life), in which the affiliation to the Christian community established by baptism is symbolically confirmed. At the same time, this "graduation" service represents an important religious-cultural act throughout the ages – both with regard to the individual person of the confirmand, the internal family system and the broader social public. The ritual act itself was perceived as a *rite of passage* in terms of biographical, religious, and civic maturity and was celebrated accordingly. This was demonstrated, for example by the fact that male adolescents were given watches or valuable writing utensils as insignia of this acquired maturity and adulthood, while female adolescents were given appropriate items of clothing or important objects for the future marital household.

1.3 Current Challenges

Confirmation work not only lives from complex theological and cultural roots, but its dynamics and practical design, including ritual practice, are also strongly connected to a series of current challenges: these relate, on the one hand, to the current conditions of young people growing up and their self-understanding and, on the other hand, to the situation of religion, faith and church in contemporary society and culture.

Regarding adolescence, a clear decline in religious socialisation can be observed over the past decades, which in turn points to the massively changing religious demographic situation in German-speaking and other European countries. This should not lead to the premature conclusion that religious aspects no longer play a role in adolescence. However, with regard to the feeling of belonging to or identifying with the church, 'believing' and 'belonging' have clearly diverged. For many young people this encounter with church practice is their first experience.

In addition, due to the specific developmental psychological conditions of adolescence, certain traditions and authorities given 'from outside' or 'from above' are perceived critically anyway. Even in the case of religious socialisation experiences in childhood, a sceptical-critical basic attitude towards church programmes must be expected for adolescence. Due to the developmental-psychological and socio-cultural conditions of adolescence, it can also be assumed that developmental steps towards critical maturity (Gräb 2004) no longer require an ecclesiastical rite of passage in the sense of a substantial rite of passage.

Finally, there is currently an increasing collision between church structures and the realities of young people's lives. This refers to the highly different time structures, as well as the life, language, and image cultures – one thinks here especially of the dynamics of digital culture – as well as independent preferences in choosing their peers and peer groups, which confronts church group formation processes with considerable plausibility requirements. In general, then, it can be said that during the confirmation period, the reality of young people's everyday lifes and their "lived" – or quasi "unlived" religion sometimes collide hard with the church's and ministers' interests and expectations with regard to young people's positive identification with the church and the "taught religion" represented by it (Koch 2020).

In addition to these challenges, the role of those who are professionally and pastorally responsible for the implementation of the respective programme has changed considerably in recent decades. For centuries, their self-image consisted primarily of conveying the central contents of the faith to the young people as strongly and convincingly as possible in the mode of catechesis and instruction. Their role in the confirmation period was thus clearly and unambiguously that of the frontally acting model of faith and life. In the usually obligatory participation of the young people in church services during the entire confirmation period, they were to experience this church practice indirectly, so to speak, or already practise the role of later regular churchgoers – and this with all the disciplinary difficulties associated with it.

In view of the ritual practice of particular interest here, the concluding confirmation service was not only the symbolic goal of the celebration of youthful maturity, but from the perspective of the pastors the ultimate climax of instruction for the mature life of faith. This was symbolised in front of all the congregation in the retrieval of the learned material, the sermon as a powerful speech to take with you on the further journey of life, the blessing of the confirmands, as well as by the symbolic exodus of the then 'confirmed' at the end of the service. The worship ceremonies thus did not have to legitimise themselves or make themselves plausible, but carried their self-evident and unquestionable institutional-authoritative meaning.

This understanding has fundamentally changed since the general social and cultural transformations of the 1960s and beyond. In the course of far-reaching emancipation tendencies, and thus also a changed role and perception of church and its personnel, the catechetical objectives have changed towards forms that are more open to experience and participation.

Accordingly, the practice of worship has also undergone a significant reforming. As already indicated, for many young people worship services are unfamiliar or even incomprehensible, both in terms of liturgical form and the forms of language used in the content. This makes it indispensable for professional staff not only to introduce the meaning and deeper meaning of liturgical events, but also to make them fundamentally plausible in their possible relevance to meaning and life. In other words, the specific meaning and history of confirmation work and the ritual practice associated with it, must be symbolised, clarified, and practised again and again as precisely as possible in view of young people's present perceptions of themselves and the world. What applies to the pedagogical dimension can consequently also be said for the ritual dimension.

This orientation in the mode of a mutual process of discovery and development between the message and the subjects of the confirmation work is consequently manifested in an increasingly participatory worship practice (Schlag 2010). This can lead to a situation, where the young people themselves not only determine the theme of the final service, but also take on considerable responsibility for shaping it. In this case, they do not simply "repeat" "given" prayers or other parts of the text. Instead, the elements of design include their own musical and textual productions, as well as sometimes even specially formulated parts of the sermon. In this way, this new balance between confirmands and staff, which is open to creative participation, is once again demonstrated for the congregation itself in a symbolic and manifest way.

2 The Relationship Between Different Aspects of Confirmation Ceremonies

2.1 Staging Patterns (Inszenierungsmuster)

The challenges outlined above lead to the need for institutionalised permanent innovation in the pedagogical and liturgical design of confirmation practice. For ritual practice, it is therefore helpful to be clear about the different dimensions of meaning of the confirmation service – which in turn can also guide other ritual elements during the confirmation period.

Thomas Klie very helpfully differentiates between four different so-called staging patterns of the baptising, forming, and confirming actions of the congregation, both for the overall practice and for the confirmation service that is to be consistently connected with it (Klie 2007). The crucial point of this differentiation is that depending on the (sometimes almost unconscious) pastoral favouritism of the respective pattern, both the objectives and the characteristics of the concrete programme – in pedagogical and ritual terms – can take on different forms:

In the sense of the *cybernetic-integrative staging pattern*, the confirmands are to undertake and experience a kind of "trial living" in the space of church and congregation through active participation in church and liturgical practice. According to this logic, the aim is to create "an overlapping field as large as possible between lived and taught religion". For the confirmation service, this entails a clear focus on the desired affiliation of the young people to the congregation. In the sense of the *life-cycle-blessing staging pattern*, confirmation is primarily understood as a "casual service of maturity", from which the concrete profile of the service is formatted less ecclesiastically than biographically. Accordingly, the confirmation service does not focus on communion and confession, but on elements of blessing and intercession. In the sense of the *catechetical-church-legal staging pattern*, there is a strong instructional orientation towards the acquisition of elementary Protestant confessional content. The reference to the historical-theological tradition, i.e., the admission to the Lord's Supper, as well as the ecclesiastical granting of the right to be a godparent, is in the foreground. In the sense of a *sacramental-ceremonial staging pattern*, the pedagogical orientation of the confirmation service is broken in favour of its liturgical dimension. The confirmation service as a form of expression of religious-symbolic communication thus takes on a performative form. The common celebration in the congregation and as a congregation comes into view as a space of experience in which life-historical and theological interpretations are closely intertwined.

Now, in view of this helpful heuristic fourfold differentiation by Klie, it should be pointed out that these different interpretations hardly occur "in pure form" in either pedagogical or liturgical practice, but rather in mixtures, which in turn are shaped by the respective expectations of the actors involved in confirmation practice. And these expectations include not only the pastoral liturgists but also the young people, their parents, and families, as well as the congregation, and not least the church boards and councils. Thus – and this is also to be noted for the ritual practice – quite different expectations and logics come together in the time of confirmation.

This justifies speaking of a plurality of expectations inherent in confirmation, which can hardly be transferred back into a one-line homogeneous horizon of meaning. In this respect, the art of this church event – to anticipate it already at this juncture – consists in aligning the respective focus in practice in such a way that as few "blind spots" and exclusion tendencies are created as possible. At the same time the question arises, whether in view of the current challenges indicated above, a stronger and clearer profile of confirmation work and the liturgical practice to be experienced and shaped in it, should be developed in general. To do this, it is helpful to look empirically at young people's experiences with and their expectations of this programme.

2.2 The Significance of Ritual Practice During the Confirmation Period and the Confirmation Service – Empirical Insights

In a comprehensive, predominantly quantitative study, the expectations and experiences of confirmands and workers in a total of 9 European countries were surveyed in the years 2012–2014. The survey was conducted at the beginning of the confirmation period (t_1), shortly before confirmation (t_2) and in retrospect about one year after confirmation (t_3). One thematic focus of these three consecutive surveys was on worship and ritual practice. In the following, some central insights will be presented, concentrating on the participating German-speaking countries Germany, Switzerland, and Austria. In the following, detailed percentage figures will be dispensed with, but the respective recognisable tendencies will be depicted.

Regarding expectations at the beginning of the confirmation period (t_1), about half of the confirmands agree with the statement "Church services are usually boring". Only about one third expressed interest in the topic "Course and meaning of Sunday services". With regard to their own attitude to church services, more than half would like "to experience services adequate for young people". However, only a quarter of confirmands – in Switzerland only a tenth – are willing "to contribute my own ideas to the services" and "to have tasks in the services (for example, do a reading)". In terms of expectations, about half said "to meet nice people in the services" and slightly less than half said "to listen to interesting sermons". A quarter of the confirmands agree with the statement: "It is unclear to me what I can expect from a worship service". As far as confirmation itself is concerned about half also expect "to have a beautiful celebration with family and friends on the day of my confirmation" and "to receive a blessing on the day of confirmation".

There is a notable discrepancy in the survey between the confirmands and those working in the church. In response to some of the questions mentioned above, which those working were asked in the same way, the importance of the practice and themes of the service is rated significantly higher overall. For example, about four-fifths of those working consider the topic "Course and meaning of Sunday services" to be central. There is an equally clear tendency for them to want to offer worship services that are appropriate for young people and to involve young people in the design of worship services. In addition, about two thirds want the young people to "get acquainted with the liturgy" – a question, which incidentally was not asked of the young people themselves.

It is interesting to compare the expectations expressed by the young people at the beginning of the confirmation period with the experiences (t_2) they articulate shortly before confirmation, i.e., in retrospect of the confirmation period: the assessment that church services are "usually boring" has practically not changed compared to the initial expectations, and the thematic interest in church services has remained more or less the same at a low level. It seems surprising, especially in comparison with the original intentions of those working in the church, as well as their perceptions at the end of the year, that – according to the confirmands – only about half have experienced youth-oriented services. In contrast, in retrospect, the workers rate both the provision of youth-oriented services and the active participation of the young people as much higher. It should be noted that the confirmands, who not only took on "tasks" but were also able to contribute their own ideas to the service, rated the services more positively overall.

It should also be noted that at the end of the year, about half of the young people tended to confirm positively that they had met "nice people" in church services, liked the music and atmosphere, could "calm down" and felt "secure in the group" and "as a part of the worship community". However, almost half also stated that it was important for them, "to get through with it as soon as possible". Four-fifths of the young people had positive expectations of the confirmation service that was about to take place.

The statements about the day of confirmation itself made by the young people one year after their confirmation (t_3) are exciting (Christensen and Krupka 2017). Again, about half agree with the statement that the day of confirmation was "one of the most important days of my life", two thirds agree with the statement "Having a beautiful celebration with family and friends was important for me" and about half agree "To receive a blessing was important for me".

Overall, both the expectations and the experiences of the confirmands show that at least the "normal" worship practice is clearly inferior to the other experiences during the confirmation period. The confirmation service is an exception here, which is hardly surprising in view of its prominent, biographical, and familial significance. And of course, the experience of being at the centre of it all as a young person is of considerable lasting significance.

Further empirical results of the study show that the confirmation period as a whole, and the church service at the end, are not experienced by young people as so important that it would really be appropriate to speak of it as a *rite de passage*. The assessment that the young people had made "an important step in growing up" through the confirmation time, was positively answered by less than half: "In all the participating countries, confirmation has lost most, but not all, of its implications for the civil status of adolescents, both within and outside the church." (Christensen and Krupka 2017, 30). It therefore seems problematic to regard confirmation itself as a decisive rite of passage.

However, it should be pointed out that, due to the specifically experience-oriented character of the confirmation period, many decisive ritual-related experiences are not made in the classic church building or in the normal Sunday service, but for example at confirmation weekends or at confirmation camps. Thus, it can be assumed that not only successful group experiences, joint activities, and camps, as well as the positive perception of church workers, are relevant for the positive overall assessment of the young people, but that these experiences also have a considerable influence on the perception of the ritual practice. In this respect, it can be reasonably assumed that celebrating, praying, and singing in the group outside of the Sunday service nevertheless facilitated positive experiences with this church practice.

3 Confirmation Ceremonies as Dialogical and Resonant Relational Events of a Theological Interpretation of Life and Religion

The historical and theological considerations, as well as the empirical findings, have shown that there is a close connection between pedagogical, liturgical, pastoral-theological and church-theoretical aspects in confirmation work and the ritual practice associated with it. If one takes up the objective of confirmation work formulated at the beginning, namely coming of age in questions of one's own faith, then it is clear that there is no need for homogenising, nor at the same time for pooling these different aspects. As a conceptual bracket for this, a definition of the *Confirmation Ceremonies as a dialogical, resonant relational event of a theological interpretation of life and religion* can be understood. This needs to be explained theologically in more detail in the following:

Religious maturity – to put it theologically – is not acquired through a specific ritual practice. Rather, this ritual event is itself a symbolic expression of the maturity experienced and practised during confirmation, which has already experienced its full expression in baptism. Theologically speaking, the experiences of confirmation combine the passive dimension of promise and the active dimension of encouragement to form a religiously significant whole of meaning. Confirmation ceremonies are thus on the one hand – with regard to their dimension of passivity – predetermined provisions of interpretation for individual life and religious practice. On the other hand – in respect to their dimension of activity – they open up a constantly new and not yet fixed resonance space for individual and at the same time group-related interpretation through the possibilities of individual co-creation.

This is based on the church- and liturgy-theoretical conviction that in the ritual itself, individuals are never only atomistically present alongside each other, but that the respective common experience contributes significantly to this resonance-open relational event. In this respect, it is of considerable importance from the point of view of ritual theory and church theory that it is precisely in the ritual that the confirmation group can experience itself both collectively as a group and together with the staff.

On the other hand, the individual family constellation (as problematic as it may be in individual cases) is of course also directly 'gathered' in this resonance space –

ultimately in the confirmation service. Finally, the congregation celebrating is also experienced as a congregation gathered in the worship space and as an interacting community. Theologically speaking, in a successful case the respective rite makes it possible to experience the congregation as a whole individually and collectively as *communio sanctorum*. In this sense, the ritual practice during the confirmation period itself represents a specific form of jointly lived religion.

Thus, confirmation work is decisively about opening up the most experience-oriented connections possible between church-symbolic practice and individual theological literacy. In a successful case, it can become clear which specific content-related message can be opened up through this symbolising act of the rite or can open itself up. Exemplarily, this could manifest itself in the confirmation service, in that the elementary significance of baptism for the understanding of the promised and given faith is made a theme (Schlag 2010).

Consequently, this already makes it necessary to practise ritual and worship during the confirmation period (Meyer-Blanck 2001). However, this also means that especially in and through ritual practice, the factually existing plurality and heterogeneity among all the actors involved must not simply be blunted. Rather, as a wealth of individual religious needs and forms of expression, this must consciously take shape and be expressed in ritual practice – which may then include the creation of individual prayers, as well as the productive-creative restaging of existing rituals. However, from the empirical results, it must be emphasised once again that a merely liturgical auxiliary function should in any case not yet be passed off as truly responsible participation. In a successful case, one could speak of a ritual-related theological productivity.

And on the part of the staff, this also makes it absolutely necessary for them to reflect again and again on their own ritual practice and its possible relevance for the realisation of a mature life of faith. The role as liturgist, preacher and hermeneutic theologian of lived and taught religion only becomes plausibly transparent and, in the truest sense of the word, can only be experienced as credible through one's own mature performance and one's own readiness for relational resonance (Beile 2016).

To conclude: From this theological point of view, the confirmation service is the public and visible expression of a many-voiced, partly ambivalent, but basically approving 'yes' of all those involved in it: the young people, their families, those responsible for this programme, as well as the whole congregation celebrating with them – and all this against the backdrop of an intensely resonant, audible and visible tradition.

This is why this church celebration represents an enormous opportunity for a theological-reformatory profile in such a way that the manifold expectations and experiences in their factual fragility and openness are included. A supposedly more coherent adjustment to secular would hardly meet the demands of this ceremony. Theologically responsibly not sweeping the complexities and fractures of life under the table, but consciously articulated – also by the young people themselves – the profile of the confirmation service differs significantly from secular youth consecration like the in the former East Germany still quite popular *Jugendweihe*.

In this respect, it is important to keep in mind this richness and the need to preserve theological tradition on the one hand, but on the other hand also to be open to elements that are appropriate for young people and also quite fresh, unconventional and surprising. In this way, the confirmation service corresponds to the experiences made during the whole confirmation time – in the best case: as an encounter with a faith tradition that is still relevant for young people today, and with a church that is open to impulses and ideas from the "next generation" in a convincing way (Simojoki, et al. 2018, 200).

4 The Contribution to Practical Theology in General

Dealing with confirmation work and its ritual references makes it clear that strong networking between the practical theological disciplines should be implemented wherever possible. In concrete terms, it becomes clear that confirmation work can by no means be adequately defined or even profiled by reflection on religious education alone. Rather, precisely because it is such a complex event, the ritual-theoretical, church-theoretical, pastoral-theological and pastoral-care aspects must be addressed integratively in the interplay of the various practical-theological disciplines and reflected upon hermeneutically and empirically in their factual context.

In addition, the challenges of confirmation work show the need for much closer cooperation between Practical Theology and Systematic Theology in the future, with regard to both dogmatic and ethical questions. Here, in the sense of a hermeneutic-pedagogical approach to ritual practice and its better understanding, perspectives of 'theological literacy' in the sense of a "lived theology", as well as the question of empowerment of the young generation – also in terms of their civil society engagement (Schweitzer et al. 2016; Simojoki et al. 2018, 109–124) – must be increasingly considered in a theological-intradisciplinary way.

It is particularly important for Practical Theology to think systemically in the area of confirmation work and beyond. Because it is the entire family and church network that is relevant for a coherent and sustainable confirmation practice – and this applies not only to the question of religious socialisation in the parental home, but also to the shared experience of worship.

In any case, it would be an indictment – with all understanding for the cultural significance of the confirmation service, which has long since changed – if at some point it were to be understood and experienced only as a civil-religious family celebration and no longer as a life-significant common celebration in the face of life given by God.

For the staging of this event, this means that the young people are naturally at the centre of all liturgical events and should experience them as such. However, theologically speaking, it is important that such a centre experience is not understood as a self-created religious experience. Rather, this worship practice is to be profiled and staged as a blessing event through which the young people can experience themselves as individually endowed by God with inalienable and inviolable dignity and be able to express this in their own feelings and words.

In this respect, if the concept of religious maturity is to be used constructively here, practical-theological reflection is needed on what life development means in the horizon of Protestant faith and what it does not mean. In any case, it would be theologically and developmentally problematic to assume a teleological understanding of this concept of maturity, according to which a new qualitatively higher state of aggregation would be established through confirmation.

Rather, such a concept only makes sense if it is understood as processual. In this respect, the development of religious maturity is not to be seen as a specific, possibly already clearly established goal. Maturity is to be understood here as an expression of the experiences with religion and faith that are to be made anew in each case, which can and should lead to ever new processes – not stages! – of interpretation on the basis of the respective individual and common experiences. However, this can and must neither undermine nor homogenise the factual plurality of different interpretations and, for example, the different patterns of staging mentioned above.

From there, it can be demanded from a practical-theological point of view that such a ritual practice is not only to be limited to the Sunday service, but can also be experienced in completely different places, right into the everyday life of the young people. Here, for example, the experience of praying together as a specific rite is such an element of experience that can remain significant far beyond the time of confirmation.

In the best case it must be reflected – e.g., in confirmation group processes – that despite all the heterogeneities and possible conflicts within the confirmation group, something like the ideal form of solidary congregation can be symbolised in the rite during the confirmation period. Of course, it should be borne in mind – and the empirical results point to this – that it is often only half of the young people who can really gain positive experiences from the confirmation period. What this means for the question of exclusion of a certain majority requires further thorough consideration and creative design, especially for those young people, who do not have positive previous experiences. In concrete cases, this has eminent pastoral implications. On the other hand, such a justice-sensitive ritual confirmation practice also has a highly relevant signal function from a social and political perspective.

In this respect, continuous reflection on the conditions and forms of convincing and life-relevant confirmation work and its liturgical-ritual practice is a challenge not only for Practical Theology, but also for the church in its self-understanding as a biographically, religiously, and publicly significant manifestation of Protestant faith and life.

Bibliography

Beile, Markus. 2016. *Herausforderungen und Perspektiven der Konfirmationspredigt: Empirische Einsichten und theologische Klärungen.* Stuttgart: Kohlhammer.
Christensen, Leise, and Bernd Krupka. 2017. "Confirmands Looking Back to Their Day of Confirmation." In *Confirmation, Faith and Volunteerism: A Longitudinal Study on Protestant Adolescents in the Transition towards Adulthood: European Perspectives*, edited by Friedrich Schweitzer, Thomas Schlag, Henrik Simojoki, Kati Tervo-Niemelä, and Wolfgang Ilg, Gütersloh: Gütersloher Verlagshaus, 30–44.
Ebinger, Thomas, Thomas Böhme, Matthias Hempel, Herbert Kolb, and Achim Plagentz, eds. 2018. *Handbuch Konfi-Arbeit.* Gütersloh: Gütersloher Verlagshaus.
Gräb, Wilhelm. 2004. "Die Konfirmation als Kasualie der Mündigkeit". In *Pastoraltheologie* 94:175–191.
Grethlein, Christian. ^{4}2001. "Konfirmation". In *Religion in Geschichte und Gegenwart.* Vol. 4, edited by Hans Dieter Betz, Don Browning, Bernd Janowski, and Eberhard Jüngel, Tübingen: Mohr Siebeck, 1558–1562.
Klie, Thomas. 2007. "Konfirmation: Konfirmation und Taufpraxis / Katechismusunterricht / Konfirmation und Jugendweihe / Inszenierungsmuster." In *Handbuch Praktische Theologie*, edited by Wilhelm Gräb and Birgit Weyel, Gütersloh: Gütersloher Verlagshaus, 591–601.
Koch, Muriel. 2020. *Jugendliche und ihre Sprache des Glaubens: Sprachliche Identifizierungspraktiken in der Konfirmationszeit.* Zürich: Theologischer Verlag Zürich.
Meyer-Blanck, Michael. 2001. "Liturgie lernen – Konfirmation feiern." In *Konfirmandenunterricht: Didaktik und Inszenierung*, edited by Bernhard Dressler, Thomas Klie, and Carsten Mork, Hannover: Lutherisches Verlagshaus, 261–281.
Osmer, Richard R. 1996. *Confirmation: Presbyterian Practices in Ecumenical Perspective.* Louisville: Geneva Press.
Osmer, Richard R., and Katherine M. Douglass, eds. 2018. *Cultivating Teen Faith: Insights from the Confirmation Project.* Grand Rapids: Eerdmans.
Schlag, Thomas. 2010. "Partizipation." In *Konfirmandenarbeit gestalten: Perspektiven und Impulse für die Praxis aus der bundesweiten Studie zur Konfirmandenarbeit in Deutschland*, edited by Thomas Böhme-Lischewski, Volker Elsenbast, Carsten Haeske, Wolfgang Ilg, and Friedrich Schweitzer, Gütersloh: Gütersloher Verlagshaus, 112–124.
Schlag, Thomas. 2010. "Wenn Glaube auf Wirklichkeit trifft: Notwendige Überlegungen zur theologischen Bildungserfahrung in der Konfirmationsarbeit." In *Konfirmandenarbeit für das 21. Jahrhundert*, edited by Thomas Böhme-Lischewski, Sönke von Stemm, and Volker Elsenbast, Münster: Comenius-Institut, 26–32.
Schlag, Thomas, Muriel Koch, and Christoph H. Maaß. 2016. *Konfirmationsarbeit in der Schweiz: Ergebnisse, Interpretationen, Konsequenzen.* Zürich: Theologischer Verlag Zürich.
Schweitzer, Friedrich, Kati Niemelä, Thomas Schlag, and Henrik Simojoki, eds. 2015a. *Youth, Religion and Confirmation Work in Europe: The Second Study.* Gütersloh: Gütersloher Verlagshaus.
Schweitzer, Friedrich, Christoph H. Maaß, Katja Lißmann, Georg Hardecker, and Wolfgang Ilg. 2015b. *Konfirmandenarbeit im Wandel: Neue Herausforderungen und Chancen: Perspektiven aus der zweiten bundeweiten Studie.* Gütersloh: Gütersloher Verlagshaus.
Schweitzer, Friedrich, Georg Hardecker, Christoph H. Maaß, Wolfgang Ilg, and Katja Lißmann. 2016. *Jugendliche nach der Konfirmation: Glaube, Kirche und eigenes Engagement – eine Längsschnittstude.* Gütersloh: Gütersloher Verlagshaus.

Schweitzer, Friedrich, Henrik Simojoki, Kati Tervo-Niemelä, and Wolfgang-Ilg, eds. 2017. *Confirmation, Faith and Volunteerism: A Longitudinal Study on Protestant Adolescents in the Transition towards Adulthood: European Perspectives*. Gütersloh: Gütersloher Verlagshaus.

Simojoki, Henrik, Wolfgang Ilg, Thomas Schlag, and Friedrich Schweitzer. 2018. *Zukunftsfähige Konfirmandenarbeit: Empirische Erträge – theologische Orientierungen – Perspektiven für die Praxis*. Gütersloh: Gütersloher Verlagshaus.

Brendan Ozawa-de Silva and Chikako Ozawa-de Silva
Contemplative Practice / Sacred Spaces / Cultural Resilience

1 Introduction

> For me, forgiveness has been the most profound act of self-compassion that I have experienced thus far. I am experiencing that when you start to understand the pain of those who cause you suffering and choose to let it go, forgiveness comes naturally. The cup of poison that I drank from for years is now officially emptied and retired. What a refreshing, liberating relief!

This opening quote was written by a former student of ours while engaging in a 200-hour retreat on the contemplative practice of Naikan, a practice originating in Japan and derived from a form of Buddhist meditation. Through this practice, this remarkable individual, to whom we shall return later, was able to overcome decades of resentment, hurt, and moral injury built up due to a ten-year long traumatic period of sexual abuse starting in early childhood that took place with the full knowledge of, and sometimes in the presence of, her own mother.

But what is perhaps even more unusual is that the practice was undertaken while this young woman was incarcerated in a maximum-security prison for the violent offense she had committed after her years of abuse. She therefore engaged in her practice without access to many of the traditional resources of sacred space places of worship, and spiritual retreat. Yet through her practice, she, and others like her, created their own sense of sacred space and thereby transformed an inhospitable setting into a place of spiritual transformation.

This chapter sets out to examine secular contemplative practices, and in particular the practice of Naikan, as particularly useful tools for spiritual growth, healing, and the treatment of moral injury. Such practices are typically engaged in within sacred spaces, such as temples, monasteries, churches, holy sites, and so on. But in the twentieth century, the definition of sacred space is changing. Increasingly, individuals are seeking alternatives to traditional institutions and traditional forms of practice, spirituality, and religiosity; in some cases, technology and our ever-shrinking world facilitate options for alternative sacred spaces. At the same time, millions of others have been forced to find alternative sacred spaces because traditional venues and communities have been closed off to them – due to war and exile in the case of refugees, for example, or due to another form of exile in the case of mass incarceration.

Whether the move to alternative sacred spaces is by choice or forced, such individuals nevertheless manage to exhibit and cultivate extraordinary resilience by creating their own, less traditional sacred spaces for the purposes of spiritual and religious practice. By examining such instances, we can learn more about the possibilities of using such practices for the treatment of moral injury and the cultivation of resilience. Moreover, we can examine the way individuals develop resilience not only individually, but by working to establish the systems and structures that support resilience. We call this 'cultural resilience': social and cultural systems, beliefs, and practices that best support individual resilience. Both individual and cultural resilience, we argue, are important for the treatment and healing of moral injury.

2 Secular Contemplative Practice

Recent years have seen a growing interest in contemplative practices that have been derived from religious traditions. The most popular of these are probably hatha yoga and mindfulness meditation, both of which are increasingly ubiquitous internationally. These practices retain a strong element of spirituality but are generally not connected to institutional religion. Unlike the original religious practices from which they are derived, which typically involved aims directed towards a future life beyond this one, these secularized contemplative practices are typically approached for this-worldly benefits. Yet these benefits can range from better health or stress-reduction to the purposes of meaning-making and personal growth.

Despite the unmooring of such practices from many of the overtly religious and metaphysical aspects of their original contexts, secularized contemplative practices are not merely raw techniques (Ozawa-de Silva 2016). Rather, they include and are informed by many aspects of contemplative theory. Indeed, they typically require such theory to be intelligible and meaningful to those who practice them. Mindfulness meditation, for example, includes a strong emphasis on the impermanence or fleeting nature of phenomena and experiences – a key Buddhist tenet, but not one that by itself requires faith in or adherence to Buddhism (Shapiro et al. 2006). Yoga, as often practiced in modern contexts, emphasizes the mind-body connection, the fundamental importance of breath and its relation to vital energies, and other spiritual dimensions of the practice. Given all this, modern secularized contemplative practices stand very much at the intersections of religion and spirituality, and of theory and practice. They should therefore be of particular interest for the study of practical theology.

In this chapter, we will examine a contemporary contemplative practice derived from the Buddhist tradition called Naikan, which is less known in the English-speaking world but popular in Japan, where it originated. In its use of sacred space to create safety and an opportunity for deep reflection and self-examination, and in its use of specific modes of memory as a tool to facilitate the reconstruction of autobiography, Naikan is a contemplative practice that also stands at another important intersection: between therapy and meditation (Ozawa-de Silva 2006). The research literature on Naikan in Japanese, English, and German, as well as the first-hand experiences and research of the authors, suggests that Naikan may be particularly suited to address issues of healing moral injury, which, we will suggest, is an affliction that pertains not only to veterans of war, but to a wide number of individuals in our modern world.

3 Moral Injury

"Moral injury" was originally coined by the psychiatrist Jonathan Shay and his colleagues to refer to the injury of moral conscience suffered by military personnel and veterans (Shay 2014). Since then, definitions continue to evolve. For the purpose of this chapter, and generally following Farnsworth et al. (2014), we define it broadly as a form of on-going suffering caused by committing, witnessing, or being the victim of an act of violence that deeply violates one's moral beliefs or expectations of how people should behave. It is often characterized by a sense of betrayal and results in condemnation of others and self, a damaged sense of oneself as a moral agent, and feelings of guilt, shame, anger, and helplessness.

In recent years, moral injury has become a topic of interest for scholars of religion, in part due to the efforts of Rita Nakashima Brock and others. The concept of moral injury is useful because it expands our understanding of traumatic events by allowing for triggering events that do not necessarily involve threats to the individual's life or physical safety. It also shifts the focus away from an often-medicalized and stigmatizing understanding of Post-Traumatic Stress Disorder (PTSD) as an individual affliction towards a consideration of the moral, social, political, and systemic dimensions of traumatic experience.

4 Contemplative Practice in Prison

Six years ago, we began teaching courses in contemplative and spiritual practice at the Lee Arrendale State Prison for women in Alto, Georgia. We are a psychological and medical anthropologist who studies mental well-being and mental illness in cross-cultural context and grew up in Japan (Chikako), and an interdisciplinary scholar of psychology, Buddhism, and contemplative practices who grew up in the United States (Brendan). We are also both practitioners in the Tibetan Buddhist tradition. Our interest in offering courses in contemplative practice, however, has never been primarily to teach Buddhist religious practices to Buddhists, and neither of us considers her- or himself to be a Buddhist spiritual teacher. Rather, we are interested in how contemplative and spiritual practices, which may have their origins in Buddhism or other religious traditions, can have benefits (therapeutic or otherwise) to individuals and communities even when offered in a secular way – meaning offered in a way that does not depend upon religious metaphysical claims and that is open to people of all, or no, religion.

We and the several co-instructors we invited to teach with us at the prison quickly realized that despite the students' strong wish to learn contemplative practices such as mindfulness, Naikan, and compassion meditation, several of the students were encountering serious obstacles in their practice. For many, focusing attention on the breath would cause anxiety and frustration. One woman occasionally got up suddenly during the meditation session to leave the room. She later explained that this was not because she did not want to meditate or disliked what we were doing. She said she desperately wanted to experience the peace and relaxation that the other women were describing, but she found it impossible to settle her mind or sit still in one place.

In hindsight this should not have surprised us. A prison is anything but a safe space. And without the establishment of a sense of safety and sacred space, how could we expect our small community to engage meaningfully in contemplative practice, especially considering that all our students had also experienced a variety of forms of trauma? As we learned more about their situations, it became clear that the traumas they had experienced had impacted their nervous systems significantly enough to make sitting still and engaging in silent meditation extremely challenging, despite their ardent wishes for the peace of mind meditation was said to offer those who practiced it.

Violent offenses, whether inflicted upon or by oneself, and especially when involving a close person or family member, are prime causes of moral injury. Such experiences are violations of moral order and trigger a breakdown in one's moral vision of the world, and therefore one's own self-evaluation as a moral individual. One's mother is supposed to be the one person in the world who will protect oneself – not the person who facilitates or passively witnesses one's abuse. The same holds for one's own perpetration of an unthinkable crime. If one comes to realize that one is capable of such action, how does that affect one's ability to feel safe among others?

Our collective journey of understanding trauma and moral injury led to the recognition that the practices we were engaging in, which had evolved from and been designed for traditional sacred spaces, needed to be adapted to fit new times and new surroundings. The focus of our time together became the establishment of a sacred space within and among ourselves, even within the confines of a prison.

5 Naikan Practice

Both the women mentioned above, and many others who faced similarly traumatic events and instances of moral injury, were taught secularized contemplative practices derived from Buddhist traditions through twelve-week courses in prison. These included: mindfulness meditation; simple restorative yoga practices; Cognitively-Based Compassion Training (CBCT), which is an analytical meditation protocol derived from the Lojong (*blo sbyong*) tradition of Tibetan Buddhism developed by

Geshe Lobsang Tenzin Negi at Emory University; Compassionate Integrity Training (CIT), developed at Life University; and Naikan, which is originally a Japanese practice derived from Shin Buddhism.

Naikan is a particularly interesting practice with regard to sacred space, because unlike many other contemplative practices, Naikan intentionally and explicitly seeks to establish a sacred, womb-like space around the practitioner both physically and spiritually. Naikan is traditionally practiced for one week, 14–16 hours a day, with the practitioner sitting behind a Japanese paper screen or in a room by themselves, to establish a "tomb and womb" environment of sensory deprivation (Ozawa-de Silva 2006). Naikan is a simple method on the surface. The practitioner contemplates three questions with regard to a significant person in one's life, such as one's mother, starting from early childhood and leading to the present day: What did I receive from this person? What did I give back to this person? What trouble did I cause this person?

The practitioner does this in two-hour sessions in a temporal sequence: for example, starting with one's mother from age zero to five, asking these three questions, and trying to recollect through one's memory. At the end of each two-hour session, the practitioner is visited by the Naikan guide facilitating the retreat. The guide asks the practitioner to give a report on what they received, what they gave back, and what trouble they caused (the three Naikan questions). The guide listens, usually without comment, and asks the practitioner what they will focus on for the next session. Then the guide leaves and the practitioner continues with the next session.

Both the physical seclusion and the non-judgmental listening by the guide facilitate the establishment of sacred space. But so, too, does the practice. Because practitioners spend around a hundred hours remembering what they received from others throughout their lives – starting with childhood when they could not offer much, if anything, in return – they gradually come to a realization that they have been supported by a seemingly infinite network of care throughout their lives. Some practitioners have described this as being surrounded by love as if sitting in the center of a mandala. This is the establishment of what could be called a spiritual sacred space of safety and care.

C., the woman mentioned above who had suffered sexual abuse in the presence of her mother, at first rejected Naikan as a practice and found it unrealistic when we offered it as a potential practice. Within two weeks or so, however, she had decided to practice it. Very shortly after that, she resolved to do 100 hours of Naikan practice on her mother – the length of a typical one-week Naikan session – by doing half an hour of practice each day for 200 days. She soon increased this to one hour per day of practice, and therefore decided to do 200 hours of Naikan, a 'double Naikan' retreat.

In C.'s journal entries prior to doing Naikan, she repeatedly wrote of her mother and the trauma of her childhood abuse. But while engaging in Naikan, and upon completing it, her narrative changed. The following quote comes after C. had engaged in a 30-day period of daily Naikan practice. She refers to the topic of self-compassion, which had been explored in a course on Cognitively-Based Compassion Training (CBCT) that she had participated in just prior to starting Naikan. In CBCT, self-compassion involves recognizing that suffering and happiness come largely from our own perspectives, attitudes, and emotional reactions, and that we have the ability to transform them and thereby emerge from suffering. C. wrote:

> Self-compassion and learning how to cultivate it is helping to free me from an inner prison emotionally and spiritually. I find that I am a lot happier, and I am more direct and decisive in my decision making. I am noticing also that I am not as easily disturbed and short of patience with others or with myself. I am genuinely enjoying the company of others and can now respect them for who they are and how they are without attempting to change them and without judgment. I can now accept their beliefs and perspectives respectfully, even if they differ from my own. [...] Learning self-compassion and how to cultivate it has given me a desire to extend compassion to others. I no longer want to be consumed with unhealthy, destructive emotions and behavior. Learning to view and interpret my past horrific childhood experiences in a different way makes me confront and acknowledge these experiences for what and how they were, yet not be controlled and overwhelmed by them. My experiences have given me a passion and desire to share my story and to be of help to those who suffer or have suffered in similar ways as I. [...] One of the things that I gained from doing the Naikan practice for 30 minutes, 30 days, is realizing that the past is already gone and can't be changed, and the future is yet to come and isn't promised to anyone. Grasping onto this reality makes me want to acknowledge my past without letting it affect and overwhelm me, accept it for what and how it was, and move on from it, instead of being stuck in it. It also makes me not want to focus on a future that isn't promised because in doing so, you miss the beauty, blessings, joy, healing, and transformation of right NOW! Learning to live my life in the present moment has made me more appreciative and mindful of my surroundings, myself, and others.

There are many important insights here. C. points out that a violation of moral order occurs within the context of expectations about reality. One assumes that people will act a certain way, but these assumptions do not reflect reality, since violations of our expected moral order do in fact happen. When one learns to see that reality and therefore stops assuming and taking for granted certain levels of decent moral behavior, that does not lead to a breakdown in one's moral universe. On the contrary, it appears to lead to a greater appreciation for the good in one's life. As C. writes, the reality she 'grasps onto' is that the past is gone and can't be changed, and the future is uncertain.

She later reported that the chief gift Naikan had given her was memory recall. Before, she had only been able to remember sadness, abuse, and disappointment in her childhood. Yet by going through the process – over two hundred hours – of remembering what her mother had given her, she began to recover memories of happiness and well-being. Her childhood had not all been abuse and pain. There were many moments of joy as well. The ability to recognize goodness and safety in one's experiences and surroundings – and not just pain, threats, and dangers – seems central to establishing a safe space and a sacred space, and has been an important topic of research in dealing with trauma.

Importantly, Naikan prompts the practitioner to remember their past from the perspective of another person – in this case, C.'s mother. This encourages empathy. C. began to see her mother not just as her mother, but as a young woman struggling to raise a child on her own. As she saw the larger context and remembered all the kindness her mother had shown her over the years, her image of her mother, and therefore her image of her own past, changed. Such changes as a result of Naikan are not limited to one individual but have been well documented in a number of publications and studies (Krech 2001; Ozawa-de Silva 2006, 2007; Reiss and Bechmann 2016).

6 Forbearance and Individual Resilience

The characteristic that comes from seeing reality, and that results in self-acceptance, courage, an ability to bear and withstand hardship and injury, and forgiveness, is called *kṣānti* (Skt) or *bzod pa* (Tib., pronounced 'so-pa') in the Indo-Tibetan Buddhist tradition. Often simply translated as 'forbearance' or 'patience,' it means an inner fortitude that allows one to bear suffering without buckling under pressure or retaliating with anger. It can also be understood as a resilience that involves not just the ability to 'bounce back,' but also the strength to withstand adversity courageously. This type of forbearance is one of the six 'perfections' that bodhisattvas (spiritual practitioners intent upon enlightenment for the benefit of all sentient beings) must practice in Mahāyāna (Greater Vehicle) Buddhism and would appear to be the key virtue of relevance in discussing moral injury. Interestingly, although there is no exact equivalent in English for *bzod pa*, it appears to be very similar to the Arabic term *hilm*, particularly as it was used in pre-Islamic and early Islamic times, which also meant forbearance and composure, and which was opposed to *jahl* or ignorance, an incapacity to use reason, and a tendency to break out in anger (Izutsu 2002).

The lasting consequences of moral injury appear to come from a difficulty in sustaining and recovering from the suffering that comes from having inflicted or having witnessed the infliction of unwarranted harm. A path to moral repair, therefore, may be the cultivation of this forbearance or *bzod pa*. In the Buddhist tradition, this is often done through practices of habituated cognitive reframing, as in Naikan. The most famous text on *bzod pa* today is the sixth chapter of Śāntideva's *bodhicāryāvatāra* (Entrance to the Bodhisattva's Way), a key text for the Buddhist Lojong (*blo sbyong*, mind training) tradition. In it, the author provides a panoply of cognitive reframing strategies to help practitioners overcome anger and ignorance and cultivate *bzod pa*. In one famous example, he asks: if we do not get angry at the stick that hits us, but rather at the person who compels the stick, why do we get angry at the person who hits us and not at the anger that compels him or her to hit us (Gyatso 1997)? The intention is to focus our blame on ignorance and the destructive emotions it results in, rather than on individual people who are the victims of their own ignorance.

Just as the body can 'remember' a physical wound long after it occurs, moral injury seems to be retained when we cannot let go of the memory of a psychological wound, a common characteristic of trauma (van der Kolk 1994). Memory is therefore a central aspect of moral injury, and secularized practices derived from contemplative traditions that engage and deal with memories may be very effective in helping people with moral injury. As C. said beautifully in one of her journal entries during her practice of Naikan, "I truly do believe that gratitude is the moral memory of mankind."

Our incarcerated fellow practitioners taught us a great deal on moral injury and its relationship to contemplative practice. Some, having learned various practices in classes with us, went on to offer classes for others in their dorms. One such student-turned-instructor wrote of the Buddhist concept of 'refuge,' itself a concept closely connected to the idea of sacred space. Just as one seeks physical refuge in a shelter in the case of a storm, or refuge in a place of safety when fleeing a place of danger, the Buddhist concept of refuge pertains to seeking true safety and protection from that which afflicts us. This safety is not to be found in a physical space, but in the Buddhas (those who have transcended sorrow and can therefore show the way to happiness), the Dharma (reality as it is, not as we ignorantly perceive it, and our own wisdom of that reality), and the Sangha (the community of practitioners). Of these, the ultimate refuge is considered to be the Dharma: reality itself, and our understanding of it.

One such student-turned-instructor wrote:

> When we reach the ability to withstand pain or seemingly bad situations with a mind that is still positive and unwavering, this is refuge – refuge within ourselves and our ability to endure and overcome. I take refuge in my own wisdom. I know that without a doubt, I have the innate potential to be happy and free from suffering in any circumstance.

This remarkable statement parallels very closely with the quote on self-compassion above, and also with the idea of cultivating *bzod pa*, the ability to withstand suffering. It seems to be a mental attitude that is the very opposite of moral injury; it is the hope and conviction that one can overcome one's present situation and future situations of difficulty and emerge with happiness. That type of moral courage would appear to be an essential ingredient in moral repair.

7 Trauma and Cultural Resilience

We have been looking at moral injury on an individual level, and there is little doubt that resilience to trauma can be cultivated at the individual level by teaching individuals not only contemplative practices but also skills of body awareness and regulation of the nervous system (Grabbe and Miller-Karas 2018; Miller-Karas 2015). But one of the characteristics of moral injury in the context of war veterans, the incarcerated, refugees, and others is the larger scale involved. Moral injury is not just about an individual being traumatized and suffering a threat to his or her moral conscience; it is about systems that enable and perpetuate such infractions. If, then, we are to look from the other perspective and ask about moral repair and resilience, are we able to also identify systemic forms of resilience? These would be institutional, cultural, or social forms of resilience that would protect against moral injury and that would facilitate healing and moral repair.

As many have recognized, it is not enough to ask individuals to be resilient as long as they live within systems that continue to be oppressive. It is therefore important that we study not just structures of oppression on a systems level, but also look at the way institutional, social, and cultural structures support and foster resilience. We call 'structural resilience' the manner in which social structures, such as laws, policies, and institutions, support resilience, whereas we call 'cultural resilience' the beliefs, practices, and values that underpin those structures.

It is possible that the Tibetan refugee population in India and Nepal provides one such example of cultural resilience. This is a population that was forced into exile following the Chinese takeover of Tibet, an occupation that involved brutal murder, rape, imprisonment, and the destruction of most of Tibet's one thousand monasteries. Some estimate that about twenty per cent of Tibet's population – or about one million Tibetans – lost their lives because of the violence that took place during this time. Despite taking an overall conciliatory attitude towards China in the hope of reaching a peaceful settlement to the Tibet issue, even the Dalai Lama has called China's occupation of Tibet a 'cultural genocide.' In addition, those who have left for India and come to the refugee settlements had to undergo very long and dangerous journeys across the Himalayas, leaving almost everything behind.

It is important to recognize that for refugee communities like the Tibetans, one of the main losses experienced is the loss of access to sacred spaces. For Tibetans, Tibet is not only the location of the most important sacred spaces of their religious tradition – monasteries, holy lakes and caves, holy mountains, sacred statues of the Buddha, the Potala palace (the traditional home of the Dalai Lamas), and a countless array of local habitats of spirits and protective deities – but Tibet itself was and is considered a sacred space as a whole by Tibetans. Prison and exile share much in common, and even have a related history as forms of punishment. Here again, therefore, we encounter the need to create a different kind of symbolic sacred space for the purpose of practice for those to whom traditional access has been barred.

Despite their losses, Tibetan refugees as a group appear to have exhibited remarkable resilience. Numerous researchers have concluded that Tibetan refugees, who are almost all Buddhist, are less prone to PTSD symptoms than other refugee survivors of torture, even given comparable traumatic experiences (Crescenzi et al. 2002; Holtz 1998; Keller et al. 2006; Terheggen et al. 2001). Based on a study with Tibetan refugees in Dharamsala, Sachs et al. write:

In light of the hardships reported by study participants, the low levels of psychological distress are particularly striking. Average symptom severity ratings typically fell between *not at all* and *a little* on standardized measures, with only 10% (n = 77) of the sample demonstrating clinically significant depression or anxiety. Among torture survivors, anxiety and depression were more common, but still occurred in only 12% (for anxiety) and 9.6% (for depression) of this subgroup. Perhaps most surprisingly, only one study participant (0.1%) had clinically significant PTSD symptoms. In short, this study suggests an unusual degree of resilience among Tibetan refugees, even those who had survived torture (Sachs et al. 2008).

Are Tibetans simply more resilient on an individual level? This is possible but unlikely. Tibetan refugees have managed to set up new spaces that can serve to support their resilience, including institutional structures and an exile society that includes political representation. But just as importantly, they have managed to bring with them into exile powerful forms of cultural resilience. Together, these structural and cultural forms of resilience have allowed them to establish a new kind of sacred space – certainly not the same as that which they had in Tibet, but one that seems to exhibit powerful benefits, nonetheless.

Sara Lewis is an anthropologist who has engaged in lengthy ethnographic research on the Tibetan refugee population in Dharamsala, India. According to Lewis, the resilience exhibited by Tibetans is not merely a product of their culture and religion in general, but the specific use of cultural coping mechanisms drawn from the Lojong tradition that serve to make their minds more "spacious" and "flexible" (Lewis 2013). These take place largely in the form of cultural idioms, rather than active engagement in practices such as formal meditation. Yet they involve a cognitive reorientation familiar in Lojong practices and Naikan practice to achieve a different perspective on the past and to let go of, or not dwell on, anger, resentment, and hurt. Lewis's ethnographic work is supported by a study of 855 Tibetan refugees in Dharamsala by Sachs et al. (2008), which found that it was coping activity that appeared to mediate the effect of trauma exposure on PTSD symptoms.

Moreover, many of the qualities Lewis describes in refugee Tibetans align closely to the idea of *bzod pa* or *hilm* (forbearance, acceptance, resilience). For example, Tibetan refugees reflect on the pervasiveness and inevitability of suffering and on existential facts such as impermanence – practices that would lead to the cultivation of an attitude of acceptance and resilience to suffering, i.e., *bzod pa*. They also reflect that the travails of this life may be transformed to a higher purpose. Three lines from the popular Lojong text "Seven Point Mind Training" read:

> When the world is filled with wrongdoing, transform all misfortunes into the path of enlightenment. Banish all blame to the single source, and towards all beings, contemplate their great kindness (Jinpa 2014).

Though brief, these lines encapsulate a range of powerful cultural beliefs that may bolster resilience among Tibetans and Buddhists: there are times when the world will be filled with suffering and wrongdoing, but misfortunes can be turned into vehicles for spiritual growth. Other human beings are not the appropriate object of blame, and when one sees this, and instead focuses blame on its true source (ignorance, in the case of Buddhism), then others appear in a different light and one can appreciate the true kindness of humanity, which has a liberating effect.

8 Conclusion

Much attention has been given to individual practices such as prayer, meditation, yoga, mindfulness, and so on. Less attention has been paid to the way such practices depend upon the establishment of a conducive space – not just a physical space, but also a symbolic space of safety, support, and nurturance. Specific practices, such as Naikan, intentionally aim to create this sacred space. C. managed to create this experience even while incarcerated, a remarkable achievement, and now that she has been released, her wish is to establish a Naikan center that can offer a space for practice to others.

As we have seen, in the case of Keyword and refugees, traditional sacred spaces are sadly inaccessible, necessitating the creation of new kinds of sacred space. The utility of such spaces, even when non-traditionally constructed, suggests to us that resilience should not be conceived of as solely the attribute of individuals. Sacred symbolic space that is conducive to resilience and spiritual growth is also created culturally through the beliefs, practices, norms, perspectives, and attitudes of multiple people. No doubt, we do see examples of incredible individual resilience in the face of structures and cultures of oppression. That does not change the fact, we would argue, that resilience is best cultivated individually, structurally, and culturally.

This may require a slight shift in perspective. It is often easier to recognize the ways in which structures – institutional and cultural – facilitate oppression and violence; but if we recognize this aspect of the importance of structures and systems, we must also recognize that the same structures and systems can foster resilience. If, instead of tolerating and perpetuating moral injury, systems are redesigned to facilitate moral repair and an intolerance for moral injury, such changes in both policy and climate can help individuals be less subject to harm and more able to recover from harm when it does happen. Work that aims to transform the lives of individuals and communities may be most effective if it seeks to introduce practices of resilience while at the same time reshaping institutions, environments, and cultures so that they best facilitate resilience on a structural and cultural level – be this in prisons, schools, hospitals, or other areas of life.

Bibliography

Crescenzi, Antonella, Eva Ketzer, Mark van Ommeren, Kalsang Phuntsok, Ivan Komproe, and Joop T. V. M. de Jong. 2002. "Effect of Political Imprisonment and Trauma History on Recent Tibetan Refugees in India." *Journal of Traumatic Stress:* 15:369–375.

Gyatso, Tenzin (Dalai Lama). 1997. *Healing Anger: The Power of Patience from a Buddhist Perspective*, trans. Geshe Thupten Jinpa. New York: Snow Lion.

Farnsworth, Jacob K., Kent D. Drescher, Jason A. Nieuwsma, Robyn B. Walser, and Joseph M. Currier. 2014. "The Role of Moral Emotions in Military Trauma: Implications for the Study and Treatment of Moral Injury." *Review of General Psychology* 18:249.

Grabbe, Linda, and Elaine Miller-Karas. 2018. "The Trauma Resiliency Model: A 'Bottom-up' Intervention for Trauma Psychotherapy." *Journal of the American Psychiatric Nurses Association* 24:76–84.

Holtz, Timothy H. 1998. "Refugee Trauma Versus Torture Trauma: A Retrospective Controlled Cohort Study of Tibetan Refugees." *The Journal of Nervous and Mental Disease* 186:24–34.

Izutsu, Toshihiko. 2002. *Ethico-religious Concepts in the Qur'an*. Vol. 1. Montreal: McGill-Queen's University Press.

Jinpa, Thupten, ed. 2014. *Mind Training: The Great Collection*. Vol. 1. Toronto: Simon and Schuster.

Keller, Allen, Dechen Lhewa, Barry Rosenfeld, Emily Sachs, Asher Aladjem, Ilene Cohen, Hawthorne Smith, and Katherine Porterfield. 2006. "Traumatic Experiences and Psychological Distress in an Urban Refugee Population Seeking Treatment Services." *The Journal of Nervous and Mental Disease* 194:188–194.

Kolk, Bessel A. van der. 1994. "The Body Keeps the Score: Memory and the Evolving Psychobiology of Posttraumatic Stress." *Harvard Review of Psychiatry* 1:253–265.

Krech, Gregg. 2001. *Naikan: Gratitude, Grace, and the Japanese Art of Self-reflection*. Berkeley: Stone Bridge Press.

Lewis, Sara E. 2013. "Trauma and the Making of Flexible Minds in the Tibetan Exile Community." *Ethos* 41:313–336.

Miller-Karas, Elaine. 2015. *Building Resilience to Trauma: The Trauma and Community Resiliency Models*. Abingdon: Routledge.

Ozawa-de Silva, Brendan. 2016. "Contemplative Science and Secular Ethics." *Religions* 7: 98.

Ozawa-de Silva, Chikako. 2006. *Psychotherapy and Religion in Japan: The Japanese Introspection Practice of Naikan*. Abingdon: Routledge.

Reiss, Wolfram, and Ulrike Bechmann, eds. 2016. *Selbstbetrachtung hinter Gittern: Naikan im Strafvollzug in Deutschland und Österreich*. Marburg: Tectum Wissenschaftsverlag.

Sachs, Emily, Barry Rosenfeld, Dechen Lhewa, Andrew Rasmussen, and Allen Keller. 2008. "Entering Exile: Trauma, Mental Health, and Coping Among Tibetan Refugees Arriving in Dharamsala, India." *Journal of Traumatic Stress:* 21:199–208.

Shapiro, Shauna L., Linda E. Carlson, John A. Astin, and Benedict Freedman. 2006. "Mechanisms of Mindfulness." *Journal of Clinical Psychology* 62:373–386.

Shay, Jonathan. 2014. "Moral Injury." *Psychoanalytic Psychology* 31:182.

Terheggen, Maaike A., Margaret S. Stroebe, and Rolf J. Kleber. 2001. "Western Conceptualizations and Eastern Experience: A Cross-cultural Study of Traumatic Stress Reactions among Tibetan Refugees in India." *Journal of Traumatic Stress* 14:391–403.

Katharina Krause
Conversion / Change / Transformation of Lifestyle

1 Introduction

"You must change your life!" (Rilke 1995). The inner voice rousing young Rilke while contemplating one of Rodin's sculptures is also meant to address the poem's reader, testing her readiness to move forward and make a new start. In traditional Protestant milieus such an openness to fundamental change would be framed in terms of Christian doctrine and addressed as the need to be born again. In postmodern spirituality, on the other hand, manifestations of this state of mind and heart seem to be the religious seeker or shopper. In recent decades, transitions within and between religious traditions, denominational contexts or spiritual milieus have drawn much interest in the scientific study of religion. Today, various academic disciplines join in the attempt to describe and interpret these different versions of conversion. Section 2 briefly depicts the branches into which this research has spread over time. In section 3 I introduce my own approach of reflecting on conversion. Here, my academic and cultural background becomes especially apparent. The case study in section 4 focuses on conversion in the sense of a (re-)vitalization of piety, which, in certain traditional Protestant milieus, is still experienced, practiced, and discussed as giving one's life to Jesus. Section 5, finally, discusses new research perspectives for Practical Theology and Religious Studies in the field of conversion.

2 Versions of Conversion

When the scientific study of religion was established at American universities at the turn of the nineteenth century, conversion was among its first subjects. Early American Psychology attempted to explain what was going on during the revivals of the so called Second and Third Great Awakening (Wulff 2002 and Zock 2006). Aiming to reach beyond Christian teaching, scholars had to develop new scientific methodology. Data was first obtained in the form of diaries, spiritual autobiographies, and letters. Leuba and Starbuck were the first to use standard questionnaires, which were based on an evaluation of conversion narratives (Leuba 1896 and Starbuck 1897). These conversion narratives, for their part, followed patterns common in evangelical and revivalist contexts. Conversion was modeled according to the *ordo salutis* in its reformed tradition. Consequently, the topos of a personal crisis being solved at the climax of the transformative event trickled down into scientific theory. An example for this is William James' well-known definition of conversion (James 1991, 157):

> To be converted, to be regenerated, to receive grace, to experience religion, to gain an assurance, are so many phrases which denote the process, gradual or sudden, by which a self hitherto divided, and consciously wrong inferior and unhappy, becomes unified and consciously right superior and happy, in consequence of its firmer hold upon religious realities.

James thought conversions to be a process, over the course of which personal priorities were rearranged. Yet, there were also other types of conversion, which, according to his informants, were experienced as highly disruptive and emotionally overwhelming. James explained these seemingly sudden conversions in terms of parapsychology. From this point of view, they could be equally understood as unfolding gradually over time. However, they did so subliminally and remained unnoticed until the point at which the converts themselves became aware.

Following Leuba, Starbuck and James, the paradigm of crisis and solution became a standard explanation for conversion which eventually led to pathologizing. Following Freud (1948), research in the tradition of psychoanalysis often was reductionist in its thinking that conversions were a rather unsuccessful attempt to repress personal conflicts. Another strand of psychological research tried to understand to what extent insecure attachment patterns influenced the convert's readiness to break former ties (Ullman 1989).

During the second half of the twentieth century, Psychology's interest in conversion began to dwindle. At about the same time, Sociology of Religion began to investigate conversion (Bruce 2006). The topic was brought to the attention during a public debate on "New Religious Movements" which had appeared on the scene in the 1960s. Suspected of brainwashing, these movements were heavily attacked by so called Anti-Cultists (Bromley 1983), accusing them of subjecting converts to great emotional stress in order to make them ripe for emotional and financial exploitation. In contrast to this conception by the Anti-Cultists, sociologists painted a different picture: that of a convert actively engaging in the religious groups' (re-)socializing influences (Wilson 1978 and Bromley and Shupe 1979). Far from being a victim of unorthodox discipling methods, these converts were seen to simply be perusing their options. Taking on the identity of a religious seeker and experimenting with different worldviews and lifestyles on the spiritual marketplace, they were seeking new ties, which might foster their personal development and help them grow beyond themselves. According to Rodney Stark and Roger Finke, this exploratory testing had its own method: converts who wanted to maximize their social, emotional, and religious capital, had to rationally balance their own interests with those of the group (Stark and Finke 2000).

Leaving undecided whether rational-choice explanations reach to the very foundation of religious practices, researchers were confronted with the fact that a path, once chosen, seemed to be far from irreversible for the convert. In this experimental climate, Peter L. Berger coined the phrase of the heretical imperative (Berger 1979). James T. Richardson, in contrast, suggested giving up the notion of conversion as a one-time experience and proposed focusing on conversion careers (Richardson 1980) instead. In his view, it was about time to announce a change of paradigm. For the old conception of a convert seized by sudden and overwhelming emotions had now been replaced by converts actively engaging in spiritual identity management.

However, also the figure of the flaneur on the religious scene turned out to be highly dependent on the ideology of religious groups or, more irritating still, of the research's design. In a meta-study, which studied the motivations and expectations attributed to converts, John Lofland and Norman Skonovd were able to show that the experimental convert was merely one out of seven different types. Alongside these active conversions were those described as either passive, intellectual, mystical, affective, coerced or revivalist (Lofland and Skonovd 1981).

In view of never-ending typologies of converts it seemed advisable to look for approaches which considered the religious group's expectations in tandem with the convert's motivations and reflect upon the correlation between these factors. Research drawing on ethnomethodology and social constructivism allowed light to be shed into a group's universe of discourse, such that conversions from and to religious milieus could finally start to be understood in terms of the group's own logics. Consequently, studies focused on conversion narratives, assuming that converts presenting themselves as members of a group were generally expected to relate experiences consistent with the group's ideology of transformation. Based on an analysis of various conversion narratives, David Snow and Richard Machalek (Snow and Machalek 1983) were able to show that participants carefully studied the group's rhetoric and opinions on the decisive transformative event, thereby gradually learning how to convincingly tell their own stories in-line with the group's language. Drawing on (Luckmann 1986), Volkhard Krech (Krech 1998) identified different narrative patterns for different religious groups, which worked like a frame whereby rather obscure feelings could be made sense of, interpreted, and finally articulated.

However, telling one's story does not imply that the narrated event has already taken place. According to Peter Stromberg (Stromberg 1993), the event of accounting for one's conversion could also be a way of making it occur. Emotions can be evoked at the very moment they are vocalized. In Stromberg's study, conversion narratives had the dual function of representation and enaction.

These and similar studies in the line of social constructionism opened doors to a change in perspective. Contrary to established opinion, the essence of conversion was no longer sought in highly individualistic and therefore inexpressible personal feelings. Rather, conversion was viewed as being culturally situated and socially shaped – the result of a group's endeavor to make meaning. This was even true for the personal crisis and its solution for it turned out to be told of only in such milieus, where conversion meant deliverance from corruption and sin and was assumed to be the only remedy of the convert's problems. Brought about, or at least supported by language, conversions were now seen as highly group-specific discourse. The ritualistic dimensions of telling one's story did not go unnoticed; nevertheless, they remained unexplored until brought to the attention by the ethnosciences. In the last three decades, one strand of the debate specialized in conversions taking place in the sequel of macro-cultural transformation (Gooren 2014). Studies on the microlevel focused on the extralinguistic realities of conversion – the ritual, bodily and artefactual dimensions of conversion gradually came into view, opening new ways of understanding conversion as culturally inflected experience and practice (Glazier 2003; Sachs and Norris 2003; Jaggi 2012).

3 Conversion as a Social Practice

As a member of a Protestant mainline church in Germany, I talked frequently with people of the same institution, who considered it important to state at some point in our conversation, that they had been born again or had given their life to Jesus. Their emphasis made it clear that what was spoken about in metaphorical terms was indeed essential to the person's identity. To me it seemed that having given one's life to Jesus or having been born again was akin to a key to a symbolic universe of its own – open for those who were willing to enter on its terms, while being firmly locked for 'the rest of the world' which, from this point of view, seemed to be on the outside and often described as being different, if not sinful. To find out more about what made people think that way, I set out to explore what I call conversionist piety. Whilst doing so, I have come to develop an approach, which might be called Conversion as a Social Practice (Krause 2018). In this framework, questions in the vein of the following could be posed:

- What exactly do people mean when they state that they are born again or have given their life to Jesus? What self-understandings are associated with these claims?
- What do people feel, or are meant to feel, when they are born again? Which experiences are accounted for, and what are the possible ways of cultivating them?
- Are there any practices which support the experience and self-concept of being born again? What are people who have given their life to Jesus expected to do?
- Does their behavior have any implications on how they treat their body? And if there is something like a 'converted body', what does it look like? Are there any artefacts involved in the process of its formation?

Conversion, as can be easily seen, is conceptualized as something multidimensional. Consequently, narratives, experiences, bodies, and artefacts are equally considered, for all of them carry and produce meaning. Whilst previous research on conversion generally focused on either of the above-mentioned aspects, the following case study holds the assumption that in conversionist contexts – as in every-day life and practice – discourse, emotion, body, and artefact are inextricably enmeshed; interwoven in a network of socially constructed meaning. Among the born-again, discourse, emotions, bodies and artefacts may take different shapes, yet they still interact reciprocally, whilst constituting what might be called the conversionist reality of 'pious universes'.

Conversion as a Social Practice draws on concepts from the sociology of knowledge, practice theory and the ethnohistory of emotions. Integrated in a cultural-sociological framework, these theoretical perspectives provide the Practical Theologian with useful tools to describe and interpret religious cultures – in this case, more specifically, conversionist cultures of discourse, emotion, and body.

With this theoretical background on the one hand, and data from my sample on the other, 'giving one's life to Jesus' or 'being born again' could be conceptualized as a process of entering into a symbolic universe. In other words, members of the conversionist milieus in my sample generate, share and pass on meaning – a knowledge in the widest sense of the word, which supports their views and ways of life. This knowledge consists of doings, sayings, and feelings. It is therefore analyzed with the help of a threefold concept, differentiating conceptual knowledge, emotional knowledge, and body knowledge. For the sake of analytical clarity, the three are described one after the other. It is important, however, to note that in the process of (conversionist) meaning-making, doings, sayings, and feelings are indissolubly enmeshed.

- *Conceptual knowledge* is *knowing about* group-specific beliefs, norms, and values, which are normally made explicit only in teaching contexts. In ordinary life, conceptual knowledge is embedded in everyday speech, in stories, proverbs or jokes. Because conceptual knowledge is essentially discourse, it can be subjected to debate.
- *Emotional knowledge* is *knowing about* and *knowing by.* What is known about are emotional repertoires – conventions and cultural agreements about how particular feelings are generated, regulated, expressed, and named. In conversionist contexts *emotional knowledge about* can be both knowledge about the experiences crucial in the event of 'being born again', and the practices of stirring them up. In contrast, *knowing by emotions* is best described as awareness. It is gained whilst engaging in emotionalizing practices. *Knowledge about*, which has transformed into *knowing by*, is highly persuasive, for it bears the evidence of personal experience, which is very difficult to call into question.
- *Body knowledge* is *knowing about* norms and techniques of the body. In conversionist milieus there are a lot of dos and don'ts, which regulate the regenerate's conduct and ways of bearing. *Knowledge about* the body merges into the body's *knowing how* as soon as these norms are transformed into routine and become visible in the body's habitus and performance. More accurately a skill than a knowledge, *knowing how* is a pre-conscious kind of knowledge is. It can therefore be called implicit or embodied knowledge. Self-evident in its nature and tacitly working within the body and out of it, it is difficult to put in words. In situations of conflict, it might even be beyond debate. For conversionist knowledge once turned into flesh and blood has become a fact speaking for itself. The same is true when it imprints itself into artefacts. Transformed into the body's materiality it enables a person to an intuitive way of being in and being aware of the world, which could be referred to as a *knowing by* the body.

Considering this, entering the symbolic universes of pious milieus does not only require picking up relevant knowledge by listening to the talk of the people. It also involves absorbing the group's views and ways of life through engaging in group-specific practices. Simultaneously they learn, how to bring conversionist realities about. Acquisition of conversionist knowledge therefore cannot be reduced to its cognitive nor to its emotional or bodily dimension, but rather is an interplay between all three dimensions.

4 Giving One's Life to Jesus. A Case Study in Humility

Objections against conversionist milieus and their believes and practices are frequently voiced, both in academic theology and in the context of the church.[1] Cultural distance proves to be helpful when trying to look upon a subject of research in a manner, that is non-judgmental from the outset. Other than that, it sharpens the eye to the unexpected. For this reason, the case study chosen here is a historical one. It draws on a rich archive of sources of various types going back to the colonies of British New England between the 1660s and the 1750s and allows for an exploration of the ways in which 'pious universes' are formed and developed over the course of three generations in different social contexts. And it sheds light on how the beliefs and practices brought to the New World by Puritan settlers were transformed into what would later be called Early Evangelicalism.

It was the wish to reform the church by reforming the people, which made the first settlers join hands and set up holy commonwealths on the shores of North America. To understand what reform meant and what giving one's life to Jesus had to do with it, it was deemed necessary to understand and, more importantly, to learn, humility, which seemed to be everything at once: a virtue, a value, an emotion, and an outward bearing and demeanor. It is therefore fitting to focus on humility in the following when describing believes and practices of New English pious milieus.

The conceptual knowledge of New English cultures of piety can be traced through various representations of the order of salvation. These are explained in theological treatises and sermons, catechisms, and manuals of devotion, but they have also found their way into spiritual (auto-)biographies and fiction. Variable in details, these versions of the *ordo salutis* are generally based on the doctrine of law and gospel. Accordingly, conversion is depicted as a turn from darkness into light. Within this framework, different emotions are arranged like the links of a

---

[1] Usually, the anti-intellectual impetus of conversionist beliefs and practices is criticized. Apart from that, missionary activities are thought to undo, what ecumenical and interreligious dialogue has achieved.

chain.[2] They are told of in conversion narratives,[3] which are usually modeled according to the following pattern: At first, the convert-to-be is depicted as an unrepentant sinner. Various evil deeds are named to prove his moral depravity. Then, a call to repent is received, which is generally ignored for some time. At some point, however, the message trickles down, triggering contrition and remorse. In this state, named humiliation, the convert pictures himself in danger of eternal damnation. Filled with terror he enters a struggle with his Maker, which ultimately involves subjecting himself to God's sovereign will. His heart is overpowered by the strong desire to receive Jesus as his savior and to entrust his life unto him. After an often long and distressing period, this is experienced as the decisive turn – humiliation is transformed into faith which is often described as coming from death to life or being born again. Unfortunately, this happy state is of short duration. Again, humility dampens the joy of salvation. This time, however, it is experienced differently. Whereas previously he was forced to act by terror and fright, the convert now for the first time thoroughly regrets his transgressions. But true repentance is soon overshadowed by scruples and doubt or, even worse, backsliding into sin. Converts are therefore expected to talk about the measures they have taken to secure their faith and to lead a sanctified life. Narratives generally end with modest statements of their success – humble declarations of humble people who have come to realize that assurance can never truly be achieved as long as they live.

Obviously, humility is addressed twice: once before uniting with Jesus and once afterwards. While at first it is very much an experience of being crushed into submission to God's will, humility after the turn is meant to be experienced as a pleasant sensation: a melting of the heart in the sight of God's love. Opening the convert's eyes to his former hardness of heart, this time, humility triggers genuine regret. Humility, as a result, is experienced as a mixed feeling, offering the convert both, sadness, and comfort.

Making mind and heart switch between darkness and light humility was highly valued and sought after. Pastors and laypeople dedicated to the salvation of souls aimed at cultivating humility through pious emotion management, involving spiritual disciplines which were also called humiliating exercises. Best known is probably the practice of hell-fire preaching. Through vivid descriptions of eternal torments preachers urged their flock to humble themselves and repent before all is lost. Congregations not yet inured against such practice and accustomed to reacting with call-and-response, translated the representations they received from the pulpit into bodily performances of mortification. Sinking to the ground, moaning, and wringing hands were common, as were tears, which were thought to be the water that rises

---

[2] A prominent example is Perkins (1595). For its reception in the New England context see Ball (1992).
[3] For examples see McGiffert (1994) and https://www.congregationallibrary.org/nehh/main (30.11.2021).

from a frozen heart that had begun to melt. Similarly, collapsing was viewed as a as bodily manifestation of dying to sin.

The impressions received in the meetinghouse were contemplated and expanded upon in the privacy of the closet or through devotional fellowship. Manuals on the art of meditation were printed and sold to the public at small cost[4] next to hymnbooks. In some places, singing schools were set up, teaching people how to engage emotionally and bodily with the feelings conjured up in hymns by Isaac Watts (Watts 1709) or Elizabeth Singer-Rowe's devotional poetry (Singer-Rowe 1737). These exercises were supplemented by techniques of the body supporting the impression that the spiritual issues ruminated upon were indeed present as tangible realities. In his spiritual autobiography, Nathan Cole describes inserting his finger into his pipe while pondering the torments of hell, hoping thereby to enter a state of humility, preparing him for receiving saving grace (Crawford 1976, 94).

Running the risk of being misused by the inexperienced or spiritually over-ambitious, humiliating exercises were not exempt from criticism. Authors of devotional literature therefore admonished their readers to practice with care else they might run the risk of going mad. Cases of spiritual melancholy were frequently reported.[5] In the face of this, opinions differed as to whether humiliating exercises were either dangerous, or whether they were simply indispensable to assist in being born again for they triggered the crucial emotions without which no saving conversion was expected to come to pass. Both, advocates, and critics were fully aware of the fact that these humiliating exercises were strongly persuasive. Engaged in skillful practice, people obtained, so to speak, intuitive access to the spiritual realities their minds and hearts were set upon: a knowledge gained through personal experience.

Yet, emotions are of a fleeting nature. It was therefore crucial to turn them into the hard facts of every-day life and practice. Expected to sanctify their lives, people who had given their life to Jesus embarked on a course of bodily transformation, which essentially consisted in making humility a habit. Eating and drinking, but also clothing and relaxing the body was done unto the Lord, turning the body into an instrument fit for his service.[6] Sanctification therefore implied not to make the body an end of itself but to carefully exert discipline and self-control in all matters of sensuality; modestly answering the body's basic needs, and vigilantly taming inappropriate appetites. An attitude of conscious self-regulation and restraint was desired, which could be described as mortification, self-denial, or humility.

In keeping with this ideal, lavish luxury and wasteful abundance were abhorred. Men and women who paraded costly clothing and fine ornaments were made to pay a penalty for making a show of pride (Shurtleff 1853, 126.183.274 f.) which, contrary to the humility and meekness of a lamb of God, exhibited discontent with one's calling

---

4 Widely read in New-England was for example Richard Baxter's *The Saints Everlasting Rest*.
5 Best known are probably the cases described in Jonathan Edwards' *Faithful Narrative*.
6 Particularly evident in Richard Baxter's *Christian Directory*, which was also very popular in New England.

and vocation. No less reprehensible were elaborate hairstyles and the use of cosmetics (Mather 1691). Wigs were fiercely attacked, not least for their time-consuming maintenance. Since time was a precious gift of the Lord, it was better dedicated to his service. For the same reason, Native American practices of community building by doing each other's hair were harshly criticized (Clark 2003, 97 f.115 f.).

Humility also had to inscribe itself into the body through nourishing. People were expected to consciously observe which quantities of food and drink supported their health, and modestly restrain themselves from consuming too much. The mindful attitude towards food, and the diligent handling of it could even be made a topic for introspection. An increasing willingness to submit to the 'duty of mortification' and exert self-discipline at the table was interpreted as a sign of growing in grace. The image of the reformed alcoholic-turned-sober, still prominent to this day, was a popular figure in missionary tracts (Brainerd 1746, 13 f.)

In the context of missions, English techniques of clothing and nourishing the body became sacrosanct. In the eyes of the missionaries, indigenous people were not only to be converted spiritually; they were to be changed in body and soul which included shaping the body according to standards of piety. For a converted body not only displayed humility; it was also thought to be a vehicle for triggering humble feelings and attitudes because "holiness in visible realities is apt to affect the World more deeply, than in Portraiture or Precept only." (Baxter 1677, 2 f.). Made material in bodies and artefacts, conversionist values, attitudes and emotions thus gained the evidence of tangible realities. Pious care of the body became looked upon as a means of grace comparable to other spiritual exercises such as praying, contemplating the scriptures, or listening to sermons.

5 Reaching Beyond

In some Protestant contexts giving one's life to Jesus or being born again is placed at the center of Christian identity. The historical case study presented here suggests that this event is connected to unique cultures of discourse, emotions, and the body. Of course, the beliefs and practices of protestant conversionist milieus today have changed significantly. However, there seems to be a certain likeness to modern Evangelical and Pentecostal spirituality, which suggests that we are dealing here with an interesting and multifaceted cultural pattern, still inspiring Christian communities, and churches worldwide. It would be interesting to trace these different versions of conversionist piety in synchrony and diachrony – and maybe even in parody.[7] The three-dimensional model of knowledge presented in this article might stimulate further empirical research. This in turn would help Practical Theology to find suita-

---

[7] See for example https://local.theonion.com/christ-reluctantly-enters-area-man-s-heart-1819575568 (30.11.2017).

ble criteria for the assessment of conversionist believes and practices and encourage church professionals to exert spiritual leadership sensibly and responsibly.

Bibliography

Ball, John H. 1992. *Chronicling the Soul's Windings: Thomas Hooker and his Morphology of Conversion*. Lanham: University Press of America.
Baxter, Richard, ed. 1677. *The Life and Death of that Excellent Minister of Christ Mr. Joseph Alleine, Late Teacher of the Church of Taunton in Somersetshire, Assistant to Mr. Newton*. London: no publisher.
Berger, Peter L. 1979. *The Heretical Imperative: Contemporary Possibilities of Religious Affirmation*. Garden City: Anchor Press.
Brainerd, David. 1746. *Mirabilia Dei inter Indicos: Or the Rise and Progress of a Remarkable Work of Grace amongst a Number of the Indians in the Provinces of New-Jersey and Pennsylvania, Justly Represented in a Journal Kept by Order of the Honorable Society (in Scotland) for Propagating Christian Knowledge. With Some General Remarks*. Philadelphia: no publisher.
Bromley, David G., ed. 1983. *The Brainwashing / Deprogramming Controversy: Sociological, Psychological, Legal and Historical Perspectives*. Studies in Religion and Society 5. New York / Toronto: Mellen.
Bromley, David G., and Anson D. Shupe. 1979. "Just a Few Years Seem Like a Lifetime: A Role Theory Approach to Participation in Religious Movements." *Research in Social Movements, Conflicts and Change* 2:159–185.
Bruce, Steve. 2006. "Sociology of Conversion: The Last Twenty-Five Years." In *Paradigms, Poetics and Politics of Conversion*. Groningen Studies in Cultural Change 19, edited by Jan N. Bremmer, Wout J. van Bekkum, and Arie L. Molendijk, Leuven, Dudley: Peeters, 1–11.
Clark, Michael P., ed. 2003. *The Eliot Tracts: With Letters from John Eliot to Thomas Thorowgood and Richard Baxter*. Contributions in American History 199. Westport: Praeger Publishers.
Crawford, Michael J. 1976. "The Spiritual Travels of Nathan Cole." *The William and Mary Quarterly* 33:89–126.
Freud, Sigmund. 1948. "Ein religiöses Erlebnis." In *Werke aus den Jahren 1925–1931*. Vol. 14, *Gesammelte Werke*, edited by Anna Freud, Frankfurt am Main: S. Fischer, 393–396.
Glazier, Stephen D. 2003. "Limin' wid Jah: Spiritual Baptists Who Become Rastafarians and Then Become Spiritual Baptists Again." In *The Anthropology of Religious Conversion*, edited by Andrew Buckser and Stephen D. Glazier, Lanham: Rowman & Littlefield Publishers, 149–170.
Gooren, Henri. 2014. "Anthropology of Religious Conversion." In *The Oxford Handbook of Religious Conversion*, edited by Lewis R. Rambo and Charles E. Farhadian, Oxford / New York: Oxford University Press, 84–116.
Jaggi, Sabine. 2012. "Konversion von Tamilinnen und Tamilen in der Schweiz zum Christentum: Einblicke in sich verändernde Beziehungen." In *Religiöse Grenzüberschreitungen: Studien zu Bekehrung, Konfessions- und Religionswechsel*. Studien zur außereuropäischen Christentumsgeschichte (Asien, Afrika, Lateinamerika) 20, edited by Christine Lienemann-Perrin and Wolfgang Lienemann, Wiesbaden: Harrassowitz, 89–114.
James, William. 1991. *The Varieties of Religious Experience: A Triumph Classic*. New York: Triumph Books.
Krause, Katharina. 2018. *Bekehrungsfrömmigkeit: Historische und kultursoziologische Perspektiven auf eine Gestalt gelebter Religion*. Praktische Theologie in Geschichte und Gegenwart 23. Tübingen: Mohr Siebeck.

Krech, Volkhard. 1998. "Religiöse Erfahrung – was oder wie?: Zur soziologischen Rekonzeptualisierung eines religionswissenschaftlichen Begriffs anhand der Analyse von Konversionsberichten." In *Religion als Kommunikation*. Religion in der Gesellschaft 4, edited by Hartmann Tyrell, Volkhard Krech, and Hubert Knoblauch, Würzburg: Ergon Verlag, 473–503.

Leuba, James H. 1896. "A Study in the Psychology of Religious Phenomena." *American Journal of Psychology* 7:309–385.

Lofland, John, and Norman Skonovd. 1981. "Conversion Motifs." *Journal for the Scientific Study of Religion* 20:373–385.

Luckmann, Thomas. 1986. "Grundformen der gesellschaftlichen Vermittlung des Wissens: Kommunikative Gattungen." In *Kultur und Gesellschaft: René König, dem Begründer der Sonderhefte, zum 80. Geburtstag gewidmet*. Kölner Zeitschrift für Soziologie und Sozialpsychologie. Sonderhefte 27, edited by Friedhelm Neidhardt, M. R. Lepsius, and Johannes Weiss, Opladen: Westdeutscher Verlag, 191–211.

Mather, Cotton. 1691. *Ornaments for the Daughters of Zion: Or, the Character and Happiness of a Vertuous Woman. In a Discourse Which Directs the Female Sex How to Express the Fear of God in Every Age and State of their Life and Obtain Both Temporal and Eternal Blessedness*. Boston: no publisher.

McGiffert, Michael, ed. 1994. *God's Plot: Puritan Spirituality in Thomas Shepard's Cambridge*. Amherst: University of Massachusetts Press.

Perkins, William. 1595. *A Golden Chaine, or, the Description of Theologie*. London: no publisher.

Richardson, James T. 1980. "Conversion Careers." *Society* 17:47–50.

Rilke, Rainer Maria. 1995. "Archaic Torso of Apollo." In *Ahead of All Parting: The Selected Poetry and Prose of Rainer Maria Rilke*, edited and trans. Stephen Mitchell, New York: The Modern Library, 67.

Sachs Norris, Rebecca. 2003. "Converting to What? Embodied Culture and the Adoption of New Beliefs." In *The Anthropology of Religious Conversion*, edited by Andrew Buckser and Stephen D. Glazier, Lanham: Rowman & Littlefield Publishers, 171–181.

Shurtleff, Nathaniel B., ed. 1853. *Records of the Governor and Company of the Massachusetts Bay*. Volume 1, 1628–1641. Boston: William White.

Singer-Rowe, Elizabeth. 1737. *Devout Exercises of the Heart in Meditation and Soliloqui, Prayer and Praise*. London: no publisher.

Snow, David A., and Richard Machalek. 1983. "The Convert as a Social Type." *Sociological Theory* 1:259–289.

Starbuck, Edwin D. 1897. "A Study of Conversion." *American Journal of Psychology* 8:268–308.

Stark, Rodney, and Roger Finke. 2000. *Acts of Faith: Explaining the Human Side of Religion*. Berkeley: University of California Press.

Stromberg, Peter G. 1993. *Language and Self-Transformation: A Study of the Christian Conversion Narrative*. Publications of the Society for Psychological Anthropology 5. Cambridge / New York: Cambridge University Press.

Ullman, Chana. 1989. *The Transformed Self: The Psychology of Religious Conversion: Emotions, Personality, and Psychotherapy*. New York: Plenum Press.

Watts, Isaac. 1709. *Hymns, and Spiritual Songs, in Three Books, I. Collected from the Scriptures, II. Composed on Divine Subjects, III. Prepared for the Lord's Supper*. London: no publisher.

Wilson, Bryan R. 1978. "Becoming a Sectarian: Motivation and Commitment." In *Religious Motivation: Biographical and Sociological Problems for the Church Historian. Papers Read at the Sixteenth Summer Meeting and the Seventeenth Winter Meeting of the Ecclesiastical History Society*. Studies in Church History 15, edited by Derek Baker, Oxford: Blackwell, 481–506.

Wulff, David M. 2002. "A Century of Conversion in American Psychology of Religion." In *Konversion: Zur Aktualität Eines Jahrhundertthemas*, Einblicke: Beiträge zur Religionspsychologie 4, edited by Christian Henning, Erich Nestler, and Walter Sparn, Frankfurt am Main, New York: Peter Lang, 43–73.

Zock, Hetty. 2006. "Paradigms in Psychological Conversion Research: Between Social Science and Literary Analysis." In *Paradigms, Poetics and Politics of Conversion*. Groningen Studies in Cultural Change 19, edited by Jan N. Bremmer, Wout J. van Bekkum, and Arie L. Molendijk, Leuven, Dudley: Peeters, 41–58.

Trygve Wyller
Diaconia / Empowering / Social Development

1 Contribution to the International Handbook of Practical Theology

The Swedish theologian Gustaf Wingren (1910–2000) inspired by his reading of Luther often referred to the church as *extra nos*. For Wingren this meant that no one owned the church spaces. They were always outside, moving, somewhere else. God is undoubtedly the subject of all churches, but the *extra nos* urges us to look elsewhere for the church; the church space is the surprise, never the limited and the well-known. More people are there, other people are there. "The Church exists for the sake of the non-Christian humanity who are outside it. This is its *raison d'être*. If instead it exists only for the sake of its members it will be in continual conflict with its indwelling Lord." (Wingren [1960] 1964, 10–11, Kristensson Uggla 2016)

In a Scandinavian historical context, this topic has been challenging theological and diaconal discussions for the last few decades. Questions include: Is diaconia also *extra nos*? What would this mean? Within Scandinavian churches and theological institutions there are, of course, many who reject the *extra nos*, arguing instead for the more classical interpretation of diaconia, limiting it to explicit church-run institutions and practices. Due to this situation, diaconia often becomes a contested arena, both practically and theoretically.

In the Scandinavian context, this tension peaked in 1850, and has since then continued to be an issue of debate. At the heart of the conflict was the Danish theologian Grundtvig, (1783–1872) who opposed pietist confessionalism and claimed God's presence in culture, history, nature and the everyday (Gregersen, Kristensson Uggla, and Wyller 2017). Pietist theologians insisted that personal conversion and the following of Jesus were the only acceptable criteria for Christian faith, and for diaconia. Grundtvig's passion for God's presence in all creation was thus rejected, and the young diaconia movement (imported from Germany) became one of the most important pietist symbols. Converted members were vital for the construction of modern Scandinavia. According to the pietists the still more secularized state and the still less confessional (Grundtvigian Danish / Norwegian) church were unable to contribute in this way. Pietists therefore built hospitals, schools and all manner of charity institutions and organizations, thus becoming one of the main contributors to the shaping of modern Scandinavia (Christoffersen 1999). The pietists were the modernizers, but the price was high: The *extra nos* motive had been lost. The paradox is that those who contributed immensely to improved justice systems, more social inclusion and more security in the created world, at the same time did not recognize that there might be a vocation in all creation and a presence *extra nos* in all life worlds.

This historical and theological tension has influenced and impacted the discussion of diaconia and diaconal practices in the Scandinavian context. The traditional conflict has been connected to how the theological and diaconal reflection influenced the political building of the welfare state, which has been the signature of Scandinavian social policy since the 1930s. The question is thus: is the ambitious goal of including all citizens in the welfare state an ambition with diaconal significance? In the Grundtvig / Wingren tradition of Lutheran creation theology, the answer must be one of confirmation. The welfare state is obviously not the church. Nevertheless, caring for the creation cannot be irrelevant to God. The Danish theologian and philosopher Løgstrup (1905–1981) famously stated that we always carry something of the other in our hands (Løgstrup 1997). Moreover, by recognizing the calling from the other we are interwoven into such an interpretation of life that comes very close to a religious interpretation.

In a historical parallel, Danish scholars – in particular Knudsen (2000) and Østergaard (2005) – have asked whether the start of the welfare state in reality was initiated with the Church ordinances during the time of the Reformation. The reformers (including Luther's close collaborator Bugenhagen, who wrote the Danish-Norwegian church ordinance) argued that the responsibility for the poor, the sick and the needy were to be transferred from the ecclesial and monastic hierarchy to the King. The King should, with mandate from the Church, take care of those with social needs. Against this backdrop, theologians and historians have claimed that there is a close and significant relation between the universal ambition of the welfare state and the Christian model of society.

The recognition of all good deeds, also those performed by the welfare state, as part of God's will and responsibility, radicalizes the question of the spaces and the agents of diaconia. Borders become open, definitions blurred, other people than the inscribed might belong, etc.

In this way, the significance of the outside and *extra nos* is an important heritage coming out of the Scandinavian interpretation of diaconia. At the same time, the *extra nos* and the outside as spaces of discovering God's presence, is an issue beyond the Scandinavian context. Today, in times of multi-religiosity, migration, and populism, the outside and the *extra nos* have become contested again, this time bringing new challenges. There are strong contemporary positions (e.g., Ward 2000, Cavanaugh 2009), who, once again, argue that the present situation requires – more than ever – a concentration of Christian identity and communities. The *extra nos* position of Wingren and Grundtvig, therefore, needs to be re-thought and to be re-connected. What kind of *extra nos* is relevant in diaconia today?

In contemporaneity it is no longer necessarily only the welfare state or the traditions of Scandinavian culture that represent the *extra nos* and the outside. The call of the others has now become calls of others who belong to different life worlds and challenging religious, cultural and political traditions; and the most challenging call does not even come from humans, it comes from the non-human, from nature.

Therefore, the spatial conflict of the *extra nos* of diaconia is both different and new at the same time. The argument of restriction, however, remains the same: Christians need to protect and develop their identity. The argument of the *extra nos* needs new creativity: How to identify an identity that is not one's own? The following will sketch out some proposals, moving to contexts beyond the well-known and the safe. The *extra nos* and the other spaces (heterotopias) must establish themselves within decolonial contexts. To make the challenge embodied: Here are some narratives from South Africa.

2 Walking the Third Space

When the Congolese refugee Nisha Mlele (name given to her for anonymity by the author) walked through the South African township where she lived one morning in early autumn 2018, the smells, colors and heat were the same as every day. However, for Nisha, this was not an average day, this was her first walk through the township since her husband had died some weeks before. As a child, Nisha and her family fled civil wars in the Democratic Republic of Congo (DRC). Her journey as a refugee, which also included years spent in different refugee camps in Tanzania, finally brought her to South Africa, where she can stay, but with no public support. A few months before the walk described above, her husband, also a refugee from the DRC, died suddenly from a brain stroke. His family suspected that the stroke was caused by injuries associated with an assault some weeks previously. In many South African regions, especially some people and leaders from the Zulu nation, the historical natives, practice violent xenophobia against other African refugees settling in Zulu areas.

That day, however, Nisha was not walking alone. She was with her pastor and the researcher, the white professor now narrating this story. Nisha attends Sunday services in the township, facilitated by the pastor, singing Swahili hymns and spending time with friends who are also refugees. During weekdays, the pastor organizes activities supporting refugees to find work, accommodation and he does advocacy work for refugees within the local municipality. In other words: He carries out classical diaconia.

Nisha's walk illustrates a symbolic *extra nos*. During one visit to Nisha together with the pastor the researcher asked whether the three of them could take a walk through the neighborhood. During all the other visits they had just been talking inside Nisha's house. The walk was primarily intended for changing context, but it turned out to symbolize a lot more. During the walk, the pastor is second in line. Nisha leads, the pastor and the researcher are behind her. The everyday belongs to Nisha.

Walking together, sensing the concrete everyday space of a South African township is everything but reflective theology. Nevertheless, the walk is a piece of spatial, heterotopic diaconia in the Foucauldian and Lefevbrian sense. The sensory level embodies what Lefevbre called the lived space. It is, no doubt, a heterotopic space, an 'other' space, also known as the third space (Soja 1996). The walkers spatialize a sensory presence, at the same time connecting and interconnecting. Renewing and confirming the lived spaces of the everyday are the God surprises of diaconia. God performs within the calling from creation.

Nisha and her every day initiate a heterotopic diaconia. It is a walk where spaces are conquered, and roles are inverted. She is symbolically in the front and the hierarchy is behind. The conventional church decenters and there is a new one emerging, *extra nos*. The walk embodies a perception of diaconia very different from the classical version initiated in the eighteenth and nineteenth century. There the subject of diaconia was the church. The Nisha walk symbolizes a situation where the church is not the only dominating subject. Nisha's lead illustrates a diaconia where ordinary people, the *extra nos*, are the most significant. The walk is, of course, facilitated and initiated by the scholar and the pastor. In this sense it still has aspects of classical diaconia. Nevertheless, the practice of it becomes different, roles are changing, church structures are less dominant, almost dissolving. There is an *extra nos* in symbolically walking.

3 The Third Space and the Church Space

In itself, God's spatial presence is not a surprise in the story of diaconia. Most diaconia narratives are about this presence, how to pursue or achieve the sacred glimpses of a more just and a more decent life, especially for the poor and the underprivileged. There is a historical tradition of a spatial diaconia, initiated in the early church. One might call this the tradition of the monastic hospital.

One historical and still visible example is the Ospedale dello Spirito Santo, situated only a few minutes' walk from St Peter's Square in Rome. Today, the eleventh-century building is a part-modern Italian hospital, part-museum, where one of the most significant hospital rooms (historically as well as theologically), can still be seen, with its huge, rectangular building and altar in the center. To the right there is the women's ward, to the left the men's ward. All beds were situated so that one could see the altar while lying on the pillow. The monastic hospital is a symbolic and thoughtful representation of many contemporary and substantial discussions of diaconia.

Historically, hospitals were organic parts of religious institutions, also in pre-Christian traditions. Greek sites show traces of specific rooms for the sick, built in connection with groups of priests or other sacred representatives of the religious site (Thompson and Goldin 1975). This tradition continued into the first Christian centuries. The hospital was either an integrated part of the monastery, or the hospital itself expanded into a total ecclesial space.

The paradox is this: The monastic hospital, for many still today holds a significant diaconal practice. It was exactly what the Protestant (Luther and Pragman [1521] 1964) reformers most wanted to impact. The monastic hospital was the opposite of the *extra nos*. Even if there were exceptions, and many different traditions developing within the Protestant (Lutheran) churches, the resurgence of hospitals in the first centuries after the radical years of the Reformation, were different from the monastic hospital from the Medieval Ages. The decisive point was: Always outside (*extra nos*) the now demolished monasteries. This is the start of the diaconia as modernity. The caring for the sick and the needy developed as manifestations of the process of differentiation, no longer chaired (and controlled) by the ecclesial hierarchy. Many hospitals, even though they were often run by Christian people or organizations, became part of what later generations would label secularization, taken to mean disconnecting from the ecclesial structures.

Modern diaconia was shaped in this context. What followed in the diaconal revival movement in the eighteenth and nineteenth century challenged the *extra nos* once again. The complaints about a decrease in the specific Christian profile of the diaconal work in institutions and churches on the one hand, and the need for a more just sharing of social goods became a starting point for the period where diaconia often stood up against what the diaconal leaders of the time labeled as secular society. The monastic hospital was not reintroduced, but a permanent tension was born. The diaconia movement was strengthening and began to contribute substantially to the construction of the modern-day western world, both in the North and in the South. Diaconia, especially in parts of Africa, China and India took on important and influential roles in the different and numerous colonies. they occupied.

When Nisha fled from DRC via Tanzania, she could have travelled to areas in Southern Tanzania. In the areas close to Lake Malawi, German missionaries from the Berliner Missionswerk, moved north from South Africa and settled at the shores of the lake in the small village of Matema. The Lutheran hospital is still there today, receiving primarily HIV and malaria patients, and cooperating with the other Lutheran hospitals further North. In the same area there are schools, churches, and villages, all impacted by Lutheran traditions and customs. The missionary diaconia contributed to the ambiguous project of modernizing and colonizing the African continent. The Berliner Mission in Matema, Tanzania is just one illustrative case of this.

The diaconal mission narrative deepens the significance of the Nisha Mlele's township walk. Nisha's walk is facilitated by a pastor and joined by a professor, but she literally walks away from them. The walk also symbolizes a shift from colonial to heterotopic and decolonial diaconia. The indigenous, originally the receivers of diaconia, turn around and perform beyond the charities. In the midst of the precarious township life there are no diaconal institutions. In this symbolic act the discussions and the tensions move in directions far away from the diaconia discussions of the nineteenth and even the twentieth century. Space, resistance, and embodied empowerment are moving to the center.

4 An Epistemological Challenge: Developing a New Discipline

In contemporary Germany, Scandinavia and elsewhere, the institutions, organizations and projects coming out of the Inner Mission context have impacted and continue to impact on the interpretation of what diaconia is. In addition, the paradox is that the Inner Mission grounded the diaconal turn of the eighteenth century and onwards, partly implying a Protestant revival of the model of the Ospedale dello Santo Spirito. The argument was that churches needed to engage more meaningfully in real-life challenges, for missionary reasons, as well as to ameliorate conditions for the poor and the sick themselves. The diaconal movement in the eighteenth and nineteenth century, was born out of this realization. The issue of the space for diaconia was central. The churches (and inner missions) should expand beyond the space of the church hospital in Rome, and from the sacramental hospital ward, move from the rather disengaged Lutheran orthodoxy, towards the urban poor and today, to the global poor.

Theodor Schäfer (Schäfer 1914) was the first to propose that there was a need to study and research what was, during his time, the increasing influence of the Inner Mission diaconia. Schäfer called this study field *Diakonik*. Schäfer's interest was to give more significance to the Inner Mission and its projects for people in social and spiritual "need".

Diakonik was meant to be a scientific study of these practices in the Inner Mission context. This word is still in use to this day. In Germany, where the discipline *Diakoniewissenschaft* is established in many universities, the field of study is often, like in Heidelberg, a branch of Practical Theology. There are also diaconal studies and professors in several European universities. In Nordic countries, there are no specific institutes for the study of diaconia like there are in Germany, but there are chairs at Universities and University colleges in Oslo, Uppsala, and Stockholm and in different Danish and Finnish institutions.

The contemporary challenge for all these kinds of diaconal studies is to move beyond the narrow field of the *Diakonik*. The issue of the outside and the *extra nos* seems difficult to pose within that context. The Nisha Mlele walk challenges the different *Diakonik* research traditions. Nisha enjoys meeting neighbors and friends after so many months absent. She reconquers a greater space.

There is no altar and no ward in Nisha's walk, but there is an obvious joy in encountering others. Neither is any direct vocation taking place. Nisha leads the walk herself, a walk of reconnecting, hugging her DRC neighbor, who seeing Nisha coming, runs to her house to tidy before her friend (and the pastor and the professor) visit. We share in the sensations of the room, the smells, the friendly voices chatting. We are, in a way, decentered from both church and vocation, and still, there are all reasons to call this diaconia. Roles are inverted, gender, power and spirituality are not in someone's specific property. It is a disruption and a decentering of what used to be called diaconia.

5 Theoretical Aspects and Concepts

One first basic criteria of the decentering is that the institutional church does not act in Nisha's name. Nisha is the actor. Not *Diakonik*, but freedom walk. Socially, one might call the context, the subaltern context. However, different from Spivak (Spivak 1988), the subaltern (Nisha) speaks a lot, sensory speaking, audible speaking, another language that is not the language initiated by the professor and the scholar, Nisha spatializes with language during the walk. This is third space; the decentering heterotopia that mirrors the surrounding spaces, as defined by Foucault (Foucault 1986).

The walk Nisha performs is an embodied spirituality, not as an instrument of transformation, but as an organic part of the transformation itself. Nisha walks spaces of justice, joy and recognition. The institutional church, the pastor, (and the professor) walking two steps behind her. Nevertheless, Nisha walks in the front, taking the space back in her social context, remaking her relations with her neighbors and friends, receiving inclusion and generosity, reclaiming the space that has been hijacked by the paradoxical xenophobia.

This implies that the traditional (colonial) binary of the religious and the secular does not make sense when trying to interpret the walk. The Nisha walk is a seemingly very secular practice, but in the context presented above it is not. More than 70 years ago, Dietrich Bonhoeffer (Bonhoeffer and Barnett 2012) criticized Karl Barth for not being aware of the *Arkandiziplin*. By that, Bonhoeffer meant that Barth was unable to see and formulate how the gospel was embodied in the world with no boasting whatsoever. What seemed secular was in fact not: it was the secret of the gospel incarnated in lived life. Nisha walks the *Arkandiziplin*.

Two generations of scholars have discussed what Bonhoeffer really intended with his Barth critique and whether the critique was fair. What matters here, however, is that Bonhoeffer's critique does make sense in the context presented above. The decentered, heterotopic diaconia as the embodied, spatial agency of people, is the diaconal praxis to look for. Here is the *Arkandiziplin*, more fruitful for the discussion of diaconia in a paradigm other than the established *Diakonik* trajectory.

The *Diakonik* tradition presupposes that diaconal practice and diaconal theology belongs to ecclesiology and grow out of it as a theological discipline. It is the church that acts, the central category in the *Diakonik* tradition. The decentering of diaconia is an act of God in the hands of humans. Sometimes it happens as an explicit part of a church, sometimes in the grey zone and sometimes just anywhere. The Nisha walk is situated in the ambiguous space in between the grey zone and the 'anywhere'. The basic point is that diaconia is a decentering, spatial act where people are connected, and justice is enhanced.

6 The Church as Event

Based on the above, diaconia is about empowerment, social transformation, and justice. Yet, those who are empowered, transformed, and enjoying expanded notions of justice are themselves working actively to achieve them. Reconstructing subjectivities within new spaces is the core element of diaconia. This performs innovation as well as ecclesial significance. In the case of Nisha, she leads the walk; the pastor and the professor come two steps behind. Nevertheless, it is the pastor, who has contributed to making the walk possible. He knows her for many years, assists her to find a small income, invites her to Sunday services and facilitates the walk on that specific day. However, Nisha walks in front, the pastor decenters.

In Protestant dogmatic, the church is an event. In Protestant theology, therefore, it is misleading to look only at the institutional side of diaconia. Diaconia embodies dogmatically what the *extra nos* is substantially about.

This is, theologically speaking, the reason why the Reformers closed the monastic hospitals in their areas. The decentering movement needed to be performed in a robust manner. In Oslo, Norway, the stones from a demolished Cistercian monastery were used for construction of the Royal castle. These were radical manifestations of a decentering reformation.

7 Decolonizing Diaconia

Based on a substantial critique of colonial power, including churches and Christendom, Catherine Walsh and Walter Mignolo (Mignolo and Walsh 2018) have developed what they call a decolonial approach. The decolonial is the explicit resistance to colonial hegemony. The decolonial focuses on bottom-up-practices, indigenous traditions, everyday local knowledges, especially in the Global South. The intention is to reestablish all under-researched and normatively insignificant practices and lifeworlds as sources of resistance and empowerment, no longer as victimized receivers of so-called colonial beneficence.

The *extra nos*, decentering, heterotopic diaconia in the example of Nisha could also be seen as part of this decolonial trajectory. The introduction to this article located the origin of the outside to a tension within Scandinavian theology and diaconia. The Nisha narrative has expanded the *extra nos* into a much larger context where it belongs today. In the decolonial context of Mignolo and Walsh, the Nisha practice is a trace of a new diaconia. The empowerment comes from a decentering of the church, intending to avoid the colonial violence of its centering. This also means that the township walk leaves the secular/sacred binary. Surpassing the classical binaries of modernity is one of the major implications of a decolonial, and heterotopic diaconia. Diaconia in this sense is very much about proclaiming and taking space, not on behalf of others, but by others (Wyller 2018).

This empowering aspect of diaconia is, however, also its theological challenge. It can be illustrated through the important and influential scholarly and activist work of the South African theologian Gerald West (West 1995, 2013). West has contributed to African liberation theologies since the last years of apartheid. Strongly influenced from the Kairos document (2010, West for many years identified with the third historical period presented in the Kairos document, the prophetic theology. Theology had to act prophetically; the churches had to be on the side of the oppressed. Church theology could not develop without prophetic practice, aiming at freedom and empowerment of people of colour and the underprivileged.

Over the last few years, West, however, has published more on what he now calls "people's theology" (West 2012). Churches are no longer the only source of theology; churches might not even have the only theological competence. There is a theology of the people, meaning that the resisting practices of the oppressed themselves are the new sources of theology.

Gerald West's theology of the people and the diaconia of the decentering church move in the same direction. The minister walking with Nisha, literally two steps behind, embodies and symbolizes a non-instrumental diaconia of the people. It is the walking, the township neighbors, the smells, and the invitations to meals, including the resistance to all violence and injustice, that is the diaconia of the people. It is diaconia because it is a church-facilitated embodied event, but at this moment, the church is at least two steps behind, leaving space for the people, for Nisha. She empowers and resists by walking, by walking *extra nos*.

However, this means that the theology of diaconia can no longer be viewed solely from a one-sided functionalistic point of view. The traditional, diaconal, functionalist contribution to church and society in itself is, of course, still important and remains one of the major contributions of the church to modern-day society. However, these practices need to be critically analyzed with regard to how much they contribute today to the decentering practices of diaconia.

The reception, the entanglement of earth, smells, expectations, colors, and voices; the pastor still two steps behind, all make this walk different from the functionalist (and colonial) diaconia. The diaconia of the Nisha walk involves Nisha taking the lead while the church (symbolized by the pastor) is reducing and almost dissolving behind her. It is Nisha in her sensible relations to the earth that is the start of a diaconia beyond colonial faces of modernity.

8 Heterotopic Diaconia

The American sociologist Rogers Brubaker (Brubaker 2017) has coined the concept of "Christianism" to label the fusion of populism and Christianity. Christianism implies that nations should avoid Muslims and other non-Christian immigrants. The Christianists claim that it is by disconnecting from non-Christians that you protect secularity, liberal freedom, LGBT rights and universal Human Rights.

The Christianist version offers one profile of Christian identity. Christian faith is preserved and protected by not allowing anyone but the faithful to be the value center of the nation. God is on your side, but this is not a God that surprises. God is in his church and the diaconia protects what it should protect.

The heterotopic diaconia is the opposite of the Christianist diaconia. The heterotopic diaconia represents another option for Christian identity. Christian performance happens also when someone like Nisha walks away from the classical center. This is the diaconia of the people (West 2012), and this is the diaconia where the Trinitarian God acts. Leaving the center in order to spatialize for others is at the core of Christianity's other identity profile.

Traditionally, the academic study of diaconia calls itself multidisciplinary. That is, in a way, true. A variety of methods and disciplines can be drawn on to analyze all the different aspects of the Nisha walk, the justice-making connected to it and the organized work following from it and leading up to it. Still, it follows from this article that diaconal studies belong to theology in a mix between ethnography, ethics, dogmatic and practical theology. Nevertheless, it also follows that the starting point does not come from above, but from the experiences and the embodied connectedness that people share and experience. This starting point is the basic, and the theology of diaconia needs to be developed and reformulated any time the smells and the injustice are new, and a new God surprise is needed.

The heterotopic diaconia is therefore not only a diaconia for the Nisha township walk. However, the important and decisive global diaconal work for justice and recognition needs to take its values from the insights of the walk. Here is the challenge for the future societal ambitions of diaconia. Colonial history has shaped the modern world. The challenge is to develop empowering structures and institutions that aim for the heterotopic, the decoloniality of diaconia.

9 Diaconia as Decolonial Counter-Conducts

This way of elaborating diaconia also points to interesting new perspectives for political theology. We can learn that from a parallel between the *extra nos* tradition developed above and the concept of counter conducts developed by Michel Foucault in the last years of his life. The walk of Nisha is a walk beyond the secular/religious binary. The church decenters, but in the *extra nos* tradition this does not mean that God is lost, on the contrary: the Nisha walk subverts the conventional, but it opens a future through Nisha's agency, "a diaconia of the people" (West 2012). The parallel is to be found exactly in this connection between resistance and blurred religion that is also present in Foucault's interpretation of counter-conducts.

Counter-conducts developed from Foucault's studies of pastoral power (Foucault 1994, 2006, 2007). Pastoral power means a practice where the abbot – since the early days of monastic history – has absolute control over the spiritual lives of the monks under him. The goal of this power was to rule the souls of the obedient. In a next step, Foucault then developed his theory of governmentality which was a prolonged pastoral power outside the monastery: "What I mean in fact is the development of power techniques oriented toward individuals and intended to rule them in a continuous and permanent way. If the state is the political form of a centralized and centralizing power, let us call pastorship the individualizing power" (Foucault 1994).

The strong and influential tradition of pastoral power was, for Foucault, the main source for how discipline, control and self-control developed in medicine, prisons, and institutions for "the mad". Foucault's seminal books on the history of medicine and the history of madness found its material, first of all, in French Catholic institutions and hospitals (Foucault 2006. However, parallel material has, of course, also been found in post-Reformation Protestant institutions (Villadsen 2011).

On this background, there is no doubt that Foucault was one of the main inspirations when Mignolo and Walsh developed their decolonial thinking. Colonial oppression involves economic and political oppression. Nevertheless, some of the main roots are in religion, especially in the traditions of pastoral power where power was executed in such a way that obedience and suppression became the norm. From this perspective, there are good reasons for Mignolo and Walsh to disconnect from religion. For them, religion belongs to the epistemological power that has mainly contributed to the colonial empire.

Nevertheless, there are traces of an opposite epistemological position in Foucault's thinking, and this is the point where the decentering *extra nos* and the radical power critique of Foucault connect in a surprising way. Foucault himself is obviously not focused on the theology of a decentering church / diaconia, but he is, implicitly very close in his late elaborations on counter-conducts (Foucault 2006, 2007). Counter-conducts are religious traditions that have a liberating and empowering aspect. Not all kinds of pastoral power are oppressive, Foucault himself found evidence of such practices in mystical, eschatological movements in the late medieval period, traces of a religiosity other than the (controlling) Christianity of modernity: "Spirituality, intense forms of devotion, recourse to Scripture, and the at least partial re-qualification of asceticism and mysticism are all part of a kind of re-integration of counter-conduct within a religious pastorate" (Foucault 2007, 229). According to Davidson (Davidson 2011) the counter conducts, originating in these marginal areas of religion have a subversive aspect, taking a position different from the ecclesial power structures. There are good reasons to call counter-conducts heterotopic, decentering practices in their context.

Nisha Mlele' s township walk does not belong to the any kind of medieval mysticism or millenaristic speculation. Nevertheless, her decentering walk is a walk beyond the religious/secular binary, leaving the hierarchy two steps behind, and constructing a new space for Nisha. It is a decolonial and diaconal counter-conduct that re-spatializes and symbolizes the decentering power.

Bibliography

Bonhoeffer, Dietrich, and Barnett Victoria, eds. 2012. *Dietrich Bonhoeffer Works: Letters and Papers from Prison.* Minneapolis: Fortress Press.

Brubaker, Rogers. 2017. "Between Nationalism and Civilizationism: The European Populist Moment in Comparative Perspective." *Ethnic and Racial Studies* 40:1191–1226.

Cavanaugh, William. 2009. *The Myth of Religious Violence: Secular Ideology and the Roots of Modern Conflict.* Oxford: Oxford University Press.

Christoffersen, Svein Aage. 1999. *Moralsk og moderne? Trekk av den kristne moraltradisjonen i Norge fra 1814 til i dag.* Oslo: Gyldendal.

Davidson, Arnold. 2011. "In Praise of Counter-Conduct." *History of the Human Sciences* 24:25–41.

Foucault, Michel. 1986. "Of Other Spaces." *Diacritics: A Review of Contemporary Criticism* 16:22–27.

Foucault, Michel. 1994. "Omnes et singulatim: Toward a Critique of Political Reason." In *Power: Essential Works of Foucault 1954–1984*, edited by Michel Foucault, New York: The New Press, 298–325.

Foucault, Michel. 2006. *Die Geburt der Biopolitik: Vorlesung am Collège de France; 1978–1979.* Frankfurt am Main: Suhrkamp.

Foucault, Michel. 2006. *History of Madness.* New York: Routledge.

Foucault, Michel. 2007. *Security, Territory, Population*, New York: Palgrave Macmillan, 191–227.

Gregersen, Niels-Henrik, Kristensson Uggla Bengt, and Trygve Wyller, eds. 2017. *Reformation Theology for a Post-Secular Age: Løgstrup, Prenter, Wingren, and the Future of Scandinavian Creation Theology.* Research in Contemporary Religion 24. Göttingen: Vandenhoeck & Ruprecht.

Heimbrock, Hans-Günter, and Trygve Wyller. 2019. "Challenging Ecclesiological Traditions." In *Reforming: Space, Body and Politics*, edited by Sivert Angel, Kirstine H. Johansen, and Auli Vähäkangas, Tübingen: IAPT Conference Proceedings, 129–136.

Knudsen, Tim, ed. 2000. *Den nordiske protestantisme og velfærdsstaten.* Århus: Aarhus Universitetsforlag.

Kristensson Uggla, Bengt. 2016. *Becoming Human Again: The Theological Life of Gustaf Wingren.* Eugene: Cascade Books.

Lefebvre, Henri. 1991. *The Production of Space.* Oxford: Blackwell.

Leonard, Gary S.D. 2010. *The Kairos Documents.* Pietermaritzburg: Ujamaa Centre for Biblical and Theological Community Development and Research.

Luther, Martin, and James H. Pragman, ed. 1964. *De votis monasticis Martini Lutheri Iudicium (A Translation of Parts III and IVa.).* Saint Louis: Concordia Seminary.

Løgstrup, Knud Ejler. 1997. *The Ethical Demand.* Notre Dame: Notre Dame University Press.

Mignolo, Walter, and Walsh Catherine. 2018. *On Decoloniality: Concepts, Analytics, Praxis.* Durham: Duke University Press.

Sander, Hans-Joachim, Kaspar Villadsen, and Trygve Wyller. 2016. *The Spaces of Others – Heterotopic Spaces: Practicing and Theorizing Hospitality and Counter-Conduct beyond the Religion / Secular Divide.* Göttingen: Vandenhoeck & Ruprecht.

Schäfer, Theodor. 1914. *Leitfaden der inneren Mission: zunächst für den Berufsunterricht in Diakonen- und Diakonissen-Anstalten.* Hamburg: Wolf Lothar Demler.

Soja, Eduard. 1996. *Thirdspace: Journeys to Los Angeles and Real-and-Imagined Places*. London: Blackwell.
Spivak, Gayatri. 1988. "Can the Subaltern Speak?" In *Marxism and the Interpretation of Culture*, edited by Cary Nelson and Lawrence Grossberg, London: Macmillan, 271–316.
Thompson, John, and Goldin Grace. 1975. *The Hospital: A Social and Architectural History*. New Haven: Yale University Press.
Villadsen, Kaspar, 2011. "Modern Welfare and 'Good Old' Philanthropy: A New Discursive Space in Welfare Policy." *Acta Sociologica* 50:309–325.
Ward, Graham. 2000. *The Cities of God*. Abingdon: Routledge.
West, Gerald. 1995. *Biblical Hermeneutics of Liberation: Modes of Reading the Bible in the South African Context*. Pietermaritzburg: Cluster Publisher.
West, Gerald. 2012. "Tracing the 'Kairos' Trajectory from South Africa (1985) to Palestine (2009): Discerning Continuities and Differences." *Journal for Theology of the Southern Africa* 143:4–22.
Wingren, Gustaf. [1960] 2006. *Gospel and Church*. Eugene: Wipf & Stock.
Wyller, Trygve. 2018. "Touching and Contamination: What the Xenophobes Want to Avoid. Reflections from a Congolese Borderland in South Africa." In *Borderland Religion*, edited by Daisy Machado, Bryan Turner and Trygve Wyller. London: Routledge, 180–196.
Østergård, Uffe. 2005. "Lutheranismen og den universelle velfærdsstat." In *Velferdsstat og kirke*, edited by Schjørring Jens Holger and Jens Torkild Bak. Copenhagen: ANIS, 147–186.

Thias Kgatla
Exorcism / Envy / Witchcraft

1 Introduction

This chapter discusses the relationship between exorcism, envy, and witchcraft in an African social setting, the reasons for their escalation and ways to combat them. An African worldview that constructs and shapes the trajectory of envy in society is examined within the theoretical framework of African epistemology, its principles of egalitarianism, and the function of exorcism.

The starting point is identifying how some African people come to know the truth and their justification of their knowledge, which is then used as a platform for envious persecution. The discussion proceeds by first examining the tenets of African epistemology as a justification for persecution and exorcism. This is followed by a consideration of the way that principles of egalitarianism could be applied negatively to justify violence in the name of corrective exorcism. Exorcism has many dimensions, such as psychology, theology, traditional religion, and sociology (Moore 1979). It posits the existence of spiritual forces (benevolent or malevolent) that sometimes trespass in places where they ought not to be by taking possession of people, who in turn cause harm to society (Moore 1979) and to the wellbeing of the person possessed and by extension to the community where the individual lives. Ending the supernatural possession is necessary as the community leaders have to ensure the wellbeing of the whole society either through rituals, use of force, or even persecution.

This chapter argues that exorcism can take another form where the exorcist needs to be exorcised of envy and the harmful beliefs that lead to the persecution of perceived foes and treating people with different qualities and possessions as somehow the same. Such maltreatment may take the form of hidden and undetected vengeance behaviour and uses the discourse of witchcraft accusations and persecution. There has not been much exploration in the literature of the methods of, and rationale for, exorcist violence. But the study of the phenomenon is crucial to account for certain crimes in society. Variables such as rumours, gossip, language and silencing, secrets/privacy and beliefs are analysed as propellers of the envy-driven persecution that justifies 'cleansing' by exorcism. As a practice supposed to rid a person of negative influences, exorcism may in fact turn into a persecuting machine that impedes development in society (Dombeck 1999). This study adopted a case study method and offers recommendations for the 'exorcism' of the evildoers themselves, namely the exorcists who are often perceived as community leaders.

2 African Epistemology

Is there such a thing as an African epistemology? The answer is that there is and it rotates on a different axis from the Western way of knowing. African people have their own way of conceptualising, interpreting and apprehending reality within the context of the African situation. The idea of an African epistemology is also based on African people's understanding of the concepts of knowledge, truth, and rationality (Udefi 2014) without mediation from Western categories of knowing. African people are complete people capable of thinking through issues and were able to reach viable conclusions without external assistance before the colonial authorities set foot on the African continent. With the arrival of Western missionaries and the colonial dispensation, African knowledge systems were disregarded, overridden, pushed into silence (Spewak 2017, 423–440; Wray 2010, 181–184) and regarded as unscientific and delusional. The arrival of the colonial powers did not advance the African quest for knowledge but instead negated it. African ways of knowing were driven underground and operated at the level of privacy and in secrecy (Fallis 2013).

Like its counterpart, Western epistemology, African epistemology has its own challenges and false beliefs that are motivated by hidden motives (Ani 2013, 295–320). As a human construct and product, any epistemological system is limited in its grasp of reality and becomes further blurred by human subjectivity. Subjectivity remains the silent enemy of all good intentions in every community. Not everything people believe to be true is true, and people may also sincerely hold false beliefs. Because of total depravity of the sin (Jer 17:9) that humans harbour, their objectivity is tainted by forces such as envy and jealousy, which to be exorcised. People kill other humans for reasons that cannot be explained in wholly rational terms, but that does not mean they are less human. Sometimes these atrocities are committed for the sake of corrective actions to get rid of evil in victims who are innocent but detrimental to societal development

The individual is inevitably seen as requiring help from others to realise or satisfy his/her basic needs. The value of collective action, mutual aid and interdependence is, therefore, stressed to ensure an individual's – and ultimately social – welfare, and for the successful achievement of the most difficult undertakings. Communalism, therefore, insists that the good of all determines the good of each individual, and that an individual finds the highest benefit – materially, morally and spiritually – in relationships with others and in working for the good of all. The promotion of communal life in African settings is in a sense the recognition of the existence of conflicts and tensions that normally emerge in individual competition, the desire to satisfy one's own needs at the expense of others, the pursuit of a selfish agenda by individuals, and the frustrations that arise when a person works on his/her own. In an attempt to improve relations, minimise competition and reduce tensions and frustration, a communal approach is adopted aimed not at eliminating individuality but at regulating it (Gyekye 1987, 88). Misbehaviour or anti-social conduct on the part of an individual would have catastrophic effects on communal harmony. Avoidance of such disruptive behaviour is sometimes the reason behind the curtailment of individualism and independence. But this curtailment of individualism often has a negative impact on development and leads to hegemony. An individual may be prevented from developing his/her skills, as is the case in Western cultures. But total control of the individual exercise of independence has negative effects, as new initiatives may not be tolerated, especially if this intolerance is further motivated by jealousy or suspicion of witchcraft.

3 Theory of Egalitarianism

Egalitarianism entails the levelling and equalizing of power relations – whether in the form of intellectual influence in society or possession. Egalitarianism as a concept comes from a political philosophy that endorses the principle of the equality of people in their social setting (Arneson 2013). It argues that people should get the same, be treated the same, be treated as equals, relate as equals, or enjoy equal social status (Wolff 2010, 335–350). Egalitarian doctrines tend to be based on the idea that all humans are equal in fundamental worth or moral status. The term egalitarianism resonates with the Christian notion that God has created all people equal and loves all human souls equally. Egalitarianism postulates that asymmetrical relationships in society should be adjusted to become more symmetrical. The 'haves' and 'have-nots' should share the available resources in such a way that an equilibrium is achieved. As a social theory on the equality of people, it is an idealist philosophy, but it has a darker flipside. Where activism for equality is premised on envy disguised as seeking egalitarianism, the project could be more dubious. In such circumstances the underlying motive for promoting egalitarianism could be envious persecution that is mainly aimed at social control by self-appointed demagogues in the community who want people to toe the line and to punish those who overstep certain boundaries (Kgatla 2000, 203).

In his chapter titled 'Fairness, Respect and Egalitarian Ethos Revisited', Wolff (2010, 335–350) argues that egalitarianism is a many-splendored thing. In some cases, however, it fails to devote sufficient attention to issues of respect and self-respect. Although egalitarianism may be animated by a vision of the good society, it could also be argued that there are other good ways of living together (Wolff 2010). Wolff (2010, 8) advances a notion of egalitarianism that is fair and respectful and includes what he calls the element of responsibility. He asserts that individuals should only be entitled to help when their plight is beyond their control (Wolff 2010, 9). It is unethical for an individual to refuse to work (out of laziness) but then also expect welfare that is sponsored by the drive towards equalisation in terms of meeting material needs. This notion is in line with what Paul says in 2Thess 3:1: 'He who does not work, neither shall he eat'. Those who are not employed through their own choice should not be morally entitled to social benefits and they have no grounds to envy those who are working to earn their living. But these structural impediments and exclusions should be exposed for what they are. Exclusion and suppression of individuals because of their abilities is anti-developmental.

The victims here include all people who do not comply with the law of negative egalitarianism. By negative egalitarianism I mean a principle by which all people are expected to be the same or identical. This illusion advocates for a situation in which people are expected to think the same and have the same views about issues. Their children must have the same education, achieve the same qualifications at a tertiary education level, drive the same cars, have the same intellect, have the same values, and consequently participate in the same mediocracy. More often than not, this equalising thinking is the trigger for envy and identifies those people who transgress the norm as the enemies of the people (Kgatla 2000, 203). Such instruments of social control are self-destructive in that they prevent any form of development in the society in the name of egalitarianism. Admired and exemplary people in society may be reduced to objects of pity (Hagedorn and Neyrey 1998, 12). Through ostracism, feuds and homicide, people are prevented from excelling in anything desirable or constructive (Hagedorn and Neyrey 1998). This insistence on the preservation of popular obedience and loyalty to the people obsessed with envy is regarded as the essential bulwark against anarchy and social disintegration (Hagedorn and Neyrey 1998). In such an environment, social tools such as rumours, gossip, and innuendo can divert wholly good purposes. What follows below is an analysis of the way that undetected envious possession can play itself out.

4 Variables in Envious Persecution

Variables such as rumours, gossip, language and silencing, and beliefs play a significant role in envious persecutions. They act to prepare, control, and direct the extent to which the persecutions may evolve. Rumours in the escalation of persecution are generated where the boundaries between what is real and unreal, false, and true become blurred (Ellis and ter Haar 2004, 27). Rumours are speculative by definition and attempt to provide people with a theory or explanation of what really happened and the agency behind why it happened. They are attempts at understanding something inexplicable by attributing causes to what had happened in order to construct an unseen world of cause and effect (Ellis and ter Haar 2004, 36). Rumours contribute to a system where loose facts are appropriated into a coherent whole to provide a viable explanation that may soothe people's souls into accepting even something awful.

Gossip is talk about absent third parties that is aimed at ruining their reputations (Hagedorn and Neyrey 1998, 12). Nycyk (2015, 18–32) describes gossip as the spreading of harmful information about others with the view to persuading listeners or readers of the gossip to change their perception of the person or thing being gossiped about. It is a power tactic that is used to shape the thinking of others negatively. Gossip may result in the stigmatisation and shaming of the targeted person(s) where their identity and reputation are judged negatively, especially where there is competition for honour and respect.

Envious persecution, as socially constructed between the persons who experience it, is shaped by cultural, historical, and political factors to serve the purpose of the powerful (Darlaston-Jones 2016, 19). In such a space some injustices such as silencing and exclusion may be committed by using aspects of language that prevent others from fully expressing or defending themselves in cases where they are falsely accused (Spewak 2017, 425–440). In a country where rights of the weak are not fully protected and advantage may be taken of them on the basis of belief or religion, language is used to defend and justify such oppressive behaviour (Spewak 2017). Silencing with a view to exclusion may be used to offend or embarrass or mute the voices of those who are the target of persecution or make their actions offensive to those who must police human rights. A woman reporting a rape case at a police station may be asked embarrassing questions to prevent or inhibit her from telling the full story of what had happened. The purpose is to make her case not admissible before a court.

Fallis (2013) argues that protecting one's own privacy is natural to every human being in order to protect themselves from invasion by outside forces seeking control over something dear to them. Blaauw (2013) concurs with Fallis (2013) that allowing others to acquire knowledge of something in another's life may lead to harming the other. But often when persecutors identify someone for persecution, they insist that the secret of such a person should be revealed in order for them to assess whether that person has a secret, which then implies they are evil. More often than not such insistence is maliciously inspired, and the privacy of the victim is violated with the sole purpose of looting, persecuting and eventually even killing such a person. The protection of one's privacy is a fundamental and inalienable human right.

5 Professional Jealousy and Envy

Ashley (2009) defines professional jealousy as 'envy-turned-bad'. It is a normal and sometimes even positive thing to envy someone else and want to be like him or her. But in general envy starts with an unflattering social comparison that leads to a perception of inferiority (Smith 2004, 42). Envy arises when someone else's advantage is perceived as unfair and threatening (Smith 2004, 46). According to Ashley (2009), envying a person who does something wonderful is normal, but when some people fail to get what they want while other people get more than they need, four fundamental questions present themselves: 1) Do they want what the successful person has? 2) Are they willing to work hard to achieve the same success? 3) Do they have the necessary skills to reach that goal? 4) How do they deal with their own failures? More often than not, negative responses to these questions gives rise to jealousy. Professional jealousy stems from a fear of failure when workers are not team orientated. In situations in which ministers are working in silos and have amassed imagined powers, they often feel disorientated (Bednarz 2012).

5.1 Ladder of Escalation of Disputes that Leads to Persecution

In this section I first analyse theories of envy in communities by providing a model that explains how envy can lead to the persecution of the people envied (see Figure 1). The ladder of the escalation of persecution is used as a model to explain how envy is precipitated and then leads to a seemingly logical conclusion that it is necessary or justifiable to inflict pain or death on victims. One event in the Old Testament and one in the New Testament are used to illustrate this point.

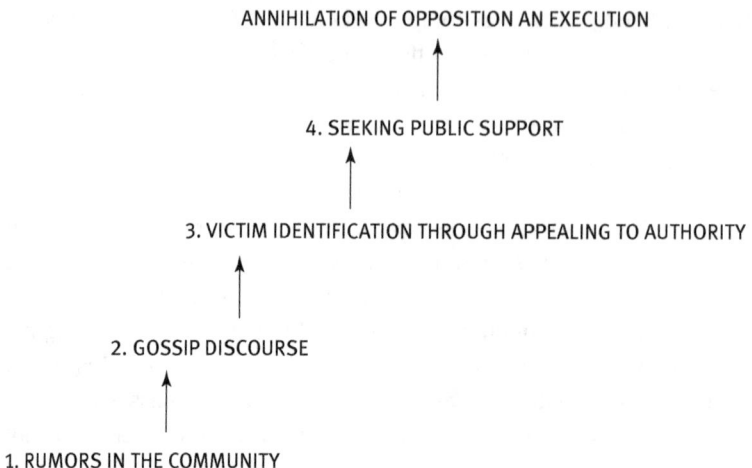

Figure 1: Foundations of Envious Persecutions, © Thias Kgatla.

In their research on witchcraft accusations and persecution in South Africa, Kgatla et al. (2003) came up with a model that explains how the escalation of disputes often leads to persecution. The model in Figure 1 is adapted from their model and used here to explain the phenomenon. The ladder starts at the bottom (level 1) and in some cases skips or even elaborates on some of the stages up to level 5. The model is universal and not limited to South Africa. Two biblical examples are used to explain how the model works: Gen 37 and Mark 15. Gen 37 and Mark 15 portray the lives of Joseph and Jesus Christ as targets of envy and describe how this envy evolved through simmering dissatisfactions, negative discourse (gossip or backbiting), victim naming, public support, annihilation of opposition and execution. The execution may take different paths depending on the circumstances. In rural communities, for example, the death penalty may be executed by mobs, while in communities where there are established civil laws, the alleged victims of persecution might be hurt physically or emotionally (as in urban areas).

In order to explain the model of persecution shown in Figure 1, I will now discuss each stage starting from the bottom to the top to elucidate the theory with examples. The work of Hagedorn and Neyrey (1998) is used to illustrate the model. Hagedorn and Neyrey (1998, 1) argue convincingly that it was out of envy that the Jews handed Jesus over to Pilate. These two scholars draw on two anthropological sources to provide a comprehensive study of what they call the 'anatomy of envy' in which they describe who envies whom, what is envied, why it is envied and how it is envied. They use the insight of Foster (in Hagedorn and Neyrey 1998) that envy has a complex structure.

5.2 Gossip Discourse

Landman (2009, 37–44) describes discourse as a grand narrative which, when a majority believes in it, starts to regulate behaviour and perceptions. Whether it is true or not, discourse has the power of legitimising how people see life. Its grave consequences include stereotyping its victims and shaping people's view of the world, while regulating a way of thinking about the matter at hand (Kgatla et al. 2003, 11). Discourse has a way of speaking about events while providing clarity on how to deal with competitors and rivals (Kgatla et al. 2003). Through 'whispering', discourse gathers its adherents, who may later become a large following (Kgatla et al. 2003). In communities, gossip discourse helps to identify the alleged 'evil doer', who should either be eliminated or ostracised from the community.

5.3 Identification of Victim and Legitimation of Persecution

The main purpose of persecution is to identify or legitimise accusation of the victim(s) (Kgatla et al. 2003, 13). Envious individuals accuse a person of wrongdoing without proof and the methods of identification and legitimisation are established. All steps that would be taken on the route to the persecution of victims are crucial as one step feeds into the other (Kgatla 2000, 84). The purpose of envious persecution is mainly to assert social control by self-appointed demagogues in the community who want people to toe the line and punish those who overstep the mark (Kgatla 2000, 203). The victims here include all people who do not comply with the law of negative egalitarianism (equalisation). This illusion advocates for a situation in which people are expected to think the same and have the same views about issues. More often than not, this kind of supposedly egalitarian thinking is the trigger of envy and identifies those people who transgress the norm as the enemies of the people (Kgatla 2000, 203). Such instruments of social control are self-destructive in that they prevent any form of development in the society in the name of egalitarianism. Admired and exemplary people in society are reduced to objects of pity (Hagedorn and Neyrey 1998, 12) through ostracism, exorcism and even homicide, stunting social development (Hagedorn and Neyrey 1998). The preservation of popular obedience and loyalty among people obsessed with envy is regarded as the essential bulwark against anarchy and social disintegration (Hagedorn and Neyrey 1998). The entire process of persecution is aimed at ensuring public support for the successful persecution. Gossip, rumours, talk about the alleged crime, confirmation of the identity of the victim(s), choosing an authoritative person for verification and support are all means of eliciting public support. In some incidents, the public support is sought with the aim of imposing mob justice, depending on the effectiveness of law enforcement in the society. The fatal flaw of the process is that it assumes accusations supported by an arbitrary positive allegation are evidence and not subjective assessments, whereas this is never the case (Taylor 2018). Based on arbitrary accusations and absurd claims, the persecutors try to justify their actions to the communities, for without their support they would feel insecure and vulnerable. The complexity of mob justice is manifestation of elements on a structural level in societies (Glad, Strömberg, and Westerlund 2010).

5.4 Authentication of the Process of Victim Identification

The intention of persecution can lie dormant in the community for a long time until the opportune moment for accusations or complaints arises (Kgatla et al. 2003, 13). In some societies, the identification of the people who are targets of envy occurs through divination (diviner or a fortune-teller), a king or chief, a psychotherapist in the society, authoritative persons in the society or through public outcries. A misguided interpretation of the law by a leader may also serve as a sufficient source for conviction. Once authority has been obtained from persons perceived to be the sources of moral authority (such as a diviner, chief, prominent leader, or church leader), execution of judgement is the next step. The process of identifying the person envied does not proceed according to universal legal principles of people being presumed innocent until proven guilty the court of law; instead, the victim is guilty as charged before trial (Kgatla et al. 2003, 27). If a trial is held, it is a mere formality that confirms the desired preconceived outcome (Kgatla et al. 2003). Therefore, envy is a malady that corrodes healthy relationships and hampers authentic social development. If it is not detected at an early stage and dealt with, it may spread like a wildfire that is difficult to extinguish at a later stage.

5.5 Annihilation of Opposition

If support for persecution is deemed insufficient, attempts are made to remove any doubts because a doubting community is not a supportive community. The exercise involves repudiating people with a different worldview and opting instead for likeminded people who would support the agenda of punishing the perceived enemies (Glad, Strömberg, and Westerlund 2010). It is therefore crucial that they annihilate any opposition to their envisaged programme. After persecuting envied persons, the persecutors would not like to live with dissonant feelings or remorse for what they have done. They do everything in their power to gloss over and justify their deeds in the name of protecting the people against evil individuals (Kgatla et al. 2003, 21). I now turn to the two biblical narratives that address the phenomenon of envy (Gen 37 and Mark 15).

5.5.1 Gen 37:3 and the Anatomy of Envy

Gen 37–50 explain how envy developed between Joseph and his brothers. In Gen 37:3 we read the story of Jacob and his preferential treatment of his son Joseph. Jacob's favouritism was demonstrated by his gift of the famous coat he gave to Joseph and this favouritism was reinforced by the unkind reports Joseph brought to his father about his brothers. Joseph was also a half-brother to Jacob's other ten sons and he earned the birth-right after Reuben, the eldest son, fell out of grace with Jacob because of his evil deed. Furthermore, Joseph had dreams that demonstrated that he had authority over his brothers, and they hated him for that (Deffinbaugh 2004). The animosity of Joseph's brothers towards him generated a bitterness that would lead to fierce persecution. Joseph's brothers waited until an opportune occasion to enact their persecution. Eventually the moment presented itself where Joseph's brothers could carry out their plans to eliminate him from their family. When his father sent him to look into his brothers, they captured him and plotted against him to put him to death.

5.5.2 Mark 15 and the Anatomy of Envy

Hagedorn and Neyrey (1998) argue that Pilate perceived that the accusers of Jesus Christ were acting out of envy when they handed Jesus over to him. High priests and religious leaders of the time were competing with Jesus for fame and civic honour. Hagedorn and Neyrey (1998) note that such honour was one of the pivotal values of ancient Israel. Honour determined people's worth, standing and reputation in the eyes of the broader public and the religious leaders of the time competed intensely for honour. Honour was perceived as a 'limited good for which they fought'. According to the Pulpit Bible Commentary of Mark 15:10, religious leaders of the time of Jesus saw that Jesus was gaining great and increasing influence over the people by the sublime beauty of his character, by the fame of his miracles, and by the power of his words. Hence, they concluded that unless he was arrested and put out of the way, their own influence would soon be jeopardised (Rigney 2014).

The chief priests were distressed at Jesus' success and His mere presence was destroying their prestige as He invaded their space of honour (Hagedorn and Neyrey 1998, 17). Jesus' recognition by the crowd was expanding at the expense of the chief priests. Jesus' honour and recognition were further dramatized by his entry into Jerusalem that enticed the people to sing Hosanna on Palm Sunday. This completely devasted the profiles of religious elites. They envied Him but they could not reach His standard. The solution to their distress was to eliminate Him. The honour of Jesus was publicly acknowledged wherever He went, and chief priests and scribes were no match for Him. They hid their envy behind a façade of care and compassion for others. In John 11:48 the religious leaders say: 'If we let him go on like this, everyone will believe in him, and the Romans will come and take away both our place and our nation'. In the same vein, the chief priest, Caiaphas, reiterated that it was better for one person to die for the people rather than for the whole nation to perish (Rigney 2014).

5.6 The Stages of Envy in Mark 15

The teachings, miracles and fame of Jesus overwhelm the chief priests and the elite of their time. Envy ensues because the praise and the acclaim of the crowds are for Jesus, while the high priests' popularity wanes. Ways are sought to discredit Jesus but when these fail, they opt to put Him to death.

Slanderous gossip is spread. They argue that 'He is possessed by Beelzebul, and by the prince of demons he casts out demons' (Mark 3:22). Pharisees would even tell those who were healed by Jesus to deny that he did in fact heal them (John 9:1–41).

Pharisees and some of the scribes send people to Jesus to entrap him in his talk (Mark 12:13). As he did his work publicly, he could be identified by the crowd that was following him.

In their entire campaign and attempt to discredit Jesus, the religious leaders of the time aimed to get public support. They sent rumours around that Jesus is disrespectful to the law of Moses and he is eating with sinners. They spare no effort to do harm to his reputation.

As the fame and the work of Jesus spread by leaps and bounds, the Pharisees and chief priests try everything in their power to regain the support of the masses until they are forced to kill Jesus. Envy remains a predictable, regular, and important element in pulling down Jesus, who is growing in fame and reputation.

Arbitrary arrest, trial and death remain the common outcomes of envy. The Jewish leaders' motives are based on love of fame and entitlement to mass praises, although their motives coincide with the overall plan of God of delivering His Son for the redemption of His people (Rigney 2014).

5.7 The Execution of the Sentence Is Abrupt and without Due Process

In the case of envy trials, as is often the case in witchcraft cases, the judges (juries) are not *crimen exceptum* (exceptional criminal judges) (Kgatla et al. 2003, 29), but activists who are propelled by envy. Often poverty, envy, frustrated aspirations and lost fame or limited opportunities for achieving fame are the hidden motives for why a person regarded by a society as successful is attacked on dubious grounds. The end goal of envious persecution is to eliminate any possibility of fairness to the other (Smith 2004, 46). It is an injustice that is flavoured by resentment towards a person who is viewed as not deserving his / her advantage over others (Smith 2004). Hostility and revulsion are defining elements of the envy; it is a defensive response to the achievements of those we reckon do not deserve the achievement or success. Depending on the epistemological lens through which cultural constructions have been shaped, the degradation of the culprit may take the form of persecution, scandalous attacks or harbouring of painful emotions that may erupt in other circumstances. If not managed, envy may hamper societal development, while masquerading as community welfare operations and even protection.

5.8 Four Axioms for the Process of Exorcism of the Exorcists

Egalitarianism often loses its utilitarian value of promoting equitable communal living to disputes that are often unexplained. Envy that is operationalized through witchcraft beliefs and persecution hides behind religious beliefs while justifying extreme violence. Wading off the demons of jealousy from the very people who are the leaders in exorcism practices may prove unattainable. The following are some guidelines for such 'exorcism from below'.

5.8.1 Knowledge of, and Respect for, Peoples' Fundamental Right to Hold Different Views, Values and Beliefs

The right to differ from others and still remain their friend is one of the basic requirements for the peaceful coexistence of human beings. In a healthy society, people venture outside of their personal boundaries to reach out to their neighbours in a spirit of acceptance. To achieve such objectives, a new educational plan to cultivate a willingness to give oneself to others by realigning one's personal identity in a way to give space to others, regardless their sex and age, should be designed (Kgatla 2007, 280–290).

5.8.2 A Comprehensive Understanding of Imago Dei

The first step in creating the right relationship with others is having a healthy relationship with oneself as a creature of God. The conflicting voices of love of neighbour and the misogyny, machismo, and sexism that men have used to inflate their sense of self should be resolved to create a way to creative coexistence. The daunting and conflicting feelings of bitterness, hate, jealousy, emptiness, and inferiority within people should be addressed by transformational education rooted in the development of a new character that accepts other people for whom they are. The next step in transcending personal and societal prejudices is coming to the realisation that humanity was created in the image of God to live and let others live for the sake of the prosperity of humankind in its entirety. Living in peace with those who constitute the 'other' implies acceptance of them, irrespective who they are and what gender they are. Healthy interpersonal relationships can be built by developing values such as honesty, responsibility, accountability, and sincerity. An educational model based on these values should be implemented to create an anti-hegemonic society (Kgatla 2007, 289).

5.8.3 Demonstrating the Role and Function of Religion in Promoting and Constructing Conflict

Religion, by its very nature, promotes values, beliefs and attitudes that may either be conflictual or character enhancing. If negative elements of religion are instilled in learners from a tender age, they are less likely to transcend them when they are grown up. Religion can leave an indelible mark, which cannot be removed at a later stage, on people's minds. Deconstructing polluted minds may prove impossible once ideas have been left to germinate in the minds of learners. Resources to fight the pandemic of patriarchal infection should be made available. Religious virtues such as love, justice, fairness, coexistence, and righteousness can be cemented in the minds of learners, if inculcated responsibly (Kgatla 2000).

5.8.4 Correcting and Resolving Political, Social, Economic, and Cultural Disputes and Conflicts

Many disputes and conflicts stemming from and creating prejudices in society emanate from fear of domination, competition for power, scarce resources, and inferiority complexes. Conversely, the desire for equality can also generate conflicts as people who have an innate talent for development may break the chain of slavery to assert themselves. In that way resistance to suppression (forced egalitarianism) may lead to a social and cultural explosion. Accusations of witchcraft may be used as a survival tool to address people's vulnerabilities, but it may also lead to insurrection. The powerful may be reminded by the less powerful to stop dominating a space, the 'haves' made aware of the need for resources by the 'have-nots'. This could be a matter of simple justice that the powerful do not want to confront. Education curricula tailored to addressing and correcting the imbalances between the rich and poor, men and women, arrogant and meek are imperative. Conflict-ridden communities would be able to attend to their problems if they were made aware of them and helped to find a way out of these problems, developing survival skills that would keep them on course towards a healthy civil society (Kgatla 2000).

6 Conclusion

The trajectory of this chapter has been the introduction to the task of dealing with 'exorcism from below', where the exorcists are themselves to be exorcised of the evil they perceive in others while it is resident within themselves. Here the discourse should be turned around and the 'hunters become the hunted'; the exorcists become the exorcised. The study is anchored in the African epistemology of 'live and let live'. A cautionary note is struck in pointing out that egalitarianism is not always value-free but may be embedded in prejudices that are life-threatening. A new balance of African communality should be adopted as the guiding star.

In the space in which these prejudices are operative, different forms of stereotyping, persecution and even death may remain unnoticed as the very sources where violence is brewed, and they need the antidote of exorcism from below. The study also reaffirmed that the understanding of exorcism should be retrieved from narrow religious and psychological confines. If viewed in totality, the methods to be employed for its eradication will be broad and comprehensive to address the whole of society. There is no 'one size fits all' or 'quick fix' when it comes to the form of exorcism discussed in this chapter. A few guidelines are suggested as ways of minimising the extent of the underlying threat of envy as externalised in witchcraft.

People need an environment that supports life: food, shelter, water, and security. In order to lead a stable life, they require resources such as land, money, livestock, water, roads, schools, employment and other necessities. They need an imaginative programme that will infuse their lives with hope and inform their vision. If these things are absent, the result is a deepening of poverty. Then distortion of social relationships, stress, and anxiety – all leading to social conflict – are bound to occur. Economic and political power, as well as cultural progress, should be restored since people want to be in control of their future and of their destiny. Early detection of societal prejudices that deny the value of life is essential if the demagogues are to be exorcised from prohibited from exercising their delinquent power.

Bibliography

Ani, Ndubuisi C. 2013. "Appraisal of African Epistemology in the Global System." *Journal of Alternation* 20:295–320.

Arneson, Richard. 2013. "Egalitarianism." *Stanford Encyclopaedia of Philosophy.* https://plato.stanford.edu/entries/egalitarianism/ (30.11.2021).

Ashley, Jennifer. 2009. "Professional Jealousy – How to Deal with it and Make it Work for you." http://jenniferonwriting.blogspot.com/2009/07/professional-jealousy-how-to-deal-with.html (30.11.2021).

Bednarz, Timothy F. 2012. "Dealing with the Five Causes of Professional Jealousy." https://majorium.wordpress.com/2012/07/05/dealing-with-the-five-causes-of-professional-jealousy/ (30.11.2021).

Blaauw, Martijn. 2013. "Introduction: Privacy, Secrecy and Epistemology." *Episteme* 10:99.

Darlaston-Jones, Dawn. 2016. *Making Connections: The Relationship between Epistemology and Research Methods*. Fremantle: University of Notre Dame.

Deffinbaugh, Robert L. 2004. *The Generations of Jacob and the Jealousy of His Sons*. A Bible Study Presented at Community Bible Chapel in Richardson, Texas: no publisher.

Dombeck, Mark. No date. "Exorcism: When it Is Appropriate." https://www.mentalhelp.net/blogs/exorcism-when-is-it-appropriate/ (30.11.2021).

Ellis, Stephen, and Gerrie ter Haar. 2004. *Worlds of Power: Religious Thought and Political Practice in Africa*. Johannesburg: Wits University Press.

Fallis, Don T. 2013. "Privacy and Lack of Knowledge." *Episteme* 10:153–166.

Glad, Robin, Åsa Strömberg, and Anton Westerlund. 2010. *Mob Justice: A Qualitative Research Regarding Vigilante Justice in Modern Uganda*. Gothenburg: University of Gothenburg.

Gyekey, Kwame. 1987. *An Essay on African Philosophical Thought: The Akan Conceptual Scheme*. Cambridge, MA: Cambridge University Press.

Hagedorn, Anselm C., and Jerome H. Neyrey. 1998. "It Was out of Envy that they Handed Jesus over (Mark 15:10): The Anatomy of Envy and the Gospel of Mark." *Journal for the Study of the New Testament* 20:15–56.

Kgatla, Thias. 2000. *Moloi ga na mmala (A Witch Has No Colour)*. Dissertation: University of South Africa.

Kgatla, Thias, Gerrie ter Haar, Wouter E. A. van Beek, and J. J. de Wolf, eds. 2003. *Crossing Witchcraft Barriers in South Africa: Exploring Witchcraft Accusations: Causes and Solutions*. Utrecht: Utrecht University.

Kgatla, Thias. 2007. "Containment of Witchcraft Accusations in South Africa: A Search for a Transformational Approach to Curb the Problem." In *Imagining Evil: Witchcraft Beliefs and Accusations in Contemporary Africa*, edited by Gerrie ter Haar, Trenton: Africa World Press, 269–292.

Moore, E. Garth. 1979. "Theories Underlying Exorcism: Theological and Psychic." *Journal of the Royal Society of Medicine* 72:220–221.

Nycyk, Michael. 2015. "The Power of Gossip and Rumour Have in Shaping Online Identity and Reputation: A Critical Discourse Analysis." *The Qualitative Report* 20:18–32.

Landman, Christina. 2009. "Calvinism and South African Women: A Short Historical Overview." *Studia Historiae Ecclesiasticae* 35:89–102.

Pulpit Bible Commentary. https://www.studylight.org/commentaries/tpc.html (30.11.2021).

Rigney, John. 2014. *When Envy Turns Deadly*. https://www.desiringgod.org/articles/when-envy-turns-deadly (30.11.2021)

Smith, Richard H. 2004. "Envy and Its Transmutation." In *The Social Life of Emotions*, edited by Larissa Z. Tiedens and Colin W. Leach, Cambridge, MA: Cambridge University Press, 43–63.

Spewak, David C. 2017. "Understanding Assertion to Understand Silencing: Finding an Account of Assertion that Explains Silencing Arising from Testimonial Injustice." *Episteme* 14:423–440.

Taylor, Kathy. 2018. "Getting the Wrong End of the Stick: The Prosecutor's Fallacy." https://www.cebm.ox.ac.uk/news/views/the-prosecutors-fallacy (30.11.2021).

Udefi, Amaechi. 2014. "The Rationale for an African Epistemology: A Critical Examination of the Igbo Views on Knowledge, Belief, and Justification." *Canadian Social Science* 10:108–117.

Wolff, Jonathan. 2010. "Fairness, Respect and Egalitarian *Ethos* Revisited." *The Journal of Ethics* 14:335–350.

Wray, K. Brad. 2010. "Introduction: Collective Knowledge and Science." *Episteme* 7:181–184.

Michel Clasquin-Johnson
Fasting / Asceticism / Feasting

1 Introduction

Fasting is one of the most universal patterns of religious behaviour. From prehistoric shamans to the mystics of our own time, the sensory deprivation provided by a fast has been used to fuel mystical experiences (Espi Forcen and Espi Forcen 2015; Rampling 1986). The most extreme form of this is fasting to the point of death, exploited as a religious exercise (*sallekhanà*) in the Jain religion (Vallely 2018; The Quint News Staff 2018) and more recently as political blackmail by figures as diverse as Gandhi, whose claim to scriptural support for his practice in the Bhagavad Gītā was somewhat far-fetched (Thomas 1974, 191), nominally religious groups like the Provisional IRA (Yuill 2007), and the purely political – as I write this, the Ukrainian dissident Oleg Sentsov lies dying in a Russian prison hospital after a 100-day hunger strike (France24.com 2018).

Fasting is not the exclusive domain of the religious elite. Various religious traditions have institutionalized a more moderate form of the practice. The most famous of these nowadays is the Muslim fast of Ramadan, which always receives considerable media attention in both Islamic (Christmann 2006) and non-Islamic countries. But fasting has a long history in the Abrahamic faiths. In Christianity, we can trace it all the way to the Apostle Paul (Yinger 2008). Jews, even secular Jews, fast over Yom Kippur (Shoham 2013, 184). The latest member of this group of religions, the Bahá'í Faith, has its own fasting ritual adapted from the Muslim one to fit in with its 19-day months (Bahai.org no date). In Hinduism, the situation is more complicated, some Hindus may fast on specific days of significance to their guru, others may do so only during a specific festival period. In Buddhism we do not find much evidence of institutionalized fasting: the monastic practice of not eating after noon, also followed by especially zealous lay followers during retreats, is not seen in that light.

But fasting has its counterpart, and in the English language we can call it by its cognate term, feasting. Where fasting has been the technique of choice of the solitary mystic, and more occasionally codified into rituals for the masses, feasting has been far more universally adopted. Sometimes the two become intermingled. The feast may precede the fast – Carnival is followed by Lent. Alternatively, the fast may precede the feast: Ramadan is followed by Eid al Fitr, but there have even been criticisms from within the Muslim world that the nightly fast-breaking during Ramadan (al-Iftar) is becoming overly commercialized and is turning the monthly fast of Ramadan into a nightly feast of Ramadan:

> In each day of the Ramadan month, thousands of visitors crammed the square before the sunset and waited until the time that daily fasting would be over. After the meals were eaten, shopping

and enjoyment of various cultural activities began. The activities included religious panels addressing different aspects of Ramadan and Islam as well as artistic performances (Sandikci and Omeraki 2007).

Does this dichotomy between religious fasting and feasting echo in our own, more secular time? I believe it does. On the one hand we are told that the developed world is experiencing an epidemic of obesity. This is not a purely western phenomenon, and it does not spare the religious. In 2016, the Bangkok Post reported that nearly half the Buddhist monks in Thailand were dangerously overweight (Charoensuthipan 2016), findings that were quickly echoed around the world (Iyengar 2016; Rosenbaum 2016; Sherwell 2016). At this point, I need to divulge that I underwent a Roux-en-Y gastric bypass some years ago.

On the other hand, we have seen the emergence of eating disorders such as anorexia nervosa and bulimia. Possibly they have always existed, but they are now common enough, or sufficiently well-recognized, to claim their own category in the DSM-V and ICD-10 (Fairburn and Cooper 2011; Limburg et al. 2018). Long regarded as mainly a female problem, there is now a belated realization that specifically male eating disorders exist and are currently not reflected in these lists (Murray et al. 2017). This male form of the problem focuses on muscularity rather than thinness but can be just as fatal.

These issues (I will not prejudge them by calling them diseases) are embedded in a social context. O'Connor (O'Connor 2000) sees them as reflecting the Protestant worldly asceticism, a fruitless pursuit of perfection demanded by middle-class society, and a search for identity in a world of ever-expanding choices. We have created a world, he argues, in which it is possible not only for anorexia to exist, but in which it can change and mutate to confound us once again:

> Once anorexia was trauma-induced: a terrible event – death, divorce, sexual abuse – fed a synergy of self-hate and ascetic escape. Now it seems increasingly trauma-inducing: adolescent risk-taking goes wrong, a trauma tempted comes to be (O'Connor 2000, 8).

Religion is part of this social context. There is some indication that religion may act as a contributing factor (Huline-Dickens 2000; Abraham and Birmingham 2008) to eating disorders, although the evidence is hardly overwhelming, and at times contradictory.[1] It is rather more obvious that westernisation is a powerful factor (Lai 2000). Religion, or at least aspects of religion, has also been used as a tool for recovery (Garrett 1997; Slyter 2012).

We will not deal with fasting as a deliberate religious or political act. What interests us here is not the Jain monk making a deliberate decision to fast unto death, nor with the political prisoner staging a hunger strike. These are issues of suicide, soteri-

---

[1] E.g., Joughin et al. 1992 report that religious beliefs increase among anorexics but decrease among bulimics.

ology, and self-sacrifice. The religious professional will be able to determine his or her religion's theological position on that and respond accordingly. The religiously-sanctioned fast stopping far short of death is also not our concern here. The health implications of these rituals are well-researched (e.g., Myers and Dardas 2017) and religious traditions generally have their own lists of exceptional cases where a fast can be interrupted or deferred. What interests us in the context of Practical Theology, as the term is understood in this volume, is the position of the person who come to the religious professional and confesses that the tension between fasting and feasting has oscillated out of control and has become a life-controlling, and life-threatening, obsession.

A full investigation of the historical development of fasting and feasting in religion such as found in Grimm (Grimm 1996) is beyond the scope of this article. Let us simply stipulate that religious professionals, and religious people generally, will encounter these patterns in daily life and need guidance on how to deal with them. In what follows I will explore possible resources from the Buddhist tradition, but that does not mean that it only applies to Buddhist situations. On the contrary, the intention is to explore how engagement with different ways of thinking about a problem can enrich our ability to deal with social issues regardless of our personal beliefs and affiliations.

The Buddhist approach to the feasting/fasting problem is to recommend the Middle Way between extreme asceticism and extreme indulgence. A balanced lifestyle, as we might say today. This references the Buddha's own history, in which he experienced extreme indulgence as a prince and extreme asceticism as a wandering ascetic. Enlightenment would not be attained until he renounced both extremes and took up a lifestyle that was still disciplined, but not life-threatening. This has been the blueprint for the Buddhist monastic lifestyle ever since. It is something of a stock Buddhist answer to all existential crises.

It sounds promising, but once we start asking questions it quickly shows it limitations. Where, exactly, are the endpoints, the limiting conditions? In the context of his own time the Buddha was a moderate, but we can hardly extrapolate that position to all times, places and social positions. What would be considered 'extreme asceticism' today? Considering the resources now available to the well-off, what would constitute 'extreme indulgence'? Then, is the Middle Way to be regarded as an exact, computable position precisely in-between these extremes or is it more of a broad area that avoids both but allows considerable vagueness at its own borders?

It is not at all clear that Middle-Way-ism was ever intended to be a universal cure to all human dilemmas. Vernezze (Vernezze 2007), for example demonstrates that the Buddhist approach to anger more closely resembles the Stoic view of Seneca than the Golden Mean of Aristotle. It *was* explicitly applied to the question of eating. In fact, the Buddha's decision to abandon self-starvation and adopt a moderate nutritional regime is one of the key moments in the Buddhist mythos. But what does it mean in practice? How can we apply it?

To get a clearer understanding of the Middle Way, we need to stop thinking of it as a static position between two extremes and see how it can act as a dynamic, metamodern (Clasquin-Johnson 2017) movement that oscillates between them while also transcending both. This will require a journey into Indian logic.

Western logic, also known as Aristotelian logic after its great systematizer, holds that there are two distinct logical states, which we can represent as A and not-A. No third possibility exists. We cannot deny that this is an immensely powerful way of looking at reality. Its descendant, Boolean logic, determines the operation of the computer on which I am typing this essay. However, it is not the only way to view reality. Two-value logic assumes the existence of an external world that can be neatly dissected into opposing pairs of values. It does not value the messiness of actual human experience. It forces our perception of an analogue world into a digital pattern.

Indian logic evolved from the study of grammar rather than mathematics. It does not attempt to separate logical relations from epistemology (Matilal, Ganeri, and Tiwari 1998, 14); on the contrary, how we come by valid knowledge is a key question in Indian thought that cannot be separated from how we can manipulate that knowledge. If we were to look at the phenomenon of feasting and fasting from the world of Indian, and specifically Buddhist, logic, the reality of a Middle Way might well become clear.

In Buddhism, there are four logical possibilities. Instead of a *dilemma*, Buddhism presents us with a *tetralemma* (Sanskrit: Catuṣkoṭi, literally, "four corners"):

- A
- Not-A
- Both A and Not-A
- Neither A nor Not-A

The first two of these are familiar enough and for our present purposes we can regard them as identical to their equivalents in western logic. The third option can be characterized as the position of 'it depends'. Is a blade of grass intelligent? It is and it is not. What is the context of the question? Compared to the sand out of which it grows, grass can be seen to send its roots down towards moisture and its leaves towards the light. There is an intelligence of a sort there. But compared to human intelligence, that of a blade of grass is sufficiently minuscule that we can feel justified in saying that grass is not intelligent. It depends. Or, to relate it to the theme of this essay, is the human ability to store excess energy as fat life-threatening? Originally, when we lived as hunter-gatherers, it might have been all that stood between us and death during a harsh winter. But today, that life-enhancing ability has become potentially life-threatening. It depends.

The fourth possibility is best explained in terms of what Ryle (Ryle 1949, 16) calls a "category mistake". It indicates that the question has been wrongly phrased, that to answer 'Yes', 'No' or even 'It depends' is wrong because the question itself makes no sense. However, Buddhist philosophy does not simply wave it away as an error. By fully integrating this corner into its system, it acknowledges the human ability to hold mutually contradictory views. Is an anorexia sufferer fat? She is neither fat nor non-fat. She sees herself as overweight despite the emaciated figure staring back at her from the mirror. This is the corner of 'Not Applicable' or 'None of the Above'.

There is no hierarchy among the four corners. No one corner is considered ultimate or even superior to the others. In fact, if we were to ask the question which one is ultimate the answer must be 'none of the above' on an even higher level of 'none-of-the-aboveness' than before. Ultimacy, enlightenment, nirvana is not a geometrical central point between the corners, it is transcendent to all four, simultaneously the center and the periphery of this four-cornered reality.

Is this way of looking at the world exclusively Buddhist? No. It has its own antecedents as far back as the Ṛg Veda, for example, the radical skepticism in RV 10.129 where it is said that "Then even nothingness was not, nor existence" and "Then there was neither death nor immortality". That it was commonly held by non-Buddhist sages in the Buddha's time is evident in the Brahmajala Sutta:

> When questioned about this or that point, he resorts to evasive statements and to endless equivocation: 'I do not take it thus, nor do I take it in that way, nor do I take it in some other way. I do not say that it is not, nor do I say that it is neither this nor that' (Bodhi 2010).

We can see similar approaches in the thinking of pre-Socratic (or should that be pre-Aristotelian?) thinkers like Democritus. In our own time, we see fuzzy logic and probability theory as other attempts to broaden the horizons of thought beyond two-value logic.

Within Buddhist Studies, the attention has mostly been on its presence in the thought of Nāgārjuna (e. g., Cotnoir 2018; Hayes 1994), but Nāgārjuna's task was to use the Catuskoti to destroy itself, leaving only Ultimacy staring us in the face. Our task here is less radical. There is also a philosophical cottage industry that has taken up the task of relating Buddhist logic to western logic (e. g., Ng 1987; Chakravarti 1980; Makino 2014). Again, this is not our concern here. We want to *apply* the logic of the "four corners" to find a practical, helpful understanding of the Middle Way between fasting and feasting. If we cannot find the extradimensional Ultimacy, perhaps we can at least find, not an exact point, between the four corners, but a broad two-dimensional area where we can understand what the sufferer is going through and reduce the suffering: an unstable, inexact, and philosophically unsatisfying, but humanly helpful Middle Way.

2 Corner 1: Feasting

Somewhat arbitrarily, we will set up feasting rather than fasting as the first corner. Feasting is overindulgence in the classical sense, the gratification of the senses, and Buddhism has a lot to say about it and advice on avoiding it (and if the reports of obese Thai monks are to be believed, not all that successfully). Overindulgence in sensual pleasure of any kind, including food, is the prime exemplar of craving (Pali: *taṇhā*). Etymologically, the word *taṇhā* is derived from the Old Sanskrit *tṛ́ṣṇā* and therefore related to the English word *thirst*.

This is such an important concept in Buddhism that it features in the Four Noble Truths as the prime factor in keeping us trapped in unenlightened reality. Three types are distinguished: *kama-taṇhā* (the craving for sensual pleasure), *bhava-taṇhā* (the craving for existence) and *vibhava-taṇhā* (the craving for non-existence).

It is obvious that craving for sensory pleasures is the main issue here. But these three types of craving are not mutually exclusive: sensory pleasure provides evidence that we exist. Craving for pleasure and craving for existence are intertwined.

In the Donapaka Sutta we are told that King Pasenadi of Kosala was used to eating a bucketful of rice at a time. The Buddha told him to have a verse recited to him at every meal.

> When a person is constantly mindful,
> And knows when enough food has been taken,
> All their afflictions become more slender,
> They age more gradually, protecting their lives. (Olendzki 2005)

The King gradually reduced his rice intake to no more than a cup-full and was reported to have become quite slim. This may well be the oldest recorded example of a reduced carbohydrate diet in history.

In the Buddhist monastic world, the classical prescription against craving for sensory pleasures (primary sexual desires, but also the pleasures of eating) is to meditate on the body (Pali: *paṭikkūlamanasikāra*), analyzing it into its constituent parts and reflecting on the unpleasantness of each part in isolation (Radich 2007, 154–55). In time, this results in a revulsion with the body's demands for sensory input. A more extreme version of this practice was the contemplation of the decomposition process of a corpse (Radich 2007, 159–164).

How can this be translated into practical terms? The Buddha did not explicitly tell the king how much rice was permissible. He trusted in the king's own judgement to determine the correct amount, and simply gave him a daily reminder in the form of a verse. The meditation on the parts of the body does not castigate the practitioner for *having* desires, it simply advises us to see the body for what it is. The strategy common to both is not to attack the act of feasting itself, not even the craving underlying it, but to let the practitioner get in touch with their own physicality, to trust in his or her own ability to perceive the reality of our physical condition and take the necessary steps to correct it.

3 Corner 2: Fasting

If craving for existence leads to suffering, then so does craving for non-existence. If anything, it is a more subtle form of craving, and here we must find the roots of anorexia. In the Buddhist analysis, this is not merely a response to peer pressure and social norms: it reflects a deep-seated desire *not to be*, a suicide in slow-motion. Suicide is regarded as an irrational act in Buddhism. "By this I do not mean that it is performed while the balance of the mind is disturbed, but that it is incoherent in the context of Buddhist teachings" (Keown 1996, 30).

However, Buddhism has little concrete to offer here. There is of course the Buddha's rejection of the extreme asceticism he had practiced in his youth, as discussed above. There are several exhortations to appreciate human life as a rare opportunity to practice meditation and attain enlightenment. But are there specific procedures? We have seen that there are specific meditative techniques to reduce the craving for sense-pleasures for those addicted to them. But there are no forms of meditation specifically designed to increase awareness of the joys of living, especially not where food is concerned. To the Buddha and the early Buddhists, desire for existence and sense-pleasures were more immediate problems than the desire for non-existence. We may wonder if Buddhism itself has strayed from its own Middle Way here.

What we certainly do not find here is any advice to 'get in touch with your body'. On the contrary, the Buddhist view is that we are excessively obsessed with our bodies, with the way they appear to others, the way they feel after a meal or during a fast. These are data points to be noted, of course. But the Buddhist view is that we need to get at far deeper-rooted tendencies in the mind to find the source of the problem.

4 Corner 3: Both Feasting and Fasting

Before we continue, no, this is not the corner where we will explain bulimia. That would be seen as feasting and fasting (of a sort) in rapid succession, and therefore also the craving for existence and non-existence competing within the person's awareness.

In this corner we can raise the question, who gets to define feasting and fasting? Is a given meal a feast or a fast? We have already seen this problem when we discussed the Middle Way. Perceptions of feasting change with time and distance. What may seem to be a depressingly non-nutritious and routine-tasting foodstuff to a Western twenty-first century urbanite, say, a slice of white bread with peanut butter, might appear as the pinnacle of decadence to a sixth century BCE Indian peasant. Not, however to the sixth century BCE Indian noble or courtier. On the other hand, amounts of food that would lead to obesity in a sedentary modern person would barely sustain a pre-modern worker who requires the energy to perform long hours of manual labor.

Feasting is about quality as well as quantity, and the perception of both these qualities is socially determined. We can therefore make no hard and fast rule at which point normal intake is "normal". Our normal may be another's feast or fast.

Let us recall the Buddha's encounter with King Pasenadi. Social convention at the time required the king to feast. What triggered the Buddha's advice? The fact that king Pasenadi was having physical difficulties walking – he is described as "replete and puffing" (Walshe 2007). It was not the feasting, but the result of the feasting that resulted in this text. The king was admonished to develop mindfulness and know from an inner awareness when "enough food has been taken" (Olendzki 2005). After losing weight through reducing his food intake (fasting, compared to what he used to consume) we are told that "on a later occasion King Pasenadi, his body in good shape, stroked his healthy limbs and fervently exclaimed: 'Truly the Blessed One has doubly shown compassion for my welfare, both in this life and in the life to come!" (Walshe 2007) While not a feast in any literal sense, metaphorically his fast had resulted in a "feast" of positive sensations.

The lesson here is that we have within us, the wisdom to know when healthy eating has evolved into unhealthy feasting, and perhaps by extension, when it has evolved into unhealthy fasting. We are taught that this mindfulness trumps the social conventions that attempt to define us and our relationship to food. Within this subjectivity we can escape from the social confusion of 'it depends' and find our own balance, our own Middle Way. Like King Pasenadi, we can be both fasting and feasting.

5 Corner 4: Neither Feasting nor Fasting

Finally, we reach the fourth possibility, the corner of 'Not Applicable'. We have already pointed out one application in the self-image of the anorexia sufferer, but there is a further dimension. Here we encounter the phenomena we earlier decided not to focus on: the hunger striker. If we focus on the hunger striker's relationship to food, we simply miss the point. The hunger striker, or the Jain who is hastening his or her death by refraining from eating, is neither feasting nor fasting. They are doing something completely different, which requires a different analysis and approach.

6 Conclusion

Let us return to the question we posed before: Is there a Middle Way to be found between feasting and fasting? How can we help people caught up in either one, or both? From the discussion above I believe we can isolate some guidelines:

1. Is the problem really food related? If the person is fasting for religious or political purposes, the relationship must occur on that level. Food is a secondary, perhaps even tertiary consideration. The hunger striker has chosen food to make a point,

but it could have been something else. For example, in Buddhism we have seen self-immolation used to bring the world's attention to the plight of otherwise forgotten people (King 2000; Yang 2011).

2. Which kind of craving is active within the person? In the Buddhist analysis, there will always be craving, unless the person is fully enlightened, in which case he or she would be counselling us! We have seen that three types are distinguished: *kama-taṇhā* (the craving for sensual pleasure), *bhava-taṇhā* (the craving for existence) and *vibhava-taṇhā* (the craving for non-existence). This is not the *only* valid Buddhist analysis. We could instead have used the "three cankers", a list that partially overlaps this one:
- Sensual craving (*kāmāsavā*)
- Craving for existence (*bhavāsavā*)
- Ignorance (*avijjāsavā*)

Or we could have used the 'three poisons of greed (*lobha*), hatred (*dosa*) and delusion (*moha*). These are different ways of restating the Buddhist message, and some are more popular in some schools of Buddhism than others. Regardless of which one we choose to work with, the underlying theme is that we need to look beneath the surface manifestation and trace the deeply rooted universal patterns in the human psyche, to analyze the problem to its most fundamental form.

3. Now comes the difficult part: empowering the person to find his or her own path. We saw this in the tale of King Pasenadi. The king was a devout Buddhist, and the Buddha could simply have ordered him to eat less. He did not. Instead, he presented a verse that caused the king to look within. The king's actions followed from that. We each have to find our own way, our own Middle Way between feasting and fasting. All that a religious professional can hope to do is to provide an initial impetus, to kickstart the process. After that, we have to let go.

There is therefore not a Middle Way. There are as many Middle Ways as there are human beings, each one unique. But Buddhism maintains that within ourselves we each have the innate wisdom to find that personal Middle Way. Gurus, holy texts, rituals, meditative exercises, and philosophies can help. I trust, for example that the above discussion has shown how a consideration of other ways of thinking can help us to break out of the shackles of dualistic thinking and take full account of the glorious messiness of our way of experiencing reality. But in the end, we are alone and must find our own Middle Way.

We will fail. That is inevitable for unenlightened beings. But we will try again. Eventually we will find a relatively stable equilibrium, the right Middle Way for that time, that place, and above all, for that person. When time, place or person changes, the process starts all over, but hopefully, with the newly gained insight, the oscillations will be more gentle. Over the years (or lifetimes, if you follow Buddhist ideas on the afterlife) the stabilization will continue, and the Middle Way will reveal itself. It will be the Middle Way of fasting, of feasting, of both fasting and feasting, and of neither fasting nor feasting.

Bibliography

Abraham, Natalia K., and Carl Laird Birmingham. 2008. "Is There Evidence That Religion Is a Risk Factor for Eating Disorders?" *Eating and Weight Disorders: Studies on Anorexia, Bulimia and Obesity* 13:75–78.

Bahai.org. No date. "Fasting." https://www.bahai.org/beliefs/life-spirit/devotion/fasting (29.11.2021).

Bodhi Bhikkhu. 2010. "Brahmajāla Sutta: The All-Embracing Net of Views." https://www.accesstoinsight.org/tipitaka/dn/dn.01.0.bodh.html (29.11.2021).

Chakravarti, Sitansu. 1980. "The Madhyamika 'Catuskoti' or Tetralemma." *Journal of Indian Philosophy* 8:303–306.

Charoensuthipan, Penchan. 2016. "Almost Half Monkhood 'Overweight'." In *Bangkok Post*. https://www.bangkokpost.com/thailand/general/897276/almost-half-monkhood-overweight (29.11.2021).

Christmann, Andreas. 2006. "An Invented Piety: Ramadan on Syrian TV." *Diskus* 4. http://jbasr.com/basr/diskus/diskus1-6/CHRISTMA.txt (29.11.2021).

Clasquin-Johnson, Michel. 2017. "Towards a Metamodern Academic Study of Religion and a More Religiously Informed Metamodernism." *HTS Teologiese Studies / Theological Studies* 73:1–11.

Cotnoir, Aaron J. 2018. "Nagarjuna's Logic." In *The Moon Points Back*, edited by Koji Tanaka, Jay L. Garfield, Yasuo Deguchi, and Graham Priest, New York: Oxford University Press, 176–188.

Espi Forcen, Fernando, and Carlos Espi Forcen. 2015. "The Practice of Holy Fasting in the Late Middle Ages." *The Journal of Nervous and Mental Disease* 203:650–653.

Fairburn, Christopher G., and Zafra Cooper. 2011. "Eating Disorders, DSM–5 and Clinical Reality." *British Journal of Psychiatry* 198:8–10.

France24.com. 2018. "Jailed Filmmaker Oleg Sentsov on Day 100 of Russia Hunger Strike." https://www.france24.com/en/20180821-jailed-filmmaker-oleg-sentsov-day-100-russia-hunger-strike-ukraine-crimea-putin (29.11.2021).

Garrett, Catherine J. 1997. "Recovery from Anorexia Nervosa: A Sociological Perspective." *International Journal of Eating Disorders* 21:261–272.

Grimm, Veronika E. 1996. *From Feasting to Fasting, the Evolution of a Sin*. London: Routledge.

Hayes, Richard P. 1994. "Nāgārjuna's Appeal." *Journal of Indian Philosophy* 22:299–378.

Huline-Dickens, Sarah. 2000. "Anorexia Nervosa: Some Connections with the Religious Attitude." *British Journal of Medical Psychology* 73:67–76.

Iyengar, Rishi. 2016. "Thailand's Monks Eat Too Much and Are Costing the Country Millions in Health Care." *Time*. http://time.com/4260641/thailand-buddhist-monks-food-obesity/ (29.11.2021).

Joughin, Neil, Arthur H. Crisp, Christine Halek, and Heather Humphrey. 1992. "Religious Belief and Anorexia Nervosa." *International Journal of Eating Disorders* 12:397–406.

Keown, Damien. 1996. "Buddhism and Suicide: The Case of Channa." *Journal of Buddhist Ethics* 3:8–31.

King, Sallie B. 2000. "They Who Burned Themselves for Peace: Quaker and Buddhist Self-Immolators during the Vietnam War." *Buddhist-Christian Studies* 20:127–150.

Lai, Kelly Y.C. 2000. "Anorexia Nervosa in Chinese Adolescents – Does Culture Make a Difference?" *Journal of Adolescence* 23:561–568.

Limburg, Karina, Chloe Y. Shu, Hunna J. Watson, Kimberley J. Hoiles, and Sarah J. Egan. 2018. "Implications of DSM-5 for the Diagnosis of Pediatric Eating Disorders." *International Journal of Eating Disorders* 51:392–400.

Makino, Tetu. 2014. "A Note on a Modified Catuskoti." *Prospectus* 17:1–18.

Matilal, Bimal Krishna, Jonardon Ganeri, and Heeraman Tiwari. 1998. *The Character of Logic in India*. Albany: State University of New York Press.

Murray, Stuart B., Jason M. Nagata, Scott Griffiths, Jerel P. Calzo, Tiffany A. Brown, Deborah Mitchison, Aaron J. Blashill, and Jonathan M. Mond. 2017. "The Enigma of Male Eating Disorders: A Critical Review and Synthesis." *Clinical Psychology Review* 57:1–11.

Myers, Pauline, and Latefa Ali Dardas. 2017. "Ramadan Fasting and Diabetes Management among Muslims in the United States: An Exploratory Study." *Journal of Muslim Minority Affairs* 37:233–244.

Ng, Yu-Kwan. 1987. "The Arguments of Nāgārjuna in the Light of Modern Logic." *Journal of Indian Philosophy* 15:363–384.

O'Connor, Richard A. 2000. "Is Anorexia a Post-Modern Asceticism?" *Anthropology News* 41:7–8.

Olendzki, Andrew. 2005. "Donapaka Sutta: King Pasenadi Goes on a Diet." https://www.accestoinsight.org/tipitaka/sn/sn03/sn03.013.olen.html (29.11.2021).

Radich, Michael David. 2007. "The Somatics of Liberation: Ideas about Embodiment in Buddhism from Its Origins to the Fifth Century C.E." Harvard: Doctoral Dissertation. https://www.academia.edu/297146/_The_Somatics_of_Liberation_Ideas_about_Embodiment_in_Buddhism_from_Its_Origins_to_the_Fifth_Century_C.E._ (29.11.2021).

Rampling, David. 1986. "Ascetic Ideals and Anorexia Nervosa". In *Anorexia Nervosa and Bulimic Disorders*, edited by George Szmukler, Peter David Slade, and Paul Harris, Amsterdam: Elsevier, 89–94.

Rosenbaum, Sophia. 2016. "Thailand's Buddhist Monks Have an Obesity Problem." *New York Post*. https://nypost.com/2016/03/15/buddhist-monks-have-an-obesity-problem/ (29.11.2021).

Ryle, Gilbert. 1949. *The Concept of Mind*. Chicago: University of Chicago Press.

Sandikci, Ozlem, and Sahver Omeraki. 2007. "Islam in the Marketplace: Does Ramadan Turn into Christmas?" In *Advances in Consumer Research* 34:610–615.

Sherwell, Philip. 2016. "Thailand's Monks Are Put on Diet and Fitness Regime amid 'Obesity Time Bomb'." *The Telegraph*. https://www.telegraph.co.uk/news/worldnews/asia/thailand/12195261/ Thailands-monks-are-put-on-diet-and-fitness-regime-amid-obesity-time-bomb.html (29.11.2021).

Shoham, Hizky. 2013. "Yom Kippur and Jewish Public Culture in Israel." *Journal of Israeli History* 32:175–196.

Slyter, Marty. 2012. "Treating Eating Disorders with the Buddhist Tradition of Mindfulness." *American Counselling Association* 32:1–12.

The Quint News Staff. 2018. "Jain Monk Tarun Sagar Passes Away, Modi Expresses Condolences." *The Quint:* https://www.thequint.com/news/india/jain-monk-tarun-sagar-passes-away-modi-leads-condolences (30.11.2021).

Thomas, Pillachira Matthew. 1974. "Twentieth Century Indian Interpretations of the Bhagavadgita: A Selective Study of Patterns." In: https://www.semanticscholar.org/paper/Twentieth-Century-Indian-Interpretations-of-the-A-Thomas/ae5f9fdd22893ea4e930d8bd1d9e9373fdd91962?p2df (30.11.2021).

Vallely, Anne. 2018. "Dying Heroically: Jainism and the Ritual Fast to Death." In *Martyrdom, Self-Sacrifice and Self-Immolation: Religious Perspectives on Suicide*, edited by Margo Kitts, New York: Oxford University Press, 182–204.

Vernezze, Peter. 2007. "Moderation or the Middle Way: Two Approaches to Anger." *Philosophy East and West* 58:2–16.

Walshe, Maurice O'Connell. 2007. "Donapaka Sutta: A Heavy Meal." *Access to Insight*. https://www.accesstoinsight.org/tipitaka/sn/sn03/sn03.013.wlsh.html (30.11.2021).

Yang, Michelle Murray. 2011. "Still Burning: Self-Immolation as Photographic Protest." *Quarterly Journal of Speech* 97:1–25.

Yinger, Kent L. 2008. "Paul and Asceticism in 1 Corinthians 9:27a." *Faculty Publications – Portland Seminary* 9. https://digitalcommons.georgefox.edu/gfes/9/ (29.11.2021).

Yuill, Chris. 2007. "The Body as Weapon: Bobby Sands and the Republican Hunger Strikes." *Sociological Research Online* 12. https://journals.sagepub.com/doi/10.5153/sro.1348 (29.11.2021).

Manuel Stetter
Funerals / Death / Grief

1 Introduction: Death in Context

Death can often be associated with an aura of objectivity. It is considered a universal phenomenon, the fundamental constant of human existence. Certainly, what death means, how societies deal with the finitude of life, and how humans react emotionally to the loss of someone, will all vary. The meanings associated with death depend on social settings and cultural contexts: the ways in which death is articulated are based on sociocultural conventions; local legislation impinges on ways of treating the dead; the abundance of different conceptualizations of the afterlife points to the diversity of how death is construed; and even the feeling of sorrow is less an anthropological fact than a socially and culturally determined variable, both in terms of mourning and in terms of grief. Hence, the putative objective fact of death never occurs detached from the sociocultural practices that shape its experience. Death is always death-in-context (Robben 2018).

In this regard, the role of the funeral is important. The set of actions funerals entail embody significant aspects of how a social formation deals with death: how death is imagined, processed, and felt emotionally. In Germany, within the field of Practical Theology over the past decades, funerary culture has received an increase in attention. There are three reasons for this increased interest. *Firstly*, the large-scale membership surveys commissioned by the Protestant Church in Germany, initially conducted in the 1970s, have continuously provided strong evidence for the relevance of funerals (Bedford-Strohm and Jung 2015). These findings stimulated further research on funerals and other rites of passage. As a result, a distinct branch of practical-theological theorizing has emerged. *Secondly*, analyzing rites of passage has proven highly instructive. A study of the funeral not only requires trans-sectoral research integrating classical practical-theological subdisciplines such as homiletics, liturgics, and poimenics. It also points to an area of action in which the traditions of the church intersect with individuals' religion, and the culturally circulating vocabularies of the spiritual. Indeed, life transitions can be regarded as religiously productive contexts of experience. Death in particular notoriously challenges people to ask for meaning or to deal with contingency and is therefore also addressed explicitly as a religious topic by many people (Bedford-Strohm and Jung 2015, 491). Deeply connected with the lived religion of individuals, their biographies, and cultural imaginations of death, social changes have an immediate impact on the ecclesial funeral practice. This alteration of the Christian burial as well as the German funerary culture as a whole has become a topos in recent years and is a *third* reason for the deepened research on death rites. Such changes arouse scientific curiosity, call for new understandings of 'what is going on' and demand the development of perspectives by means of which religious actors can reflect on their actions.

It is against the backdrop of this discursive setting in the German context, that I am reflecting on funeral practice. Such reflection is, of course, always influenced by one's own personal experiences of funerals. In addition, my descriptions include participant observations that I was able to conduct during field research at a funeral home in southern Germany. For four weeks I had the opportunity to accompany the funeral staff and to observe how they deal with the deceased and the bereaved.

In what follows, I have chosen to emphasize the funeral practices of the Protestant Church. This, of course, is not possible without addressing the plural funerary cultures in which they are embedded. In fact, as a theory of lived religion, Practical Theology should not be reduced to funeral rites of organized religion. Rather, it has to reflect the broad field of death-related practices and to explore its religious dimensions.

2 Dynamics in the Field

2.1 Tendencies

The current dynamics of funerary culture are diverse and emerge at various levels. To gain a first idea of these changes, it is helpful to concentrate on some rough lines of development.

In the wake of modernization, treatment of the dead has experienced an increasing *professionalization*. An expert culture has evolved around death, shifting processes from within the private sphere to the institutional environment of the health care system; and funeral specialists support the bereaved as well. This increased contact with public institutions and professionalized agents has been constitutive of the encounter with death. Within this expert culture, however, distinctive alterations have occurred. Promoted by the hospice movement, for instance, or the rise of so-called alternative funeral directors, a kind of counterculture has been established aiming at a more autonomous reappropriation of the funeral, and a new involvement of the bereaved in its process as a whole (Lüddeckens 2018).

The institutionally underpinned 're-privatization' process bears upon a further tendency in the funeral field. As with other areas of life, the 'last things' have also become *individualized* (Meitzler 2016, 138). This touches not only on the notions of death or the choice of interment, burial sites, and ceremonial rites, but above all, on the specific criteria that guide these very choices. As thanatological studies prove in many ways, a funeral is often arranged in such a way as to represent the remembered personhood of the deceased, as well as the kind of relationship the bereaved have maintained with the dead person. The funeral is understood as a practice that will reflect something of the specific way of being in the world of the bereaved and of the deceased. It has become an eminent medium of (post mortal) identity construction.

Such personalized funerals demand and evoke a diverse set of options. Indeed, funerary practice has become *differentiated*. Anyone who has to arrange a funeral today will face a number of questions when sitting in the consultation room of an average urban funeral home: earth burial or cremation, cemetery or forest resting place, pastor or religiously unaffiliated speaker, live music or sound system. This list goes on. It indicates that on the one hand funerals are less and less defined by given matters of course, and that on the other hand, the ecclesiastical funeral is located in a field in which several actors are operating.

A great proportion of the knowledge guiding people's decisions concerning funerals derives from the media. New forms of media offer a variety of possibilities of quickly informing oneself and making direct comparisons between options. Certainly, it is not information that is the most relevant factor of the *digitization* of the sepulchral. More important is online communication which opens new spaces of grief and remembrance. Virtual cemeteries or social network memorials explore languages of bereavement which differ from established expressions of grief and allow for a redistribution of agency in respect of mourning (Cann 2016, 105–131).

These tendencies are connected with a number of phenomena each calling for further comprehensive studies. Hereinafter, three of these phenomena are singled out selectively.

2.2 Concretizations

2.2.1 Funeral Homes

Within the field of funerals and funeral care, there are a number of different actors. It is funeral directors in particular who have gained prominence in recent years. Their work once used to focus on the transportation of the dead, the preparation of the corpses, and the selling of coffins, but now their range of services has expanded considerably. Correspondently, most funeral directors see themselves as experts in ritual and as grief counselors, or, as the owner of the funeral home I gained insight into put it: "What we do is actually a sort of life counselling." The modern funeral home therefore integrates functions which for a long period had typically been attributed to religious institutions, with their practices of spiritual care and liturgies of death.

Regarding the funeral ceremony itself, the funeral directors' "performative agency" (Krüger et al. 2005, 20–22) does not involve consulting alone. They are directly responsible for the basic constituents of the ceremony. This applies to the spatial environment, especially when the ritual proceeds in the mourning hall of the funeral home with its specific architecture and figural accouterment. This also applies, however, to the "spacing" at other locations (Löw 2016, 134–136). Alongside florists, the funeral directors create a ritual space by arranging candles, wreaths, and other ritual items such as personal mementoes provided by the bereaved or large-sized portraits of the deceased, which are frequently placed on a scaffold next to the coffin or urn. Even though these material components do not unfold their ritual effects beyond their practical usage, they cannot be regarded as mere décor. As ritual and material studies show, place, space, and objects have an important effect on the ritual experiences of participants including their spiritual dimensions (Hallam and Hockey 2001).

The emphasis funeral directors have placed on questions of grief work not only lead to an expansion of aftercare services and a new ethic of counseling; the re-ritualization of caring for the dead, too, calls for exploration. Indeed, the corpse has been revalued inside the funeral industry. As I was able to witness at the funeral home I worked for, many funeral firms actively promote encounters with the prepared dead body and offer in-house rooms for this purpose. They account for these intimate contacts as constitutive of a wholesome grieving process and even ascribe religious qualities to them. The corpse turns into an "intermediator of transcendence" (Kahl 2013).

Although this enlargement of services cannot be reduced to economic principles alone, the practice of the funeral directors is of course shaped by the commodification of death (Akyel 2013). This does not only mean that a funeral has its price, but that the funeral field is determined by entrepreneurial behavior including service consciousness, advertising strategies, product innovation, content profiling, or customer orientation. A customer role is adopted by the bereaved, too, when they use the services of independent ritual guides and funeral speakers (Lüddeckens 2018, 112). In Germany, the number of such non-ecclesial funerals has been growing. Not least due to the entrepreneurial logic of their action, they contribute to a handling of the funeral that is quite different from the ways a traditional institution is used to operating in the funeral context.

2.2.2 Virtual Bereavement

With the spread of the internet, new spaces of mourning have emerged. They represent a broader process resulting in an unbundling of burial site and grieving place, although online memorials frequently comprise various references to the gravesite. Of course, virtual bereavement is regularly entangled with offline mourning practices (Offerhaus 2016). Nevertheless, it is precisely the potential distance from other areas of social life which makes virtual practices attractive to many mourners. Such spaces provide them with the possibility of gaining visibility as mourners even when the social environment commands the end of grief, or if their mourning is not acknowledged due to other socially established regimes of feeling (Doka 1989).

In the following, a short example will illustrate some aspects discussed in the current discourse on virtual bereavement. It refers to a memorial site S. created two days after her husband died on the 16th of October 2014. The site presents an obituary, pictures, and videos, and allows visitors to sign a book of condolences or to light a candle and leave a message. In the context of the fourth anniversary of her husband's death S. writes:[1]

> 'four years ... / for four years you have been with the angels / and it seems to me that it had just happened [...] / for you it has been a release from all of your pain / for me it has been the loss of my big love, / the love of my life / I miss you so much / I will always love you.' [16 October 2018]
>
> 'Congratulations on our fourth wedding day. / I hope you had a nice day up there / I miss you so terribly. [...]' [10 October 2018]
>
> 'After almost four years you have already been living in another world, I still love you as in the beginning when we met and I miss you more with each day that goes by but with each day that goes by I come closer to you I'm looking forward to seeing you again [...]' [30 July 2018]

There are three remarkable aspects. *Firstly*, the language employed is deeply personal and emotional. The motives of love and of missing, which also belong to the standard discursive repertoire of traditional obituaries, where they are commonly used in coined phrases, are accomplished in an informal and emotionalized manner. This, *secondly*, is due to the pragmatic character of these posts. It is the dead person who is addressed; the posts stage the deceased as a direct dialogue partner. The mourning practice evident here centers on the maintenance of "continuing bonds" – a key concept in recent thanatological research – rather than alluding to a successive detachment from the deceased (Klass et al. 1996). *Thirdly*, in just a few words, the messages convey a specific imagination of the afterlife. The deceased is situated in 'another world' populated with 'angels,' a world with consistently positive connotations promising 'release' and 'nice day[s]' which will also be the place for a future reunion of the now separated. This topography of the beyond draws upon repertoires of popular afterlife myths that feed on Christian tradition. Certainly, these vocabularies are appropriated autonomously, and, more importantly, are not used to profess an abstracted, general belief in the hereafter, but to interpret experiences associated with the loss of a particular person. Borrowing a phrase from Claudia Venhorst (Venhorst 2013): The eschatology noticeable here is a 'lived eschatology', embedded in lifeworld practices of grieving and related to a specific person.

2.2.3 Disaster Rituals

The previous examples have focused upon practices which are not directly affiliated with the organized church. The third example will now refer to a field of action in which the religious institutions adopt an important function besides their classic funeral rites. In the wake of several disasters that have shaken broad sections of German society in recent years, Practical Theology has started to address the role

---

1 https://www.gedenkseiten.de/peter-grimm/kerzen/ (30.11.2021; translation MS).

churches play in public rituals following such catastrophes (Kranemann and Benz 2016).

Where death assumes the form of a disaster there is a need for social practices which allow for collective remembrance and sympathy. As well as spontaneously emerging grassroots memorials, it is through official commemorations that a society will respond ritually to a tragic event (Post 2016). In Germany, these ceremonies are mostly performed as ecumenical services organized by the Protestant and Catholic Church and frequently combined with an act of the state in some way or other. It is in this ceremonial encounter between the ideologically neutral state and Christian churches, that the specific liturgical challenges of post-disaster rituals become apparent.

Situations of disaster can call for a language in which the secular state is not versed. Churches, however, are still considered social actors with access to such a vocabulary. In the case of a commemoration which firmly addresses civil society, this vocabulary has to be converted into ritual practices appealing to a pluralized public. Gestures, singing, symbols, readings, and orations result at best in an overall context that opens a space accessible not only to an inner-ecclesial milieu but also to the relatives of the victims, whatever their worldviews might be, and to a compassionate society being confronted with the fragility of human existence and social order. It might indeed be this shared experience of contingency which induces disaster rituals. Catastrophes like the Germanwings crash in 2015 threaten the fundamental trust social life is based upon and call for a reassurance of solidarity and its meaning.

The memorial service held in the Cologne Cathedral after the Germanwings disaster contributed to this function. A small wooden angel bearing the motto 'to hold and to be held' was handed to different representatives sitting in the pews: to a relative representing the bereaved 'as a sign of condolence;' to the Spanish Minister for the Interior representing the Spanish victims' kin 'as a sign of our attachment;' to the French transport minister representing the people who helped the bereaved in the French Alps 'as a note of thanks,' and so on.[2]

This act can be read as a ritualized attempt not only to assert the value of solidarity but to *enact* it. What had been challenged by the catastrophic event became visualized and transposed into an emotionally touching, or – to cite Durkheim (Durkheim 1995) – an 'effervescent' scene. Not only did the wooden angel symbolize holding by means of its shape, the people offering this holding held an important function, as 'the angels surrounding us.' However, and this is the interesting point here, the angel offered further symbolic traces: verbally presented as a symbol for deceased loved ones, its shape also resembled a cross. It is through the ambiguity of the symbolic act that diverse functions of a memorial service can be transferred. The shared values of a social formation are performed, drawing on symbolic images

---

[2] Cf. https://www.youtube.com/watch?v=wZZ3XKLy1_0 (30.11.2021)

from a Christian vocabulary to describe death, yet all the while being open to multiple interpretations and meaning making.

3 Dimensions of the Ecclesial Funeral

The ecclesial funeral is part of this broader sepulchral culture and has to be approached against this background. In particular, there are three perspectives guiding the practical-theological discourse on funerals: It is regarded as a form of pastoral accompaniment; it involves interpretative practices framing the experiences caused by death; and it is a ritual performance making the radical transitions associated with death perceptible (Roth 2007). These aspects cannot be isolated from each other; they are entangled and together constitute the process of the funeral.

3.1 Listening to the Bereaved

This already applies to the preliminary conversation the minister will have with the bereaved relatives of the deceased. For a short time, the minister literally enters the lifeworld of the bereaved and becomes a transient entity in their grieving process. This meeting will not be utilized to expound a supposed authoritative meaning of the funeral, or to advise the bereaved of the stipulated order of the funeral liturgy, rather, the encounter with the religious professional can become an occasion for the bereaved to attempt to make their own interpretations of their situation and to participate in the design of the ritual.

The meanings articulated within this conversation with respect to death, the life of the deceased, the relationship to them, or the bereaved person's state of mind, do not commonly take on an elaborated form. Instead, they end up being embedded in for example short narratives, bodily expressions of emotion and sorrow, the showing of a photograph. In short, they are incorporated in the whole practice of meeting the pastor on this specific occasion. In this sense, the entire encounter can be understood as what Alois Hahn (Hahn 1995) has called a 'generator of biography.' With this concept he tries to account for the insight that addressing oneself does not stem from a 'natural instinct,' but bears on particular 'institutional inducements.' These situational contexts do not only facilitate practices of self-reflection, but they also shape them. They determine their pragmatic function, semantic focus, and factual media. There are several typical structures shaping the interpretations communicated here: time limitations; apprehensions over the portrait of the deceased being respectable; the encounter with the pastor itself – who, despite his or her attentiveness and care, may well still be regarded as part of an institution; the focus on the preparation of the ritual, to name but a few concerns.

Regarding the preparation of the funeral service, this preliminary conversation is the place for negotiating performative agency. Who has the right and power to decide on the ritual is not fixed. Rather, it has to be negotiated and renegotiated. Consequently, the agency of the pastor should not be regarded as something fundamentally corresponding to her due to ecclesial authority or social conventions. Instead, it should be regarded as something that arises from the encounter with the bereaved, through companionship and competence regarding matters of ritual. Ritual competence is distinct from acquaintance with the ready-made liturgical scripts and their implementation. It comprises knowing diverse repertoires of ritual actions, the ways in which they work in the mode of their performance, and how they can be made productive for the needs of the people asking for the ritual. Ritual competence therefore always means to work *with* the people involved, through the process of "co-constructing" (Kelly 2008, 66–117).

The dialogue prior to the funeral touches on all three abovementioned dimensions. Their entanglement results in both an encounter in its own right, experienced as helpful by the bereaved, and in a conversational situation facilitating a ritual that can be experienced as personalized.

3.2 Funeral Oratory

Discursive practices are key elements of dealing with death. The *laudatio funebris* has a long history involving an abundance of different manifestations (Eybl 1996). And today the rhetoric of death still ranges from obituaries to sermons, as well as postings in the realm of virtual grieving.

As empirical findings show, the funeral sermon itself can be performed very differently (Weyel 2015). In all its variations, however, it might be concerned with the configuration of three basic relations: It refers to the *dead* and addresses the *living* by combining *biographical* and *eschatological* perspectives and performing *individual spiritual* and *public cultural* functions.

Whoever rises to speak in the context of a funeral faces the challenge of articulating a specific life. As with every biographical work, this articulation is an interpretative endeavor and as such, is constructive in nature. In the interest of meaning-making, the retelling of a life makes selections, sets relevancies, and establishes intelligible relations. The funeral oration is itself such an interpretation, transforming the course of the deceased's life into a meaningful, coherent story. As a biographic realization of a life that has come to an end, this interpretation takes place in an eschatological perspective. The funeral oration is concerned with the 'last things' not in the sense that it formulates a conclusive interpretation immune from being augmented, corrected, or challenged by other interpretations, but in the dual sense, that it claims meaning for a finished life and thus is confronted with the question of how to imagine a post-mortal future. Whereas traditional Christian imaginaries of the afterlife are not usually focused on individual biographies, the foregoing observations have indicated that current references to the beyond are often bound to the deceased person in question. This gives rise to the homiletical challenge of associating traditional images with the individual person in such a manner as to yield personalized eschatological images (Quartier 2011, 129–142), or, alternatively, of "reinventing" vivid and maybe "bold" images out of the biographic contexts of the deceased (Grimes 2000, 275–282).

The biographical and eschatological interpretations do not take place in a sphere of free expression but are located in a specific communicative setting. They are addressed to a certain audience. The number of participants should not obscure the fact that the audience of an ordinary funeral ritual is diverse and, above all, that the funeral is quite similar to a disaster ritual, in that it takes place within the heterogeneous context of culturally circulating patterns of construing death and reconstructing life. Hence, in addition to a word of comfort for the directly affected, it also contributes to a public understanding about the finitude of life (Weyel 2015, 124). This does not mean that the oration has to loosen its relation to the particular bereavement or has to seek refuge in abstract assertions. On the contrary, the understanding about the finitude of life occurs through the medium of interpreting a particular life. The oration is at once *referring* (to the historical life of a person) and *exemplifying* (a 'general' that can be adopted) (Stetter 2018, 181–206). It opens a space of self-interpretation by interpreting the life and death of another and thus reflects the structure of self-understanding in general which does not consist in a monologic introspection, but always proceeds via a "detour", as Ricoeur (Ricoeur 1991, 80) puts it.

3.3 Ritualizing Death

The funeral oration is part of a set of complex ritual practices. Due to its distinctive communicative possibilities, it can be distinguished from other segments of this "set of doings and sayings" (Schatzki 2002, 73). However, it should not be seen in isolation. Indeed, inspired by recent ritual studies, Protestant Theology has reasserted the ineluctable relevance of the performativity of the funeral. Through acts of stylizing, dramaturgical arrangement, and setting framing cues, a sphere of action is put forth that suspends everyday behavior and opens a space in which the transitions associated with death can find a condensed expression (Platvoet 1995, 33–34).

As *practice*, the ritual is thereby more than just an expression of preexisting feelings or a representation of ulterior meanings. The experience provoked by death and the interpretation bestowed on it are integrated in the practices being performed including its material dimensions: the artefacts, spaces, and bodies present.

In the case of the funeral, it is the corpse itself that ranks high in the "hierarchy of ritual things" (Bräunlein 2014, 247). Covert in the coffin or cremated in the urn, the dead body is the performative center of the funeral. However, one may assess the agency of things more precisely, the corpse can be regarded as a 'participant' of the funeral practice, shaping its actions as much as its actions influence its impact (Hirschauer 2004). In the ensemble of ritual objects, the coffin or urn is positioned in such a manner that it catches the attendants' eyes, as it is ordinarily placed in the center. At significant moments in the funeral, the celebrants face the coffin or urn, for example when the pastor enters the scene, moves to the urn, and bows in front of it. The funeral ritual often (but not necessarily) entails practices that mobilize the coffin or urn: the coffin may be solemnly processed in by pall bearers; the urn is carefully carried out maybe by one of the mourners; if the interment follows the funeral the coffin or urn leads the mourners to the burial site where it is lowered slowly into the grave.

Even this description demonstrates that ritual dealings with the coffin or urn give the corpse a special, if not sacred status. Coffin and urn are not dealt with as if they were mere wooden or ceramic containers. They are dealt with as if they embody something beyond the object: the presence of the deceased person. By means of its practices related to the corpse, the funeral ritual thus confers the deceased with a specific presence and thus produces a space in which both the invisible 'last passage' of the deceased and their relation to the bereaved can be experienced.

The example of the corpse indicates that it is the actual ritual practice involving discourses as well as objects, spaces, and bodies, that constitutes the experience of death and its interpretation in the funeral performance. The interpretation is not something additional; and the feelings are not simply expressed (Scheer 2012). They are inherent in the complex practical arrangements. Moreover, the example gives emphasis to the central meaning of the actual person who died. Whatever the funeral tries to provide for the mourners, whatever it contributes to a cultural understanding of the fragility of life and an imagination of the hereafter in general, it achieves that only through its relation to the death of a unique person.

4 Conclusions: The Funeral in Context

As the preceding considerations indicate, it is not only death that is a contextual phenomenon. Three concluding remarks shall concretize this aspect once more outlining some consequences this contextuality has for the practical-theological research on funerals.

As seen, the ecclesial funeral is located in a field that is occupied by various actors. There are the funeral directors, who understand the funeral as a spiritual and ritual service for the customers; there is the growing presence of independent ritual designers promising individualized ceremonies that meet the needs of the mourners; and there are the bereaved themselves, claiming authority in questions of funeral design and exploring autonomous ways of grieving and remembrance. Against this backdrop, funerals are an instructive case for reflecting on the church and its practical-theological understandings. The funeral obviously requires a conduct that is in tension with a church, regarding itself as an institution by analogy with the state. Conversely, vocabularies of market and competition seem inadequate, too, to describe the current social place of the church and its self-understanding properly.

To gain more clarity here, it seems necessary to me not to map the field by means of strong preconceived categories such as 'ecclesial' / 'non-ecclesial', 'religious' / 'worldly', 'traditional' / 'alternative' or 'institution-based' / 'independent'. Rather, the field of the funeral should be researched as a common field describing its various forms, following the routes of its diverse actors, and exploring similarities, differences, and mutual ritual transfers.

As has become clear, the ecclesial funeral is situated in the sense that it is motivated by particular biographic situations, bound to the loss of a unique person, and performed in specific practical settings. Consequently, the religious implications of funerals, too, become accessible only in this embeddedness. Practical-theological research can therefore consist not solely in applying general concepts of religion to funeral practices. Rather, these theoretical preunderstandings Practical Theology naturally relies upon are at best shaped in such a manner as to stimulate empirical research by providing a conceptual framework that helps to uncover relevant phenomena and interesting relations, thus allowing for instructive questions as well as unexpected findings. With respect to the funeral, this means that concepts of religion focusing primarily on beliefs and a "catalog of immaterial ideas and ideologies" (Engelke 2015, 32) are not really capable of revealing the religious dimensions of death-related practices (Kjærsgaard 2017, 113–114). In the case of funerals, religion has to be explored as something that is deeply entangled with biographic experiences, that show up in narrative constructions of a completed life and in acts of transcending, that are mediated by the deceased, and that are produced in practices integrating discourse as well as objects, spaces and bodies.

Finally, the ecclesial funeral can be regarded as a contextual phenomenon insofar as it is only one part in the grieving process of the bereaved, as well as in the overall context of death-related practices. Given that a funeral cannot be detached from this broader context, a Practical Theology of funerals should actually unfold as a Practical Theology of death-related practices. In dialogue with other thanatological studies, it refers to the sociocultural practices that generate death, and what it means for us, focusing on its religious dimensions as well as its ecclesial involvements.

Bibliography

Akyel, Dominic. 2013. *Die Ökonomisierung der Pietät: Der Wandel des Bestattungsmarktes in Deutschland*. Frankfurt / New York: Campus.

Bedford-Strohm, Heinrich, and Volker Jung, eds. 2015. *Vernetzte Vielfalt: Kirche angesichts von Individualisierung und Säkularisierung*. Gütersloh: Gütersloher Verlagshaus.

Bräunlein, Peter J. 2014. "Ritualdinge." In *Handbuch materielle Kultur: Bedeutungen, Konzepte, Disziplinen*, edited by Stefanie Samida, Manfred K.H. Eggert, and Hans Peter Hahn, Stuttgart / Weimar: J.B. Metzler, 245–248.

Cann, Candi K. 2016. *Virtual Afterlives: Grieving the Dead in the Twenty-First Century*. Lexington: University Press of Kentucky.

Doka, Kenneth J. 1989. *Disenfranchised Grief: Recognizing Hidden Sorrow.* Lexington: Lexington Books.
Durkheim, Emile. 1995. *The Elementary Forms of Religious Life.* New York: The Free Press.
Engelke, Matthew. 2015. "The Coffin Question: Death and Materiality in Humanist Funerals." *Material Religion* 11:26–49.
Eybl, Franz. 1996. "Funeralrhetorik." In *Historisches Wörterbuch der Rhetorik.* Vol. 3, edited by Gert Ueding, Tübingen: Max Niemeyer, 478–484.
Grimes, Ronald L. 2000. *Deeply into the Bone: Re-Inventing Rites of Passage.* Berkeley / Los Angeles: University of California Press.
Hahn, Alois. 1995. "Identität und Biographie." In *Biographie und Religion: Zwischen Ritual und Selbstsuche,* edited by Monika Wohlrab-Sahr, Frankfurt am Main: Campus, 127–152.
Hallam, Elizabeth, and Janny Hockey. 2001. *Death, Memory and Material Culture.* Oxford / New York: Berg.
Hirschauer, Stefan. 2004. "Praktiken und ihre Körper: Über materielle Partizipanden des Tuns." In *Doing Culture: Neue Positionen zum Verhältnis von Kultur und sozialer Praxis,* edited by Karl. H. Hörning and Julia Reuter, Bielefeld: transcript, 73–91.
Kahl, Antje. 2013. "Our Dead are the Ultimate Teachers of Life: The Corpse as an Intermediator of Transcendence: Spirituality in the German Funeral Market." *Fieldwork in Religion* 8:223–240.
Kelly, Ewan. 2008. *Meaningful Funerals: Meeting the Theological and Pastoral Challenge in a Postmodern Era.* London / New York: Mowbray.
Kjærsgaard, Anne. 2017. *Funerary Culture and the Limits of Secularization in Denmark.* Zürich: LIT.
Klass, Dennis, Phyllis R. Silverman, and Steven L. Nickman, eds. 1996. *Continuing Bonds: New Understandings of Grief.* New York / London: Routledge.
Kranemann, Benedikt, and Brigitte Benz, eds. 2016. *Trauerfeiern nach Großkatastrophen: Theologische und sozialwissenschaftliche Zugänge.* Neukirchen-Vluyn: Neukirchener Verlagsgesellschaft.
Krüger, Oliver, Michael Nijhawan, and Eftychia Stravrianopoulou. 2005. "'Ritual' und 'Agency': Legitimation und Reflexivität ritueller Handlungsmacht." *Forum Ritualdynamik* 14:1–34.
Löw, Martina. 2016. *The Sociology of Space: Materiality, Social Structures, and Action.* New York: Palgrave Macmillan.
Lüddeckens, Dorothea. 2018. "Alternative Death Rituals in Switzerland: Building a Community of Shared Emotions and Practices." *Journal of Contemporary Religion* 33:107–121.
Meitzler, Matthias. 2016. "Postexistenzielle Existenzbastelei." In *Die Zukunft des Todes: Heterotopien des Lebensendes,* edited by Thorsten Benkel, Bielefeld: transcript, 133–162.
Offerhaus, Anke. 2016. "Begraben im Cyberspace: Virtuelle Friedhöfe als Räume mediatisierter Trauer und Erinnerung." In *Die Zukunft des Todes: Heterotopien des Lebensendes,* edited by Thorsten Benkel, Bielefeld: transcript, 339–364.
Platvoet, Jan. 1995. "Ritual in Plural and Pluralist Societies: Instruments for Analysis." In *Pluralism and Identity: Studies in Ritual Behaviour,* edited by Jan Platvoet and Karel van der Toorn, Leiden / Köln: Brill, 25–51.
Post, Paul. 2016. "Current Post-Disaster Ritual: An Exploration of Established, Absent, and Emerging Repertoires: National and International Perspectives." In *Trauerfeiern nach Großkatastrophen: Theologische und sozialwissenschaftliche Zugänge,* edited by Benedikt Kranemann and Brigitte Benz, Neukirchen-Vluyn: Neukirchener Verlagsgesellschaft, 51–75.
Quartier, Thomas. 2011. *Die Grenze des Todes: Ritualisierte Religiosität im Umgang mit den Toten.* Berlin: LIT.
Ricoeur, Paul. 1991. "Narrative Identity." *Philosophy Today* 35:73–81.
Robben, Antonius C. G. M. 2018. "An Anthropology of Death for the Twenty-First Century." In *A Companion to the Anthropology of Death,* edited by Antonius C. G. M Robben, Hoboken: Wiley, 15–40.

Roth, Ursula. 2007. "Bestattung." In *Handbuch Praktische Theologie*, edited by Wilhelm Gräb and Birgit Weyel, Gütersloh: Gütersloher Verlagshaus, 51–75.

Schatzki, Theodore. 2002. *The Site of the Social: A Philosophical Account of the Constitution of Social Life and Change.* University Park: Penn State University Press.

Scheer, Monique. 2012. "Are Emotions a Kind of Practice (and is it that what Makes them Have a History)? A Bourdieuan Approach to Understanding Emotion." *History and Theory* 51:193–220.

Stetter, Manuel. 2018. *Die Predigt als Praxis der Veränderung: Ein Beitrag zur Grundlegung der Homiletik.* Göttingen: Vandenhoeck & Ruprecht.

Venhorst, Claudia. 2013. "Lived Eschatology: Muslim Views on Life and Death: Preliminary Practices." In *Changing European Death Ways*, edited by Erin Venbrux, Thomas Quartier, Claudia Venhorst, and Brenda Matthijssen, Berlin: LIT, 259–281.

Weyel, Birgit. 2015. "Lebensdeutung: Die Bestattungspredigt in empirischer Perspektive." In *Praktische Theologie der Bestattung*, edited by Thomas Klie, Martina Kumlehn, Ralph Kunz, and Thomas Schlag, Berlin / München: Walter de Gruyter, 121–139.

Cas Wepener
Holy Supper / Meal / Sharing Food

1 Searching for a Balanced (Practical Theological) Diet

Feeding more than one person at a time has become a complicated enterprise in many contexts. When it comes to food, people have diverse preferences and tolerances, which renders cooking and serving a meal for more than one person fairly demanding. If, in addition, people come from different cultural and religious backgrounds, this adds further challenge, as etiquette or taboo should be taken into consideration. One might picture a modern version of the miracle of the loaves and fishes where Jesus multiplied the food and fed the crowd (Matt 14:13–21; Mark 6:31–24; Luke 9:12–17; John 6:1–14), to be met with responses such as: 'no thank you, not for me, I am wheat intolerant with an iodine deficiency', not to mention the gourmands for whom the fish is not fresh enough and who would ask the disciples for extra virgin olive oil to dip the bread in and a pinch of dill for the fish. Of course, there are also the ethically-conscious who would be taking out their cards (Basson 2011, 5–6) to see whether the fish is on the endangered species list before deciding whether or not to eat it.

In spite of this challenge today, hosts – which include religious communities – still try their best to satisfy the needs and preferences of their guests, and to cook and lay a table where all (or at least many) can be simultaneously accommodated. And not only accommodated, but also nourished with a healthy, balanced meal. They do this because they realise the potential of the meal to not only feed people and serve their bodily needs, but also to reconcile, to raise ecological awareness, and touch them in ways that a sermon or a prayer alone cannot (Wepener 2010). In this regard, the warning of Catherine Bell in respect to eating habits and table etiquette is significant: "they are eminently open to manipulation, appropriation, and nuance; in matters of etiquette and ritual, people do not just follow rules" (Bell 1997, 144). The practice of sharing food can deeply impact people's health, relationships, understandings of ecclesiology, as well as ecology. Eating, therefore, including ritualised eating such as taking the sacrament of the Lord's Supper in the Christian tradition, is a practice that should be open for criticism (Grimes 1990, 18).[1]

At the Stellenbosch University[2] in South Africa where I teach Practical Theology, one of my challenges is to develop and teach modules in Practical Theology that accommodate students from a very wide range of backgrounds. This teaching challenge

---
[1] According to Grimes (1990, 18): "Ritual criticism is the interpretation of a rite or ritual system with a view to implicating its practice."
[2] Previously I taught at the University of Pretoria where my task was similar.

OpenAccess. © 2022 Cas Wepener, published by De Gruyter. This work is licensed under the Creative Commons Attribution-NonCommercial-NoDerivatives 4.0 International License.
https://doi.org/10.1515/9783110618150-028

is akin to the challenge of cooking for a diverse group of people, not to just keep them satisfied by catering to all their preferences, but to accommodate them and to ensure that all receive a balanced and nutritious practical theological diet that will sustain them within the contexts they will be working. One of the modules focusing on Liturgy and Homiletics that I developed and that I teach, takes cooking, eating and the table as a central theme and uses it as a *leitmotiv* throughout the module. It is a theme with which a great diversity of students can be accommodated in one curriculum space. The challenge is to open up a transcultural space by means of a hermeneutics of culture, in which eating habits are seen as part of lived religion, and thus of culture (Gräb 2017; Weyel 2014). The module is empirically grounded in the realities regarding commensality, from which the students and lecturer come, and includes eating practices from churches and wider society. It builds on these practices and fosters an appreciation and critical understanding beyond one's own religious-cultural borders.

In this chapter, I will discuss this particular module which is specifically aimed at laying the table for a transcultural approach towards Practical Theology with the potential to also become trans-religious in future given the developments regarding Faculties of Theology in South Africa.[3] The module and its development should however be placed in a very specific transitional and (post)colonial socio-political context, namely South Africa 28 years after the advent of democracy. In the next section I will unpack this context, a context to which I as lecturer belong, and also my relation to the theme of the module, which is a relation on both an academic and personal level. Thereafter I will briefly outline our students in relation to the context and theme of eating, focusing on their liturgical backgrounds as pertaining to food and eating, followed by a description and discussion of the module.

The description of the module, which is closely connected to my own story, will shed light on the theme of this chapter, 'Holy Supper / Meal / Sharing Food' from a transcultural perspective, showing that, when it comes to food and eating, students vary whilst also sharing habits and tendencies (Tisdale 2008, 75–89). Eating as a part of lived religion is experienced by all students, in their own idiosyncratic ways, as well as in shared ways.

2 Eating and the Table in (Post) Apartheid South Africa

The table and commensality, or the absence thereof, has a particular history in South Africa. One can begin to tell this story from many different places, but one possible beginning for the theme of the celebration of the holy meal in South Africa, is the meeting

---

[3] Recently the names of the Faculties of Theology at the University of Pretoria and the University of the Free State was changed from Theology to that of Theology and Religion.

of the Dutch Reformed Synod in the year 1829. This synod also first raised the so-called 'colour problem', and the question of whether people of colour – who were accepted as members of the Churches through confession and baptism – would receive the Lord's Supper together with born Christians (Kriel 1961, 55). In other words, at this meeting, Christians were discussing whether black and white Christians should eat and drink together in the same building and at the same table when they celebrated the Lord's Supper or whether they should do so at separate tables in separate buildings. A decision was not taken in 1829. Instead, the landmark and tragic decision on the matter was taken twenty-eight years later. During the meeting of the synod in 1857, the topic of a separate service again found itself on the agenda, with many votes both in favour and against such a decision. A proposal was accepted with a large majority. An extract from this proposal reads as follows:

> The Synod deems it desirable and scriptural that our members from the Heathen, be admitted and inducted to our existing congregations, especially where this can be done; but where this regulation, because of the weakness of some, the promotion of the matter of Christ among the Heathen established, or yet to be established, will enjoy their Christian privileges in a separate building or establishment. (Gereformeerde Kerk 1857, 60; Loff 1983; Vosloo 2017; Wepener 2002)

Thus, in the nineteenth century in South Africa, the holy meal of the Christian faith, the Lord's Supper, served as one of the main stimuli for the founding of separate churches on account of racial differences. The phrase "the weakness of some" (Gereformeerde Kerk 1857, 60) is a reference to the weakness of those who did not see their way open to partake of the sacrament together. Here, a decision regarding a liturgical ritual (sacrament) deeply influenced ecclesiology and this filtered through into larger society, just like the societal context itself had influenced these decisions. The origin and development of the policy of apartheid can of course be traced back to many provocations, however, for this chapter it is important to note that one important factor was the decision of 1857 on the celebration of the Lord's Supper. Thus the (un)holy meal and (not) sharing of food has a close relationship with apartheid. Over the course of time, the separate celebration led to the establishment of separate churches along racial lines.

Just as (the absence of) eating together played a role in what later became known as apartheid, the table and commensality has also been an important practice during the era of the transition to democracy before and after 1994, the year in which the country had its first democratic election and Nelson Mandela became President. Studies have been carried out on the role of eating and the table in the struggle for justice (De Gruchy and Villa-Vicencio 1983; Wallis and Hollyday 1989; Wepener 2011) as well as in building up the country by means of generating certain kinds of social capital and also promoting social cohesion (Wepener 2019). However, this prevailing ambivalence regarding eating together and also not eating together within the South African context, past and present, forms part of the context in which and for which the particular module discussed in this chapter was developed. Another critical aspect of this context is the wide cultural and Christian denominational diversity at the Faculty of Theology and Religion at the University of Pretoria and the Faculty of Theology at Stellenbosch University.

With this historical and contextual background in mind, I now move to discuss the students who study Theology and who attend the abovementioned module. I will also discuss their lecturer. I will focus on the religious and cultural contexts pertaining to food and eating from which the students and lecturer hail. I will begin with a description of myself as a white middle-aged male lecturer who is also an ordained minister in the Reformed tradition.

3 The Cultural and Religious Background of the Lecturer and the Students

I am a white male, born in 1972 in South Africa. The National Party with their apartheid policy was at that time the ruling party, with John Vorster as prime minister. Our family were members of the Dutch Reformed Church, a denomination that supported the policies of the ruling political party and that celebrated the Lord's Supper at least four times a year. We were, economically speaking, a fairly typical middle-class family. When I ate, in church and elsewhere, I ate with white people from a roughly similar socio-economic background. This was supported by many apartheid laws. After school, I studied at Stellenbosch University completing my studies in 1998 and was thus a student when our country underwent radical political change. In Stellenbosch however, not much changed in the first years after 1994 as it did in some other parts of the country. We were white Afrikaans-speaking students, with white male Dutch Reformed lecturers in the theological Faculty. The greatest culinary borders we ever crossed as students, were when taking another white person on a date to a restaurant (something most of us could afford). Of course, there were some exceptions to the rule. However, in light of South African racial demographics, and in light of the prevalence of the monocultural tables at which we dined, these exceptions were so rare that they are hardly worth mentioning.

I taught at the University of Pretoria between 2010 and 2019 and since 2019 at Stellenbosch University, and my experience on a Sunday differs vastly from my experience during the rest of the week. Most Dutch Reformed congregations still only have white members. Worship on a Sunday in these churches, which includes communion services, is still "the most segregated hour" (Luther King Jr. 1960)[4] of the week, whilst borders are crossed in other spaces during the rest of the week. My church reality is still a kind of apartheid experience which is strongly juxtaposed to my experiences during the rest of the week. As one of my children at the age of five aptly remarked during a worship service: "Why are there only white faces in this place?" He asked this question, because,

---

[4] Following a statement by Martin Luther King Jr., "The most Segregated Hour in America,", https://www.youtube.com/watch?v=1q881g1L_d8 (30.11.2021).

just like my students, his Monday to Saturday experience of Pretoria – at school, at home, at leisure – was that of cultural diversity.

The students who register for the Practical Theology modules in Pretoria and Stellenbosch were almost all born after 1994; they truly represent the South African demographics with regard to ethnicity and come from a wide variety of ecclesial traditions, including African independent, (neo)Pentecostal, Charismatic, Reformed, Lutheran, Methodist, Anglican, Roman Catholic, to name some. Their experiences regarding the celebration of the Lord's Supper / Communion / Mass in their churches of course vary. Readers may be familiar with the weekly celebration in churches such as the Roman Catholic, Anglican, and Lutheran Churches, from which several students come, and the liturgies are comparable to the way they are celebrated in Europe and North America for example. There are also several students from churches belonging to the Reformed family. In these churches, the Lord's Supper is celebrated only four times a year.[5] In some African independent churches, to which a number of the students belong, Communion is celebrated only once a year, and in many Charismatic and Pentecostal churches, when Communion is included in worship, it is seen as an addendum to the main worship service, served after the benediction has been pronounced, and it is not compulsory, with few people attending (Denny and Wepener 2013).

Painting a picture of commensality in such broad strokes in the churches that students are affiliated to is not too difficult, and as lecturer I have tried to attend church services in most, if not all, of the churches our students come from. Painting a picture of their eating habits at home or in public, is however much more difficult. One of the aims of the module is to let students themselves bring descriptions of their eating habits, in church and beyond, into the module to open up a transcultural space.

This very brief description of the eating habits of the students and their lecturer may look fairly insignificant, but when it comes to the theme of food and eating habits, it is quite significant. To quote the South African philosopher Martin Versfeld (Versfeld 1983, 38) from his book *Food for Thought. A Philosopher's Cookbook*: "Nothing is more indicative of who we are than our food and table customs". We are what and how we eat, when eating alone or together. This was true in 1998 in Stellenbosch; it is still true in 2022 in Pretoria and Stellenbosch and this basic truth is critical for understanding why the above-mentioned module in Practical Theology was developed for a post-apartheid and post-colonial South African context (Venter and Tolmie 2013). South Africans can learn to lay their tables as spaces for justice and reconciliation, but this is a conscious choice that must be made, and in which Practical Theology and fields such as Liturgical Studies, can play a significant role. In the

---

5 Over the past decades the Liturgical Movement also reached (parts of) South Africa and there has been a call for a more frequent celebration. However, there has been very little success in this regard and the tendency seems instead to move in the direction of even fewer celebrations.

next section several pedagogical practices and curriculum themes from the module are selected and discussed.

4 Making Room at the Table, Making Room in the Module

Broadly speaking, the module consists of two main phases. Firstly, a liturgical phase, focusing on worship and ritual, and more specifically on food, eating and the table. The second half of the module focusses on homiletics and speech and the same focus is kept. Throughout the course of the semester, students read a variety of prescribed texts, whilst, importantly, being exposed to practices in the course of the module.

After the first lecture during which the outlines of the module are sketched and basic theoretical concepts are explained, the class visits Echo Youth Development[6]. Echo has a long-established practice of eating as a community on a Monday evening with all who would like to join them in the larger community. They make a fire, volunteers bring food, and everyone is welcome. Around the fire with a hotdog, bunny chow or a bowl of curry in your hand, you meet people and cross many boundaries: age, nationality, level of education, income etc. For many students, this is their first experience of this kind, and the experience informs and inspires the rest of the module and almost all discussions.

Throughout the course of the semester, students must also keep a food journal and describe when, where, with whom, and what, they eat. During the course of the module students get the opportunity to present the content of their journals to the rest of the class. For the students, this is a learning opportunity to reflect on the impact of their eating habits, on for example the ecology and economy, but also to gain exposure to the practices of others (Bass 2012, 51–60). Passionate debates often ensue: some feel that discussions regarding the sourcing of ethical food and supporting fair trade is an elite hobby of the rich who can afford it, and that the focus should rather be on hunger and inequality; whilst others disagree and deem it an important theme, as everyone's eating habits impact the poor and the earth. The theme of an ethics of eating is thus dealt with and importantly, food and eating are linked to the issue of poverty in South Africa, as well as to the potential of commensality for social development and the generation of social capital (Wepener and Cilliers 2010, 417–430). What also surfaces are issues pertaining to privilege, which is closely connected to South Africa's colonial and apartheid past and some students then, for the first time, realise that they are actually white (Beaudoin and Turpin 2014, 251–270). Other students have similar experiences as they discover who they are in conversation with students from different backgrounds.

---

6 Cf. http://www.echoyouth.co.za/ (30.11.2021).

In addition to the weekly lecture and reading material, we also take a tour of our university campus during lunch time, looking specifically at how the students eat on campus. We do this in a very informal way by just observing what is happening on campus. However, as soon as you take food and commensality as a lens, a whole new picture comes into view. There are very specific cultural borders separating those who eat in relatively expensive cafés and restaurants, those who get cheaper food at fast-food outlets, those who bring their own food to campus and those who visit a food scheme for students. This experience is ideal for introducing the history of the table and commensality in the Christian tradition with a specific emphasis on the Lord's Supper.

The unfortunate history regarding the celebration of the Lord's Supper in South Africa is introduced, as well as a broader overview regarding the celebration of the Lord's Supper in two thousand years of liturgical history. Here students learn about similarities and differences regarding the development of theology and practice in their own denominational tradition and that of other traditions. The various names for the sacrament of the table such as Mass, Eucharist, Communion, Lord's Supper etc. are introduced in order to deepen this discussion (Caspers, Lukken, and Rouwhorst 1995).

Throughout the module, anthropological material, especially from the domain of Ritual Studies, is read in combination with theological material (Grimes 2010, 77–88). Ronald Grimes for example shows how practices in the Christian tradition are often orientated on consuming and communicating, which include for example Mass (consuming) in the Roman Catholic tradition and preaching (communicating) in the Protestant tradition. This is probably true for the North American context in which he operates but is true only for some of the students. It does not pertain to those students coming from African Independent churches and (neo-)Pentecostal churches (Wepener 2014, 82–95). Important anthropological reading material is that of Mary Douglas regarding meals and dirt.

Douglas defines dirt as being matter out of place and shows that such a definition implies "a set of ordered relations and a contravention of that order" (Douglas 1966, 44). She also writes that "where there is dirt there is system" (Douglas 1966, 44). Douglas explains that the ways in which humans and societies behave towards dirt or 'matter out of place' is the fact that the dirt is "likely to confuse or contradict our cherished classifications" (Douglas 1966, 45). She also explains how those things in society that do not fit our ordered systems and classifications are potential "powers and dangers" (Douglas 1966, 62) threatening our sense of order. And in this regard, she remarks that "Ritual recognises the potency of disorder" (Douglas 1966, 117). Students are challenged to recognise how (holy) meals were used in this regard during the time of apartheid, how this still happens in our churches and society, and how rituals of purity and taboo relating to dirt are important in upholding a certain social structure (Douglas 1971, 61–81).

A last aspect of the module that can be mentioned here, is the part towards the end when students get the opportunity to develop and preach a sermon. The module under discussion in this chapter builds on previous modules in Practical Theology and the students are familiar with homiletical theories and approaches of scholars such as Zimbabwean Eben Nhiwatiwa, South Africans such as Johan Cilliers and Hendrik Pieterse and American Thomas Long. This is thus an existing repertoire of homiletical works to which chapters are added and some are revisited (Cilliers 2004; Nhiwatiwa 2012; Long 2005; Pieterse 2001). For this assignment they must choose a pericope from Luke or Acts pertaining to commensality and also make explicit the context in which they will preach the sermon, particularly with regard to socio-economic realities (Corley 1993; Heil 1999; Love 1995; Malina and Rohrbaugh 1992; Neyrey 1991, 361–387; Pater 2018, 137–148). The module ends with the preaching of these sermons, followed by the lecturer, a guest and the students critiquing each sermon.

Whilst listening to the sermons it becomes clear that students learn a lot regarding the meaning of meals in their own culture and tradition, but also in that of fellow students with different backgrounds. They realise that they still mostly eat with people of the same background. And that those times in which they do come together and cross borders, are also mostly around food. They learn that in South Africa, one can assume one knows who one is, but that one does not fully know until forced to critically look inside one's own lunch box. And that the same applies to understanding more about other people through looking at their lunch boxes. They learn that colonialism and apartheid are technically gone, but that they do actually still remain. White students, and a small portion of students from the new black elite, drink sparkling mineral water, skinny cappuccinos and eat Greek salads, whilst a number of their classmates get lunch from a food scheme on campus. The picture is bleak, but it is a lot better than it was 28 years ago. They also learn that they eat together with people from other backgrounds far more than I and my generation did, not to mention the generations before us. This is very positive and happens from Monday to Saturday. However, worship services on a Sunday in South Africa still remain to a large extent the most segregated (racially and socio-economically) hour of the week in many traditions. Students argue in their sermons for the importance of sharing food for the future of our country, not only at the sacrament of the Lord's table, but also the "casual sacramentality" of the cup of tea, the sacrament of the pie and a coke, the sacrament of the pap and the braai (Klomp and Barnard 2018, 15–31).

5 Still Searching for a Balanced (Practical Theological) Diet

The theme of the module discussed in this chapter is the same as the title of this chapter: Holy Supper / Meal / Sharing Food. And the aim when I developed the module was not only to impart knowledge regarding this theme to students, but to create the possibility of a transcultural practical theological encounter where there is space for a variety of students (and the lecturer) where a transcultural hermeneutic can be developed with regard to this theme. In this way I believe a balanced practical theological diet should be developed, a diet or menu that fits the context of a post-apartheid and post-colonial South African context where the legacy of our past is still clearly visible.

The title of the chapter 'Holy Supper / Meal / Sharing Food' portrays an ideal. A chapter on this theme from a South African perspective can to a large extent also be titled 'Unholy Supper / Fast / Not Sharing Food' or in more positive terms 'Striving towards the Holy Supper / Meal / Sharing Food'. Basic to a transcultural and trans-religious approach to Practical Theology is the understanding that all people are like all other people, like no other people and like some other people. All people eat and cook their food and it is therefore a practice that reflects this truth. People all also have their very unique ways in which they prepare their food and eat it. And of course, there are groups of people who cook and eat in similar ways. This is also true regarding the students sitting at the table of the Practical Theology module. The menu of the curriculum is not always what can be termed high cuisine, but the hope is that there will at least be a bite or two for everyone, that no student will leave hungry and that it will assist in giving students (and the lecturer) a balanced practical theological diet.

Bibliography

Bass, Dorothy. 2012. "Eating." In *The Wiley-Blackwell Companion to Practical Theology*, edited by Bonnie Miller-McLemore, Malden: John Wiley & Sons, 51–60.
Basson, Janine. 2011. "Not All Seafood is Equal." *South African Journal of Science* 107:8–10.
Beaudoin, Tom, and Katherine Turpin. 2014. "White Practical Theology." In *Opening the Field of Practical Theology: An Introduction,* edited by Kathleen Cahalan and Gordon Mikoski, Lanham: Rowman & Littlefield, 251–269.
Bell, Catherine M. 1997. *Ritual: Perspectives and Dimensions.* New York: Oxford University Press.
Cahalan, Kathleen, and Gordon Mikoski, eds. 2014. *Opening the Field of Practical Theology: An Introduction.* Lanham: Rowman & Littlefield.
Caspers, Charles, Gerard Lukken, and Gerard Rouwhorst. 1995. *Bread of Heaven: Customs and Practices Surrounding Holy Communion: Essays in the History of Liturgy and Culture.* Liturgia Condenda 3. Kampen: Kok Pharos.
Cilliers, Johan. 2004. *The Living Voice of the Gospel.* Stellenbosch: SUN Press.
Corley, Kathleen. 1993. *Private Women, Public Meals: Social Conflict in the Synoptic Tradition.* Peabody: Hendrickson.
Douglas, Mary. "Deciphering a Meal." In *Myth, Symbol and Culture*, edited by Geertz Clifford, New York: W.W. Norton & Company, 61–81.
Douglas, Mary. [1966] 2007. *Purity and Danger: An Analysis of Concepts of Pollution and Taboo.* London / New York: Routledge.
De Gruchy, John, and Charles Villa-Vicencio, eds. 1983. *Apartheid is a Heresy.* Cape Town: David Philip.
Denny, Lindie, and Cas Wepener. 2013. "The Spirit and the Meal as a Model for Charismatic Worship: A Practical-Theological Exploration." *HTS Theological Studies* 69:1–9.
Echo. "About Us: Echo." http://www.echoyouth.co.za/ (01.12.2021).

Esler, Philip, ed. 1995. *Modelling Early Christianity: Social-Scientific Studies of the New Testament in its Context.* London: Routledge.
Geertz, Clifford. 1971. *Myth, Symbol and Culture.* New York: W.W. Norton & Company.
Gereformeerde Kerk. 1857. *Handelingen der Negende Vergadering van de Synode der Gereformeerde Kerk van Zuid-Afrika.* Cape Town: G. J. Pike.
Grimes, Ronald. 1990. *Ritual Criticism: Case Studies in its Practice, Essays on Its Theory.* Colombia: University of South Carolina Press.
Grimes, Ronald. ³2010. *Beginnings in Ritual Studies.* Waterloo: Ritual Studies International.
Heil, John. 1999. *The Meal Scenes in Luke-Acts: An Audience-Oriented Approach.* Monograph Series 52. Atlanta: Society of Biblical Literature.
Klomp, Mirella, and Marcel Barnard. 2018. "Dagelijkse kos: Het verband tussen de keukentafel en avondsmaaltafel in de hedendaagse cultuur." In *Rond de tafel: Maaltijd vieren in liturgische contexten.* Meander 17, edited by Mirella Klomp, Peter-Ben Smit, and Iris Speckmann, Heeswijk: Berne Media, 15–31.
Kriel, Johannes. 1961. *Die geskiedenis van die Nederduitse Gereformeerde Sendingkerk in Suid-Afrika, 1881–1956.* Pretoria: Doctoral dissertation.
Loff, Chris. 1983. "The History of a Heresy." In *Apartheid is a Heresy*, edited by John de Gruchy and Charles Villa-Vicencio, Cape Town: David Philip, 10–23.
Long, Tom. ²2005. *The Witness of Preaching.* Louisville: Westminster John Knox.
Long, Thomas, and Leonora Tisdale, eds. 2008. *Teaching Preaching as a Christian Practice: A New Approach to Homiletical Pedagogy.* Westminster: John Knox Press.
Love, Stuart. 1995. "Women and Men at Hellenistic Symposia Meals in Luke." In *Modelling Early Christianity Social-Scientific Studies of the New Testament in its Context*, edited by Philip Esler, London: Routledge, 208–220.
Luther King Jr., Martin. 1960. "The Most Segregated Hour in America." https://www.youtube.com/watch?v=1q881g1L_d8 (01.12.2021).
Malina, Bruce, and Richard Rohrbaugh. 1992. *Social Science Commentary on the Synoptic Gospels.* Minneapolis: Fortress Press.
McMinn, Lisa. 2016. *To the Table: A Spirituality of Food, Farming, and Community.* Grand Rapids: Brazos Press.
Miller-McLemore, Bonnie, ed. 2012. *The Wiley Blackwell Companion to Practical Theology.* Malden: John Wiley & Sons.
Neyrey, Jerome. 1991. "Ceremonies in Luke-Acts: A Case of Meals and Table-Fellowship." In *The Social World of Luke-Acts. Models for Interpretation*, edited by Jerome Neyrey, Peabody: Hendrickson Pub, 361–387.
Nhiwatiwa, Eben. 2012. *Why we Preach: Preaching in the African Context.* Nashville: Discipleship Resources International.
Nhiwatiwa, Eben. 2012. *How we Preach: Preaching in the African Context.* Nashville: Discipleship Resources International.
Old, Hughes. 2002. *Worship: Reformed According to Scripture.* Louisville: Westminster John Knox Press.
Pater, Jonathan. 2018. "Aan tafel met armen, slaven, zieken en zondaren: Maaltijd en gemeenschpsideaal in het evangelie van Lukas." In *Rond de tafel: Maaltijd Vieren in Liturgische Contexten.* Meander 17, edited by Mirella Klomp, Peter-Ben Smit, and Iris Speckmann. Heeswijk: Berne Media, Uitgeverij Abdij Van Berne.
Pieterse, Hennie. 2001. *Preaching in a Context of Poverty.* Pretoria: UNISA Press.
Stringer, Martin. 2005. *A Sociological History of Christian Worship.* Cambridge: Cambridge University Press.

Tisdale, Leonora. 2008. "Exegeting the Congregation." In *Teaching Preaching as a Christian Practice: A New Approach to Homiletical Pedagogy,* edited by Thomas Long and Leonora Tubbs Tisdale, Westminster John Knox Press, 75–89.
Venter, Rian, and Francois Tolmie, eds. 2013. *Transforming Theological Knowledge: Essays on Theology and the University after Apartheid.* Bloemfontein: SUN Press.
Versfeld, Martin. 1983. *Food for Thought: A Philosopher's Cook-Book.* Cape Town: Tafelberg.
Vosloo, Robert. 2017. "On the Lord's Supper: The 'Welcome Table', Exclusion and the Reformed Tradition." In *Reforming Memory: Essays on South African Church and Theological History,* edited by Robert Vosloo, Stellenbosch: African SUN Media, 239–254.
Wallis, Jim, and Joyce Hollyday, eds. 1989. *Crucible of Fire: The Church Confronts Apartheid: Essays by Leading South African Christians 1980–1990.* Maryknoll: Orbis Books.
Wegman, Herman. 1991. *Riten en mythen: Liturgie in de geschiedenis van het christendom.* Kampen: Kok.
Wepener, Cas. 2002. "Still Because of the Weakness of Some? – A Descriptive Exploration of the Lord's Supper in South Africa, 1948–2002." *Jaarboek voor liturgie-onderzoek* 18:139–158.
Wepener, Cas. 2010. *Aan tafel met Jesus.* Wellington: Bybelmedia.
Wepener Cas, and Johan Cilliers. 2010. "Ritual and the Generation of Social Capital in Contexts of Poverty." In *Religion and Social Development in Post-Apartheid South Africa: Perspectives for Critical Engagement,* edited by Ignatius Swart, Hermann Rocher, Sulina Green, and Johannes Erasmus, Stellenbosch: SUN Press, 417–430.
Wepener, Cas. 2011. "Liminality: Recent Avatars of this Notion in a South African Context." *Jaarboek voor liturgie-onderzoek / Yearbook for Liturgical and Ritual Studies* 27:189–208.
Wepener, Cas. 2014. "Liturgical 'Reform' in Sub-Saharan Africa: Some Observations on Worship, Language and Culture." *Studia Liturgica* 44:82–95.
Wepener, Cas. 2019. "Eating and Drinking: Measurements and Recipes for Social Capital." In *Bonding in Worship: A Ritual Lens on Social Capital Formation in African Independent Churches in South Africa.* Liturgia Condenda 30, edited by Cas Wepener, Ignatius Swart, Gerrie Ter Haar, and Marcel Barnard. Leuven: Peeters Press.
Weyel, Birgit. 2014. "Practical Theology as Hermeneutical Science of Lived Religion." *International Journal of Practical Theology* 18:150–159.
White, James. ³2000. *Introduction to Christian Worship.* Nashville: Abingdon Press.

J. Kwabena Asamoah-Gyadu
Initiation Ceremonies / Incorporating / Identity Formation

1 Introduction

This article examines processes of initiation from the viewpoint of traditional non-Western cultures. We consider practices relating to both the African religio-cultural and Christian contexts. Rites of passage encompass ritual processes that accompany the transitions of life from one social status to another. In non-Western contexts, the changes in human life are usually interpreted through religious ideas and therefore, these transitions are marked by ritual; hence the reference to "rites of passage." Although Africans have practiced these rites of passage since antiquity, their academic study with the discipline of anthropology is attributed to the Belgian scholar Arnold van Gennep ([1909] 1960). He defined the total ritual processes as constituted in three phases: first, the original status; second, a liminal period in which candidates are in between statuses; and third, the conferment of a new status on the candidate. Perhaps, one of the most important things we have learnt from anthropologists with respect to rites of passage is the importance of the "liminal periods" during which the candidates experience a sense of *communitas*, that is, an "intense awareness of being bound together in a community of shared experience" (Davies 1994, 4).

Africa is a culturally diverse and multiethnic continent. This means descriptions of rites of passage provided here only serve as a generalized picture, but one I hope which is still representative of what these rites are and why they are performed. Traditional non-Western cultures are noted for their sense of the presence of the supernatural in everyday life and the dependence of human wellbeing and flourishing on the maintenance of harmonious cosmic relationships. Some key features of indigenous religions include belief in a Supreme Being who is creator, provider and sustainer of the universe and whose representatives in the earthly realm of existence include small community-owned deities. There is also a general worshipful reverence for clan ancestors – the "living-dead" as John Mbiti refers to them – whose beneficent presence may be invoked at appropriate times as needed (Mbiti 1989). These ancestors are also the custodians of public morality and initiation rites and traditional festivals are designed to celebrate them as part of the African world. Africans have strong worldviews of mystical causality in which evil is caused by malevolent spirit powers such as witches. Initiation rites, accompanied by religious sacrifices therefore constitute important means by which humans sustain relationships with the world of spirits or even seek to live in harmony with the ancestral worlds for existential benefits and blessings. Such harmonious relationships are enhanced through the performance of rites of passage.

2 Initiation Rites and Rituals

In Africa, tensions often arise between Christianity and traditional religions over the appropriateness or not of various initiation rites. African traditional religions regard rites of initiation as being important for human wellbeing, communal identity, spiritual security, and wholeness. These rites have embedded in them processes and ends directed towards human flourishing. Initiation rites serve as means of pastoral care because refusal to perform them, it is believed, could lead to negative ontological consequences not just for the individual, but for the family too. Religious specialists – male and female clan elders, diviners, seers, and priests – preside over initiation rites because they are adept at performing them in prescribed and appropriate ways.

African Christians, especially those belonging to the evangelical and Pentecostal/charismatic traditions, frown on initiation rites, damning them as sources of spiritual contamination and inimical to human flourishing (Meyer 1996, 214). Thus, practices of exorcism in these newer streams of Christianity include deliverance from demonic spirits who intrude into lives through initiation rites. The educational value of rites of passage – which some scholars lament that Africans have drifted from – lays emphasis on character building, respect for the self, family, and community (Opoku-Agyeman 2012, 97). Tensions emerge between indigenous cultures representing tradition and Christianity, and representing change, because in traditional Africa, human beings are spiritually incomplete and vulnerable in terms of belonging and identity without the appropriate traditional rites of initiation. Indeed, some misfortunes, physical deformities, and illnesses, are explained in terms of punishments from ancestors for the neglect or even improper performance of initiation rites. Christians generally contest the performance of these same rites on account of their being considered inconsistent with biblical teaching.

In the religious context, initiation ceremonies consist of the rites and rituals through which human beings solicit the help of transcendent powers for holistic living and cosmic harmony. James L. Cox defines "ritual" as "a repeated and symbolic dramatization directing attention to a place where the sacred enters life thereby granting identity to participants in the drama, transforming them, communicating social meaning verbally and non-verbally and offering a paradigm for how the world ought to be" (Cox 1998, x). There are, Cox notes, "correct and incorrect ways of performing rituals which determine their efficacy as sources of transformative power" (Cox 1998, x). Rituals as defined by Cox come with certain general characteristics and they include the fact that: first, they point towards sacred realities through acts and symbols; second, they are repeated according to fixed patterns; third, they occur within sacred and sacralized spaces; fourth, they provide shared identity for participants and foster a sense of community; fifth, they operate within symbolic modes of communication; and sixth, they have a transformative power (Cox 1998, 60).

Initiation rites also take place at specific sacred spaces and sites recognized by the community, that is, mountains, forests, river sites or shrines, and they are normally held out of public view. It is during these liminal periods of seclusion that the candidates are educated in social obligations and responsibilities associated with the status to which their age entitles them. In African traditions, there is rarely doubt about who one is, because identity formation is always a crucial part of education (Opoku-Agyeman 2012, 97). Initiation ceremonies are constituted by religious 'rites' and the way they are coordinated through words and symbols is what gives them their ritual character. Our discussion is restricted to initiation and its associated ceremonies occurring within African traditional religious contexts and its intersections with Christian pastoral practices in Africa. Getting the timings, procedures and processes right is considered critical to the effectiveness of these initiation ceremonies.

3 Christianity Encounters Tradition

In both the biblical and African cultural traditions, initiation ceremonies are critical to living. Funerary rites in the Old Testament were important for ushering the dead peacefully into the realm of the ancestors. Similarly, among the Igbo Amasiri of southeastern Nigeria, funerary rites ensure smooth transitions into the spirit world. If these rites are not performed, the deceased, it is feared, return as ghosts to trouble living relatives (Obinna 2013, 6). In the African Christian context some of these initiation ceremonies – the dedication of infants, circumcision, and baptism – have been adopted in relation to the confession of faith and church membership. God instituted circumcision as a sign of his covenant with Israel through Abraham (Gen 17:9–14). Those who failed to observe the rite were to be cut off from among the people of Israel. When Jesus was born, not only was he circumcised, but Jesus was also taken to the temple where the designated sacrifices as outlined by Moses were offered in fulfillment of tradition: a pair of turtledoves or two young pigeons (Luke 2:22–23).

African traditional and Christian initiation rites are both driven by certain pastoral objectives. We have already mentioned their importance as sources of moral instruction and socialization. Child-naming ceremonies, for example, exist both as a means of socio-cultural integration and moral education. Rites of puberty are performed for similar reasons and in most cases, they prepare the initiates for the assumption of adult responsibilities such as marriage. All these pastoral activities are supposed to have implications for moral character formation, health, wholeness, flourishing and communal wellbeing. It is not uncommon for convulsion in infants, for example, to be explained in terms of the neglect of rituals meant to establish them firmly among the living. When such rituals are overlooked, infants are said to be caught between the physical and spiritual realms representing life and death, or between the communities of the living and the dead but not settled in either of the two.

Mercy A. Oduyoye notes how puberty rites are performed to make young people members of both their immediate families and extended communities as they take on adult responsibilities. Oduyoye laments the dehumanizing aspects of initiation ceremonies but does not discount their importance in the holistic development of women in African societies (Oduyoye 1995, 9–24). Certain aspects of traditional widowhood rites for example, have been cited as demeaning women. However, the symbolic principle of spiritually severing relationships with deceased spouses through widowhood rites serve important pastoral purposes in removing fear from surviving spouses and restoring them to proper functioning order following bereavement.

Christian attitudes towards initiation rites range from outright denunciation as demonic to various attempts to 'Christianize' such ceremonies because, as we have noted, traditionally they are seen as being inconsistent with biblical faith. In many African communities, missionaries created the Christian quarters, called *Salems* in places, where members of the church lived separately, away from the 'heathens' to prevent them from patronizing traditional initiation rites and the services of priest-healers. The other part of the town thus became 'pagan' or 'heathen' quarters. Traditional rules and regulations were not applicable at *Salem* and those who lived there were forbidden from undergoing traditional initiation rites or participating in any festivals. Despite the Christian denunciation of initiation rites, it is well known that in times of desperation the services of traditional priest-healers are also patronized by Christians (Soyinka 2012, 110–111).

4 Initiatory Rites of Passage and Ancestors

Initiation rites or life-cycle rituals, as they are sometimes referred to, are associated with religion and culture because they are carried out in fulfilment of ancestral obligations. The presence of ancestors is invoked during critical moments in the history of communities such as festivals, calamitous occasions, and initiation ceremonies. Whether we are talking about naming, circumcision or other puberty rites, marriages, or funerals, the ancestors play a critical role and indeed, the rites performed are those that must have been orally scripted by them.

Akan communities for example, 'feed' their ancestors during festivals and through rituals of libation prayer and, as occasions demand, these ancestors are invited to participate in whatever celebrations are in place. During libation pouring, a representative list of ancestral names would be mentioned, and their blessings solicited for general communal wellbeing and flourishing. The most important point is that not only is the presence of the ancestors invoked during the performance of initiation and other ceremonies, but the process of becoming an ancestor itself is an initiatory one that requires elaborate rites and rituals.

5 Select Initiation Ceremonies

Humanitarian and communal values are very important to African societies. The aims behind initiation ceremonies thus include the affirming of communal belongingness through moral instruction on roles in society. The values of godliness, respect, honor, moral integrity, hospitality, humility, gratitude, and a strong sense of community are all highlighted during initiation ceremonies. We now consider just a select few of the most common initiation ceremonies in African societies:

5.1 Child Naming Ceremonies

In the Akan traditions, naming new infants takes place on the eighth day of birth. When babies survive the first week of birth, it is a sign that they have come to stay and are formally initiated into the life of the living. Early in the morning on the eighth day, the immediate families of the couple together with members of the community gather wearing bright apparel, signifying the mother's victory in childbirth. Childbirth signals victory for families because infertility is considered a curse. The child is laid on the lap of the family elder and the initiation rites are conducted with water and some liquor. The officiants dip an index finger into the water and the liquor alternatively and let a drip of each fall onto the tongue of the baby accompanied by the words: "[Name] if you say it is water, let it be water; and if you say it is drink, let it be a drink." After three drops of each liquid, the rest of the liquor is passed round for each member of the community present to take a sip and pronounce a blessing on the child.

Child-naming here is not merely a ceremony for giving the name to a newly born infant. It is also a period of moral education in which the child is instructed to learn to distinguish truth from falsehood. The ritual of naming initiates the child to the essence of truthful and discreet speech, the need for care, truth, firmness, and social sensitivity in the exercise of the spoken word. As the child reacts differently to the tastes of water and liquor "the child thereby demonstrates potential sensitivity to the vagaries of social experience, and the need to comply with the cultural rules of communication" (Yankah 1995, 46–47).

The name is an identity marker that links the newly born infant to a particular family, clan, or ethnic group. The names chosen tells stories. It links individuals to families; indicates the day of the week in which the child was born; shows where the child falls in the lines of births; and tells the circumstances surrounding the birth of the child. In some societies, infants also receive "tribal marks" which like names, connect individual persons to larger communities. An infant's umbilical cord may be buried on the family compound as an act that connects this person spiritually to a community. Thus, unlike in Western contexts, Africans do not hail from where they are born. People connect to ancestral homes depending on whether families practice patrilineal or matrilineal systems of inheritance.

5.2 Circumcision

Circumcisions mark the transition of boys and girls from infants into boyhood and girlhood and prepare them for active sexual life. Traditional circumcision rituals have largely been discontinued. Circumcision, whether for boys or girls marked the natural order of growing up. In the Sene-Gambia regions of West Africa, *Kunang* is the name given to this surgical rite. Circumcision required sequestration in the bush for varying numbers of weeks and the rite was at once a test of bravado and a preparation for one's teenage years. In the bush, and away from public view, the rite is a test of individual endurance and back home, the circumcision was a communal celebration of coming of age (Sanneh 2012, 53, 54).

5.3 Puberty

Initiation rites of puberty are related to fecundity, marriage, and childbirths. Female initiation ceremonies among the Chewa of Malawi are considered very important because they are also the contexts for sex and moral education (Phiri 1998). Isabel Phiri identifies four stages in puberty ceremonies. The first, which marks the transition between girlhood and womanhood is called, *chinamwali cha nkangali* and takes place on reaching puberty. The second is performed on reaching the age of marriage and the third involves newlyweds receiving matrimonial counsel on their union. The fourth, *chinamwali cha chisamba* deals with issues around pregnancy and the sorts of taboos and observances associated with childbirth. These initiations of transition from puberty to marriage take place under the tutelage of the officially recognized traditional women who were required to be adept at moral norms, customs, and beliefs of Chewa society (Phiri 1998, 133).

In Ghana both the Krobo and Asante have elaborated nubility rites for girls that prepare them for marriage and motherhood. Female initiation rites are embedded in cultural notions about cleanliness, pollution, and what it means to be a woman in, and to be part of, a particular society (Steegstra 2005, 1). Peter Sarpong, a Catholic archbishop, and anthropologist says he prefers the expression "nubility" to "puberty" because "they are a means whereby Ashanti girls are introduced into the adult society of their sex and are given access to marriage both as a sexual union and as a social institution" (Sarpong 1977, x). A good portion of the period of the nubility rites are devoted to instructing the neophyte on lessons in sexual development, marriage and tribal traditions involving the female gender. The rites are held after first menstruation, but it takes about three consecutive menstrual periods to go through the rites. There is a moral side to the performance of Ashanti nubility rites as the girls are supposed to remain virgins until they have gone through them.

In Ashanti tradition, the girl is given a bath of ritual cleanliness and the eating of ritual eggs as a sign of life. Her hair is cut in a prescribed style and the hairs kept in the crack of a wall and sealed.[1] Part of the ritual bath takes place in the river with an elderly woman. The officiant dips the neophyte three times in the water and committing her wellbeing into the custody of the river deity. From this point, the girl's new life begins. She is reclothed in traditional handwoven *kente* cloth, puts on new sandals and is given a loincloth, which is tucked in the strings of precious beads with which her waist has been adorned (Sarpong 1977, 30). Following these riverside ceremonies, the initiand is carried home ceremoniously.

She takes her seat in public, usually at the family compound as the community comes around to congratulate the girl and shower her with gifts. Finally, the Ashanti girl must go through the *anoka* (touching the mouth), in which the traditional festive food of mashed yam with eggs are used in touch her lips three times before eating a few morsels. The prayerful declarations that are made as various food items are used to touch the mouth of the girl are very instructive: the mashed yam and egg, "this is what God created first"; pepper, "may you never taste misfortune"; salt, "may you always be happy and hear news as sweet as salt'; elephant's skin, "may you have many children"; and so on and so forth. Ultimately, these are prayers of goodwill for success in life, marriage, and childbirth (Sarpong 1977, 33–34).

5.4 Chieftaincy

In African societies, chieftaincy has continued to exist alongside modern political systems of government. Traditional chiefs govern on behalf of the ancestors. The installation of chiefs consists of very elaborate religious rites and rituals that are meant to achieve two things: first, to confer on the candidate the blessing of the ancestors; and second, to sacralize their personality leading to a life of prescribed taboos. A chief should not see corpses; strike anyone or be struck; eat in public; walk barefooted; and on no account must his buttocks touch the ground. Indeed, among Akan tribes, the easiest way to de-stool chiefs is either to remove their sandals in public or to forcibly place their buttocks on the ground when performing some public function. In other words, certain forms of public humiliation de-sacralize chiefs, rendering their positions as representatives of the ancestors untenable.

When the candidate for chiefship is identified, they are placed in quarantine for prescribed periods of time. The quarantine period is for instruction on the role of

---

[1] This is done so that if the girl passes away in another geographical location and the family is unable for some reason to receive the dead body, the head and pubic hairs could be used in the performance of funeral ceremonies.

chiefship and the ancestral ceremonies required to carry out the functions of the position. The chief is the moral, political, and religious leader of the community with responsibilities that require wisdom, probity, and a deep knowledge of traditional customs. Every step of the process requires prayer through libation pouring and the candidate is taken to a stool room of the ancestors where various rites and rituals including sacrifices involving the blood of sheep are undertaken. They swear oaths to be truthful and honest in their dealings with the ancestors and pledge not to undermine the sacred customs bequeathed by these ancestors. On the day of inauguration, the chief also swears publicly to protect the community and serve them in truth, honesty, and integrity. The installation of the chief involves lowering the candidate three times on the stool of the ancestors whose name they will bear and from then on, the candidate's real name is dropped as they adopt what the Akans refer to as a 'stool name'.

One of the most important roles of the chief is to be the main celebrant of traditional festivals through which African communities acknowledge their ancestors. The rituals of installation, which legitimizes the position of the chief, signals the transformation of the personality of the candidate. This transformation from an ordinary mundane personality into an extraordinary sacred individual is what legitimizes one's position. Religious and political power are said to be invested in the person of the Oba of Benin. The Oba mediates between the two worlds envisioned by the people of Benin and communicates with both the visible world of human beings, *agbon,* and the invisible world of deities and spirits, *erinmwi*. The Oba is said to personify the living realities of spiritual beings and deities and in his awe-inspiring personality, presides over the agrarian festivals through which gratitude is expressed to the ancestors for their provision (Kaplan 2000, 116–117).

The taboos that we have outlined in connection with chiefship act as the regulative principles that protect the office of the chief from abuse and defilement (Akrong 2006, 196). Among the Akan of Ghana, the title of *Nana* is conferred on newly installed traditional chiefs. This is the same title that the ancestors bear and so among the Akan, the ancestors are referred to collectively as *nananom* and that is how they are addressed during libation prayer. The status of the chief as a sacred personality or a *de jure* ancestor implies that anytime his actions contradict the norms and values that regulate his office, he *ipso facto* ceases to be a chief and must be de-stooled (Akrong 2006, 198).

5.5 Priesthood

The initiation into priesthood begins when the spirit of a deity takes possession of individuals indicating a calling into cultic duties. The modes of calling into priesthood include inexplicable illnesses, sudden possession by the deity or disappearance into forests. Each of these modes of calling is a means to an end (Ekem 2008, 49). The training that follows a certified calling ushers the candidates for priesthood into the mystical world of the deities in whose services they have been called. The process of initiation which occurs at the end of training at a shrine includes rituals that covenant the life of the priest to that of the deity and this means priests, like chiefs, live by certain taboos depending on the religious identity of the deity to be served. Priests serve in mediatory capacities to bring communication from the supernatural realm into the physical realm and offer sacrifices on behalf of communities to the deities. Their functions include divination and medical services.

From an African pastoral perspective, genuine religion is about salvation or liberation that occurs within daily life (McKenzie 1997, 525). It is not for nothing that among the Yoruba of Nigeria, the priest-diviner is referred to as the *Babalawo*, the 'father of secrets' because they are the ones who bring information and answers to existential questions from the spiritual to the physical realm. The popularity of the healing and prophetic roles of traditional priests and diviners has its equivalent, especially within African initiated Christianity. In traditional thought, the pastoral roles of priests include the supply of therapeutic and other sacramental substances that people use to protect themselves against evil. In the traditional world, rain and fertility, wellbeing, long life, protection from evil and helping women in childbirth are some of the issues that the priests deal with (McKenzie 1997, 527–528).

6 Initiation Ceremonies of Incorporation and Identity

African rituals constitute powerful and effective modes of religious expression and are critical to both incorporation and identity formation (Grillo 2012, 112–126). People are communal beings and cannot belong without going through proper processes of incorporation through the prescribed rites of initiation of their society. In other words, initiation rites constitute forms of pastoral care within traditional societies. It is the reason why these initiation rites are always an occasion for bringing the living and the living-dead together as one community. It shows how a strong sense of community is required for the maintenance of social and psychological stability in human life. Cosmic harmony through the performance of appropriate rites is needed for human wellbeing and flourishing in traditional African societies.

A study of three Bantu peoples, the Bashi of central Kivu in the Congo, Rwanda and Burundi revealed that participation in a common life is the main basis of family, social, political life and religious institutions and customs. Life is lived in the communion of its members. The "vital union" has been described as the non-negotiable link that unites both the living and the living-dead in a vertical and horizontal relationship. It is said to result from "a communion of participation in the same reality, the same vital principle, which unites a number of beings with one another" (Mulago 1996, 138). The primary concern of the Bantu, life, is both empirical and super-empirical because it encompasses life beyond the grave and the two remain inseparable (Mulago 1996, 139).

On the traditional front, therefore, non-Western cultures have inherited elaborate ancestral initiatory religious rites and rituals by which members of the society are made communal beings because individualism such that known in the West is considered inconsistent with traditional philosophical understandings of modes of being. Further, although there are social sides to initiation ceremonies, primarily, they have a religious orientation. The pragmatic nature of African religions means they are oriented towards the view that humans must vigilantly maintain harmonious relationships in both this-worldly and other-worldly realms for prosperity (Grillo 2012, 112). The African worldview asserts the "ontological primacy" of the community, which means, "the reality of the communal world takes precedence over the reality of individual life histories" (Gyekye 1997, 37). African philosopher Kwame Gyekye argues that human beings are born into societies and cultures and this communitarian conception of the person implies that community life is not optional, but obligatory (Gyekye 1997, 38). What distinguishes a community from a mere association of individuals is the sharing of a common way of life and of values (Gyekye 1997, 42).

In traditional Africa, initiation ceremonies are related to concepts of power. Africans live in a spirit world, a world associated with power, health, protection and mystical knowledge for survival and vitality. Thus, especially in quests for success that relate to leadership, ownership of property and survival, it is not uncommon to seek initiation into traditional secret societies in search for the securities from supernatural realms. Fisherfolk seek protection against hazardous and perilous fishing expeditions and farmers seek spiritual protection against dangerous forest creatures. Hunters seek the help of medicine men or enroll in cults that provide fortification against bullets, for, it is not uncommon for competitors to "mistake" one another for game. Some opt for powers that enable them to vanish at the sight of danger with the recitation of appropriate incantations. All these modes of acquisition of mystical power require one form of initiation or another.

The acquisition of these powers often requires ingesting medicines by eating, swallowing, or inserting them through the anus. If one's traditional vocation requires the use of a powerful vision of sight, the liquid preparation may be dropped into the eyes. Most of these processes require initiation ceremonies, that also must be renewed periodically for the supernatural powers to retain their potency. Stephen Ellis and Gerrie ter Haar also document instances in which modern African politicians enroll in secret societies in search of security and for the spiritual leverage needed to protect them and give them whatever advantages they seek over competitors, opponents, and enemies (Ellis and ter Haar 2004, 75–88). Thus, "secret rituals are a feature of initiation into societies that are considered repositories of esoteric knowledge and power that are often regarded as mainstays of morality and social order" (Ellis and ter Haar 2004, 81).

Exclusivity is critical to initiation ceremonies that relate to the membership of secret societies. Secret societies – whether local or imported – Ellis and ter Haar note, impress on members during their initiation a sense that they are gaining access to forms of knowledge to which others are not privy. These initiation rites incorporate acolytes "into a transcendental world of power" (Ellis and ter Haar 2004, 84). In other words, in these initiatory ceremonies, access to power and privileged information requires the observance of certain ethics of secrecy in the performance of duties.

In addition to the rites of transition, Africa is also home to many secret societies.[2] Medicine cults have for example been part of traditional African cult systems for generations. The membership of these cults requires prescribed initiation ceremonies. Gabon, for example, has a secret society called Njobi which is a traditional-style religious exclusive patriarchal society. There is also Bwiti, known in many parts of Central and Western Africa. Here, in these secret societies, the patriarchs of the community "govern community affairs and interact with the spirit world" (Ellis and ter Haar 2004, 77).

7 Christianity and Initiation

Despite their acknowledged importance, some of the initiation rites and sacred customs discussed here have either lost their significance or undergone various changes under pressure from the forces of modernization, democratization, urbanization, and the influence of Christianity. Phiri writes that the initiation of Chewa women in Malawi was considered among Presbyterian missions to be 'pagan' and 'sinful'. Chewa girls and their families were therefore counseled to pull out of these traditional rites in favor of Christian initiation rites developed by the church and devoid of any of the rituals associated with the traditional culture (Phiri 1998, 135, 136). Among the Bafodea Limba of Northern Sierra Leone, the circumcision rite takes place within the context of male secret societies, but today, Christians will circumcise boys at a modern clinic, a change that upholds tradition but strips it of its sacredness (Ottenberg 1994, 364).

In Ghana the tensions between tradition and Christianity are felt within chieftaincy (Asante 2006, 234). The installation of traditional chiefs tends to be very much a religious affair involving clan ancestors and rituals associated with local deities. The debate on whether a traditional chief can be a Christian or not continues to rage. In many Christian traditions, a chief could be in church, but may not be allowed to participate in Holy Communion. According to the churches in which chiefs are excluded from Communion, initiation rituals of chiefship put candidates in situa-

---

[2] In the colonial era several secret societies originally set up for Western elites, accepted into members some African compatriots. Masonic and other lodges therefore became part of African life attracting the new local elites and these became contexts in which the powerful and influential of African societies met to do business and plan political activities.

tions of double allegiance – ancestors and Christ – and therefore chieftaincy is deemed to compromise allegiance to Christ.

Initiation ceremonies are not limited to traditional societies and new religious movements. Although they may not be described as "initiation" as such, there are several ceremonial transitions that occur in the lives of Christians as part of the requirements for their belonging to the church. A number of these like baptism and confirmation take place at the beginning of life and at the point of entry into adulthood respectively. These rites came with the missionary package of what it means to be a member of a church. However, in Africa, churches have sought to use them as initiation rites that mark a person or family's renunciation of traditional religion and the embracing of faith in Christ. At the beginning of the missionary era, the parents of infants brought for baptism were required to provide a 'Christian name' and in case they did not have one, the pastor or priest had a list for families to choose from.

Baptism has gradually developed as an initiation ceremony for children of Christians. Confirmation in the historic mission denominations has also developed in many African contexts as a Christian alternative to rites of puberty. This is because in Africa, Christian conversion has often meant breaking with the African past in traditional religion. Traditional initiation rites have in Christian discourses been presented as linking or tying individual and families to a spirit world that is considered demonic and dangerous. African traditional names, as a result of their linkages with dead ancestors and not in a few cases with the deities that made pregnancy possible, were considered 'satanic' or 'demonic'. The so-called 'Christian names' many of which come from the Old Testament – Joseph, John, Samuel, Benjamin, Elijah, Elisha, Jeremiah, Peter, Andrew and the like – have either replaced traditional names or were used as first name as a mark of conversion to faith in Christ.

8 Conclusion

African religions are not inscribed in canonical texts but lived out in embodied experiences. Thus, the rites and rituals we have discussed constitute symbolic reenactments of human aspirations and the importance of flourishing as a critical definition of what abundant life means. The communal nature of these initiation rites –whether Christian or traditional – and their relationship with the transcendent powers are indicative of the important role that the supernatural plays in African life and existence. That communities believe that the non-performance of initiation rites could lead to negative mystical consequences means that traditional worldviews are not that easily discarded in the attempts to replace them with Christian ones.

Anthony Ephirim-Donkor who is traditional chief and a scholar in African traditional religions bemoans the fact that in child naming ceremonies, the liquor used is now replaced with soda drinks by Christian communities. His claim is that by this change, neonates are denied their first psychosocial rite of sharing in the long continuum of an ancient Akan rite (Ephirim-Donkor 2011, 93).

Traditionalists bemoan the way Christianity has displaced traditional sacred initiation rites. The observation that Christian groups arbitrarily demonize traditional rites and replace them or usurp the powers of traditional families in the performance of naming and puberty rites is a valid one. In the formulation of pastoral practices and strategies for example, the intersection between the biblical material and the traditional beliefs ought to be accessed carefully to reformulate and regurgitate these initiation rituals in ways that respect human rights and also help those who have opted for the Christian faith to still fulfill their responsibilities towards the communities in which they are nurtured.

References

Akrong, Abraham. 2006. "Religion and Traditional Leadership in Ghana." In *Chieftaincy in Ghana: Culture, Governance and Development*, edited by Irene K. Odotei and Albert K. Awedoba, Accra: Sub-Saharan Publishers, 193–212.

Asante, Emmanuel. 2006. "The Relationship between the Chieftaincy Institution and Christianity in Ghana." In *Chieftaincy in Ghana: Culture, Governance and Development*, edited by Irene K. Odotei and Albert K. Awedoba, Accra: Sub-Saharan Publishers, 231–246.

Cox, James L. 1998. "Ritual, Rites of Passage and the Interaction between Christian and Traditional Religions." In *Rites of Passage in Contemporary Africa*, edited by James L. Cox, Cardiff: Cardiff Academic Press, viii–xx.

Davies, Douglas. 1994. "Introduction: Raising the Issues." In *Rites of Passage*, edited by Jean Holm with John Bowker, London: Pinter Publishers, 1–9.

Ekem, John D. K. 2008. *Priesthood in Context: A Study of Priesthood in Some Christian and Primal Communities of Ghana and its Relevance for Mother-Tongue Biblical Interpretation.* Accra: Sonlife.

Ellis, Stephen, and Gerrie ter Haar. 2004. *African Worlds: Religious Thought and Political Practice in Africa.* Oxford / New York: Oxford University Press.

Ephirim-Donkor, Anthony. 2011. *African Spirituality.* Lanham: University Press of America.

Gennep, Arnold van. [1909] 1960. *Rites of Passage.* Chicago: University Press.

Grillo, Laura S. 2012. "African Rituals." In *The Wiley-Blackwell Companion to African Religions*, edited by Elias Bongmba, West Sussex: Wiley-Blackwell, 112–126.

Gyekye, Kwame. 1997. *Tradition and Modernity: Philosophical Reflections on the African Experience.* Oxford: Oxford University Press.

Kaplan, Flora Edouwaye S. 2000. "Some Thoughts on Ideology, Beliefs, and Sacred Kingship among the Edo (Benin) of Nigeria." In *African Spirituality: Forms, Meanings and Expressions*, edited by Jacob K. Olupona, New York: Crossroad Publishing, 114–151.

Mbiti, John S. ²1989. *African Religions and Philosophy.* London: Heineman.

Meyer, Birgit. 1996. "Modernity and Enchantment: The Image of the Devil in Popular African Christianity." In *Conversion to Modernities: The Globalization of Christianity*, edited by Peter van der Veer, London / New York: Routledge, 199–230.

McKenzie, Peter. 1997. *Hail Orisha: A Phenomenology of a West African Religion in the Mid-Nineteenth Century.* Leiden: Brill.

Mulago, Vincent. 1969. "Vital Participation." In *Biblical Revelation and African Beliefs*, edited by Kwesi Dickson and Paul Ellingworth, Maryknoll: Orbis Books, 137–158.

Obinna, Elijah. 2013. "Ritual and Symbol: Funeral and Naming Rituals in an African Indigenous Community." In *Critical Reflections on Indigenous Religions*, edited by James L. Cox, Surrey: Ashgate, 159–174.

Oduyoye, Mercy Amba. 1995. "Women and Ritual in Africa." In *The Will to Arise: Women, Tradition and the Church in Africa*, edited by Mercy Amba Oduyoye and Musimbi R.A. Kanyoro, Maryknoll: Orbis Books, 9–24.

Opoku-Agyeman, Jane Naana. 2012. "Writing for the Child in a Fractured World." In *Reader in African Cultural Studies: Essays in Honor of Ama Atta Aidoo*, edited by Anne V. Adams, Oxfordshire: Ayebia Clarke Publishing, 86–87.

Otttenberg, Simon. 1994. "Male and Female Secret Societies among the Bafodea Limba of Northern Sierra Leone." In *Religion in Africa: Experience and Expression*, edited by Thomas D. Blakely, Walter E.A. van Beek, and Dennis L. Thomson, London: James Currey, 363–387.

Phiri, Isabel Apawo. 1998. "The Initiation of Chewa Women of Malawi: A Presbyterian Woman's Perspective." In *Rites of Passage in Contemporary Africa*, edited by James L. Cox, Cardiff: Cardiff Academic Press, 129–145.

Sanneh, Lamin. 2012. *Summoned from the Margin: Homecoming of an African*. Grand Rapids: William B. Eerdmans.

Sarpong, Peter K. 1974. *Ghana in Retrospect: Some Aspects of Ghanaian Culture*. Accra: Ghana Publishing Corporation.

Sarpong, Peter K. 1977. *Girls' Nubility Rites in Ashanti*. Accra: Ghana Publishing Corporation.

Soyinka, Wole. 2012. *Of Africa*. New Haven / London: Yale University Press.

Steegstra, Marijke. 2005. *Dipo and the Politics of Culture in Ghana*. Accra: Woeli Publishing Services.

Yankah, Kwesi. 1995. *Speaking for the Chief: Okyeame and the Politics of Akan Royal Oratory*. Bloomington / Indianapolis: Indiana University Press.

Faustino Cruz
Leadership / Embodied Knowledge / Resistance

1 Introduction

Our common life as theological educators is rooted in a locus of reflective practice that seriously demands embodied leadership for resistance: the workplace. In the United States, workplace bullying is a hidden and silent epidemic. It has been a pervasive and growing leadership challenge even within higher education. Imagine suffering from gastric discomfort each time you shared a space with a disruptive, cantankerous student. Recall the day when you chose to work from home to avoid colleagues who publicly criticized your work, ignored you in the hallways, and sarcastically insinuated that your tenure and promotion were contingent upon their political machinations. Remember feeling deep isolation and despair, perhaps while ruminating on toxic thoughts that kept you awake all night. When your body spoke, were you prepared to listen? This critical reflection examines how embodied knowledge serves as a mobilizing source of resistance for transformation, particularly in contesting faculty incivility and bullying in the workplace. I argue that by embodying knowledge and choreographing resistance, we become effective agents of adaptive change inspired to create academies grounded in ethical principles and moral values.

2 Transformational Leadership

Bernard Bass (1985) identifies four constitutive elements of transformational leadership. In an earlier work, I have summarized and appropriated them as follows:
- Intellectual stimulation – leaders demonstrate how to say "no" to the world as it is by systematically challenging the status quo; promote creative innovation; model critical thinking and generative decision making; and explore multiple and new ways of meaning-making that sustain a dynamic learning community.
- Individualized consideration – leaders advance the holistic growth and integration of each person-agent through effective mentoring and coaching, practice empathetic ways of listening, and promote sound interpersonal relationships that support an inclusive sense of identity and belonging in the organization.
- Inspirational motivation – leaders articulate a shared vision that inspires others to act intentionally, engaging both head and heart.
- Idealized influence – leaders reveal the ethical principles and moral values in which their transformative practices are grounded, by embodying virtues such

as respect, trust, charity, integrity, collaboration, and justice (Cruz 2015, 1311–1312).

Transformational leaders view leadership as a process of conversion, underscoring their primordial role as animators of adaptive and generative change (Barrett 2012; Boyatzis and McKee 2005; Kouzes and Posner [1987] 2012). They regard followers as persons-in-relationship who seek holistic integration, thereby framing human or organizational situations through the prism of their priorities, core values, and practices (Markham 1999). Accordingly, transformational leaders allow others to lead. As a result, they form among followers future leaders as moral agents for the common good (Cruz 2015, 1311). One essential practice of transformational leadership is constructing embodied knowledge.

3 Embodied Knowledge

French philosopher Maurice Merleau-Ponty compares embodied knowledge to typing on a keyboard without looking at the keys. When we touch type, he explains, we neither have to know where each letter is in relation to the other keys nor to develop a conditioned reflex for a specific key upon seeing it (Merleau-Ponty [1945] 2005, 166). He argues that it is *knowledge in our hands*, a way of knowing that demands an intentional bodily exertion that cannot be objectified. Typists can distinguish where letters are on the keyboard, just as we can identify our limbs in relation to other body parts, introducing a "knowledge of familiarity that does not provide us with a position in objective space" (Merleau-Ponty 2005, 166).

Building upon Merleau-Ponty's phenomenology, Japanese philosophical psychologist Shogo Tanaka defines embodied knowledge as a phenomenon in which the body knows how to act without any deliberation – like riding a bicycle (Tanaka 2013, 47). He asserts that, to perform such act, there is "no need to verbalize or represent in the mind all the procedures required" (Tanaka 2013, 48). The knowledge constructed is somehow imprinted in one's body, and the act is performed unconsciously. The knowing subject is the body and not the mind. More concretely, the knowing subject is the lived body – the embodied mind that engages in embodied knowing (Tanaka 2013, 48).

Thus, embodied knowledge is lived knowledge; it is unlike scientific knowledge that is clearly objectified. Some examples include basic bodily movements such as breathing, walking, or running; use of tools such as playing with a tennis racket, eating with a fork and spoon, or playing the piano; spatial behaviors such as differentiating front-back, left-right, and top-down; and non-verbal behaviors such as maintaining physical distance, emoting feelings with facial expressions, or gazing at a person in a conversation (Tanaka 2013, 52). What are some of the implications of embodied ways of knowing for embodied pedagogies?

Asian American educator, dancer, and sociologist Hui Niu Wilcox maintains that when we apply embodied ways of knowing, we "signal an epistemological and pedagogical shift that draws attention to bodies as agents of knowledge production" (Wilcox 2009, 105). Consequently, we affirm our body's capacity to know. Embodied ways of knowing incorporate subjugated perspectives from underrepresented enclaves such as women, indigenous groups, and communities of color that contest, resist, or give witness to notions of objectivity, dualism, and hierarchies. Embodied knowers affirm the body's complex relationship with subjectivity; accordingly, they interface bodily ways of knowing, lived experience, and performance (Wilcox 2009, 105).

Moreover, Wilcox presents qualitative evidence to prove that embodied pedagogies form communities of belonging and foster inclusion by contesting Eurocentric and androcentric systems of knowledge production grounded in a body-mind binary (Wilcox 2009, 104). She declares that, to advance such pedagogies, we must develop alternative models of knowledge production that (a) resist the intersectional dualisms and hierarchies of mind-body, male-female, and white-other; and (b) acknowledge the body's ability to know. Drawing from the work of feminist theorist Elizabeth Grosz (1993), Wilcox emphasizes that "the body is not just another thing or object to be controlled and studied"; for "it is in and through our bodies that we experience the world and develop consciousness" (Wilcox 2009, 106). To illustrate, she purports that in the civic arena, activists use embodied pedagogies to provide emotional access to science-based information and to mobilize for social change. She animates artists, activists, and educators to utilize embodied ways of knowing in forging creative alliances and transforming radically their work, institutions, and systems of meaning making – where the body is at the very core of knowledge production (Wilcox 2009, 104).

Lamentably, U.S. higher education still bifurcates the mind and body, and theological schools are not sheltered from this predicament. For instance, in some seminaries, we still attempt to delineate clearly the limits and boundaries of intellectual, spiritual, human, and pastoral studies – rather than aspiring for a more holistic or integrative approach. Wilcox warns that, whenever we perpetuate this dichotomy, we replicate the very system of power that we aim to resist. We find ourselves in such an impasse, particularly when we privilege the texts and contexts prescribed by the canons of our degree programs, extricate teaching and learning from real life, or exclude anything that happens outside the classroom, or any embodied knowledge constructed in the classroom from the curriculum. If we insist that only thoughts count, we essentially frame knowledge as disembodied; concomitantly, we assert that, when the body thinks and articulates a thought, it is essentially irrelevant (Wilcox 2009, 107). As a result, selected popular paradigms of critical pedagogy are still too theoretical and disembodied, while attributing power struggles in the academy to socio-historical contexts. Wilcox elucidates that this problem makes it difficult for some educators teaching from the trenches to assess the effectiveness of some theories when put into practice (Wilcox 2009, 106). Let us explore how embodied practices support choreographies of resistance, particularly in contesting faculty incivility and bullying in the academy.

4 Choreographies of Resistance

Research on workplace bullying is fairly recent, and not much has been written prior to 2000. In one of the earliest comprehensive studies on faculty incivility, Darla Twale and Barbara De Luca write on the rise of the academic bully culture (Twale and De Luca 2008). While recognizing that the general literature on workplace bullying defines the phenomenon in various terms, they emphasize that bullying is fundamentally characterized by actions: verbal, indirect, or passive. Bullying is "*a voluntary deviant behavior that is deliberate and systemic, and departs from positive workplace norms*" (Twale 2018, 8). The target of bullying has limited space, time, or option to flee the physical setting, avoid the personal provocation, or evade potential social interaction with the bully. On one hand only bullies know their intent to bully the target. On the other hand, the target does not have to name the experience as bullying (Twale 2018, 9).

In a 2014 study of U.S. health care workers, more than 50 % of survey respondents confirm having been targets of bullying, and 80 % have witnessed bullying behaviors in the workplace. Bullying has affected about 23 % of university faculty and staff, as well as public school teachers. Among department chairs or heads, 59 % recognize faculty incivility as a pandemic leadership challenge. Worse still, 25–50 % of the time, administrators are the perpetrators, and in at least 38 % of the cases, targets are bullied by co-workers (Twale 2018, 4). Unfortunately, there are currently no studies on workplace bullying in U.S. theological schools.

However, participants at various faculty development seminars, academic conferences, and facilitated professional support groups – during my tenure as dean at three graduate schools for nearly fifteen years – have attested by way of anecdotes and personal testimonies that explicit forms of workplace bullying are common. Seminary bullies may be senior faculty who unknowingly (not having done reflective work in therapy and spiritual direction) remain insecure about their professional status in the university or guild, despite their scholarly publications, promotion in rank and tenure, popularity as teachers, compensation and benefits, or formal administrative and ecclesial appointments. They usually cannot let go of previously held positions of power and prestige, like some recalcitrant emeriti pastors-in-residence who oblige their successors to minister in their shadows and perennially disrupt any attempts of incumbent administrators to lead effectively and introduce adaptive change. For instance, they may perceive any curriculum revision, reframing of faculty and staff appointments, or new recruitment initiative to be a malicious critique of what they had either accomplished or not. Some demonstrate diffused or unfocused anger expressed at academic meetings, social events, or even at worship services. They target through disruptive micro-aggressions or dramatic expressions of rage.

Many exhibit narcissistic and other ego-dystonic behaviors that may warrant mental health intervention. In a case study that I present at the end of this chapter, I attempt to capture some of the critical issues and challenges of workplace bullying encountered by theological educators and their implications for embodied leadership. What do targets generally experience, and when are actions considered bullying?

Targets of bullying express knowledge through the body, which manifests itself through stress related physical disorders. For an action to be considered bullying, it must be executed as a complex pattern of negative behaviors rather than an isolated occurrence. Such action may include abuse, cruelty, threats, mocking, rancor, oppression, hostility, ostracism, exclusion, and marginalization. On a micro level, bullying includes: (a) inaction, such as silent treatment, withdrawal, or withholding things from the target; (b) subtle action, such as interrupting, glaring at, or eye rolling directed toward the target; and (c) manifested action, such as shouting, blaming, humiliating, name calling, or criticizing the target. On a social or macro level, bullies use tactics that attack or denigrate a target's reputation such as name calling, rumor mongering, or overt public humiliation. Moreover, bullies may live through feelings of personal inadequacy, professional jealousy, or the inability to control negative behaviors as a result of more serious mental health issues (Twale 2018, 7–10). In every social system, beginning with the family, persons are socialized to bully. For this reason, no workplace is immune from this dilemma.

Did you ever wonder what happened to the playground bullies at your grammar school? Twale concurs with other scholars who are strongly convinced that playground bullies have all become adults and that, deplorably, some are today's notorious academic bullies. She writes:

> Bullying may result when faculty members believe their institution fails to meet their needs. According to the theory of work adjustment, dissatisfaction precipitates maladjustment and resulting negative behaviors. Bullies may use these feelings to attack colleagues and the administration. Administrators may simply rate these negative behaviors as unsatisfactory work performance rather than label them bully behaviors. Lack of knowledge about bullying on the part of administrators translates into mishandling the situation and avoiding the consequences of bullying (Twale 2018, 11).

At every faith-based, ecclesial, and academic institution in which I have ministered, there has been at least one bully and a target. In some cases, bullies targeted in a mob, a circle of bully allies who preyed on unsuspecting and vulnerable targets such as junior non-tenured faculty, international students, women, and staff of color. The digital age has increased the methods and frequency with which we communicate using social media; consequently, bullies no longer rely simply on face-face encounters to traumatize their targets (Twale 2018, xii–12). A threatening email written in a belligerent, rude prose is a common example. An academic bully culture ineluctably creates a toxic, vitriolic, and hostile work environment.

R. Kent Crookston, in his book *Working with Problem Faculty*, alerts us that bullies "often operate behind closed doors or cloaked in the confidentiality of a group", such as on a rank and tenure committee, and "from a position of seniority or hierarchy", such as full professors who have served as former deans and department chairs, aware that "their prominence, rank, or connections [...] serve as effective cover for their maneuvers" (Crookston 2012, 132). Their targets may develop stress related physical and emotional disorders such as high blood pressure and depression, and demonstrate poor self-esteem, lower institutional commitment and satisfaction, burnout, resentment, impaired concentration, and compromised safety in the workplace (Crookston 2012, 133).

Furthermore, bullying imposes additional burden to the organization. It builds strained peer relationships manipulated by dystonic mobs and clicks. It leads to habitual absenteeism, accelerated employee turnover, sub-standard levels of work productivity, and higher human resource related expenditures such as healthcare cost. It threatens institutional reputation through legal action (Lester 2013, vii–xi). Let us examine some of the legal issues and challenges.

Labor and employment law professor Kerri Stone explains that, under U.S. federal or state law, bullying behavior as such is lawful. She clarifies that anti-discrimination statutes (Civil Rights Act of 1964), as several courts have interpreted, are not civility codes designed to promote collegiality, compassion, or morality in the workplace. On the contrary, "they exist to combat class-based discrimination with respect to the terms and conditions on one's employment" (Stone 2013, 88). Stone states that bullying is deemed actionable only if it "amounts to or may be seen as amounting to discrimination based on a protected class such as race, religion, sex, age, disability", and so forth (Stone 2013, 88). Bullying may also result in individual and/or employer liability insofar as it falls within the category of an actionable tort. In common law jurisdictions, a tort is a civil wrong – such as assault or defamation – that causes someone else to suffer loss or harm resulting in a legal liability for the tortfeasor or the person who commits the tortious act (Stone 2013, 88). The legality of bullying challenges the limits and boundaries of academic tenure.

Susan Taylor, a scholar of organizational leadership in higher education, writes that academic freedom and tenure are new topics in workplace bullying literature (Taylor 2013, 23–40). She explores how job security may effectually support and perpetuate faculty incivility, in light of how higher education comprehends academic freedom and tenure.

The American Association of University Professors, in its *1940 Statement of Principles on Academic Freedom and Tenure*, upholds that a tenured appointment is an indefinite appointment, i.e., "after the expiration of a probationary period, teachers or investigators should have permanent or continuous tenure, and their service should be terminated only for adequate cause, in case of retirement for age, or under extraordinary circumstances because of financial exigencies" (AAUP 1940, 2018). This provision ensures that no tenured faculty may be terminated without due process. The organization also declares that lack of collegiality should never be considered when adjudicating personnel matters.

Collegiality must only be evaluated within the parameters of teaching, scholarship, and service; this policy makes it difficult for targets of bullying to seek redress. However, AAUP emphasizes that in some cases, there are legitimate issues worthy of investigation and evaluation, e.g., malfeasance (meaning any illegal or improper behavior) or professional misconduct (AAUP 2006, 40). More concretely, obstructing the ability of colleagues to carry out their normal functions, engaging in personal attack, or violating ethical standards are legitimate issues worthy of investigation and evaluation (Taylor 2013, 36; Gula 2010). Still, tenured faculty who bully are difficult to terminate.

Since bullying is not illegal and does not fall under any of the federal protected categories, human resource departments and ombudspersons often resort to mediation and other negotiation methods to address complaints. Given their limited options, they end up leaving most cases of unresolved, often perpetuating a faculty culture of normal abnormality and chronic resignation. Common responses include: there is not much we can do; this too shall pass; that is just the way she is; or let's just wait until he retires in three years. Confronted by an acute leadership challenge, what role must academic leaders play to change systematically such a dystonic status quo?

5 Saying "No" to the Academy as it Is

Reflecting within her context as director of the office of academic integrity at the University of California San Diego, Tricia Bertram Gallant observes that once administrators have recognized a wrongful behavior, they typically introduce rules to clarify what behaviors are inadmissible or even illegal. Subsequently, they establish policies and protocols for managing perpetrators. She argues that, when administrators primarily focus on the victim-perpetrator aspect of a complaint, they might ineluctably privilege institutional compliance. Consequently, they fail to facilitate, support, and form ethical persons and organizations (Gallant 2013, 104). She claims that articulating shared standards and establishing policies for dealing with undesirable behaviors can be helpful; however, to be successful, such strategies must be part of a larger organizational vision to support ethical conduct "that is honest, transparent, and accountable to higher order principles (such as do more good than harm)", even, "when there may not be a law or rule to guide behaviors, or when there may be no known resolution to conflicting interests, needs or demands" (Gallant 2013, 104). Her vision calls for the creation of an ethical academy in which bullying will find no place to thrive (Gallant 2013, 105). Such locus of practice inspires constituents to produce embodied knowledge – both personal and collective—that forms and sustains a culture of embodied resistance – one that says "no to the academy as it is." For theological schools, this leadership practice demands building a community grounded in virtue ethics.

Roman Catholic moral theologian Richard Gula identifies the constitutive elements of virtue ethics in his book *Just Ministry: Professional Ethics for Pastoral Ministers*. He writes:

> In virtue ethics, we turn to the character of a moral exemplar as the ultimate court of appeal for what constitutes the good life, or the life of a fully flourishing person. Christians know something about what it means to be human, to be good and to live the good life because we have seen it in Jesus. Christian morality regards the life of discipleship, or being conformed in the image of Christ, to be the best life for us to live. The long tradition of following Christ (imitatio Christi) echoes this feature of virtue ethics. In Christian virtue ethics, we turn to Jesus to see whom we are called to be, to know what constitutes good character, what counts as virtuous behavior, and what the good life looks like (Gula 2010, 48).

What happens when we intentionally seek the 'good life' in our graduate schools, departments, and seminaries—the same 'good life' that we aspire for our students? I am cognizant that we require students to meet ethical and professional standards prescribed for graduation, ordination by judicatories, or licensure and certification by regulatory boards. I know that, at least in my institution, students with an A or 4.0 grade point average (GPA) could still be dismissed from a degree program for failing to embody good character. Yet, we do not impose the same standards on ourselves due to certain unearned privileges that rank, tenure, or academic freedom might have bestowed upon us. We fail to model the way for our students to live out our core vision of professional and pastoral leadership, a practice that embodied leaders must articulate through adaptive action. Therefore, as theological educators, we must strive to become embodied leaders for resistance by committing ourselves to the good life. How do we go about this?

Within our communities of belonging and accountability, we must promote creative innovation, critical thinking, faithful discernment, and generative decision making in order to rebuild our enervated, dysfunctional academies targeted by workplace bullies. We must facilitate the holistic growth and integration of each of our constituents (*cura personalis*) through effective mentoring and coaching. We must listen with empathy, maintain sound interpersonal relationships, and support a diverse yet inclusive sense of identity to dismantle the biases and prejudices that divide us. We must articulate a shared vision that inspires others to embody knowledge and choreograph resistance, acting prophetically with both head and heart. We must reveal the ethical principles and moral values in which our teaching, scholarship, and service are grounded, by embodying virtues that in the Jesuit Catholic tradition reside in solidarity, service, and justice (Cruz 2015, 1311–1312). Ultimately, our mission is to breathe forth and live the good life.

6 A Case Study

Catherine was a first-generation Asian immigrant and a vowed member of a Roman Catholic religious order. The graduate school where she had taught for six years appointed her academic dean, a month after she was granted tenure and promotion in rank as Associate Professor of Theology and Practice. At 43, she was the youngest member of the faculty. This case study depicts her struggle and survival as a target of workplace bullying within an academic institution committed to "educating the whole person".

The seminary president appointed Catherine as academic dean upon the unanimous and enthusiastic recommendation of the core faculty. While she had only been recently tenured, her previous experience as an effective parish and health care administrator, as well as her demonstrated excellence in teaching and scholarship, made her an obvious candidate for leadership. She was very articulate, imaginative, passionate, and engaging, particularly as a public speaker. Her empathy and deep concern for the over-all formation and welfare of the students were remarkable. She embodied the school's vision of educating for solidarity, service, and justice. She was collegial in her teaching, scholarship, and service. However, her experience of moving into a new role as dean was quite traumatic.

Catherine's predecessor – a religious priest who had been on the faculty for more than 25 years – was given a sabbatical to facilitate her transition. There were three other senior colleagues, two white females and a white male, all of whom supported and mentored her during pre-tenure. Catherine never expected incivility to dominate her school.

Each time Catherine facilitated a faculty meeting, the senior faculty would sit together on one side of the room and criticize every idea or change she introduced. They would either interrupt or engage in side talks whenever she spoke, and usually avoided any eye contact. Once, Catherine sent an email to confirm an academic policy change that had already been carefully vetted by the faculty, only to receive a cantankerous response from one of the female senior professors. Since the entire faculty was copied on that response, it triggered a series of negative comments from other senior professors, including her predecessor, each one explicitly questioning her competence to serve as dean. Catherine chose not to respond to the messages. Subsequently, each junior faculty spoke to Catherine in private to offer her support and affirmation. One of them explicitly described what he had witnessed at meetings and online as "bullying". Finally, Catherine had a name for what she had been struggling with.

Now, Catherine could even claim that she had also been bullied behind closed door. The same female senior faculty who wrote the cantankerous email yelled at her on two occasions about administrative decisions that Catherine's predecessor had made regarding faculty workload and course scheduling. Perhaps for cultural reasons, Catherine found it difficult to challenge verbally anyone older than she.

While not accepting culpability, she would simply reply in a low tone of voice, "I'm sorry," in an attempt to diffuse the conflict. Since that encounter, she found herself avoiding her colleague at all costs, even to the point of taking the back exit when leaving the building to make sure they didn't meet in the hallway. Each time Catherine heard that woman's voice – or any voice similar to hers – she would hide in her office sheltering herself from a perpetrator. Her entire body would tense up.

After working in such a toxic environment for six months, Catherine developed a serious form of acid reflux, which triggered chronic cough and inflamed her vocal cords. Her speech was impaired; she had to go to a therapist to learn how to speak again. She remembered a friend saying, "you really lost your voice there". Losing her voice convinced her that she must explore other employment options. At the end of the academic year, she gave up tenure and the privilege to lead. She has since accepted a job at another institution on a modified tenure-track contract.

Reflection questions: How can practical theologians utilize embodied ways of knowing to resist the hidden and silent epidemic of workplace bullying in higher education? What is the role of an academic leader in this case?

Bibliography

American Association of University Professors. 2006. *Policy Documents and Reports*. Baltimore: Johns Hopkins Press.
American Association of University Professors. 2018. "Tenure." https://www.aaup.org/issues/tenure (01.12.2021).
American Association of University Professors. "1940 Statement of Principles on Academic Freedom and Tenure." https://www.aaup.org/report/1940-statement-principles-academic-freedom-and-tenure (01.12.2021).
Barrett, Frank. 2012. *Yes to the Mess: Surprising Leadership Lessons from Jazz*. Cambridge: Harvard Business Review Press.
Bass, Bernard. 1985. *Leadership Performance Beyond Expectations*. New York: The Free Press.
Boyatzis, Richard E., and Annie McKee. 2005. *Resonant Leadership: Renewing Yourself and Connecting with Others through Mindfulness, Hope, and Compassion*. Boston: Harvard Business Press.
Crookston, R. Kent. 2012. *Working with Problem Faculty: A 6-Step Guide for Department Chairs*. San Francisco: Jossey-Bass.
Cruz, Faustino M. 2015. "Transformational Leadership." In *Encyclopedia of Christian Education*, edited by George Thomas Kurian and Mark A. Lamport, Lanham: Rowman and Littlefield, 1311–1312.
Gallant Bertram, Tricia. 2013. "The Ethical Dimensions of Bullying." In *Workplace Bullying in Higher Education Working*, edited by Jaime Lester, New York: Routledge, 104–120.
Grosz, Elizabeth. 1993. "Bodies and Knowledges: Feminism and the Crisis of Reason." In *Feminist Epistemologies*, edited by Linda Alcoff and Elizabeth Potter, New York: Routledge, 187–215.
Gula, Richard. 2010. *Just Ministry: Professional Ethics for Pastoral Ministers*. New York / Mahwah: Paulist Press.
Kouzes, James M., and Barry Z. Posner. [1987] 2012. *The Leadership Challenge*. San Francisco: Jossey-Bass.
Lester, Jaime, ed. 2013. *Workplace Bullying in Higher Education*. New York / London: Routledge.

Markham, Donna. 1999. *Spiritlinking Leadership: Working through Resistance to Achieve Organizational Change*. Mahwah: Paulist Press.

Merleau-Ponty, Maurice. [1945] 2005. *Phenomenology of Perception*, trans. Collin Smith. London / New York: Routledge Classics.

Stone, Kerri. 2013. "Workplace Bullying in Higher Education: Some Legal Background." In *Working with Problem Faculty: A 6-Step Guide for Department Chairs*, edited by Jaime Lester, San Francisco: Jossey-Bass, 87–103.

Tanaka, Shogo. 2013. "The Notion of Embodied Knowledge and its Range." *Encyclopadeia* 37:47–66.

Taylor, Susan. 2013. "Workplace Bullying: Does Tenure Change Anything? The Example of a Midwestern Research University." In *Workplace Bullying in Higher Education*, edited by Jaime Lester, New York: Routledge, 23–40.

Twale, Darla J. 2018. *Understanding and Preventing Faculty-on-Faculty Bullying*. New York: Routledge, 2018.

Twale, Darla J., and Barbara M. De Luca. 2008. *Faculty Incivility: The Rise of the Academic Bully Culture and What to Do about it*. Jossey-Bass Higher and Adult Education Series. San Francisco: Jossey-Bass.

Wilcox, Hui Niu. 2009. "Embodied Ways of Knowing, Pedagogies, and Social Justice: Inclusive Science and Beyond." *NWSA Journal* 21:104–120.

R. Simangaliso Kumalo
Pulpit / Power / People / Publics

1 Introduction

To the disappointment of many Marxists in Africa, who believed that religion is a sleeping pill for the oppressed masses, religion has proven that it is more complex than that. Asserting this point even more firmly, the Catholic Theologian Hans Küng observed that "Religion has proven that it can be not only a means of social appeasement and consolation but also […] a catalyst of social liberation: and this without that revolutionary use of force which results in a vicious circle of ever-new violence" (Küng 1992, 13). As a result, the church's participation in the political life of Africa in the contemporary era is ambivalent and a cause for intense debate and discussion. Any discourse on the place of Practical Theology in Africa conjures images of large crowds listening to powerful sermons from high pulpits, being influenced spiritually or politically. Africa as a whole, East, West, North and South is indeed highly religious with a total number of 599 million Christians (Johnson 2018). It is important to note that religion in Africa is not necessarily a private matter, but it is freely lived and practiced in the public realm. For the purpose of this article, I will be referring predominantly to the southern region of southern Africa/South Africa in particular, as it is one of the largest economies and most Christian country in the continent, with almost 87% of its population of 58 million people professing to be Christian (Schoeman 2017, 2). South Africa is inhabited by people from many different countries of the continent, who come as refugees, migrant workers, and students. The country therefore is a melting pot of cultures and religions from all over the continent. I start by defining Practical Theology and governance. The main aim of this paper is to explore the contribution of Practical Theology in the political life of Southern African society with the aim of enhancing good governance and wellbeing of all people. Then I move to discuss the church's participation in politics during the pre- and post-independence period. This is followed by a discussion of a few practical strategies to be taken to address the place of governance in the field of Practical Theology.

James Cochrane and his colleagues defined Practical Theology as: "That disciplined, reflective theological activity which seeks to relate the faith of the Christian community to its life, mission and social praxis" (Cochrane, De Gruchy, and Petersen 1991, 2). In a nutshell Practical Theology focuses on the "study of human actions that serve the transmission of God's discourse to man [sic], in which people function as intermediaries" (Eybers et al. 1978, 268). It is about how the church – through its teachings that come through messages preached from pulpits – influence people to realize the mandate and power they have to shape political decisions. By 'public' we are referring to the social realm, where both the church and government influence people. The public is important for the church and theology because as Allan Boesak puts it "the Christian faith in Jesus Christ is public. It is public because Jesus of Nazareth, took on public form when he became a human person, and because his life was lived in public servanthood and vulnerability in obedience to God." (Boesak 2005, 3) By governance we mean:

> a particular set of initiatives to strengthen the institutions of civil society with the objective of making government more accountable, more open and transparent, more democratic (Minogue 1997, 21).

Practical Theology or religion is one of the key sets of initiatives that can be employed to strengthen good governance, for it to be more accountable, open, transparent, and democratic as Minogue observes in this definition; whilst arguing for the significance of the church for good political practice. Politics is built on secular assumptions about the world, people power and institutions and these will not always be in continuity with the theology and mission of the church. Politics and governance are secular disciplines with their own meanings, rituals, values, languages, and assumptions. These need to be carefully evaluated before they are applied to the discipline of Practical Theology whose main subject and concern is the church and the kingdom of God. Drawing from insights shared by Stephen Patterson I argue that politics or governance has its own faith assumptions, but these need to be brought into a creative synergy with Practical Theology (Patterson 2004, 90). The boundaries of Practical Theology go beyond the confines of the church, but extend to society at large, where this discipline can be used to analyze the world and provide fresh insights. It is for this reason that my proposal in this paper is that governance must be taken seriously and understood as a key component of the church's life and mission.

Despite growing secularization in the contemporary world, there is an interesting development in countries in Southern Africa, where religion continues to influence and shape political processes and practices. It continues to break out of the private realm where western secularists had pushed it to. Michael Walzer notes that: "Liberal and left secularists may once have hoped for total exclusion: not only in the religiously motivated militants but also the sentiments and doctrines that motivate them would play no part in political decision making" (Walzer 2007, 147). Those assumptions have not worked in much of Africa, where both politics and religion are treated as two sides of the same coin, which is the total wellbeing of people. This is because generally African culture which means the traits such as values, norms and practices by some African people which distinguishes them from others) and religious life is seen as holistic rather than in compartments especially because human beings too are a combination of qualities, as Setiloane observes "a person is something divine, sacred, weird, holy; all qualities" (Setiloane 1978, 13). Politics, Power and Public are all secular terms. At a glance they have nothing to do with the discipline of Theology, let alone Practical Theology and the ministry of the church. However, as countries continue to struggle with issues of democracy, good governance, attainment of the common good, the church has to ask the question, what is our role in the leadership; management and development of society and those are questions of Practical Theology.

2 Pre- and Post-Independence Political Participation of the Church

This essay explores the challenges that politics and governance pose for the church's participation in democracy formation in African societies. The beginning of the twentieth century saw germination and growth of the seed of African nationalism. This came with the growth of the number of mission school educated elites who were becoming teachers, lawyers, priests, clerks, and authors. This period saw the emergence of political organizations, started and led by African leaders most of whom were leaders in the church both lay and clergy, but also in political organizations or groups. These mission school graduates most of whom were sent overseas by church related institutions to study destabilized the colonial rule in most African countries, by campaigning for the freedom of their people. A good example of this is Kwame Nkrumah, the first president of Ghana, the first African country to gain independence. Nkrumah was motivated and shaped by Christianity in his early years, as a result he studied theology at Lincoln University and Seminary (Nkrumah 2002, 30). Robert Vinson noted that there was an encounter between Africans in the diaspora and those from the continent which "encouraged the growing idea among Africans and African Americans that they are of the same race, bound together in a programme of transnational racial uplift" (Vinson 2012, 107). This emphasizes the fact that the churches through their educational institutions enabled interaction between continental Africans and Africans in the diaspora, which enabled political exposure and awareness of their situation.

At the heart of the colonial system of governance was the fact that even though the Europeans formed a tiny minority of the population compared to the Africans who were the majority by far, the political and economic power to make decisions remained with them and served their interests. The church collaborated with those who viewed Africans as inferior and instituted paternalistic methods of relating to them, in the name of mission and expression of the love of God for them. The churches were "servants of power" meaning the colonial system (Cochrane 1987). So, whilst in pre-colonial African communities, a person's status in society was determined by membership to the clan and loyalty to the royal house, with the arrival of the Europeans, through the help of the church, a person's worth and dignity was determined by their colour, economic status, and allegiance to Christianity (Meintjes 2020). So, discouraging African Christians from political participation was meant to sustain the dominance of the Europeans who continued to rule African communities even though they remained tiny minorities. This led to some influential African religious leaders also shunning politics and declaring their churches apolitical. A good example of this is the Zion Christian Church (ZCC) which is the largest African Independent Church in South Africa, which declares itself to be apolitical. Haynes notes that: "The church, however, took a rather apolitical stance in relation to apartheid and to the position of non-whites in the society. This was largely because its leaders perceived that their role was predominantly religious and spiritual rather than political" (Haynes 1996, 177).

As a result, even after the end of colonial rule and the emergence of independence in most African countries, Christians were reluctant to participate in the political governance of their countries especially the ordained. This matter was compounded by the fact that after independence as John Gatu observed, Christian leaders "[i]nherited the very churches and governments that were against African freedoms" (Gatu 2006, 132). A good example of this is Archbishop Tutu's utterances during the emergency of democracy in South Africa. He told his biographer John Allen that, "[h]e had been an interim political leader, standing in for the real political leaders. Now that role is over. He was a pastor, not a politician and had no intention of entering politics" (Allen 2006, 314). Whilst the churches had been very active in the development of mission schools and better education for African people, such institutions did not prioritise political education, governance, and the importance of a conscientized electorate in order to sustain democracy for all people. Practical Theology as practiced in the life of the churches or taught in Seminaries did not explicitly include political education from a church perspective. They would claim to be above politics. Mugambi correctly notes that: "It is important to appreciate that some missionaries claimed to be either 'neutral' or 'above' politics and therefore justified their refusal to support anti-colonial struggles emphasizing 'salvation' rather than 'liberation' (Mugambi 2002, 23).

Interestingly enough, as more black Africans became Christians and received education through mission schools, they were dissatisfied with the political systems that deprived them of basic rights and equality with white people, and the churches that ignored their experiences of political oppression. Racism within education and Christianity from the churches and the mission schools implicitly opened up their eyes to pervasive racism and domination perpetuated by the colonial governments which in many cases was also being assisted by some of the progressive churches. The same churches that laid the foundation for political apathy amongst Africans which in a sense would confirm Marx's predictions, became catalysts for political resistance in most African countries. As a result, in most African countries the struggle for independence was pioneered and led by mission school educated elites (Hughes 2011).

3 Pulpit, People and Power

The changing impact of politics in African states became most evident when countries such as Ghana, Zambia, Mozambique, Zimbabwe, Botswana, and lastly South Africa became democratic. The work that had been carried out by mission school elites, who were also Christians or at least sympathetic to the church in the struggle for liberation ensured that these leaders were viewed positively and drawn into forming the new governments. These newly liberated countries needed a pool of educated and conscientised leaders to help with the reconstruction of their countries and most of these were found in the church. They led the struggle and now they needed to put into practice the values and strategic vision of a free, independent, and democratic society that they had been calling for. A neo-colonial, form of democratic government, built around three P's, pulpit, people and power. Church leaders including bishops, theologians joined government as cabinet members, heads of department, parliamentarians, and advisers. Thus, the teaching of the church on good governance, equality, development, the common good, service and work ethic were transferred into the new governments meaning that Practical Theology was again thrust into the public realm. For instance, the Rev Frank Chikane who was the General Secretary of the South African Council of Churches during the years of the struggle against apartheid who later became the Director General in the Office of the President in South Africa, is an example of a church leader who became the most powerful official of government in democratic South Africa and saw the synergy between church and politics. Mookgo Kgatla observes that:

> Chikane was not only a servant leader within Pentecostal ranks. He was also a servant in government because of the position he held as the director general in the presidency. For Chikane, there is a very thin line that divides the secular and the sacred. He did not see anything wrong with being a Pentecostal and being involved in a secular job. On the contrary, this involvement increased his influence in society and the church. This influence has opened doors for a relationship between the church and government (Kgatla 2018, 13).

This is just one example of how people in many countries in Southern Africa are connecting the pulpit and politics in the public realm in the post-colonial era. It is also an example of how the discipline of Practical Theology continues to be important for governance and politics in Africa. However, there seems to be a lack of intentionality in exploring this interface. As a result, whilst most of the people in government are committed and practicing Christians, many African governments are still faced with challenges of corruption, instability, poverty, poor governance and in some cases of being undemocratic despite holding regular elections.

4 The Church and Governance

During the colonial era, English-speaking mainline churches dominated the political landscape in most countries in Africa. These were the churches that supported and led the struggle for independence and mobilized financial support from their sister churches in European countries. However, during the independence era Pentecostal churches mostly from the USA burst into the scene and dominated the religious landscape. They replaced the European originated churches in most of the ecumenical bodies and their theology which is not progressive and tends to lean towards the prosperity gospel became more prominent. This is noted by Paul Gifford in the Ghanaian context, who observed that the "mainline churches [...] remain significant bodies. Nevertheless, in the two decades we are especially considering (1979–2002) they have in many ways been eclipsed by something quite new, the charismatic sector" (Gifford 2004, 23). He continues to note that the prosperity theology of these charismatic mainly Pentecostal Churches is spreading throughout Africa. He said that "[w]e has seen how widespread this prosperity theology has become in Africa. It's preached at length in the newer churches, and these beliefs are ritually enacted, with collections and offerings. They are enforced by countless testimonies" (Gifford 2004, 335).

There has been a proliferation of ministries set up by foreigners from other African countries and citizens. These are proponents of the prosperity gospel and don't pay much attention to the contribution of the church to the political life of the countries, but rather promote the support of the men or women of God, leading to the growing number of extremely rich pastors some of whom are actually richer than their churches and their converts. This brand of church has thrown a spanner to the wheel of progressive church-state political engagement because it is aligned with the "pro-capitalist economic"[1] agenda and prosperity type of gospel. The focus of this type of religion is on drawing people's focus away from the public towards a privatised form of faith that promises to enrich the individual both spiritually and economically. It also shifts people's attention away from the needs of their context and the resources that can be gleaned from African traditional religions and culture to materialistic forms of Christianity. This form of Christianity does not add value to the identity of people in Africa nor does it contribute to their quest for development: socially, economically, and politically. It benefits those who embrace a culture of consumerism, ignoring the plundering of the environment and the need of holding governments accountable as a prophetic role of the church. This is exacerbated by the fact that its Practical Theology is imported from outside the African continent. Making this critique of the prosperity gospel, Gifford observed that "faith theology that is heard so widely in Africa was not devised in Africa" (Gifford 2004, 337).

---

[1] I have borrowed this term from my friend Roderick Hewitt (2014).

Therefore, it is not surprising that Practical Theology's contribution to good governance, if any, is limited.

5 Developing Afro-Centric Practical Theologies of Governance

As seen from the earlier discussion, theologies that came with the missionaries did not address the issue of the role of the church in the governance of society. They tended to be aloof towards politics, encouraging Christians to leave politics with politicians because Christianity itself was a colonial project because it "came to Africa through extensive and intensive contacts between Africa and Europe" (Bongmba 2016, 25). Elsewhere I noted that "theologies that came with the missionaries, that continue to be taught in the churches today, are Eurocentric" (Kumalo 2015, 171). This is because at worst they were sympathizers of imperialism and at their best they were just paternalistic towards Africans (Elphick 2012).

For the church to make a tangible contribution in the development of good governance in Africa, it needs to develop a variety of practical theologies of governance and democracy to guide its participation in the deepening of democracy for the African nations. These theologies must emanate from the experience of continued exploitation of the African people and their natural resources be they human or natural as a result of neoliberal economies and multi-national companies. A theology of governance needs to encourage participation in political processes such as elections, debates, campaigns as part of citizen responsibility and witness to the fact that God stands for justice. Aquiline Tarimo has noted that, "political organizations cannot ignore the role of religion. Religion plays the role of formation of attitude and character. It is unfortunate that the public sphere, the place where we debate public policy, is hostile to religion" (Tarimo and Manwelo 2008, 103).

A Practical Theology of governance would give us the foundational motivation for responding to these concerns. It would teach us that "this earth belongs to the Lord with all that is in it" (Ps 241). So, God is the head of the earth as a household, which is a just, democratic home where all are equal and are to be treated with dignity. Such Afro-centric practical theologies of governance will also need to draw insights and experiences from African traditional forms of leadership with emphasizes community, equality, hospitality, sharing and *ubuntu* (humanness), which is a deep sense of interdependency and belonging together (Shutte 2001, 12).

6 An Eco-Theology to the Injustices of the Politics of Development

There is a huge negative impact to the environment by policies of economic development that are passed by African governments through their political actors. These policies have allowed the cutting down of trees, pollution of rivers and burning of fossil fuels, which has led to climate change, unpredictability of weather patterns, drought, natural disasters, and escalated poverty. There is a need for the church to develop a pro-active eco-theological understanding of its ministry especially with regard to the policymakers. Humanity living in harmony with the environment has always been part of African culture and religion. Kaoma asserts that "As Africans, we pride ourselves as the daughters and sons of the soil. Therefore, the destruction of the Earth means our own death and ultimately life, as we know it" (Kaoma 2015, 3). But modernity and industrialization has alienated the community from the environment. The teaching of the church brought with it the doctrine of dominion where people were told that God had given them the earth and all that is in it for their exploitation and pleasure (Gen 1:28). This theology of anthropomorphocentricism gave theological justification to environmental injustice, thus depriving political leaders of a message of caution when passing policy, so that they could remain pro-environmental. Kapya Koama has observed that "the future of the African continent depends on how Christians and politicians move to address the recurring ecological crisis" (Kaoma 2015, 24).

7 The Church as an Agent of Democracy and Good Governance

Another area of life that call for the church's intervention is to facilitate servant-leadership formation that equips people both lay and clergy with skills to act as agents of a culture of democracy and human rights for all people starting from the home to the church, local society, and national government. Emmanuel Ngara observed that "if leaders are needed for the church in Africa today, there is an even more desperate need for leaders in the secular sphere" (Ngara 2004, 10). The church can contribute by producing servant leaders for the sake of good governance. It is the norm for the Christian community to care for one another so that all can experience life in its fullness and that should be the main aim of governance. In their seminal work on the History of the church in Africa Bengt Sundkler and Christopher Steed (2000, 6) asserted that:

> Reception of the Gospel is, on the deepest level, an expression of African peoples' conscientization' by which they rise to a new awareness, a new consciousness kindled by faith in Jesus Christ and his message, I have come that they may have life and have it more abundantly (John 10:10).

Seen from this perspective, the church has the capacity to conscientize people to appreciate freedom, good governance, and promotion of peoples' holistic wellbeing. Governments can legislate and run educational campaigns on democracy and rights, but they need the assistance of the church in inculcating a culture of democratic practice in people. So, the church can be an agent of democracy and human rights, through its justice ministries and Christian education classes, that can be developed through the discipline of Practical Theology.

8 Re-Examining the Guiding Principles of Governance

The guiding principles of governance in the African continent are built on the separation of religion from politics, relegation of faith into the private realm, whilst leaving politics to the public. It is the role of the church to identify those areas that need to be guided by Christians or at least religious principles that would add value in the guidance to good politics that promote life, rather than deny it. If the church and institutions of theological education are to engage seriously with the challenges of bad governance in African nations, then a practical theological revision is important in the development of leadership both for the church and the nation. African countries have a history of unrest, "coup d'état" and leaders who do not want to leave power, as a result of a culture of patrimonialism and personality cults that are embodied by leaders. Bhekithemba Mngomezulu notes that: "From the bad side, one factor that is glaringly knitting the African continent together is the issues of African leaders who, once elected, or once they forcefully ascend to power, literally refuse or only grudgingly agree to leave office" (Mngomezulu 2013, xx). The church can emphasize shared and rotational leadership. Reminding leaders that the greatest is not the one who is serving, but the masses who are being served. These principles will change the ethic of self-serving leadership to one that emphasises servanthood.

9 Participating in the African Renaissance

Recent years have seen the rise of African leaders wanting to promote the development of the continent and freeing themselves from economic dependency from the West. This is coupled with the quest to retain and promote all that is African, other than always consuming ideas from the rest of the world especially the West. Presidents like Ian Khama of Botswana, Thabo Mbeki of South Africa, Jakaya Kikwete of Tanzania and Paul Kagame of Rwanda advocated what is known as "African solutions for African problems (Nathan 2013). This belief in the regeneration of Africa was first sparked by Pixley ka Isaka Seme in an award-winning speech at Columbia University in 1906, when he prophesied the "[r]egeneration of Africa." (Ngqulunga

2017, 26). This quest for the regeneration of Africa includes an appreciation of African culture, its systems of governance and spirituality. The church must join the politician's attempts at affirming Africa as an important role player in global development issues. The Ghanaian African Theologian Kwesi Dickson was amongst the first to observe that religion "cannot escape the necessity of being incarnated in African culture" (Edusa-Eyison 2013, 95–119). Edusa-Eyison takes the conversation further by emphasizing the push for theology in Africa to concern itself with political renewal. He observed that:

> Churches began discussing political issues, and subsequently were informed. Therefore, theology in West Africa does not concern itself only with the cultural issues: it also addresses political and social issues. Indeed, theology must be helped to think in theologically relevant ways (Edusa-Eyison 2013).

In many African countries the church – through Practical Theology – is one of the institutions that can add weight to the government's programmes of appreciating the heritage and resources that come from the African context. If the church supports those calls by giving them a theological rationale many people will participate in those programmes.

10 Conclusion

In this article, I have argued that there is fresh focus on the interface between the discipline of Practical Theology and the governance of society in Africa. I have argued that Practical Theology must be employed to help us study, understand and even perfect the governing of society instead of it being shunned because we want to honour the doctrine of separation of church and state. Despite the lack of recognition and appreciation, the interface between Practical Theology and governance, as well as the significance spirituality of politics in Africa is growing. With the emergence of independence in most African countries there has been a realization that the two cannot be kept apart. They need to inform each other. Politics is becoming more and more important for the future development of democracy and freedom of the African people as well as faith, for Africans remain religious. So, these two realms are bound to connect and move closer to each other. There is a need for Practical Theology to embrace its role in the shaping of politics in the African continent. In their research on the interface between Christianity and politics in Africa, Bengt Sundkler and Christopher Steeds are among many other intellectuals who have concluded that these two are interlinked and refuse to be separated and thus should not be separated. It is for that reason that I agree with Küng's assertion that Karl Marx's prediction of religion being an opium of the oppressed masses has been proven wrong in most African countries where churches have contributed to the struggle for freedom and rights of people, though with ambivalence and not without ambiguities. The facts show that in Africa, politics are religious, and religion is political, therefore Practical Theology to continue its endeavours to find its place in the public realm so that it can contribute to the development of good governance in this continent.

Bibliography

Allen, John. 2006. *Rabble-Rouser for Peace: The Authorized Biography of Desmond Tutu*. London: Rider Books.
Boesak, Allan. 2005. *The Tenderness of Conscience: African Renaissance and the Spirituality of Politics*. Stellenbosch: SUN Press.
Bongmba, Elias K. 2016. "Christianity in North Africa." In *The Routledge Companion to Christianity in Africa*, edited by Elias K. Bongmba, New York: Routledge, 25–44.
Cochrane, James R. 1987. *Servants of Power*. Johannesburg: Raven Press.
Cochrane, James R., John W. De Gruchy, and Robin Petersen. 1991. *In Word and Deed: Towards a Practical Theology for Social Transformation*. Cluster Studies 1. Pietermaritzburg: Cluster Publications.
Edusa-Eyison, Joseph M. 2008. "Kwesi A. Dickson: The Bible and African Life and Thought in Dialogue." In *African Theology in the 21st Century: The Contribution of the Pioneers*. Vol. 2, edited by Bénézet Bujo, Nairobi: Paulines Publishers, 93–123.
Elphick, Richard. 2012. *Equality of Believers: Protestant Missionaries and the Racial Politics of South Africa*. Scottsville: University of KwaZulu-Natal Press.
Eybers, Ian H., Adrio König, John Stoop, and D. Roy Briggs. ²1978. *Introduction to Theology*. Pretoria: Church Booksellers.
Gatu, John. 2006. *Joyfully Christian, Truly African*. Nairobi: Acton Publishers.
Gifford, Paul. 2004. *Ghana's New Christianity: Pentecostalism in a Globalizing African Economy*. London: C. Hurst & Co.
Haynes, Jeffrey. 1996. *Religion and Politics in Africa*. London: Zed Books.
Hewitt, Roderick. 2014. "Sun, Sand, Rum and Reggae: The Challenge of Tourism for Church and Society in the Caribbean." In *Deconstructing Tourism: Who Benefits? A Theological Reading from the Global South*, edited by Caesar D'Mello, Wati Longchar, and Philip Mathew, Kolkata: Programme for Theological Cultures in Asia / SCEPTRE, 80–95.
Hughes, Heather. 2011. *The First President: A Life of John L. Dube, Founding President of the ANC*. Johannesburg: Jacana Media.
Johnson, Todd M., Gina A. Zurlo, Albert W. Hickman, and Peter F. Crossing: "Christianity 2018: More African Christians and Counting Martyrs." *International Bulletin of Mission Research* 42:20–28.
Kaoma, Kapya J. 2013. *God's Family, God's Earth: Christian Ecological Ethics of Ubuntu*. Kachere Books 65. Zomba: Kachere Series.
Kaoma, Kapya J. 2015. *The Creator's Symphony: African Christianity, the Plight of the Earth and the Poor*. Dorpspruit: Cluster Publications.
Kgatla, Moogko S. 2018. "Servant Leadership: The Style of Frank Chikane from Early Life to the Presidency of Thabo Mbeki." *Studia Historiae Ecclesiasticae* 44:1–17.
Kumalo, Simangaliso R. 2015. "The Role of the Church in the 21st Century: Towards an Afrocentric Church." In *Pastoral Care in a Globalized World: African and European Perspectives*, edited by Herbert Moyo, Pietermaritzburg: Cluster Publications, 169–178.
Küng, Hans. 1992. *Credo: The Apostles' Creed Explained for Today*. London: SCM.

Meintjes, Sheila. 2020. *In the Shadow of the Great White Queen: The Edendale Kholwa of Colonial Natal 1850–1906*. Pietermaritzburg: Natal Society Foundation.
Minogue, Martin. 1997. "The Principles and Practice of Good Governance." *British Council Briefing on Law and Governance* 4:2–11.
Mngomezulu, Bhekithemba. 2013. *The President for Life Pandemic in Africa*. London: Adonis & Abbey.
Mugambi, Jesse. 2002. *Christianity and African Culture*. Nairobi: Acton Publishers.
Nathan, Laurie. "African Solutions to African Problems: South African's Foreign Policy." *WeltTrends: Zeitschrift für internationale Politik* 92:48–55.
Ngara, Emmanuel. 2004. *Christian Leadership: A Challenge to the African Church*. Nairobi: Paulines Publications Africa.
Ngqulunga, Bongani. 2017. *The Man Who Founded the ANC: A Biography of Pixley ka Isaka Seme*. South Africa: Random House.
Schoeman, Willem J. 2017. "South African Religious Demography: The 2013 General Household Survey." *HTS Teologiese Studies / Theological Studies* 73:1–7.
Setiloane, Gabriel M. 1986. *Introduction to African Theology*. Braamfontein: Skottaville Publishers.
Shutte, Augustine. 2001. *Ubuntu: An Ethic for a New South Africa*. Pietermaritzburg: Cluster Publications.
Sundkler, Bengt, and Christopher Steed. 2000. *A History of the Church in Africa*. Cambridge: Cambridge University Press.
Tarimo, Aquiline, and Paulin Manwelo. 2008. *African Peacemaking and Governance*. Nairobi: Acton Publishers.
Walzer, Michael. 2007. *Thinking Politically: Essays in Political Theory*. New Haven: Yale University Press.
Vinson, Robert T. 2012. *The Americans Are Coming! Dreams of Liberation in Segregationist South Africa*. Ohio: Ohio University Press.

Mahmoud Abdallah
Pilgrimage / Journey / Practice of Hajj

1 Introduction

"And perform the pilgrimage and the pious visit in the service of God" (Sura 2:196). Pilgrimage (Arabic *Hajj* or *Hadj*) stands for a journey to a specific place at certain times with the aim of approaching a specific transcendent and does not constitute a unique feature of Islam. In Islam, pilgrimage is not only a means of "existential healing" and a possibility to make religion fruitful for atheists (de Botton, 2012, 273) and thus interwoven with one's own biography, but it is a duty that every Muslim of full age, health and financial capacity has to perform (Sura 3:97). For pilgrimage in Islam, there is an occasion (Sura 22:28), a fixed place (Sura 3:96–97) and a fixed period (Sura 2:197), a series of fixed components and stations (*arkān*, 2:198–200), a prehistory (Sura 2:127), a practical development (Sura 22:29–32), a religious and social responsibility (Sura 22:36–37) and a social and emic perception (Sura 22:34–35), a cultural imprint and a social openness (Sura 14:37), a liberating side and a couple of restrictive consequences. The Muslim rulers were thus supposed to secure the pilgrims' caravans and ensure the practice of the ritual, so that we can think of it as an institutionalized access from the very beginning. Moreover, this ritual takes Muslims back to the birthplace of their prophet and their faith and is directly associated with Abraham. Accordingly, the pilgrimage in Islam has been booming right from the start. *Hajj* can convey an important contribution to historical research of Muslim societies, such as a glimpse into life practices of Muslims today (Peters 1994; Long 1979), into their lives over 1400 years ago (Doughty 1888; Faroqhi 2002), into the lives of Arabs before Islam ('Alī 2001; Conrad 1987), i.e., into the period up to 622, etc. Furthermore, *Hajj* is equally considered an interesting source for travel stories (Begum 1909; Maltzan 1989) and also provides an important basis for interfaith dialogue and coexistence. Isabella Schwaderer classifies pilgrimage in Christianity as a metaphor for late modern religiosity (Schwaderer 2019, 105). However, since pilgrimage has been consistently popular in Islam, it is necessary to ask: How have the social, cultural, religious, economic, and political dimensions of pilgrimage changed in late modernity? I usually treat the ritual of pilgrimage, as a Muslim theologian living and teaching in Germany, from an internal Islamic perspective in my seminars. In this article, it is also very important for me to look at the phenomenon from an external perspective. Nevertheless, some personal experiences regarding the course of *Hajj* will be included here. This paper aims at showing how pilgrimage is being practiced in Islam today and at reflecting on the ritual in modernity from different, especially theological, religious, and anthropological perspectives.

2 Basics to the Ritual of Hajj in Islam

Because Islam does not understand pilgrimage as peripheral devotion, the ritual as a practiced form has not lost its importance over time, but it gets a place within the communities, and is considered the spiritual peak to which a religious Muslim aspires. Muslims living in Germany basically have two options for carrying out the pilgrimage: they either travel from Germany (often with a transfer within an Islamic country) or they apply for a pilgrimage visa in the countries of their origin. The decisive factors here are often the prices and whether a vacation is subsequently planned in the country of origin. The religious communities not only support their members in organizing the pilgrimage and ceremoniously welcome them back, but the ritual also becomes the subject of Friday sermons and religious speeches (*Vaz*) for a longer period of time. Muslims have founded pilgrimage offices exclusively for this purpose, which take care of all the bureaucratic matters and organize a 'pilgrim guide'. The role of these offices increased after efforts in recent decades to institutionalize pilgrimage, such as Saudi Arabia's strict requirement that pilgrims enter the country through an approved tour company. The pilgrimage offices must also ensure that visitors leave the country on time. Thus, the group leader has a double task: he takes care of the religious education of the pilgrimage and must prevent anyone of the group from being left behind for which he is allowed to collect and keep the travel documents. There are further rules for converts. They must first prove that they have become Muslims, and some Muslim communities can assist with this. However, these people often travel to an Islamic country and obtain confirmation from the religious authorities there (e. g., al-Azhar in Egypt). This 'institutionalized' approach to the ritual has not changed the liveliness of the pilgrimage and the variety of offerings during this time. Pilgrims also get the opportunity to attend teaching circles of renowned scholars in the pilgrimage sites and to decide for themselves the appropriate personal and religious spirituality.

The number of pilgrims is mainly determined by Saudi Arabia.[1] The Saudi Ministry of Hajj and Umrah is responsible for the planning and implementation of this ritual. As the competent authority, it determines the annual numbers of pilgrims and their international composition in cooperation with the Organization of the Islamic Cooperation (OIC).[2] The ministry which meanwhile offers the information on its website in three languages (Arabic, English, and French) wants to ensure that the ritual is performed as calmly, swiftly, unhindered, undisturbed and in accordance with the law as possible. For this purpose, it constantly oversees building projects in Mecca, provides pilgrims with sufficient information, and thus quite strongly con-

---

[1] In 1908, there were 173.000 (Ochsenwald 1984, 61); in 2019 2.4 million completed the *Hajj*. The number of pilgrims from Europe was 5% (Ministry of Islamic Affairs, Dawah and Guidance 2019).
[2] The percentage of pilgrims for each country is 1% of the total national population, and this agreement can still be revised every 10 years (Organization of the Islamic Cooperation, no date).

trols the entire course of the ritual. As a practice, it does not matter from where one arrives. One does not have different pilgrimage routes and places in Islam but only one place where the different routes and carriers have to go to: Mecca. The mosque in Mecca is called the Ancient House or *al-Ka'ba* (Kaaba) in Islam.

There are two types of *Hajj* in Islam, the major one, known as *al-Hajj* which can only be performed in the month of *Dhu al-Hijjah*, the last month in the Islamic calendar. The second one is the minor pilgrimage, called *'umrah*, a pilgrimage that is much less demanding ritually and financially, in terms of time and space, and can be undertaken at any time throughout. When performing the *Hajj*, there are three possibilities: 1. *Hajj ifrād* (literally, sole pilgrimage), i.e., the pilgrim intends to perform only the *Hajj* ritual; 2. *Hajj tamattu'*, i.e., the pilgrim intends and plans to do the *'umrah* first, then to perform the *Hajj*. In the interim period between the two rituals, the pilgrim leaves the *Iḥrām* state (state of holiness) and all forbidden actions due to the *Iḥrām* state become permitted again during this period, hence the name *tamattu'* (literally: enjoyment), and 3. *Hajj qirān*, (literally, to connect); during this pilgrimage, as in the second case, the pilgrim performs *Hajj* and *'umrah*, but both with an *Iḥrām* state and one intention (*nīya*), with no pause in between. A person who is unable to perform the pilgrimage is not obligated to do so, however if he/she did do it, the pilgrimage has its validity. For the pilgrimage, there are four main indispensable locations (*arkān*), seven obligatory components (*wağibāt*) and other recommended but voluntary acts (*sunan*). Thus, the precept in Islam is that a person who wishes to make the pilgrimage must learn what is permitted and/or prohibited therein before entering the course. The following picture is to show the Stages of *Hajj*.

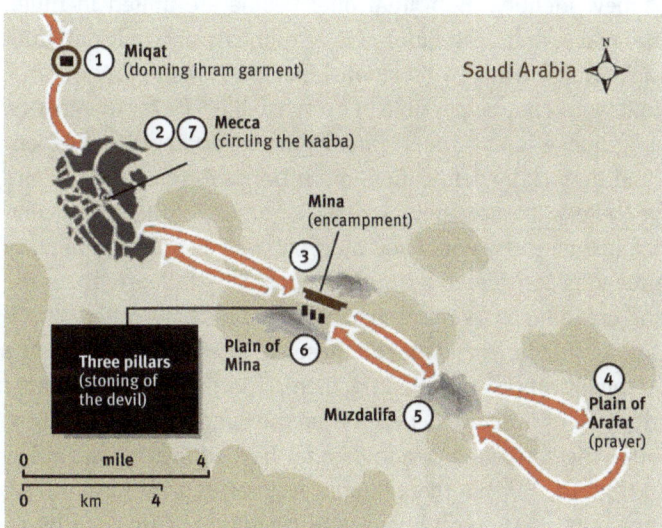

Image 5: Hajj Locations and Rites; Hajj1.ar.svg; Creative-Commons-Linzenz, © Ascetic Rose; retrieved from https://de.wikipedia.org/wiki/Datei:Hajj_locations_and_rites.png (incorporated without modifications).

3 Together across Borders – Pilgrimage as an Image of the Ummah

The pilgrimage in Islam is characterized by a very high level of interest in spiritual experience but is not to be understood as a search for the meaning of life caused by modernity, or as a pure search for spiritual depth. In Islam, pilgrimage is not a "biographical program" (Kurrat 2012, 162). This means that a Muslim does not make his/her decision to go on pilgrimage based on a biographical situation, even if this cannot be ruled out. For example, while statistics of the Pilgrims' Office in Santiago de Compostela mention that in 2018 around 10% of pilgrims were explicitly non-religious (Schwaderer 2019, 100), Muslims perform the ritual out of the religious conviction that they must obey this religious commandment. There are also religious regulations that must be observed for this. Sura 2:197 literally warns against unethical acts and quarrels. A kind of asceticism occurs through the reduction of clothing, equipment and everyday actions, a process of 'experience of separation'. In order to prepare the people to open themselves up to new experiences, the pilgrimage has its own rules, and it is a clear departure from what is customary under Islamic law and the fixed structures of the individual. Thus, it is forbidden to dress up normally, to shorten the hair or to cut fingernails (Sura 2:196), likewise sexual intercourse, hunting and slaughtering animals are inadmissible. Permitted, on the other hand, are everyday practices that are natural, so that permission seems unnecessary, such as ablution, trading, using a parasol or money belt. This new order gives place for acceptance of the others as things that need getting used to are reduced to the minimum and establishes a new identity, a spiritual one. People are united in ritual, dress, supplication, time, place, and destination. Class, ethnicity and cultural affiliation recede into the background, whereby "relationships of trust can grow within a protected atmosphere that would not be possible in everyday life." (Schwaderer 2019, 102; o.t.) Accordingly, pilgrimage is not a mere ritual practice and spiritual experience that is physically and financially demanding, but it brings forth a new community. Through pilgrimage there is the possibility to have a glimpse of the global community of Muslims, since nowhere else could you meet so many people in one place at a time. So, the pilgrimage is considered a unique opportunity to learn about the plurality of the world and creation, as well as to learn that people have different customs, values, cultures, and upbringings and that all these are to be respected and one has to make space for them without questioning them. The pilgrimage not only brings together an uneducated or illiterate Bedouin from the Sahara desert, an IT expert from the U.S., a housewife who often does not go far beyond the borders of her village, a career woman from the EU, but there happens a "detachment from the everyday world with its previous status positions, sociostructurally characteristics as well as cultural […] affiliations" (Zinsmeister 2016, 366; o.t.). A new communality emerges outside of established social norms and dominant structures, although the bond to it remains temporary. Nevertheless, these different temporary forms of communalization "contribute decisively to the subjectively perceived success of the pilgrimage" (Schwaderer 2019, 101; o.t.) and are considered an important basis for travel narratives. In the process, pilgrims adopt different norms and social structures, bring them back home, and develop them further.

The new community resembles the Muslim Ummah and is considered its image, replacing it for a moment at the same time. It offers an open and new space for self-awareness. Its members are united not only by spirituality and religious identity but are entitled to mutual support. They do this, among other things, by tolerating, accepting, and giving space to the other. 'Giving place' is a central aspect of the pilgrimage – both physically and mentally. Even before the journey, it is necessary to plan for the other. As a pilgrim, the traveler should think about providing for fellow pilgrims who might have little or nothing. Strong people must make room for weak and sick people, men must make room for their wives, younger people must make room for elders, locals must make room for guests, and with this consideration/accommodation one creates a place for oneself on the bench of healed souls and humble selves. After the pilgrimage, the pilgrims must not keep the whole sacrificial animal for themselves, but they ought to share in those in need (Sura 22:28). On the other hand, each pilgrim competes with the others for a place in the popular locations (Peters 1994, 14–19; al-Azraqī 2003), so that every year numerous people fall victim because of the crowd of pilgrims (BBC 2006). In search of salvation for oneself and others, one creates a place for oneself only by granting a place to others (ummah members). In doing so, one experiences the connection of the visible with the invisible and thus "a MORE – [...] a feeling of being with God" (Zinsmeister 2016, 369), which – despite the bad experiences by some – reserves the pinnacle of spirituality and pastoral activity to the pilgrimage in the Muslim perception.

4 Between Religion and Society – Pilgrimage as Social Practice

The pilgrimage is a demonstration of the unity, brotherhood, and equality of all Muslims. From all professions, social classes, and strata, from every corner of the world, Muslims gather in Mecca, dress in the same simple manner, abide by the same rules, say the same supplications (in the same language), at the same time, in the same place, in the same order, and with the same goal. There is no arrogance or 'nobility,' but humility and devotion. "You are all made of Adam and Adam is made of earth," the speakers echo all the time. Since this is a ritual duty, the main motive for this gathering is basically the relation to the transcendent. However, if we look at this practice more closely, it is obvious that social differentiation is strongly present during the pilgrimage, despite all attempts to create 'unity'. At this point one can agree with Schwaderer that in the practiced form of pilgrimage "the relationship of subjects to themselves, to the natural and social environment and to transcendence can be explained" (Schwaderer 2019, 96; o.t.).

The pilgrimage becomes a ceremony in everyday life, in which an incredible number of actors of the social environment participate. The everyday and social handling of the pilgrimage differs from one social environment to another and is related to the nature of the subject, but the pilgrimage shapes the whole scene in society during the pilgrimage months, so that the material, physical and spiritual aspects of the pilgrimage overlap. The so-called 'period of pilgrimage', in which one can apply for a place, is officially announced. The time of the pilgrimage evokes a 'state of emergency' in most Muslim countries. For the state it is not only a logistical and infrastructural challenge, but also a medical and medial one. In addition to securing necessary personnel and infrastructure such as transportation and waiting rooms at airports, short broadcasts, info-commercials to educate the people about health measures, administrative regulations, and religious-spiritual acts (in) the pilgrimage are produced and broadcast on various channels. In addition, the important information is provided to the pilgrims as a 'pilgrimage book' and MP3 audio file. The governments of the Islamic states thus show special attention to this ritual and occasionally try to instrumentalize it politically, so that the boundary between profane and sacred resp. pilgrimage and politics cannot be clearly grasped. On the one hand, some common pilgrims receive audiences with high officials, heads of government or state (Wazārat al-awqāf wa al-shu'ūn al-islāmīya 2020), on the other hand, high officials (often judges, military, and police officers) and important personalities (this is the case in many countries) are favored with a pilgrimage and exclusive care and accommodation programs are organized for this group. This use of the ritual as a political tool goes back into history (Peters 1994, 109; Slight 2015; Ryad 2016). It suggests, therefore, that Islamic cultural circles have used pilgrimage to bring about a kind of sacralization of public space and a 'recall of the gods'.

This 'to relating' of the state to the pilgrims and to the natural environment ties in with the social image and social imprint of the practice. One does not only perform a ritual, one visits the city and mosque of the prophet and the graves of his great companions, is a circulating phrase. As soon as people learn about a person who is going to participate in the pilgrimage, this is considered an occasion for celebration. Relatives, neighbors, acquaintances, and friends explicitly express their congratulations, gather at the person's home, paint or inscribe his house with motifs of the pilgrimage, hang up white flags on the roof of the house and accompany him to the airport. A pilgrim's return from the ritual is usually likewise received in celebration. At the end of the pilgrimage the highest Islamic holiday begins, namely the Feast of Sacrifice. On this 4-day festival, sacrificial animals are slaughtered, with only one-third of the flesh kept for oneself and the rest given to the ill and poor. This feast marks the theological and social conclusion of the pilgrimage and is not reserved for pilgrims but is celebrated by Muslims all over the world. The pilgrim is given the honorary title of Hājj (for men) or Hājjah (for women), which means more prestige and social advancement. With this festival, the pilgrimage session comes to an end, previously forbidden things are allowed again, and one returns to normality.

5 Pilgrimage as a Spiritual Practice in Modernity

The pilgrim status begins with entering the *Iḥrām* area, about 20 kilometers around Mecca. There the pilgrims have to do ablution (*ghusl*), put on the pilgrim robe and declare the intention (*nīya*) to start the pilgrimage. However, many pilgrims put themselves into the *Iḥrām* state out of joy already in the homelands, thereby also claiming certain freedom that would not be imaginable outside the *Iḥrām* state. The abolition of borders thus takes place not only at the place of pilgrimage, but already on the way there.

In the practiced form of pilgrimage in the modern era, the Quranic image of pilgrimage which links the ritual with traveling caravans and mounts (Sura 22:27) disappeared. Instead of this classical image, the Muslims today have several transportation options to answer God's call: they can travel by car, ship and/or airplane. These are not merely time-related or indicative of practical diversity due to local proximity or distance, but also express social and economic differences. Nevertheless, some individuals keep insisting on making the journey there on foot, spending months and years on the road to do, so sometimes making it into the headline. One can interpret this as kind of rebellion against modernity, which seems to marginalize the spirituality of the pilgrimage in favor of the practice. This is also an attempt to experience God in a different way at this place, and indeed "often one feels deeply moved, even inspired" (Zinsmeister 2016, 363; o.t.).

The competition among Muslim states in Saudi Arabia for more places for their citizens also characterizes the practice in the modern era. Demonstrating good relationship, political influence, economic advantages, population numbers, etc. become commonplace. The pilgrim delegations usually mark themselves with the flags of their home countries in order to recognize each other. The preacher on the day of the most important event of the pilgrimage, namely the standing at 'Arafah (*waqfa-t'arafāt*), is an object of this competition in order not to miss this honor. But the social differentiation (and demarcation) also includes the pilgrims themselves. Despite similarities in dress and pilgrimage route, major differences occur in treatment, accommodation, care, and recognition. Pilgrims from wealthy regions often expect (and receive) different perceptions than those from poor areas. Muslims from Europe are treated according to European standards, while their co-believers from China or India have divergent experiences. Rich believers can afford a panoramic view of the holy site in Mecca and Medina; their financially constrained fellow pilgrims, on the other hand, have to live miles away from the mosque.

Social differentiation also affects the duration of the pilgrimage. As modern society increasingly pressures people and measures them by their achievements, it is no longer possible to preserve the classic image of pilgrims, where the ruler has pilgrims brought to Mecca under his supervision. However, the conviction that in this place "life is fuller, richer, deeper, more rewarding, more admirable, and to a great extent what it should be" (Zinsmeister 2016, 363; o.t.) has not lost its value. Therefore, many ways are developed to allow more people to practice the ritual. State pilgrimage, for example, is about pilgrimage being organized by the state for its lower- and middle-class citizens for little cost. In addition, there is the tourist pilgrimage (touristic stands here for an upgrade of the service performances), which is organized by travel agencies – as usual in the tourism sector (Thurner 2012) – one's specific wishes are gladly considered for an additional fee. For the elites of society, there is also the businessmen' pilgrimage ('businessmen' here is to indicate the time pressure), a pilgrimage that lasts on average for a few days only. This social vibrancy and the multitude of possibilities regarding the spiritual experience, as well as the essential role in religious and political identity formation, should gain depth in further studies of pilgrimage in modernity. The development of various practical forms of pilgrimage may vary regionally, but nevertheless shows that the classical ritual has been able to preserve its role as a transcendental experience that takes place within the framework of "traditional religious spaces and conventional patterns" (Schwaderer 2019, 98; o.t.) despite fundamental social change and invites us to observe the phenomenon of how pilgrimage gains a new quality in modernity.

6 Pilgrimage as Life Transformation: A Place between Hope of Forgiveness and Hope for Change

In Islam, studies on the attractiveness of the pilgrimage for biographical reasons are still lacking but some aspects from studies on the same topic within Christianity can be transferred to the ritual in Islam. In his study on the biographical significance of pilgrimages on the Way of Saint James, Christian Kurrat identifies five biographical starting situations: as a balancing of life, as a means to processing a crisis, as a time-out, as a transition between two stages of life, or as a signal for a new start (Kurrat 2012, 179). Within an Islamic context it is mainly the last two motivations that can be of relevance. During the *Hajj*, the image of the prophet's farewell pilgrimage is reactivated, so that the ritual often initiates a new start and is perceived by the social environment as a transition between two phases of life.

At the very end of his own – and only pilgrimage in March 632, the Prophet Mohammed addressed his fellow pilgrims and contemporaries at the end of the ritual with the most famous sermon in Islam ever, which has gone down in history under the name of Farewell Sermon (*khutbat al-wadāʿ*). In this sermon, the Prophet addressed religious, social, ethical, legal, economic, and family issues. Among the most succinct passages are the paragraphs in which he announces a definitive break with certain past actions because they contradict to Islamic teachings, such as charging interest, carrying out acts in the name ofblood vengeance, and class society: "And verily, every interest is abrogated. [...] And verily, every blood debt (*damm*) from the time of *ğāhilīya* is abrogated [...] know that every Muslim is the brother of the Muslim and that Muslims are brothers and sisters (among themselves)" (Ibn Isḥāq/Rotter 2004, 250). The clear break with the *ğāhilīya* in this sermon is transferred to the pilgrimage, as it is considered a break with one's bad habits, the announcement of a new chapter in the pilgrim's life and actions, the labor of the birth of a new person who comes into the world with the completion of the ritual (cf. Al-Ajarma, 2021). This meaning is confirmed by a prophetic tradition that states: "Whoever performs the pilgrimage without having performed coitus or committed sacrilege will return [as sinless] as on the day his mother gave birth to him" (Bukhārī, Hadith no. 1737). Thus, pilgrimage also begins with breaking up with the structures of everyday life and an openness to join a new kind of community and to embrace a new identity.

Breaking with old habits is an important feature of pilgrimage, but similarities with pilgrimage in Christianity can be attributed more to the second type of pilgrimage, *'umrah*, especially in terms of motivations and starting situations. Although it has fixed forms, it is, on the one hand, selectable, not fixed in time, offers a certain flexibility, and, on the other hand, can be performed as a kind of time-out or "in the case of biographical turns in life or in situations of personal crisis, re-actualized" (Pollack 1996, 82; o.t.). *Hajj* can be performed belatedly for the souls of the deceased and as an apology/admonition to parents and loved ones, it can also be performed by proxy. Hybridization, that is, the combination of religious practice and leisure or vacation, would be a lived practice in *'umrah*. In the case of the *Hajj*, hybridization is not ruled out in principle, but is unusual. If one assumes hybridization, this applies at best only to the local people and should be enjoyed with reservation.

The fact that pilgrimage is accompanied by the will and willingness to break with the past and to join a new form of community still plays a crucial role today and has practical, social, and theological consequences. The perception of the pilgrimage as 'setting back the works attitude' leads to the social attitude of tending to postpone pilgrimage until an advanced age is reached. In practice, the perspective and hope are directed towards social change and nothing less than a social rebirth. The Muslim's accomplishment or failure in stopping bad habits and practices after the pilgrimage on the one hand enhances or strains social prestige while it is on the other hand interpreted as showing divine acceptance or rejection of the pilgrimage. Society expects a certain social role from pilgrims; one should become (more) friendly and helpful to one's social environment, appear (more) modest, mild, mannered, prudent, etc. As a carryover to a new stage of life, the pilgrimage is accompanied by the willingness to modify and change roles, but to do so without giving up one's own identity is a challenge that occurs only after having taken part in the ritual.

The pilgrimage does not have any decisive biographical meaning as a starting situation within a before-and-after narrative, yet the pilgrimage itself is considered a biographically significant point. Accordingly, the pilgrimage can have parallels with life transformation after all, it is because through the ritual that the different phases of individual and social change can become (more) conscious. This is especially observable in the case of converts for whom the new type of community of Muslims plays an important role. In addition, it is obvious that converts may perform the ritual because they have experienced a life crisis, seek to reach new spiritual depths, or as they are simply fascinated by the spiritual fullness – but also the physical demands – of pilgrimage. Converts want to let it be known that with the pilgrimage the past is "negated, canceled or eliminated" (Turner 1995, 69; o.t.). Numerous examples confirm how the pilgrimage can uncannily transform the lives of some converts. It will suffice to briefly mention, as an example, the well-known American activist Malcolm X, who decided to abandon racist attitudes and leave the 'Nation of Islam' based on his experience with pilgrimage. Malcolm X, who acted out of conviction that Islam favors blacks, encountered in pilgrimage a 'community of equals' that does not distinguish master from slave. Initially embracing Islam in the hopes to counter the anti-black racism he encountered in the United States with an ideology pushing for black superiority over whites, he soon learned and embraces the Islamic principles of equality regardless of notions of race or ethnicity.

Thus it can be summed up with Schwaderer: the pilgrimage is "a multi-layered affair in which inner-subjective levels intersect with social dynamics and the experiences of meaning through sensuality. The existential experience of limits, but also of the enjoyment of one's own corporeality, of overcoming obstacles, and the conscious reduction of comforts make pilgrimage" (Schwaderer 2019, 106; o.t.) an unrivaled opportunity for self-perception as well as the perception of others and an experience countering the ordinariness of everyday life. Throughout history some people even completed the pilgrimage even without becoming Muslims (Peters 1994, 223–228). This promotes a critical reflection on the practiced form of pilgrimage beyond one's own religious and cultural boundaries.

7 Historical and Cultural Background of the Pilgrimage

When the Qur'an speaks of the pilgrimage, it speaks of "known months" (*ashhurun ma'lūmāt*) without mentioning them by name. Al-Qurṭubī (1964, vol. 2, 405) concludes that the pilgrimage months were known enough to the recipients in the Arabian Peninsula at that time so that mentioning them by name in the Qur'an was unnecessary.

Pilgrimage as a pre-Islamic practice should not be a new finding although the period of pilgrimage before Islam remains controversial. There is some disagreement among scholars about whether the pilgrimage took place in fall or whether it was associated with spring ('Alī 2001, vol. 11, 348–349).

Before Islam, there was not one single pilgrimage site on the Arabian Peninsula but in addition to Mecca, the Arabs had established other pilgrimage sites some of which were already in the vicinity of Mecca. Since Islam has retained some rituals of the pre-Islamic pilgrimage, cultural similarities should not come as a surprise. Recognizing that pilgrimage was a central link between religion and society in the Hijaz (Ochsenwald 1984, 58), Islam took it up and added modifications. Before Islam, there also was the so-called 'silent pilgrimage,' meaning that pilgrims did not talk during the pilgrimage (al-Qasṭallānī 1996, vol. 6, 175). Before Islam, there also were two options for practicing *ṭawāf* around the house: one could perform the *ṭawāf* completely unclothed or perform it clothed ('Alī 2001, vol. 11, 364). Taking off clothes is as a metaphor for putting away one's sins, breaking up with the past and of the will to start a new chapter of life; a gesture that is anchored in Islam, as shown above. Before Islam, the practice of pilgrimage was not uniform, the Quraysh tribe, for instance, kept certain rites and places for themselves where other clans were not allowed to go while others included certain places and actions among the rites of the *Hajj* which were not recognized as such by the Quraysh. This practice can be reflected to some extent in contemporary practice, as Shi'ite pilgrims associate and occasionally delineate locations and add certain acts to the *Hajj* (al-Aṣfahānī 1373 AH, 55–58).

The appreciation and special status of the Holy Mosque was also part of the practice in the pre-Islamic period. Each tribe was therefore entrusted with a task during the pilgrimage, to facilitate the pilgrims to perform the ritual. Facilitation became an Islamic precept, over time, the principle of relief has flown into an individual, social, cultural, and political attitude and practice, as shown above.

From these remarks it can be summarized: Pilgrimage is considered a transcultural spiritual encounter in which space and time are transformed into transcendence, offering a space for the diversity of people and their actions, cultures, and spiritual practices. For the salvation of souls, pilgrimage in Islam experiences continuous popularity and thus deserves proper attention and hermeneutical discussion within the context of (practical) theology.

Bibliography

al-Aṣfahānī, 'Abbās. 1373 AH. Tabyiyn fiqh shi'at ahl al-bayt fī ba'ḍ al-masā'il al-muhimma. Iran: no publisher.

al-Azraqī, Abū al-Walīd Muḥammad ibn Aḥmad. 2003. *Akhbār Makka wa-ma ǧā'a fīha min al-athār*, edited by 'Abdulmalik ibn Dahīsh. Mecca: Maktabat al-Asdī.

al-Bukhārī, Muḥammad b. Ismā'īl. 2000. *Al-Ǧāmi' aṣ-ṣaḥīḥ*. Kairo: Jam'iyat al-Maknaz al-Kabīr.

'Alī, Ǧawād Muḥammad. 2001. *Al-Mufaṣṣal fī tarīkh al-'Arab qabl al-Islām*. 20 Vols. Beirut: Dār aṣ-Ṣāqī.

al-Ajarma, Kholoud. 2021. "After Hajj: Muslim Pilgrims Refashioning Themselves." In *Religions* 12:36. https://www.mdpi.com/2077-1444/12/1/36 (01.12.2021).

al-Qasṭallānī, Abū al-ʿAbbās Shihāb ad-Dīn Aḥmad b. Muḥammad. 1996. *Irshād as-sārī li-sharḥ ṣaḥīḥ al-Bukhārī*. 10 Vols. Cairo: al-Maṭbaʿah al-kubra al-amīrīyah.

al-Qurṭubī, Muḥammad b. Aḥmad. 1964. *Al-Ǧāmiʿ li-Aḥkām al-Qurʾān*. 20 Vols. Cairo: Mūʾsasat ar-risāla.

BBC. 2006. *Hundreds Killed in Hajj Stampede*. http://news.bbc.co.uk/2/hi/middle_east/4606002.stm (01.12.2021).

Begum, Nawab Sultan Jahan. 1909. *The Story of a Pilgrimage to Hijaz*. Calcutta: Thacker, Spink & Co.

De Botton, Alain. 2012. *Religion for Atheists: A Non-Believer's Guide to Uses of Religion*. London: Hamish Hamilton.

Doughty, Charles Montagu. 1888. *Travels in Arabia Deserta*. Cambridge: Cambridge University Press.

Faroqhi, Suraiya. 2002. *Herrscher über Mekka: Die Geschichte der Pilgerfahrt*. München / Zürich: Artemis & Winkler.

Ibn Isḥāq, Muḥammad. 2004. *As-Sīra an-nabawīya*, trans. Gernot Rotter. Kandern: Spohr.

Kurrat, Christian. 2012. "Biographische Bedeutung und Rituale des Pilgerns." In *Pilgern gestern und heute: Soziologische Beiträge zur religiösen Praxis auf dem Jakobsweg*, edited by Patrick Heiser and Christian Kurrat, Münster / Berlin: LIT, 161–191.

Long, David Edwin. 1979. *The Hajj Today: A Survey of the Contemporary Makkah Pilgrimage*. Albany: State University of New York Press.

Maltzan, Heinrich von. 1989. "Meine Wallfahrt nach Mekka." In *Alte abenteuerliche Reiseberichte*, edited by Gernot Giertz, Berlin: Neues Leben.

Ministry of Islamic Affairs, Dawah and Guidance, Kingdom of Saudi Arabia. 2019. *al-Kitāb al-iḥṣāʾy lil-ʿām al-mālī 1440–1441*. https://www.moia.gov.sa/Statistics/DocLib/MOIA_1440_1441.pdf (01.12.2021).

Ministry of Hajj and Umrah. 2019. *Hajj 1440 bi-lughat al-arqām*. https://www.haj.gov.sa/ar/News/Details/12360 (01.12.2021).

Ministry of Hajj and Umrah. 2021. https://www.haj.gov.sa/ (01.12.2021).

Ochsenwald, William. 1984. *Religion, Society, and the State in Arabia: The Hijaz under Ottoman Control: 1840–1908*. Columbus: Ohio State University Press.

Organization of the Islamic Cooperation. No date. https://www.oic-oci.org/home/?lan=en (01.10.2021).

Peters, Francis Edward. 1994. *The Hajj: The Muslim Pilgrimage to Mecca and the Holy Places*. Princeton: University Press.

Pollack, Detlef. 1996. "Individualisierung statt Säkularisierung? Zur Diskussion eines neueren Paradigmas in der Religionssoziologie." In *Religiöse Individualisierung oder Säkularisierung: Biographie und Gruppe als Bezugspunkte moderner Religiosität*. Veröffentlichungen der Sektion Religionssoziologie in der Deutschen Gesellschaft für Soziologie 1, edited by Karl Gabriel, Gütersloh: Kaiser / Gütersloher, 57–85.

Ryad, Umar. 2016. *The Hajj and Europe in the Age of Empire*. Leiden Studies in Islam and Society 5. Leiden / Boston: Brill.

Schwaderer, Isabella. 2019. "Pilgern – eine religionswissenschaftliche Einordnung eines zeitgenössischen Phänomens." In *Theologie der Gegenwart* 26:95–106.

Slight, John. 2015. *The British Empire and the Hajj: 1865–1956*. Cambridge, MA / London: Harvard University Press.

Thurner, Ingrid. 2012. "Destination Mekka: Die Pilgerfahrt der Muslime als Tourismusereignis." In *Kulturfaktor Spiritualität und Tourismus: Sinnorientierung als Strategie für Destinationen*. Schriften zu Tourismus und Freizeit 14, edited by Hans Hopfinger, Harald Pechlaner, Silvia Schön, and Christian Antz, Berlin: Erich Schmidt, 115–142.

Turner, Victor. 1995. *Vom Ritual zum Theater: Vom Ernst des menschlichen Spiels*, trans. Sylvia M. Schomburg-Schreff. Frankfurt am Main: Campus [Engl. 1982. *From Ritual to Theatre: The Human Seriousness of Play: Performance Studies Series*. New York: Performing Arts Journal Publication].

Wazārat al-awqāf wa al-shu'ūn al-islāmīya. 2020. *Al-lağnah al-malakīyah lil-Hajj tu'lin 'an istirğā' maṣārīf al-Hajj wa al-iḥtidifāẓ 'ala natā'iğ al-qur'ah*. http://www.habous.gov.ma/pelerinage/ (01.12.2021).

X, Malcolm. 1992. *The Autobiography of Malcolm X*. New York: Ballantine Books.

Zinsmeister, Stefan. 2016. "Pilgern – Möglichkeit einer lebensdienlichen Aktualisierung der Beziehung des Menschen zu Gott." In *Lebensdienlich und überlieferungsgerecht: Jüdische und christliche Aktualisierung der Gott-Mensch-Beziehung: Festschrift für Heinz-Günther Schöttler*, edited by Johannes Först and Barbara Schmitz, Würzburg: Ergon, 359–371.

Theo Pleizier
Praying / Pastoral Care / Spirituality

1 Introduction

A Dutch newspaper reported that the sales of books on praying during the COVID-19 pandemic has increased compared to the previous year. Based upon a list of these bestsellers, the newspaper concludes that books on praying are hard to find and that our houses have started to become more like monasteries. The crisis of the pandemic has indeed sparked urgent questions for many: 'what is the meaning of life?' 'what if I become ill?' or 'what happens when I die?'. Praying is a central feature of religion in general and of Christianity in particular (Meyer-Blanck 2019). This article is interested in exploring the following: When do people pray, what do people pray about, to whom do people pray and what do people do when they pray?

This practical-theological essay on praying departs from two paradoxical observations. First, there is something distinctly religious about praying yet praying is not an exclusively religious practice. Empirical studies in secular spirituality show a decrease in interest in prayer (Zuckerman, Shook, and Fuller 2017), but praying is not confined to those who affiliate with religion. Post-secular approaches view prayer as

> The place into which I pour my despair and out of which I drag my often elusive, often reluctant hope; it is the space into which I spiral, as well as the connection that rescues me there; it is the transformative work in which I am compelled to engage [...]. The connection I find in this place is essential to my being, but what it is to/with/by which I connect, I am not able to say. (Vosper 2014, introduction)

Second, praying is not phenomenologically unique to Christianity. Yet it determines the Christian religion in all its aspects. Praying is a source for doing theology (Muis 2021), its history and practice are as rich as Christianity itself (Meyer-Blanck 2019) and as a practice of 'addressing God' Christian prayers articulate an understanding of a Triune God (Coakley 2013). Christian praying is thus a source for understanding the Christian religion though praying is not a unique practice to Christianity.

In this chapter I present a Protestant (Reformed) and Western-European (Dutch) perspective to Christian praying. The Reformed tradition is known for its 'free prayers'; a spirituality that runs deep in post-Reformation European approaches to prayer. According to nineteenth-century thinkers like Friedrich Schleiermacher, William James, and Friedrich Heiler, praying expresses religious awareness and constitutes religious experience.

In contemporary Protestant religious cultures, however, praying is an ambiguous practice. On the one hand, it is connected to institutionalised and ecclesial Christianity, following the classic principle *lex orandi, lex credendi*. It expresses the nature of a specific religion and thus has an institutional aspect, ecclesial and denominational.

On the other hand, the praying subject is free to access God without mediation of the church. Praying is foremost a spiritual practice to be found everywhere rather than being bound to ecclesial practices.

Christians pray on many occasions. To explain this, John Calvin distinguishes between 'personal prayer' and 'public prayer' (Calvin Institutes III.20). These two types of praying continue to shape practical-theological research, both with respect to prayer in the personal context (Lunk 2014) and in the context of worship (Baschera, Berlis, and Kunz 2014). Within the Reformed tradition and following Calvin, a specific 'third' type of prayer emerged. This type of prayer is neither strictly personal nor mainly public but concerns a type of 'pastoral praying'; pastoral, not in the setting of worship, but in the setting of care and counselling, for instance praying for the sick and the dying, even if one does not believe in God.

This 'third' type of prayer challenges the limited perspectives of this essay: Reformed theology and the secularised European culture. First, pastoral praying in times of illness and death gave rise to specific 'scripted' textbooks on prayer in the Reformed tradition. Next, praying in times of illness and death is an important topic for research and reflection in studies on palliative care, including interreligious care practices and secular or non-religious spiritual care. Further, pastoral prayer is a helpful case to reflect upon significant theological topics such as divine presence and religious performativity. These theological topics resonate with Reformed theology and the practical-theological study of praying, as we will see.

The structure for the essay is as follows. First the case of pastoral praying in times of illness and death is introduced. This will be done through sketching an empirical situation.

Next, the case is studied from three different perspectives. The contextual perspective presents pastoral praying in its historical origins (the Reformed context) and its contemporary realities (the secular West). A comparative analysis adds examples from other contemporary Christian traditions. Interdisciplinarity broadens the conversation by including sociology and psychology of religion, two natural conversation partners of practical theology.

Finally, we consider the practical-theological implications by applying three different concepts: performativity, religious language, and divine presence. The essay closes with a reflection on the contribution of practical theology to understand the major concept of 'religion' in view of the specific practice of praying.

2 A Case of Pastoral Praying

Pastoral praying is a central practice in pastoral ministry:

> A parish minister visits a parishioner who has recently been diagnosed with a terminal illness. The pastor has a longstanding relationship with the parishioner; the parishioner's family partly belongs to the church; some members of the family left the church while others joined another

denominational church. The parishioner's family has lived in the village for a few generations and at the moment the family is in doubt whether the ill father should be moved to a hospital in a nearby city or should spend his final weeks at home, supported by palliative aid. The minister is not used to praying at every pastoral occasion as some of her colleagues would do. She does not shy away from praying either and considers pastoral prayer as one of the ways in which pastoral care can transcend interhuman conversation. At this particular moment of visiting the ill person, however, it feels appropriate for the minister to ask the parishioner whether he wants to pray. After he expresses his desire to do so, she formulates an *extempore* prayer, picking up themes from the conversation such as the fear for the unknown territory of death, the sadness of the moment, contemplating the coming departure, and the dilemma of staying at home or moving to a health-care facility. The prayer contains hints of gratitude towards God, because of the medical aid and the loving family; yet the tone is mostly intercessory, a call for help from God, to be present during this final stage in the parishioner's earthly life and to provide spiritual support in preparing for death. The pastor does not pray for returning health let alone for physical healing. Yet her prayer reflects nonetheless faith in God's active involvement in this person's life that soon will end in death and move into a state beyond death. There is still much to be asked for, when it no longer feels theologically appropriate to pray for physical health.

In a first practical-theological analysis, this empirical incident of an all-too-familiar scene for many pastors contains *multiple* religious practices. Praying is only one practice among others, such as the practice of hospitality, of preparing for death, of being church, or as practicing lived religion.

First, pastoral care is a practice of hospitality. Based upon a trinitarian structure in the hospitality of God, Neil Pembroke describes pastoral care as a practice that creates a space in which another person feels at welcome in a dialectic of unbounded and bounded openness (Pembroke 2006).

Further, in times of death, pastoral care is part of a broader practice of preparing for death and practicing the art of dying well (*ars moriendi*); a religious practice that is shared among religions but obviously reflects different values, convictions and eschatologies (Choudry, Latif, and Warburton 2018).

Next, pastoral care interacts with devotional practices, both individual and communal. The pastor engages with the individual spirituality of the parishioner without losing sight of communal spirituality; the religious community that the pastor represents and to which the parishioner belongs. This makes pastoral care, particularly in the moment of praying, an *ecclesial practice*. It is a practice in which 'church', or the body of Christ is expressed, experienced, and practiced.

Finally, in pastoral praying, religious convictions, such as beliefs concerning God's active involvement in the world, are actualised. How God's presence in the praying moment is experienced depends upon various theological conceptualisations. These conceptualisations also shape the expectations of those who pray during praying. Does the praying subject(s) believe in God's ability to bring about change in the situation of the praying subject? In other words, praying is a practice of 'lived theology' or perhaps even better: 'lived religion'.

Hence, pastoral praying in times of illness and death is part of an integrated whole of religious practices. Practices such as hospitality, dying well, devotion, being-church, and lived religion require a separate analysis and are expressed in many other ways than in prayer. The fact of the interrelatedness of religious practices demonstrates that the concept of practice in practical theology is a complex concept.

3 Contextual Aspects of Pastoral Praying

Personal prayer, according to John Calvin, is about making petitions and expressing gratitude towards God:

> In asking and beseeching, we pour out our desires before God, seeking both those things which make for the extension of his glory and setting forth of his name, and those benefits which conduce to our own advantage. In giving thanks, we celebrate with due praise his benefits towards us, and credit to his generosity every good that comes to us. (Calvin, Institutes III, 20.28)

Calvin values private prayer higher than public prayer. He addresses the 'dangers' of public prayers as they run the risk of turning prayer into public religious display. Public and private prayer, however, remain intimately connected. The person who does not show an interest in worship and public prayer, demonstrates a lack of valuing private prayer and vice versa. Calvin's exposition of private and public prayer follows the sections that contain his criticism of intercession by the saints and his insistence on the necessity of Christ praying for us. Calvin's critique of human intercession runs deeply into Reformed devotional practice. Later Reformed theologians such as the seventeenth century Dutch Reformed theologian Gisbertus Voetius in his treatise on religious devotion (Voetius *Exceritia pietatis*, 1664, chapter 4) also stress the importance of personal prayer instead of relying on prayer by other human beings.

On the other hand, pastoral visitation is a typical Reformed invention in pastoral ministry. Especially in times of sickness and death. Pastoral prayer in times of death was an important topic in the guidance of pastors in the times of the Reformers. Beyond the almost exclusive practice of free personal praying, Calvin's colleagues, like Heinrich Bullinger and Theodore Beza, instructed local pastors by providing them with prayerbooks and other liturgical forms to be used in pastoral practice. Beza's prayer 'On the visitation of the sick' (*Household Prayers* 1603) contains a brief theology of suffering and a pastoral approach towards the sick. Not only do these prayers connect Protestantism with the Medieval church, but they also influenced later Presbyterianism greatly. R. Milton Winter closes his overview on praying in the Presbyterian tradition with the observation that "prayers for the sick have evolved from highly introspective and penitential exercises which attribute sickness and affliction to the chastisement of God to sensitive intercessions and sacramental orders which blend prayers for physical healing with concerns for sexual health, spiritual well-being and emotional wholeness." (Winter 1986, 153) These historical and contextual examples influenced contemporary practices of pastoral praying in three ways.

First, the emphasis on private prayer in Western Christianity reoccurs strongly in Friedrich Schleiermacher's modern insistence on the free subject which seems to make pastoral care superfluous. Even for the sick and dying, Schleiermacher starts his reflections with a warning of superstition in view of the sacrament. The Reformed insistence of personal prayer is felt in the background. Beza's prayer for the sick was written to be used at home as pastoral guidance, but the praying subject is not necessarily the pastor (Manetsch 2013, 291–93). Modern pastoral care, starting with Schleiermacher, appears to be a true heir of Protestantism: pastors help parishioners to pray for themselves.

Second, contemporary pastoral care practices such as 'mutual pastoral care' move beyond the central role of the ordained minister and the professional pastor. It highlights the role of fellow parishioners in pastoral practice that includes praying for the sick (de Vries 2018). Between private and public prayer, praying is done in the personal sphere, but not just privately. Next to professional pastors, lay pastors and fellow believers engage in pastoral praying.

Thirdly, the secular Western context seems to challenge the practice of praying in times of illness. Yet in healthcare contexts, praying appears to be one of the practices that chaplains mention when they are asked how they shape *interreligious* spiritual care (Liefbroer and Berghuijs 2019). Interdisciplinary studies also show that prayer has positive effects on health in times of illness; that social workers engage in pastoral praying; and that there is a significant health effect of praying in relation to various mental and physical diseases (Hodge 2007). Hence, pastoral praying remains a lively practice, both in ecclesial and in secular contexts.

4 Comparative Perspectives

The COVID19-pandemic exemplifies how in Western-European societal discourse illness and death are dealt with both medically and politically. Religious practices, such as pastoral work, seemed irrelevant at best or problematic at worst. Generally, opportunities to pray for the ill and the dying depended on most situations on local decisions and hospital policies. This defines the first comparative perspective to pastoral praying in an ecclesial context: spiritual care in interreligious and multi-religious public contexts

Chaplains pray with patients, with detainees and with soldiers. Public praying, however, is a contested practice in an overly secular environment such as the army. Grace Kao demonstrates a skeptical attitude towards prayer in military command settings and points to the problem of "ceremonial deism" versus the need to "manage *which* religious or civil religious interpretation or even form [of prayer] ought to prevail" (Kao 2010, 601). In pluralist and multireligious contexts in health care, however, this is very different. In situations of palliative care, for instance, to pray with the terminally ill is one of the primary religious interventions for chaplains (Nolan 2011). In his study on spiritual care at the end of life, Steve Nolan reports how chaplains comfort the dying by praying with them. Praying is embedded in a conversation about the 'what' and 'who' to pray for. For instance, in the case of 'Phoebe': the 86 years old woman who is dying asks the chaplain to pray for her 'leaving the world.' The prayer that the chaplain prays is simple, it contains scripted language, yet it is very personal and relates to Phoebe's lived experience:

> Loving God, Thank you for your love, and thank you for your love to Phoebe down through the years. I ask that you will be with her now as she is ready to come back to you. Give her peace and courage and hold her in your arms. Amen. (Nolan 2011, 75)

Spiritual care takes place in a context in which pastors and chaplains meet people from all walks of life, with or without religious affiliations. Research in healthcare situations, however, shows that praying for the (mentally) ill seems to be most beneficial when nurses and others who pray with patients do so from a similar religious background (Yoon et al. 2018).

The fact that illness and death has become 'disenchanted' and thus secularised in the Western world, also invites another comparative perspective to the scene. Without neglecting medical science, treatments and therapies, non-Western Pentecostal movements demonstrate another attitude to illness, health, and healing.

Pentecostal and charismatic spiritualities criticise a typical Western European divide of the personal and the public. Praying for personal healing is part of corporate worship, and pastoral praying is often done in a public environment, such as in a church building, among fellow believers and through mass media channels such as radio (Blanton 2015). Traditional Pentecostal praying practices entail a distinctive material aspect, such as prayer cloths or anointed handkerchiefs. Blanton describes the interactions between the anointing of pieces of cloth, prayers of the congregation and the materiality of the Holy Spirit as pieces of fabric become a tangible presence of God's healing power. Being prayed for, is more than an individual, spiritual experience. It involves the community of faith through the 'exchange of hands', when the anointed pieces of cloth are shared among the believers: "through the palpation of the cloth's texture, its physical properties signal both a tactile immediacy for the handler and a simultaneous awareness that other hands have also experienced this textured surface of prayer." (Blanton 2015, 59) In his theological analysis of practices of healing within Pentecostalism, Mark Cartledge stresses a soteriological motif, namely that "healing is in the atonement." Physical healing is an aspect of "freedom from any burden in life that brings 'dis-ease' with oneself, one's neighbor, and God." (Cartledge 2015) In the comparative perspective of Pentecostal and Charismatic spiritualities, the material aspect evokes the nature of 'reality' in pastoral prayer. There is something going on between God and our lives, and the material aspect makes this tangible and therefore empirically real.

5 Interdisciplinary Views

Both comparative perspectives illustrate how practical-theological analysis interacts with psychological and sociological views. It clarifies the empirical orientation of practical- theology: the study of human phenomena in relation to the divine.

Religious practices display an intricate interaction between interhuman communicative processes and a divine-human dynamics (Pleizier 2010). The social and the religious are not separated. This means that theology does not simply provide another interpretative perspective of a certain phenomenon. Theology particularly looks for a dynamic between humans and God *within* social and psychological communication processes between humans. Hence, pastoral praying is as much an anthropological as a religious practice. The anthropological analysis aims to reconstruct the social and psychological aspects, while practical theology provides a reconstruction of these aspects by asking how it exemplifies and transforms the many possible dynamics, relationships, energies and interactions between God and humans. Hence, theological concepts are needed to study religious practices and dynamics (Immink 2014). Despite the fact that ontologically the order might be different, epistemologically and thus methodologically the analysis of divine-human dynamics follows the social and psychological descriptions. Though psychology and sociology of praying represent different domains of study, practical-theologians need to reflect on the anthropological in which religious practices are empirically situated.

The comparative perspective raises both psychological and sociological issues. For psychologists, praying is a coping-strategy. Praying in times of illness and death triggers many studies of the beneficial effects of praying for human health and coping mechanisms. A recent study in mental healthcare affirms the positive effects of praying (van Nieuw Amerongen-Meeuse et al. 2020). Further, psychologists developed a model that explains praying as a psychological mechanism for inward, outward, and upward connections (Ladd and Spilka 2006). Inward praying is about examination of the self; outward praying concerns interhuman connections; upward praying centers on the divine-human relationship. The model relates attitudes towards death and mechanisms of coping to the extent that prayers are a means of spiritual connectivity, "a form of teamwork and not instances of self-centred solitude" (Ladd and Spilka 2006, 245). The psychological study of praying, however, primarily focusses upon the health-related effects of personal praying and praying for others (intercessory prayer), rather than on practices of praying that involve spiritual care givers, such as pastors and chaplains, which confines the study of praying to personal devotion (Spilka and Ladd 2012).

Sociologists broaden the scientific approach of praying. A study of Pentecostal-charismatic prayer ('soaking prayer') shows that in a kind of non-verbal prayer that is mostly meditative, groups of people open their hearts and minds to God's love, they ask each other what they think God is telling them. There appears to be a clear relationship between participating in soaking prayer and social engagement. Research demonstrates significant correlations between high frequencies of prayer, and social engagement as well as a strong sense of compassion and altruism (Wilkinson and Althouse 2013). In comparing several sociological studies on prayer, Linda Woodhead comments that while "prayer varies enormously according to social group and level of religious formation and commitment", topics such as illness / health and death / bereavement are surprisingly on the top of the list of prayer requests in cathedrals. Perhaps this is due to the fact that cathedrals represent the liminal space between time and eternity "in which the boundary between life and death is thin?" Woodhead wonders (Woodhead and Giordan 2015, 216). In her analysis she stresses the variety of prayer from a sociological perspective: variations in content, varied addressees, emotions, embodiments and uses. Finally, she identifies three common aspects: from formalised to less scripted prayer; less a bodily routine than a personally-meaningful experience; and praying as 'accessing God,' God is a very real presence while this does not imply that accessibility rules out transcendence (Woodhead and Giordan 2015, 221–224).

In sum, anthropological research shows that praying is a complex psychological and social phenomenon. It is in need of theological analysis, as Giordan and Woodhead imply when they write that praying "takes place within the relational dynamics between Higher Power and the subject who begs. It is within this relationship that the elements that make praying effective emerge, beyond the material realization of what is begged for." (Giordan and Woodhead 2013, 3)

6 Practical Theological Analysis: Performativity, Religious Language and Divine Presence

Practical theology develops theological theories of religious practices. The specific contribution of practical theology consists in its articulation of non-reductive, theological and situated accounts of religious practices such as pastoral praying. It is *non-reductive* in relation to psychological theories of coping, in other words: pastoral praying is not sufficiently explained with the help of the psychological concept of coping. It is *theological* in articulating the divine-human dynamics in praying and thus applying theological concepts to understanding the phenomenon of pastoral praying. And lastly, it is *situated* with respect to the fact that practices are always located in time, place, tradition and with concrete actors that act within the permeable boundaries and cultures of specific religious communities and cultures. A practical theological approach thus needs its own scientific openness towards the phenomenon being studied, while acknowledging the validity and value of knowledge that is produced in comparative, historical and anthropological studies.

In the case of praying in situations of illness or in times of death, a practical-theological account for instance entails the simple open question: 'what happens when we pray?' This question has three aspects: *performativity, religious language*, and the theme of *'God's presence'*.

Religious performativity is a central concept in contemporary practical-theological discourse to understand the nature of religious practices (Schirr 2018; Immink 2014). It conveys the idea that the religious effect of a practice is inherent in the practices itself: religion happens in doing. Praying with a parishioner in the final stage of life, for instance, evokes rest for the soul, trust in God, hope for the unknown things to come. These are all inner 'effects' of praying, generated *in* the act of prayer.

Performativity connects embodiment, aesthetics, community, and intentionality. In concrete bodily actions (embodiment), people direct their minds towards something or someone (intentionality), using linguistic or other artistic devices (aesthetics) and in doing so, they shape relationships (community). Or as Gerrit Immink puts it: "language, gestures and rituals do not only serve to describe or to convey information, but also to set things in motion. In this vein practices bring-into-practice their intrinsic goods and values. What they aim for happens in the enactment." (Immink 2014, 131) The notion of performativity focusses the practical theological analysis less on that what is external to the practice, such as societal transformations or political effects, but calls for an analysis of the practice as such. The idea of 'performativity' locates the effect in the actual practice; a notion that was already hinted upon in sociological studies of prayer (Woodhead and Giordan 2015).

The internal effect of praying is also implied in psychological theories that approach prayer in terms of coping strategies. Indeed, prayer may help severely ill patients to cope with medically unchangeable conditions. Religious performativity, however, includes other notions of understanding the inner 'effects' of praying, such as 'community' and 'intentionality.' In pastoral praying, the one who is prayed for experiences a strengthened relationship with the pastor who prays and the religious community that the pastor represents: pastoral prayer constitutes and shapes an instant religious community. Further, in praying, the minds of the those who pray are directed towards God, the One who is addressed in prayer (Immink 2014).

Next, two other questions help to unfold its conceptual potential for a deeper theological analysis of praying: 'how do we pray?' (The language and embodiment of praying) and 'to whom do we pray?' (The religious addressee in praying). This opens up two other areas of praying: *religious language* and *divine presence*.

Praying is naturally associated with the use of (religious) language. Obviously, praying is broader; it takes place in silence, and the practice of praying is an embodied practice, which is particularly exemplified in various types of 'bodily praying' such as Christian Yoga, the contemplative Jesus-prayer, or meditations of the cross (Koll 2007). Praying, however, may be considered to be the most appropriate example of religious language: language addressed to the divine takes us to the heart of religion. Yet this has many empirical forms: words, phrases, shorter and longer texts, responses that include multiple praying subjects, corporate prayers prayed with a larger group, received 'texts', or scripts that create fixed praying patterns – predominantly in corporate worship services, or free expressions of the praying subject, ex tempore formulated. Among these linguistic aspects, the difference between 'scripted prayers' and 'free prayers' is particularly significant in the case of pastoral praying.

Reformed tradition with its emphasis on 'free' prayer as guided by the Spirit in the moment, is particularly charged with a critique of scripted praying. Yet reality is more complex. Theodore Beza compiled a selection of prayers. These 'scripted prayers' include a prayer on the visitation of the sick; a prayer that according to Scott Manetsch in his study on Reformed pastoral ministry, reflects the Reformed view on human suffering, divine providence and pastoral consolation:

> Since it has pleased you, O just and merciful Father, to visit this poor sick person with your rod, afflicting him for his offenses, as he himself has confessed, we beseech you that… he may with quiet obedience bear your visitation, submitting himself willingly with all his heart to your holy will. May he trust that you strike him, not as a severe judge, but as a most merciful Father, whereby he may learn to rest his whole trust and assurance in your love, you who are the Author of his life. (quoted in Manetsch 2013, 292)

Scripted prayer clearly has two aspects. First, the language conveys a shared spiritual identity. "[M]erciful Father", "God's holy will", "trust and assurance in God's love", these references to God do not emerge from pious minds of individual praying subjects. The fact that they are part of a script entails that they resonate with a confessional identity; in praying this script the praying minds become directed to the reality that is expressed: God's mercy, God's faithfulness, or God's power. The script exemplifies how God is addressed in prayer. The identity expressed in Beza's prayer entails a Trinitarian theology, as it addresses God as Father and Creator (Author of life), taking its starting point in the traditional Christian threefold structure of addressing God as Father, Son and Spirit. Scripted prayer also explicates an ecclesial aspect of praying: the religious community ('church') not only expresses its faith, but in praying the prayer of the church the praying subjects actually 'are' church. The script of the prayer thus entertains the relation between the praying subjects. Scripted prayer communicates confessional identity, it defines praying subjects as belonging to the same religious community and it demonstrates various modes of ecclesial praying.

Pastoral prayers are often a mixture of situated personal references with scripted elements. Margriet van der Kooi-Dijkstra, a Dutch protestant health-care chaplain reports a prayer during a small-scale pastoral meeting for the anointing of Anne[1] who is terminally ill:

> God, very much has been good, and there is an abundance of love in this house; not just this afternoon; so it was in Anne's life. And we also know that you are short of us, and we are short of each other. We love, but not like you, and often not at all. We are indifferent and slow at all times when it counts. You are a God who knows just that: after all, you made us yourself. Forgive whatever gets in the way in view of each other and you. (van der Kooi-Dijkstra and van der Kooi 2017, 129)

---

[1] Anne is the name of the sick woman in the reported case.

Likewise, another pastor in the hospice who prays with 'Joe' in the face of death stresses God's love and God's presence in all circumstances and for all involved:

> God, thank you for being with us right now. We confess that we don't understand why things happen the way they do. We don't understand why illness comes into our lives, but we do know that you walk every path of life with us. Remind Joe that you are walking with him right now. Remind Joe that you love him, no matter what he is going through. I also pray for Joe's family. Give them your strength as they care for Joe. God, we thank you that you never leave us, that you never forsake us, but you love us. We trust you and pray this in your name. Amen.[2]

These two examples demonstrate how praying constitutes a dialogue; between humans, the sick person and the pastor who offers a prayer, and between humans and God. This dialogue is also a dialogue that involves spiritualities. The pastor who prays with Joe in the hospice stresses divine acceptance and God's love. The language is more generally religious. The pastor who prays with Anne touches more explicitly upon Christian understandings of God: The One who knows, the Creator who made us as bearers of God's image, and the One we need to rely upon for forgiveness. In praying, the presence of God is evoked, a loving presence, a forgiving presence, and a presence of the One who knows our frailty and our faults, and who can be trusted not to leave us.

The two aspects of performativity, religious language, and the presence of God, point to a specific internal effect of praying. Religious practices such as praying also have external effects: they motivate people to act in a certain way, the "politics of prayer" (Cocksworth 2018). Another type of consequences is of crucial theological importance, namely the issue of divine action. Especially in times of illness questions emerge like does God change our world after prayer, or does God bring about physical or mental health? These aspects can only be assessed within religious traditions. Interreligious conversations need to take into account the various answers given by various culturally embedded types of Christianity or by different religious traditions.

7 Praying, Practical Theology and the Study of Religion

There are two ways to look at religion, according to philosopher Merold Westphal: religion as means and as end. "The believing soul", he writes, "resists the reduction of the religious life to utility, expediency, and the instrumental" and this does not apply to Christianity only. To illustrate religion as an end in itself, Westphal gives

---

[2] https://www.crossroadshospice.com/hospice-palliative-care-blog/2017/may/04/prayers-for-the-dying-a-prayer-for-hospice-patients/ (30.11.2021).

the example of songs. Songs of praise, like many Psalms, should be seen as gifts to God. We praise God, because it is appropriate to do so (Westphal 1984, 129). If there is one practice, however, that seems to fit the approach of religion as a means for something else, one might think of praying. On the one hand, petitionary prayer, the form of prayer in which the believer approaches God with a request, intends to improve the situation of the believer. Praying functions as a means of improving life and of coping with difficulties or of achieving salvation. On the other hand, however, Westphal argues, praying counts foremost as an example of "useless self-transcendence." Praying has an intrinsic value and is a prime example of a religious practice that directs "the self's attention away from itself" (Westphal 1984, 138–139). Thus construed, in praying, the relationship between God and humans is at stake; a relationship that is an end in itself and thus "useless". It refers beyond the praying subject and becomes a "self-transcending" phenomenon. In this vein, praying defines the nature of religion.

The practical theological study of religion challenges the engagement of the researcher. Empirical methods such as theological action research clarify this engagement for the sake of research and this methodological branch particularly brings into focus how a practical theological study of praying blurs a neat distinction between religion and theology. The study of praying thus contributes to the much-needed integrity of prayer and theology after theology's disintegration in modernity, with its different motifs and aspects as analysed by Sarah Coakley, Rowan Williams, and John Webster among many others (Cocksworth 2018). When practical theologians start studying praying, as Butler persuasively argues, the utmost consequence is that practical theological methodology "has the potential to be prayer" (Butler 2020), a position that ultimately redefines the nature of practical theology as the theological analysis of religious practices as instances of 'doxology,' practices aimed to glorify God.

Bibliography

Baschera, Luca, Angela Berlis, and Ralph Kunz. 2014. *Gemeinsames Gebet: Form und Wirkung des Gottesdienstes*. Zürich: Theologischer Verlag Zürich.

Blanton, Anderson. 2015. *Hittin' the Prayer Bones: Materiality of Spirit in the Pentecostal South*. Chapel Hill: The University of North Carolina Press.

Butler, James E. 2020. "Prayer as Research Practice? What Corporate Practices of Prayer Disclose about Theological Action Research." *Ecclesial Practices* 7:241–257.

Calvin, John. 1960. *Institutes of the Christian Religion*, edited by John T. McNeill, trans. Ford Lewis Battles. Louisville: Westminster Press.

Cartledge, Mark J. 2015. *The Mediation of the Spirit: Interventions in Practical Theology*. Grand Rapids: William B. Eerdmans Publishing Company.

Choudry, Mohsin, Aishah Latif, and Katharine G. Warburton. 2018. "An Overview of the Spiritual Importances of End-of-Life Care Among the Five Major Faiths of the United Kingdom." *Clinical Medicine* 18:23–31.

Coakley, Sarah. 2013. *God, Sexuality and the Self: An Essay 'On the Trinity'*. Cambridge: Cambridge University Press.

Cocksworth, Ashley. 2018. *Prayer: A Guide for the Perplexed*. New York: T&T Clark.

Giordan, Giuseppe, and Linda Woodhead. 2013. "Introduction: Prayer in Religion and Spirituality." In *Prayer in Religion and Spirituality*. Vol. 4, *Annual Review of the Sociology of Religion*, edited by Giuseppe Giordan and Linda Woodhead, Leiden: Brill, 1–8.

Hodge, David R. 2007. "A Systematic Review of the Empirical Literature on Intercessory Prayer." *Research on Social Work Practice* 17:174–187.

Immink, Gerrit. 2014. "Theological Analysis of Religious Practices." *International Journal of Practical Theology* 18:127–138.

Kao, Grace Y. 2010. "Mission Impossible: 'Nonsectarian' Prayer in the Military Chaplaincy." *Political Theology* 11:577–606.

Koll, Julia. 2007. *Körper beten: religiöse Praxis und Körpererleben*. Stuttgart: Kohlhammer Verlag.

Ladd, Kevin L., and Bernard Spilka. 2006. "Inward, Outward, Upward Prayer: Scale Reliability and Validation." *Journal for the Scientific Study of Religion* 45:233–251.

Liefbroer, Anke I., and Joantine Berghuijs. 2019. "Spiritual Care for Everyone? An Analysis of Personal and Organizational Differences in Perceptions of Religious Diversity Among Spiritual Caregivers." *Journal of Health Care Chaplaincy* 25:110–129.

Lunk, Johanna. 2014. *Das persönliche Gebet: Ergebnisse einer empirischen Studie im Vergleich mit praktisch-theologischen Gebetsauffassungen*. Leipzig: Evangelische Verlagsanstalt.

Manetsch, Scott M. 2013. *Calvin's Company of Pastors: Pastoral Care and the Emerging Reformed Church, 1536–1609*. Oxford / New York: Oxford University Press.

Meyer-Blanck, Michael. 2019. *Das Gebet*. Tübingen: Mohr Siebeck.

Muis, Jan. 2021. *The Implicit Theology of the Lord's Prayer: A Biblical and Theological Investigation*. Lanham: Fortress Academic.

Kooi-Dijkstra, Margriet van der, and Kees van der Kooi. 2017. *Goed gereedschap is het halve werk. De urgentie van theologie in pastoraat en zielzorg [Good Tools are Half the Battle. The Urgency of Theology in Pastoral Care]*. Utrecht: Boekencentrum.

Nieuw Amerongen-Meeuse, Joke C. van, Arjan W. Braam, Christa Anbeek, and Hanneke Schaap-Jonker. 2020. "'Beyond Boundaries or Best Practice' Prayer in Clinical Mental Health Care: Opinions of Professionals and Patients." *Religions* 11:492.

Nolan, Steve. 2011. *Spiritual Care at the End of Life: The Chaplain As a 'Hopeful Presence'*. London: Jessica Kingsley Publishers.

Pembroke, Neil. 2006. *Renewing Pastoral Practice: Trinitarian Perspectives on Pastoral Care and Counselling*. Aldershot / Burlington: Ashgate Publishing.

Pleizier, Theo. 2010. *Religious Involvement in Hearing Sermons: A Grounded Theory Study in Empirical Theology and Homiletics*. Delft: Eburon Academic Publishers.

Schirr, Bertram J. 2018. *Fürbitten als religiöse Performance: Eine ethnographisch-theologische Untersuchung in drei kontrastierenden Berliner Gottesdienstkulturen*. Leipzig: Evangelische Verlagsanstalt.

Spilka, Bernard, and Kevin L. Ladd. 2012. *The Psychology of Prayer: A Scientific Approach*. New York: Guilford Publications.

Voetius, Gisbert. 1996. *De praktijk der godzaligheid [The Practice of Piety]. Ta Asketika sive Exercitia pietatis (1644)*, edited by C.A. de Niet, Utrecht: De Banier.

Vosper, Gretta. 2014. *Amen: What Prayer Can Mean in a World Beyond Belief*. New York: HarperCollins.

Vries, Reijer J. de. 2018. "Models of Mutual Pastoral Care in the Footsteps of Martin Luther." *NTT Journal for Theology and the Study of Religion* 72:41–56.

Westphal, Merold. 1984. *God, Guilt, and Death: An Existential Phenomenology of Religion*. Bloomington: Indiana University Press.

Wilkinson, Michael, and Peter Althouse. 2013. "Pentecostal-Charismatic Prayer and Social Engagement." In *Prayer in Religion and Spirituality*. Vol. 4, *Annual Review of the Sociology of Religion*, edited by Giuseppe Giordan and Linda Woodhead, Leiden: Brill, 221–241.

Winter, R. Milton. 1986. "Presbyterians and Prayers for the Sick: Changing Patterns of Pastoral Ministry." *American Presbyterians* 64:141–155.

Woodhead, Linda, and Giuseppe Giordan. 2015. *A Sociology of Prayer*. Burlington: Ashgate Publishing.

Yoon, Seok Joon, Sang-Yeon Suh, Sun Hyun Kim, Jeanno Park, Yu Jung Kim, Beodeul Kang, Youngmin Park, Jung Hye Kwon, Kwonoh Park, Dong Wook Shin, Hyeon Jeong Kim, Hong-Yup Ahn, and David Hui. 2018. "Spiritual Well-Being among Palliative Care Patients with Different Religious Affiliations: A Multicenter Korean Study." *Journal of Pain and Symptom Management* 56:893–901.

Zuckerman, Phil, John R. Shook, and Robert C. Fuller, eds. 2017. *Secular Spirituality*. Oxford / New York: Oxford University Press.

Sunggu Yang
Preaching / Hermeneutics and Rhetoric / Religious Speech

1 Introduction: Preaching in the Age of Globalization

In this age of globalization, preaching is a highly sophisticated theological practice of religious communication. Its complexity is due mainly to ongoing global integration, interaction, and reaction among different cultures, sub-cultures, ethnic groups, ideologies, theologies, generations, religions, and social trends. Here, 'global' refers to the way in which one can easily and simultaneously encounter such complex interactive phenomenon in almost every ecclesial community around the world. This globalized context of ecclesia creates unique opportunities and challenges for the practice of Christian preaching, the ultimate aim of which is the proclamation of God's Kingdom coming on Earth in its most generic sense. Such opportunities include (a) preaching as locus of intracultural and transcultural communication of the Gospel, (b) preaching as dialogical stimulant for reconciliation and possible resolution of social conflicts, (c) preaching as prophetic exposure to the multiple dehumanizing effects of globalization, (d) preaching as most effective venue for projecting voices from social margins, and (e) preaching as culmination of multireglious or transreligious conversation. On the other hand, preaching faces challenges such as (a) becoming an advocate for oppressive powers and privileged voices, (b) lacking the theological or hermeneutical foundations needed to exegete the complex multicultural context, (c) adopting the tendency to exclude non-Christian values and other belief systems, and (d) losing its eschatological vision at the dawn of utopian globalism.

Figures like James R. Nieman, Thomas G. Rogers, Eunjoo Kim, Justo L. González, Pablo A. Jiménez, and Kwok Pui Lan see the era of globalization as presenting more opportunities than challenges for preaching. They all contend that preaching can have more liberating power and influence when we enlist the best of globalization, when we caution against its pitfalls, and finally alter its cultural, political, and ideological trajectory from a healthy Christian point of view. Their thoughts can be summed up as five areas for further exploration: preaching as a transcontextual enterprise, a postcolonial enterprise, a multi-religious enterprise, an eco-feminist enterprise, and a digital and glocal enterprise. Rather than being mutually exclusive, these five areas are closely interlocked but have different foci.

One's perception of globalization cannot help but rise from one's specific cultural or contextual experience of it. In my case, I experienced it as an Asian American. This chapter will demonstrate my Asian American interpretation of globalization, either implicitly or explicitly – especially, in Preaching as Multi-religious Enterprise.

2 Preaching as Transcontextual Enterprise

James R. Nieman and Thomas G. Rogers in *Preaching to Every Pew: Cross-Cultural Strategies* (Nieman and Rogers 2001) draw significant homiletic attention to the multicultural and interreligious situations of congregations today. Noting the inevitable nomadic nature of the world's population (North America in particular), they identify four cultural frames that generate diversity within congregations: ethnicity, class, displacement, and different religious beliefs. The preacher therefore faces the urgent task of understanding the cultural diversity of each congregation that results from these four cultural frames and of developing preaching strategies that embrace, celebrate, and promote that diversity. Noteworthy is their interreligious concern on ways that may foster both a pastoral form of pluralism and a distinctive growth in Christian faith. They suggest that innovations in a collaborative and conversational homiletic will help the cross-cultural preacher carry out these emerging tasks.

Yet Eunjoo Mary Kim in *Preaching in an Age of Globalization* identifies a crucial downside to the cross-cultural method Nieman and Rogers endorse – although she acknowledges its merits – and moves the contextual homiletic conversation a step forward. Labeling their method as 'intracontextual', she notes that it focuses only on the contextual complexity of North American local congregations, ignoring their external relations to global contexts (Kim 2010) – a lacuna given local congregations' deep entanglement in global affairs. Instead, she proposes a transcontextual homiletic and hermeneutic. Here transcontextual means a congregational situation deeply intertwined with both local and global issues.

Since Kim suggests that what is most at risk is our dehumanization, to preach on the restoration of genuine humanity must be a high priority. To that end, she suggests three interrelated conceptions of preaching practice: preaching as the formation of a shared identity, as a nurturing apperception, and as strategic planning (Kim 2010, 54–63). Of these, the homiletic application of "apperception" is most crucial. Apperception is "conscious perception with full awareness" (Morris 1975, 63), a "uniquely human capacity of knowing" (Lehmann 1995, 23), which enables one to perceive and pursue one's true humanity. Preaching must nurture this unique human faculty of apperception in the mind of the listener experiencing dehumanization in the transcontextual environment, both within and beyond church walls.

Given the complicated existential and social reality of transcontextuality, Kim urges preachers to develop what she calls a "kaleidoscopic" practice of preaching that is "thoroughly contextual by transcending the local context in an effort to embrace the larger world as the context for preaching" (Kim 2010, xii). For such transcendence and embrace, the preacher must recognize dehumanization on both local and global levels simultaneously. Kim herself does not explore specific topics of dehumanization (see sections below), yet her perception of preaching as transcontextual enterprise is surely universally applicable today.

3 Preaching as Postcolonial Enterprise

Postcolonial criticism, as Emmanuel Y. Lartey explains, refers to "the study of how the colonized made use of and transcended [various] colonial strategies in order to articulate and assert their dignity, self-worth and identity, and to empower themselves" (Lartey 2015, ix). The result of that criticism should be "life-enhancing and constitutively opposed to every form of tyranny, domination, and abuse [...] [along with] non-coercive knowledge produced in the interests of human freedom" (Said 1991, 28). This practice of postcolonial criticism has been widely adopted by homileticians and preachers in their efforts to deconstruct dehumanizing colonial powers and influences within their own national, global, and migratory contexts. For them, the notion of postcolonial or liberative preaching is in their very essence.

Púlpito, by Justo L. González and Pablo A. Jiménez, gives perhaps the best example of postcolonial preaching in the Hispanic American context. González and Jiménez note that the bicultural and bilingual immigrant situation has had a huge impact among Hispanics, and that this has led to their severe marginalization and oppression in North America. To address the people's status of colonial repression, the Hispanic pulpit first approaches Scripture as "the liberating text" or "readings of resistance" with an eschatological hope (González and Jiménez 2005, 43). When the Hispanic preacher reads the Bible, "he or she finds a message written by and for the marginalized and the oppressed" (González and Jiménez 2005, 44). The preacher then seeks the points of contact between the social location of the listening community today and that of the text. Finally, the preacher speaks a message of change, resistance, liberation, and hope through the hermeneutical "correspondence" between today's community and that of the text (González and Jiménez 2005, 44). González and Jiménez believe that other ethnic or racial groups under other forms of colonial oppression can easily adopt this postcolonial homiletic in their particular cultural situations.

Kwok Pui Lan does exactly this, but in an innovative way. She defines postcolonial preaching as "a locally rooted and globally conscious performance that seeks to create a Third Space so that the faith community can imagine new ways of being in the world and encountering God's salvific action for the oppressed and marginalized" (Kwok 2015, 2). If the methodology by González and Jiménez has a from-negative-to-positive ethos and dynamic – simply put, "we have bad news now, but will have good news eventually!", Kwok's has a from-positive-to-positive hermeneutical orientation; that is, "we as marginalized have a great potential now, which will give birth to a new reality!" She sees the locus of oppression and marginalization as the seedbed for fresh imagination for the new world, that is, the "third space" (Bhabha 1994, 1).[1] People of

---

[1] Homi Bhabha is considered to have coined the term *third space* based on his postcolonial notion of *hybridity*, which Kwok adopts in her writing. He notices that people oscillating between the colonizer's hegemonic-cultural authority and the person's initial cultural orientation come to formulate a hy-

undue privileges, biases, and oppressive powers have lost the power of imagination needed to build a new reality. This imagination is now found only in the hopeful calls from the outcast and oppressed for a New Heaven and a New Earth. It is they who have the potential to overturn the colonial status quo.

Recently, Sarah Travis introduced a Trinitarian decolonizing homiletic that is more doctrinal, ecclesial, and theo-centric compared to those proposed by Kwok, González, and Jiménez above. Decolonizing preaching, she contends, should generate a "perichoretic space", in which the preacher and the listening community encounter the triune God of perfect harmony, mutual respect, and unconditional self-giving (Travis 2014, 60–63). That sacred encounter enables people of the ecclesial community to strive for the same triune harmony, respect, and self-giving in this world as their resistance and liberation against the colonizing reality.

In the era of globalization, all these contributors to postcolonial homiletics acknowledge that postcolonial considerations of preaching will have to go on, as colonialism in its new forms (e.g., (neo)capitalism, neo-Nazism, racism or white supremacy, ultranationalism, etc.) still continue to appear as major forces of distortive social and individual formation.

4 Preaching as Multi-Religious Enterprise

As briefly mentioned above, Nieman and Rogers proposed a pastoral way of considering multireligious preaching. Their proposal is for a dynamic interreligious dialogue embedded in the practice of preaching that leads to a respectful form of pluralism and continuing growth in Christian faith. I showcase how this respectful form of pluralism and continuing growth in Christian faith has been actualized in the Korean American immigrant context (Yang 2016). I have realized that for the Korean ethnic community in particular, preaching as a multi-religious enterprise has helped weaken hostility and unexamined biases among people of different religions within the same ethnic group. I excavate five socio-ecclesial codes and related styles that frame multireligious faith fundamentals of Korean American Protestants and the resulting preaching practice. They are:

---

brid identity that is new to the former two, though emerging and taking certain characteristics from both. This new hybrid identity appears as disruption and displacement of the existing colonial powers, which cannot fully grasp the new cultural thrust and creativity of the hybrid people and thus dismiss it by their typical universal cultural claims. Translated politically or sociologically, hybridity becomes a key source of protest, subversion and reconstruction of colonial-hegemonic society. Where the existing-exclusive colonial status quo is subverted, people of hybrid identity newly create the more inclusive third space that "initiates new signs of identity, and innovative sites of collaboration and contestation." As an additional note, homiletician Johan Cilliers from South Africa makes brilliant use of the concept of third space in his argument for an aesthetic and liberative liturgical space based on Edward W. Soja's ideas, see Johan Cilliers (2016).

1. *The Wilderness Pilgrimage Code:* This code is strongly backed by Sang Hyun Lee who finds the Abraham story in the Hebrew Bible as *the* narrative upon which Asian American Christians have constructed their own version of the "pilgrimage-in-the-wilderness" story as the community's ontological narrative ground. He writes (Lee 2001, 61–64), "The Abrahamic obedience to God's call has been invoked in the Asian American church. The challenge is to see the Asian immigrants' *de facto* uprootedness as an opportunity to embark on a sacred pilgrimage to some God-promised goal, and therefore to believe that life as strangers and exiles can be meaningful."
   - The Allegorical-Typological Narrative Style
   - The Eschatological-Symbolic Narrative Style
   - The Illustrative-Utilitarian Narrative Style
2. *The Diasporic Mission Code:* The evangelical mission's work with both co-ethnic groups and other ethnic groups has been strong ever since the Korean American church's conception in America (Warner 2001, 30; Tan 2008, 57–64; Park 2001, 57–64). It is no wonder then that the Mission Community code has been one of the most fundamental ingredients of the practice of Korean American preaching. According to various sociological studies, this evangelical trend is being rapidly intensified among most Asian American churches (Tan 2008, 143–61).
   - The Internal Otherness Style
   - The Ironic Reverse Style
   - The Identification Partnership Style
3. *The Confucian Egalitarian Code:* Confucianism is an unavoidable socio-religious force in Asia which has taken certain bicultural mutations in the Asian American context and has fundamentally influenced the constructs of Korean American faith in deep theological relation with the other codes.[2] Although there seems to be only one rigid form of Confucian practice in the Korean American church (under the patriarchal leadership of the male elder pastor), in reality there have been several recent variations in style, two of them being most widely accepted and practiced.
   - The God the Father Style
   - The Mother as Good Mentor Style

---

[2] In Asia, Confucianism is now practiced as a 'religion' on three levels. First, formal institutionalized Confucianism is performed as a "glorious" tradition by a variety of loosely connected Confucian institutions. Second, Confucianism is practiced by individual households in the form of patriarchal ancestor worship in keeping with the Confucian family model. Third, individual Confucian followers in broader society, even though they do not perceive themselves as formal Confucian practitioners, represent and practice the general Confucian culture or its value system and philosophy. In a practical sense, and in terms of socio-cultural norms, the third level is the most influential Confucian social factor that comes to construct the basic Asian/Asian American mindset today (Hongkyung 2007, 163–176).

4. *The Buddhist Shamanistic Code:* In today's religiously pluralistic Asian and Asian American contexts, Buddhism and Shamanism, both of which have existed for thousands of years as key folk religions, often intermingle with each other and generate certain widely-accepted religious practices (Hongkyung 2007, 22–33). Even though most contemporary Asian people might not identify themselves as strictly Buddhist or Shamanist, their everyday practice of social relations, popular mindset, and religious thinking are still under significant influence from both traditional religions. Thus, it was inevitable that when Christianity first arrived in East Asia, it had to (and still has to) go through some notable enculturation or inter-religious process in the Asian context.[3] Accordingly, certain religious aspects of Buddhism and Shamanism have been migrated or integrated into Korean American Christianity.
   - The Eco-Rhythmic Community Style
   - The Buddhist Shamanistic Supernatural Style
5. *The Pentecostal Liberation Code:* As Allan Anderson observes, it is no exaggeration to say that most contemporary Asian Protestant churches are evangelical Pentecostal or at least have been largely influenced by the Pentecostal movement (Anderson 2014, 123–34).[4] Thus, it is only natural that when these Pentecostal Asian Christians come to America they set up similar 'Spirit-led' churches across denominations – regardless of ethnic groups. Their Pentecostal characteristics, of course, appear most vividly in their communal worship services. In these services, worshippers emphasize and seek out the strong presence of the Spirit through a variety of liturgical mediums, depending on their particular contexts and congregational needs, such as audible prayer, a Praise and Worship band, speaking in tongues, charismatic leadership or pastoral preaching. What is most intriguing in this code is that worship within the Pentecostal Liberation Code acts as a space wherein facets of all four aforementioned codes converge and are integrated into a single practice, especially in the practice of preaching. The people's Pentecostal spirituality takes on a strong flavor of (spiritual) liberation, given their socially oppressive *wilderness* situation in America.

---

[3] A good Korean example of this is found in Kim (2008, 142–146).

[4] While the Chinese Pentecostal movement supported by the western Pentecostal missionaries has been active from 1907 in the main land and now has about a fifty-one million population through the underground church connection, not many Korean or Korean American churches were evangelistic or Pentecostal when Korean churches first began to form. These were aided by mostly non-Pentecostal foreign missionaries in the late 19th and early 20th centuries. However, rather suddenly throughout the late 1980s and all of the 1990s, the evangelistic Pentecostal trend was popularized and intensified throughout most Korean denominations when the Americanized revivalist Praise and Worship movement hit (Joo 2005, 484–491). Japanese Pentecostalism still remains relatively small, but is rapidly increasing in its influence and population (Shew 2005, 487–508).

- The Pure Spirituality Style
- The Prosperity Living Style
- The Liberative Style

While all five codes demonstrate in one way or another the multireligious formation of Korean American faith and preaching practice, the Confucian Egalitarian code and the Buddhist Shamanistic code are the most explicit. These two codes are the end-products of the inculturation of missionary-delivered western Christianity into Confucian ideology-based, Buddhist-Shamanistic Korean society over the past century. Through the interaction with Confucianism, which upholds family values and superior education, the Korean Christian pulpit has become a place of familial community building and spiritual teaching. For that reason, the images of father and mother as respectful teachers and mentors in the community are of unmistakable importance in their faith life.

Furthermore, historical interaction with Buddhism, which emphasizes meditative prayer practice and ecological harmony, and Shamanism, which is both truly humanitarian and supernatural, have left an indelible imprint on the practice of Korean preaching. Meditative preaching is almost always expected at early morning services that typically begin at 5:30am. On Sunday mornings, messages that address basic human needs (food, health, wealth, childbearing, connection, security, etc.) are particularly welcome, especially when they invoke supernatural power to help meet these needs.

Korean Americans are *Koreans* living in *North America*. Thus, it is no wonder that their Christian faith and preaching is formulated through the active interactions of two disparate cultural and religious backgrounds. After all, Korea is the only nation on earth that celebrates the birthday of Buddha and that of Jesus as national holidays with absolutely no conflict about it in society. Thus, preaching as a multi-religious enterprise is never foreign to Korean preachers and their listeners, even if both parties do not recognize it on a conscious level. This is an extremely plausible form of religious pluralism that cultivates both unique growth within Christian faith as well as respect for other religions. I think that through creative variations, this model could be adopted in other ethnic or cultural groups in North America as well as around the world.

5 Preaching as Eco-Feminist Enterprise

The exploitation of the natural world and obstacles to women's welfare have emerged as fatal issues of globalization and thus as prime concerns for preaching in the last couple of decades. Eco-feminism as the ideological foundation for the advocacy of the natural world and women "sees a connection between the exploitation and degradation of the natural world and the subordination and oppression of women. It [...] takes from the green movement a concern about the impact of human activities on the non-human world and from feminism the view of humanity as gendered in ways that subordinate, exploit and oppress women" (Mellor 1997, 1). Eco-feminists especially recognize patriarchal dominance over both the environment and women as the connecting point between the two. Maria Mies and Vandana Shiva point out that "everywhere, women were the first to protest against environmental destruction" (Mies and Shiva 2004, 334).

A quarter of a century earlier, Christine M. Smith paved the way for preaching from a feminist perspective, though not yet eco-feminist. She criticized traditional male-dominant homiletic tendencies of autonomy, authority, individuality, and detachment while valuing female emphasis on authenticity, communality, intimacy, and interdependence in ecclesial life and preaching. These feminine qualities, incorporated into preaching practice, she believed, can "create a quality of humanness that is so persuasive and honest that it calls people into connection and solidarity" (Smith 1989, 48). Smith's rather mild feminist approach to feminist preaching developed into a more progressive one in her *Preaching as Weeping, Confession, and Resistance: Radical Reponses to Radical Evil* (Smith 1992). In particular, Chapter 3. "Breaking Silence Exposes Misogyny" is worth reading, as it proposes detailed homiletic strategies to resist and overcome destructive and evil social and domestic practices against women.

In the twenty-first century, Leah D. Schade further developed Smith's feminist discourse to the eco-feminist dimension in her *Creation-Crisis Preaching: Ecology, Theology, and the Pulpit*. Schade, like earlier eco-feminists, acknowledged the historical-patriarchal connection between the destruction of nature and oppression of women in the current globalized world. Attacks on and degradation of vulnerable women easily transfers to the irreversible hurt on Mother Nature and vice versa. For instance, in many parts of the world, when nature suffers from corporate evil activities, women's burdens are doubled or tripled (for example, dumping industry-related hazardous chemicals into rivers forces indigenous women who rely heavily on those rivers for drinking water, washing, and food supply to leave their native homes and workplaces). Given the urgent eco-feminist situation, Schade hopes that preaching practice can serve as a sacred medium to "help listeners find common ground for communicating about how we may proclaim God's word of justice, hope, reconciliation, and healing for the Earth's community, inclusive of humanity" (Schade 2015, 35). For this homiletic purpose, Schade proposes three generic eco-feminist approaches to environmental preaching: consciousness-raising, calling for specific action, and deep transformation coupled with sustainable change (Schade 2015, 47–50).

For the foreseeable future, at least in the global North, such eco-feminist concerns will remain one of the most critical issues that the Christian pulpit should address as we now face unprecedented environment disasters and many old and new forms of misogynist oppressions (for example child pornography, human trafficking, sexual abuse, commercialization of sex, neo-capitalist slave labor, the social glass ceiling, etc.). More than ever, the pulpit is expected to provide continuing resistance and ultimate hope in unique ways.

6 Preaching as Digital and Glocal Enterprise

Since the 2000s, the digital and internet revolution has transformed how the Christian church operates and how the Gospel message is communicated. This has brought both benefits and problems. Given the formidable digital revolution of human communication, Keith Anderson, in his *Digital Cathedral: Networked Ministry in a Wireless World*, proposes an ecclesial model of the "digital cathedral" (Anderson 2015). Rather than simply suggesting that churches of the digital age should go completely online, he calls on churches to open their eyes to and practice "an expansive and holistic understanding of church – one that extends ministry both into digital and local gathering spaces" (Anderson 2015, 20). In other words, he is calling for a comprehensive digital ecclesiology that may better serve this new age's communicational demands in both digital and local spaces.

Following Anderson's cue, Casey Sigmon proposes the innovative idea of "homilecclesiology" (Sigmon 2017, 142) as a readily applicable possibility for preaching to the highly networked audience of today. Homilecclesiology is a compound word comprised of homiletic and ecclesiology. By this novel term, what she proposes is a digital homiletic of all believers that can preach "beyond the limits of the liturgical event, sanctuary space, and face-to-face encounter" within the digital space (Sigmon 2017, 142). This kind of digital preaching should be fundamentally cooperative, bilateral, and intimate while at the same time "radically horizontal, fluid, and spontaneous", as all these qualities are innate characteristics of digital communication. In short, preaching should become a communal and participatory event in a democratic digital space. Thus, Sigmon encourages churches to use the three most influential and user-friendly digital platforms for this preaching purpose: Facebook, Twitter, and Instagram. These platforms are not ethically neutral spaces, yet when used wisely and with caution, she acknowledges that they can prove themselves as effective digital homiletic channels for today's people. One of the greatest benefits of this digital homilecclesiology is that the preacher's message can instantly reach countless different cultural, racial, gender, and national groups on a global scale, through translation if necessary. Then, ideally, preaching can function as a catalyst for global harmony, racial reconciliation, cultural exchange, and even rigorous interreligious dialogue.

However, no matter how timely and persuasive Sigmon's argument looks, one thing is undeniable; digital communication means weak ecclesiality. Cyber communities will likely never replace the intimate relationality of conventional offline communities. Yet excellent online preaching can still stir frequent and very positive digital interactions among participants. For this reason, emerging ecclesial communities are blending their cyber activities and those offline in a balanced way, preaching being one of those activities. Certain communities from the outset intentionally form themselves as a 'glocal' mosaic[5] of different cultural, racial, gender, and national groups, just as their online preaching reaches out to those groups, with no physical limits (DeYmaz 2013).[6]

Mark DeYmaz contends that the multiculturalism of the church should not be recognized as a novel goal of the church today, as indeed it is the biblical mandate. Citing Acts 2 and many other parts of the Scripture, he realizes that multiculturalism was engraved into the life of the church from very early on (DeYmaz 2013, 3–39). We may now be returning to the original multicultural formation of the church, thanks to the digital revolution. For many racially and culturally divided – if not segregated – congregations today, homilecclesiology and its supplemental multicultural ecclesiality may be able to serve as a vital aid for their hopeful future.

7 Conclusion

The best preaching practice in the age of globalization is, at its core, to be collaborative, liberative, and dialogical, as most of the figures mentioned in this chapter would agree. Global preaching should also rely on a multireligious rhetoric that speaks the truth in love far beyond the church walls. Thankfully, with the digital revolution and internet connecting all parts of the earth, there is now virtually no place where a preacher's word cannot be heard. The five streams of global homiletics also show that there are fatal dehumanizing challenges that may easily squash the proclamation of the good news of the Gospel. Therefore, there is no guarantee that the preacher's word will be well-received (as has so often been the case in human history). What is then expected of the preacher is to be swift and wise, to seize the opportunities of the new era for the maximum homiletic use. This new era calls for deeper wisdom and proactive engagement of the preacher in every possible way, to present the living Word of Christ at both the local and global levels in the best possible ways.

---

5 The term glocal (or glocalization) is a combination of global and local, indicating a socio-cultural and economic phenomenon wherein distinction between local and global is blurred due to the vibrant interaction between the two. Local still remains local and so does global. Yet, their amalgamation is now inseparable. See Robertson 2002, 25–44.

6 DeYmaz believes that multi-ethnicity of the church should not be a goal of the church's mission but a starting point and foundation of the church. One excellent example of this kind of multi-ethnic and multicultural ecclesial philosophy is actualized in Village Baptist Church in Oregon, USA. The Village Church has under its roof several churches or fellowships, as they call themselves, from different ethnic groups, including Chinese, Korean, East Indian, Hispanic, and Caucasian. Every Sunday, the main worship service is provided in three different languages: English, Korean, and Spanish. Although the primary vocal language for worship is English, pastors from ethnic groups share in the preaching. For more information about this church, visit http://www.vbconline.org/ (30.11.2021).

Bibliography

Anderson, Allan. 2014. *An Introduction to Pentecostalism: Global Charismatic Christianity.* Cambridge / New York: Cambridge University Press.
Anderson, Keith. 2015. *Digital Cathedral: Networked Ministry in a Wireless World.* New York: Morehouse Publishing.
Cilliers, Johan. 2016. *A Space for Grace: Towards an Aesthetics of Preaching.* Stellenbosch: Sun Press.
Bhabha, Homi K. 1994. *The Location of Culture.* London: Routledge.
DeYmaz, Mark. 2013. *Building a Healthy Multi-Ethnic Church: Mandate, Commitments and Practices of a Diverse Congregation.* San Francisco: Jossey-Bass.
González, Justo L. and Pablo A. Jiménez. 2005. *Púlpito: An Introduction to Hispanic Preaching.* Nashville: Abingdon Press.
Joo, Seung-Joong, and Kyeong-Jin Kim. 2005. "The Reformed Tradition in Korea." In *The Oxford History of Christian Worship*, edited by Geoffrey Wainwright and Karen B. Westerfield Tucker. Oxford / New York: Oxford University Press, 55–69.
Kim, Eunjoo M. 2010. *Preaching in an Age of Globalization.* Louisville: Westminster John Knox Press.
Kim, Hongkyung. 2007. "A Party for the Spirits: Ritual Practice in Confucianism." In *Religions of Korea in Practice*, edited Robert E. Buswell Jr., Princeton: Princeton University Press, 163–176.
Kim, Sebastian C. H. 2008. *Christian Theology in Asia.* New York: Cambridge University Press.
Kwok, Pui Lan. 2015. "Postcolonial Preaching in Intercultural Contexts." *Homiletic* 40:8–21.
Lartey, Emmanuel Y. 2015. *Postcolonializing God: An African Practical Theology.* London: SCM Press.
Lee, Sang Hyun. 2001. "Pilgrimage and Home in the Wilderness of Marginality: Symbols and Context in Asian American Theology." In *Korean Americans and Their Religions: Pilgrims and Missionaries from a Different Shore*, edited by Ho-Youn Kwon, Kwang-Chung Kim, and R. Stephen Warner, University Park: Pennsylvania State University Press, 484–491.
Lehmann, Paul. 1995. *The Decalogue and a Human Future: The Meaning of the Commandments for Making and Keeping Human Life Human.* Grand Rapids: Eerdmans.
Mellor, Mary. 1997. *Feminism & Ecology.* Washington Square: New York University Press.
Mies, Maria and Vandana Shiva. 2004. "The Subsistence Perspective." In *The Feminist Standpoint Theory Reader: Intellectual and Political Controversies*, edited by Sandra Harding, New York: Routledge, 333–338.
Morris, William, ed. 1975. *The American Heritage Dictionary of the English Language.* Boston: American Publishing Co.
Nieman, James R., and Thomas G. Rogers. 2001. *Preaching to Every Pew: Cross-Cultural Strategies.* Minneapolis: Fortress Press.
Park, Soyoung. 2001. "The Intersection of Religion, Race, Ethnicity, and Gender in the Identity Formation of Korean American Evangelical Women." In *Korean Americans and their Religions: Pilgrims and Missionaries from a Different Shore*, edited by Ho-Youn Kwon, Kwang-Chung Kim, and R. Stephen Warner, University Park: Pennsylvania State University Press, 193–208.
Robertson, Roland. 2002. "Glocalization: Time-Space and Homogeneity-Heterogeneity." In *Global Modernities,* edited by Roland Robertson, Scollt Lash, and Mike Featherston, London: Sage Publications, 25–44.
Said, Edward W. 1991. *The World, the Text, and the Critic.* London: Vintage.
Schade, Leah D. 2015. *Creation-Crisis Preaching: Ecology, Theology, and the Pulpit.* Saint Louis: Chalice Press.

Shew, Paul T. 2005. "Pentecostals in Japan." In *Asian and Pentecostal: The Charismatic Face of Christianity in Asia*, edited by Allan Anderson and Edmond Tang, Baguio City: APTS Press, 395–412.
Sigmon, Casey. 2017. "Engaging the Gadfly: A Process Homilecclesiology for a Digital Age." PhD Dissertation. Vanderbilt University. https://ir.vanderbilt.edu/handle/1803/11258 (30.11.2021).
Smith, Christine M. 1989. *Weaving the Sermon: Preaching in a Feminist Perspective*. Louisville: Westminster John Knox Press.
Smith, Christine M. 1992. *Preaching as Weeping, Confession, and Resistance: Radical Responses to Radical Evil*. Louisville: Westminster John Knox Press.
Tan, Jonathan Y. 2008. *Asian American Theologies*. Maryknoll, NY: Orbis Books.
Travis, Sarah. 2014. *Decolonizing Preaching: The Pulpit as Postcolonial Space*. Eugene: Cascade Books.
Warner, R. Stephen. 2001. "The Korean Immigrant Church as Case and Model." In *Korean Americans and Their Religions: Pilgrims and Missionaries from a Different Shore*, edited by Ho-Youn Kwon, Kwang-Chung Kim, and R. Stephen Warner, University Park: Pennsylvania State University Press, 71–94.
Yang, Sunggu. 2016. *Evangelical Pilgrims from the East: Faith Fundamentals of Korean American Protestant Diasporas*. New York: Palgrave MacMillan.

Herbert Moyo
Priestly Office / Spirit Mediums / Pastoral Care

1 Introduction

The Priestly Office, the concept of Spirit Mediums and the practice of Pastoral Care have contextual spiritualized meaning and relevance among the Ndebele people of Matabo in Zimbabwe. Matabo is an area in the Midlands province of Zimbabwe bordering Matabeleland South Province (Moyo 2019, 114–124). In Matabo, mainly among the Ndebele people the functional understanding of the Priestly Office is synonymous with the traditional understanding of the role of spirit mediums who give answers to challenges beyond human comprehension. Spirit mediums are caregivers to individuals and communities in response to that which is mainly spiritual and mysterious to normal human beings. In the mind-set of one with a traditional understanding of a person called by God as a priest, then the priestly office becomes an avenue for caregiving to people on issues beyond human comprehension. To fully understand the characteristics of an ideal pastoral caregiver (the priest) in Matabo one needs to understand the traditional understanding of a spirit medium and *Sangomas*[1] among the Ndebele. The term 'priest' is not popular in my area of research, people use the word *Umfundisi*. *Umfundisi* is a Ndebele word directly translated to mean 'the teacher'. In Matabo the English reference to *Umfundisi*, is Pastor. The Priestly office in this chapter will be interchangeably referred to as pastoral office or *Umfundisi*. It is also common for people to refer to mainline church (Lutherans, Seventh Day Adventists, Church of Christ, and Brethren in Christ) ministers as priests or Reverends (commonly shortened to Rev) while ministers from other ministries[2] (Victory Fellowship, Oasis of Life, Assemblies of God and Living Waters) are referred to as pastors. However, both groups are referred to as *Umfundisi* in isiNdebele. This chapter seeks to explore and expose the popular understanding of the role of the pastoral office amongst the Ndebele which explains the appetite for miracle working pastors popularly known as 'man of God'.[3] This chapter is a result of an ongoing research project on how miracle healing attracts people and seemingly people do not

---

[1] *Isangoma* is also referred to as *Isanuse*. Both words refer to one with spiritual powers to see beyond human comprehension. One who can operate and communicate at the spiritual realm.
[2] Ministries refers to new churches being formed across Southern Africa who are filled with the Holy Spirit. They conduct their services mainly in tents. The majority of their membership are people who are transferring from mainline churches or those who worship in mainline churches and then visit the ministries for spiritual based solutions to challenges.
[3] At present we do not have what people popularly call 'the woman of God' for female pastors or and priests.

question the instructions by pastors leading to drinking of petrol, eating snakes, eating grass and many other behaviours that people would not do under 'normal' circumstances. What is it that makes people from all social levels of society accept instructions from pastors without questioning? Why do people seemingly shelve their rationality when dealing with pastors mainly from new church movements popularly known as 'Ministries'? This ongoing study started in 2017 in Matabo and surrounding areas. I have gathered data so far from 31 church leaders and 217 church members. Preliminary findings indicate that, at a conceptual level, amongst the Ndebele, there is no separation between Christianity and Traditional African Religions, people of Matabo prefer a 'man of God' with power. This means a priest who is overtly filled with the Holy Spirit and can act like a spirit medium or a *Sangoma* of the people by telling and foretelling people's needs and expectations. The Ndebele will flock to pastors who express their Christianity using African concepts of spirits and salvation from present afflictions such as misfortune, poverty, sickness, and spiritual attacks. The priest must demonstrate *amandla* (power). Pastors then demonstrate power through such acts as spraying people with insecticides, raising the dead, offering portions for luck, speaking in tongues, talking directly to Jesus to get immediate answers for the congregants, anointing with oil, deliverance sessions, praise worship, healing crusades, fasting and prayers, visions and prophecies that respond to the everyday needs of Africans.

In Matabo, I have observed and confirmed through interviews and informal discussions that in most cases pastors that are overtly filled with the Holy Spirit are relevant to the socio-spiritual needs of the Ndebele than pastors that are not filled with the Holy Spirit. Pastors from mainline churches or traditional churches such as the Lutheran Church, Seventh Day Adventists Church, Brethren in Christ, and Church of Christ are viewed as not filled with the Holy Spirit. Mainline church pastors are general viewed as divorced from the spiritual existential needs of their members. Members of these churches do come to their churches for a normal Sunday or Saturday service, but when they meet spirit related pastoral needs, they visit the pastors of the Ministries that are filled with the Holy Spirit. I fact amongst the Ndebele, all of life's needs have a spiritual dimension hence the argument by Clement Osunwokeh (2014, 166)[4] that "[r]eligion indeed makes a tremendous impact on the social, political and economic life of the Africans." The spiritual dimension is central in deciding which pastors to go to in times of need. Some churches do not have the spirit. For example, about 133 of my participants concurred that there is no Holy Spirit in the Lutheran Church. Participants in this research project who know that I am a pastor openly told me that there is no spiritual healing from the Lutheran church because

---

[4] Clement Osunwokeh writes from a Nigerian perspective. Interestingly, though Nigeria and Zimbabwe are miles apart, the understanding of the position of a priest is related. African Traditional religious understanding of traditional priests/priestess contributes to how society perceives a Christian priest.

the pastors of the Lutheran church do not have the Holy Spirit. They said that Lutheran pastors and those of other mainline churches 'are dry'.

This chapter will start by expositing the Ndebele people of Matabo and their context. This will be followed by an exposition of the characteristics of a spirit medium. The spirit medium phenomenon will be used as a theoretical frame of reference for the Ndebele's understanding of the priestly office. The chapter will go on to explain the behaviour of performing miracles by the church ministries in contemporary Matabo and the reasons for the behaviour of both the priests and the recipients of the services of priests. The chapter also demonstrates the concept of priestly dignity in the worldview of the Ndebele people of Matabo. The chapter concludes by pointing to the type of priest that is ideal for the people of Matabo.

2 The Ndebele People of Matabo and their Context

The Ndebele people of Zimbabwe are in the majority descendants of Zulus who travelled northwards from South Africa in the nineteenth century. They belong to the bigger group of the *Nguni* tribes, which includes groups such as the Zulu, the Xhosa, and the Swati. In 1823, Chief Mzilikazi Khumalo had a conflict with King Shaka Zulu over the spoils of war in KwaZulu-Natal, South Africa. As a result, Mzilikazi travelled north with his regiment and their families. Eventually Mzilikazi settled in Zimbabwe, becoming the king of the Ndebele. The name 'Ndebele' comes from the Sotho people who called them 'Matabele', which means 'people of the shields', in reference to the shields of war that these Zulus carried. As these Zulus travelled northwards, their vocabulary became richer (or polluted) by picking words from the tribes with which they interacted. Therefore, the Ndebele of Zimbabwe speak what some people would call corrupted Zulu. Ndebele has more vocabulary than contemporary Zulu.

Some Ndebele people do belong to the church, and they respect church-based rituals such as baptisms, funerals and marriages. However, when the Ndebele meet challenges, they do seek for pastoral care from Priests. For many Christians, pastoral care is viewed as an important aspect when one meets challenges in life, but it is not the only way. At night congregants can go to other faith-based healers such as pastors from other denominations (especial the newer charismatic healing ministries) and traditional spirit mediums including sangomas (King 2012). In a way, they will still be seeking for spiritual pastoral care, only that it will be away from their denomination.

Pastoral care is related to the works of a shepherd to a flock (Louw 1998, 21). According to Patton (2005, 107), "pastoral care is part of practical theology which focuses on pastoral practices" on human events as they make sense of their context. Patton further argues that in the ministry of pastoral care, people care for each other because they are aware that God cares for them all in their given context (Patton 2005, 107). Pastoral care is the central role of Priests in Matabo in both Christianity and African Traditional Religions.

Besides pastoral care from the church, the Ndebele people as religious beings find it difficult to make a distinction between their Ndebele culture and African Traditional Religion(s). The Ndebele are religious beings in that religion permeates one's life from the womb until life after death (Moyo 2019, 115). There is no life outside the influence of religion. Religion "is the total traditional world view with all the values and beliefs" (Moyo 2019, 115). In most cases religion means the presence and the influence of God, ancestors, and the spirit world. For the Ndebele it is difficult to pick out behavioural patterns in which a Ndebele person can then say this is culture and this other one is religion. In fact, what we have is a human being living their life in a particular way that makes them who they are. It is then up to those interested in categorising issues to say this is religion and this other is culture. This cultural way of living culture and religion does not need to convert or proselytise, one is conceived and born into the religion (Bozongwana 1983). It does not wait for a person to grow up so that they can learn how to read about the religion from some kind of 'Holy Book'; its strength is that it is a lived religion.

The Ndebele cosmology is composed of both visible and invisible spirit beings which have influence on living human beings which are appeased using rituals and living life according to acceptable social norms and values, which can be described as a cultural way of life or religious way of life of good relationships (Bozongwana 1983). The life of the Ndebele resonates with argument of Mbiti, that human life is composed of life forces that people constantly interact with influencing the course of human life for good and for evil (Mbiti 1970). In the Ndebele worldview, the unborn, the living-living and the living-dead are all part of the constellation of the living spirits (Moyo 2019, 116). A Kenyan scholar, Ndeti, argues that the community "extends beyond the living members of the clan and tribe. It incorporates those who have died and those who are yet unborn. [...] [The individual] is a physical representative of the dead, living and unborn. Thus [the individual] is a community incorporating three principles – life, spirit, and immortality" (Ndeti 1972, 114).

Life amongst the Ndebele is highly rooted in this kind of cosmology and worldview, making it very difficult to separate culture from religion and God. Laleye (1981) is of the view that the African traditional cosmology is dynamic. It recognises and integrates the duality of the mind and body, magic and rationality, order and disorder, negative and positive powers, and individual and communal consciousness. Family relationships, communal relationships and relationships with strangers are part of the religious observances to continual appease the spirit world. When things do not work out in life one is forced to seek an understanding of their relationship with the spirit world. This understanding of God and ancestors borders around theology of retribution. God and ancestors are happy, and they bless those who relate well to others and the environment. On the contrary those who do not relate well will be cursed through misfortune and ill-health. A good priest needs to understand this worldview and have the power to connect with the spirit world.

3 The Concept of Religious Hybridity in Matabo

The Ndebele people of Matabo who have converted into Christianity still participate in African Traditional Religious practices of the community such as contributing funds to the annual entourage that visits the rain goddess in Matopos hills – eNjelele.[5] The majority of the Ndebele population have intricately brought together aspects of culture and Christianity to a whole new way of doing Christianity. It is now very difficult to separate Ndebele cultural practices from Christian practices. They have formed a hybrid type of religion. They are practicing a form of Christianity that is uniquely Matabo type. The priestly office is then understood from a hybrid worldview that mixes African Ndebele worldviews with Christianity. Priests from mainline churches are viewed as directly opposed to the African cultural practices as they favour western cultural practices in their mentality and practice of ministry. On the other hand, African Initiated church pastors favour African cultural practices in their pastoral practices. Nonetheless, broadly speaking, both sides see the priest as a spirit medium who can perform extra ordinary acts through the Holy Spirit in the name of Jesus Christ of Nazareth.

In Matabo, the priestly office is multifaceted and depends on contextual religious traditions, cultural practices, and environmental conditions. The priestly office can align itself with the fundamentals of the religious spiritualties of the context or may be continuously seeking to oppose the local cultural and religious traditions. In both instances, one cannot understand the spirit medium until one understands the hybrid worldview of Matabo. A priest in the context of Matabo must understand the local cultural behavioural patterns and religious ecumenism (or syncretism) that links all religions in an individual. The priest must be transcultural and trans-religious in nature thereby allowing Christians to live their Christianity in the auspices of their *Nguni* cultural nuances. The ideal priest should be able to navigate the space between Christianity and cultural practices that can be said to be African traditional religious practices. Christianity in particular and religion in general is experienced as discursive cultural practices. The priestly office is that of navigating the socio-economic and political challenges as well as the joys of people in context and offer spiritual based responses to such. In Matabo the priestly office is a spiritual office where people receive answers to issues that are beyond human comprehension through the priest's spiritual connection with God or the gods. To understand the Ndebele worldview on priesthood one must understand the concept of spirit mediums.

---

5 Njelele is the name of the hill housing the rain goddess. The 'e' in eNjelele stands for 'in'.

4 The Spirit Medium Phenomenon

Spirit mediums are both women and men who are blessed by the possibility of being possessed by the spirit of an ancestor (at times referred to as the Living dead). The process leading to one being possessed by the spirit of an ancestor varies from one family to another or from one village to another. This is because African Traditional Religions are not monolithic even within the same tribal grouping such as the Ndebele. In Matabo community there are two common ways of becoming a spirit medium. The most common is that the spirit of the ancestor chooses whomever it wants. Whoever is chosen by the spirit can become aware of such a calling through becoming sick in strange ways that defy diagnosis by western medical practitioners. The person may also have strange dreams and visions that normal will become fulfilled to show that the ancestors (*abaphansi, izinyoka* or *amadlozi* as they are referred to in isiNdebele) are visiting the person. This eventually leads to an existing spirit medium telling the family of the sick person or the sick person directly that he/she is being invited by the *amadlozi / abaphansi* to become a spirit medium.

The second route to becoming a spirit medium for *amadlozi* is through appointment by the family. The family may see the mannerisms or physical characteristics of a family member that reminds them of an ancestor and decide to nominate that individual to be a spirit medium for the family. A ritual is then performed to invite the spirit of the ancestor to use the individual as a spirit medium. In both the above cases the individual then goes through a form of training (*Ukuthwasa*) from an experienced spirit medium. In other words, becoming a spirit medium comes through a calling to this ministry. The calling can be direct to the person, or it can be through others as in the case of family members identifying an individual as suitable to be a spirit medium. The training by an experienced spirit medium which may involve going to specific shrines equips the trainee with the tools of the trade.

A spirit medium can be a community seer, healer, or *isangoma / isanuse*. This becomes a form of a vocation for the medium. The spirit medium is a respected figure because he / she represents the presence of the spirit world. When possessed by the spirit the incumbents do not speak their own mind but the mind of the ancestor. The spirit medium is a connection between the living and the living dead. Disrespecting the spirit medium is tantamount to disrespecting the living dead. The spirit medium is consulted for spiritual issues that are seen to permeate all of life. The voice of the spirit medium is the voice of the gods and therefore cannot be opposed. Spirit mediums command respect in all sectors of the community in Matabo. This includes Christians who still fear the perceived power of the spirit mediums. Besides respect there is also fear of the spirit mediums as they may invite the wrath of the spirit world against anyone who does not respect them. So, all the Christians can do is to avoid the wrath of the spirit mediums by respecting them.

If individuals, families, and communities are confronted by spiritual issues that are believed to be hidden from normal human beings, they consult the *Sangoma*. The

Sangoma then uses spiritual powers to unravel that which is hidden from normal human beings. People do not consult a *Sangoma* before exhausting their human abilities. In Matabo the *Sangoma* is consulted when human wisdom has failed. According to the Ndebele, that which defies human wisdom, will according to the Ndebele be pointing to the spiritual nature or supernatural nature of the phenomenon requiring the services of one with supernatural powers.

5 Sources of the Dignity of a Priest in Matabo

Through the tradition of the missionaries, African Christians, especial in the mainline churches value the ritual of ordination (*Ukugcotshwa kukamfundisi*) which in the traditional sense means the anointment of the priest. According to Clement Osunwokeh (2014), the priestly office in itself carries some level of dignity for the office bearer. Dignity is supposedly conferred on the priest during ordination. For the people of Matabo one who is ordained carries the power of the spirit world. Ordination sets one apart from the rest of humanity to a level next to the gods.

The Priest is not a "normal" human being; he/she is dignified in a manner that borders on fear of the connection of the priest to the spirit world. The priest carries both blessings and curses hence the fear or veneration of the individuals in this office. The priest is the one who speaks to God or gods on behalf of society. Clement Osunwokeh says that society "understands the priest as a sacred person, set apart by ordination and in possession of special sacramental power and is often described as 'another Christ (*alter Christus*)'" (Osunwokeh 2014, 169). This resonates with the traditional African understanding of priesthood where a person is set aside and apart by the ancestors or gods to connect the living to the spirit world. The priest usually carries the character of the gods. A priest is the epiphany of the gods. In this way, a Christian priest in Matabo is expected to be the epiphany of Christ. This means the priest must speak and act with spiritual authority. The priest can earn respect and dignity for performing miracles and extra ordinary acts. In this way the priest will be demonstrating power (*amandla*). *Amandla* confirms the priest's connectedness with the gods. Without *amandla* the priest is not as accepted as the one viewed as possessing unique extra ordinary power

The character and acts of the priest, as noted above, must resemble those of Jesus Christ or of the Apostles of Jesus Christ. The life of the priest must be exemplary of what the priest represents. The priestly office demands integrity in daily life and pastoral practice. In African politics there is some level of corruption that is cancerous. Pastoral integrity calls the priest to be a model of sacrificial veracity through living according to the principles of the Kingdom of God that is governed by values such as love, honesty, and integrity. This calls for the ethics of morality and holiness in the life of the priest. The priestly office is dignified if it manifests the divine presence of the Lord Jesus Christ. In the world of the 'Ministries' priestly dignity is manifested through the presence of the Holy Spirit which enables the priest to speak in tongues and perform miracles. Being filled by the Holy Spirit and performing miracles to respond to the needs of society makes the priest worthy in the community. Priestly dignity is worthiness in the eyes of society ascribed to a priest because of what they offer to the community. The priest must bring salvation to the community in the here and now. Surely Africans in general and the Ndebele in particular do understand the eschatological meaning of salvation as espoused by the mainline churches, however a priest makes positive impact if they can save people in their present day needs in the socio-economic and political needs of society. The Ndebele are inclined towards present salvation than salvation located in the unknown eschatological future of the church.

Dignity varies from denomination to denomination. There is a tendency in Matabo for people to view their own priest as the real priest compared to priests from other denominations. Therefore, the dignity of a priest may be located only in the membership of his/her denomination. There is also the possibility of people offering selective dignity depending on their needs from different priests belonging to different denominations. Presently, the most social popular priests are from Pentecostal and charismatic churches and ministries because they are regarded spiritually powerful. The power of *Umfundisi* is based on the ability to demonstrate being filled with the Holy Spirit enabling one to perform extra ordinary events such as healing in the name of Jesus Christ. The spiritual functionality and connectedness to Christ by the *Umfundisi* is equal to dignity.

Umfundisi must remain connected to Christ for authenticity. All mysterious and strange performances by *Umfundisi* must be done in the name of Jesus Christ or the Holy Spirit to avoid being viewed as a magician. The source of the dignity of the *Umfundisi* is the Christ (Osunwokeh 2014, 169). *Umfundisi* is the dwelling place of the Christ and is therefore expected to perform the miracles that Jesus Christ performed during his earthly sojourn. In contemporary Matabo a priest who does not perform extra ordinary acts is viewed as not being filled by the Holy Spirit. Therefore, pastors perform miracles and ask their congregants to perform extra ordinary acts as a way of responding to the religious worldviews of the context. A priest must be Christ like but at the same time must be like the spirit mediums who are able to respond to extra ordinary human needs. Osunwokeh says that *Umfundisi* shares the dignity of Christ "…which no earthly instrument could alter; mankind, nature, luck or fate. All through his earthly life the divine will of the Father was upheld, and the dignity remained intact…This is also a dignity which is not determined by his human person, possession, and state but by his essence as a priest '*alter Christus*'" (2014, 170).

In the Ndebele worldview a spirit medium or *Sangoma* is a representative figure of the gods or ancestors (Wreford 2005; Jonker 2008). The spirit medium is endowed with the powers of the gods as long as they are filled by spiritual powers. Similarly, when the Ndebele see *Umfundisi* they imagine seeing God the Christ through the *Umfundisi*. The *Umfundisi* is also viewed as a representative figure of the presence of the Christ. As a result of the above Osunwokeh (2014, 170) argues that "So, it is logical to conclude that there is no other basis, no other point of reference that can be adduced for priestly dignity other than the highly dignified priesthood of Christ that a priest shares. So, one may conclude [...] that there is one priesthood, that is Christ and that there is one source of the priesthood that is Christ" (2014, 170).

6 Conclusion

The hybridity nature of Christianity in Matabo creates a particular type of a priest who should be able to respond to the needs of people whose cultural underpinnings have intertwined Christianity with African Traditional Religious beliefs and practices into an inseparable reality. Armed with this understanding we are beginning to have priests (pastors) who are keen to perform miracles such as raising the dead, giving people material and monetary prosperity in the name of Jesus. In the African context of the Ndebele, salvation is in the here and now and therefore priests are struggling to make Christianity offer salvation from the socio-economic and political challenges in the here and now. Priests are also responding to the Ndebele's inherent belief in spirits by performing exorcisms and deliverance services. The priest is a spirit medium endowed with the power of the Holy Spirit among the Ndebele people of Matabo.

Bibliography

Bozongwana, Wallace. 1983. *Ndebele Religion Customs*. Mambo Press: Gweru.

Gehman, Richard J. 1989. *African Traditional Religion*. Nairobi: East African Educational Publishers Ltd.

Jonker, Ingrid. 2008. *A Study of How a Sangoma Makes Sense of Her 'Sangomahood' through Narrative*. Pretoria: Doctoral dissertation. https://repository.up.ac.za/handle/2263/26475 (01.12.2021).

King, Brian. 2012. "We Pray at the Church in the Day and Visit the Sangomas at Night: Health Discourses and Traditional Medicine in Rural South Africa." *Annals of the Association of American Geographers* 102:1173–1181.

Laleye, Issiaka-Prosper. 1981. "La Personnalité Africaine: Pierres d'attente pour une Société Globale." In *Combats pour un Christianisme Africain*, edited by Vincent Mulago, Ngindu Mushete, and Gérard Buakasa Tulu Kia Mpansu, Kinshasa: Faculté de Théologie Catholique, 137–147.

Louw, Daniel J. 1998. *A Pastoral Hermeneutics of Care and Encounter: A Theological Design for Basic Theory, Anthropology, Method and Therapy*. Cape Town: Lux Verbi.

Mbiti, John S. 1970. *Concepts of God in Africa*. London: SPCK.

Mbiti, John S. 1989. *African Religions and Philosophy*. Westlands: East African Educational Publishers Ltd.

Moyo, Herbert. 2014. "Dual Observances of African Traditional Religion and Christianity: Implications for Pastoral Care in the Pluralistic Religious Worldview of the Ndebele People of Malabo in Zimbabwe." *Journal of Theology for Southern Africa* 148:115–132.

Moyo, Herbert. 2019. "The Ritualization of Death and Dying: The Journey from the Living Living to the Living Dead in African Religions." In *Death and Dying: An Exercise in Comparative*

Philosophy of Religion, edited by Timothy D. Knepper, Lucy Bregman, and Mary Gottschalk, Cham: Springer, 115–124.

Ndeti, Kivuto. 1972. *Elements of Akamba Life*. Nairobi: East African Publishing House.

Osunwokeh, Clement I. 2014. "Priestly Dignity in the African Religious Context." *International Journal of Social Science Research* 2:166–178.

Patton, John. 2005. *Pastoral Care: An Essential Guide*. Nashville: Abingdon.

Wreford, Jo T., 2005. *Ukusebenza neThongo (Working with Spirit): The Role of Sangoma in Contemporary South Africa*. Cape Town: Doctoral dissertation. https://open.uct.ac.za/handle/11427/14073 (01.12.2021).

Harold D. Horell and Mai-Anh Le Tran
Religious Formation / Educating / Religious Knowledge

1 Introduction

The field of religious education offers a wide variety of approaches for forming people to understand religious beliefs and practices and educating about religion(s) and the religious dimensions of life. Is this wide variety a lush, fruitful garden or an overgrown one that is an impenetrable jungle? While it may seem to some to be an identity jungle or jumble, this brief historical account and conceptual analysis shows that the field of religious education is an abundant and even overflowing garden, offering rich resources for envisioning religious formation and education.

Written from the perspective of two religious educators working in the United States who have been deeply involved in the Religious Education Association, a North American-based yet internationally oriented academic organization, this entry explores the history of the modern religious education movement that began in the United States. We will consider how, after the founding of the Religious Education Association in 1903 and the subsequent emergence of religious education as an academic field of study, most of the early twentieth century religious educators adopted a humanistic educational perspective in exploring the religious dimensions of personal and social life. We will also discuss an effort in the mid twentieth century to reground approaches to religious education in theology, how this led to what some have considered to be an 'identity crisis' in the field of religious education, and then consider one significant response to this crisis. Based on our historical review of the development of religious education, we will offer a typology for understanding contemporary approaches to religious education. Our aim is to show how those who are interested in issues of religious formation and education, once they become familiar with the interplay of humanistic and theological perspectives within the field of religious education, can learn to see the pathways through the religious education garden and gain access to its fruit.

2 The Original Vision of the Field of Religious Education

In 1902, then-President of the University of Chicago William Rainey Harper issued a "Call for a Convention to Effect a National Organization for the Improvement of Religious and Moral Education Through the Sunday School and Other Agencies" (REA Archives no date). In February 1903, Harper's call for a convention brought together in Chicago three thousand persons from the United States, Canada, and four other countries, and led to the founding of the Religious Education Association (REA). The aims of the new organization were to improve the religious formation and education of Sunday schools, draw attention to the need for improvements in moral and religious education not only in congregations but in homes, public schools, and other agencies, and bring together scholars from educational and religious / theological / biblical fields of study to work collaboratively to generate research that could guide religious and moral instruction in a more intentional and academically rigorous manner (REA 1903, 237–239).

At the time of its founding, the field of religious education was part of the ongoing development of liberal theology. In fact, as historian Sidney E. Ahlstrom pointed out, "[a] revised estimate of the purpose and power of religious education" was "a vital element" in the liberal theology movement in the early to mid-twentieth century United States (2004, 761). Most of the founders and first-generation researchers in religious education, including such significant religious education theorists as George Albert Coe, Harrison S. Elliott, William C. Bower, and Sophia Lyon Fahs, grounded their work in liberal theology, most notably, in beliefs in the imminent presence of God in human personal and social life, the importance of human freedom, the capacity for altruistic action, and the importance of religious and moral education aimed at nurturing a capacity to care about others and the common good of society. Additionally, the Social Gospel movement was "a submovement within religious liberalism" (Ahlstrom 2004, 786). Some of the Social Gospel theologians contributed to the religious education movement, and many religious educators adopted the Social Gospel belief that authentic Christianity is guided by a commitment to social reconstruction.

There was a second significant influence on the development of the religious education movement. The movement was shaped by what Ahlstrom has called the high tide of humanitarian reform, that is, the reform campaign in the United States from the first half of the nineteenth to the mid twentieth century that focused on removing impediments to personal and social development (Ahlstrom 2004, 637). The reforms of this humanitarian campaign that had the greatest impact were the education crusade of Horace Mann that led to the development of the common school movement, and the "crusade to gain fuller rights for women and to give them a larger role in the countries life" (Ahlstrom 2004, 640–644, quote from 641). The campaign also included efforts to reform hospitals and prisons and to promote world peace (Ahlstrom 2004, 644–647).

Based on its central role in the ongoing development of liberal theology and absorption of the energetic spirit of humanitarian reform movements, the founders of the field imagined research in religious education leading to what Dean Frank Knight Sanders of Yale Divinity School called revolutionary advancements. Sanders kicked off the Second Annual Convention of the REA in March of 1904 with great zeal and confidence. He described the association's organizational character as "varied," "many-sided," yet strongly "centralized" and "federated," and its work as possessing the potential to invigorate the investigation and formation of religious life in multiple domains. "The field is limitless and inviting," Sanders declared (1904, 3). Sanders and other first generation religious education researchers imagined religious educators contributing to efforts to promote the religious and moral development of persons, teach about religion in private and public schools and other social contexts, form people in religious beliefs and practices within families and religious communities, and educate people to understand the role of religion in public life. Most of the founders of the Religious Education Association were North American, white, male, mainline Protestants, and they sought to create an organization that would welcome women as well as men into the field of religious education and would have an international reach in uniting people of all races, religions, and nationalities in a shared effort to foster the religious development of humanity. To what extent these founding aspirations were actualized through inclusive practices and perspectives is subject for another discussion. (The wide scope of the interests of the founders of the REA is evident in the proceedings of the founding convention, see REA 1903.)

The founders of the REA envisioned religious education as a field at the crossroads of education and religion/theology. However, two concerns led the majority of first-generation religious education theorists to place greater emphasis on education than theology. First, in addition to being inspired by the humanitarian campaign of that era, Coe and the other scholars of the field at the time were interested in the then-influential theories of teaching, learning, and curriculum development that were grounded in the humanistic perspective of the seventeenth to nineteenth century Age of Enlightenment in Europe. They were also influenced by John Dewey's educational philosophy. Dewey posited that all education should be experiential and focused on equipping people for life in society. Hence, Coe and most of the first generation of researchers in religious education focused more on education than theology because they wanted to incorporate what they considered to be valuable insights from modern educational theories and approaches into the educational efforts of churches, synagogues, and other religious bodies (Coe 1919, 3–10; Elliott 1940, 34–62).

Second, Coe sought to distance himself as much as possible from his own theological convictions in order to view religion as a human universal and to investigate religious beliefs and practices with the disinterested eye of an objective, scientific observer (1916, ix–xv). Due in large part to the influence of Coe, many of the early religious education theorists thought that if they could step back from their personal theological convictions and the theology of their religious community, they could work together to understand how parents, religion teachers in schools, Sunday school teachers, and other religious education practitioners within and beyond religious communities could teach people to understand religion(s) from an objective viewpoint and nurture religious growth as the culminating aspect of human development. (The understanding of religious education presented here developed between 1903 and 1950. It is expressed in its fully developed form in Elliot 1950, 195–202.) Additionally, Coe thought the church needed to be reformed and updated if it were to thrive in the modern era. He envisioned the "Christian tradition" as a "living being" but as "one needing surgery" (1916, xii–xiii). Following Coe's lead, many of the first-generation researchers in religious education were interested in teaching people to step back from their theological convictions and examine them critically so they could, to use Coe's image, provide surgical treatments for the illnesses afflicting the religious bodies of which they were a part.

3 The Original Vision Challenged

From the beginning, the founding vision of the field of religious education was challenged, with its underlying liberal theological convictions being the most frequent target of critique. In the 1930s, growing concerns about what came to called liberal religious education were expressed in Norman Egbert Richardson's *The Christ of the Classroom* (1931) and Walter Scott Athearn's *The Minister and the Teacher* (1932), and the liberal theological presuppositions that undergirded the religious education movement received a blistering critique in Elmer G. Homrighausen's *Christianity in America: A Crisis* (1936). A tipping point was reached after H. Shelton Smith offered a sharp and detailed critique of liberal religious education in *Faith and Nurture* (1941). Stated briefly, critics argued that liberal religious educators did not attend fully enough to the limitations of human finitude, the reality of sin, human beings need for and dependence on God, and the distinctiveness of the revelation of God in Christianity, including, and for many, especially in Christian Scripture. The significant shift that took place at this time led to the increasing use of the term 'Christian education'. Rather than focusing on the religious development of humanity, many religious educators now focused on how Christian communities formed and educated people, especially children, in Christian faith.

Several decades of development in the field of religious education were then encapsulated in Randolph Crump Miller's *The Clue to Christian Education* (1950). Miller argued that as Christian educators balanced concerns for theology and education, theology must always come first. From a theological perspective, Christian educators should consider the relationship between God and learners and then consider what curriculum would best nurture the ongoing development of this relationship (1950, 5). Frank E. Gaebelein's *The Pattern of God's Truth* (1954) and Lewis Joseph Sherrill's *The Gift of Power* (1955) also made important contributions to the field of religious education during this era. While they offered differing approaches to Christian education, they grounded their views in the shared conviction that Christian education must begin with an openness or receptivity to God's redeeming truth and power at work in the lives of fallible and sinful persons and communities. Like Miller, Gaebelein and Sherrill placed Christian theology at the center of Christian education. However, they went beyond Miller in showing that in addition to drawing insight from the academic field of education, Christian educators can utilize resources from depth psychology, philosophy, the study of the arts, and a wide range of other fields of study in nurturing people to be open and responsive to the presence of God in their lives.

The critiques of liberal religious education and the development of Christian education enabled the field of religious education to continue to evolve and adapt to the social and cultural changes of that took place in the first half of the twentieth century. They also ensured that the field of religious education remained rooted in the theological perspectives of mainline North American Christian denominations that were primarily white and middle class. Still, they did not dampen entirely the expansive and inclusive founding vision of the field. Additionally, questions about the nature and purpose of religious education continued to be raised, and the field was plunged into an identity crisis. To consider how religious educators responded to this crisis we can look ahead to one effort to mark the semi-sesquicentennial of the founding of the REA.

4 *Who Are We?* Reimagining Religious Education

In 1978, on the 75th anniversary of the REA, Professor of Religion and Education John H. Westerhoff III of Duke University Divinity School edited a collection of essays from twenty-one contributors to chart the identity crisis in the academic guild of religious education. Titled *Who Are We? The Quest for a Religious Education* (1978), the volume offered a topography of the diverse and richly textured scholarly landscape of religious education as it had developed from the founding of the REA to that point in time. In the introductory and concluding essays of the collection, Westerhoff argued that the identity crisis in the field could be overcome if religious educators remembered the history of the religious education movement and refined and then reaffirmed the expansive founding vision of the field.

In his introductory essay, Westerhoff summarized the expansive vision of religious education developed by the first generation of religious education researchers, noting that the founders of the REA sought "to broaden the nation's understanding of religious education, and to generate new thought in this foundational aspect of national life" as well as to reach out "ecumenically and internationally" (Westerhoff 1978, 2). He added that the founding vision of the field had not been realized fully and that the members of the REA were still mainly "older liberal intellectuals." Yet, he also noted that the organization had benefited from "the gradual addition of women, blacks, Roman Catholics, Jews, and Canadians" (Westerhoff 1978, 3), and that at that time "significant numbers of Jewish, Roman Catholic, and Protestant educators comprise the REA" (Westerhoff 1978, 3). Westerhoff suggested that religious educators should work to realize the founding vision of the field more fully, and that this effort could enable them to contribute to efforts to fashion national "unity and purpose" in the face of new socio-cultural, economic, and political realities (Westerhoff 1978, 2).

In his concluding essay, Westerhoff affirmed the continuing importance of the founding aim of the Religion Education Association to unite people interested in the intersection of education and religion. Reflecting the concerns voiced about liberal religious education over the preceding seventy-five years, Westerhoff added that religious education researchers needed to examine educational approaches critically from a religious perspective. He wrote:

> Education is an intentional, valuable, long lasting, interpersonal activity of the whole person which involves knowing and understanding in depth and breath. The religious is concerned with the depth dimension of life, people's ultimate concerns and commitments, and the search for the transcendent. Insofar as any educational effort deals with patterns of belief or commitment concerning goodness, truth, or beauty it is religious. In one important sense, then, all education is religious. Similarly, a concern for religion implies a critical look at education. (Westerhoff 1978, 264)

In accord with the founding vision of the field, Westerhoff also called for religious educators to renew their commitment to educating people about the world's various religions in order to prepare them to address issues of religion in public life responsibly. And he noted the importance of education about Christian, Jewish, and Humanist worldviews, religious education in church and synagogue schools, and catechesis (which is education to embrace the beliefs and practices of a religious tradition) (1978, 266–272).

Additionally, Westerhoff suggested one significant revision to the founding vision of the field of the religious education. In accord with the critics of liberal religious education, Westerhoff called religious educators to center their religious education outlooks in theology. He wrote: "Our crisis of self-understanding and our fuzziness of identity is essentially theological" (Westerhoff 1978, 6).

In discussing the theological foundations of religious education, Westerhoff, drawing insight from Ian Knox' *Above or Within?*, asked: "does God *erupt* into human affairs from within the world itself, or does God *irrupt* into human affairs from above and outside the world?" (Westerhoff 1970, 7). Westerhoff's response was, essentially, "both." Taking into account the theological beliefs of liberal religious educators and the critiques of these beliefs that had been voiced during the preceding fifty years, he posited that religious educators should balance a sense that God reveals Godself by being present to humanity through the natural world and everyday life experiences (God's immanence) with a sense that God also reveals Godself supernaturally as Other (God's transcendence).

The eighteen chapters of *Who Are We?* support the analysis Westerhoff presents in his introductory and concluding essays. Chapters 1 through chapter 9, originally published from 1903 to 1953, document the original vision of the religious education movement and the shift from a focus on human religiousness to an emphasis on the theological foundations of education in faith. In the latter part of the book, the especially noteworthy chapter by Olivia Pearl Stokes connects efforts to educate in the Black Church with the religious education movement. Stokes proposed a teaching-learning process for black ethnic church schools that is based on Paulo Freire's problem-posing approach to education (Stokes 1978, 218–234). In Stokes's essay, and the editorial decision to include it, we detect the trace of a distinctive stream of not a liberal but rather a *liberationist* orientation for religious education, one that critiques both liberal religious education and theo-centric Christian education's inattentiveness to the plight of minoritized persons and communities facing oppressive social realities. Stokes is one of only two women who contributed to *Who Are We?* – while the REA sought to welcome women into the religious education guild from its founding onwards, it was not until the 1970s that gender inclusivity began to emerge with notable momentum in the field. Essays by Gerald Sloyan and Alvin I. Schiff tell the stories of education in faith in Catholic and Jewish communities, respectively, and how these efforts intersect with the inclusive vision of the field of religious education (1978, 123–132, 181–192). The remaining chapters in the last half of the book present various proposals offered from 1965 to 1974 for envisioning the interplay of religion and education in efforts to form or educate religiously.

Who Are We? expressed the spirit of the times, and this spirit has continued to hold sway in religious education. Most religious educators from then till now have opted to continue to work from the broad and inclusive understanding of religious education that was first articulated by the founders of the Religious Education Association in 1903. Most religious educators have also situated the field of religious education in relation to the field of theology. The most significant development since the publication of *Who Are We?* has been the rise of practical theology as a field of study that has had a pervasive influence in the ongoing development of religious education. In the next section we will explore the ongoing development of the religious education movement from the 1970s to the present by looking at three distinct, although somewhat overlapping, types of contemporary approaches to religious formation and education.

5 Present-day Approaches to Forming and Educating Religiously

A typology is a way of categorizing similar things, in this case, similar approaches to religious formation and education. While there are a range of religious educational approaches of each type, approaches of each type have similar features, not unlike the family resemblances of a lush garden's flora and fauna.

The first type consists of a group of approaches that envisions religious education as an interdisciplinary field of study closely *aligned with* practical theology. Religious educational approaches of this type situate religious education in relation to theology and balance religious/theological and educational modes of analysis. They view the field of religious education as a continuous effort from 1903 to the present to understand the religious dimensions of the human person and/or the human longing for God, to explore the fundamental dynamics of teaching and learning, and bring these two together in considering how best to educate in faith. In *Who Are We?* Westerhoff presents one of the early sketches of this type. Classic articulations are expressed in Thomas H. Groome's *Christian Religious Education* (1980), Mary Elizabeth Moore's *Education for Continuity and Change* (1988), Charles R. Foster's *Educating Congregations* ([1994] 2006), and more recently, Boyung Lee's *Transforming Congregations Through Community* (2013). A fairly recent expression of this type that subsumes religious education within practical theology as a distinctive educational subfield of theology was presented by Hyun-Sook Kim. Kim pointed out that liberal theologian Friedrich Schleiermacher thought of practical theology as the 'crown' of theology; he claimed that all other theological sub-disciplines should support the efforts of practical theologians to educate people to integrate their theological beliefs into their everyday lives (Kim 2007, 419–420). Kim added that Schleiermacher's vision of practical theology was never realized, and she suggested that the field of religious education emerged as a way of redefining practical theology and reclaiming a focus on educating in faith as being a central concern of the field of theology (Kim 2007, 420–421, 431). Kim also suggested that it is now time for religious education to return home by relocating itself within practical theology (Kim 2007, 431–433). Overall, type one contemporary approaches consider how educational theories and methods that have been used in the past can be refashioned or further developed in the present and future to nurture a viable theological understanding of life and the world.

The second type is a group of approaches that envision religious education as a multi-disciplinary rather than interdisciplinary field of study *integrated within* practical theology. The approaches to religious education developed by Gaebelein and Sherrill, who were mentioned earlier, as well as the approach of C. Ellis Nelson (1967), are forerunners of this type. Approaches of this type situate religious education in relation to theology, balance theological analysis with an effort to use the resources of the field of religious education as well as those found in other fields of inquiry to encourage full personal and social development within specific life contexts. One expression of this approach is found in the work of Richard Robert Osmer.[1] Osmer identified himself as a religious educator and practical theologian. He defined practical theology as "that branch of Christian theology that seeks to construct action-guiding theories of Christian praxis in particular social contexts" (Osmer 2005, xiv). Osmer eschewed what he calls a generic, or single focus model of religious education (Osmer 2005, xiii). Instead, he has opted for a multi-disciplinary approach, stating that "multidisciplinary thinking marshals the perspectives and analysis of many fields to understand complex, dynamic systems out of the rec-

---

[1] For brief accounts of other expressions of this approach see the biographies of Hulda Niebuhr, Nelle Morton, and other significant mid-twentieth century religious educators in Barbara Anne Keeley's *Faith of our Foremothers* (1987).

ognition that no single frame or perspective can adequately understand everything going on in such systems" (Osmer 2005, 60–61).

In contrast to approaches of the first type, approaches of the second type have a heightened concern for religious education as a multimodal and multi-faceted mode of inquiry; they are less concerned with defining religious education as a distinct and historically continuous field of academic and pastoral inquiry that can be distinguished from other fields, such as pastoral care and counseling, pastoral leadership, and ethics, by an intentional, interdisciplinary focus on human religiousness and human learning. For instance, Osmer's primary focus is on using multiples lenses of analysis to explore "Christian praxis in particular social contexts." (Osmer 2005, xiv) Then, he draws insight from educational and religious educational as well as other modes of analysis to discuss ways of refashioning the teaching ministry of Christian congregations in these contexts. According to Osmer, after using multiple modes of analysis to understand the dynamics of life in specific life contexts, practical theologians can discuss the goals of the teaching ministry of congregations in those contexts in terms of handing on the teachings of Scripture and tradition, providing moral formation, and equipping Christians to discern the Spirit's guidance in their lives (Osmer 2005, 54–55). Osmer envisioned efforts to realize the goals of the teaching ministry of congregations being animated by a willingness and desire to participate in the theo-drama of the continual unfolding of God's actions through the church (Osmer 2005, 203–236).

Another example of a multimodal and multi-faceted, type two approach is found in *Religious Educators are the Future* by Dori Baker and Patrick B. Reyes. They highlight the work of religious educators who are "re-purposing their religious traditions" to address pressing "matters of human existence" by combing an educational perspective with other modes of analysis in hybrid perspectives (Baker and Reyes 2020, 1). According to Baker and Reyes, "[r]eligious educators heal the world." They "tether religious education to matters of human existence," as they consider issues "from climate change to mass incarceration, from racism to international immigration" (Baker and Reyes 2020, 1). As envisioned by Baker and Reyes, religious education encompasses "faith leaders" ministering in the "streets" and "educators and activities" who address a wide range of issues and needs in a vast array of contexts in ways that form and educate people to view their lives from a faith perspective (Baker and Reyes 2020, 1). Additionally, Baker's and Reyes's approach could be delineated further as a distinctive subcategory of type two approach in that it sustains the liberationist orientation advanced by the previous generation (Stokes 1982; Freire 2018) and stands alongside more recent works by Anne Streaty Wimberly (2005), Allen Moore (1988), Yolanda Smith (2004), Daniel Schipani (1988), and Evelyn Parker (2017). In their focus on pressing human needs, these theorists show how the spirit of the humanitarian reform campaign of the early twentieth century and the theology of the Social Gospel continue to inform the ongoing development of the religious education movement.

The third and least common type of contemporary approaches to religious education envisions religious education as an educational field of inquiry and practice, and calls religious educators to *resist or reframe the turn to theology* in religious education. One expression of a type three approach is found in the work of James Michael Lee, who first presented the approach in fully developed form in *The Shape of Religious Instruction* (1971). Lee argued that religious instruction, like all other modes of education, needs to be based on scientific studies of teaching and learning. He contended that when theology trumps educational science, religious education too often becomes a form of religious imperialism or religious indoctrination. Like Coe and other early twentieth century religious educators, James Michael Lee thought religious educators need to distance themselves from the field of theology if they want to teach people to reflect critically on their theological convictions and those of their religious community.

The third type also includes the approaches developed by those whom Kieran Scott has labeled "reconceptualist" religious educators, a group which includes, most notably, Maria Harris and Gabriel Moran (Scott 1984, 333–337; see also Harris and Moran 1998). Based on the claim that the complex and polyvalent religious experiences of persons and groups have not and can never be explored fully in any theological system, the reconceptualists reject Miller's contention that theology is the key to religious education. Instead, they call on religious educators to develop an educational language for naming, reflecting on, and learning from religious experience. In *Teaching and Religious Imagination* (1987), Maria Harris offered one model for how this can be done. She discussed the connection between religious experiences and the imagination and uses the language of teaching to show how religious educators can guide people to reflect on and learn from imaginative experiences in ways that can enable them to become more aware of the religious dimensions of life.

Like Coe and other first-generation religious education theorists, the reconceptualists call religious educators to step back from their particular theological commitments and those of their religious communities. However, as Moran contends, they do not aspire as Coe did to view religion from a scientific, objective, and totally disinterested perspective. Rather, Moran argued that religious education is "neither proselytization nor antiseptic observation" (Moran in Westerhoff 1978, 237). Religious educators should, according to Moran, begin with a deep interest in religious knowing, that is, in exploring various ways people learn about religion and learn to be religious throughout the life cycle (what Moran calls lifelong learning) and in all aspects of life, including family life, work, leisure or recreation, as well as in education that takes place in schools (what Moran calls life-wide education) (Moran 2016, 214–231).

In conclusion, in *Who Are We?* Westerhoff suggested that education is valued because it "involves knowing and understanding in depth and breath." He then claimed that "the religious is concerned with the depth dimension of life," and that all education is religious insofar as it deals with this depth dimension, and especially with issues of "goodness, truth, and beauty." Westerhoff also noted that a concern for balancing educational and religious outlooks has been central to the religious education movement since its founding (Westerhoff 1978, 264). The three types of contemporary approaches to religious education that we have described continue the effort to balance concerns for education and the religious. However, each type envisions this balancing in a different way. What we have described as type one contemporary approaches envision forming and educating religiously as a process, essentially, of theological education, with religious educators beginning with clearly discernible interests in one or more aspects of education in faith, which they approach from a theological perspective that is developed through an alignment with the subfield of practical theology. Type two contemporary approaches are grounded in the efforts of those whose primary academic affiliation is with the field of practical theology, and who as practical theologians, and in some instance also as liberation theologians, address issues of educating in faith. They combine an effort to develop a theological understanding of the depth or religious dimension of life in particular personal and social contexts with a concern for constructing multi-disciplinary approaches for educating for deep religious understanding and religious praxis in these contexts. Type three approaches begin with the premise that the depth / religious dimension of life is dynamic, complex, and polyvalent and can be known most fully through an intentional educational process.

As stated earlier, while a professional society like the Religious Education Association aspires in its aims to be international and interreligious, many of its membership are scholars of *Christian* religious education. Thus, while they may be scholars who adhere to approaches of all three types proffered above, and while there is a continuum of positions demarking the preferential options for the religious/theological versus educational concerns, there is a shared assumption that the foundation of Christian religious educational work is a commitment to understanding the depth dimension of life in the light of the saving and liberating life of Jesus the Christ. Religious education theorists of other faith traditions ground their work in other worldviews and belief systems (e. g., Judaism, Islam, Buddhism). Part of the richness of religious education is that it provides a forum for people of differing religious traditions to discuss the intersection of education and religious sensibilities.

We propose that the field of religious education be envisioned as a verdant garden dotted with fruit of many kinds and colors. There are differing religious educational needs in the diverse life contexts of our contemporary world, and we suggest that with its rich variety of nourishing fruit, the field of religious education has much to offer those who can navigate the pathways of its garden. We also propose that religious education scholars seek a fuller sense of the history of the religious education movement and explore more fully the strengths and limitations of various ways of providing religious formation and education so that they can guide people through the religious education garden. The perceived identity crisis in the field of religious education festered because religious educators too often do not have a clear enough sense of how the distinctive identity of the field has developed over the course of the past nearly 120 years. Additionally, developments in the field of religious education over the past seventy plus years suggest that religious education may be best situated as a theological discipline, a generative co-conspirator with practical theology. However, an understanding of the history of the field also suggests that religious educators should include in their approaches to religious formation and education an intentional, educational concern for teaching people to reflect critically on the religious dimensions of life and on their theological convictions and those of their religious community. At the same time, this history suggests that it is not easy to bring together a theological (theo-centric) perspective and an educational concern for human religious development and liberation. While religious education may find a home within theology, religious educators – at least those who have an expansive sense of the religious dimensions of personal and social life – may never be fully at home there. And it may not be such a terrible plight.

Finally, we have discussed the religious education movement that began in the United States in 1903. From its start, this movement has sought to expand and become ecumenically Christian, inter-religious and international, and since the latter part of the twentieth century the movement has connected with traditions and contemporary efforts to educate religiously in various faith traditions and contexts throughout the world. Today, the Christian religious education garden discussed in this essay is ever more verdant within the biodiversity of multifaith and interfaith expressions of religious formation and education. It is also ever strengthened by better attunement to how liberationist religious education advances both theological and ontological freedom for human societies and the created world. If we could unleash our imagination and explore the varied pathways through the contemporary religious education gardens, we would have at our disposal rich resources for faith formation and education.

Bibliography

Ahlstrom, Sidney E. 2004. *A Religious History of the American People*. New Haven: Yale University Press.
Athearn, Walter S. 1932. *The Minister and the Teacher: An Interpretation of Current Trends in Christian Education*. New York: Century.
Baker, Dori, and Patrick B. Reyes. 2020. "Religious Educators are the Future." *Religious Education* 115:1–9.
Coe, George A. 1916. *The Psychology of Religion*. Chicago: University of Chicago Press.
Coe, George A. 1919. *A Social Theory of Religious Education*. New York: Charles Scribner's Sons.
Elliott, Harrison S. 1940. *Can Religious Education Be Christian?* New York: Macmillan.
Elliott, Harrison S. 1950. "Reflections of a Religious Educator." *Religious Education* 45:195–202.
Foster, Charles R. [1994] 2006. *Educating Congregations: The Future of Christian Education*. Nashville: Abingdon.
Freire, Paulo. 2018. *Pedagogy of the Oppressed: 50th Anniversary Edition*. New York: Bloomsbury Academic.

Gaebelein, Frank E. 1954. *The Pattern of God's Truth*. Colorado Springs: Association of Christian Schools.
Groome, Thomas H. 1980. *Christian Religious Education: Sharing our Story and Vision*. San Francisco: Harper and Row.
Harris, Maria. 1987. *Teaching and Religious Imagination*. San Francisco: Harper and Row.
Harris, Maria, and Gabriel Moran. 1998. *Reshaping Religious Education: Conversations on Contemporary Practice*. Louisville: Westminster John Knox.
Homrighausen, Elmer G. 1936. *Christianity in America: A Crisis*. New York: Abingdon Press.
Keeley, Barbara A. 1997. *Faith of our Foremothers: Women Changing Religious Education*. Louisville: Westminster John Knox.
Kim, Hyun-Sook. 2007. "The Hermeneutical Praxis Paradigm and Practical Theology." *Religious Education* 102:419–436.
Lee, Boyung. 2013. *Transforming Congregations through Community: Faith Formation from the Seminary to the Church*. Louisville: Westminster John Knox.
Lee, James M. 1971. *The Shape of Religious Instruction*. Mishawaka: Religious Education Press.
Miller, Randolph C. 1950. *The Clue to Christian Education*. New York: Charles Scribner's Sons.
Moore, Allen J. 1988. *Religious Education as Social Transformation*. Birmingham, AL: Religious Education Press.
Moore, Mary E. 1988. *Education for Continuity and Change: A New Model for Christian Religious Education*. Nashville: Abingdon.
Moran, Gabriel. 2016. *Missed Opportunities: Rethinking Catholic Traditions*. Bloomington: Universe.
Nelson, C. Ellis. 1967. *Where Faith Begins*. Richmond: John Knox.
Osmer, Richard R. 2005. *The Teaching Ministry of Congregations*. Louisville: Westminster John Knox.
Parker, Evelyn. 2017. *Between Sisters: Emancipatory Hope out of Tragic Relationships*. Eugene: Wipf & Stock.
Religious Education Association. 1903. *Proceedings of the First Annual Convention, Chicago, February 10–12, 1903*. Chicago: Executive Office of the Association.
Religious Education Association Archives. RG 74 A. No date. New Haven: Yale Divinity School Library.
Richardson, Norman E. 1931. *The Christ of the Classroom: How to Teach Evangelical Christianity*. New York: Macmillan.
Sanders, Frank K. 1904. "The President's Annual Address. Paper Read at Second Convention of the Religious Education Association, in Philadelphia." (unpublished).
Scott, Kieran. 1984. "Three Traditions of Religious Education." *Religious Education* 79:327–339.
Schipani, Daniel S. 1988. *Religious Education Encounters Liberation Theology*. Birmingham, AL: Religious Education Press.
Sherrill, Lewis J. 1963. *The Gift of Power*. New York: Macmillan.
Smith, H. Shelton. 1941. *Faith and Nurture*. New York: Charles Scribner's Sons.
Smith, Yolanda, Y. 2004. *Reclaiming the Spirituals: New Possibilities for African American Religious Education*. Cleveland: Pilgrim.
Stokes, Olivia P. 1982. "Black Theology: A Challenge to Religious Education." In *Religious Education and Theology*, edited by Norma Thompson, Birmingham, AL: Religious Education Press, 71–99.
Westerhoff, John H., ed. 1978. *Who Are We? The Quest for Religious Education*. Birmingham, AL: Religious Education Press.
Wimberly, Anne S. ²2005. *Soul Stories: African American Christian Education*. Nashville: Abingdon.

Marcel Barnard, Johan Cilliers and Cas Wepener
Rituals / Liturgies / Performances

1 Introduction

There is good reason to introduce the cultural-anthropological notion of ritual into practical theology. As we have shown elsewhere[1], the notion forces the researcher who uses the notion to be constantly aware, not only of his or her own cultural roots, but also of the anthropological and cultural contexts in which the rituals he or she investigates are performed.

1.1 Ritual and its Cultural and Anthropological Context

The notion of ritual finds its origin in cultural anthropology rather than in (practical) theology. It is, however, obvious that a religion without rituals is not conceivable. Burnt paper offerings in Chinese ancestral worship, the hajj to Mecca in Islam, the Passover Seder in Jewish religion, the Eucharist or the Holy Supper in Christianity, they are just as many rituals, even though each religion still has separate indications for those rituals. Since this handbook examines religious practices related to specific cultural contexts and positions, the cultural-anthropological notion of ritual presents itself as a very suitable one. Ritual is indeed determined by its anthropological and cultural context, and this also holds true for religious ritual. That does not exclude that denominational, ecclesiological, and theological notions also play a role in the design of religious ritual, but that is not the primary focus of this chapter.

1.2 The Contexts of the Authors and the Contexts Investigated

Although as authors of this article we work in different continents – Europe and Africa – we are all three white and male, to a high degree trained in Western methodologies and theologies, and teach at academic theological institutions that have Protestant, mainly Reformed, roots. However, the institutions we work at – and we ourselves – have developed extensively ecumenically speaking over the past decades. Moreover, we are ordained ministers in established Protestant Churches in the Netherlands and South Africa. Thus, we write from particular perspectives, in

---

[1] This chapter is based on and partly taken over from Barnard, Marcel, Johan Cilliers and Cas J. Wepener. 2014. *Worship in the Network Culture. Liturgical Ritual Studies. Fields and Methods, Concepts and Metaphors*. Liturgia Condenda 28. Leuven / Paris / Walpole: Peeters. The article therefore does not pretend to offer original research.

the awareness that this is only one option among others. More so, we are well aware that our perspective is a very dominant perspective, that all too often has outstripped or overpowered other perspectives.

Nevertheless, we were part of a team that researched worship practices of an African Independent Church, which have hardly been academically studied before (Wepener et al. 2019). The songs of the congregation, the dancing feet circling around in the Xhosa hut, the sermons of the pastor, the evil spirits that fled the power of the Holy Spirit, the talking drums and the sonorous sound of the vuvuzelas, and the smell of the burning herbs in the worship space, were almost never before presented to the wider academic community of practical theologians. We aimed to introduce these churches and their members to the academic discourse of Liturgical Studies. Thus, our project challenged the nature of practical theology and Liturgical Studies and their more Western and ecclesial interests. In the research project, we worked closely with people from those churches and the culture in which they are embedded. In other words, we chose an academic research practice of transcultural and, in a sense, transreligious understanding. By doing so, we did not forget our own localities and positions, nor did we cherish the naïve illusion that our report of the investigation would bridge all cultural differences. We identified the culture of the described worship as rich traditional, rural African (Wepener 2015).

On the other hand, we also focused our attention on an annual meeting in a hypermodern hospital somewhere in the Netherlands commemorating people who died in that hospital over the last year. Relatives came to the meeting and wrote the names of their deceased loved ones on a stone, which was laid on a table with all the other stones during the meeting, while the names of the deceased were called. The presiding chaplain said that the collecting of the stones had its parallel in people collecting their memories and thoughts "with the wish that memory will give power for the future" (Barnard, Cilliers, and Wepener 2014, 23). Here it was much more our intention to make clear how religiosity takes shape in highly secularized societies. Consequently, the culture that determined the ritual was therefore mainly identified as a secular one. It is no coincidence that a new ritual is 'invented' in such a context (Hobsbawm and Ranger, 1999).

In another research project, conducted by principal investigator Dr. Rima Nasrallah from Beirut, we learnt of the experiences of Lebanese women from Maronite or Orthodox backgrounds who married a reformed husband (Nasrallah 2015). Abiding to Lebanese norms, they became reformed by marrying, that is to say, nominally. However, in reality they developed a unique and hybrid spirituality mixing different traditions and dynamically moving between them. Icons, rosaries, and a Bible are found in the same room. The women celebrate the three holy days of Easter in for instance the Orthodox Church but visit the reformed church on Sunday. "The physical objects and ritual acts are used to complement the highly verbal and cerebral spirituality they meet in the Protestant church. On the other hand, the Reformed emphasis on scripture and theological reflection is laid as a background for the elaborate repertoire of spiritual expression they have developed", writes Nasrallah (2015).

Incense-burning and singing protestant hymns go hand in hand. Here culture is understood as hybrid.

In all cases, ritual is an adequate term to describe the religious act and the symbols that accompany them. We would say that a ritual is Christian liturgy when Christian sources and beliefs play a role in a ritual practice.

2 Culture and Cult; Ritual Criticism

In this section we discuss the relationship between culture and religious rituals, that is, the relationship between culture and cult. They can both be described as play in the sense of coming into contact with an outside. The close connection between culture and cult requires a critical approach to ritual practices: rituals confirm, but can also criticize, existing social, political, and religious practices.

2.1 Culture and Cult as Play

It is characteristic of humans to reach out to the outside world, eventually even to a world beyond the empirically observable. The Dutch phenomenologist and theologian van der Leeuw calls this reaching out playing. He says:

> Man is playing man. His whole life is nothing but an attempt to reach out of himself, to come into contact with something outside. He wants to play something. Breathing (…), eating (…), growing food (…), fighting (…), hunting, dressing, creating an image (…) are slightly different than just the product; they are a game and represent communication with the 'outside' according to certain rules. They are the origin of culture, but also of religion: while man cultivates (*colere*, culture) the world, he civilizes ('bildet') himself: while he civilizes himself, he also cultivates the world (van der Leeuw 1949, 249–250).

So, playing means reaching beyond you, breaking open a closed reality. In this play, two worlds or domains come together, and this is indicated by the notion of 'symbolizing'. The word symbol – from the Greek word συμβάλλειν – literally means bringing together. Playfully we enter into contact with another outside of us, and that game takes place according to agreed rules. The world is only accessible by means of playing, or, by means of symbols. The main symbol is language through which we know the world. If we write the other outside of us that we enter into contact with in a lowercase letter, we call the game culture. If we write Other with an uppercase letter, we call it cult. Culture and cult are in line with each other. "Inspiration and revelation, symbol and sacrament, culture and worship, poetry and prayer, art and religion are connected by all kinds of routes, although they are also separated by certain borders" (Barnard, Cilliers, and Wepener 2014, 41).

2.2 A Ritual-Critical Approach

Before we go on to explain some central notions, we will first make a comment about the relationship between ritual and culture that has direct consequences for how practical theologians study rituals.

Not every outside movement is in accordance with the holy texts of a religion, not every communication with the outside involves faith accordance to that religion. In other words, there are continuities as well as discontinuities between culture and religion, as famously elaborated for Christianity by H. Richard Niebuhr in his book *Christ and Culture* (1951) in five "typical answers" (Niebuhr [1951] 2001, 39–44): Christ against culture – which claims the exclusive authority of Christ and "resolutely rejects culture's claim to loyalty" (Niebuhr 2001, 45); the Christ of culture – which accommodates Christ to culture and identifies him with a specific culture; Christ above culture – which is neither anti-cultural nor accommodating, but searches for a synthesis of Christ and culture (roughly the roman-catholic position); Christ and culture in paradox, – which wants to honor and distinguish both "loyalty to Christ and responsibility for culture" (roughly the Lutheran position) (Niebuhr 2001, 149); and Christ the transformer of culture, which sees culture as "under God's sovereign rule, and that the Christian must carry on cultural work in obedience to the Lord" (roughly the reformed position) (Niebuhr 2001, 191). Even when rituals are critical of a specific culture, they take their symbols, language, and movements from that culture: "the stream of worship flows in the bed of culture, prayer is performed by way of poetics, the sacraments employ symbols, religion translates itself into the language of the arts" (Barnard, Cilliers and Wepener 2014, 41; Lutheran World Federation, 1996, 1998).

Niebuhr's 'typical answers' can be applied to Christian rituals, but we should bear in mind that Christian reality is nowadays more complex than fitting in five – or six, or seven, or eight – 'typical answers'. First, Niebuhr's model counts with established church traditions, which are declining in the world. His 'typical answers' may be of some use in practical research that is rooted in denominationally oriented institutions, but we should bear in mind that Christian rituals are often liquefying. Second, an accurate observation, description and analysis of a ritual as it is performed in practice often carries more nuanced and complex 'answers'. After all, human actions are always muddier than the theoretical and theological beliefs and convictions humans claim to adhere to: people do not always do what they claim to do. Third, in late-modernity hyper-diversity and hyper-complexity, also in rituality, prevent an easy classification of practices. The well-known scholar in Ritual Studies, Ronald Grimes points out that certainly in the European and American West, where institutions are losing power, old rituals are radically adapted to the times, and new rituals are consciously cultivated or invented. He speaks of ritualizing in this context:

> Unlike rites, ritualizing does not typically garner broad social support; it seems too innovative, dangerously creative, and insufficiently traditional. So deliberate ritualizing happens in the margins and is alternatively stigmatized and romanticized. Since ritualizing implies the invention of a tradition, it can feel contradictory, because traditions are not supposed to be inventible. Whereas rites depend on institutions and traditions, ritualizing, at least in the European American West, appeals to intuition and imagination. However, when sustained, ritualizing may eventuate in rites, with their own attendant institutions and power struggles. (Grimes 2000, 29)

Practical theologians therefore as a rule do not assess rituals that they investigate primarily from 'typical answers' but rather start from questions such as: What is going on in this or that ritual practice? How can we understand it? How do participants in rituals themselves perceive the rituals? Do they experience them as religious, and if so, in what sense? (Post 2000; Stringer 1999).

These questions result in critical rather than in 'typical' answers. This critique acts on two levels.

Firstly, it affects the level of the research itself. How are ritual practices approached academically? All too often, religion is explicitly or implicitly equated with Protestant faith and reduced to beliefs, while neglecting its physical, spatial, temporal, and material aspects. As rituals are embodied practices, they ask for researchers to immerse themselves in the rituals, in other words, for an empirical approach. As researchers we felt the heat in the Xhosa hut in which the African Independent Church conveyed, we smelled the sweat of the dancing Christians, we felt the talking drums thumping in our stomachs. That is the primary way in which we must become acquainted with the ritual to at least understand something of it (Jennings 1996). In other words, ritual theory and theorizing about rituals always go back to the practically performed rite itself (Grimes 2014, 165–184; Kreinath, Snoek, and Stausberg 2006).

In addition, the perspective of academic research is all too often white, male, and European or American. This of course relates to which universities, institutes and churches have the most resources and which research is funded. This leads to a lack of diverse perspectives. A ritual-critical approach can critique ritual practices and/or culture, for example from the perspective of people without power, and from groups living under oppression. For example, feminist methodologies can seek to navigate this, along with Participatory Action Research (PAR), which makes the investigated group of people co-researchers and co-owners of the study and thus breaks the subject–object division between researcher and researched and aims towards emancipation. In the descriptions of research projects that we introduced in the opening section of this chapter, Nasrallah's (2015) study of Lebanese women's experiences gave voice to a group of women who had previously had no voice on this subject because their actual ritual practices were not desirable objects of inquiry from the perspective of the powerful established traditional churches. Obviously, their 'answers' were not 'typical' in the sense in which Niebuhr spoke about it (Niebuhr 2001, 39–44). On a different level, the Participatory Action Research in and with the described African Independent Church contributed to the growth of the dignity of its members who felt proud to be part of a research project and of their church and worship being raised on a wider podium.

Methodological approaches can also draw on human rights, focusing on human dignity, or on postcolonialism to critique actual ritual practices. All too often rituals trample on human dignity and prosperity. You only have to think of the notorious Nazi rallies to know that political rituals can reinforce or propagate clearly abject ideas. Below we will see how sacramental theology in the Dutch Reformed Church in South Africa during apartheid was driven by racist motives. That brings us to the second level of critique.

Secondly, critique of rituals affects the level of ritual practice itself. Which values and conflicts of values do rituals refer to? Who determines what a ritual looks like? How do rituals themselves exercise power? Could they be seen to manipulate people or empower them? Description and analysis on the level of the ritual practice itself may reveal unbalanced gender relations in specific rituals, or a predominant role of adults in children's rituals, for example.

Rituals can also be critiqued from specific theological or even ecclesiastical positions. Cas Wepener (see the chapter on 'Holy Supper / Meal / Sharing Food' in this volume) gives a good example when critiquing divided Eucharistic practices in so-called white and so-called colored churches. The strong link between cult and culture showed a fight between 'the Christ of culture' and 'the Christ against culture' (Niebuhr 2001, 83–115; 45–82). Wepener criticizes this separated practice simply from the word of Jesus about approaching the altar while remembering that your brother has a grievance against you: "First go and make peace with your brothers; then come back and offer your gift" (Matt 5:23). He then proceeds by quoting the Bible as it is referred to in the liturgical form in the Dutch Reformed tradition during the distribution of bread and wine: the body and blood of the Lord are given "to a complete reconciliation of all our sins" (Barnard, Cilliers, and Wepener, 2014, 349–350). On a less dramatic level, we have criticized the abundance of words that are often common in protestant worship, to the degree of a "merely outward show of cliché", from the conviction that God is present "in absence" and that the word of God is born out of silence (Barnard, Cilliers, and Wepener 2014, 159). The church service is not merely Christian information and entertainment, God must be prayed to, and is not naturally present. This requires an attitude of expectation, silence, and prayer (Barnard, Cilliers, and Wepener 2014, 159). Obviously, both the examples given in this section of Holy Supper during apartheid and the description of silence as the womb of language could also be approached from political and cultural perspectives, viz. human rights, and anti-racism, and an all too noisy culture that we live in.

Summarizing what we have said about ritual criticism we quote Ronald Grimes:

> Criticism involves discovering, formulating, utilizing, and questioning presuppositions and criteria. It is an exercise of judgment that makes value-commitments and value-conflicts overt. Unlike theory, the aim of which is to explain, criticism aims to access. And unlike interpretation,

which is the effort to understand in general, criticism is an attempt to understand specifically in the service of practice.

Ritual criticism is the interpretation of a rite or ritual system with a view to implicating its practice. Because ritual criticism is itself a practice, it implies a politics and an ethic, as well as an aesthetic or poetics. Because the practice of criticism recontextualizes rites in a way that makes overt their means of negotiating and utilizing power – no matter how that power is conceived, sacralized, or explained – one cannot escape its conflictual nature (Grimes 1990, 15–16).

3 Key Notions

In this section we will discuss the notions that have already emerged in the description of ritual practices in rural Africa, the secularized Netherlands, and multi-religious Lebanon with which we began this chapter: ritual, symbol, and performance. The order in which we discuss these notions may seem somewhat illogical at first glance. Because a ritual consists of symbols, symbol acts and symbol language, we must first remember what a symbol is. Furthermore, it is important to remember that rituals never exist in the abstract but are always performed; rituals are practices. Finally, in the wake of Ronald Grimes, we look at qualities or elements of rituals.

3.1 Ritual as Assemblies of Symbols, Symbolic Language, Symbolic Acts

Rituals can be described as an assembly of symbolic acts, symbolic language, and symbols. The Eucharist is a ritual, its symbolic acts are taking, breaking, sharing, eating, etc.; its symbolic language is "This is my body" (Matt 26:26; Mark 14:22; Luke 22:19; 1Cor 11:24), and the symbols are bread and wine. Because rituals are a composition of symbols, acts and language, they always include the physical existence, the body. This holds true for all language, which is spoken and toned with the throat, vocal cords, tongue, lips, and cavities in the head, or read with the eyes, or heard with the ears.

As it has been said, the world and certainly the world of religions is only accessible through play, or through symbols. We mention several qualities of the notion of symbol and, as a consequence, of ritual. When we do so in this section, the notion of symbol is seen as inclusive of symbolic language and acts (Lukken 2005, 16–27).

First, symbols have a community-forming quality (Chauvet 1995, 112). Symbols are culturally determined. For a specific group (a people, a club, a church community) they are the expression of what binds them together; they are identifying signs. In the example we just gave, bread and wine are signs of recognition for the Christian church. Like the water of baptism, the Paschal candle, a well-known hymn, or the Bible. The French theologian Louis-Marie Chauvet writes:

> These words, gestures, objects, people *transport us immediately into the world of Christianity to which they belong;* each of them, because it belongs to the order of Christianity, immediately 'symbolizes' our relation with Christianity. Like every group, the Church identifies itself through its symbols, beginning with the formulation of the confession of faith, called appropriately the 'Symbol of the Apostles' (Chauvet 1995, 112).

Now these are culture-transcending symbols that apply to the vast majority of Christian traditions. However, there are also more regional symbols. For many in the western world, the organ will be a symbol that has become inextricably linked to the church and the world of faith. It is quite possible that the same applies to the talking drums and vuvuzelas in an African Independent Church. That means, *secondly*, that symbols presuppose participation. Only when we participate in the game, do the symbols have meaning. Water only has meaning in baptismal liturgy when it is related to the participant who is involved in celebrating the liturgy. So only when water is related to the baptismal formula 'I baptize you …' and to the great water narratives from the Bible: the flood, the baptism of Jesus in Jordan. If I place myself outside that narrative and remember that water is in fact no more than H_2O, the meaning is gone. From this follows a *third* characteristic of a symbol, namely that it acquires its meaning from the entire symbol system of which it is a part (Chauvet 1995, 114). To stay in the same example: water isolated from the baptismal ritual no longer has any symbolic value. Conversely, a symbol within the symbolic order calls for the whole of that order. *Fourthly*, symbols, like works of art, are gratuitous and are of no use, they are not part of an economic, financial, calculative, utilitarian, functionality. In the chapter on Aesthetics in this volume, we quoted Martin Heidegger's passage about the farmer's shoes as Van Gogh painted them. We said that an open-minded vision of the pair of shoes grants passage to being itself. In other words, the work of art, like every symbol, "*touches what is most real* in our world and allows it to come to its truth" (Chauvet 1995, 117):

> the work of art, like all symbolic work, shows what the truth is: not something already given beforehand to which one has to adjust oneself with exactitude, but rather a 'making-come-into-being', an 'advent' which, like a 'fugitive glimpse', gives itself only in simultaneously "holding itself back' in a sort of 'suspense' to the person who, against every utilitarian tendency, knows how to respect the 'vacant place' where it discloses itself (Heidegger, quoted at Chauvet 1995, 117).

Analogously, in the celebration of the Eucharist, the breaking of the bread grants passage to Christ for whoever approaches him with an open mind. From this follows a *fifth* characteristic of a symbol. From a void 'another' discloses itself on me that escapes the laws of utility-driven life. Thus, the symbol "assign[s] a place to the subject in its relation to others" (Chauvet 1995, 119); it "imposes a law of reciprocal recognition between subjects" (Chauvet 1995, 118), – be this subject a human or a divine, an animal or even a work of art (Barnard, Cilliers, and Wepener 2014, 325–326). *Sixth* and lastly, a symbol must be distinguished from a sign. A sign points to the utilitarian world: the word Amsterdam on a traffic sign points to the city of Amsterdam, the colour red in the traffic light indicates for vehicles to stop.

3.2 Performance

Rituals share their key dimension with theatre, drama, and spectacle: "the deliberate, self-conscious 'doing' of highly symbolic actions in public" (Bell 1997, 160). This is the performative dimension of ritual. In the context of practical theology, this performative dimension of rituals is especially important: performances are practices, acts, and these are the objects of practical theology. Catherine Bell mentions four qualities or aspects of performances. First, she states, "performances communicate on multiple sensory levels" (Bell 1997, 160): there is always an aesthetic dimension in the manner that the senses are involved in ritual performances (see Barnard's chapter on 'Aesthetics and Religion' in this volume). As we indicated above, this has consequences for the methods with which we study rituals. Researchers in Ritual Studies themselves enter the ritual field to immerse themselves in the rituals with all their senses. In other words, the study is empirical in nature, and theory follows empirical observation and analysis of the data. Second, performances are always set apart from ordinary life; there is 'the dynamics of framing':

> Intrinsic to performance is the communication of a type of frame that says, 'This is different, deliberate, and significant – pay attention!' By virtue of this framing, performance is understood to be something other than routine reality; it is a specific type of demonstration. [...] Although this overt identity is make-believe, by virtue of the way in which the theatrical framework set his words and deeds off from day-to-day reality, the performance is credited with the ability to convey universal truths by means of an experience not readily accessible elsewhere (Bell 1997, 160).

Third, Bell says, "such frames not only distinguish performance as such, they also create a complete and condensed, if somewhat artificial world" (Bell 1997, 160). Although the ritual is entirely connected to the culture in which it is performed and, as a rule, also derives its symbols from it, it is nevertheless separate from it. It is precisely in this connection and distance between ritual and culture that the identification and criticism of culture takes place. From here it is only a small step to the next dimension of performance that Bell mentions. Fourth, performances shape the world, because they give meaning to their world and present it in a meaningful and coherent, albeit simplified, form. Here the possible transformative power of performances is on the scene (Driver 2006). Lastly, closely linked to the previous quality, in performances people actively reflect on their community and society (Bell 1997, 75).

3.3 Qualities or Elements of Rituals

There are many definitions and descriptions of ritual (to name a few: Grimes 1990, 13–15; Grimes 2014, 237–241; Lukken 2005, 13–147; Rappaport 1999, 23–68; Snoek 2006). Many scholars, including those mentioned above, prefer not to present a strict definition of ritual, but rather to give several qualities or elements or characteristics that a practice to a greater or lesser extent may meet. Per consequence, that practice is more or less a ritual.

> Ritual is not a 'what', not a 'thing'. It is a 'how', a quality, and there are 'degrees' of it. Any action can be ritualized, though not every action is a rite (Grimes 1990, 13).

The qualities that Grimes lists are not exclusive for rituals. Think in this regard for instance of symbol and performance as we have discussed above. Rituals are symbolic, but not every symbol or symbolic act is a ritual. Rituals have a performative dimension, but not all performances are rituals. In this sense statements about rituals are provisional. Consequently, we must put in perspective the two characteristics that we discussed above, symbolic and performative. They *are* of particular importance within a theological discourse but have no *exclusive* significance for rituals.

To not make it unnecessarily complicated, we limit ourselves here to Grimes 1990 and 2014. In 1990, Grimes speaks of qualities of ritual, and he distinguishes fifteen clusters, each of which is subdivided into three to six qualities; he contrasts them with what rituals are not. It is striking that the "performed" and "symbolic" qualities are only two of the fifteen (Grimes 1990, 14). As mentioned, they are of outstanding importance for a theological discourse, because religion always reaches out to an outside and therefore always symbolizes. Moreover, practical theology focuses on practices and for that reason performance is an important quality in the context of this handbook.

Qualities of Ritual (Grimes 1990, 14)

- Performed, embodied, enacted, gestural (not merely thought or said)
- Formalized, elevated, stylized, differentiated (not ordinary, unadorned, or undifferentiated)
- Repetitive, redundant, rhythmic (not singular, or once-for-all)
- Collective, institutionalized, consensual (not personal or private)
- Patterned, invariant, standardized, stereotyped, ordered, rehearsed (not improvised, idiosyncratic, or spontaneous)
- Traditional, archaic, primordial (not invented or recent)
- Valued highly or ultimately, deeply felt, sentiment laden, meaningful, serious (not trivial or shallow)
- Condensed, multilayered (not obvious; requiring interpretation)
- Symbolic, referential (not merely technological or primarily means-end oriented)
- Perfected, idealized, pure, ideal (not conflictual or subject to criticism and failure)
- Dramatic, ludic (i.e., play-like) (not primarily discursive or explanatory; not without special framing or boundaries)
- Paradigmatic (not ineffectual in modeling either other rites or non-ritualized action)

- Mystical, transcendent, religious, cosmic (not secular or merely empirical)
- Adaptive, functional (not obsessional, neurotic, dysfunctional)
- Conscious, deliberate (not unconscious or preconscious)

It is certain that now, thirty years after the publication of this schema, some negative qualities ('a ritual is not...') are valued differently. Ritualizing has become an important feature of ritual practice and as a consequence, of Ritual Studies. Increasingly, especially in the Western world, many rituals are becoming more personal, improvised, and idiosyncratic, recently invented, and determinately secular. An example is the ritual in the Dutch hospital that we described in the introduction to this chapter.

In 2014, Grimes discerns seven of what he calls 'elements' of rituals: actions, actors, places, times, objects, languages (written, words spoken on and off stage, creeds, etc.), and groups (referring to social, political, economic domains) (Grimes, 2014, 237–241). For each of those elements, Grimes asks very practical "sample research questions" that relate to the empirical reality of the rite (Grimes, 2014, 237–241). To give some examples: "Are some actions more important than others?"; "Who enacts? Who witnesses?"; "Who sits beside whom? Who walks behind whom?"; "How does time unfold within the ritual itself?"; "To what times does the ritual refer of allude?"; "How are ritual texts handled?"; "What social dimensions or discriminations are in force?" (Grimes 2014, 237–241). These are very practical questions, but at the same time these elements also refer to discourses that are conducted in the humanities and in practical theology. Many of Grimes' elements indeed refer to accents and turns that, consecutively or, depending on the author, simultaneously come to the fore in the humanities and in practical theology: the action-based approach; the anthropological turn, that put humans first; the spatial turn, that primarily looks at space and place; the material turn, that starts from material elements in religion; and the language turn as it was proposed by post-modern philosophers in the wake of Heidegger. In other words, Ritual Studies, and practical theology in so far it is concerned with rituals, are embedded in broader humanistic academic discourses.

4 Contribution to Practical Theology in General

Religions have many dimensions. Glock and Smart discern six dimensions: the intellectual, ideological, and cognitive dimension, the dimension of social ethics, the institutional dimension, the aesthetic dimension, the psychic dimension and the ritual dimension (Auffahrt and Mohr 2006, 1611–1612). These dimensions often overlap, as we have seen in this chapter. The question of power in rituals touches on the dimension of social ethics. The aesthetic and sensual are important dimensions of rituals. Rituals are often initiated and also determined by institutions. Yet the ritual dimension of religion also has something very specific. In its countless qualities or elements, the ritual as a coherent whole of symbols, symbolic acts and symbolic language pre-eminently grants passage to being, to the divine, and eventually to God. In this way it touches on what is most real in religion and allows it to come to its truth. It is no coincidence that rituals are often understood as the most central elements of a religion (Girard 2013). It is also no coincidence that in Christianity, worship forms the core of the community, its beliefs, and practices. A well-known statement says: *lex orandi lex credendi*, which can be translated as: what one prays is also what one believes. And another dictum says: the church is known by its feasts, meaning that it is known by the liturgy. In that sense it can be argued that the study of rituals forms the core of practical theology.

Bibliography

Auffahrt, Christoph, and Hubert Mohr. 2006. "Religion." In *The Brill Dictionary of Religion*. Vol. 3, Leiden / Boston: Brill, 1607–1619.
Barnard, Marcel, Johan Cilliers, and Cas J. Wepener. 2014. *Worship in the Network Culture: Liturgical Ritual Studies: Fields and Methods, Concepts and Metaphors*. Liturgia Condenda 28. Leuven / Paris: Peeters.
Bell, Catherine. 1997. *Ritual: Perspectives and Dimensions*, New York / Oxford: Oxford University Press.
Chauvet, Louis-Marie. 1995. *Symbol and Sacrament: A Sacramental Reinterpretation of Christian Existence*. Collegeville: The Liturgical Press.
Driver, Tom. 2006. *Liberating Rites: Understanding the Transformative Power of Ritual*. Charleston: BookSurge.
Girard, René. [1972] 2013. *Violence and the Sacred*. London: Bloomsbury Academic.
Grimes, Ronald L. 1990. *Ritual Criticism: Case Studies in its Practice, Essays on its Theory*. Studies in Comparative Religion. Columbia: University of South Carolina Press.
Grimes, Ronald L. 2000. *Deeply into the Bone: Re-inventing Rites of Passage*. Berkeley / Los Angeles: University of California Press.
Grimes, Ronald L. 2014. *The Craft of Ritual Studies*. Oxford / New York: Oxford University Press.
Hobsbawm, Eric, and Terence Ranger. 1999. *The Invention of Tradition*. Cambridge: Cambridge University Press.
Jennings, Theodore W. 1996. "On Ritual Knowledge." In *Readings in Ritual Studies*, edited by Ronald L. Grimes, Upper Saddle River: Prentice Hall, 324–334.
Kreinath, Jens, Jan A. M. Snoek, and Michael Strausberg, eds. 2006. *Theorizing Rituals: Issues, Topics, Approaches, Concepts*. Leiden / Boston: Brill.
Leeuw, Gerardus van der. 1949. *Sacramentstheologie*. Nijkerk: Callenbach.
Lukken, Gerard. 2005. *Rituals in Abundance: Critical Reflection on the Place, Form and Identity of Christian Ritual in our Culture*. Liturgia Condenda 17. Leuven / Dudley: Peeters.
Lutheran World Federation. 1998. *Chicago Statement on Worship and Culture: Baptism and Rites of Life Passage*. Geneva: Lutheran World Federation.
Lutheran World Federation. 1996. *Nairobi Statement*. https://worship.calvin.edu/resources/resource-library/nairobi-statement-on-worship-and-culture-full-text (01.12.2021).
Nasrallah, Rima. 2015. *Moving and Mixing. The Fluid Liturgical Lives of Antiochian Orthodox and Maronite Women Within the Protestant Churches in Lebanon*. http://theoluniv.ub.rug.nl/153/1/NasrallahR_MovingandMixing_18febr2015.pdf (01.12.2021).
Niebuhr, H. Richard. [1951] 2001. *Christ and Culture*. New York: HarperCollins.

Post, Paul. 2000. "Interference and Intuition: On the Characteristic Nature of Research Design in Liturgical Studies." *Questions Liturgiques* 81:48–61.
Rappaport, Roy. 1999. *Ritual and Religion in the Making of Humanity.* Cambridge Studies in Social and Cultural Anthropology 110. Cambridge: Cambridge University Press.
Snoek, Jan A. M. 2006. "Defining Rituals." In *Theorizing Rituals: Issues, Topics, Approaches, Concepts*, edited by Jens Kreinath, Jan A. M. Snoek, and Michael Strausberg, Leiden / Boston: Brill, 3–15.
Stringer, Martin D. 1999. *On the Perception of Worship.* Birmingham: Birmingham University Press.
Wepener, Cas J. 2015. "Burning Incense for a Focus Group Discussion: A Spirituality of Liminality for Doing Liturgical Research in an African Context from an Emic Perspective." *International Journal of Practical Theology* 19:271–291.
Wepener, Cas J., Ignatius Swart, Gerrie ter Har, and Marcel Barnard, eds. 2019. *Bonding in Worship: A Ritual Lens on Social Capital Formation in African Independent Churches in South Africa.* Liturgia Condenda 30. Leuven: Peeters.

HyeRan Kim-Cragg
Holy Scripture / Hermeneutical Practice / Oral Literature

1 Locating a Transcultural Transreligious Experience: A Testimony

I was born into a Christian family in South Korea where Buddhism, Confucianism and Shamanism are alive and well. Despite the plurality and close proximity of such diversity, significant religious conflicts were in fact rare. Although the church and society were patriarchal and indeed, sexism was strong, my family upbringing was quite liberating. I observed my parents playing non-normative gender roles; my dad was gentle and caring, while my mom was a local leader working for the municipal office. I received a non-gender stereotypical feminist education at home, even if my parents did not realize what they were doing or name it as such.

I was raised a Catholic (baptized and confirmed). I still remember the white bishop from the US presiding at my confirmation celebration in the Catholic parish. I understood neither why he was there, nor did I know how to articulate the western Christian mission legacy at that time. But I vividly remember sensing his superior status. Almost four decades later, this formative experience has helped me unpack my own internalized white supremacy and racism and has further sharpened my analysis of colonialism and American Christian imperialism in Korea and across the globe.

Later, during my high school years, I decided to move to a Protestant denomination. I went to a Presbyterian church where my minister was the first ordained woman in her denomination. The late Rev. Yang Jung Shin founded the congregation in 1978 after she was ordained in 1976. She was blind but had managed to study theology in the US and medicine in Japan. She was a well-educated preacher. Her homiletic performance, which included the presence of a male elder helping her stand in the pulpit, and her eloquent speech which she delivered whilst touching a braille sermon manuscript has left its mark on my own understanding of preaching, and pastoral leadership in light of gender and disability. In a church that is still male-dominated and not much more sensitive to disability than it was in the 1980s, this memory stands out as a moment where I was able to glimpse a new preaching world of possibilities.

Since those days with Rev. Yang I have had the opportunity to study the Bible as Christian Holy Scripture[1] in seminary and have learned that the relationship between women and the Bible is a problematic one. There are a significant number of gender-biased references (e. g. women being silent in the church). As a scholar, gender issues have been a critical lens through which I have come to view religion, leadership, and society. That is why I have argued that the Bible is not the literal Word of God but must be interpreted in a way that reflects the context in which it was written and in conversation with our own contemporary context and culture (Beavis and Kim-Cragg 2017). During my seminary studies, I also learned that many churches (and seminaries) are doing the opposite, believing, and teaching that the Bible is the infallible Word of God and that to challenge that doctrine is deemed heretical. This rigid stance is in part due to a colonial teaching of Christian supremacy. Our colonial and patriarchal contexts continue to inform the way we read the Bible. Biblical literacy and biblical relevancy, thus, serve as heuristic keys for preaching in particular and practical theology in general when approaching the Bible as a whole. I remain convinced that when we hold the text in tension with the realities of our lives, the Holy Spirit continues to use it and to speak through it to us.

As a young adult I left Korea to pursue doctoral graduate studies in Canada. In the years since, Canada has become a home. This transnational migration experience has brought me different transcultural and transreligious experiences. It has enabled me to encounter Indigenous people, the original inhabitants in Canada and their religious, cultural, and spiritual practices. In this paper, I attempt to raise some issues pertinent to Indigenous people of the Americas[2] including how they received and resisted the teaching of the Bible. I will talk about this in terms of agency and epistemology, examining how their particular life experiences and received wisdoms are intricately connected to their view of sacred texts.

While in Canada I have also been given opportunities to meet people who practice Islam, the fastest growing religion in Canada.[3] While there were a few Muslims in Korea while I was there, I have never had close contact until I moved to Canada. I have come to believe that a respectful relationship with Muslims is another crucial task of Christian practical theology. For this work, practical theologians are called to cultivate transcultural and transreligious perspectives.

In short, these life experiences have shaped me as a Korean Canadian postcolonial feminist homiletician engaging with Scriptures. I believe lifting up my story as testimony is important because it establishes a preaching tradition, a tradition

---

[1] Holy Scripture will be used to encompass the sacred texts of Judaism, Christianity, Islam, and Indigenous people, although the Bible will be used interchangeably when it refers to Christianity.
[2] From the indigenous perspective, the demarcation of North, Central, South America is the scarred evidence of colonial legacy. The Americas are one, an undivided shared hemisphere for Indigenous people (Taylor 2003, xiii).
[3] In reference to the article: http://nationalpost.com/news/canada/survey-shows-muslim-population-is-fastest-growing-religion-in-canada (30.11.2021).

that is practiced by many women preachers who have wrestled with Scripture (Florence 2007). Taking upon this tradition, I will examine the Bible's tendency to be used to oppress others in colonial patterns of relationship. But in doing so I will not lose sight of the Bible as a tool for resistance and transformation. I will also examine the agency of Indigenous people and Muslim communities in interpreting their respective sacred teachings, rites, and texts, while examining the use of the Bible as a living tradition that is "still in the making" (Hess 2012, 300).

2 Critical Issues Emerged from the Testimony

My particular context described above affirms the need for homiletics as a subdiscipline of practical theology to take lived experiences seriously. It affirms practical theology as a theory of lived religion that informs and is informed by praxis. Praxis here is understood as a holistic and non-binary theoretical, conceptual interaction involving ongoing critical reflections with cultural and historical experiences, circumstances, and conditions. Praxis involves interrelated descriptive, interpretive, normative, pragmatic, and strategic dimensions (Schipani and Schertz 2004, 438). Practical theology as a critical hermeneutical process involves conscious, concrete, and reflective examination and assessment, analysis and action towards liberation and transformation of individuals and communities. Keeping this theological praxis of practical theology in mind, I seek to raise three interrelated issues of Holy Scripture as a source of preaching and practical theology.

The first issue is the uninformed totalitarian interpretation of the Bible and its use in the colonial mission. Historically the Bible has been used as a tool to suppress local religions and their syncretic practices. But this approach is not yet a thing of the past. It continues to shape Christians all over the world today. While the period of colonialism did come to a close, its modes of being still haunt us. Hence, a postcolonial engagement of the Bible is a useful hermeneutical approach for practical theology (Couture et al. 2015, 2).

Another issue related to the first revolves around the ways in which Indigenous peoples in the Americas view sacred texts and what they can teach about the sacred knowledge contained therein. To this end we will examine European Christian epistemology, which privileges literary knowledge over indigenous epistemology based on orality and performative knowledge. This examination leads us to explore how Christian Scriptures are more than written texts. It allows us to extend non-literary texts as part of sacred texts that are embodied and practiced in preaching, ceremonies, and storytelling.

The other related issue on the nature of sacred texts – beyond literary culture – leads to a rediscovering in both Hebrew and Christian Scriptures of prayer practices as a vital means of shaping Christian identities and Christian communities. A study of the formation of the Bible affirms that Jewish Christian Scripture is not a single book but a multiple set of texts that encourages the formation of faith communities through liturgical performative practices (Kee et al. 1997). Holy Scripture of Islam, particularly in the recitation of the Qur'an through *Salat* prayer, is also used performatively as a bodily practice and as an event for the sake of enhancing individual and communal religious life (Haeri 2013).

3 Three Aspects of Holy Scripture

3.1 Holy Scripture as a Tool to Both: Oppress and Resist Oppression

The Bible in Christianity is an ambivalent source of preaching; it is both "liberating and oppressive" (Travis 2014, 109). There is a tendency toward imperialism in the Bible as much as there is a practice of creative resistance against it (Dube 1998, 234). Yet, the Bible is often propagated as "the transcendental text which all people in all cultures at all times in all circumstances should obey" (Tolbert 1998, 176). Instead of holding the ambivalent aspects of the Bible in tension, some interpreters of the Bible have seen it as normative and have claimed to be justified in this view through an objective reading of the biblical text. Armed with the universal authority of the Bible, ideologically charged and ungrounded biblical interpretations have had violent and harmful effects. Such authoritarian and normative interpretations have influenced people's beliefs about controversial issues such as abortion, gender roles, race, and sexuality that in turn have led to discrimination and oppression (Brown 2012, 378).

During the eighteenth, nineteenth and twentieth centuries, the Bible was used as a tool to conquer in many parts of the world. The reason why we need to pay attention to this particular period is because what happened then still impacts the way in which we read the Bible today. The Bible continues to be used to legitimatize war and violence. Such foundational faith stories as those in Exodus and Joshua have fueled the political rhetoric of conquest (Tamez 2016, 8–9) and continue to contribute to the conquest rhetoric in our own time. It is also during the colonial heyday of the nineteenth and early twentieth century that the Bible traveled the world. A civilizing and colonial mission was accelerated through the dissemination of the printed English Bible to every corner of the world at the expense of local and indigenous languages (Heller and McElhinny, 2017).

There are a couple of examples to exert its western colonial power through spreading the Bible as Christian language and its supremacy. The first account comes from the British Bible Society Report *The Book about Every Book* published in 1910:

> Not only the heathen, but the speech of the heathen, must be Christianized. Their language itself needs to be born again. Their very words have to be converted from foul meanings and base uses

and baptized into a Christian sense, before those words can convey the great truths and ideas of the Bible. (Tran 2017, 63)

The second account was made in 1942 by a member of the Rockefeller family William Cameron Townsend, who lived in the post-colonial era of the twentieth century. It explicitly delineates the connection between Christianity, Capitalism, and Colonialism:

> Who will open Tibet, or claim the last acre of the Amazon, the hills of central India, the jungles of Borneo, the steppes of Siberia—the merchant or the missionary? When the war is over, let us take the Sword of the Spirit and march. (Taylor 1998, 117)

Cameron Townsend was also the founder of Wycliffe Bible Translators and carried the Bible to 'Bibleless tribes' (i.e., indigenous people of Guatemala) while supporting local military dictators to wipe out indigenous resistance Suppression of local, colonized, and indigenous languages and cultural practices was brutal in many cases around the world. Such suppression was justified in part by the logic of Christian superiority and European white racial purity. Many local, colonized, and indigenous cultures and religions were demonized as impure, barbaric, and satanic. The colonial project not only destroyed indigenous knowledge but also distorted it by fetishizing it as primitive and inferior, incapable of progress. These view of non-western peoples and their cultures has been coined Orientalism (Said 1978).

However, the so-called 'Bibleless tribes' of indigenous people have not passively surrendered. One recent example of resistance occurred in 1992 when a group of indigenous people return the Bible to the Pope, marking the five hundredth anniversary of the conquest of their lands by Europeans. The Bible was accompanied by a letter which read:

> We, Indians of the Andes and America, decided to take advantage of John Paul II's visit to return to him his Bible because in five centuries it has given us neither love, nor peace, nor justice. Please, take your Bible and give it back to our oppressors, because [...] the Bible was imposed upon America with force: European culture, language, religion, and values. (Tamez 2016, 10)

Other examples of the practice of resistance are found in the practice of popular or communitarian reading of the Bible in which Indigenous people assert their agency to interpret the text for themselves. This particular hermeneutical practice influenced by liberation theology has one unapologetic principle: "No biblical theme can be used to discriminate against or oppress another" (Tamez 2016, 12). Such a principle is also reflected in other minoritized groups' reading practice in which they read their suffering and resistance experiences into the biblical stories. There is no dichotomy or hierarchy between context and text, theory and practice, conceptual idea and lived experience, when engaging with the Bible. Moreover, it affirms that the biblical interpretation starts with the daily life of the community which is conducive to a practical theological approach. This interpretative stance decenters academia of homiletics and its coveted method of historical criticism while returning the authority to the believing community as agent of biblical interpretation for sermon making in terms of "sharing the Word." (Rose, 1997)

To say that the Bible serves as a tool of oppression is not to deny the importance of the Bible as a tool of resistance and liberation. Without question, readers and communities of faith who have suffered from oppressions have also found the Bible to be a source of freedom and hope. Many contemporary readers have identified with people in the Bible by associating their experiences with the exiles in Babylon, and their lives as the conquered and colonized communities. Such identification makes the ancient text relevant to today's world, enabling a transcultural approach to Bible reading in practical theology (O'Connor 1998, 328). Instead of viewing a multiplicity of biblical interpretation as a threat to monolithic theological orthodoxy, practical theology entertains an openness to the ambivalent role of the Bible as both liberating and oppressive.

In short, a hermeneutical use of the Bible as a source of practical theology affirms that the Bible does not speak with one voice or one language, nor does it call for one interpretation. Even familiar texts can take on an unfamiliar hue. There are conflicting voices within the text itself and within the interpretive community (Kim-Cragg 2018, 81–105). Therefore, to approach the Bible is to appreciate a "multiaxial frame of reference" (Donaldson 1996, 8), recognizing a multiplicity of meanings embedded in the text, with interpretations arising from the multiplicity of readers' experiences and contexts. From transcultural and transreligious perspectives, this view of the Bible for preaching becomes obvious. Embracing the truth that the Bible was written in different languages in different periods and must be interpreted in a way that considers and recognizes these differences, is part of this approach compatible with a transcultural and transreligious approach that this volume seeks.

3.2 Holy Scripture as Oral Literature

During the colonial period, missionaries often used Scripture to preach to Christianize Indigenous people by denying and dismissing their religious wisdom, language, and knowledge. This practice was grounded in the association of wisdom and knowledge with written language: and the Bible was thought to be the one and only written source of the highest divine revelation of Christianity.

Many European philosophers and theologians have considered western literary-centered epistemology as superior to non-western non-literary epistemology. Georg Wilhelm Friedrich Hegel, for example, said that knowledge as art (religion included) must include signs that consist of drawing and symbols with meanings therein (Hegel 1975). One without the other is not considered as full knowledge. If the knowledge only consists of signs, it is not strictly an epistemology. It is not quite knowledge, remaining "the coming-into-being of knowledge" (Spivak 1999, 41). Hegel downplays Eastern religious sacred texts from Persia, India, and Egypt as deviations from true knowledge because, according to him, they only display signs. For Hegel, these non-European religions are absent of content that can be used to construct history.

That is where a claim that Africa has no history came from. Such claim was prevalent in missionary fields in the Americas. When the friars arrived in the Americas in the fifteenth and the sixteenth century, they claimed that the Indigenous peoples' past had disappeared because they had no writing, thus no history, and no knowledge (Taylor 2003, 16). The privileging of literacy over orality was reinforced by the colonial project. People without writing systems from European standards were seen as less civilized and incapable of progress. The colonialists never doubted that history was predominantly determined by writing and that writing is a sure evidence of true knowledge.

As a performance studies scholar, Diana Taylor demonstrates how embodied practices rooted in indigenous worldviews are themselves ways of knowing. These practices construct knowledge. Challenging western colonial epistemology's over-dependence on literary and historical writings, she offers indigenous performed and oral knowledge as a counterpoint. Taylor reveals the limit of western epistemology, where "writing has become the guarantor of existence itself" (2003, 16). Western epistemology exclusively based on writings is limiting, she argues, having had a relatively short history in its development. Walter Ong supports Taylor's point by saying, "the relentless dominance of textuality in the [western] scholarly mind is shown by the fact that to this day no concepts have yet been formed for effectively, let alone gracefully, conceiving of oral art" (Ong 1982, 10).

On the contrary, oral art as an ancient and enduring way to communicate knowledge has been developed and enhanced by many Indigenous communities. Marie Battiste, a Mi'kmaw Indigenous scholar from Canada, for example, argues that there were sophisticated symbolic forms of Algonkian literacy. "The Mi'kmaq are among those indigenous peoples who have had a unique history of symbolic writing that began well before letters and orthographies were introduced" (Battiste 2016, 124). Though their writings were different from European writings, these Indigenous groups had developed a highly valued writing system as codices that contain the mixture of letters and drawings as oral art. However, the primary mode of knowing and the chief medium of transmission of knowledge, including the spiritual / religious, for Indigenous people were through embodied performance often involving orality.

Wade Davis as an anthropologist and ethnographer, describes orality performed by Penan people in Malaysia:

> Writing, while clearly an extraordinary innovation in human history, [...] permits and even encourages the numbing of memory. Oral traditions sharpen recollection, even as they seem to open a certain mysterious dialogue with the natural world [...] the Penan perceive the voices of animals in the forest. [...] Entire hunting parties may be turned back to camp by the cry of a bat hawk. [...] This remarkable dialogue informs Penan life in ways that few outsiders can be expected to understand. (Davis 2009, 175)

The inaccessibility of this knowledge to those who are outside the oral culture may lead them to resist acknowledging it as true knowledge. It was inaccessible to colonial invaders, for example, who heavily relied on literary writings. For those eager to exert control, it was troubling to find themselves locked out of the realm of indigenous knowledge. It was even harder to capture and subdue it because once it was performed, it existed only in the hearts and minds of those who understood it. Oral and embodied knowledge relies on the agency of participants, in their memory and their performance. This is key to their ability to resist colonialism.

The insight gleaned from indigenous epistemology practiced as both writing, drawing, and orality offers important implications for homileticians who study Holy Scripture. Sacred texts do not have to rely on dichotomies such as literary/oral, meaning/sign. Written texts are not necessarily superior to oral or performed texts. What is illuminated here is that sacred texts that belong to indigenous peoples are both literary and oral, written and ritualized, printed, and performed. These modes of Holy Scripture are all sources of practical theology in transcultural and transreligious contexts.

Argued elsewhere, Holy Scripture offers both literary and oral, written, and ritualized knowledge. Holy Scripture as story is presented in various forms, including myths, apologies, poems, songs, letters, narratives, and parables. God captured in the Bible is encountered not only through intellectual and cognitive knowing but in experiential and relational knowing. However, there is a challenge to fully appreciate the Bible in this way because the very terms 'The Bible' etymologically meaning 'book' in Greek, and 'Scripture' etymologically meaning 'writings' in Latin, have exclusive literary connotations (Kim-Cragg 2012, 15).

To counterbalance the heavy influence of literary tradition of the Bible, the oral tradition should be emphasized. Kwok Pui-lan is helpful in this regard. To her, the Bible as Christian Holy Scripture is a "talking book" (Kwok 1995, 40). This rather contradictory description of the Bible is not surprising in Asian contexts where multireligious and interreligious conversations are as natural as breathing. People living in religious pluralistic cultures learn to talk to and talk with and talk about different religions, and their sacred texts as a way of navigating their religiously pluralistic contexts. A conversational posture is a necessity and not a luxury as a pluralistic religious practice for people in Asia. For people in Africa, too, reading the Bible is about "talking to a talking book" (Dube 1998, 243). As a postcolonial scholar, Kwok suggests that the dialogical practice involved in a conversational posture is necessary for a postcolonial imagination that "attempts to bridge the gaps of time and space, to create new horizons, and connect the disparate elements of our lives into a meaningful whole" (Kwok 1995, 13). Oral hermeneutics provides us with a way to criticize and counterbalance the dominant western method of historical biblical criticism.

For those of us who are preoccupied with Holy Scripture as 'a collection of literary books' Kwok and Dube's treatment of Holy Scripture as 'a talking book' can be confusing. Obviously, concepts such as 'oral literature' are confusing. However,

Ong reminds us, "writing from the beginning did not reduce orality but enhanced it" (Ong 1982, 9). Thus, literacy and orality should not be in competition or opposition but viewed as complimentary and relational. In short, a task of practical theology – and preaching in particular – is to search for ways in which our approach to Holy Scripture can contain both elements of literacy and orality as they are performed by preachers lifting up the experiences of ordinary people in their communities of faith. This search includes a preacher's self-critical scanning of our *de facto* practice of according authority only to the written text in Christian religious teaching and spiritual practice.

In fact, Christians may gain new or renewed insights, through closely looking at the Bible, especially the formation of some of the Hebrew texts and the Gospels, as they discover evidence that Jewish and Christian sacred texts were created and mainly used for storytelling (orality) and various liturgical practices including bodily prayers (performance) for the formation of Christian community. Such evidence is not limited to Jewish and Christian Scripture but includes Muslim Scripture also. The final section will examine these aspects of sacred texts.

3.3 Holy Scripture as Performative for the Formation of the Community of Faith

The formation of the Jewish Bible is closely related to the formation of the people of Israel. After the monarchy disappeared, identity for Jews was provided through the priests who brought them together to worship. For this purpose, the Psalms were compiled while other wisdom texts such as Proverbs and Ecclesiastes were edited. According to Howard Clark Kee, there are two themes running in the formation of the Bible: First, that there is a people of God, and, second, that they have been spoken to by God (Kee et al. 1997, 5–7). The formation of the Bible can be seen as a response to the perceived need to communicate and reflect these themes.

The formation of the Jewish community necessitated various rituals. Biblical writings in the form of praise, poetry, epics, petition were incorporated into a body of liturgical materials in part because the work of compiling, editing, and expanding was done by priestly leaders of Israel (Newman 2018, 9). The need for prayer practices for the sake of the community required a move from oral narratives to written forms. Although the Hebrew Bible was circulating in written form, it was learned by heart through hearing and speaking (Allen 2008, 101).

Similar to, but to a lesser degree than, the formation of the Hebrew Bible, the New Testament writings were also collected and complied for a particular purpose connected to preaching, instruction, and worship. For example, the letter to Hebrews was understood as a homily, a pastoral sermon for those who faced hardship and persecution (Beavis and Kim-Cragg, 2015). The gospel tradition that contains the deeds and words of Jesus was circulated and preserved orally before it was produced in written form (Kee 1997, 447). Writings were undertaken to extend the spoken word, given that literacy ranged from 2 to 15 percent (Allen 2008, 101) in the first century. One should make no mistake that these writings did not exist as completed written materials before the editors complied and arranged them. The editors were interested in preserving these oral traditions in ways that could function for the life of the early Christian communities. Once again, the symbiotic interplay between oral and literary aspects of Christian Scripture is evident.

That biblical texts had originally been preserved orally points to the performative function of Holy Scripture. Prayers were recited from the Bible and teachings of the Bible were spoken. A need for written materials arose by the end of the first century, when the Jesus movement took root and Christian messages were scattered in various areas, to diverse cultures and among diverse people. These diverse early Christians were under pressure from different political authorities connected to the Roman Empire and felt a need to affirm their Christian identity in a way that was distinct from Greek philosophies and other popular religions. Such texts as *Didache* that has several biblical references (Matt. 7:13–14, John 14:4–6) was produced in the early second century and contains detailed instructions and practices of "baptism, prayers, fasting, and the Eucharist to be performed within the life of the community" (Kee 1997, 565) where the interplay between Christian worship and Holy Scripture has been made explicit. This early understanding was reiterated by Ruth Duck: "At the center of Christian worship is the word of God as witnessed in Scripture and incarnate in Jesus Christ. [...] From greeting to benediction, the words of Scripture are interwoven with our contemporary prayers and testimonies" (Duck 2013, 125).

Turning to Islam, the concept of *Salat* helps us make connections between the religious practices of both faiths connected to prayer. *Salat,* meaning worship in Arabic, includes the reading of *suuras*, meaning chapters, from the Qur'an. Selected Qur'anic verses are recited five times every day and it is an obligatory duty for every Muslim as one of five pillars of Islam, to include these in the daily discipline of prayer. One can see the interplay between literacy and orality being in the practice of *Salat*. *Salat* is also a bodily prayer which, depending on the time of the day, involves four body postures: standing, bending forward with hands on knees, prostrating, and sitting (Haeri 2013, 8). *Salat* is a speech event, an encounter between "a seemingly timeless text" and the voice of "its present performer" who enacts it (du Bois 2009, 31). In this musical kinesthetic event, openness to the voice of Allah in the Qur'an is modelled and practiced, while multiple meanings embedded in these texts emerge for those who do the prayer (Gade 2002). These meanings are generated through the practice of repetition. This recitation practice offers the possibility of creativity in terms of how this repeated act ushers in the openness of iteration in the advent of new meanings.

For Jewish, Christian, and Muslim traditions, reading in the form of recitation of sacred texts is "an experience; it occurs; it does something; it makes us do something" (Fish 1980, 32). In this regard, Holy Scripture is performative as much as preaching is performative; it is not a fixed entity but an event. The Bible is not a bounded private object but a participatory public practice that does not let the readers or reciters stay still. That is why literature is and can be called a "kinetic art" (Fish 1980, 25). This particular understanding of Holy Scripture is an important counter point to monolithic interpretations with literary emphasis that exclude and incite violence, as discussed in the first and the second sections. The insight of the Holy Scripture as performative is instructive to preaching and serves to enhance the well-being of communities of faith.

4 Conclusion

We have examined three issues of Holy Scripture as sources of practical theology using an autobiographical narrative method in light of preaching and performative life of religious communities. This examination has elucidated how the Christian Bible has been used as a tool to both oppress and resist, by tapping into indigenous wisdom, indigenous experiences of colonization and indigenous agency. It has lifted up a nuanced and holistic epistemology of the Bible beyond literal ways of knowing. Once Holy Scripture is understood and acknowledged as oral literature, we can also discover performative aspects of sacred texts that are enacted and preached individually and collectively for the sake of the formation and transformation of various faith communities. Holy Scripture for Jews, Christians, and Muslims presents deep and difficult questions about faith and life. Therefore, engaging Holy Scripture in practical theology, especially homiletics, is an invitation to an aural, oral, and literary event of bringing sermon to life, an event that does not define answers but seeks questions to liberate the faithful to embark on a pilgrimage for wisdom in ways that are kinesthetic and sensory.

Bibliography

Allen, Ronald J. 2008. "Performance and the New Testament in Preaching." In *Performance in Preaching: Bringing the Sermon to Life*, edited by Jana Childers and Clayton J. Schmit, Grand Rapids: Baker, 99–116.

Battiste, Marie. 2016. "Mi'kmaw Symbolic Literacy." In *Visioning a Mi'kmaw Humanities: Indigenizing the Academy*, edited by Marie Battiste, Sydney / Nova Scotia: Cape Breton University, 123–148.

Beavis, Mary Ann, and HyeRan Kim-Cragg. 2015. *Hebrews: Wisdom Commentary*. Collegeville: Liturgical Press.

Beavis, Mary Ann, and HyeRan Kim-Cragg. 2017. *What Does the Bible Say? A Critical Conversation with Popular Culture*. Eugene: Cascade.

Brown, Michael Joseph. 2012. "Biblical Theology." In *The Wiley-Blackwell Companion to Practical Theology*, edited by Bonnie J. Miller-McLemore, Malden: Wiley-Blackwell, 377–385.

Couture, Pamela, Robert Mager, Pamela McCarroll, and Natalie Wigg-Stevenson, eds. 2015. *Complex Identities in a Shifting World: Practical Theological Perspectives*. International Practical Theology 17. Zürich: LIT.

Davis, Wade. 2009. *The Wayfinders: Why Ancient Wisdom Matters in the Modern World: CBC Massey Lectures*. Toronto: Anansi Press.
Donaldson, Laura. 1996. "Postcolonialism and Bible Reading." *Semeia* 75:1–14.
Dube, Musa. 1998. "Go Therefore and Make Disciples of All Nations (Matt 29:19a): A Postcolonial Perspective on Biblical Criticism and Pedagogy." In *Teaching the Bible: The Discourses and Politics of Biblical Pedagogy*, edited by Fernando F. Segovia and Mary Ann Tolbert, Maryknoll: Orbis, 224–246.
Duck, Ruth. 2013. *Worship for the Whole People of God: Vital Worship for the 21st Century*. Louisville: Westminster John Knox.
Bois, W. John du. 2009. "Interior Dialogues: The Co-Voicing of Ritual in Solitude." In *Ritual Communication*, edited by Gunter Senft and Ellen Basso, London: Berg Publishers, 317–340.
Fish, Stanley. 1980. *Is There a Text in this Class: The Authority of Interpretive Communities*. Cambridge: Harvard University.
Florence, Anna Carter. 2007. *Preaching as Testimony*. Louisville: Westminster John Knox.
Gade, Anna M. 2002. "Taste, Talent and the Problem of Internalization: A Qur'anic Study in Religious Musicality from Southeast Asia." *History of Religions* 41:328–368.
Haeri, Niloofar. 2013. "The Private Performance of 'Salat' Prayers: Repetition, Time, and Meaning." *Anthropological Quarterly* 86:5–34.
Hegel, Georg W. F. 1975. *Aesthetics: Lectures on Fine Arts*. Vol 2., trans Thomas M. Knox. Oxford: Clarendon Press.
Heller, Monica, and Bonnie McElhinny. 2017. *Language, Capitalism, Colonialism: Toward a Critical History*. Toronto: University of Toronto.
Hess, Carol L. 2012. "Religious Education." In *The Wiley-Blackwell Companion to Practical Theology*, edited by Bonnie J. Miller-McLemore, Malden: Wiley-Blackwell, 299–307.
Kee, Howard Clark, Eric M. Meyers, John Rogerson, and Anthony J. Saldarini. 1997. *The Cambridge Companion to the Bible*. Cambridge: Cambridge University.
Kim-Cragg, HyeRan. 2012. *Story and Song: A Postcolonial Interplay between Christian Education and Worship*. New York: Peter Lang.
Kim-Cragg, HyeRan. 2018. *Interdependence: A Postcolonial Feminist Practical Theology*. Eugene: Pickwick.
Kwok, Pui-lan. 1995. *Discovering the Bible in the Non-Biblical World*. Maryknoll: Orbis.
Newman, Judith. 2018. *Before the Bible: The Liturgical Body and the Formation of Scriptures in Early Judaism*. Oxford: Oxford University.
O'Connor, Kathleen. 1998. "Crossing Borders: Biblical Studies in a Trans-cultural World." In *Teaching the Bible: The Discourses and Politics of Biblical Pedagogy*, edited by Fernando F. Segovia and Mary Ann Tolbert, Minneapolis: Fortress, 322–337.
Ong, Walter. 1982. *Orality and Literacy: The Technologizing of the Word*. New York: Methuen.
Rose, Lucy Atkinson. 1997. *Sharing the Word: Preaching in the Roundtable Church*. Louisville: Westminster John Knox.
Said, Edward. 1978. *Orientalism*. New York: Vantage Books.
Schipani, Daniel, and Mary Schertz. 2004. "Through the Eyes of Practical Theology and Theological Education." In *Through the Eyes of Another: Intercultural Reading of the Bible*, edited by Hans de Wit, Louis Jonker, Marleen Kool, and Daniel Schipani, Indiana: Institute of Mennonite Studies, 437–451.
Spivak, Gayatri C. 1999. *A Critique of Postcolonial Reason: Toward a History of the Vanishing Present*. Cambridge, MA: Harvard University.
Tamez, Elsa. 2016. "The Bible and the Five Hundred Years of Conquest." In *Voices from the Margin: Interpreting the Bible in the Third World*, edited by Rasiah S. Sugirtharajah, Maryknoll: Orbis, 1–18.

Taylor, Diana. 2003. *The Archive and The Repertoire: Performing Cultural Memory in the Americas.* Durham: Duke University.

Taylor, Mark Lewis. 1998. "Reading from an Indigenous Place." In *Teaching the Bible: The Discourses and Politics of Biblical Pedagogy,* edited by Fernando F. Segovia and Mary Ann Tolbert, Minneapolis: Fortress, 117–136.

Tolbert, Mary Ann. 1998. "A New Teaching with Authority: A Re-evaluation of the Authority of the Bible." In *Teaching the Bible: The Discourses and Politics of Biblical Pedagogy,* edited by Fernando F. Segovia and Mary Ann Tolbert, Minneapolis: Fortress, 168–189.

Tran, Mai-Anh. 2017. *Reset the Heart: Unlearning Violence, Relearning Hope.* Nashville: Abingdon.

Travis, Sarah. 2014. *Decolonizing Preaching: The Pulpit as Postcolonial Space.* Eugene: Cascade.

Dalia Marx
Sacred Times / Rites of Passage / The Talmudic Ritual for Awakening

1 Introduction

Many attest to the fact that the very first moments after awakening may determine their mood and wellbeing for the rest of the day. The way one separates oneself from sleep and from the nocturnal realm and greets the new day can be revealing. This is why many cultures and religions ascribe special importance to this particular transition. In this paper, I will explore what the sages of the Talmud have to say on this liminal moment. I will focus on the early morning ritual, described in the last chapter of Tractate *Berakhot* in the Babylonian Talmud, the tractate dealing with liturgical matters. Current Jewish practices in part divert from the Talmudic one and I will briefly relate to them in an excursus.

2 The Morning Ritual as a Miniature Rite of Passage

The Talmudic Morning Blessings ritual was intended to help the individual cope with the transition from the nocturnal domain into the day. One may consider it as a miniature rite of passage, a term coined by Arnold van Gennep (van Gennep 1960). Rites of passage are a category of rituals performed during a person's transition from one stage, state, or status to another. They mark this transformation and, no less importantly, they effect it. Van Gennep identified three components that can be found in every rite of passage: each includes a situation of disconnection or separation from the former status; a state that was later referred to by Victor Turner as the liminal stage, in which the actual transition occurs (Turner 1964); and a third state, the incorporation and entry into the new status.

According to Turner, a person undergoing a rite of passage who is in the liminal stage constitutes a kind of 'primordial matter' that has lost its previous form and has not yet acquired a new form (Turner 1969, 94–97). He or she are effectively simultaneously present in two contrary states, and yet does not belong to either. The ritual permits the individual to experience the structured and controlled breaking of cognitive forms and conventional perceptions; in a "moment within and outside time" (Turner 1969, 96), the individual stands without identity, status, or property, in what Turner calls "sanctified poverty" (Turner 1967, 98–99). The function of this period of time (which may be extremely brief) is that it creates a state in which the individual is removed from the routine flow of their life and is given an opportunity to examine the reality they have come to take for granted. Accordingly, this time may be marked by reflection and creative thought.

Turner emphasizes that the purpose of rites of passage is not to create a subversive experience liable to erode the existing order of life. On the contrary: the successful completion of the rite of passage will lead the individual into an acceptance and embrace of the new state they have entered. In other words, the chaotic nature of the liminal state is actually intended to affirm the structure from which the individual has departed and the structure into which they will enter (Turner 1964).

The attempt to apply the theory of rites of passage, which usually refers to dramatic, acute, and irreversible transitions relating to key stages of life (birth, sexual maturation, the forming of spousal partnership, and death) to the recitation of the Morning Blessings in accordance with the instructions in the Talmud – a routine and daily task – is certainly far from simple. It must be admitted that, in the vast majority of cases, awakening in the morning is not accompanied by a crisis in either the clinical or the existential sense of the word. In contrast to the individual undergoing a rite of passage in the context of the life cycle, the daily transition between day and night is generally muted and mundane. However, the location of the Morning Blessings within the framework of the Talmudic discussion of blessings recited on occasions of crisis may testify to the manner in which these were perceived by the Rabbis. I shall now attempt to suggest why transformational qualities may be identified in the Talmudic Morning Ritual, and why it may be considered a repeated and miniature rite of passage.

It is often suggested that rituals are created as a response to a genuine human need, reflecting the challenges presented by life. I would argue that the Morning Ritual, as presented in the Talmud, seeks to address such a moment of crisis – the point of transition between the nocturnal domain of sleep, which is characterized by a lack of control and discernment, and the diurnal domain of awakening, characterized by the demand for control, restraint, and the capacity to create categories and distinctions. Awakening in the morning, therefore, is a routine occurrence, yet one that may be experienced as a minor crisis.

What, then, is the nature of the crisis that may be involved in sleep? A person who sleeps undergoes an experience that is somewhat similar to that of one who is dead and indeed they can appear to be dead to an observer. Like the dead person, a person who is asleep is exempt from the commandments, since they are no more than a body whose soul is inactive and, perhaps, not even present within them. On going to sleep, people submit themselves to uncertainty. They are no longer the masters of their own thoughts and dreams; they have no control over their bodies, and no real certainty that tomorrow the sun will shine; alternately – they have no certainty that they themselves will awaken from their sleep. The person retiring to sleep – willingly, in most cases – removes his or her clothes and the other symbols of social status and identity as an alert being with conscience and the ability to choose, and hence, to an extent, waives his or her very aliveness. The concept of the separation of body and soul during sleep was elaborated in depth in the *Zohar* and in later Kabbalistic thought, but the kernel of this concept may already be found in the late *rabbinic literature*. For example, the following, attributed to Rabbi Alexandri:

> When one lends new things to a person of flesh and blood, he [the borrower] returns them worn and torn; but the Holy One, blessed be He, is given them worn and torn and returns them new. Know that the laborer works all day, and his soul is tired and worn, and when he sleeps, he returns his soul to the Holy One, blessed be He, and it is deposited with Him, and in the morning it returns to his body as a new creation, as it is written: New every morning, abundant is your faith (Lamentations 3). We believe and acknowledge that You return our souls at the [time of the] resurrection of the dead. (*Midrash Tehillim* 22:2 [ed. Solomon Buber])

Going to sleep at the close of the day is a human reflection of the changing seasons of nature, mimicking (at least on the symbolic level) the death that comes at the close of life. The perception of sleep as resembling death, or even having some of the characteristics of death, is reflected in several sayings of the Rabbis, the best known of which is, "Sleep is one-sixtieth of death" (bavli *Ber.* 57b). Human curiosity about what happens to our body and soul during sleep, and the anxiety this question may arouse, are somewhat analogous to human curiosity about what happens to our body and soul after death, and this similarity underlies the rituals relating to sleep. Sleep is described as containing the taste of death, and the impurity of the sleeping person is often likened to that of the dead (Moelin 1979, 23), underscoring the status of the Morning Ritual as symbolizing (or creating) a divide between the world of the living and the world of the dead. The Rabbis are aware that the awakening human is no longer a denizen of the nocturnal realm but has also yet to take his or her place in the diurnal one. The blessings in the Morning Ritual accompany each of the normal morning actions, helping the individual to gradually return to his state as an active, conscious human.

Rabbinic prayer seeks to provide protecting shelter to those who need this in any situation and in every transition in the passing of the day, the year, and the life cycle. Equally, prayer constitutes the arena in which the worshippers cope with their existence, their surroundings, and their Creator. The Morning Ritual constitutes one plank in this structure, by which the liturgy accompanies those who observe it into situations of dilemma and conflict and supports them through perils and transitions.

If the person going to sleep is afraid of the loss of control and of death (whether symbolic or actual, since, as discussed, sleep is perceived as a microcosm of death), then on awakening, the individual feels – or, at least, is encouraged to feel – a sense of relief and gratitude that they have been guarded through sleep and into awakening. Nevertheless, I would argue that this is also a time of crisis that may be accompanied by anxieties.

I believe that at least three kinds of anxiety might face the person awakening from sleep, and assuaged by the Morning Ritual; all three relate to the fact that this ritual is recited at a liminal point in time: Anxieties relating to the sleep from which the individual has just awoken, to nightmares or unresolved dreams, and to aspects of the separation from the world of sleep – a fetal and primordial world whose essence does not lend itself to simple explanations or rational analysis. One may also experience anxieties relating to the new day and the need to cope with leaving the private, domestic realm to enter the public one. And finally, one may have anxieties of an existential nature: as order is restored and creation is renewed in the morning, questions may emerge regarding the fragile nature of this order, its disturbance and cessation, the disappearance of divine providence, or the fear of being unworthy and inadequate in one's actions and hence undeserving of divine mercy. If we employ Turner's terms, consciousness is *structure* while sleep is a *liminal state*, as illustrated in the following figure:

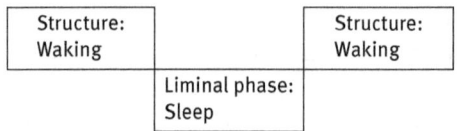

Figure 2: Sleep as Liminal State.

Sleep is a liminal state since the conventional divisions of functions, status, and so forth do not apply when one is asleep. The borders of sleep consist of falling asleep and awakening, but during its course, the sleeper is in a structureless state of an extreme nature. Man and woman, free person and slave, Jew, and Gentile, the mighty and the lowly – all are equal in standing and status as they sleep.

In a way, sleep defies all definitions of category and structure. Yet it may also be perceived as a structureless structure, since it is clearly defined and limited. When we add the ritual relief provided at both ends of the night, we see that, in addition to sleep, another level of liminality is present: the ritual designed to lead the individual from the state of being awake to that of sleep (the recitation of the bedtime *shema*) and from sleep to awakening (the Morning Ritual). These two rituals, both of which are presented in the same Talmudic discussion, serve as guards, as it were, at the borders between the two realms. More accurately, perhaps, they may be described as border stations through which those who recite the blessings pass from one realm to the other (Zerubavel 1993, 5–20). This is reflected in the following figure:

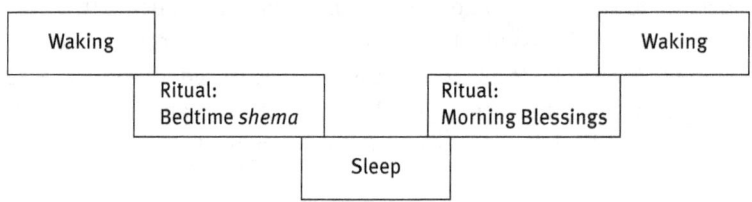

Figure 3: Talmudic Morning Ritual.

This figure also requires elaboration. The reality of human life as it progresses is not simply linear, but also cyclical, advancing in a kind of spiral. Just as both extremities of sleep are wrapped in rituals, so the period of awakening is marked at its beginning by the Morning Ritual, and at its end by the recitation of the *sh'ma* before going to bed.

According to the biblical stories of the creation, the original state of the world was one of chaos, which out of and in opposition to which God established His world (this terminology appears in Psalm 136, and thereafter in the blessing for standing upon the ground in the Morning Ritual, see below). Similarly, the initial state of the human is latent and passive; against this, the person reciting the blessings resume and, in a way, recreate their talents, capabilities, and regain their identity through actions and their verbalization in the blessings. Just as the daily setting and rising of the sun is perceived by the Rabbis as corroborative evidence of the existence of God and, no less importantly, of God's merciful providence, so, I would argue, is the daily miracle of awakening from sleep and from miniature or symbolic death.

3 The Talmudic Ritual of Awakening

According to the Mishnah (the first Jewish legal compendia, redacted around 220 in the Land of Israel), the first liturgical text recited in the morning is *Sh'ma Yishrael* (a central liturgical unit comprised of three biblical paragraphs, encased with liturgical blessings). It seems, that the sages of the Mishnah, the *Tana'im*, did not know of any liturgy preceding it. The *Sh'ma*, a statement Jews are required to recite twice daily at least, is the closest statement to a creed in the Jewish tradition (Kimelman 2001). Apparently, later authorities around the fifth century (the last generators of the *Amoraim*), may have felt that the *Sh'ma*, text which requires the acceptance of the yoke of Heaven and of the commandments, was too mentally and spiritually demanding a text for the tender moments of transition between sleep and awakening. They believed that the worshippers needed liturgy that would help them to gradually rise up for the new day. The ritual they developed is one that involves the body and soul, aiming to help one get the worshipper ready for the new day (Marx 2008).

The core of the morning blessings appears in the framework of a *suggiah* (a Talmudic discussion) on the blessings one should recite when entering a dangerous place such as a foreign city, and on those recited upon leaving those places in peace. The 'entering' in our case, which is the last part of the *suggiah*, is not into a place but, rather, to a state, that of sleep, and the departure of it is wakefulness. As mentioned above, sleep was considered by the rabbis as 'one sixtieth of death', and a special prayer, the bedtime *sh'ma* is specified when entering this state. The Morning Blessings, the most elaborate part of the *suggiah*, is the response upon 'exiting' from this dangerous place (Marx 2007).

The first blessing in this collection, *Birkat Neshamah* (the blessing regarding the soul) opens with the words: "My God, the soul that you have given me is pure," rather than the blessing traditional formula ("Blessed are You, Eternal our God"). This may attest to its antiquity (even though it appears for the first time in the Talmud). This is an optimistic statement, it declares that our soul, the source of our very being, is pure and good. The implication is that human existence is good at its core and therefore we can strive to do good. There is some debate about the actual meaning of the conclusion of the blessing: "Blessed [...] who restores souls to dead corpses", with different opinions regarding whether this refers to the mercy of the 'daily resurrection' of waking up, or to the resurrection of the dead at the end of time (Petuchowski 1981). This ambiguous language may plausibly suggest both interpretations.

Birkat Neshamah is followed by a collection of short blessings. Rabbi Sa'adia Ga'on (882–943, Egypt and Babylon) called this collection *Birkhot Hape'ulot* (The Blessings Over Activities), since each one of them is recited while performing a routine morning activity. Here are the blessings as they appear in the Talmud:

Upon awakening one should say: "My God, the soul which You have bestowed in me is pure. You formed it within me, You breathed it into me, and You preserve it within me. And You will take it from me and restore it to me in the time to come. As long as my soul is within me, I give thanks to You, Eternal, my God and God of my ancestors, Ruler of all worlds, Sovereign of all souls. Blessed are You, Eternal, Who restores souls to dead bodies."

On hearing the sound of the rooster [crowing], one should say: "Blessed Who gives understanding to the rooster to distinguish between day and night;"

When opening the eyes, one should say: "Blessed, Who gives sight to the blind;"

On straightening and sitting up, one should say: "Blessed, Who releases the imprisoned;"

When dressing, one should say: "Blessed, Who clothes the naked;"

Upon standing up, one should say: "Blessed, Who straightens the bent;"

On stepping on the ground, one should say: "Blessed, who spreads the earth above the waters;"

Upon walking, one should say, "Blessed, Who prepares the steps of man;"

When putting on one's shoes, one should say: "Blessed, Who has provided me with all my needs;"

On fastening one's belt, one should say: "Blessed, Who girds Israel with might;"

When pulling a cape over one's head, one should say: "Blessed, Who crowns Israel with glory;"

When putting on the tsitsit (fringed garment), one should say: "Blessed, Who has sanctified us with the commandments and commanded us to wrap ourselves with tsitsit;"

On placing the tefillin (phylacteries) on the arm, one should say: "Blessed, Who has sanctified us with His commandments and commanded us to put on tefilin;"

When [placing the tefillin] on the head, one should say: "Blessed, Who has sanctified us with His commandments and commanded us concerning the commandment of *tefillin*;"

On washing one's hands, one should say: "Blessed, Who has sanctified us with His commandments and commanded us regarding the washing of hands;"

On washing one's face, one should say: "Blessed, Who removes sleep from my eyes and slumber from my eyelids. [And] may it be Your will, Eternal my God, to accustom me to the study of Your Torah and to let me adhere to Your commandments. And bring me not into the grasp of sin, nor into the grasp of iniquity, nor into the grasp of transgression, nor into the grasp of trial, nor into the grasp of disgrace. And turn my inclination to submit to you, and keep me far from an evil person and from an evil companion, and make me hold fast to the good inclination, and to a good companion in Your world, and grant me today and every day favor, kindness, and compassion in Your eyes and in the eyes of all those who see me, and bestow bountiful kindness upon me. Blessed are You, Eternal, who bestows bountiful kindness upon His people Israel" (Bavli, Ber. 60b).

These Talmudic blessings accompany the routine activities of the morning from the moment of waking up, indeed, even before opening the eyes, ascribing them with holiness, there follows the increasing awareness of one's surroundings (the blessing on hearing the crowing of the rooster), opening the eyes ("Who gives sight to the blind"), stretching out ("Who releases the imprisoned") etc. It seems that the Talmud is citing an abridged form of the full blessing formula, "Blessed are You, Eternal, Ruler of the Universe, who [...]", which was known to all. The first blessings have a universal character (e.g., the two blessings cited above), while the later blessings have more particular nature (e.g., "Who girds Israel with might"). This carries over to the blessings over the commandments (over the tsitsit, Tefillin and ritual hand washing) that follow.

4 The Narrative of the Talmudic Morning Ritual

The blessings as presented in the Talmud are occasional blessings, that is, ones recited upon performing specific actions (in this case, the ordinary actions of the morning). Accordingly, the assertion that they are constructed in a quasi-narrative form does not relate to the original manner of their performance, but rather to the manner in which they are presented in the Talmudic discussion.

The blessing over the restoration of the soul, the first of the Talmudic Morning Ritual, offers thanks for the return of the soul with morning. It is recited when the individual awakens in their bed, their eyes still closed, not yet confronting the external world. This blessing draws an explicit analogy between awakening from sleep in the morning and the expectation of awakening from death at the End of Days, "You will take my soul from me, to restore it to me in the time to come," (Petuchowski 1981). In the next blessing, recited upon hearing the rooster crow, the awakening person relates to the wisdom that the Creator has implanted within the natural world ("Who gives understanding to the rooster.") The worshipper gradually emerges from the primal state of sleep and, to the accompaniment of the blessings, becomes a responsible and active being. While the blessing over the rooster's discerning of dawn relates to the human sense of hearing, the next blessing relates to the sense of sight and the opening of the eyes as one awakens ("Who gives sight to the blind,").

Through reciting the Morning Blessings, the awakening person passes from blindness to sight; is liberated from the shackles of body at sleep ("Who releases the bound,"); moves from a raw, naked state to one in which s/he he may move about freely in public ("Who clothes the naked,"); from lying on their bed to standing in an upright position ("Who straightens the bent,"); from involuntary to voluntary motion ("Who spreads the earth over the water"); and self-ambulation ("Who prepares the steps of man"); and from being unable to care for themselves (and indeed requiring nothing), to being aware of their needs and able to go out and tend to their livelihood ("Who provided me with all my needs").

These blessings, and the actions over which they are recited, thus gradually lead the reciter from the nocturnal, primal, and passive state into the diurnal, dynamic, and active one. Their recitation encourages awareness of the body and of physiological capabilities. They also draw the individual, to employ the terminology the anthropologist Claude Levi-Strauss, from nature to culture (Levi-Strauss 1963, 1). While asleep, the human is no more than a shell, a body strewn helplessly on a bed. Through awakening, dressing, and bathing, the human gradually becomes an enculturated, civilized being. It should be noted that the reference so far is to culture in general; these blessings do not explicitly contain any particularistic Jewish dimension (beyond their redolent use of biblical language) and could be recited by any individual.

Now begins the next significant stage in the transition: the transformation of the awakening person into a Jew. On fastening one's belt and putting on a cape, two blessings are recited that emphasize the reciter's membership amongst the Jewish people ("Who girds Israel with might" and "Who crowns Israel with glory.") These 'Jewish' blessings mark out the restructuring of the personality and the body of the reciter. What is perceived as Jewish in these blessings is not the mere action of fastening a belt or putting on a cape, neither of which were exclusive to Jews; rather the language of the blessings is particularistic, affirming the awakening person's reconstitution as a Jew.

The unit continues with four blessings relating to the commandments of donning *tsitsit* (*fringed garment*), *tefillin* (phylacteries) of the arm and of the head, and the washing of hands). The principle behind these blessings is, to a large extent, the opposite of the blessings over occasional actions. In the latter, the routine 'mundane' action acquires a religious status through the addition of the blessing. In the case of the blessings over performance of the commandments, the blessing accompanies an action that has no independent meaning outside of its religious dimension. Just as the recitation of the blessings over generic actions reaffirms and demonstrates human capacities and capabilities, so the particularistic blessings reaffirm and demonstrate Jewish identity, as manifested and modeled in the commandments and their associated blessings.

The Talmudic early morning ritual ends with a blessing thanking God "Who removes sleep," in which the worshipper expresses the completion of the process of awakening and renewed creation by washing their face. This blessing begins and ends in the blessing formula ("Blessed are You [...]"). It is significantly longer than the other blessing over activities, as it includes a supplication for preservation and protection from evil forces outside the home: "May it be Your will, Eternal, my God, to accustom me to the study of Torah [...] and keep me far from an evil person and from an evil companion, and make me hold fast to the good inclination and to a good companion in Your world." The action with which the blessing is associated is washing the face – preparing the public aspect of the body that was hidden during the night.

5 The Complex Meaning of the Talmudic Morning Blessings

Though modest in length, the Morning Ritual addresses diverse aspects of life. I shall illustrate the broad fields of meaning created by the blessings by examining one in particular, "Who gives sight to the blind," which is recited when one opens the eyes in the morning. As with the other blessings, this short blessing would seem to allude to several aspects that must surely have been apparent both to those who formulated these blessings and to those who used them:

- *Awakening* – Thanksgiving for the mere ability to open one's eyes. The person awakening from sleep, who was as good as blind while sleeping, offers thanks for the restoration of sight that comes with the awakening.
- *Birth* – As mentioned above, the Rabbis perceived sleep as a miniature experience of death. Accordingly, upon awakening the reciter of the blessings is likened to a newborn baby (i.e., *Lev. Rabbah* 14:2). Just as the baby, while still a fetus in its mother's womb, can hear vague sounds, and perhaps even see blurred shadows, so a sleeping person sees only dream images. The regaining of sight in the morning appears to symbolize reemergence into the world and the potency of the awakened and active individual.
- *Creation* – After Adam and Eve have eaten of the fruit of the Tree of Knowledge, it is said "And the eyes of them both were opened, and they knew that they were naked" (Gen 3:7). The insight they are granted relates to their sight and constitutes the realization of a hitherto dormant potential. The opening of the eyes and the capacity for sight (and, on an extended level, 'insight') are associated with understanding and with the capability of discernment. Light is perceived not only as part of creation, but also as testimony to creation. Thus sight, or better, the ability to perceive light, is also a testimony to creation.
- *Moral Awakening* – The image of blindness is often used to denote moral blindness (i.e., Is. 42:16–19; 43:8). The opening of the eyes may be perceived symboli-

cally as awakening from a state of moral blindness (and, perhaps, symbolic death), as suggested in the following *midrash:*

> There is no sorrow so great and no torment so burdened and difficult as blindness... And when [God] comes to heal the world, He begins with none other than the blind, as it is said, *God opens the eyes of the blind* (Ps 146:8). And who are the blind? Those generations that walk in the Torah like blind people, as it is said: *We grope for the wall like the blind* (Isa 59:10). All read and know not what they read, repeat and know not what they repeat. But in the time to come: *Then the eyes of the blind shall be opened* (Isa 35:5) (*Midrash on Pss*, 146:5 [ed. Solomon Buber]).

The act of opening one's eyes in the morning may thus be likened to a reenactment of a moral awakening, and hence a commitment to a proper and sober life.

- *Awakening as an Allusion to Future Redemption* – If sleep is perceived as a miniature form of death, awakening from sleep is likened in metaphoric terms (and perhaps even in metonymic ones) to the resurrection of the dead. Accordingly, we may likely identify in the action of opening the eyes of the blind eschatological allusions to the future, as evident, for example, in the *midrash* quoted in the previous paragraph.

These interpretations, which relate to diverse layers of understanding and consciousness, seem to be present simultaneously (though not necessarily consciously) in the formulation of the blessing, and are not mutually exclusive. Indeed, they are intertwined and support one another: the opening of the eyes, an almost instinctive physiological act, is testimony of God's mercy to those He has created; symbolic daily creation recalls the primal creation of the world and the creation of life through human birth and, in the same manner, the eschatological expectation of rebirth after death.

Even if it cannot be expected that this plethora of meanings was regularly present in the consciousness of most worshippers, these meanings would seem to lie on the margins of their awareness, and among the images through which they interpret their being and their daily experiences. The same multivocal and multilayered quality may be seen in the remaining blessings, manifested in their concrete, cosmic, and eschatological fields and in the simultaneous connection between a primordial beginning and eschatological end.

As mentioned above, this liturgical rubric is included in the ninth and last chapter of Tractate *Berakhot* of the Babylonian Talmud. This chapter deals with event-specific and occasional blessings, rather than prayers that must be recited every day. The occasional nature of the Morning Blessings may be inferred by its location among the event-specific liturgical utterances. Perhaps the redactors of the Talmud did not intend to specify a fixed unit but to give examples of blessings one may recite over daily activities. Be that as it may, this collection of blessings is designed to help those just waking up in the morning to revitalize their bodies and souls anew after their hours of sleep.

6 Excursus: Post-Talmudic Early Morning Ritual

The first Jewish prayer books appeared in the 9th–10th centuries, that is, about three centuries after the redaction of the Talmud. The early morning ritual depicted in them is rather different than the one described in the Talmud.

During the early Islamic period, concern was raised by rabbinic authorities in Babylon that the hands of the awakening person might have become ritually impure during sleep. A responsum of Rav Natronai Gaon, quoted with certain changes in *Seder Rav Amram*, acknowledges the Talmudic teaching but adds: "But because of impurity [of the hands], this is the rule: once a person has awakened from his sleep, he may not recite even a single blessing until he has washed his hands". (*Responsa of Rav Natronai*, 107; cf. *Seder Rav Amram Gaon*, 2). Thus, upon awakening, the worshipper was now required to wash their hands and attend to their bodily needs before reciting all blessings together as a complete sequence rather than singly, upon performing each individual morning action. The custom of reciting the Morning Ritual as a single unit in the synagogue (or at home) has since been the practice of most Jewish communities.

Over time, the blessings of the Morning Ritual came to be viewed as a required list of blessings, part of the one hundred blessings a Jew is required to recite each day; they no longer belonged to the category of occasional blessings. Does this mean, therefore, that the entire content of this article is no longer relevant to today's worshippers as they recite the Morning Ritual? That is, has any affinity between the sequential blessings in the synagogue and the Talmudic Morning Ritual, which seeks to transfer the reciter in practical terms from the nocturnal domain to the diurnal domain, been broken? I would suggest that the connection with these actions indeed remains at least on the connotative level, or, at least, through the study of the sources, even if the blessings are no longer recited in the manner in which they were originally cast.

Further, as is often the case, Jewish liturgical units, originally concise, tend to absorb many components and become rather large pieces. The Morning ritual is no exception to the rule. Post-Talmudic authorities wedded the blessings over activities, with three blessings framed in a negative form, thanking God who "did not make me a gentile, a woman and a boor/slave" (Kahn 2011). Unlike the blessings over actions, these blessings already appear in tannaitic literature (Tosefta Ber. 6:8). As far as we know, they were not originally connected to any morning ritual, and hence are not fully within the scope of this current discussion. However, the two clusters of blessings appear alongside each other from the earliest *siddurim* in our possession onwards, as part of the Morning Ritual. These blessings are disconcerting many contemporary Jews who replace them with positive and non-discriminatory formulations (Tabory 2001).

Many more rubrics were added along the generations to the early morning ritual, such as a symbolic Torah study, recitation of biblical and rabbinical passages concerning the Temple sacrifices, poems, supplications and more (Elbogen 1993, 3–9).

Even if the spirit of daily creation and rebirth is weakened when the blessings are recited in the manner as a fix list, which is necessarily immediately after awakening, that has now become customary, it still flows within them, helping the individual to set down roots in their daily reality, after a night of sleep.

Bibliography

Buber, Solomon. 1885. *Midrash Tanchuma*. https://www.sefaria.org/Midrash_Tanchuma_Buber (01.12.2021).

Elbogen, Ismar. 1993. *Jewish Liturgy: A Comprehensive History*, trans. Raymond P. Scheindlin. New York: The Jewish Publication Society.

Gennep, Arnold van. 1960. *The Rites of Passage*, trans. Monica Vizedom and Gabrielle Caffee. Chicago: University of Chicago Press.

Kahn, Yoel. 2011. *The Three Blessings: Boundaries, Censorship, and Identity in Jewish Liturgy*. New York: Oxford University Press.

Kimelman, Reuven. 2001. "The Shema' Liturgy: From Covenant Ceremony to Coronation." *Kenishta* 1:9–105.

Levi-Strauss, Claude. 1963. *Structural Anthropology*, trans. Claire Jacobson and Brooke Grundfest Schoepf. New York: Basic Books.

Marx, Dalia. 2007. "One who Enters a Capital City: Prayers in Liminal Moments." *Jewish Studies* 44:105–136 (in Hebrew).

Marx, Dalia. 2008. "The Morning Ritual (*Birkhot Hashahar*) in the Talmud: The Reconstructing of Body and Mind through the Blessings." *Hebrew Union College Annual* 77:103–129.

Moelin, Jacob. 1979. *Responsa of the Maharil*. Jerusalem: Mekhon Yerushalayim.

Petuchowski, Jakob. 1981. "Modern Misunderstandings of an Ancient Benediction." In *Studies in Aggadah, Targum and Jewish Liturgy, in Memory of Joseph Heinemann*, edited by Ezra Fleischer and Jakob Petuchowski, Jerusalem / Cincinnati: Magnes Press, 45–54.

Tabory, Joseph. 2001. "The Benedictions of Self-Identity and the Changing Status of Women and of Orthodoxy." *Kenishta* 1:107–130.

Turner, Victor. 1964. "Betwixt and Between: The Liminal Period in Rites de Passage." *The Proceedings of the American Ethnological Society* 4–20.

Turner, Victor. 1967. *The Forest of Symbols: Aspects of Ndembu Ritual*. Ithaca: Cornell University Press.

Turner, Victor. 1969. *The Ritual Process: Structure and Anti-Structure*. Chicago: Aldine Publishing Company.

Zerubavel, Eviatar. 1993. *The Fine Line: Making Distinctions in Everyday Life*. Chicago / London: Chicago University Press.

Henry Mbaya and Cas Wepener
Sacrifice / Violence / Isitshisa

1 Introduction

The word sacrifice is still used in most parts of the world to denote, for example, sacrifice on behalf of family and children (Schreurs 2001), but the practice of the ritual killing and burning of a human or animal has all but disappeared in most countries of the world. However, there are also parts of the world in which sacrifice, as the ritual killing and burning of an animal, is still a core part of the culture and of the liturgical praxis of churches (Mbaya 2019). This is the case in certain African Independent Churches (AIC) in South Africa. This chapter will focus on one such church: the Corinthian Church of South Africa (CCSA) and will begin with a description of the actual ritual killing and burning of animals as sacrifice. The chapter will then present theories on sacrifice – from both Western and African perspectives – to attempt an interpretation of this event.

Both authors of this chapter attended the sacrifice in question as participatory observers. They also conducted several interviews and focus group discussions regarding this particular sacrifice and other smaller sacrifices conducted in this church with members and leaders of the CCSA. During one workshop hosted by the authors of this chapter, they presented a description of this sacrifice to an academic audience comprised of scholars from both Africa and Europe. Whilst listening to the description and looking at the photographs of a heifer being killed and afterwards burnt to ashes, one of the participants who was from a Western European secular context exclaimed: "But this is against the Enlightenment!"

The aim of this contribution is to not only describe and better understand sacrifice and violence embedded in ritual action, but also foster at least some transcultural appreciation for this practice in line with the core values of the Handbook.

2 The 'Pilgrimage' to Umlazi

Every year on the last Saturday of October, thousands of members of the CCSA, from almost every corner of the country, converge at Unit 2 of Umlazi Township close to Durban in the province of KwaZulu-Natal, South Africa. They participate in the annual pilgrimage to attend the ritual burning of the sacrifice, which in IsiZulu is called *Isitshisa*, a marked day on the calendar. The pilgrims arrive in buses, taxis (minibuses), cars; and nearly all are dressed in golden-like attire; with slings hanging over their shoulders. The colours make them conspicuous in the late afternoon, and sunset of the October sky. Most of the men wear turbans and are bearded, some carry sticks.

Umlazi Unit 2 is similar to other Black South African townships. Most people who live in this township are materially poor: they do menial jobs in Durban city, and in some suburbs in the city. Umlazi is mostly comprised of shacks, with some middle-income houses scattered here and there. It is here that the main Church of the Corinthians is situated.

As one enters the church, an area of about 200 metres in length and 80 metres in width, there is a festive feeling in the air: people sing and dance endlessly, others beat drums and play trumpet-like instruments and hornets *(imibhobho)*. Many members are dripping in sweat in the heat of spring in this sub-tropical part of the country. Others are seated or stand chatting around the church building.

Amidst all the loud singing and dancing in the building, it is almost impossible to conduct a conversation and understand one another. The singing and the talking, the chatter, and the sound of the *imibhobho* is deafening. The smell of meat cooking and roasting on the open fire behind the church building fills the air. This smell blends with the pungent smell of incense for which a shrub *(impepho)* is used.

Umlazi, the headquarters of the CCSA, seems to mean to the Corinthians what 'Mecca' might mean to Muslim people, or what 'Jerusalem' might mean to Jewish and Christian people. However, in the South African context, and to some extent, to the Corinthians, Umlazi has become similar to what Moria outside Polokwane is to the members of the Zionist Christian Church (ZCC), under Bishop Barnabas Lekganyane that is visited annually at Easter by millions of ZCC members (Müller 2011).

A question which naturally comes to mind is: what attracts all these people to this place? What motivates them to congregate here every year? And why particularly do they come to Umlazi? We obtained answers to these questions by means of interviews and focus group discussions.

To the Corinthians, this space is special; it is here where the church founder, Johannes Richmond, established his ministry, and the spirit of the founder is believed to reside in this Church (Wepener 2019). It is also a place where the founder's widow, Bestina Richmond, who was the archbishop at the time of our visits, was performing her duties and was thus present during the *Isitshisa*.

This rectangular Church building, situated at the northern end of the ground, nearly a hundred meters in length, and thirty meters in breath is the centre of the gathering; the very centre of ritual worship and service. It is like a shrine, symbolising the presence and authority of the late archbishop, as his staff is kept there. On this occasion the church is fully packed, with almost no space to move as soon as you step through the door.

It is important to note, that the church grounds surrounding the building are also a relevant ritual space during the performance of *Isitshisa*. Behind the building, at the eastern end of the church, a group of mostly women cook mutton in three-legged pots on an open fire. There are others, washing pots and plates, and men slaughtering sheep. The smoke blows all around the church building, and some of it finds its way into the church – since the windows are open.

Around 6pm, the worshippers sing and dance in circles. The church officials seem to sit according to hierarchy at the one end of the building – with the wife of the founder and current archbishop elevated above them. Then come the bishops and other dignitaries including the secretaries (*oonobhala*).

Inside the Church, different rituals take place at the same time. Jean Richmond, the daughter of the founder and the principal secretary, stands at the centre of the church. A long line of ladies and girls sing and dance as they carry food items, such as oranges, packets of rice, beans, potatoes, on their heads – making their way to the secretary, where after they put it down, the secretary records the items in the book. These items are presented to poor people in Umlazi the following day.

While these food presentations take place, the ordination of the clergy attracts particular attention. The rite entails the smearing of goat's blood in the hands of the ordinands, and the stewards. The founder's staff, and then the Bible, is placed for a while on the head of each ordinand, while some words are spoken. This rite goes on for many hours.

At about 11.30 pm, a brown heifer is led inside the church through the West door by four men and is taken to the centre of the building. There it is blessed by a senior bishop. Immediately after that, in a procession, the heifer is led slowly and solemnly outside through the Western door of the Church. As this happens, the singing and blowing of the hornets increases. The atmosphere is electric. Outside the church, a fire burns on a large altar built of stones.

Around midnight, the heifer's throat is slit, and the animal is placed on a large fire on the altar. As this happens, the singing gets louder and louder. A red cloth is suspended over the fire while the heifer burns. The large amount of smoke and the smell of burning flesh fills the whole area. The heifer remains on the altar burning into ashes, as people continue to sing and pray. This ritual killing and burning is the *Isitshisa*, the burning of the heifer, the climax of the worship service.

Subsequently, the ashes from *Isitshisa* after the service are shared amongst the priests of the various local congregations for later usage. The *Isitshisa* is however not the only sacrifice done in the CCSA. According to one priest during an interview:

> There are also times we go to the mountains and there we make a fire and burn a chicken or sheep or small lamb as an offering. It is our culture as Corinthian Church people. If you remember the offering that Abraham and Isaac did on the mountain – we follow that culture. The reason for that is that we sometimes have visions that lead us to go and perform that ritual at the mountain. (See also Mbaya 2019; Wepener and ter Haar 2014; Wepener and Meyer 2012)

The *Isitshisa* concludes at midday on the Sunday with a communal meal. During this meal, blind people from Umlazi are brought to the church where they share in a meal with the Corinthians and are presented with gifts. This meal, and gifts, just like the sacrifice of the heifer, were instituted by Johannes Richmond.

During the rest of the liturgical year until the next *Isitshisa* the ashes are used by priests to conduct a variety of rituals. Most of these rituals are, according to the leaders and members, aimed at healing and cleansing, especially with regards to rituals pertaining to death.

This case study described a sacrifice in an AIC in current day South Africa in which members perform an annual slaughtering and burning of a heifer as well as numerous smaller animal sacrifices over the course of the year. In what follows, we present theories pertaining to sacrifice and violence. However, first a word about the authors of this chapter on whose participatory observation this description is based.

3 The Authors

As authors, we had various degrees of closeness to the service that we observed. Firstly, and importantly, the authors are both, amongst other things, ordained ministers in their respective church traditions (Anglican and Dutch Reformed). Right from the outset, the leaders of the CCSA made it clear that they would only allow us to conduct the research in their congregations, to participate, observe, and conduct interviews and focus groups, if we had been ordained with the laying on of hands. Had we not been, we would probably have not been allowed to carry out this research at all.

In the first meeting with the leader of the CCSA and the congregation in Phepheni, they expected the project leader (Wepener) to stand up and pray aloud before they gave their final approval (Wepener and Barnard 2010). Thus, in spite of the fact that the authors are in very different ecclesial and liturgical traditions to that of the CCSA, permission was sought from the leaders of the CCSA to do the research. We reassured them that the researchers would approach the data in a theological and fairly open-minded way and with transcultural sensitivity for a repertoire of liturgical practices which they knew would possibly be fairly new to us.

There are similarities and differences between the authors of this chapter. Both are ordained and academics. The first author is Malawian/South African, and an Anglican priest. He is specialised in Church History and Missiology. The second author is a white South African. He is a Dutch Reformed minister and is specialised in Practical Theology and specifically Liturgical- and Ritual Studies. Our various ways of looking at *Isitshisa* helped us to focus on different aspects and afterwards compare notes in order to provide a thicker description. In what follows, we will particularly focus on the ritual killing and burning of the heifer and the other 'smaller' sacrifices by members over the course of the year.

4 Sacrifice

Etymologically 'sacrifice' comes from the Latin *sacrificium* (sacred action) or *sacer facere* (to make holy). It is important to distinguish it from 'offer', which is derived from *operari* (to serve God through works) (Bell 1997, 112; Drexler 2006, 1658). There is however some overlap in the meaning of sacrifice and offering. Catherine Bell (1997, 112) explains that certain theories make a distinction between sacrifice and offering, arguing that in sacrifice the object sacrificed is sanctified.

Foci of these theories of sacrifice vary: from sacrifice as gift/exchange, as divining, as connecting, as meal, as communicative act, and as purifying (Bell 1997, 111–114; Mbiti 2008, 59; Schreurs 2001, 220). In the light of the *Isitshisa* as a case study, René Girard's theory on sacrifice and violence, as well as theories of sacrifice by scholars of African religion and philosophy will be discussed. As South Africans, we understand violence in a broad sense, such as the violence of colonialism, the violence of apartheid, deliberate physical violence that includes acts such as murder and death as a form of violence within an African cosmology. Sacrifice, as ritual act is itself a form of violence. René Girard ([1972] 2018, 34) states: "Violence is the heart and secret soul of the sacred" and Girard's theory specifically makes a connection between violence in society and the violence of ritual sacrifice.

4.1 René Girard on Sacrifice and Violence

In *Violence and the Sacred* Girard (2018) writes that societies are inherently violent. This violence can build up over time so that it overflows in a community like a dam overflowing its walls, ending in catastrophe. In sacrifice, the society then deflects upon a victim the violence that would have otherwise spread among its members (Girard 1996, 241). However, sacrifice can serve to stop the rising tide and channel the violence (Girard 1996, 245). The inherent violence in society is thus redirected in the act of sacrificing. A victim outside the confines of the society is chosen, and serves to repress the inherent strife, jealousy, in-fighting, thus "protect[ing] the entire community form its own violence" (Girard 2018, 8, 105). The aim of the sacrifice is to stop the potential gulf of violence and to establish harmony in society as well as to strengthen social fibres (Girard 2018, 9, 106).

Violence, in this case, ritual violence in the form of sacrifice, is thus utilised to stop violence in society. Sacrifice as violent ritual in other words substitutes the real thing and "Thus the circle closes" (Mack 1987, 9; see also Schreurs 2001, 221). "Only violence can put an end to violence, and that is why violence is self-propagating" (Girard 1996, 252). Violence from his perspective can also be contaminating, and thus sacrifice also plays a role in this regard as he sees death as "nothing more than the worst form of violence that can befall men" (Girard 1996, 255). Sacrifice can thus also serve to curb the contagion, which can include death.

A concept in Girard's (2018: chapter 4; Girard 1986) scholarship that should also be included here, is scapegoating. Scapegoating is the act of 'sacrificing' one victim instead of many. This identification has an impact on the bonding of the group who now feels more united than before. "The alien threat displaces everything else; internal quarrels are forgotten. A new unity and comradeship prevails" (Girard 1987, 90).

He writes how the scapegoating phenomenon thus has a real impact on the society, specifically on social cohesion, as the death of the scapegoat is followed by "a new mood of harmony and peace" (Girard 1987, 91). He suggests the importance of seeing how a scapegoat has power, because even though the person might have been (for example, in Medieval Europe) burnt on a pyre, people would have believed the person to possess powers that could be utilised for good or bad means (Girard 1987, 94). Here one can think of the utilisation of the ashes of the *Isitshisa* in many rituals of the CCSA and the social and spiritual capital and spiritual power that is generated through participation in the performance of *Isitshisa* (Mbaya 2019; Wepener and ter Haar 2014).

Of particular significance for us is Girard's discussion of sacrifice in cultures where the ancestors or living dead play a significant role and where they are seen as "founders, guardians and, if need be, disruptors of the cultural order" (Girard 2018, 290). *Isitshisa* is performed within an African spiritual ontology in which the living dead play an important role influencing the livings' daily lives for good or for evil. When the ancestors are unhappy with the living, they, in the words of Girard (2018, 290) "incarnate violence"; however, they do not want to destroy the community, and are "willing once more to accept the homage of their descendants; they cease to haunt the living and withdraw to their usual retreats." It is in this regard that ritual observances which include sacrifices play an important role. According to Girard (2018, 290–291) death is the ultimate violence and funereal rites play a large role here. Girard (2018, 291) states that death contains the germ of life. The death of the heifer and other animals and the ritual use of their ashes contain the germ of life in the CCSA as it is used in cleansing and healing rituals. These insights gained from Girard's theory on sacrifice and violence are helpful to come to an interpretation of the sacrifices performed in the CCSA.

4.2 Sacrifice in African Thought

The phenomenon of sacrifice is highly complex, and Girard's theory should be read alongside other insights, and for our purposes, alongside insights from scholars of African religion. *Isitshisa* clearly fits within an African ontology. In this regard, and like the discussion by Girard, Zahan (2000, 10–14) confirms the importance of the so-called cult of the ancestors for understanding ritual sacrifices across the African continent. Sacrifices play a role in appeasing the ancestors who can for various reasons become upset with the living. However, libations precede bloody sacrifices, as the libations are used to start a trade with the ancestors, whereas the sacrifice forms the high point "in their quest and their wat, engaging the living, in a radical fashion, and the dead in their obligation to reply favourably" (Zahan 2000, 12). He also emphasises the importance of blood in the sacrifice as a symbol of life.

The African cosmology within which sacrifices such as *Isitshisa* should be appreciated, consists of the world of the Spirit and the spirits which form part of the lives of humans. In Africa, the spirit world is not seen as a metaphor for reality, but as an integral part of reality (Ellis and Ter Haar 2004, 51). According to Jacob Olupona (2011, xvii) the divine realm interpenetrates daily experiences of humans in such a way that religion, culture, and society are very closely interrelated. It is within this spiritual ontology which consists of an intricate and delicate network of relationships between the worlds of humans and those of the spirits, that sacrifice in Africa should be understood. This also becomes clear in the work of John Mbiti.

According to John Mbiti (2008, 58) sacrifice is in Sub-Saharan Africa one of the most common acts of worship, with number of examples. He makes the distinction between sacrifice in which animal life is destroyed, and offerings in which food or items are presented. For Mbiti both (just) slaughtering as well as slaughtering and burning in African custom will thus come under this definition of sacrifice. He (Mbiti 2008, 59; 1999) explains that the ontological balance or equilibrium that should exist between God, humans, the deceased ancestors, and the cosmos, is sometimes disrupted. According to Mbiti (2008, 59), sacrifice serves to assist in re-establishing the desired equilibrium within this spiritual ontology as misfortune is the result of such an imbalance.

Chinaka Nwachukwu's (2018, 141–157) thoughts are closely related to the work of Mbiti. Nwachukwu (2018, 143, 153) states for example: "The visible and the invisible coexist in a constant cycle of harmonization made possible through prayers, sacrifices, and appeasements" and that "survival in the world of the living depends on meaningful access to the resources of the supernatural world." There are many kinds of sacrifice, such as expiation, petition, thanksgiving to ward off evil, and they are practised at various occasions, such as at life passages, with the new yam celebration, or after disasters, but all are aimed at influencing God through the deities and spirits as messengers of God (Nwachukwu 2018, 144–145). Elochokwu Uzukwu (1983, 277–278) points to the fact that sacrifice is often part of reconciliation rituals in Africa which links to Zahan. What is also meaningful in Nwachukwu's (2018, 156) contribution is his observation that "the time has come when the West must allow Africans to present our experiences of God and his revelation within our own history and culture" and suggestions on how sacrifice can be integrated in a meaningful way in Christian liturgy in Africa. This chapter would like to align with the values expressed by Nwachukwu and hope that this exploration of the *Isitshisa* can assist in fostering a transcultural and transreligious appreciation of these religious practices.

In the light of the South African case study as well as these theories, we will now endeavour to do an interpretation of the *Isitshisa*.

5 Interpretation

In light of Girard's theory, the sacrifice of the heifer in the *Isitshisa* is aimed at stopping the spread of death as a form of violence. *Isitshisa* as sacrifice should thus be understood as an act of violence aimed against the spread of the violence of death within the CCSA and amongst its members. The case study also showed how afterwards, the ashes are used ritually to assist in preventing the spreading of the contagion (see also Douglas 2008) of death; it is clear that the ashes from this sacrifice are believed to possess certain powers. CCSA members who attend a funeral are cleansed afterwards by means of a ritual washing in which ashes are mixed with water. Girard's insights are helpful to see how this sacrifice assists in curbing certain forms of violence, here specifically the threat of the violence of death.

Apart from curbing the spread of violence, the sacrifice, and specifically the use of a scapegoat (the heifer), assists in fostering group cohesion, or in the words of Girard, to foster the social fabric of the group. In a large-scale research project regarding the role of religious rituals in social capital formation in an AIC (Wepener et al. 2019) it became clear that the liturgical rituals of the CCSA fosters mostly bonding capital as a subset of social capital amongst its members. The core ritual, which is almost the epicentre of the ritual activities of the CCSA, is the *Isitshisa*. This sacrifice thus supports bonding capital among members of the CCSA and a heightened kind of bonding is established in the group when the scapegoat is removed from their midst and sacrificed. It is important here to recognise the scapegoat mechanism and surrogate victim at work in the ritual sacrifice by means of the heifer and how it fosters bonding during the service in Umlazi. On the other hand, it is also significant that members and leaders, after attending *Isisthisa*, take the ashes back to their congregations for ritual usage, the spiritual capital they have accumulated during the service with CCSA back home, and share with those who did not attend the *Isitshisa* (Wepener and Ter Haar, 2014).

The *Isitshisa* should also be understood and appreciated in light of the work of scholars of African religion, within a spiritual ontology aimed at serving equilibrium. There are many forces (violence?) that continuously disrupt equilibrium, and sacrifices (and libations) that play a vital role in restoring this equilibrium. However, in Africa, not only should an equilibrium be maintained between the living, but also between the living and the living dead (Wepener 2021).

In many African traditional religions, blood is symbolically very significant. "[It] symbolises and expresses life", so Magesa asserts (1997, 110). Magesa goes on to note that "Blood has a very high concentration of the power of life, so much so that it is often identified with life itself." Precisely because of its high symbolic value, it plays a critical role in ritual sacrifices. Blood functions in initiation rites as a symbol of bonding envisaged to occur between the initiate, the land, and the community. Mbiti (1991, 75) puts it like this: "The blood which is shed during the physical operation binds the person to the land and consequently to departed members of his society. It is said that the individual is alive, and that he or she now wishes to be tied to the community and people, among whom he or she has been born as a child."

Magesa furthermore asserts that, "[c]onsequent are the many taboos surrounding blood as well as the function of sharing blood in cementing blood-pacts or blood-friendships, and in assuring transitions through the critical stages if life" (Magesa 1997, 162). Similarly, the symbolic significance of blood in bonding relates to cementing personal relationships. Mbiti (1969, 212) states that, "Formal oaths are used as another method of establishing and maintaining good human relationships. They are oaths which people mystically make together, the best known being the one which creates what is rather loosely referred to as 'blood-brotherhood'" (Mbiti 1969, 212). Mbiti highlights the significance of the oath as follows, "This oath places great moral and mystical obligations upon the parties concerned; and any breach of the covenant is dreaded and feared upon to bring misfortunes [...] death, suffering, if broken" (Mbiti 1969, 212). However, perhaps the widest use of blood as a symbol denoting the essence of life relates to animal sacrifice.

Thus, Mbiti (1991, 63) asserts that, "The practice of presenting sacrifice and offering to a deity or spirits is found almost all over Africa. It is a critical dimension of African tradition and cultures". He goes on to elaborate saying "By this practice material and physical items are offered to god and other spiritual beings. This act marks the point where the visible and invisible worlds meet and shows man's intention to project himself into the invisible world" (Mbiti 1991, 63). However, Magesa highlights the significance of blood in the efficacy of sacrifice offering to the Supreme Being, ancestors, or spirits. He notes that, "Sacrifices and offerings gain value because of what the items represent. The one offering identifies self with the offering by touching it before it is dedicated and offered. In this respect, the offerer becomes the sacrificial victim" (Magesa 1997, 203).

The significance of the offering lies in the offerer identifying themselves with the sacrificed victim. In other words, the blood, (life) of the sacrifice seems to represent the life of the one sacrificing. As Magesa (1997, 203) states, "It is the offerer who gives him- or herself in propitiation or expiation, and in this way asks to be reintegrated properly into the order of the universe". Magesa underscores the most pragmatic rationale behind sacrifices in Africa which affirm the claims made by the African scholars above. He states, "The fundamental meaning of sacrifices and offerings lies in their efficacy to restore wholeness. If wrongdoing causes a dangerous separation of the various elements of the universe, sacrifices and offerings aims to re-establish unity and restore balance. [...] [s]acrifices and offerings have their goal 'to give the cosmos dynamic continuity.'" (Magesa 1997, 203)

6 Conclusion

Sacrifice as an act of ritual violence in the context of the CCSA involves violence directed at the violence of death and in service of the ideals of peace and equilibrium. In addition, the restoration of equilibrium is a kind of healing, as its aim is the restoration of relationships, with and between the living and the living dead. This restoration can also be called reconnection, as the sacrifice assists participants to be reconnected with those around them in renewed and restored relationships, but also and importantly their relationship with the spirits of the ancestors. These relationships form within an African worldview a delicate web of connections (Wepener 2021). Sacrifices play an important role in maintaining relationships in this web and also, when they get disrupted by the violence of death, to restore these relationships.

Bibliography

Bell, Catherine. 1997. *Ritual: Perspectives and Dimensions*. Oxford: Oxford University Press.
Douglas, Mary. [1966] 2008. *Purity and Danger: An Analysis of the Concepts of Pollution and Taboo*. London: Routledge.
Drexler, Josef. 2006. "Sacrifice." In *The Brill Dictionary of Religion*. Vol 2., edited by Kocku von Stuckrad, Leiden / Boston: Brill.
Ellis, Stephen, and Gerrie ter Haar. 2004. *Worlds of Power: Religious Thought and Political Practise in Africa*. London: Hurst & Company.
Girard, René. [1972] 2018. *Violence and the Sacred*. London: Bloomsbury Academic.
Girard, René. 1986. *The Scapegoat*. Baltimore: The Johns Hopkins University Press.
Girard René. 1987. "Generative Scapegoating: Discussion." In *Violent Origins: Ritual Killing and Cultural Formation*, edited by Robert G. Hamerton-Kelly, Stanford: Stanford University Press, 73–145.
Girard, René. 1996. "Violence and the Sacred: Sacrifice." In *Readings in Ritual Studies*, edited by Ronald L. Grimes, Upper Saddle River: Prentice Hall, 239–256.
Mack, Burton. 1987. "Introduction: Religion and Ritual." In *Violent Origins: Ritual Killing and Cultural Formation*, edited by Gerald Hamerton-Kelly, Stanford: Stanford University Press, 1–70.
Magesa, Laurenti. 1997. *African Religion: The Moral Traditions of Abundant Life*. New York: Orbis.
Mbaya, Henry. 2019. "Isitshisa: Appreciating a Ritual Sacrifice." In *Bonding in Worship: A Ritual Lens on Social Capital Formation in African Independent Churches in South Africa*. Liturgia Condenda 30, edited by Cas Wepener, Ignatius Swart, Gerrie ter Haar, and Marcel Barnard, Leuven: Peeters, 193–208.
Mbiti, John S. [1969] 2008. *African Religions and Philosophy*. Gaborone: Heinemann.
Mbiti, John S. 1999. "Hearts Cannot be Lent! In Search of Peace and Reconciliation in African Traditional Society." *The Princeton Seminary Bulletin* 20:1–10.
Müller, Retief. 2011. *African Pilgrimage: Ritual Travel in South Africa's Christianity of Zion*. Farnham: Ashgate.
Nwachukwu, Chinaka S. 2018. "Indigenous Igbo Worship in Nigerian Churches." In *Traditional Ritual as Christian Worship*, edited by Daniel Shaw and William R. Burrows, Maryknoll: Orbis, 141–157.
Olupona, Jacob, ed. 2011. *African Spirituality: Forms, Meanings and Expressions*. New York: The Crossroad Publishing Company.
Schreurs, Nic. 2001. "Offeren." In *Ritueel bestek: Antropologische kernwoorden van de liturgie*, edited by Marcel Barnard and Paul Post, Zoetermeer: Uitgeverij Meinema, 217–222.
Uzukwu, Elochukwu E. 1983. "Reconciliation and Inculturation: A Nigerian (Igbo) Orientation." *African Ecclesiastical Review* 25:277–278.
Wepener, Cas. 2019. "The Life of Founder Bishop Johannes Richmond: The Invention of Tradition and Social Cohesion in the CCSA." In *Bonding in Worship: A Ritual Lens on Social Capital Formation in African Independent Churches in South Africa*. Liturgia Condenda 30, edited by Cas Wepener, Ignatius Swart, Gerrie ter Haar, and Marcel Barnard, Leuven: Peeters, 91–111.
Wepener, Cas. 2021. "The Practice of Ritual Sacrifice and the Role of Religion in Development: A South African Practical Theological Exploration." *Stellenbosch Theological Journal* 7:1–18.

Wepener, Cas, and Esias E. Meyer. 2012."The Liturgical Inculturation of the Priestly Understanding of Cleansing in the Corinthian Church of South Africa (AIC) with Special Emphasis on the Book of Leviticus." *Religion & Theology* 19:298–318.

Wepener, Cas, and Gerrie ter Haar. 2014. "Sacred Sites and Spiritual Power: One Angel, Two Sites, Many Spirits." In *Sacred Sites, Contested Grounds: Space and Ritual Dynamics in Europe and Africa*, edited by Paul Post and Philip Nel, Trenton: Africa World Press, 89–104.

Wepener, Cas, and Marcel Barnard. 2010. "Entering the Field: Initiating Liturgical Research in an AIC." *Acta Theologica* 30:192–210.

Wepener, Cas, Ignatius Swart, Gerrie ter Har, and Marcel Barnard, eds. 2019. *Bonding in Worship: A Ritual Lens on Social Capital Formation in African Independent Churches in South Africa*. Liturgia Condenda 30. Leuven: Peeters.

Zahan, Dominique. 2011. "Some Reflections on African Spirituality." In *African Spirituality: Forms, Meanings and Expressions*, edited by Jacob Olupona, New York: The Crossroad Publishing Company, 3–25.

David Plüss and Dorothea Haspelmath-Finatti
Singing / Embodiment / Resonance

1 Introduction

Singing is a basic mode of human expression. The sound of a nursed baby is a form of singing. Children spend much of their time at school and at home singing. And many adults sing, alone or in a choir, just for fun or at a professional level. Everybody listens to singing voices in different styles – on the radio, online or during live concerts.

But what are people doing when they sing? How do they experience singing and what is its effect? What is the significance of singing in religious contexts like worship? Is it possible to identify a religious significance of singing even in a non-religious context, like a football match in a stadium?

In the following chapter, we present and analyse three cases of singing in different religious situations and modes. Then, we deepen central aspects by referring to relevant theories. In the last part, we conclude with the central insights for research and teaching in the field of Practical Theology.

2 Cases of Religious Singing and Analyses

2.1 The Singing Parish of Pitasch

2.1.1 Case 1

When parishioners of the Reformed Church of Pitasch sing, they still sing the old reformed four-part chorales. Pitasch is a small village in the Val Lugnez high in the Swiss mountains. The parishoners' choir is small as well. There are just a handful of voices supporting the singing during Sunday morning worship. The chorales are performed *a capella*. There is no organ in the little chapel. Four-part singing has a long and important tradition not only in Pitasch but also in the whole Val Lugnez. The surrounding Surselva is primarily Catholic. Perhaps the conservation of this custom is partly due to a different liturgical and church tradition from the surroundings, and an attempt to cultivate a Reformed spiritual identity. In any case, the tradition of four-part singing is well practiced. The singers do not have to tediously read their part in the hymnbook – they know it by heart. The principal of the council of the elders begins the singing. The pastor is only permitted to lead the chorales if the principal is absent (Plüss 2015).

Four-part singing is part of the Reformed Church's worship tradition. Since the eighteenth century, schoolteachers have rehearsed the four voices with their pupils and have supported the parishioners' singing during Sunday morning worship.

2.1.2 Four-Part Singing as Connection of the Different: Analysis 1

What is going on in Pitasch? And why is this little singing parish high up in the Swiss mountains interesting to explore?

Four-part singing is an old and important tradition in the Reformed churches of Switzerland. In the 1770s, the composer Johann Friedrich Reichardt wrote to his friend Johann Wolfgang von Goethe after a Reformed worship in Zurich: "I was never more impressed than through the four-part singing in Zurich. The whole Reformed parish sings the common psalm four-part melodies referring to notes. Girls and boys sing soprano. Adults sing alto and the elderly men tenor and bass. Whoever knows our German chanting has no idea of the dignity and power of this four-part singing supported by hundreds of people of every age. I was really in a totally new mood, my heart was so full and my chest so tight, I felt so good and was moved to tears" (Scholl 2001, 152).

The singing of Pitasch stands in this old Reformed tradition, inspired by the Protestant Reformation of the sixteenth century and as well by Pietism and the Enlightenment. The mode of singing in Pitasch can be interpreted as a form of lived Theology (Marti 2014, 36). It performs, in an impressive way, the theological axiom of the priesthood of the baptized. The parish answers the Word of God through prayers and hymns.[1] The parish has a central role in the worship, not only standing on the sideline. For the pastor, room for manoeuvre is limited.

The importance of four-part singing in the Reformed Church of Switzerland is surprising, since Huldrych Zwingli and Heinrich Bullinger in Zurich forbade singing during worship to avoid distraction from meditation and the heresy of meritorious work. However, John Calvin allowed and even promoted the singing of psalms. He asked scholars for a translation of the Psalter from Hebrew into French to put the psalms in verses and encouraged composers to create new and appropriate melodies for psalm singing. In 1537 he wrote: "It is a thing most expedient for the edification of the church to sing some psalms in the form of public prayers by which one prays to God or sings His praises so that the hearts of all may be roused and stimulated to make similar prayers and to render similar praises and thanks to God with a common love" (Calvin 1954).

Although Calvin promoted only one voice singing in worship and four-part singing at home and in school, the latter has been practiced in worship since the six-

---

[1] See Martin Luther in the Sermon held in the Schlosskirche of Torgau on 5 October 1544, the so-called "Torgauer Formel", Luther (1931).

teenth century. Not only did it become important for the Reformed Church in French-speaking countries, but since the seventeenth century, it became popular in German-speaking countries, in the Netherlands, Scotland, Poland, Hungary, before becoming practise worldwide.

This important tradition within the Reformed Church has undoubtedly inspired the small parish of Pitasch. It is said to be conserved in its pure form due to the diaspora. In the Reformed Church, the congregation is central. It is the main liturgical actor, assisted by the pastor and the school teacher, who leads the singing. The singing of psalms has been a central liturgical act since the sixteenth century. The most important aspects of this act are that:

1. The congregation's singing is the *performance of liturgical agency*, the charge of the priesthood of the baptized. The congregation is active and supports the service. No substitution by an ordained priest is possible for this task. During Reformed worship, the congregation stands up to sing and to say the Lord's Prayer. Standing before God is an expression of reverence in many Christian traditions. In the Reformed Church, it is a form of heightened action, in addition to reception and attendance.
2. Singing is a *performance of community* (Klomp 2021). The first song transforms the different attenders at church into a community, into the holy priesthood and the body of Christ. Singing is a transformative action. It transgresses the assumed distinct limitations of a person and joins them to others. There are very few situations nowadays that allow for the experiencing of community in such an intensive and evident way as through the act of singing together.
3. Singing is or should be *performing and hearing*. It is simultaneously doing and receiving. The sound space of the other voices is open for entrance. It receives the individual and encourages them to participate. Through participation, one's own voice connects and melts with the voices of the others. Group singing only works if all the singers keep up the synchrony of singing and listening.
4. Singing is a thoroughly *bodily action* (Klomp 2011). It is performed by one's vocal cords and resonates not only through the cranial bone but through the whole body, supported by the midriff (Adelmann 2018). Singing is not dependent on reflexion or on a secondary expression of a thought.
5. Singing is an *individual expression*. The voice is like a fingerprint. We can discern voices easily and identify a well-known person in the dark or without seeing them in a crowd of speaking people. Every person's voice is composed of their own tone, colour and articulation. The four-part singing of the parishioner of Pitasch is an articulation of plurality in connection.
6. Four-part singing should be *harmonious*. The four voices are different in tone, pitch and melody. They can differ in rhythm and create moments of tension and disharmony. But they come together in a more or less complex manner and create a common sound, groove and atmosphere which is connected to religious motives, stimulates religious emotions and often resonates much longer than the message of the sermon.

2.2 Taizé Meeting in Basel

2.2.1 Case 2

Following Christmas 2017, the brothers of Taizé were invited to the traditional European Youth Meeting which took place in Basel, Switzerland.[2] 15,000 young people from all over Europe and beyond gathered together in the old medieval churches of Basel. They sat in densely packed pews and on the floor, to be quiet together and sing in the rather chilly and gloomy rooms, illuminated only by candles at the front of the church near the Communion table. Taizé involves singing short, simple songs together, by heart, over and over again, the same song, melody and words. Nobody counts how often the participants repeat the song. With every single song they enter a shared mood and world. The ongoing singing generates a shared flow. Prayer doesn't have to be explained at this moment but is experienced and evident for all the participants. Anyone unfamiliar with the songs of Taizé merely repeats them over and over. Taizé means singing and praying through repetition. The songs of Taizé are all in different languages. Participants therefore sing in foreign languages they may know a little or not at all. This multilingualism of singing and praying is characteristic of Taizé. It is a widespread prayer and singing movement which reaches many young and also elderly people and integrates different confessions and spiritual styles, more traditional parishioners as well as distant members of the church.

2.2.2 Singing as a Ritual: Analysis 2

Taizé was and still is a youth movement (Kubicki 1999), attracting young people from different European countries, cultures and denominations. But what is the reason for its success?

The most famous elements of Taizé, which are also export products, are the songs, songbooks and CDs of Taizé songs. What is particularly interesting for this study, and which aspects of singing mentioned above are to be differentiated or deepened?

1. First, singing is the *liturgical core element* in Taizé prayers. Taizé liturgies contain a lot of songs in a row, times of silence and Bible readings. But are mainly comprised of singing.
2. The *repetition of songs is striking*. Participants repeat the songs about seven or twelve times, with nobody counting. As mentioned above, it doesn't matter if the songs or the language are known or not. The singers enter in the song and participate through repetition. The repetition of the songs is more than repetition; it is like chewing dry bread, which develops its taste all the more. The ar-

---

[2] Cf. http://www.taizebasel.ch (30.11.2019).

ticulation of a song grows and moves by repetition and the singing experience grows and moves with it.
3. Taizé songs are *short and simple* in content and melody. They are mostly Bible based and contain liturgical speech acts like praise or thanks, confession or calling. The content of the song is quite important but it is not to be memorized or reflected upon. It becomes melody and rhythm, voice and gesture, atmosphere and emotion. This aspect could be one of the reasons for the popularity of Taizé.
4. The melody and mood of the songs seem to be even more important than the words. Foreign languages – including Greek and Latin – create a separate space, a *heterotopos* (Foucault 1991). A somehow sacred atmosphere seems to be created by the foreignness of the songs. Intelligibility in a cognitive sense is no condition for up-to-date and attractive forms of religious practice.
5. Whereas it is primarily young people who visit Taizé or the Youth Meetings and sing Taizé songs, their melodies and modes are not in the style of the familiar pop culture but rather in a simple orthodox style. They represent a *counterculture* to everyday life and everyday music.
6. Joining in the singing of Taizé songs seems to be a kind of *resonance* in a bodily sense rather than of understanding and reflexivity (Rosa 2016, 109–115).
7. Compared with Pitasch, we can see that four-part singing is also important for Taizé. The reasons are presumably the same. The liturgical structure in both cases is rather loose. In contrast to Pitasch, there are impulsive elements of participation especially in small groups. Taizé seems to be even more democratic than the Reformed liturgy and singing.

2.3 Charismatic Singing

2.3.1 Case 3

We are in the Sunday evening worship of the Vineyard Church at 5 pm in the old city of Bern, Switzerland.[3] There is no clear beginning to the worship service, no formal liturgical entrance, but rather an informal start with a welcome and long introduction by an elderly couple. They speak about the holiday to Croatia that a group from the congregation went on together. Events of the coming weeks are mentioned and special guests introduced. The parishioners are still entering, greeting and hugging each other, and looking for free chairs. About 300 people are gathering. All the chairs seem to be occupied. The liturgical leaders – so-called moderators – are on stage together with a band. The stage is illuminated; the room of the parish is shaded. Then, the moderators call for the congregation to stand up for worship and the band begins to play: four guitars, drums, an electric piano and a lead singer, six

---

[3] Cf. https://www.vineyard-bern.ch/home/ (30.11.2021).

men and a woman, all about 35 years old. The band plays several well-known and some self-written worship songs in a row. Most of the band members play their instruments and sing with clear voices. The parishioners try to join in. Some songs are easy to join in with because of the repetition of short phrases. Others are quite challenging. The texts of the songs are projected on a screen behind the band. Some songs are chorused with the parish; some are performed by the worship band. When the parishioners sing, they do it in one voice. The congregation is standing; some raise their hands, others teeter, leave their chairs and move around. The intensity of singing and worshiping seems to grow the closer one is to the band and the stage. The worship music played by the band is amplified, loud and fills the room easily. The voices of the people join in, but they can't build up to a proper singing body.

2.3.2 Singing till Ecstasy: Analysis 3

Praise songs are central to charismatic services (Versteeg 2001; Ingalls 2018). While the Roman Catholic mass is focused on the Eucharist and the Protestant service on the Gospel in the sermon, the Pentecostals and Neo-Charismatics meet God through singing. Singing is a kind of sacrament in the Pentecostal churches and the Charismatic movements. The intensity of the gathering culminates during singing. The presence of God through the Holy Spirit is expected, and is experienced by the congregation when the band is playing and people are standing up, singing and moving around. Since Pentecostal churches and Charismatic movements are growing in Europe and worldwide – even in Roman Catholic and Protestant congregations – and ecstatic singing is a core element of their worship, we have to consider this phenomenon carefully.

1. Most of the neo-charismatic worship songs are structured in verses and chorus like the songs in Pitasch. The chorus is often well known and sung by heart. In contrast to Taizé and Pitasch, the *rhythm* of the songs is accented and excites an immediate bodily and emotional experience.
2. Charismatic songs are *part of pop culture*. They do not try to be different like in Taizé, but aim to be a part of everyday life.
3. This pop cultural accommodation is linked with the *ecclesiology* of the Neo-Charismatics. The church should not be separated from the 'world' but rather be a part of it. The intention is to be a Greek for the Greeks and a Jew for the Jews. Unchurched people should be reached with the Gospel of Christ. Accommodation in style is a means to attain this goal. The praise-and-worship music is part of these ecclesiological and missiological strategies to reach people.
4. *Emotions are expressed and intensified* in charismatic worship. Whereas in Pitasch emotions are not expressed at all and in Taizé they are transformed by repeated singing and moments of silence, in the Vineyard, worship emotions are not only allowed but are stimulated. Melodies, rhythms and live instruments viv-

ify emotions; worship leaders and other parishioners seem to express their inner feelings and desires, encouraging the others to do the same. Charismatic singing is emotional singing. Melodies and words are simply the media to give an authentic expression to one's own desire or gratitude, love and adoration of God.

5. The expression of melody and words is intensified and individualized by *bodily gestures*. The worshipers are standing up, moving and even swinging with their whole body, eyes closed and hands reached outwards and upwards. Some leave their seats to have more space in which to move. There is a set of worship gestures in neo-charismatic worship, but there is no choreography of the performance. The gestures are rather extemporized by individuals.

6. There is a *climax* in the charismatic worship expressed by singing or speaking in tongues, weeping or laughing, clapping hands or being quiet. The climax is prepared and accompanied by the musicians and the worship leader. The instruments continue to play and the leader sings in tongues or prays quietly. It is a form of *collective, stimulated and cultivated religious ecstasy*.

7. When *religious experience* comprises a touching event, expression (of emotions) and (language-based) interpretation (Jung 2000, 135–149; Plüss 2008, 247–257), the Neo-Charismatic worship is a strong expression of religious experience. While the congregations in Pitasch and Taizé express their religious experiences in a rather ritualized and discreet way, the Neo-Charismatics in Bern allow and express strong emotions, tears and joy.

3 The Theoretical Concept: Brain, Body, and Environment as 'Open Loops'

Why do human beings sing on their own and in community? Singing in joint worship provides an experience that is simultaneously individual and communal. Here, we suggest an anthropological approach to the question of singing. Singing is a human activity that conjoins body and mind, the individual and the many, in an exemplary way.

Recent anthropological research delves into the rich complexity of the human mind-and-body-relationship that is paramount to activities such as singing. Studies in Anthropology, evolutionary Biology and Neuroscience are continuously developing an ever-deeper understanding of the complex interrelatedness of the physical and mental aspects of life. The model proposed here comes from the dialogue between Theology and Natural Sciences as suggested by Markus Mühling in his book "Resonances" (Mühling 2014). Mühling presents the model of 'open loops', as developed in neuroscience and in niche construction theory, and introduces the concept into Systematic Theology. As we suggest, this model can help us to understand the role of worship singing.

3.1 The Model: Brain, Body, and Humankind as 'Open Loops'

As a systematic theologian, Markus Mühling engages with recent research in the two fields of brain studies and evolutionary theory: The epistemological concept of the "ecological brain" (Mühling 2014, 71–85) overcomes theories that describe the brain as representing or depicting reality by using specific brain areas for specific activities. As an alternative to these models, Mühling introduces the "ecological brain" theory. Here, the functions of the brain appear to be interrelated not only with the entire body, but also with the environment.

Further, the topic of interrelatedness is not only to be found in concepts of brain studies, but also in evolution theories. While the Darwinian theory is based on the adaptation of individuals to pressures of selection, more recent concepts now focus on kinds of interactions called "niche construction" activities (Mühling 2014, 144–166). Not only do organisms change and adapt to pressures, but the environment also changes and is changed by numerous influences.

Both theories, the "ecological brain" and the "niche construction", are described as open systems, or "open loops" (Mühling 2014, 81).

Here, we propose taking Mühling's 'open loops' as a way of describing what happens in the context of worship singing. Mühling's theory of the brain and the body can illustrate the personal experience of singing: While singing, our brain functions within the body, words are pronounced, melodies are brought forth while the sound already reaches our ears, and our bodies receive the sounds, through vibrations. We produce and receive emotions while singing. Our brain functions as an 'open loop', in connectivity with the entire body and with the environment. We breathe in and out while singing. Through singing, we can physically experience that we receive faith. We are moved and even altered.

The Niche Construction Theory can also illustrate the communal experience of worship singing: We sing within our church community. However, in singing, a Christian community is all 'open loops': In singing, our community is linked to the other church communities, to humankind and creation. Through singing, we praise God as one church. We already live what we are to become.

The two parts of Mühling's model can now be illuminated by recent research in different fields of the Human Sciences. Here we present some examples that might prove relevant for Practical Theology.

3.1.1 Music as Scaffolding of Language

The use of language and language learning are traditionally understood as brain-centred activities. Protestant Theology, over the centuries, has understood itself as centred in the 'word' dimension of faith and in human intellectual activities, and thus without much need for the physical dimensions of life and faith, such as singing. The aesthetic strands of worship were seen as little more than decoration, beautiful, but unnecessary, and potentially even misleading. However, recent anthropological research shows that human language cannot exist apart from its musical dimensions.

Thus, music can be described as a kind of 'scaffolding' for language acquisition. In their study *Music and Early Language Acquisition* (Brandt, Gebrian, and Slevc 2012), researchers Anthony Brandt et al. put forward the hypothesis that music precedes language in human development. The researchers came up with a proposed definition for music: "Music is creative play with sound; it arises when sound meets human imagination" (Brandt, Gebrian, and Slevc 2012, 3).

Speech uses sound in a creative way, but differing from music, speech is referential, is symbolic and is used for communication. However, "while speech is symbolic, sound is the bearer of the message" (Brandt, Gebrian, and Slevc 2012, 3).

The authors show how children, while learning to speak a language, play with sounds. "Infants use the musical aspects of language (rhythm, timbral contrast, melodic contour) as a scaffolding for the later development of semantic and syntactic aspects of language" (Brandt, Gebrian, and Slevc 2012, 3).

Young children listen to their mothers' voices. Parents use their voices in a more musical way when speaking to their children than when speaking to adults. What children can grasp at first is the 'music of the speech', the prosody. Only later, they become able to discern the referential features of language. While learning to speak, young children practice their repertoire of musical language features. Then, as they develop, they learn to insert the referential meaning of language into this musical 'scaffolding'.

As the authors make clear, music is necessary and central to human development. It is learned and trained. However, music does not serve a clearly defined purpose. Music is non-referential. As 'creative play' music can be understood as a gift to the human being and to humankind. The gift is the necessary prerequisite for the other purpose-led human activities, such as the use of language.

With Brandt and his colleagues, we could say: In language acquisition and in speaking, the brain can be understood as a 'loop' that is open to the body in its entireness. Singing, then, might be called an 'open-loop-activitiy' that links music and language, the brain and the body.

3.1.2 The Ritual and the Story: Intertwinements

In his ground-breaking book *Il corpo di Dio. Vita e senso della vita* (Bonaccorso 2006) the Italian liturgist Giorgio Bonaccorso outlines the development of the understanding of the relationship between 'body and mind' or 'brain and body' in concepts of Theology, Philosophy, Psychology and Neuroscience. He demonstrates how recent studies are continuously uncovering increasingly complex networks of inner (between brain and body) and outer (between human beings and the environment) relations. As a liturgist, Bonaccorso demonstrates how embodied liturgical practices, precisely when engaging with a rich variety of aesthetic and cognitive strands, can augment the chance of experiences of transcendence. While activities such as the contemplation of a work of art, the listening to the song of one voice, or to the reading a religious story, can already arouse feelings of oneness with the environment, the possibility of such experiences of transcendence grows as the number of aesthetic and cognitive strands increases.

Drawing on findings from Bonaccorso's research, we might conclude that worship singing engages a number of such strands. Joint singing connects a variety of voices and musical expressions, even more so when there is four-part singing or the involvement of instrumental music. The presence of the other singers, the architectural features and further artwork in the worship space, Biblical readings or a sermon – are all aesthetical and cognitive strands of experience. Together, these liturgical features contribute to growing chances of transcendental experiences.

Through liturgical activities such as singing, the human brain functions as an 'open loop', in connection with the body, and the body functions as an open loop, interconnected with the human and non-human environment. Singing can bring forth experiences of transcendence. Singing can be the place where believers can experience faith. However, there is no 'automatism'. What liturgical activities can provide is a prominent 'space of possibilities'[4] for such experiences.

3.1.3 Joint Music Making Promotes Helpful Behaviour

Michael Tomasello and Sebastian Kirschner, scientists at the Max Planck Institute for Evolutionary Anthropology in Leipzig, Germany, explored the effects of joint music making in four-year-old children. They compared the behaviour of two groups of children with nearly equal tasks and with "the same level of social and linguistic interaction"(Kirschner and Tomasello 2010, 354); the only difference between the two playful activities was that one group, but not the other, used music. As a result, the study made clear that joint music making "increases subsequent spontaneous cooperative and helpful behaviour" (Kirschner and Tomasello 2010, 354). Singing promotes social bonding.

As the study shows, the chance to find the readiness for mutual help in the participants is higher in the music-making group than in the 'non-singing' group. However, helping is not the necessary consequence of the joint singing experience. The experience only increases the probability. The children do not sing in order to then help each other. By contrast, when they sing, they experience themselves as a group, joined through the activity of singing, and then they spontaneously help each other. Their singing itself is an aimless activity.

---

4 In German "Möglichkeitsraum", cf. Ricœur 1974.

Here, it becomes clear that joint singing widens the 'space of possibilities' for spontaneous prosocial behaviour. Singing can not only promote experiences of faith and transcendence, but can also change behaviour. The singing community can experience: what Theology calls sanctification, can actually be observed. A community where prosocial behaviour grows out of singing might also be of help to the wider environment. What anthropologists call 'niche construction' can actually be experienced.

3.2 The Theory Model of 'Open Loops' and the Case Studies

Here, we suggest the model of 'open loops' as a possibility for understanding the apparent importance of singing for the worshiping community more deeply, as described in the case studies. What follows here are some exemplary observations.

In the context of Reformation history and Protestant Theology, the importance of singing often seems to have come as a surprise. The Reformation rediscovered the 'word' as the decisive dimension for the Christian faith, and for Theology. In consequence, Zwingli and Bullinger in Zurich forbade singing during worship. Why, then, did Calvin so soon re-establish singing? Why did four-part singing spread so fast in the Reformed churches in Europe and then worldwide? The Taizé community and the Neo-Charismatic Vineyard churches have roots in the churches of the Reformation and their word-centred theologies. Why, then, is singing so important in their liturgies?

The open-loop model suggests that the human brain relies on the entire body and on the environment in order to function. Recent studies indicate that singing is fundamental to speaking. While Reformation theologians may not have been aware of these circumstances, the congregations intuitively longed for singing as the basis for the all-important word dimension of faith, and subsequently the musical aspects of the biblical Psalm words unfolded in unexpected beauty in Reformed worship traditions.[5]

As the Roman Catholic liturgist Bonaccorso outlines, a variety of aesthetic and cognitive strands in liturgical actions augment the chances for transcendental experiences. Calvin remarked that "the hearts of all may be roused and stimulated to make similar prayers [...] and thank God with a common love" (cf. 2.1.2.). One eighteenth century witness of Reformed four-part singing found himself moved to tears

---

[5] This refers to one surprising experience: at her very first visit to the Zurich University Faculty of Theology in Autumn 2018, Dorothea Haspelmath-Finatti, as a Lutheran minister and liturgical scholar, participated for the very first time in a Swiss Reformed worship service. It was a university service, prepared by students of Practical Theology, but open to the public. Here, the congregational four-part-singing was strikingly beautiful. The singers, who were not professional singers, seemed to listen carefully to the other voices while singing their own parts. Their voices blended together in an exceptional way.

through this very special worship experience (cf. 2.1.2.). Both cases speak of experiences of transcendence and transformation through communal singing. In our times, the ritual use of short phrases of biblical content, as in Taizé, can lead to feelings of oneness. Singing can lead to ecstasy, like in Charismatic worship. Both can be understood as examples of experiences of transcendence, where strands of aesthetic and cognitive acts are interwoven.

As further research finds, singing can benefit community. The singing community can be 'open loops' to the environment. The century witness speaks of his own wellbeing as brought forth by the experience of singing. Calvin speaks of the oneness of the congregation and of the edification of the church through the singing of Psalms. One might observe that the word 'edification' is not far from the term 'niche construction'.

4 Consequences for Practical Theology

What follows from the above analysis on singing and embodiment for Practical Theology in general? We present our conclusions in short paragraphs:
1. Practical Theology in our German-speaking context is *text-oriented* and often *text-limited*, due to Protestantism and a text-focused culture and science. In contrast, religious praxis and experience – like singing and embodiment – are much more than text and language. Therefore, description and interpretation should contain the multifaceted aspects of a phenomenon: texts and spoken (or sung) words, performance and the body, emotions, images and rhythm.
2. Although singing and embodiment are constitutive human and religious elements, they are not common topics of research and teaching in German-speaking Practical Theology (recent exceptions: Klomp 2011, Kaiser 2017, Kühn 2018). This is also true for all forms of (religious) emotions. Since Practical Theology reminds other fields of Theology of the present 'lived religion', these aspects have to be focused on, although the methodological approach is not easy to manage since there are no established methods to analyse singing, embodiment and emotions.
3. *Religious individualization* is becoming the core focus of German-speaking Practical Theology, whereas group forms or aspects of religion seem to be old-fashioned. Regarding singing and embodiment, they can illustrate the fact that *religion is a social phenomenon* and illuminate the ways in which religious persons can benefit from collective religious practice. Research on singing reminds Practical Theology of the strong and vivid connection between social and individual aspects of religion.
4. Our reflections show that *case studies* are helpful to explore central aspects of neglected (or new) religious phenomena. We described and analysed the three examples of singing only very roughly. To deepen the analysis of singing and em-

bodiment, it would be helpful to do a "thick description" (Geertz 1973), and a methodologically reflected analysis of the cases.
5. We tried to show that the cases are rooted in their own *history* and genesis. We are convinced that Practical Theology should not ignore historical aspects in order to better understand religious and ecclesial phenomenon in the present, even after the 'empirical turn' in the 1970s in the German-speaking context.
6. It is fruitful to have a first-hand analysis based on the cases before introducing theory models in the field. We neither opt for pure inductive research like Grounded Theory (Strauss and Corbin 1990) nor for a deductive procedure based on theoretical or theological principals but for an *abductive procedure* (Peirce 1965, 171), reflecting on cases and theories – like the two focusses of an ellipse – at the same level and time.
7. A basic method of Practical Theology is the *method of comparison*. If we compare cases, theories and theological interpretations, we can discover the complexity of a phenomenon, its differences and structures. The selection of cases and theories has to be well considered and explicitly justified. However, it is not possible to cover the whole field or to eliminate the dependence on our point of view and our own cultural and personal limitations.

Bibliography

Adelmann, Winfried. 2018. "Vom Gesang 'hinter dem Lied'." *Liturgie und Kultur* 9:16–25.
Bonaccorso, Giorgio. 2006. *Il corpo di Dio: Vita e senso della vita*. Assisi: Citadella Editrice.
Brandt, Anthony, Molly Gebrian, and L. Robert Slevc. 2012. "Music and Early Language Acquistion." *Frontiers in Psychology* 3:1–17.
Calvin, John. 1954. "Articles Concerning the Organization of the Church and of Worship at Geneva Proposed by the Ministers at the Council, January 16, 1537." In *Theological Treatises*, trans. John K. S. Reid. Philadelphia: Westminster Press, 47–55.
Foucault, Michel. 1991. "Andere Räume." In *Aisthesis: Wahrnehmung heute oder Perspektiven einer anderen Ästhetik*, edited by Karlheinz Barck, Peter Gente, Heidi Paris, and Stefan Richter, Leipzig: Reclam, 34–46.
Geertz, Clifford. 1973. *The Interpretation of Cultures*. New York: Basic Books.
Haspelmath-Finatti, Dorothea. 2014. *Theologia Prima: Liturgische Theologie für den evangelischen Gottesdienst*. Arbeiten zur Pastoraltheologie, Liturgik und Hymnologie 80. Göttingen: Vandenhoeck & Ruprecht.
Ingalls, Monique. 2018. *Singing the Congregation: How Contemporary Worship Music Forms Evangelical Community*. New York: Oxford University Press.
Jung, Matthias. 2000. "Religiöse Erfahrung: Genese und Kritik eines religionsphilosophischen Grundbegriffs." In *Religionsphilosophie: Historische Positionen und systematische Reflexionen*, edited by Matthias Jung, Michael Moxter, and Thomas M. Schmidt, Würzburg: Echter, 135–149.
Kaiser, Jochen. 2017. *Singen in Gemeinschaft als ästhetische Kommunikation: Eine ethnographische Studie*. Wiesbaden: Springer.
Klomp, Mirella. 2011. *The Sound of Worship: Liturgical Performance by Surinamese Lutherans and Ghanaian Methodists in Amsterdam*. Leuven: Peeters.

Klomp, Mirella. 2021. "Ecclesioscapes: Interpreting Gatherings around Christian Music in and outside the Church: The Dutch Case of the 'Sing Along Matthäuspassion'." In *Studying Congregational Music: Key Issues, Methods, and Theoretical Perspectives*, edited by Andrew Mall, Jeffers Engelhardt, and Monique Ingalls, Abingdon: Routledge.

Kubicki, Judith Marie. 1999. *Liturgical Music as Ritual Symbol: A Case Study of Jacques Berthier's Taizé Music*. Leuven: Peeters.

Kühn, Jonathan. 2018. *Klanggewalt und Wir-Gefühl: Eine ethnographische Analyse christlicher Großchorprojekte*. Stuttgart: Kohlhammer.

Kirschner, Sebastian, and Michael Tomasello. 2010. "Joint Music Making Promotes Prosocial Behavior in 4-Year-Old Children." *Evolution and Human Behavior* 31:354–364.

Luther, Martin. 1931. D. *Martin Luthers Werke, Weimarer Ausgabe. Kritische Gesamtausgabe*. Vol. 49, Stuttgart: Metzler, 588–615.

Marti, Andreas. 2001. *Singen – Feiern – Glauben: Hymnologisches, Liturgisches und Theologisches zum Gesangbuch der Evangelisch-reformierten Kirchen der deutschsprachigen Schweiz*. Basel: Friedrich Reinhardt.

Marti, Andreas. 2014. *Wie klingt reformiert? Arbeiten zu Liturgie und Musik*. Zürich: Theologischer Verlag Zürich.

Mühling, Markus. 2014. *Resonances: Neurobiology, Evolution and Theology: Evolutionary Niche Construction, The Ecological Brain and Relational-Narrative Theology*. Göttingen / Bristol, CT: Vandenhoeck Ruprecht.

Peirce, Charles Sanders. ³1965. *Pragmatism and Pragmaticism*. Vol. 5, Collected Papers. Cambridge: The Belknap Press of Harvard University Press.

Plüss, David. 2008. "Religiöse Erfahrung zwischen Genesis und Performanz." *Zeitschrift für Theologie und Kirche* 105:242–257.

Plüss, David. 2015. "Wo ereignet sich Gemeinde? Gemeindegesang und reformiertes Selbstverständnis." *Musik & Gottesdienst: Zeitschrift für evangelische Kirchenmusik* 69:222–232.

Ricoeur, Paul. 1974. "Philosophische und theologische Hermeneutik." In *Metapher: Zur Hermeneutik religiöser Sprache*, edited by Paul Ricoeur and Eberhard Jüngel, München: Kaiser, 24–45.

Rosa, Hartmut. 2016. *Resonanz. Eine Soziologie der Weltbeziehung*. Frankfurt am Main: Suhrkamp.

Scholl, Hans. 2001. "Aimez-vous Goudimel?" *Musik & Gottesdienst: Zeitschrift für evangelische Kirchenmusik* 55:138–153.

Strauss, Anselm L., and Juliet Corbin. 1990. *Basics of Qualitative Research: Grounded Theory Procedures and Techniques*. Newbury Park: SAGE Publications.

Versteeg, Peter Gerrit Albert. 2001. *Draw me Close: An Ethnography of Experience in a Dutch Charismatic Church*. Amsterdam: no publisher.

Daniel S. Schipani
Spiritual Care / Counselling / Religious Coping

1 Introduction

The content of this chapter stems from my work as a practical theologian engaged in teaching, supervision, and research and in spiritual caregiving practice. Further, that work has been enriched in diverse contexts in which I lecture and enjoy collegial collaboration in Canada, the United States, Latin America,[1] and Europe.[2] One common, general observation correlates the transition in nomenclature – from 'pastoral' to 'spiritual' care – increasingly explicit in health care centers and educational programs, with ongoing sociocultural developments in religion and spirituality in late modern societies as highlighted below.

Attention to the related processes of deinstitutionalization and pluralization helps us to appreciate the significance of social changes taking place in our times while also illumining the challenges and opportunities of caregiving in multifaith and multicultural contexts.[3] 'Deinstitutionalization' refers to the process in which the traditional religious institutions, especially Christian, lose control over the religious and spiritual dimensions of society and culture. 'Pluralization' refers to the increasing diversity of religious and spiritual traditions and perspectives. 'Multifaith' is here used descriptively to denote the presence of a plurality of faith traditions (that is, religious and non-religious, such as Humanism) in a given social context; it should not be confused with 'interfaith', a term that connotes dynamic interaction between persons of different faith traditions.

Connected to deinstitutionalization and pluralization we encounter more and more frequently people self-defined as "spiritual but not religious" (Mercadante 2014) together with increased religious and spiritual fluidity and hybridity (Bidwell 2018). Further and, to some extent, in response to those trends within the overarching socio-economic and cultural globalization process underway, we also recognize the presence of religious fundamentalism (Antoun 2008; Armstrong 2001). This is the

---

1 Those countries include Argentina, Brazil, Colombia, Dominican Republic, Cuba, Guatemala, Mexico, Paraguay, Puerto Rico, and Uruguay.
2 Visiting scholar and lecturer, VU University Amsterdam; active member of the *Gesellschaft für interkulturelle Seelsorge und Beratung-Society for Intercultural Pastoral Care and Counseling*; and the *International Association for Spiritual Care*.
3 Major recent books in these areas include the following: Federschmidt, Hauschildt and Schneider-Harpprecht (2002); Schipani and Bueckert (2009); Weiß, Federschmidt and Temme (2010); Schipani (2013); Schipani, Walton, and Lootens (2018); Noth and Kohli Reichenbach (2019); and Snodgrass (2019).

case especially, though not exclusively, among Christians and Muslims, including specific challenges to counseling, chaplaincy, and psychotherapy as spiritual care work.[4]

It is with awareness of such complex and challenging realities that I invite the readers to reflect on spiritual care. I do so by employing a practical theology framework with its fourfold epistemological structure and methodological dimensions: empirical-descriptive, interpretive, normative, and pragmatic-strategic.[5] That structure and those dimensions characterize the case study method as a way of doing qualitative empirical research (Schipani 2014).

The remainder of this chapter has two main sections. The first one consists of a case study from chaplaincy practice; it is the story of an atheist caregiver who discovers the value of prayer in an interfaith encounter. That chaplain's testimony is examined as an exercise of practical theology. The second section of the chapter addresses the search for common ground in spiritual care as a discipline. It does so by highlighting unique contributions of spiritual caregivers and the necessary place and role of interdisciplinary perspectives; it also proposes a four-dimensional framework for spiritual care theory and practice.

2 Case Study: An Atheist Prays with Hospital Patients and Relatives

Sally Fritsche's reflection on her personal story and her vocation as a spiritual caregiver (2018) supplies an interesting window to the promise and possibilities of a transcultural and transreligious approach to spiritual care. Following the excerpt that documents her transforming encounter with the family of a dying man will be a brief analysis of her experience:

> Meeting Ernesto was the beginning of a shift in my feelings on how an atheist might pray. [...] It was one of my first shifts as a chaplain at Brigham and Women's Hospital in Boston, and a nurse called to say that a Catholic man was nearing the end of his life, and his family wanted someone to come say some prayers. I was the only chaplain on call, so I went. The small hospital room was crowded with easily 15 people, Ernesto's bed in the center. His wife was there, his children and cousins and brothers, his grandchildren. I was prepared to hold their sadness and anger, to offer support and affirmation of their grief. But I couldn't imagine how I was going to pray. I didn't want to lie to these people. They want me to talk to God for them, but won't a prayer from me be empty? Won't the words come out meaningless? Won't it feel like a lie on my tongue? But a dozen pairs of teary eyes turned to me. I invited everyone to gather close and reach out for each other and, together, we prayed the Hail Mary, the Our Father, and prayed for whatever

---

[4] For example, Muslim practical theologian Nazila Isgandarova (2019) addresses the challenge of certain implications of Islamic fundamentalism in connection with domestic violence.
[5] The fourfold epistemological structure and methodological dimensions and tasks of practical theology are well described and illustrated by Richard Osmer (2008).

comes next to come with peace and overwhelming love. And those prayers, those prayers were far from empty. I came into the room wanting to help and expecting to feel helpless. I came with skepticism, ready to say the words of Catholic prayers if they wanted them, but not expecting those words to come from my heart, or to become a truly spiritual experience. But joining my voice with the sobs of those at their father's deathbed, and saying the words, "Our Father, who art in heaven ..." I didn't have to believe we were talking to God to see something real in that. Those prayers were deeply healing, not just for the believers in the room, but for me, too. (Fritsche 2018)

2.1 Description

Sally Fritsche is an atheist chaplain who grew up Unitarian Universalist. She had been encouraged to experiment with prayer, meditation, and different kinds of spirituality:

> I went to church, to mass, to Hindu temple, to synagogue, and to my mid-Missouri town's lone mosque. And [...] I loved it. I loved religion wherever I found it. I coughed through the incense, fumbled the right-to-left prayer books, and soaked in the powerful peace that can happen when faith communities come together. The problem was, when I looked honestly into my own heart, there just wasn't any 'religion' there in the way I had been taught to think about it. When it comes down to it, I lack, quite simply and sincerely, any belief in God, an afterlife, or anything not earthly, observable. [...] I never intended to be an atheist, but here I am. My love of religion, my commitment to religious community, and my personal atheism exist side by side, deep and unforced, beliefs that I find written into my very bones. (Fritsche 2018)

Sally has always loved religion but has never prayed as a religious practice. She always viewed prayer critically and had been convinced that she could never pray. It would be expected, therefore, that prayer and praying would present a special challenge both personally and professionally. Again, in her own words:

> Given my non-belief, prayer has never meant a lot to me. Can an atheist pray? Or perhaps more importantly, why would an atheist want to? [...] when I came to terms with my lack of belief in God, I never felt like I was missing out on much by missing out on prayer. Even the more thoughtful approaches to prayer haven't gotten through to me. [...] [W]ith no God, what's the difference between prayer and just reflecting on a concept in the privacy of your own head? And when I need help, or want to express gratitude, it would feel silly to turn to a listening ear I don't believe actually exists. Why pray when no one's there to hear me? So, prayer, I've gradually come to realize, just isn't for atheists like me. And that's fine. There are other ways I connect to the sublime and the sacred, but without a belief in God, prayer can't really be one of them. (Fritsche 2018)

2.2 Interpretive Analysis

Sally recognizes that her encounter with Ernesto and his Catholic family was a turning point for her, both vocationally and professionally. She discovered that she can actually pray meaningfully and, in her words, "from the heart" in ways that are timely and effective. Let us consider what was going on, and why, by listening to her own way of making sense of the experience:

> So what, exactly, was happening when I prayed for Ernesto and his family? This isn't a conversion story about an atheist who sees the error of her ways and the power of the Lord. I wasn't praying to any God, but I was praying. And there was something powerful happening in that room. Something about the end of a life, the family's intense need, the connection formed when they reached for me, the chaplain, asking me to carry their sadness and their hopes, asking me to help them put it all into words and to tell their God what they need. Ernesto and his family were the first people I prayed for in the hospital, but they were far from the last. In my work as a chaplain, I have become almost comfortable offering sincere prayers for peace, for healing, and for God's presence in patients' lives. I had thought that my own theology would get between us and turn those prayers into lies. But when I open my mouth, the particulars of my own beliefs become enormously unimportant. [...] [W]hen I am praying for a patient in the hospital, it's not about me. The prayer is theirs, and I am just the conduit for their deep need. [...] Their prayers flow between us in those terrible moments of loss and diagnosis and anxiety, and I speak them into the world. Not for God to hear, as far as I am concerned, but for us to hear. I never thought I could truly pray because there's no one listening. But here, someone is listening. Those words of gratitude and love and hope are heard by those who most need to hear them. Heard by Ernesto, and his family, and by me. Those prayers are powerful, and those prayers were prayed by an atheist. (Fritsche 2018)

2.3 Evaluation

In light of Sally's testimony, we might say that the encounter with Ernesto's family mobilized her compassion and passion as a spiritual caregiver. She was able to engage that family spiritually and connect with them deeply and in their (not her!) terms. In her reflection of spiritual practice, Sally focused on the nature and the role of prayer. She says:

> Christian prayer is different from Muslim prayer, is different from Buddhist prayer, is different from Jewish prayer. And I hadn't thought atheist prayer was a thing that could exist. But this, speaking aloud the prayer of another and lending my voice and the strength of my heart to the belief of someone who needs to feel their God listening, this I can do. The prayer that I pray is an articulation of our connection, a deep investment in the lives and beliefs of fellow human beings. Prayer cannot bring water to parched land, nor mend a broken bridge, nor rebuild a ruined city, but prayer can water an arid soul, mend a broken heart, and rebuild a weakened will. [...] [S]ometimes, being in community is more important than being in agreement. [...] I no longer run from prayer. I am learning something. Can an atheist pray, and why would she want to? After today, let the answers to these questions be a little less clear, and let us remember how it can feel to pray the prayers of others with our whole hearts, to stop trying, for half a breath, to make a prayer fit neatly into our theology, and just let it come. To open ourselves up to some change, to pray heartily, and to learn something. (Fritsche 2018)

It is apparent that the caregiving situation was transformational for the spiritual caregiver. Sally became a better chaplain! Significantly, she reports having experienced healing. Regarding vocational growth, Sally experienced enhanced understanding, deepening "therapeutic love", and strengthened professional competence. In other words, the assessment of Sally's spiritual caregiving competence may be seen in light of a normative framework of holistic competence, as follows: academic-interdisciplinary formation and growth (competencies of 'knowing'), personal formation (competencies of 'being'), and professional formation and growth (competencies of 'doing').[6]

The account of Sally's caregiving encounter with Ernesto's family illustrates key features of appropriate and effective spiritual care practice. Regarding the action and content of her praying, we might say that, for the care receivers, they were both "psychologically functional" and "theologically appropriate" (van Deusen Hunsinger 1995, 130–145); they were fitting as far as the family's religious beliefs and spiritual practices were concerned. Put in terms of the psychology of religion and spirituality, the chaplain had facilitated 'positive religious coping'.[7] The relationship that was co-created by caregiver and care receivers made it possible for those experiencing anticipatory grief to create meaning in the face of Ernesto's impending death, to garner emotional control, to acquire comfort by virtue of a sense of closeness to God, and to achieve closeness with each other. Actually, all of those outcomes are indicators of what we might call healthy spirituality. That claim calls for further discussion of the place and role of interdisciplinary views in psycho-spiritual assessment, as proposed below.

3 Interdisciplinary Perspectives on Psycho-Spiritual Assessment

One way of exploring the question of 'healthy' and 'toxic' spiritualities consists in studying them with an interdisciplinary approach that includes psychological and theological norms, as suggested in the diagrams that follow. Readers should keep in mind that on this point I write explicitly as a Christian practical theologian. My practice and theory of spiritual care always reflect my theological grounding, including normative claims regarding the nature of reality and of human wholeness, health and healing, and related concerns. In reality, all spiritual caregivers must competently address and respond to those and related questions whether or not they identify with a given religious tradition, as in Sally's case. Even though we (spiritual caregivers) will not impose our normative views and criteria on care receivers, our normative criteria will always be operative in all forms of assessment and therapeutic approach.

---

[6] For a presentation of a competency profile including formation pedagogies, see Schipani (2017b, 134–144).
[7] The categories 'positive religious coping' and 'negative religious coping' are described and illustrated thoroughly in Kenneth I. Pargament's work (1997; 2007).

It is precisely because of that grounding that I deem the outcome of Sally's care for Ernesto and his family as 'theologically adequate' while focusing on the religious faith and the response of the care receivers. Furthermore, I can also assess Sally's work theologically from my perspective. In light of my theological framework (especially Christological and Pneumatological theology), I view and interpret it as an event in which Sally became a partner, not only with Ernesto's family, but also with the Spirit of God, regardless of her desire for or awareness of such partnership. It is also possible that Ernesto's family considered Sally as an instrument of divine grace in light of their Christian faith.

Depending on the epistemological place given to theology (or another worldview and ethical framework) in connection with psychology, theological criteria and judgment may determine *a priori* that some spiritualities can never be 'healthy' even if they are psychologically functional (integrating), as in the case of options [2] and [6] in the diagram below. Conversely, theological norms may determine that certain spiritualities are 'healthy' (or faithful, from a certain theological perspective) despite their possibly being psychologically dysfunctional, as in options [3] and [7] in the diagram. It is obvious that spiritual care providers must always be able to assess spirituality and to help people access their spiritual resources in the direction of healthy integration (for instance, by moving beyond 'negative religious coping'). (Schipani 2017a, 82, including diagram)

Table 1: Norms and Criteria for Interdisciplinary Assessment, © Daniel S. Schipani.

	theologically adequate	theologically inadequate
psychologically functional	1. life-giving, community-building spiritualities	2. spiritualities connected with "Prosperity Gospel," or with fundamentalism
	3. spiritualities that see the self-limiting Divine as a benevolent partner in one's suffering and in one's healing process; God is closely present with compassion, in solidarity. *Positive religious coping:* emotional-spiritual comfort; strength, peace	4. spiritualities that see a micromanaging God as one who "knows better... has a plan for my life... is testing me... I suffer here but will be compensated in heaven... I've been chosen for this test" *Positive religious coping:* meaning and purpose clarified; "blessing in disguise"
psychologically dysfunctional	5. prophetic spirituality confronted as antipatriotic	6. spirituality of People's Temple that led to mass suicide
	7. spiritualities that see God as "just and wise, and has made us free.... We face the consequences of that freedom [accident, illness]" *Negative religious coping:* increased sense of vulnerability, weakness, diminished hope	8. spiritualities that see a micromanaging God as one who "is punishing me... has abandoned me... I'm not worthy of God's love" *Negative religious coping:* increased angst, guilt, isolation, despair

4 Application

4.1 Interdisciplinary Understanding of a Spiritual Care Practice

We can apply the same kind of analysis to our spiritual care practices (Schipani 2017a, 83). Let us consider, for instance, the case of praying during a counseling session or a hospital visit and let us assume that the prayer was either requested by the patient or gladly welcomed when offered by the spiritual care provider. Of course, there are many ways of praying wisely for a care receiver whether in a counseling setting or in a health care center. We might say that, in all instances, prayers, blessings, or our words of support and guidance in the face of crisis should be sources of comfort or healing; they must communicate a deep spiritual-theological truth (e. g., the sustaining presence of Grace, however understood or defined, in all circumstances). At the same time, such prayer must be mentally and emotionally helpful (e. g., by fostering trust and hope in the face of anxiety and fear, by including the health care team and the family, etc.). Regretfully, there are also harmful ways of offering care, as suggested below with some simple examples in the chart with psychological and theological norms and criteria (cases 2, 3, 4):

Table 2: Assessment Applied to Prayer with Care Receivers © Daniel S. Schipani.

	theologically adequate	theologically inadequate
psychologically functional	1. prayer that elicits a sense of grace and activates emotional and spiritual resources of the patient and family	2. prayer that momentarily alleviates anxiety and fear by persuading one that quick healing is available
psychologically dysfunctional	3. prayer that elicits a sense of grace and activates emotional and spiritual resources of the patient and family	4. prayer that associates one's medical condition with God's judgment and condemnation

4.2 Common Ground and the Unique Contribution of Spiritual Caregivers

Literature on spiritual care across traditions and cultures allows us to identify common ground regarding both practice and theory. One can experience something similar in multicultural and multifaith collegial conversation and collaboration. It is not a question of finding some common (minimum) denominator shared by everybody; distinctness and difference must be duly recognized. Common ground cannot be explained only in terms of similar clinical training or formation of caregivers. Rather, common ground can be appreciated as actually reflecting the reality of the holy ground of human encounter created in spiritual caregiving situations, as illustrated in our case study. Indeed, those encounters normally deal with fundamental needs, questions, potential, and resourcefulness that point to transcultural and transreligious issues of meaning, connectedness, vocation, and mystery; in short, the very concerns of the human spirit through the ages.[8]

Another general observation has to do with the central place and role of wisdom in diverse traditions basically understood as both a way of life and discernment of the journey forward in the face of life challenges and struggles (Boelhower 2013). That is, spiritual care tends to be shaped as a dialogical-hermeneutical process involving a normative body of existentially pertinent knowledge together with the contextually pertinent resources of the people involved in the process.[9] In all cases, holistic formation of spiritual caregivers include work on several sets of competencies, as already indicated.[10]

4.3 Core Competencies Identified

Two special core competencies – 'bilingual proficiency' and a four-dimensional view – must be highlighted. The unique contribution of spiritual caregivers within any health care team is that they need to view and work with the care receivers holistically while primarily engaging them psychologically as well as spiritually. Therefore, spiritual caregivers must develop the core competency of 'bilingual proficiency' in terms of understanding the languages and resources of psychology and spirituality / theology (or non-theological worldviews, as in the case of Humanism and Buddhism) and employing such understandings and resources in spiritual assessment and all other verbal and nonverbal (e. g., rituals) caregiving practices.

The spiritual caregiver's main function is to connect persons in crisis to their (the care receivers') spiritual resources and community. Given the plurality of sociocultur-

---

[8] This affirmation implies several claims I make, as follows: (1.) We are human because we are spiritual beings (i.e., spirit is the essential dimension of being human). (2.) Spirituality can be understood as how our spirit manifests itself in ways of searching or longing for, experiencing ('inner' sense), and expressing ('outer' manifestations) in interrelated realms: meaning, truth seeking, wisdom; faith; relatedness and communion with others, nature, oneself, the Divine; and life orientation, purpose. The claim that those dimensions of spirituality – meaning, communion, purpose – name fundamental (or existential) experiences and expressions of our human spirit is based on consistent confirmation stemming from various sources such as these: my clinical work and supervision, analysis of sacred texts, cultural anthropology, and comparative studies including literature in the fields of pastoral and spiritual care, and spiritual direction in particular.
[9] I offer a reframing of pastoral counseling along those lines in *The Way of Wisdom in Pastoral Counseling* (Schipani 2003). In that book I argue that the biblically grounded Jewish-Christian wisdom tradition consists in a way of doing practical theology which can help redefine the counseling process and its overarching goals. Recent texts representing different traditions can also be viewed as wisdom-focused even though they don't share similar theological grounding, cf. Giles and Miller (2012); Rassool (2016); Friedman and Yehuda (2017).
[10] See annot. 6 above regarding academic-interdisciplinary, personal, and professional sets of competencies.

al and religious variables at work, caregivers will normally be faced with situations that present either commonality, complementarity, or contrast and even conflict. This issue can be helpfully considered with the aid of three concentric circles of interreligious spiritual care representing three categories of situations that can be addressed: (1.) 'common (universal) human experience', in which the caregiver functions primarily as *companion*; (2.) 'interconnected spiritual practice', in which the caregiver functions as *representative of the sacred*; and (3.) 'particular religious spiritual practice', in which the caregiver functions primarily as *resource agent* who relates (and often refers) care receivers and their families to their spiritual communities and resources (Grefe 2011, 49–53).[11] The diagram that follows represents the opportunities and challenges of intercultural and interfaith care we face in our time (Schipani 2017a, 81). Specific illustrations may include situations like these: a Protestant caregiver cares for a grieving Jewish family in the hospital; a Humanist female chaplain blesses the stillborn baby of a Catholic couple; a Buddhist caregiver helps a young man in despair and unable to pray; a Muslim therapist counsels another Muslim woman suffering depression (somehow connected with spousal abuse and religious instruction); a Jewish chaplain offers a Jewish ritual (washing hands) to a non-Jewish grieving husband and son; etc. Therefore, spiritual caregivers must be able to work with hermeneutical, communicative, and tradition-specific competencies.

In all cases, competent spiritual caregivers seek to engage in holistic care. Further, spiritual care that is intentionally and consistently offered and reflected upon as a spiritual health discipline also calls for a four-dimensional view of reality, as explained below. In other words, this discipline must function as a special form of *intercultural* care and counseling (Sue et al. 2019) with explicit consideration to normative frameworks regarding the nature of reality and of human wholeness (Schipani 2013, 149–166).

4.4 A Four-Dimensional Framework

Psychotherapeutic and psychiatric approaches normally assume a two-dimensional view involving the self (or selves, in the case of couples, family, or group therapy) and the lived world. The recent and ongoing 'recovery' of spirituality in health care and, especially, counseling, and psychotherapy includes emphasis on spiritual assessment (Richards and Bergin[1997] 2005, 219–249), engaging clients' spirituality (e. g., beliefs, sources of meaning, and hope, etc.) during therapy (Miller 2000; Pargament 2013), and integration of spirituality into the therapeutic process (Alten and Leach 2009) including issues and practices (e. g. meditation, prayer, sacred readings,

---

11 The diagram of three concentric circles comes from the work of the Sri Lankan theologian Wesley Ariarajah (1999) in connection with interfaith worship. He visualizes the possibility of interfaith worship as a public form of interreligious prayer with the use of analogous concentric circles. Dagmar Grefe was first inspired by Ariarajah's model as documented in her book.

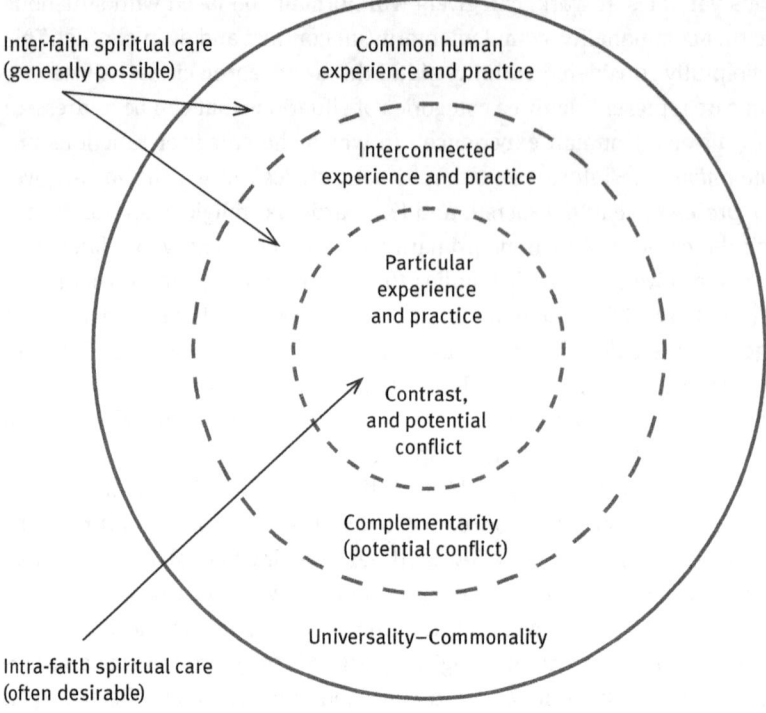

Figure 4: Three Circles of Spiritual Care, © Daniel S. Schipani.

Plante 2009). This is a welcome development. However, much is still missing in terms of clinical research and theoretical reflection, to say nothing of the arena of caregiving practice as such. A large majority of clinicians and theorists simply collapse the spiritual into the psychological and do not recognize the distinct place and function of the spiritual self and its inseparable connection to the psychological self. In any event, the relationship between the psychological and the spiritual self can be further understood in light of the contribution of the late practical theologian James E. Loder. In his words: "Being human entails environment, selfhood, the possibility of nonbeing, and the possibility of new being. All four dimensions are essential, and none of them can be ignored without decisive loss to our understanding of what is essentially human" (Loder 1989, 69). For Loder, the four dimensions of human existence are the self, the lived world, the Void, and the Holy. The 'Void' is the third of the fundamental four dimensions of human existence: human existence is destined to annihilation and the ultimate absence of being. The many faces of the Void include existential loneliness, despair, and death. The 'Holy' constitutes the fourth dimension of human existence which has, by the power of the Spirit of God, the capacity to transform the other three dimensions (Loder 1989, 80–91). My adaptation of the model follows below as four-dimensional framework for spiritual care (Schipani 2013, 165; 2017b 132).

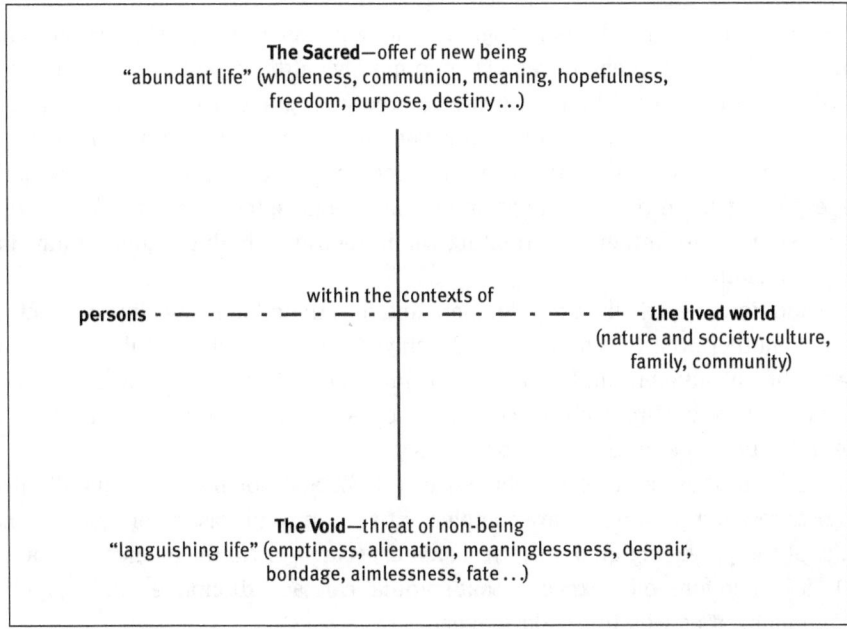

Figure 5: A Four-Dimensional Framework for Spiritual Care, © Daniel S. Schipani.

Applied to Sally's caregiving encounter with Ernesto and his Hispanic Catholic family, the model can help us to identify several spiritual and theological issues in addition to those normally accounted for with an exclusive psychological / social science framework. By focusing on that family's religious spirituality with theological lenses, a number of issues may be explored, such as: a sense of mystery connected with images of God and divine will; the face of evil in ultimate separation and suffering; experience of divine presence and grace in the face of death; need for forgiveness and reconciliation related to unfinished business with the dying person; a deep bond between biological and spiritual family (the faith community); and grieving well while mobilizing internal and external spiritual resources.

5 Conclusion: The Way Forward

In the face of rapid social change, there is a felt need for designing new programs aimed at the formation of competent professional spiritual caregivers working in (late) modern and increasingly secular and multifaith contexts. At the same time, it is another priority to care well for those persons who represent particular religious traditions, including 'hybrid' and 'fluid' spirituality, and those who identify themselves as non-religious spiritual people. Indeed, there is an evolving twofold movement in that direction, particularly in Europe, Canada, and the United States. On the one hand, in addition to programs associated with the Christian faith, we now find others connected with different religious traditions, such as Jewish, Islamic, and Buddhist. They can prepare caregivers primarily, although not exclusively, for *intra-faith* spiritual care.[12] In many instances, those programs also seek to equip students for *interfaith* work carried out from the perspective of their tradition. On the other hand, new initiatives are also emerging that focus primarily on interfaith care, especially in university settings and medical centers; they can also offer the option for students to further their training within their own faith tradition, if any, including Humanism.

In addition to curriculum development and the strengthening of clinical practice as such, another priority is to focus on the specific dynamics of intercultural and interfaith clinical supervision. This agenda includes both the variables involved in the supervisory relationship itself as well as the consideration of group dynamics that foster intercultural and interfaith competency.

Finally, all those and related challenges call for additional work in quantitative empirical research as a necessary complement and, in some cases, corrective to the results of the prevailing qualitative research especially in North America (Liefbroer 2020). It is therefore to be expected that spiritual care as a discipline will be significantly enhanced as well in the days ahead.

Bibliography

Ahmed, Sameera, and Mona M. Amer, eds. 2012. *Counseling Muslims: Handbook of Mental Health Issues and Interventions.* London: Routledge.

Alten, Jamie D., and Mark M. Leach, eds. 2009. *Spirituality and the Therapeutic Process: A Comprehensive Resource from Intake to Termination.* Washington: American Psychological Association.

Antoun, Richard T. ²2008. *Understanding Fundamentalism: Christian, Islamic, and Jewish Movements.* Lanham: Rowman & Littlefield.

Ariarajah, Wesley S. 1999. *Not without my Neighbor. Issues of Interfaith Relations.* Geneva: World Council of Churches Publications.

Armstrong, Karen. 2001. *The Battle for God: A History of Fundamentalism.* New York: Random House.

Bidwell, Duane R. 2018. *When One Religion Isn't Enough: The Lives of Spiritually Fluid People.* Boston: Beacon Press.

Boelhower, Gary J. 2013. *Choose Wisely: Practical Insights from Spiritual Traditions.* New York: Paulist Press.

Deusen Hunsinger, Deborah van. 1995. *Theology and Pastoral Counseling: A New Interdisciplinary Approach.* Grand Rapids: Eerdmans.

---

[12] For example, several important texts have been published recently by Muslim caregivers addressing Muslim populations primarily (Ahmed and Amer 2012; Rassool 2016; Isgandarova 2019). Similarly in the case of intra-faith Jewish spiritual care (Levits and Twerski 2012; Friedman 2015).

Federschmidt, Karl, Eberhard Hauschildt, Christoph Schneider-Harpprecht, Klaus Temme, and Helmut Weiß, eds. 2002. *Handbuch Interkulturelle Seelsorge*. Neukirchen-Vluyn: Neukirchener Verlag.
Friedman, Dayle A., ed. ²2015. *Jewish Pastoral Care: A Practical Handbook from Traditional and Contemporary Sources*. Woodstock: Jewish Lights.
Friedman, Michelle, and Rachel Yehuda. 2017. *The Art of Jewish Pastoral Counseling: A Guide to All Faiths*. London / New York: Routledge.
Fritsche, Sally. 2018. "An Atheist's Prayer." https://hds.harvard.edu/news/2017/07/17/sally-fritche-atheist's-prayer (30.11.2021).
Giles, Cheryl A., and Willa B. Miller, eds. 2012. *The Arts of Contemplative Care: Pioneering Voices in Buddhist Chaplaincy and Pastoral Work*. Sommerville: Wisdom.
Grefe, Dagmar. 2011. *Encounters for Change: Interreligious Cooperation in the Care of Individuals and Communities*. Eugene: Wipf & Stock.
Isgandarova, Nazila. 2019. *Muslim Women, Domestic Violence, and Psychotherapy: Theological and Clinical Issues*. New York / London: Routledge.
Levits, Yisrael N., and Abraham J. Twerski, eds. 2012. *A Practical Guide to Rabbinic Counseling*. Woodstock: Jewish Lights.
Liefbroer, Anke I. 2020. *Interfaith Spiritual Care*. Amsterdam: Doctoral dissertation. https://research.vu.nl/en/publications/interfaith-spiritual-care (30.11.2021).
Loder, James E. ²1989. *The Transforming Moment*. Colorado Springs: Helmers and Howard.
Mercadante, Linda A. 2014. *Belief without Borders: Inside the Minds of the Spiritual but not Religious*. New York: Oxford University Press.
Miller, William R., ed. 2000. *Integrating Spirituality into Treatment: Resources for Practitioners*. Washington: American Psychological Association.
Noth, Isabelle, and Claudia Kohli Reichenbach, eds. 2019. *Spiritual Care and Migration*. Pastoral and Spiritual Care Across Religions and Cultures 2. Göttingen: Vandenhoeck & Ruprecht.
Osmer, Richard R. 2008. *Practical Theology: An Introduction*. Grand Rapids: Eerdmans.
Pargament, Kenneth I. 1997. *The Psychology of Religion and Coping: Theory, Research, Practice*. New York: Guilford Press.
Pargament, Kenneth I. 2007. *Spiritually Integrated Psychotherapy: Understanding and Addressing the Sacred*. New York: Guilford Press.
Pargament, Kenneth I., ed. 2013. *APA Handbook of Psychology, Religion, and Spirituality*. Washington: American Psychological Association.
Plante, Thomas G. 2009. *Spiritual Practice in Psychotherapy: Thirteen Tools for Enhancing Psychological Health*. Washington: American Psychological Association.
Richards, P. Scott, and Allen E. Bergin. ²2005. *A Spiritual Strategy for Counseling and Psychotherapy*. Washington: American Psychological Association.
Rassool, G. Husein. 2016. *Islamic Counselling: An Introduction to Theory and Practice*. London / New York: Routledge.
Schipani, Daniel S. 2003. *The Way of Wisdom in Pastoral Counseling*. Elkhart: Institute of Mennonite Studies.
Schipani, Daniel S., ed. 2013. *Multifaith Views in Spiritual Care*. Kitchener: Pandora Press.
Schipani, Daniel S. 2014. "Case Study Method." In *The Wiley-Blackwell Companion to Practical Theology*, edited by Bonnie J. Miller-McLemore, Chichester: Wiley-Blackwell, 91–101.
Schipani, Daniel S. 2017a. "Many Faiths, One Human Spirit." *Vision: A Journal for Church and Theology* 18:76–85.
Schipani, Daniel S. 2017b. "Pastoral and Spiritual Care in Multifaith Contexts." In *Teaching for a Multifaith World*, edited by Eleazar S. Fernandez, Eugene: Pickwick Publications, 134–144.
Schipani, Daniel S., and Leah D. Bueckert, eds. 2009. *Interfaith Spiritual Care: Understandings and Practices*. Kitchener: Pandora Press.

Schipani, Daniel S., Martin Walton, and Dominiek Lootens, eds. 2018. *Where are We? Pastoral Environments and Care for Migrants: Intercultural and Interreligious Perspectives*. Düsseldorf: Gesellschaft für interkulturelle Seelsorge und Beratung / Society for Intercultural Pastoral Care and Counseling.

Snodgrass, Jill, ed. 2019. *Navigating Religious Difference in Spiritual Care and Counseling: Essays in Honor of Kathleen J. Greider*. Claremont: Claremont Press.

Sue, Derald W., David Sue, Helen A. Neville, and Laura L. Smith. ^{8}2019. *Counseling the Culturally Diverse: Theory and Practice*. Hoboken: John Wiley and Sons.

Weiß, Helmut, Karl H. Federschmidt, and Klaus Temme, eds. 2010. *Handbuch Interreligiöse Seelsorge*. Neukirchen-Vluyn: Neukirchener Verlag.

Volker Küster

Storytelling / Minjung Theology / Identity Formation

1 Introduction

Storytelling, or narrativity, made its appearance on the theological scene in the 1970s. While in Western Academic Theology it remained negligible and only gained some momentum in Religious Education, it flourished in the emerging contextual Theologies in the Global South. I will therefore start from the margins and put storytelling into an intercultural perspective. Since the medium is the message (Marshall McLuhan) I will begin with some of the stories that have been told mainly by Asian theologians. They come from the underside of his/her story and re/construct it from below. A practice that has become known as "oral history" in other academic disciplines. After a short mapping of the discourse in Intercultural Theology (2.), and the focus on Asian story Theologies in particular (3.) I will turn to Western reflections on the significance of Story for Theology (4.).

2 Storytelling in Contextual and Intercultural Theology

Storytelling seems to be a particularity of Asian Theologies, with Suh Nam-Dong, one of the founding fathers of South Korean Minjung Theology, and Taiwanese theologian Choan-Seng Song, as pioneers. Latin American Theology of Liberation on the other hand has its roots in the *lectura popular,* Bible-reading in the basic Christian communities. Ernesto Cardenal's *The Gospel in Solentiname* (Cardenal 1976–1984) documenting the communal interpretation of the Gospel stories by his congregation of peasants on the shore of Lake Nicaragua is a well-known example. In South Africa, Itumeleng J. Mosala with his Biblical hermeneutics from the perspective of Black Theology (Mosala 1989) and Gerald O. West with his *ordinary reader approach* (West 1995; esp. 175–238) and the *Ujamaa Center for Biblical and Theological Community Development and Research* at the University of Kwazulu-Natal (UKZN) went in a similar direction. Yet when Allan Boesak for instance reads *Revelations* in the light of his prison experience under the Apartheid regime (Boesak 1987), or Elsa Tamez interprets Paul's prison experience in the context of poverty and oppression in Latin America (Tamez 1993), the relation between Biblical stories and real life stories – be it individual or collective – is at stake in the background.

First generation African Inculturation Theology practiced neither storytelling nor contextual Bible reading.[1] Contrariwise Musimbi Kanyoro in her *Introducing Feminist Cultural Hermeneutics* (Kanyoro 2002) shows how African patriarchal values reinforce patriarchal Biblical texts and vice versa, in a narrative way. Musa W. Dube tries to develop postcolonial hermeneutical tools by analyzing the Spirit (*semoya*) reading of African Instituted Churches (Dube 2000, 115–117; Dube 2001). Both belong to the third generation of African theologians many of which are Biblical scholars who try to reread Biblical texts in the light of African contexts and life experiences on an academic level.

This short overview already demonstrates that across Latin America and Africa biblical stories are the entry point for contextual Theologies which relate them in a hermeneutic circle to the lifeworld of the people. As we will see in the next part, in Asia theologians often enter the hermeneutic circle between text and context through the life stories, both lived and fictional, of their people. Therefore, not all Asian Theology is necessarily story Theology but most of story Theology is Asian, with its epicenter in North-East Asia. An exception to be mentioned here are women in North American Diaspora Theologies who obviously independently from Asian Theologies have used the storytelling method. Ada María Isasi-Díaz (1943–2012), the neoterist of Mujerista Theology, uses Hispanic women's life stories in her work *En la Lucha* (Isasi-Díaz 2004) gathered through ethnologic interviews to analyze the plight of her protagonists. Delores S. Williams (*1937), one of the mothers of Womanist Theology introduces novels in her *Sisters in the Wilderness* (Williams 1993) to describe the predicaments of black women. This has become a common strategy in Womanist Theology up until today.

3 Storytelling in Asian Theologies

Minjung Theology, the South Korean Brand of Liberation Theology,[2] is methodologically based on storytelling as is the work of Choan-Seng Song and other major Asian theologians. In what follows I offer a close reading of their appropriation of stories and ask for commonalities and differences as well as tracing possible interactions among them.

---

[1] An exception is John Mbiti (1971), who has been professionally trained in New Testament exegesis.
[2] The Sino-Korean word consists of two syllables Min (people) and -jung (mass), so Minjung Theology is a 'Theology of the people'. Minjung Theologians however claim that it is untranslatable because of the particular Korean experience.

3.1 Theology as Story-Telling – Suh Nam-Dong (1918–1984)[3]

Suh Nam-Dong's article under the same title has become his theological will, published posthumously in English translation in a special issue of the CTC-Bulletin (Suh 1984/85a) on story, that was edited in his honor. The vision of *history* as a *confluence of two traditions* ("the Minjung tradition in Christianity and the Korean Minjung tradition" [Suh 1983a, 177]) proclaimed by him and his use of *story* are the two foci of Suh's methodological framework. Story-telling is his method of choice for doing Theology, in the particular context of Korea in the 1970s and 1980s, a country divided between a ruthless communist regime in the North and a military development dictatorship closely aligned with the US in the South. Many Korean Christians living in the South, including most Minjung Theologians themselves, had fled the communists in the North after World War Two. Park Chung Hee then based his military dictatorship ideologically on strict anti-communism. Different from Latin American Liberation Theology, Marxist analysis therefore did not seem to be an option for first-generation Minjung theologians. Yet Suh is using materialist language and insists on sociological analysis. I will offer an inventory of the different genres of stories Suh is using and analyze how he is appropriating them.

Suh Nam-Dong introduces three different genres of stories in his articles under consideration: *classics* from late eighteenth century Yi-Dynasty (1392–1910), *contemporary literature* from the 1970s and *real-life stories* from the same period. All three genres are appropriated to articulate and analyze the suffering (*han*) of the minjung.

– The *real-life stories* are supposed to illustrate the han of the minjung and the *priesthood of han* of those Christian pastors and social activists who work among them. Minjung events like the self-immolation of the textile worker Chun Tae-Il (1948–1970) who was protesting against the inhuman working conditions of female textile workers in Seoul's Pyonghwa market, were a wakeup call for intellectuals like Suh Nam-Dong, who even happened to be an eye-witness. As a consequence of this story, Suh advocated for a *Hyonjang* church that is present among the minjung (Suh 1983a, 68).[4] As a matter of fact this was already practiced by the Urban Industrial and Rural Mission (UIM/URM). Suh is referring to the story of Ms. Kim Kyong-Suk from the Y.H. Trade Union who was killed by the police during a demonstration. In the case of brother Oh Won-Chun from the Catholic Farmers' Association, the story goes that he was captured, beaten and kept in solitary confinement.

– The han of the minjung is also expressed in *Contemporary literature*. Yun Hyong-Kil describes, in *Rainy Season* (*Changma*), the rifts going through nearly every

---

[3] These thoughts have been first presented at a symposium to commemorate Suh Nam-Dong's centennial in Seoul on September 10th, 2018, at Yonsei University.
[4] In Annotation 2 Suh compares the Hyonjang church to the Basic Christian Communities in Latin America: "Hyonjang Church is a Christian koinonia engaged in a social movement. The term may be translated as 'field church' or 'church on the spot.'"

Korean family that were caused by the Korean War and the division of the country. In a mytho-poetical way the author describes the resolving of han, and the reconciliation between two old women living together as in-laws in a traditional Korean house complex. Kim Chi-Ha's *Story of the Sound* is about an underdog who is eventually thrown into prison and is crippled by his torturers. The chunk of his body that is left rolls against the walls of the prison cell creating a sound of han that is widely heard. Kim's *Chang Il-Dam* is a Korean one-man opera (*pansori*) about a Jesus figure who teaches how to overcome han. In *God's Bow* (*Shingung*) written by Chon Seung-Se a shaman takes revenge by killing a rich man who ruined her life by taking everything away from her during a ritual he had requested her to perform.

- This leads us to the *Classics* from earlier epochs that are supposed to refer to the han of the minjung in Korean *history* in particular the social grievances of the Confucian Yi-dynasty. Suh is referring to the story of the Buddhist Monk Jee-Sung, the protagonist of an eighteenth century short-story from Ahn Sok-Kyong's *Sapyobyolijb* who ransoms two children from an impoverished Confucian scholar who wants to take them as a substitute for the debts of his servants who died without paying him back. Suh, in comparing the Buddhist monk's redemptive act with Jesus and how he made the blind man see in John 9, clearly champions Jesus as more subversive and persistent in criticizing the system and the powers that be.

Central to Suh's approach is his interpretation of the classical story of *The Bridegroom of Ahndong* from *Dongsangki'chan*, a collection of satirical writings. It is about Ahn-Gook, the son of a high-ranking Confucian scholar from Seoul who fails to learn how to read and write from early childhood days. Completely frustrated, the father sends his son to an uncle who serves in the province in Ahndong to get him out of his sight for good. The uncle also fails in engaging his nephew in reading and writing, and after some time decides to marry him off to the daughter of a minor provincial official. The latter however is suspicious why the son of a high-ranking official should wish to marry his daughter. When he finally hears about the reasons for the desperation he agrees to the marriage because he still regards it as prestigious for his family.

The daughter on her part then also tries to motivate her husband to join her father and the other learned men around him in the pleasures of intellectual life but fails initially as well. Against the Confucian convention she eventually decides to try to teach her husband by telling him stories that are related to the *history* of the country and the classics. She manages to catch his attention by her innocent question of whether he would 'like to hear a story or two'. For the first time in his life Ahn-Gook gets excited about learning and eventually asks her, where all these wonderful stories come from. When she tells him that he can find them in books, the ban is broken, and he eagerly learns how to read and write.

The problems at stake here are the Confucian educational system and the social stratification that comes with it as well as the subjugation of women. Suh acknowledges that as well but nevertheless puts the emphasis on the opposition between written letters and oral stories and misses the *tertium comparationis:* that being the patriarchy. My close reading of the story and Suh's reception reveals one of the pitfalls of Minjung Theology, namely, to have seen the agency of women but never making it theologically explicit. This led to a certain skepticism among Korean women theologians regarding Minjung Theology. Next to cultural hermeneutics and class analysis, feminism is the third theoretical tool that must be applied in interpreting this story.

Contemplating the different genres of stories that Suh is using, it turns out that there are different issues under consideration regarding *real-life stories* and *contemporary literature* on the one hand and the *classics* on the other. In the first case the question is whether there is a difference between so-called real and fictional stories. As far as Suh is concerned obviously there is none, they are both chosen as evidence for the han of the minjung. Methodologically he speaks of social analysis and sociology of literature respectively. The cultural-religious context of the *classics* is shaped by Confucianism and Buddhism and the historical distance to the feudal and patriarchal society must be taken into account. With these stories in mind two questions are called for regarding Suh's appropriation: (1.) how can cultural hermeneutics (Kanyoro 2002), class analysis and other theoretical tools help to bridge the historical gap? (2.) What exactly is the *tertium comparationis* between the classical stories and the contemporary lifeworld of the Minjung?

3.2 Minjung Theology on Story

Storytelling proves to be a core concept throughout Minjung Theology (Küster 2010a; Suh 1984/85). Hyun Young-Hack describes Theology as *rumor mongering*. In situations of oppression, like for example under the military dictatorship in Korea, rumors, stories told in secret, became the preferred medium of communication, a strategy that can easily lean on the Bible.

> Jesus was the worst and the most notorious rumormonger, telling the people that the Sabbath was made for human beings, not the other way around; that the Kingdom belongs to the poor rather than to the wealthy, and that he would rise up from the dead. He drank, ate, and chatted with the sinners and prostitutes, and became the source of insidious rumors. He himself was the rumor. He had to pay for it with his life (Hyun 1984/85, 47).

New Testament scholar Ahn Byung-Mu accordingly identifies different social groups of transmitters of the Jesus event. The stories of Jesus' life and death have been communicated as rumors by the Galilean minjung (ὄχλος) that followed Jesus, while the ancient church interpreted his death and resurrection as κήρυγμα.

> Therefore, the story about Jesus must have been transmitted secretly by those who knew him intimately. This type of tradition sociologically speaking, is *rumor*. Rumor expresses the effort on the part of the minjung of Jesus to transmit the real facts of the Jesus-event; and it is also the medium through which the minjung try to understand their own position in society. The political authorities, however, regard such rumors as an expression of rebellion, and consider rumor-mongering as dangerous minjung behavior (Ahn 1984/85, 30–31).

Kim Yong Bock points to the collective aspect of the shared stories as the *social biography* of the minjung:

> At present, the only way to understand the social biography of the Minjung is to approach it through dialogue and involvement with the Minjung and through the minjung's telling of their own story [...] Social biography encompasses the minjung's subjective experiences as well as objective conditions and structures and societal power relations (Kim 1984/85, 70–71).

In the footsteps of Suh Nam-Dong David Kwang-Sun Suh describes theologians and Christian social activists as the *Priesthood of han* who resolve the suffering of the minjung by creating space for their stories to be told.

> We are called into the priesthood of han to articulate the cries and groanings of the people in the language of theology, sociology, statistics, socio-economic analysis, and in poetry, drama, songs paintings and sculpture (Suh 1984 / 85, 62).

The writings collected in the CTC Bulletin in honor of Suh Nam-Dong are good examples for the confluence of two traditions he envisioned. The various authors read the Jesus stories in the light of their Korean experience and the stories of minjung and vice versa. Initially the minjung stories and the Biblical stories are read *contrapuntally*,[5] sometimes they are intertwined or a minjung story becomes transparent for the Jesus event and vice versa.

3.3 Choan-Seng Song

Choan-Seng Song (*1929) is certainly the Asian theologian whose name became almost synonymous with storytelling and who has also been engaged in a dialogue with Minjung Theology and Suh Nam-Dong in particular. over the course of his long career, Song published numerous books, all functioning according to the same pattern. He usually starts with telling a story, not necessarily Asian, it can also be Biblical or even *Alice in Wonderland* or *Cinderella*. Song explicitly refers to the hunger of his two daughters for stories (Song 1984, ix). His young daughters illustrated one of his books with children's sketches related to the stories he is telling (Song 1984, ix). The Taiwanese theologian then associates freely with his experiences

---

5 A term I adopt from postcolonial critic Edward Said (Küster 2018).

in the ecumenical movement and his theological knowledge, and references Biblical stories, with a strong predilection for Jesus. In the later part of his career the Biblical stories become more and more dominant over Asian stories.

There are few theoretical and methodological reflections detectable in Song's writings. When it comes to terminology, he remains rather vague. Even though his compatriot Shoki Coe (1914–1988), who in a sense holds the copyright on the term contextualization, is a sort of theological godfather to Song, he only mentions these discourses in passing. He develops his own private jargon when he speaks of "transposition" from Israel to Asia etc. (Song 1982, 16–17)[6]. Song himself states:

> [T]heological method is something of an after-thought [...] For me theology is like storytelling. The story unfolds itself as you tell it. It moves in all directions. It may even stray into byways. But this is the excitement of telling stories. A story grows and expands. It leads to new terrains and depicts new scenes. If this is what our storytelling is like, how much more so is God's storytelling! [...] The method of storytelling is in the telling of stories. (Song 1999a, 2)

At the same time, Song, similarly to Suh is interested in a Theology of history since his dissertation on comparing Barth and Tillich's view on revelation and man's religion (Song 1965, 1984). In an extensive review of Choan-Seng Song's early writings, Suh Nam-Dong criticizes a divergent understanding of "revelation". Suh distinguishes between the infra-structure and super-structure of revelation, a terminology that has Marxist overtones. Theologically, the relationship between revelation and history is at stake among the two.

Song's account of his participation in a 1984 conference on Minjung Theology in Seoul allows a fictitious dialogue between the two. Regarding the questions raised on the understanding of revelation Song laconically qualifies this as a matter of emphasis not substance and problematizes the term "infra-structure" (Song 1984, 17–18). Song interprets Minjung Theology as a Theology of the cross in a very socio-historical way. His own *Tears of Lady Meng* is probably as close as one can get to Minjung Theology from another contextual background (Küster 2010b). Song is a strong advocate of a Taiwanese political Theology and Liberation Theologies in general. Concurrently Song deals not only with Confucianism and Buddhism, which Suh regards as "supra-structure" (Suh 1984/85b, 14), but also with folk culture and folk religion like Shamanism. As a matter of fact, he refers several times to Korean minjung culture and religion in his writings. In their methodological use of story as well as in their theological take on *his*tory Suh Nam-Dong and Choan-Seng Song seem to be soulmates rather than antagonists.

---

6 Cf. for similar spatial metaphors Koyama (1985) or Panikkar (1987).

3.4 Kosuke Koyama and Kwok Pui-Lan

Even though Kosuke Koyama (1929–2009), another icon of Asian Theology, does not use the term *story* programmatically, but only rather in passing (Koyama 1974a, 206), he and Choan-Seng Song are like twin brothers in the way that their careers have developed internationally and in their doing of Theology (Küster 2011; Koyama 1985). Their writing style is narrative and their way of thinking associative. Koyama discloses more of his autobiography, he reflects on his mission work in Thailand, his experiences of war and nationalism in his home country Japan as well as his work in the ecumenical movement in Asia and worldwide and his own cosmopolitan life between countries and continents. While Choan-Seng Song's Theology is Jesus-centered and operates within a Trinitarian framework, Koyama's Theology, due to his Lutheran background, is cross-centered. Both combine an interest in a Theology of history (Koyama 1974a, 22–23, 52) with an interest in narrative Theology. The title of Koyama's classic *Waterbuffalo Theology* is a metaphor for his kenotic approach to "re-root" (Koyama 1974a, 118) Biblical texts and theological ideas in the Asian context "from below" (Koyama 1974a, viii). Similar to Song, Koyama prefers a private terminology but is well aware of the contextualization debate. His theological program of "neighbourology" (Koyama 1974a, 89–94) in a nutshell reads as follows:

> On my way to the country church, I never fail to see a herd of waterbuffoloes grazing in the muddy paddy field. This sight is an inspiring moment for me. Why? Because it reminds me that the people to whom I am to bring the gospel of Christ spend most of their time with these waterbuffaloes in the rice field. [...] They remind me to discard all abstract ideas, and to use exclusively objects that are immediately tangible 'Sticky-rice', 'banana', 'pepper', 'dog' [...] (Koyama 1974a, 39).

Second-generation Asian Woman Theologian Kwok Pui-Lan (*1952) propagates a historical, dialogical and postcolonial imagination. She occasionally refers to the story-approach of first-generation Asian male theologians. Applying the method of feminist New Testament scholar Elisabeth Schüssler Fiorenza, Kwok reconstructs the stories of Chinese Bible women and demonstrates that there has been local, female agency in spreading the Christian faith in China beyond the Western missionary project. In her work, Kwok skillfully combines storytelling with rewriting *her*story. At the same time, she wants to read the Biblical stories in the context of other sacred texts of Asian religions and de/construct the impact of Western colonial Christianity:

> The term *dialogical imagination* describes the process of creative hermeneutics in Asia. [...] It is highly imaginative, for it looks at both the Bible and our Asian reality anew, challenging the historical-critical method, presumed by many to be objective and neutral (Kwok 1995, 13).

> '[P]ostcolonial imagination' refers to a desire, a determination, and a process of disengagement from the whole colonial syndrome, which takes many forms and guises (Kwok 2005, 2–3).

An intervention that must be taken into consideration in all this is Gayatri Spivak's famous article *Can the Subaltern Speak?* (Spivak 1988) that raises the question of representation. The contextual theologians introduced here for their part try to create a space for the stories of the poor and oppressed to be heard. They rewrite his/herstory story by pointing out their subjectivity and local agency.

4 Story and the West

While Minjung Theology with its slogan "people as the subjects of history" (Commission on Theological Concerns 1983) content-wise still belongs to the project of modernity, its methodology already shifts into the direction of *The Postmodern Condition*. The famous title of Jean Francois Lyotard's (1924–1998) report to the Canadian government (Lyotard 1984) is of interest here mainly because of the language game he created. Lyotard postulates the end of the Meta narratives of Modernity like Enlightenment, Marxism etc. and propagates the power of local narratives instead, which are championed by contextual Theologies. At present we are experiencing the return of the Meta narratives in its worst form. Trump's "Make America great Again" is symptomatic for the new nationalistic chauvinism that is swamping the world. While on the other hand, unfortunately, narratives like enlightenment, democracy, human rights etc. seem to have lost their radiant power.

4.1 Western Theologians on Story

While contextual theologians from Asia do storytelling, western academic theologians tend to reflect theoretically on the possibilities of storytelling.[7] In Germany in the 1970s the linguist and literary critic Harald Weinrich (*1927), and the Catholic founding father of a new political Theology Johann Baptist Metz (1928-2019), were advocating what they called "narrative theology" in two short but influential articles in *Concilium* (Metz 1973, Weinrich 1973). In his methodological and theological reflections, Metz opts for a narrative Theology that keeps alive the "dangerous memory" of the suffering of victims, the poor and oppressed. He formulated this new political Theology after Auschwitz and has been in solidarity with Latin American Liberation Theology from its very beginnings.

Dietrich Ritschl (1929–2018) and Hugh O. Jones, consider "story as raw material of Theology" (Ritschl and Jones 1976, translation by V.K.). Consequently, Ritschl regards contextual Theologies not "Theology" in the real sense of the word. Already in 1974 Gerhard Ebeling had pointed out the lack of "experience" as a theological

---

[7] An exception is Hollenweger (1979–1988), one of the founding fathers of Intercultural Theology that is a collection of stories with little theoretical reflection.

category (Ebeling 1975). As a Lutheran Theologian he criss-crossed the Barthian neglect of all things contextual and oriented himself toward human life experience. He introduced the theological notion of *experience with the experience* (Ebeling 1975, 25) of God's presence in human lifeworlds.

In the footsteps of Karl Barth's Neo-Orthodoxy, the post-liberal Yale school represented by theologians like Hans Frei (1922–1988), George Lindbeck (1923–2018) and Stanley Hauerwas (*1940), developed a different take on "narrative theology" from Metz and Ebeling that "rejects both the traditional Enlightenment appeal to a 'universal rationality' and the liberal assumption of an immediate religious experience common to all humanity" (McGrath 2017, 78). Over against Metz who wants to relocate the church in the enlightenment project and his pathos that the *dangerous memory* of the suffering of Christ has a political impact on society and includes the memory of the suffering of the victims of oppression and terror, they argue for an internal communication process within the church, in narrative form following the model of much of the Biblical texts.

> I am persuaded that historical inquiry is a useful and necessary procedure but that theological reading is the reading of a *text*, and not the reading of a *source*, which is how historians read it. Historical inquiry, while telling us many useful things, does not tell us how we are to understand the text as texts (Frei 1992, 11).

Narrative Exegesis on its part diverges from historical critical exegesis with its interest in the Biblical texts in their current form. Its proponents apply methods like New Criticism, close reading or reader response criticism (Erbele-Küster 2014). They refer to the classical hermeneutical positions behind the text (narrator), in the text (narrative structures and functions) and in front of the text (reader response).

In the late 1980s, early 1990s in Practical Theology Wilhelm Gräb (*1948), Henning Luther (1947–1991), and others propagated a life story approach that focused on the Re/construction of one's identity through telling one's life story. Gräb (1998) applied the story approach to rites of passage like baptism, confirmation, wedding and funeral. Theologically he saw these as events of justification of individual human life stories. Henning Luther (1992) also deals with the individual subject and how human life stories are under permanent deconstruction and reconstruction. Over against the more communal approach of Contextual Theology, "people as the subject of history", they emphasize the subjectivity of his/herstory. Still it is the subject in front of God and fellow human beings. The single most important philosophical contribution to the subject under discussion is the oeuvre of Wilhelm Schapp (1884–1965) that has never been translated into English. According to Schapp (1953; 1959) human beings are enmeshed in stories. Storytelling is an anthropological constant that needs an audience. In a similar way Paul Ricoeur's (1913–2005) philosophical anthropology is centered on the concept of *narrative identity*.

Ultimately, Practical Theology today seems to have a more pragmatic take on story, in the sense of Dietrich Ritschl's understanding as raw material. The empirical turn in Practical Theology has led to research based on quantitative and qualitative interviews regarding people's life stories. A link between Practical Theology and Contextual as well as Intercultural Theology could be the use of story in healing from trauma. At the same time, this could also be a way for intercultural exchange between Asian Theologies and Liberation Theologies in Africa and Latin America. Post-conflict societies are still overshadowed by past suffering. Contextual Theologies can create safe spaces for storytelling and allow the subaltern to find their own voice as well as overcoming trauma.

4.2 Aesthetic Resistance – Pussy Riot Against the New Meta Narratives

Coming back to Lyotard's distinction between stories and meta narratives once more, I want to have a side glance on contemporary popular culture. The Russian feminist artist collective Pussy Riot became known in the West through their *Punk Prayer*, an event in the Cathedral of Christ the Savior, the central church of the Russian-Orthodox Church, in Moscow in 2012. Some of their members stormed into the Trump Tower in New York City in 2017. With subversive statements they protested the man-to-man friendship of Putin and Trump. A theater play and the video *Make America Great Again*[8] targeted the nationalism and chauvinism of the two. In the clip Nadezhda Tolokonnikowa poses as Anchor-woman of a fake CNN newscast covering Trump's success in the elections. She also appears as Trump in the Oval Office, with legs spread on the presidential desk and cowboy boots. Later, in a Sado-Maso scene, her barely dressed body is measured by two clones of Trump in police uniforms checking if she fulfills Trump's ideals of what a woman's body should look like. She is branded according to the way in which she embodies different stigmatized minorities discriminated against by Trump.

Pussy Riot direct a new dimension of political Theology in public space. Their theological interventions are opposing the alliance of the Russian-Orthodox Church and State, Kyrill I and Putin are both targets of their critique. Not only has the text of the Punk prayer, but also statements during the lawsuit shown that they draw from Christian faith (Pussy Riot! 2012, 23.29–32).[9] Furthermore they apologized after the event in the Cathedral of Christ the Savior explicitly in case they should have hurt religious feelings, but not for their attempt to remind the church of its genuine mission.

Social media and YouTube are platforms of storytelling in the twenty-first century. They often function in the same way as the rumor mongering practiced by the

---

[8] https://www.youtube.com/watch?v=s-bKFo30o2o (30.11.2021). A sequence from the video was shown as introduction to the lecture at Yonsei University, cf. Küster (2021).
[9] Maria Aljochina was a volunteer in orthodox youth work (Willems 2013, 50).

Minjung movement. Trump himself ran his presidency via Twitter and tries to denounce and silence his critics by labeling their subversive voices as fake news. Yet stories like the ones created by and around Pussy Riot remain to be subversive to dominant discourses and meta-narratives.

5 Conclusions

- Story(telling) is an anthropological constant. Human beings live in and by their stories. Storytelling constitutes their identity.
- Story always is a re/construction be it real-life or fictional. Stories vary with the context they are told in. Human beings develop different visions of their life in the course of time.
- Storytelling often reveals the underside of his/herstory. Contextual Theologies share this approach, also known as oral history with other disciplines of humanities.
- In Theology the issue at stake is the link between the Biblical stories and stories of human life experience. They can be correlated in different modes: read contrapuntally, intertwined, or as 'experience with the experience'.
- A good story is the theology in itself rather than its raw material. Marshall McLuhan's (1911–1980) famous catchphrase "The medium is the message" points to form, not to content. Yet stories can be interpreted theologically by identifying the plot and points of comparison as well as the generative themes they contain.
- In contextual Theologies, story goes with social analysis and cultural hermeneutics. The stories told already constitute a form of social biography. They often imply a critical view on the life circumstances in a given society.
- Story is subversive to dominant discourses and meta-narratives.

Bibliography

Ahn, Byung-Mu. 1984/85. "The Transmitters of the Jesus-event." *CTC Bulletin* 5–6:26–39.
Boesak, Allan. 1987. *Comfort and Protest: The Apocalypse from a South African Perspective.* Louisville: Westminster John Knox Press.
Cardenal, Ernesto. 1976–84. *The Gospel in Solentiname.* 4 Vols. Maryknoll: Orbis.
Commission on Theological Concerns of the Christian Conference of Asia, ed. ²1983. *Minjung Theology: People as the Subjects of History.* Maryknoll: Orbis.
Dube, Musa W. 2000. *Postcolonial Feminist Interpretation of the Bible.* St. Louis: Chalice Press.
Dube, Musa W. 2001. "Fifty Years of Bleeding: A Storytelling Feminist Reading of Mark 5, 24–43." In *Other Ways of Reading: African Women and the Bible*, edited by Musa W. Dube, Atlanta: Society of Biblical Literature, 50–60.
Ebeling, Gerhard. 1975. "Die Klage über das Erfahrungsdefizit in der Theologie als Frage nach ihrer Sache." In *Beiträge zur Fundamentaltheologie, Soteriologie und Ekklesiologie.* Vol. 3, edited by Gerhard Ebeling. Tübingen: Mohr, 3–28.

Erbele-Küster, Dorothea. 2014. "A Short Story of Narratology in Biblical Studies." In *Religious Stories We Live By: Narrative Approaches in Theology and Religious Studies*. STAR 19, edited by R. Ruard Ganzevoort, Maaike de Haardt, and Michael Scherer-Rath, Leiden / Boston: Brill, 75–87.
Gräb, Wilhelm. 1998. *Lebensgeschichten, Lebensentwürfe, Sinndeutungen: Eine praktische Theologie gelebter Religion*. Gütersloh: Kaiser / Gütersloher Verlagshaus.
Frei, Hans Wilhelm. 1992. *Types of Christian Theology*. New Haven: Yale University Press.
Hollenweger, Walter. 1979–1988. *Interkulturelle Theologie*. 3 Vols., München: Kaiser.
Hyun, Young-Hack. 1984/85. "Theology as Rumor-Mongering." *CTC Bulletin* 5–6:40–48.
Kanyoro, Musimbi R. A. 2002. *Introducing Feminist Cultural Hermeneutics: An African Perspective*. IFT 9. London: Sheffield Academic Press.
Koyama, Kosuke. 1974. *Waterbuffalo Theology*. Maryknoll: Orbis.
Koyama, Kosuke. 1985. *Mount Fuji and Mount Sinai: A Critique of Idols*. Maryknoll: Orbis.
Küster, Volker. 2001. *The Many Faces of Jesus Christ: Intercultural Christology*. Maryknoll: Orbis.
Küster, Volker. 2010a. *A Protestant Theology of Passion: Korean Minjung Theology Revisited*. SIST 4. Leiden / Boston: Brill.
Küster, Volker. 2010b. "Lady Meng Revisited: Doing Political Theology with Asian Stories of Suffering and Hope." *Theologies and Cultures* 7:49–62.
Küster, Volker. 2011. *Einführung in die Interkulturelle Theologie*. UTB 3465. Göttingen: Vandenhoeck & Ruprecht.
Küster, Volker. 2021. "Konfessionskunde im Kontext interkultureller Theologie". In *Konfessionskunde im 21. Jahrhundert. Bestandsaufnahmen, Herausforderungen, Perspektiven*, edited by Mareile Lasogga and Michael Roth, Leipzig: Evangelische Verlagsanstalt, 166–180.
Kwok, Pui-Lan. 1995. *Discovering the Bible in the Non-Biblical World*. Maryknoll: Orbis.
Kwok, Pui-Lan. 2005. *Postcolonial Imagination and Feminist Theology*. Louisville: Westminster John Knox Press.
Luther, Henning. 1992. *Religion und Alltag*, Stuttgart: Radius Verlag.
Lyotard, Jean François. [1979] 1984. *The Postmodern Condition: A Report on Knowledge*. Theory and History of Literature 10, trans. Geoff Bennington and Brian Massumi. Minneapolis: University of Minnesota Press.
Mbiti, John S. 1971. *New Testament Eschatology in an African Background: A Study of the Encounter between New Testament Theology and African Traditional Concepts*. London: Oxford University Press.
Isasi-Díaz, Ada María. 2004. *En la Lucha. In the Struggle: Elaborating a Mujerista Theology*, Minneapolis: Fortress Press.
Kim, Yong-Bock. 1984/85. "Theology and the Social Biography of the Minjung." *CTC Bulletin* 5–6:66–78.
McGrath, Alistair E. [1991] 2017. *Christian Theology: An Introduction*. Chichester / Malden: Wiley, Blackwell.
McLuhan, Marshall. 1964. *Understanding Media: The Extensions of Man*. New York: McGraw-Hill.
Metz, Johann Baptist. 1973. "Kleine Apologie des Erzählens." *Concilium* 9:334–341.
Mosala, Itumeleng J. 1989. *Biblical Hermeneutics and Black Theology in South Africa*. Grand Rapids: Eerdmans.
Ritschl, Dietrich, and Hugh O. Jones. 1976. '*Story*' *als Rohmaterial der Theologie*. München: Kaiser.
Ricoeur, Paul. 1984–88. *Time and Narrative*. 4 Vols., Chicago: University of Chicago Press.
Ricoeur, Paul. 1992. *Oneself as Another*. Chicago: University of Chicago Press.
Panikkar, Raimundo. 1987. "The Jordan, the Tiber and the Ganges." In *The Myth of Christian Uniqueness: Toward a Pluralistic Theology of Religions*, edited by John Hick and Paul Knitter, Maryknoll: Orbis, 89–116.

Pussy Riot. 2012. *Pussy Riot! Ein Punkgebet für die Freiheit*. Hamburg: Edition Nautilus.
Schapp, Wilhelm. 1953. *In Geschichten verstrickt: Zum Sein von Mensch und Ding*. Hamburg: Richard Meiner.
Schapp, Wilhelm. 1959. *Philosophie der Geschichten*. Leer: Gerhard Rautenberg.
Song, Choan-Seng. 1965. *The Relation of Divine Revelation and Man's Religion in the Theologies of Karl Barth and Paul Tillich*. New York: no publisher.
Song, Choan-Seng. 1981. *The Tears of Lady Meng: A Parable of People's Political Theology*. Maryknoll: Orbis.
Song, Choan-Seng. 1982. *The Compassionate God*. Maryknoll: Orbis.
Song, Choan-Seng. 1984. *Tell Us Our Names: Story Theology from an Asian Perspective*, Maryknoll: Orbis.
Song, Choan-Seng. 1999a. "Five Stages toward Christian Theology in the Multicultural World." In *Journeys at the Margin: Toward an Autobiographical Theology in American-Asian Perspective*, edited by Peter C. Phan and Jung Young Lee, Collegeville: Liturgical Press, 1–21.
Song, Choan-Seng. 1999b. *The Believing Heart: An Invitation to Story Theology*. Minneapolis: Fortress Press.
Suh, David Kwang-Sun. 1984/85. "Called to Witness to the Gospel Today: The Priesthood of *Han*." *CTC Bulletin* 5–6:57–65.
Suh, Nam-Dong: 1983a. "Historical References for a Theology of Minjung." In *Minjung Theology: People as the Subjects of History*, edited by the Commission on Theological Concerns of the Christian Conference of Asia (CTC-CCA), Maryknoll: Orbis, 155–182.
Suh, Nam-Dong. 1983b. "Towards a Theology of Han." In *Minjung Theology: People as the Subjects of History*, edited by the Commission on Theological Concerns of the Christian Conference of Asia (CTC-CCA), Maryknoll: Orbis, 55–69.
Suh, Nam-Dong. 1984/85a. "Theology as Story-telling: A Counter-theology." *CTC Bulletin* 5–6:4–11.
Suh, Nam-Dong. 1984/85b. "Cultural Theology, Political Theology and Minjung Theology." *CTC Bulletin* 5–6:12–15.
Spivak, Gayatri Chakravorty. 1988. "Can the Subaltern Speak?" In *Marxism and the Interpretation of Culture*, edited by Cary Nelson and Lawrence Grossberg, Chicago: University of Illinois Press, 271–313.
Tamez, Elsa. 1993. *The Amnesty of Grace: Justification by Faith from a Latin American Perspective*. Nashville: Abingdon Press.
Weinrich, Harald. 1973. "Narrative Theologie." In *Concilium* 9:329–333.
West, Gerald O. 1995. *Biblical Hermeneutics of Liberation: Modes of Reading the Bible in the South African Context*. Pietermaritzburg: Cluster / Maryknoll: Orbis.
Willems, Joachim. 2013. *Pussy Riots Punk-Gebet: Religion, Recht und Politik in Russland*. Berlin: Berlin University Press.
Williams, Delores S. 1992. *Sisters in the Wilderness: The Challenge of Womanist God-Talk*. Maryknoll: Orbis.

Rima Nasrallah
Symbolizing / Meaning / Ambiguity

1 Introduction: Faced with Symbols

In the obscurity of the Maronite cave of Saint Anthony in North Lebanon an array of cooking pots is displayed upside down on the humid rocks. Placed on top or underneath them are fragments of letters, pictures, and items of babies' clothing. The pots are all different, varying in size and shape. The lady in charge of the gift shop at the monastery explained that these pots are left there in prayer by believers who wish to conceive children. "Why pots?" I asked. The shop keeper stared at me in silence obviously unsettled by my question. "Pots symbolize the womb" she answered as she placed her hand on her own abdomen with a hint of disbelief at my ignorance.

The shop keeper is a native of the area and possess inside knowledge of this traditional practice. To her, the very question is absurd: The pots belong to the cave and *clearly* symbolize wombs yearning to be filled. The symbol is not questioned: rather, it is accepted, taught, elaborated on, and handed down from generation to generation. To the extent that it becomes 'invisible'. As she walks into the cave every evening to put out the candles, the ever-growing pile of pots appears as a continuation of the grey rocks. They are objects of familiarity and comfort, of certainty and of clarity. Though the question of the intruder is answered, it is at the same time silenced and dismissed.

Our faith systems rest on symbols – material, ritual and linguistic. Some of them are common and unchallenged like the breaking of the bread, or the use of water for purifying and cleansing. However, despite their depth and surplus of meaning, repetition and habitude run the risk of rendering silenced certain symbols. Many have remarked how with time these symbols tend to flatten out and shrink, making of the loaf of bread, a crumb and of the bath, a droplet (see Guiver in Gordon-Taylor and Day 2013). Yet, these are not the only symbols in our life of faith. A more intricate body of symbols built into our everyday life buttresses our relationship with God and defines our understanding of life and its meaning (de Haardt 2013). Many of these practices and objects are passed on across generations, and are adopted without hesitation, and one inhabits them and performs them without a second thought, until a question arises. What are those activities and objects and why are they part of our faith system? Why pots? Why candles? Why kneeling?

Desire for certainty and for comfort leads one to dismiss these questions and silence the interrogation. However, my thesis is that it is precisely this question, this moment of uncertainty and ambiguity, that brings the symbol to life and gives it its meaning as it leads the performer of the symbol into becoming.

This chapter looks at what happens to symbols such as these pots when a question arises. In other words, when they are taken out of their faith systems and subjected to a different system of belief and inquiry that does not share in these symbols. To do so I consider a particular group of Lebanese women who socially and religiously move in and out of the various matrices of meaning that faith weaves. These women originally come from Antiochian Orthodox Churches (Atiyyeh 2005; Hunt 2007) or Maronite Churches (McCallum in O'Mahony and Loosley 2010, 25–40; Galadza 2007, 291–391) and have joined the Lebanese Protestant Churches (Badr 2005) by virtue of marriage. Every year, it is through marriage, that many new female members of the congregation are added to the tiny Reformed Church in Lebanon. The great majority of these women come from these Eastern Churches. Bound by their own social obligations and abiding by tradition, these women must then join their husbands' church, where they are expected to act as Protestant congregants, without any official initiation or prior exposure to the Reformed faith and tradition.

By joining the Reformed Church, these women never completely leave their mother church, nor do they convert to the new tradition, but they keep moving – physically and virtually – between the two and in-between the two or three traditions (Nasrallah et al. 2012, 270–284). They could participate in the Orthodox liturgy on Wednesdays and the Protestant service on Sundays, they could celebrate Easter with the Maronites and Christmas with the Reformed or visit Orthodox pilgrimage sites and Reformed conferences. The constant movement and exposure to both (or more) traditions translates itself in creative ways in the liturgical lives of these women, and the way in which they manage and perceive objects and rituals as they redefine and reconstruct their own liturgical lives (Nasrallah et al. 2016).

Like the shop keeper in the monastery of Saint Anthony, these women grew up in homes and families where certain objects are considered normal and certain rituals are simply part of daily life. "Media are intrinsic to religion" (Meyer 2006, 12) in general, and each religious tradition has its own set of objects, practices and linguistic symbols or media; symbols that point to some further reality and connect on a deeper level of existence. Yet, unlike the case of the shop keeper, the objects and rituals of the women considered here are constantly put in question, as a radically different spirituality presses itself upon their faith life.

2 Women in-between Traditions

To understand what happens to the liturgical lives[1] of these women and the matrix of symbols in this particular situation, ethnographic methods were used. Along with their public practices of faith, their private and domestic practices were investigated. Participant observation, in-depth interviews, discussions, filming, and spiritual biographies were collected to understand what these women do to reach out and commu-

---

[1] By liturgical lives we refer to worship practices that are not confined to the walls of the church, see Barnard, Cilliers, and Wepener (2014).

nicate with God. Public and private, formal, and everyday practices were all taken into consideration. This study benefited from developments within the social and cultural sciences in order to understand why certain people do, what they do as they communicate with God.

A rich array of practices emerged as each woman displayed or described what she does, where she goes and what she possesses. What is distinctive in the mother traditions of these women is that they are all intrinsically highly symbolic. Rooted in the Syriac tradition, the Maronite spirituality embraces the symbolic and remains close to the material world; the world is seen as creation transformed, as inspired by Ephrem the Syrian and is appreciated in its materiality. As for the Antiochian Orthodox tradition, with its focus on the incarnation in approaching the material and performative world, liturgical rituals as well as Icons and objects, are seen as window into heaven or the divine world. The women considered here grew up in homes where mothers and grandmothers decorated the domestic space with a multitude of holy objects. They witnessed priests sprinkling and blessing these objects. As children, they were taken to visit monasteries, light candles, kneel in front of altars and sample sweets baked for feasts. These "normal" practices and "authorized" (Meyer 2011a, 27) objects are "transmitted and shared" from generation to generation. Many of the women owned Icons, images, or statues that were given to them by their mothers. Most decorate their homes or cook according to recipes learned at home. However, these acquired objects and learned practices do not exactly copy or repeat what had been learned as a child or what is practiced by other members of the family. In their new liturgical environment, these women have their own way of dealing with objects and their own way of practicing rituals. I mention some examples here:

Greek Orthodox Nada does not have an elaborate home altar as the one in her mother's or sister's home. Instead, she owns one Icon of the Theotokos hung over a door and a number of small souvenirs such as a rosary, a cross, and a bottle of oil collected from monasteries. These objects migrate from one place to another periodically, disappear in a drawer to then be replaced by other objects. The collection is complemented by a Van Dyke Bible[2] and a few leaflets from the local Protestant church. Every time she acquires a new object, she waits, thinks, and rethinks where to place it, only to move it again or even throw it away.

Maronite Lara elaborated her own censing ritual at home. She retained some traditions from her childhood, introduced new ones and merged Protestant teachings on censing practices. While she cooks food for religious feasts, she is selective and creative in how to do it. She does not observe all the Maronite fasts, instead she adapts the fasting menu to her own family's needs and wishes, sometimes even neglecting an entire fasting season. Although she grew up praying with the rosary regularly, she now uses it to decorate her mirror and occasionally glances at it while conversing with God in a more 'Evangelical' manner.

---

[2] The van Dyke Bible is the official Arabic Protestant translation.

Looking in their homes, or at their practices, one sees similar themes from their mother churches, that have been adapted or that have evolved. Their collection of items is always changing, and their rituals vary. There is movement and dynamism in these symbolic practices and objects as well as a degree of discomfort, particularly as the women explain and perform to a Protestant researcher, or in front of their Protestant husbands.

3 Disorientation and Reorientation

3.1 Disorientation

Inherited practices and objects tend to 'disappear' in the piety of people. Icons and objects merge with walls and furniture; rituals flow with the rhythm of the day and the year. The signifier merges with the substance it signifies, creating a synthesis, as Birgit Meyer puts it, which veils the material and physical aspect of a symbol. "On the other hand, objects and rituals 'appear' if this synthesis is cracked" (Meyer 2011b, 63).

In other words, the symbol and the thing symbolized become one when taken for granted, yet when the synthesis between the two is challenged, the symbol and the thing symbolized, or the world it orients its user towards, begin to separate. As a result, one ends up with a useless object or an empty ritual: a handful of ashes, a deformed candle, or an aesthetically displeasing image. When the "synthesis is cracked" the symbol stops working (Morgan 2011, 142).

Despite recent developments within Protestantism that hold a revised position towards media or symbols present in other Christian traditions[3], traditionally and in the Lebanese context, Protestantism seems to suggest a direct relation with God which can only be obstructed by objects and rituals (Meyer 2012, 26). Ever since its advent in the nineteenth century, Lebanese Protestantism has challenged objects and rituals in the life of Eastern Christians. The images, pilgrimages and home rituals of Middle Eastern women fell under attack by American and British missionaries who dismissed these as "superstitious" and depicted the women as "hopeless subjects of missionary labour" (Jessup [1873] 2005, 47). This attitude continues today, within two forms of Protestantism (Sabra 2001, 101–115): a Pietist form as well as a Cultural form. Inheriting Enlightenment values, cultural Protestantism dismisses objects and rituals based on an assumption that we only know through our minds (Meyer and Verrips 2008, 20–30), not our bodies nor our emotions. Pietist Protestantism on the other hand does not wholly reject emotions, but it has been critical of emotions depicted in the lives of the Virgin Mary, or the Saints. The women considered here have interacted with these attitudes within their husbands' Church. The

---

[3] Knowing that the Protestant tradition like all other religious systems is built on symbols as well: material, ritual, and linguistic even if they look, feel, and sound different.

Protestant approach that claims to be a direct relationship with Christ alone, be it through the mind (cultural) or thorough the heart (pietist) clashes both with the incarnational and performative Orthodox attitude, as well as with the anthropological material Maronite position. The emphasis on 'direct relationship' creates dissonance in the women's daily practices. The objects and practices emerge as 'indirect' or 'mediated' relationships, and the women are suddenly confronted with the material and physical aspects of their symbolic world.

The objects and practices are thus defamiliarized or demystified. Subjected to the Protestant logic and discourse, these symbols become insignificant and the women whose faith is expressed through them lose their direction and become – at least temporarily – disoriented (Chauvet 1995, 86).

The collections of things and practices lose their charm and in a sense their power to communicate with the divine and establish connections. The more the role of the human hand is obvious, the weaker their claim to offer truth (Latour 2002, 18). However, despite their emergence as highly questionable if not dangerous things, they are not discarded or eliminated. On the contrary, this situation of estrangement from their symbols triggers the women into experimentation, in a quest for reorientation. The objects and rituals, though questioned and now confronting the women with a possible uselessness or even obstructiveness, are re-evaluated.

3.2 Reorientation

Though the synthesis between object and what it symbolizes is broken, the objects are rarely totally emptied of their 'holiness'. Under the Protestant tradition's questioning and challenging gaze, one starts seeing the wood, the paint, the metal hooks and even the dirt covering an icon. It is, after all, wood and paint made by a human hand and bought with money. The ritual starts to feel repetitive, and even religious words and terms become confused. However, the women refuse to consider that it is *just* wood and paint. There remains something more than just the wood and paint, the wax and wick, oil, and cotton, that make up the objects. However, that 'something more' is not totally identified with the object or practice, nor is it taken for granted.

In an attempt to connect with that 'something more', the women resort to experimenting with varying their rituals and moving their objects around their homes.

It was observed for example that Leena, one of the respondents, changed the configuration of her home altar more than five times within four years. With every change there was a logic inspired both by the Protestant discourse as well as Leena's own developing convictions. Certain Icons were dismissed, others incorporated, and some acquired a more prominent and central place. The logic guiding this experimentation is dynamic, as interaction with the Protestant sola scriptura and solus Christus alternates with visits to Orthodox monasteries or Maronite Churches.

In the same way, many women vary their home rituals. They introduce new elements, change the order, try different postures, and say other words. By trying out different rituals, combining a candle with a Bible or censing the home whilst chanting a Protestant hymn, the women attempt to find a new way of reaching the divine, whose contours are being drawn and redrawn as new insights are glimpsed in the tensions within the various traditions. Objects and rituals are changed and altered all the time. They are restless and unresolved. And it is through these movements and this ambiguity that they start to address the women in a more pressing manner and to draw attention towards something beyond them.

This movement, or flux, is reminiscent of Bruno Latour's concept of de-freeze-framing. While discussing images in art, science and religion, Latour restates the second commandment of the decalogue not as a destruction of images but rather as a refusal of what he calls freeze-framing. By freeze-framing, Latour means "extracting an image out of the flow, and becom[ing] fascinated by it, as if it were sufficient, as if all movement had stopped." (Latour 2002, 26). In Latour's logic, active images are moving images, while frozen or stable images invite idolatry. He claims that frozen images – mental or physical – attract attention to themselves rather than point beyond themselves. In addition, Latour and many with him (Morgan, Meyer) remind us that there is no such thing as a world without images, without media or without symbols. No matter how iconoclastic one is, one destroys a symbol only to replace it with a different one, sometimes from a different category only to treat it in the same way, i.e., to be fascinated by it to the point of a new form of 'idolatry'. Idolatry is that moment when one totally confuses the referent with that which it points to, so that words or objects are seen to 'contain God' or rituals to 'control the divine presence' (Saliers 1984, 38).

On the other hand, Latour discusses how it is only when images are broken, when their constructed nature is revealed, that they start pointing away from themselves. 'Broken' images are images that can address the onlooker, the user, by deflecting the gaze towards what is beyond the image. With this in mind, we notice that the women in question are addressed through this questioning of their images, and through the variation and movement of their symbolic objects and practices. Here, it is not an iconoclasm that attempts to wipe away all images, but a continuous appraisal and reappraisal of existing objects and practices. This variation redirects the attention, as Latour points out, but it is also a means of discovery and knowledge. In a similar way, Theodore W. Jennings, writing about ritual knowledge, believes that ritual knowledge is activated through variation. "If there is no variation in the ritual performance, we would have to conclude that there is here neither search nor discovery but only transmission and illustration of knowledge gained elsewhere and otherwise" (Jennings 1996, 326).

Changing the place of their objects, varying their rituals, the women are working out the new meaning of their symbols. Their homes become transformed into laboratories or workshops of liturgical experimentation or tinkering (Grimes, Latour, Lévi Strauss, Barnard, and others). The ambiguity around the meaning of their objects and their validity, the challenge launched towards their practices, as well as their own changing convictions, keep the objects and rituals moving and flowing, they thus acquire an ever-renewed meaning, and address the user by their ambiguity: of presence and absence, construction, and truth.

4 Power in Ambiguity

The thesis is, consequently, that these symbols are (re)made active *because* of their ambiguity not *despite* of it. Objects in general are potent, they can even talk (Datson 2004) particularly through their very ambivalence. According to Sheryl Turkle, "objects help us make our minds, reaching out to us to form active partnerships" (Turkle 2007, 308). Yet these collections and rituals have their own potency in their brokenness and movement. And it is in this particular aspect that they are interesting to us. In the liturgical lives of these women, they become their theology,[4] they provide for the experience of God's presence, they form the women, and they create connections.

The objects featuring in the loose collections or organized altars of the women are classically tools for worship and ritual. The practices are mostly borrowed from what Rappaport calls 'canonical practices' (Rappaport [1979] 1999), i.e., formal and stylized practices seen in historically established settings. However, the women in this case pick and choose objects and rituals as they see fit and then mix items and practices that are not normally encountered together. By doing this, the women change the 'original' meaning of the symbols and create their own new system of meaning while remaining conscious of the provisional nature of this meaning. The symbols have been challenged, the signifier and the substance signified have separated and any new meaning is temporary. Yet, the search is on.

Through changing and varying, through choosing and mixing, the women 'reason' about important doctrinal concepts, not through words and reflective actions, but through redefining their relations to certain objects and their place in their life: by symbolizing.

These, literally 'handmade' theologies, take several shapes in the various arrangements of the collections. Every woman forms her own theology through her selection of objects, through what she leaves out and what she places at the centre of a collection, and how she performs certain practices. The fact that most of these arrangements keep changing form and display is a sign that these theologies are always in the making, but also that God is not understood as static but rather as dynamic and involved.[5] With each move and variation, a phase of the development of these theologies is seen but is never conclusive.

---

4 Theology understood as pondering, reasoning, and discussing God.
5 See more on movement and sacramentality in Brown and Loades (1995).

Saying that these objects and rituals are a form of theology might seem alien to a culture that is conditioned to think of theology as an academic discipline expressed with words and verbal language. Yet, when material objects, practices and performance are perceived as symbols of the same category as words and language, one can appreciate that, just as we reason with language, we also reason by manipulating objects and performing actions (Johnson 2007). These are in the words of Don Saliers "an expression and a vulnerable exposure of what we believe about God and the world, and what we are prepared to live and die for" (Saliers 1982, 37).

Instead of words on paper, this theology is 'written' or formed with objects and movements which define who God is and how God works through their quality, be it natural objects, aesthetic objects, objects related to healing, personal objects, etc. In these changing *bricolages*, the women express their own dynamic understanding of God. He can be at the same time Holy and Other in Orthodox Icons, as well as feminine, human, and tender in images of the sacred heart (Morgan 2008) and/or also a crucified saviour testified to in a displayed Bible, or an empty cross. Latour reminds us that "if the medium is the message, slightly different types of media (and mediation) will produce enormous differences in types of messages" (Latour 1998, 424). If the arrangements of the women and the quality and selection of objects is always changing it is also the message, the theology that is changing.

Not only do the women 'write' their theology with these material and performative symbols, but they also experience God's presence through them in a certain way. Many theologians as well as cultural theorists (Meyer, Morgan, Latour) have discussed how media, images, or symbols 'allow' the experience of God's presence since they are understood as holding their referent within them. Symbols can be "crucibles of experiences and places of epiphany" (Saliers 1982, 40).

Yet, looking at the situation at hand, these symbols seem to also work sacramentally because of their ambiguity in an interplay of presence and absence. This understanding of sacramentality is similar to that proposed by Louis Marie Chauvet's theology of sacramentality as expressed in *Symbol and Sacrament* (Chauvet 1995) and borrows from Paul Ricoeur's conception of presence in absence.

Hence, on one level "*sensational forms* [...] make the transcendental sense-able" (Meyer 2006, 9) and "they effect or make present what they mediate." (Meyer 2012, 26) This is particularly pertinent since most of the objects are pictures, they make the divine present in a more visual way. David Morgan comments on pictures of Jesus, saying: "the picture is taken as a medium that generates the spiritual presence of Jesus through a mutual gaze of seeing and being seen" (Morgan 1998, 7).

However, on another level – a more theological level – in the experience of the women we are considering, presence is not automatic and unquestioned. The synthesis between God and the objects, as explained earlier, is cracked. God is not essentially, incarnationally, or salvifically merged with the objects. The objects are superfluous and optional for God, Christ is everywhere in the conviction of these women and does not need objects. But still, the women would propose that God can be 'seen' in these objects because of the challenge of his absence. It is in the uncertainty and 'optionality' that God is present for the women rather than in the certainty and familiarity of the medium. As Latour says: "the more human-work is shown, the *better* is their grasp of reality, of sanctity, of worship [emphasis original]" (Latour 2002, 18).

Instead of destroying the symbol, questioning it and reconsidering it makes it active. The women try not to trap God's presence in the objects, yet God is there. It is in the cracks, the 'brokenness' of the objects that God seems to be simultaneously present and absent. These material objects, these "ordinary everyday matters can also be as meaningless as always and nevertheless offer a view of something else" (Brinkman 2012, 43). The ambiguity then functions in a sacramental and generative way.

In addition, these ambiguous symbols play a role in forming selves and leading into becoming. Not only is God experienced as present, but the women are also led into becoming present in the face of ambiguity. Meyer reminds us that media "organize vertical encounters of religious subjects with the transcendental" but they also "induce a particular sense of the self and one's being in the world – if you wish a particular identity" (Meyer 2006, 21). Moreover, it is said that "we construct images, but images also construct us" (Brinkman 2012, 51).

The women experience with all their senses the texture, smell, colours, and taste of their objects which both enchant and disturb them. They enchant them with their beauty and holiness and disturb them with their 'profanity'. And it is this unease, this estrangement before meanings previously assumed as understood, that forms the subjects and leads them into becoming: as subjects who become agents in the makeup of their own liturgical lives. Tradition is no longer a guarantee for certainty; on the contrary, personal decisions concerning the most 'trivial' of things should be constantly taken. Objects are questioned, rituals examined, and the meaning of systems is put under construction. Church, tradition, or community cannot assist in meaning-giving. The women are forced to be 'present', not as spectators or users but totally present in the face of another presence (or absence). All this creates agency,[6] responsibility, and ownership of one's symbolic system of faith.

Moreover, this personalized and dynamic symbolic system built with objects, rituals and elements of discourse gleaned and redefined through the interaction with various liturgical and symbolic worlds, helps in establishing connections. In these *bricolages*, these women work out their lived experiences, the inherited historical traditions as well as their social networks in relation to God and their faith. Scholar Kay Turner emphasizes that in a home altar a woman "assembles a highly condensed, symbolic model of connection by bringing together sacred images and ritual objects, pictures, mementos, natural materials and decorative effects which represent different realms of meaning and experience – heaven and earth, family and deities, nature and culture, Self and Other" (Turner 1999, 27). In the case of the women in this research we see this 'symbolic model of connection' as well. In the collections and rit-

---

[6] It is proposed that altar-making in the home gives women agency in Eastern Churches in general, see Weaver (2011).

uals, connections are established between all the aspects of one's life and between the various traditions the women belong to.

The women's 'broken' images and symbols direct them to what is beyond, to God. These same images and symbols create subjects who are open to the reality and presence of God in ambiguity. Yet, the connections are not only vertical. All aspects of the lives of these women find connections through these personal and dynamic symbolic systems. When one brings into contact elements from different liturgical traditions in one home altar; when one connects family history with images of the sacred, when one brings items of the past with practices from the present, connections are established. Many women cherish images that once hung in grandparents' homes, they decorate these with pictures of their children, bringing together different generations through the image. Some have shown altars where elements collected during pilgrimages live side by side with books brought from Protestant Churches as well as gifts received at the occasion of a wedding, baptism, or confirmation. They become one collection where a van Dyke Bible can sit next to a statue of the Virgin Mary from a Maronite church, and a bag of holy oil from an Orthodox Monastery.

Many of the items in the collections are gifts from family members and friends and as Marcel Mauss says, "gifts retain something of their givers" (Turkle 2007, 312). They are also connected to certain events. Some come from weddings, baptisms, feasts, funerals, or medical operations. They connect the women spatially to these different spaces and pilgrimage sites. A lady explained "I visit places and experience things and collect. Now what to do with these things? I put them in the *altar*...this remind me of this place and that remind me of that [...]." This connecting of various types of images and objects helps create and organize memory (Morgan 2011).

In the same line, Birgit Meyer explains that "to many people, religious sensory regimes allow them to make sense of – and regain their senses in – our increasingly fragmented and distracted world" (Meyer 2006, 23). Yet, what is fascinating in these 'religious sensory regimes' or symbolic systems of faith, is that they are not stable and not obvious and self-explanatory. They are constantly put into question and reconsidered, activating the power of the symbolic.

5 Conclusion

If only, some say, we could do *without* any images. How much better, purer, faster our access to God, to nature, to truth, to science could be! Others respond: "Alas (or unfortunately), we cannot do without images, intermediaries, mediators of all shapes and forms, because this is the only way to access God, Nature, Truth and Science'" (Latour 2002, 16). In this chapter, I have attempted to show how symbols, in the form of objects, practices, or even words permeate our lives. Through the example of the women who live their liturgical lives in-between liturgical traditions and therefore different symbolic systems, I have shown how symbols become active or 'living' when challenged or put into question. What I have described is an example of a response to the 'breaking' or challenging of one's symbols by re-discovering new meanings in ambiguity. When the symbols are challenged, they emerge as objects or movements that are external to their referent, to the divine. Yet, the freedom to appropriate them, to select and adapt them, is found, and through this, new symbolic meanings are created.

Ambiguity unleashes the power of the symbol rather than destroying it. My thesis is therefore that it is the job of theologians to keep symbols in the realm of the ambiguous and unstable, lest they become fixed 'idols'. To do so, theology should engage with the everyday life of believers, tracing the systems of symbols that are built into their world and stirring the waters. The challenge that theology should present is not aimed at destroying symbols, but rather at keeping them moving, 'de-freeze-framing' them, revealing their ambiguity in order to make them active in the lives of believers, as partners towards faith rather than as objects of faith.

Bibliography

Atiyyeh, George. 2005. "The Rise of Eastern Churches." In *Christianity: A History in the Middle East*, edited by Habib Badr, Beirut: Middle East Council of Churches, 293–316.
Badr, Habib. 2005. "Evangelical Missions and Church in the Middle East: Lebanon, Syria and Turkey." In *Christianity: A History in the Middle East*, edited by Habib Badr, Beirut: Middle East Council of Churches, 715–726.
Barnard, Marcel, Johan Cilliers, and Cas Wepener. 2014. *Worship in the Network Culture: Fields and Methods, Concepts and Metaphors*. Liturgia Condenda 28. Leuven / Dudley: Peeters.
Brinkman, Martien E. 2012. *Jesus Incognito: The Hidden Christ in Western Art since 1960*. Amsterdam / New York: Radopi.
Brown, David, and Ann Loades, eds. 1995. *The Sense of the Sacramental: Movement and Measure in Art, Music, Place and Time*. London: SPCK.
Chauvet, Louis-Marie. 1995. *Symbol and Sacrament: A Sacramental Reinterpretation of Christian Existence*, trans. Patrick Madigan and Madeleine Beaumont. Collegeville: The Liturgical Press.
Datson, Lorrain, ed. 2004. *Things that Talk: Object Lessons from Art and Science*. New York: Zone Books.
Elkins, James, and David Morgan, eds. 2009. *Re-Enchantment*. New York / London: Routledge.
Galadza, Peter. 2007. "Eastern Catholic Christianity." In *The Blackwell Companion to Eastern Christianity*, edited by Ken Parry, Malden / Oxford: Blackwell Publishing, 291–318.
Grimes, Ronald. 2010. *Ritual Criticism: Case Studies in its Practice, Essays on its Theory*. Waterloo: Ritual Studies International.
Gordon-Taylor, Benjamin, and Juliette Day, eds. 2016. *The Study of Liturgy and Worship: An Alcuin Guide*. Collegeville: Liturgical Press.
Haardt, Maaike de. 2013. *Raam op het Zuiden: Religie en Spiritualiteit in het Alledaagse*. Zoetermeer: Meinema.
Haardt, Maaike de, and Anne-Marie Korte, eds. 2002. *Common Bodies: Everyday Practices, Gender and Religion*. Münster: LIT.
Hunt, Hannah. 2007. "Byzantine Christianity." In *The Blackwell Companion to Eastern Christianity*, edited by Ken Parry, Malden / Oxford: Blackwell Publishing, 73–93.
Jennings, Theodor W. Jr. 1996. "On Ritual Knowledge." In *Readings in Ritual Studies*, edited by Ronald Grimes, Upper Saddle River: Prentice-Hall, 324–334.

Jessup, Henry. [1873] 2005. *The Women of the Arabs.* https://www.gutenberg.org/files/17278/17278-h/17278-h.htm (01.12.2021)

Johnson, Mark. 2007. *The Meaning of the Body: Aesthetics of Human Understanding.* Chicago / London: University of Chicago Press.

Latour, Bruno. 2002. "What Is Iconoclash? Or Is There a World Beyond the Image Wars?" In *Iconoclash Beyond the Image Wars in Science Religion and Art,* edited by Bruno Latour, and Peter Wiebel, Karlsruhe: ZKM and Cambridge, MA / London: MIT Press, 14–37.

Latour, Bruno. 1998. "How to be Iconophilic in Art, Science and Religion." In *Picturing Science Producing Art,* edited by Carrie Jones and Peter Galison, London: Routledge, 418–440.

Meyer, Birgit. 2006. *Religious Sensations: Why Media, Aesthetics and Power Matter in the Study of Contemporary Religion.* Amsterdam: Vrije Universiteit, Inaugural Lecture.

Meyer, Birgit. 2011a. "Mediation and Immediacy: Sensational Forms, Semiotic Ideologies and the Question of the Medium." *Social Anthropology* 19:23–39.

Meyer, Birgit. 2011b. "Medium". *Material Religion* 7:58–64.

Meyer, Birgit. 2012. *Mediation and the Genesis of Presence: Towards a Material Approach to Religion.* Utrecht: Utrecht University, Inaugural Lecture

Meyer, Birgit, and Jojada Verrips. 2008. "Aesthetics." In *Key Words in Religion, Media, and Culture,* edited by David Morgan, New York, London: Routledge, 20–30.

Morgan, David. 1998. *Visual Piety: A History and Theory of Popular Religious Images.* Berkley / Los Angeles / London: University of California Press.

Morgan, David. 2008. *The Sacred Heart of Jesus: The Visual Evolution of a Devotion.* Amsterdam: Amsterdam University Press.

Morgan, David. 2011. "Thing." *Material Religion* 7:140–146.

Nasrallah, Rima, Heleen Murre-van den Berg, and Marcel Barnard. 2012. "Kinetics of Healing." *Studia Liturgica* 42:270–284.

Nasrallah, Rima, and Marcel Barnard. 2013. "Taking Liberties: The Fluid Liturgical Lives of Orthodox and Maronite Women within the Protestant Church in Lebanon." *Journal for Eastern Christian Studies* 65:97–119.

Nasrallah, Rima, Martien E. Brinkman, Heleen Murre-van den Berg, and Marcel Barnard. 2016. "Rearranging Things: How Protestant attitudes shake the objects in the piety of Eastern Christian Women." *Material Religion* 12:74–95.

O'Mahony, Anthony, and Loosley Emma, eds. 2010. *Eastern Christianity in the Modern Middle East.* Abingdon: Routledge.

O'Mahony, Anthony, ed. 2004. *Eastern Christianity: Studies in Modern History, Religion and Politics.* London: Mellsende.

Rappaport, Roy A. 1979. *Ecology, Meaning and Religion.* Richmond, CA: North Atlantic Books.

Sabra, George. 2001. *Fi Sabeel el Hiwar el Maskouni, and Maqalat Lahoutiya Injilia.* في لاهوتية إنجيلية سبيل الحوار المسكوني: مقالات [*Towards the Ecumenical Dialogue: Evangelical Theological Essays.*] Beirut: Clarion Publishing House.

Saliers, Don. 1984. "Symbols in Liturgy: Tracing the Hidden Languages." *Worship* 58:37–49.

Tamen, Miguel. 2001. *Friends of Interpretable Objects.* Cambridge / London: Harvard University Press.

Turkle, Sherry, ed. 2007. *Evocative Objects: Things we Think with.* Cambridge / London: MIT Press.

Turner, Kay. 1999. *Beautiful Necessity: The Art and Meaning of Women's Altars.* London: Thames Hudson.

Weaver, Dorothy C. 2011. "Shifting Agency: Male Clergy, Female Believers, and the Role of Icons." *Material Religion* 7:394–419.

Auli Vähäkangas and Kirstine Helboe Johansen
Wedding Ceremonies / Blessings / Partnership

1 Personalization and Renewal of Tradition

In the Nordic setting, as in any organized society, marriage is a central social and religious institution, but the Nordic setting is distinctive in that most of the population belongs to the national Lutheran churches. Historically, the Nordic countries constituted homogeneous spaces regarding religion due to little inward migration, and the Lutheran Churches used to be the state religion/church, also known as the "religion of the throne" (Bruce 2000, 34). Despite increased migration, worldview plurality and secularization, the national churches continue to perform many public roles in the Nordic countries, but they are no longer all-encompassing religious-cultural institutions. This change is also witnessed in a decrease in church life-cycle rituals – among them church weddings. According to Norwegian sociologist Inger Furseth and her Nordic colleagues:

> A dramatic decline has taken place in church weddings, which amounts to less than half of all marriages in Sweden, Denmark, Norway, and Finland in 2013 – 2014. Since the late 1980s, church weddings have dropped by 33% points in Finland, 28 in Sweden, 22 in Norway, and 15 in Denmark. (Furseth et al. 2017, 47)

Nevertheless, in the Nordic countries, a church wedding continues to be both a religious ceremony and a legally binding marital contract (Christoffersen 2010).

The theological research on marriage has been quite limited during recent decades. From the 1970s onwards, the discussions of cohabitation (Trost 1979; Hafstad 1994) and remarriage of divorcees were hot debates in the Nordic Lutheran churches and societies (Finnäs 1997). Discussions on cohabitation and remarriage seem not to be relevant any longer and the current research is no longer focusing on these topics. In the 1990s, there are a few examples of journals dealing with issues regarding marriage in various Nordic countries. An issue of the journal *Social Compass* from 1991 deals with marriage in Finland. In response to a new ritual for church weddings, the Swedish journal *Svenskt Gudstjänstliv* (Swedish Worship-life) published an issue on church weddings in 1992. Nevertheless, these examples are exceptions; marriage was not widely researched in the 1990s.

In the next century, the interest of Nordic researchers turned to homosexual relationships (Pètursson 2014; Johansen and Pedersen 2015; Christensen 2013; Lindberg 2016), and research interest in same-sex unions and marriages seems to continue (Hellqvist and Vähäkangas 2018; Metso and Kallatsa 2018). All Nordic countries acknowledge same-sex marriages, Sweden, and Iceland as early as 2009, the Faroe

Islands the latest in 2017. By way of rather different decision processes, the established churches in Sweden (2009), Denmark (2012) and Norway (2016) all perform same-sex marriage rituals, whereas the Finnish church discusses the need for and regulation of a ritual for same-sex marriage (Hellqvist and Vähäkangas 2018; Metso and Kallatsa 2018). The Faroe church has yet to embark on this discussion.

Recent research on heterosexual marriage has mainly focussed on Lutheran theological perspectives on body and sexuality and, among other things, marriage as a theological metaphor (Gerle 2015). The research on heterosexual marriage ritual in contemporary Nordic societies has been very limited (Jarnkvist 2011; Johansen 2015; 2017).

The strong Lutheran heritage in the Nordic context and the above-discussed lack of research shows how necessary it is to study marital rituals in the Nordic countries. The aim of this article is to introduce our studies on nuptial rituals in two Nordic countries, Finland, and Denmark, and to discuss personalization and renewal of ritual tradition through these cases. Additionally, we will discuss approaches and methods utilized in them. Before going deeper into these studies, it is necessary to introduce some basic theories on personalized rituals.

2 Meaningful Rituals

Rituals adhere to tradition, but they are not static. Rather, all rituals contain an aspect of change (Grimes 2010, 12). Inspired by anthropologist Michael Houseman, Johansen uses the term 'new rituals', which are characterized by creative adaptation, and continues the analysis: "the scholarly interest in life-cycle rituals takes into account the fact that churches are placed in modern, secularised societies populated by people who relate individually to religion according to their own decisions and considerations" (Johansen 2019, 485).

Following her study of the personalization of post-mortem rituals, Ramshaw (2010) points out how personalization may facilitate the ability of a ritual to meet the most important requirements of the people involved. She further writes:

> This equation of 'meaningful' with 'personal' is a giveaway of postmodern culture. When people are not embedded in a tradition-bearing community, the rituals of such a community do not seem to speak to their personal experience, the private world that is the locus of meaning making. A ritual is likely to be meaningful to the extent that it is personally constructed or tailored to one's own experience (Ramshaw 2010, 172).

In the Nordic context with its tight bonds between the Lutheran churches and traditional culture and national identity, church weddings are still a strong signal of traditionalism. A church wedding is a ritual with a long history; it takes place within an established church and it conforms with traditional family values of monogamous partnership (Jarnkvist 2011; Johansen and Pedersen 2015; Johansen 2017). At the same time, recent studies of both heterosexual and same-sex marital rituals show

how marital rituals are constructed as personalized rituals to fit an individual situation (Johansen 2017).

In the following we introduce our respective studies: first, Johansen's research on heterosexual weddings. Heterosexual weddings constitute most marital rituals, but they have been subject to very little research. Second, Vähäkangas' research on same-sex prayer rituals. Same-sex marital rituals are a minority but recently they have been the main topic of marital research due to theological discussions and inventions of new rituals in recent years.

3 Traditional and Personal Wedding Rituals in Denmark (Kirstine Helboe Johansen)

How do bridal couples describe their expectations of a church wedding? What characterizes their relationship to the established wedding liturgy? How do pastors understand a church wedding and the established wedding liturgy? With such questions as my guide, in 2012 I embarked on a research project to examine preparatory wedding conversations between pastors and heterosexual wedding couples in Denmark. I selected eight pastors (male / female, younger / older, urban / rural parishes) and they made agreements with one or two bridal couples within the selected time period. In all, thirteen bridal couples participated. All pastors and wedding couples gave their consent to participate in the research project and research outcomes are published without names and places. The research was conducted in a combination of observations and follow-up interviews with both pastors and wedding couples. I am myself a theologian, educated primarily within an Evangelical-Lutheran tradition and I am also member of the Evangelical-Lutheran church in Denmark, but I have received no pastoral training and I am not ordained. In this project, my position helped me side primarily with the perspective of the bridal couple and their guests, and I used my experience as wedding guest to urge them to elaborate certain aspects. First, I observed the preparatory conversation between pastor and bridal couples during which they go through the wedding ritual, select hymns, and talk about the wedding and the couple's reasons for wanting a church wedding. These conversations lasted about an hour or an hour and a half and usually took place in the pastor's office, sometimes with a short visit to the sanctuary. Immediately after this conversation, I interviewed the bridal couples about their expectations of the wedding ritual and asked them to elaborate on issues regarding the ritual that came up during the conversation. Finally, after having observed all the bridal couples of a given pastor, I went back to conduct an interview with the pastor regarding his or her understanding of the wedding ritual and asked him or her to elaborate on issues that came up during the conversations. All observations and interviews were audio recorded, transcribed, and coded.

The theoretical framework guiding the research project consisted predominantly of a combination of ritual theories that allowed me to examine how church rituals and the understanding of church rituals are transformed and re-orientated. The hypothesis was that it is not only people's ideas about religion and values that are undergoing changes, but also their understanding of and expectations to religious practices are subject to similar changes. To build this argument, I combine both well-established ritual theories such as those of Roy Rappaport (1999) and Catherine Bell (1997) and younger ritual theories dealing with new-age rituals such as those of Michael Houseman (2007) (Johansen 2017). My interest was to investigate whether wedding rituals were anticipated mainly as established and fixed or mainly as an individually constructed.

In the analysis of the material, the bridal couples group into two main approaches to the wedding ritual. Both groups agree that a church wedding is something special, and both groups agree that a church wedding is an important tradition, but they differ in the degree to which they think of the ritual as something they construct individually. One group tends to value church wedding as part of tradition and to argue for their own choice of church wedding as a wish to be part of tradition. A groom expresses himself in this way: "When your children are baptized and you expect them to have their confirmation, then you use the church anyway. Even though we are not strong believers [...] this is the place to turn. When it is a big thing, then the church is there." And a bride explicitly asks for a wedding ritual that is traditional: "Yes, it is all of it ... and that is why you cannot begin to rewrite it or anything, because the church is something very traditional, so you cannot change that, then it would not be the same [...]."

The other group has a slightly different approach. They also wish to have a traditional church wedding, but they emphasise that it was a conscious choice. They had considered whether and to what degree it was the right thing for them before they chose it. A groom expresses this understanding when he says: "It is important [for us] that it is in a church and therefore, it is personal in the sense that it is something we have chosen, and we have chosen the hymns. A big part of it kind of follows the procedures and that is fixed beforehand, but it is us that chose the package. We know that a big part of the package, 80 per cent of the package, was there. We could choose it or not, but we chose it."

Thus, it is evident in both groups that a church wedding is attractive as tradition, but among the second group, tradition is only attractive in a personalised version. In the words of Ramshaw (2010) as cited above, meaningful is personal – in this study, also when it comes to traditional wedding rituals.

4 Personalized Same-Sex Prayer Rituals in Finland (Auli Vähäkangas)

This section narrates Vähäkangas' study of same-sex couples' experiences in connection with a prayer ritual conducted over their registered partnerships and focuses on the pre-legal context of same-sex marriage in Finland. Homosexuality, or more precisely the question of LGBTI (lesbian, gay, bisexual, transgender, and intersex) church members is an internally divisive issue for the Evangelical Lutheran Church of Finland (ELCF), with an extensive discussion on the role of LGBTI church members taking place from the 1990s up to the present day. The Pastoral guidelines of the ELCF simply indicate that the ritual can involve a prayer with the registered couple and for them. Blessing of a partnership or any other rituals, which could be interpreted as marital rites, should not be conducted (*Pastoral guidelines* 2011). Despite these delineations, the discussion regarding homosexual members of the ELCF continued even after the Pastoral guidelines of 2011 were given, but no new official guidelines have been provided since the legalization of same-sex marriage.

The data comprises interviews with ten people in 2015. Pseudonyms are used when referring to the interviewees. Unlike many who have written on this subject, Vähäkangas is a heterosexual woman with no direct experience of same-sex partnerships. The interviewees seemed to accept her conducting this study, even though she is not part of the same-sex community. Additionally, Vähäkangas is an ordained pastor of the ELCF which the pastors participating knew in advance. She introduced herself as a researcher from the Faculty of Theology, but I did not hide her pastoral identity either.

The name of the ritual emerged from the interviews and was vividly discussed in them. The name used in the Pastoral guidelines of 2011 is 'prayer with and for' the registered same-sex couple, but the interviewees expressed a dislike for this long and complicated name. Some called it a wedding, most labelled it a blessing of a registered partnership and a few simply called it a prayer ceremony. Hanna and her partner had met through girl scouts and chose to call their ceremony 'woodland – a picnic of love'. They explicitly excluded any traditional elements of a wedding in the ritual but expressed a desire to have an official blessing of their partnership. The reason for avoiding nuptial symbolism was their personal wish to keep the ritual as simple as possible. Hanna further elaborates the idea of a blessing and human value: "For me it's personally enough to have my faith and the feeling that I was created this way and that I have a purpose and my life has a meaning, as does my relationship, and we are blessed and as valuable as others." Hanna considered that the pastor, her colleague in the same parish, followed the Pastoral guidelines too closely.

An important part of the action in the ritual was the speech and prayers by the pastor. The interviewees remembered these as the most important part, as this involved the pastor indicating, to both the couple and the congregation present, an acceptance of same-sex partnerships. Heikki elaborates: "That speech when she spoke about our life, our home and partnership, work, friends and all of our life [...] So, all of our guests were crying and also for me that speech was something that I will remember forever." Heikki explained how they were standing on a rock in their garden and the pastor preached, "God is like a rock, as eternal as love is." The metaphor of the rock was very powerful to Heikki because the pastor had chosen a metaphor from his own precious garden to make it especially personal.

Maja and Ritva as well as Sari and Kirsi called their ritual a wedding. In the wedding of Maja and Ritva, the rite took place as a modified wedding ritual of the ELCF, whereas the rite used in the wedding of Sari and Kirsi was modified from the rite of a blessing of a marriage. In both rituals, exchanging of rings was central. Both female couples were actively involved in the rainbow worship community and in their weddings, a special nuptial object, a rainbow-coloured *ryijy* was used. A *ryijy* is a traditional Finnish woven craftwork, a large wall mat, on which the bridal couple traditionally stand during a religious wedding ceremony. The rainbow-coloured ritual elements celebrated the same-sex nature of the partners while also acknowledging their inclusion within the Lutheran tradition. In other words, these rainbow-coloured objects straddled both the resistance and the conformity aspects of a ritual, as they were simultaneously strongly personalized ritual objects tailored for a small rainbow community in a ritual acknowledging the Lutheran tradition.

The most important elements of rituals were ones personally tailored to the couple themselves. The feeling of being accepted and being the focus of the ritual were important. Most of the participants of this study were well acquainted with the Lutheran liturgy, hymns, and other traditions of the church. However, tailored experiences maintained their position as the most meaningful for them. Personalization of a ritual brings the therapeutic or pastoral care element to it. This personalization is possible only when the facilitators, pastors in the case of this study, were willing to conduct personalized rituals and did not follow the restrictions of the Pastoral guidelines of 2011.

One aspect that made the same-sex rituals in Finland very different from each other was that the only given guidelines, the Pastoral guidelines of 2011, did not include a clear rite for conducting such a ritual; rather they only gave a list of restrictions on which things not to include in a same-sex prayer ritual. This left it quite open to the couples and pastors concerned to plan a very personalized ritual even after the guidelines were given.

5 Marriage as Tradition and as Broker of Renewed Family Values and Legal Rights

As our two cases show, marriage and church wedding are both – and at the same time – an icon of tradition and traditional values and a broker of renewed family values and legal rights. Johansen's case shows how a church wedding is seen as and chosen for its status as traditional wedding and therefore also as part of a wider tradition that takes you through important moments in life: childbirth, adolescence, family building and death, but also points to how one group of bridal couples emphasizes their own personalization of the ritual. Vähäkangas' case illuminates how nuptial rituals are also part of renewing tradition and moving both church and society in their construction of values.

Thereby, Vähäkangas' research further supports the general insight that the understanding and legal regulations of marriage have been an important part of the transformation of moral values and legal rights both with respect to gender equality and the acknowledgement of same-sex relations. Beginning with Martin Luther's transformation of marriage from sacrament to social order, Finnish jurist Anu Pylkkänen (2010) argues that the liberalization and equality of women is closely connected to the reformation – and to some extent secularization – of marriage law. In the same way, the acknowledgement of same-sex marriage with the inclusion of a church wedding ritual is not only an extension of the ritual to include other forms of marital partnerships but also a symbol of the (re)negotiation of family values and alternative lifestyles as well as of the understanding of marriage. This negotiation and transformation takes place at different levels: as pastors' engagement in the public debate on same-sex marriage (Christensen 2013), as statements in administrative consultations before legal changes (Johansen and Pedersen 2015), and in the personal adaptation of the ritual (Vähäkangas 2019).

Literature on rituals over same-sex marriage reveal that some elements in the same-sex rituals were understood to show conformity, whereas others show resistance. Bell sees the relationship between conformity and resistance as the fundamental dimension of rituals in which the following of an old tradition or the making of new traditions is the dividing issue (Bell 1997, 145). Lash studied same-sex marriage rituals among Canadian Jews and concluded that those rituals which differed from heterosexual weddings and included various same-sex objects were rituals of resistance and those rituals most closely following the liberal Jewish traditions were rituals of conformity (Lash 2012). The division between resistance and conformity was not, however, very clear in the same-sex rituals studied by Vähäkangas, as some of the rituals included both elements. There was some resistance found but the findings stress more the importance of following the Lutheran traditions. In many cases, it was a question of adaptation of rituals to a personal situation, which did not indicate any clear resistance. Implicitly, rituals always carry in them both the transformation and the continuation of traditions which are then negotiated by the community or individuals concerned. Hüsken and Neubert write: "Not only are rituals frequently disputed; they also constitute a field in which vital and sometimes even violent negotiations take place" (Hüsken and Neubert 2012, 1).

This balancing of continuation and transformation, of conformity and resistance, comes to almost subtle expression in Johansen's study of wedding couples. One group emphasizes continuation of and conformity with tradition; their wish is to have a wedding as it – in their opinion – has always been. But though the other group is drawn to a traditional wedding, their insistence on personalizing the ritual shows their resistance to being dominated by tradition – tradition is invited into their lives, not the other way around, and this also points to this group as brokers of transformation and renewal. They do not wish to create a new ritual, but they reject pure conformity and insist on transforming the ritual for their purposes. Due to the double affiliation of the studied same-sex couples, they produce more complex forms of conformity and resistance. The religious couples represent a minority in the mainstream same-sex culture and in this way express resistance towards the same-sex culture by following the heterosexual nuptial traditions. Most of the participants interpret religious ceremonies as partly against mainstream gay culture. Ganzevoort, van der Laan, and Olsman (2011, 221) share a similar finding that gay Christians had to negotiate their double affiliation with both Christian and gay culture. This double affiliation is further confirmed by Bos (2017, 188–189), according to whom same-sex culture aimed to be rebellious against all institutions and marriage was interpreted as an outdated and patriarchal institution that bred inequality. These findings indicate the need for renewal and a need for keeping the Lutheran traditions.

Transformation was an essential aspect in the narrated rituals both from Denmark and from Finland, but, additionally, the results indicate the importance of continuation of tradition to the couples concerned. That said, to reiterate, the most important traditions are personalized. This means that the traditions themselves are perpetuated, while ensuring that they hold particular significance for the people involved.

6 Conclusion and Reflections on Methodology

As the two cases and cited literature indicate, the study of wedding rituals may be approached from different angles and therefore also by utilization of different methods depending on what kinds of topics one wishes to research. These different approaches may be grouped roughly into three categories according to their field of interest.

Wedding rituals can be studied at *text level*. This might be conducted as a legal investigation of the relationship between marriage ritual and marriage law (Pylkkänen 2010), as historical and dogmatic examinations of the meaning and conduct of marriage rituals during church history (Bible readings, prayers, hymns, ritual orders) or as liturgical and ritual enquiries into the liturgical construction of the marriage ritual.

Wedding rituals may also be studied at the *discursive level:* How, why and in what contexts do people engage in reflections on what the marriage ritual is or should be? Who engages in these discussions? And what kind of understandings do they express? One approach to such an investigation is document analysis by which one might gain insight to positions in different kinds of public discourses (e. g., Christensen 2013; Johansen and Pedersen 2015). Another approach utilizes interview methods to enter into the ways the individuals involved think and feel about the wedding ritual (Vähäkangas 2019; Johansen 2015; 2017; Jarnkvist 2011).

Wedding rituals might also be studied as performed *church practices*. One approach could be quantitative mappings of the number of weddings, wedding traditions, wedding couples etc., but one might also apply anthropologically inspired methods such as participant observation. The study of the wedding ritual as church practice includes both preparations leading up to the wedding ritual (such as wedding fairs; conversations between pastor and wedding couples; preparations in church, among other things, decorating the sanctuary; communicative acts on homepages and in folders); and the ritual performance itself (what is done, what is sung, how do they dress, how do they sit). This approach is still highly under-researched.

The most central finding of our studies shows that Nordic couples wish to have personalized wedding rituals that at the same time follow the Lutheran traditions quite closely. This indicates that both conformity and resistance, continuation, and renewal of tradition, seem to be important to those Nordic couples who have opted to have a church ritual over their partnership. We cannot compare legal points of view between these studies because the Finnish case did not involve legalization of same-sex partnerships in the church. In the Danish situation, legalization of marriage was also seen to be an essential part of the ritual, and same-sex couples in Finland hope that this will be the future situation in the ELCF as well.

Our chapter additionally reveals that there is very little research on marital rituals in the Nordic countries, and we would request students of theology to focus on the issue in various Nordic institutions. We see that studying marital rituals is inspiring and through it, we can find out central aspects of renewal and conformity in Nordic families, churches, and societies.

Bibliography

Bell, Catherine. 1997. *Ritual Perspectives and Dimensions*. New York: Oxford University Press.
Bos, David J. 2017. "'Equal Rites Before the Law': Religious Celebrations of Same-Sex Relationships in the Netherlands, 1960's–1990's." *Theology & Sexuality* 23:188–208.
Brodd, Sven-Erik. 1992. "Äktenskapets sakramentalitet – til frågan om äktenskapets teologiska motivering." *Svenskt Gudstjäntliv.Kyrkbröllop Tro og Tanke* 67:81–99.
Bruce, Steve. 2000. "The Supply-Side Model of Religion: The Nordic and Baltic States." *Journal for the Scientific Study of Religion* 39:32–46.
Christensen, Henrik Reintoft. 2013. "Tavshed og kald. Præsters deltagelse i den offentlige debat om homoseksuelle vielser." ["Silence and Vocation: Pastors' Participation in the Public Debate Regardign Same-Sex Marriages."] In *Ytrings – og informationsfrihed til genforhandling* [Renegotiation of Freedom of Speech and Information], edited by Ejvind Hansen, Copenhagen: Hans Reitzel Publishers, 69–92.
Christoffersen, Lisbet. 2010. "State, Church and Religion in Denmark: At the Beginning of the 21st Century." In *Law and Religion in the 21st Century – Nordic Perspectives*, edited by Lisbet Christoffersen, Kjell Å Modéer, and Svend Andersen, Copenhagen: DJØF Publishing, 145–161.

Finnäs, Fjalar. 1997. "Social Integration, Heterogeneity, and Divorce: The Case of the Swedish-speaking Population in Finland." *Acta Sociologica* 40:263–277.
Furseth, Inger, Lars Ahlin, Kimmo Ketola, Annette Leis-Peters, and Bjarni Randver Sigurvinsson. 2017. "Changing Religious Landscapes in the Nordic Countries Since the 1980s." In *Religious Complexity in the Public Sphere*. Palgrave Studies in Religion, Politics, and Policy, edited by Inger Furseth, London / New York: Palgrave Macmillan, 31–80.
Ganzevoort, R. Ruard, Mark van der Laan, and Erik Olsman. 2011. "Growing up Gay and Religious: Conflict, Dialogue, and Religious Identity Strategies." *Mental Health, Religion and Culture* 14:209–222.
Gerle, Elisabeth. 2015. *Sinnlighetens Närvaro: Luther mellan kroppskult och kroppsförakt*. Stockholm: Verbum.
Grimes, Ronald L. ³2010. *Beginnings in Ritual Studies*. Waterloo: Ritual Studies International.
Hafstad, Kjetil. 1994. "Marriage in Theological and Church Debate." *Studia Theologica* 48:150–163.
Hellqvist, Elina, and Auli Vähäkangas. 2018. "Experiences of (Mis)Recognition of Same-Sex Partnerships in the Evangelical Lutheran Church of Finland." *Exchange* 47:258–281.
Holte, Ragnar. 1992. "Vigselgudstjänstens teologi och liturgy." *Svenskt Gudstjäntliv 67 / Kyrkbröllop Tro og Tanke* 9:63–80.
Houseman, M. 2007. "Menstrual Slaps and First Blood Celebrations: Inference, Simulation and the Learning of Ritual." In *Learning Religion: Anthropological Approaches*, edited by David Berliner and Ramon Sarró, New York / Oxford: Berghahn Books, 31–48.
Hüsken, Ute, and Frank Neubert. 2012. "Introduction." In *Negotiating Rites*, edited by Ute Hüsken and Frank Neubert, New York / Oxford University Press, 1–17.
Jarnkvist, Karin. 2011. *När jag gifter mig ska jeg göra det på riktigt*. Umeå: Umeå University.
Johansen, Kirstine Helboe, and Helene Helboe Pedersen. 2015. "The Power over the Marriage Ritual: Positions in the Administrative Consultation Prior to the Implementation of Same-Sex Marriages in the Evangelical-Lutheran Church in Denmark." *Journal of Church and State* 58:731–752.
Johansen, Kirstine Helboe. 2015. "When Religion and Spirituality Converge in Ritual: Weddings within the Church of Denmark." In *Complex Identities in a Shifting World: Practical Theological Perspectives*. International Practical Theology 17, edited by Pamela Couture, Robert Mager, Pamela McCarroll, and Natalie Wigg-Stevenson, Wien: LIT, 53–63.
Johansen, Kirstine Helboe. 2017. "Weddings in the Church of Denmark – Traditional and Modern Expectations of an Efficacious Ritual." In *Christliche Rituale im Wandel: Schlaglichter aus theologischer und religionswissenschaftlicher Sicht*, edited by Hans Gerald Hödl, Johann Pock, and Teresa Schweighofer, Göttingen / Wien: Vandenhoeck & Ruprecht, 65–86.
Johansen, Kirstine Helboe. 2019. "'There is Something Special about the Church': a Study of Wedding Couples in the Evangelical-Lutheran Church in Denmark." *Practical Theology* 12:483–496.
Lash, Shari Rochelle. 2012. "Jewish Same-Sex Weddings in Canada: Rituals of Resistance or Rituals of Conformity?" In *Negotiating Rites*, edited by Ute Hüsken and Frank Neubert, New York: Oxford University Press, 161–176.
Lindberg, Jonas. 2016. "Renegotiating the Role of Majority Churches in Nordic Parliamentary Debates on Same-Sex Unions." *Journal of Church and State* 58:80–97.
Metso, Pekka, and Laura Kallatsa. 2018. "Contemporary and Traditional Voices: Reactions to Same-Sex Marriage Legislation in the Evangelical Lutheran Church in Finland the Orthodox Church of Finland." *Exchange* 47:230–257.
Evangelical Lutheran Church of Finland. 2011. *Pastoraalinen ohje vapaamuotoisesta rukouksesta parisuhteensa rekisteröineiden kanssa ja heidän puolestaan*. [Pastoral Guidelines on the Prayer with and for those Who Have Registered their Same-Sex Relationship.] http://sakasti.

evl.fi/sakasti.nsf/0/A78B3114D64D8273C22577030039EE08/$FILE/PASTORAALINEN-OHJE.pdf (30.11.2021).

Pètursson, Pètur. 2014. "Religion and Politics – The Icelandic Experiment." *Temenos* 50:115–135.

Pylkkänen, Anu. 2010. "Feminism and the Challenge to Religious Truth on Marriage: The Case of Nordic Protestantism." In *Law and Religion in the 21st Century – Nordic Perspectives*, edited by Lisbet Christoffersen, Kjell Å Modéer, and Svend Andersen. Copenhagen: DJØF Publishing, 525–545.

Ramshaw, Elaine. 2010. "The Personalization of Postmodern Post-Mortem Rituals." *Pastoral Psychology* 59:171–178.

Rappaport, Roy A. 1999. *Ritual and Religion in the Making of Humanity*. Cambridge, MA: Cambridge University Press.

Trost, Jan. 1979. *Unmarried Cohabitation*. Västerås: International Library.

Vähäkangas, Auli. 2019. "Conformity and Resistance in Personalized Same-sex Prayer Rituals in Finland." *Theology & Sexuality* 25:81–97.

Part III: **Theoretical Approaches towards a Global Practical Theology**

Jun'ichi Isomae
Anthropology of Religion

1 Introduction

Recently, anthropology of religion has made substantial impacts on religious studies and theology. Anthropology of religion was originally motivated by Western scholars' interest in non-western, namely non-Judeo-Christian traditions. Western anthropologists categorized them as religion and non-religion judging on whether or not they held explicit similarities with Judeo-Christianity, especially Protestantism. This lead Western anthropologists, on the one hand, to reflect on the unique characteristics of their own Judeo-Christian tradition, and on the other hand, to treat their own tradition as the civilized superior to the 'uncivilized' others. This was of course bound up in the West's colonial project in the non-West (Masuzawa 2005, 107–121).

A relevant representative work is Talal Asad's critique on religion as a modern notion. He analyzes the Protestant definition of Islam and Catholicism as religions. The problem of the Protestant notion of religion, according to Asad, is its belief-centric and privatized nature, which is also a core component of religion as a modern notion (Asad 1993, 1–17).

The Protestant notion of religion is a product of the secularization of society in which the dichotomy of religion and the secular divides the private and public spheres. Here religion is designated only for the private sphere. According to Hannah Arendt, this is an intimate dimension of human activity where people are deprived of social rights (Arendt 1958, 58–71). In the public sphere, on the contrary, people are granted social rights. Obviously in secular society the public sphere is deemed more valuable than the private sphere. The division of the public and the private itself does not directly mean secularism. If this division, however, presumes the priority to public sphere because it is considered secular, it should be called secularism (Asad 2003, 1–17).

The Western notions of secularism and religion as facets of modernization permeated through non-Western societies as a way to avoid the threat of colonization. Western empires required non-western countries to show evidence of Western civilization, via constitutional law and freedom of (Christian) religion. Many societies in the Global South challenged the dichotomy of civilized vs non-civilized forwarded by the West. For example, in Japan, the system of State Shinto emerged as a reaction to the Western dichotomy of the religious and the secular. The Japanese government defined the ideology associated with State Shinto and the Japanese Emperor (*Tennō*) beyond this dichotomy, because it was described as neither religious nor secular (Isomae 2014, 25–67). In this way, Shinto's belief-centric character was lost, and it became instead a form of popular religion under the totalitarian system of State Shinto.

In this chapter, I would like to examine the ideology of Shinto in modern Japan to explore the negotiating process between the Western definition of religion and non-Western religious practice through the case of Fushimi Inari Shrine in Kyoto (Isomae 2017, 87–102).

2 Beyond Belief-Centric Religion

At the tall red Shinto gate (*Torii*) of the Fushimi Inari Shrine in Kyoto, you will find on your right the Shrine[1] worshipping former Shinto priest, Kada no Azumamaro (1669– 1736). He was active in the Tokugawa period (1603–1867) as a priest of the Fushimi Inari Shrine. In the modern period, he came to be extolled as one of the four great men of native learning (*Kokugaku*) in Japanese, or the 'Learning of the Imperial Land'. In this sense, he reveals a dimension of the Fushimi Inari Shrine in the early modern period which is different from the world of popular belief where people would eat roasted sparrow and quail in front of the shrine gate and go on to the pleasure quarters nearby after pilgrimage. He stood for a divergence of the Shrine from the world of popular religion.

Upon climbing the slope while leaving that Shrine behind, you come to the famous sequence of the red Torii gate. In fact, the Fushimi Inari Shrine enshrines the Inari Mountain as its divine object of worship, as the mountain is shaped like the abode of the *kami*[2]. With this mountain in the background, numerous *kami* have been worshiped here including Kannon Bodhisattva. These *kami* had forms decided by human beings but the *kami* themselves, just like the Inari Mountain, did not utter a single word. Precisely due to this silence, it had been an important concern of pilgrims and believers to figure out what kind of *kami* were to be discovered here. Into the Meiji period (1668–1912) when policies of separating the *kami* from the Buddha (Ketelaar 1993, 122–139) were implemented, numerous red Shinto gates were donated by believers and erected to form a pilgrimage path, and various rock altars that could not be assimilated into the State Shinto structure were constructed.

Along the path on the western side of the Inari Mountain all the way to its top is a succession of religious constructions: numerous rock altars (*Otsuka*) inscribed with names of businesses and human individuals such as "The Mainichi News Paper Company" and "The Grand Shrine of Great Sight", and Daoist temples enshrining the Inari gods, goddess of still-born children, and the "kami of crown of head" (Smyers 1998, 150–183).

---

[1] The Shrine is the name of the building to worship Shinto Gods and Goddess to be distinguished from Christian churches and Buddhist temples.
[2] Kami is the name of Gods and Goddess in Shinto symbolizing the essences of nature, mountains, trees, sky, sea and so on. It can be thought of as another side of Buddhist Hotoke (Gods and Goddess). Kami is distinguished from the monotheistic Christian God.

As such, Fushimi Inari can be understood as a space continuously pluralized through the existence of rock altars and refusing to be homogenized either in terms of the kami enshrined or those who enshrine. Fushimi Inari in the modern period, while being an Imperial Shrine, was not reducible to Shrine Shinto which was incorporated into the State Shinto system (Hardacre 1991, 21–41). The plurality of space is not unrelated to the activities of the Inari confraternities affiliated with the Inari Shrine which were connected to folk religions.

Despite the activities of the Nativist scholar Kada no Azumamaro, it is in the modern period, when State Shinto was created, that rock altars increased and enriched the beliefs of Fushimi Inari. It is the believers of rock altars and waterfall practitioners who supported these various religious facilities on the Inari Mountain inside and outside the shrine compound and expanded the beliefs of these facilities. There, the kami enshrined were never homogenized. Actual Fushimi Inari beliefs were pluralized by pilgrims and believers.

3 Healing as the Practice of Subjectification

Fushimi Inari Mountain is a metaphor of God which is always expanding through religious practice. Here I introduce one example of an Inari believer who founded his own Shinto church in Aichi Prefecture. He was famed to be good at healing diseases. The act of healing has often been dismissed as superstition in modern societies. Here, however, I would like to evaluate it as religious practice of subjectification. In this chapter, I will move beyond the belief-centric notion of Protestantism defined by Asad (Asad 1993, 55–80) and examine the notion of religion as a practice of subjectification.

The Shinto Fushimi Inari Great Tōyō Church (at the Futagawa Fushimi Inari Shrine) in Toyohashi City of Aichi prefecture is another example of the proliferation of meaning in the process of regional expansion of Inari beliefs. The Great Tōyō Church started its religious activities as one sect of the Shinto religions, the Shinto Jikkō-kyō, after its founding leader, Urano Katsuyasu, received a branch spirit from the Fushimi Inari Shrine in 1910. Both the Sect Shinto, which traced its origin to the Mount Fuji confraternity, and the Fushimi Inari were deeply connected to mountain asceticism. As such, they shared one religious tradition. Because Urano was a religious person belonging to the Religion Bureau of the Ministry of Education, he did not need a license to become a Shinto priest.

In 1927 he moved to Futagawa, one of the post towns on the highway between Tokyo and Kyoto, and built a hall at the foot of a mountain and gave the peaks on the mountain the same set of names as those of the Inari Mountain: Mount of First Peak, Mount of Second Peak, Mount of Third Peak, etc. On each mount, he set up *iwakura* ('god's abode') that corresponded to the rock altars of Fushimi Inari and at each one, he enshrined spirits from various lineages. Katsuyasu, who was born in Shinshiro City of the Aichi prefecture, once received training in mountain asceticism and in the Ontakekyō religion that were popular in the Mikawa region.

Katsuyasu was a charismatic figure with good looks and an impressive presence. It is said that many followers were moved to tears by his voice during praying. It is said that through the mediation of his charismatic character, illness was cured. During the treatment, however, the kami enshrined at god's abode on the mountain of his town, Ōiwa, also very likely played a vital role by connecting heaven with humans.

As such, Katsuyasu shared a world of heterogeneous beliefs in common with the folk believers commuting to Fushimi Inari. The kami and spirits in that world sometimes protected believers whilst also bringing about disasters. It is said that when Katsuyasu went to the local Mountain, Ontake, for practice, fellow believers travelling with him became possessed by the kami and suddenly started to jump up and down. It is not unusual for popular religion founders, often called 'living gods', to be possessed by this kind of heterogeneous kami or spirits. As an example, here, how to incarnate and control an unknown kami that possessed oneself became a question that tests the skill of the possessed.

Treatment of illness was something Sect Shinto founders of the late Tokugawa and Meiji periods, such as Nakayama Miki of Tenrikyō and and Deguchi Nao of Ōmotokyō, as well as early modern mountain ascetic practitioners like Ontakekyō, excelled at. Illness treatment was based on a broad religious tradition tracing back to premodern times in Japan. Katsuyasu converted people in pleasure quarters, private store owners, and dentists who wished for the treatment of illness and business prosperity, into followers, and his believer base was able to expand not just in Toyohashi but also to Hamamatsu and Yokohama where he once worked.

Shimazono Susumu uses the term "amalgamation religion" to refer to this world of popular religious activities, a world mixing *kami* with Buddhist deities, where religious leaders revered powerful *kami*, spirits, or locally active *kami* and Buddhist deities, and connected with each other across regions (Shimazono 2004, 3). These practices cannot be fully encompassed by modern concepts of Shinto or Buddhism and were attempts to reconfigure the subjectivity of practitioners and followers through corporeally based communications with the *kami*.

Here Katsuyasu was preaching that ethics following the laws of the universe would be rewarded in this life. Treatment of illness was for Katsuyasu not simply an act for this worldly benefit but also an act of self-reflection on how to transform one's way of life through the relationship with the *kami*. This was the same with Fushimi Inari's ascetic practitioners. When the subject of illness treatment shifted from individuals to society, these acts would turn into subjectivity-reconfiguring "world renewal" attempts preached by Deguchi Nao and Nakayama Miki.

Katsuyasu's case shows certain features specific to the religious groups which operated locally and independently without being assimilated into a centralized religious structure. Inoue Nobutaka calls this "long-legged cup model" (Inoue 1991, 124–127). Ontakekyō and the Fushimi Inari Shrine provided social spaces for the popular religious practitioner Shigeno, who was given the freedom to fill the space as she wished.

Anne Bouchy observed that "their characteristic is not to theorize practice which contrasts with many attempts to decorate waterfall practice with polished Shinto or Buddhist doctrines" (Bouchy 2009, 91). Without sticking to doctrine, it became possible for individual practitioners to freely incorporate meanings which developed from their practice into established religious frameworks. When this un-institutionalized belief world entered society, however, its risked being re-appropriated by established social powers.

Accommodative inclusion and the State Shinto system are two sides of the same coin. Departure from that inclusive framework would mean no official recognition and could lead to arrest: charged with harbouring dangerous thoughts. Popular religions described by Inoue as the "long-legged cup model" did have the tolerant tendency to include any popular religion as its branch, but at the same time they needed a minimum qualification of doctrine and organization to meet legal criteria of official religious systems. In the case of the popular religions of Deguchi Nao and Nakayama Miki as portrayed by Yasumaru Yoshio, when their worldviews conflicted with the worldviews of the emperor system state, they would be punished by the state. The form of freedom in the State Shinto system was conditional and precarious, as Yasumaru has pointed out (Yasumaru 1987, 209–213).

In the overlap of the state and the world of popular beliefs, and manifestation of the *kami* could appear through the channel of the emperor. These were the overwhelming structures of Sect Shinto consolidated under the State Shinto system. On the other hand, popular desires for illness recovery and business prosperity were made to overlap with the imperial universe.

If amalgamated religions want to give up pursuit for this worldly benefit and deepen their faiths by contemplating ethical ways of life while maintaining their religious praxis, certain mediums that connects them to the universal become necessary. In modern Japan it was the emperor system, which in its embodiment of both the nation-state and the empire played the role of the channel for universalization. Here, it is difficult to differentiate publicness from the state, or the state from the nation because the emperor system served all public functions. It is not possible to understand State Shinto and the world of popular beliefs as two completely different things or as an official position and a real intention. Rather, we need to explore why religious believers were able to formulate their subjectivity whilst maintaining a subtle balance between their religious practice and the emperor system.

As the third leader of the Great Tōyō Church, Urano Tomoyasu, told me, believers live their life by "revering the heaven and prostrating before the earth." But what does the heaven mean here? Very likely, in pre-war Japan, the answer did not manifest as an either–or choice between state power and *kami* of the populace.

Popular religions emerged one after another during the late Tokugawa and Meiji periods to provide salvation to people suffering from contradictions of modern capitalism. If they chose to critique the logic of exploitation of the modern state, like Nakayama Miki and Deguchi Nao, they would lose their social space and be expelled as heterodoxy. On the other hand, when they focused on dissolving people's anxiety arising from modern capitalism, like Katsuyasu has done, there existed a possibility in pre-war Japan of a channel through which they could universalize their local belief world into the public space of the modern nation-state by proactively stepping into the space of the emperor-system.

As such, the simplistic binary perspective of choosing between the emperor-system and popular belief cannot grasp pre-war worlds of belief. We should ask rather whether the spiritual metaphor, either as Amaterasu (ancestral Goddess of royal family) or the Inari *kami*, came to shape the subjectivity of the believer by making it identify with the *kami* or Amaterasu, or whether that subjectivity, formulated via that metaphor, was also able to objectify that power of identification.

The question is whether subjectivity, in reliance it is upon the *kami*, hardens or transforms itself via the *kami*. This is a question about the technique of subjectivity formation. Both humans and the *kami* continue to transform. At question it was how to believe in the *kami* and what the nature of that belief was.

4 Purified Body and State Power

Against the government's policy of secularization of Shinto, religious right-wingers started to religionize Shinto. They challenged the dichotomy between religion and the secular as well as the separation between public and private spheres. Their approach to Shinto may be seen as part of the movement of 'public religion'.

Recently the notion of "public religion" is estimated positively by scholars (i.e., José Casanova) to go beyond the limitation of private-sphere religion (Casanova 2008, 102–103). The case of Shinto in modern Japan, however, has revealed the problems of public religion, as it fostered a homogenization of plural voices in the public sphere by a one and only religion. By expanding the religious sphere into the public sphere, the system of State Shinto homogenized the Japanese society and fostered totalitarianism in the 1940s.

Edward Said has advocated "secular criticism" and argues that only secular intelligence can critique society objectively (Said 1983, 24–30). On the other hand, Talal Asad and Gauri Viswanathan have advanced "religious criticism". For them, religious speeches and actions can be used to interrogate social values (Asad 2008, 605; Viswanathan 1998, 45–47). The case of Japanese Shinto, however, both the positive and negative sides of religious criticism are shown in terms of a way to relocate human subjectivity; on the one hand to heterogenize secular subjectivity, on the other to be homogenized under state authority.

The second leader of the Great Tōyō Church, Shirai Kiichirō conducted practice at Toga Shrine which was a site of much religious practice. He married into the Urano family as in February 1935 and entered the Shintisto University, Kokugakuin, in October that same year.

The Toga Shrine enshrines the tutelary *kami* of the area. Up to the early modern period, the shrine was called "the Great Toga Bodhisattva" and enshrined the medicine Buddha Bhaisajyaguru with a Buddhist temple affiliated with it as steward temple. Like the Great Fushimi Inari Shrine, the Toga Shrine had prosperous confraternities and activities from the early modern to the Meiji periods. In the backyard area of the shrine are sites of extreme mountain ascetic practice and in the interior compound are huge cedar trees reaching into the sky. Near the interior compound is the place of seclusion practice where Yoshiyasu used to stay overnight. This shrine is like the Fushimi Inari Shrine in valuing practice as a form of belief. Yoshiyasu enshrined an earthly *kami*, which is different from the imperial gods, and managed confraternities (Isomae 2012).

In these two respects, Yoshiyasu maintained beliefs by refusing to be domesticated by the State Shinto. In this sense, he must have met expectations of the first leader Katsuyasu. At that time, Shinto priests reportedly stayed at the Toga Shrine for about a month for practice. It is said that during Yoshiyasu's practice stay, he experienced a variety of uncanny phenomena such as Tengu running at the ceiling, thunder sounding without rain, and a procession of lamp-carrying foxes in the valley.

Yoshiyasu's spiritual power manifested as the power to see dreams. When he was a middle school student, he once stepped over a snake on a mountain trail without giving it a second thought. The snake followed him to his home and coiled itself beside Yoshiyasu. That night the snake appeared in his dream and complained that its practice to become *kami* had been hindered by being stepped over. Now it had to rectify its practice, so it asked Yoshiyasu also to practice as a priest and enshrine it as *kami*. This was how Yoshiyasu started his practice at the Hongusan, the well-known place of religious practice.

One day, in practice, Yoshiyasu entreated the snake to manifest itself. Then in a dream he saw the snake again, and the snake told him that "if I show you my entire body you will be shocked" and then manifested itself as a huge dragon covered in golden scales., It is said that the Inari family crest was painted on the dragon's body.

The dragon became the tutelary *kami* of Yoshiyasu and started to be enshrined as the White Lady Dragon *Kami* on the mountain of the Great Tōyō Church. The dragon then reappeared in Yoshiyasu's dream telling him that thanks to Yoshiyas's effort it had become a *kami* thereby ascending to heaven. For Yoshiyasu the snake *kami* is the messenger of the *kami* connecting heaven with humans.

For Yoshiyasu who had been working as a priest at the Toga Shrine, it was not so easy to cure believers' illnesses with a spiritual power like that of Katsuyasu nor was it so easy to provide counselling for people's life problems. But then there came a turning point. One day, Yoshiyasu talked to his teacher at the Kokugakuin University and made the decision to study the purification ritual by water (*misogi*) under the tutelage of Yukihiro Tadasu, the once-priest of the famous big Shinto Shrines. Yoshiyasu participated for the first time in the water purification ritual at the Fushimi Inari Shrine at the end of 1941.

The Manchurian Incident took place when Yoshiyasu married into the Urano house in 1931. Then in 1937 the Sino-Japanese War broke out, followed by the start of the Pacific War at the end of 1941. In the social context of imminent war, Patriotic Corps was organized at the Kokugakuin University in 1941, and students in Shinto Studies of the university started to perform water purification at the Meiji Shrine and at other shrines. Water purification practices became widespread in the Shinto circle and then spread across Japanese society.

It was Kawatsura Bonji, born in Ōita prefecture in 1913 and Yukihiro's teacher, who systematized the water purification ritual. Upon receiving divine revelation in South Japan, Kawatsura went to Tokyo and preached "the unity of all teachings" and "all gods as one" as a Shinto specialist of "despiritualized Shamanism" (Tsushiro 1990, chap. 4). In particular, Kawatsura emphasized purification praxis rather than doctrine. His teaching with its emphasis on praxis spread not only in Japan but also to Manchuria and the Korean Peninsula.

His supporters included prominent figures such as the politician Hiranuma Kiichirō who was vice-president of Kokugakuin University, professor Kakei Katsuhiko of the Faculty of Law of the Tokyo Imperial University who promoted an 'All Teachings Returning to One' Shinto, Imaizumi Sadasuke, chairman of the Association for Revering the Ise Shrine (*Jingu Hōsai Kai*) and the navy, and so on. With his emphasis on the bodily practice of water purification, Kawatsura's Shinto differed from the stances of the scholars in the Shinto Studies department of Tokyo Imperial University and Kokugakuin University which either followed the traditions of Western philosophy or Kokugaku philological studies.

Like Katsuyasu, Kawatsura placed an emphasis on bodily practice. At the same time, he tried to dovetail popular practice with *Kojiki* and *Nihon shoki* mythological metaphors to provide substance to intellectualized Shinto terminology while systematizing popular beliefs. For the Great Tōyō Church, the essence of Kawatsura's teaching was first and foremost 'correcting spirit'.

> All things in the universe including humans have a pearl in their bodies. This is the fundamental straight spirit (ultimate potential consciousness) and has the same quality as the *kami*. With this spirit, every human possesses the thought about the *kami* [...]. We pray to the kami through this innermost correcting spirit. (Kanatani 1941, 170)

Putting the spirit to exercise was the water purification practice. For that purpose, it is important to foreground the metaphor of *Amenominakanushi no kami* ('the Central God of the Heaven').

Kawatsura held that the fundamental ontological nature of human being and the universe is called *Amenominakanushi no kami* in Japan, *Shangdi* in China, *Buddha* in India, and *God* in the UK and the U.S. He wanted to pose Shinto as a world religion, as a universal phenomenon in smooth and flexible relationship with Christianity, Buddhism, or Islam, rather than as an ethnic religion.

Amaterasu Ōkami is the imperial ancestor enshrined at the Ise Shrine which provided the mythological basis for the claim of Japanese emperors being living gods. According to current Great Tōyō Church leader Tomoyasu, this kind of *kami*, with its concrete features, cannot become the original *kami* of the universe. Where the State Shinto system erred was to present Amaterasu Ōkami as an original kami. Rather, by relying on a content-void *kami* named as *Amenominakanushi no Kami* ('Center God of Heaven'), which has no personality nor can be called an imperial ancestor, Shinto can be relieved of any ethnic nationalist feature. Here, the Great Tōyō Church dramatically transformed from an illness-treating popular religion of Katsuyasu's time to a Shinto of the water purification ritual connected to *Amenominakanushi no kami*.

Here, the popular belief in Tengu experienced by Yoshiyasu at a local Shrine was also transformed into the role of spiritual guru in the systematic religious world. According to Tomoyasu, the Great Tōyō Church's encounter with the belief of Kawatsura rendered the messenger *kami* such as the dragon *kami* and Tengu dispensable. "Revelation" delivered by these medium *kami* was also negated as of this world, and no longer given positive meaning.

The importance of understanding laws of the universe and living a life in accordance with those laws came to be the central teaching of Kawatsura. Illness arose from mistakes in one's life when one went against the universe's laws. When one realized this deviation, illness would be cured naturally. As a result, illness treatment came to be reconceived as a derivative phenomenon. Tomoyasu told me personally that "the teaching of the master Kawatsura did not respond to personal problems but rather emphasized guidance by following laws of the universe."

Amenominakanushi no Kami, however, remained a metaphor that constituted one side of the coin with the other side being the public space of the emperor-system state, insofar as the *kami* was written into *Kojiki* and *Nihon shoki* mythologies, the origin and ancient history of the Japanese Royal family, to secure the unbroken imperial genealogy starting from Amaterasu. In fact, regarding the emperor-system state, Kawatsura asserted that "the world is broad, and countries are numerous, but the Great Japan is the only state and ethnic nation that developed, based on a unity of the *kami* and the land, an unbroken genealogy tracing back to the sun goddess Amaterasu" (Kawatsura 1940, 8). He then asserted that Shinto held the key to save humanity.

These assertions of Kawatsura reflected the complicated social conditions of the time and cannot be reductively understood as meaning that Shinto was some universal phenomenon transcending nationalism. The Japanese empire of the time was sustained by the two-layer structure of a mono-ethnic Japanese nation-state and a multi-ethnic nation-state concerned with its relationship with colonies. Multi-ethnicity can function to affirm imperialist domination if the Japanese ethnic nation was located at the central position of excellence.

If the hypostatization of such a centre were negated, however, it was possible for certain universality to emerge. Would the state open itself up to plural public spaces, or would public space end up being assimilated by state power? Kawatsura died in 1929, before Japan plunged into the Asia-Pacific War. He was unable to see the bankruptcy of the ambiguous logic embodied in imperialism, his life coming to an end when the two-layer structure of universalist and nationalist maintained its subtle balance.

The question was how Kawatsura's successors would interpret his teachings. His multivalent teachings contained the danger of departing from Kawatsura's original intention and segmenting into new discourses in East Asian political conditions.

In 1939, the tenth anniversary of the death of Kawatsura was commemorated at the Military Officers' Club neighbouring the Yasukuni Shrine. The head priest of the Fushimi Inari Shrine until 1936, Takayama Noboru, presided over the commemoration event. Prime Minister Hiranuma who promoted the national mobilization system and Mizuno Rentarō, the director of the National Shinto Priest Association, offered prayers. The following year, the Imperial Rule Assistance Association was founded and in 1941, the water purification ritual was adopted by the association as the method for national training.

The water purification ritual was promoted not just in Japan but also in colonies including the Korean Peninsula. On the other hand, at the Fushimi Inari Shrine the water purification ritual site, the Pure and Bright House, was erected in as early as 1934 thanks to the effort of Takayama Noboru, the head priest of the Fushimi Inari Shrine. The purpose of the creation of the house was motivated by the contribution of the Fushimi Inari Shrine to the State Shinto system, rather than to folk religion, through the water purification ritual.

In 1924 Takayama banned construction of a new rock altar at Fushimi Inari and in 1927, he created the Inari confraternity. Shimazono Susumu observes: "the Inari confraternity gathered together various communities of devotion to the Inari *kami* and directed it toward where shrines intended in order to counter the critique since the Taisho period of the thesis that Shinto shrines were non-religious facilities" (Shimazono 2004, 7).

Takayama attempted to situate the Inari Mountain as the space for swearing loyalty to the imperial *kami* by way of the water purification ritual, rather than the space of interaction with a plurality of *kami* through divine possession. Whilst being a bodily practice, the *misogi* purification ritual of Kawatsura came to be contrasted with the belief of the Fushimi Inari Mountain practitioners.

Takayama studied at the Institute of Imperial Classics, the predecessor of Kokugakuin University, and worked as the head priest of major shrines such as Nogi Shrine. It can be assumed that he played an important role in dovetailing the shrine-as-non-religion thesis of the Ministry of the Interior and established Shinto shrines with the popular water purification ritual advocated by Kawatsura. The intellectual pillar of this dovetailing was Imaizumi Sadasuke, Chairman of the Association for Revering the Ise Shrine. Conflating the emperor-system state with the principles of the universe, Imaizumi reinterpreted Kawatsura's Shinto thought as centring on the emperor to make it comply with the conditions of the time.

As Akazawa Shirō has pointed out, they were "nationalists who succeeded the non-State-Shinto tradition" (Akazawa 1985, 96–97). They used the same metaphor of imperial *kami* as that of bureaucrats in the Ministry of the Interior but aimed at the expansion and transformation of the national subject fit for national mobilization, to be achieved through bodily practice that took seriously the human spirit which was ignored by the imperial metaphor. It was no longer possible to constitute the national subject capable of meeting the difficulty of the time with purely doctrinal inculcation.

Yukihiro who taught Kawatsura's teaching to Yoshiyasu was also a Shinto specialist actively promoting Kawatsura's water purification ritual during this period. Yukihiro's work, *Misogi Ritual Practice Guide*, had the endorsement of Hiranuma Kiichiro, the preface of Imaizumi Sadasuke, and the afterword of Takayama Noboru, and was appended with *guidelines to the Misogi Practice at the Central Training Institute of the Imperial Rule Assistance Association*. In the Guide, Yukihiro stated, "during the crisis of our imperial nation, we must revive the spirit of the imperial nation and realize the unified spirit of Japan by practicing the water purification ritual which is the mysterious movement resulted from the enactment of one's nature" (Yukihiro 1943, 3).

It is true that in Kawatsura's teaching there existed the possibility for a belief subjectivity, which refused assimilation by the nation-state, to emerge from the overlapping space of the emperor-system state and popular belief. If the emperor system was not used for private interest, the centre would maintain its balance and serve the whole collectively. Here one notices the possibility of the emperor system as a 'selfless apparatus', the possibility first envisioned by Motoori Norinaga. When the emperor was used to serve a particularistic interest group, the decentred centre articulated by Kawatsura may be hypostatized. When retracing the historical process of such a hypostatization in pre-war Japan, we come to understand that church-state separation introduced in the post-war period, its evaluation aside, is an institution to prevent the *kami* from coming to the foreground through the mediation of the state.

With the effort of Kawatsura, Takayama, Imaizumi and Yukihiro, the bodily practice of purification ritual became an indispensable training for many Shinto priests. The practice of the water purification ritual popular among today's shrines was systematized during this period although their names were forgotten because of defeat in war. The bodily practice of water purification as a technology of subject constitution saw phenomenal development in the second decade of the Showa Period (1925–1989).

5 Shinto as World Religion

The third leader of the Great Tōyō Church, Tomoyasu, from 1954, received instruction from Toda Yoshio, a graduate in religious studies from the University of Tokyo, and others at Kokugakuin University, and progressed to third year in the master's program while practicing yoga under the guidance at the Yoga Association. When Yoshiyasu died in 1971, Tomoyasu followed the footprint of his father in the water purification practice of Kawatsura under the guidance of the Miizukai Society to learn the teaching of the straight spirit and the unity of the universe. Returning Kawatsura's teaching to its original focus on *Amenominakanushi no kami,* Tomoyasu in the post-war period intended to go beyond wartime imperialism as well as the post-war mainstream stance of Shinto being an ethnic religion. Precisely because post-war Japan lost its colonies, for Tomoyasu it was important to transcend self-ethnocentrism by opening Shinto up to other ethnicities and nations.

Then Tomoyasu attempted to establish an open subjectivity, without being limited to its interiority, through bodily practice, while renouncing statism. Because bodily practice refuses to be assimilated into the political structure of church-state separation, which divided state and religion into the public and private spheres, it represents a chance of relativizing both institutions of church-state unity and church-state separation. Through the deepening of bodily practice, a channel opens up for establishing a subjectivity of belief which resists identification with the state or *kami* and also refuses to be devoured by one's own subjectivity.

The *kami* itself, however, remains unchanged and remains the subjectivity unable to materialize. *Kami* as the other that refuses segmentation and materialization turns into the subjectivity calling upon humans to act. Depending on how the voice is heard by humans, the form of existence of the *kami* itself changes as the form of human society changes. In a given historical context, humans give name to *kami* and make it manifest in society by way of thought and bodily practice. The words of Tomoyasu, "Praying to Heaven and Prostrating before the Earth," which was told to me personally, demonstrate a stage of belief reached by the leaders of Great Tōyō Church after going through difficult times. The Fushimi Inari Mountain, today as in the past, continues to be the womb engendering diverse subjectivities of belief.

Here I would like to conclude this article by explaining how anthropology of religion has developed Asad's critique on the Protestant notion of religion. Following Asad's argument, the critique of the notion of religion opens the gate to the discussion on religious subjectification which is totally distinguished from a secular one. For Asad, religion as a method of subjectification breaks the boundaries between the religious and the secular and bridges the sphere of the private and that of the public.

In terms of Asad's critique, it is now obvious the Western secularism coupled with a Protestant notion of religion is not universal all over the world. It questions the superiority of secular subjectification, basing on the binary thinking that the West is civilized whereas the non-West is uncivilized. Anthropology started to presume this binary division, on the other hand nowadays, it has turned to reflect its own locality of each tradition without prejudice of evolutionism like with the notion of 'world religions'. It can be a method opening the gate to recognize the diversity subjectification beyond the dichotomy of the West and non-West.

However, I do not claim that public religion is right whilst private religion is wrong. Under the Japanese emperor system, public religion had served as a governmental means to establish totalitarian homogeneity in society by mobilizing both public discourse and bodily emotion. On the other hand, public religion also ushers religious plurality to challenge homogeneity. Therefore, the function of public religion is principally ambivalent, and may lead to either heterogeneity or homogeneity, or both.

Lastly, the structure of religious subjectification is composed of subject, mystical Other and transference of emotion. A mystical Other may play the crucial role in constructing individual subjectivity, depending on whether one takes a secularist or religionist standpoint. If one takes the secularist standpoint, individual subjectivity does not need a mystical Other because rational subjectivity is independent of the other's gaze. From the standpoint of religionist subjectification, however, individual subjectivity was necessitated by the gaze of the mythical Other (Lacan 1973, 203– 263). Individual subjectivity must always negotiate with the gaze of the mythical Other to renew itself.

Needless to say, Asad's argument on religious subjectification comes from Michel Foucault's notion of the technology of the self. But the Foucauldian argument lacks a religious dimension, as it deals only with individual subjectivity not collective subjectivity (Foucault 2005, 491–505). Adding Lacanian theory of the mythical Other to Foucauldian subjectification allows us to expand the theory of religious subjectification from the private sphere into the public sphere.

The case of Japanese modern religions leads us to the discussion on the degree of religious freedom under State Shinto, a public religion system. What kind of freedom or tolerance does a public religion system provide? What is the possibility and impossibility of public religion? The history of Shinto as an imperial religion provides ample examples of how to rethink the boundaries defined by Western-centric notions of world religion and national religion (Masuzawa 2005, chap. 3).

Bibliography

Akazawa, Shirō. 1985. *Kindai Nihon no Shisō Dōin to Shūkyō Tōsei*. Tokyo: Azekura shobo.
Arendt, Hannah. 1958. *The Human Condition*. Chicago / London: The University of Chicago.
Asad, Talal. 1993. *Genealogies of Religion: Discipline and Reasons of Power in Christianity and Islam*. Baltimore: Johns Hopkins University Press.
Asad, Talal. 2003. *Formations of the Secular: Christianity, Islam, Modernity*. Stanford: Stanford University Press.
Asad, Talal. 2008. "Reflections on Blasphemy and Secular Criticism." In *Religion: Beyond a Concept,* edited by Hent de Vries, New York: Fordham University Press, 580–609.
Bouchy, Anne. 2009. *Kami to Hito no Hazama ni Ikiru – Kindai Toshi no Josei Fusha*. Tokyo: University of Tokyo Press.
Casanova, José. 2008. "Public Religion Revised." In *Religion: Beyond a Concept*, edited by Hent de Vries, New York: Fordham University Press, 101–119.

Foucault, Michel. 2005. *The Hermeneutics of the Subject: Lectures at the Collège de France, 1981–1982*. New York: Picador.
Hardacre, Helen. 1991. *Shinto and the State, 1868–1988*. Princeton: Princeton University Press.
Inoue, Nobutaka. 1991. *Kyōha Shinto no Keisei*. Tokyo: Kōbundō.
Isomae, Jun'ichi. 2012. "Discursive Formation around 'Shinto' in Colonial Korea." In *The Religion and Culture Web Form*. Chicago: Divinity School at University of Chicago. https://voices.uchicago.edu/religionculture/2012/09/29/discursive-formation-around-shinto-in-colonial-korea/ (30.11.2021).
Isomae, Jun'ichi. 2014. *Religious Discourse in Modern Japan: Religion, State and Shinto*, trans. Galen Amstutz and Lynne Riggs. Leiden: Brill.
Isomae, Jun'ichi. 2017. "Revering Heaven and Prostrating before the Earth: History of the Shinto Fushimi Inari Great Toyo Church." In *Religion, Politik und Ideologie: Beiträge zu einer kritischen Kulturwissenschaft*, edited by Michael Wachutka, Monika Schrimpf, and Birgit Stämmler. München: Iudicium, 87–102.
Kanatani, Makoto. 1941. *Kawatsura Bonji-senseiden*. Tokyo: Misogikai-sezarenmei.
Kawatsura Bonji. 1940. *Nippon Koten Shingi*. Vol. 1, Tokyo: Kawatsura Bonji Sensei Jyushunen Kinenkai.
Ketelaar, James. 1993. *Of Heretics and Martyrs in Meiji Japan*. Princeton: Princeton University Press.
Lacan Jacques. 1981. *The Four Fundamental Concepts of Psychoanalysis: The Seminar of Jacques Lacan Book XI*, trans. Alan Sheridan. New York / London: W. W. Norton & Company.
Masuzawa, Tomoko. 2005. *The Invention of World Religions: Or, How European Universalism Was Preserved in the Language of Pluralism*. Chicago / London: University of Chicago Press.
Said, Edward. 1983. *The World, the Text, and the Critic*. Cambridge, MA: Harvard University Press.
Shimazono, Susumu. 2004. "Inari Shinkō no Kindai." *Ake* 47:2–13.
Smyers, Karen Ann. 1998. *The Fox and the Jewel: Shared and Private Meanings in Contemporary Japanese Inari Worship*. Honolulu: University of Hawaii Press.
Tsushiro, Hirofumi. 1990. *Chinkon Gyōhō-ron – Kindai Shinto Sekai no Reikon-ron to Shintai-ron*. Tokyo: Shunjusha.
Viswanathan, Gauri. 1998. *Outside the Fold: Conversion, Modernity, and Belief*. Princeton: Princeton University.
Yasumaru, Yoshio. 1987. *Deguchi Nao*. Tokyo: Asahi Shimbun sha.
Yukihiro, Tadasu. 1943. *Misogi Rensei Dokuhon*. Tokyo: Sozosha.

Ulrike E. Auga
Gender Studies

1 Introduction

Feminist research experienced some delays in its development regarding the concept of gender: a notion only absorbed by feminist theology at the start of the 1990s. This was followed by an important change in theory construction. The presuppositions underpinning gender research are mostly poststructuralist, and work with the methodology of deconstruction. Gender theory is in a constant state of self-development, with ripple effects on the diverse landscape of Gender Studies and theology.

These effects have not yet been sufficiently reflected theologically. However, an expression of these developments has been seen in the increasing use of the term *gender-conscious theology*, which breaks away somewhat from the narrower focus of women's perspectives but centralizes gender justice as a goal within the church, and theology more broadly. The inclusion of gender questions within scientific theology as well as within the work of the church has remained controversial. In the ecumenical context in particular, the debate has been contentious. In disputes with papal pronouncements, the issues of the ordination of women or the churches' position on LGBTIQ* more generally are particularly at stake. There are fundamentalist backlashes in all religions and Christian denominations but also progressive developments and e.g., many of the Protestant theologies and churches are increasingly making greater efforts to become more inclusive.

My own approach stems from a feminist, postcolonial, post-secular position within Protestant Theology in Germany where I teach as a professor and where I am an ordained minister in the Protestant church in Berlin. I was a cofounder of – and work as acting president of – the International Association of the Study of Religion and Gender. This is an important organization that finds itself at the intersection of research in religion and in Gender Studies, inside as well as beyond the discipline of theology.

This article addresses some of the main developments in gender theory and their effects on the study of religion and theology. It also explores historical milestones and the nuances of the word 'woman' as well as looking at feminism(s) in their relation to religion. Feminist Liberation Theologies of the twentieth–twenty-first century are also acknowledged. Then, gender theory is introduced, distinguishing the terms sex and gender. Kimberlé Crenshaw's concept of intersectionality is also elaborated upon. Then, the chapter turns to poststructuralist approaches in the analysis of gender and sexuality, exploring notions such as sexuality, biopolitics and epistemology from Michel Foucault's oeuvre. His work remains foundational for Gender, Sexuality, Queer and Transgender Studies, including for Judith Butler who developed the concept of gender as a discursive, performative category of knowledge production and laid the basis for Gender Studies as we know it today. The chapter shows further advances in the discipline of Biology and the deconstruction of sex and diverse sexualities. Lastly, the text turns to Queer Studies and Religion, their theorisation but also to Queer Theology and Precarious (Postcolonial) Sexualities. It underlines the importance of Transgender Studies and Religion and elaborates particularly on Gender, Religion and Postcoloniality. Furthermore, Gender and Postsecular Theory are highlighted as fields where new developments bring about a shift in the concept of representation. Saba Mahmood's understanding of resistance (2012) led gender, postcolonial, postsecular theory to shift from representation to the analysis of subject formation, agency, and human flourishing. The conclusion discusses the influence of the New Material turn for Gender Studies and Theologies.

2 Historical Milestones

2.1 Women – Atheism – Feminism

Like many other emancipatory movements, the feminist struggle for women's rights in Europe has historically taken an agnostic or atheist position and can thus be seen as a secular struggle. European feminism in its beginnings was heavily influenced by the Enlightenment critique of religious dogma and clerical authority. Existentialist feminism (de Beauvoir [1949] 1989) and Marxist or socialist feminism (Davis 1981) also greatly influenced second-wave feminism. The feminist thought system was thus based on Enlightenment rational and secular argumentation, as opposed to authoritarianism and orthodoxy. Feminist politics in general combine rational arguments with political activism, towards a just society. The secularist heritage for feminism contained the idea that there needed to be separation of church from state in matters of faith and ethics. Some hold the idea of an opposition between religion as belonging to the private sphere, and political citizenship as taking place in the public domain. Agency or political subjectivity in this framing is therefore placed only in the public sphere. Furthermore, the private-public sphere divide is used to construct a gendered hierarchy of 'female' as belonging to tradition and 'religion' in the private sphere, and 'male' as progressive and belonging to the public sphere. In Continental Europe, anticlericalism, and a critique especially of the patriarchal heritage of main strands of the Catholic church have been brought forward by the European left, and emancipatory movements (de Beauvoir 1992).

2.2 Twentieth and Twenty-First Century Feminist Liberation Theologies

Concern about discrimination by the church and society at large, against people pertaining to particular religious minority communities, led to various resistance movements, including that of liberation theology. In the Americas, liberation theology began with the "option for the poor", addressing issues of poverty and class in ecclesial practice itself. The African American Civil Rights Movement (1954–1968) stimulated Black theology first in the U.S. and then worldwide. Feminist liberation theology developed in the context of the women's movement which demanded equal rights for women and men. However, some realised that marginalisation can be multi-dimensional and that there is no "equality" based on shared experience. Concerns therefore differed within these resistance movements. Consequently, Black-identified Womanist theology emerged, as well as Mujerista theology, focusing on the discrimination of Latin American women*. Several indigenous liberation theologies concerned with issues specific to first nations peoples were also born. The acknowledgement of diverse, heterogeneous experiences is important, but analysis must go beyond essentialized constructions of race, class, gender, sexuality, nation, and religion.

Important Christian feminist liberation theologians include Elisabeth Schüssler Fiorenza, Rosemary Radford Ruether, Carter Heywood, Lisa Isherwood, Musa Dube, Kwok Pui-lan. Several generations of scholars continue to work in the AAR Feminist Liberation Theology Network, in the AAR Women's Caucus (Elizabeth Ursic) and WATER (Mary Hunt, Bernadette Brooten). An important author in Jewish Theology and Gender is Susannah Heschel.

2.3 The Controversy over Difference

Difference feminism starts from an essentialized notion of binary gender. A difference feminist approach, particularly discussed in Europe, was developed by Italian Diotima thinkers who strove to overcome the phallocratic gender order through a feminine conceptualization of gender order. Luce Irigaray also holds to an a priori thinking of femininity and masculinity.

Equality feminism is oriented towards the political-legal idea of equality. It is accused of overlooking the construction of gender hierarchy in universalist discourses that also include law. Wendy Brown's illustration of the paradox of rights, also discussed by Joan Scott (1996) became prominent when the rights discourse gained momentum amongst the left, feminist, Black, LGBTIQ* and other movements. According to Brown, it is paradoxical that on the one hand, the more specific rights are characterised as rights for women, the more they establish an ever more precise, essentialized definition of 'woman' which reinforces subordination. On the other hand, the more 'gender neutral' a given right is, the more it privileges men because the universal position is not neutral, but masculine. To be addressed as a legal subject ultimately reinforces essentialized marginalisations (Brown 1995, 420–434).

So-called difference feminism and equality feminism are not in themselves sufficient to dismantle epistemic violence in the context of gender and religion.

2.4 The Concept of Intersectionality: History and New Approaches

Intersectionality analyses forms of injustice connected to gender. There is a significant inconsistency between the emergence of this term in North America and in Europe. In North America, the notion of 'multiple intersecting differences' has been influential since the 1990s, while in Europe the discussion entered the feminist mainstream 15 years later (Essed 1991; Yuval-Davis 1997).

The term 'intersectionality' was coined 1989 in Kimberlé Crenshaw's famous article *Demarginalizing the Intersection of Race and Sex: A Black Feminist Critique of Antidiscrimination Doctrine, Feminist Theory, and Antiracist Politics*. Here, Crenshaw compares the discrimination of Afro-American women with a car accident at an intersection: If a Black woman is harmed because she is in the intersection, her injury could result from sex discrimination or race discrimination (1989, 149). She states that the anti-discrimination laws in the US are useful mechanisms to oppose discrimination because of sex or race.[1] However, these mechanisms are not sufficient to cover the specific, intersectional discriminations that black women as a group experience.

Crenshaw also encourages an intersectional critique of sexism and racism in feminist theory and black movements. The intersectionality of gender, race and class has since been referred to as 'triple oppression'. Today, the interest has shifted to the analysis of how the intersection of gender, race, class, nation, sexuality, (dis)ability, age, species etc. influences a particular object of study (Hancock 2007, 251–252).

These categories are also eminent in historical contexts, such as in Denise Kimber Buell's study (2001) of the intersection of race and Christianity during the first Christian centuries. In my work since 2012 onwards, I have proposed an understanding of religion as a discursive, intersectional category of knowledge production, because religion had been neglected in Gender Studies. The understanding of religion as intersectional category is connected with an attempt to deessentialize and disidentify gender, religion and further intersectional categories. Overall, it is suggested to understand the categories neither in an essentialized way nor as simple social categories but as categories of knowledge production. To overcome epistemic violence connected to them it is suggested to deconstruct and to deessentialize them as well as to overcome identitarian presumptions ad therefore to disidentify the categories.

---

[1] Precursors of Crenshaw's notion of intersectionality are Hull, Bell-Scott, and Smith (1993) and Anzaldúa (1987).

3 Poststructuralist Approaches in the Analysis of Gender and Sexuality

3.1 Sexuality, Biopolitics, Epistemic Order, Confessionalism – the Work of Michel Foucault

The work of Michel Foucault, specialist in the history of systems of thought, is in many respects foundational for Gender, Sexuality, Queer and Transgender Studies. For Foucault, knowledge is always a form of power. Power is not an object but rather, a network. Defining the epistemic subconscious of a period as *episteme*, he writes: "In any given culture and at any given moment, there is always only one *episteme* that defines the conditions of possibility of all knowledge" (Foucault 1970, 168). He describes the way in which an historical period considers particular presuppositions to be immutable and true – such as the idea of identity in the 19th and 20th century – and thus how 'epistemic violence' is produced through the exclusion of other ideas. Foucault describes the changes in systems of thought and points out the arbitrary character of orders in 'western' knowledge production.

In *History of Sexuality* (1990, 57), he elaborates two ways of producing 'the truth' about human sexuality:

> Historically, there have been two great procedures for producing the truth of sex. On the one hand, the societies [...] which endowed themselves with an 'ars erotica'. In the erotic art, truth is drawn from pleasure itself, understood as a practice and accumulated as experience; pleasure is not considered in relation to an absolute law of the permitted and the forbidden, nor by reference to a criterion of utility, but first and foremost in relation to itself; it is experienced as pleasure, evaluated in terms of its intensity, its specific quality, its duration, its reverberations in the body and the soul [...]. [Western] civilisation possesses no ars erotica. In return, it is undoubtedly the only civilisation to practice a scientia sexualis; [...] to have developed over the centuries procedures for telling the truth of sex which are geared to a form of knowledge-power strictly opposed to the art of initiations and the masterful secret: I have in mind the confession.

The confession is the general standard governing the production of the 'true' discourse on sex. Because sexuality is not a matter of repressed essences, there can be no liberation of sexuality.

In 1984, Foucault wrote a history of the desiring subject and personal and sexual subjectivity, looking at the 'use of pleasure' and 'care of the self', in both Greek and Christian traditions.

Foucault's lectures *On the Government of the Living* were partly the intended fourth volume of the *History of Sexuality* to appear under the title *Confessions of the Flesh*. Published in 2012, the lectures explain the historical foundations of the obedience of the Western subject. Foucault locates these foundations in the connections between obedience and confession within early Christianity. In his genealogy of confession, he underlines that the 'West' developed a concept of confession as 'liberation', which does not work in other contexts. As empirical research shows, the demand and wish to 'come out' publicly is a typical Western construct. The problem is that in order to confess, to seek to know, and to produce 'the truth' concerning oneself, this amounts to a submission (Foucault 2014).

Foucault postulates a non-essentialist understanding of gender and sexuality, arguing for a more nuanced constructivist view. Furthermore, he also has a non-essentialist perception of religion. By following Foucault, one can see how religion can also be understood as discursively constructed, and how the notions of gender, sexuality and religion are intertwined.

3.2 Gender as a Discursive, Performative Category of Knowledge Production – Judith Butler

Carol Hageman-White (1984) has shown that the classification of human beings in 'men' and 'women' represents a problem as it presupposes that there are (only) two sexes and imagines sex as something natural and stable, situated beyond society. Joan W. Scott (1986) has established gender as a category of historical analysis.

With Judith Butler's thought (1990 and 1993) the discussion shifts from 'woman' and a critique of the construction of social gender to a critique of any idea of gender as substance. Butler shows that both sex and gender are culturally determined. Butler applies John L. Austin's theory of performativity to the production of gender. She argues that gender has a cultural meaning which is ascribed to the human body, but not an inherent attribute of personhood or subjectivity (Austin 1962). The meaning of gender is, in her view, inseparable from the cultural and political constructs in which it is produced and maintained. She argues, following Austin, that gendering is a re-iterative, performative process through which a gender is ascribed to an individual. The performativity of gender is not related to an individual act but rather to the long, repetitive process through which discourse effectively produces the gender which it pretends to simply name that: "There is no gender identity behind the expressions of gender; [...] identity is performatively constituted by the very expressions that are said to be its results." (Butler 1990, 25)

Butler argues that traditional thinking including some strands of feminism which look to a natural, 'essential' notion of the female, or sex and gender generally, are wrong. Butler begins by questioning the categories of 'woman' and 'man' and asks who is included and who decides about the inclusion or exclusion. Butler showed how gender is a reiterated social performance rather than the expression of a preceding reality.

The intention of Butler's deconstructivist approach is not the achievement of any kind of identity, but the undoing of gender as an essentialized, biological category. Yet gender does not only function regressively, but also productively. Thus, performativity is studied as a productive act of subject formation in relation to the category of gender. One of the consequences of a deconstructed and deessentialized notion of gender is the denaturalisation of kinship and the emphasis on care in the description of terms such as 'sexuality' or 'marriage' (Butler 2000).

3.3 Biology and the Deconstruction of Sex – Diverse Sexuality

Since Thomas Laqueur's study (1990) on the history of gender from Antiquity to Freud, it has also become clear that the biological opposition between 'men' and 'women' was established not before the Enlightenment. Before, the model of one gender that can take two different forms was prevalent in 'Western' thought. Numerous historical and contemporary empirical examples for fluid ideas of gender can be found. New insights in biology show that the human body does not conform to one of two binary genders, but rather is situated on a continuum (Maurer 2002, 87–88). The biological sex binary is questioned because, on the one hand, subjects change their gender within their lifetime and, on the other hand, because biological gender is understood as a multidimensional continuum (chromosomal, gonodal, hormonal, genital, morphological/phenotypical) that is formed in subjects in interrelation with the respective environment.

Biologist Hans-Juergen Voss underlined that the species homo sapiens did not consist of two complementary genders, but that countless genders existed (Voss 2010, 2012a, 2013; Sweetapple 2018). Voss thus ties in with the work of the historian of science Helga Satzinger as well as the biologist and gender researcher Anne Fausto-Sterling. In his volume *Intersexuality – Intersex* he comments critically on the opinion of the German Ethics Council of 2012 about the situation of intersex people in Germany. He criticized the Ethics Council for adhering to a framing of intersex as a disease, and "that central concerns of intersex activists, like surgical and hormonal intervention in early childhood to refrain, are not included in his recommendations" (Voss 2012b, x).

In Germany, in December 2018, the Federal Constitutional Court (BVerfG) extended both legally and socially recognised gender categories of 'male' and 'female' with the addition of a new category of 'diverse' with the Act on the Amendment of Information to be entered in the Register of Births.

4 Queer Studies and Religion

4.1 Theory

Queer critique is not an identitarian approach, but a critique of the essentialization of gender, sexuality and of heteronormativity. It implies a consequent epistemological critique, which allows new perspectives on minority discourses. One of the central aspects of queer analysis is its potential for the deconstruction of categories.

Queer concepts developed out of the poststructuralist critique of gender, especially Butler's deconstruction of the notion of gender. Queer critique is "a point of departure for a broad critique that is calibrated to account for the social antagonism of nationality, race, gender, and class as well as sexuality" (McClintock et al. 1997, 90).

A number of ideas of queer theory can usefully be applied to theology and religious studies: a) the new focus on subject formation and agency; b) the disidentification of violent concepts of identity of which José Esteban Muñoz writes that "[d]isidentification is meant to be descriptive of the survival strategies the minority subject practices in order to negotiate a phobic majoritarian public sphere that continuously elides or punishes the existence of subjects who do not conform to the phantasm of normative citizenship" (Muñoz 1999, 4); c) Gilles Deleuze's and Félix Guattari's queer assemblage which goes beyond collectivities with their exclusions (Ferguson 2004, 4; 2005); d) the concept of 'queer collectivity' and its political potential which is linked to the idea of queer utopia; e) queer of color concepts (Roderick Ferguson) and queer diaspora approaches (Muñoz) with their critique of capitalism. Ferguson laments the blind spots in Marxist thinking regarding gender, sexuality, and race: "Queer of color analysis extends women of color feminism by investigating how intersecting racial, gender, and sexual practices antagonize and/or conspire with the normative investments of nation states and capital." (Ferguson 2004, 4) Based on Adrienne Rich's early queer of color critique, Ferguson's approach learns from Aihwa Ong's analysis of capital and transnationalism that "[t]he reproduction of racialized gender and sexual regulations [...] facilitate the production of global capital." (Ferguson 2004, 136)

Not only are gender and sexuality regulated, but everybody's life is affected by regulations through the nation state and capital. I argue for the integration of the critique of biopolitical effects and their counter-discourses into queer critique. Foucault used the concept of biopower / biopolitics to describe a competitive life-or-death rationale in the biopolitically regulated state, which claims that either "we" or the "others" (but not both) could survive. This counts for both capitalist and socialist competitive regimes (Foucault 1997). Consequently, in such a society only the body which makes profit has a value. The weak or ill body as well as dissident sexuality are enemies within the collective body. Individual and collective reproduction are intertwined. The other human body is understood as a racialized, essentialized "other".

Under neoliberal conditions there is a shift within the nation state. Homonationalism, for example, (REF e.g., Puar 2007) describes the phenomenon that certain queer subjects – mostly financially well off – are included in the nation state granting certain rights (marriage, service in the army) on the costs of the construction of the presumed homophobic Muslim 'other'. That counts also for the acceptance of certain queer subjects in some Christian communities. Therefore, it is important not only to grant rights but to ensure they do not merely shift exclusions (Auga and Hawthorne 2017).

4.2 Queer Theology and Precarious Postcolonial Sexualities

Queer Theology scrutinizes societal discourses to overcome heteronormativity and epistemic violence in dominant and liberation theologies and in society influenced by symbolic orders. The beginning of Queer Theology is especially connected with the late Argentinian theologian Marcella Althaus-Reid (2000, 2003). Althaus-Reid worked in the footsteps of classical theories of liberation in Latin America, combining them with queer theory. She applies Paulo Freire's *Pedagogy of the Oppressed*, which gives agency to marginalized people in grassroots communities in Latin America, to theology and uses this approach in marginalized contexts in Scotland. She claims that Queer Theology is an undertaking oriented toward base communities, be it in dissident medieval women's communities or in soup kitchens in Brazilian favelas staffed by transvestites. Queer Theology analyses how throughout the history of Christianity, excluded subjects try to achieve agency and self-representation, and how they actualise the Christian narrative through that process. Althaus-Reid writes (2000, 89): "It is a fight for representativity, for a person reading theology to be able to be interpellated by the text, that is, by saying 'it is me; I recognise myself in this situation.'"

Another important representative of Queer Theology is the Welsh theologian Lisa Isherwood. In her study *The Fat Jesus: Christianity and Body Image*, Isherwood (2008) deals with marginalized bodies: the overweight, poor, persons of color or with the body of the planet itself. She focuses on conservative Christian eschatologies and how they form alliances with neoliberal exploitation. She responds with creative resistance by re-reading forgotten theologumena such as *energeia*, *dynamis*, and *emanatio*. With Isherwood, it becomes clear again that Queer Theology has an interest in embodiment theory as well as in ecological and cosmological questions.

Also, Linn Marie Tonstad (2017) applies critical queer theory to theology. In her book *God and Difference*, she argues against difference feminisms and the subsuming of several identitarian LGBT theologies under Queer Theology.

5 Transgender Studies and Religion

Over the last twenty years Transgender Studies have increasingly come into focus (Stryker and Whittle 2006; Stryker and Aizura 2013). Melissa Wilcox (2020) offers an introduction to Queer and Transgender Studies in Religion. The international interdisciplinary research group Queering Paradigms, attached to the independent Intersectional Center for Inclusion and Social Justice, led by Bee Scherer publishes cutting-edge material. Scherer (2009–2020) focuses in particular on gender, sexuality, transgender theory and Buddhism.

6 Gender, Postcoloniality, and Religion

6.1 The History of Postcolonial Theory and Religion

In postcolonial contexts, there has been a great deal of suspicion of 'Western' missionaries and universalistic theologies. Concurrently, the religious practices of indigenous peoples have often been dismissed as 'superstitions' by the 'Western' canon. Many anti-colonial theories draw on Marxist ideas, set within an atheist philosophy. Nevertheless, throughout the history of resistance, there have always been alliances with theological approaches which were also resisting hegemonic imperial power structures. Until today, however, one can observe a certain sense of uncertainty or ambiguity in the relationship between postcolonial theory, feminist theory and religion.

On the one hand, this can be seen in the fact that religion often does not appear as a category of analysis in postcolonial theory. In addition, the understanding of religion is all too often based on essentialized, naturalized (fundamentalist) framings, rather than contextualized through a deconstructionist analysis. However, the relationship between religion and post-colonial theory is shifting. Religion is no longer seen as mainly a place of patriarchal violence but also more as enabling agency and human flourishing.

Today, the connection between Gender Studies and Postcolonial Studies is very close and influences the study of religion. The deciphering of epistemic violence and with it the de-essentialization of categories is a crucial task in the scholarship of Edward Said and Gayatri Chakravorty Spivak, and a major strategy in postcolonial theory per se. Said criticizes the construction of the essentialized 'other' as a violent act known as 'othering'. Essentialism reduces and 'others' the subject (Isherwood and Harris 2013; Quiros 2011). It presumes an (inferior) ontological subject a priori (Holliday, Kulmann, and Hyde 2010, 2). This essentialization is often connected with categories of knowledge through which 'nation', 'ethnicity', 'race', 'class', 'gender', 'ability', and 'religion' are characterised as homogenising descriptions of a group. Notions of group 'identity' are in danger of falling into the trap of 'othering' and becoming essentializing concepts.

Another important concept addressed in postcolonial theory is that of individual and collective representation. Spivak discusses the position of the subaltern (woman), who cannot speak and represent herself because of the epistemic violence of colonial discourse endemic in legal structures and in patriarchal formations of local traditions. However, to speak *for* somebody can be an act of objectification if the agency of the oppressed subject is not acknowledged.

Spivak's critique of epistemic violence is highly relevant for theology (Moore and Rivera 2011). However, her essentialist notion of religion remains problematic (Auga 2015, 49–68).

As for research in theology, Kwok Pui-lan (1995, 40) argues that it is determined by 'Western', white, male perceptions of the 'correct' understanding of the text. The relationship between Europe's colonial expansion and the historical-critical method is not made transparent (Pui-lan 2006, 62). Some critics claim that the historical-critical method itself subjugated 'local' readings of biblical texts which are based on different understandings of history or a different relationship between politics and religion. Elisabeth Schüssler Fiorenza argues along the same lines that the question surrounding this method is a battle about domination in an as such unjust academic system (Fiorenza 1992, 180).

In her book *Toward a Postcolonial Feminist Interpretation of the Bible*, Musa Dube (2000, 15) highlights how the Christian biblical religion has been "unique in its imperial sponsorship". She goes on to describe the way in which the Bible emerged in a colonial context and has been used for the purposes of subjugation up until today, but that at the same time, it also contains anti-colonial strands that go beyond its colonializing influence. Dube also discusses postcoloniality, ethics, and feminism. She shows the influence of religion and biblical interpretation on African women and their oppression. Together with indigenous religions, Christianity in many parts of Africa still supports patriarchal systems. Dube (2002, 100–120) tries to decolonize religious practices with hybrid strategies and hybrid spaces. The term hybridity is widely used in postcolonial theory. According to Homi Bhabha – who introduced the notion of hybridity to describe the margin where different cultural contexts come into contact with the aim to unsettle all stable identities that are constructed around oppositions such as inclusion or exclusion – hybridity offers a release from singular identities and essentializations around race, class, nation or gender. Bhabha underlines the value of a continuous being 'in-between-spaces' and hybridization of all cultural contexts (1994).

The field of systematic or dogmatic theology is criticized because as a coherent dogmatic system it often carries exclusive, universalist structures. Today, these fields are further developed as 'constructive theology' by theologians like Sallie McFague, Catherine Keller, Serene Jones, Stefanie Knauss, Laurel Schneider, and others (Jones and Lakeland 2005). Their focus reaches beyond truth claims about the interpretation of dogmatic sentences, looking at theological and ethical issues from an individual perspective and experience, and discussing issues such as the question of the survival of the world facing environmental problems, of love under globalized conditions, of trauma in a violated world, or the inclusion of visual arts in theological approaches in search of new open languages.

6.2 Postcolonial Imagination, Multitude, and the Critique of Neoliberalism

Kwok Pui-lan (2010) has been an important voice since the beginnings of postcolonial theology. She stresses the necessity of a postcolonial imagination and how this is especially relevant for theology. The questions she shares with the work of Janet Jakobsen and Teresa Forcades i Vila are: How will we, as feminist theorists, philosophers, theologians, and ethicists living in a postcolonial world, deal with neoliberalism in the future? What is our vision for society?

The perception of the public sphere and resistance within it is changing in decisive ways (Chatterjee 2004; Appadurai 2013). This has influenced the emergence of the field of public theology as a further development of political and liberation theology. Here faith-based protest, as well as biopolitics and counter-discourses to empire, come to the fore.

Mayra Rivera's work draws on Latin American Studies and poststructuralism (Rivera 2007; Keller, Nausner, and Rivera 2004). Her essay *A Labyrinth of Incarnations: The Social Materiality of Bodies* (2014) connects traditional (feminist) liberation theologies with insights from poststructuralist philosophy and postcolonial theory. Furthermore, it draws on the theoretical turns towards materiality and affect for developing a theology of corporality beyond the 'body'. Rivera suggests that the explorations of social-material incarnations should characterize a new phase in theologies of the body. She suggests concepts for future interpretations which could overcome the epistemic violence attached to notions of the 'body', which has been sexualized, racialized, and perfectionized able body in dominant societal and theological discourses.

7 Gender and Postsecular Theory

Contrary to mainstream research, José Casanova contradicts the assumption of an indissoluble connection between secularization and modernity as well as the prognosis of a loss of importance for churches (Casanova 1994). The idea that religion would fade turned out to be false. Rather, new ideas of the concept of religion and secularity have been generated (Jakobsen and Pellegrini 2008). In the postcolonial context it becomes particularly clear that a new discursive concept of religion and secularity is needed. In addition, the focus is on the connection between religion and agency. Within postcolonial and postsecular theory, religion and secularity can be understood as discursive categories. In addition – against previous reservations – subjective deessentialized religious experiences can be conceptualized as a contribution to the radical social imaginary and to the establishment of a society based on connections of solidary (Auga 2020, 45–244, 314–339).

Tomoku Masuzawa (2005) shows in *The Invention of World Religions* that the concept of secularity arises in 'Western' thinking to defend a binary of secularity versus religion.

Saba Mahmood's (1962–2018) study *Politics of Piety: The Islamic Revival and the Feminist Subject* (2012) became a turning point in several debates on religion. In her anthropological study of grassroots piety movements in Cairo, Mahmood questions secular-liberal principles as a goal of resistance. One conclusion of her investigation is that the women in these movements receive their subject formation, agency, and human flourishing beyond 'Western' (feminist) values of freedom and autonomy. In this way, Mahmood expands Foucault's notion of discourses of resistance and Butler's views on performativity. She emphasizes that power to act can also be developed in the exercise of norms and not just in resistance to dominant discourses. Consequently, religion must also be understood as a practice that opens new possibilities and can enable agency. As a result of these debates within interdisciplinary feminist and postcolonial resistance, the focus has shifted from representation to subject formation, agency, and human flourishing.

Postcolonial scholars including Talal Asad and Saba Mahmood formed an alliance with deconstructivist feminist theorists including Wendy Brown and Judith Butler via a research forum at the University of Berkeley, which published some of their debates. They opposed portraying the secularized 'West' as being more enlightened than most of the world and all religions, and Christianity as being 'more rational' than Islam, and questioned the secularism of analysis, criticism, epistemology and science of the 'Western' academy. The answer to the question 'Is Criticism Secular?' given by Asad, Butler, Brown, and Mahmood was negative. Indeed, they showed how religious practices and the concept of religion can be places where new knowledge can arise (Asad, Brown, Butler, and Mahmood 2009). The epistemic subordination of the category of religion is a legacy from Marx which has been carried forward in the early theorizations of Jürgen Habermas and Gayatri Chakravorty Spivak (Auga 2020; 2018, 92–115; Auga and Schirr 2014, 37–54).

Another possible fruitful approach is to study gender and religion as categories within the analysis of the broader concept of diversity, as theorized by Monika Salzbrunn. To understand religious and ethnic minorities in contemporary urban complexities the interdependence of gender and religion is central (Reuschke, Salzbrunn, and Schönhärl 2013).

8 Conclusion

In my research, I specify the epistemological positioning of religion and gender. In gender research, gender as a discursive performative category has been released from the assumption of an essentialized, natural, identitarian core. In cultural theory, the modern concepts of culture, nation, etc. were seen to have been imagined, essentialized and naturalized (Anderson 1996; Hobsbawm and Ranger 1983). In gender research, the construction of gender is understood as intersectionally overlapping with the categories of race, nation, class, ability. I add religion to this debate as an intersectional category and developed religion as 'situated knowledge' following Donna Haraway (Auga 2020, 1–32; Haraway 1988, 575–599). In my approach, gender, religion, and secularity are understood not only as social and historical categories of analysis, but also as categories of knowledge production. Thus, the epistemic violence that threatens through essentialization, naturalization, "othering" and exclusion, can be averted.

Finally, I would like to mention some new developments. Historically, some strands of theology have operated rather 'material-phobically.' Protestant Christianity in particular has imparted upon theology a privilege of the soul over the body and belief over practice, in line with the difference between a disembodied God and the inanimate world. Like all other human, social, and natural sciences, religious studies imported these theological dualisms into a purportedly secular modernity, mapping them onto the distinction between a 'rational', 'enlightened' Europe on the one hand and an 'emotional', 'traditional' and 'animist' non-Europe on the other.

The New Materialisms currently flowing through cultural, feminist, political, and queer theories seek to displace human privilege by attending to the agency of matter itself. Far from being passive or inert, they show us that matter acts, creates, destroys, and transforms – and, as such, is more processual (Haraway 2016; Barad 2007; Braidotti 2013).

What is matter, how does it materialise, and what kind of universe or sorts of worlds are enacted in its varied entanglements with divinity? While both theology and religious studies have over the past few decades come to prioritise the material contexts and bodily ecologies of more-than-human life, recent debates have set forth a multi-vocal conversation between religious studies, theology, and the body of New Materialism. In response to this mutual connectedness, the growing complexity of our entanglements takes on a consistent ethical texture of urgency (Keller and Rubenstein 2017). While theorists of materialism often assume that science and religious thought are at odds, work has begun which demonstrates that a sophisticated understanding of theology and religion enriches our understanding of materiality in its full liveliness and complexity. A focus on materiality, in turn, alters and enriches theologies.

Bibliography

Althaus-Reid, Marcella. 2000. *Indecent Theology: Theological Perversions in Sex, Gender and Politics*. London: Routledge.
Althaus-Reid, Marcella. 2003. *The Queer God*. London: Routledge.
Anderson, Benedict. 1996. *Imagined Communities: Reflections on the Origins and Spread of Nationalism*. London: Verso.
Anzaldúa, Gloria. 1987. *Borderlands / La Frontera: The New Mestiza*. San Francisco: Aunt Lute Books.
Appadurai, Arjun. 2013. *The Future as Cultural Fact: Essays on the Global Condition*. London / New York: Verso.
Asad, Talal, Wendy Brown, Judith Butler, and Saba Mahmood. 2009. *Is Critique Secular? Blasphemy, Injury, and Free Speech*. Berkeley: University of California Press.
Auga, Ulrike E. 2018. "Dekolonisierung des öffentlichen Raumes: Eine Herausforderung von Bonhoeffers und Spivaks Konzepten von Widerstand, Religion und Geschlecht." In *Postkoloniale Theologien II: Perspektiven aus dem deutschsprachigen Raum*, edited by Andreas Nehring and Simon Wiesgickl, Stuttgart: Kohlhammer, 92–115.
Auga, Ulrike E. 2020. *An Epistemology of Religion and Gender: Biopolitics – Performativity – Agency*. London / New York: Routledge.

Auga, Ulrike, and Bertram Schirr. 2014 "'Do not Conform to the Patterns of this World': A Postcolonial Investigation of Performativity, Metamorphoses, and Bodily Materiality in Romans 12." *Feminist Theology* 23:37–54.

Auga, Ulrike E., and Sian M. Hawthorne. 2017. "Homonationalism and the Challenge of Queer Theology." In *Gender: God*. Macmillan Interdisciplinary Handbooks: Gender Series, edited by Sian M. Hawthorne, Farmington Hills: Macmillan Reference USA, 367–383.

Austin, John L. 1962. *How to Do Things with Words: The William James Lectures Delivered at Harvard University in 1955*. Oxford: Oxford University Press.

Beauvoir, Simone de. [1949] 1989. *The Second Sex*, trans. H. M. Parshley. New York: Vintage.

Beauvoir, Simone de. 1992. *The Force of Circumstance*. New York: Paragon House.

Bhabha, Homi K. 1994. *The Location of Culture*. London and New York: Routledge.

Braidotti, Rosi. 2013. *The Posthuman*. Cambridge: Polity Press.

Brooten, Bernadette. 1996. *Love Between Women: Early Christian Responses to Female Homoeroticism*. Chicago: Chicago University Press.

Brown, Wendy. 1995. *States of Injury: Power and Freedom in Late Modernity*. Princeton: Princeton University Press.

Buell, Denise K. 2001. "Rethinking the Relevance of Race for Early Christian Self-Definition." *The Harvard Theological Review* 94:449–476.

Butler, Judith. 1990. *Gender Trouble: Feminism and the Subversion of Identity*. London: Routledge.

Butler, Judith. 1993. *Bodies That Matter*. New York: Routledge.

Butler, Judith. 2000. *Undoing Gender*. New York: Routledge.

Casanova, José. 1994. *Public Religions in the Modern World*. Chicago: University of Chicago Press.

Chatterjee, Partha. 2004. *The Politics of the Governed: Reflections on Popular Politics in Most of the World*. New York: Columbia University Press.

Crenshaw, Kimberlé. 1989. "Demarginalizing the Intersection of Race and Sex: A Black Feminist Critique of Antidiscrimination Doctrine, Feminist Theory and Antiracist Politics." *University of Chicago Legal Forum* 1:139–167.

Davis, Angela. 1981. *Women, Race and Class*. New York: Random House.

Dube, Musa W. 2002. "Postcoloniality, Feminist Spaces, and Religion." In *Postcolonialism, Feminism and Religious Discourse*, edited by Laura Donaldson, and Kwok Pui-lan, New York / London: Routledge, 100–122.

Dube, Musa W. 2000. *Postcolonial Feminist Interpretation of the Bible*. St. Louis: Christian Board of Publication.

Essed, Philomena. 1991. *Understanding Everyday Racism: An Interdisciplinary Theory*. Thousand Oaks: SAGE Publications.

Ferguson, Roderick A. 2004. *Aberrations in Black: Toward a Queer of Color Critique*. Minneapolis: University of Minnesota Press.

Ferguson, Roderick A. 2005. "Racing Homonormativity: Citizenship, Sociology and Gay Identity." In *Black Queer Studies: A Critical Anthology*, edited by Johnson Patrick and Mae G. Henderson, Durham: Duke University Press, 52–67.

Foucault, Michel. 1970. *The Order of Things: An Archaeology of the Human Sciences*. New York: Pantheon Books.

Foucault, Michel. 1990. *The History of Sexuality. An Introduction*. Vol. 1. New York: Random House.

Foucault, Michel. 1997. *Il faut défendre la société: Cours au Collège de France 1975–1976*. Paris: Seuil.

Foucault, Michel. 2014. *On the Government of the Living: Lectures at the Collège de France 1979–1980*.

Hagemann-White, Carol. 1984. *Sozialisation: Weiblich-männlich?* Opladen: Leske / Budrich.

Hancock, Ange-Marie. 2007. "Intersectionality as a Normative and Empirical Paradigm." *Politics and Gender* 3:248–254.

Haraway, Donna J. 1988. "Situated Knowledges: The Science Question in Feminism and the Privilege of a Partial Perspective." *Feminist Studies* 14:575–599.
Haraway, Donna J. 2016. *Staying with the Trouble: Making Kin in the Chthulucene. Experimental Futures.* Durham: Duke University Press.
Hobsbawm, Eric, and Terence Ranger. 1983. *The Invention of Tradition.* Cambridge: Cambridge University Press.
Holliday, Adrian, John Kullman, and Martin Hyde. 2010. *Intercultural Communication: An Advanced Resource Book.* London: Routledge.
Hull, Gloria T., Patricia Bell-Scott, and Barbara Smith, eds. 1993. *But Some of us Are Brave: All the Women Are White, All the Blacks Are Men: Black Women's Studies.* New York: The Feminist Press at CUNY.
Isherwood, Lisa, and David Harris. 2013. *Radical Otherness: Sociological and Theological Approaches.* Durham: Acumen.
Isherwood, Lisa. 2008. *The Fat Jesus: Christianity and Body Image.* London: Seabury Books.
Jakobsen, Janet R., and Ann Pellegrini, eds. 2008. *Secularisms.* Durham: Duke University Press.
Jones, Serene, and Paul Lakeland, eds. 2005. *Constructive Theology: A Contemporary Approach to Classical Themes.* Minneapolis: Fortress Press.
Keller, Cathrine, and Mary Rubenstein, eds. 2017. *Entangled Worlds: Religion, Science, and New Materialisms.* Transdisciplinary Theological Colloquia. New York: Fordham University Press.
Keller, Cathrine, Michael Nausner, and Mayra Rivera, eds. 2004. *Postcolonial Theologies: Divinity and Empire.* Atlanta: Chalice Press.
Kimber Buell, Denise. 2001. "Rethinking the Relevance of Race for Early Christian Self-Definition." *The Harvard Theological Review* 94:449–476.
Kwok, Pui-lan. 1995. *Discovering the Bible in a Non-biblical World.* Maryknoll: Orbis.
Kwok, Pui-lan. 2005. *Postcolonial Imagination and Feminist Theology.* Louisville: John Knox Press.
Kwok, Pui-lan, ed. 2010. *Hope Abundant: Third World and Indigenous Women's Theology.* Maryknoll: Orbis Books.
Laqueur, Thomas W. 1990. *Making Sex: Body and Gender from the Greeks to Freud.* Cambridge, MA: Harvard University Press.
Mahmood, Saba. 2012. *Politics of Piety: The Islamic Revival and the Feminist Subject.* Princeton: Princeton University Press.
Masuzawa, Tomoko. 2005. *The Invention of World Religions or, How European Universalism Was Preserved in the Language of Pluralism.* Chicago: University of Chicago Press.
Maurer, Margarete. 2002. "Sexualdimorphismus, Geschlechterkonstruktion und Hirnforschung." In *Wie natürlich ist Geschlecht? Gender und die Konstruktion von Natur und Technik,* edited by Ursula Pasero and Anja Gottburgsen, Wiesbaden: VS Verlag für Sozialwissenschaften, 65–108.
McClintock, Anne, Phillip B., José E. Muñoz, and Trish Rosen, eds. 1997. In *Queer Transexions of Race, Nation, and Gender.* Social Text. Duke University Press: Durham, 52–53.
Muñoz, José E. 1999. *Disidentifications: Queers of Color and the Performance of Politics.* Minneapolis: University of Minnesota Press.
Puar, Jasbir. 2007. *Terrorist Assemblages: Homonationalism in Queer Times.* Durham: Duke University Press.
Quiros, Luis. 2011. *An Other's Mind.* Bloomington: Author House.
Reuschke, Darja, Monika Salzbrunn, and Korinna Schönhärl, eds. 2013. *The Economies of Urban Diversity: Ruhr Area and Istanbul.* London: Palgrave Macmillan.
Rivera, Mayra. 2007. *The Touch of Transcendence: A Postcolonial Theology of God.* Westminster: John Knox.
Rivera, Mayra. 2014. "A Labyrinth of Incarnations: The Social Materiality of Bodies." *Journal of the European Society of Women in Theological Research* 22:187–198.

Scherer, Bee, ed. 2009–2020. *Queering Paradigms Series*. Oxford: Peter Lang.
Schüssler Fiorenza, Elisabeth. 1992. *But she Said: Feminist Practices of Biblical Interpretation*. Boston: Beacon.
Scott, Joan Wallach. 1986. "Gender: A Useful Category of Historical Analysis." *The American Historical Review* 91:1053–1075.

Scott, Joan Wallach. 1996. *Only Paradoxes to Offer: French Feminism and the Rights of Men*. Cambridge, MA: Harvard University Press.
Stryker, Susan, and Aren Z. Aizura, eds. 2013. *The Transgender Studies Reader*. Vol. 2, London / New York: Routledge.
Stryker, Susan, and Stephen Whittle, eds. 2006. *The Transgender Studies Reader*. Vol. 1, London / New York: Routledge.
Sweetapple, Christopher, ed. 2018. *The Queer Intersectional in Contemporary Germany: Essays on Racism, Capitalism and Sexual Politics*. Gießen: Psychosozial Verlag.
Voss, Heinz-Jürgen. 2010. *Making Sex Revisited: Dekonstruktion des Geschlechts aus biologisch-medizinischer Perspektive*. Bielefeld: Transcript.
Voss, Heinz-Jürgen. 2012a. "Sex in the Making – A Biological Approach." In *Double Blind*, edited by Marion Denis, Berlin: Revolver Publishing, 90–99.
Voss, Heinz-Jürgen. 2012b. *Intersexualität – Intersex: Eine Intervention*. Münster: Unrast.
Voss, Heinz-Jürgen. 2013. *Geschlecht: Wider die Natürlichkeit*. Stuttgart: Schmetterling Verlag.
Wilcox, Melissa. 2020. *Queer Religiosities: An Introduction to Queer and Transgender Studies in Religion*. Lanham / Boulder: Rowman & Littlefield.
Yuval-Davis, Nira. 1997. *Gender and Nation*. Thousand Oaks: SAGE Publications.

R. Ruard Ganzevoort
Cultural Hermeneutics of Religion

1 Introduction

If religion is understood as a cultural and culturally embedded phenomenon and if practical theology is understood as a culturally sensitive and contextual reflection, then a hermeneutical approach is at the heart of the practical theological endeavour. This chapter explores this hermeneutical character and places it in a transcultural and transreligious context. The chapter focuses on lived religion in culture and sees the formalised and institutionalised traditions from the vantage point of people's practices and experiences. Firstly, I position myself within the field of practical theology and discuss various layers of culture and lived religion. Then I attend to the specifics of a hermeneutical approach. Lastly, I ask what this implies for practical theology as cultural hermeneutics, offering the concrete example of the European public discourse on refugees.

2 Practical Theology

As it quickly becomes clear from the contributions in this volume, there is a wide variety of what counts as practical theology. In previous research in which I undertake a survey of the discipline at that moment in time (Ganzevoort 2009), I suggest that beneath the different and competing approaches to practical theology and the distinct parameters on which they rest, a clear, common ground can be discerned. The common ground is in my view the understanding of practical theology as the *Hermeneutics of Lived Religion*.

I define *religion* as the transcending patterns of action and meaning embedded in and contributing to the relation with the sacred (Sremac and Ganzevoort 2019). Transcending here means not limited to the specific situation but reaching 'beyond' or responding to what is experienced as coming from 'beyond' (Ganzevoort 2006). This primarily functional definition seeks to avoid both false negatives – excluding new and idiosyncratic forms of religiosity due to a bias toward established traditions – and false positives – including traditional forms of religion even when there is in fact little transcending momentum or relation with the sacred. The relation with the sacred, however understood or culturally construed, is at the heart of practical theology. The focus on *lived* religion distinguishes practical theology methodologically

---

Note: Valuable comments to earlier versions were given by Marianne Moyaert, Johan Roeland, and Srdjan Sremac.

from other theological disciplines. Whereas other disciplines take 'text' or 'idea' to be the primary object of analysis, practical theology focuses on praxis (Ganzevoort and Roeland 2014). Obviously, these materials overlap and intersect – praxis includes and refers to texts and ideas, and vice versa – but the primary focus determines the methodologies and the perspective (and vice versa). The hermeneutical dimension, crucial to any theological approach in my view, will be discussed in more detail below.

On this common ground of practical theology, many different versions of practical theology have been developed, based on the different choices on four parameters (Ganzevoort 2009): 1) the *object*, running the gamut from religious clergy through the faith community and the religious traditions to culture and society; 2) the *method*, approaching praxis empirically, phenomenologically, critically, constructively, or dialogically; 3) the role of the *researcher* as participant, consultant, referee, or observer; and 4) the *audience*, being primarily the academy, the church, or society (Tracy 1981). Although the usage of term 'practical theology is commonly restricted to (Western) Christianity, scholars from other religious backgrounds have explored how it can also function to describe parallel approaches in their context (Carter 2018; Isgandarova 2014; Trinlae 2014).

My own approach to practical theology is of course influenced by my own social location. I was raised in a protestant, middle-class, Dutch, intellectual environment. I have lived in different locations in both the Netherlands and Surinam. I have worked as a church minister, academic, academic administrator, hotel owner, and politician (and usually simultaneously). I have worked and lived with colleagues, students, friends, and partners from different cultural and religious backgrounds – and am myself inspired by several of those. I am a father of six and a grandfather of five and I identify as gay (and increasingly as middle-aged). I have experienced great joys as well as intense grief. In other words: I cannot be categorised by simple labels, as probably nobody can. I am privileged in some respects and disadvantaged in others. I can only acknowledge the fact that my perspective is multi-layered, inconsistent, and not universal and that my particular vantage point can and should always be critiqued.

This awareness has contributed significantly to my social-constructionist perspective in practical theology (Ganzevoort 2004, 2006). Meaning and truth are ingrained in social interactions and dependent on culturally determined understandings and power relations. I will develop this topic further in the sections below.

3 Culture, Lived Religion, and the Sacred

It is not the intention of this chapter to provide an in-depth discussion on the concept of culture. My broad and plural understanding of culture incorporates two particular types of differences. On the one hand my conceptualisation includes what we usually call 'intercultural' encounters, for example between people from Europe, Africa, and Asia (Lartey 2006). As mobility and migration increase, more and more contexts are becoming internally diverse, challenging notions of multiculturalism and interculturalism (Elias and Mansouri 2020) and moving into a situation of religious and cultural superdiversity, especially in post-secular cities. Although all these concepts are contested (Sealy 2018), they commonly point to the cultural differences rooted in different societies.

The second notion of difference refers to the differences between so-called high culture, popular culture, and folk culture. Although these categories can and should critiqued, they offer a helpful theoretical model to reflect on cultural expressions. These three connected but distinguishable cultural repertoires co-exist in many cultural contexts and interact across those contexts (Lynch 2005). High culture circles around original cultural creations with identifiable authors (like Bach's cantatas or Garcia Marquez's novels). Folk culture refers to traditional, often local, expressions, handed down the generations (including local crafts and decoration styles). Popular culture is characterised by mediation and usually has strong appeal in very diverse contexts. These distinctions should not be taken as absolute but as a lens to understand cultural dynamics. When the souvenir shop at the Louvre museum sells Mona Lisa coffee mugs, high culture moves into popular culture. When artists make innovative creations using traditional Aboriginal techniques, folk culture moves into high culture. And so on. Religion can be expressed in all three of these dimensions and in their interactions.

Both types of cultural differences and their intersections are relevant for a transcultural approach to practical theology. It is a simplification to assume that the intercultural differences are more fundamental than the differences between high, folk, and popular culture, especially in a globalised world. The cultural elites in many contexts share a preference for globalised high culture, especially when it represents the historical Western repertoire, as found in museums, opera houses, and universities. Popular culture is perhaps even more proliferated across cultural contexts and in many contexts the appropriation of popular culture from elsewhere is a sign of being modern. This is equally true for the commercial success of McDonald's and Starbucks in emerging economies as it is for western youth cultures embracing Eastern meditation and Caribbean or Africanised music styles. In the field of religion, clear examples of this globalised influence are the popular culture-based worship style of Hillsong, originating in Australia and now popular in many non-western countries (Klaver 2021), or the more classical shapes of Orthodox liturgy attended by post-secular westerners (Herbel 2014).

Religion is in my view a specific part of culture and of these cultural differences and repertoires. My definition used the phrase "patterns of action and meaning" which refer to this broader definition of culture. The specifying element is the relation with the sacred. This relatively open term can be defined by a particular tradition or take an idiosyncratic shape, but it at least represents a centre around which one's life gravitates and a presence that evokes awe and passion. This is not a matter of value judgement: the sacred – and one's relation with it – can be life-giving and creative, or it can be toxic and destructive. The question whether for example soccer fandom can count as religion, can now be answered in a nuanced way: for a particular fan it can certainly take on these religious qualities of a relationship with what is sacred, although for many it will just be pleasure. Similarly, however, traditional practices like attending prayers in the mosque or temple can be religious but are not necessarily so.

Lived religion refers to what people – alone or together – experience, do, and construe in their relationship with the sacred. The repertoires of the cultural and religious traditions facilitate them by providing narratives and rituals, prescribed behaviours, and material forms and places. The concrete practices that can be studied in practical theology are therefore by definition the outcome of complex and multilayered negotiations of the actors with the available repertoires, the normative audiences they encounter, their understandings of the sacred, and so on. An example may serve to demonstrate this.

In a qualitative study among young Dutch and bicultural women who got pregnant before their 20th birthday, we explored how young women navigate the moral arena when they are confronted with a teenage pregnancy and which role the embodiment of pregnancy plays in the construction of social meanings (Cense and Ganzevoort 2019). Normative discourses influence the stories these young women tell about their pregnancies. Social, cultural, and religious norms play an important role in the construction of the meaning of their teenage pregnancies, but so do their embodied experiences. One woman explained: "I went through a very difficult period. So, although my boyfriend did not agree, I had an abortion. My parents still do not know. They would find it horrible if they ever found out. My boyfriend and I had a lot of conflicts over it, but well, in the end it was me who had to choose as it was in my body. It was a hard decision to make, as I am a Christian myself. To tell you the truth I felt I did not have the right [...]. And I was afraid I would regret it later. But when I look back now, I feel sorry, but I also feel it was the right thing to do for me then."

To understand this woman's story, it doesn't suffice to ask for 'the' Christian view of abortion or the liberal Western perspective on self-determination. The concrete outcome and the meaning this has in her story has to do with the complexities of her biography, the normative framework of her parents and her boyfriend, the moral repertoire of her Christian tradition, and so on. We described this as the storyscape in which she finds herself, the multi-layered narrative world provided by her polyvalent social context. This storyscape consists of narrative repertoires and cultural normativity present in the story as well as in the audience. The narrator is constantly navigating this storyscape, that is: negotiating possible meanings that can account for her experienced reality vis-à-vis her audience (Ganzevoort 2017b). What is at stake in this woman's story is her sense of purpose and identity, her commitment to her tradition, her view that she did not have the right to have an abortion, and so on. All these elements can be indications of what is sacred to her. All of them are strongly related to the cultural and religious context in which she navigates her story. To understand her story then, is to understand what precisely is sacred to her – and to those around her – and how she engages with that.

This is not only the case for the extraordinary instances of intense suffering or moral dilemmas. It also holds for much more common everyday practices and experiences. We can assume to know what it means to have one's new-born baptised or circumcised by asking for the normative theological views of one's tradition, or the formal views of academic theologians. However, these may be different from the espoused (what people say they believe and do) and operant (what they actually believe and do) theologies (Ward 2017). Religious post-birth rituals may have multiple possible meanings, for example, of divine grace, gratitude, obedience, joining the covenant, testifying to one's faith, strengthening the community, fear of social disapproval, magical protection, family customs, or something else entirely. Whether the significance of the praxis is related to the sacred or not, cannot be decided beforehand.

Lived religion is culturally embedded, just as the sacred texts and places in religious traditions are embedded in their cultural context. It is usually easier to see to what degree specific religious practices are culturally determined when that culture is further removed from one's own in time or space. Many European or American protestants may feel that an African ecstatic worship service with drums, dancing, and spiritual trance for example, is more culturally defined than their own quiet sitting in the pews listening to a sermon. Both, however, are cultural patterns determining body postures and movements that directly affect our limbic system and foster particular experiences that are construed as religious. For this reason, Tweed (2006, 54) refers in his definition of religions to "organic-cultural flows that intensify joy and confront suffering." His definition further speaks of human and suprahuman forces and describes the aim of religions as "[making] homes and [crossing] boundaries".

This 'crossing and dwelling', as Tweed calls it, is an important final dimension of cultural dynamics and especially of the religious dimension of culture. Religion, in a Durkheimian sense, is one of the fundamental social institutions, providing structure and a sense of collective consciousness. It allows for humans to build a socially inhabitable world, which means: a place where they can dwell. Religion also offers the elements to symbolise this dwelling, including ritual times and spaces that differentiate the sacred from the profane. But religion does not only support the dwelling-character of culture; it also challenges its structures and status quo by crossing boundaries and inviting individuals to break out of prescribed norms and behaviours. Examples here are religious trance, carnivals, and pilgrimages. Often these two roles of religion are connected. Pilgrimages, for instance, are movements (crossings) towards a specific place (dwellings). Sometimes their connection remains ambivalent. Monasteries are places of dwelling for the monks but crossings for the visitors. Religion, in sum, validates cultural structures and values but also challenges them, and it takes a nuanced and critical reading of religious and other cultural practices to understand them.

4 Hermeneutics of Force and Meaning

Precisely this search for understanding is the essence of the hermeneutical approach. Its starting point is the hermeneutical awareness that a full and direct understanding of the other – be it a text or another person – is not possible because we have no complete access to the intentions and the inherent layers of meaning. This awareness is denied in some romanticising or fundamentalist naïve circles but is commonly accepted in the field of practical theology (Brown 2012).

As a theory of interpretation, hermeneutics was originally applied primarily to ancient texts so that it could also be understood as the theory of exegesis. With Schleiermacher, Dilthey and others, the focus broadened to include the intentions of the author as well as the historical context of the text. Gadamer's interest in the role of the reader in construing meaning so that the text-reader interaction became a central point of attention, added another perspective. More importantly for practical theology, however, has been the contribution of Paul Ricoeur, who articulated how meaningful action can be interpreted as a text (Ricoeur 1981). He shows that – similar to texts – actions, once performed, take on a meaning that is partially independent from the actor and their intentions. The significance of the action stretches beyond the original situation, making it a kind of 'open work' of which the meaning remains undecided because each observer can add their own, new interpretations.

This focus on text has been criticised because it can easily downplay embodied dimensions. A textual reductionism can become too cognitivist and distort our view of the essential dynamics of religions as if they are primarily about texts and ideas. Moyaert (2017) acknowledges the risk of this 'textualisation' of the world when the metaphor of action as text becomes too dominant but argues that the model is still helpful to understand symbolic mediation in ritual action. She claims that Ricoeur's fundamental combination of distanciation and appropriation is present not only in the cognitive mode of reading a text but also in the embodied, physical mode of participating in ritual. This broadening of the model is necessary to make it useful for an analysis of the material/physical dimensions of lived religion.

To understand the practices of lived religion, we need a hermeneutical approach that accounts for cultural embeddedness and intercultural differences. A helpful distinction in that regard is found in the threefold *mimesis* as Ricoeur (1984–1988) calls it, building on Aristotle. The first mimesis is the *prefiguration* or the 'world behind the text'. This includes the pre-understandings, intentions, and competences of the author and the reader (or the actor and the audience) and their cultural backgrounds. The second mimesis is the *configuration* or the 'world in the text'. This includes the content, structure, symbolism, and everything that is part of the text or the praxis itself. The third mimesis is the *refiguration* or the 'world in front of the text'. This includes the possibilities that are presented to the reader and that (s)he can envision, contemplate, and respond to.

With this threefold mimesis, the possible meanings of every practice can be gauged in these three worlds. When asking about the meaning of a movie, for example, we can read interviews with the director or the actors to establish their intentions or compare the movie to the book or the events it may be based on. We can also focus on the movie itself by analysing the structure, narrative, use of camera, light, and music, internal references, and recurring symbols and metaphors. Or we can interview the audience to find out how the movie affects people. There is no necessary priority for one of these meanings as if the 'true' meaning of the practice is found in either the intentions, or the action itself, or its effects. Obviously, one may prefer one of those, just like one may prefer an ethical approach that highlights the intentions, the factual action, or the consequences. For a culturally sensitive hermeneutics of lived religion, it is necessary in my view to pay attention to all three and ask specifically about the concordances and discordances between them. If the audience reads something very different in the text, movie, or performance than the author, director, or performer intended, this is where fruitful conversations can commence. This juxtaposition will therefore serve to develop intercultural understanding because it allows the voices and interpretations of multiple sides to be heard.

It also challenges us to add a critical dimension to the encounter, or a hermeneutics of suspicion, following Ricoeur's depiction of the work of Marx, Freud, and Nietzsche. At this point, it is interesting to note Ricoeur's (1970) interpretation of Freud's semantics of desire, consisting of the two different languages of force and of meaning. This interpretation is an important element in the application of hermeneutics to practical theology, as Gerkin (1984) already pointed out, because it precludes an overly cognitivist or idealist approach to hermeneutics (or narrative for that matter). A critical hermeneutics should not only attend to meanings attributed to practices and experiences, but also to the interpersonal and structural power dynamics and the subconscious psychological forces and neurological processes, notably in the limbic functions of the human brain. Critical contributions based on this hermeneutics can be recognised in for example feminist, postcolonial, queer, and empire studies.

The importance of the critical hermeneutics of force and meaning becomes clear when we look at the concrete example of traumatic experiences incurred from structural violence like racism, a matter of much debate in decolonial discussions and the protests known as *Black Lives Matter* (Mitchell and Williams 2017). Notwithstanding contextual particularities which make the debate about race and power different in for example the United States, South Africa, or the Netherlands, the dynamics of force and meaning operate in each of these contexts. Given the historical background of slavery and injustice and the remaining social inequalities, it would be misleading to limit our interest only to the level of meanings and neglect the level of force. That would suggest that we can have a simple exchange of different views without acknowledging the differences in power and privilege that are the resultant of this historical background. Not acknowledging those differences in fact benefits the status quo and those privileged by it. Similarly, ignoring the traumatic effects and the forces of traumatisation affecting one's possibilities to think, speak, and act, constitutes new violence and injustice. The meanings attached to black and white bodies play out in the forces of structural power and violence available to each. The meanings attributed to that power, depend on the power positions of each actor, as can be seen in the contested terms like brutality, rioting, protest, and so on.

This critical hermeneutics of force and meaning is essential for the understanding of lived religion in its cultural context. It acknowledges the multiplicity of meanings which remain fundamentally open to reinterpretation. It allows for the various voices brought to the conversation to be heard. It also considers the contestation of these interpretations that are themselves subject to power, authority, and cultural dominance.

5 Practical Theological Hermeneutics of Culture

How do these insights contribute to a practical theological hermeneutics of culture? In other words, how do practical theologians deploy their perspective with regard to cultural and intercultural practices? In the remainder of this chapter, I will demonstrate this practical theological hermeneutics of culture by focusing on the specific case of the recent refugee crisis and especially the public discourse around it in Western Europe (Ganzevoort 2017a). This case provides interesting material because it concerns the encounter of cultures and religious traditions as well as cultural expressions on different levels. For this purpose, I consider media outlets and social media platforms as cultural practices that are produced, mediated, and consumed.

At the heart of the European refugee crisis is the Syrian civil war, which started in 2011. As a result, more than half of the 22 million population had to leave their homes. One quarter was internally displaced, and one quarter crossed into other countries where they applied for asylum or were forced to stay in refugee camps, especially in Turkey, Lebanon, and Jordan. In search of better chances, a substantial number tried to flee to Europe through the sea passage to Greece where the overcrowded camps on islands such as Lesbos became a symbol of the humanitarian disaster taking place. An icon of this narrative was the dramatic 2015 picture of three-year-old Alan Shenu (or 'Kurdi') whose body was found on the Turkish coast of Bodrum after he and most of his family drowned when the small inflatable and overcrowded boat they had been travelling in, capsized.

The public discourse responding to this crisis can be found in newspapers, television talk shows, and social media. Central actors are of course politicians and public influencers, but also spokespersons for humanitarian and religious organisations. The stories of the asylum seekers themselves are seldom heard (for an exeption see Derks and Sremac 2020).

The storyscapes emerging in this situation are highly contested and mutually excluding. On the one hand, the right-wing populist frame posits refugees as a threat to European society. They are generally assumed to be Muslim, overlooking the religious diversity among them or treating the Christian refugees as the only acceptable exceptions. The situation in their home country is downplayed, whether this is Syria or elsewhere. The conflicts and fires in reception camps are taken as evidence that they are uncivilised and dangerous. The risks they take by fleeing or boarding small boats with their children are seen as proof of their irresponsibility. The frame is exacerbated by politicians claiming that Islam is not a religion but a political ideology and that the "asylum-tsunami" is threatening our values, our welfare state, and our peaceful and tolerant society. Young male asylum refugees are portrayed as potential jihadi terrorists or at least a sexual danger for women and children, dubbed 'rapefugee' by anti-Islam-organisation PEGIDA. Al Jazeera (2016) reported:

> Dutch anti-immigrant politician Geert Wilders has handed out self-defence sprays to women fearful of what he described as "Islamic testosterone bombs". [...] The Freedom Party leader said that, if elected, he would "close the borders immediately and have no more asylum seekers. We just cannot afford to have more". "The Dutch people in a big majority don't want it. [...] It makes our people and women more unsafe," Wilders added.

Wilders and the likes play out a rhetorical trope well known from historical forms of racial and religious ostracization, especially targeting Black and Jewish men (Bonjour and Bracke 2020). This trope sees the refugee as the male, dominant, hypersexualised, animalistic, and violent intruder, and Europe as the pure, innocent, vulnerable woman. The female body, ostensibly protected by the politician with self-defence sprays, is a symbol for the body of the nation that should be protected from desecration and defamation.

The storyscape on the other side is no less explicit about the European values that need to be protected, but they identify an entirely different threat. For them, Europe is all about hospitality and inclusion and the influx of refugees as the victims of violence constitutes primarily a moral responsibility to offer care and protection. Here the storyscape is filled with historical tropes like the immigration of the Sephardic Jews in the 16th century and the Huguenots in the 17th and 18th. These groups were welcomed in Amsterdam and other cities proud of their religious freedom and equally eager to attract commercial and intellectual high-potentials, and bolster Dutch identity against the Spanish Catholic oppressor. In this idealised storyscape, cultural diversity is embraced, and the iconic refugee is a child. Centuries later, this storyscape results in the political decision to grant a general 'Children's Pardon' to young asylum seekers who matched certain criteria.

Based on my theoretical explorations in this chapter, we can now further probe into these two storyscapes from the perspective of practical theology as cultural hermeneutics of lived religion. This leads to the following observations, each warranting further research.

First, the competing storyscapes focus on cultural conflicts and values. One storyscape depicts this in the style of the clash of civilisations, the idea that conflicts after the cold war will be mostly cultural and religious by nature (Huntington 1996).

The other approaches it as an intercultural encounter in which the refugee is a migrant who makes the intercultural encounter possible. In both cases, there is a narrative of victims, perpetrators, and bystanders. The narrators differ on who is the real victim, but both narrators portray themselves as the saviour and protector of those victims (Ganzevoort 2017a). This application of the drama triangle turns the concrete issues into a value conflict that takes on cosmic proportions. It is no exaggeration to suggest that it has become a conflict about the question of what is sacred in Europe's identity.

Second, religion plays a significant role in these storyscapes. Not only are the refugees categorised as Muslims, but the European culture is in return portrayed as Judeo-Christian, sometimes adding the humanist and Enlightenment tradition (Nathan and Topolski 2016). Downplaying Europe's grim history of persecution of Jews and religious dissenters and the cruelties of colonialism, this self-identification based on religious heritage serves to build and uphold an image of tolerance and human rights as the quintessential nature of Europe (Kluveld 2016). Usually, this self-identification is more secular than religious and often it excludes Islam as 'the other'. It serves primarily to mark the boundaries of European cultural values and implies less of a return to or revaluation of the religious traditions themselves. The lived religion in which this narrative functions, is therefore also primarily a civil religion, as Bellah ([1967] 2005) described with reference to Rousseau. It aims to protect for example Christmas and Easter as European Christian feasts without much interest in the religious meanings that underpin them. It is important that shops and companies use the word Christmas rather than 'winter' in their advertisements, much more than any reference to Jesus.

Religion also plays a role in the competing storyscape of the pro-refugee movement. Although this movement consists of convinced atheists and agnostics as well as religious people, there are some remarkable cases of explicitly religiously inspired interventions. One of these cases is the "church asylum" that was offered from October 26th, 2018, until January 30th, 2019, in the Protestant Church of the Hague. Building on old traditions and the constitutional protection of religious worship against state interventions, the church held a continuous service with alternating preachers and worshippers that lasted 2,307 hours. During this time the Christian Armenian family Tamrazyan lived in the church building, protected by this ongoing worship. The family had come to the Netherlands as refugees and permission to stay had been granted to them, but the state kept appealing the decision to grant asylum. When their application to the Children's Pardon was denied and they were at the point of being evicted, the church stepped in and used its religious right (successfully) to protect this family and (unsuccessfully) to press the government to develop more welcoming policies. Although this church action was criticised by some as being too political, it was at least also a clear example of lived religion, using the traditional ecclesial institution and structures. Their daughter, Hayarpi, wrote a collection of mostly Christian poems that was published afterwards.

A kindred campaign was the initiative "We gaan ze halen" ("Let's bring them here"). In 2018 this crowdfunded grassroots movement, led by young post-evangelical theologians, bought a bus, and drove from the Netherlands to Greece to pick up asylum seekers and bring them to the Netherlands. In 2020 they rented an airplane and flew to Athens to collect 189 refugees from the burnt down refugee camp Moria on Lesbos. In both cases they had to return without a single refugee, but the campaigns attracted much media coverage and challenged the public opinion. The message of "We gaan ze halen" is never explicitly religious but instead foregrounds the language of human rights and European values, but the inspiration of the founders and many supporters is a typical post-secular lived religion.

Third, although the whole case of Europe's response to refugees is about power and justice, the critical hermeneutics advocated above invites us to reflect on the fact that the voice of the asylum seekers themselves is hardly heard, Hayarpi Tamrazyan being one of the exceptions. The right-wing anti-immigration groups as well as the 'refugee protectors' are articulate and well able to access (social) media platforms, but the refugees are more the object of their rhetoric than narrators with their own voice. How they experience these conflicts and how their lived religion plays a role in coping with the situation and with the hostilities they encounter, therefore remains mostly absent from our understanding.

6 Conclusion

This chapter has described practical theology as a hermeneutical discipline with culturally embedded lived religion as its object. A critical hermeneutical approach toward culture and the implicit or explicit religious practices in it allows us to understand the multi-layered meanings and the often-competing narratives (storyscapes) as well as the power dynamics operant in these intercultural encounters.

Bibliography

AlJazeera. 2016. "Wilders: Migrant Men Are 'Islamic Testosterone Bombs'." *Al Jazeera*, 23.01.2016. https://www.aljazeera.com/news/2016/1/23/wilders-migrant-men-are-islamic-testosterone-bombs (30.11.2021).

Bellah, Robert N. [1967] 2005. "Civil Religion in America." *Daedalus* 134:40–55.

Bonjour, Saskia, and Sarah Bracke. 2020. "Europe and the Myth of the Racialized Sexual Predator: Gendered and Sexualized Patterns of Prejudice." https://www.europenowjournal.org/2020/12/07/europe-and-the-myth-of-the-racialized-sexual-predator-gendered-and-sexualized-patterns-of-prejudice/ (30.11.2021).

Brown, Sally A. 2012. "Hermeneutical Theory." In *The Wiley-Blackwell Companion to Practical Theology*, edited by Bonnie J. Miller-McLemore, Chichester: Wiley-Blackwell, 112–122.

Carter, Erik C. 2018. "Finding the Voice of Judaism within Practical Theological Research." *Practical Theology* 11:67–78.

Cense, Marianne, and R. Ruard Ganzevoort. 2019. "The Storyscapes of Teenage Pregnancy: On Morality, Embodiment, and Narrative Agency." *Journal of Youth Studies* 22:568–583.

Elias, Amanuel, and Fethi Mansouri. 2020. "A Systematic Review of Studies on Interculturalism and Intercultural Dialogue." *Journal of Intercultural Studies* 41:490–523.

Ganzevoort, R. Ruard 2004. "What you See Is what you Get: Social Construction and Normativity in Practical Theology." In *Normativity and Empirical Research in Theology*, edited by Johannes A. van der Ven and Michael Scherer-Rath, Leiden: Brill, 17–34.

Ganzevoort, R. Ruard 2006. "The Social Construction of Revelation." *International Journal of Practical Theology* 8:1–14.

Ganzevoort, R. Ruard. 2009. "Forks in the Road When Tracing the Sacred: Practical Theology as Hermeneutics of Lived Religion." Keynote at the *International Academy of Practical Theology*, Chicago. http://citeseerx.ist.psu.edu/viewdoc/summary?doi=10.1.1.489.9830 (30.11.2021).

Ganzevoort, R. Ruard. 2017a. "The Drama Triangle of Religion and Violence." In *Religion and Violence: Muslim and Christian Theological and Pedagogical Reflections*, edited by Ednan Aslan and Marcia Hermansen, Wiesbaden: Springer, 17–30.

Ganzevoort, R. Ruard. 2017b. "Naviguer dans les récits: Négociation des histoires canoniques dans la construction de l'identité religieuse." In *Récit de soi et narrativité dans la construction de l'identité religieuse*, edited by Pierre-Yves Brandt, Paulo Jesus, and Pascal Roman, Paris: Éditions des Archives Contemporaines, 45–63.

Ganzevoort, R. Ruard, and Johan H. Roeland. 2014. "Lived Religion: The Praxis of Practical Theology." *International Journal of Practical Theology* 18:91–101.

Gerkin, Charles V. 1984. *The Living Human Document: Re-visioning Pastoral Counseling in a Hermeneutical Mode*. Nashville: Abingdon.

Herbel, D. Oliver. 2014. *Turning to Tradition: Converts and the Making of an American Orthodox Church*. New York: Oxford University Press.

Huntington, Samuel. 1996. *The Clash of Civilizations and the Remaking of World Order*. New York: Simon & Schuster.

Isgandarova, Nazila. 2014. "Practical Theology and its Importance for Islamic Theological Studies." *Ilahiyat Studies: A Journal on Islamic and Religious Studies* 5:217–236.

Klaver, Miranda. 2021. *Hillsong Church: Expansive Pentecostalism, Media, and Global Cities*. Cham: Palgrave Macmillan.

Kluveld, Amanda. 2016. "Secular, Superior, and Desperately Searching for its Soul: The Confusing Political-Cultural References to a Judeo- Christian Europe in the Twenty-First Century" In *Is there a Judeo-Christian Tradition? A European Perspective*, edited by Emmanuel Nathan and Anya Topolski, Boston: De Gruyter, 267–284.

Lartey, Emmanuel Y. 2006. *Pastoral Theology in an Intercultural World*. Werrington: Epworth.

Lynch, Gordon. 2005. *Understanding Theology and Popular Culture*. Oxford: Blackwell.

Mitchell, Christine M., and David R. Williams. 2017. "Black Lives Matter: A Theological Response to Racism's Impact on the Black Body in the United States." *Studia Historiae Ecclesiasticae* 43:28–45.

Moyaert, Marianne. 2017. "Ricoeur and the Wager of Interreligious Ritual Participation." *International Journal of Philosophy and Theology* 78:173–199.

Nathan, Emmanuel, and Anya Topolski. 2016. *Is there a Judeo-Christian Tradition? A European Perspective*. Berlin / Boston: De Gruyter.

Ricoeur, Paul. 1970. *Freud and Philosophy: An Essay on Interpretation*. New Haven: Yale University Press.

Ricoeur, Paul. 1981. "The Model of the Text: Meaningful Action Considered as a Text." In *Hermeneutics and the Human Sciences*, edited by John B. Thompson, Cambridge: University Press, 159–183.

Ricoeur, Paul. 1984–1988. *Time and Narrative*. Vol. 2, trans. Kathleen Blamey and David Pellauer. Chicago: University of Chicago Press.
Sealy, Thomas. 2018. "Multiculturalism, Interculturalism, 'Multiculture' and Super-diversity: Of Zombies, Shadows and Other Ways of Being." *Ethnicities* 18:692–716.
Sremac, Srdjan, and R. Ruard Ganzevoort. 2019. "Trauma and Lived Religion: Embodiment and Emplotment." In *Trauma and Lived Religion: Transcending the Ordinary*, edited by R. Ruard Ganzevoort and Srdjan Sremac, Cham: Palgrave Macmillan, 1–14.
Tracy, David. 1981. *The Analogical Imagination: Christian Theology and the Culture of Pluralism*. New York: Crossroad.
Trinlae, Bhikshuni L. 2014. "Prospects for a Buddhist Practical Theology." *International Journal of Practical Theology* 18:7–22.
Tweed, Thomas A. 2006. *Crossing and Dwelling: A Theory of Religion*. Cambridge, MA: Harvard University Press.
Ward, Peter. 2017. *Introducing Practical Theology: Mission, Ministry, and the Life of the Church*. Baker Academic.

Hans-Günter Heimbrock
Phenomenology

1 Introduction

Philosophy has been all through the centuries one of the most prominent disciplines to which theology relates, partly in dialogue, partly in concurrence. Philosophical phenomenology, after its arrival in the first decades of the twentieth century was an influential movement within the entire field of philosophy. Its main intersection with theology was with philosophical theology (Heidegger [1927] 1970), subsequently disappearing from interdisciplinary exchange for a significant length of time. Renewed theological interest in dialogue with philosophical phenomenology in the US, as well as in Germany, was prepared over the course of the re-discovery of the experiential nature of religion and faith as well as the empirical turn that Practical Theology took. Eventually it became an inspiring source of methodological innovation for empirical research in Practical Theology. Within contemporary French philosophy there is growing interest in the phenomenological analysis of religious experience (Chrétien and Courtine 1992), whether this really is a veritable "theological turn of phenomenology" (cf. title of Janicaud and Courtine 2000) will be evidenced through future developments.

2 The Phenomenological Movement

The word 'phenomenology' dates to eighteenth-century philosophy. For a long time, a rather Platonist meaning of the concept was popular. Phenomena were understood to be things as they appear to the human senses, rather than things as they are in themselves. In the twentieth century, phenomenology – as the most elaborated theory of phenomena – opposed this rather dualistic model. Likewise, phenomenologists contested the epistemological assumption that one could make sense of phenomena only by putting them into a mental frame, called 'interpretation'.

The overall theoretical orientation of phenomenology can be summarised in four points (Zahavi 2019):
- As a particular theory of knowledge, it contributes to clarifying concepts such as truth, evidence, reason.
- It develops an understanding of the human subject as an embodied basis of experience and knowing it offers a frame for the Humanities and Social Sciences.
- It provides a sharp critique on objectivism and scientism; it clarifies the scope of scientific knowledge.

– It contributes to analyses which are relevant for the empirical study of concrete phenomena like the experience of aesthetics, speech, encounter with foreign cultures and many others.

Phenomenology was developed by Edmund Husserl (1859–1938) as a "descriptive psychology" (Husserl [1900] 1970) but it has been developed throughout the 20th and early 21st centuries in various specifications, such as a transcendental philosophy of consciousness (Mohanty 1985), an ontological analysis of existence (Heidegger 1962), a phenomenology of the social world (Schütz 1967), and also a phenomenology of religion (van der Leeuw [1933] 1978 and Waardenburg 1978). Subsequently it has been taken up by many academic disciplines (Embree 1997). The following pages present a rough sketch focusing on key concepts, taking up some of Husserl's ideas as well as further philosophical developments after Husserl.

2.1 "The Principle of Principles"

Husserl tried to focus exclusively on the givenness of things. The phenomena that are initially given are not our intellectual categories, nor the discursive language in which we describe an experience. Husserl posited that we gain knowledge in the human mind about objects in reality followed his critical call to go back to the things themselves. This inherited posture of phenomenology is still little understood as regards the elementary and crucial question: what are data? The heart of phenomenological epistemology reflects on how to get knowledge from data, consistent with the very basic and essential idea of Husserl's philosophy about data. In his rather essentialist language, Husserl describes this with the word 'givenness'. This can be called an experiential start because his point of departure is an experience that is given to a human being. For Husserl, the structure of intentionality is basic, the "principle of principles", as he called it, is "that every originally presentive intuition is a legitimizing source of cognition, that everything originally (so to speak in its 'personal' actuality) offered to us in 'intuition' is to be accepted simply as what it is presented as being, but also only within the limits in which it is presented there." (Husserl 1983, 44).

To recover this quality, to step back from secondary causal explanations of reality to primary 'givenness', Husserl developed a set of methodical steps in reflection, including description, variation, and eidetic and transcendental reduction. The task is to approach living reality in the best possible manner, not preoccupied by a specific filter, called a scientific hypothesis. The overall phenomenological program that emerges can be summarized thus: "Through phenomenology, a significant methodology is developed for investigating human experience and for deriving knowledge [...]. One learns to see naively and freshly again." (Moustakas 1994, 101)

2.2 Embodied Perception

Phenomenological epistemology deepened further into the specific relation between knowledge about "data" and human beings as knowing subjects. Husserl's perceptual approach to reality implied a heavy critique of the intellectualistic and dualistic model common in his world – a model that posited 'objective data' on one side and a perceiving subject on the other. Instead, Husserl applied the two corresponding concepts 'noesis' and 'noema', pointing at the perceptive mental process and at the perceived object of conscious experience as two sides of a coin. 'Reality outside there' is only accessible for human knowing by way of a subject. And knowing is no mere naming of sensual perceptions with verbal concepts but is intimately connected to perceptions as the first layer of meaning-giving activities. Nevertheless, Husserl's approach remained dominantly consciousness-centered.

After Husserl, the phenomenological concept of perception was deepened by many followers. The French phenomenologist Maurice Merleau-Ponty (1908–1961) elaborated a broader and less idealistic concept of human existence, including especially its bodily rootedness. Based on philosophical as well as empirical arguments, Merleau-Ponty drew on a specific concept of human perception as bodily perception: "The perceiving mind is an incarnate mind" (1962, 4). Merleau-Ponty also described the specific ambiguity of simultaneously having a body and being a living body; this suggests a distinction between the body as object (in German, *Körper*) and the body as a living subject (in German, *Leib*), the latter implying that the body is also the subject of perception. The human body-subject with its emotions, desires and sensations might well be mediated by physical and social conditions. Nevertheless, the body is the basis for, and the transcendental prerequisite of perception, and thus of any knowing about ourselves and objects within the world. The body itself can never be perceived fully, never be reduced to a pure object.

This rooting of the concept of perception in corporality has been described as a 'perceptive turn' of philosophy induced by phenomenology. Merleau-Ponty's essential proposition is thus: "The world is that which I perceive […]." (Merleau-Ponty 1968, 8)

2.3 Life-World

One of the programmatic concepts of phenomenological epistemology Husserl presented incompletely only in his almost latest, nevertheless most influential texts entitled *The Crisis of European Sciences and Transcendental Phenomenology* (Husserl [1936] 1970). It was the idea of a "science of the life-world". Corresponding to the notion of perception is the phenomenological way to perceive and conceive of reality from a life-world perspective. In Husserl's sense, this aims at a pre-scientific encounter with the world, "the world in which we are always already living, and which furnishes the ground for all cognitive performance and all scientific determination"

(Husserl, [1936] 1970). Life-world precedes any conceptual structuring of reality by naming this reality with human language. In this way, reality appears to us first as a whole, as a 'gestalt', before we distinguish different pieces in conscious mental activities. Life-word is "the world in which we are always already living, and which furnishes the ground for all cognitive performance and all scientific determination" (Moran 2000, 15).

The concept of life-world provides a way to reflect more precisely on Husserl's key principle of givenness. The particular reality that is given in the senses does not only vary in terms of content, but also in the possibility that this reality might have different qualities. Some objects in reality sometimes appear quite clear to the senses and consciousness. Some objects intuitively appear as a profiled gestalt. Others are less profiled, only at the periphery of our senses, nevertheless still perceived and registered. This peripheral perception might happen for a long time in one's life, and then suddenly, due to circumstances, change entirely. At such a time, the perception might press itself to the foreground of our perceptions. Such everyday pre-conscious experience of situations, scenery, and circumstances attach themselves to people in different ways. A particular life-world experience might lead one person to the overall feeling of being in a normal and well-known surrounding; it might even provide a deep emotional and cognitive sense of being at home. For somebody else, the same situation, or a similar interaction with this situation, might give a preconscious feeling of displeasure, tentativeness, sureness, or even estrangement. These phenomena are not without relevance to empirical approaches to reality.

As the German philosopher Hans Blumenberg (1920 – 1996) has showed in detail, reflecting on one's life-world means stepping back from the self-evident and basic givens of life (Blumenberg 2010). To think of the life-world subjectively is not, however, to circumvent the context, for this is one's horizon or a form of life praxis. Neither does this approach restrict thinking in a narrow, circumspect way. Rather, reflecting on life world stimulates further knowledge by encouraging people to reflect on the blind spots of their perceptions. Further, the unusual and extraordinary are grounded in the usual, in everyday life. The life-world is the universal horizon toward which meaning aims. In this sense, the life-world may be the object of theoretical criticism, or a source to critique the sciences and scientific methods when they either ignore life or become imperialistic towards life. In the development of theory, the concept can also function as a critical advocate in favor of a subject and against an institution.

The overall interest in the life-world perspective can be characterized as "seeking to describe rather than to explain, in valuing interpretation rather than 'objective truth', in opposing reductionism while focusing on intentionality, coherence, and intelligibility, and in assuming a fundamental pre-reflective, non-rational part of experience, which is consciously available to the person" (Aden 1990, 911).

2.4 Lived Experience

Phenomenological epistemology contributed to the theory of experience focussing on its pre-scientific roots. The empirical approach to reality in social scientific research usually follows the experiential ideal in terms of collecting data as detached objects, which are gained independently from the researching subject. Referring back to the world of experience in the life-world approach relates to the self-evidences and pre-reflexive familiarities in everyday life described by late Husserlian theory (Husserl [1936] 1970).

The life-world perspective emphasizes the relational aspect of experience. In the relational approach to the empirical way of focusing on 'lived experience' there is a more open and more contextual understanding of reality. Reality is not to be described without the individual's involvement on the level of experience, as well as on the level of theoretical description. Furthermore, it contains *ab ovo* elements, which are spontaneous, irregular, faults, and slips, unexpected, and even strange. Similar to the detached model of experience, 'lived experience' as a theoretical construct, converges in the non-positivist stance that states that reality is not simply that 'which is the case'. However, "things look rather different when we get to the roots of experience where things *become* what they could be" (Waldenfels 2004). In the relational approach, the empirical basis is conceived of as something "given" from beyond the perceiving individual, and only accessible through sensual experience of a human subject, being involved in the experiential process.

2.5 Culture: Home World and Alien World

Somehow in correspondence to developments of pluralization and advanced diversity in late modern societies, phenomenology participated in reframing the understanding of cultural conditions and patterns of human life-worlds beyond the traditional binary of 'we – them'. During the last decades French and German phenomenologists especially, such as Levinas, Derrida, Foucault and Waldenfels made major contributions to developing a phenomenological theory, attempting to theorise towards a phenomenology of the inter-subjectivity and of the experience of the alien. From the very beginning, phenomenology as philosophy of consciousness has struggled with a basic epistemological weakness, that is: if every knowledge is given to me in my own senses, how to come to the experience of the other? Decisive for an enlarged phenomenological understanding of intercultural experience was a differentiated description of life-world. Not only beyond, but also within the world of self-evidences and pre-given certainties, people stumble about experiences of otherness. Reflecting on the encounter of the subject with the other does not only provide insight into the ambiguous conditions and limits of intercultural experience, however, it leads to the awareness of otherness within oneself, the intertwinement of one's own world and the alien (Waldenfels 1998).

2.6 On Normativity

Despite some superficial critiques against a 'pure descriptive' status of a phenomenological approach to reality, it is quite impossible to overlook the value-laden character of phenomenology. It would be an error to identify the phenomenological way to reality with a 'neutral' stance stripped of any norms. Phenomenology, although using the method of 'bracketing out' for some steps of description, is based on normative ground, and its specific methods have normative implications. A normative basis is already given when research work starts with a life-world approach. Because life-world means at least two elements, first the ensemble of elements given through the senses, and second, a meaningful world to the perceiving subject. Everyday life is not neutral or random in terms of values, and structures of order. One can see that it is not only ethical judgments that contain a particular world view. Even observing and describing sensual perceptions through body and mind carries a particular understanding of life; a particular meaning; a world of self-evidence or an encounter with the extraordinary, the strange, or sometimes with the holy. Thus, life-world is a foundational basis for normativity.

3 Researching Lived Experience

As indicated above, Husserl and his followers developed a set of methods for philosophical inquiry. Although these authors constantly related to the theories and research praxis of empirical disciplines of their age, they did not invent methods for empirical research. Phenomenology itself was not intended to serve as a tool for empirical research in a contemporary meaning. However, methodological elements of phenomenology have been picked up for improving and enlarging the scope of qualitative empirical research in many disciplines, like sociology, ethnography, religious studies, educational science, language studies, social geography, environmental studies among others.

But to avoid misunderstandings; there is no pure 'phenomenological method' for empirical research. There are only some characteristic elements for a research approach that follow phenomenological theory, or better, a research 'habit'. It can be indicated briefly by some characteristics.

3.1 Perceptions in the Field

Proceeding with research in a life-world perspective asks for one to enter a situation in everyday life as a concrete setting, as a field; it might be even in the field of dreams. In such a field, the scenery has a spatial as well as temporal structure. A 'field' is an unknown and unstructured terrain, which a researcher enters bodily and mentally, gets involved in, and may meet known or unknown images, visions, and occurrences. It is not completely pre-established as a static entity. It is rather a dynamic interactive space where people will develop their own connections and contexts. Doing research then starts with the researcher's suspicion that he or she initially has to unfold the very object of research because he or she does not know everyday life completely.

3.2 The Researcher as Self-Reflecting Subject

The emphasis on the subject's involvement has a crucial impact on the research process. It asks for an actual research praxis in which the researching human being perceives his or her research field not only as distinct object, but also of being involved in the research scenery as mind-body subject. Ethnography points in this direction by offering rules for the method of participant observation. But usually, it keeps the awareness of the researcher to cognitive or emotional responses. The phenomenological impulse, however, moves the researcher-subject further.

3.3 Interpretation and Representation

Phenomenology opens an unlimited multitude of horizons, against which you could study the phenomenon. Nevertheless, every research project must come to a temporary end and to formulate insights. Phenomenologists (as well as ethnographers and psychoanalysts) hold that discovering reality is not refining data in the sense of mere reproductions or secondary structuring, independent of other methodical activities. Both approaches to research include a constructive element within the scientific, hermeneutic activity; thus, they reveal something that is not simply a 'matter of fact'. Rather they have to represent 'what takes place' in its quality of 'lived experience'. Thus, the problem of representation in phenomenological research is vibrant. There is a need for a specific use of language, called 'phenomenological description', narratives and stories are important and appropriate elements. "A successful description is made visible with words, it helps us to see, what we would not see without it." (Waldenfels 2001, 67) And there is no exact and final interpretation of life.

3.4 The Methodological Paradox

Scientific validity of any research is based on methodical ways to get knowledge that can be controlled and used or falsified. Applying this principle to a research methodology based on phenomenology leads to a fundamental paradox. The approach sketched above essentially insists on the openness of the concept of religion against every attempt to take too much control of the subject matter by way of foreclosing, or fore ordaining the results, through using narrow definitions from the beginning. But how can this be objectified and controlled in a research process? How do we organise a research routine to approach the unexpected and the strange? It is evident that it cannot be planed completely if the method does not risk to exclude the very object.

This argument is a strong warning against the 'technisizing' of the phenomenological method in any other empirically oriented discipline. Out of this necessary objection, it follows that this phenomenological attitude can never – neither methodologically nor conceptually – substitute for the exactness of scientific knowledge or of logical concepts. However, its "precise imprecision" (Moxter 2001, 92) is not an epistemological deficiency; instead, it is a plus for method and research. In principle this is in accordance with a theological understanding of reality according to a spiritual perception of reality as an open process.

The main contribution of phenomenology to the logic of empirical sciences is an anti-positivist notion. It stresses the interconnectedness between collecting data and meaning-giving activities. Further, it underlines the core role of the subject in gaining knowledge. Opposite to the ideal of objectivism, it stresses the conviction that the subjective view of experience, and hence any experiential-based research, is not a fault but rather a necessary part of the nature of knowledge. Dermot Moran states it in even more emphatic language "Subjectivity must be understood as inextricably involved in the process of constituting objectivity." (Moran 2000, 15)

Approaching the research situation from the perspective of 'lived experience', it is about the 'me' in experience, but it also challenges to ask back upon this 'me' in the subject-perspective; its boundaries and intertwinements. If experience, fully understood, is relational, there is next to inter-subjective relations of otherness also an *internal relation*. The phenomenological analysis of experience also sharpens our eyes to the reverse of the active position: experiences sometimes are also doing something to us. It emphasizes the perspective for those layers of reality, where the subject is inter-active, interwoven with reality, affected, touched, and perhaps even overwhelmed by things that happen. It includes sometimes even inactive, more passive elements, elements described by medical scholars like Victor von Weizsäcker and F. Buytendijk as "pathic behaviour" (von Weizsäcker 1947; Buytendijk, 1956).

4 Empirical Theology

Phenomenology in several theological disciplines played a major role in elaborating on programs of 'Empirical Theology' (cf. for a comprehensive overview Heimbrock 2011).

4.1 The 'Chicago School' of Empirical Theology

A model explicitly called 'Empirical Theology', which drew heavily on phenomenology, was first developed in the 'Chicago School' in the 1960s and 1970s of the twentieth century (Meland 1969). All this happened long before the issue appeared on the agenda of European Practical Theology. Not denying the traditional theological notion of transcendence, this movement shared with other types of Empirical Theology the overall conviction that God's presence is immanent to human beings in experience. The overall intention of his Empirical Theology method was "to take seriously the empirical situation as a source of grace" (Rogers 1990, 121).

The movement took its departure beyond Dilthey's categories of explanation and interpretation, starting with other conceptual tools for religion, faith and experience, like the notion of 'lived experience'. Referring to Schleiermacher and to pietistic traditions, the systematic theologian Bernhard Meland sharpens both the very empirical basis of faith and the reflective task of theology as a theoretical endeavour. Theological thinking about faith and experience cannot escape the necessity to distinguish between faith embedded within the vital immediacy of 'lived experience' and its attempt to conceptually clarify this experience to communicate about it on the grounds of rationality. Further on, Meland holds that an adequate theological understanding of faith starts by acknowledging "faith as a structure of experience" (Meland 1953, 183). This supposes that the vital essence of theological notions like revelation, forgiveness and grace is aiming at resonance in human experience and thus not treated exhaustively if reduced to "simply linguistic realities" (Meland 1969, 293).

Meland called his approach empirical realism. The model argues that theology could and should profit from this type of reflection on reality, which distinguishes language and reality, as well as semantic and logical explications from the awareness of an immediacy of lived experience. In a particular sense, his perspective defines the practical mission of theology as an academic discipline, which aims at "carrying the act of faith beyond linguistic preoccupations to an experience of grace and judgment within this vital immediacy" (Meland 1969, 305).

His programmatic question, "Can Empirical Theology Learn from Phenomenology?" (Meland 1969, 283), explicitly marks a theoretical link between empirical realism and a life-world based theory of experience. A bridging link is identified in Husserl's 'stream of thought'. Nevertheless, Meland followed the turn from a conscious-centred transcendental type of phenomenology of the younger Husserl towards a bodily-oriented thinking of his French pupil Merleau-Ponty.

To promote the notion of 'lived experience' as a theoretical tool for the praxis of faith as lived experience, theology must sharpen the understanding of the nature of experience. In consequence, in Meland's way of describing the quality of experience, the engagement of faithful people is not only mirrored by presented objects as content, but also focuses on the experiential side of faith as a particular responsiveness, which he called "appreciative consciousness" (Meland 1953). This basic concept of his theological method, as he put it himself, "can best be understood as an orientation of the mind which makes for a maximum degree of receptivity to the datum under consideration on the principle that what is given may be more than what is immediately perceived, or more than one can think" (Meland 1953, 63). The particular intention of Empirical Theology was to define this quality as a central element of theological reflection, in order to avoid theological as well as epistemological objectivism against human experience.

Without any anti-rational bias, he states, "Theologians must reckon with the fact that their intellectual undertaking is motivated by objectives that differ decidedly from those of scientist. The scientist pursues knowledge of his world with a view to controlling" (Meland 1934, 199 f.). In his view, the theologian's interest is not to control the world by gathering distinct data according to the rationale of exact science, but rather to prepare worship, to open life to the mysterious structure of reality.

4.2 The Empirical-Phenomenological Model of Practical Theology

Within Practical Theology in Europe as well as in the US during the last five decennia one finds many attempts to pick up impulses from phenomenology to broaden the empirical interest of theology, to enrich research methods and even to reshape the scope of the whole discipline of Practical Theology. First attempts were done in pastoral psychology (Aden 1990; Park 2014). The interest in experience and the theological task to regain contact with lived life played a major role in reconstructing and promoting a type of Empirical Theology called the empirical-phenomenological model (Dinter, Heimbrock, and Söderblom 2007).

Essential in this model is to pick up the specific phenomenological way to reflect about the 'pre-givenness' of reality in the human mind-body perception, the lifeworld perspective, and to transform this impulse into research strategies. This way of doing theological research is interested in the study of 'lived religion'. It does not start with an explicit and completely predefined normative basis of a concept of faith, from which it would draw the findings of research, nor does it simply pretend to collect observations in a neutral way. 'Living religion' like religion in general, is used here in accord with a broad consensus in more recent theories of religion; it is used as a strategic concept. While it does include things in reality that are associated with religion, as everyday language might presume, it simultaneously points to specific perspectives on life. This enables empirical theologians to study the different qualities of subjects' involvement in, and entanglement with, everyday life and culture, as well as their religious meanings.

During the last two decades this methodological orientation has opened up Practical Theological research perspectives on two levels:

Firstly, it helped to initiate the study of a wide range of material research objects related to everyday experiences which had up until then been neglected, like dreams, healing movements, aesthetic expressions, the enjoyment of listening to music, intense body experiences, phantasy and virtual reality, and many others. Phenomenology, in this way, is helpful for theology to avoid a "clericalisation of practice" (Farley 1983). This helped to open up a perspective in Practical Theology that looked to an analysis of the culturally shaped forms and symbolic representations of life. In clear contrast to the religious studies' discipline of the 'phenomenology of religion' a lifeworld approach does not deal with distinct 'religious things', but always starts and ends up with a broad perspective on life, connected to everyday culture. Phenomenology in the broad sense inspires theological education and sharpens our eyes to look more closely at familiar, everyday experiences.

Secondly, and concerning the scope of the whole discipline of Practical Theology, it contributed to re-consider the basic concept of 'practice'. Following the overall epistemological question of phenomenology, how people are related to reality in their concrete life-world encounter, Practical Theology contributed to a broader concept of practice beyond pure activity. Many experiences – such as being touched by a specific atmosphere, being open to an experience of disclosure, being caught by the 'flow' of experiences and other religious or cultural phenomena – reach beyond the category of practice; they cannot be fully identified as activities of a particular individual or community. Responding to such phenomena, one Practical Theologian even proposed defining religion as the human experience of the impossibility of action, becoming aware of God's action at the limits of human activity (Josuttis 1985).

The concepts of action and praxis in Empirical Theology still require further clarification to compare anthropological insights about religion as human activity to the classical theological notion of God's actions.

For both however, doing research on particular material objects as well as reflecting on the formal objects of Practical Theology from the perspective of the empirical-phenomenological model, it is inevitable to take up the dynamic relation between reality under research and the perceiving and interpreting subject, who is 'doing' theology.

The contribution of the empirical-phenomenological model of Practical Theology to theology in general is to keep contact with – and reflect upon – religious life in congregations as well as with the culture Christians are participating in. If the task of Christians is to take part in God's ongoing creation of the world, Empirical Theology contributes some intellectual tools to reconstruct this process. Practical Theology focusing particularly on 'lived experience' helps theology in general to profile its indispensable role within the academy. In times when 'life sciences' are on the rise in terms of popularity, there is an additional need to communicate the surplus of theological theory to the interpretation of humankind. Our epistemological reasoning provides secular arguments to enlarge an understanding of life and reality beyond restricted ideals of natural scientific objectivity.

After almost half a century starting of 'hard' empirical research in theology today, phenomenology might become a helpful partner for theology to open up a new interdisciplinary discourse on fundamental concepts like 'reality' and 'life'. Its epistemological reasoning provides secular arguments to contest an understanding of reality that is bound to modern ideals of conceiving reality according cause and effect, quantitative or even determinative correlations. The phenomenological notion of 'otherness' within life in itself is not 'natural theology' or an empirical proof for the theological proposition of God's transcendence. However, it could be in service of an understanding of reality in accordance with a theological interpretation of life beyond the categories of cause and effect, in its dynamic and mysterious structure.

Bibliography

Aden, LeRoy. 1990. "Phenomenological Method in Pastoral Care." In *Dictionary of Pastoral Care and Counseling*, edited by Rodney Hunter, Nashville: Abingdon Press, 911–912.
Blumenberg, Hans. 2010. *Theorie der Lebenswelt*. Berlin: Suhrkamp.
Buytendijk, Frederik. 1956. *Allgemeine Theorie der menschlichen Haltung und Bewegung*. Berlin: Springer.
Chrétien, Jean-Louis, and Jean-François Courtine. 1992. *Phénoménologie et théologie*. Paris: Criterion.
Dinter, Astrid, Hans-Günter Heimbrock, and Kerstin Söderblom. 2007. *Einführung in die Empirische Theologie*. Göttingen: Vandenhoeck & Ruprecht.
Embree, Lester, ed. 1997. *Encyclopedia of Phenomenology*. Dordrecht: Kluwer Academic Publishers.
Farley, Edwin. 1983. "Theology and Practice Outside the Clerical Paradigm." In *Practical Theology*, edited by Don Browning, San Francisco: Harper & Row, 21–41.
Heidegger, Martin. [1927] 1970. *Phänomenologie und Theologie*. Vol. 9, *Heidegger Gesamtausgabe*. Freiburg: Klostermann.
Heidegger, Martin. 1962. *Being and Time*, trans. John Macquarrie and E. Robinson. New York: Harper and Row.
Heimbrock, Hans-Günter. 2011. "Practical Theology as Empirical Theology." *International Journal of Practical Theology* 14:153–170.
Husserl, Edmund. 1970. *Logical Investigations 1*, trans. John N. Findlay. London: Routledge.
Husserl, Edmund. 1983. *Ideas Pertaining to a Pure Phenomenology and to a Phenomenological Philosophy*, Vol. 1, trans. Fred Kersten. Dordrecht: Klüwer.
Husserl, Edmund. [1936] 1970. *The Crisis of European Sciences and Transcendental Phenomenology*, trans. David Carr. Evanston: Northwestern University Press.
Janicaud, Dominique, and Jean-François Courtine. 2000. *Phenomenology and the 'Theological Turn': The French Debate*. New York: Fordham University Press.
Josuttis, Manfred. 1985. "Zu einigen handlungstheoretischen Anfragen an die Liturgiewissenschaft." In *Kommunikation und Solidarität*, edited by Hans-Ulrich von Brachel and Norbert Mette, Fribourg: Exodus Verlag, 231–239.
Leeuw, Gerardus van der. 1978. *Religion in Essence and Manifestation: A Study in Phenomenology*, trans. John E. Turner. New York: Harper & Row.
Manen, Max van. 2011. *PHENOMENOLOGYONLINE*. http://www.phenomenologyonline.com/ (29.11.2021)
Manen, Max van. 1990. *Researching Lived Experience: Human Science for an Action Sensitive Pedagogy*. New York: State University of New York Press.
Meland, Bernhard E. 1934. "The Appreciative Approach in Religion." *Journal of Religion* 14:194–204.

Meland, Bernhard E. 1953. *Faith and Culture*. New York: Oxford University Press.
Meland, Bernhard E., ed. 1969. *The Future of Empirical Theology*. Chicago: Chicago University Press.
Merleau-Ponty, Maurice. 1962. *Phenomenology of Perception*, trans. Colin Smith. London: Routledge.
Merleau-Ponty, Maurice. 1968. *The Visible and the Invisible*, trans. Alphonso Lingis. Evanston: Northwestern University Press.
Moustakas, Clark. 1994. *Phenomenological Research Methods*. London: Sage Publications.
Mohanty, Jitendra Nath. 1985. "Transcendental Philosophy and the Hermeneutic Critique of Consciousness." In *The Possibility of Transcendental Philosophy,* edited by Jitendra Nath Mohanty, Dordrecht: Kluver, 223–246.
Moran, Dermond. 2000. *Introduction to Phenomenology*. London / New York: Routledge.
Moxter, Michael. 2001. "Die Phänomene der Phänomenologie." In *Religion als Phänomen: Sozialwissenschaftliche, theologische und philosophische Erkundungen in der Lebenswelt,* edited by Wolf-Eckart Failing, Hans-Günter Heimbrock, and Thomas Lotz, Berlin: De Gruyter, 85–95.
Park, Hee-Kyu Heidi. 2014. "Toward a Pastoral Theological Phenomenology: Constructing a Reflexive and Relational Phenomenological Method from a Postcolonial Perspective." *Journal of Pastoral Theology* 24:1–21.
Rogers, Delores Joan. 1990. *The American Empirical Movement in Theology*. New York: Peter Lang.
Schütz, Alfred. 1967. *The Phenomenology of the Social World,* trans. George Walsh and Frederik Lehnert. Evanston: Northwestern University Press.
Waardenburg, Jacques. 1978. *Reflections on the Study of Religion*. Den Haag: Mouton.
Waldenfels, Bernhard. 1998. "Homeworld and Alienworld." In *Phenomenology of Interculturality and Life-World,* edited by Ernst Wolfgang Orth and Chan-Fai Cheung, Freiburg / München: Karl Alber, 72–88.
Waldenfels, Bernhard. 2001. "Phänomenologie der Erfahrung und das Dilemma einer Religionsphänomenologie." In *Religion als Phänomen: Sozialwissenschaftliche, theologische und philosophische Erkundungen in der Lebenswelt,* edited by Wolf-Eckart Failing, Hans-Günter Heimbrock, and Thomas Lotz, Berlin: De Gruyter, 63–84.
Waldenfels, Bernhard. 2004. "Bodily Experience between Selfhood and Otherness." *Phenomenology and the Cognitive Sciences* 3:235–248.
Waldenfels, Berhard. 2011. *Phenomenology of the Alien*. Frankfurt am Main: Suhrkamp.
Weizsäcker, Viktor von. 1947. *Der Gestaltkreis: Theorie und Einheit von Wahrnehmen und Bewegen*. Stuttgart: Georg Thieme.
Zahavi, Dan. 2019. *Phenomenology: The Basics*. London: Routledge.

Emmanuel Y. Lartey
Postcolonial Studies in Practical Theology

1 Introduction

A huge disconnect exists between the orthodox, official theology of the ruling classes of religious institutions on the one hand, and the living faiths of believers on the other. Official church dogma is often not what most Christians live by. Whereas official statements emphasize the 'purity' of the faith, most Christians in the pews and practitioners of other living religious faiths, live what can be described as a mixed, pragmatic version which is a combination of orthodoxy and heterodoxy, official teaching and local cultural practices, religious understandings, and experiential realities. This phenomenon is observable in most if not all faith traditions. Christian systematic theology has focused on the statements of faith (creeds, councils, and doctrines) of officialdom and the writings of recognized authority figures whereas many practical theologians have by and large grappled with the lived experience and daily-life faith of ordinary believers. This historic divide has been the case down through the years and arguably lies at the heart of the reason for the Councils and Creeds of Early Christianity, whose primary purpose was to clearly define the core, essential, pure, and true faith to which all believers were to be directed and by which heresies could be detected and expunged, corrected, or punished. An example of this in contemporary times takes the form of the conflicts and controversies between purists who insist on the exclusive claims of Christian doctrine and the 'multiple religious belonging' that characterize the lives of many Christians. It is also evident in postcolonial studies in practical theology.

In this chapter I shall be focusing on the practical theological disciplines of pastoral theology and pastoral care in tracing the trajectory of postcolonial criticism in the work of practical theology, especially emphasizing the work of those whose cultural and historical heritage, like my own, is traceable to the African continent.[1] Pathways in postcolonial thought and practice typically seek to enhance an engagement with the cultural heritage of the formerly colonized in ways that lift up subjugated knowledge for the purpose of a more authentic future in which suppressed ways of being and knowing are represented and clearly articulated at the table of all pastoral theology.

---

[1] See Lartey (2018, 79–97). In this chapter, as in that one, for the purposes of brevity and focus, I stay within the discipline of pastoral theology understood as exploring the theological underpinnings, implications, and practices of pastoral care and counseling as a sub-discipline of practical theology. Practical theology, as a whole, I would define as encompassing the four disciplines of Religious Education, Liturgy and Worship, Homiletics, and Pastoral Theology.

I write from the region of the United States of America which is referred to as the Deep South where for the past nineteen years I have lived, taught, researched, and provided pastoral care and counseling. I was born in Ghana, then known as the Gold Coast, in the dying years of British colonial rule on the African continent. My own experience growing up, living, and teaching in Africa, and then studying and teaching for over a decade in Britain, and now since 2001 here in the United States, informs everything I have to say and has had a marked influence on my perspectives and views. Moreover, I have had the honor and privilege of travelling internationally and engaging in research and study in different parts of the world, including extensively in Africa, in Europe, in Asia, the Caribbean and South America. My experience has typically been in intercultural communities located in the various countries I have worked in. Coming from a minority ethnic group in my home country, and then sharing the life space and existential realities of minorities – Black British, African Americans and people of color – has given me a particularly keen sense of the experience of being marginalized. However, as a professor and religious leader, privilege and power have not been absent from my experience as well. In this regard marginalization and recognition, oppression and valuing, resentment and respect, rejection, and acceptance, have in curious ways been the hallmarks of my existence and social location.

Since the mid-1980s a steady stream of works from pastoral theologians have embraced and operated through a lens that has been described as 'intercultural'. In this approach a concerted effort is made to seriously promote a dialogical and interactive study and practice of ministry and pastoral care, drawing upon theories and practices from different cultures. The underlying premise of this effort is equal respect for all cultures and all people as bearing the image and likeness of God. The *modus operandi* of intercultural pastoral care and counseling has entailed respectful dialogue between participants from different geographic and social locations in which each purport to learn from the other. If all people are created in and bear the image of God, then all have a contribution to make in the presentation of the God of all creation and in the care of all humanity. It goes without saying that if there is to be genuine intercultural interaction among pastoral practitioners there indeed needs to be recognition and respect for each participant's cultural and religious heritage. Such however was not the case from the beginnings of interaction between Europeans and peoples of the rest of the world. When Europeans ventured out of their shores beginning in the fifteenth century CE it was in a mode of conquest and control of trade, economics, culture, and religion. European civilization sought dominated and imposed its own values on all everywhere it went. European imperialism and colonialism were fuelled by views of superiority and patronage.

The colonial project with its inherently oppressive and de-facing characteristics in relation to cultures different from itself has left the partners in intercultural interaction who originate from the former colonies unable to truly engage the colonizers and their descendants from an equal epistemological, sociological, and political base. Psychiatrist and political activist Frantz Fanon perhaps most clearly analyzed the deleterious effect of colonialism upon Africans. In *The Wretched of the Earth*, a seminal text which, although predating formal designations of 'postcolonial criticism', articulates very well the core values of postcolonial thought, Fanon declared, "Colonialism is not satisfied merely with holding a people in its grip and emptying the native's brain of all form and content. By a kind of perverted logic, it turns to the past of the oppressed people, and distorts, disfigures and destroys it." (Fanon [1961] 1990, 169) As Sugirtharajah, a towering figure in postcolonial studies, puts it in language that describes lingering images of Africa that persist even today, "for colonialism the vast continent of Africa was a 'haunt of savages' replete with 'superstitions and fanaticisms', and was held in contempt and cursed by God." (Sugirtharajah 2002, 17)

The task 'postcolonializing'[2] activities seek to accomplish entails critique, validation, recovery, and construction. They aim to facilitate the formerly colonized person's authentic participation in scholarly as well as pragmatic engagement. As critique, postcolonial criticism uncovers the logic of colonialism's constructions of the colonized and demonstrates its inadequacy and misrepresentation of the people and cultures encountered. It also critiques the hegemony and 'control over' that is embedded in much of the discourse of relations between nations and cultures. Because of the pervasive, often pernicious, and latent power of the colonial project upon the personhood of the colonized, an important aspect of postcolonial criticism and one of its objectives is the 'de-colonizing' of the thought, theory, and practice of colonized experience. As validation, postcolonial interpretations of the realities of the colonized re-value their humanity and begin to underscore and strengthen the formerly colonized people's capacity for authentic selfhood. The task of recovery undertaken in postcolonial studies entails a process of re-appropriation of subjugated knowledge and epistemology. Such recovery requires both historical and constructive research and crafting. Subjugated knowledge needs to be re-appropriated, validated and put to work in the construction of new realities, theories, and practices able to forge a new consciousness and new orientation to life for all in the future. Postcolonial criticism thus requires both courage and creativity.

2 What Do We Mean by Postcolonial?

The term *postcolonial* has many and varied usages in different disciplines. It points more often not merely to a chronological ordering of relations in reference to what follows the colonial, but rather as a discourse about existing orientations and in critique of ongoing international relational realities. Generally, it is employed in an attempt to capture two particular features of international relations historic and contemporaneous. First, postcolonial studies have been about an analysis of the

---

[2] A term I coined to express an ongoing activity as opposed to a static state, see Lartey (2013).

various strategies employed by colonizers to construct images of and to exercise dominance over the colonized. This form of study undertaken mostly by scholars from the historic colonizing nations can and has been very sharply criticized.[3] Second, postcolonial criticism has referred to the study of the agency of the colonized in making use of and transcending colonial strategies of dominance, subjugation and demeaning in order to articulate and assert their dignity, self-worth and identity, and to empower themselves. Sugirtharajah, whose work has been pioneering in the field of postcolonial Biblical and Asian studies, describes postcolonial criticism "as signifying a reactive resistance discourse of the colonized who critically interrogate dominant knowledge systems in order to recover the past from the Western slander and misinformation of the colonial period." (Sugirtharajah, 2002, 13) This way of using the term has led to a flurry of studies and texts mostly by nationals of the former colonized nations. It is important to note that in this latter way of analysis the critique has included that of the 'colonized' themselves and the ways they have at times internalized the images and projections of their interlocutors, as Sugirtharajah puts it postcolonial criticism "also continues to interrogate neo-colonizing tendencies after the declaration of independence." (2002, 13)

3 Postcolonial Criticism in Pastoral Theology and Care

One of the first publications in the field of pastoral theology and pastoral care to engage in a critique of colonial anthropological presuppositions in pastoral care was my doctoral dissertation, *Pastoral Counselling in Inter-cultural Perspective: A Study of Some African (Ghanaian) and Anglo-American Views on Human Existence and Counselling* (Lartey 1987). In this pioneering work African anthropological conceptions are utilized in a critique of Euro-American foundations of pastoral care and counseling. This early critical work that played a leading role in the formulation of an intercultural paradigm of pastoral care and counseling predated the explicit usage of the term 'postcolonial' in the literature of practical theology. Perhaps the first work to explicitly refer to postcolonial theory and practice in the sense we have outlined was *Pastoral Care from a Third World Perspective: A Pastoral Theology of Care for the Urban Contemporary Shona in Zimbabwe* (Mucherera 2001). Mucherera identifies the existence of deep psychological and spiritual scars needing healing within his formerly colonized Zimbabwean compatriots. Psychiatrist Frantz Fanon's answer to the scars of colonization was a call to Africans to recover their history and reassert their identity, dignity, and culture (Fanon 1990). Mucherera, as had Lartey before him, called for pastoral caregivers with "integrative consciousness" (Mucher-

---

[3] For a detailed summary of the most trenchant critiques see Moore-Gilbert (1997, 5–33).

era, 2001, 175) by which he meant caregivers who understood both the traditional African and the western worldview and able to integrate these in treatment modalities.

Mucherera's second monograph *Meet me at the Palaver* (2009) in true postcolonial vein, lifts up a tried and tested ancient African approach to communal conflict management and education – the village gatherings referred to as 'palavers' – and demonstrates how African wisdom operates more adequately in dealing with the HIV/AIDS pandemic plaguing the continent than individualistic Western logocentric approaches. Drawing on holistic communal narratives and oral story-telling modes of communication Mucherera takes seriously African attention to spirit, body, and mind, in quest for healing of souls.

Pastoral theologians made a significant turn towards the postcolonial in the mid-2000s. The *Journal of Pastoral Theology* has in recent years regularly featured articles that represent postcolonializing discourse. The Society of Pastoral Theology's 2007 annual study conference held in San Juan, Puerto Rico, had as its main theme "Doing Pastoral Theology in a Post-Colonial Context." Articles generated from this conference published in the Journal of Pastoral Theology address very squarely the complex and intriguing postcolonial relations within the South, Central and North American context. This conference was itself evidence of the desire on the part of members of the Society for Pastoral Theology, most of whom are US nationals, to engage decidedly in and seek to study long standing postcolonial pastoral theological theories and practices promulgated by Central American peoples. In that issue (2007) of the Journal of Pastoral Theology Professor Héctor López-Sierra pointing to the subversive survival skills (la *brega*) and resilience of Hispanic Caribbean religious subjects, speaks of their need to "reinvent ourselves" (López-Sierra 2007, 60). In the midst of the liminality and hybridity of the Hispanic Caribbean lived experience he argues that "one of the results of that *brega* has been to make our myths and customs survive through the subaltern worldviews and practices of popular religions, spirituality, and multiple religious belongings or 'affiliations' of the peoples" (López-Sierra 2007, 61). He further points to a postcolonial methodology in which his people

> raise an 'ironic syncretic voice' that starts with the criticism and deconstruction of Iberian-European and North American hegemonic God-talk and ends by subverting the institutionalized story of 'official' Christianity from the hybrid and 'syncretic rhetoric' of 'popular' religion, spirituality, and contemporary socio-cultural knowledges. (López-Sierra 2007, 61)

As López-Sierra shows Hispanic-Caribbean postcolonializing pastoral theology has been going on "ironically" for a long time. Its two-fold methodology both clear and intriguing is as follows:

- Criticize, deconstruct, and subvert the Iberian-European and North American hegemonic God-talk
- Utilize "the hybrid and syncretic rhetoric of official Christian ecclesial establishment discourse and tradition, 'popular' religion and spirituality, and contemporary psycho-socio-cultural knowledge." (López-Sierra 2007, 77)

Such deconstructive and constructive strategies are present in all forms of postcolonial pastoral theology and pastoral care.

Postcolonializing God: An African Practical Theology was published in 2013 in which I explore historic examples of postcolonializing activities undertaken by different leaders of colonized and formerly colonized peoples. These activities are discernible, if latent, in much of African Indigenous (independent) Christianity and latterly more so in the religious pluralism that is evident in the growth of mystical and interreligious movements on the African continent and in the diaspora. In direct reference to pastoral care, I raise the centrality of spirituality, the crucial function of building healthy communities and the transformation of cultures that continue to be key goals of postcolonial pastoral practice, about which more will be found later in this chapter. That same year Melinda McGarrah Sharp offered a work based on her experience as a Peace Corp volunteer in Suriname, South America. Titled *Misunderstanding Stories: Towards a postcolonial pastoral theology* (McGarrah Sharp 2013). Sharp addresses a very real challenge embedded in encounters across cultures unexplored in earlier works, namely misunderstandings and conflicts. Drawing thoughtfully on resources from pastoral theology, ethnography, and postcolonial studies she provides a valuable resource for relating across cultural difference especially where conflict and misunderstanding rises to the fore. An important methodological recognition that is common to both Mucherera with reference to Zimbabwe (East Africa) and Sharp in reference to Surinam (South America) is the pursuit and exploration of narrative as a significant analytic category highly valued within the subjugated knowledge repertoire and practice of colonized people across the world

In terms of methodologies of pastoral theological research and engagement with the agency of post-colonial subjects, Hee-Kyu Heidi Park demonstrates the twofold action of postcolonial criticism in first, unearthing the epistemological assumptions and reductive essentializing tendencies in phenomenology, and second, in constructive mode, drawing on feminist standpoint theory, indigenous research and postcolonial theories to propose "a pastoral theological phenomenology that allows the postcolonial person, as a person characterized by hybridity and mimicry, to reflect on the power dynamic within the self and to stand on the bracket as his or her standpoint." (Park 2014, 3–14) Postcolonial critical studies make room for the complexity of postcolonial experience to find both authentic standpoint and voice at the table.

In a similar postcolonial turn Congolese American pastoral theologian Fulgence Nyengele engages in what is a third feature of postcolonial study, namely the articulation and enhancement of subjugated knowledge. Nyengele lifts up subjugated knowledge in the form of the Southern African Zulu concept of *Ubuntu* bringing it in critical dialogue with the recently articulated discipline of positive psychology "to recover African ancestral wisdom and put it to the positive service of the world" (Nyengele 2014, 4–28). A significant recent example of this turn to subjugated knowledge and to *Ubuntu* precisely in the field of Practical Theology was the 2015 International Academy of Practical Theology's conference which was held in Pretoria, South Africa. Twenty-two thoughtful papers from the conference containing reflections on *Ubuntu* as it relates to justice, personhood and human dignity in Southern Africa as well as across the globe are contained in the book titled, *Practicing Ubuntu: Practical Theological perspectives on Injustice, Personhood and Human Dignity* (Dreyer et al. 2017).

Korean American theologian Hee-An Choi in *A Postcolonial Self: Korean Immigrant Theology and the Church* (2016) extends postcolonial discourse into the realm of the experience of minorities within the US western colonial metropolis. As Sugirtharajah, following Madsen argues, "since a sense of commonality runs through the writings of the Third World and American minority writers based on experience of 'imperial domination, cultural catastrophe, genocide, and erasure' (Madsen 1999, 11) there is no justification for excluding their texts" (Sugirtharajah 2002, 35) from considerations of postcolonial discourse. Choi explores how Korean immigrants work to create a different identity in response to life in the United States. She discusses how a Korean ethnic self differs from Western norms. She then examines theological debates over the concept of the independent self, and the impact of racism, sexism, classism, and postcolonialism on the formation of this self. The book concludes with a look at how Korean immigrants, especially immigrant women, cope with the transition to a US culture which includes prejudice and discrimination, and the role the Korean immigrant church plays in this. Choi's work provides an illuminating analysis of postcolonial Korean experience and acts as a resource for postcolonial Asian American pastoral care and counseling.

Postcolonial Practice of Ministry: Leadership, Liturgy and Interfaith Engagement edited by systematic theologian Kwok-Pui Lan and pastoral theologian Stephen Burns (2016), a ground-breaking text exploring various aspects of practical theology and ministry through postcolonial lenses, was published in 2016. This comprehensive collection of essays, international in scope, covers the various disciplines of practical theology and includes chapters on the "Dynamics of Interfaith Collaborations in Postcolonial Asia" (Tan 2016), "Womanist Interfaith Dialogue: Inter, Intra, and All the Spaces in Between" (Harris 2016), "Table Habits, Liturgical Pelau, and Displacing Conversation" (Jagessar 2016), and "Church Music in Postcolonial Liturgical Celebration" (Lim 2016). The first section of the book, headed, "Pastoral Leadership" contains illuminating pastoral theological articles by Emmanuel Lartey, Melinda Sharp, Mona West, and Stephanie Mitchem, all engaging in postcolonial critical discourse in the arena of the spiritual care of individuals and communities.

4 Themes in Postcolonial Practical Theology

In terms of postcolonial practical theology, three main thematic issues are discernible. These are
- Voice
- Epistemology
- Praxis

4.1 Voice: Can the Subaltern Speak?

Spivak's poignant question[4] draws attention to the complex realities of the silencing and the silence of the economically dispossessed. The issue clearly is not simply the physical ability of the subaltern to speak but rather whether they are given the space or the permission to voice their own views or whether western intellectuals will be the only ones permitted to speak on behalf of the dispossessed and colonized. In postcolonial practical theological discourse four types of speaking by the formerly colonized are recognized and discussed. These are mimicry, improvisation, innovation, and polyvocality. An intriguing example of all these ways of speaking, or perhaps 'seeing' (to use the framing vision – 'opting for an optic' – adopted in the book) is contained in the text *Christian Worship: Postcolonial Perspectives*, co-authored by Michael Jagessar and Stephen Burns (2014). Jagessar and Burns provocatively describe their book as offering "an unsystematic, fragmentary, piecemeal and unfinished – and yet for us challenging, unsettling, exciting and rewarding – shared insight into numerous and ongoing conversations about the shape, style and future of Christian worship." (Jagessar and Burns 2014, x) They write "for participants and presiders in Christian worship, to invite questions, directions and consideration of how liturgical theology and practice needs in certain respects, in different situations, to be chastened, expanded and re-visioned in conversation with postcolonial perspectives." (Jagessar and Burns 2014, xi) Postcolonial perspectives and practices of imitation, improvisation, creativity, and polyvocality are clearly in evidence in liturgical theology and practice.

4.1.1 Imitation

Imitation (Homi Bhabha's 'mimicry') in which the colonized speaks in the very form and 'voice' of the oppressor, in my experience is adopted as a strategy to fulfil different objectives. Being able to reproduce the colonizer's speech 'to the letter' convinces

---

4 Spivak's oft-quoted essay with the title, "Can the Subaltern Speak?" was first published in Cary Nelson and Lawrence Grossberg's *Marxism and the Interpretation of Culture* (1988).

the colonizer that the colonized, far from being incapable, incompetent, or even subhuman, actually possesses all the capabilities of the colonizer. However, as Bhabha argues, mimicry because it always contains an element of mockery, remains menacing to the colonizer always causing uncertainty as to what the colonized is actually trying to convey, and ominously suggesting that the colonized may actually have had an edge over the colonizer (Bhabha 1984, 86). The colonized can 'play the oppressor's part'. Mimicry as a strategy for the subversion and overthrow of colonialism has become a post-colonial way of life, that at times far exceeds even the practice during the colonial period. In Africa we are left especially in the churches with the repetition of the doctrines and negative attitudes of the colonizers towards all things African to the detriment and neglect of these rich traditions. Many of the traumas suffered by persons of African descent result from inauthentic imitation of the discourse and belief patterns foisted upon Africans during colonization. Mimicry as a postcolonializing strategy needs reconsideration for its potential to subvert the crucial tasks of recovery and uncovering of subjugated knowledge can render it counter-productive. Mimicry functions as a defense mechanism needed for the protection of vulnerable souls yet often masking the painful reality of inauthentic existence. Pastoral caregivers and counselors seek to promote the authentic selfhood of clients and parishioners. In this task though they often have to plough on through and work with the subtilties and defenses of mimicry.

4.1.2 Improvisation

In improvisation persons utilize whatever they can find at hand to make the most of an inadequate situation. Improvisation is the creed of the slave, the colonized, the un-free, who must make the most of whatever they can lay their hands on or have access to. The colonized, slaves, and people kept under domination have used incredible skills to improvise. Improvisation is the art of survival. Improvisation is the 'muddling through' that is the lived experience of so many former colonized people. Improvisation in music, art and literature bears witness to the ingenuity and social fortitude of the oppressed. In terms of the colonial experience, it seems to me that the colonized and especially the enslaved utilized improvisation to good effect as a survival strategy. As the need arose for the formulation of ceremonies at times especially of gathering, slaves no doubt used whatever was at hand, and whatever they could call to memory in the crafting of rituals of encouragement, memorial, and renewal. With limited resources of education in the languages of the colonizer, the colonized were still able, as for instance in the establishment of Independent Indigenous churches on the African continent and in the Caribbean and elsewhere, Black churches and other Black spiritual movements, to form social institutions that resembled those of the colonizers whilst infusing them with the philosophies and cultural content of their African heritage.

Improvisation as a colonial and post-colonial activity differs from mimicry in that it includes substantial content from the cultural heritage of the colonized. As a postcolonializing exercise improvisation goes much further than imitation. It entails a degree of independence and unconcern with the gaze of the colonizer. In the early days of slavery it happened mostly away from that gaze. In colonialism it took place decidedly in contexts in which the influence of colonizers was very limited. Thus, improvisation became a significant strategy of the free in which their dignity and capabilities were expressed and endorsed from within themselves and their own communities. Improvisation continues to be a significant postcolonializing activity, but that of those whose resources in both colonial and indigenous terms, are limited. So long as access and opportunity remain limited improvisation will continue to be an important feature of the postcolonial discourse in practical theology.

4.1.3 Creativity

In creativity the colonized have great facility in both their own arts and those of the colonizer. The creative person has inner freedom that is borne of confidence in different spheres and fields of knowledge. Mucherera referred to this as 'integrative consciousness' (2001). Such confidence comes from a variety of sources. The creative person is neither afraid of the sanctions of an authority nor has anxiety at the gaze of any legitimizing forerunner. Creativity is what postcolonial pastoral theology craves and calls for. Innovation is the language of postcolonial practical theologians that have attained maturity. Postcolonial practical theologians are increasingly finding their own authentic voice and are thus more able to make substantial contributions to the disciplines and practices of practical theology. They call for and produce new forms of being, institutions and practices. They weave together disparate materials into innovative forms and practices. Moving beyond improvisation which implies utilizing the leftovers and whatever is available in and from the colonial project in the formulation of structures that implicitly are temporary, creativity requires the generation and utilization of new practices, methods and material in the development and promotion of substantially different forms of activity that go beyond the status quo inherited or established as standard by colonizers. This is what Héctor López-Sierra has referred to as "reinventing of self" (López-Sierra, 2007, 60).

4.1.4 Polyvocality

Postcolonial practical theologians recognize, operate out of and highly value *polyvocality*. They recognize and encourage many voices to speak and be heard on the subjects under consideration. Never satisfied with solely one perspective on any subject, the postcolonial pastoral theologian actively seeks out voices other than their own, especially submerged, ignored or rejected voices, to be invited to the table, and there to articulate their own authentic voice. Subjugated voices with submerged often despised knowledge are given room at the postcolonial table. Educated, middle-class, liberal, progressive voices are not the only ones invited to speak. Nor is there an attempt to silence the speech of the uneducated, differently able, or different. Such recognition and encouragement are vital to the postcolonial project. It is precisely the silencing, suppression, denial, or ignoring of voices because of their difference from the dominant ones, that has led to the need for postcolonial activity.

4.2 Epistemology: How Do we Know What we Know?

Questions such as the following are being addressed. What specifically do the colonized know and how different is it from western knowledge? What does postcolonial or de-colonial practical knowledge really look like? Four features of postcolonial practical epistemology are apparent.

First, it is recognized that postcolonial activities in practical theology need to be *counter-hegemonic*, insurgent even subversive in nature and character. That is to say that postcolonial practical theology operates out of a counter-hegemonic epistemology. Such ways of knowledge by their very nature call into question hierarchy, dominance, and hegemony in human relations. Where patterns of dominance have solidified into oppressive structures that stifle or threaten to squeeze the life out of clients, postcolonial pastoral theologians actively support insurgency and may be deemed subversive by the powers that be. They essentially problematize, disrupt, and attempt to subvert dominant structures with a view to the establishment of more equable relations between and amongst people. Through recognition of domestication on the part of many who suffered the brutal suppression and selective valorizing processes of colonialism, and of the nature of domesticated discourse, it is possible to discern counter-hegemonic patterns and strategies sometimes deeply embedded within domesticated discourse. It is also possible to recognize more overt forms of counter-hegemonic activities in which existing structures are being torn down.

Second, postcolonial practical theology is politically *strategic*. In other words, it brings into critical focus the dialogical nature of relations between theory and practice, and results in actions with transformative intent in the world. I have described this kind of knowledge in line with liberation theologians as "praxiological or practical-and-theoretical with an action-for-change orientation." (Lartey 2013, xvi) The kind of knowing referred to here is knowledge gained through action. An example of this that is being utilized in pastoral care and liturgical reform is dance and rhythmic movement. Drawing upon ethnographic research I have engaged in with African religious healers, elaborated on in a chapter titled, "Knowing through Moving: African Embodied Epistemologies", I write about African embodied ways of knowing self, other and God. With reference to the Anlo-Ewe people of South-East Ghana and Togo, I explain how "*proprioception*, the term used to describe the sensory information that contributes to the sense of position of self and movement, seems to mark the key to human ontology and epistemology in African traditional and African Diasporan religious practice" (Lartey 2016, 102). As I listened intensely and participated in the rituals and practices of African religious practitioners, what has been fascinating for me is that in place of a logo-centric, word-based theory from which is derived particular healing and care practices, African priest healers seem to know through a different means, one more bodily, more incarnational, and especially more kinesthetic. Movement, rhythm, and dance are for them powerful symbols and signals that are cathartic in themselves and also convey important messages that can assist in calling the desired states of being into existence.

Third, postcolonial practical knowledge recognizes its *hybridity* and participation in multi-dimensional discourses and practices. Such knowledge is intrinsically *variegated* and *plural*. *Diversity* is a hallmark, characteristic feature, and desired end of postcolonial practical theological processes. As such they are *messy*, (Jagessar and Burns's 'unsystematic') in that they question and disrupt sharp and clear boundaries between materials, recognizing the often-arbitrary lines of demarcation that are drawn, and calling for attention to complexity and *metissage* in the approach to all matters. Sharp demarcations and neat contents are not to be found in postcolonializing discourse and practices. They are therefore also and always ambiguous and at times contradictory, full of contestation and controversy, wary of over-privileging any one form over all others.

Fourth, postcolonial practical theology is *dynamic* in nature. Epistemological dynamism recognizes that issues are in a constant state of change and flux. As such postcolonial practical theologians attempt to engage in analyses that reflect time, change and movement. Analyzing moving structures can be daunting. However, recognizing that social reality is inevitably fluid is a sign of maturity not to be rejected.

4.3 Praxis: What Does Practical Theology Look Like When it Is Informed by Postcolonial Theory and Practice?

Postcolonial practical theology is definitely oriented towards the 'action' dimension of the 'action-reflection' couplet characteristic of practical theological discourse. Postcolonial practical theologians are wary of discourse that ends with an aesthetically pleasing statement that may not realistically change anything on the ground. They are suspicious of theoretical abstractions that leave power imbalances and inequalities in the distribution of goods, services, and materials intact in the real world. In this regard the praxis-orientation of Liberation Theology continues to be attractive across postcolonial practical theological disciplines. To this end, postcolonial practical theologians recognize the importance of and work towards transformation of communities.

4.3.1 Building Healthy Community

Whereas colonial models of pastoral care and counseling tend to focus upon individuals and their intro-psychic processes, postcolonial pastoral care and counseling emphasizes the deeply *interactional, interpersonal,* and *intersubjective* nature of the human persons. Postcolonial pastoral theologians emphasize the social and global nature of all phenomena and encourage approaches to subjects that engage interactively with all people's experience in the discourse on any subject. Put in another way, postcolonial practical theologians tend to engage analytically and relationally with the agents as well as the practices they wish to critique and transform. Relationality is valued especially when it is set within an ethical framework of equality and respect.

Postcolonial pastoral care ultimately is about community building. A central motivation for postcolonial approaches to pastoral care is a communal relational one. One of the downsides of the drive for the autonomous, self-directed, personally morally responsible, rational, logic-centered individual envisaged and imposed by the westernizing colonial social agents was the loss of community and the socially and relationally integrated persons that traditional African morals upheld. This is not an argument for one to replace the other which sadly was the effect of colonialism. Had there been a greater respect for the communal values of the colonized a better balance would have been sought between the rugged rational individual and the socially responsible communal person. Postcolonial pastoral counseling is directed at the fostering of communities within which acts of care and counseling have meaning and significance, and within which persons may thrive as individuals as well as participants in relational networks to which they may contribute. Pastoral practices and pastoral counseling are the natural outflow of these communities of care. Healthy communities – like healthy families – produce healthy people. Individuals who receive excellent pastoral counseling and whose inner lives are repaired only to return into unwholesome social circumstances will soon be re-infected and need to return for individual therapy. It is the growth of healthy societies that will lead to the stabilization of healthy persons. An individual cannot be well in a society that is toxic and that allows illness to fester. As such there is the need for attention both to the care of individuals and the care of communities if there is to be an encompassing delivery of health.

The aim of postcolonial pastoral care is the cultivation of communal spaces in which all people can be safe, nurtured and empowered to grow. The focus on individual therapy to the exclusion of communal care follows the pattern of an ineffectual colonialism. Postcolonial pastoral care sets individual therapy within a community building paradigm that privileges the growth of persons as social beings and communal participants who seek the well-being of total groups. Pastoral care givers by virtue of their recognition of the importance of communal space and communal resources will be in the forefront of the struggle for safety in community. They seek to establish and often transform ecclesial spaces into places of safety for all persons at risk of molestation, violence, discriminatory or oppressive practices of any sort. This frequently means a keen eye for potential danger evident in the social climate. Aware of the fact that societies can be manipulated and mobilized in ways that are oppressive of minority groups, they keep alert to social and public policy making processes for any hints of legislation that could prove harmful to certain groups. They mobilize resources for the provision of safe houses for women at risk of violence, and the staffing of such premises with suitably trained personnel. They engage in the political processes of the communities in which they work and often advocate in the interest of disadvantaged and marginalized groups. This means that a crucial part of the postcolonial pastoral care giver's art is listening for the voices of the marginalized of whatever kind. Such voices are frequently very loud by their absence. So pastoral care givers will be attuned to the voices of the silenced and the silence of the voiceless. Pastoral care giving includes advocacy for social justice. And pastoral care givers do not shy away from participating in and engaging the political process in the interest of the creation of humane communities. The goal of pastoral care is always the creation of healthy communities in which *all persons* can live humane lives. Human dignity is premised upon social institutions and processes of nurture and growth.

4.3.2 Transforming Cultures: It Takes the Whole World

Postcolonial pastoral care has ultimately to do with the transformation of cultures. Postcolonial pastoral theologians see pastoral care, when it is fulfilling its true vocation, as functioning as a liberating human activity, in line with divine activity. As such it aims at changing underlying assumptions about human communities, about divine presence and activity, and about human well-being. Accordingly, postcolonial pastoral care aims not merely at the personal transformation of individuals, but rather at changing the total ecology of the world, the nature of relations between and amongst peoples. Communities, and therefore individuals, are set within cultures. Whole cultures can promote and maintain healthy communities which in turn nurture individuals who are well. Cultures, in which the signs, symbols, tendencies, ideologies and covert assumptions are disrespectful of human persons and death-dealing, cannot produce healthy communities. Communities that result from the postcolonial pastoral care activities and practices referred to do bear the hallmarks and characteristics of health, safety, and human dignity, interpersonal, communal, and inter-communal well-being.

5 Conclusion

Postcolonial practical theologians are charting a path in their different disciplines in which the upliftment of the forgotten, denied, suppressed, marginalized, and subjugated is front and center. Their aim is not merely to supplant or replace western forms of the disciplines but rather to be authentic partnering voices in what needs to be a global phenomenon in which voices from throughout the world are able to contribute their wisdom and where such contributions are valued and respected. Postcolonial practical theology operates under a vision of empowered communities of the oppressed former colonialized peoples of this world. This vision of global responsibility inspires postcolonial theorists and practitioners to recover subjugated knowledge and to revalue silenced people. The table can be enriched. The practical theological disciplines can be more relevant to a world that is diverse and polyvalent, not by a one-size-fits all monolithic endeavor but instead by a polyvocal, communal, respectful practice of the care of persons.

Bibliography

Baldwin, Jennifer, ed. 2016. *Sensing Sacred: Exploring the Human Senses in Practical Theology and Pastoral Care*. New York: Lexington Books.
Bhabha, Homi. 1984. *The Location of Culture*. London / New York: Routledge.
Choi, Hee-An. 2015. *A Postcolonial Self: Korean Immigrant Theology and Church*. New York: State University of New York Press.
Dreyer, Jaco, Yolanda Dreyer, Edward Foley, and Malan Nel, eds. 2017. *Practicing Ubuntu: Practical Theological perspectives on Injustice, Personhood and Human Dignity*. International Practical Theology 20. Zürich: LIT.
Fanon, Frantz. [1961] 1990. *The Wretched of the Earth*, trans. Constance Farrington. London: Penguin Books.
Harris, Melanie L. 2016. "Womanist Interfaith Dialogue: Inter, Intra, and All the Spaces in Between." In *Postcolonial Practice of Ministry: Leadership, Liturgy and Interfaith Engagement*, edited by Pui-Lan Kwok and Stephen Burns, Lanham: Lexington Books, 199–214.
Jagessar, Michael N. 2016. "Table Habits, Liturgical Pelau, and Displacing Conversation." In *Postcolonial Practice of Ministry: Leadership, Liturgy and Interfaith Engagement*, edited by Pui-Lan Kwok and Stephen Burns, Lanham: Lexington Books, 91–107.
Jagessar, Michael N., and Stephen Burns. 2014. *Christian Worship: Postcolonial Perspectives*. London / New York: Routledge.
Kwok, Pui-Lan, and Stephen Burns, eds. 2016. *Postcolonial Practice of Ministry: Leadership, Liturgy and Interfaith Engagement*. Lanham: Lexington Books.
Lartey, Emmanuel. 1987. *Pastoral Counselling in Inter-cultural perspective: A Study of Some African (Ghanaian) and Anglo-American Views on Human Existence and Counselling*. Frankfurt: Peter Lang.
Lartey, Emmanuel. 2013. *Postcolonializing God: An African Practical Theology*. London: SCM.
Lartey, Emmanuel. 2016. "Knowing through Moving: African Embodied Epistemologies." In *Sensing Sacred: Exploring the Human Senses in Practical Theology and Pastoral Care*, edited by Jennifer Baldwin, New York: Lexington Books, 101–113.
Lartey, Emmanuel. 2018. "Postcolonializing Pastoral Theology: Enhancing the Intercultural Paradigm." In *Pastoral Theology and Care: Critical Trajectories in Theory and Practice*, edited by Nancy J. Ramsay, Oxford: Wiley Blackwell, 79–97.

Lim, Swee-Hong. "Church Music in Postcolonial Liturgical Celebration." In *Postcolonial Practice of Ministry: Leadership, Liturgy and Interfaith Engagement*, edited by Pui-Lan Kwok and Stephen Burns, Lanham: Lexington Books, 123–136.

López-Sierra, Héctor E. 2007. "Towards a Spanish-speaking Caribbean, Postcolonial, Macro-ecumenical, and Trans-pastoral Practical Theological Method." *Journal of Pastoral Theology* 17:57–81.

Madsen, Deborah L. 1999. "Beyond the Commonwealth: Post-Colonialism and American Literature." In *Post-Colonial Literatures: Expanding the Canon*, edited by Deborah L. Madsen, London: Pluto Press, 1–14.

McGarrah Sharp, Melinda M. 2013. *Misunderstanding Stories: Toward a Postcolonial Pastoral Theology*. Eugene: Pickwick Publications.

Moore Gilbert, Bart J. 1997. *Postcolonial Theory: Contexts, Practices, Politics*. London / New York: Verso.

Mucherera, Tapiwa N. [2001] 2005. *Pastoral Care from a Third World Perspective: A Pastoral Theology of Care for the Urban Contemporary Shona in Zimbabwe*. Research in Family and Religion 6. New York: Peter Lang.

Mucherera, Tapiwa N. 2009. *Meet me at the Palaver: Narrative Pastoral Counseling in Postcolonial Contexts*. Eugene: Cascade Books.

Nelson, Cary, and Lawrence Grossberg, eds. 1988. *Marxism and the Interpretation of Culture*. Urbana: University of Illinois Press.

Nyengele, M. Fulgence. 2014. "Cultivating Ubuntu: An African Postcolonial Pastoral Theological Engagement with Positive Psychology." *Journal of Pastoral Theology* 24:1–35.

Park, Hee-Kyu Heidi. 2014. "Toward a Pastoral Theological Phenomenology: Constructing a Reflexive and Relational Phenomenological Method from a Postcolonial Perspective." *Journal of Pastoral Theology* 24:1–21.

Spivak, Gayatri C. 1988. "Can the Subaltern Speak?" In *Marxism and the Interpretation of Culture*, edited by Cary Nelson and Lawrence Grossberg, Urbana: University of Illinois Press, 271–313.

Sugirtharajah, Rasiah S. 2002. *Postcolonial Criticism and Biblical Interpretation*. Oxford: Oxford University Press.

Tan, Jonathan Y. 2016. "Dynamics of Interfaith Collaborations in Postcolonial Asia: Prospects and Opportunities." In *Postcolonial Practice of Ministry: Leadership, Liturgy and Interfaith Engagement*, edited by Pui-Lan Kwok and Stephen Burns, Lanham: Lexington Books, 167–181.

Geir Sigmund Afdal
Practice Theory

1 Introduction

The last decades, new understandings of social and material practices have emerged. It is a heterogeneous process; the changes are taking place within different academic disciplines and traditions, and the various contributions understand practices in somewhat different ways. Still, it is possible to talk about a 'practice turn in social theory' and of 'practice theories' as one collective movement.

In this article, I will give an overview of 'practice theories' and discuss possible implication for the understanding and research of religion. I argue that practice theory is a heterogeneous concept but characterized by a certain social ontology. This social ontology has significant consequences for the understanding of religion. The argument is developed in three steps. First, I situate contemporary practice theories. Secondly, I discuss different understandings of explicit 'practice theories'. Thirdly, I analyze a practice theory approach to religion as a reaction to three separations; between practice and theory; between social practices and individual agents; and between practices and normativity.

Religion is a heterogeneous concept, including very different practices and phenomena. Intercultural and interreligious processes add to the complex and changing character of religion. This chapter is a contribution to a discussion of how to develop the complex, changing and processual character of religion.

2 Situating Practice Theories

Having a background in religion and academic degrees in theology and then moving to the field of education, one of my interests is the intersection between the fields. In this chapter, I move from practice perspectives that are influential in educational science over to religion, and then analyze what they do to the conception of religion.

Giving attention to human practice is of course not new. Much attention has been given to the 'theory-practice'-gap. In a much-sited work, Schön (1983) argues for the value of practical knowledge and reflection-in-action. Schön's context is the relationship between professional practitioners and research, or more precisely, the lack of relationship: "Practitioners and researchers tend increasingly to live in different worlds, pursue different enterprises, and have little to say to one another," he claims (Schön 1983, 308). There is a rift and gap between theory-producing research and the practical knowledge of professional practitioners. Theoretical knowledge is abstract and general, and cannot account for situations of uncertainty, instability, uniqueness, and conflict in practitioners' everyday life. Practitioners' knowledge is mainly tacit, theoretical knowledge is unable to account for practical situations and experiences.

Interestingly, Schön (1983, 280) argues that one of causes of the problem is the separation of thinking from doing. Thought is understood as prior to action, and action as implementation of thought. In professional practices doing and thinking is complementary, he argues.

Other contributors to the discussion of the theory-practice-relation draw on Aristotelian perspectives, emphasizing phonetic, moral knowledge as different from both technical, practical knowledge on one hand and epistemic, theoretical knowledge on the other (Dunn 1993). Many of these contributions are critical to trusting a combination of scientific, epistemic evidence and technical, instrumental rationality in public sectors like health and education.

Practice theories should also be situated in other philosophical traditions. Dewey ([1938] 1986) and pragmatism argues that there is no foundation of knowledge beyond practice, and that reflections are constituted in practical habits. Wittgenstein (1997) understands language as language-game, which means that language should be understood in use and in light of the practices of which it is a part. The interwoven character of language and social practices is also elaborated by Taylor:

> The situation we have here is one which the vocabulary of a given social dimension is grounded in the shape of social practice in this dimension; that is, the vocabulary would not make sense, could not be applied sensibly, where this range of practices did not prevail. And yet this range of practices could not exist without the prevalence of this or some related vocabulary (Taylor 1985, 34).

The close relationship between practice on one hand and language use and theorizing on the other, resembles the one Schön is arguing for, but the argument is more general. It is worth noting that while practice in Schön is by and large understood individually, Taylor argues for practices as social and collective.

Despite differences between the different accounts above, social practices are given a key role in understanding human and social affairs. Practices are often discussed in relation to theory and language, and all authors argue against theory having primacy over practice and for a dynamic relationship.

In the social sciences, Giddens (1984) and Bourdieu (1977) emphasize the importance of practices, and in the 1980s and 1990s research in several fields took what could be called a "practice turn" (Schatzki et al. 2001). Practices had a key role in these studies – often more implicit than explicit. In some cases, the term 'practices' was used, in others it was referred to 'activities' or 'networks'. Many of these research fields worked separate from each other. It seems that studying social and material practices and working with practices as a unit of analysis was a general trend. The concept of practice was more used than theorized, but by putting practice in the forefront, a new understanding of social practices emerged. In this context four different traditions are interesting.

The first practice-oriented tradition is situated in moral philosophy, famously argued in MacIntyre's *After Virtue* ([1981] 1985). MacIntyre (1985, 187) argues that human beings are participants in social practices, and that these social practices have internal goods and standards of excellence. This means that through participation in these activities moral virtues are shaped and developed. The moral is not restricted to autonomous, rational deliberation and choice, it is an aspect of social practices. Such an account does not end in social determinism, the individual navigates through her stories about herself, where she comes from, where she is going and who she is and wants to be.

Secondly, sociocultural and –material approaches of learning and knowledge expanded the understanding of learning from individual, cognitive processes to distributed, situated collective practices. In *Situated Learning* Lave and Wenger (1991) argue against learning as acquisition, the idea that processes of learning are the same all over – the cognitive acquiring of abstract knowledge, which in turn is used in choices of action. Through ethnographic studies they argue that learning is taking place through participation in practices; one learns to be a tailor in the social practice of tailoring. Cognition is taking place in action and interaction. Learning should be understood as a collective and relational process and learning processes must be seen in light of the practices where they take place. There is no general theory of learning; learning is situated. Learning is an aspect of social practices, not abstract, internal cognitive processes. Several authors argue that cognition is distributed between human and material-symbolic actors in practices (Hutchins 1996). Cognition is not an internal property; it is a relational process happening in-between actors. In an academic context one can argue that a researcher is thinking with her articles, computers, and research community. Cultural psychology (Cole 1996) understands human behavior and cognition as aspects of cultural practices, which means that one cannot understand the individual apart from different cultural, social, historical, and situated practices.

Thirdly, authors used many of the same perspectives in organizational studies. Wenger developed the idea of situated learning to a broad theory of *Communities of Practice* (1998), of how participating in a community of practice is connected to identity- and meaning-making-processes. Participation in a community of practice constitute who I am and how I make sense of experiences. Several of these researchers are influenced by Vygotsky (1986) and his idea of mediation. Vygotsky argued that human cognition is mediated by cultural tools, and therefore constituted by and in cultural practices (see also Wertsch 1998). Also building on the work of Leont'ev (1978), Engeström (1987) and others developed Cultural Historical Activity Theory (CHAT). An activity is different from an action in the sense that it is collective, it has a history, and it has a direction and affective drive towards something. Furthermore, activities use different kinds of material and symbolic tools, and they are constituted by divisions of labor and different sets of rules. Mediation is important in understanding activities – the idea that tools, rules, and division of labor constitute affordances and restrictions of what is happening in the activity. Human agency is understood as constituted and conditioned – a middle position between full individual autonomy on one hand and social, structural determinism on the other.

Fourthly, a large and heterogeneous research tradition emerged in the same period, called the Actor Network Theory (ANT). Starting with laboratory and science studies, Latour (2005) and many others (Law; Callon; Knorr Cetina) developed ANT to a general sociological theory. It is a 'sociology of associations', in the sense that it starts 'in the middle of things', in practices, and then analyzes the different parts and how they are associated and related. The relations are not understood causally in the sense that one variable effects another in certain ways, but as translations and mediations. The different associations and relations create networks, and these networks expand the space and time of a 'community of practice'. In a network, actors can be connected to things and persons in distant spaces and times. Furthermore, networks create time and spaces in a different way than regional space and time. Famously, material things are understood as actors on the same level as human beings. Agency is understood radically relational, "an actor is what is made to act by many others" (Latour 2005, 46) – agents are understood as collectively assembled actants. Practices are therefore not primarily social, they are also natural and material, or more exact material-social hybrids. Practices are neither 'communities', like a church choir. To understand a church choir, one has to trace the various material and social connections – across space and time – of which it is made.

3 What Is a Practice Theory?

As mentioned, the theories above are less theories of practice than theories where the conception of practice has a key role. The similarities between these contributions and others, have led authors to formulate explicit theories of practice.

A crucial text is the anthology *The practice Turn in Contemporary Theory* (Schatzki et al. 2001). Several key authors in the development of the new generation of practice theory have contributed to the book: Knorr Cetina, Thévenot, Swidler, Bloor, Lynch, Rouse – and not least, Schatzki. In his introductory chapter, Schatzki discusses what characterized the practice turn, across quite different research traditions:

> In social theory, consequently, practice approaches promulgate a distinct social ontology: the social is a field of embodied, materially interwoven practices centrally organized around shared practical understandings. This conception contrasts with accounts that privilege individuals, (inter)actions, language, signifying systems, the life world, institutions/roles, structures, or systems in defining the social. These phenomena, say practice theorists, can only be analyzed via the field of practices. (Schatzki 2001, 3)

The practice turn is an ontological one – practices are understood as the "primary generic social thing" (Schatzki 2001, 1). Practice theory is an alternative to individual explanations, methodological individualism, and homo economicus on one hand

and structural explanations, methodological holism, and homo sociologicus on the other (Reckwitz 2002, 244). The social is not explained as individual rational choices or individual intentions, nor as consequences of external, abstract structures. The generic social thing is more than the individual actor and less than universal structures, it is the nexus of everyday, collective, historical, material, embodied social practices (Hui, Schatzki and Shove 2017). It is imperative to understand social practices as an *analytical* and not only *empirical* concept. The practice turn does not mean to do more study on social, collective practices, and less on individuals and institutions. It means that individuals, institutions, and everything else are understood as social practices. The ontological character of practice theories means that: "[…] such phenomena as knowledge, meaning, human activity, science, power, language, social institutions, and historical transformation occur within and are aspects or components of the field of practices" (Schatzki 2001, 2).

Reckwitz (2002) locates practice theories within the broad tradition of cultural sociology, which is an alternative to purpose oriented, individualistic sociologies on one hand and norm, structural oriented sociologies on the other. Practice theories distinguish themselves from three other forms of cultural sociology: mentalism, textualism and intersubjectivism. While mentalism focuses on the internal, cognitive meaning-making, textualism is outward-looking and look for how external discourses and linguistic practices order the social world. Intersubjectivism is searching for an interactional, communicative, objective mentalism. This means that practice theories are related to, but different from, theories of meaning-making, discourses, and interaction.

How, then, do practice theories understand 'practice' or 'practices'? Reckwitz argues for a distinction between practice in the singular and practices in the plural. 'Practice' is simply the doing and the action mode of being human, in contrast to theory or thinking. "Practices", however, are "routinized type[s] of behavior which consists of several elements, interconnected to one other: forms of bodily activities, forms of mental activities, 'things', and their use, a background knowledge in the form of understanding, know-how, states of emotion and motivational knowledge" (Reckwitz 2002, 249). Examples of practices vary from rearing practices and political practices to cooking practices and the practice of brushing teeth. Religion is another example of practices. Practices are sets of doings, but also include sayings and meaning making. The relationships are turned on their heads: Discourses and meaning-making do not create practices, discourses are parts and aspects *of* practices.

Schatzki (1996, 89) understands practice as "a temporally unfolding and spatially dispersed nexus of doings and sayings". Taking teaching practice as an example, it consists of a complex blend of ways of doings and ways of sayings. The practice of teaching has a past, present, and future – it is constituted and evolves in time. At the same time a teaching practice is prior to and more than the individual teacher. The teacher enters a teaching practice, participate in it and negotiate the practice. But teaching practice can never be understood by researching the individual teacher. The practice is prior to the practitioner. Furthermore, a teaching practice is dispersed in space. Teaching takes place in the classroom, but not only so. Political, economic, and legal regulations are constitutive parts of teaching. Teaching takes place in numerous contexts, in workplaces, sports and the family. Furthermore, the teaching in the classroom is extended by the students and by material tools like books, calculators or computer software to other spaces and activities (Schatzki 2010). This means that practice theory does not only study local micro-phenomena or delimited practices. Practices are connected with other phenomena, stretching in time and space.

In his introduction of practice theories in the context of organizational studies, Nicolini (2013) identifies five characteristics of practice theories. The following is my own elaboration of these characteristics. First, practice theories understand activity and performance as primary in social life. That is, practice theories are processual. Practices are unfolding and evolving more than they are essentialized 'things'. This does not exclude processes of reification, that for instance valuing in social processes may be reified as values or that meditating may be reified to meditation. The point is that processes are primary, and the analytical context of reifications. The processual and performative character is connected to the production of social practices. The practice of politics is producing policy, the practice of teaching is producing learning, the practice of religion is producing religion. Practices have a drive towards something, a drive which have affective character and involve questions of value. Schatzki calls this the teleo-affective structure of practices, and CHAT understands the 'object' in an activity in somewhat the same way. Secondly, material things and bodies are fundamental to practices. Through the conception of habitus, Bourdieu shows how social practices are inscribed in the bodies of people. The teacher take part in the teaching practice through the habituation of the body. Cognitive sense-making does not happen prior to, but in bodily participating. Cognition is constituted by habitus, not a separate and independent faculty. The same goes for material things, artefacts, and tools. Material things are not separate instruments for human will and actions, things make people act. Furthermore, material objects are integrated in human practice to such extent, that they are extensions of agents (Wertsch 1998). Thirdly, practice theories understand individual agency as constituted, not as full autonomy or determined. On the one hand, individual agency cannot be understood apart from social practices; on the other hand, the practice does not determine the actor. She is constantly negotiating, maneuvering, and expanding. Fourthly, practice theories offer a certain view on knowledge. Knowledge not limited to epistemic knowing-that, but also includes know-how, practical knowledge. Knowledge is connected to taking part in the practice, knowing what and how to do in practices. Knowledge in processual, knowing, not only reified. This does not mean that knowledge is limited to certain ways of knowing within a practice. Practices are knowledge-producing, knowledging (Nonaka and Takeuchi 1995). Knowledge is not only represented, but re-presented, translated and transformed (Latour 2005). Knowledge as product is not separated from the production of knowledge. This means that knowledge is distributed within practices, in-between humans and in-between humans and material objects. Fifth, all social practices are characterized by issues of power, conflict, and politics. Even the 'purest' social practices – the laboratories and natural sciences – are characterized by human interest, deep conflicts and power-relations. There is no reason to think that these characteristics of production will not affect the product. The same goes for practices of religion. There are few reasons to think that power-relations and impure production of religion will not affect religion as product.

Further characteristics could be added. Practice theories as a distinctive social ontology has been mentioned. This ontology can further be described as *flat, relational,* and *processual.* According to Schatzki (2016, 29) "[a] flat ontology holds that everything there is to phenomena of some general sort is laid out on one level of reality". This means that there are no a priori social and analytical levels, like the global, institutional and the person level – or macro, meso and micro. Furthermore, practices are neither located at the everyday, local level – as different from institutions. As mentioned, social practices are an analytical as well as an empirical concept. The social consists of a nexus and bundle of different practices, Schatzki uses the concept of 'plenum' to indicate that all the bundles of practices are at the same level and potentially related. This leads to the relational ontology in practice theories. In quite different ways, authors like Engeström, Latour and Taylor argue against atomism and for understanding the world as associations. An individual, an object or a phenomenon cannot be understood in isolation. Relations are not external contexts of a person, a person is acting, feeling, and thinking in response to someone or something. Furthermore, a person appropriate symbolic and material tools in acting, in the sense that the person would be different without these tools. Human life and society are a network of relations, and through these relations and associations, actors are gradually changed, transformed, or translated. This translating character of relations shows the processual character of practice theory ontology. According to practice theories, social-material phenomena should be understood in use and in motion. Human and material actors are what they are in relations – and in motion.

4 Three Purifications and Religion as Practice

This section will discuss one last characteristic of practice theories in the context of the conception of religion. In general, practice theories draw on pragmatism and their a-dichotomous approach. We have already seen that there is no dichotomy in practice theory between actors and structures, between the individual and the social, between knowledging and knowledge, between autonomy and determinism, between theory and practice and between language and practice. There is neither a dichotomy between facts and values, between is and ought, the descriptive and the normative. Latour (1993) argues that using dichotomies like these, enables purification, which in turn is a key aspect of an account of the modern. The problem, he argues, is that in real life all these things are mixed:

> By all means, they seem to say, let us not mix up knowledge, interest, justice and power. Let us not mix up heaven and earth, the global stage and the local scene, the human and the nonhuman. 'But these imbroglios do the mixing', you'll say, 'they weave our world together!' 'Act as if they didn't exist' the analyst replies (Latour 1993, 3).

Practice theory works from the assumption that the confused masses, the hybrid mixes, the imbroglios, exist. Furthermore, the hybrids are more and different than the sum of pure forms (Latour 1993, 78). The analysis does not start with purified structures, agents, nature, or society, but with mixed practices and the nexus of practices. That is, analysis does not assume or aim for foundational truths, it starts in the middle of things. In the following, I will discuss what the unpurified notion of the individual, language and normativity means for the understanding of religion.

4.1 The (Un)purified Religious Individual

Separating the individual agent from hybrid practices, means that religion can be located in the pure agent. In the study of religion, this is done in several ways. The most (in)famous is understanding religion as beliefs, for instance Tylor's definition of religion as 'belief in spirits'. McKinnon (2002) argues that with the collapse of structural functionalist theory, functional definitions of religion seemed less plausible. Despite criticism, there was a comeback of substantial definitions, and the key role of beliefs in the understanding of religion. There are several alternatives for what kind of beliefs that qualify as religious – superhuman being, supernatural assumptions or transcendent reality (McKinnon 2002). In his genealogy of religion, Smith (1978) argues for religion as a modern concept and for the priority of 'faith' over religion. There are similarities between faith, Tillich's ultimate concern and meaning making in psychology of religion. McKinnon argues that faith is not an improvement from belief; faith resembles protestant intellectualism. Anyhow, faith, ultimate concern and meaning making are concepts which locate religion in the individual. The individual is in the foreground and the social in the background; the social is an external context, and the individual agent is generic in understanding religion.

I argue that practice theory locates religion in social and material practices. More so, religion should be understood as practice, not something that is practiced. Religion does not exist beyond or prior to practices. To rephrase Schatzki, religion is a temporally unfolding and spatially dispersed nexus of doings and sayings. There is no essence of religion beyond how religion is done and made as practice. This does not exclude the extensive processes of reification in religion. In a practice theory perspective, these reifications are not essences. Reification can only be understood as an aspect of practices.

Understanding religion as practice is different from conceiving religion as tradition. Religion is the empirical, hybrid practice, not a normative, prescriptive tradition. Furthermore, religion often takes place in the nexus between different practices.

Religion may be done in a political speech, in a hospital or in gym (Bender et al. 2012). This means that a practice approach to religion does not limit religion to faith communities of practice. The practice of meditation may be understood as hybrid religion; the mix of health, body, mental processes, ways of doing and saying, internet websites, books, and movies, work out stuff and so on. Religion does not have to be pure to be religion. But it is a practice. The same goes for a funeral. A funeral is a nexus of different practices: the practice of human separation, the practice of the funeral agency, the practice of the professional pastor, the practice of grief, the practice of singing, of commemorating, of preaching, and so on.

A lot of important work has been done in sociology of religion on the individualization of religion, in the sense that people are less concerned about religious traditions and construct autonomous religiosity and spirituality (McGuire 2008). The argument here is that the active constructing religious individual does not require methodological individualism. Meditation and healing practices, for example, are not pure constructions of the individual – they are social and material practices. Actors are participating in and actively maneuvering in nexus of practices. Still, understanding the practices are necessary to analyze the maneuvering of individual actors.

4.2 (Un)purified Religious Language

Secondly, practice theory is arguing against a purified conception of language, where language is separated from social practices. I understand language broadly here, including texts, discourses, and theory. Texts and language have of course always played a significant part in several religions. There is a long tradition in religious studies and theology for treating texts as primary source to religion, that is, the meanings of texts are interpreted prior to investigating texts in use in religious practices. Independent of an outsider or insider perspective, religious texts are often understood as expressions of religious universes and sacred ontologies. That is, the development and content of religions can be traced through (historical critical) interpretations of texts. The point here is that meaning of texts is created prior to use. The meanings of texts are applied to practice, not created in religious practices. This may also be combined with a realist view of language as representation, that language represent religion in different (good or bad) ways. The empirical rejoinder is of course: Where do we find this real religion? And who decides what religion really is?

The separation of language from practice may be understood in light of western, protestant religion, emphasizing the particular role of religious scriptures and preaching, and how this religious mode shaped the general understanding of religion in a variety of disciplines (Asad 1993, Bender et al. 2012). Understanding religion as beliefs in sociology of religion and meaning making in psychology of religion, gives primacy to language as the key mode of religion. Inter-actions, rituals, materials, and practices are phenomena that can be explained by beliefs and meaning making, not vice versa.

Understanding religion as practice does not oppose language and action, giving primacy to one or the other. "Practice theories must stress that 'language exists only in its (routinized) use'" (Reckwitz 2002, 255). Doings and sayings are parts of social practices, and nexuses of practices, as are material objects and human actors. This means that texts, language, and discourses should be understood and analyzed in use. Texts are not transporters of a religious content, but mediating artifacts in the practice of religion. Texts and language are used in practices to do and produce things, and to create meaning of the doings and productions.

This leads to a radical symmetry between all the elements and aspects of practices. One element cannot be used a priori to explain other elements and processes, like rituals, affective climate, interactions, the materials in use, and so on. Only empirical studies of religious practices, nexuses and networks can trace the role of the different subjects and objects, what is frequently used, what is not and how religion is made, by whom and what, with which tools and affective direction and production.

A practice theory approach to religion starts, as mentioned, in the middle of things, in the imperfect and blended doings of religion. The focus of analysis are the relations and associations between the different and heterogeneous elements. This requires a radical relational and flat ontology in the study of religion, in the sense that neither texts, language, faith or belief are located at another and separate analytical level than practices.

4.3 (Un)purified Religious Normativity

Thirdly, normativity is frequently purified and separated from how things are done. The issue of normativity is discussed in several contexts, of course. With reference to religion, one may ask what is good and bad about religion, or how is a certain religion done properly, or what is ethically good and right, or how do we decide what is true knowledge. In this context, I want to discuss the use of the transcendence / immanence dichotomy in order to normatively argue what religion 'really' is or ought to be.

The dichotomy is expressed in a variety of ways and embedded in everyday discourses. Armstrong (2001, ix) is an example:

> Very often, priests, rabbis, imams, and shamans are just as consumed by worldly ambition as regular politicians. But all this is generally seen as an abuse of a sacred ideal. These power struggles are not what religion is really about, but an unworthy distraction from the life of the spirit, which is conducted far from the maddening crowd, unseen, silent, and unobtrusive.

Framing religion in such pure and dichotomous terms is not unusual. On the one hand, there is a sphere of "real" religion, on the other, the worldly sphere, regular and maddening. Real religion, the transcendent, can connect with the worldly, the immanent, but only in the form of the internal, unseen, and silent – as individual faith. Nongbri (2013, 19) comments: "Religion is not political, not concerned with current events; it is about 'the heart'. [...] religion is thought to be divorced from history. Thus, in this view, 'religious *traditions*' have '*external* histories', but there is something timeless and ahistorical about religion." Religion and God becomes the "crossed-out God of metaphysics" (Latour 1993, 33) on one hand and in the inner soul and faith of the individual on the other. Real religion is pure metaphysics and pure faith, while the practice of religion is impure representation.

Invoking a separation between this and another world, immanence, and transcendence, is – for understandable reasons – frequently done in the conception of religion. One sophisticated, and currently widely used, definition of religion is Lincoln's (2006, 1). He describes four domains of religion, and the two first are:

> (1) A discourse whose concerns transcend the human, temporal and contingent and that claims for itself a similarly transcendent status, (2) a set of practices whose goal is to produce a proper world and/or proper human subjects, as defined by a religious discourse to which these practices are connected.

Religion is understood primarily as discourses, which in turn produce goals and directions for practices. Language is given primacy to practice, as discussed above. Furthermore, these religious discourses are about what transcends the contingent, mundane, and everyday life, and the discourses get a transcendent status. Lincoln's definition indicates interest in everyday religious practices, communities, and institutions. Simultaneously, everyday religion is given an analytical frame of transcendence, and transcendence as something different and separated from, the mundane and immanent.

The question is whether much of what we would consider religion in everyday life fits within an understanding that gives primacy to transcendence. My claim is that much of what we would consider more or less religious is not driven by discourses or conceptions of transcendence. As mentioned, a funeral is a nexus of practices, actors, materials, and meanings. A funeral is the un/holy mix of money, everyday professional work, stories about everyday life, strong affect, and bodies in tears, singing, preaching, flowers and a coffin. This practice is not driven by a discourse of transcendence, it is driven by several things. And the funeral constitutes and gives meaning to several things. One could of course argue that only certain aspects are religious, not the entire funeral. That would lead to endless purification of what counts as "real" religious. Furthermore, it would miss the empirical point that a funeral may actually involve transcendence in another mode than a pre-given one. Transcendence may be produced in the funeral, as an expansion of the everyday life of participants. Transcendence may be understood not in dichotomy with immanence and as referring to metaphysics and a super-natural sphere:

> It is the conception of the terms 'transcendence' and 'immanence' that ends up being modified by the moderns' return to nonmodernity. Who told us that transcendence had to have a contrary? We have never abandoned transcendence – that is, the maintenance in presence by the mediation of a pass (Latour 1993, 128).

I argue that a practice theory approach understands normativity and transcendence as aspects of practices, not as separated and purified entities. Transcendence may be an aspect of religion, but it is not a necessary or primary condition. Transcendence is produced in religious practices, in interaction and in discourses that are parts of the practices, not by discourses separated from and prior to religion as practice.

5 Impure Religion

In this article, I have given a broad account of practice theories. These theories understand practice not only as the doing mode of human affairs, but as an ontological category in the conception of society. My main claim in the second part of the article has been that giving practices a generic role has several consequences for the understanding of religion, many of which conflict with traditional and current conceptions in the different disciplines of religion. The ambition has not been to give a new definition of religion, but to discuss how religion can be understood as practice, as different from 'the practice of religion'. In sum, I argue for impure religion – that there never was, and never will be, pure religion.

Bibliography

Armstrong, Karen. 2001. *Islam: A Short History*. London: Phoenix.
Asad, Talal. 1993. *Genealogies of Religion: Discipline and Reasons of Power in Christianity and Islam*. Baltimore: Johns Hopkins University Press.
Bender, Courtney, Wendy Cage, Peggy Levitt, and David Smilde, eds. 2012. *Religion on the Edge: De-centering and Re-centering the Sociology of Religion*. Oxford: Oxford University Press.
Bourdieu, Pierre. 1977. *Outline of a Theory of Practice*. Cambridge, MA: Cambridge University Press.
Cole, Michael. 1996. *Cultural Psychology: A Once and Future Discipline*. Cambridge, MA: Harvard University Press.
Dewey, John. [1938] 1986. "Logic. The Theory of Inquiry." In *The Later Works 1925–1953*. Vol. 12, edited by Jo Ann Boydston, Carbondale: Southern Illinois University Press, 1–2.
Dunn, Joseph. 1993. *Back to the Rough Ground*. Notre Dame: University of Notre Dame Press.
Engeström, Yrjö. 1987. *Learning by Expanding: An Activity-Theoretical Approach to Developmental Research*. Helsinki: Orienta-Konsultit.
Giddens, Anthony. 1984. *The Constitution of Society: Outline of a Theory of Structuration*. Cambridge: Polity Press.
Hui, Allison, Theodore Schatzki, and Elizabeth Shove. 2017. *The Nexus of Practices: Connections, Constellations, Practitioners*. London: Routledge.
Hutchins, Edwin. 1996. "Learning to Navigate." In *Understanding Practice: Perspectives on Activity and Context*, edited by Seth Chaiklin and Jean Lave, Cambridge: Cambridge University Press, 33–63.
Latour, Bruno. 1993. *We Have Never Been Modern*. Cambridge, MA: Harvard University Press.
Latour, Bruno. 2005. *Reassembling the Social: An Introduction to Actor-Network-Theory*. Oxford: Oxford University Press.

Lave, Jean and Etienne Wenger. 1991. *Situated Learning: Legitimate Peripheral Participation*. Cambridge: Cambridge University Press.
Leont'ev, Alexei. 1978. *Activity, Consciousness, and Personality*. Englewood Cliffs: Prentice Hall.
Lincoln, Bruce. ²2006. *Holy Terrors: Thinking about Religion after September 11*. Chicago: University of Chicago Press.
MacIntyre, Alasdair. ²1985. *After Virtue: A Study in Moral Theory*. London: Duckworth.
McGuire, Meredith B. 2008. *Lived Religion: Faith and Practice in Everyday Life*. New York: Oxford University Press.
McKinnon, Andrew M. 2002. "Sociological Definitions, Language Games, and the 'Essence' of Religion." *Method & Theory in the Study of Religion* 14:61–83.
Nicolini, Davide. 2013. *Practice Theory, Work, and Organization: An Introduction*. Oxford: Oxford University Press.
Nonaka, Ikujiro, and Hirotaka Takeuchi. 1995. *The Knowledge-Creating Company*. New York: Oxford University Press.
Nongbri, Brent. 2013. *Before Religion: A History of a Modern Concept*. New Haven: Yale University Press.
Reckwitz, Andreas. 2002. "Toward a Theory of Social Practices: A Development in Culturalist Theorizing." *European Journal of Social Theory* 5:243–263.
Schatzki, Theodore. 1996. *Social Practices: A Wittgensteinian Approach to Human Activity and the Social*. Cambridge: Cambridge University Press.
Schatzki, Theodore, Karin Knorr Cetina, and Eike von Savigny, eds. 2001. *The Practice Turn in Contemporary Theory*. London: Routledge.
Schatzki, Theodore. 2001. "Introduction: Practice Theory." In *The Practice Turn in Contemporary Theory*, edited by Theodore Schatzki, Karin Knorr Cetina, and Eike von Savigny, London: Routledge, 1–14.
Schatzki, Theodore. 2010. *The Timespace of Human Activity*. Lanham: Lexington Books.
Schatzki, Theodore. 2016. "Practice Theory as Flat Ontology." In *Practice Theory and Research: Exploring the Dynamics of Social Life*, edited by Gert Spaargaren, Don Weenink, and Machiel Lamers, Abingdon: Taylor and Francis, 28–42.
Schön, Donald A. 1983. *The Reflective Practitioner: How Professionals Think in Action*. New York: Basic Books.
Smith, Wilfred C. 1978. *The Meaning and End of Religion*. New York: Harper & Row.
Taylor, Charles. 1985. *Philosophy and the Human Sciences: Philosophical Papers 2*. Cambridge: Cambridge University Press.
Vygotsky, Lev. 1986. *Thought and Language*. Cambridge: MIT Press.
Wenger, Etienne. 1998. *Communities of Practice. Learning, Meaning and Identity*. Cambridge: Cambridge University Press.
Wertsch, James. 1998. *Mind as Action*. New York: Oxford University Press.
Wittgenstein, Ludwig. 1997. *Filosofiske undersøkelser*, trans. Mikkel B. Tin, Oslo: Pax.

Tõnu Lehtsaar
Psychology of Religion

1 Introduction

The psychology of religion can be defined as a branch of psychology explaining human religiosity and spirituality using psychological methods and theories. The essence of the psychology of religion is explained in the presentation of the 36th division of the American Psychological Association (APA 2018). This Division, the Society for the Psychology of Religion and Spirituality, promotes the application of psychological research methods and interpretive frameworks to diverse forms of religion and spirituality; encourages the incorporation of the results of such work into clinical and other applied settings; and fosters constructive dialogue and interchange between psychological study and practice on the one hand and between religious perspectives and institutions on the other.

The term 'psychology of religion' is in the process of change. It is increasingly being replaced with the term 'psychology of religion and spirituality'. For both religiosity and spirituality, the belief and/or the experience of the divine is essential. Religiosity refers to the form of spirituality having a certain doctrine, organized practice, and organizational affiliation. Spirituality is primarily oriented towards experience and personal transformation. Conceptualization and measurement of these realities is one of the research subjects of contemporary psychology of religion.

Another development during the past decades has been a rise in intercultural and interreligious studies. Several basic concepts of the psychology of religion, such as religious development, religious orientation, religious values and religious (de)conversion, have been studied from comparative perspective. At the same time, we should recognize that there in no one single cultural psychology of religion. Very different culturally sensitive approaches can be gathered under this general term (Belzen 2010).

Working as the staff counselor-chaplain at the university provides an excellent opportunity to apply knowledge of the psychological side of religion. The focus of any kind of counseling process is on human experiences, problems, and behaviour. All the theoretical concepts and research data serve as tools to interpret these experiences and behaviour. Therefore, an eclectic approach can be applied using the theories and empirical knowledge that are best suited to a particular counseling case.

2 Religion from a Psychological Perspective

As we know, the word 'religion' means different things to different people. There is no consensus on this concept among psychologists of religion. By and large, there have been two types of approaches. The first relates to one particular characteristic where religion is defined based on one variable. This variable can be, for example, the experience of the holy, the practice of prayer or of certain beliefs. In this conceptual framework, one possibility is to perceive as religious everything in the human psyche and/or behaviour that is related to a deity or to a higher power.

The other approach is multidimensional: treating religion as a combination of different dimensions. This approach goes back to Glock (1962) and has been modified by various authors. The dimensions of religion are experiential, ideological, ritualistic, intellectual, and consequential. The dimension of belonging was added to this list later.

The experiential dimension of religion refers primarily to religious feelings concerning a religious experience. The number of feelings accompanying a religious experience is not limited. It could range from love to fear and from awe to despair. From psychology of religion's early inception, the role of the experiential dimension of religion was emphasized. In many cases, the existence, intensity, and type of feeling are perceived as criteria for true religion.

The ideological dimension primarily concerns the beliefs one has. This dimension refers to the intellectual side of religion, to what it is that is believed. Psychologically speaking, how strongly a particular belief is held and what the practical implications on the behaviour are, are held as important. Beliefs express the essential teachings of a religion. Beliefs also define the purpose of humankind, the meaning for the divine perspective. Beliefs may also hold practical recommendations and implications for everyday life.

The ritualistic dimension refers to a set of repeated symbolic behaviours that bear religious meaning. The main social function of rituals is the provision of social cohesion and stability. On the individual level, rituals satisfy the need for belonging and identity. Celebration of weddings, funerals, and the birth of a first child are just a few examples of the rituals practiced. Religious rituals usually have some specific characteristics: they symbolize the presence of the divine, help people involved get closer to God, and entrust people to God's care even after the ritual is over.

The knowledge dimension refers to the information one has about their religion. On one end of the spectrum, it is possible to practice a religion without any particular knowledge of its meaning. On the other, an individual may be extremely competent in religious teachings and practices.

The consequential or effect dimension refers to the impact of religion on human behaviour in general. Areas like moral decision-making, coping with stress, well-being and health behaviours have been studied. One of the characteristics of one's religiosity is the number of areas of life influenced by religion.

The belonging dimension means emotional and formal membership of a religious group, movement, or organization. There are religious organizations and movements with very loose membership based on the feeling of solidarity. In others, the membership may be very formal. Belonging can follow or precede religious conversion. In all cases, the sense of 'we' is an important part of belonging.

The dimensions of religion may form very different combinations in one's life. It is possible that one dimension is prevalent and others less represented. For example, a person can be religious just because of strong beliefs and have only superficial religious feelings. Another person may have several intense religious experiences without any particular knowledge or ideological reasoning.

These dimensions provide a theoretical framework for interreligious studies as well. This means that different religious traditions, movements, and practices between different cultures or within one culture can be studied based on these categories. For example, religious dedication or religious fundamentalism can have similar psychological characteristics despite their ideological and ritualistic dimensions being very different.

3 Psychological Theories and Studies of Religion

Psychological studies of religion can be split into two areas: methodological and theoretical. For the psychology of religion, these two categories are essential because the psychology of religion uses the methods of psychology and psychological theories to design the research and interpret the data gathered. The following is a brief overview of the methods and theories used.

The psychological methods used in the psychology of religion as a social science can be broadly divided into two large groups: qualitative and quantitative research methods (Weathington, Cunningham, and Pittenger 2010). These methods concern methods of data collection and data interpretation. These methods can also complement each other, through mixed methods. For example, interviews (a qualitative method) can be analyzed using quantitative content analysis. For both methods, the two criteria of scientific research, reliability, and validity, must be guaranteed.

The most widely used qualitative method in the psychology of religion are interviews, observations, biographical analyses, case studies and analyses of personal documents. The popularity of qualitative methods is grounded in the fact that a person's religion – as well as the social occurrences of religion (rituals and movements), can be studied in their individuality to a sufficient level of detail and depth. The prime concern with qualitative methods is that the power of generalization is relatively low and that reliable qualitative methods are relatively expensive to use.

One of the most popular quantitative research methods in the psychology of religion is the use of surveys. As a result of the wide use of this method, a remarkable number of correlational relationships between different aspects of religion and religiosity have been gathered. The drawback is that we cannot always give meaningful interpretation to the data that arises.

One way to overcome the lack of theories in the field of the psychology of religion is to use other psychological theories explaining intra-psychological phenomena or human behaviour. For the psychology of religion, it means that planning the research and interpreting the data gathered is carried out based on a general theoretical understanding of the human psyche and behaviour. The following is a description of five different psychological traditions – psychodynamic, cognitive, neuropsychological, evolutionary, and positive psychology – and of their impact on the psychology of religion (Nelson 2010; Wulff 1997).

In the *psychodynamic or psychoanalytical approach*, one's personality and behaviour are seen as essentially determined by unconscious drives. Unconscious material is heavily influenced by the events of early childhood. Emotional and psychological problems are often rooted in conflicts between the conscious and unconscious mind.

The impact of psychoanalysis on the psychology of religion can be condensed into three fields. First, the terminology of psychoanalysis can be used in describing religious phenomena. For example, religion can be described as a protective system, or hiding a sin as a result of a defense mechanism. Second, particular theoretical approaches for describing religiosity have been developed. For example, according to Attachment Theory, the image of God can be treated as an attachment figure. Third, psychoanalysis has a remarkable impact on pastoral counseling, where the analytical conversation has been used as therapeutic tool.

The *cognitive approach* to the psychology of religion studies the relationship of religion to higher mental processes, such as attention, language use, memory, perception, problem solving, and thinking. It involves investigation of the role and impact of religion on internal mental states and processes. One of the main issues here is the question of specifically religious mental processes. The general point of view is that psychologically there are general human phenomena, like thinking or feeling, and religious thinking is a subcategory of these phenomena. What makes one's psychological process sacred is its relation to religion in general or to a person's category of the sacred, or otherworldly. From this perspective, religion has a meaning-giving and attributive character.

Under the cognitive approach, religious beliefs, religious doubts and struggles, religious feelings, religious motivation in decision-making, religious moral reasoning and religious motivation have been studied.

The *neuropsychology of religion* primarily deals with neurophysiological correlates of religious experiences and religious behaviour. These explanations are based on a general neuropsychological understanding of the localization of psychological processes in the human brain and the relation of brain activity to different types of human behaviour.

The three fields of neuropsychological studies of religion, which are developing rapidly, are as follows. First, the localization of religious experiences in the human brain. The main conclusion of the research is that it depends on the type and character of a religious experience. The type of experience can be mystical, ecstatic, intuitive, purely emotional, or rational. Second, the impact of psychedelic drugs on religious experience. Third, the relation of distractions of neurological functioning and mental illnesses to religious experiences and religious behaviour. The main conclusion is that religious experiences and behaviours have their representations in the human brain, drugs can facilitate religious experiences and religion can have diverse effects on mental functioning, from a balancing effect to a situation where religious practices can also be a source of mental dysfunction.

The *evolutionary psychology of religion* is a relatively new branch of the psychology of religion. Evolutionary psychology is a theoretical approach to psychology attempting to explain the adaptation of useful mental and psychological traits as functional products of natural selection. Alongside memory, patterns of social behaviour, models of thinking and decision-making, religion too can be interpreted from the evolutionary perspective.

One of the main ideas of the evolutionary approach is that only the behaviours of functional experiences will be maintained through the process of natural selection. The fact that religion has existed in all human cultures prompts the question about its evolutionary functionality. To answer this broad question, evolutionary psychology categories are used to explain the role and functionality of religion. Terms like adaptation, inference system, functional behaviour and universal patterns are used. In short, the evolutionary psychology of religion is focused on how evolution has shaped the religious mind and religious behaviour.

The *positive psychology of religion* is related to a humanistic understanding of human behaviour. It is a scientific approach to studying human thoughts, feelings, and behaviour with a focus on strengths. Positive psychology is a perspective, an approach to studying positive experiences (happiness, inspiration), positive states of mind and traits (gratitude, compassion) and applying positive principles in professional behaviour (spiritual leadership, supportive coaching models).

In positive psychology, the virtues leading to well-being are listed. These are wisdom and knowledge, courage, humanity, justice, temperance, and transcendence. The last item encompasses spirituality with all its dimensions, including religiosity. Apart from the essence of religiosity, which is to enhance one's well-being and happiness, its different aspects, such as its relation to health behaviours, coping, finding meaning, prosocial behaviour, well-being, and happiness, are studied in the context of positive psychology.

In concrete research, one of the major psychological approaches can be used as a framework for research design and data analysis. Another option is to use a synthetic approach, in which different schools are employed to explain the phenomena investigated. For example, to gain a better understanding of someone's religious experience, both psychoanalytical and neuropsychological categories can be used.

4 Research Subjects in the Psychology of Religion

The psychology of religion is about bringing explanation to three interrelated areas. First, how is religion related to the intrapsychic processes? Second, what is the impact of a person's religiosity on their behaviour? Third, how are people of different ages developing in religious terms (religious development)? These three broad fields – intrapsychic processes, behaviour and development – can be considered the main focus of the psychology of religion.

4.1 Religion and Intrapsychic Processes

Religion and intrapsychic processes have been studied under the cognitive psychology of religion. Among others, religious experiences, specifically religious phenomena have attracted attention throughout the history of the psychology of religion. Since the times of William James (1842–1910), the experiential dimension of religion has been considered by several scholars to be the root and centre of a person's religion. This means that on the personal level one's religious experiences play an important role in their religion.

In his classic work "Varieties of religious experience", William James ([1902] 1958, 42) defined religious experience as "feelings, acts and experiences of individual men, in their solitude, so far as they apprehend themselves to stand in relation to whatever they may consider the divine". He did not find religious experiences to be 'supernatural', but rather a natural fact of human life. In James' interpretation, religious traditions developed around individuals who had deep religious experiences. Consequently, personal religious experiences lie at the heart of religion.

Rudolf Otto ([1917] 1950) argued that there is one common factor to all religious experience irrespective of cultural background. He identifies this factor as the 'numinous'. The numinous cannot be strictly defined as it is that by which all religious experiences are defined. The numinous can only be evoked or awakened in the mind. The numinous is a realm or dimension of reality that is mysterious, awe-inspiring, and fascinating. According to Otto, the best expression for the numinous is the Latin phrase *mysterium tremendum* – a magnificent mystery. The mystery is the 'Wholly Other', which is beyond apprehension and comprehension.

Informative for understanding the structure of a religious experience are the studies of Karl Girgensohn (1921) which are based on the use of the method of experimental introspection. He asked the subjects to read different religious texts and recorded their reports of internal experiences. As a result, he described the structure of a religious experience as consisting of primary and secondary components.

The primary components of a religious experience are intuitive thinking and the ego function. Intuitive thinking is vague and unformulated, uncontrollable, and unrepeatable, and is associated with feelings of pleasure and displeasure. The ego function means that a person's ego has to take a stand when confronted with a religious reality. The secondary components are images and the will. Images were the 'mental pictures' the respondents reported to have seen during the reading of the text. The will is a result of the ego function and refers to a new attitude in terms of greater commitment to and identity with the religious reality.

Essentially, religious experience means a person experiencing something called the divine. The divine is understood differently by different persons and in different religious traditions. During a mystical experience, one feels as though they have been touched by some higher or greater truth or power. This may occur inside or outside a religious setting or religious tradition.

According to Pahnke (1971), the main characteristics of a mystical experience are as follows: (1) unity – a sense of cosmic oneness, (2) transcendence of time and space, (3) a deeply felt positive mood, (4) a sense of sacredness, (5) noetic quality – a feeling of insight or illumination, (6) paradoxicality – a person may realize that he/she is experiencing, for example, "an identity of opposites," yet it seems to make sense at the time, (7) alleged ineffability (8) transience – the experience passes, (9) persisting positive changes in attitudes and behaviour.

According to Paloutzian (2017, 250), religious experiences differ along several dimensions, such as ordinary versus unusual, frequent versus infrequent, pre-belief versus post-belief, mystical versus earthly, discrete versus continuous, and explainable versus unexplainable. All this shows the variety of possible religious experiences.

4.2 Religiosity and Behaviour

The relationship between one's religiosity and behaviour covers different fields, such as religion and helping behaviour, religion and moral decision-making, religion and health behaviour, the impact of religion on purposeful action, religion and coping. There are some forms of behaviour that can be called religious behaviour. The essence of such types of behaviour is addressing the divine relationship or carrying religious meaning. A good example thereof is prayer.

The relation between religion and helping behaviour raises the question of whether religious people are more helpful than non-religious people. The empirical results of the studies in this field are controversial. In their classic "Good Samaritan" experiment, Darley and Batson (1973) found that in a situation where someone needs help, one's being in a hurry has more bearing on helping behaviour than religious orientation and actual thoughts (religious or non-religious).

A sweeping generalization about religion and pro-social attitude would be that most of the religious traditions cultivate pro-social attitudes; most religious people say that they are rather helpful. Despite vivid examples like Mother Theresa, today's empirical research has not attested to the greater helpfulness of religious compared to non-religious people.

Religion and moral decision-making have been studied in relation to different forms of behaviour. For example, religious people are more critical of teasing than non-religious people. Their moral decisions are based on their religious value system. Religious people tend to be more conservative compared to general tendencies in a society.

According to Nelson (2010, 313), studies on connections between religion, spirituality and health show a moderate correlation between religious involvement and better health status. A positive effect is found at both the individual and the group level. The prevalent opinion is that religion has an indirect impact on health. It means that not religion as such but a religiously motivated lifestyle, e.g., taking care of the body as a temple of God, results in a healthy way of life.

Religion can drive purposeful human action in different ways. One of the main processes in this area is sanctification as a psychological process through which aspects of life take on a spiritual quality and significance. Respondents can describe the process with expressions like 'God played a role in the development of this striving', 'I experience God through this striving', and 'this striving reflects what I think God wants for me'. Apart from religious pursuits, religion can also satisfy general human needs, such as the need for status and acceptance, curiosity, social contact, and idealism. The studies in this field can be generalized into the statement that the function of religion cannot be reduced to a naturalistic set of human motivations. The sacred component of religion requires that religious motivation be appreciated and investigated on its own terms.

A coping strategy is the thoughts and actions we use to deal with a threatening or stressful situation, e.g., action taking, planning, or seeking emotional support. Religion can serve as a coping strategy. In stressful situations, people tend to be more religious than in times of tranquility. There are various means of using religion for coping with the stress of the life. According to Pargament et al. (2015), the methods of religious coping can be divided into five groups. These are as follows: the religious methods of coping to find meaning, to gain mastery and control, to gain comfort and closeness to God, to gain intimacy with others and God, and to achieve life transformation.

One of the purely religious forms of behaviour is prayer, generally understood as a dialogue between a human and God. Under the psychology of religion, the dimensions, types, and psychological effects of prayer have been studied. In addition, the category of God's image as a subjective understanding of God is connected with studies on prayer. It appears that prayer has at least three dimensions: awareness, including concern for others and self-awareness; upward reaching, search for meaning, of experiences of inner peace, and outward reaching, including petitionary prayer.

The psychological effects of prayer depend on different variables like the characteristics of the image of God or religious orientation. It is possible to distinguish the effects of prayer on the individual and the group level. On the individual level, prayer increases awareness of one's self, needs and motives. Further, prayer supports one's faith and hope. Prayer also helps to verbalize internal feelings and find meaning for actions and life in general. On the group level, the practice of joint prayer increases the group's cohesiveness and its centeredness on religious values.

The correlation between religiosity and behaviour may manifest itself on different levels. For example, religion can provide a motivation, meaning or goal for acting. In some cases, e.g., religious ritual or prayer, we can talk about purely religious behaviour.

4.3 Religious Development

Religious development has been studied from three different perspectives. First, religious development is understood as a lifelong phenomenon. Under this perspective, religious development has been studied in childhood, adolescence, adulthood, and old age. In addition, theories of lifelong religious development covering the entire span of human life have been developed. The second perspective concerns some concrete aspects of one's religious development, such as conversion, apostasy or the turning points in the process of religious development.

Religious development in childhood has been investigated from different angles. For example, it has been found that religious socialization of children depends on the caring attitude and religious harmony between parents. Children experience God in everyday situations, not necessarily in religious settings. For children, prayer and the image of God develop from the fantasy stage toward a more individualistic and reflective stage.

Religion in adolescence is mainly influenced by the development of abstract thinking. The image of God is more conceptualized; the spiritual dimension of life requires a satisfactory explanation. Typical to adolescence are religious doubts. As to religious socialization, the role of the family decreases and the influence of peers, friends, and school increases.

Most of the studies on religiosity have been conducted on adults. Special attention has been paid to the religiosity of the elderly. Ties with the religious community change and various values are reassessed in a more reflective manner. An invariable subject is the attitude toward approaching death. Studies of the relationship between death anxiety and religiosity have controversial results. The general understanding is that death anxiety is alleviated not so much by religious beliefs as by confidence in one's worldview in general.

There are two more well-known theories of lifelong religious development. These are James Fowler's theory of faith development and Fritz Oser's and Paul Gmünder's theory of the stages of religious judgment. In his theory, Fowler (1981) defines faith as a universal quality of human meaning-making. Faith describes the underlying meaning-making process used by all people regardless of their beliefs or cultural tradition. The faith development theory conceptualizes this psychological process of meaning-making in seven stages. The highest stage is called universalizing faith, at which people are detached from any ideology, living their values like Mother

Theresa or Dietrich Bonhoeffer. Fowler suggests that these stages are the same regardless of whether individuals are aligned with a religion or are non-religious.

Oser and Gmünder (1991) understand religious judgment as the way in which an individual reconstructs his or her experience from the point of view of a personal relationship with the Ultimate (God). Religious development is concerned with the age-related, meaning-making qualities of this reconstruction. Religious judgements can occur in any context but have special importance during times of crisis. The authors describe six stages of religious judgement starting with the stage of absolute heteronomy, where God is active and the human being reactive, and ending with the stage of intersubjective religiosity, where God can be seen in all commitments, and loyalty to the Ultimate is shown in relation with others.

One of the specific phenomena of religious development studied is that of conversion. The main motive for conversion can be intellectual, where a person intellectually comes to the assurance of the existence of God; mystical, where conversion is a result of a supernatural experience; and social, where a person converts because of social pressure or demand. Based on the speed of conversion, distinction can be made between sudden conversion and gradual conversion. One question relating to conversion is whether conversion changes personality. The answer is that there are changes on the general level of functioning, like ultimate concerns and the goals of life. There may also be changes in mid-level functioning, such as concrete goals and instrumental values. The main characteristics of personality, such as openness to experience, conscientiousness, extraversion, agreeableness, and neuroticism or will, remain the same.

Current psychological studies are investigating the phenomena of spiritual transformation and apostasy, or deconversion. Spiritual transformation denotes changes in one's meaning system in relation to the sacred. Deconversion (Streib et al. 2009) can be described through different trajectories, such as secularizing exit, oppositional exit, religious switching, integrating exit, privatizing exit or heretical exit. There are also cultural differences between North America and Europe. In North America, religious deconversion is interpreted as a personal spiritual change, and in Europe more as a change of religious tradition.

5 Contribution of the Psychology of Religion to Practical Theology

Historically, practical theology has been a church-related subdiscipline of theology. Today, practical theology is becoming increasingly independent, focusing more on religious practices inside and outside the church. Therefore, practical theology is incorporating disciplines like the psychology of religion, the sociology of religion, psychotherapy, and communication theory.

Based on Richard Osmer's (2008) approach, it is possible to develop a framework for practical theological interpretation by focusing on four key questions:
- What is going on? (descriptive-empirical task)
- Why is this going on? (interpretative task)
- What ought to be going on? (normative task)
- How might we respond? (pragmatic task)

The object of these questions is similar to the psychology of religion and practical theology – a living human document.

The psychology of religion can contribute to these tasks in different ways. It provides a solid empirical basis of human experiences and practices. These data are interpreted in psychological terms, but practical theology can give a larger, religious meaning to the knowledge gathered. Although the psychology of religion is not normative *per se*, the categories of functional and dysfunctional religiosity can be applied in pastoral care and counseling. The psychology of religion can provide conceptual and evidence-based arguments for solving practical problems in people's lives and in church practice.

Finally, one of the greatest deficits in the psychology of religion is the theory. Despite tremendous amounts of correlative data, psychometric results, experimental and observational data, it still lacks a systematic approach to putting these parts together. The situation in the psychology of religion has been called a "cry for theory" (Paloutzian and Park, 2005). Hopefully, one day the friendship between research-based psychology of religion and philosophically orientated practical theology will lead to such a theory.

Bibliography

American Psychological Association. 2018. http://www.apadivisions.org/division-36/about/index.aspx (29.11.2021).
Belzen, Jacob A. 2010. *Towards Cultural Psychology of Religion: Principles, Approaches, Applications*. Dordrecht: Springer.
Darley, John M., and Daniel C. Batson. 1973. "From Jerusalem to Jericho: A Study of Situational and Dispositional Variables in Helping Behavior." *Journal of Personality and Social Psychology* 27:100–108.
Fowler, James W. 1981. *Stages of Faith: The Psychology of Human Development and the Quest for Meaning*. San Francisco: Harper & Row.
Girgensohn, Karl Gustav. 1921. *Der seelische Aufbau des religiösen Erlebens: Eine religionspsychologische Untersuchung auf experimenteller Grundlage*. Leipzig: S. Hirzel.
Glock, Charles Y. 1962. "On the Study of Religious Commitment." *Religious Education* 57:98–110.
James, William. [1902] 1958. *The Varieties of Religious Experience*. New York: The New American Library.
Nelson, James M. 2010. *Psychology, Religion and Spirituality*. New York: Springer.
Oser, Fritz, and Paul Gmünder. 1991. *Religious Judgment: A Developmental Perspective*. Birmingham: Religious Education.

Osmer, Richard R. 2008. *Practical Theology: An Introduction*. Grand Rapids: Eerdmans.

Otto, Rudolf. [1917] 1950. *The Idea of the Holy: An Inquiry into the Non-Rational Factor in the Idea of the Divine and its Relation to the Rational*. London: Oxford University Press.

Paloutzian, Raymond F. ³2017. *Invitation to the Psychology of Religion*. New York: Guilford Press.

Paloutzian, Raymond F., and Crystal L. Park. 2005. "Integrative Themes in the Current Science of the Psychology of Religion." In *Handbook of the Psychology of Religion and Spirituality*, edited by Raymond F. Paloutzian and Chrystal L. Park, New York: Guilford Press, 3–20.

Pahnke, Walter. 1971. "The Psychedelic Mystical Experience in the Human Encounter with Death." *Psychedelic Review* 11:3–20.

Pargament, Kenneth, Gene G. Ano, and Amy B. Wachholtz. 2015. "The Religious Dimension of Coping: Advances in Theory, Research, and Practice." In *Handbook of the Psychology of Religion and Spirituality*, edited by Raymond F. Paloutzian and Chrystal L. Park, New York: Guilford Press, 560–579.

Streib, Heinz, Ralph W. Hood, Barbara Keller, Rosina Marth Csöff, and Christoph F. Silver. 2009. *Deconversion: Qualitative and Quantitative Results from Cross-Cultural Research in Germany and the United States of America*. Göttingen: Vandenhoeck & Ruprecht.

Weathington, Bart L., Christopher J. L. Cunningham, and David J. Pittenger. 2010. *Research Methods for the Behavioral and Social Sciences*. Hoboken: John Wiley & Sons.

Wulff, David. M. ²1997. *Psychology of Religion: Classic & Contemporary*. New York: John Wiley & Sons.

Bonnie J. Miller-McLemore
Religion and the Social Sciences

1 Introduction

Of all the entries in the *International Handbook*, this chapter deals with one of the broadest and, dare I say, most important questions: How do practical theologians engage religion and social science? I say 'broadest' and 'most important' because the rise of social science lies at the heart of practical theology's modern ascent, and social scientific analysis shapes almost all practical theological endeavors. Nearly all the chapters in the third part of this book deal with particular sciences (e.g., anthropology of religion; psychology of religion; sociology of religion). In fact, most chapters in the book as a whole display the value of social science in analyzing specific concepts (e.g., family; media) and practices (e.g., conversion; fasting). Despite the challenges in using social science, it remains an essential partner in practical theology, comprising a basic approach to the study of religion and, as I will argue, an essential component of practical theology's twentieth-century rebirth and continued growth.

Engagement with social science raises all sorts of questions for practical theologians, however. How should we approach them? What *is* social science? What *is* religion? What kind of knowledge comes from each discipline or practice? What does theology gain from social science, and what, if anything, does religion and theology have to offer? Does social science have hidden values that demand analysis? Is it complicit with religion in imposing colonialist assumptions in its study of the 'other'?

Although this essay will not answer these questions exhaustively, it provides initial tools for addressing them. The main focus is to show how the rise of social science sparked a rejuvenation of practical theology and became one of its most important theoretical approaches. I begin with a description of the growth of social science in the United States, focusing on psychology. I then turn to an analysis of methods, brief illustration, and a few of the dilemmas. In a way, this chapter provides a meta-theory for a challenge that implicitly faces all the contributors to the *Handbook* and all practical theologians – how to relate religion and social science in doing practical theology.

2 Context: What Personal and Historical Perspectives Shape This Approach?

Standing in a lecture hall filled with psychology professors and students in 1977, I struggled to make my college senior project comprehensible. In talking about the intersection of religion and psychology in hospital ministry, I might as well have been on Mars. My campus – a small liberal arts college in the Midwest – exemplified a state of affairs that is still prevalent forty years later in social science departments of most universities around the United States. People harbor lingering suspicion about religious belief or incomprehension of religion as a valuable academic subject. This situation remains a problem not only for practical theologians but also for all scholars in religion.

Although I majored in psychology, it was not my psychology professor and advisor but a favorite religion professor who grasped my intersectional interests in religion and psychology and recommended that I spend ten weeks in a Clinical Pastoral Education (CPE) program for my senior off-campus project. So, for a quarter of my final year of college, I was the sole twenty-year-old among two elderly Catholic sisters and four Protestant clergymen doing the yearlong chaplain residency to retool for a second career outside the parish. They adopted me into supervisory seminars like a mascot, and I absorbed new ideas, reading some of the earliest efforts to connect religion and psychology by David Roberts (1950) and Albert Outler (1954). Little did I know that terms like *pastoral counseling* had only been coined a few decades earlier by pioneering figure Seward Hiltner (1949). Although an unofficial unit in CPE as a college senior turned out to be a great, even life changing experience, putting 'ministry' and 'therapy' together did not translate easily to faculty and peers back home in the psychology department. Honestly, I am not sure that I understood myself how they related to one another except that both areas seemed convinced that they possessed truths about human behavior and how to make people and the world better.

So, what exactly does the engagement of religion and social science in practical theology entail and why is it important? As my story suggests, I bring only one perspective, but it is emblematic of what was percolating in the United States between the mid-twentieth century and the 1980s with ongoing implications for today.[1] As an undergraduate in the 1970s, I rode the last great wave of psychology's US heyday. Only a couple decades earlier, during the 1950s and 1960s, pastoral counseling was the "glamour discipline" of theological education (Patton 1990, 851), a glorified position in theological and religious studies that it has lost in recent decades.

Fascination with psychology in the United States had begun with Freud's *Interpretation of Dreams* at the turn of the twentieth century and his trip to Clark Univer-

---

[1] For a contrast, see Schweitzer (1999) on Germany.

sity in 1909. Freud came with Carl Jung on invitation from G. Stanley Hall. Hall had earned the first US doctorate in psychology at Harvard in 1878 and studied with William James who taught the nation's first psychology class. Even as James spearheaded a new department in the 1870s, he remained skeptical about psychology as a discipline.[2] However, in contrast to its lukewarm European reception, psychoanalysis took the United States by storm. Cultural critics like Philip Rieff claimed a "triumph of the therapeutic" – a conversion from previous "character ideals" of "political man," "economic man," and "religious man" that had dominated earlier societies to the rise of "psychological man" (1963, 8–11). The new ideal was marked by what Freud himself called an "analytic attitude," a kind of detached "anti-doctrine" that reduced human aims to the "private needs of private man" (Rieff 1963, 11–12).

So began the earliest US efforts to study religion and social science as a practical theological endeavor. A small but powerful array of early leaders, such as Roberts, Hiltner, Lutheran neo-orthodox scholar Paul Tillich, and humanist psychologists Rollo May, Erich Fromm, and Carl Rogers, gathered regularly in New York City to engage new psychological ideas, and Tillich and Reformed theologian Reinhold Niebuhr explored in their writing psychoanalytic hypotheses about desire, guilt, and anxiety. Gradually, this "culture of psychology," as Don Browning (1980; 1987) dubbed it, infiltrated almost all theological schools, leading to new classes in pastoral care and new openings for professors with expertise in psychology, counseling, and chaplaincy. Hence, when I arrived at the University of Chicago Divinity School in 1978 to study with Browning, a doctoral area called *Religion and Psychological Studies* was thriving, even though, tellingly, it no longer exists today. Scholars familiar with Browning's practical theology work may be less familiar with his earlier contributions in psychology and religion (e.g., 1966, 1973).

This interdisciplinary enterprise at the University of Chicago had roots running back nearly a century when Chicago's President William Rainey Harper, a Baptist churchman, had joined liberal Christian leaders concerned that theology had "lost touch with the new social context" (Gilpin 1996, 86). Both Harper and Charles Eliot at Harvard insisted that theology had a place in the university, but only if it heeded the "modern spirit of science" in Rainey's words (Gilpin 1996, 87). Rainey participated in what historian Clark Gilpin describes as the wider "American experience" – "the transition from theology done in the context of nationally established churches to theology done in the context of religious pluralism and the separation of church and state" (Gilpin 1996, xiii). The University of Chicago, including its new Divinity School established by Harper, became known for its receptivity to social science. It is in this context that Tillich (1951) advocated for a meditational relationship between experience and gospel in the early 1950s; Hiltner (1958) made a case for an even more mutual interchange in the study of "living documents" via psychology

---

[2] "This is no science," James remarked about psychology, "it is only the hope of a science," cited by https://psychology.fas.harvard.edu/people/william-james (29.11.2021).

in the late 1950s and 1960s; and Catholic revisionist David Tracy (1975) modified Tillich's correlational approach to allow for a stronger constructive voice for secular sources in the 1970s.

In other words, by osmosis as much as conscious recognition, I benefited in my studies from sweeping developments in religion and social science. Even in the minority as a woman, I found a place in predominantly white institutions for my early curiosities about why people do what they do. Not surprisingly, when doing a book review years later, I wondered why the editors of *Converging on Culture: Theologians in Dialogue with Cultural Analysis and Criticism* (Brown, Davaney, and Tanner 2001) thought the turn to cultural analysis in systematic theology was so innovative. As I finished a dissertation in the mid-1980s on modern dying at the intersection of religion, medicine, and popular psychology, Browning, himself a Hiltner student at Chicago, was busy working with colleagues to create a new doctoral area of practical theology whose position in the school was also short-lived.

In summary, practical theology's late-twentieth-century rejuvenation owes a great deal to the flourishing of modern social science, especially psychology. Indeed, practical theology might not have become the prominent discipline of today without the social science growth that preceded and ran alongside its own revival. Influenced by figures, such as James and Freud in psychology and Karl Marx, Max Weber, Michel Foucault, and Pierre Bourdieu in sociology and anthropology, social scientists of the nineteenth and twentieth centuries – many of whom also doubled as philosophers – developed empirical methods dedicated to the investigation of persons, places, and politics. With the rise of these sciences, practical theologians found precisely the intellectual tools needed to analyze human behavior regarding religion. The avid interest among practical theologians in the human sciences continues unabated up to today. Resources in psychology and sociology have been especially useful in understanding persons in society and in informing individual care and social ministries.

Of course, attraction to social science has not been unique to practical theologians. Other scholars in religion also adjusted their primary intellectual partnerships throughout the twentieth century. Biblical, historical, and doctrinal theologians, for example, turned from philosophy, literature, and history to social science to expand their disciplinary capabilities. Some scholars describe this interest in psychoanalysis, anthropological fieldwork, statistics, and other subspecialties as a "turn to culture" (see Tanner 1997; Brown, et al. 2001).

Social science, however, has been uniquely important for practical theologians because of our professed interest in everyday religious practice and activity. Understanding lived religion and lived theology as enacted and not simply as believed or professed requires disciplines especially attuned to empirical observation and analysis. Moreover, to grasp the complexity of the distinctive subject matter of practical theology – realities such as how people worship, how parents treat children, how religious communities confront poverty – requires multiple resources beyond theology. In fact, most practical theologians believe that the subjects that we study cannot be adequately understood via one narrow discipline alone.

In grounding exploration of human life in social science rather than philosophy and history, practical theologians shifted attention from human nature as comprised by universal characteristics to more dynamic aspects of human living. While most twentieth-century systematic theologians focused on metaphysical matters such as free will or the nature of God, debating them philosophically, practical theologians raised different kinds of questions about personal, social, and historical actualities that shape religious conviction and action. In so doing, practical theologians initiated a new approach to theological anthropology that shifted attention from abstract depictions of body and soul to features such as behavior, experience, and practice that vary greatly from context to context. Although still invested in understanding human and divine nature, suddenly a whole new range of material became available for study across a rich cross section of human interaction.

3 Method: How Do Practical Theologians Engage Religion and Social Science?

How, then, should practical theologians engage religion and social science?[3] Ian Barbour, a physicist who taught religion in a private liberal arts college in the upper Midwest, offers a useful portrait of the options. From the 1960s on, he focused his energy on science and religion, culminating in reception of the Templeton Prize in 1999. Concerned about sustaining faith in what he saw as a science-dominated world, he began his 1966 book *Issues in Science and Religion* asking, "Is the scientific method the only reliable guide to truth? Is man [sic] only a complex biochemical mechanism?" (Barbour 1966, 1) Three decades later, in *Religion and Science* (1997), he inquires, "What is the place of religion in an age of science? How can one believe in God today?" (Barbour 1997, xiii) Although he is more adept in showing what religion has to gain from science than the reverse, and he attends primarily to 'hard' sciences, telling the history through big men (mostly white) and big ideas, he still challenges the view of science as wholly other than religion and therefore supposedly the "most reliable path to knowledge" (Barbour 1966, 4). More important for my purposes, his typologies still prove fruitful in grasping different ways to relate the two enterprises.

In Barbour's 1966 book, which some credit as creating the science-religion field, he describes three responses to modern science: theologians who draw sharp contrasts (e.g., neo-orthodox theology, existentialism, and linguistic analysis); those who draw parallels (e.g., liberal and process theology); and those who argue that theology and even God's existence can be derived from science (e.g., natural theology). Linguists, for example, distinguish between science and religion as different language games serving divergent social functions, a position that George Lindbeck (1984) developed into postliberal theology and that resembles neo-orthodox theolo-

---

[3] For a more fulsome treatment, see Miller-McLemore (2011).

gian Karl Barth's claim from the 1930s that the technical knowledge of science can neither contribute nor conflict with revelatory truth. Barbour himself represents a position somewhere between his second and third groupings. In contrast to those who see science and religion as "*strongly contrasting enterprises* which have essentially nothing to do with each other [his emphasis]" (Barbour 1966, 1), he sees science as "a more human enterprise" and theology as a "more self-critical undertaking" than commonly understood (Barbour 1996, 4).

Two books later, Barbour turns these observations into a tighter four-part model, describing in detail fours positions: conflict, independence, dialogue, and integration. Although biblical literalism and scientific materialism seem like opposites, they share basic commonalties typical of *conflict* models. They both "seek knowledge with a sure foundation" and believe that science and theology make competing exhaustive explanatory claims about reality. Hence, "one must choose between them" with only one yielding valid truths (Barbour 1997, 78). Today, John Milbank's *Theology and Social Theory* and Richard Dawkins's *The God Delusion* represent provocative opposing examples.

Independence models also place science and religion in separate spheres but less antagonistically, "as totally independent and autonomous," each with "its own distinctive domain and its characteristic methods," as Barbour observes. "Each must tend to its own business and not meddle in the affairs of the other" (Barbour 1997, 84). He locates the mid-twentieth century theologies of Barth and Rudolf Bultmann in this approach as well as more contemporary postliberal theologies influenced by Wittgenstein's linguistic analysis. For those such as Lindbeck, religious language recommends an entire "way of life [...] a set of attitudes [...] particular moral principles" transmitted through religious communities (Barbour 1997, 87), whereas scientific language merely predicts and explains. Tillich's neo-orthodox correlation falls partially in this camp because he argues that science provides insight into questions of existence, but answers come only from Christian doctrine.

By contrast, both *dialogue* and *integration* see science and religion as more akin than different, with science less objective and religion less subjective than presumed. Religion offers reasonable interpretations of human experience, using methods similar to science, and science involves presuppositions and moral commitments similar to religion. Scientific data are always theory-laden, subject to interpretation and creative imagination, and religion can be judged by scientific criteria (e. g., coherence, fruitfulness). In contrast to *dialogue*, *integration* argues for an even broader metaphysics that encompasses science and religion within a greater whole. Both liberals and conservatives who appeal to this position see as possible and desirable a larger combination of truths. Barbour himself finds science suggestive in formulating doctrines of creation and human nature and grasping divine 'influence', as he might say in process philosophy terms. Inversely, some evangelicals unite scripture and psychology under the belief that "all truth is God's truth, wherever it is found" (Carter and Narramore, 1979, 13). *Dialogue* seeks no such synthesis or unity. It emphasizes the differences between science and religion, even as it hopes to find ways each arena might influence the other.

Barbour's typology makes the distinctions sound more pristine than they are. Even he combines tenets from three of the four positions in his own approach (e.g., see 1997, 105). Practical theologians display a similar complexity not only internally as individuals but also within the discipline. Many agree with South African scholar Jaco Dreyer's (2012) argument for a respectful disciplinary pluralism. Most disciplines, he observes, are "characterized by instability, multiple traditions and intradisciplinary diversity" (Dreyer 2012, 41). Since diversity is "inherent" (Dreyer 2012, 35), the best response in Dreyer's view, is to see disciplinary differences as "opportunity for 'productive intellectual dialogue'" – a "dialogic pluralist response" – rather than melding differences into a common framework – a "unitary response" – or merely accepting but largely ignoring disciplinary conflicts – a "pluralist response" (Dreyer 2012, 49).

Measured by the sheer number of typologies created to depict different ways to do theological reflection in relationship to science and culture, practical theologians demonstrate a keen interest in the problem of the science-religion relationship, perhaps more than colleagues in other disciplines. Indeed, we might even say that we obsess about such questions. Typologies on bridging experience (including the sciences) with religious convictions are rampant in our literature, put forth by those in diverse political and confessional positions.

Catholic missiologist Stephen Bevans ([1992] 2002), for example, creates out of his missionary work seven models for engaging the cultural context (translation, anthropological, praxis, synthetic, transcendental, and countercultural). Meanwhile, evangelical theologian Charles Scalise (2003) proposes five models to help ministry students bridge seminary and congregations (correlational, contextual, narrative, performance, and regulative). Two years later, British Protestant scholars Elaine Graham, Heather Walton, and Frances Ward (2005) offer seven methods of theological reflection for those within and beyond the academy (pastoral, literary, postliberal, congregational, correlational, liberationist, and contextual). And these three examples are just the short list! Dreyer names several others. Dutch scholar Gerben Heitink describes the normative-deductive, hermeneutical-mediative, empirical-analytical, political-critical, and pastoral-theological as marking a division that he says "coincides [...] with that proposed by others" (Heitink 1999, 171) a few decades earlier, such as German scholar Norbert Mette. Others in the 1990s depicted the different currents more simply. In the United Kingdom, Paul Ballard and John Prichard name four models: applied, critical correlational, praxis, and habitus (1996, 57–68); and Dutch practical theologian Gijsbert Dingemans (1996) distinguishes four paradigms: clerical, church, liberation, and individual.

Of course, none of these treatments single out social science. Social science is often subsidiary to broader questions about how to engage culture, the humanities, and other facets of modernity. Nonetheless, social science still figures prominently as one of the most important conversation partners with which practical theologians get entangled in our effort to understand everyday life. Each model must come to terms with how to regard social science, from those who see it as "ancillary" (Heitink 1999, 171) to those who see it as absolutely requisite and constitutive, including empirical practical theologians who suggest that we "be fully conversant" in its methods (Heitink 1999, 174).

Many practical theologians, regardless of intellectual and confessional stance, adopt some form of correlation, which explains why Tracy has remained a pivotal figure. Years ago, he proposed a "revisionist theology" to respond not only to the "modern scientific disenchantment" with religion but also the "postmodern disenchantment" with science. This second "disenchantment with disenchantment" (Tracy 1975, 10) need not lead us back to a nostalgic restoration of pre-modern belief. Rather he aspires to a richer kind of conversation between science and religion that contributes to what he and others have called *public theology* or a continued commitment to making Christian faith intelligible for a wider non-Christian public while also using non-Christian resources to enrich Christian faith.

Correlational models come under regular scrutiny, of course. Two of Tracy's doctoral students – Mark Kline Taylor and Rebecca Chopp – go on to use liberation theology to modify without completely negating its viability. In the late 1980s and early 1990s, they questioned Tracy's view of human experience as universal and his distinction between experience and tradition as two separate poles. Their versions of correlation privilege –*"those excluded or absent from the conversation"* in Taylor's words (1990, 64) – shift the aim in using social science from cognitive debate and objective empirical analysis to transformative practice, what Chopp calls a "critical praxis correlation" (1987, 132) and Taylor calls "cultural-political theology" (1990, 23) aimed at improving the condition of the marginalized. Other scholars challenge correlational categories and practices from anthropological, post structural, and decolonial perspectives. Katherine Tanner (1997), having studied under Lindbeck at Yale, suggests that Christian theology is not a philosophical enterprise that stands above culture requiring correlation with secular sources but "a culture-specific activity" (Tanner 1984, 64). More recently, Carmen Nanko-Fernandez argues from a "Latinamente" perspective that "handy [correlational] frameworks" reflect an "obsession with method" in practical theology, separating elements like experience and tradition that "some of us never experienced [as] divorce[d]" (Nanko-Fernandez 2013, 39). Claire Watkins (2015), Director of the Theology and Action Research Network in England, uses Belgian theologian Lieven Boeve's (2007) critique of correlation to argue for a non-correlational approach of "interruption" and "recontextualization". Even Tracy (2011) revisits his model over three decades later and suggests a return to aesthetic and spiritual disciplines to dispel modern dichotomies such as theory and practice.

Nevertheless, although a correlational model has come under justified critique from a variety of angles, its usefulness in organizing research projects, course syllabi, and even social justice efforts endures. It is difficult for anyone, even those who adopt models of conflict, independence, or interruption, to avoid entirely some semblance of religion-science correlation. More important, correlation presumes and demands dialogue, and dialogue places particular demands on the sciences, asking scientists to take religion seriously and to recognize when their own constructs expand beyond scientific parameters into the territory of theology, ethics, and philosophy. Dialogue occurs (or should occur) when religion makes claims about human experience that put it in the realm of science, when science becomes more than science, when science becomes dogmatic, or when science and religion hold competing visions of the good life. In genuine conversation, there is presumably no last or ultimate word.

4 Illustration: How Does Religion and Social Science Work as a Theoretical Approach?

What can one know from the perspective of religion and social science? At this point, a concrete illustration may prove more fruitful than further theoretical argument about history and method.

In a class on theology and social science several years ago, I assigned a few chapters from my book, *Let the Children Come: Reimagining Childhood from a Christian Perspective* (Miller-McLemore 2003), to illustrate the use of religion and psychology in doing practical theology. But I was still surprised when friend and colleague Mary Fulkerson told me that she wished her Duke Divinity School colleagues would read it. Like a fish in water, I hardly notice the fluidity that I presume between religion and social science. But Fulkerson has taught for most of her career at an institution where virtue ethicist Stanley Hauerwas's suspicion of the secular social sciences has reigned, especially the much maligned 'therapeutic'. Critics blame psychology for fostering individualism, encouraging divorce, spoiling children, and much more. By contrast, the two institutions at which I have taught sustain long histories of respect for social science and progressive causes. My first teaching appointment, Chicago Theological Seminary, appointed Graham Taylor to head the school's new department of *Christian sociology* in 1892 and hired Anton Boisen in the 1920s to teach psychology of religion. Graham founded the profession of social work; Boisen founded CPE.

The methods in psychology and religion that I use in *Let the Children Come* already shaped my first book on death and dying (Miller-McLemore 1988), another complex human experience that, similar to childhood, a cohort of social scientists had begun to examine and appropriate in the mid-twentieth century. In both works, I examine prominent life phases – facing our end on one hand and raising children on the other – and, to understand them, I weave together social science, psychology in particular, and contemporary and historical theology. In *Let the Children Come*, I urge theologians to quit "picking on psychology" for promoting the "me generation" (Miller-McLemore 2003, 26) and take it more seriously when trying to understand children's needs. "If any discipline has given children a fresh voice and special place, it is psychology" (Miller-McLemore 2003, 27). It is ironic and even sad to note that the "study of children became a respectable science at about the same time that interest in children [...] waned among Christian scholars" (Miller-McLemore 2003, 28). Major psychologists such as Freud's own daughter Anna, Erik Erikson, and Robert Coles have spent hours upon hours with children, crediting them with deeper thoughts than children can put into words.

What then is learned from psychology? Psychology has the capacity to take us inside children's lives with an uncanny empathy often missing in theology. I turn to Alice Miller who uses object relations theory to show how parents almost unavoidably misuse their children to gratify their own narcissistic desires, leaving children with "false selves" vulnerable to losing a sense of their own needs. Psychology "corrects Christianity" by insisting that "adults take the child's point of view" (Miller-McLemore 2003, 39). Psychology shows the damage caused by lofty Christian ideals (e.g., a sacrificial godhead, sinfulness, obedience, submission, honoring parents), that often play out in harmful ways in the lives of real people, especially children, and it disproves truths that many Christians assume: "that strong feelings are dangerous, that a child's will must be broken, that tenderness is harmful and order and strictness are good for children, that thinking less of oneself fosters altruism" (Miller-McLemore 2003, 44).

What are some of the limits of psychology, however, and what might psychologists learn from religion? Although emotionally astute, psychology promotes implicit normative visions (e.g., children as innocent), all the while failing to grasp children's moral and religious complexity. Even though many Christians find Augustine's views of sexuality and sin problematic, he did understand better than most contemporary psychologists why people do the distorted things they do in progressively insidious ways as they mature from children to adults. Even children and youths are fallible and prone to turning in on themselves. Classic Christian frameworks, such as Augustine's in the fourth century or leader of the Radical Reformation Menno Simons in the early 1500s, grasp how iniquity evolves from near innocence in childhood to an ever-greater complicity as children move into adulthood. The likes of Augustine and Simons allow for an "incremental accretion of responsibility" on the part of children, youths, and young adults, making an important "place for human frailty, mistakes, destructive failures, and the need for amends and grace" (Miller-McLemore 2003, 67–68). Of course, it still took a psychologist, Bruno Bettelheim (1985), to challenge Christian distortions of discipline by reminding us of the term's root, *disciple*, and noticing that Jesus invited obedience through alliance and invitation rather than chastisement and force. In this instance, Bettelheim confirms that religious traditions bear valuable ideas. In short, study of children illustrates a basic religion-science premise: "If Christian theology has erred on the side of moral mastery and condemnation, psychology errs on the said of moral naïveté" (Miller-McLemore 2003, 50).

5 Concerns, Debates, and Suspicions: What Are Some Problems with the Approach?

I conclude by briefly naming three challenges that arise in engaging religion and social science in practical theology. These are not the only debates, but they assume a certain primacy. First, in most academic settings, social science knowledge reigns over religious knowledge, which is often ignored, misunderstood, or suspected of subjective and even proselytizing biases. The so-called dialogue is largely one-directional, from religion to the sciences, and rarely the other way. Genuine partnership has never existed. Social scientists either fail to recognize theological scholarship or doubt its validity and relevance. This unfortunate dynamic leaves both disciplines bereft of what could be engaging interactions around several issues.

A second challenge centers around the tension between fact and value, empirical description and normative interpretation. Despite general acceptance of the postmodern maxim that all knowledge is shaped by power and context, many scholars still regard scientific knowledge as somehow above the fray, more objective and rational than religious knowledge. We prize the quantifiable over the qualitative and prefer arguments based on repeatable empirical experiment over those built around single cases (see Flyvbjerg 2006). Some practical theologians, such as Heather Walton (2014), turn away from social science because it cannot access knowledge that only becomes apparent through creative arts, and many more have noticed how science perpetuates racism and sexism. But few have sustained the kind of moral and religious evaluation of social science's implicit assumptions that Browning modeled in his early work and others, such as Jeremy Carrette (2007), have pursued. Fewer still have extended a decolonial critique to our use of social science, which was essentially co-constructed with colonialism. Most practical theologians simply go on using social science even as we admit that it can perpetuate Western imperialism.

Third, interdisciplinarity presents inherent challenges. "Interdisciplinarity is constitutive of practical theology", as Joyce Ann Mercer asserts (2016, 163); the very subjects that we study require "deft engagement of multiple fields of knowledge and methods of study." However, our interdisciplinary aspirations also threaten our validity. Scholars in more rigidly defined areas accuse us of lacking disciplinary identity and expertise, and we ourselves reach unsurprising limits, knowing enough about other disciplines to be dangerous and not enough to wield their tools and insights wisely or well. As theologians we can never know enough to use social science as well as we should, and we fall prey to allowing social science to control our own terms until any unique theological perspective falls to the wayside.

Despite these hazards, engaging religion and social science remains absolutely core to practical theology regardless of where scholars, students, and ministers stand on a variety of issues. Social science helped resurrect practical theology as an arena of study, and it will remain at the forefront of practical theological research, teaching, and practice.

Bibliography

Ballard, Paul and John Pritchard. 1996. *Practical Theology in Action: Christian Thinking in the Service of Church and Society.* London: SPCK.
Barbour, Ian G. 1966. *Issues in Science and Religion.* New York: Harper Torchbooks.
Barbour, Ian G. 1997. *Religion and Science: Historical and Contemporary Issues.* New York: Harper Collins.
Bettelheim, Bruno. 1985. "Punishment vs. Discipline." *The Atlantic* 256:51–59.
Bevans, Stephen. [1992] 2002. *Models of Contextual Theology.* Maryknoll: Orbis.
Brown, Delwin, Sheila Greeve Davaney, and Kathryn Tanner, eds. 2001. *Converging on Culture: Theologians in Dialogue with Cultural Analysis and Criticism.* New York: Oxford University Press.
Boeve, Lieven. 2007. *God Interrupts History: Theology in a Time of Upheaval.* New York: Continuum International.
Browning, Don. S. 1966. *Atonement and Psychotherapy.* Philadelphia: Westminster.
Browning, Don. S. 1973. *Generative Man: Psychoanalytic Perspectives.* Philadelphia: Westminster.
Browning, Don. S. 1980. *Pluralism and Personality: William James and Some Contemporary Cultures of Psychology.* Lewisburg: Bucknell University Press.
Browning, Don S. 1987. *Religious Thought and the Modern Psychologies.* Philadelphia: Augsburg Fortress.
Carter, John D., and S. Bruce Narramore. 1979. *The Integration of Psychology and Theology: An Introduction.* Grand Rapids: Zondervan.
Carrette, Jeremy. 2007. *Religion and Critical Psychology: Religious Experience in the Knowledge Economy.* London / New York: Routledge.
Chopp, Rebecca S. 1987. "Practical Theology and Liberation." In *Formation and Reflection: The Promise of Practical Theology*, edited by Lewis S. Mudge and James N. Poling, Philadelphia: Fortress, 120–138.
Dingemans, Gijsbert D. J. 1996. "Practical Theology in the Academy: A Contemporary Overview." *The Journal of Religion* 76:82–96.
Dreyer, Jaco. 2012. "Practical Theology and Intradisciplinary Diversity: A Response to Miller-McLemore." *International Journal of Practical Theology* 16:34–54.
Flyvbjerg, Bent. 2006. "Five Misunderstandings about Case-Study Research." *Qualitative Inquiry* 12:219–245.
Gilpin, W. Clark. 1996. *A Preface to Theology.* Chicago: University of Chicago.
Graham, Elaine, Heather Walton, and Frances Ward. 2005. *Theological Reflection: Methods.* London: SCM.
Heitink, Gerben. 1999. *Practical Theology.* Grand Rapids: Eerdmans.
Hiltner, Seward. 1949. *Pastoral Counseling.* New York: Abingdon-Cokesbury.
Hiltner, Seward. 1958. *Preface to Pastoral Theology.* Nashville: Abingdon.
Lindbeck, George. 1984. *The Nature of Doctrine: Religion and Theology in a Postliberal Age.* Philadelphia: Westminster.
Mercer, Joyce Ann. 2016. "Interdisciplinarity as a Practical Theological Conundrum." In *Conundrums in Practical Theology*, edited by Joyce Ann Mercer and Bonnie Miller-McLemore, Leiden: Brill, 163–189.
Miller-McLemore, Bonnie J. 1988. *Death, Sin and the Moral Life: Contemporary Cultural Interpretations of Death.* Atlanta: Scholars Press.
Miller-McLemore, Bonnie J. 2003. *Let the Children Come: Reimagining Childhood from a Christian Perspective.* San Francisco: Jossey-Bass.

Miller-McLemore, Bonnie J. 2011. "Cognitive Neuroscience and the Question of Theological Method." *Journal of Pastoral Theology* 20:64–92.
Nanko-Fernandez, Carmen. 2013. "Held Hostage by Method? Interrupting Pedagogical Assumptions – Latinamente." *Theological Education* 48:35–45.
Outler, Albert. 1954. *Psychotherapy and the Christian Message*. New York: Harper.
Patton, John. 1990. "Pastoral Counseling." In *Dictionary of Pastoral Care and Counseling*, edited by Rodney J. Hunter, Nashville: Abingdon, 849–854.
Rieff, Philip. 1963. "Introduction." In *Therapy and Technique*, edited by Sigmund Freud, New York: Macmillan, 7–26.
Roberts, David. 1950. *Psychotherapy and a Christian View of Man*. New York: Scribner.
Scalise, Charles. 2003. *Bridging the Gap: Connecting What you Learned in Seminary with what you Find in the Congregation*. Nashville: Abingdon.
Schweitzer, Friedrich. 1999. "Practical Theology, Contemporary Culture, and the Social Sciences: Interdisciplinary Relationships and the Unity of Practical Theology as a Discipline." In *Practical Theology: International Perspectives*, edited by Friedrich Schweitzer and Johannes A. van der Ven, Frankfurt am Main: Peter Lang, 307–321.
Tanner, Kathryn. 1997. *Theories of Culture: A New Agenda for Theology*. Minneapolis: Fortress.
Taylor, Mark Kline. 1990. *Remembering Esperanza: A Cultural-Political Theology for North American Praxis*. Maryknoll: Orbis.
Tillich, Paul. 1951. *Systematic Theology*. Vol. 1. Chicago: University of Chicago.
Tracy, David. 1975. *Blessed Rage for Order: The New Pluralism in Theology*. New York: Crossroad.
Tracy, David. 2011. "A Correlational Model of Practical Theology Revisited." In *Religion, Diversity, and Conflict*, edited by Edward Foley, Berlin: LIT, 49–61.
Walton, Heather. 2014. *Writing Methods in Theological Reflection*. London: SCM.
Watkins, Claire. 2015. "Practising Ecclesiology: From Product to Process. Developing Ecclesiology as a Non-Correlative Process and Practice through the Theological Action Research Framework of Theology in Four Voices." *Ecclesial Practices* 2:23–39.

Ana Thea Filipović
Religious Education

1 Introduction

Reflection on religion in the context of education touches upon many aspects of the relationship between faith and learning, faith, and personal growth, of ways of becoming Christians, religious socialization, communication of faith experience and shaping of religious knowledge, as well as of learning religion in the public space of schools. The dialectic tension in the relationship between substance and function, faith content and its role in education, formation, development and maturing of persons and communities, is being articulated in a specific way in each of the aforementioned aspects. The semantics of the individual terms always holds historic and contextual connotations. Ecclesial-theological normativity and lived practice of religious formation dialectically connect in hermeneutics as an attempt to understand and interpret practice on the background of the changes articulated in the relationship between Church and society, proclamation and culture, transmission of faith and interests, needs and experience of subjects of religious socialization, initiation, and formation. In that attempt to understand and interpret, what comes in focus is the interdisciplinary communication between practical theology and religious education and other sciences, in particular humanistic and social.

2 Can Faith Be Learned?

In Christian theology, faith and rational thinking, as well as faith and learning, support and complement each other (FR 5). Faith is born in a person as a fruit of grace, which anticipates and supports the person's free acceptance and trust in the truth, prompted by the Holy Spirit (DV 5). As an undeserved gift of God's love, faith cannot be produced or extorted, even with the most efficient learning methods. At the same time, it is weaved into the process of human growth, maturing and learning. In these processes that last throughout the human life, action is required by which a person goes through trials, obstacles, doubts, insecurities, questioning and discovering, advancing towards a deeper knowledge of God, a greater security of faith and a more encompassing love as the basic attitude in life, which stems from faith. Human beings have the capacity for religious learning that needs incentive in order to grow.

Education and formation are required to progress towards mature faith. Faith needs education so it does not stray into fundamentalism, but rather continue to develop in the context of personal and social challenges. Religious education and formation help deepen the insight that connects rational and intuitive knowledge of God, faith, and action, individual and community, faith and culture, Church, and the world. On the other hand, education cannot exclude a person's faith. Faith has its place in education because it promotes the growth of the whole person, it encourages the person to realize him/herself in communion with others, and in relation to God as the giver of life and creator of the world. As such, faith offers the ultimate horizon for human learning, because it directs it towards a life that is meaningful. The dialectic relationship between faith as a gift and a free response from human beings, and faith as a process of learning, guards every teacher of faith and leader of religious educational processes from absolutizing and manipulating. Each person has its own biography of faith, which profiles itself not only through help received from others, but also through resistance towards what is given by religious educators and teachers (Filipović 2011, 30–35; Englert 2007, 11–13).

The context I am writing from on religious education is the Catholic Church in Croatia, where the dominant perspective in theology is that of the institutional Church. Observing the practice of Christian formation and education from a perspective of the institutional Church, the focus will firstly be on processes of becoming Christian and continuing education in faith within the frame of pastoral care of Christian communities, and secondly on religious education in public schools.

3 Christian Formation and Education in Processes of Becoming Christians and Continuing Growth in Faith

The need for Christian formation comes out of the process character of discipleship and following Christ. According to the New Testament as the basic document of the Christian faith, faith is understood as a dynamic process, as a path of growth and progress towards maturity, as relationship with God that needs to be nurtured, purified, and deepened (Matt 13:23; 2 Cor 10:15; Phil 1:25; Col 1:10; 2 Pet 3:18; Eph 4:13; 1 Cor 3:2–3). Important phases of faith development and becoming Christian can be recognized in the practice of the historical Jesus and in the evangelization activity of the first Christian communities; from conversion as the elementary decision for Christ, to joining the Church and continuing growth in faith. The three important points of that process are: listening to the proclamation of the Gospel, faith in Jesus as the Son of God and acceptance of his teaching, and finally following Christ through joining the Church (John 4:4–42; Acts 2:37–41).

Since the maturing in faith is a lifelong task, it requires continuing encouragement and formation which accompanies believers throughout their life. Religious and faith education are important, not only for the development of the Christian identity of individual believers, but also for the building up of Christian communities (DCG 56, 142–147). From the beginnings of Christianity until today, we can recognize two main ways of becoming Christian and Christian formation: the model of catechumenate and religious socialization. In contemporary pluralist contexts, besides these two models, there are diverse forms of religious formation and education that meet and respond to the needs of the people today.

3.1 Christian Initiation through Catechumenate

At the end of the second century, following the practice of evangelization testified in the New Testament and the Early Church, the institution of catechumenate is developed, as a structured itinerary of becoming Christians. The Christian initiation into faith and life of the community within the frame of catechumenate is understood as a holistic, existential, and communal process of learning and teaching faith, guided by bishops, priests or deacons. Its basic phases are: accepting catechumens interested in Christian faith, first proclamation of the history of salvation and listening to the Word of God, conversion, change and scrutiny of life, catechesis of initiation with a focus on learning the *Lord's prayer* and the *Creed*, and finally joining the Church through celebrating the sacraments of initiation: baptism, confirmation and Eucharist. What follows after is mystagogy as a deeper interpretation of received sacramental signs with the goal of strengthening the person in their Christian life and walking in faith with the community of faithful (Dujarier 1984).

The Second Vatican Council (1962–1965) with its renewing impulses, encouraged a rediscovery of catechumenate (SC 64–65; AG 14) and contributed to the promotion of Christian adult faith formation, based on catechumenal experiences (EN 44; DCG 90–91). Catechumenate as an initiation and formation process was broadened to include persons who have been baptized, but were not raised in faith, or who have not received all sacraments of Christian initiation (OICA, chapter IV and V). The catechumenal model was an inspiration to the catechetical formation of adult believers in general, and specifically of those who have grown apart from faith, and needed to be reinitiated (CT 44), as well as for the catechesis of children who have been baptized and needed to finish the process of Christian initiation. Since in the countries with Christian tradition most children are still baptized, but do not have serious faith education, a need is perceived for a sort of "post-baptismal catechumenate" for the Christian initiation of children and preadolescents, which also includes children who are not baptized, who are catechumens in the full sense (CT 19). This process requires rediscovery of the first proclamation, practice in Christian life, catechumenal path of purification and enlightenment, connection of liturgy and life, appropriate spiritual accompaniment and joining small groups within a local church community (Morante 2002, 254–255).

Catechumenate for adults obtained new significance in former socialist countries of Europe after the collapse of communist regimes and rule of atheism as the official worldview, in 1989/1990. Since in the times of state repression faith was defamed and considered a private matter, religious education happened in the family and in parish communities, and catechumenate for adults was rare. With the change in the social system many adults, especially in cities, asked to join the Church by baptism, or to finish the Christian initiation, because they might have been (secretly) baptized as children. In contact with those who have been raised as atheists or just cultural traditional believers, new questions were raised in relation to appropriate forms of evangelization, catechesis, and continuing education in faith in those countries.

Catechumenal models of becoming Christian stand and fall with the meaning of the church community as the basic subject that gives strength to Christian initiation. Church as a place of the coming of the Kingdom of God and place of learning of elementary Christian experiences and life according to the Gospel has a central meaning in shaping of the Christian identity. The Christian community which gathers, listens to the Word of God, celebrates its faith and lives by faith, is an appropriate environment from which and to which the catechumenal itinerary leads (DCG 69–70; 91; 254). What is meant under the term community is for mostly the irreplaceable local Church led by the bishop. Within a community there are various responsibilities that need to be assumed according to the ministries and charisms (DCG 219–232). According to the experience of the ancient catechumenate, lay ministries in the Church held great importance (e.g., sponsorship), but were gradually extinguished as the process of clericalization of Church began to take place. Especially important were the catechists, who interpreted and testified faith to catechumens, not just as "professionals", but as those baptized and mature in faith, who have been called and sent as representatives of the community to accompany catechumens (Alberich 2002a, 243). Today still, the formation of catechists represents one of the greatest challenges for the Church in every local context.

Often the catechumenal processes in a community happen on the margins of church community life, and are considered secondary activities, done by designated individuals. That is why small communities are important, communities that accompany catechumens before and after catechumenate. Besides the parish community, today there are in different contexts various Catholic institutions, organizations, movements, and basic church communities that practice faith formation. The Church recognizes the importance of those small Christian communities for the adult faith formation, as well as for the development of lay leadership in religious formation (DCG 253; 261–264). In many local churches, there are new ecclesial movements with a distinct catechumenal mission in relation to those not baptized, and Christians on the margins of traditional Church affiliation. Ecclesial movements promote a new image of the Church and a new model of being Christian as someone who isn't Christian just by tradition, but by their own choice; they mediate the experience of community, discover the ministries of the Church anew and revalorize laity. However, they often lack the capacity to dialog with contemporary society, to be part of the culture, but also to be part of the parish community as a whole (Alberich 2002b, 265).

The rootedness of catechumenate in the Christian community as its base and bearer, mostly remains an ideal. The practice of church communities shows that Catholics have difficulty with quality of communal life (EG 98–100). The lack of authentic and living community, which testifies and lives out its faith, is one of the reasons for the crisis of credibility in relation to catechumenal models of initiation. If there are no living communities, newly baptized believers gradually move away from the Church (Alberich 2002a, 246–247). The incapacity of the Church today to truly be a community seems to be as an ecclesiological problem, which has repercussions on evangelization and religious formation.

3.2 Religious Socialization

The second form of becoming Christian is weaved into the processes of socialization in faith. The model of catechumenate and model of religious socialization today often intertwine and happen simultaneously within Christian communities. Introduction into Christianity through religious socialization began with the acceptance of Christianity as a legitimate religion in the Roman Empire based on Constantine's edict in 313, i.e., formal state religion, based on Theodosius' decree in 380. It was followed also by the baptizing of barbaric nations in Europe at the end of the ancient period and during the medieval period (Elias 1993, 12). With the practice of baptism of newborns, western Christianity gradually began introducing a time separation between sacraments of Christian initiation. First, there was a delay in receiving the sacrament of confirmation because it needed to be done by the bishop, and nineth century testimonies say that the sacrament of Eucharist was also delayed and separated from baptism. Before receiving those sacraments, at the age of 7 or so, when a child is capable to at least understand the important points of what it is receiving, teaching of elementary knowledge about faith is introduced within the frame of family and parish catechesis (Caspani and Sartor 2008).

Catechetical sermons on Sundays and feast days served as religious education for adult believers. Since literacy was low in the Middle Ages, catechetical instruction relied on visual representation of salvation history scenes depicted in churches and cathedrals, as well as on sacral sculptures and stations of the cross, all commonly called the Paupers' Bible (lat. *Biblia pauperum*) (Fleck 2011, 25). There was a visible gap between theological thought which developed in the newly founded universities of that time, which individual persons dealt with, and the popular Christian culture, overwhelmed by folk beliefs, existential questions, fears and hopes of people, which put the focus on the topics of duty, sin, repentance, preparation for death and eschatological realities. There was a need for abstracts of faith and simple handbooks, which were used for catechetical teaching focused on interpreting the basics of Christian faith: Creed, commandments, and good deeds (Gianetto 2002, 64).

Cultural shifts and political movements contributed to the emergence of the Reformation at the beginning of the sixteenth century, which in turn greatly influenced religious education and formation in the Roman Catholic Church. The Reformation established the catechism as the basic handbook for faith education, and its widespread distribution was made possible by the invention of printing press and increase in literacy among the common folk. In the Catholic tradition, catechisms are created as a response to Luther's and Melanchthon's catechisms, and most often are counter-reformational in doctrine. Catechism as a literary form was focused on adopting doctrinally correct formulated faith knowledge, and it defined catechetical formation of children and adults from the middle of the sixteenth century until the middle of the twentieth century. Important parts of the catechism are: Creed, sacraments, commandments, and prayer, while the order of individual parts differs depending on the author. The catechism influences the content and method of the catechetical instruction, which focuses on gaining religious knowledge and prefers the form of questions and answers. Parish catechesis organized after the Council of Trent (1545–1563), was focused on interpreting and learning the truths of faith by heart, while the practice of Christian life was learned through religious socialization. Besides memorizing key elements of Christian doctrine, catechesis included narration of salvation history, and stressing examples of important figures of the biblical faith and Church history as role models one should look up to, be inspired by and imitate (Braido 1991).

The industrial revolution brought about new social and cultural changes, which, together with pedagogical development, put into question the suitability and efficiency of religious education focused on learning of abstract faith knowledge. That model, leaning on the "social catechumenate" and rural culture in which the Church was fitted during the century, had to give place to new ways of evangelization and education in faith in growing worker communities and urban areas (Gianetto 2002, 69). From the end of the nineteenth century until the Second Vatican Council, the Catechetical movement promoted and advocated for a determined step away from the catechism and memorizing of dogmatic definitions, but towards catechesis as a living activity. It became more and more evident that the shift in society required holistic faith formation. Inspired by the kerygmatic theology, the Catechetical movement rediscovered the strength of the Christian proclamation (Jungmann 1953). Catechesis turned from preoccupation with systematic religious knowledge towards the existential meaning of the Christian message. That turn was based on the insight that there is a need for Christian formation which will help believers live the reality of Christian faith by drinking at the fount of their personal encounter with Christ in his Word, despite a lack of support or in spite of societal pressures. Processes of religious education since then have been marked by attempts to adjust to new societal and cultural circumstances in which believers live and grow.

Processes of religious learning are questioned in relation to the requirements of a certain developmental age, life experience and varying life situations, and critical life events. Maturing in Christian faith is connected to maturing in humanity. It is evident that faithful must be accompanied in their specific circumstances and phases in life and helped to connect faith and contemporary rational thought. The connection between faith and experience follows wider theological discussions on the principle of correlation (Paul Tillich, Karl Rahner, Edward Schillebeeckx and others), which are religious-educationally and didactically transposed and developed in various models, from multi-correlational and abductive to hermeneutically communicative (Filipović and Lehner-Hartmann 2016, 194). Various catechetical textbooks and materials published after the Second Vatican Council are focused on questioning and reflecting on life in light of faith. Latin American liberation theology and catechesis turn the focus to the social dimension of the Gospel message (the International Catechetical Week in Medellín in 1968; EG 176–285). Respecting the church experience on other continents raises awareness of the necessity of contextualization and inculturation of catechesis and faith formation. Furthermore, it recognizes their contribution to the integral development of persons (EN 1975).

Catechesis, religious and theological formation of adult faithful has the central place in catechetical theory almost since the 1960s. Adult religious learning includes various kinds of knowledge, according to which various forms and processes of religious education and faith formation are directed. After the Second Vatican Council stressed the importance of the priesthood of all baptized believers, adult faithful became more interested in deepening their faith. Besides theological reasons, that was also prompted by the insight into the necessity of lifelong learning in various fields of life in modern society. Continuing, lifelong adult catechesis is considered today as a basic form of catechesis in the Roman Catholic Church (CT 43), even though its realization in practice remains more of a postulate than a reality. The new awareness of lay faithful as subjects of catechesis in the post-council period contributed to the awareness of catechetical responsibility of the whole Christian community for catechesis. Adult believers feel responsible for the catechetical formation of their children, as well as new adult community members (Fleck 2011, 29).

In the new church and pastoral context there is visible dialectical tension between anthropologically oriented theology and magisterium in catechetical mediation. As a response to the pluriformity of theological thinking, at the beginning of the 1980s there was a need in some circles in the Church for an authoritative definition of Catholic teaching in the form of an adult catechism, which prompted the creation of *The Catechism of the Catholic Church* in 1992. The Catechism for youth, Youcat, published in 2011, attempts to express faith in a language understandable to youth, encourage discussion on faith and confront today's way of thinking to the faith of the Church. Today it is obvious that processes of religious education and formation are happening in plural contexts.

3.3 Religious Education and Formation in Contemporary Plural Contexts

The question of becoming Christians and continuing growth in faith is incorporated into a wider pastoral plan today and it considers the specificity of each local church context (Derroitte 2000). Because of changed circumstances various ways of Christian initiation and continuing formation are required for specific groups and different categories of believers, their religious needs, and possibilities. That prompted the creation of various evangelizational and catechetical projects more adjusted to the life of people in growing urban areas, as a call to a community of the faithful and encounter with the faith tradition of the community, and as a call to an active participation in the life of the Christian community (e.g., Alpha course, Night Fever, adult faith pathways, spiritual exercises in everyday life). Various biographies and situations of faith and life of individuals require differentiated forms of religious formation, as well as cooperation between professional and volunteer catechists, who become involved based on personal responsibilities and gifts. Regarding the content of faith, believers are not asked to obey blindly, but to reflect, be attentive and contextually understand faith. Self-awareness of the faith of the Church meets the subjective understanding of faith of individual believers as carriers of church life and partners in shaping of a new faith language (Exeler 1966, 277–282). Knowing and understanding faith is embodied in concrete historical becoming of persons in the community.

Religious socialization in the family, parish, Catholic educational institutions, and organizations is no longer understood as a one-way process of the transmission of faith and internalization by the receiver of Christian values and norms that govern a certain community. Through social processes of individualization and pluralization, the relationship between the individual and the collective has radically changed. The authority of traditional social institutions and relationships i.e., social class, Church, family, neighborhood, was gradually weakened in favor of the autonomy of the individual who sets personal goals and wants to realize him/herself as a unique person. In a plural society, there is a decrease of fixed roles and undisputable norms that need to be internalized. Contemporary theories of socialization stress individualization as the core of socialization. Religious education and formation are also done in dynamic tension between promoting the growth of persons in their uniqueness and their integration into community (Vermeer 2010, 105–107).

Catechesis and faith education is today increasingly understood as intergenerational communication and learning of faith (Amherdt 2017). Formative processes in a community happen in interpersonal sharing of religious knowledge and experience, in an atmosphere of trust and respect, to recognize the meaning of faith in one's own life context. Older and younger members in the community enrich each other with their perspectives and experiences. The model of Family catechesis (span. *Catequesis familiar*), developed in Chile in the 1960s, and brought to some European church contexts (Filipović 2011, 129–133), and the model of Shared Christian practice, which moves from experience towards faith and from faith again towards experience (Groome 2011, 299–338), are examples of didactic concretization of the forementioned ideas.

Processes of religious education and faith formation today happen through formal and informal channels, and life circumstances become a place of religious learning. In the process of Christian initiation and faith education, essential importance further on is placed on family as the "house Church" where one becomes Christian in the midst of everyday experiences. Family needs support in order to accompany its members on the path of maturity in faith, especially in those dimensions which cannot be delegated, i.e., answers to children's religious questions, and building the relationship with God and image of God in connection to relationships in the family (Scharer 2000, 115–136; Filipović and Lehner-Hartmann 2016).

Besides the Christian community and family, which continue to hold the most important role in religious education and formation, there are other agents, such as Christian organizations, Catholic educational institutions (kindergartens, schools, universities), Catholic media, etc. The new media of social communication give new possibilities of religious education and faith formation. Their development, which in former socialist countries went hand in hand with the development of freedom of religious expression, opened many doors and opportunities to gain deeper religious knowledge and more incentive for spiritual life. Pilgrimages and organized Christian gatherings and meetings for youth and adults also hold within themselves elements of faith formation. However, religious education in public schools within the frame of school education, holds a special place.

4 Religious Education in School

School, as a social institution, promotes intellectual, cultural, ethical, and social development of students in answering the challenges of the new media, shifts in the labor market and questioning its own contribution to the communal life in growingly plural and multicultural societies. Religious education in schools has since the 1970s been profiled as a subject that is, with its goals and methods, adjusted to modern schools. Religious content is no longer a subject of school teaching due to its objective truth, but rather because of the understanding of European culture, which is permeated with Christian heritage, and because of the meaning of religion for the individual and society (Synodenbeschluß: Der Religionsunterricht in der Schule [1974]; 1998). After the collapse of opposing ideologies of the West and the East, interest in religion is questioned in relation to its contribution to the interpretation of the human experience and the shaping of a personal value system.

Religion and religious world view in religious education is put to the test of critical rationality. Care for transmission of Christian values, which was for a long time, due to the role of Christianity in the development of the school system in Europe, the dominant goal of religious education in schools, is broadened to include a holistic care of human maturing, with a focus on the meaning of spirituality and religiosity in the lives of the people. Even in the model of confessional religious education, the content of Christian revelation is expanded to the broadest horizon of research of religion, and the role of religion is questioned in confrontation with the greatest challenges of the times and context. This is didactically shaped by connecting theological and anthropological goals and contents (didactics of correlation), by putting emphasis on the contribution of religion in finding the meaning of life and providing the motif of hope (Roebben 2011).

Religious education as a school subject contributes to the gaining of specific hermeneutical and critically reflexive skills that students need to develop a personal and social identity. To achieve this, religious education today, more than focusing on doctrinal aspects of religious traditions, focuses on personal narratives of believers, with which children and youth can identify. Through the encounter and critical confrontation with those narratives, students are invited to think about the way in which believers experience and live their faith, and to discover that each path of faith is a personal construction. Doing so, they will also question their own way of life and oppose stereotypes. The broader religious tradition is not just a subject being taught, but a means of interpretation, questioning and nurturing personal faith or worldview in encounter with others (Jackson 2002; Cush and Robinson 2014, 6–7). Faith or personal worldview develops through encounters and confrontations with the faith of the Church, with the faith of other people from history and the present, and with one's own spiritual and religious practice, gained knowledge and experiences.

A discussion on the requirements of the truth in various religions contributes to the development of critically reflexive skills as well. That requires readiness of the students to rationally question faith and values to become autonomous persons. Educational confrontation with diversity in religious education (especially in non-confessional models of religious education, but also in confessional) invites students to think critically about their own and others' religious, cultural and ethics traditions and backgrounds. If capacity for rational thought and decision making is to be promoted, religious standpoints need to be confronted also with secular counterarguments. Through that, religious education also shows its educational role in developing basic values of a democratic society, such as equality, freedom of speech, tolerance, and nondiscrimination, which secure social cohesion necessary for the flourishing of diversity (Vermeer 2010, 108–115).

Pluralization of society and dialogical openness towards other religions also change the goals of religious education. Religious education in schools was, for a long time in schools across Europe, considered a means of religious socialization, introducing individuals into the life of a certain religious community, i.e., Church (education in religion/learning religion). However, in countries with stronger religious pluralization, the focus was, already since the beginning of the 1970s, put on a neutral phenomenological approach and learning about religion. Today, depending on the socio-religious situation and tradition in certain countries of Europe, the most dominant models are those of learning through religion in confessional religious education and learning from religion in confessionally neutral versions of religious education (Kaupp 2019, 577; 582–585). Transformation of religious education in schools follows the transformation of religion in society. In many former communist countries, after the fall of communism, confessional religious education became an important place of religious socialization, which is attended by most students. In the meantime, it became conceptually adjusted to social shifts and requirements of modern schools in a global and plural world (Filipović 2011, 187–214).

5 Mutual Questioning of Religion and Education

Christian education and formation processes as social practice are weaved into historical structures of understanding faith and Church, and their significance in the political and social community. The pyramidal ecclesiology of division of the Church on clerics and laypeople, which is still dominant in many church and theological contexts and practices, even though the Second Vatican Council highlighted an ecclesiology of communion, has direct consequences on the understanding and practice of learning faith. Clericalization of the Church, which puts great power into the hands of the clerics, with all further mechanisms of exclusion and suppression, is an obstacle to a communal and intergenerational communication of faith, to the strengthening and the flourishing of catechetical ministries and charisms, and to the opening of new paths of learning faith in today's circumstances.

That is also reflected in the capability of theology for dialogue with other sciences. Methodologies of sciences relevant for critical thinking on education are a multifaceted challenge to today's religious education and practical theology. They point to the fact that a perspective influences the perception of practice and show that there are many interpretations of religion that can conflict with the dominant discourse or dominant ecclesial practice in a certain context (Cush and Robinson 2014, 8–9). That helps to perceive the fact of the social construction of knowledge and to discover the connection between knowledge and power (Michel Foucault). Connected to the theological thinking of the Second Vatican council, those methodologies help recognize the Church's involvement in the logic of power, which is diametrically opposed to the Gospel values, and uncover the oppressive structures within the educational processes. The deconstruction of power leaves space for questioning of hegemonic and exclusive (colonial, patriarchal and other hierarchically normative) perspectives and their involvement in the structuring of religion in a certain context. The uncovering of mechanisms of dominance that hinder the development of pluralism and communion is necessary to develop awareness of and sensitivity to the basic equality of all faithful. That enables one to read anew the sources and tradition, to read the Bible with the eyes of the oppressed, marginalized, unjustly treated, so that the liberation power of the Biblical message for promotion of justice, nondiscrimination and diversity in the Church and society can come to the fore (Reddie 2006).

Opposing the so-called objective knowledge and the meaning of a certain knowledge for individuals and social communities, is considered overcome in religious education and other education sciences today. Contemporary education theories are distancing themselves from the illuminist separation of theory and practice, substance, and function, and are aspiring towards holistic understanding of knowledge, which ties together education and formation, practice and reflection, knowledge, and wisdom. Critical thinking and discerning which leads to balance, maturity, and wisdom, is inherent to education (Groome 2011, 115–120). In that return to integrality, religion and education come together performing the task of humanizing the individual and society.

Knowledge is constituted in multiple communication processes, which in a context of Christian theology means: in the encounter with the basic documents of faith and tradition of the Church, but also in the encounter with contemporary sciences, cultures and persons, with other religious traditions and spiritualities. The formative processes, not just in school, but in the Christian community, must open spaces and hold tension between tradition and context, between the message and understanding, between universality and particularity, between unity and diversity. The dialectic tension between faith and culture, tradition and contemporary context, content, and function of faith, is reflected also in religious language. Traditionally religious language in religious education in school was more implicit, while in catechesis and continuing faith formation in a Christian community more explicit, relying on Christian sources and tradition. In the cultural horizon of postmodern consciousness, characterized by the abandoning of universal systems of meaning, where truth is not understood metaphysically but rather as an encounter that influences the transformation of a person, interaction is necessary between two languages in all education processes.

Today, the ability of the Church and religious education processes to be plural is especially put to test. It is necessary to conceptually and methodically valorize it and turn it into models of action (Riegel 2016). There is a need for a hermeneutical toolkit that will meet the heterogeneity of participants in educational and formative processes, as well as answer the intersectional interdependence of certain characteristics of their identities.

Bibliography

Alberich, Emilio. 2002a. "La catechesi di iniziazione." In *Andate e insegnate: Manuale di Catechetica*, edited by Istituto di Catechetica, Facoltà di Scienze dell'Educazione, Università Pontificia Salesiana–Roma, Torino: Elledici, 239–248.

Alberich, Emilio. 2002b. "Catechesi e re-iniziazione." In *Andate e insegnate: Manuale di Catechetica*, edited by Istituto di Catechetica, Facoltà di Scienze dell'Educazione, Università Pontificia Salesiana–Roma, Torino: Elledici, 262–267.

Amherdt, François-Xavier. 2017. "La catéchèse intergénérationnelle et communautaire – entre les générations et au sein de la communauté." *Bildungsforschung* 1:1–15.

Braido, Pietro. 1991. *Lineamenti di storia della catechesi e dei catechismi: Dal "tempo delle riforme" all'età degli imperialismi (1450–1870)*. Torino: Elledici.

Caspani, Pierpaolo, and Paolo Sartor. 2008. *Iniziazione cristiana: L'itinerario e i sacramenti*. Bologna: Edizioni Dehoniane.

Cush, Denise, and Catherine Robinson. 2014. "Developments in Religious Studies: Towards a Dialogue with Religious Education." *British Journal of Religious Education* 36:4–17.

Derroitte, Henri. 2000. *La catéchèse décloisonnée: Jalons pour un nouveau projet catéchétique*. Bruxelles: Lumen Vitae.

Dujarier, Michel. 1984. *Breve storia del catecumenato*. Torino: Elledici.

Elias, John L. 1993. *The Foundations and Practice of Adult Religious Education.* Malabar: Krieger Publishing.
Englert, Rudolf. 2007. *Religionspädagogische Grundfragen: Anstöße zur Urteilsbildung.* Stuttgart: Kohlhammer.
Exeler, Adolf. 1966. *Wesen und Aufgabe der Katechese: Eine pastoralgeschichtliche Untersuchung.* Freiburg / Basel: Herder.
Filipović, Ana Thea, and Andrea Lehner-Hartmann. 2016. "Reflections on Theories of (Catholic) Education from the Perspective of Practical Theology." In *Catholic Approaches in Practical Theology: International and Interdisciplinary Perspectives*, edited by Claire E. Wolfteich and Annemie Dillen, Leuven / Dudley: Peeters, 185–206.
Filipović, Ana Thea. 2011. *U službi zrelosti vjere i rasta osoba: Katehetska i religijskopedagoška promišljanja u suvremenom kontekstu.* Zagreb: Glas koncila.
Fleck, Carola. 2011. "Katechese in Geschichte und Gegenwart." In *Handbuch der Katechese: Für Studium und Praxis*, edited by Angela Kaupp, Stephan Leimgruber, and Monika Scheidler, Freiburg / Basel: Herder, 21–38.
Gianetto, Ubaldo. 2002. "La catechesi nella storia: dagli inizi fino al rinnovamento conciliare." In *Andate e insegnate: Manuale di Catechetica*, edited by Istituto di Catechetica, Facoltà di Scienze dell'Educazione, Università Pontificia Salesiana–Roma, Torino: Elledici, 59–80.
Groome, Thomas H. 2011. *Will There Be Faith? A New Vision for Educating and Growing Disciples.* New York: Harper Collins.
Jackson, Robert. 2002. *Religious Education: An Interpretive Approach.* London: Hodder and Stoughton.
Jungmann, Josef Andreas. 1953. *Katechetik: Aufgabe und Methode der Religiösen Unterweisung.* Freiburg / Basel: Herder.
Kaupp, Angela. 2019. "Catholic Religious Education in Germany and the Challenges of Religious Plurality." In *Global Perspectives on Catholic Religious Education in Schools.* Vol. 2, *Learning and Leading in a Pluralist World,* edited by Michael T. Buchanan and Adrian-Mario Gallel, Singapore: Springer, 575–587.
Morante, Giuseppe. 2002. "L'iniziazione cristiana dei minori." In *Andate e insegnate: Manuale di Catechetica*, edited by Istituto di Catechetica, Facoltà di Scienze dell'Educazione, Università Pontificia Salesiana–Roma, Torino: Elledici, 248–262.
Reddie, Anthony. 2006. "Telling a New Story: Reconfiguring Christian Education for the Challenges of the Twenty-First Century." In *Education, Religion and Society: Essays in Honour of John M. Hull*, edited by Dennis Bates, Gloria Durka, and Friedrich Schweitzer, London: Routledge, 115–127.
Riegel, Ulrich. 2016. "Pluralisierung." In *WiReLex*, edited by Mirjam Zimmermann and Heike Lindner, https://www.bibelwissenschaft.de/de/wirelex/das-wissenschaftlich-religionspaedagogische-lexikon/lexikon/sachwort/anzeigen/details/pluralisierung/ch/f1aa48954ac313e5c351008b83006ecd/ (29.11.2021).
Roebben, Bert. 2011. *Religionspädagogik der Hoffnung: Grundlinien religiöser Bildung in der Spätmoderne.* Münster: Lit-Verlag.
Scharer, Matthias. 2000. "Das 'geheiligte' Fragment: Annäherungen an eine Theologie der Familie." In *Gottesbeziehung in der Familie: Familienkatechetische Orientierungen von der Kindertaufe bis ins Jugendalter*, edited by Albert Biesinger and Herbert Bendel, Ostfildern: Schwabenverlag, 115–136.
Vermeer, Paul. 2010. "Religious Education and Socialization." *Religious Education* 105:103–116.

Roman Catholic Church Documents

AG Ad gentes. Decree on the Church's Missionary Activity. Second Vatican Ecumenical Council, December 7, 1965.
CT Catechesi Tradendae. Apostolic Exhortation of John Paul II, October 16, 1979.
DV Dei Verbum. Dogmatic Constitution on Divine Revelation. Second Vatican Ecumenical Council, November 18, 1965.
DCG Directorium Catechisticum Generale. Ad normam decreti, Sacred Congregation for the Clergy, August 11, 1997.
EG Evangelii gaudium. The Joy of the Gospel. Apostolic Exhortation of Pope Francis, November 24, 2013.
EN Evangelii nuntiandi. Evangelization in the Modern World, Apostolic Exhortation of Pope Paul VI, December 8, 1975.
FR Fides et Ratio. Encyclical Letter of Pope John Paul II to the Bishops of the Catholic Church on the Relationship between Faith and Reason, September 14, 1998.
OICA Ordo Initiationis Christianae Adultorum, Typis Polyglottis Vaticanis, 1972.
SC Sacrosanctum concilium. Constitution on the Sacred Liturgy, Second Vatican Ecumenical Council, December 4, 1963.
Synodenbeschluss. 1998. "Der Religionsunterricht in der Schule." In *Texte zu Katechese und Religionsunterricht*. Bonn: Sekretariat der Deutschen Bischöfe, 127–160.

Anita Louisa Cloete
Religious Literacy

1 Introduction

This article focuses on religious literacy and how it relates to religious education as a key element and foundation. The first section engages the scope and focus of religious education, arguing mainly for the interrelatedness of cognitive and relational aspects. The following section delves into the complexity of context and the dynamic nature of religion as represented in religious plurality. Approaches, mainly from the work of Jackson (2005), are proposed as viable options to engage with plurality as key component of both religious education and religious literacy. I would like to address religious literacy and the connection with religious education within a specific context to illustrate some of these complexities, limitations, and opportunities around both. I choose to focus on South Africa because it is an interesting case in point for several reasons, one being the context I am familiar with. Moreover, it presents an interesting case regarding the complexities of religious pluralism, as religion was used to dehumanise during apartheid, but now, with a multi-religious approach, it is viewed as an important role player in building a united South Africa (Du Plessis 2016, 237). Ntho-Ntho and Nieuwenhuis (2016, 236) confirm that the aim with the religious policy, especially of the governing party, the African National Congress (ANC), was to cherish and celebrate diversity in South Africa. Although I choose to focus on religious literacy within the South African context, I also engage with other conversation partners from the UK and USA to broaden the discussion.

2 Religious Literacy

Richardson (2017, 373) refers to the definition offered by Prothero (2007, 15) that postulates that religious literacy is: "The ability to understand and use in one's day to day life, the basic building blocks of religious traditions – their key terms, symbols, doctrines, practices, sayings, characters, metaphors and narratives". I would like to argue that an understanding of religious education is central in understanding religious literacy. The outcomes of religious education to a certain extent represent religious literacy, as will become clear in the following discussion. Religious literacy is more than knowledge that only values individuals' religious views and experiences; an encounter (relationship) with the religious other is essential. Therefore, knowledge about religions and interaction with different religions seems to be vital. Religious literacy has an individual character as well as a community focus. It implies that knowledge gained through religious education leads to the expectation that individuals will be empowered to express certain attitudes such as tolerance towards other religions and people from other religions and, in doing so, to appreciate diversity. Religious education is, therefore, value-laden and geared towards instilling certain values in learners, like respect for others, their religion, and opinions, in order to live in harmony in a diverse, pluralistic society. Considering such an understanding of religious literacy, Kumar (2006, 273) argues that "religious education in South Africa is not only a human rights issue but also a moral issue".

3 Assets and Limitations of Religious Literacy as an Essential Part of Religious Education

Gallagher (2009, 208) from the USA also refers to the work of Prothero (2007) because he believes the book "makes a strong case for minimal religious literacy as essential requirement for effective citizenship". However, he contends that Prothero focuses too much on the *what* (content) and too little on the *how*. The how and why of religion refers to the dynamic nature of religion. Gallagher (2009, 208) states that "To be literate about religion one needs to know something about religious dynamics, mechanics and processes – the how of religion". This implies an understanding is needed of why religion persists after all these years, defying predictions about the decline of religion known as secularisation, which proposes that religion will not have a prominent place in society and people's lives.

Motivation for religious education to promote and enhance religious literacy in several public spaces like schools, rests on certain prerequisites like mutual respect to understand each other's ethical frameworks, which, in turn, are informed by religion. For ethical dialogue to be possible, an understanding of diverse religious perspectives is needed. Religious literacy is often limited to being merely information about religion, resulting in this aspect being over-emphasised at the cost of other important aspects (Richardson 2017, 364). Considering this challenge, Richardson (2017, 365–366) argues that the limited cognitive focus of religious literacy could be countered by including a focus on communicative encounters with others. He explains the focus on relationality by making a distinction between weak and strong relationality. According to this understanding, knowledge only about religion represents a weak relationality. He continues to clarify weak relationality versus strong relationality by considering three positions, namely:

- *Atomism vs. relational recognition:* This perspective assumes that individual entities (individuals or organisations) are self-contained, while relational recognition suggests that there is no person until there are at least two persons. This means that the individual is only recognised in relation to the other.
- *Abstractionism vs. situated activity:* This perspective warns against the abstract understanding of entities which implies some form of decontextualisation. In terms of religious literacy, it entails discarding or even denying the contextual

nature of religion by assuming it universal applicability. A strong relational perspective would emphasise the relational and contextual nature of religion.
- *Objectivism vs. value-ladenness:* According to objectivism, it is possible to have neutrality and objectivity, a perspective which is value or bias free. A strong relational approach acknowledges that such objectivity and neutrality is not possible, as the very act of communication brings us into a thickly value-laden context.

Considering these views concerning weak or strong relationality in the process of religious education to obtain religious literacy, it becomes evident that the act of education is not neutral or objective. This implies that one cannot teach about religion (facts and content) without an encounter with the religious other. This encountering refers to an experience where involvement of more faculties than just the cognitive function is needed (Richardson 2017, 373).

Gallagher (2009, 209) attempts to respond to a similar question on what religious education for religious literacy could look like, considering the context in which it occurs and how that context will shape (enhance or inhibit) our efforts. These could include different contexts like schools, congregations/churches, theological training, and within the family. Gallagher (2009, 209–210) presents a few factors that may impact on religious literacy, namely:
- Religion education courses, especially in higher education, often have a narrow scope and therefore depth is forfeited.
- Despite the narrowness of the scope, it is often the only religion education course (module) students will ever take and should therefore have more depth as it cannot be assumed that students will continue with the subject.
- Although students may have religious experience, they are often ill-informed or uninformed about religion and therefore do not have the capacity to think about religion critically.

4 Religious Literacy and Plurality

Plurality is an important aspect when exploring religious education and religious literacy. Jackson (2005) gives an important and helpful overview in his book *Rethinking Religious Education and Plurality: Issues in Religious Diversity and Pedagogy* (2004), focusing primarily on religious education amidst plurality. His understanding of plurality is informed by the Norwegian scholar Geir Skeie (1995, 2002), who distinguishes between traditional and modern plurality. He also identifies plurality as a descriptive concept versus plurality as a normative concept. Plurality as a descriptive concept entails how we describe and interpret plurality and the stance we take when making that judgment (Jackson 2005, 3). The traditional understanding of plurality refers to empirical, observable cultural diversity like the movement of migrants between different countries and the emergence of new religious movements. Modern or postmodern plurality relates to the intellectual climate, characterised by fragmentation, individualisation, and the privatisation of religion. It is important to take note of the intertwined relationship between traditional and modern plurality (Jackson 2005, 2–3).

The question is how we can respond to plurality, to shape religious literacy. This is the key focus of the overview presented by Jackson (2004, 2005), who identifies six responses followed by critique and suggestions on how to enhance these approaches to serve religious literacy better. The different responses could be summarised as follows:

- *A nostalgic response* attempts to return to the good old days by denying the existence and impact of plurality, for example offering religious education only from a Christian perspective, accepting Christian indoctrination. However, such an approach is not sustainable considering the changes and diversity brought about by globalisation.
- *Privatisation of religious education* takes place when schools take on a specific religious character. This places religious education in the private or semi-private sphere, and the religious character of the school and the underlying values permeate all the education offered at the institution. Learners in such schools are isolated from other voices and opinions; core values in a globalised world – like social justice, which includes religious tolerance – might not be addressed.
- *Normative postmodern pluralism* opposes the study of religions because it is viewed as an oppressive construction. It rejects textbooks, preferring children's personal stories of faith. This view is, however, not realistic and withholds from children the opportunity to scrutinise and question the religious views presented to them.
- *Religion as discrete system* promotes religious literacy by identifying and arguing for a specific religious or non-religious position. Although this approach assists learners in justifying their own positions, it portrays religion as a discrete system, disregarding the diversity of experiences of learners.
- *The interpretive approach* acknowledges plurality and allows learners to find their own positions through debate about religious plurality. In this process learners' own religious beliefs and values serve as sources in reflexivity where learners are encouraged to reflect on their own way of life and how they encounter difference.
- *Religious education in relation to multicultural (intercultural relationships)* advocates for the removal of religious education from the school curriculum because society is deeply secular. However, this position is rejected, and it is argued that it could be mutually beneficial to bring together religious diversity and specialisation in the field of religion and education for democratic citizenship, and intercultural and values-led education.

5 Religious Literacy in South Africa

During 2003, the democratic government started to implement the *National Policy on Religion and Education*, which provides a framework to work towards unity in diversity, specifically around religion as a core focus. Moreover, the policy aims to prevent discrimination on the grounds of religion and this focus was integrated as part of a school subject called Life Orientation. The government opted for a non-confessional multi-religious approach for presenting religious education in schools. This secular approach is the opposite of the confessional approach that was followed under the apartheid government, in which Christianity was viewed and nurtured as the dominant religion in society, including in schools (Nogueira-Godsey 2016, 229). This policy was well-intended as part of a bigger dream/aspiration of making a new start in South Africa with the constitution as the cornerstone of the newly founded democracy. Despite the good intentions of this policy, it has proven to have serious limitations in terms of implementation. The policy was intended to prevent religious discrimination, but several cases were reported where religious discrimination was experienced, be it wearing a nose ring with religious undertones or having dreadlocks that are associated with Rastafarians (Nogueira-Godsey 2016, 230–231).

The questions that came to the fore are, how should a secular approach to teaching religion be implemented, what does it entail, and are people trained for this? Does this assume that people can be objective when teaching religion? Meaning, can they distance themselves from their own religious experience, views and practices when presenting religious education? The response to these questions will depend largely on the understanding of religion. Moulin (2011, 313) engages with similar questions and argues that responses are often informed by different epistemological conceptions.

Nogueira-Godsey (2016, 231–232) has undertaken research in South Africa regarding teachers' views on their preparedness and experiences as religious educators. Some important findings are that teachers have poor knowledge and skills of the subject in general, and specifically about religions other than their own and consequently a superficial understanding of the purpose of the subject. Related to this is the lack of engaged textbooks and relevant training on how to utilise appropriate approaches to teach from a multi-religious viewpoint. Moreover, they feel that there are unreasonable expectations of them to promote diversity and pluralism. Ntho-Ntho and Nieuwenhuis (2016, 239) describe these expectations very well, stating that it is expected of schools "to mediate between old and new systems, creating a social, intellectual, emotional, behavioral, organizational and structural environment that reflects a sense of acceptance, security and respect for people with different values, cultural backgrounds and religious traditions".

Some of the feedback also confirms that teachers are not aware of their own subjectivity which causes them to rely on the presumably dominant religion in their specific contexts/cultures. Considering these findings, Nogueira-Godsey (2016, 232) concludes: "The educational curricula in South Africa have not sufficiently addressed the subjectivities that have been created in these spheres nor have they acknowledged the assimilations between the Christian confessionalism and democratic values under the banner of a multi-religious approach." Another important aspect of the implementation of the *National Policy on Religion and Education* is an expectation that principals implement the policy and fulfill a mediating role when conflicts arise because of different religious interests. This implies that principals implement the policy according to their interpretation of it, which could potentially cause conflict with parents and other stakeholders, which they are responsible for resolving (Ntho-Ntho and Nieuwenhuis 2016, 237).

Moulin (2011) has carried out similar and relevant research on religious students' experience of religious education in the contemporary non-confessional religious education approach in the United Kingdom. Moulin (2011, 316–319) reports that one of the significant findings was that respondents believed their tradition was stereotyped by the way the lessons were presented. This stereotyping of their tradition is counterproductive in terms of the outcomes of religious education, which are to enhance knowledge and respect for (all) religious traditions, as lack of this leads to ignorance and disrespect. More examples were presented where Christian students reported for instance how communion was treated as an outdated practice. Likewise, being a believer was introduced as following a set of rules instead of as a relationship. Jewish students perceived that the complexity of their religious tradition, including the diversity of identities, was not considered in how it was portrayed. Interestingly, students also felt that due to the unscientific nature of religion, not everything can be explained and understood in a logical way, for example the miracles of Jesus. Others explained that during Religious Philosophy classes it is necessary to step back as a believer, as you don't necessarily believe what is said about your religious tradition. These findings confirm the central role that teachers play in the experience of students during religious education. Teachers' lack of knowledge of other religions together with their own religious beliefs interfere with how they present religious traditions other than theirs.

Research on religious education in two other African countries, namely Malawi and Ghana, correlate with the conclusions in the foregoing discussion. Matemba and Addai-Manunkum (2019, 155) are of the opinion that religious misrepresentation in a context of religious pluralism in sub-Saharan African is a topic that is not receiving the attention it should. They use the theory of selective tradition from the work of Michael Apple ([1993] 2000, [1979] 2004) as a framework to interpret the empirical data gathered to address the challenge of misrepresentation of religions. The theory of selective tradition postulates that education is not neutral but rather that it is embedded within the messy politics of culture and as such cannot always be regarded as serving the common good. Central to their arguments and findings are the ideas concerning choices on what to include, exclude and 'misclude' (included but misrepresented) (Matemba and Addai-Manunkum 2019, 156). In both Malawi and Ghana, Christianity, Islam, and African Indigenous Religions (AIR) are presented as part of a multi-faith curriculum in religious education. Christianity is still the most common religion that seems to dominate the views of both educators and students, creating a fertile ground for discrimination towards and misrepresentation of other religions (Matemba and Addai-Manunkum 2019, 162).

Their most important findings are that although both educators and students are aware of religious diversity both in the classroom and in wider society, they still fail to recognise and respect religious others. Instead, they express feelings of superiority over other religions and therefore demonise religions such as Hinduism, Buddhism, Judaism, and Rastafarianism (Matemba and Addai-Manunkum 2019, 164). One of the main contributing factors to this misrepresentation and mistreatment of religious others is the limited scope of religions presented that creates a culture where other minor religions are judged and viewed as undesirable.

Kumar (2006, 274) points out that religious pluralism raises the question of representation, in other words which religions are included, which are excluded, and how those included are approached and presented. These are important questions, especially if religious literacy implies an appreciation of diversity that reaches beyond mere knowledge but, importantly, includes certain values and attitudes such as respect. Another important issue Kumar (2006, 282–283) raises pertaining to South Africa, is the interrelatedness of religion and race. Religious education in South Africa must deal with another layer of complexity as both religion and race on their own are complex, but when combined even more so. Although the South African constitution separates religious and racial discrimination, the ideal in terms of religious education is finding a balance between national unity and religious and personal laws.

6 Religion as the Subject of Religious Literacy

A multi-religious approach instead of a confessional approach seems to the obvious choice, not only in South Africa but also in other parts of the world, as became evident in the discussion above. In my view a central question is: What understanding of religion is worked with in religious education, as this relates directly to how religion is presented in the educational process. The previous paragraph alluded to the complexity of religion and race in South Africa. Should religion be viewed/approached as a phenomenon amongst many histories and daily lives of people? Kumar (2006, 280) notes that the method of phenomenology is attractive to universities in South Africa but also warns that this approach has serious limitations. Citing the work of Kay (1997) on Piaget (1972) about the phenomenological approach to religion, Kumar (2006, 288) summarises the critique of this approach as requiring a removal of prejudice and the self, upon entering the experience of the other.

Drawing primarily on the work of Herder (1969, 1993, 2006), Czobor-Lupp (2017) makes a valuable contribution in terms of how religion could function as an emancipatory power within religious education. Czobor-Lupp (2017) argues primarily that

Herder's understanding of religion is of importance to make a constructive contribution, especially regarding religious literacy. This understanding of religion rests on an anti-dualist account of religion that emphasises the continuity between religion and reason. Furthermore, such a conceptualisation of the relationship of continuity between religion and reason is embedded in a certain conception of culture, including language and imagination. To see religion as not opposing reason opens the possibility for religion to act as an emancipatory agent, instead of being viewed as irrational and a source of violence. Herder's work is in response to and as critique of the Enlightenment when a narrow and abstract understanding of religion developed. He views the basis of religion not as divine revelation but rather as human witnessing. Therefore, human experience, feelings, and language are important aspects of religion (Czobor-Lupp 2017, 242). Subsequently, the affective and the cognitive operate in tandem in this understanding of religion. Czobor-Lupp (2017, 253) reaches a helpful conclusion regarding this understanding of religion in relation to religious education when she states: "Individuals that thus developed their humanity, as an expression of both their freedom and their love, of both reason and faith, are aware that, when engaged with dialogue across cultures, a moment might arrive when the firm ground provided by their certainties and truths are shaken and start dissolving: when their reason reaches its limits." This means that engaging with religion in an educational setting is not only a cognitive exercise, but the affective side makes provision for vulnerability instead of dogmatism and despotism. Being vulnerable implies having the ability to not only accept the unknown and uncertainty, but also being prepared to live with this. In this process faith and love may have the power to keep the dialogue ongoing. A question related to the understanding/view of religion is whether religion could have a secular appeal? Or is the better question not whether we should still work with these differentiations of secular and sacred?

Another important factor is the proliferation of new religious movements today, which makes being inclusive a daunting and almost impossible task. Although New Religious Movements (NRM) is not a new concept, the study thereof is (Introvigne 2016, 1). Despite a lack of agreement on the definition, it has become an accepted concept of which the broad definition is viewed as strengthening the research field instead of weakening it. The term is quite broad, including groups with both explicit and not overtly supernatural ideologies, while religion is defined by two approaches, namely groups that explicitly refer to themselves as religious and groups that look like other religious movements (Introvigne 2016, 13–14). A related term is Invented Religions (IR), which are primarily defined in terms of their characteristics, of which the most important one is their rejection of established religious movements and existing historical tradition and having a fictional basis (Cusack 2016, 291). Moreover, "[i]nvented religions fit newer models of religion that emphasize story, play, creativity, and the importance of meaning-making, both individual and collective" (Cusack 2016, 295). Whilst invented religions do not want to have any connection with established religion movements, new religious movements do. In the words of Adogame (2016, 236), "The interface of religious culture of sub-Saharan Africa with globalization needs to be located against the backdrop of the interlocking relationship and mutual enhancement of the various old and new religions rather than in any unilateral perspective." African New Religious Movements (ANRM) are therefore closely linked to the specific cultures from which they emerge, for example the African Initiated/Independent Churches (AIC's) and the African Pentecostal/Charismatic Churches.

Lived Religion (LR) is the last description of religion I would like to focus on, as it is increasingly becoming the focus of practical theology. As the term "lived" suggests, lived religion refers to the everyday, practical, and popular. This kind of religion is informed by what people believe and how they express such beliefs in words or deeds (ways of living) in their everyday life. Therefore, people's actions, especially choices and experiences, are the focus of lived religion, and not institutionalised forms of religion. This, however, does not mean that what people do and believe and practise in their everyday life has nothing to do with institutionalised religion. To the contrary, a realistic view of lived religion includes at least three interacting components, namely official religion, folk religion, and individual religion, which constitute what individuals believe (Bowman 2016, 254). These new movements emphasise the dynamic, contextual, and cultural nature of religion as continuously changing and transforming instead of being static. Moreover, it underscores the diversity of religion and within religions, something often underplayed or ignored in religious education.

A question I also found worth engaging with is, who should present religious education? As the previous discussion clearly indicated, the role of the educator is key to what is taught and how it is taught and experienced. In South Africa, religious education is part of a subject called Life Orientation; religion does not necessarily have a prominent focus and is presented by teachers who do not receive adequate training in this regard. Moreover, this subject is not taken into consideration to qualify for university admission, which could create the impression among learners that it is not important. Despite this, the issue of who is teaching religious education is central – should it be someone who receives professional training in religion education; should they belong to and be an active participant in a faith tradition? Any response to these questions could produce its own set of challenges. As already discussed, both teachers and learners misrepresent and even marginalise and demonise religions other than their own. Despite these challenges I suggest that we engage with them, especially considering the great expectation of religious literacy in South Africa.

A final aspect that needs to be acknowledged regarding religion and its complexity, is power as an integral part of religion. We tend to think about religion as purely positive and constructive. However, history has proven how destructive religion can be, particularly in South Africa, where apartheid was justified by religion. A fairly general description of religion is as a meaning-making process that is value laden, expressed through different practices signifying a religious identity. Religion as power, however, is often neglected, not only in our description of religion, but also due to secularisation theories' emphasis on the loss of the social power of religion. According to Woodhead (2011, 134) "Religion indicates where power lies (in forces of both good and evil), allows people to enter into relation with it by understanding it, revering it, worshipping it, appeasing it, drawing upon it, manipulating it, railing against it, mediating upon it, making offerings to it, and falling in love with it." Woodhead (2011) argues for a broad understanding of religion – not only in research. But such a rich understanding of religion should also be presented as part of religious education to cultivate more balanced and informed religious literate citizens.

7 Conclusion

I would like to return to the definition of religious literacy cited earlier in the article that includes aspects like everyday living, understanding of religious language (symbols, practices etc.). Considering the elements in the definition, religious literary is more than knowledge and therefore more than being religiously educated. An attitude that is informed by certain values are some of the concrete characteristics of a religiously literate person. Moreover, such attitudes and values, such as respecting different religions could not be obtained through knowledge only, but rather through exposure to religious others. The expectation is that religious literacy will make a difference in everyday living, resulting in responsible citizenship. The aim of religious literacy therefore is not only focused on the individual but holds the broader community in mind and is about how we live together.

The relationships between religious literacy and religious education received ample attention. Challenges and limitations experienced in religious education directly impact on religious literacy. From both teachers' and students' responses it became evident that although religion is a much-needed subject with even greater expectations, especially in South Africa, it is certainly not without serious challenges. Respondents, students, and teachers gave valuable data concerning their experiences of religious education from their different vantage points that seem to suggest that you cannot distance yourself from your own religious views and experience while engaging in a multi-religious approach.

Objectivity in terms of religious stance from the educators and students involved in religious education therefore does not seem possible. Therefore, knowledge of, coupled with respect for, other religions is paramount, otherwise skewed/negative presentations ensue. The expectations of religious education to shape religious literate citizens is high, especially in South Africa, which could allude to a simplistic understanding of religion on the one hand, but at the same time points to the positive power religion holds. Therefore, this article argues for a broad and balanced view of religion as basis for religious education. No education is neutral; this includes religious education where choices become more complicated in a context of religious plurality. The politics of knowledge, the intrinsic power of religious positions, and the experience of those involved in the education process are key elements that influence how religions are presented and perceived through religious education. It is not necessarily clear what approach(es) is / are used in South Africa to facilitate a multi-faith approach to religious education. Underlying a multi-faith approach is the idea of inclusiveness, but as discussed this is not easy for various reasons. As became clear from the research in South Africa, Malawi and Ghana, Christianity still seems to have a dominant position in these societies as well as in religious education.

Bibliography

Adogame, Afe. 2016. "African New Religious Movements." In *The Bloomsbury Companion to New Religious Movements*, edited by George D. Chryssides and Benjamin E. Zeller, London: Bloomsbury Publishing, 235–251.

Apple, Michael. [1979] 2004. *Ideology and Curriculum*. New York: Routledge Florence.

Apple, Michael. [1993] 2000. *Official Knowledge: Democratic Education in a Conservative Age*. London: Routledge.

Bowman, Marion. 2016. "Vernacular / Lived Religion." In *The Bloomsbury Companion to New Religious Movements*, edited by George D. Chryssides and Benjamin E. Zeller, London: Bloomsbury Publishing, 253–269.

Cusack, Carole. 2016. "Invented Religions." In *The Bloomsbury Companion to New Religious Movements*, edited by George D. Chryssides and Benjamin E. Zeller, London: Bloomsbury Publishing, 291–295.

Czobor-Lupp, Mihaela. 2017. "Herder on the Emancipatory Power of Religion in Religious Education." *The Review of Politics* 79:239–261.

Du Plessis, Georgia. 2016. "Apartheid, Religious Pluralism and the Evolution of the Right to Religious Freedom in South Africa." *Journal of Religious History* 40:237–260.

Gallagher, Eugene. 2009. "Teaching for Religious Literacy." *Teaching Theology and Religion* 12:208–221.

Herder, Johann G. 1969. "Journal of my Voyage in the Year 1769." In *Herder on Social and Political Thought*, edited by Frederick M. Barnard, Cambridge: Cambridge University Press.

Herder, Johann G. 1993. "Ideas toward a Philosophy of History." In *Against Pure Reason: Writings on Religion, Language and History*, edited by Marcia G. Bunge, Eugene: Wipf and Stock Publishers, 50–54.

Herder, Johann G. 2006. "On Image, Poetry, and Fable." In *Selected Writings on Aesthetics*, edited by Gregory Moore, Princeton: Princeton University Press, 357–382.

Introvigne, Massimo. 2016. "Introduction." In *The Bloomsbury Companion to New Religious Movements*, edited by George D. Chryssides and Benjamin E. Zeller, London: Bloomsbury Publishing, 1–21.

Jackson, Robert. 2004. *Rethinking Religious Education and Plurality: Issues in Religious Diversity and Pedagogy*. London / New York: Routledge.

Jackson, Robert. 2005. "Rethinking Religious Education and Plurality: Issues in Religious Diversity and Pedagogy." *Religion & Education* 32:1–10.

Kay, William. 1997. "Phenomenology, Religious Education and Piaget." *Religion* 32:275–283.

Kumar, Pratap. 2006. "Religious Pluralism and Religious Education in South Africa." *Method & Theory in the Study of Religion* 18:273–293.

Matemba, Yonah, and Richardson Addai-Mununkum. 2019. "'These Religions Are No Good – They're Nothing But Idol Worship': Mis/representation of Religion in Religious Education at Schools in Malawi and Ghana." *British Journal of Religious Education* 41:155–173.

Moulin, Dan. 2011. "Giving Voice to 'the Silent Minority': The Experience of Religious Students in Secondary School Religious Education Lessons." *British Journal of Religious Education* 33:313–326.

Nogueira-Godsey, Elaine. 2016. "Country Report: Recent Observations on Religion Education in South Africa." *British Journal of Religious Education* 38:229–235.

Ntho-Ntho, Albertina, and Jan Nieuwenhuis. 2016. "Religion in Education Policy in South Africa: A Challenge of Change." *British Journal of Religious Education* 38:236–248.

Piaget, Jean. 1972. *Insight and Illusions of Philosophy*. London: Routledge and Kegan Paul.

Prothero, Stephen. 2007. *Religious Literacy: What Every American Needs to Know – And Doesn't*. New York: Harper Collins.

Richardson, Michael. 2017. "Religious Literacy, Moral Recognition, and Strong Relationality." *Journal of Moral Education* 46:363–377.

Skeie, Geir. 1995. "Plurality and Pluralism: A Challenge for Religious Education." *British Journal of Religious Education* 17:84–91.

Skeie, Geir. 2002. "The Concept of Plurality and its Meaning for Religious Education." *British Journal of Religious Education* 25:47–59.

Woodhead, Linda. 2011. "Five Concepts of Religion." *International Review of Sociology* 21:121–143.

Paul Post
Ritual Studies

1 Introduction

1.1 Setup

In this contribution, ritual acts and performances are explored from the perspective of the multidisciplinary platform of Ritual Studies (Post 2015). This chapter argues that this is of use – perhaps necessity – for anyone directly or indirectly involved in religious practices. I seek to provide material for a critical attitude both 'internal' via reflection on the nature and essence of ritual acting, and 'external' via study of current cultural dynamics that lead to ritual transformation.

The design of this contribution is threefold: (a) It asks: what is ritual? A simple question that on closer inspection turns out to be less straightforward to answer. It seeks to address the phenomenon of the ritual act as well as the study of it. (b) The second part deals with the ambiguities, paradoxes, and ambivalences of rituals. Precisely due to their complex and ambivalent nature, rituals are elusive, unpredictable, and confusing, as well as being exciting and dynamic. (c) The third part shows how rituals are influenced by trends in a specific cultural context, in this case (post)modern Western-European society. It also brings in a critical perspective, known as Ritual Criticism (Post 2013b; Post and van der Beek 2016). I conclude with a note on ritual in times of corona. Ultimately, the purpose of this chapter is to offer a critical lens with which to explore ritual acting as a dominant form of religious practice.

1.2 Ritual Studies

This chapter is framed by the perspective of Ritual Studies, an interdisciplinary platform for ritual research which emerged in the USA in the mid-1970s. Ritual Studies is characterized by an open 'canon' of themes, a strong theoretical foundation, a cross-cultural and comparative perspective, and an academic tradition which produces book series, journals, congresses, research programs (Post 2015; Grimes 2014).

Although Ritual Studies can, to a certain extent, be characterized as transcultural and trans-religious, a critical note needs to be added regarding the term 'transcultural'. Although the tradition of theorizing (Kreinath, Snoek, and Stausberg 2009) and analysing ritual is comparative in nature and therefore could be said to be transcultural, some suggest that rituals should only be studied fully in specific anthropological and cultural contexts. Outside of these contexts, theorizing rituals is based on academic conceptual presuppositions, including that of the 'semantic trap'. Concepts always have a load and a history. There are many studies in the *Begriffsgeschichte* tradition that provide critical insights into the concept of ritual (Buc 2009; Boudewijnse 1995).

It is also important to signal how, in current Ritual Studies, attention is strongly focused on the dynamics, change and transformation processes shown by studies on sharing ritual (Post 2019a), failing ritual (Hüsken 2007), denying ritual (Hüsken and Seamone 2013), contesting ritual (Post, Nel, and van Beek 2014), postponing ritual (Faro 2015), negotiating ritual (Hüsken and Neubert 2012), and the absence of ritual (Post and Hoondert 2019). I will pursue this focus on transformation and dynamics in this contribution.

2 How to Define Ritual?

2.1 "Juggling Clouds"

Ritual is one of those words or concepts that is particularly difficult to define. Words such as landscape, magic, religion, superstition are too: we immediately know what they refer to, we can immediately picture them. But when it comes to forming an adequate description or giving a definition, it becomes more difficult. The search for a description of these types of words is akin to juggling clouds. In addition, there is another aspect that makes it particularly difficult to find a conclusive description of ritual.

2.2 Worn Images and Frames

Ritual has been surrounded by a series of ideas that seem to steer the direction of a description in advance as a kind of 'frame'. This steering can sometimes be misleading. I will now briefly explore and demystify some assumptions, ideas, and expectations regarding ritual (I will use ritual, rituals, rites, ritual acts, ritual performances interchangeably):

Ritual is connected to tradition; it has an unchanging and fixed character. Ritual is not made, but rather it is inherited, and passed down through history. *Quod non*.[1] Indeed, ritual can just as easily be created anew, it can emerge or disappear.

Rituals are always repeatable. *Quod non*. There are also unique rituals that only occur once.

Ritual is always connected to religion. *Quod non*. Apart from the issue of what exactly is to be understood by the term religion itself, ritual is by no means always religious. There are many secular rituals.

---

[1] Meaning: which not / that is not true.

Ritual is always a collective act, connected with community. *Quod non.* Ritual can be performed by individuals.

Ritual is of necessity something beautiful, good, and healthy. *Quod non.* Despite the subjective nature of these adjectives, ritual can also be ugly, unhealthy, and undesirable, and it can also fail to meet its aims.

Rituals are associated with major events, such as feasts and festivals, weddings, and funerals. *Quod non.* There are many small, unseen rituals that occur every day within the private sphere.

Ritual is always, above all, meaningful. It is symbolic in nature, referring to something or someone external; it is thus meant to contain multiple deep layers of meaning. *Quod non.* Many ritual experts emphasize the self-referential nature of ritual, ritual does not always refer to something outside of itself, often the performance itself is of central importance.

Ritual should always be a nicely balanced self-contained whole. *Quod non.* Often ritual is a colourful hybrid fusion of very different parts and units. Like for religion per se, the default situation of ritual is that of 'syncretism'. I like to make a comparison here with the children's toy Lego: ritual could be seen as being made up of many individual Lego bricks. Describing or analysing a ritual is thus like playing with Lego, attempting to make something out of disparate pieces. One must have an eye open for the composite character of a ritual and try to find the most important units of which it is made up.

This does not make seeking an adequate definition any more straightforward. Nevertheless, ritual does still call for such an attempt. Just as with any academic project, in the study of ritual, we must systematically and critically work towards a definition which possesses a certain general validity (Grimes 2014, 185–197[2]).

2.3 A Working Definition

Let me put my cards on the table and present my working definition as I have developed it over the years, I have been studying ritual. For me, ritual is:

> a more or less repeatable sequence of action units which take on a symbolic dimension through formalization, stylization, and their situation in place and time. On the one hand, individuals and groups express their ideas and ideals, their mentalities, and identities through these rituals, on the other hand the ritual actions shape, foster, and transform these ideas, mentalities, and identities. (Post 2015, 6)

Instead of extensively elaborating on this description, I will put it into perspective. I am suggesting that I have demarcated ritual clearly with this working definition. But

---

[2] The online Appendix 1 contains definitions of ritual: http://oxrit.twohornedbull.ca/wp-content/uploads/2013/04/grimes-craft-appendixes.pdf (29.11.2021).

that is by no means my intention. I used to try to make my conceptual description of ritual as broad as possible, so that it would be open to all kinds of practices and repertoires that I also wanted to include. This working description is for me an indication of what I call core ritual, or 'full ritual,' but which does not necessarily exclude other types of acts from having a ritual dimension. That is why I now speak of 'ritual' as well as 'ritual-like' acts in addition to ritual, I see practices with a ritual dimension. This is not necessarily in line with how Ronald Grimes describes 'ritualizing', as being performance that is 'still wet behind the ears': still developing into a fully-fledged ritual whilst not yet culturally accepted or framed as a ritual (Grimes 2014, 192–193). I see my thinking in this respect as being more in line with how Catherine Bell presents ritual practice and behaviour that has a ritual dimension, alongside 'full ritual' (Bell 1997, 138–169). As an example, let me refer to collective performances after a natural disaster or a terrorist attack. In these contexts, we see all kinds of practices that wish to express compassion, solidarity as well as anger and protest at the injustice or loss. We see how cities all over the world express their solidarity, for example, by installing landmarks with lasers and LED lights in the colours of the country where the attack or disaster took place. We might see people getting tattoos out of a collective compassion (Cadell et al. 2020). For example, after the Manchester Arena attack in 2017 during a performance by Ariana Grande, it became popular to get a tattoo of a bee, as this is the symbol of Manchester. These are all acts which have a commemorative and ritual character, but the question remains: are they 'full rituals'?

2.4 Qualities of Ritual

Not everyone within the field of Ritual Studies is happy with this search for a definition of ritual, even if it is only a provisional and working description. Many academics decide to walk a different path and instead look for a series of 'qualities of ritual', characteristics, dimensions or functions that together provide an image of what ritual is and what it is capable of. There are all kinds of lists of qualities or dimensions in circulation (see Lukken 2005, 35–74; Post et al. 2003, 41–42). Here is a list of some of them:

Ritual relieves and channels emotions and feelings.

Ritual marks and honours, it makes us think about major events, and makes us stop to pay attention. According to Jonathan Z. Smith, paying attention and situating are the basic components of ritual acting: "Ritual is, first and foremost, a mode of paying attention. It is a process for making interest. [...] It is this characteristic, as well, that explains the role or place of a fundamental component or ritual: place directs attention." (Smith 1987, 103)

Ritual positioning or situating works through this marking. It places us and events on the axis of the past, present, and future. In this way, ritual has an 'anamnetic' character.

Ritual also has an ethical side: "One could say that as ritual is a source and norm for a humane perspective on life [...] so ritual is also the source and norm of authentic human action [..]." (Lukken 2005, 69) Ritual is never for free, it is 'a dangerous game'. The apostle Paul emphasizes this in his letter to the Corinthians (1 Cor 11) when he points to the fact that sitting at the Christian ritual meal is not without its obligations. A separation between the rich and the poor disrupts a solidarity-based community.

As already noted in my working definition, ritual is expressive. It enables us to express our feelings, ideas, dreams, ideals, and ultimately what is 'sacred' to us. The range of expressions is wide: from anger and compassion to protest and displeasure.

Ritual is also related to incantation and exorcism. It is a means to ban evil, to implore salvation and healing. This is perhaps the ultimate basic layer of any ritual act: coping with contingency and banning evil.

Ritual is also an act of condensation that enables us to bring together enormously complex feelings, ideas or ideals into a simple act or symbol.

Many points to the socializing function of ritual. If you want to transform a school, sports club, or a nation into a group, into a collective or community, then you ensure they have rites and symbols: a club song, a flag, a logo, an anthem, shared meals. Rituals are thus what define the in-group. The founder of sociology Émile Durkheim elaborated on this perspective in an exemplary and very influential way (Durkheim 1964 [1915]).

And finally, a general quality often remains unmentioned: ritual creates a break, a moratorium. Rituals give us a break and the opportunity for 'recreation'. Without rituals, without feasts, without marking the axes of years and lives, our existence would be an uninterrupted staccato note. Rituals are therefore connected to leisure time and contrast with everyday life. It is precisely in this setting that we see concepts like 'asylum' and 'heterotopia' in relation to ritual: ritual as 'other space' in contrast to daily space and life (Foucault 2005, cf. Post 2010, 100–111).

Thus, ritual enters the picture through certain characteristics and functions. The idea is that the more of these characteristics and functions that can be assigned to a certain action, the more akin to a ritual it is.

2.5 Dynamic Playing Field

We have previously highlighted that rituals are definitely not traditional in the sense of being invariable through place and time. On the contrary: rituals are extremely dynamic and changeable. To get a closer look, it is important to see the wider playing field, which is extremely complex due to the strong contextual dynamics of ritual acts. The use of a schematic representation often helps me to bring some clarity: it allows us to see the playing field of ritual repertoires. A ritual repertoire is a set of ritual practices that display a certain coherence in terms of design, participation, cause, or context.

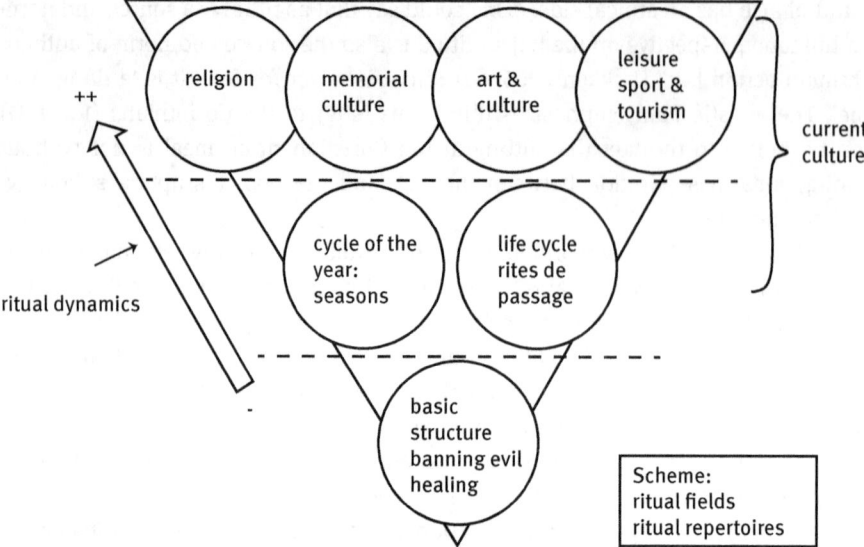

Figure 6: Scheme of the Ritual Playing Field with Fields and Repertoires © Paul Post.

I present three layers in the inverted triangle. At the base is the basic structure of ritual practices that seems more or less constant through place and time. As mentioned, this concerns banning evil, the prophylactic and apotropaic function of ritual, healing, and coping. I can refer here to many scholars in Ritual Studies, for example Martin Stringer who ultimately sees ritual and religion as being connected by "intimate relationships with the non-empirical other" through ritual practices based on the need to "cope pragmatically with everyday problems." (Stringer 2008, 113–114)

A middle layer comprises two large repertoires, two important ritual fields that we encounter everywhere, but in changing forms. It concerns the rituals on the axis of life, the rites of passage from birth to death, and those on the axis of the year, usually determined by the calendar, lunar or solar, or a combination of both that in turn are the basis of a ritual annual calendar. Ritual Studies' authors such as Arnold van Gennep, Victor Turner and Émile Durkheim focused their scholarship on this layer.

In addition, at the upside of the inverted triangle there is the current playing field of ritual repertoires. This is a very dynamic field and looks very different in different places in the world. I offer a general outline of the situation of contemporary Western European culture where I see four major ritual domains with recognizable and dominant ritual repertoires (Post 2011, 13–59; Post 2013a, 149–158). As said, here we see the greatest dynamic shifts: rituals coming and going, changing form, content, and context, we see 'ritual transfer' and we witness all kinds of appropriations and transformations.

2.6 Current Playing Field

I wish to focus on four areas or fields in this section. Firstly, the domain of religion. Despite the idea that Europe is largely deemed to be secular, religion is quietly thriving. And indeed, the closure, demolition and repurposing of many church buildings, whose parishes had been declining sharply in number – particularly in the Netherlands and the UK (contexts with which I am most familiar), suggest a marginalisation of churchgoing. However, when the terrain is looked at more closely, it appears that many new church buildings are in fact being built and set up. This could be due to the growth of urban spaces and cities and an increase in migration. The image is thus one of a balancing effect: fewer traditional churches on the one hand and an increase in newly built churches on the other (Post and Hoondert 2019, 57–59).

Secondly, I wish to focus on the vibrant domain of memorial culture in contemporary Western European society: that of remembering and honouring the past through rituals. I refer to funeral rites, and the commemorative culture of the first and second World War. It is interesting to see here how wide the scope of memorial culture is. After an accident or attack, after death and destruction in the public domain, we see all kinds of grassroots rituals: flowers being laid, candlelit vigils, letters and written eulogies left to commemorate losses, including road-side memorials to loved ones killed in traffic accidents. But there are also these ritual markings that occur decades after the event in question, this could be referred to as postponed ritual. We witness this with WW1 and WW2 events, and with Holocaust memorial culture. For example, the *Holocaust Mahnmal* in Berlin was only opened in 2005 after decades of debates over its complex and sensitive historical context.

A third domain is that of art and culture. The world of theatre, museums, monuments, and heritage is a ritual playing field of its own that is constantly changing.

And finally, there is the field of leisure culture with the important subfields of sport and tourism.

As already indicated, these distinct zones or ritual-sacred fields are especially important to allow us to visualize current ritual dynamics, to indicate the broad playing field or environment in which rituals are situated. In my view, contextualisation is indispensable for understanding and studying religious and ritual practices.

Through exploration of these different fields mentioned above, we gain a better view of the tensions and overlaps between them, as well as how the other layers and repertoires in the diagram interact with each other. The diagram helps me to predict which ritual repertoires will be successful in terms of participation and absorption in the culture, and which are, or will become, marginal. The success of the Camino de Santiago, the medieval pilgrimage route to Santiago de Compostela, is directly linked to the fact that its ritual is bound up in almost all the fields and layers represented in my schema (Post, Pieper, and van Uden 1998). The Camino de Santiago is an example of a ritual that is broadly and deeply anchored in culture and tradition. Whereas many religious liturgical rituals, especially those of traditional churches, seem to withdraw into their own religious domains and thus have fewer or no roots in other domains. Newly emerging often Pentecostal and evangelical liturgy tends to explicitly seek connection with other sacred fields for this very reason.

A final important observation about ritual dynamics is the fact that that dynamic itself might be characteristic of current rituals. In our network culture there is a constant flow between and through the fields and layers. Ritual is a flow that constantly changes its core. There is no single core or centre. An abbey or monastery in modern western Europe is still very much a religious centre of prayer and contemplation, but at the same time, it will be a place for relaxation, tourism for historical appreciation, or an experience in nature.

This section has attempted to understand and unpack what we mean by the term ritual. In the next section, we consider the ambiguous nature of rituals, their ambivalences, and paradoxes.

3 Ritual Ambivalences

Rituals are ambiguous and ambivalent (Post and Hoondert 2019). This is part of their 'nature'. I am not suggesting here that this nature is independent of context, of time and place, culture, and society. It is precisely in these contexts that ambivalence takes shape and therefore ritual always changes in emphasis due to the socio-cultural context at play. Here I do not mean to say that there is a dichotomy or a fixed gap, but rather that there is an interplay. Because of their ambivalent nature, rituals are difficult to categorise and understand, they are elusive, largely uncontrollable, and even unplannable. Religious authorities in particular have often had difficulty with this aspect: rites are not subject to control mechanisms. A common attempt at control is that of written scenarios, directives, and instructions. But ultimately, ritual is always the act itself, the one-off performance. This elusiveness makes rituals complex to understand and describe, as it renders them exciting and attractive at the same time.

I now briefly mention some of these ambivalent aspects.

3.1 The Traditional and the New

There is the tension between ritual as a given tradition on the one hand and as a newly made act on the other. Ritual certainly has the aura of being stored in and handed down from tradition. That is why rituals are repeatable and recognizable or might be seen as being outdated routines. For young people in particular, their traditional aspect can make them seem boring and old-fashioned. This sense of sameness and repetition therefore calls for new forms to be made, it calls for creativity and innovation to freshen and update rituals to the current context and climate. Notwithstanding, the idea that rituals are 'centuries old' traditions is often erroneous, and itself a social construct. Eric Hobsbawm writes of this labelling as 'invention of tradition' (Hobsbawm and Ranger 1992; Post 1996). Let us take the Christmas tree as an example of an object which does not in fact go directly back to a tree cult of the ancient Germans but is rather a late nineteenth-and twentieth-century 'bourgeois' invention that spread from and through many European countries via German housemaids.

3.2 Rituals as Cold and Warm

Rituals can be seen as being simultaneously 'cold', by being connected to critical reason, and 'warm', via being connected to emotion and empathy. They are both Apollonian and Dionysian. Sometimes the search for a good feeling predominates, the cherishing of the idyll in the ritual, for example like a comforting 'warm bath'. Sometimes, however, ritual becomes very cool and detached, clean, purified. As with all ambivalence, a call for balance and harmony can easily be made. I think this can sometimes simplify the issue: it is more a matter of dealing with these kinds of ambivalences and nuances in different contexts and situations, of learning to live with them. Where does a funeral perish in exalted expression of individual or collective emotion, and where does a cooler, more sanitised detachment dominate?

3.3 The Individual and the Community

A third ambivalence is that of the individual and the community. We constantly struggle with this tension in our rituals. To take the example of the funeral-as-ritual, the (post)modern funeral liturgy focuses on the deceased person in question and their group of mourning relatives. It seems that even in this type of ritual, it is a challenge to navigate the dominance of a 'culture of self' alongside a desire for a sense of the collective or the social group. We often possess a strongly idealized image of community, as being a solid, locally bound group (the image of the German *Gemeinschaft*), instead of as an assemblage, a flowing, incidental, and instantaneous community, but still a community no less (cf. the Spanish, Italian *assemblea*). I see this idea reflected in the popularity of the pilgrimage route to Santiago de Compostela. The pilgrim starts with an individual project, leaving family, home, and local community in search of a personal quest. But that individual then meets others and becomes part of the community of fellow pilgrims. We also see this ambivalence reflected in online communities. Communities in cyberspace, for example, are formed by groups of individuals who share a passion or interest (Post and van der Beek 2016). One can therefore be part of quite different communities that are characterized by the interplay of the individual and the larger community.

3.4 Grand and Small

There is also the interplay of grand and small ritual. Often ritual is connected to feasts and ceremony rites, especially those on the axis of life: from birth through marriage, to death and dying. This type of ritual contains some drama and abundance. But small daily rituals are being rediscovered and appreciated. On closer inspection, ritual practice is often a combination of the two forms, grand and small: there may be a prominent concentrated ritual, with small rituals surrounding it. Again, to draw on the example of a funeral, which has a concentrated group celebration in a church or crematorium, but around it there will be all kinds of small rituals at home, in the hospital or elsewhere, before and after the central funeral ceremony.

3.5 Idealism and Reality

Rituals often find themselves in a tension between the reality of their possibilities and limitations, and an idealisation of what they would like to look like, particularly for rituals pertaining to rites of passage, such as weddings and funerals. The media has played a role in this, for example through depictions of weddings and funerals of members of the royal family and celebrities. This has created for many a standard to which to aim. As a result, local celebrations can often feel mediocre or downright disappointing in comparison to the grandiose televised events. Maybe they were not able to afford a professional choir for the service, or they may not have found the right pastor with sufficient competences in the field of speech and performance to deliver the ceremony.

3.6 Inclusive and Exclusive

Ritual is both inclusive and exclusive. It is inviting, accessible, hospitable, but also closed, exclusive. These two poles are important for the character of a ritual: the interplay of form and content in what we call ritual configurations. A Veda ritual, for example, is for most people inaccessible and exclusive in terms of both form and content. A Pentecostal celebration may be more open in its form. Everyone is welcome, with modern popular music, projectors, accessible language. But the content can be very exclusive, a very strict message on religious doctrine, ethics, gender, and sexuality. But, as we will see in our brief description of current ritual trends, we are increasingly seeing a configuration of openness and inclusiveness both in form and content: rituals that are open spaces that people can appropriate and fill by themselves.

3.7 Symbolic and Diabolic

Rituals are symbolic but can also be diabolic. This duality is often forgotten, but rituals are not only and always beautiful and good – they can be devilish like the rituals orchestrated in detail at the annual rally of the Nazi party in Nuremberg in the 1920s and 1930s. Rituals can mask or legitimize discrimination and oppression.

3.8 Useless and Useful

Another ambivalence is seeing ritual as a useless action, or instead as a powerful instrument or act. Any reflection on ritual tends to end up struggling with this paradox. Huizinga (1949 [1938]) strongly emphasizes its 'useless' dimension. For him, cult and ritual are directly related to play, and the playing of man is in line with that of a child or an animal. It is just for fun. It contrasts with efficiency, productivity and the search for end-results that now characterizes and dominates human actions. However, other ritual scholars argue that the basic dimension that we already indicated in our scheme is that of incantation. Rituals are productive, are powerful tools that allow humans to cope with setbacks and contingencies, they keep us going in a world of dangers and evil. I think there is no 'useless / useful trap' (Wepener et al. 2019, 27–46), but rather, that they are two sides of the same coin. Are rituals not powerful coping mechanisms precisely because they are of a different order? (Post 2019b, 73–76)

4 Some Current Ritual Tendencies and Trends

In a third and final part, we explore how rituals are influenced by external trends and events. Rituals do not exist in a vacuum, they are not independent of time and place, of cultural, social, economic, and political contexts, tendencies, and trends. Because of these external stimuli, rituals change, they inculturate or are put under pressure. General trends in culture also lead to trends in rituals. Sometimes this will directly affect the ambivalences mentioned above.

I illustrate this process through a few topical trends that I have identified in the western European context (Post 2019c). In addition, I also provide a brief critical evaluation. By doing so I introduce more explicitly an important perspective of Ritual Studies, namely that of Ritual Criticism (Post and van der Beek 2016). Ritual study is never only descriptive or analytical but has a critical function and task as well. This criticism can be informed and oriented in different ways. It can focus on the ritual performance, the acting competence, or the lack thereof at the level of the presentation, the 'craft' of performing the ritual. Or it can focus on norms and values, on political or religious ideology. Recently, the importance of authenticity in ritual acting is emerging, along with insights informed by research as presented in Ritual Studies. In the following presentation of trends, I will include Ritual Criticism.

4.1 'Casualization'

A first trend with a direct impact on rituals in my context, which is that of the Netherlands, is what I call 'casualization', the advancement of a casual approach to ritual that manifests itself primarily in the external design, but I think goes deeper and expresses something about our attitude towards the sacred. During funeral ceremonies I often see that people no longer dress specifically for the event, but are instead dressed casually, maybe in jeans and an old sweater. We see the same with cremation. The ashes of the deceased loved one might be collected on a bicycle, and the urn might then be placed on a windowsill along with an array of indoor pot plants. The design of ritual spaces is also a sign of this casualization. The interior of modern crematoria or rooms of silence hardly differs from trendy home furnishings: warm colours, casual chairs, and couches where you can lounge.

This is not the place to elaborate on the tendency of what can be called the 'domestication' of ritual. However, referring to Martin Stringer I see a relation with the above mentioned warm emotional side of ritual and 'an increasing sense of comfortableness and intimacy' in ritual acting in a global setting of discourses of consumerism and individual well-being. Stringer notices in contemporary Christian worship in both England and the United States: "carpets on the floor, a crèche for the children, PowerPoint technology providing reassuring images, language that does not offend, and music aimed to speak to our emotions and calm us down." (Stringer 2005, 239)

4.2 'Eventization' and 'Festivization'

A second trend widely recognized is that of 'eventization' and in direct relation to it, 'festivization.' Large events, especially feasts and festivals, are on the rise. The calendar of festivals in the Netherlands has never been this full (at least before the corona pandemic). Rituals are seen by many as being a special event that requires a great effort This has been the case for a long time, especially when it comes to those rites of passage that are known as 'four-wheel moments', for example when a pram is present during the celebration of a birth or baptism, when a limousine is used to drive to the wedding ceremony or funeral and graveyard.
Disasters and commemorations of terrorist attacks, as well as many funerals, are increasingly being held in special event locations or in the public domain. For example, the phenomenon of The Passion, the re-enactment of the Christian passion story through popular music on the streets of a big city, which in the Netherlands has been an enormously popular event every Maundy Thursday since 2011. This modernised version of the passion play originated as a musical TV special in Manchester in 2006.

Rituals are in danger of being overgrown and subsumed by the general tendency of festivization, of the expanding culture of feasts and festivals.

This befits two points of analysis. Firstly, there is the question of what the notion of feast represents in our culture (Post et al. 2001). A feast is based on three main elements: a contrast with or break from everyday life; an underlying reason for the celebration; and a sense of solidarity community, as feasting is not something one tends to do alone. Questions can be asked about the latter two aspects. Is there always a good reason, do we always know what or who we are celebrating? And is there necessarily a solidary group involved?

Here it is necessary to highlight again that ritual acting does not only and always exist in the great gesture of an event or feast. The small ritual is also important.

4.3 Uselessness under Pressure

As we highlighted previously, one of the fundamental dimensions of ritual is that it is determined by the so-called uselessness of play. In a society where there is always a demand for utility and productivity, for efficiency and for results, the uselessness of ritual is under threat. This pressure directly impacts our ritual acting. The Camino de Santiago, the Way of Saint James, for example, like many other pilgrimages, is increasingly being turned into a sponsorship challenge to raise money for a good cause (Post and van der Beek 2017).

4.4 Explosion of the Singular and the Unique

In his richly descriptive and analytical book, German cultural sociologist Andreas Reckwitz points to 'the explosion of the special and unique.' (Reckwitz 2017, 7) In the lifestyle of an emerging wealthy middle class, the idea of the special and the unique plays a major role. This manifests itself in eating, in celebrating rites of passage, traveling, education, designing and furnishing a home and garden, and similarly online, designing the homepage of your website and how you come across on social media. For some of these areas of life, experts may be hired, who, in the same way as curators of museum exhibitions, make life appear special and unique. The ritual is also impacted by this. In the German-speaking world, *rent-a-pastor.com* has been operating with great success (Saß 2019). It is an agency where you hire a pastor / celebrant for a wedding or funeral that presents itself as offering something both special and unique.

4.5 Explaining Rituals

Another emerging trend is that of explanation and commentary. Old city centres are full to the brim of signs outlining the history of particular buildings, how old it is, which architect built it, etc. I see such signs on a large scale when out in nature, signs labelling different species of tree, birds, small mammals, and insects etc. As a people we are becoming increasingly didactic. This pertains also to rituals. For example, during a ritual, the pastor may constantly explain what they are doing, what it means, where it comes from. This is disastrous for ritual. That you light a candle and that it gives light needs no explanation, the act in itself is sufficient. My colleague Walter van Beek once aptly stated: "In a functional ritual, catechesis is superfluous, for an incomprehensible ritual it comes too late." (van Beek 2007, 49)

4.6 Basic Sacrality

Finally, I mention the rise of what I have come to call basic symbolism or basic sacrality in ritual (Schippers 2015). A lot could be said about this. However, I will limit myself to a straightforward description. Due to all kinds of circumstances, such as the diversity of our globalized network culture, rites and symbols arise that are often very open and basic. Here I refer also to ritual spaces as open spaces, which are opening up more and more to a wider variety of appropriations and recasting (Post 2019b) from the established sacred fields. This can be either recasting of existing ritual sites or of entirely new ones. Richard Meier envisaged such a recasting in the much-discussed design of the Holy Year's Jubilee Church in Tor Tre Teste on the outskirts of Rome. It is a white open space, open for more focused religious appropriations, but also for more general and individual spiritual ones in the well-known tradition of new spiritual spaces that potentially started with the Rothko Chapel in Houston (consecrated in 1971). It could be said to be an open hermeneutic space. We see the same in the recasting of an old building in the canal zone of Amsterdam under the initiative Huub Oosterhuis, as a new form of ritual space. The motto of this building, which is called *De Nieuwe Liefde* (New Love) is: "a centre for study, contemplation and debate; a space for spirituality and religion; a stage for poetry, music and theatre."[3] These are exactly the four fields I distinguished in my scheme of ritual repertoires. However, the space is not restricted to being filled only with white: on Sunday the alternative Christian 'Dominicus Community' appropriates a colourful neogothic church in Amsterdam in their own way: they use the space by sitting facing both directions. The recasting of the old Augustinian church in the centre of Eindhoven as the 'Domus Dela Ceremony House' is also striking in this context. The

---

[3] Denieuweliefde.com (29.11.2021). Recently it has become a cultural center for language and words (literature, poetry, spoken-word etc.).

space is open for a variety of ceremonies, from music performances to weddings and funerals and conferences.

Rituals and symbols often become open spaces to be filled. Here once again, the Camino de Santiago is an example. The pilgrimage journey is literally a space or vessel to be filled by the pilgrims themselves, through the very act of walking – stepping into, and through, the space. Ritual acting, often consists of basic, archetypal symbols: the sun, light, a tree, a woman, water, earth, fire. It can derive its identity through small details (Post 2013a). Indeed, 'God is in the details' (Mies van der Rohe).

5 Coda: Rituals in Times of Corona

I completed this chapter during the corona epidemic in April 2020. In this crisis it has become clear what the position of rituals is in society and how topical many observations in this contribution turn out to be.

First and foremost, the position of rituals appears to be ambivalent. On the one hand, the Netherlands is the main context I have experienced, rituals appear to be both a weak and a soft force. Rituals are not listed as 'vital processes' such as those of the medical sector, food supply, police, education etc. Funerals and cremations do of course attract attention, but not directly through the role of ritual experts, pastors, and ritual counsellors. But on the other hand, there are signs that people experience the role of rituals more acutely now that they are not so self-evident. There has been plenty of creativity in the absence of more formal rituals when such rituals have become impossible due to social distancing.

Against the background of what I have presented on ritual and Ritual Studies, I conclude this chapter with some observations about rituals in the time of the corona virus. My observations are preliminary and provisional because a balanced description, analysis and evaluation can only take place after some time has passed, at a certain distance.

Firstly, three aspects that concern the 'nature' of ritual have become very striking. I mention the physical, embodied, and tactile dimension of ritual acting. The necessary practice of social distancing has far-reaching consequences for an embodied ritual performance. At the same time, the dimension of healing and coping has come to the fore. And thirdly, partly connected to the first two elements, ritual creativity not only reshapes those existing but now impossible rituals, but creativity is especially manifest in all kinds of practices which have a ritual dimension, as 'ritual-like' performances. People sing to each other from balconies, express solidarity, hope, appreciation, and compassion by applauding together.

Existing tendencies are being put under pressure, and this is when often undervalued or forgotten aspects of ritual can emerge. We are now confronted with the fact that many communal rituals must be cancelled, rearranged, and postponed. People begin to appreciate that in addition to grand rituals, there can also be smaller rituals, at home, in a small circle of friends, family or neighbours. Performing rituals live, as major events is now impossible. The Passion was cancelled, commemorations were called off or postponed. And above all, the media is used to mediate rituals which have begun to be conducted and streamed online. Liturgy, for example is now live-streamed: the celebration is recorded and transmitted from an empty church.

The situation is challenging and a debate about what might constitute 'online ritual' (Post and Hoondert 2019) has ensued. As well as those rituals which are recorded and uploaded for an online audience, 'cyber rituals', which are live-streamed, only exist virtually. Discussion of the pros and cons of online rituals is topical, especially in a Christian context. Questions abound, such as: Can you celebrate the Lord's Supper online at home, by having bread and wine in front of the computer screen? Does this appropriately shape the Christian community, or is that only reserved for a 'real' in-person gathering and not for a 'virtual' one? Here again ritual ambiguity manifests itself. On the one hand, there has been a tendency for some time to see the liturgical meal in relation to food and drink culture of the surrounding cultural context, and on the other hand, we are rediscovering the ritual dimension of food and drink in our culture (Klomp, Smit, and Speckmann 2018).

All in all, rituals during the time of the corona virus, show the dynamics of rituals in the making, and indicate that ritual practices always ask for ritual critique. This contribution is in essence meant as a plaidoyer for approaching ritual – and practices with a ritual dimension – as a form of 'dangerous play' that requires a critical attitude.

Bibliography

Beek, Wouter van. 2007. *De rite is rond: Betekenis en boodschap van het ongewone*. Inaugural Lecture Tilburg University. https://scholarlypublications.universiteitleiden.nl/handle/1887/13000 (29.11.2021)

Bell, Catherine. 1997. *Ritual, Perspectives and Dimensions*. New York / Oxford: Oxford University Press.

Boudewijnse, Barbara. 1995. "The Conceptualization of Ritual: A History of its Problematic Aspects." *Jaarboek voor liturgie-onderzoek* 11:31–56.

Buc, Philip. 2009. *The Dangers of Ritual: Between Early Medieval Texts and Social Scientific Theory*. Princeton: Princeton University Press.

Cadell, Susan, Melissa Reid Lambert, Deborah Davidson, Carly Greco, and Mary Ellen Macdonald. 2020. "Memorial Tattoos: Advancing Continuing Bonds Theory." *Death Studies*. 46:132–139.

Faro, Laurie M.C. 2015. *Postponed Monuments in the Netherlands: Manifestation, Context, and Meaning*. Tilburg: Doctoral Dissertation. https://research.tilburguniversity.edu/files/15024988/Faro_Postponed_28_01_2015_emb_tot_28_01_2017.pdf (29.11.2021).

Durkheim, Émile. [orig. French 1915] 1964. *The Elementary Forms of the Religious Life*. London: George Allen & Unwin.

Foucault, Michel. 2005. *Die Heterotopien / Der utopische Körper*, trans. M. Bischoff. Frankfurt am Main: Suhrkamp.

Grimes, Ronald L. 2014. *The Craft of Ritual Studies*. Oxford: Oxford University Press.

Hobsbawm, Eric, and Terence Ranger. 1992. *The Invention of Tradition*. Cambridge: Cambridge University Press.

Hüsken, Ute. 2007. *When Rituals Go Wrong: Mistakes, Failure, and the Dynamics of Ritual*. Numen Book Series 115. Leiden: Brill.

Hüsken, Ute, and Frank Neubert. 2012. *Negotiating Rites*. Oxford: Oxford University Press.

Hüsken, Ute, and Donna Lynne Seamone. 2013. "The Denial of Ritual and its Return." *Journal of Ritual Studies* 27: Special Issue.

Huizinga, Johan. [orig. Dutch 1938] 1949. *Homo Ludens: A Study of the Play-Element in Culture*. London: Routledge.

Klomp, Mirella, Peter-Ben Smit, and Iris Speckmann. 2018. *Rond de tafel: Maaltijd vieren in liturgische contexten*. Meander 17. Heeswijk-Dinther: Berne Media.

Kreinath, Jens, Jan Snoek, and Michael Stausberg. 2009. *Theorizing Rituals*. Vol. 1, *Issues, Topics, Approaches, Concepts*; Vol. 2, *Annotated Bibliography of Ritual Theory, 1966–2005*. Leiden: Brill.

Lukken, Gerard. 2005. *Rituals in Abundance: Critical Reflections on the Place, Form, and Identity of Christian Ritual in our Culture*. Liturgia Condenda 17. Leuven / Dudley: Peeters.

Post, Paul. 1996. "Rituals and the Function of the Past: Rereading Eric Hobsbawm." *Journal of Ritual Studies* 10:91–108.

Post, Paul. 2010. *Voorbij het kerkgebouw: De speelruimte van een ander sacraal milieu*. Heeswijk: Abdij van Berne.

Post, Paul. 2011. "Fields of the Sacred: Reframing Identities of Sacred Places." In *Sacred Places in Modern Western Culture*, edited by Paul Post, Arie L. Molendijk, and Justin Kroesen, Leuven / Dudley: Peeters, 13–60.

Post, Paul. 2013a. "From Identity to Accent: The Ritual Studies Perspective of Fields of the Sacred." *Pastoraltheologische Informationen* 33:149–158.

Post, Paul. 2013b. "Ritual Criticism: Een actuele verkenning van kritische reflectie ten aanzien van ritueel, met bijzondere aandacht voor e-ritueel en cyberpilgrimage." *Jaarboek voor Liturgieonderzoek / Yearbook for Liturgical and Ritual Studies* 29:173–199.

Post, Paul. 2015. "Ritual Studies." *Oxford Research Encyclopedia of Religion*. http://religion.oxfordre.com/view/10.1093/acrefore/9780199340378.001.0001/acrefore-9780199340378-e-21 (29.11.2021).

Post, Paul. 2019a. "Sharing Ritual Religious Space: Mapping the Field from a Ritual Studies Perspective." In *Zukunftsraum Liturgie: Gottesdienst vor neuen Herausforderungen*, edited by Peter Ebenbauer and Basilius Groen, Wien: LIT, 87–104.

Post, Paul. 2019b. *Rituele herbestemming als recasting: Rituele dynamiek voorbij inculturatie en syncretisme*. Valedictory lecture, Tilburg University. https://research.tilburguniversity.edu/en/publications/recasting-ritual-rituele-dynamiek-voorbij-inculturatie-en-syncret (29.11.2021).

Post, Paul. 2019c. "Ein Panorama der Ritualdynamik: Bereiche und Trends." In *Provozierte Kasualpraxis: Rituale in Bewegung*. Praktische Theologie heute 166, edited by Ulrike Wagner-Rau and Emilia Handke, Stuttgart: Kohlhammer, 21–43.

Post, Paul, Jos Pieper, and Marinus van Uden. 1998. *The Modern Pilgrim: Multidisciplinary Explorations of Christian Pilgrimage*. Liturgia Condenda 8. Leuven / Dudley: Peeters.

Post, Paul, Gerard Rouwhorst, Louis van Tongeren, and Ton Scheer. 2001. *Christian Feast and Festival: The Dynamics of Western Liturgy and Culture*. Liturgia Condenda 12. Leuven / Dudley: Peeters.

Post, Paul, Ronald L. Grimes, Albertina Nugteren, Per Petterson, and Hessel J. Zondag. *Disaster Ritual: Explorations of an Emerging Ritual Repertoire*. Liturgia Condenda 15. Leuven / Dudley: Peeters, 2003.

Post, Paul, Philip Nel, and Walter van Beek. 2014. *Sacred Spaces and Contested Identities: Space and Ritual Dynamics in Europe and Africa*. Trenton: Africa World Press.

Post, Paul, and Suzanne van der Beek. 2016. *Doing Ritual Criticism in a Network Society: Online and Offline Explorations into Pilgrimage and Sacred Place.* Liturgia Condenda 29. Leuven / Dudley: Peeters.

Post, Paul, and Suzanne van der Beek. 2017. *Onderweg met een missie: Verkenning van de opkomende trend om te lopen, fietsen, pelgrimeren met een missie of een goed doel.* Camino Cahier 1. Utrecht: Camino Academie. https://www.caminoacademie.nl/camino-cahiers/camino-cahier-1-onderweg-met-een-missie/ (29.11.2021).

Post, Paul, and Martin Hoondert. 2019. *Absent Ritual: Exploring the Ambivalence and Dynamics of Ritual.* Ritual Studies Monograph Series. Durham: Carolina Academic Press.

Reckwitz, Andreas. 2017. *Die Gesellschaft der Singularitäten: Zum Strukturwandel der Moderne.* Berlin: Suhrkamp.

Saß, Marcell. 2019. "Rent a Pastor? Beobachtungen zur Ritualpraxis im Zeitalter der Digitalisierung." In *Provozierte Kasualpraxis: Rituale in Bewegung.* Praktische Theologie heute 166, edited by Ulrike Wagner-Rau and Emilia Handke, Stuttgart: Kohlhammer, 131–140.

Schippers, Inez. 2015. *Sacred Places in the Suburbs: Casual Sacrality in the Dutch VINEX-District Leidsche Rijn.* Netherlands Studies in Ritual and Liturgy 16. Dissertation: Tilburg University.

Smith, Jonathan Z. 1987. *To Take Place: Toward Theory in Ritual.* Chicago / London: University of Chicago Press.

Stringer, Martin. 2005. *A Sociological History of Christian Worship.* Cambridge: Cambridge University Press.

Stringer, Martin. 2008. *Contemporary Western Ethnography and the Definition of Religion.* London / New York: Continuum.

Wepener, Cas, Ignatius Swart, Gerrie ter Haar and Marcel Barnard. 2019. *Bonding in Worship: A Ritual Lens on Social Capital in African Independent Churches in South Africa.* Liturgia Condenda 30. Leuven / Dudley: Peeters.

Federico Settler
Sociology of Religion

1 Introduction

Sociology of religion represents the various theories and methodologies through which the relationship between religion and social science is explicated. Although relatively new in the academy, the field came to prominence through the work of Durkheim and Weber as they sought to account for the role and meaning of the church in producing and sustaining social networks, social relations as well as norms related to beliefs. Most commentators in religion, theology and sociology today will trace the sociology of religion to the early 1900s, with specific reference to the social theories that saw religion as shared symbols that informs and shapes the moral order within society. Despite the fact that much of sociology of religion, historically rests on sociological theories about protestant Christian orthodoxy, people's affiliation and participation in the church as a social institution, the relation of social science to religion's companion discipline, theology, has generally been marked by suspicion and ambivalence. In the same year that Durkheim published his *Elementary Forms of Religion*, American theologian Guy Talbot (1915) published an essay titled "the relation between sociology and theology" that was driven by one basic questions: What level of sociological knowledge is required to shape Christian practice? Talbot's reticence is palpable and signals the ambivalence and suspicion that would for the next 100 years characterize the relationship between theology and sociology. Despite some laudable attempts to see what sociology has to offer theology (Gill 1978; Marty 1981; Martin, Mills, and Pickering 2003), theologians, have largely remained cautious about permitting sociological knowledge too much space in determining Christian social practice.

Notwithstanding theology's apparent ambivalence towards social science, faith communities have generally relied on sociological analysis to craft political, environmental, and developmental theologies – such as black theology in the USA and South Africa, liberation theology in South America, and dalit theology in India. Although these Christian traditions operate within a neo-Weberian paradigm in that it imagines religion as coupled with national moral interests, they nonetheless represent a break with theology's suspicion of social science insofar as they significantly rely on Marxian analysis to show that God is on the side of the poor. Recently, practical theology has assumed similarly reflexive and critical postures as a discipline (Osmer 2011; Lartey 2012), and increasingly look toward sociology of religion as a sub-discipline to collaborate with. If practical theology draws on sociology of religion for expanding its theoretical and methodological repertoires, it cannot rely on traditional sociological assumption about religion as either in decline or thriving in late modernity. As a postcolonial scholar, doing sociology of religion starts with the lived patterns from everyday life and embodied practices of religious persons, which in turn promises to potentially free practical theology from primarily caring about communities of believers, to caring for communities in need, wherever they are located regardless of their beliefs, practices, and relationship to institutional religion.

2 Origins and Disciplinary Horizons of Sociology of Religion

For more than 100 years, sociology of religion has been concerned with the study of religious institutions, beliefs, and practice – a largely a western academic enterprise concerned questions such as: How do people live religious lives? What do religious people do? Ad why do religious people do what they do? Why do they do what they do, in the way that they do it?

Sociology of religion is a field of inquiry concerned with the social formations of religion – through examining its manifestations of religious organizations or faith communities, as well as with how such faith communities give expression to their belief. Sociologists of religion are also concerned with how religious beliefs effect behaviors and decisions, as well as people's orientations towards society. Historically, these questions have been pursued through social science methods such as quantitative surveys that give indications of social trends and patterns in religious affiliation and preferences, while through more qualitative studies sociologist offer insights into motivation and behaviors related to religious beliefs. Thus, we can see that in general sociologists measure religiosity by asking people about their religious beliefs, their membership to religious organizations, and attendance at religious services, and then measure how such patterns inform social behavior. Regardless of whether one takes a quantitative or qualitative approach, the sociology of religion is generally interested in the following questions:
- How are religious institutions organized?
- What is the nature and extent of religious affiliation in a society?
- How does religion affect social change? And how does social change effect religious behavior?
- What influence does religion have on social institutions, such as political or educational institutions?
- How are religious beliefs and factors related to other social factors like race, age, gender, and class?

There is widespread agreement that modern sociology, and by association sociology of religion, has its origins in Emile Durkheim's 1897 *The Study of Suicide* wherein he explored the differing suicide rates among Protestants and Catholics. About the same time, Karl Marx and Max Weber, in their attempts to offer social scientific accounts of social life, also looked at religion and its influence in other social institutions and norms. While the continuing relevance of these early classical accounts are contested, most sociologists regard this heritage as a valued resource insofar as it provides an archaeology of the prevailing ideas about the relationship between religion and sociology. As such I will briefly introduce their respective views on the relation between religion and social science.

Emile Durkheim advocated a functionalist perspective of society because for him religion was a cohering force in society insofar as it provided an explanatory frame around which people organized and formed collective beliefs and practices. It is through building a sense of belonging (affect) and collective consciousness (belief) that, for Durkheim, religion produces a sense of cohesion. Max Weber, on the other hand, saw religion as a resource that upheld and sustained other social institutions. In this regard, religious beliefs are seen to provide a cultural and explanatory framework that supported the legitimacy and function other social institutions, such as the family, church, or economy as the base units of society. Unlike, Durkheim and Weber who focused on the various ways that religion contributes to the cohesion of society or social institutions, Karl Marx saw religion as a social force that sustained class division in industrial societies – through ritually dissolving conflict and resistance to oppression. Marx saw religion not simply as a tool for class oppression, but as an imaginative field that blinded people to unequal social stratification, which religion and religious authorities explained as divinely sanctioned.

What these classical sociological approaches to religion have in common, is their concerns with the patterns of power and status in European religious contexts of the late 1800s and early 1900s, and how these related to and reinforced social organization. Now, while the field of sociology is hugely indebted to these classical thinkers, sociology has become increasingly preoccupied with processes by which people become religious, as well as the historical and contextual forces that frame the making, and practices of religion. As such most sociologists agree that religious beliefs and practices emerge in different social and historical contexts, and in this sense Durkheim, Weber and Marx were products of their context, but they nonetheless charted the development of a field concerned with understanding of religious institutions, belief, and practices as socially constructed, and provoked critical questions about the relationship between religion and other social institutions and practices.

3 (Religion / Theology and the) Conceptions of Social and Public Life

Since the 1960s sociology of religion has been particularly concerned with deepening sociological knowledge about religious affiliation and conversion, changing rates of church attendance, religiously inspired political activism, the emergence of new religions, and secularization – epitomized by the work of David Martin, Robert Wuthnow, Robert Bellah and Peter Berger. Their work marked a return to prominence for the sociology of religion by using religion as a lens through which to understand modernity. These scholars like their predecessor were confident about the decline of religion, and out of this scholarship developed into two main approaches in the sociology of religion: *secularization approach*, and *market approach*. Although both traditions have a history of being focused on North American or European Christian-centered notions of religion, the former relies on large empirical studies related to the apparent decline in affiliation and participation in churches, while the latter is more focused on the motivation and rates of conversion from one Christian tradition to another, or the proliferation of congregational forms, patterns, and practices. While the first takes the institutional church and levels of participation as a measure of stable belief and its inevitable decline, the second take satisfaction, affect and belonging as a measure of the persistence of religious beliefs despite the apparent fracturing of broad-based religious institutions, or national churches into locally organized and led, faith communities.

With respect to Berger who has made a substantial scholarly contribution to the secularization approach, Linda Woodhead noted that "under the pressure of the pluralizing force of modernity the 'sacred canopy' becomes precarious vision. A central conclusion was that pluralism leads inevitably to secularization. Berger's vision of secularization theory endorsed the view that there is an intrinsic link between modernization and secularization" (Woodhead 2001, 2). While Berger in the later part of his academic career held to the view that pluralism has a corrosive effect of western social organization, he offers a qualifying note on the relationship between pluralism and secularization and writes that "I would now say that pluralism affects the *how* of religious belief, but not necessarily the *what*." (Berger 2001, 194) In this regard, Berger is not unlike his peers in offering some qualification to early secularization theses, and thus conceded that the decline of institutional religion or the state church, as is the case of much of Northern Europe, does not necessarily translate into people not being religious. Religious authority and taken-for-granted religious values have been supplanted with new ways of being religious and new ways of expressing religious beliefs.

Unlike the pessimistic orientation of the secularization approach to religion, the *market approach* offers an account of religious vitality in the modern era. It is often presented as a remedial theory to the failure of secularizations theorists to account for the persistence of religion. Primarily located in the North American context, this approach challenges secularization theory's argument that religion is a poor fit in the modern world, and advocates argue that it is not so much that religion has declined, but that the nature of belief and religious affiliation has changed – particularly in those non-European contexts where national churches have been intimately embroiled with the state and national identity, such as was the case in Germany or Norway, until very recently. In explaining the market approach to religion, Edgell posits that modernity "creates the conditions that foster religious privatization, pluralism, and voluntarism, causing religion to thrive—and, ironically, to retain much of its public significance" (Edgell 2012, 249). In this approach, the *market* was used as a metaphor for the choice and patterns of self-organization, initially seen to be occurring in American religious life, but later also included those societies where religious authorities are uncoupled from the nation-state, and where religious affiliation is largely voluntary. For example, instead of simply relying on church membership and participation as the primary measure of religious solidarity, changing religious patterns and organization could be said to be as much the result of "soft city-dwelling life that reduces group feeling" (Spickard 2000) or the inability of faith communities to adapt to the changing family patterns and needs among its constituents (Smith et al. 2013).

Obviously, this particular approach to religious life applies equally to religious life beyond America, such as in countries like Brazil, the Philippines or Uganda – where religion has been thriving for decades but received little attention from sociologists of religion. The North American focus of market theory was born out of attempts to explain the seemingly changing fortunes of institutional religion, not as a decline, but as a failure to supply the religious goods required by the market – and in so doing, like secularization approaches, it fails to consider sociological theories of religion in transnational context, thus re-producing theories about the religious behaviors and practices of North America and Europe, as if universally applicable.

Numerous efforts have been advanced to theoretically expand the field through developing, for example, critical sociology of religion (Smith et al. 2013), feminist sociology of religion (Nason-Clark and Neitz 2001; Neitz 2014), lived religion (Ammerman 2012) and non-western perspectives in the sociology of religion (Spickard 2017). Despite the enormous contribution of the field to understanding of religion religious, life choice and behaviours, it is now widely agreed that much of sociology of religion has developed through privileging "empirical studies of [European and] American Protestantism, especially White evangelicalism, to the relative neglect of non-Western, Catholic, and non-Christian religious experiences and practices" (Edgell 2012). The point here is that social science entanglement with religion is not innocent, and more often than not it is deployed in the promotion of very clear ideological ideas related to human life, diversity, and freedom.

For example, social scientific surveys such as the 2010 report of Pew Research Forum on Religion and Public Life, *Tolerance and Tension: Islam and Christianity in Sub-Saharan Africa* offered some interesting comparative national data. David Chidester and I noted that despite 74% of South Africans reporting that religion is very important in their lives, the survey nonetheless showed a high rate of religious illiteracy. For example, in this survey, 76% of Christians in South Africa say that they do not know very much or nothing at all about Islam and yet 63% of Christians say that despite not knowing much about Islam, they can conclude that Christianity and Islam are "very different." What we found was that while ignorance does not entail prejudice, it does not preclude respondents from drawing conclusions about other religions (Chidester and Settler 2010). In order to fully understand and present the data, we aggregated the Pew results against several local studies regarding the intersection of religion with race and gender, leading us to conclude (a) that working with religion in the South African context means working in a context where people care intensely about religion, (b) that social science approaches must be oriented to elaborating the lived experience of religious persons, (c) that studies in religion cannot be divorced from political and material histories of racial and gender exclusion.

Similarly, while Bertelsmann's 2013 survey on religion and cohesion in Germany reported a steady decline in religiosity – with only 25% of Christians reporting religion as important in their public lives – when coupled with a changing religious demography due to the recent influx of migrants from more religious regions such as North Africa, and the Middle East, a change of public culture and policies related to religion may be necessary. Neighboring countries, such a France and Switzerland, saw it necessary to respectively, introduce legislation regarding Muslim women's choice to wear the *niqab* in public, and the building of minarets in a seeming regulation of religious architecture and life. What this example shows is the changing nature and landscape of the sociology of religion – a departure from North American and European parochial studies being treated as universally relevant and a move towards a sociology of religion that takes seriously issues of race, class, gender and sexual diversity in both design and analyses.

The transnational migration of people has had a tangible impact on religious mapping of the world, as well as expanded ideas about religion, and orthodoxies within religious traditions. While on the one hand, Israel is contending with African Jews and how their claims to settlement disrupt ideas of Zionism, and on the other hand, the centers of Pentecostalism are seen to be located in Asia, Latin America and parts of Africa – and yet religion and theology continue to look to Europe and North America when it comes to resolving questions about the nature, definition, and classification of religiosity. Asad (1993), Adogame and Spickard (2010), Huwelmeier and Krause (2011) have argued and illustrated how when people move transnationally, they take their religions, belief, and practices with them. Firstly, this suggests that the transnational movement of people, not only enhance religious diversity but that it potentially reforms the ideas about and taxonomies of religion. Secondly, it necessitates a shift in social reception and recognition of religion as not so much in decline but rather variously as privatized (Jose Casanova), commodified (Talal Asad) and / or vicarious (Grace Davie).

What I suggest here is that the sociology of religion offers insights and information that are used to make determinations about the extent of religiosity in a general population, affinity to religious authority, the degrees of secularizations in a society but also significantly, that it has emerged as a field that helps us expand the definitional boundaries and contestations over what constitutes religion, about who possess religious authority especially with respect to the embodied experiences of religion, and the activation of religion in the everyday life. It is precisely because of my location as a scholar of color from the global South that questions of authority, the material and the embodied are coupled with issues of religious belonging and practice. In contexts outside North America and Europe, concerns with the religiosity, and people's material struggles are generally inseparable.

4 Theoretical Orientations in the Sociology of Religion

The changing landscape and orientation in the sociology of religion necessitate new ways to imagine of sociology of religion in response to criticism leveled at it. In seeking to move beyond the imaginative regimes of secularization and market approaches, I will now proceed to a discussion where sociology of religion is framed as concerned with (1) institutions, behaviors, and beliefs; (2) embodied and intersectional experiences of religion; and (3) religion in everyday life. This schema is an attempt to present nuanced ways in which sociological practice are already entangled in the fields of religion and theology, as well as to point to the interesting ways that it might be deployed to better understand religion as institutional, embodied, and mundane.

4.1 Institutions, Beliefs, and Practices

Notwithstanding the range of critiques that have been levelled at both the secularization and market approaches for their privileging of institutional religion, the practice of taking people's contact with religious institutions as a basic measure of religiosity remains widespread and useful. Thus, despite disagreement about the ontological orientation towards religion in society, most sociologists view survey data about relations to institutional religion, changing practices and beliefs as critical for understanding the link between religion and societal patterns. For example, in 2008 Berger, Hunter and Schlemmer published a study, *Under the Radar*, with the Centre for Development and Enterprise in South Africa, which sought to ascertain the relation between Pentecostal teaching and economic behavior, and what impact this might have on socio-economic development in the society at large. Despite the innovative nature of this study, it too relied on a series of assumptions that proximity to religious authority and participation in the life of the religious community is a reliable measure of religiosity. Elsewhere, Grace Davie (2010) has demonstrated that while data might indicate low religious participation in the activities of a religious organization, that this does not necessarily reflect an equivalence in the strength of connectedness. She argues that despite declining number, the relatively small number of active members are religious on behalf of an absent but invested majority. What is very useful about Davie's work is that she separates belief from belonging and in so doing she decenters institution of religions as the center of inquiry, to focus our attention instead on the relation to, and the strength of our connections (affect) related to institutional religion. Thus, there continues to be value in thinking through the relationship between membership and affiliation, especially where it is done in conjunction with the changing nature of people's relation to institutional religion.

In addition to the narrow, often congregational focus of sociology of religion, the field has for some time been under pressure to respond changing religious geographies and religious diversities, both within the West and transnationally. Talal Asad's critique of the supposedly universalist assumptions about religion in social science approaches noted that "what appears to [social scientists] today to be self-evident, namely that religion is essentially a matter of symbolic meaning linked to ideas of general order [...] is, in fact, a view that has a specific Christian history. From being a concrete set of practical rules attached to specific processes and power, religion has come to be abstracted and universalised" (Asad 1993, 29). Thus, new inflections in traditional sociology of religion have also been borne out of interreligious contact and diversity, as well as incorporating different models of social organization. One such example is Spickard' recent book, *Alternative Sociologies of Religion: Through Non-Western Eyes* (Spickard 2017, 26) in which he elaborates non-western approaches, such as ritual and communal virtue (Confucian) and group feeling (Ibn Khaldun) as principles of social organization and social change that might point to different of ways measuring religiosity.

Thus, sociology of religion today seeks to do more than understand how religious beliefs, practices, and institutions operate as forces of social change, but also represent those religious practices, innovation, and beliefs that occur outside of, and independent of religious authorities. Further, critical examinations of religious institutions not only map trajectories of the sacred in society but it also shows how religious organizations connect with the felt needs and beliefs of people regardless of their connection, or of the strength of their connection to institutional religion.

4.2 Embodied and Lived-Experience

While sociology of religion has traditionally focused on religious institutions as sites of inquiry, the accompanying religious practices have often been viewed as those embodied performances related to institutions and beliefs. Jonkers and Sarot suggest "the human body is always involved in the concepts and practices of religions" (Jonkers and Sarot 2013, 2), and although this focus on the body for many signaled the privileging of lived religious experiences, it still relies on assumptions about the neutrality and universality of religious experience. While social science approaches to religion have strong explanatory potential, both market and secularization approaches to the study of religion are inclined to de-historicize and decontextualize social phenomena, and in so doing offer accounts of embodied religion, without ever referencing issues of gender, race, class, and sexual diversity.

Acutely aware of the implicit assumptions of the supposed gender-neutrality that has accompanied sociology of religion, Linda Woodhead (2009) and Mary Jo Neitz (2014) among others, variously problematized the inadequate ways that issues of gender and sexuality have been attended to in sociology of religion. While drawing on church membership and participation data; they respectively highlight the gender variables related to affiliation and participation (institutions), shifting attitudes in religious education as well as factors that inform women's participation in faith communities. Neitz reminds us of the implicit patriarchal bias in traditional approaches to the sociology of religion, and suggest that although "survey research in North America and Europe repeatedly shows that women are more likely to be members of and participants in religious groups [... and that ...] women use religion as a resource for acting in their own behalf, and women also more frequently the object of regulation by religions" (Neitz 2014, 513) such data is seldom utilized as meaningful in explanatory accounts of significant religious change in society.

As such, I argue that when engaging embodied or lived religious experiences, we must be vigilant of the tendency to uncoupled it from critical discourses related to gender, race, class, and sexuality. Similarly, Anthony Pinn (2010) argues that black theological thought has been intimately connected with embodied black experiences through history, especially in the United States. For example, in comparing two (one white and one black) evangelical Christian congregations' narratives of stewardship and God's sovereignty, Peifer, Ecklund, and Fullerton (2014, 373) found that while there was little "evidence to suggest that religious beliefs foster different environmental attitudes across the two congregations," they found that race coupled with socio-economic status do impact on the degree of environmental apathy. Thus, to simply present or extract information about religious change in society based simply on people's religious affiliation and participation without due recognition of people's subjectivity regarding gender, race, sexuality, and class would likely present an incomplete and skewed picture of social and religious life.

What these examples point to is the manner in which embodied accounts of religion, or encounters with religion help us better understand, and hopefully incorporate a more diverse range of religious experiences in the general population. Embodied accounts of religion, when not obscured by presumed religious normativity in Europe and North America, enables as to ask such questions as: What does the embodied or lived experience Muslim women migrants reveal about protestant practices of reception and hospitality in Norway? By centering the embodied and lived experience, sociology of religion opens the possibility of disrupting and expanding normative modes of religious being, organization, and exchange.

4.3 Everyday Life

This brings me to the third orientation in the sociology of religion, namely the engagement with everyday life. Everyday religion was brought to prominence through the work of Nancy Ammerman (*Everyday Religion* 2006) and Meredith McGuire (*Lived Religion* 2008), and it has since enjoyed much attention in the sociology of religion because of its exploration of religion in outside religious institutions, privileging of everyday life as site of religious knowledge and experience, and engaging religious work and expressions in popular and material culture – such as music, painting dance, and film (Flanagan 2007; Morgan 2010).

Religion and theology scholars like Ammerman, McGuire, Houtman, and Meyer have sought to explain the relationship between everyday life, routines practices and the changing nature of spirituality. Nancy Ammerman (2006, 4) writes that "If the strength of religion is measured by orthodoxy of belief, regularity of attendance, and the ability of traditional religious institutions to enforce their norms, much of the world is very secular indeed." She goes on to argue that an exploration of the everyday reveals of more widespread and diffused engagement with religion and spirituality through popular culture. Similarly, Vanhoozer, Anderson, and Sleasman (2007) in *Everyday Theology* argue that all person possesses a degree of cultural literacy that enables them to read and interpret the world through their faith. In this text, scholars explore popular cultural phenomenon as wide-ranging as fantasy funerals, volunteerism, megachurch architecture, the internet, music, and movies.

However, when material religion outside Europe or North America is discussed, it is often coupled with histories of animism and totem (Harvey 2014), or superstition and gullibility (Settler 2018) or trauma and violence (Boesak 1984; Gebara 1999; Rajkumar 2011) – the latter being most persistent in Christian liberation theologies. Privileging the traumatic and dramatic as a basis for political theologies obscures everyday life and the accompanying religious experiences among the vulnerable. Through drawing our attention to religion and everyday life, the late Marcella Althauss-Reid reminded us that political theologies such as black and liberation theology (with its adamant critique of material relations), rose to prominence at the expense of sexuality, and everyday life experiences in the global South. Althauss-Reid in *Indecent Theology* (2000) suggests that liberation theology had become domesticated, and she uses the figure of the woman lemon vendor from Peru – women who do not wear underwear under their skirts – to show how the examination of an everyday life situation can simultaneously make visible what cannot ordinarily be seen and reveal what is expected to be hidden. The image of the lemon vender – a convergence of sexuality and economics – brings us back to those 'other' everyday realities that have not enjoyed the attention of religion and liberation theology scholars, by virtue of those everyday life realities being regarded indecent, illicit, and deviant.

Thus, this focus on everyday life helps us to better understand religion *wherever* it happens and in whatever way that it manifests, instead of trying to explain why it no longer occurs in the places and ways that we had become accustomed to, or inherited. As sociology of religion looks to new sites of religious meaning-making we begin to ask questions such as: What are the things around which the religious self-organize? This opens new registers for measuring religious feeling and participation, through an uptake in new modalities of the sacred such as collective action to public tragedy (e.g., terror attacks) or social campaigns such as #arabspring, #blacklivesmatter or #metoo.

4.4 Conclusion and Implications for Practical Theology

One of the questions posed at the start of this essay was: What level of sociological knowledge is required to shape Christian practice? This question queries the relationship between practical theology and the sociology of religion, and social sciences more generally. While Kieran Flanagan (2007) in his *Sociology into Theology* argues for critical reflexivity as a way to lessen the distance between the two fields, and Richard Osmer (2008) in his *Practical Theology: An Introduction* proposes four tasks (empirical, interpretative, normative and pragmatic) both rely heavily on social sciences competencies in order that practical theology, despite its Christian particularity, might contribute to the common good in society. In a similar vein, Emmanuel Lartey's *Postcolonializing God: New Perspectives in Pastoral and Practical Theology* (2012) further asserts the need for taking sincere accounts of socio-economic and historical realities of faith communities. Taking the lived reality of Africa as his point of departure, Lartey calls for religious actors to assume a counter-hegemonic posture in relation to the coloniality of knowledge, power and religious practice in religion and theology.

Edgell (2012) has argued that for the relationship between sociology of religion and practical theology to be fruitful, we must proceed from fundamentally different ideas about religious authority, affinity and changing participation in religion in the late modern world. While market and secularization approaches have dominated in the sociology of religion, both approaches have become insufficient as accounts or theories related to the changing global map of religion and theology. The changing religious landscape as well as salient critiques from critical feminist, race, and queer studies, has disrupted ideas about what schemas are suitable for understanding religion in society.

While the relationship between sociology of religion and practical theology has been one marked by suspicion, these fields are both oriented to giving account (sociology) and offering meaning (practical theology) that rely on 'real' accounts of various life worlds. While new social scientific accounts of religious life outside faith organizations threaten to decenter the church or religious authorities more generally, it offers religious stakeholders (faith leaders and laity) access to whole new fields of sociological inquiry, self-description, and religious practice. It challenges faith communities to engage people, not as redeemable subjects – requiring that people be a certain kind of subject, as a prerequisite to benefit from practical theological or Christian social practice. Instead, it promises to open the possibility for care across religious beliefs, as well as to produce religious discourses of accompaniment, where religion is visible in the embodied, everyday lives of people.

From my perspective as a scholar shaped by traditions of decoloniality, this privileging of the body and the everyday, with its apparent decentering of the church and religious authority, also demands that we let go of the idea of faith organizations as stable communities into which new members are incorporated, but rather to move to a self-understanding a precarious communities defined by postures of discomfort.

This produces the possibility of redeeming religion through disruption, discomfort and queering to open the category of religious belief, work, and practice beyond the normative, to disrupt our ideas what we regard as the center of religious knowledge and practice by looking to everyday life, and to privilege the body in religious scholarship and reflection, work, and practice. Thus, the encounter between practical theology and sociology of religion, where it takes seriously the embodied experiences of power in everyday life, as much as it does the institutional, allows precarity, ambivalence and discomfort to emerge as a meaningful analytical and theological resources for understanding affinity, affect and meaning related to religion in the general population.

Bibliography

Adogame, Afe, and Jim Spickard. 2010. *Religion Crossing Boundaries: Transnational Religious and Social Dynamics in Africa and the New African Diaspora.* Leiden and Boston: Brill Press.

Althauss-Reid, Marcella. 2000. *Indecent Theology: Theological Perversions in Sex, Gender, and Politics.* London, New York: Routledge.

Ammerman, Nancy, ed. 2006. *Everyday Religion: Observing Modern Religious Lives.* Oxford: Oxford University Press.

Asad, Talal. 1993. *Genealogy of Religion.* Baltimore: John Hopkins University Press.

Berger, Peter L. 2001. "Postscript." In *Peter Berger and the Study of Religion*, edited by Linda Woodhead with Paul Heelas and David Martin, London: Routledge, 189–198.

Boesak, Allan. 1984. "Black Theology and the Struggle for Liberation in South Africa." *Monthly Review* 36:127–137.

Chidester, David, and Federico G. Settler. 2010. "Hopes and Fears: A South African Response to REDCo." *Religion & Education* 37:213–217.

Davie, Grace. 2010. "Vicarious Religion. A Response." *Journal of Contemporary Religion* 25:261–267

Davie, Grace. 2013. *The Sociology of Religion: A Critical Agenda.* London: Sage Publishing.

Edgell, Penny. 2012. "A Cultural Sociology of Religion: New Directions." *Annual Review of Sociology* 38:247–265.

Flanagan, Kieran. 2007. *Sociology in Theology: Reflexivity and Belief.* London: Palgrave MacMillan.

Gebara, Ivone. 1999. *Longing for Running Water: Ecofeminism and Liberation.* Fortress Press.

Gill, Robin. 1978. *Theology and Social Structure.* Oxford: Mowbrays.

Harvey, Graham. 2014. *The Handbook of Contemporary Animism.* Oxon: Routledge.

Houtman, Dick, and Birgit Meyer. 2012. *Things: Religion and the Question of Materiality.* New York: Fordham University Press.

Huwelmeier, Gertrud, and Kristine Krause. 2011. *Traveling Spirits: Migrants, Markets and Mobilities.* London: Routledge.

Jonkers, Peter, and Marcel Sarot. 2013. *Embodied Religion: Proceedings of the 2012 Conference of the European Society for Philosophy of Religion.* Utrecht: Ars Disputandi.

Lartey, Emmanuel. 2012. *Postcolonializing God: New Perspectives in Pastoral and Practical Theology.* London: SCM.

McGuire, Meredith B. 2008. *Lived Religion: Faith and Practice in Everyday Life.* Oxford: Oxford University Press.

Martin, David, John Mills, and William Pickering, eds. [1980] 2003. *Sociology and Theology: Alliance and Conflict.* Leiden: Brill

Marty, Martin. 1981. *The Public Church*. New York: Crossroads Press.
Morgan, David. 2010. *Religion and Material Culture: The Matter of Belief*. New York: Routledge.
Nason-Clark, Nancy, and Mary Jo Neitz, eds. 2001. *Feminist Narratives and the Sociology of Religion*. Walnut Creek: AltaMira Press.
Neitz, Mary Jo. 2014. "Becoming Visible: Religion and Gender in Sociology." *Sociology of Religion* 75:511–523.
Osmer, Richard R. 2011. "Practical Theology: A Current International Perspective." *HTS Teologiese Studies / Theological Studies* 67:1–7.
Osmer, Richard R. 2008. *Practical Theology: An Introduction*. Grand Rapids: Eerdmans.
Pinn, Anthony. 2010. *Embodiment and the New Shape of Black Theological Thought*. New York: NYU Press.
Peifer, Jared, Elaine Howard Ecklund and Cara Fullerton. 2014. "How Evangelicals from Two Churches in the American Southwest Frame their Relationship with the Environment." *Review of Religious Research* 56:373–397.
Rajkumar, Peniel. 2011. *Dalit Theology and Dalit Liberation: Problems, Paradigms and Possibilities*. London: Routledge.
Settler, Federico G. 2018. "Race and Materiality in African Religious Contexts." *Journal for the Study of Religion* 31:36–56.
Center for Development and Enterprise. 2008. *Under the Radar: Pentecostalism in South Africa and its Potential Social and Economic Role*. https://www.cde.org.za/wp-content/uploads/2018/07/Under-the-radar-Pentecostalism-in-South-Africa-and-its-potential-social-and-economic-role-CDE-Report.pdf (01.12.2021).
Smith, Christian, Brandon Vaidyanathan, Nancy Tatom Ammerman, José Casanova, Hilary Davidson, Elaine Howard Ecklund, John H. Evans, Philip S. Gorski, Mary Ellen Konieczny, Jason A. Springs, Jenny Trinitapoli and Meredith Whitnah. "Roundtable on the Sociology of Religion." *Journal of the American Academy of Religion* 81:903–938.
Spickard, James. 2017. *Alternative Sociologies of Religion: Through Non-Western Eyes*. New York: New York University Press.
Spickard, James. 2000. "Fashioning a Post-Colonial Sociology of Religion." *Journal of Church, Religion, and Society, Norway* 13:113–127.
Vanhoozer, Kevin, Charles A. Anderson, and Michael J. Sleasman. 2007. *Everyday Theology: How to Read Cultural Texts and Interpret Trends*. Grand Rapids: Baker Academic.
Vopel, Stephan. 2013. *Religionsmonitor 2013*. Gütersloh: Bertelsmann Stiftung.
Woodhead, Linda. 2001. "Introduction." In *Peter Berger and the Study of Religion*, edited by Linda Woodhead, Paul Heelas and David Martin, London: Routledge, 1–8.
Woodhead, Linda. 2009. "Old, New, and Emerging Paradigms in the Sociological Study of Religion." *Nordic Journal of Religion and Society* 22:103–121.

Terry A. Veling
Theology of Religion

1 Introduction

Theology may be the least helpful discipline to explore the enduring presence of religion in human societies and cultures. After all, theology is a religious discipline and may be too closely attached or implicated in that which it seeks to study. Maybe disciplines such as philosophy or psychology or anthropology or sociology are better suited to address the question of religion – at least they can maintain a certain objective distance of 'studying religion', without necessarily being implicated or religiously oriented themselves.

On the other hand, maybe theology is well suited to address the question of religion in human cultures because it shares in the phenomenon it seeks to understand, without the stricture of science's 'objectivity'. Standing within a subject-matter of inquiry can often lead to better understandings than standing 'aloof' and objectively detached.

To stand 'within' something means we are implicated in our inquiry. This can often lead to better results of understanding than when we attempt to be distanced and analytical observers. My approach in this essay is not a scientific one – a 'study of religion' – my approach is a theological one, which means that religion need not only be studied from the 'outside', but can also be fruitfully understood from the 'inside'.

2 The Smell of Religion

In the Australian film, *Kenny*, the title character operates a portable toilet rental company. In one of the scenes, he climbs into a large effluent-holding tank that needs cleaning. After some minutes he emerges and exclaims: "There is a smell in here that will outlast religion!"

Religion is one of the most complex words in the English language. All human history has carried the "smell" of religion – for both good and for ill. Religion is sometimes opposed to the word "secular," often with the assumption that the secular world promotes tolerance and freedom, while religion promotes war and conflict. However, secular society has also played its part in promoting war and conflict. Think of the (now common) mantra, 'the war on terror', presumably aimed at defending freedom and democracy. As Walter Benjamin (1968, 256) suggests, "There is no document of civilization which is not at the same time a document of barbarism."

In other words, neither the secular nor the religious world is free of stain or blemish, and it seems pointless separating the two as if in competing worlds.

While I appreciate many of secular culture's values (I do not, for example, want to live in a theocracy), I do not think that secularism is the bastion of all virtue and religion the source of all evils. There are many fine secularists out there promoting the wellbeing of humanity, just as there are many fine religious people promoting peace and goodness. As Jewish philosopher Emmanuel Levinas (1990, 186–187) notes: "The separation of men into the religious and non-religious does not get us very far. It's not at all a question of a special disposition which some possess, and others lack."

The fact that the two – the secular and the religious – have been placed asunder in our Enlightened age seems to me misguided – part of the problem rather than the solution. Indeed, it is interesting to consider that the word 'secular' was initially derived from religious language, framed, for example, within the understanding that the kingdom of heaven (*divinitas*) is directly related to the conditions of living on earth (*saeculum* or *humanitas*). According to this theological conception, the religious and the secular (heaven and earth, if you like) are directly related and implicated, rather than split into competing worlds. "Humanity is the knot in which heaven and earth are interlaced," Abraham Heschel (1955, 103) says. Indeed, Heschel notes that religious language has always struggled with the claims of these two 'realms':

> The life of man is embroiled in earthly concerns, but his soul opens somewhat to heavenly matters. He is therefore obliged to speak in two tongues, one entirely earthly, the other entirely heavenly. He must, perforce, use two types of idioms. Moreover, he must search for the place where heaven and earth embrace. Language is a ladder set on earth whose head reaches heaven – it is both all earthly and all heavenly. (2010, 234)

Religious people who neglect their earthly condition (and the earthly humanity of others) are probably not very religious at all. Indeed, this may be religion's greatest temptation – idolatry – which the Hebrew prophets constantly rallied against. Amos, for example, derides false worship: "I hate, I despise your feasts, and I take no delight in your solemn assemblies … Let justice roll down like waters, and righteousness like an ever-flowing stream" (Amos 5:21; 24). And Isaiah speaks of the true fasting that pleases God: "Is it not to share your food with the hungry and to provide the poor wanderer with shelter – when you see the naked, to clothe them, and not to turn away from your own flesh and blood?" (Isaiah 58:7–8)

In other words, a religious tradition that cannot connect with the world and humanity is probably worshipping something false. St John puts it best: "Those who say, 'I love God,' and hate their brothers or sisters, are liars; for those who do not love a brother or sister whom they have seen, cannot love God whom they have not seen" (1 John 4:20).

Jesus was no great lover of religion. Indeed, he was often a quintessential critic of false religion. His problem was not with sinners – those who may have lost their way for one reason or another – his problem was with hypocrites, people who heap-up burdens on others: "They tie up heavy, cumbersome loads and put them on other people's shoulders, but they themselves are not willing to lift a finger to move them"

(Matt 23:4). Jesus admonishes those who announce their good deeds for all to see and prefers those whose actions are secretive. "Then your Father, who sees what is done in secret, will reward you" (Matt 6:4).

Many of my young undergraduate students are suspicious of religious institutions that seem disconnected from their own experience and the world around them. I often hear them say, "I am spiritual, but I am not religious." Or, if you like, "I am religious without being religious." I admire their honesty. They feel a need and desire to affirm spirituality, yet they also feel a large disconnect between their own experience and what 'religion' has to offer.

I doubt this is something new. Sixty years ago, Heschel was already noting that religion can sometimes be its own worst enemy. Rather than blame secularism for the demise of religion, Heschel (1955, 3) says we need to look at the lack of creativity and relevance of our own faith traditions:

> It is customary to blame secular science and anti-religious philosophy for the eclipse of religion in modern society. It would be more honest to blame religion for its own defeats. Religion declined not because it was refuted, but because it became *irrelevant, dull, oppressive, insipid*. When faith is completely replaced by creed, worship by discipline, love by habit; when faith becomes an heirloom rather than *a living fountain*; when religion speaks only in the name of authority rather than with the voice of compassion – its message becomes meaningless.

The ill health of religion is attributable to its dearth of creativity. Non-creative religious traditions lead to fundamentalism, irrationalism, and dogmatism – upon which the sources of war and conflict feed. Healthy religious traditions are attributable to the richness of creativity. Creative religious traditions lead to peace, healing, newfound wisdom – they draw on the sources of love and beauty.

Of course, it would be easy at this juncture to note that secularism also has its own 'demons' to face, that it has not lived up to its own ideals of peace, tolerance, and freedom. Levinas (2007, 121) puts this most starkly in his indictment of Western thought in the wake of the Holocaust and other tragedies of the twentieth century:

> The history of modern Europe attests to an obsession with ... an order to be established on universal but abstract rules [...] while undermining or forgetting the uniqueness of the other person, whose right is, after all, at the origin of all rights, yet always a new calling. The history of modern Europe is the permanent temptation of an ideological rationalism, and of experiments carried out through the rigor of deduction, administration, and violence. A philosophy of history, a dialectic leading to peace among men – is such a thing possible after the Gulag and Auschwitz?

It seems there is no pure or faultless secularism or religiosity. The ultimate measure, for Levinas, is not whether one is secular or religious, but whether one is able to respond to the face of another – or, if you like, to my fellow human being – and, I would add, to all living creatures who share our planet. "I do not wish to talk in terms of belief and non-belief," Levinas (1986, 18) writes.

> *Believe* is not a verb to be employed in the first person singular. Nobody can really say *I believe* – or *I do not believe* for that matter – that God exists. The existence of God is not a question of an individual's soul uttering logical syllogisms. It cannot be proved. The existence of God [...] is the sacredness of man's relation to man through which God may pass.

Of course, even as Levinas dismisses bland religiosity, he nevertheless still refers to God. This word, which in the Jewish tradition cannot be pronounced, nevertheless retains a meaning for Levinas. In what sense? He writes:

> I am thinking in effect of a God who is bored to be alone. It is Christian too. I do not say that it is uniquely Jewish. It is a God whose grandeur, whose justice and *rachamim* (mercy) you see everywhere. You see his humility; it is a God who comes down [...] who has not negated the finite and who has entered into the finite. [...] This means it is a God who has sent you the other human being. [...] It is the constitution of society [...] there is a human being sent toward the other human being. That is my central thesis and consequently it is this structure that is divinity. (1989a, 107)

For Levinas, the constitution of society (secularism, if you like) is dependent on the humility of God, who enters our world from on high and makes us mindful of (or sends us) the other person to care for. When speaking to Christian audiences, Levinas often referred to chapter 25 of Matthew's Gospel: "in so far as you did this to one of the least". Of this passage he says:

> The relation to God is presented there as a relation to another human person. It is not a metaphor; in the other, there is a real presence of God. In my relation to the other, I hear the word of God. It is not a metaphor. It is not only extremely important; it is literally true. I'm not saying that the other is God, but that in his or her face I hear the word of God (2001, 171).

3 Humanising Our World Is Divinising Our World

Many people seem to be able to appreciate the love of parent and child, or the love of brothers and sisters, or the love between partners – even the love of one's neighbour. Yet they struggle to appreciate the love of God. I've often felt that the ordinary loves of our lives are the very essence of God's love. As soon as we link human love with divine love, we divinise our world and humanise our relationships. Human love incarnates divine love, and divine love ignites or inspires human love. This is the theological understanding of religion, whereby divine and human love are interlaced and invested with each other, rather than alienated in separate and disconnected realms.

A person with secular sensibilities, it seems to me, is interested in humanising our world, and stands against all forms of dehumanisation. I imagine that a person with authentic religious sensibilities would share this vision for humanity. There is perhaps nothing worse than a spirituality that cannot accommodate humanity. Rather, it is our spiritual duty to become human. This "becoming human" is not a task we set ourselves to achieve; rather, it is a task given us by divine life. Everything *of God* is ultimately concerned with everything *of humanity*. To hallow God's name is to hallow each other. "I consider the human person," Martin Buber (1965, 70) says, "to be the irremovable central place of the struggle between the world's movement away from God and its movement towards God." *Divinitas* can never be separated from *humanitas but* must always be related in their mutual concern. As it is with God, so too with us. As it is in heaven, so too on earth (Veling 2005).

It seems appropriate that the first book of the Bible is called *Genesis* or *Bereshit*. In the beginning God did not create religion, God created the world, which means that God created plants and animals and the starry sky and you and me. This is God's primary revelation – not religion. If religion means anything, then it means I am caught up in this bundle of life and that my existence is not solitary; rather it is relationally implicated. Religion is a matter of living relations between us. The duty of religious faith is to 'humanise' our world or to 'personalise' our world, to overcome the world of 'It' and welcome the presence of 'Thou'. This is also what it means to 'divinise' our world – hallowing each other and each created life as sacred and holy. The fact that *I* learn to say *You* – this is the religious.

4 Trapped in Immanence

Over sixty years ago, Buber (1957, 224; 226) perceptively wrote: "The theories of seeing-through and unmasking, both the psychological and the sociological, have become the great sport among men." As such, we end up in a world of mistrust and suspicion, rather than mutual recognition and dialogue.

In an insipid, narcissistic culture, Levinas helps us feel again *what it is to be addressed*. His writing comes to us as a constant prophetic appeal that is deeply shaped by the Hebraic tradition. According to this tradition, freedom does not reside in my authentic subjectivity; rather, freedom is *subjected* to an exteriority – the exteriority of God and the exteriority of my neighbour (Chalier 1995, 7). A self that is founded on autonomous subjectivity alone – free and above all constraints – is a 'self-sameness', an *egoism* (or even worse, a potential 'totalitarianism'). For Levinas (1969, 88) existence *for itself* is not the ultimate meaning; rather, it is existence *for the other*. The other addresses me and calls into question my existence:

> Can the Same welcome the Other, not by giving the Other to itself as a theme (that is to say, as being) but by putting itself in question? Does not this putting in question occur precisely when the Other has nothing in common with me, when the Other is wholly other, that is to say, a human Other? When, through the nakedness and destitution of his defenseless eyes, he forbids murder and paralyzes my impetuous freedom? [...] This putting into question of the Same by the Other is a summons to respond [...] the responsibility that empties the I of its imperialism and egoism. (Levinas 1996, 16–18)

What matters is not so much the 'Here I am' that is the declaration and assertion of my existence, but the 'Here I am' that is the response of my existence to the call and claim of the other. "The word I means here I am," writes Levinas (1991, 114). The priority here is not with the I constituting itself, but with the call of the other who asks after me, who asks me to be, not for myself alone, but also for the "stranger, the widow, and the orphan." This calling into question of my existence by the presence of the other constitutes my identity as a response-ability and answer-ability. As Adriaan Peperzak (1986, 211–212) suggests, "In the ethical 'experience', the ego of I think discovers itself as I am obliged ... not I think, I see, I will, I want, I can, but 'me voici' (Here I am)."

Levinas is converting the 'I think, therefore I am' of modern, Western thought into the 'Here I am' (Hebrew: Hinéni) of biblical, prophetic response. "The I loses its hold before the absolutely Other, before the human Other, and can no longer be powerful" (1996, 17). Relinquishing the power to say I, however, is not the annihilation of the I; rather, it is the election of the I as chosen and responsible before the face of God and neighbour. "I am," says Levinas, "as if I had been chosen" (1993, 35).

According to Levinas, much of the religious soul in the West has been captured by a type of 'immanentism', whereby any talk of God's otherness or revelation or transcendence seems offensive to our intelligence. We are allergic to transcendence. "But the paradox of faith," writes Jacques Derrida (1995, 63) "is that interiority remains 'incommensurable with exteriority'." The inner world is no match for the transcendence of exteriority. If the event of religious faith is not to be dissolved into psychology, withdrawn into inwardness, deadened by sameness, reduced to the innate processes of socialization, or lost in an all-absorbing immanence, then it must be aligned with an elsewhere and an otherwise, with revelation. Levinas found an exit from self-enclosed being that allowed him to move toward being-open-to-the-other. What he perceived in this radical movement of transcendence he later named the 'face' – the one who is other than me and exterior to myself. With the revelation of the face, he realized that the world is not structured by indifference and impersonality, but by the "gleam of exteriority or of transcendence in the face of the Other" (1969, 24).

Revelation punctures the circle of immanence and arrives instead as a magnificent message. Especially for the prophetic traditions of Judaism and Christianity, attention to the voice of the other is always a pivotal moment in the announcement and advent of God. Levinas helps us realize again that we are personal, living, relational beings – that our lives are not so much self-sufficient and self-made projects; rather, we are answering, responding subjects.

Much attention in spiritual life is given to the interior life. No doubt this is important. Yet Levinas also brings a deep appreciation for the exterior life. He writes: "The exteriority of discourse cannot be converted into interiority. The interlocutor can have no place in an inwardness; he is forever outside. The relationship between separated beings does not totalize them; it is an 'unrelenting relation', which no one can encompass or thematize. [...] For no concept lays hold of exteriority" (1969, 295).

Revelation establishes a relation with exteriority. "This exteriority – unlike the exteriority which surrounds man whenever he seeks knowledge – cannot be transformed into a content with interiority; it remains 'uncontainable', infinite, and yet the relation is maintained" (Levinas 1989b, 207).

Levinas privileges you before me, you above me, you in front of me. Paul Ricoeur (1998, 170) evokes similar associations: *Anteriority* – before me; *Superiority* – above me; *Exteriority* – in front of me. According to *Ricoeur*, these three references delineate the religious. It is interesting that he does not speak of *interiority* or within me. Our interior worlds will never be the full measure of all that lay outside ourselves, in front of us and beyond us.

Monotheism is not afraid or embarrassed to speak in the name of 'thou', 'you', the 'Most High', the orphan, widow, stranger. Monotheism is a vigorous and infinite exposure to what is other in our life – God, neighbour, creation – none of which originate in me or are purely internal to me. Exteriority is necessary if we are to experience what is required of us, or what we are called to serve and dedicate our lives to. Exteriority is necessary even to know that we are loved, that *another* loves me. Our twofold lives (call and response, commandment and obedience, being chosen and choosing) are directly attributable to the monotheistic insight that "the Lord our God, the Lord, is one" – unique, irreplaceable, original, existing – the singular one who binds us in relation rather than the all-absorbing one who assimilates us in sameness. Levinas (1998, 31) writes: "Forty centuries of monotheism have had no other goal than to liberate humanity from their own obsessive grip." "*Shema yisra'el!*"

The miracle of exteriority is the miracle of having another to love; it is the miracle of relation, the miracle of living in each other's presence. "In ethical and religious terms: you will have someone to love, you will have someone for whom to exist, you cannot be just for yourself" (Levinas 1998, 113).

All of life – each and every life – is tied to another life. We do not exist – cannot exist – on our own. We are bundled together in life – with all that is living and shares time with us. We are bundled together with every living creature, with all the natural world. We are bundled together with friends and family, with neighbours and strangers, with the rich and the poor, with the just and the unjust. We are bundled together with writers and artists, texts and traditions, saints and prophets. We are bundled together on this beautiful blue earth, under a night sky – the wheat and the chaff together. And in the midst of all this life, there is an abiding mystery – there is "my relationship to you" (Veling 2014).

5 God Is Personal and Relational

Commenting on his translation of Martin Buber's *I and Thou*, Walter Kaufmann (1970, 26) writes: "God cannot be spoken of, but God can be spoken to. God cannot be seen, but God can be listened to. The only possible relation with God is to address him and to be addressed by him, here and now." For most people of faith, God is not a theory or a problem, a treatise or a dogma, a speculation or a doctrine, a *this* or a *that*. God is the one who hears our prayers, more than the one we talk about. It is more important to speak to God rather than about God. "Go into your room and shut the door and pray to your Father who is in secret" (Matt 6:26). For most people, God is their deepest and most secret hope, the one they talk to, the one they pray to, the one who listens and understands. In speech, as also in prayer, "we do not just think of the interlocutor, we speak to him" (Levinas 1998, 32).

Amidst the hardships of life, God is the miraculous one. God can do what seems impossible, can change what seems hopeless, can soften even the hardest heart. God is personal, relational, mysterious, and intimate.

The world is propelled by many impersonal forces, forces that we ourselves have made, forces that make the world go round – economic systems, political structures, laws and jurisdictions, programs, and agendas – what St. Paul calls "the rulers, the authorities, the powers of this age" (Eph 6:12; 1 Cor 2:6).

To speak of life's inherent personality is difficult. John Macmurray, a Scottish philosopher writing in the 1930s, raised his voice in the name of personality, yet he always found his task frustrating. "It is a shallow civilization we've got," he wrote in a letter to a friend, "people don't seem to know what I mean when I talk about a *personal* life. 'What's the use of it?' is what they ask" (1992, xi). Speaking of the personal life, he writes: "It is amazing how blind we are to this simplest and commonest of all our fields of experience, and to the way it determines and conditions all the others. The last thing we seem to become aware of in our conscious reflection is one another and the concrete ties that bind us together in the bundle of life" (1992, 153).

To think about personality – to write and speak of it – is difficult because personality doesn't like to be called an 'it' at all (Veling 2013). Personality is not a concept, something that can be conceptualized or pinned down (or even less, something that can be utilised), because personality refuses to be treated as a 'thing'. Nevertheless, Erazim Kohák (1984, 126) attempts a definition of sorts, saying that personality "is the decision to treat the Person, the Person-al mode of being, as the ultimate metaphysical category." He goes on to say that personality is concerned with relationships between us, relationships that are marked with respect and responsibility for each other and for the world in which we live. Personality reminds us that moral and interpersonal categories of love, care, and goodness lie at the very heart of life.

According to the Russian religious philosopher, Nikolai Berdyaev, most of us live somewhat unthinkingly in the context of social arrangements and cultural norms that shape the way we live in the world. Yet personality is the exception to all of this:

> In human personality there is much that is generic, belonging to the human race, much which belongs to history, tradition, society, class, family [...] much that is 'common'. But it is precisely this which is not 'personal' in personality. That which is 'personal' is original [...] Personality is the exception, not the rule. The secret of the existence of personality lies in its absolute irreplaceability, its happening but once, its uniqueness, its incomparableness. (1944, 23–24)

That which is personal is original, which is to say that human personality is not interchangeable, but rather incomparable and unique. Berdyaev calls this the secret of existence that belongs to each and every person. It is a secret because no human personality can ever be fully known by systems of thought, or subsumed by social processes, or reduced to any other form of contingency or conditioning.

Levinas (1993, 117–118) cites a Talmudic passage that plays on the image of minting coins: "Behold man, who strikes coins with the same die and gets coins all alike; but behold the Holy-Blessed-Be-He, who strikes all men with the die of Adam and not one is the same as another." Human beings are not like minted coins, interchangeable and alike; rather, human beings are incomparable and unique. This incomparableness reveals the trace of God in humanity.

Personality is the exception, not the rule. Personality asks us to think exceptionally rather than routinely. Personality requires an almost saintly attention to the often unnoticed – the singular one amidst the multitude. There may well be a hundred, but there is also the one. Personality asks us to act with the exceptional in mind, rather than according to customary norms or conventions. Personality represents a great difficulty for anyone who seeks all-encompassing theories or all-embracing standards. Even before the law and the court of justice, there is always the exceptional one. Personality is not made to measure or made to fit. Rather, it is immeasurable and cannot be contained.

"The Sabbath was made for humankind, and not humankind for the Sabbath" (Mark 2:27). This is a key principle in both the Jewish and Christian traditions. Like a good rabbi, like a person well-schooled in the Torah, Jesus was always sensitive to the exception before the law. Jesus gave preference to the errant one, rather than to the righteous or law-abiding one. He spoke of leaving ninety-nine behind to go in search of the one who had strayed (Matt 18:12). He preferred the exceptional one rather than the well-placed or well-positioned one (Luke 18:9–14). He often came to the defense of the one accused before the law, as with the woman "caught in adultery" (John 8:1–11). He "welcomed sinners and ate with them" (Luke 15:2).

Liberation theologian, Gustavo Gutièrrez, maintains that human beings are most prone to inflicting violence upon others precisely when the other person is considered as anything but human – indeed, as a 'non-person'. History abounds with examples, and the times have not changed very much. We continue to depersonalise and dehumanise our fellow human beings. "The majority of peoples today are still non-persons," Gutièrrez says, "they are not even considered as human persons" (1992, 272). I am often reminded, for example, of a striking image from a civil rights march of the 1960s, where African American men are walking down the streets with placards declaring, "I am a man."

Catholic theologian, Edward Schillebeeckx (1987, 174) tells us that "the great symbol of the human as *imago Dei* is the one permissible image of God that is not an idolatry." To disparage the human person or any living creature is to make a mockery of God, rather than to respect the image of God. I recall attending a Passover meal with a family in Jerusalem. One of the readings during the meal was the following passage from the Psalms, which made quite an impression on me:

> Their idols are silver and gold,
>   the work of human hands.
> They have mouths but do not speak,
>   eyes but do not see.
> They have ears but do not hear,
>   noses but do not smell.
> They have hands but do not feel,
>   feet but do not walk,
>   and no sound rises from their throats.
> Their makers shall be like them,
>   all who trust in them.
> (Ps 115:4–8)

God is not to be identified with dead and lifeless things, with idols that have no soul, no sense of the human, no living *personality*. God is not a faceless, impersonal God, but the God who is face-to-face, the God of the living. The personal and the relational have everything to do with the holiness of life.

"To sense the sacred," Abraham Heschel says, "is to sense what is dear to God" (1965, 49). The concerns of God are personal. If not, then I don't know how we can speak of God's relationality, or God's communication, or God's justice and mercy. These concerns are either matters of personal concern, or empty 'matter-less' theories. It is difficult for systems and constructs to capture these concerns because much of our systematic and abstract thought is empty of personality. Our ways of thinking and systematising often take their shape in the impersonal worlds of detached thought and rational knowledge. We always think about, about, about ... and what is personal eludes us. Personality can only be experienced in relational encounter, yet most of our lives are distracted by the structures and routines of impersonal existence. It takes an attentive soul and a responsive awareness to embrace God's personal concerns.

The concerns of God are personal. They are concerns that are ever focused on the lost and the last, the unnoticed and the little one. In every crowd, in every bureaucracy, in every managerial and administrative system, God sees the personal one, and lifts this one up, beyond the dark forces of impersonal being. Even when thronged by the crowds, Jesus never failed to notice the one who stands out, the one silenced and shunned by the crowds, like the blind beggar sitting by the road (Mark 10:46–51).

The concerns of God are personal. They are the concerns of dignity – the dignity of each human person and every living being – not as pieces in a system or players in a grand scheme – but as personal, living entities – unique and irreplaceable. God's concerns are the concerns of loving relationships, whereby we nurture friendship and respect – hallowing each other and each created life as sacred and holy.

Attention to the beauty and singularity of personality magnifies, rather than diminishes, our apprehension of the Divine. There is a holy spark in every living creature and every human being. Can we say that the ocean has personality? I'm sure a seafarer would say so – not only of the ocean, but of the wind as well. The geologist and the sculptor know the personality of rock and granite. The farmer and the gardener know the personality of soil and plants. The conservationist knows the personality of rainforests and wetlands. Indigenous people have long taught us that there is spirit and personality in all living creatures – in earth and sky, in land and ocean, in the natural ecologies of life that sustain us all.

As Martin Buber (1970, 57–58) notes, personality also finds expression in the natural world. "I contemplate a tree," he writes. In doing so, "I can assign it to a species"; "I can overcome its uniqueness"; "I can dissolve it into a number." In all these ways, "the tree remains my object and has its place." However, Buber continues, "it can also happen, if will and grace are joined, that as I contemplate the tree, I am drawn into a relation, and the tree ceases to be an *It*. The power of exclusiveness has seized me." Personality is concerned with all that addresses and reveals itself to me in its "thou-like" originality.

If we could let go of our arrogance, perhaps we could see that there is friendship in creation. Think of birds, for example. They are perhaps one of our shiest creatures, born of the air and distant to us, which is perhaps why I especially love it when they draw close and display amazing trust across the barrier of our strangeness, as though there were some primal part of them that recognized creation's friendship. I love this capacity for friendship expressed in the wild and the untamed. Communion in creation is a wonderful gift, if only we could listen and be attentive, if only we could believe that there are, as George Steiner (1989) reminds us, "real presences" in life, real signs of vitality and personality.

God's personal love means that people of different creeds, people of different nationalities, people of different social and economic backgrounds can share friendship. It is not that the differences between us do not matter; indeed, they are the basis for the infinite variety of relationships that can be shared in our interpersonal lives. Yet when we cling to our differences or guard them in fear, we lose sight of God's love and are living instead in a world of labels and name-calling: you are this, you are that; they are this, they are that. Love helps us to find joy in living together, to seek mutual understanding, to share experience, to express and reveal ourselves to one another. This is all that is required of us – to put down our swords, surrender our defenses, and share in the spirit of friendship which is the essence of the personal and spiritual life.

Bibliography

Benjamin, Walter. 1968. *Illuminations*, edited by Hannah Arendt. New York: Schocken Books.
Berdyaev, Nikolai. 1944. *Slavery and Freedom*, trans. R. M. French. New York: Charles Scribner's Sons.
Buber, Martin. 1957. *Pointing the Way: Collected Essays*, ed. and trans. Maurice Friedman. New Jersey: Humanities Press International.
Buber, Martin. 1965. *Between Man and Man*. New York: Collier.
Buber, Martin. 1970. *I and Thou*, trans. Walter Kaufmann. Edinburgh: T. & T. Clark.

Chalier, Catherine. 1995. "The Philosophy of Emmanuel Levinas and the Hebraic Tradition." In *Ethics as First Philosophy: The Significance of Emmanuel Levinas for Philosophy, Literature and Religion*, edited by Adriaan Peperzak, New York: Routledge, 3–12.

Derrida, Jacques. 1995. *The Gift of Death*, trans. David Wills. Chicago: University of Chicago Press.

Gutièrrez, Gustavo. 1992. "Bartolomé de Las Casas: Defender of the Indians." *Pacifica* 5:263–273.

Heschel, Abraham. 1955. *God in Search of Man: A Philosophy of Judaism*. New York: Farrar, Straus and Giroux.

Heschel, Abraham. 1965. *Who is Man?* Stanford: Stanford University Press.

Heschel, Abraham. 2010. *Heavenly Torah: As Refracted through the Generations*, ed. and trans. Gordon Tucker with Leonard Levin. New York: Continuum.

Kaufmann, Walter. 1970. "I and You: A Prologue." In *I and Thou*, trans. Walter Kaufmann, Edinburgh: T. & T. Clark, 7–48.

Kohák, Erazim. 1984. *The Embers and the Stars: A Philosophical Inquiry into the Moral Sense of Nature*. Chicago: Chicago University Press.

Levinas, Emmanuel. 1986 "Dialogue with Emmanuel Levinas." In *Face to Face with Levinas*, edited by Richard A. Cohen, Albany: State University of New York Press, 13–33.

Levinas, Emmanuel. 1969. *Totality and Infinity: An Essay on Exteriority*, trans. Alphonso Lingis. Pittsburgh: Duquesne University Press.

Levinas, Emmanuel. 1989a. "Interview with Emmanuel Levinas." *Philosophy and Theology* 4:105–118.

Levinas, Emmanuel. 1989b. *The Levinas Reader*, edited by Sean Hand. Oxford: Blackwell.

Levinas, Emmanuel. 1990. *Difficult Freedom: Essays on Judaism*, trans. Sean Hand. Baltimore: John Hopkins University Press.

Levinas, Emmanuel. 1991. *Otherwise than Being or Beyond Essence*, trans. Alphonso Lingis. Dordrecht: Kluwer Academic.

Levinas, Emmanuel. 1993. *Outside the Subject*, trans. Michael B. Smith. Stanford: Stanford University Press.

Levinas, Emmanuel. 1996. *Basic Philosophical Writings*, edited by Adriaan T. Peperzak, Simon Critchley, and Robert Bernasconi. Bloomington: Indiana University Press.

Levinas, Emmanuel. 1998. *Entre Nous: Thinking-of-the-Other*, trans. Michael B. Smith and Barbara Harshav. New York: Columbia University Press.

Levinas, Emmanuel. 2001. *Is It Righteous to Be? Interviews with Emmanuel Levinas*, edited by Jill Robins. Stanford: Stanford University Press.

Levinas, Emmanuel. 2007. *In the Time of the Nations*, trans. Michael B. Smith. London: Continuum.

Macmurray, John. 1992. *Reason and Emotion*. London: Faber and Faber.

Peperzak, Adriaan. 1986. "Some Remarks on Hegel, Kant, and Levinas." In *Face to Face with Levinas*, edited by Richard A. Cohen, Albany: State University of New York Press, 205–218.

Ricoeur, Paul. 1998. *Critique and Conviction: Conversations with Francois Azouvi and Marc de Launa*, trans. Kathleen Blamey. Cambridge: Polity Press.

Schillebeeckx, Edward. 1987. *The Schillebeeckx Reader*, edited by Robert Schreiter. New York: Crossroad.

Steiner, George. 1989. *Real Presences*. Chicago: University of Chicago Press.

Veling, Terry A. 2005. *Practical Theology: On Earth as It is in Heaven*. Maryknoll: Orbis Books.

Veling, Terry A. 2013. "The Personal and Spiritual Life: All Too Human, All Too Divine." *The Way* 52:7–21.

Veling, Terry A. 2014. *For You Alone: Emmanuel Levinas and the Answerable Life*. Eugene: Cascade Books.

Jaco Beyers
Theories of Religious Communication

1 Introduction

Communication is not a uniquely human characteristic; but it is a fundamental social building block of human society. Over time, symbolic signs have evolved into spoken symbols. In this regard, Njoku (2017, 50) refers to Aristotle's comment that the human ability to utilise language is an indication of creative intelligence, differentiating humans from other living beings. This same intelligence ("creative spark", Fuentes 2017, 243) led to the creation of religion in various cultural forms. The anthropologist Agustín Fuentes indicates how language most probably came into being when the first humans required the need to communicate with one another and expressed meaning by way of mutual agreement on the significance of signs (Fuentes 2017, 214). The origin of language can be linked to the existence of dance, music, and storytelling (Fuentes 2017, 239.242). Sign language most likely preceded spoken language (Fuentes 2017, 78). The development of religion is, according to Fuentes, closely linked to the development of symbols as a means of communication.

Language as a form of human self-expression became a means of controlling reality by naming and labelling experiences of reality (Njoku 2017, 50). Since humans started communicating through language, humans have critically reflected on the nature of language itself. The condition for effective communication is that the sender and receiver of the message reach the same understanding. Over time, communication became more complex, as the plethora of theories on communication attests to.

Religious communication includes different configurations of communication:
- The transcendent and immanent
- Members of the same religious system
- Members of different or no religious system
- Religion as a communicative system within society

Part of religious communication is the ambiguity of naming the unnameable and speaking to and about the unseeable, or as Luhmann (2002, 232) says, the "Unzugängliches" (that which is inaccessible). Religious communication can be deemed to entail speaking about the unspeakable, although the unspeakable "speaks".

The very nature of religion comes into focus. Religion is in essence a communicative action. Communication between transcendence and immanence constitutes a vertical line of communication. Communication between religions and society constitutes a horizontal line of communication. The ambiguity lies therein that all religious communication is in fact communication about transcendence.

Commenting on theories of religious communication requires awareness of three presuppositions: what is meant by the term theory; what is the definition of communication, and what is religion.

1.1 Theories, Models and Approaches

Theory can be described as the reflection and collection of knowledge on processes or events to explain phenomena. In simple terms, Griffin, Ledbetter, and Sparks (2015, 2) explain theory as making sense of the world. Theories are informed hunches that are systemic in nature (Griffin, Ledbetter, and Sparks 2015, 4). This description of theory indicates speculative attempts based on gained knowledge by scholars, to formulate multiple explanations of reality. In order to grasp the concept of theory better, metaphors that describe theories in terms of nets, lenses or maps, can aid understanding (Griffin, Ledbetter, and Sparks 2015, 5). Theories address questions and problems and present multiple possible solutions and answers based on experiments, indicating relationships between solutions.

Theories on communication abound. The most popular theories range from theories on Mass communication (McQuail 1994), Cross-cultural communication to philosophical theories of communicative action (Habermas 1981 and 1983), to technological theories on communication (Gadamer 1981). Not many theories on religious communication exist, and not all talk about communication in the same fashion, making them difficult to compare. This contribution will focus on Social System Theory, Phenomenology and Material Religion for theories on religious communication.

McQuail and Windahl (1981, 13) indicate that the most basic understanding of communication is to answer the questions related to 'Who? Says What? In which Channel? To Whom? With what effect?' This model is attributed to the theory of Harold D. Lasswell. Njoku (2017, 51) confirms that this understanding of communication is linear. A message is carried by a sender onwards towards a receiver. There is, however, no control mechanism to determine if the correct meaning has reached its intended destination. McQuail and Windahl (1981, 14) acknowledge that this model can be effective in mass communication. A variation on the linear theory by Lasswell is discussed by McQuail and Windahl (1981, 16–18). Shannon and Weaver expanded on Lasswell's theory by adding the element of 'noise' to disrupt the process of conveying information. The point of the linear model is to illustrate how information that has been changed into signals by a transmitter is passed on to a receiver which constructs a message from the signal. Successful communication occurs when the meaning produced at the destination corresponds to the meaning intended by the transmitter. Correspondence between meanings is the goal of communication (McQuail and Windahl 1981, 18). By adding another element in order to determine if the received meaning corresponds with the intended meaning, a new model is created.

The circular model attributed to Osgood and Schramm (McQuail and Windahl 1981, 19) implies that the sender and receiver are engaged in similar activities of encoding and decoding a message. By checking if the received meaning is similar to the intended meaning, feedback is given in order to ensure successful communication. This model implies that the participants in communication are viewed as equals, both able to encode and decode messages. Both are considered to be 'in the know' – having valid and worthwhile messages to be exchanged. This is an important element, as missionaries in the past may have considered the receivers as unequal communication partners with no valid or worthwhile message to give, in conveying the Christian message. This resulted in a monologue; a one-way delivery of messages. A third possible model is created by the theory of F.E.X. Dance when he identifies the limitations of the circular model (McQuail and Windahl 1981, 20). Dance indicates how a message returned to its sender does not return in the same form that it departed from. Communication is dynamic. Participants in communication develop knowledge of a topic as they exchange information. The message is influenced through the very process of conveying it. The participants in communication progressively detangle and assign meaning in an ever-expanding manner. This has implications for how religious communication is perceived: the message changes as it passes through processes and is handled by different participants. The question then arises whether the message does in fact remain congruent to the meaning originally assigned to it.

By reflecting on what theory is, we are already creating a theory on theory. In what follows, a theory on communication and a theory on religion will be presented before discussing several existing theories of religious communication.

1.2 Communication

Communication is a multi-faceted concept. Griffin, Ledbetter, and Sparks (2015, 6) when discussing definitions of communication, reach the conclusion that it is perhaps impossible to define communication comprehensively. What is however possible is to indicate the essential elements of communication. Griffin, Ledbetter, and Sparks (2015, 6–7) indicate the following essentials of communication: communication is a process of creating and interpreting messages. Many disciplines are interested in studying communication. So too is theology. Although other disciplines such as psychology, sociology, anthropology, linguistics, literature, political sciences, and religious studies only intersect with the study of communication, scholars of communication remain focussed on the study of communication. In this regard, the other disciplines broaden the way in which communication is viewed. Communication can be presented in many different mediums (i.e., texts, art, words, songs, poems, symbols, speeches, gestures, events, dance, etc.).

As indicated, communication can be defined in many different ways. Communication can be the action on others, the interaction with others and a reaction to others (McQuail and Windahl 1981, 3). For Kelly (1981, 227) communication is the sharing of meaning. The sender and receiver of the message in communication assigns the same meaning to the message. Religion is a carrier and transmitter of a message.

1.3 Religion

A definition of the concept of religion is notoriously difficult. In fact, it is considered by some to be totally impossible (Caputo 2001, 1).

Several scholars have therefore argued against the use of the term religion. Smith (1991, 50) suggests discarding the term religion altogether. His argument is that the term religion is misleading, confusing, and unnecessary and hampers the understanding of people's faith and traditions. Instead, Smith (1991, 53 footnote 2) suggests it would be more appropriate to talk about "cumulative traditions". Olson (2011, 16) indicates how Jean-Luc Marion referred to religion as a "saturated phenomenon". With this, Marion implies that religion has an excessive nature and therefore religion becomes invisible in its excessiveness. The result is that there is no single concept that captures the essence of religion (Olson 2011, 16).

The concept of religion has proved to have a limited application. Smith argues (1991, 52) that Western culture has determined the way religion is perceived and what can be deemed religious. Western researchers have over centuries determined the field of religion by providing names for the world religions. The methods of studying religions are mainly due to historic Western scholarly processes. As Chidester (2017, 75) summarises, "religion is a modern invention, a Western construction, a colonial imposition or an imperial expansion."

The point of departure of viewing religion can either be deemed as from beneath or from above. Religion as from beneath reflects an understanding that religion does in fact start with human agency. Humans project images of power, hope and comfort to facilitate coping with human existence. Religion from above is typical bipolar, and even tri-polar. This approach assumes the existence of an autonomous spiritual sphere. Humans merely become aware of the presence and influence of the spiritual sphere (transcendence). The human relation to the spiritual sphere constitutes two separate spheres, the sacred and the profane. The moment in which good and evil are envisaged as belonging to the spiritual sphere, the addition of the human entity changes this into a tri-polar construct.

As to the relation of the above to the beneath, Stoker (2012, 6–8) discusses the various ways in which the transcendent and immanent can relate to one another. This will become important when discussing communication between God and humans. This communication takes on cultural forms.

> Religion is not an entity or a field of entities but an aspect of human experience which has specific historical and cultural expressions. Religion as religiousness is the individual human being's response to what it discerns to be the most comprehensive powers of its environment. Re-

ligion as historical tradition is the corporate and symbolic expression of that discernment rendered into forms of repetition, transmission, institution. (Farley 1988, 66)

As to Farley's analysis it becomes clear that monolithic blocks or entities named as religion do not in fact exist. What do exist, however, are contextual expressions of human responses to that which is considered to exist outside of human existence. This confirms the dualistic understanding of the nature of religion. It also confirms varying meanings attached to expressions as determined by contexts. What is considered as religious in one context may not be considered as such in a different context.

The concept of religion tends to call to mind a structured system of beliefs, with a specific and wide-ranging vocabulary Smith (1991, 52) includes terms such as piety, reverence, faith, devotion and God-fearing. Chidester (2017, 76) suggests including related terms such as superstition and magic, heresy and infidelity, secularism, and irreligion into this lexicon.

For the discussion here the following definition of religion is considered a working definition. Sundermeier (1999, 17) defines religion as the communal response of society when becoming aware of transcendence and responding to it in ethics and rituals. This definition of religion has its root in the social behaviour of human beings and acknowledges the impact of religion and society as systems acting upon one another. The definition assumes the existence of transcendence and accounts for its interaction with reality. Religion is, according to this definition, presented as a human response (communication) and thereby implies that religion is man-made although the impetus lies elsewhere. The expressions of religion in terms of ethics and rites are culturally determined. This definition attempts to present a balanced view of religion as it accounts for the interaction and exchange of messages between the transcendent and the immanent.

Religion is expressed in various ways. Several theories have been identified over time. For an exhaustive discussion on the different theories on language in religion, see Walter Capps (1995, 209–265).

Religious communication can be reduced to refer to ways in which Christians convey the Christian message to others in order to lead to a commitment to Christianity (conversion). In this regard, the work by Pierre Babin (1991) is a good example. Babin (1991, 29.188) considers the particular challenges Christians encounter in dealing with electronic media as a means of communication. The message Christians want to convey should consist of correct and relevant symbols (Babin 1991, 163) to enable others to comprehend the Christian message. At times, he suggests, the mere presence, even if silent, of Christians in society can convey a message of care (Babin 1991, 90).

Communication from Christianity to other religions or non-religious persons is, although important, not the main focus of this contribution. Religious communication can be categorised as intra-religious (internally within a religious system), inter-religious (between religions) and trans-religious (communicating to society). The focus of this contribution is to discuss variations on intra-, inter- as well as trans-religious communication as highlighted by the theories in Social Systems, Phenomenology and Material Religion.

2 Social System Theory

Social System Theory has as its goal the study of the relationships between a system and its environment (Pace 2011, 206). The changes in a system and its environment are studied, especially the affect the changes have on other systems (Pace 2011, 221). In effect, the focus is on changing forms and changing consequences (Beyer 2009, 99). A system is considered a system from the moment in which it produces communication (Pace 2011, 222). The seminal work of Talcott Parsons (Parsons 1951) sheds light on the origin of Social System Theory. Parsons (1970, 831) indicates how his research was focussed on analysing how society interacts and develops within a cognitive framework. His thoughts on this were especially influenced by Durkheim, Weber and Freud (Parsons 1970, 874).

Religion is considered as a system functioning within society besides and in relation to other systems such as the judicial, health care, financial, education and government systems (Luhmann 2002, 14). Religion is a system of means of communication endeavouring to simplify the meaning humans ascribe to reality (Pace 2011, 206). Pace (2011, 225) considers religion to be a unique system in that it serves a reassuring purpose with regard to human fears and concerns, which ensures the continuation of religion. Religion is constantly interpreting the relationships between God, humans and reality and disseminating this interpretation. It is clear that religion excels as a communicative system in mediating the exchange of information between God and human beings (Pace 2011, 210). The ability of religions to adapt and evolve also enables their longevity. Pace (2011, 226) considers that the most effective way religions impart communication is through rituals. Niklas Luhmann emphasised the role of rituals in religious communication.

In discussing religion, Luhmann emphasised the understanding of rituals as key to understanding religion (Beyer 2009, 100). Rituals are a form of communication: "Rituals are processes of important ceremonial communication [...]" (Luhmann 1984a, 9). The essential issue with Luhmann would then be to ask how the changing relations between religion and other systems affects communication between systems and how it affects the nature of religion.

In attempting to answer this question, Luhmann's theory on communication needs to be scrutinized. For Luhmann (1984b, 193–201) communication is the fundamental component of society. Society is made up of communication. Communication is not a characteristic of society. Rather, communication leads to sociality. Luhmann can be suspected of reducing society to the function of communication. Society only exists because communication exists. As to the relation of religion and communication Luhmann (1998, 137) clearly states that religion is only able to exist in society due to the fact, that religion is communication. Beyer (2009, 104) however remarks that Luhmann never gave a clear description as to what he considers to be religious communication.

For Luhmann there are three elements constituting communication: information, utterances and understanding (Beyer 2009, 101.106). All three need to be present in order for communication to take place (Beyer 2009, 101). Should communication stop, society will stop existing (Beyer 2009, 101).

As to religious communication, Luhmann (1997, 232) departs from an understanding of religion as consisting of two constitutive elements: the transcendental and the immanent. Luhmann left behind in his writings a quite ambiguous description of religious communication. At times it is clear that rituals are presented as the norm of religious communication (Luhman 1984a, 9) but then again in several writings by Luhmann[1] he indicates the impossibility of communication between gods and humans. It seems as if Luhmann emphasised that religious communication is only possible through human agency (Beyer 2009, 104). Communication from the gods (transcendence) seems to have become obsolete and impossible in Luhmann's view.

The problem for Luhmann is that God becomes the unobservable observer (1997, 69), the one which cannot be seen but who is participating in communication. The second problem related to this is that Luhmann indicates that it is impossible to differentiate between the information and the utterance in communication from God. The self-revelation of God in fact causes the utterance (revelation) to be the information. The real question according to Beyer (2009, 107) is rather to what extent a non-human participant in communication can be considered an actor within society. Luhmann is not arguing against the possibility of supernatural communication, but rather highlighting the problem with the indivisibility of utterances and information when it comes to communication from God. The messenger in fact is the message.

Ritual and myth are considered to be at the core of religious communication (Beyer 2009, 107). Luhmann (1997, 236) states that ritual does not differentiate between information imparted and the performed action of the utterances made. The utterance becomes the message. The correct performance of the ritual is the message. The conclusion Beyer (2009, 105) draws from this is that Luhmann is emphasising the paradox of communication through something that is not communication. The unique nature of religion should account here for the unique form of religious communication.

A critical analysis of Luhmann's theory indicates that society cannot only be perceived as a function of communication. Communication should rather be viewed as a function of society, establishing, and reaffirming society. An even more apt description would be that communication creates and affirms community among members of society. This community extends beyond the boundaries of those physically present. Through rituals, connections with the past and with the deceased, as well as connections to future generations to whom traditions will be imparted, are forged, and reaffirmed.

---

[1] Compare the complete list of references to Luhmann's writings in Beyer (2009, 113–114).

Luhmann (1997, 645) alludes to this principle when he indicates how myths attempt to make the unfamiliar familiar. Myths refer to already existing knowledge. By a repetition of this known knowledge, myths create solidarity; they do not solely function to convey information.

Beyer (2009, 109) concludes by summarising Luhmann's theory of communication by identifying two types of communication: paradoxical communication from the unobservable and thus non-communicative, and secondly the communication about the paradoxical communication which consists of interpretation and commentary. Understanding is the end result of communication for Luhmann.

In summary, for Luhmann, communication consists of utterances, information and understanding. There are non-human participants in religious communication; whereby the unobservable communicate in an ostensible manner. Humans are unable to differentiate between the utterances and information in the revelation from gods. The revelation is in fact the information. Rituals and myths therefore become the mediums of communication.

3 Phenomenological Approach

Studying different forms of religious communication is dependent on a phenomenological approach, identifying and analysing the different phenomena (i.e., rituals, myths, etc.) which facilitate communication.

Phenomenology is based on the philosophical ideas of Edmund Husserl. For Husserl, the point of engaging with reality is to make things as they appear speak for themselves (Krüger 1982, 16). To prevent the observer from subjectively mitigating meaning, the bias of the observer should be removed (known as *epoché*) to reach an understanding of that which is encountered. An inter-subjectivity replaces an objectification in the relation of the observer engaging with the essences of the object (Krüger 1982, 17).

The historian of religions[2], Mircea Eliade, introduced a theory on the origin of religion with implications for understanding religious communication. For Eliade (1987, 14) it is clear that reality is to be divided into sacred and profane spheres. The key to understanding religion is the way in which the sacred (transcendent) communicates to or manifests in the world (the immanent). The term 'hierophany' is key to understanding this process of communication (Eliade 1987, 9). Hierophany is the manifestation of the sacred in ordinary objects and the only way in which humans become aware of the sacred (Eliade 1987, 11).

For Eliade, the sacred is unknown and unknowable but mediates knowledge through manifestation in space and time. The hierophanies are the mundane objects

---

[2] Eliade is often referred to as a 'phenomenologist' as well. Compare John Clifford Holt's remark in the introduction to (Eliade 1996, xiii).

which become channels by which the sacred is communicated to humans. Hierophanies take on many different forms varying from nature (i.e., trees or mountains) to sacred texts (i.e., Bible, Qur'an), visions and dreams and can even be through human beings (i.e., shamans, prophets or holy people). Discerning the meaning of the hierophany requires a clear choice in order to distinguish the element from its surroundings (Eliade 1996, 13). The hierophanies are captured in myths within traditions and are dramatized in rituals. Interpreting myths and rituals are essential to understanding communication (Eliade 1987, 63). Let us compare in this regard Luhmann's understanding of rituals. Traces of the sacred (transcendent) are left behind in the mundane (immanent) world. Religion, therefore, is the complex phenomena resulting from the human experience of the sacred and giving expression to this experience.

Interpreting and discerning the meaning of the hierophany requires knowledge of the symbolic. Symbols only make sense in an environment where there is an agreement on their meaning (Fuentes 2017, 214). Symbols are assigned meaning within a certain community, in this case a religious community. This causes symbols to be understood from within the contexts in which they function. The meaning of the communication through symbols is therefore only available to the initiates of the religious community. As an outsider, the meaning can only be accessed through the interpretation provided by the insider. Religious communication is therefore only possible through consensus in a particular community.

Eliade, contrary to Luhmann, assumes that communication is possible reciprocally between transcendence and immanence. Eliade emphasises the communication by the gods imparted to humans through the hierophany. Luhmann (2002, 329.335) refers to such revelation as mysterious communication which requires interpretation in order to convey it into common religious communication. Revelation creates the problem that the utterance and information cannot be differentiated. The utterance is the information: the revelation is the message. What is required according to Luhmann is the interpretation of the utterance in order to reach meaning.

For Luhmann, the requirement remains that interpretation of the utterance through ritual, mythical or revelatory actions is necessary. Only through interpretation can the meaning be conveyed, enabling successful communication. Conveying the interpretation is considered as normal communication and not religious communication (Beyer 2009, 109).

Eliade emphasises the understanding of the symbolic sphere in which the hierophany is presented. Understanding the symbols facilitates understanding the hierophany. The symbols become the means of communication between the transcendent and immanent, conveying meaning between the two spheres of the sacred and the profane.

4 Material Religion

The ways in which religion is studied change as new approaches and methods are discovered. David Chidester (2017, 74) has indicated that in the future, the study of religion needs to orientate towards the material study of religion. Material religion is much more concerned with the "material conditions of possibility" for understanding the human need for expressing religion (Chidester 2017, 76; 2018, 3).

Houtman and Meyer (2012, 11) see the turn to material religion as a "corrective" to the one-sided Protestant emphasis on studying solely beliefs in religion. Keane (2008, 115) calls for a shift "away from beliefs and towards practices." Material religion expands the understanding of religion in order to include "the social life mediated in feelings, things, places and performances" (Morgan 2010, 12). Religion is not only that which is captured in texts and doctrines. Religion is mostly visible and audible in its everyday expression, or as it is popularly referred to as "lived religion" (Hazard 2013, 59 footnote 2). The emphasis is on studying expressions framed by the social construction of the sacred. The focus of material religion is then on embodiment and belief (Morgan 2010, 13). Focussing on more than utterances of belief would imply that we also consider human behaviour, feeling, intuition and images in everyday existence as expressions of and communication in religion. Religion no longer becomes the symbolic representation but includes the symbols and its world of reference (Morgan 2010, 5).

Keane (2008, 114) indicates how material religion wants to give recognition to the fact that we do not have access to ideas. Humans only have access to ideas once they are mediated by signs which can then be repeated. These semiotic forms are in the public domain, they are repeatable and visible and open to interpretation. It is clear to Keane (2008, 114) that these characteristics do not mean that the signs will necessarily communicate the same meaning every time or in every context in which they are used.

Religion is the cultural expression of an awareness (communication) between the transcendent and immanent. The origin of religion most probably lies within the evolutionary growth of the human psyche. Human self-awareness gave the spark to externalise objects and surroundings from the individual. This alienation from surroundings was exacerbated by the projection of beings that are higher than human. Thus, a dualistic reality was created; a reality co-inhabited by humans and spirits. Fuentes (2017, 197) attests to this distinction between humans and "an ultimate reality". He argues that humans have always behaved as if there is a transcendent or supernatural reality with which communication is possible. This communication is by way of symbols. This has already been alluded to earlier in this discussion.

Hazard (2013, 60) indicates the approach of studying religion in terms of symbols. She departs from the anthropologist Clifford Geertz's definition of religion as being comprised of a system of symbols. The implication, then, is that the outward appearances of religion (such as in shrines, dances, amulets, portraits) are in fact outward symbols communicating inward religious meaning. Material objects thus embody and communicate something else, representing religious essences (Hazard 2013, 60). Studying religion, in this case its material effects, makes the scholar a semiotician – one who reads and decodes symbols in order to glean – and impart – some meaning.

Religion is mediated concretely in order to make it visible, present and tangible. Houtman and Meyer (2012) identify the following as concrete instances of material religion through which communication is possible:
- Objects like relics, amulets, garments, images sculpted or painted, written words and architectural designs;
- Feelings and sensory experiences like seeing, hearing, smelling, tasting and touching;
- Bodily actions like gestures, rituals, ceremonies, and festivals.

Hazard (2013, 59 footnote 4) adds to the above list: space, body, art and visual culture, emotion, technology, media, popular culture, architecture and film, as additional ways in which religion communicates. The function of studying these sensory perceivable elements is to come to an understanding of how the practices of religious mediation effect the presence of entities in the world (Houtman and Meyer 2012, 6).

Religious beliefs are thus not only communicated in texts. Studying visual expressions of religion contribute to the communication process. Art may of course be perceived as having a function of religious communication (Apostolos-Cappadona 2017, 32). Religious art may have in some cases a pedagogical function to educate and remind adherents of religious doctrines. The meaning of art, however, is only discerned by the initiated who understand the symbolic meaning of elements in art. Religious art is therefore to be viewed contextually.

Studying material objects conveying religious meaning may end up as a positivistic endeavour, focussing only on the immanent. In this regard Bruno Reinhardt (2016, 75) evaluates material religion critically as only relying on the immanent at the cost of the transcendent. The corrective would be to view material religion as the means and not the goal. The materiality becomes carrier of the message, rather than being the message itself.

5 Conclusion

Identifying theories on religious communication is a non-exhaustive process. Religious communication takes place on different levels whether internal, external or across religious borders. Communication can be between the transcendent and immanent or on a horizontal level where religions communicate to society. This contribution attempted to present three theories of religious communication. Social System Theory, Phenomenology and Material Religion, however, do not function in absolute isolation from one another. They can be viewed as inter-related. Material forms of religion, like the various rituals, can be phenomenologically viewed as functioning as mediums of communication within a social environment.

Myths and rites are forms of communication. They convey a certain understanding of a worldview and explanation as to why things are the way they are. Myths as a narrative of a relation between humans and the transcendental convey a message which can be described as 'holy history'. The rite associated with the myth is the expression and re-enactment of the myth. Myths and rites can bring about social cohesion by binding society to the past while simultaneously engaging with future generations and expressing the relation with the transcendent. Religion as one system among many can influence society by functioning coherently to provide meaning to reality.

Bibliography

Apostolos-Cappadona, Diane. 2017. *Religion and the Arts: History and Method.* Leiden: Brill.
Babin, Pierre. 1991. *The New Era in Religious Communication.* Minneapolis: Fortress Press.
Beyer, Peter. 2009. "Religion as Communication: On Niklas Luhmann, The Religion of Society (2000)." In *Contemporary Theories of Religion: A Critical Companion*, edited by Michael Stausberg, London: Routledge, 99–114.
Capps, Walter H. 1995. *Religious Studies: The Making of a Discipline.* Minneapolis: Fortress Press.
Caputo, John. 2001. *On Religion.* London: Routledge.
Chidester, David. 2017. "Beyond Religious Studies? The Future of the Study of Religion in a Multidisciplinary Perspective." *Journal for Theology and the Study of Religion* 71:74–85.
Chidester, David. 2018. *Religion: Material Dynamics.* California: University of California Press.
Eliade, Mircea. [1957] 1987. *The Sacred and the Profane: The Nature of Religion.* San Diego: Harcourt Brace & Company.
Eliade, Mircea. 1996. *Patterns in Comparative Religion.* London: University of Nebraska Press.
Farley, Edward. 1988. *The Fragility of Knowledge: Theological Education in the Church and the University.* Philadelphia: Fortress Press.
Fuentes, Agustín. 2017. *The Creative Spark: How Imagination Made Humans Exceptional.* New York: Dutton.
Gadamer, Hans-Georg. 1981. *Reason in the Age of Science.* London: MIT Press.
Griffin, Em, Andrew Ledbetter, and Glen Sparks. 2015. *A First Look at Communication Theory.* New York: McGraw-Hill Education.
Habermas, Jürgen. 1981. *The Theory of Communicative Action.* Vol. 1. Boston: Beacon.
Habermas, Jürgen. 1983. *The Theory of Communicative Action.* Vol. 2. Boston: Beacon.
Hazard, Sonia. 2013. "The Material Turn in the Study of Religion." *Religion and Society: Advances in Research* 4:58–78.
Houtman, Dirk, and Birgit Meyer, eds. 2012. *Things: Religion and the Question of Materiality.* New York: Fordham University Press.
Keane, Webb. 2008. "The Evidence of the Senses and the Materiality of Religion." *Journal of the Royal Anthropological Institute* 14:110–127.
Kelly, James C. 1981. "A Philosophy of Communication." *Communicatio Socialis: Zeitschrift für Medienethik und Kommunikation in Kirche und Gesellschaft* 14:223–231.
Krüger, Jakobus S. 1982. *Studying Religion.* Pretoria: Unisa.

Luhmann, Niklas. 1984a. *Religious Dogmatics and the Evolution of Societies*, trans. Peter Beyer. Lewiston / New York: Edwin Mellen Press.
Luhmann, Niklas. 1984b. *Soziale Systeme: Grundriss einer allgemeinen Theorie*. Frankfurt am Main: Suhrkamp.
Luhmann, Niklas. 1997. *Die Gesellschaft der Gesellschaft*. Frankfurt am Main: Suhrkamp.
Luhmann, Niklas. 1998. "Religion als Kommunikation." In *Religion als Kommunikation*, edited by Hartmann Tyrell, Volkhard Krech, and Hubert Knoblauch, Frankfurt am Main: Ergon, 135–145.
Luhmann, Niklas. 2002. *Einführung in die Systemtheorie*. Heidelberg: Carl Auer Systeme Verlag.
McQuail, Denis. 1994. *Mass Communication Theory: An Introduction*. London: Sage Publications.
McQuail, Denis, and Sven Windahl. 1981. *Communication Models for the Study of Mass Communications*. London: Longman.
Morgan, David. 2010. *Religion and Material Culture: The Matter of Belief*. New York: Routledge.
Njoku, Francis O. C. 2017. "Philosophy of Communication, Culture and Mission." *Journal of Communication and Religion* 40: 49–71.
Olson, Carl. 2011. *Religious Studies: The Key Concepts*. London: Routledge.
Pace, Enzo. 2011. "Religion as Communication." *International Review of Sociology* 21:205–229.
Parsons, Talcott. 1951. *The Social System*. New York: Free Press.
Parsons, Talcott. 1970. "On Building Social System Theory: A Personal History." *Daedalus* 99:826–881.
Reinhardt, Bruno. 2016. "'Don't Make It a Doctrine': Material Religion, Transcendence, Critique." *Anthropological Theory* 16:75–97.
Smith, Wilfried C. 1991. *The Meaning and End of Religion*. Minneapolis: Fortress Press.
Stoker, Wessel, and Willie L. van der Merwe, eds. 2012. *Looking Beyond: Shifting Views of Transcendence in Philosophy, Theology, Art and Politics*. Amsterdam: Rodopi.
Sundermeier, Theo. 1999. *Was ist Religion? Religionswissenschaft im theologischen Kontext*. Gütersloh: Gütersloher Verlagshaus.

Contributors

Dr. Abdallah, Mahmoud (1976), teaches Pastoral Care at Zentrum für Islamische Theologie at Eberhard Karls Universität Tübingen; recent publications include *Theologie des Zusammenlebens. Christen und Muslime beginnen einen Weg* (2017, co-edited with Bernd Jochen Hilberath); *Islamische Seelsorgelehre. Theologische Grundlegung und Perspektiven in einer pluralistischen Gesellschaft* (2022).

Dr. Adam, Júlio Cézar (1972) is Associate Professor for Practical Theology at Faculdades EST São Leopoldo / RS; recent publications include *Mindfulness e espiritualidade como estratégica de enfrentamento em situações de crise* (2021, co-authored with Clairton Puntel); *(De)coloniality and Religious Practices: Liberating Hope* (2021, co-edited with Valburga Schmiedt Streck and Claúdio Carvalhaes).

Dr. Afdal, Geir Sigmund is Professor of Religious Education at MF Norwegian School of Theology; recent publications include Negotiating Purity and Impurity of Religion and Economy: An Empirical Contribution to Kathryn Tanner's Christianity and the New Spirit of Capitalism (2020, co-authored with Maria Ledstam); Two Concepts of Practice and Theology (2021).

Dr. al-Khatib, Mutaz (1976) is Associate Professor of Islamic Ethics and coordinator of th MA in Applied Islamic Ethics MA program at the College of Islamic Studies, and the Research Center for Islamic Legislation & Ethics (CILE), Hamad Bin Khalifa University, Doha; recent publications include *Qabūl al-Ḥadīth* (*The Reception of Ḥadīth*, 2017); *Islamic Ethics and the Trusteeship Paradigm: Taha Abderrahmane's Philosophy in Comparative Perspectives* (2020, co-authored with Mohammed Hashas); *Ḥadīth and Ethics Through the Lens of Interdisciplinarity* (2022 ed.).

Asamoah-Gyadu, J. Kwabena, PhD is President and Baeta-Grau Professor of Contemporary African Christianity and Pentecostal Theology at Trinity Theological Seminary, Legon, Ghana; recent publications include *Christianity in Ghana: A Postcolonial History* (2018); *Christianity and Faith in the Covid-19 Era: Lockdown Periods from Hosanna to Pentecost* (2020).

Dr. Auga, Ulrike E., is Professor of Theology and Gender Studies at Humboldt-Universität zu Berlin and Universität Hamburg; recent publications include *Resistance and Visions – the Contribution of Postcolonial, Postsecular and Queer Theory to Theology and Religious Studies* (2014, co-edited with Sigríður Guðmarsdóttir and Stefanie Knauss); *An Epistemology of Religion and Gender. Biopolitics – Performativity – Agency* (2020).

Barnard, Marcel, PhD (1957) is Professor of Practical Theology and Liturgical Studies at the Protestant Theological University Amsterdam and extraordinary Professor of Practical Theology at Stellenbosch University, South Africa; recent publications include *Worship in the Network Culture. Liturgical Ritual Studies. Fields and Methods. Concepts and Metaphors* (2014, co-authored with Johan Cilliers and Cas Wepener); *Bonding in Worship. A Ritual Lens on Social Capital Formation in African Independent Churches in South Africa* (2019, co-edited with Cas Wepener, Ignatius Swart, and Gerrie ter Haar).

Beyers, Jaco, PhD (1971) is Associate Professor of Religious Studies and Head of the Religious Studies Department Religion Studies at the University of Pretoria, South Africa; recent publications include *Perspective on Theology of Religions* (2017); *Understanding the Other: An Introduction to Christian and Jewish Relations* (2017).

Bowers Du Toit, Nadine, PhD is Associate Professor of Theology and Development in the Department of Practical Theology and Missiology at the University of Stellenbosch, South Africa; recent publications include *Does Faith Matter? Exploring the Emerging Value and Tensions Ascribed to Faith Identity in South African Faith-Based Organisations* (2019) and *Faith, race and inequality among youth in South Africa: Contested and contesting discourses for a better future* (2022).

Cilliers, Johan, PhD (1954) is Professor Emeritus of Practical Theology at Stellenbosch University, South Africa; recent publications include *Preaching Fools: The Gospel as a Rhetoric of Folly* (2012); *Timing Grace. Reflections on the Temporality of Preaching* (2019).

Dr. Litt et Phil Clasquin-Johnson, Michel (1960) is Professor of Religious Studies and Arabic at University of South Africa; recent publications include *Towards a Metamodern Academic Study of Religion and a More Religiously Informed Metamodernism* (2017); *Religion and Autism: Integrating the Person with Autism into a Community* (2020).

Dr. Cloete, Anita Louisa is Associate Professor of Practical Theology at Stellenbosch University, South Africa; recent publications include *Unstoppable: A Critical Reflection on the Socio-Economic Embeddedness of Technology and the Implications for the Human Agenda* (2019); *Interdisciplinary Reflections on the Interplay between: Religion, Film and Youth* (2019).

Cruz, Faustino, PhD (1961) is Dean and Professor of Practical Theology at Graduate School of Religion and Religious Education at Fordham University; recent publications include *Theological Education as Praxis: Pastoral and Practical Theology in a Globalized World* (2019); *Immigrant Faith Communities as Interpreters* (2019).

Dr. Dillen, Annemie (1978) is Professor of Pastoral and Empirical Theology at the Faculty of Theology and Religious Studies at Katholieke Universiteit Leuven and Extraordinary Researcher at the Faculty of Theology, North-West University, Potchefstroom, South Africa; recent publications include *Catholic Approaches in Practical Theology. International and Interdisciplinary Perspectives* (2016; co-edited with Claire Wolfteich); *Discovering Practical Theology. Exploring Boundaries* (2020, co-authored with Stefan Gärtner).

Filipović, Ana Thea, PhD (1961) is Professor of Religious Education at the Catholic Faculty of Theology at University of Zagreb; recent publications include *Neu lernen Kirche zu sein. Synodalität im Kontext der Jugendsynode* (2019); *Theory and Practice of Recognition and its Meaning for and in Religious Education* (2021).

Dr. Ganzevoort, R. Ruard (1965) is Dean and Professor of Practical Theology at Vrije Universiteit Amsterdam and research fellow at the University of the Free State, Bloemfontein, South Africa; recent publications include *Lived Religion and the Politics of (In)Tolerance* (2017, co-edited with Srdjan Sremac); *Trauma and Lived Religion. Transcending the Ordinary* (2019, co-edited with Srdjan Sremac).

Dr. Gräb, Wilhelm (1948) is Professor Emeritus of Practical Theology at Humboldt-Universität zu Berlin and Extraordinary Professor at the Theological Faculty of Stellenbosch University, South Africa; recent publications include *Predigtlehre. Über religiöse Rede* (2013); *Vom Menschsein und der Religion. Eine praktische Kulturtheologie* (2018).

Ha, Jaesung, PhD (1967) teaches Practical Theology at Korea Theological Seminary; recent publications include *Guidelines for Lay Pastoral Counseling* (2019); *Trauma, Scapegoating, and Community Narratives: A Study of Covid-19 Trauma and Rebuilding of Community* (2021).

Dr. Haspelmath-Finatti, Dorothea teaches Liturgical Studies at Universität Wien; recent publications include *Theologia Prima – Liturgische Theologie für den evangelischen Gottesdienst* (2014); *Homo Cantans. On the Logic of Liturgical Singing* (2019).

Dr. paed. Heimbrock, Hans-Günter (1948) is Professor Emeritus for Practical Theology and Religious Education at Goethe-Universität Frankfurt; recent publications include *Eco-Theology. Essays in Honor of Sigurd Bergmann* (2021); *Riskante Sätze: Von Gott reden* (2021, edited with Jörg Persch).

Dr. Horell, Harold D. is Associate Professor of Religious Education at Fordham University Graduate School of Religion and Religious Education; recent publications include *Remembering for our Future: Affirming the Religious Education Tradition as a Guide for the Religious Education Movement* (2018); *Thomas H. Groome*. http://www.talbot.edu/ce20/educators/catholic/thomas_groome/.

Isomae, Jun'ichi, PhD (1961) is Associate Professor of Religious Studies at International Research Center for Japanese Studies; recent publications include *Japanese Mythology: Hermeneutics on Scripture* (2010) and *Religious Discourse in Modern Japan: Religion, State, and Shintō* (2014).

Johansen, Kirstine Helboe, PhD (1977) is Associate Professor for Church History and Practical Theology at Aarhus University's School of Culture and Society; recent publications include *Transforming Churches: The Lived Religion of Religious Organizations in a Contemporary Context* (2019, co-authored with Marie Vejrup Nielsen); *There is Something Special about the Church: A Study of Wedding Couples in the Evangelical-Lutheran Church in Denmark* (2019).

Dr. Kgatla, Thias is Professor Emeritus of Missiology at the University of Pretoria, South Africa; recent publications include *Addicts of Gender-Based Violence: Patriarchy as the Seed-bed of Gendered Witchcraft Accusations* (2020); *Born into a World of Hostility and Contradiction: The Role of Mary-Anne Elizabeth Plaatjies-Van Huffel in URCSA* (2021).

Dr. Khalfaoui, Mouez is Professor for Islamic Law at Zentrum für Islamische Theologie at Eberhard Karls Universität Tübingen; recent publications include *Pluralism and Plurality in Islamic Legal Scholarship* (2021); *Islamisches Recht, Scharia und Ethik: Eine europäische Perspektive* (2022).

Dr. Kim-Cragg, HyeRan is Timothy Eaton Memorial Church Professor of Preaching at Emmanuel College of Victoria University at Toronto; recent publications include *Interdependence: A Postcolonial Feminist Practical Theology* (2018); *Postcolonial Preaching: Creating a Ripple Effect* (2021).

Dr. Krause, Katharina (1984) teaches Practical Theology at Evangelisch-Theologische Fakultät, Eberhard Karls Universität Tübingen; recent publications include *Bekehrungsfrömmigkeit. Historische und kultursoziologische Perspektiven auf eine Gestalt gelebter Religion* (2018); *The Social Practice of Being Born Again. Historical and Cultural-Sociological Perspectives on Conversionist Piety* (2020).

Dr. Dr. h.c. Küster, Volker (1962) is Professor of Comparative Religion and Intercultural Theology at Johannes Gutenberg-Universität Mainz; recent publications include *The Many Faces of Jesus Christ. Intercultural Christology* (2001); *God / Terror. Ethics and Aesthetics in Contexts of Conflict and Reconciliation* (2021).

Kumalo, R. Simangaliso PhD is Professor for Public Theology and History at University of KwaZulu-Natal, South Africa; recent publications include *Pastor and Politician: Essays on the Life of John Langalibalele Dube. The First President of the African National Congress* (2012); *Religion and Politics in Swaziland: The Contributions of Dr J. B. Mzizi* (2013).

Lartey, Emmanuel Y., PhD, DD (Honoris Causa) (1954) is Methodist Bishop and Charles Howard Candler Professor of Pastoral Theology and Spiritual Care at Candler School of Theology, Emory University; recent publications include *Postcolonializing God: An African Practical Theology* (2013); *Postcolonial Images of Spiritual Care: Challenges of Care in a Neoliberal Age* (2020, co-edited with Hellena Moon).

Dr. Psych. Lehtsaar, Tõnu, PhD Education (1960) is Professor of Psychology of Religion at University of Tartu's School of Theology and Religious Studies; recent publications include *Väike vaimuraamat. Karismaatiline usupraktika vaatleja pilgu läbi* (engl.: *A Small Book on Spiritual Subjects: Charismatic Christian Practices as Perceived by An Observer* 2021) and *Forms and Roots of Contemporary Religiosity in Estonia. Occasional Papers on Religion in Eastern Europe* (2021, co-authored with Kaido Soom).

Doc. Masarik, Albin, PhD (1959) is Professor for Practical Theology and Head of Department of Theology and Christian Education at Matej Bel University, Slovakia; recent publications include *Grieving with Hope: Selected Aspects of Funeral Sermons* (2017) and *Transformation of Human in Christ* (2019).

Rabbi Marx, Dalia, PhD is the Rabbi Aaron Panken Professor of Liturgy and Midrash at Hebrew Union College-JIR Jerusalem; recent publications include *From Time to Time: Journeys in the Jewish Calendar* (2018); *Tfillat HaAdam, the Israeli Refom Prayer Book* (2020); *Durch das Jüdische Jahr* (2021).

Dr. Mbaya, Henry is Professor of Church History at Stellenbosch University, South Africa; recent publications include *Resistance to and Acquiescence in Apartheid: St. Paul's Anglican Theological College, Grahamstown, 1965–1992* (2018).

Miller-McLemore, Bonnie J., PhD is E. Rhodes and Leona B. Carpenter Professor Emerita of Religion, Psychology, and Culture at Vanderbilt University Divinity School and Graduate Department of Religion Vanderbilt University; recent publications include *Christian Theology in Practice: Discovering a Discipline* (2012); *The Wiley-Blackwell Reader in Practical Theology* (2019).

Moyo, Herbert, PhD is Associate Professor of Theology and Religious Practices in Africa at University of KwaZulu-Natal's School of Religion, Philosophy and Classics, South Africa; recent publications include *The Apostles, One Church and One Human Race: The Apostles' Diaries of David S. Phakathi and Jim S. Ndlovu* (2019); *Zimbabwean Illegal Migrants in South Africa and the Problem of Stateless Children* (2020).

Dr. Nasrallah, Rima (1976) is Assistant Professor of Practical Theology at Near East School of Theology; recent publications include *Oriental Orthodox Young Adults and Liturgical Participation:*

A Matter of Identity (2020, co-authored with Ronelle Sonnenberg); *The Armenian Genocide Commemoration: A Dynamic Demand of Memory* (2021).

Dr. Ozawa-de Silva, Chikako is Senior Lecturer at the Center for Contemplative Science and Compassion-Based Ethics at Emory University; recent publications include *Toward an Anthropology of Loneliness* (2020, co-authored with Michele Parsons) and *The Anatomy of Loneliness: Suicide, Social Connection, and the Search for Relational Meaning in Contemporary Japan* (2021).

Dr. Ozawa-de Silva, Brendan, is Senior Lecturer at the Center for Contemplative Science and Compassion-Based Ethics at Emory University, recent publications include *Secular Ethics, Embodied Cognitive Logics, and Education* (2014); and *Religion, Spirituality, and Mental Health: Towards a Preventive Model Based on the Cultivation of Basic Human Values* (2014).

Dr. Pleizier, Theo (1975) is Assistant Professor of Practical Theology at Protestant Theological University Groningen; recent publications include *Religious Involvement in Hearing Sermons* (2010); *Spiritual Formation in Local Faith Communities* (2022, co-authored with Pembroke, Neil, Ewan Kelly, William Schmidt, and Jan Albert van den Berg).

Dr. Plüss, David (1964) is Professor of Homiletics, Liturgy and Practical Ecclesiology at Universität Bern; recent publications include *Gottesdienst als Textinszenierung. Perspektiven einer performativen Ästhetik des Gottesdienstes* (2007); *Lehrbuch Liturgik* (2021, co-authored with Alexander Deeg).

Dr. Post, Paul (1953) is Professor Emeritus of Ritual Studies at Tilburg University's School of Humanities and Digital Sciences; recent publications include *Absent Ritual. Exploring the Ambivalence and Dynamics of Ritual* (2019, co-edited with Martin Hoondert); *Handbook of Disaster Ritual. Multidisciplinary Perspectives, Cases and Themes* (2021, co-edited with Martin Hoondert, Mirella Klomp, and Marcel Barnard).

Dr. Probst, Hans-Ulrich (1988) teaches Practical Theology at Evangelisch-Theologische Fakultät, Eberhard Karls Universität Tübingen; recent publications include *Fußball als Religion. Eine lebensweltanalytische Ethnographie* (2022).

Dr. Robinson, Matthew Ryan, PhD (1982) leads the area for Intercultural Theology in the Protestant Theological Faculty of the Rheinische Friedrich-Wilhelms Universität Bonn; recent publications include *Redeeming Relationship, Relationships that Redeem: Free Sociability and the Completion of Humanity in the Thought of Friedrich Schleiermacher* (2018); *Theology Compromised: Schleiermacher, Troeltsch and the Possibility of a Sociological Theology* (2019, (2019, co-authored with Evan F. Kuehn); *What Does Theology Do, Actually? Observing Theology and the Transcultural* (2020, co-edited with Inja Inderst).

Dr. Razu, Indukuri John Mohan is Professor of Social Ethics at South-East Graduate School of Theology (SEAGST) Manila, columnist, and social activist; recent publications include *Ethics of Inclusion and Equality, Politics and Society* (2018); *Ethics of Inclusion and Equality, Economy, Education, Religion* (2018); *Ethics of Inclusion and Equality, An Indian Anthology of Cases* (2020).

Dr. psych. Schipani, Daniel S., PhD is Professor Emeritus of Pastoral Care and Counseling at Anabaptist Mennonite Biblical Seminary and Affiliate Professor of Pastoral and Spiritual Care at McCormick Theological Seminary and San Francisco Theological Seminary; recent publications include *Multifaith Views in Spiritual Care* (2013); *Manual de Psicología Pastoral: Fundamentos y*

Principios de Acompañamiento (2018); *Camino de Sabiduría: Consejería como Cuidado Psico-espiritual* (2020).

Dr. Schlag, Thomas (1965) is Professor for Practical Theology at Universität Zürich; recent publications include *Zukunftsfähige Konfirmandenarbeit. Empirische Erträge – theologische Orientierungen – Perspektiven für die Praxis* (2018, co-authored with Henrik Simojoki, Wolfgang Ilg, and Friedrich Schweitzer); *Interreligiöses Lernen im öffentlichen Bildungskontext Schule. Eine theologisch-religionspädagogische Annäherung* (2018, co-authored with Jasmine Suhner).

Dr. Settler, Federico, Prof. (1970) is Associate Professor of Sociology of African Religions at University of KwaZulu-Natal's School of Religion, Philosophy and Classics, South Africa; recent publications include *Curating Violence: Reflecting on Race and Religion in Campaigns for Decolonizing the University in South Africa* (2019); *Race, Hospitality and Phantasies of Benevolence* (2021).

Dr. Stetter, Manuel (1981) teaches Practical Theology at the Faculty of Protestant Theology, Eberhard Karls Universität Tübingen; recent publications include *Die Predigt als Praxis der Veränderung. Ein Beitrag zur Grundlegung der Homiletik* (2018); *Die Sozialität der Trauer. Erfahrungen des Verlusts im Zeichen der Pandemie* (2021).

Dr. phil Sumiala, Johanna (1971) is Associate Professor of Media and Communication Studies at University of Helsinki; recent publications include *Mediated Death* (2021); *Digital Religion – A Methodological Approach* (2022).

Dr. Swart, Ignatius (1965) is Professor at the Department of Religion and Theology at the University of the Western Cape, South Africa; recent publications include *African Initiated Churches and Development from Below: Subjecting a Thesis to Closer Scrutiny* (2020); *Stuck in the Margins? Young People and Faith-based Organisations in South African and Nordic Localities* (2021, co-edited with Auli Vähäkangas, Marlize Rabe, and Annette Leis-Peters).

Dr. Tran, Mai-Anh Le is Associate Professor of Religious Education and Practical Theology at Garrett-Evangelical Theological Seminary; recent publications include *Reset the Heart: Unlearning Violence, Relearning Hope* (2017).

Dr. Treiber, Angela is Professor of European Ethnology and Cultural Analysis at Catholic University of Eichstätt-Ingolstadt; recent publications include *Migration übersetzen. Alltags- und Forschungspraktiken des Dolmetschens im Rahmen von Flucht und Migration* (2020, co-edited with Kerstin Kazzazi and Marina Jaciuk); *Körperkreativitäten. Gesellschaftliche Aushandlungen mit dem menschlichen Körper* (2021, co-edited with Rainer Wenrich).

Dr. Ukah, Asonzeh is Professor of Christianity and African Religions, Chair of Religious Studies and Director of the African Centre for Religion, Ethics and Society at the University of Cape Town, South Africa; recent publications include *Prosperity, Prophecy, and the COVID-19 Pandemic: The Healing Economy of African Pentecostalism* (2020); *Apocalyptic Homophobia: Freedom of Religious Expression, Hate Speech, and The Pentecostal Discourses on Same-Sex Relations in Africa* (2021).

Dr. Vähäkangas, Auli (1967) is Professor of Practical Theology at University of Helsinki; recent publications include *Searching Missing Theology in the Nordic Practice Discussion* (2021); *The Search for Meaning in Life Through Continuing and/or Transforming the Bond to a Deceased Spouse in Late Life* (2021, co-authored with Suvi-Maria Saarelainen and Jonna Ojalammi).

Dr. Veling, Terry A. teaches in the Faculty of Theology and Philosophy at the Australian Catholic University; recent publications include *Someone to Love, Someone Like You: Poems of Divine and Human Love* (2020).

Dr. Walton, Heather is Professor of Theology and Creative Practice at the School of Critical Studies of the University of Glasgow; recent publications include *Writing Methods in Theological Reflection* (2014); *Not Eden: Spiritual Life Writing for this World* (2015); *Invitation to Research in Practical Theology* (2018 co-authored with Z. Bennett, E. Graham and S. Pattison).

Dr. Wepener, Cas (1972) is Professor or Practical Theology at Stellenbosch University, South Africa; recent publications include *Die reis gaan inwaarts. Die kuns van sterwe in kreatiewe werke van Karel Schoeman* (2017); *Bonding in Worship. A Ritual Lens on Social Capital Formation in African Independent Churches in South Africa* (2019, co-edited with Ignatius Swart, Gerrie ter Haar, and Marcel Barnard).

Dr. Weyel, Birgit (1964) is Professor of Practical Theology at Eberhard Karls Universität Tübingen; recent publications include *Praktische Bildung zum Pfarrberuf. Das Predigerseminar Wittenberg und die Entstehung einer zweiten Ausbildungsphase evangelischer Pfarrer in Preußen* (2006); *Netzwerkanalyse – ein empirisches Paradigma zur Konzeptionalisierung von religiöser Sozialität? Überlegungen zur wechselseitigen Erhellung von empirischen Methoden und praktisch-theologischen Konzepten* (2013).

Dr. Wyller, Trygve (1950) is Professor Emeritus of Contemporary Theology and the Study of Christian Social Practice at University of Oslo and Honorary Professor at the School of Religion, Philosophy and Classics at the University of KwaZulu-Natal, South Africa; recent publications include *Decolonial Counter-conducts? Traces of Decentering Migrant Ecclesiologies* (2018); *Embodied Spiritualities: Methodologies, Practices, and the Issue of Generous Christianities* (2021).

Yang, Sunggu A., PhD is Associate Professor of Christian Ministries at George Fox University and Director of the Margaret Fell Scholars Program; recent publications include *King's Speech: Preaching Reconciliation in a World of Violence and Chasm* (2019); *Arts and Preaching: An Aesthetic Homiletic for the 21st Century* (2021).

Images, Figures and Tables

Images

Image 1: Taturo Atzu, The Garden Which is Nearest to God (2015), printed with friendly permission of Museum De Oude Kerk, Amsterdam —— 20

Image 2: Christian Boltanski, NA (2017), printed with friendly permission of Museum De Oude Kerk, Amsterdam —— 21

Image 3: Giorgio Calò, Anastasis (2018), printed with friendly permission of Museum de Oude Kerk, Amsterdama —— 23

Image 4: Dietrich Bonhoeffer, Letters and Papers from Prison; SCM-Edition 1973 in possession of the author, © Heather Walton —— 48

Image 5: Hajj Locations and Rites; Hajj1.ar.svg; Creative-Commons-Linzenz, © Ascetic Rose; retrieved from https://de.wikipedia.org/wiki/Datei:Hajj_locations_and_rites.png (incorporated without modifications) —— 419

Figures

Figure 1: Foundations of Envious Persecutions, © Thias Kgatlas —— 332
Figure 2: Sleep as Liminal State © Dalia Marx —— 512
Figure 3: Talmudic Morning Ritual © Dalia Marx —— 512
Figure 4: Three Circles of Spiritual Care, © Daniel S. Schipani —— 556
Figure 5: A Four-Dimensional Framework for Spiritual Care, © Daniel S. Schipani —— 557
Figure 6: Scheme of the Ritual Playing Field with Fields and Repertoires, © Paul Post —— 748

Tables

Table 1: Norms and Criteria for Interdisciplinary Assessment, © Daniel S. Schipani —— 552
Table 2: Assessment Applied to Prayer with Care Receivers © Daniel S. Schipani —— 553

Index of Names

Ahlstrom, Sidney E. 468
Al-Qurṭubī, Muḥammad b. Aḥmad 426
Allen, John 408
Althaus-Reid, Marcella 623
Anderson, Allan 450
Anderson, Keith 453
Arendt, Hannah 205, 601
Aristotle 61, 343–345, 638, 678, 787
Asad, Talal 31, 164, 186, 601, 606, 612f., 627, 766
Ashley, Jennifer 331
Athearn, Walter Scott 470
Austin, John L. 620
Azumamaro, Kada no 602f.

Babiš, Andrej 264
Baker, Dori 475
Barbour, Ian 707–709
Barth, Karl 319, 567, 570, 708
Bass, Bernard 393
Battiste, Marie 501
Beauvoir, Simone de 616
Bell, Catherine 367, 489, 525, 593, 746
Berger, Peter 32, 189, 302, 764
Bertram Gallant, Tricia 399
Beza, Theodore 434f., 440
Bhabha, Homi 447, 625, 668f.
Blaauw, Martijn 331
Blumenberg, Hans 650
Boddló, Marican 269–271
Bonhoeffer, Dietrich 47–49, 53, 319
Bower, William 468
Brooten, Bernadette 617
Brown, Wendy 617f., 627
Browning, Don 61–63, 66, 68–70, 72, 117f., 705f., 713
Brubaker, Rogers 321
Buber, Martin 779, 781, 785
Bucer, Martin 277
Bugenhagen, Johannes 314
Bullinger, Heinrich 434, 534, 544
Butler, James E. 442
Butler, Judith 51, 615, 620f., 627

Calvin, John 432, 434, 534, 544f.
Campbell, Heidi 83, 195, 201f.
Cardenal, Ernesto 561

Cartledge, Mark 436
Casanova, José 198, 606, 626
Castell, Manuel 198
Chauvet, Louis-Marie 17–18
Chi-ha, Kim 564
Chidester, David 150f., 206, 765, 790f., 796
Chikane, Frank 409
Choi, Hee-An 667
Chung-hee, Park 563
Cilliers, Johan 374, 448
Coakley, Sarah 442
Cochrane, James 405
Coe, George Albert 468–470, 476
Cole, Nathan 308,
Cox, James L. 380
Crenshaw, Kimberlé 618
Crookston, R. Kent 397

Dalai Lama 198, 297
Deleuze, Gilles 622
Descartes, Renes 250
Dewey, John 469, 678
DeYmaz, Mark 454
Dickson, Kwesi 414
Dilthey, Wilhelm 236, 638, 655
Domingo Raphael 158, 165f.
Douglas, Mary 373
Dube, Musa W. 562, 617, 624
Durkheim, Émile 75, 207f., 213, 251, 358, 637, 747f., 762f., 792

Ebeling, Gerhard 569f.
Edusa-Eyison, Joseph 415
Eisenlohr, Patrick 201
Eliade, Mircea 212f., 794f.
Elliott, Harrison S. 468
Ellis, Stephen 388
Ephirim-Donkor, Anthony 390

Fallis, Don 331
Fanon, Frantz 662–664
Farnsworth, Jacob 291
Finke, Roger 302
Fischer, Andreas 263
Foster, Charles R. 474
Foucault, Michel 319, 322f., 613, 615, 619f., 622, 626, 651, 706, 727

Index of Names

Frankl, Victor 63
Frei, Hans 570
Freire, Paulo 473, 623
Freud, Sigmund 302, 621, 639, 704–706, 712, 792
Fritsche, Sally 548–551, 557
Fuentes, Agustín 787, 796

Ga'on, Sa'adia 514
Gadamer, Hans-Georg 66, 69, 638
Gaebelein, Frank E. 470, 474
Gandhi, Mahatma 341
Ganzevoort, Ruard 124, 143 f., 186, 188
Gaon, Natronai 519
Gatu, John 408
Geertz, Clifford 30 f., 33, 545
Gennep, Arnold van 178, 379, 509, 748
Gifford, Paul 410
Girard, René 525–527
Girgensohn, Karl 696
Gogh, Vincent van 488
González, Justo L. 445, 447
Goto, Courtney 53 f.
Gräb, Wilhelm 143, 170, 172–174, 177, 183–187, 189, 192, 221, 225, 227, 570
Grimes, Ronald 373, 484–487, 490 f., 746
Grimm, Veronika E. 343
Groome, Thomas H. 474
Grosz, Elizabeth 395
Grundtvig, Nikolai Frederik Severin 314 f.
Guattari, Félix 622
Gula, Richard 400
Gundlach, Thies 59
Gyekye, Kwame 388

Haar, Gerrie ter 388
Habermas, Jürgen 113, 165, 197 f., 237, 627, 788
Hagedorn, Anselm C. 332, 335
Hageman-White, Carol 620
Hahn, Alois 359
Haraway, Donna 52 f., 627
Harper, William Rainey 467
Harris, Maria 476
Hauerwas, Stanley 570
Haynes, Jeffrey 408
Hegel, Georg Friedrich Wilhelm 500 f.
Heidegger, Martin 17 f., 488, 491
Heschel, Abraham 776 f., 784
Heschel, Susannah 617

Heydrich, Reinhard 261, 264
Heywood, Carter 617
Hitler, Adolf 264
Homrighausen, Elmer G. 470
Hume, David 209
Hunt, Mary 617
Husserl, Edmund 251, 648–652, 655, 794
Hyong-Kil, Yun 563
Hyun, Young-Hack 565

Isasi-Díaz, Ada María 562
Isherwood, Lisa 617, 623

James, William 301 f., 431, 705 f.
Jenkins, Todd 146–149, 150–152, 154
Jiménez, Pablo A. 445, 447
Jones, Hugh O. 569
Jones, Serene 625

Kagame, Paul 413
Kant, Immanuel 13
Kanyoro, Musimbi 562
Kaoma, Kapya 412
Katsuyasu, Urano 603 f., 606
Kawatsura, Bonji 608–612
Kearney, Richard 25
Kee, Howard Klark 503
Keller, Catherine 625
Kgatla, Mookgo 408
Khama, Ian 413
Khumalo, Mzilikazi 459
Kiichirō, Hiranuma 608
Kiichirō, Shirai 606–608
Kikwete, Jakaya 413
Kim, Eunjoo Mary 445 f.
Kim, Hyun-Sook 474
Kirschner, Sebastian 542
Klie, Thomas 280
Knauss, Stefanie 625
Knox, Ian 472
Knudsen, Tim 314
Kooi-Dijkstra, Margriet van der 440
Koyama, Kosuke 568 f.
Krech, Volkhard 303
Kriss-Rettenbeck, Lenz 30 f.
Küng, Hans 405, 414
Kurrat, Christian 424
Kwok, Pui Lan 445, 447 f., 502, 568 f., 617, 624

Landman, Christina 333
Lanštiak, Ladislav 273
Laqueur, Thomas 621
Lartey, Emanuel Y. 447, 664, 771
Latour, Bruno 80, 580–583
Lee, Boyung 474
Lee, James Michael 476
Lee, Sang Hyun 449
Leeuw, Gerardus van der 483
Lekganyane, Barnabas 522
Leuba, James 301f.
Levinas, Emmanuel 651, 776–783
Lewis, Sara 298,
Lindbeck, George 570
Loder, James E. 556
Lofland, John 303
Løgstrup, Knud Ejler 314
Long, Thomas 374
López-Sierra, Héctor 665f., 670
Luca, Barbara de 396
Luckmann, Thomas 32, 36, 185, 227
Luhmann, Niklas 75, 77, 787, 792–795
Luther King, Martin Jr. 370
Luther, Henning 188, 570
Luther, Martin 314, 593, 721
Lyon Fahs, Sophia 468
Lyotard, Jean Francois 569

Machalek, Richard 303
Magesa, Laurenti 528f.
Mahmood, Saba 616, 626f.
Malcom X 426
Mandela, Nelson 369
Marx, Karl 408, 414, 627, 639, 706, 762f.
Masuzawa, Tomoku 626
Mbeki, Thabo 413
Mbiti, John 379, 460, 527–529
McFabue, Sallie 625
McGarrah Sharp, Melinda 666
Meland, Bernhard 655f.
Merleau-Ponty, Maurice 394, 649, 655
Metz, Johann Baptist 569f.
Meyer, Birgit 578–584
Mies, Maria 452
Mignolo, Walter 320, 323
Miller, Randolph Crump 470
Mngomezulu, Bhekithemba 413
Moore, Allen 475
Moore, Mary Elizabeth 474
Moran, Gabriel 476

Morgan, David 578–584, 794
Mosala, Itumeng 561
Mucherera, Tapiwa N. 664–666, 670
Mugambi, Jesse 408
Mühling, Markus 539f.
Muñoz, José Esteban 622

Nāgārjuna 345
Nakashima Brock, Rita
Nam-Dong, Suh 561, 563–566
Nasrallah, Rima 482
Ndeti, Kivuto 460
Negi, Geshe Lobsang Tenzin 293
Nelson, C. Ellis 474
Ngara, Emmanuel 412
Nhiwatiwa, Eben 374
Niebuhr, H. Richard 484f.
Nieman, James R. 445f., 448
Nkrumah, Kwame 407
Nolan, Steve 435
Nwachukwu, Chinaka 527
Nyengele, Fulgence 666

Oduyoye, Mercy A. 382
Olupona, Jacob 527
Ondrejčin, Ján 272
Osmer, Richard Robert 474f.
Osunwokeh, Clement 458f., 463f.
Otto, Rudolf 696

Park, Hee-Kyu Heidi 666
Parker, Evelyn 475
Parsons, Talcott 792
Patterson, Stephen 406
Philipp, Landgrave of Hesse 277
Phiri, Isabel 384, 389
Pieterse, Hendrik 374

Radford Ruether, Rosemary 617
Reckwitz, Andreas 681, 755
Reichardt, Johann Friedrich 534
Rich, Adrienne 622
Richardson, James 302,
Richardson, Norman Egbert 470
Richmond, Johannes 523
Ricoeur, Paul 50, 361, 570, 582, 638f., 781
Rilke, Rainer Maria 301
Ritschl, Dietrich 569
Rivera, Mayra 626
Rodríguez, Encarnación Gutiérrez 42

Roeland, Johan   143 f., 186, 188
Rogers, Thomas G.   445 f., 448
Ryle, Gilbert   344

Sachs, Emily   297 f.
Said, Edward   499, 606, 624
Saliers, Don   582
Salzbrunn, Monika   627
Sanders, Frank Knight   468 f.
Sarpong, Peter   384 f.
Schade, Lea D.   452
Schäfer, Theodor   318
Schapp, Wilhelm   570
Schatzki, Theodore   680–684
Scheerer, Bee   623
Schiff, Alvin I.   473
Schipani, Daniel   475
Schleiermacher, Friedrich Daniel Ernst   16–18, 25, 221 f., 234–241, 431, 435, 474, 638, 655
Schneider, Jan Tom   265, 272
Schneider, Laurel   625
Schüssler Fiorenza, Elisabeth   617
Schwaderer, Isabella   417, 421, 426
Scott, Kieran   476
Seme, Pixley ka Isaka   413
Sen, Amartya   97–98
Seneca   343
Sentsov, Oleg   341
Setiloane, Gabriel   406
Shay, Jonathan   291
Sherrill, Lewis Jopseph   470, 474
Shimazono, Susumu   604
Shin, Yang Jung   495 f.
Shiva, Vandana   452
Sigmon, Casey   453
Singer-Rowe, Elizabeth   308
Skonovd, Norman   303
Sloyan, Gerald   473
Smith, Christine M.   452
Smith, H. Shelton   470
Smith, Yolanda   475
Snow, David   303
Song, Choan-Seng   561 f., 566 f.
Spivak, Gayatri C.   319, 569, 624, 627, 668
Starbuck, Edwin   301 f.
Stark, Rodney   302
Steed, Christopher   412, 414
Stokes, Olivia Pearl   472 f.
Stone, Kerri   398

Stringer, Martin   748, 754
Stromberg, Peter   303
Sugirtharajah, Rasiah S.   663 f., 667
Suh, David Kwang-Sun   566
Sundkler, Bengt   412, 414
Swart, Ignatius   99

Tamez, Elsa   561
Tanaka, Shogo   394
Tarimo, Aquiline   411
Taylor, Charles   51, 69, 165, 169, 334, 678, 683
Taylor, Diana   501
Taylor, Susan   398
Thiselston, Anthony C.   70 f.
Tillich, Paul   17, 25, 66, 68, 186, 567, 684, 705 f., 708, 722
Tomasello, Michael   542
Tomoyasu, Urano   605
Tonstad, Linn Marie   623
Townsend, William Cameron   499
Travis, Sarah   448
Troeltsch, Ernst   147, 237 f.
Turkle, Sheryl   581
Turner, Victor   37, 178 f., 426, 509 f., 512, 748
Tutu, Desmond   408
Twale, Darla   396 f.

Ursic, Elizabeth   617
Uzukwu, Elochokwu   527

Venhorst, Claudia   357
Vernezze, Peter   343
Versfeld, Martin   371
Vinson, Robert   407
Voetius, Gisbertus   434
Vorster, John   370
Voss, Hans-Jürgen   621

Walsh, Catherine   320, 323
Walzer, Michael   406
Weber, Max   75, 82 f., 147, 213, 706, 761–763, 792
Webster, John   442
Wepener, Cas   147, 369, 486
West, Gerald O.   321, 561
Westerhoff, John H.   471 f., 474, 476 f.
Westphal, Merold   441 f.
Weyel, Birgit   143 f., 152, 170, 174, 219, 221, 227

Wilcox, Hui Niu 395
Wilcox, Melissa 623
Williams, Delore S. 562
Williams, Rowan 442
Wimberley, Anne Streaty 475
Wingren, Gustaf 313f.
Winston, Diane 197f.
Winter, R. Milton 434

Wittgenstein, Ludwig 678, 708
Woodhead, Linda 438f.

Yoshiyasu 607–612

Zulu, Shaka 459
Zwingli, Huldrych 534, 544

Index of Subjects

Academia 41, 70, 157, 164, 499
Academic freedom 398
Adolescence 278, 593, 699
Aesthetics 189, 439, 488, 648
Africa / African 145, 147, 149f., 190, 205, 209, 213, 215, 317, 327f., 339, 380, 383, 387, 389f., 405–407, 410–414, 458, 460, 465, 501, 521, 525f., 528, 571, 625, 637, 661–663, 666, 732, 765, 771
Agency 5–7, 55, 80, 89f., 94, 97–99, 199, 201, 251, 322, 330, 355, 361, 496, 499, 502, 535, 565, 583, 616, 622–624, 628f., 664, 666, 680, 682, 685, 755, 793
Air disaster 263, 265
Ambiguity 358, 575, 580–585, 624, 758, 787
Ancestor 211, 379–382, 386, 460, 462, 464, 514, 526, 529, 609
Animal 6, 147, 159, 420–422, 488, 501, 521, 523, 526, 753, 779
Annihilation 332, 334, 556, 780
Anniversary 263f., 357, 499, 610
Anthropology 379, 481, 539, 542, 554, 570, 601, 612, 706f., 775
Anxiety 51, 58, 292, 298, 339, 511, 550, 553, 606, 670, 699, 705
Apartheid 55, 96, 99, 150, 321, 369f., 374, 409, 486, 525, 561, 731, 735
Applied science 222
Archive 206, 215, 306
Artefact / Artifact 228, 250–259, 304, 309, 361, 682, 686
Arts 13–17, 25f., 470, 484, 704, 713
Asceticism 323, 342f., 347, 420, 603
Asia 147f., 172, 215, 449f., 502, 562, 568f., 635, 662, 667, 766
Assets 89, 97, 732
Authority 31, 64, 69, 71, 113, 130, 137f., 165, 198, 200–202, 210f., 214, 239, 332, 334f., 360, 362, 418, 452, 484, 498, 503, 522, 606, 616, 640, 670, 724, 764, 766f., 771, 777
Autobiography 290, 308, 568
Autoethnography 54f.
Autonomy 169f., 452, 626, 680, 682f., 724

Banal religion 199f.

Baptism 13, 170, 177, 275–277, 283f., 369, 381, 390, 487f., 719, 721
Belief 14, 25, 36, 67, 96, 110, 129, 147, 186, 199, 207–209, 252, 298, 309, 327f., 337, 363, 379, 410, 413, 433, 465, 468, 472, 485, 549, 601, 603, 606f., 684, 691f., 710, 739, 762, 767f., 796
Bereavement 58, 356, 382, 438
Bible 63f., 98, 123, 137, 486f., 496–505, 523, 537, 562, 582, 584, 625, 727
Biography 3, 65, 111, 171, 290, 359, 417
Biopolitics 615, 622, 626
Birth 18, 65, 120, 125f., 140, 383f., 425, 517, 692, 754
Blessing 171, 276, 279, 280, 282, 286, 379, 382, 385, 463, 509–520, 553, 577, 587, 591
Blood 24, 132, 140, 147, 305, 386, 398, 425f., 511, 523, 526, 528f., 776
Body 7, 13, 18, 38, 49, 53, 54, 100, 103, 106, 109–114, 134, 146f., 151, 189, 192, 223, 250, 252, 269, 290, 296, 304f., 308f., 346f., 356, 361, 393–395, 397, 402, 433, 460, 487, 504, 510f., 513, 516, 535, 538–542, 544, 554, 564, 571, 588, 606f., 619–626, 628, 636f., 640f., 649, 652, 656f., 665, 682, 685, 698, 707, 768, 771, 797
Born again 212, 301, 304, 305–309, 498
Buddha 296f., 343, 347, 451, 602, 608
Buddhism 90, 290–293, 295, 299, 341, 344, 346f., 349, 450f., 477, 554, 565, 567, 604, 608, 623, 737
Bullying 393, 396–399, 401f.

Camino 749, 755, 757
Catechesis 276, 278, 472, 719–724, 728, 756
Catechism 277, 721–723
Catechumenate 720–722
Catholicism 120, 188, 190, 601
Ceremony 177, 265, 268, 272f., 276, 284, 355, 383, 390, 422, 587, 591, 752
Chaplaincy 119, 265, 548, 705
Charismatic 38, 66, 148, 151, 172, 207, 214, 371, 380, 410, 436, 450, 459, 464, 537–539, 544, 604, 739
Chieftaincy 385, 389f.

Children 15, 53, 84, 119, 123–125, 161, 178, 184, 226, 264, 271, 277, 330, 370, 385, 390, 470, 486, 521, 533, 541f., 548, 564, 575, 577, 584, 590, 602, 641, 699, 706, 711f., 719, 722f., 726, 734, 745, 754
Christian practice 187, 224, 461, 724, 761, 771
Church 6, 14, 19f., 24, 47, 57, 62f., 67, 69, 75f., 143, 177, 223, 262, 280, 313f., 407, 450, 523, 615, 719f.
Church member 64, 66, 76
City 149f., 513, 522, 756
Civil religion 205, 207–209, 642
Civil rights 99, 398, 617, 783
Cognitive 66, 295, 298, 306, 491, 502, 509, 537, 542, 638, 650, 679, 694, 710, 732, 738, 792
Collaborative research 76
Colonialism 89, 91, 205f., 374, 448, 495, 497, 499, 502, 642, 662f., 669–671, 673f., 713
Comfort 64, 267, 270, 307, 361, 436, 551, 552f., 575, 698, 790
Commemoration 261, 558, 610
Commemorative 261, 749
Commensality 368f., 371–374
Common ground 178, 452, 548, 553, 633f.
Communication 17, 29, 41, 52f., 61 187, 189, 195, 437, 445, 453, 484, 541, 570, 665, 700, 717, 724, 728, 784, 787–789, 791, 794
Communion 13f., 254, 280, 370f., 387, 389, 536, 554, 718, 727, 736, 785
Community 17, 37, 62, 66, 69, 75, 82, 95, 122, 140, 198, 212, 222, 235, 284, 296, 327, 383, 426, 439, 543, 679, 723
Competence / Competency 175, 321, 360, 401, 554, 558, 752f.
Complexity 1, 3, 33, 51, 103–105, 191, 219, 334, 446, 484, 539, 545, 628, 666, 672, 706, 712, 737
Confession 66, 177, 277, 280, 369, 381, 452, 488, 537, 619
Confessionalism 62, 313, 619, 736
Congregation 19f., 65, 76, 174, 276, 436, 446, 482, 495, 524, 535, 537f., 544, 561, 576, 591
Contemplative 13, 126, 289–293, 439
Conversion 40, 51, 65, 82, 131, 301–305, 313, 390, 394, 550, 691–693, 699f., 703, 705, 718f., 763f., 791

Coping 40, 171, 177, 298, 437–439, 547, 551f., 643, 692, 695, 698, 747, 753, 790
Corona 743, 754, 757f.
Correlation 118, 186, 252, 303, 698f., 708, 710f., 722, 725
Correlational 68, 118, 693, 706, 709f., 722
Covid-19 pandemic 77, 431
Creation 61, 106, 110f., 137–140, 174, 176f., 243, 253, 264, 283f., 299, 313f., 399, 420, 452, 511–513, 517f., 540, 577, 610, 657, 662, 674, 708, 723, 781, 785
Crisis 77, 301–303, 412, 424–426, 431, 452, 467, 470f., 477, 510, 553f., 611, 640, 649, 720, 757
Cultural anthropology 29, 32–35, 37, 41f., 481
Culture 5, 14f., 29–31, 41, 61, 81, 93f., 126, 131, 133, 178, 183f., 186, 196, 218, 226, 250–252, 257, 353, 382, 396, 406, 413, 460f., 482–484, 516, 582, 588, 594, 633–637, 738, 748f., 770

Death 20, 63, 177, 262, 332, 339, 343, 353, 359, 361, 412, 432f., 436, 511, 518, 524, 526, 528, 557, 699, 721, 748
Decolonial 53, 89, 144, 315, 317, 320, 322, 710, 713
Decolonizing/Decolonization 93, 100, 320, 448
Democracy 129f., 136, 211f., 368f., 407, 412f., 569, 775
Desire 14, 33, 53, 63, 173, 196, 294, 307, 328, 347, 552, 568, 591, 639, 665, 751, 777
Development 77, 81, 89f., 92–94, 96–99, 138, 149, 172, 189, 195, 197f., 213, 223, 237, 241, 314, 327, 330, 333, 338, 343, 368, 406, 412f., 469f., 473, 541, 558, 615, 650, 685, 699, 718, 767
Diaconia 91, 313, 316f., 320–322
Dialogue 25, 52, 69, 117, 119, 156, 158, 184, 188, 220, 276, 357, 360, 417, 441, 448, 539, 566, 662, 667, 691, 708, 738
Digital 81, 397, 445, 453f.
Digital religion 195, 201f.
Digitalization / Digitisation 75, 80, 355
Disaster 90, 261, 263, 265, 357f., 412, 452, 527, 604, 640, 746, 754
Disaster rituals 357f.

Index of Subjects

Discourse 1, 7f., 15, 24f., 29, 41, 84, 89, 130, 135, 156, 209, 303, 327, 333, 452, 482, 490f., 572, 617, 622, 636, 665, 667, 669, 672, 686f., 727
Diversity 123, 129, 133, 146, 184, 187, 214, 227, 368, 371, 423, 427, 446, 495, 547, 612, 627, 641, 651, 672, 719, 726, 728, 731, 733f., 736, 766
Divination 334, 387
Drugs 695
Dutch Reformed 369f., 434, 486, 524
Dying 63, 90, 134, 177, 341, 432f., 435f., 548, 557, 662, 706, 711, 752

Eating 137, 308, 336, 342, 346, 348, 367–369, 371f., 385, 394, 458, 483, 487, 755
Ecclesiology 77, 80, 84, 90, 319, 367, 369, 453, 538, 727
Eco-feminist 445, 451f.
Economy 149, 151, 160, 189, 206f., 215, 372, 763
Education 47, 90, 95, 99, 110, 117, 123f., 138, 148, 155, 159–161, 166, 170, 215, 221, 223, 225, 234, 241, 285, 330, 372, 381, 384, 395, 398, 413, 418, 451, 467–478, 495, 657, 665, 669, 677, 704, 717f., 722, 725f., 731–741, 755, 769
Effervescence 189, 358
Egalitarianism 327, 329f., 333, 338f.
Elderly 90, 95, 385, 534, 536f., 699, 704
Embodied 5, 13, 35, 40, 52, 54, 56, 66, 254, 315, 319, 321f., 390, 394f., 401f., 413, 439, 485, 490, 497, 501f., 541, 610, 636, 638, 647, 649, 671, 680f., 724, 757, 762, 766, 768f., 771
Embodied knowledge 7, 305, 393f., 502
Emotion 13, 207, 304f., 307, 359, 537, 613, 681, 751, 797
Empirical studies 75, 94, 431, 686, 764f.
Empirical theology 238, 654–657
Epistemic violence 618f., 623f., 626f.
Epistemology 103 191, 327f., 339, 496f., 500–502, 505, 615, 627, 648f., 651, 663, 668, 671f.
Eschatology 357
Essentialization 3, 621, 624, 627
Ethics 103–105, 109, 117, 121, 208f., 236, 322, 372, 389, 399f., 463, 491, 604, 616, 621, 625, 711, 726, 752, 791
Ethnography 229, 257, 322, 652f., 666

Ethnology 29, 33–37, 229, 251
Eucharist 17, 19, 23, 373, 481, 487f., 504, 538, 719, 721
Eurocentrism 220
Europe 6, 14, 29, 38, 95, 144, 146f., 150f., 169, 197, 214, 423, 431, 469, 499, 501, 536, 543, 616, 618, 642, 763
Evangelicalism 196, 306, 765
Evangelization 718–722
Everyday 15, 17, 25, 32, 40, 42, 55, 68, 81, 84, 143, 173, 176, 186, 190f., 197, 257, 286, 305, 420, 450, 537f., 577, 583, 585, 637, 650f., 656, 683, 687, 692, 699, 706, 710, 739f., 755, 766, 769f.
Everyday life 10, 55f., 68, 81, 174, 176, 186, 188, 190f., 197, 227, 286, 379, 420, 422, 425f., 472, 537f., 575, 585, 650–653, 656, 687, 692, 710, 724, 739, 747, 755, 766f., 769f., 772
Everyday religion 185, 687, 769
Evolution 113, 237, 540, 695
Execution 261, 332, 334, 336
Exorcism 147, 327, 337, 339, 380, 747

Faith 19, 32, 36, 66, 172, 211, 222, 276, 286, 290, 307, 390, 406, 448, 451,
Faith-based organizations 91–93
Family 117, 119, 125, 159, 174, 207, 237, 277, 281, 285, 315, 380, 432f., 460, 462, 548, 550, 552f., 583, 592f., 606, 642, 699, 721, 724
Fasting 341, 347–349, 458, 504, 577, 776
Feasting 341, 345, 347–349
Fieldwork 33f., 243, 706
Film 178, 200, 770, 797
Food 90, 125, 309, 339, 346, 348, 367, 371, 375, 385, 451, 486, 523, 757f., 776
Football 178, 254, 533
Forgiveness 65, 123, 264f., 289, 295, 424, 441, 557, 655
Freedom 6, 36, 78, 97f., 109, 132, 136f., 159–162, 165, 169, 185, 212, 229, 236, 241, 319, 321, 398, 407, 414, 423, 447, 468, 552, 557, 585, 601, 604, 613, 626, 641, 670, 725f., 738, 765, 775, 777, 779
Funeral 178, 268, 270, 353–355, 359, 362f., 528, 570, 685, 687, 749, 571f., 754f.

Genocide 135, 297, 667, 805

Global North 89, 91f., 98, 100, 144–146, 148, 152, 452
Global South 4, 89, 91–94, 98–100, 144–146, 148–150, 152, 172, 201, 320, 561, 601, 766, 770
Glocal 445, 453f.
Governance 61, 130, 132, 206f., 210, 405–415
Good Life 104, 106, 237, 400, 711
Gossip 327, 330, 332–334, 336

Habit 31, 35, 38, 65, 156, 235, 295, 297, 306, 308, 367f., 371f., 398, 425, 575, 652, 667, 678, 682, 709, 777
Heritage 5, 19, 150, 192, 207, 314, 414, 616, 642, 661f., 669f., 725, 749, 763
Hermeneutics 3, 7, 33f., 63–66, 68–71, 184, 188f., 192, 234, 258, 368, 502, 561f., 565, 568, 572, 633, 638–641, 643, 717
Heterotopia 315, 319, 747
Holism 89, 93, 681
Holy Spirit 24, 38, 172f., 436, 458f., 461, 463–465, 482, 496, 538, 717
Homiletics 353, 368, 372, 448, 454, 497, 499, 505
Human flourishing 97, 173, 240, 380, 616, 624, 626f.
Human rights 96, 107, 129, 134–140, 159–162, 165, 322, 331, 391, 412f., 486, 569, 642f., 732
Humility 306–309, 383, 421, 778
Hybrid 202, 448, 461, 475, 482f., 557, 625, 666, 680, 684f., 745
Hybridity 29, 41f., 77, 80, 171, 189f., 425, 461, 465, 547, 625, 666, 672

Ideology 130, 132, 135, 137, 155, 161, 165f., 303, 426, 451, 601f., 641, 699, 753
In-between 8, 81f., 343, 576, 584, 625, 679, 682
Incarcerated 289, 296, 299
Inculturation 149, 451, 562, 723
India 129–135, 137, 139, 156, 201, 297f., 317, 344, 347, 423, 454, 499f., 608, 761
Indigenous 53, 94, 98, 189f., 309, 317, 320, 379f., 395, 452, 496–502, 505, 617, 624f., 666, 679f., 736, 785
Individualization 171, 177, 184, 189, 223, 227, 544, 685, 724

Initiation 119, 379–384, 386–391, 528, 576, 620, 717, 719–721, 723f.
Integration 64, 158, 170f., 226, 323, 330, 333, 381, 393f., 400, 442, 445, 552, 555, 622, 708, 724
Intercultural 8, 119, 241, 555, 558, 561, 571, 630, 634f., 638–640, 642f., 651, 662, 664, 677, 691, 734
Interdisciplinarity 105, 151, 195, 205, 225, 291, 432, 435, 437, 473–475, 548, 551–553, 623, 627, 647, 657, 705, 713, 717, 743
Interfaith 155, 417, 478, 547f., 555, 558f., 667
Intersectionality 93f., 100, 395, 615, 618, 623, 627, 704, 728, 767
Islamic law 104f., 156, 158f., 162–164, 420

Jealousy 328, 329, 331, 337, 397
Jerusalem 249, 522, 783
Jewish prayer 519, 550
Jews 341, 513, 516, 519, 538, 593, 641f., 766

Knowledge 2f., 6f., 14, 16, 34, 37f., 52f., 56, 98, 103, 110, 114, 225f., 238f., 251, 254, 271, 305f., 328, 388, 393–395, 497, 499–502, 618f., 627, 647f., 654, 663, 666f., 671f., 677–679, 681f., 691f., 713, 717, 722, 727, 731, 736, 740, 761, 771, 788, 794
Korean churches 62, 68–72

Language 130f., 133, 173f., 278f., 303, 319, 330f., 438–441, 487, 500, 536, 540f., 582, 678, 685f., 738, 787
Leadership 78f., 148, 393f., 399, 413, 667
Lebanon 575f.
LGBTIQ* 591, 615, 617
Liberation 100, 146, 190f., 409, 447f., 450, 478, 499, 561–563, 569, 571, 617, 623, 626, 709, 723, 770
Liberal theology 468
Life cycle 174, 176, 178, 476, 510f., 748
Life rituals 176, 179
Life writing 50, 57f.
Lifeworld 252, 256, 258, 652
Liminality 512
Liturgical practice 280
Liturgical studies 371, 482
Liturgy 368, 488, 513, 527, 537, 589, 750f.
Lived religion 79, 81, 118–120, 125, 127, 143f., 146, 169, 171, 173f., 183f., 186–

188, 190, 192, 227, 233, 257, 353 f., 368, 433, 633, 643, 739
Lord's Supper   277, 369, 373, 486
Loss   263, 268 f., 357
Lutheran Church   458, 587

Marginalization   92, 97, 447
Margins   151, 720
Marriage   62, 121 f., 177, 384, 587 f., 591, 593 f.
Mass media   200
Material culture   249–252, 257
Material religion   252, 796 f.
Material turn   251
Materiality   36, 255, 577, 626, 628
Maturity   277, 283, 286
Meal   347, 368
Meaning   15, 33, 36 f., 55, 63 f., 66 f., 171 f., 176, 187, 189, 192, 200, 206, 253 f., 256, 258, 279, 488, 502, 504, 517 f., 575, 581, 583, 636, 638 f., 681, 685, 692, 699, 788 f., 795, 797
Media   82, 195–197, 199–202, 582, 640
Mediation   200, 679
Mediatization   82, 195, 199 f.
Meditation   290, 292, 308, 347
Medium   457, 461 f., 582
Membership   75 f., 78 f., 389, 693
Memorial site   266
Middle way   344, 349
Midrash   518
Migration   152
Military memorials   262
Mining disasters   263, 267, 270
Miracle   147, 457, 464
Mishnah   513
Models   156, 161, 695, 708 f., 722, 726, 788
Modern culture   171, 177 f.
Monastic traditions   317
Moral   72, 111 f., 185, 209, 216, 250, 291 f., 294–296, 381, 400, 468, 517 f., 679, 712
Movements   99, 242, 302, 617, 626, 720, 738
Multi-religious   448
Multiplicity of meanings   500
Museum   13 f., 24 f., 635
Muslim   134, 156, 160, 162 f., 166, 198, 211, 341, 417 f., 423, 496
Myth   164, 613, 794, 798

Narrative   50 f., 62, 66 f., 254, 303, 449, 515, 569 f., 636

Network Theory   80 f., 174, 680
Neuropsychology of religion   694
Nigeria   211 f., 387
Nordic countries   318, 587

Objects   14, 30 f., 208, 249–259, 356, 482, 489, 575–585, 592, 648–657, 794 f., 797
Offline religion   81, 202, 356, 453
Online religion   81–83, 202, 215, 355 f., 401, 453, 758
Ontology   14, 526–528, 672, 677, 683
Orality   501, 503
Oral literature   502, 505
Orthodox   39 f., 68 f., 76, 175, 184, 200, 215, 240, 261, 272, 318, 482, 500, 537, 570 f., 576 f., 579, 582, 584, 616, 635, 661, 705, 707, 761, 766, 770

Participant observation   33, 243, 354, 576, 595, 653
Participatory   229, 235, 279, 453, 485, 504, 521, 524
Pastor   62, 65 f., 174, 226, 265, 272, 307, 315, 320, 355, 390, 396, 408, 410, 433–436, 439, 441, 457–459, 465, 533 f., 589, 591 f., 752, 755, 757
Pastoral care   380, 387, 433, 435, 457, 459, 592, 661 f., 664, 666, 673 f.
Pastoral counseling   673, 694, 704
Pastoral ministry   64, 184, 190, 223, 432, 434, 440
Pastoral theology   69, 71, 661, 664–666, 670
Pedagogical   54, 275 f., 280
Pentecostal   38, 148–152, 172, 242, 436 f., 450, 464, 538, 752
Performance / Performativity   51, 280, 361, 380, 382, 439, 464, 489 f., 504 f., 535, 620, 682
Persecution   270 f., 330–333
Phenomenology   251, 394, 647 f., 651 f., 655, 657, 794
Philosophy   13, 647
Piety   39, 304
Pilgrimage   417–427, 449, 521, 749, 757
Play   483, 487, 753 f.
Poetry   55, 191
Politics   47, 53, 130–132, 166, 205–216, 406, 409, 413 f., 616, 736, 740
Popular culture   571, 635
Popular religion   39 f., 605, 665

Postcolonial 191f., 447, 562, 568, 616, 624–626, 661, 663–675
Postcolonial theory 624
Postsecular theory 57, 626
Poverty 90–95
Power 98, 100, 110, 138, 199, 206, 216, 323, 338, 380, 388–389, 407, 458, 463, 487, 581, 619, 639f., 683, 727, 739f.
Practice theory 224, 677, 680–683, 688
Praxis 497, 634, 672
Prayer 431–442, 450, 497f., 504, 511, 536, 548–550, 553, 698f.
Preaching 445–454, 495–497, 503–505
Priestly office 457, 461, 463
Priest 386f., 457–459, 461, 463–465
Professional 262, 271, 354, 677f.
Protestant 36f., 38, 208, 276, 309, 342, 434f., 578, 601, 627f.
Protestant church 76f.
Psychoanalysis 302, 694
Psychology 648, 679, 691–701, 704f., 711f.
Psychology of religion 551, 691–701, 711f.
Public sphere 155f., 197–199, 601, 616, 626
Public theology 100, 118, 626, 710
Purification 80, 607–612, 683

Qualitative research 54, 56, 75, 84f., 227, 257f., 395, 548, 558, 571, 636, 652, 693, 713, 762
Quantitative research 75, 85, 163, 281, 558, 571, 595, 658, 693, 762
Queer studies 616, 621, 771
Queer theology 616, 623

Race 96, 398, 407, 426, 469, 498, 617f., 622, 624f., 627, 639, 737, 762, 765f., 768f., 771
Racism 124, 408, 426, 448, 475, 486, 495, 618, 639, 667, 713
Racist 215, 426, 486, 618
Reflexivity 34, 49, 54, 228, 537, 734, 771
Reformed 151, 301, 369–371, 431f., 434f., 440, 481f., 484, 486, 524, 533–535, 537, 543, 576, 705
Refugee 21, 289, 297–299, 315, 405, 633, 640–643
Relationality 75, 83, 121, 453, 673, 732f., 784
Religiosity 14, 25, 32, 35f., 39–41, 81, 95, 119, 125, 150, 163, 183, 185, 187f., 190f., 196, 200f., 255, 301, 323, 417, 482, 633, 685, 691f., 694–697, 699–701, 725, 762, 766–768, 777f.
Religious development 469f., 478, 496, 691, 699f.
Religious education 117, 123f., 155, 159–161, 223f., 285, 418, 467–478, 561, 661, 717–719, 721–728, 731–741, 769
Religious plurality 38, 129, 214, 613, 731, 734, 740
Religious practice 3–8, 35, 38–40, 42, 56, 78, 80f., 125, 165, 170, 176, 186, 191, 196–198, 202, 215, 219, 221–223, 226–228, 249–252, 257f., 289–291, 302, 425, 433–435, 437–439, 441f., 461, 481, 483, 502, 527, 537, 544, 549, 602f., 605–607, 624f., 637, 672, 685–688, 695, 700, 706, 743, 768, 771
Religious studies 2, 6, 8, 14f., 31, 37, 144f., 150f., 174, 228, 237, 243, 250, 301, 601, 622, 628, 652, 657, 685, 691, 704, 789
Research 2f., 8, 35f., 54–56, 75f., 80–85, 107f., 118–120, 151f., 162f., 173f., 184f., 195–197, 199–203, 223–229, 233, 239–243, 250–258, 301–304, 353f., 484–486, 539–542, 587–590, 651–654, 656f., 677–680, 691, 693–697, 735f.
Resilience 121, 123, 205, 289f., 295–299, 665
Resistance 47, 72, 99, 201, 318, 320–322, 338, 393, 396, 399f., 408, 447f., 452f., 497–500, 571, 592–595, 616f., 623f., 626f., 664, 763
Rhetoric 54, 135, 212, 303, 360, 445, 454, 498, 643, 665f.
Rite of passage 3, 178f., 277f., 282, 353, 379f., 382, 509f., 570, 748, 752, 754f.
Rites 178, 186, 249, 284, 286, 353f., 357, 367, 379–391, 419, 427, 485, 487, 490f., 523, 526, 528, 591f., 744, 749f., 752, 754–756, 791, 798
Ritual 6f., 13–17, 35–38, 82, 147, 160f., 169–172, 176–179, 197f., 206–208, 257f., 275–286, 341, 355–363, 367, 372f., 379–391, 417–427, 459f., 462f., 481–492, 509–513, 515, 517, 519–529, 536, 541, 555, 575–583, 587–595, 607–611, 636–638, 669, 685f., 692f., 743–758, 791–795, 797f.
Ritual criticism 367, 483, 486f., 743, 753f.

Ritual studies   361, 373, 484, 489, 491, 524, 743f., 746–748, 753–755
Ritualizing   361, 484f., 491, 746
Rumor   322, 397, 565f., 571

Sacralization   253–255, 257–259, 422
Sacrament   17–19, 25f., 120, 177, 277, 367, 369, 373f., 434f., 483f., 538, 581–583, 593, 719, 721f.
Sacred   13, 16, 39, 41, 62, 139, 150f., 158f., 186–188, 205f., 208f., 211–216, 252–255, 257f., 289–294, 296–299, 316, 380f., 386, 389, 409, 448f., 463, 496f., 502–505, 509, 524f., 549, 554f., 557, 582–584, 633–637, 685f., 697f., 749f., 768, 778f., 784, 790, 794–796
Sacrifice   6, 69, 123, 147, 271, 343, 379, 381, 386f., 422, 520f., 523–529
Same-sex marriage   209, 587f., 591, 593
Sanctification   308, 543, 698
Scripture   62–66, 68–72, 99, 137, 157, 161–164, 212, 214, 323, 447, 470, 482, 495–505, 685, 708
Sect   95, 130, 147f., 603, 605
Secularization   49, 55, 77, 95, 120, 143–145, 152, 155, 163f., 169, 171, 189f., 197–200, 205, 213, 227, 317, 587, 593, 601, 606, 626, 732, 740, 763–768
Secularism   14, 57, 131, 155f., 161–164, 167, 189, 207, 223, 601, 612, 627, 776–778, 791
Self-understanding   2, 78, 173, 177, 225, 228, 240, 243, 275, 278, 286, 304, 340, 361f., 472, 771
Sexism   337, 495, 618, 667, 713
Sexuality   69, 72, 120–123, 125, 127, 189, 209, 498, 588, 591, 615, 617–623, 712, 752, 768–770
Sharia   155, 158–160, 163–165, 211f.
Signs   22, 35, 165, 228, 487, 500f., 674, 719, 756f., 785, 787, 796
Sitz im Leben   33
Slaughtering   420, 522, 524, 527
Sleep   47–49, 57, 405, 509–513, 515–520
Sociability   233–237, 239, 241, 243
Social capital   89, 94–97, 369, 372, 528
Social constructionism   303
Social practice   30, 76, 83, 191, 227f., 253, 256, 258, 304f., 358, 421, 677–679, 681–683, 685f., 727, 761, 771

Social science   105, 151, 243, 251, 255, 257f., 557, 647, 678, 693, 703–707, 709–711, 713, 761–763, 765f., 768, 771
Sociality   75, 77, 79, 81–84, 169, 226, 792
Society   30f., 36, 40f., 61f., 68f., 72, 99f., 120, 130–136, 162, 172, 178, 183–186, 189f., 195–200, 205–211, 213, 227f., 262f., 321, 327, 329f., 333f., 337–339, 357f., 373, 383f., 387–389, 406–409, 421–425, 451, 458, 468f., 525–528, 565f., 604–606, 608, 612f., 634, 640f., 683f., 688, 722–728, 761–763, 767–769, 771, 777f., 791–793, 797f.
Sociology   3, 29, 36, 75, 80f., 83, 143, 185f., 208, 305, 327, 437, 565f., 652, 680f., 706, 711, 747, 761–763, 771f., 789
Sociology of religion   7, 39f., 75, 100, 148, 184–186, 195, 197, 199, 213, 228, 302, 685, 700, 703, 761–772
South Africa   6, 47–50, 53, 57, 89, 93, 96–99, 144f., 149–152, 215, 315–317, 321, 332, 367–375, 405, 408f., 413, 459, 481, 486, 521f., 524f., 527, 561, 639, 667, 709, 731f., 735–737, 739–741, 761, 765–767, 772
Space   7f., 13f., 19, 40, 49f., 53–55, 57f., 81f., 150f., 155f., 159–161, 190f., 212f., 228f., 280, 283f., 289–294, 296–299, 314–321, 337–339, 355f., 361–363, 370f., 380f., 419–422, 447f., 453, 542f., 571, 603–606, 609–611, 625, 637, 673, 682, 751f., 756f.
Speech act   71, 537
Spirit   16, 24, 131f., 139, 172f., 250, 297, 379–381, 386, 388–390, 440, 450, 457–465, 475, 482, 496, 499, 526f., 529, 538, 552, 556, 562, 603f., 608, 611f., 684, 717, 785, 796
Spiritual   13f., 24, 40, 42, 51, 62–65, 92f., 95–97, 124f., 147–149, 170–175, 208f., 250, 272, 289–291, 293–295, 301–303, 306–310, 327f., 355f., 380–383, 386–388, 420, 422–424, 426f., 432–437, 450f., 457–459, 461–464, 526–529, 547–558, 606–609, 669, 698–700, 724–726, 756, 777f., 790
Spirituality   40f., 117, 119f., 123–126, 170, 183–185, 289f., 301, 319, 414, 421, 431, 433, 450f., 482, 549, 551f., 554f., 557, 576f., 665f., 691, 725, 770, 777f.

Subjectivity 70, 169f., 228, 328, 348, 395, 569f., 604–606, 611–613, 616, 619f., 654, 735, 769, 779
Suffering 58, 61–67, 70, 73, 91, 190f., 198, 261, 289, 291, 294–298, 345, 347, 393, 434, 440, 499, 529, 552, 557, 563, 566, 569–571, 637
Superstition 37, 40, 435, 603, 624, 663, 744, 770, 791
Symbol 15f., 18, 30f., 38, 78, 135, 155f., 159–161, 171f., 176–178, 186, 199, 202, 208, 243, 253, 255–258, 358, 380f., 483f., 487–490, 500, 528f., 541, 575f., 578–585, 593, 639–641, 672, 674, 732, 740, 746f., 756f., 783, 787, 789, 791, 795–797
Syncretism 189f., 461, 745
Systems 31, 33, 67, 77, 98, 103, 129, 132, 138, 158f., 162, 164–166, 192, 200, 210, 290, 292, 297, 299, 313, 328, 373, 385, 389, 395, 414, 445, 474f., 477, 501, 540, 575, 583–585, 605, 619, 625, 664, 680, 728, 735, 782–784, 791f.

Taboo 120, 124, 254, 367, 373, 383–387, 528
Talmud 509–519, 783
Tetralemma 344
Theatre 178, 489, 749, 756,
Theocracy 205, 207–212
Theory 7, 30, 76–81, 118, 199f., 205, 219–221, 225–229, 251, 290, 329, 485, 489, 539f., 545, 548, 615f., 621–627, 638, 647, 651f., 663, 671f., 677–688, 699, 700f., 710–712, 727, 736, 764, 788f., 792–794
Theory-practice-gap 7, 677f.
Thick description 33, 545
Things 7, 35–38, 42, 58, 80, 208, 249–259, 361, 579, 583f., 647f., 656f., 680–682, 686f., 770, 784, 794–796
Tradition 1–3, 6, 8, 36–38, 42, 51, 66–68, 70, 82, 111f., 114, 169–171, 178f., 183f., 186–189, 196f., 250, 285, 291f., 297–299, 319, 322f., 381–385, 388–391, 458–461, 485, 497, 502, 513f., 533–536, 547, 558, 575–580, 583f., 588–595, 633–637, 642, 655, 669, 678–680, 697, 710, 720, 726–728, 736, 743f., 749f., 777–779
Tragic events 261–263, 267, 270

Transcendence 24, 33, 179, 188, 252, 356, 427, 438, 442, 446, 542–544, 655, 686–688, 780, 791
Transfiguration 51, 253–255
Transformation 8, 76f., 90, 99, 123f., 169–171, 177, 289, 303f., 319f., 386, 393, 424, 497, 509, 516, 544, 593f., 666, 672, 674, 681, 700, 726–728, 743f.
Transgender studies 615–619, 623
Trauma 56, 125, 292–298, 342, 571, 625, 770
Tribe 385, 427, 459f., 499

Ultimate 15, 207, 211, 345, 453, 684, 700, 711, 796
Universality 62, 65f., 72f., 233, 556, 609, 728,
University 117, 124, 220–226, 396, 558, 691, 739

Values 14, 34, 40, 64, 67–69, 93–97, 169f., 177f., 190, 207–209, 309, 337f., 383, 387f., 393, 406–409, 460, 486, 562, 588, 592f., 626, 641–643, 662f., 683, 691, 699f., 724–727, 731f., 734–740, 764
Victim 48, 124, 138f., 261–273, 291, 328–334, 358, 525–529, 641f.
Violence 54, 94f., 120–127, 135, 320f., 327, 525–530, 618f., 624–627, 640f., 674
Vocation 52, 212, 309, 314–319, 388, 462, 548, 555
Volkskunde 29–36

War 63–65, 124, 261–273, 289–291, 459, 498f., 563–568, 605–612, 640f., 775–777
Wedding 177, 570, 587–595, 754f.
Wisdom 53, 61f., 296, 348f., 463, 500–505, 665–667, 727
Witchcraft 327–339
Women 52–55, 62–64, 94–97, 124–126, 160, 264, 382–384, 387, 395–397, 451f., 471–473, 482–485, 496f., 562–568, 576–584, 615–626, 636, 641, 769f.
Worship 16–19, 147f., 279–286, 370–374, 432–434, 450, 481–486, 503f., 513–519, 522f., 533f., 581–583, 602, 635–637, 642, 668, 776f.

www.ingramcontent.com/pod-product-compliance
Lightning Source LLC
Chambersburg PA
CBHW081821230426
43668CB00017B/2339